The British Bomber since 1914

A Panavia Tornado GR1, ZA412/FZ of No 16 (Bomber) Squadron, blasts over the photographer with afterburners lit and wings in the fully-swept position. Aircraft of this type, with crews from seven RAF Tornado squadrons, were flown with great skill and courage during Operation Desert Storm of 1992, in the vital runway denial attacks on Iraqi air bases.

The British Bomber since 1914

Francis K Mason

PUTNAM

ALSO BY FRANCIS MASON IN THE
PUTNAM SERIES

Hawker Aircraft since 1920
The British Fighter since 1912

© Francis K Mason 1994

First published in Great Britain in 1994 by
Putnam Aeronautical Books, an imprint of
Brassey's (UK) Ltd,
33 John Street,
London WC1N 2AT

British Library Cataloguing-in Publication Data
Mason, Francis K. (Francis Kenneth), 1928—
The British Bomber since 1914
I. Title
623.7

ISBN 0 85177 861 5

Book designed and typeset by the Author in
Ehrhardt and Rockwell with Apple®
Macintosh® SE, using MicrosoftWord©,
Aldus PageMaker© and MacDraft©.
Acknowledgement is made to C A Mason.
Printed and bound in Great Britain by
Butler & Tanner Ltd, Frome

CONTENTS

INTRODUCTION

Whatever verdict historians and moralists of the distant future, no longer constrained by personal experience and familiarity, consider appropriate on the bombing aeroplane of the twentieth century, one fact is incontestable: it represented the most powerful weapon in the arsenals of the belligerent nations in two World Wars, potentially decisive in the first and demonstrably so in the second.

Despite being conceived in times of international tranquility, the flying machine was inevitably doomed to become a weapon of war, for such is the short-sighted ingenuity of mankind — whatever the motives, be they aggression or survival in the face of it. International war may be the result of failed diplomacy, but it is also a product of human greed and the fear of uncontrolled tyranny. Unfortunately wars in the twentieth century have become a reality too quickly for any genuine understanding to be gained of the ultimate cost in human life, and the breakup of social structures they engender.

During the lifespan of the bombing aeroplane even the accepted rules of warfare, for so long observed to a greater or lesser degree, were almost wholly abandoned. The assumed ability of the bomber to deliver a decisive attack has rendered obsolete the traditional declaration of war, for such a declaration would not only eliminate the essential element of surprise but would invite pre-emptive action — itself potentially decisive.

Central to the principle of aerial bombardment was the Douhet doctrine, an uncompromising strategic philosophy expressed after the end of the First World War by the Italian, General Giulio Douhet (1869-1930): that with the advent of air power the bomber is all-powerful, against which there is no sure defence, and that, this being so, the traditional arms can provide only a screen. This was a logical doctrine to express so soon after the end of the most destructive war of modern times, in which fruitless battlefield stalemate had resulted in enormous casualties, and huge naval fleets had turned tail the moment a major sea battle had threatened, in order to preserve 'a fleet in being'; only unrestricted submarine warfare by Germany had come close to becoming a decisive factor in the War.

Thus a logical corollary of Douhet's gospel was the acceptance of *la guerre totale*, the air assault upon the very fabric, social and industrial, of an enemy nation, a precept pursued by Trenchard — though not fully realised by his Independent Force of bombers at the end of the War.

It was *because* the Armistice intervened to prevent the full bomber offensive from developing against German industrial towns and cities remote from the Western Front, that the full import of Douhet's doctrine remained a subject for debate rather than a proven strategy for a further quarter-century.

Germany, however, was to be less reticent, having achieved disproportionate apprehension among the fragile British civilian population, after three long years of enervating privations, not to mention its untried metropolitan defences, with what was, after all, a very small force of medium and heavy bombers. Although beyond the scope of this book, it is worth mentioning that the martial policy of *Schrechlichkeit* ('frightfulness') from the air came to dominate German preparations for the subjugation of Europe under the Nazis, and was central to their *Blitzkreig* operations in the Spanish Civil War, and in Poland, the Low Countries, France and elsewhere during the Second World War.

What has been suggested by latterday pacifists — but competently refuted by historians — was that Sir Arthur Harris resorted to *Schrechlichkeit* with his bomber offensive in the last eighteen months of the Second World War, even though he passionately believed in his bomber force's ability to destroy the Germans' will to continue waging war. He later argued, with justification, that being deprived of the necessary number of heavy bombers, he was prevented from achieving that aim. Paradoxically, for those on the ground, the difference between a British raid employing 'area bombing' tactics upon a city wherein lie numerous strategic targets and a raid, such as that on Coventry in November 1940 by the *Luftwaffe*, is nothing less than academic. Be that as it may, there can be little doubt but that the repeated blows by the heavy bombers of Harris' Command contributed more than any other single fighting arm to the ultimate capitulation of Germany.

* * *

In August 1914 Britain went to war ill-prepared to engage in any significant air operations either in support of her expeditionary force being transported to mainland Europe or against the German Imperial Navy. Between them the Royal Flying Corps and the Royal Naval Air Service could muster a total of 179 aeroplanes, compared with about 1,500 French and 1,000 German military aircraft. Commanded by Maj-Gen Sir David Henderson, the full uniformed strength of the RFC on 4 August 1914 was just 2,073 officers and other ranks.

The RFC, not yet three years old, despatched five squadrons to France during the first two months of the War, equipped with a motley collection of aeroplanes, none of which was officially armed with a gun, and all of which were certainly unable to carry bombs. The job of their pilots was strictly confined to eyeball reconnaissance over the advancing German armies, striking deep into Belgium and France.

The first bombing attacks, launched by line squadrons against targets thought to be directly associated with enemy forces in the field, were flown in mid-March 1915 during the bloody attack on Neuve Chapelle but, owing to the makeshift nature of the bomb installations, these proved of little effect and were held by the Army to be ample justification of its lack of trust in the bombing aeroplane.

Nevertheless, such raids continued to be ordered by Corps Headquarters in France until fast-increasing casualties, occasioned by the bombers' inability to defend themselves, forced the War Office to take steps to obtain aeroplanes designed from the outset to carry both bombs and at least a token defensive gun armament.

The first truly efficient light bomber to reach the RFC squadrons in the field was Geoffrey de Havilland's Airco D.H.4, arguably the best light bomber in the world during the Kaiser's War. Unfor-

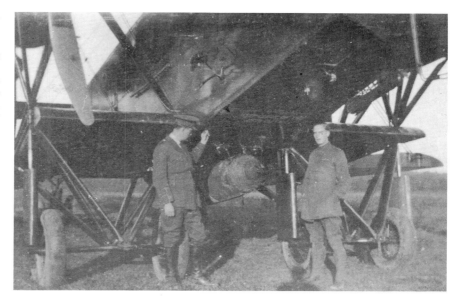

A contrast in big bombs, each the most destructive weapon of its day — half a century apart, yet both carried by Handley Page bombers. Upper photo: A 1,650lb SN bomb carried on Gledhill slips beneath a Handley Page O/400, probably in 1918. Lower photo: Trials of the Blue Steel stand-off nuclear weapon at Boscombe Down with Victor B.2R/BS, XL158, of No 139 Squadron in 1961. (Both photos: A J Jackson Collection)

tunately it was not ready for flight until mid-1916, and did not enter operational service for a further year, by which time the British Army had fought countless major battles and suffered appalling losses. In due course about 1,500 examples of the D.H.4 were produced, joining twenty-five squadrons, of which ten served in France and six in the Mediterranean theatre.

The D.H.9 followed before the end of 1917 but, on joining the Service, was severely criticised by Maj-Gen Hugh Trenchard and others on account of its lack of superiority over earlier aircraft owing to an unreliable engine. However, modified with either the Rolls-Royce Eagle or Liberty 12 engine, the D.H.9A (the famous 'Nine-Ack') gave excellent ser-vice with the RAF during the last six months of the War and for many years afterwards.

The Heavy Bomber

While the War Office had unquestionably dragged its heels in reaching a decision to procure purpose-designed tactical bombers, another line of reasoning on the use of bombing aircraft had been conceived as early as December 1914 at the Admiralty under Commodore Murray F Sueter, Director of the Air Department. Although not argued initially as a paraphrase of the Royal Navy's traditional strategic rôle in war, it was but a short step from the heavy bomb-carrying long-range patrol aircraft to a similar type of heavy bomber; the purpose of the latter was seen as the ability to perform heavy raids against the enemy's harbours and shipbuilding dockyards, and ultimately the Germans' major centres of munitions manufacture and land communications. This was indeed radical thinking, for little was known in Britain at that time concerning the air war in Eastern Europe which embraced raids by very large Russian and German bomb-carrying aeroplanes.

The choice of manufacturer to build

Britain's first very large heavy bomber fell logically on Frederick Handley Page, whose factory had started producing a large aeroplane intended to attempt a non-stop crossing of the Atlantic before the War. From these early deliberations was born the O/100, a predominantly wooden aeroplane of much greater size than any other previously built in Britain and capable of carrying no fewer than sixteen 112lb bombs — roughly the same as half an RFC squadron of light bombers, and over twice the distance. And it is pertinent to mention that the Admiralty's O/100 prototype first flew in December 1915 at roughly the same time that the War Office was deciding against any proposal to engage in strategic bombing, while cancelling the production of its first twin-engine aeroplane capable of carrying bombs.

It is likely that, had not an acrimonious dispute arisen over the respective rôles played in the processes of aircraft

procurement — born of jealousies involving the Admiralty's Air Department and the Army's Royal Aircraft Factory, and involving the manner in which manufacturing contracts were awarded to commercial companies — the Admiralty's O/100 and O/400 heavy bombers could have been supplied to the RNAS as well as the RFC much sooner by means of wider sub-contracting and common flight test facilities.

The matter was settled largely as a result of daylight attacks by German bombers on London and south-east England during the summer of 1917. Almost overnight the entire concept of strategic bombing, inevitably exposing the civilian population — the electorate — to the delivery of explosive bombs, became of highly emotive political consequence, a connotation with the heavy bomber that has persisted ever since.

The public outcry that followed the scarcely opposed bombing attacks on

London forced the British government to set up a Committee, chaired by the South African General Jan Smuts, to examine the illogical division of responsibilities between the Admiralty and the War Office for the air defence of the British Isles. It recommended the establishment of a single air service, integrating the Royal Flying Corps and the Royal Naval Air Service under a separate Air Staff and Air Ministry. Not only did this bring the aircraft defence forces under a single authority, but it unified the planned strategic bomber force under the same Ministry.

The O/400, an efficient heavy bomber capable of carrying up to 2,000lb of bombs, including a single bomb which weighed 1,650lb, came to provide the Royal Air Force's bombing muscle in the last six months of the First World War. Indeed, it formed the backbone of Sir Hugh Trenchard's Independent Force that was intended to undertake a systematic strategic bombing campaign against Germany, and was just getting into its stride when the Armistice was signed.

Thus, when peace arrived, strategic use of the bombing aeroplane had been made by the air forces of Britain, France, Germany and Italy; and it was the Italian general Douhet who formally theorised the philosophy that the strategic bomber was the *raison d'être* of air power, and that the heavy bomber had it within its power to bring about the collapse of a hostile nation by attacking its entire structure, economic and social, if not the military. Moreover, as if to emphasise the validity of this philosophy, Britain possessed, at the time of the Armistice, the Handley Page V/1500, a four-engine heavy bomber, capable of lifting up to 7,500lb of bombs and of reaching Berlin from its base in Norfolk.

Trenchard's postwar preoccupation with the bomber was not enthusiastically received by a nation so recently itself a victim of *la guerre totale*; nor had British bomber airmen been accorded the plaudits for gallantry as had those who had fought in fighters and become household names. It was universally hoped that never again would the bombing aeroplane be unleashed against towns and cities far from the ground battle.

Yet Trenchard it was who was to use bombers — such as the Vickers Vimy and the D.H.9A — to demonstrate the value of an independent Royal Air Force, and secure its survival in the face of powerful opposition from the Admiralty and War Office, intent on appropriating the meagre financial resources being made available for an air service. Had it not been for the survival of the Royal Air Force in the 1920s as a Service independent of the Royal Navy and the Army, it is unlikely that there would have been an autonomous Fighter Command in 1940 to gain survival of Britain, or a strategic Bomber Command in 1943 with which to take the war back to the people of Germany.

And it is worth recording here that, not only did Bomber Command during the Second World War suffer higher casualties (55,000) in relation to the number of fighting men engaged than any other branch of Britain's fighting forces, with one exception, but it was also the only branch of those forces which was in uninterrupted offensive action against Germany from the first day of the War until the the last, again with one exception. The exception in each case was the submarine service of the Royal Navy.

* * *

Turning to the more specific contents of this book, which closely follows the pattern adopted in the companion work on British fighters[1], no attempt has been made to confine the subject matter to those aircraft employed in, or intended solely for bombing duties in the generally accepted sense. Indeed, relatively few such aeroplanes existed. At the outset, most British aircraft designed for offensive operations were designed to carry a torpedo, and by their nature were capable of being, and frequently were adapted to carry bombs as an alternative. For the purpose of this work, therefore, the torpedo is regarded as a variation of the bomb that is dropped into the water before continuing on its way to the target. In any case, torpedo-carrying aeroplanes were for many years formally referred to as 'torpedo bombers'.

The terms heavy, medium and light bomber gained general currency during the interwar years and sufficed as being self-explanatory up to a point, persisting until after the Second World War. With the advance of technology, however, they became increasingly misleading: for instance, the Vickers Wellington, undeniably a 'heavy bomber' by the standards of 1939, was by 1944 scarcely on a par with the famous Lancaster-Halifax-Stirling trio of 'heavy bombers' but, by the criterion of bomb load carried, was comparable with those versions of the Mosquito — otherwise a 'light' bomber — which carried a 4,000lb bomb all the way to Berlin.

The category 'bomber-transport' originated in the 1920s as a subterfuge as much to secure treasury appropriations for dual-capability aircraft as to ensure compliance with requirements issued to the aircraft industry. To begin with, emphasis tended to rest upon the troop-carrying or 'transport' aspects of the Specification, with scope for adaptation as a bomber; such examples were provided by the Bristol Bombay and Handley Page Harrow (the former being a transport that was occasionally used as a bomber, and the latter being a bomber in its own right before being overtaken by technology and then employed exclusively as a transport).

This implication of duality of purpose persisted in most Specifications issued for heavy bombers almost up to the Second World War, and brought forth such aeroplanes as the Manchester and Halifax bombers of the War period. The Manchester's design was less compromised by the secondary requirement for troop-carrying (and came to be developed into the classic Lancaster); the Halifax, despite adopting four Merlin engines at an early stage of design, was much less outstanding as a heavy bomber — to some degree on account of its bomb bay restrictions, brought about by the 'transport legacy' — and, ironically, was to finish its Service life as a troop transport, in much the same way as its forerunner, the Harrow.

Excluded from this book are those aircraft which, although capable of carrying bombs as a matter of course, were designed from the outset for the maritime reconnaissance rôle. For many years and during the Second World War this duty was performed almost exclusively by flying boats, the reconnaissance aspect of their rôle being confined to the search for and reporting of the presence of enemy surface or underwater naval craft. During the War they were armed with depth charges (or depth bombs) while engaged in the Battle of the Atlantic on convoy protection duties. They were joined, during the War, by land-based aircraft — often heavy bombers, but not on account of their outstanding suitability for this task but more because of their ready availa-

---

[1] *The British Fighter since 1912*, Putnam, London, September 1992.

bility and the critical nature of the war at sea. This book therefore excludes such aircraft as the Short Sunderland, but includes those like the Whitley, Wellington, Halifax and Lancaster, bombers in their own right, making passing mention of their work in the maritime reconnaissance rôle. The Avro Shackleton, flown almost exclusively in the MR rôle, was however employed very briefly as a bomber aircraft in exceptional circumstances, and is therefore included.

If the classification of light, medium and heavy bombers was losing its meaning before the end of the Second World War, the introduction of the 'strategic' bomber was intended to imply a very heavy bomber of intercontinental range capacity and was introduced to differentiate between the American B-17/B-24 generation of so-called heavy bombers and the B-29 Superfortress, which devastated Japan in 1945. The 'strategic' description lost its exclusive implication of large aircraft size and long range with the introduction of in-flight refuelling which, for instance, enabled British bombers of the V-force — 'medium' bombers if compared with the huge B-36 and B-52 bombers of the USAF — to achieve theoretically unlimited sortie ranges.

Thus, when referring to the various bomber classifications mentioned above, the terms used reflect those to which the aircraft could reasonably be regarded as belonging at the time they entered service.

At the other end of the scale, there has to be a subtle differentiation between the light bomber and the fighter-bomber. The former is assumed to be an aircraft whose principal rôle is to carry bombs at the time of design and therefore has a rightful place in this work, even though its manœuvrability and gun armament may be such as to be adequate to engage in close combat with opposing fighters (as exemplified by the Mosquito Mark VI). The latter classification is what the term suggests: a fighter on which bombs may be hung so as to provide increased tactical support; such adaptations have been made on almost every fighter produced since the early years of the Second World War, and are described in the Fighter companion to this book.

The same applies to the torpedo-fighter, such as the Beaufighter (the 'Torbeau'), Sea Mosquito, Firebrand and Wyvern, and, for consistency, it is again necessary to regard the torpedo as a 'water bomb', and like the fighter-bomber, these aircraft are regarded as strike *fighters*, and their fortunes when armed with torpedoes are recounted in the Fighter book.

Acknowledgements

Grateful acknowledgement is made to the courteous and long-suffering staffs at the Public Record Office at Kew, and the Royal Air Force Museum at Hendon; their patience and encouragement has been reassuring as one continues to learn of repeated acts of mindless administrative vandalism by captains of industry, and narrow-minded bureaucrats, who dismiss and dispose of the priceless artefacts of our heritage as just so much waste paper. They will know to whom I refer — if the cap fits — and history itself will pass judgement.

Fortunately, there are so many others who go out of their way to assist the historian, and I'd like, in particular, to record my thanks to Roger Hayward, Terry Heffernan, Harry Holmes, Jeff Jefford, George Jenks, David Kamiya, Alec Lumsden, Graham Mottram, Bill Taylor, Rod Taylor and Brian Wexham for their help during the preparation of this book. And I must also express my gratitude to those dozen or so individuals who assisted me in locating original research material relating to that hitherto elusive weapon, the Capital Ship Bomb; it is a pity that space limitations in a book, which has to embrace so many aspects of aviation, have limited me to little more than the briefest commentary on this important, though abortive, project. The helpful advice which I was fortunate to be given, has at least served to place the weapon in its correct perspective — I believe for the first time in published form.

In the important matter of providing photographs for this book, old friends have again come to my rescue, namely Chris Ashworth, Jim Colman, Peter Green, Philip Holmes, Roger Jackson, Derek James, Tim Mason, Eric Morgan, David O'Keane, Alan Park, Bruce Robertson and Ray Sturtivant, as well as a number of former copyright owners, the use of whose pictures is acknowledged. My sincere thanks to them.

Finally, I should express my gratitude to Conway Maritime Press Ltd, and to Julian Mannering in particular, for affording me permission to refer to the wide range of Putnam books whose prestigious record of aviation history is second to none, and to their eminent authors.

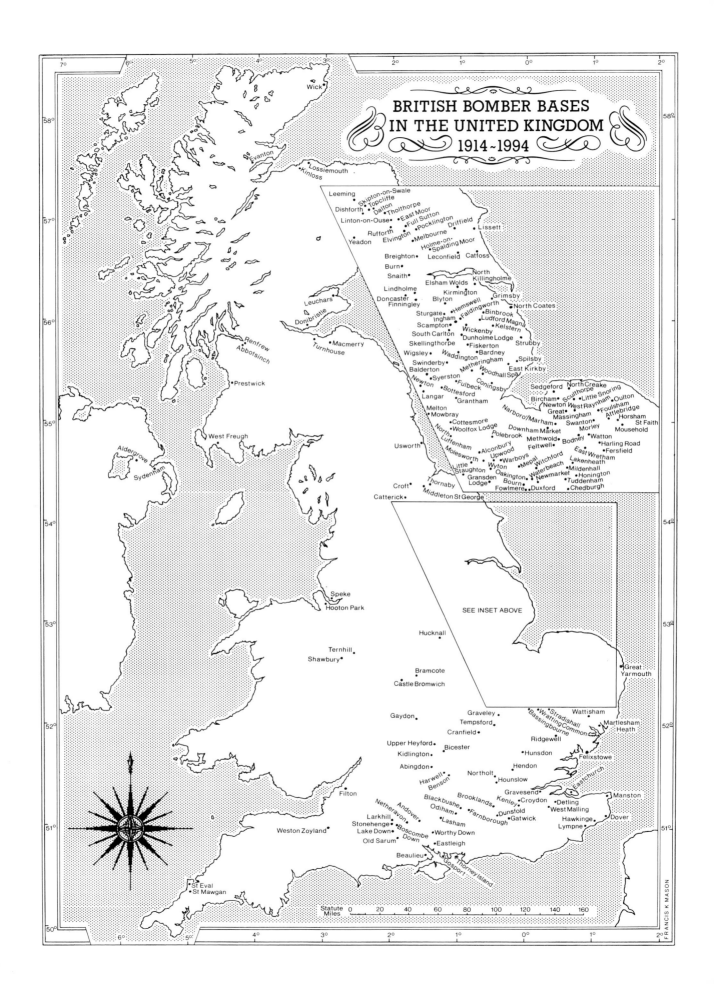

BRITISH BOMBER BASES
IN THE UNITED KINGDOM
1914~1994

1. BOMBER BEGINNINGS

'I hope these new mechanic meteors will prove only playthings for the learned and the idle, and not be converted into new engines of destruction to the human race, as is so often the case of refinements or discoveries in science.'

Letter from Horace Walpole to Sir Joseph Banks, 1783, the year in which a hot air balloon rose aloft in France for the first time bearing human beings.

The delivery of ballistic missiles against an enemy is almost as long established as warfare itself. Furthermore, the indiscriminate involvement of the civilian population does not constitute a prerogative of the twentieth century: siege artillery, notoriously unpredictable in its accuracy, found its origins in the Roman *ballistae*. The history of warfare is littered with examples of wanton vandalism and bloodshed by mankind — made the more horrific by the progressive introduction of black powder, explosives, grapeshot, canister and shrapnel.

It was inevitable that, with the appearance of the flying machine, the military would come to recognise its value as a means of bringing the 'artillery' closer to its target. And, although Count von Zeppelin (1838-1917), experimenting with the very large dirigible during the first decade of the twentieth century, demonstrated the feasibility of carrying explosive weapons over long distances, it was not until the Italo-Turkish War of 1911-12 that the first such weapons were delivered in a small aeroplane against enemy forces in the field when, flying a German Etrich *Taube* on 1 November 1911, Giulio Gavotti released three 4.4lb grenades over a Turkish encampment near Tripoli in Libya.

With the creation of the Royal Flying Corps in 1912, and the establishment of Military and Naval Wings within the Corps, came qualified recognition in Britain of the potential value of aeroplanes in warfare. Simultaneously formed were the Central Flying School, its staff being assembled at Upavon from the former Army Air Battalion, and the Royal Aircraft Factory at Farnborough, Hampshire — formerly the Army Aircraft Factory. The Military Wing was to consist of seven squadrons, each with twelve aeroplanes.

Admirable though the plans for a new aviation Service seemed on paper, no thought had been given to the age-old jealousies that existed between the War Office and Admiralty and, so long as the personnel of each Wing and the procurement of their equipment would be paid for by their respective ministries, joint command of the Corps by the War Office and Admiralty was simply unacceptable to the latter, especially as the Senior Service was, as yet, unable to formulate its own plans for the operational use of naval aeroplanes.

The first recorded 'bombing' trials by a British aeroplane were conducted in March 1912 by the Naval Wing when a number of weighted objects — not bombs *per se* — were carried and dropped at Eastchurch in order to establish the effects their release had on the aircraft's handling and performance. These were followed in 1913 by trials with a Short seaplane (probably an S.41) which was flown over a series of ground explosions produced by charges of different weights to determine the lowest heights at which an aeroplane might release various bombs without suffering damage. The pilots engaged in these trials were Lieut Charles Rumney Samson RN (later Air Cdre, CMG, DSO, AFC, RAF) and Lieut Robert Hamilton Clark-Hall RN (an aircraft armament specialist and later Air Marshal Sir Robert, KBE, CMG, DSO, RAF), both pioneer pilots of the greatest renown in the annals of early maritime aviation.

While the Army persisted in its opinion that the likely value of the military aeroplane would be confined to battlefield reconnaissance, the Admiralty continued to express keen interest in aerial bombing, as well as supporting experiments to mount aerial torpedoes on seaplanes. Short Bros of Eastchurch and the Sopwith Aviation Company were becoming established as the Admiralty's principal aircraft contractors, being joined by J Samuel White of East Cowes and A V Roe & Co of Manchester in 1913. Though not expressly a formal contractor to the Admiralty at that time, the British & Colonial Aeroplane Company of Bristol had been working on a promising aircraft design with obvious military applications, the T.B.8, and it quickly attracted naval attention. This two-seat aeroplane was displayed at the Paris *Salon de l'Aéronautique* in November 1913 equipped with a rotary bomb rack capable of mounting twelve 10lb bombs and with a prismatic bomb sight in the front (observer's) cockpit.

Twelve T.B.8s were ordered for the RFC shortly before the War, but these were diverted to the RNAS, and three accompanied the Eastchurch squadron to Belgium, one of them bombing German gun positions at Middelkerke on 25

Among the most widely used light bombs of the First World War were the 20lb Hales, of which eight are shown here loaded under the wings of a B.E.2E with an RFC Squadron in the Middle East. (Photo:C Huston)

November 1914 with hand-dropped 20lb Hales bombs[1].

The Royal Navy

Returning to the original decision to employ aeroplanes on offensive operations, the Admiralty plans awaited the outcome of trials being conducted by Sidney Vincent Sippe (later Sqn Cdr, DSO, OBE, RNAS) with the Avro Type D seaplane, equipped with floats developed by Cdr O Schwann RN (later Air Vice-Marshal Sir Oliver, KCB, CBE, RAF) at Barrow. During April 1912 these trials confirmed the feasibility of marine aeroplanes with Sippe's successful take-off and flight from seawater, results which immediately suggested all manner of applications to the operations of warships at sea, not least as extensions to their offensive capabilities.

From the outset the Admiralty envisaged seaplanes as being the means of delivering torpedoes against enemy ships, to whose vicinity they would be brought by specially adapted tenders, Indeed, it was a Short 'Folder' — so called on account of its folding wings to facilitate accommodation ashore and aboard ship — flown by Sqn Cdr A M Longmore at Calshot on 28 July 1914, that launched the first torpedo to be carried by a seaplane in Britain[2].

Some months later, floatplanes were produced capable of carrying loads comprising relatively small bombs (often adaptations of naval 6-inch shells with tailfins welded on) as an alternative to the torpedo, the latter in its early form being a weapon that weighed no less than 810lb and, soon afterwards, slightly more than 1,000lb. These aeroplanes came to be termed 'torpedo bombers', a classification that remained in currency for many years.

For the purpose of this work, therefore, it appears logical to regard the torpedo as being a form of bomb whose final journey towards its target is made submerged in water, rather than being a ballistic trajectory.

Although a great deal of work on aerial torpedoes was carried out at the behest of the Admiralty, and relatively large numbers of torpedo bombers came to be ordered and built, scarcely any use was made of their torpedoes by the Royal Naval Air Service during the First World War, and the limited, but surprisingly successful use of the aerial torpedo during the Dardanelles campaign of 1915 was not repeated during the War.

Instead the RNAS, recognising the age-old strategic responsibilities of the Royal Navy, adopted the bomb as the most operationally flexible weapon for use against both ship and shore targets; and aircraft, formerly intended to carry a torpedo, were quickly adapted to make possible the loading of bombs, ranging in weight from 10lb to 112lb.

Meanwhile, the Admiralty had requisitioned and set about converting a number of cross-Channel and Isle of Man steamers (the *Empress, Engadine, Riviera, Ben-My-Chree, Manxman* and *Vindex*) as seaplane carriers, each capable of carrying three or four seaplanes. The world's first aircraft (seaplane) carrier to be completed as such was HMS *Ark Royal*, 7,020 tons, which joined the fleet early in 1915 and could carry up to eight seaplanes. Isolated bombing raids by aircraft from these ships were attempted against enemy land targets, culminating in the attack against Cuxhaven on Christmas Day 1914 which caused no material damage but prompted the Germans to move part of their fleet eastwards through the Kiel Canal to escape further attention by British naval aircraft.

Undoubtedly Charles Samson was the most famous of the British naval pilots of the early war months. As a lieutenant he had pioneered, in a British aeroplane, take-offs from a platform laid over the bows of a battleship in January 1912. Promoted acting commander, he was appointed the first commanding officer of the Naval Wing of the RFC later that year and, after the outbreak of war in August 1914, took the Eastchurch squadron to Antwerp whence a number of offensive sorties was flown by naval airmen. These culminated in the famous attack by Sqn-Cdr Spenser Grey and Flt-Lt Reginald Lennox Gregory Marix against the Zeppelin sheds at Cologne and Düsseldorf on 8 October. Samson commanded a squadron of naval land-planes sent to the Dardanelles, arriving at Tenedos in March 1915, and it was one of these, flown by Samson himself, that dropped the first 500lb bomb on Turkish fortifications — the heaviest such weapon used up to that time.

Indeed, the lack of German shipping targets at sea suggested that a better policy for the RNAS would be to concentrate its offensive efforts on bombing — in effect, strategic bombing — rather than keeping relatively large numbers of torpedo-carrying seaplanes standing by in case enemy ships were sighted at sea. And such bombing attacks, to achieve worthwhile results, implied that not only were larger and more powerful bomb-carrying aircraft needed, but that larger formations should be launched. Even before the end of 1914 the Admiralty had stated its interest in obtaining a large bomber, capable of performing long-duration sorties for both long distance heavy raiding and for extended coastal patrols while carrying a heavy load of bombs, and approached Frederick Handley Page to discuss such an aircraft. Within a year Handley Page, who had shortly before the War begun building a large single-engine aircraft for an attempt to fly the Atlantic non-stop and was well-known for his advocacy of the large aeroplane for carrying heavy loads, produced his O/400 prototype heavy bomber for the Admiralty. In this machine lay the seeds of a true British strategic bomber.

The Army

In contrast to the Admiralty, the War Office failed to appreciate the full potential of the military aeroplane. To many senior staff officers, steeped in the traditions of hand-to-hand fighting and the cavalry charge, aeronautics were a closed book, an innovation worthy of no more attention that that accorded to the handling of observation balloons, bridge building, mining and sapping — the

---

[1] In August 1914 Britain's only aerial bombs amounted to twenty-six Hales 20lb TNT-filled weapons, stocked at Eastchurch. Frederick Marten Hale, born in 1864, was one of the world's leading explosive experts at the outbreak of the First World War, having engaged in the manufacture and testing of high explosives, and in torpedo and artillery research since 1895. He was the inventor of the Hale Rifle Grenade, and his 20lb aerial bombs, patented on 26th January 1914, were the only such weapons available in any quantity to the British and French forces during the first seven months of the War. He also invented the first aerial depth charge for anti-submarine operations in November 1914, and pioneered armour-piercing weapons.

[2] A conflicting claim, attributed to Oswald Short and quoted by C H Barnes in his *Shorts Aircraft since 1900* (Putnam, 1967), is that Gordon Bell made the first successful torpedo drop on the previous evening. J M Bruce, writing in *Aeroplane Monthly*, March 1987, page 149, advances cogent reasoning that Longmore, referring to his own contemporary records, was almost certainly correct in his claim. As Commandant of RNAS Calshot, argues Mr Bruce, he would have been aware of any successful torpedo drop from one of his aircraft on the previous evening.

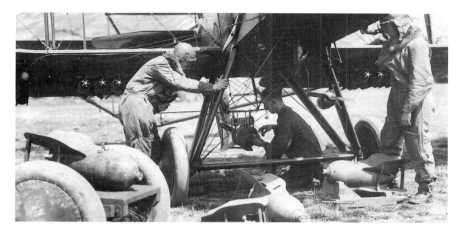

Pilot and observer watch an armourer load a 112lb bomb on their F.E.2B; either six or eight 20lb Cooper bombs are also being carried under the wings. (Photo: via Bruce Robertson).

realms of the Royal Engineers, concerned with supporting the fighting echelons. This attitude persisted, even though many of those fighting men had, at their own expense, learned to fly; yet those men — relatively junior in rank — were among the first to volunteer for transfer to the Royal Flying Corps on its creation in 1912.

Symptomatic of this lack of staff appreciation were the regulations governing the Military Trials of August 1912, held on Salisbury Plain to decide on the best military aeroplane competing under a set of formal operating parameters. Not only did the regulations omit any requirement for a competing aeroplane's military load, offensive or defensive, but they specifically excluded any aeroplane designed under official sponsorship. The declared winner, the Cody biplane, offered not the slightest development potential and already represented an outmoded approach to the flying machine, constituting an impossible liability owing to its fragility and unreliability under military service conditions. Fortunately it enjoyed little further official attention. By contrast, the Royal Aircraft Factory's B.E.2 — designed by Geoffrey de Havilland and therefore excluded from the official results as ineligible — was probably the best all-round aeroplane in the Trials within the narrow limits examined.

In the event it was particularly ironic that it was to be the B.E.2C that, *three years later*, was to be used frequently for tactical support bombing over the cauldron of the Western Front. The lack of attention paid by the War Office during those three years to the provision of operational aeroplanes, capable of carrying guns and/or bombs, and the contrasting appearance of German fighting

scouts (the Fokker monoplanes) over the Western Front in mid-1915, tragically demonstrated for all to see the results of the War Office's dereliction in the years prior to the Great War.

When measured numerically against the carnage suffered by the opposing armies in the trenches of France, the Allied casualties in the air during 1915 were minuscule. Nevertheless, so deep-rooted was the War Office's lack of perception of the real requirements of a fully combat-capable aeroplane that it was not until mid-1916 that such aeroplanes — fighters and bombers — began to carry British insignia into the skies over France. Indeed, the password among those whose job it was to formulate the Army's requirements for operational aeroplanes during 1914 and 1915 was *adaptability*, the application born of necessity of guns and bombs to aircraft not originally conceived with any armament in mind, *whether or not it compromised that aeroplane's chances of survival in air combat.*

As a consequence, aircraft whose performance was unremarkable by the standards of 1915, even without armament, such as the B.E.2C and F.E.2B, had become fatally anachronistic by 1916 when flown with bombs, and were all but powerless to survive when confronted by the German fighting scouts.

That is not to suggest that, when the RFC squadrons were called on to commence bombing attacks as a regular adjunct to their reconnaissance duties over the ground fighting in March 1915, the Army held any significant stocks of aerial bombs. As already stated, the RNAS held the only bombs — just twenty-six 20-pounders — at the beginning of the War. The 20lb Hales weapon was urgently ordered into production, as

were Hales 10lb and 100lb bombs, together with 100lb and 112lb RL weapons (developed by the Royal Laboratory at Woolwich Arsenal). The Royal Aircraft Factory developed a 336lb fragmentation bomb, this being the intended weapon to be carried by the Factory's R.E.7, itself a reconnaissance machine adapted for bombing work. Heavier bombs, such as the 520lb light case and the 550lb heavy case weapons, also appeared before the end of 1915, although these were as yet academic owing to the absence in service of any RFC aeroplane sufficiently muscular to lift them. The RNAS Short Type 184 was still the only aeroplane capable of carrying a bomb heavier than the 336lb bomb just mentioned, although the War Office had taken belated steps to order dedicated bombing aircraft, none of which would enter service until well into 1916.

The one bright glow on the horizon, illusory as it later transpired, emanated from the firm which de Havilland had joined shortly before the War, namely the Aircraft Manufacturing Company at Hendon. He it was who created the D.H.1 and D.H.2 fighters, and now set in train the design of two new bombers, the D.H.3 and D.H.4. These aircraft represented the fruits of original reasoning and, not before time, ended the frustrations of adaptation. Design work on the D.H.3, with which this chapter ends, began in mid-1915 and, by the standards of the day, it was a remarkably proficient aeroplane. Though not speci-fically termed a bomber, it would certainly have been employed as such, had the planned production gone ahead. Even before the first prototype had been completed, however, the War Office stepped in and cancelled its production contract on the grounds that strategic bombing of German industrial towns was superfluous and that, in any case, the twin-engine bomber was impractical, an opinion that disclosed the lack of communication that existed between the War Office and Admiralty — especially so, considering that the Handley Page O/100 was nearing completion for the RNAS!

Bristol T.B.8

It is generally accepted that the first British aeroplane to carry bombs aloft did so in 1914. Only vestiges of circumstantial evidence remain to support claims that the event occurred in the previous year[1]. As explained in the introduction to this chapter, weighted objects had been dropped from a Short aeroplane in 1913 to examine the effects on handling and performance of the aircraft on being suddenly relieved of its warload.

At the British and Colonial Aeroplane Company the Franco-Romanian designer, Henri Coanda, had since 1912 been developing military monoplanes and biplanes for the British and foreign governments, and early in 1913 produced a central-float seaplane, which attracted the British Admiralty's attention. It was, however, to be a land biplane that came to be ordered as the T.B.8, this being converted from a Coanda monoplane and first flown with the naval serial number 43 on 12 August 1913. At the same time a Romanian Coanda monoplane was returned to Filton for conversion to T.B.8 biplane configuration, and returned to Romania in October, equipped with a simple bomb rack. It is not known for certain, however, whether this aeroplane carried a bomb into the air before the end of 1913, although suggestions have been made that it did so.

The success with which the first T.B.8 conversion progressed through its initial trials encouraged British & Colonial to build further examples from scratch, and the first of these was completed with flying controls in the rear cockpit only, the front cockpit being equipped with a prismatic bomb sight and a bomb release trigger. Twelve small bombs of 10lb weight were attached to a cylindrical carrier, located in the lower fuselage immediately forward of the cockpit. Actuation of the trigger released the lowest bomb and automatically rotated the carrier so as to bring the next bomb into the release position. A trip ratchet in the trigger gear enabled

One of the relatively small number of genuine T.B.8 bombers was No 153 which had, prior to its purchase by the Admiralty, displayed a rotating bomb rack and prismatic bomb sight at Paris before the end of 1913. (Photo:A J Jackson Collection, dated January 1914)

the observer to release all twelve bombs as a salvo if desired.

Although this T.B.8 is generally accepted as having flown before the end of 1913 there is no evidence that it had carried bombs, yet it was displayed with full bomb gear at the Paris *Salon de l'Aéronautique* during December. Another example was demonstrated to the French army in March 1914, flying with a 'useful' load of 715lb, suggesting that at least on that occasion the bombs were being carried.

The Admiralty, in the meantime, had purchased the 'Paris' aeroplane which now carried the naval number 153. Shortly afterwards the War Office ordered twelve improved examples, with ailerons in place of wing warping, but these aircraft were transferred to Admiralty charge in October 1914 as Nos 1216-1227.

On the outbreak of war the Eastchurch Squadron, under Squadron Commander Charles Samson, left for France, among its complement of aircraft being a single T.B.8 — the 'Paris'

aeroplane, No 153. This was, however, to be damaged in a gale at Ostend in September, and was returned to Eastchurch the following month. Two other T.B.8s were sent to the Squadron in October, one of them making a bombing attack on German gun batteries at Middelkerke on 25 November 1914.

Although two further orders, each for a dozen aeroplanes, were placed later, the aircraft was deemed to be too slow for further operational use, and it is believed that the above attack was the only offensive sortie flown by the T.B.8. Instead, it was considered to be an ideal 'school' aircraft, and by early 1915 the remaining aircraft were being delivered to RNAS training units at Newcastle-on-Tyne, Gosport and Hendon.

---

[1] A photo survives showing a Coanda B.R.7 biplane at Larkhill, dated July 1913, with a mechanic nearby holding a light bomb; this has been suggested as indicating that the aircraft carried the weapon on that date, but no substantiating record has come to light to indicate that the B.R.7 ever carried a bomb.

Originally ordered as a bomber for the RFC, this T.B.8 was one of those transferred to the RNAS as a trainer. (Photo: GSL/JMB Collection)

Type: Single tractor engine, two-seat, two-bay biplane

Manufacturer: The British & Colonial Co Ltd, Filton and Brislington, Bristol.

Powerplant: One 50 or 80hp Gnome, 60 or 80hp Le Rhône, or 100hp Gnome *mono-soupape* engine.

Dimensions: Span, 37ft 8in; length, 29ft 3in; wing area, 450 sq ft.

Weights: Tare, 970lb; all-up, 1,665lb.

Performance: Max speed, 75 mph at sea level; endurance, 2 hr.

Production: Total Service aircraft built: 41: Admiralty Nos 43, 153, 916 (previously War Office No 620), 948 (previously War Office No 614), 1216-1227, 8442-8453 and 8562-8573.

Summary of Service: T.B.8s served with the Eastchurch Squadron during 1914; as trainers they later served with No 1 (Naval) Squadron at Newcastle-on-Tyne, No 2 (Naval) Squadron at Gosport and the RNAS Training School, Hendon.

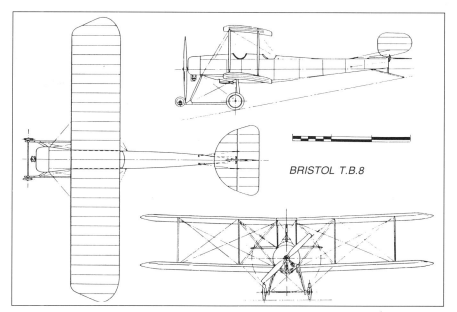

BRISTOL T.B.8

Short Folder Seaplanes

Following the visit by the American pioneer pilot, Wilbur Wright, to Europe in August 1908, the Leysdown-based manufacturer Short Bros acquired the British licence rights to construct a small number of Wright *Flyers* and, during the next four years, embarked on the production of original tractor and pusher aeroplanes to the orders of various British private owners. By 1912 the Board of Admiralty had become sufficiently interested in the potential of the float-equipped seaplanes, which were being advocated by Horace Short, to order a number of Short aeroplanes for the newly-established Naval Wing of the Royal Flying Corps.

Early in 1913 Horace Short drew up and patented a system whereby the wings of his seaplanes could be folded aft, thereby enabling them to be accommodated aboard naval vessels. Thereafter Shorts' Eastchurch works on the Isle of Sheppey became almost exclusively engaged in building a range of twin-float biplanes equipped with two-bay folding wings, the first being allocated the naval serial numbers 81 and 82 (Short S.63 and S.64 respectively), powered by 160hp Gnome engines. Four others, Nos 119-122, entered service at the RNAS Station, Isle of Grain, in May and June 1914.

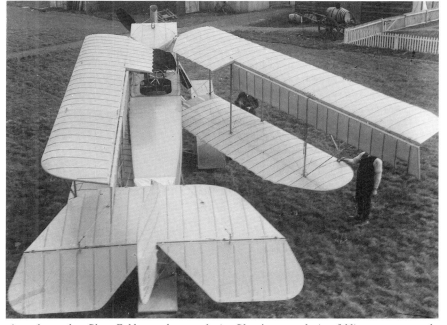

An early two-bay Short Folder seaplane employing Short's patented wing-folding system; note the single-acting ailerons which conveniently permitted the necessary clearance of the tail unit when folded. (Photo: A J Jackson Collection)

Following successful participation by No 81 in naval manœuvres during July 1913, when it operated from HM Seaplane Carrier *Hermes*, Shorts produced three examples of a new version with three-bay wings, Nos 89, 90 and 186, and the last of these was with the Calshot Flight, commanded by Sqn-Cdr A M Longmore, RN (later Air Chief Marshal Sir Arthur, GCB, DSO, RAF), during the Royal Naval Review at Spithead on 18-22 July 1914. Immediately after the

Review, the First Lord of the Admiralty, Winston Churchill, discussed with Longmore the possibility of adapting a Short Folder, No 121, to deliver an aerial torpedo. (The Sopwith Special Seaplane and Type C, see page 19, had been fitted with a 14in naval torpedo some months earlier, but the weapon had not yet been flown by these aircraft.)

Within a week Horace Short had completed the necessary drawings and new cross-beams had been fitted be-

Three-bay Short Folder No 120 at the RNAS Station, Westgate, in about September1914. It had previously been at Calshot where it had been flown on 21 July with a dummy torpedo, weighing little more than 500lb; as far as is known it never flew with the real 810lb weapon, but this was said to have been due to a recalcitrant engine. No 120, carrying bombs and flown by Flt-Lt Arnold John Miley RN, accompanied the raid against Cuxhaven on Christmas Day, 1914. (Photo: via J M Bruce)

tween No 121's floats to enable a torpedo to be carried on crutches, clear of the water, and on 28 July the first torpedo drop by a British aircraft was made by Longmore at Calshot. (Although Longmore reported that he made the first drop on this day, an account, written long afterwards by Oswald Short, claimed that Gordon Bell, the company's staff pilot, had made a drop on the previous evening, albeit only after two attempts to coax the Gnome-Short into the air. (See page 14, footnote 2)

None of the Short Folders was ever used to deliver a torpedo against the Germans after the outbreak of the First World War, although at least two other aircraft were modified to carry the weapon. The Admiralty decided instead to depend on aerial bombs; in any case the Gnome-powered Folder was unable to take off with its second crew member while carrying the torpedo.

Two Folders, Nos 119 and 120 (flown by Flt-Cdr Robert Peel Ross RN [later Air Cdre, DSO, AFC, RAF], and Flt-Lt Arnold John Miley RN [later Gp Capt, OBE, RAF], respectively) accompanied HMS *Engadine* for the bombing attack against Cuxhaven on Christmas Day 1914. Three other Folders, Nos 811, 814 and 815, powered by 100hp Gnome *monosoupape* engines, also took part in this raid (Short Admiralty Type 74, see below).

Nos 120-122 were shipped to Durban in 1915 aboard the armed liner *Laconia* for operations against the German light cruiser *Königsberg*, trapped in the Rufiji delta, but, in the hot humid climate prevailing, proved incapable of taking off with bombs.

Type: Single-engine, two-seat, two- or three-bay biplane torpedo-carrying seaplane.
Manufacturer: Short Brothers, Eastchurch, Isle of Sheppey, Kent.
Powerplant: One 160hp Gnome 14-cylinder rotary engine driving two-blade propeller.
Dimensions: Span, 56ft 0in; length, 39ft 0in; wing area, 550 sq ft.
Weights: Tare, 2,400lb; all-up (with 14in torpedo), 3,830lb
Performance (without torpedo): Max speed, 78 mph at sea level; climb to 3,000ft, 5 min 30 sec; endurance, 5 hr (about 30 min with torpedo).
Armament: No gun armament. Four 112lb bombs or one 810lb Admiralty torpedo.
Prototype and Production: Admiralty No 81, first flown by Cdr C R Samson in July 1913. Total of nine 'Folders' built, Nos 81, 82, 89, 90, 119-122 and 186. No 121 first flown with torpedo by Sqn-Cdr A M Longmore on 28 July 1914.
Summary of Service: Short Folders served at RNAS Stations at Isle of Grain, Westgate and Calshot, and aboard HM Seaplane Carriers *Engadine*, *Empress* and *Riviera*. Three aircraft served with the RNAS detachment to Niororo Island, East Africa, in operations against German light cruiser *Königsberg* in 1915.

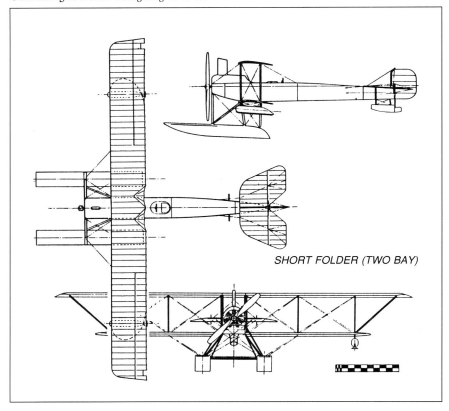

SHORT FOLDER (TWO BAY)

Short Admiralty Type 74

As was a fairly common practice at the time, the Short Admiralty Type 74 Seaplane took its designation from the serial number of a representative production example, in this instance the

first such aircraft completed.

Bearing a marked resemblance to an earlier Short design, the Biplane No 42, though initially with three-bay non-folding wings, the Type 74, No 74, was first flown by Gordon Bell on 4 January 1914, being followed by Nos 75-80 during the next four weeks. Powered by 100hp Gnome ten-cylinder rotary engines, the Type 74 followed the customary Short construction of box-girder fuselage with aluminium nose panels, ply-covered cockpit panels and fabric-covered rear fuselage. However, despite the successful use of double-acting ailerons in earlier aircraft, Shorts reverted to the single-acting type in the Type 74.

These first seven Type 74 seaplanes served with the RNAS at Grain and Dundee during 1914, four of them taking part in the Royal Naval Review at Spithead in July. They were followed by eleven further 100hp Gnome-powered examples, Nos 180, 182, 183 and 811-818 — the latter batch being equipped with folding wings. Unlike the earlier 'Folders', none was converted to lift a torpedo, owing to the lack of engine power; instead they were adapted to carry a pair of bombs, usually of 100lb or 112lb.

Three of the 100hp Gnome Folders, Nos 811 (Flt-Lt C H K Edmonds), 814 (Flt Sub-Lt V Gaskell-Blackburn) and 815 (Flt-Cdr D A Oliver) took part in the raid against the Zeppelin sheds at

Cuxhaven on Christmas Day 1914; however, the pilots failed to find their intended targets, and attacked other installations along the Kiel canal with only limited success.

Type: Single-engine, two-seat, three-bay biplane coastal patrol twin-float seaplane.
Manufacturer: Short Brothers, Eastchurch, Isle of Sheppey, Kent.
Powerplant: One 100hp Gnôme ten-cylinder rotary engine driving two-blade propeller.
Dimensions: Span, 57ft 0in; length, 39ft 0in; wing area, 580 sq ft.
Weights: Tare, 2,100lb; all-up, 2,700lb (without bombs).
Performance: Max speed, 65 mph at sea level; endurance, 5 hr (45 min with light load).
Armament: No gun armament. Bomb load of up to two 112lb bombs carried externally.
Prototype and Production: Admiralty No 74 first flown in January 1914 by Gordon Bell, followed by seventeen similar examples, Nos 75-80, 180, 182, 183 and 811-818 (the last eight with folding wings). Nos 811, 814 and 815 accompanied HM Seaplane Carriers *Arethusa*, *Engadine* and *Riviera* for bombing raid against Cuxhaven on Christmas Day, 1914.

An early Admiralty Type 74, No 76, without folding wings; this type was adapted in 1915 to carry up to a pair of 112lb bombs. (Photo: via J M Bruce)

Sopwith Special (No 170) & Type C

Whether or not Italian pioneering work on aerial torpedo-dropping, dating from 1912, in any way influenced the British Admiralty, has not been positively established. It is, however, recorded that a discussion paper was prepared by Lieut D H Hyde-Thomson RN in 1912, setting down suggested parameters for the use of aerial torpedoes; this was submitted to the Admiralty torpedo establishment and eventually reached Capt Murray Fraser Sueter RN (later Rear-Admiral, CB, MP) of the Air Department at the Admiralty. In 1913, as a direct result of this paper, the Admiralty invited the manufacturers Sopwith, Short and White to produce prototype torpedo-carrying seaplanes. These were to become the Sopwith Special, the Short Type 184 and the Wight Type 840 (listed chronologically — although, by means of adaptation, a Short Folder was to be the first

British aeroplane to air-drop a torpedo, see page 18).

Until relatively recently there has been much confusion regarding early Sopwith torpedo-carrying seaplanes, to some extent caused by surviving company records which suggest that *all* seaplanes ordered by the Admiralty before the First World War, and powered by the 200hp Canton-Unné fourteen-cylinder water-cooled radial engine, mounted horizontally (purchased in France, and later manufactured in Britain as the Salmson 2M.7), were referred to as Type Cs. There was certainly a Short Type C powered thus, but it was not equipped to carry a torpedo. A surviving Sopwith company photograph was captioned to illustrate a large four-bay seaplane with Canton-Unné engine as a Type C aeroplane. The accuracy of this caption had never been questioned until recent research indicated that the photograph in fact depicts the Sopwith Special, No 170, apparently designed by R J Ashfield, an aircraft intended to lift a 14in torpedo weighing 810lb. Indeed, this was the

first British aeroplane designed and built with the specific object of carrying a torpedo.

According to Sqn-Cdr Longmore, commanding NAS Calshot, No 170 arrived on or about 1 July, and was assembled within about five days. Engine runs and some taxying trials, however, disclosed that 'extensive' modifications would be needed before the aircraft would succeed in taking off with the torpedo. To begin with, it was found that the engine was not giving full power, and a new engine was fitted, but even when the torpedo was removed the aircraft still refused to take off. Thus, it was to be the Short No 121 that first took off and launched a torpedo on 28 July.

There is no doubt but that the Short Folder was a superior aircraft and, although the Sopwith Special eventually managed at least one flight with pilot (Flt-Cdr J L Travers), passenger and a full load of fuel on 7 November, it never succeeded in lifting a torpedo. At the end of that month, in a belief that No 170 might be usefully employed as a bomber, the seaplane was being fitted

The photograph of the Sopwith Special Seaplane, referred to in the text and which for many years was said to depict the Sopwith Type C. The aeroplane appears to be moored alongside the Sopwith workshops at Woolston, up-river from Calshot. (Photo: A J Jackson Collection)

with an experimental bomb rack, but it is not known whether it was ever flown with this for, early in January 1915, the Canton Unné engine was being stripped down for inspection at Calshot. At about the end of April the Special was removed from RNAS charge and during the following weeks it was finally dismantled.

Unfortunately very little information of a reliable nature survives about the Sopwith Type C, other than reference to three such aircraft, Nos 157-159, in the RNAS equipment lists; these seaplanes (and the six Short Type Cs, Nos 161-166) were categorised as 'bomb-carriers'

with folding wings, wireless equipment and a defensive gun. However, there is no evidence that the Sopwith Type Cs ever flew with a bomb load and, as they do not appear to have undergone trials with the RNAS at Calshot, there are no surviving records of flight trials.

Type: Single-engine, two-seat, four-bay biplane, twin-float seaplane designed to carry a torpedo.

Manufacturer: The Sopwith Aviation Co Ltd, Kingston-upon-Thames, Surrey.

Powerplant: One 205hp Canton-Unné (Salmson) fourteen-cylinder, water-cooled, radial engine mounted with crankshaft vertical and driving two-blade propeller through extension shaft and gearbox.

Dimensions: Span (upper wing) 66ft; (lower wing) 58ft; length, 36ft; wing area, 785 sq ft.

Weight: Max all-up, 4,324lb (design estimate)

Performance: No records traced.

Armament: Provision to carry one 810lb 14in Whitehead torpedo. No gun armament. (Neither torpedo nor gun believed to have been flown)

Prototypes: Special Seaplane, No 170, first flown during September 1914. Three Sopwith Type Cs are believed to have been constructed (Nos 157-159), but no flight details have been traced.

Short Admiralty Type 135

The absence of a reliable British aero-engine in the 200hp class before the First World War, and the unreliability of the two-row 160hp Gnome, prompted the Admiralty to purchase examples of the water-cooled Canton-Unné radial engines being built under a Swiss licence at the French Salmson factory at Billancourt. Two versions, a nine-cylinder single-row radial of 135hp and a fourteen-cylinder two-row radial of 200hp, were considered, with the object of obtaining a licence for production by the Dudbridge Ironworks at Stroud, Gloucestershire. Accordingly, two Short seaplanes, Nos 135 and 136, were ordered by the Admiralty in 1913, these being powered by the 135hp and 200hp engines respectively; although almost identical, the latter aircraft was slightly the larger.

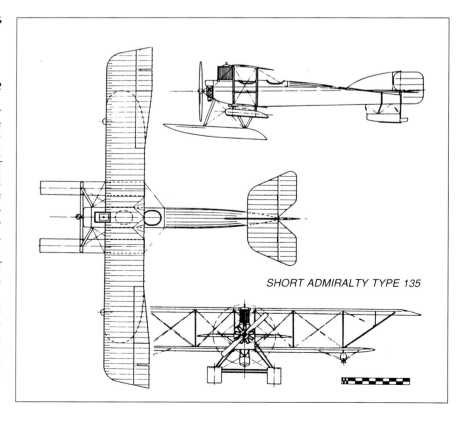

SHORT ADMIRALTY TYPE 135

Anticipating a regular supply of the British-built engines, the Admiralty purchased relatively few of the Salmson engines from France, and no production of these seaplanes — intended largely as engine test-beds — was ordered. (In the event, the first Dudbridge engines did not materialise until 1916, by which time several excellent British engines were being produced.)

Known as Short Admiralty Type 135s, the two prototypes were built at Eastchurch during the spring of 1914, No 135 being delivered to Grain in July; No 136 followed in September. They were two-bay biplanes with strut-braced, extended upper wings incorporating single-acting, inversely-tapered ailerons.

Both aircraft were generally liked by their pilots and, adapted to carry two 112lb bombs each, took part in the Cuxhaven raid on Christmas Day, 1914. No 135 suffered engine failure on its return flight, and was abandoned after

ditching; the pilot, Flt-Lt Francis Esmé Theodore Hewlett RN (later Gp Capt, DSO, OBE, RAF), flying solo, was rescued. No 136 returned safely, flown by Flt-Cdr C F Kilner with Lieut Erskine Childers as observer, having also carried out a reconnaissance of the German Fleet in the Schillig Roads.

No 136 was shipped to the Dardan-

elles aboard the new seaplane carrier, HMS *Ark Royal*, in February 1915 but, after being damaged by enemy gunfire, suffered collapse of its undercarriage on return from a sortie two months later; immersion in the salt water prevented the engine from running reliably there-after.

Type: Single-engine, two-seat, two-bay biplane, twin-float patrol bomber seaplane.
Manufacturer: Short Brothers, Eastchurch, Isle of Sheppey, Kent.
Powerplant: No 135. One 135hp Salmson nine-cylinder single-row water-cooled radial engine. No 136. One 200hp Salmson fourteen-cylinder two-row water-cooled radial engine.
Dimensions: Span, 52ft 0in (No 136, 54ft 6in); length, 39ft 0in (No 136, 40ft 0in); height, 12ft 6in; wing area, 530 sq ft (No 136, 570 sq ft).
Weights: No 135. Tare, 2,700lb; all-up, 3,400lb. No 136. Tare, 3,000lb; all-up, 3,700lb.
Performance: No 135. Max speed, 65 mph at sea level. No 136. Max speed, 72 mph at sea level.
Armament: No gun armament. Normal bomb load either two 112lb or four 65lb bombs carried on underwing racks.
Prototypes: Two, RNAS Nos 135 and 136. No 135 first flown in July 1914, 136 probably in September 1914. Both seaplanes took part in the abortive attacks on Cuxhaven on 25 December; No 135 ditched and was lost, but No 136 accompanied HM Seaplane Carrier *Ark Royal* to the Dardanelles in February 1915. No production.

Shown at Belfort, the three Avro 504 single-seat bombers which attacked the Zeppelin works at Friedrichshafen on 21 November 1914, from left to right, Nos 873, 875 and 874. A fourth, No 179 (flown by Flt Sub-Lt R P Cannon) broke its tail skid and was unable to take part in the raid. Just visible under the fuselage of No 873 are its four 20lb bombs, carried for the attack. (Photo: via J M Bruce)

Avro Type 504 Bombers

Originating in 1913 as a much improved development of the Type 500, the Avro 504 attracted small pre-War orders by both the War Office and Admiralty, the former contracting for twelve aircraft in the summer of that year, and the latter for a total of five aircraft during the months immediately before the out-break of war. A small number of RFC 504s accompanied No 5 Squadron to France, but these were used primarily for reconnaissance and gun attacks on ground targets.

The last four of the pre-War 504s ordered by the Admiralty were not completed, and six War Office aircraft

were transferred to Admiralty charge. Three of these (Nos 873-875) together with the original naval aircraft (No 179) were formed into a special bombing flight and, flying from Belfort in south-east France on 21 November 1914, Nos 873 (flown by Flt-Lt S V Sippe), 874 (Sqn-Cdr E Featherstone Briggs) and 875 (Flt-Cdr John Tremayne Babington, later Air Marshal Sir John Tremayne KCB, CB, DSO), set out to bomb the airship sheds at Freidrichshafen on the shores of Lake Constance. Each aircraft carried four 20lb bombs under the fuselage and several bombs scored direct hits on their target, while another hit the hydrogen plant which blew up, causing extensive damage on the airship station. No 874 was shot down, but the other two 504s returned safely. No 873 later served with No 1 Squadron, RNAS, taking part in two bombing attacks on Ostend early in

1915, and hit two U-boats in a raid on a submarine depot near Antwerp on 24 March that year.

The engine most widely used in the Avro 504 was the 80hp Gnome, and considerable orders were placed for subsequent versions of the aircraft, the 504A being the first major production version for the RFC, though relatively few examples were used as bombers. The much-modified 504B was built in quantity for the RNAS, being most easily identified by its large, unbalanced rudder hinged to a long, fixed dorsal fin. Production of the 504C was undertaken by Avro and the Brush Electrical Engineering company. While the majority of 504 variants were employed as training aircraft, conversions to carry bombs were made on an *ad hoc* basis, and the single-seat 504C was a dedicated anti-airship aircraft, being equipped with a

No 3315 was an Arvo 504C single-seat bomber, built by The Brush Electrical Engineering Co Ltd, Loughborough, and is shown carrying a 65lb bomb under the fuselage. Note the low aspect ratio fin and unbalanced rudder, favoured by the Admiralty on its later 504s. (Photo: The Brush Collection)

Lewis gun and able to carry 20lb or 65lb bombs. In place of the front cockpit, which was faired over, there was an extra fuel tank which enabled the aircraft to remain airborne for up to eight hours. A small number of 504As and Bs served at Aboukir and Imbros, several of these being used occasionally as bombers, but primarily for reconnaissance and coastal patrol.

The Avro 504E, also a naval variant but powered by a 100hp Gnome *monosoupape*, featured cockpits moved further apart to counter the movement of cg caused by installing an extra fuel tank between the cockpits. At least one 504E was equipped to carry light bombs beneath the fuselage, possibly for anti-Zeppelin attack.

Type: Single-engine, two-seat, two-bay tractor biplane modified as light bomber.
Manufacturer: A. V. Roe & Co. Ltd., Clifton Street, Miles Platting, Manchester.
Powerplant: One 80hp Gnome seven-cylinder air-cooled rotary engine driving two-blade propeller.
Structure: All-wood, wire-braced box girder fuselage structure and two-spar wings.
Dimensions: Span, 36ft 0in; length, 29ft 5in; height, 10ft 5in; wing area, 330 sq ft.
Weights: Tare, 924lb; all-up, 1,574lb.
Performance: Max speed, 82 mph; climb to 3,500ft, 8 min 30 sec; endurance, 2 hr.
Armament: No gun armament; bomb load normally comprised up to four 20lb bombs.
Prototype: None. First flight by a bomb-carrying Avro 504 was by Sqn Cdr E. Featherstone Briggs, RNAS, in No 874 during the attack on airship sheds at Friedrichshafen on 21 November 1914; the aircraft was shot down during this flight.
Production: Seven Avro 504s modified for use as bombers by the RNAS, Nos. 179 and 873-878. Served operationally with RNAS. Eastchurch Squadron, Special Bombing Flight, RNAS, and No 1 Squadron, RNAS.

Short Admiralty Type 166

The first purpose-designed torpedo-carrier produced by Shorts was the Admiralty Type 166, which retained the 200hp Salmson engine of the Type 135 and embodied the arched cross-struts between the floats incorporated in the modified Folders to mount the torpedo. The first six production aircraft, Nos 161-166, were just beginning construction at Eastchurch when war broke out on 4 August 1914, just over a week since No 121 had first dropped a torpedo — such was the Admiralty's determination to press ahead with this air-dropped weapon without further delay.

The Type 166 featured Shorts' customary wire-braced wooden box structure in the fuselage and single-acting ailerons were fitted but, unlike the Type 135s, the outer wing extensions were wire-braced by kingposts located im-

No 166 being hoisted outboard from the seaplane carrier Ark Royal *at Mitylene, Greece, in 1916.* (Photo: Imperial War Museum)

mediately above the outboard interplane struts; the two-bay wings were made to fold using the Short patented system, but it had been found that the sloping struts supporting the wing extensions possessed little clearance with the tailplane in the folded position, with a risk of damage; hence the decision to revert to extensive wire bracing with kingposts instead. The Type 166 also introduced a much-enlarged fixed fin, and retained the ungainly vertical radiator block on top of the nose, a feature of most Salmson-powered aircraft and one which would have interfered with the pilot's line of sight during a torpedo attack.

The six Short-built Type 166s were the only examples to give service with the RNAS during 1915 and, as far as is known, were never flown in service with torpedoes. Instead they remained at home naval air stations until, in November that year, five of them were shipped in HMS *Ark Royal* to the Eastern Mediterranean. They were used to good effect, bombing enemy gun batteries at Salonika and spotting for the monitors HMS *Raglan* and *Roberts*. Two of them, Nos 163 and 166, were later converted to landplanes for operations from RNAS Thasos.

By 1916 Short Bros were heavily engaged in production of later aircraft so that, when the need arose for further Type 166s, an order for twenty aircraft (Nos 9751-9770) was placed with Westland Aircraft Works at Yeovil. On completion of the seaplanes they were moved by train to Hamble where they were test flown by Sidney Pickles on behalf of Shorts. Being no longer required to carry torpedoes, these 166s reverted to the straight cross-struts between the floats and, equipped with wireless and armed with a Lewis gun on the rear cockpit, were fitted with racks to carry up to three 112lb bombs. At least one of them, No 9754, was flown as a landplane at Thasos, while another, No 9758, is known to have still been on charge with 'A' Squadron, RNAS, at Thasos in February 1917.

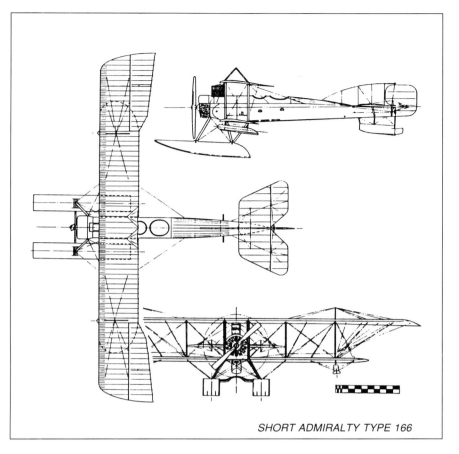

SHORT ADMIRALTY TYPE 166

Type: Single-engine, two-seat, two-bay biplane, twin-float torpedo-bomber reconnaissance seaplane.

Manufacturers: Short Bros, Eastchurch, Kent; Westland Aircraft Works, Yeovil.

Powerplant: One 200hp Salmson fourteen-cylinder water-cooled two-row radial engine.

Dimensions: Span, 57ft 3in; length, 40ft 7in; height, 14ft 0¾in; wing area, 573 sq ft.

Weights: Tare, 3,500lb; all-up, 4,580lb.

Performance (with two 112lb bombs): Max speed, 62 mph at sea level; service ceiling, 8,200ft; endurance, 1¾ hr; max endurance without external load, 4 hr.

Armament: Provision to mount one Lewis gun in rear cockpit. Bomb load of up to three 112lb bombs or one 810lb 14in Admiralty torpedo (the latter not employed operationally).

Prototype and Production: A total of 26 Type 166s was built, Nos 161-166 by Short Bros in 1914-15, and Nos 9751-9770 by Westland during 1916.

Summary of Service: Type 166s served in the bombing rôle with HM Seaplane Carrier *Ark Royal* at Salonika at the end of 1915 and with 'A' Squadron, RNAS, at Thasos in 1916; they also served at RNAS, Calshot.

Short Admiralty Types 827 & 830

As early as 1912 both the War Office and Admiralty had expressed concern that no British engine manufacturer was yet working on an engine which promised high power with reliability. During the following year Louis Coatalen at the Sunbeam Motor Car Company was commissioned by the Admiralty to start on an adaptation of his successful 3-litre racing car engine, producing a V-8 of 150hp (later named the Nubian) and a V-12 of 225hp. The first examples of these engines, roughly equivalent in power and weight to the Salmson nine- and fourteen-cylinder water-cooled radials (which were being purchased in small numbers from France, see page 20), were not ready by the outbreak of war. In anticipation of deliveries, however, the Admiralty had during the early summer of 1914 ordered twelve new seaplanes from Short Bros — similar in most respects to the Type 166; six of them (Nos 819-821 and 828-830), referred to as Admiralty Type 830, were powered by the 135hp Salmson, while Nos 822-827, the Type 827, featured the 150hp Sunbeam Nubian.

By the time these seaplanes were being completed at the end of 1914, the Admiralty was beginning to express a preference for bombs, and neither the Type 827 nor 830 had provision to carry torpedoes. Moreover, despite its slightly inferior performance, it was the Type 827, with its indigenous Sunbeam en-

Left: *An Admiralty Type 827 off the German East African coast, probably one of those sent to Mombasa in July 1915 for operations against the* Königsberg *in the Rufiji delta.* (Photo: via J M Bruce)

Below:*A Type 830, No 1344, at an RNAS Station in Britain.* (Photo: Fleet Air Arm Museum)

gine, that was selected for the greater production, sub-contracts being placed with Brush Electrical Engineering, Parnall and Sunbeam for a total of 72 aircraft, in addition to 30 further examples from Shorts, which switched production from Eastchurch to Rochester.

Following shipboard trials by Nos 824 and 826 with HMS *Campania* in June 1915, Type 827s began delivery to the RNAS Stations at Calshot, Dundee, Grain, Great Yarmouth and Killingholme, being equipped to carry a pair of 112lb bombs for coastal patrol duties.

When Lowestoft and Southwold were shelled by warships of the German High Seas Fleet in April 1916, a Short 827 was among the British seaplanes which attacked the enemy ships with bombs.

Three Short 827s were shipped to East Africa to spot for British naval guns operating against the German warship *Königsberg* trapped in the Rufiji delta, but arrived too late to take part; they were therefore sent on to Mesopotamia where two of them, converted as landplanes with wheel undercarriages, flew bombing attacks on the Turkish forces advancing on Kut in December 1915.

Another epic involved the use of four Short 827s, Nos 3093-3095 and 8219, which were handed over to Belgian volunteers who, in March 1916, were opposing German colonial forces on Lake Tanganyika. Dismantled and transported overland to Lake Tongwe, they were assembled and flown in May, and two months later bombed the German lake cruiser *Graf von Goetzen* in port at Kigoma, leading to the surrender of the town three days later.

At home, Short 827s remained in service until late in 1918.

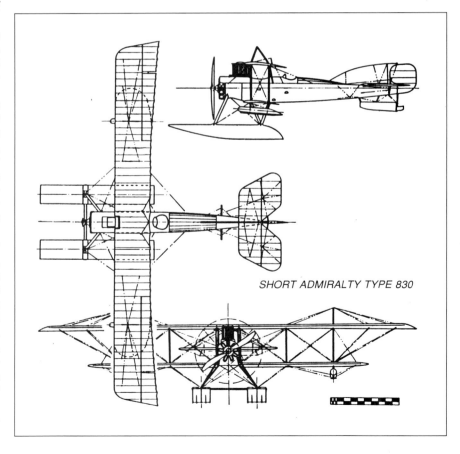

SHORT ADMIRALTY TYPE 830

Type: Single-engine, two-seat, two-bay biplane, twin-float reconnaissance bomber seaplane.

Manufacturers: Short Brothers, Rochester, Kent; The Brush Electrical Engineering Co Ltd, Loughborough; The Fairey Aviation Co Ltd, Hayes, Middlesex; Parnall & Sons Ltd, Eastville, Bristol; The Sunbeam Motor Car Co Ltd, Wolverhampton.

Powerplant: Type 830. One 135hp Salmson water-cooled radial engine. Type 827. One 150hp Sunbeam (later Nubian) eight-cylinder water-cooled in-line engine.

Dimensions: Span, 53ft 11in; length, 35ft 3in; height, 13ft 3in; wing area, 506 sq ft.

Weights: Type 830. Tare, 2,624lb; all-up, 3,324lb; Type 827. Tare, 2,700lb; all-up, 3,400lb.

Performance: Sunbeam. Max speed, 61 mph. Salmson. Max speed, 70 mph; climb to 2,000ft, 10 min 25 sec; endurance, 3½ hr.

Armament: Provision to mount one Lewis gun on rear cockpit. Bomb load of two 112lb or four 65lb bombs carried on underwing racks.

Prototypes and Production: The Type 830 (Salmson) appeared before the Type 827 (Sunbeam), the first 830s being flown and delivered to the RNAS at the end of 1914. Production of the Type 830 was 19 aircraft, all built by Short Bros (Nos. 819-821, 827[1]-830 and 1335-1346). Total of 827s was 107 aircraft: Short, 35 (Nos 822-826, 3063-3072 and 3093-3112); Brush, 20 (Nos 3221-3332 and 8230-8237); Parnall, 20 (Nos 8218-8229 and 8250-8257); Sunbeam, 20 (Nos 8630-8649); Fairey, 12 (Nos 8550-8561).

Summary of Service: Short 827s and 830s served on patrol and bombing duties at RNAS Stations Calshot, Dundee, Grain, Great Yarmouth and Killingholme; others were shipped to East Africa with HM Armed Liner *Laconia*, and operated from *Laconia*, *Himalaya* and *Manica*, flying with No 8 Squadron, RNAS; Short 827s operated in the Mediterranean at Otranto, Italy, and from HM Seaplane Carrier *Ben-my-Chree*.

---

[1] No 827 was test flown with both Sunbeam and Salmson engines; therefore it was at one time a Type 827.

Wight Twins

The boat-building company of J Samuel Wight & Co Ltd, sited in the Isle of Wight at East Cowes, had entered the aircraft manufacturing industry in 1912 with its acquisition of the services of Howard T Wright as designer. By mid-1914 at least three of Wright's seaplane designs had been built and exhibited, and the company had established itself as one of the three prime contractors to the Admiralty.

All the above aircraft were single pusher-engine aircraft, classified as unarmed reconnaissance seaplanes, the last being a large two-seater powered by a 200hp Salmson fourteen-cylinder radial. Seven examples were ordered by the Admiralty, one of which was shipped to the Dardanelles aboard HMS *Ark Royal* in 1915.

Wright's next essay was, for its time, an exceptionally large aeroplane, originally built as a landplane and almost certainly intended from the outset to carry a torpedo or bombs. With five-bay wings spanning 117 feet, the aircraft

This view of the Wight Twin landplane provides a good impression of its great size as well as illustrating the central crew nacelle then included. (Photo: C H Barnes Collection)

featured twin fuselages each with a 200hp Salmson water-cooled radial engine at the front; the two-man crew was accommodated in a small central nacelle. Like the Short aircraft, previously described, the Wight Twin's wings were designed to fold rearwards.

This first Wight Twin suffered an accident early in 1915, resulting in substantial damage to the crew nacelle, engine installations and undercarriage. The company, however, persevered with

the project, producing a twin-float prototype at the behest of the Admiralty — almost certainly employing most of the components of the crashed landplane. The wings evidently remained unchanged, as did the biplane tail unit and long parallel-chord fins with rectangular cutouts between the two horizontal surfaces. The crew nacelle was deleted and a cockpit provided in each fuselage well aft of the wings. The Salmson engine installations were revised to be enclosed within the contours of the front fuselage bays, the two-blade propellers being driven through extension shafts.

Very long three-step main floats were located beneath the fuselages, these being considered of sufficient length to avoid

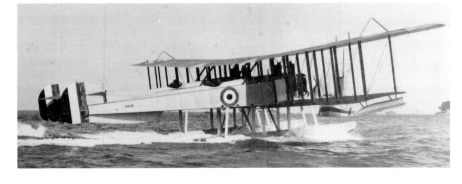

The third Wight Twin, No 1451, showing the two cockpits, set well aft of the wings; note also the wings of unequal span, with kingpost bracing to support the large upper wing overhang. (Photo: GSL/JMB Collection)

The Wight Twin seaplane, No 1451, at East Cowes with an 18in torpedo mounted beneath the lower wing centresection. (Photo: The Royal Aeronautical Society)

the need for tail floats; cylindrical outrigger floats were mounted directly below the outboard interplane struts, and double-acting ailerons were fitted on upper and lower wings.

This aircraft, given the naval serial number 187, was destined from the start to carry a torpedo, contemporary photographs showing it carrying the 1,100lb Admiralty Mark IX weapon beneath the lower centre wing section. It seems likely from these pictures that difficulty would have been experienced in taking off with the torpedo in anything but the calmest water conditions without submersing the tail, and the two further

Wight Twin seaplanes, Nos 1450 and 1451 (ordered in 1915) featured longer float struts so that the aircraft rode higher on the water. The vertical tail

surfaces were completely revised with much smaller triangular fins and long, nearly parallel chord ventral fins.

No 1450 was delivered to RNAS Felixstowe and 1451 to Calshot where torpedo drops were achieved, although it was quickly realised that the aircraft were badly underpowered — being incapable of leaving the water when carrying a torpedo and a full fuel load.

Type: Twin-engine, two-seat, five-bay biplane, twin-float torpedo-carrying seaplane with twin fuselages.
Manufacturer: J Samuel White & Co, East Cowes, Isle of Wight.
Powerplant: Two 200hp Salmson (Canton-Unné) fourteen-cylinder two-row, water-cooled, radial engines driving two-blade tractor propellers through extension shafts.
Dimension: Span, 117ft. Further details of dimensions, weights and performance not traced.
Armament: Provision to carry one Whitehead Mk IX 18in torpedo of 1,100lb nominal weight; no provision for guns.
Prototypes: Three, Nos 187, 1450 and 1451. No 187 was originally completed and flown as a landplane in 1914. Nos 1450 and 1451 underwent Service trials at RNAS Felixstowe and Calshot respectively. No production.

Sopwith Admiralty Type 860

Experience with the early torpedo-carrying seaplanes had demonstrated to two of the three main Admiralty contractors that the smaller Salmson and Sunbeam engines were inadequate to enable torpedo-carriers to lift off the water when carrying full fuel load. After the unsuccessful attempts by the Sopwith Special No 170 to lift a torpedo into the air in August 1914, its manufacturers decided to produce a smaller aircraft, powered by the 225hp Sunbeam (later named the Mohawk). In the meantime Sopwith persevered with another of its seaplanes, No 138 (also powered by a 200hp Canton Unné engine), and on 29 August 1914, flown by Longmore, this machine succeeded in lifting and launching an 810lb torpedo at Calshot.

Continuing frustration with the recal-

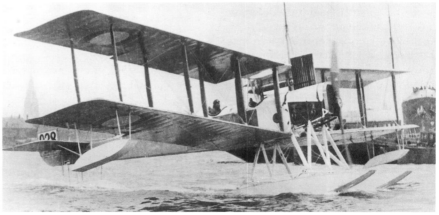

An Admiralty Type 860, No 928 of the second batch, featuring three-bay wings with square tips. (Photo: A J Jackson Collection)

citrant Canton Unné engine encouraged Sopwith to adopt the 225hp Sunbeam, at the time the most powerful engine available to the RNAS; no prototype of the new aircraft was built as such, a total of 22 examples of this aircraft being ordered during the autumn of 1914. All but four were completed between December that year and

early in 1915. The first ten examples were numbered 851-860, and were referred to as Admiralty Type 860s (although confusion was compounded when the RNAS equipment list erroneously referred to them as Type 157s, suggesting that they were a production batch of Sopwith Type Cs). The first flight by a Type 860 with a torpedo was made by

Type 860 No 931 at the RNAS Station, Great Yarmouth in August 1915; this example featured two-bay wings of unequal span, braced by kingposts, curved wing tips, and a rectangular rudder. A suggestion that this machine flew North Sea patrols has not been confirmed. (Photo: Stuart Leslie)

Victor Mahl, a Sopwith pilot, at Calshot on 27 January 1915.

The big Sunbeam engine, driving either a two- or four-blade propeller, featured a frontal radiator and a prominent stack of twelve vertical exhaust pipes extending upwards immediately forward of the upper wing. The single-step main pontoon floats were attached by long struts to the lower fuselage longerons, the 14in torpedo being carried on crutches at the centre of the cross-bars between the floats (when the aircraft was at rest on the water the torpedo was partly submerged). A single tail float was provided, as well as stabilising wingtip floats.

Folding wings of at least three alternative designs appeared on the production aircraft; the original three-bay wings of equal span were fitted with double-acting ailerons on upper and lower surfaces. Some aircraft were fitted with two-bay wings of unequal span with ailerons on the upper wing only; the outboard upper wing extensions were wire-braced with kingposts, but some aircraft featured outwardly raked struts in place of interplane wire bracing. At an early stage in production the fin, originally a small triangular structure, was enlarged to incorporate a curved leading edge. Further redesign resulted in a rectangular fin being fitted.

The Sopwith Type 860 was flown from the rear cockpit, a surprising feature of this aircraft having regard for its torpedo-dropping rôle. The observer's cockpit was located beneath a large aperture in the upper wing centresection, suggesting that it was intended to mount an upward firing Lewis gun — though no evidence has been found to suggest that this was ever fitted, despite being called for in the original Admiralty purchase order.

Production Type 860s are said to have been test flown from the Solent and subsequently served briefly with the RNAS at Grain, though without much distinction. The greater experience gained by Short Bros in numerous aspects of naval seaplane design inclined the Admiralty to favour that company's parallel project, the Type 184 (see page 31), which was to become one of the outstanding British seaplane bombers of the First World War. Certainly the Sopwith aircraft never launched a torpedo in anger.

Type: Single-engine, two-seat, two- or three-bay biplane, torpedo-carrying twin-float seaplane.
Manufacturer: The Sopwith Aviation Co Ltd, Kingston-upon-Thames, Surrey.
Powerplant: One 225hp Sunbeam Mohawk twelve-cylinder, water-cooled, in-line engine driving a two- or four-blade propeller.
Dimensions, Weights and Performance: No records traced.
Armament: Provision to carry one 810lb 14in Whitehead torpedo. Provision may have been made to mount a Lewis gun above the observer's cockpit.
Prototypes and Production: Total of 22 aircraft ordered, Nos 851-860 and 927-938, but four (Nos 833, 834, 836 and 837) not completed. No 851, possibly regarded as the prototype, is believed to have first flown in December 1914.
Summary of Service: At least three Sopwith Type 860s were flown at the RNAS Station, Isle of Grain, in 1915, and two may have been present during the Dardanelles campaign that year.

Air Department Type 1000

The brainchild of the eccentric engineer, Harris Booth, the massive A.D.1000 possessed a wing span only marginally less than that of the Wight Twin, but was certainly much heavier. The Admiralty's Air Department was, in 1914, headed by Capt Murray Fraser Sueter, who had been an influential advocate of the aerial bomb and torpedo, and who gave his authority for the design of a large seaplane capable of carrying a single 810lb 14in naval torpedo or an equivalent weight of bombs.

Booth's design, like Howard Wright's Wight Twin, was of the twin-fuselage configuration, but in other respects differed radically. Unlike the Twin the A.D.1000 was conceived as a seaplane from the outset, and therein lay the likely reason for its manufacture being undertaken by J Samuel White, whose boat-building factory was equipped to handle large craft and possessed slipways to a sheltered anchorage. Moreover, if nothing else, Booth recognised the importance of providing engines of sufficient power for his huge aeroplane (where others had failed), and selected three 310hp Sunbeam twelve-cylinder water-cooled engines — then the most powerful under development. Thus the A.D.1000 theoretically possessed more than twice the power of the Wight Twin.

The A.D.1000 was an all-wooden, four-bay biplane with unequal-span wings, kingposts being used for wire-bracing the upper wing extensions which carried single-acting ailerons; the choice of this layout clearly demanded a very heavy internal wing structure. The big engines were located at the forward ends of the twin fuselages and at the rear of the central nacelle. The latter structure also accommodated the five-man crew,

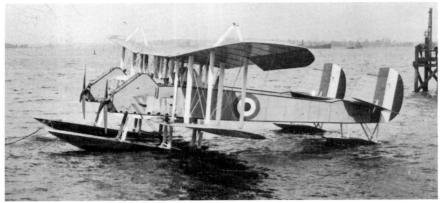

The A.D. Type 1000, No 1358, moored at East Cowes in 1915. Unlike the Wight Twin seaplane, which abandoned the central crew nacelle, the Type 1000 retained this extraordinary structure until the aircraft was broken up. (Photo: via Stuart Leslie)

its nose resembling a domestic conservatory with upwards of forty panes of glass, and no concession to drag limitation. The torpedo or bomb load was to be suspended from the lower wing which passed beneath both the fuselages and the central nacelle. The twin main floats were attached by struts to the lower longerons of the fuselages, as were the twin tail floats. There was little to suggest that this float gear would have been adequate to support the enormous machine on any but the calmest water.

The A.D.1000 was completed at Cowes in the spring of 1915, but was never flown. The Sunbeam engines (later to become the Cossack) were installed with their four-blade propellers. At that time, however, the engines had never flown, and doubt must have been expressed about the efficiency of the cooling system and its extraordinarily cumbersome radiator installation, to say nothing of the float structure's strength. The aircraft was transported to Felixstowe and was almost certainly broken up there in 1916.

Type: Four-bay, five-crew bomber/torpedo-bomber biplane seaplane with one pusher and two tractor engines, central crew nacelle, twin main floats and twin tail floats.
Manufacturer: J. Samuel White & Co. Ltd., Cowes, Isle of Wight, to the design of Harris Booth of the Air Department, Admiralty.
Powerplant: Three 310hp Sunbeam (later named Cossack) 12-cylinder water-cooled in-line engines driving four-blade propellers, two driving tractor propellers at the front of the twin fuselages, and one driving a pusher propeller at the rear of the central crew nacelle.
Dimensions: Span, 115ft.
Armament: Designed to carry a bomb load of approximately 800lb, or one 810hp 14in Admiralty torpedo.
Prototype: Seven examples ordered, but only one, No 1358, completed and delivered to Felixstowe, but not flown. No production.

Royal Aircraft Factory R.E.5 and R.E.7

Despite the reluctance of the War Office to recognise aerial bombing as a prescribed rôle for the aeroplane in service prior to the First World War, the fact that no such rôle was undertaken regularly by the RFC in France during 1914 was attributable as much to the absence of suitable aircraft as to the absence of any significant stock of aerial bombs. Indeed, the only stock amounted to twenty-six 20lb Hales bombs held by the RNAS at the outbreak of War. It is true that the Bristol T.B.8 had been ordered for the RFC, ostensibly as a bomber, but this order was transferred to the RNAS when war was declared.

The first aircraft considered as adequately powerful to lift pilot, fuel and bomb(s) was the Royal Aircraft Factory's R.E.5, by 1914 a promising member of the 'Reconnaissance Experimental' category of aircraft that had originated in 1912 as a derivative of the B.E.2. The latter aircraft, in its developed forms,

A standard R.E.5, powered by a 120hp Austro-Daimler engine driving a four-blade propeller, and with wings of equal span. (Photo: Real Photographs Co, Neg No 807)

also came to carry bombs as a matter of necessity early in 1915 (see page 34), and the only reason that in this work the R.E.5 ante-dates the B.E.2 lies in the work carried out during 1914 to examine the likelihood of the R.E.5 being capable of carrying bombs in service, although the distinction of it being the first to do so is extremely tenuous.

The R.E.5, like its immediate predecessor, the R.E.3, was powered by the 120hp Austro-Daimler water-cooled in-line engine, and was ordered into production by the War Office 'off the drawing board' in December 1913, the cost of the 24 aeroplanes (less engines) being subscribed by a windfall payment by the Admiralty in return for the transfer of all Army airships to the Navy at that time. Thus the R.E.5 was among the first Factory aircraft actually built in quantity at Farnborough, instead of

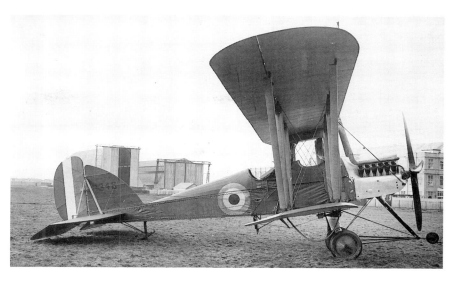

R.E.7, No 2348, in standard form powered by a 150hp R.A.F. 4A engine, and featuring twin cockpits. What appears to be a 20lb bomb may be seen under the starboard wing. This aeroplane was later modified with a third cockpit and provision to carry the 336lb bomb (see the photograph on page 30). (Photo: Royal Aerospace Establishment, Neg No 1049 dated 8 January 1916)

being subcontracted to a commercial manufacturer.

The first R.E.5 (there was no prototype *per se*) was completed before the end of January 1914, being a two-bay, two-seat biplane with equal-span wings; construction was of mixed metal tube and spruce with fabric covering. Ailerons were fitted to upper and lower wings, and the unbalanced rudder was hinged to a triangular fin; a conventional twin wheel and skid undercarriage was standard.

The 5th, 6th, 12th and 13th aircraft were completed as single-seaters with upper wings extended in span to 57ft 2½in, the large tip overhang being braced by additional outward-raked pairs of interplane struts. These aircraft were often referred to — though unofficially — as R.E.5As and were intended for high altitude work, and Norman Spratt, a Factory pilot (later Gp Capt, RAF), climbed No 380 to a height of 18,900 feet on 14 May 1914.

Beardmore-built Austro-Daimler engines with strengthened crankshafts proved to be more reliable than the imported examples, and an R.E.5 thus powered was retained by the Factory to investigate the carriage of bombs, and was flown with various loads of jettisonable weights for investigation of performance penalties and effects on handling. Although these trials were performed before the War, they were largely academic for, as already stated, real bombs were in acutely short supply.

By the outbreak of war about 15 R.E.5s and 5As had been completed, and a few of these accompanied the RFC squadrons to France. One example, allocated to the RNAS, was flown to Dunkerque by Sqn-Cdr A M Longmore on 27 September. Three days later Longmore carried out a bombing attack on Courtrai railway station but, as the aircraft was without bomb racks, Long-more's observer carried the small, improvised French bombs in his cockpit, dropping them over the side when above the target!

As far as can be determined, RFC R.E.5s did not fly true bombing sorties until 26 April 1915, when a pair of these aircraft from No 7 Squadron, accompanied by seven B.E.2Cs of No 8 Squadron, flying from St Omer, set out to attack German troop trains near Ghent. Thereafter such attacks became fairly commonplace (though the first regular bombing attacks by RFC aircraft had in fact commenced a month earlier, see the B.E.2C, page 34). In the course of one R.E.5 attack on 31 July, Capt John Aidan Liddell of No 7 Squadron was mortally wounded in the thigh by ground fire. His aircraft was hit and dropped out of control, the throttle and control wheel being smashed. In great pain, Liddell managed to regain control and crash landed on a Belgian aerodrome, thereby saving the life of his observer. Liddell was awarded the Victoria Cross, only to succumb to his wounds shortly afterwards.

The R.E.7

R.E.5s continued in limited operational service until the autumn of 1915, by which time most of the survivors from the original batch of 25 aircraft were being relegated to training duties. A new version, the R.E.7, was coming into service, an aircraft that retained the big Beardmore engine and took no significant account of performance advances made by other in-service aircraft since the beginning of the War.

However, stemming largely from pre-war work done to determine the bomb-carrying potential of the R.E.5, already referred to, the R.E.7 was intended from the outset to carry a single 336lb bomb, designed and developed at the Royal Aircraft Factory. This bomb, which was

first flown experimentally on an R.E.5A, was 4ft 11½in long, and was classified as a heavy case (HC) weapon, containing only 70lb of compressed or cast TNT.

Unlike the R.E.5, all R.E.7s were contract-built by commercial manufacturers, namely the Austin Car Company, the Coventry Ordnance Works, D Napier & Sons and the Siddeley-Deasey Motor Car Company, a total of 252 being built. The aircraft featured the long-span upper wings of the R.E.5A, and first reached No 21 Squadron in July 1915, then forming at Netheravon. In September that year No 12 Squadron, already flying B.E.2Cs and R.E.5s at Natheravon, received in addition a few R.E.7s and moved to St Omer on the 6th.

Owing to delays in manufacturing the Factory's 336lb bomb, No 12 Squadron's R.E.7s were flown as escort fighters but, with the observer/gunner occupying the front cockpit beneath the upper wing, were quickly found to be quite unable to counter the new German Fokker monoplane scouts, then in full cry over the Western Front.

When No 21 Squadron brought its full complement of R.E.7s to France in January 1916, both it and No 12 were transferred to special reconnaissance work in preparation for the major Allied offensive which was to be launched on the Somme in July that year.

As No 12 Squadron gave up its R.E.7s to re-equip with F.E.2Bs, No 21 received new R.E.7s powered by the 150hp R.A.F. 4A — an engine that was some 100lb lighter than the Beardmore — and in June began operations with the 336lb bomb, flying from Fienvillers. During the period between 30 June and 9 July the Squadron flew 29 bombing sorties,

R.E.7 No 2348 after modification as a three-seater and carrying the 336lb bomb. The aircraft also appears to have reverted to the 160hp Beardmore engine. (Photo: Royal Aerospace Establishment, Neg No 7644 dated 8th August 1916)

each with the big bomb, against targets at St Sauveur, Bapaume and Cambrai, often with spectacular results. On at least two other occasions the R.E.7s each carried two 112lb and six 60lb bombs.

Despite these belated successes the bombing career of the R.E.7 was destined to be shortlived, and in August No 21 Squadron, the only operational unit to be fully equipped with the type, was withdrawn from operations to re-equip with the B.E.12. The great majority of R.E.7s were retained at home for training purposes. Some attempts were made to improve their performance, and among the engines experimentally fitted for this purpose were the 190hp Rolls-Royce Falcon and the 250hp Rolls-Royce III. Two aircraft, Nos 2299 and 2348 (built by Napier and Siddeley-Deasey respectively) were modified as three-seaters, with an extra cockpit with Lewis gun mounting added aft of the pilot in an effort to improve the aircraft's ability to defend itself. Predictably the extra weight of gun and gunner only served to reduce the aircraft's very poor performance yet further.

The truth had yet to dawn on the War Office in early 1916 that engines of greatly improved power/weight ratios were essential if bomb loads of effective powers of destruction were to be carried by aircraft with the slightest chance of survival in the face of superior enemy fighters.

The accompanying table refers to the R.E.7.

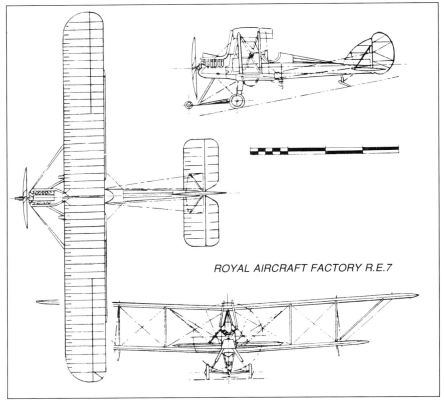

ROYAL AIRCRAFT FACTORY R.E.7

Type: Single-engine, two-seat, two-bay biplane corps reconnaissance bomber.

Manufacturers: The Austin Motor Co (1914) Ltd, Northfield, Birmingham; The Coventry Ordnance Works Ltd, Coventry; D Napier & Sons Ltd, Acton, London; The Siddeley-Deasy Motor Car Co Ltd, Park Side, Coventry.

Powerplant: One 120hp Beardmore; 160hp Beardmore; 150hp R.A.F. 4A. Experimental installations: 190hp Rolls-Royce Falcon; 250hp Rolls-Royce Mk III (284hp Eagle III); 200hp R.A.F.3A; 225hp Sunbeam.

Dimensions: Span, 57ft 2in; length 31ft 10½in; height, 12ft 7in; wing area, 548 sq ft.

Weights: 160hp Beardmore. Tare, 2,285lb; all-up, 3,290lb. 150hp R.A.F. 4A (with 336lb bomb). Tare, 2,170lb; all-up, 3,449lb. 190hp Falcon. All-up, 3,280lb.

Performance: 160hp Beardmore. Max speed, 91 mph at sea level,

83 mph at 10,000ft; climb to 10,000ft, 31 min 50 sec. 150hp R.A.F.4A (with 336lb bomb). Max speed, 85 mph at sea level. Service ceiling, 6,500ft. Endurance, 6 min.

Armament: Standard aircraft were provided with a single 0.303in Lewis machine gun on the front cockpit. Capable of carrying one 336lb R.A.F. bomb, or two 112lb and four 20lb bombs.

Prototype: None. First production aircraft probably first flown in May-June 1915.

Production: A total of 252 R.E.7s was built: Coventry Ordnance Works, 50 (Nos 2185-2234); Austin, 52 (Nos 2235-2286); Napier, 50 (Nos 2287-2336); Siddeley-Deasy, 100 (Nos 2348-2447). Nos 2241, 2242, 2260 and 2364 were transferred to the RNAS.

Summary of Service: R.E.7s served with Nos 12 and 21 Squadrons, RFC, over the Western Front during 1915-16, and with Nos 6,9,19, 37, 38, 49 and 60 Squadron, RFC, in the United Kingdom between 1915 and 1917.

Short Admiralty Type 184

The launching of the original Short Admiralty Type 184, No 184, at Rochester in March 1915, with a 14in torpedo in position between the floats. (Photo: via R C Sturtivant)

When approached by the Admiralty's Air Department in September 1914 to tender proposals for a torpedo-carrying seaplane powered by the 225hp Sunbeam engine (as were Sopwith and J Samuel White), Horace Short proposed submitting a development of his abortive 1913 Circuit of Britain seaplane, which had been withdrawn owing to a lack of power from its 100hp Green engine. Within a few months two prototypes, Nos 184 and 185, were ordered from Short Bros.

The Short Admiralty Type 184 was not significantly larger than the former aircraft but, with more than twice the power available, could be strengthened considerably so as to lift a much greater weight. The equal-span, three-bay wings were of high aspect ratio and featured large-area, single-acting ailerons on the upper surfaces only. The wing folding arrangement was improved, the entire folding and locking operation being carried out by the pilot in his cockpit by means of a hand-operated winch and lever-controlled locking bar in the rear

fuselage. The fuselage structure was the customary four-longeron box-girder of spruce members with wire bracing, the longerons extending forward to the front of the engine which itself was carried on pressed-steel cross frames.

The sprung floats were not mounted directly on the attachment struts but were slotted so as to ride vertically relative to the front and rear cross-members, being retained by stout elastic cords. Wingtip and tail floats were fitted, the latter including a small water rudder linked to the main rudder, this being a balanced surface with large fin.

The upper wing was inversely tapered from the aircraft centreline to two-thirds of semi-span, and of parallel chord outwards thereafter; the lower wing was entirely of parallel chord. Apart from the front fuselage, the whole airframe was fabric-covered.

An evaluation batch of ten further Short 184s was ordered before the prototypes flew in about March 1915. Early flights by Nos 184 and 185 disclosed the need to improve the lateral control, the large-area single-acting ailerons making the seaplanes almost unmanageable while taxying downwind, with the result that rubber cords were fitted to retain the ailerons in the neutral position, except when actuated by the pilot; this did not prove to be a complete remedy, and ailerons were then added to the lower wings, being connected to the upper surfaces by cables. Trials with bombs and torpedoes were also carried out, and

Standard Short-built Short Type 184 No 8076 with 240hp Sunbeam engine, illustrating the manner of carrying the bomb load of four 100/112lb bombs on a centreline beam. Unlike the early examples, this aircraft has double-acting ailerons. (Photo: GSL/JMB Collection)

Sage-built Improved Type 184, N1616, powered by a 260hp Sunbeam engine, probably at Newlyn, seen with a pair of 100/112lb bombs — often carried during coastal patrol sorties. (Photo: GSL/JMB Collection)

No 184 was at some point fitted with an unbalanced rudder, although this is said to have been 'an improvisation rather than a modification'.

Meanwhile, conversion of a number of Isle of Man packet steamers into seaplane carriers had been put in hand, and on 21 May 1915 one of these, *Ben-my-Chree*, sailed from Harwich for the Dardanelles with the two Short 184 prototypes embarked (as well as a spare airframe, unassembled, and two Sopwith Schneiders), arriving at her destination on 12 June. On 12 August Flt-Cdr Charles Humphrey Kingsman Edmonds (later Air Vice-Marshal, CBE, DSO, RAF), flying solo in No 184, torpedoed and sank a Turkish transport off Gallipoli — only to be told that the ship had already been damaged by a submarine; five days later this pilot torpedoed another Turkish transport, leaving it on fire, and on the same day Flt-Cdr George Bentley Dacre (later Air Cdre, CBE, DSO, RAF), flying No 186, had to alight in the Straits with a failing engine; however, he sighted a large enemy tug, which he torpedoed while taxying on the water. He was then able to fly back to *Ben-my-Chree*.

These were the only successes with torpedoes achieved by Short 184s, principally on account of the difficulty they had in taking off with a heavy load in the hot, humid conditions of the Aegean. Instead, the seaplanes were employed, like the other Shorts, in bombing and gunnery spotting work. For the former, bombs were carried in tandem on a long beam attached beneath the fuselage which incorporated shackles for up to four 65lb or two 100/112lb bombs; with these

loads the 184 could at least carry a two-man crew aloft as well as a somewhat greater fuel load. Indeed, on 8 November 1915 Edmonds and Dacre bombed a railway bridge at Maritza in Bulgaria, a round trip of over 200 miles.

By this date, and probably encouraged by the isolated achievements of the Short 184s in the torpedo attack rôle, the Admiralty had placed what were, for the time, large orders for the aircraft. However, Shorts became fully extended after receiving a contract for 75 aircraft, and further orders, totalling 78 Type 184s, were placed with five other manufacturers. In addition to twelve ordered from Mann, Egerton of Norwich, a further ten two-bay derivatives of the basic Short 184 were built as the Mann, Egerton Type B (see page 71).

At about this time it was a Short 184 that first dropped a 500lb bomb during trials with the Short-built No 8052. On 8 May 1916 this weapon was dropped at Kingsnorth from 4,000 feet using a special bombsight designed by Lieut R B Bourdillon and Henry Thomas Tizard (later Sir Henry, GCB, AFC, FRS); it is said that the redoubtable Cdr C R Samson was the pilot on this occasion, before being posted to the Mediterranean.

In June 1916 Cdr Samson was given command of *Ben-my-Chree* as well as two smaller seaplane carriers, *Anne* and

Raven II, for operations in the Eastern Mediterranean. Realising that the Shorts of his small force were severely handicapped by the need to operate only in the cooler temperatures of the early morning and late evening, Samson had one of his aircraft extensively modified by reducing the lower wing span, removing the outboard interplane struts, replacing the cylindrical wingtip floats by small planing hydrofoils, and reducing the tail fin area. Samson, who claimed that these modifications resulted in a seven-knot speed increase, was ordered to Aden to locate and destroy the German raider *Wolf* at large in the Indian Ocean early in 1917. The modified Short made numerous search patrols until, at the end of March that year, the floats collapsed in a heavy swell and the seaplane sank.

Short 184s were despatched to Mesopotamia in February 1916 to serve with an RNAS detachment operating from the Tigris at Ora; at one time they were used to drop supplies to the beleaguered garrison at Kut, each aircraft being loaded with about 200lb of containers.

In home waters 184s flew many patrols over the Channel and North Sea, and HM Seaplane Carrier *Engadine* embarked two Short 184s with the Battle Cruiser Squadron prior to the Battle of Jutland on 31 May 1916. One of the Shorts, flown by Flt-Lt F J Rutland RN, with Asst Paymaster G S Trewin RN, as observer, was used to shadow an enemy force of light cruisers and destroyers, their position and course being transmitted back to the British fleet. This was history's first occasion on which an aeroplane was used in a major fleet action.

No 8073 was a 'Dover' Type 184, originally built by Shorts and modified as a single-seat bomber. Up to nine 65lb bombs could be carried, suspended vertically in the space normally occupied by the front cockpit. (Photo: Stuart Leslie)

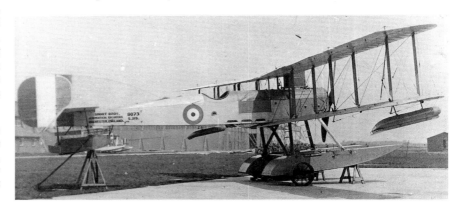

Type: Single-engine, two-seat, three-bay biplane, twin-float torpedo-bomber patrol seaplane.

Manufacturers: Short Brothers, Rochester, Kent; The Brush Electrical Engineering Co Ltd, Loughborough; Mann, Egerton & Co Ltd, Prince of Wales Road, Norwich, Norfolk; The Phoenix Dynamo Manufacturing Co Ltd, Bradford; Robey & Co Ltd, Lincoln; Frederick Sage & Co Ltd, Peterborough; S E Saunders Ltd, East Cowes, Isle of Wight; The Supermarine Aviation Works Ltd, Woolston, Southampton; Westland Aircraft Works, Yeovil, Somerset; J Samuel White & Co Ltd, Cowes, Isle of Wight.

Powerplant: One 225hp, 240hp or 260hp Sunbeam engine; 275hp Sunbeam Maori III; 300hp Sunbeam Manitou; 250hp Rolls-Royce (Eagle IV); 240hp Renault.

Dimensions: Span, 63ft 6¼in; length, 40ft 7½in; height, 13ft 6in; wing area, 688 sq ft.

Weights: Standard Type 184. Tare, 3,500lb; all-up, 5,100lb. Improved Type 184. Tare, 3,703lb; all-up, 5,363lb.

Performance: Standard Type 184. Max speed, 75 mph at 2,000ft. Improved Type 184. Max speed, 88 mph at 2,000ft; climb to 2,000ft, 8 min 35 sec; service ceiling, 9,000ft; endurance, 2¾ hr.

Armament: Single Lewis gun on rear cockpit, later provided with Scarff or Whitehouse ring mounting. A 810lb 14in torpedo could be carried between the floats, or a bomb load comprising one 520lb or 500lb bomb, four 112lb or 100lb bombs or one 264lb and one 100lb bomb carried on external racks; single-seat bombers could carry nine 65lb bombs internally.

Prototypes: Two, Nos 184 and 185, both probably first flown at Rochester in March 1915; both flown operationally at the Dardanelles.

Production: A total of 944 Short 184s, excluding prototypes, was built: Short, 115 (Nos 841-850, 8031-8105, N1080-N1099 and N1580-N1589); Brush, 190 (N1660-N1689, N2600-N2659, N2790-N2819, N9060-N9099 and N9260-N9289); Mann, Egerton, 22 (Nos 8344-8355 and 9085-9094[1]); Phoenix, 62 (Nos 8368-8379, N1630-N1659 and N1740-N1759); Robey, 256 (Nos 9041-9060, N1220-N1229, N1260-N1279, N1820-N1839, N2820-N2849, N2900-N2949, N9000-N9059, N9140-N9169 and N9290-N9305); Sage, 82 (Nos 8380-8391, 9065-9084, N1130-N1139, N1230-N1239, N1590-N1599 and N1780-N1799); Saunders, 80 (Nos 8001-8030, N1140-N1149, N1600-N1624 and N1760-N1774); Supermarine, 15 (N9170-N9184); Westland, 12 (Nos 8356-8367); White, 110 (1240-1259, N2950-N2999 and N9100-N9139). Orders for 159 further aircraft were cancelled at the end of the War.

Summary of Service: Short 184s operated from the following seaplane and aircraft carriers: HMS *Ark Royal, Anne, Ben-my-Chree, Campania, Empress, Engadine, Furious, Nairana, Pegasus, Raven II, Riviera* and *Vindex,* and from HM Light Cruisers *Arethusa* and *Aurora.* They also served in the bombing, coastal patrol and anti-submarine rôles at the following RNAS Stations in the United Kingdom: Westgate (becoming No 219 Squadron, RAF, on 1 August 1918), Dover (No 233 Sqn), Newlyn (No 235 Sqn), Cattewater (Nos 237 and 238 Sqns), Torquay (No 239 Sqn), Calshot (No 240 Sqn), Portland (No 241 Sqn), Newhaven (No 242 Sqn), Fishguard (No 245 Sqn), Seaton Carew (No 246 Sqn), Hornsea Mere (No 248 Sqn), Dundee (No 249 Sqn), and Bembridge (No 253 Sqn); and overseas at Alexandria, Egypt (Nos 202, 269 and 270 Sqns), Oudezeele, France (No 229 Sqn), Cherbourg, France (No 243 Sqn), Otranto, Italy (Nos 263 and 271 Sqns), Suda Bay, Crete (No 264 Sqn), Gibraltar (No 265 Sqn), Mudros, Aegean (No 266 Sqn) and Kalafrana, Malta (No 268 Sqn). They served on the East Indies Station, and with the RNAS Detachment, Basra, Mesopotamia, as well as the Torpedo Training School, Felixstowe.

([1]) The latter batch of ten aircraft, being modified to the design of Mann, Egerton as Type B aircraft, is also listed under the entry for the Mann, Egerton Type B, see page 71.

General recognition that the Type 184 was a fundamentally sound aeroplane and popular with its crews, so long as it was required to fly in no more than fairly docile weather and water conditions, prompted the Admiralty to pursue development of the aircraft with progressively more powerful engines. Some aircraft were fitted with the 240hp Sunbeam, while one example, Short-built No 8104, was powered by a 250hp Rolls-Royce Eagle, but no wartime production with the latter engine followed (although some aircraft, supplied to Estonia after the War, were so powered). Short 184s also appeared in production with 240hp Renault 12-cylinder water-cooled in-line engines, and some were powered by the 275hp Sunbeam Maori III. However, the best and most popular version was said to be the 260hp Sunbeam Maori I-powered Dover Type 184, so called on account of it being used primarily at the Dover Patrol stations at Newhaven and Cherbourg. The engine installation of this version featured a flat frontal honeycomb radiator immediately behind the propeller. Full-travel, double-acting ailerons were fitted on upper and lower wings, and wingtip floats of improved shape were intoduced.

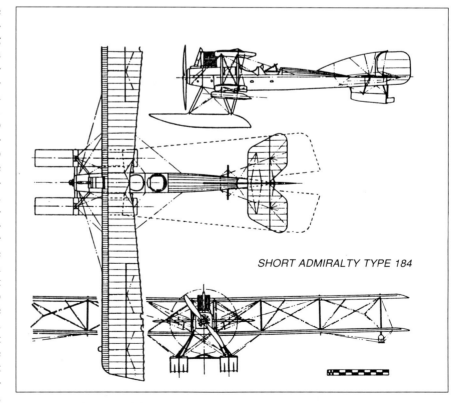

SHORT ADMIRALTY TYPE 184

When rigged with Rafwires throughout, in place of stranded cables, the aircraft was officially referred to as the Improved Type 184, and was the subject of late production orders.

The Short Type 184 remained in

service after the Armistice (even though 159 aircraft were cancelled at the end of the War), being widely used for mine-spotting over coastal waters, and a small number was embarked in the carrier HMS *Pegasus* for service at Archangel in 1919. A few were sold to Chile, Estonia, Greece and Japan.

Royal Aircraft Factory B.E.2C/E Bombers

A B.E.2C single-seat bomber of No 2 Wing, RNAS, at Imbros. This aeroplane, shown carrying 20lb Hales bombs on racks under the engine and fuselage amidships, was the first to bomb Constantinople, flying from Imbros. The identity of the two naval pilots is not known. (Photo; via J M Bruce)

It has been shown that by the end of 1914 the RNAS had deployed a number of seaplanes capable of carrying bombs or torpedoes, and had already demonstrated its ability to strike targets with the relatively small bombs then at its disposal, although as yet no success had attended the use of the aerial torpedo.

In France the RFC with the British Expeditionary Force was deployed in the field with a heterogeneous collection of aircraft whose pilots were charged with general reconnaissance duties over and immediately beyond the German lines. None of the aircraft hitherto built under War Office contracts had been equipped to carry bombs.

The onset of aerial combat in the skies over the Western Front during the winter of 1914-15, rudimentary as it was in both tactics and weapons, was but an inevitable presentiment of a more ominous turn of events, and the first recorded raid by the RFC with aerial bombs — as distinct from hand grenades, or adaptations thereof — appears to have been launched on 11 March 1915 by three B.E.2As of No 4 Squadron, then based at St Omer, against the railway junction at Lille, 38 miles distant; none of the aircraft returned to base, all having succumbed to engine failure.

The Royal Aircraft Factory B.E.2 variants were the best of the aircraft taken to France by the RFC with Nos 2 and 4 Squadrons in 1914. Designed by Geoffrey de Havilland, the B.E.2 prototype had first flown in 1912, when it was seen to be the best aeroplane attending the Military Trials of that year (though ineligible to be declared the winner). Powered by a 70hp Renault in-line engine driving a four-blade propeller, the B.E.2 was a two-bay biplane of wire-braced wooden construction with fabric covering. Lateral control on the early B.E.2s was by means of wing warping; there was no fin and the rudder was unbalanced.

The B.E.2 and 2A had attracted adverse comment on account of a lack of protection from the slipstream for the observer, who occupied the front cockpit, and the B.E.2B, produced in small numbers, introduced increased fuselage decking around the two cockpits.

The next B.E.2 variant, and the most famous and longest-serving, was the B.E.2C, of which a single example accompanied the RFC to France in August 1914. Early production aircraft retained the 70hp Renault, but this engine had provided the basis of a new design produced at the Royal Aircraft Factory that was to emerge as the R.A.F.1 of 90hp. Unfortunately the prototype engine, installed in an experimental B.E.2 at the Factory, was lost when it caught fire and the aircraft crashed, killing Edward Teshmaker Busk. This pilot was the Assistant Engineer (Physics) at Farnborough, and had been largely responsible for much of the investigation and improvement of aircraft stability in flight, improvements that were to be incorporated in the new B.E.2C.

This version retained the fuselage of the B.E.2B but introduced new wings with marked stagger and ailerons on upper and lower surfaces. A new tailplane was fitted to the rear fuselage between the upper and lower longerons, and a

No 1738, a Bristol-built B.E.2C with a 90hp Curtiss OX-5 engine, a conversion probably made by Frederick Sage & Co Ltd. (Photo: Imperial War Museum, Neg No Q 66958)

steel-framed, triangular fin was added forward of the rudder.

Deliveries of production B.E.2Cs were slow to build up, and by the date of the raid against Lille, mentioned above, only 13 of this type had reached the seven RFC squadrons on the Western Front. And it was in a B.E.2 or 2A of No 2 Squadron that Lieut William Barnard Rhodes-Moorhouse won the first Victoria Cross to be awarded to a British airman; on 26 April 1915 he succeeded in dropping his 100lb bomb on Courtrai railway station from 300 feet and, although mortally wounded, brought his aircraft back to his own base at Merville to make his report. One of the first bombing attacks made by the B.E.2C was that by Lieut Lanoe G Hawker (later also to win the Victoria Cross), who attacked a German airship shed at Gontrode on 19 April.

It was soon after these early bombing attacks by the RFC that the first German Fokker monoplane fighters began appearing over the Western Front, aircraft that possessed remarkable manoeuvrability for that time; they were, moreover, armed with a synchronized machine gun capable of firing through the propeller arc. The B.E.2s, on account of the stability for which they were applauded while performing bombing and reconnaissance duties, and their lack of agility, were to suffer mounting losses, and it soon became normal prac-

---

Type: Single-engine, single/two-seat, two-bay biplane, as used as support light bomber.

Manufacturers: Sir W G Armstrong, Whitworth & Co Ltd, Gosforth, Newcastle-upon-Tyne; Barclay, Curle & Co Ltd, Whiteinch, Glasgow; William Beardmore & Co Ltd, Dalmuir, Dunbartonshire; The Blackburn Aeroplane & Motor Co Ltd, Olympia, Leeds; The British Caudron Co Ltd, Cricklewood, London, NW2; The British & Colonial Aeroplane Co Ltd, Filton, Bristol; The Daimler Co Ltd, Coventry; William Denny & Bros, Dumbarton; The Eastbourne Aviation Co Ltd, Eastbourne; The Grahame-White Aviation Co Ltd, Hendon, London NW9; Hewlett & Blondeau Ltd, Clapham, London; Martinsyde Ltd, Brooklands, Surrey; Napier & Miller Ltd, Old Kilpatrick; Ruston & Proctor & Co Ltd, Lincoln; Vickers Ltd (Aviation Dept), Knightsbridge, London; The Vulcan Motor & Engineering Co (1906) Ltd, Southport, Lancashire; G & J Weir Ltd, Cathcart, Glasgow; Wolseley Motors Ltd, Birmingham.

Powerplant: B.E.2C. 70hp Renault; 90hp R.A.F.1A; 105hp R.A.F.1B; 105hp R.A.F.1D; 90hp Curtiss OX-5; 150hp Hispano-Suiza. B.E.2D. 90hp R.A.F.1A. B.E.2E. 90hp R.A.F.1A; 105hp R.A.F.1B; 150hp Hispano-Suiza; 75hp Rolls-Royce Hawk.

Structure: Fuselage of wire-braced wooden box girder construction, wooden twin-spar wings; fin and rudder of steel tubular frame construction. Engine part-cowled with aluminium sheet panels, cockpit decking plywood-covered, the remainder of the aircraft fabric-covered.

Dimensions: B.E.2C. Span, 37ft 0in; length, 27ft 3in; height, 11ft 1½in; wing area, 371 sq ft. B.E.2D. Span, 36ft 10in; length, 27ft 3in; height, 11 ft 0in; wing area, 371 sq ft. B.E.2E. Span, 40ft 9in; length, 27ft 3in; height, 12ft 0in; wing area, 360 sq ft.

Weights: B.E.2C. Tare, 1,370lb; all-up (eight 20lb bombs), 2,142lb. B.E.2E. Tare, 1,431lb; all-up (two 25lb bombs), 2,080lb.

Performance: B.E.2C (R.A.F.1A). Max speed, 77 mph at sea level, 69 mph at 10,000ft; climb to 5,000ft, 9 min 10 sec; service ceiling, 10,000ft. B.E.2E (R.A.F.1A). Max speed, 90 mph at sea level.

Armament: A single Lewis machine gun was sometimes carried on a spigot mounting aft of the rear cockpit. When flown as a single-seat bomber, the B.E.2C could carry up to two 112lb bombs or smaller bombs up to an equivalent weight.

Production: A total of 3,430 B.E.2C, B.E.2D and B.E.2E aircraft was built (including rebuilds). Of these, 1,256 B.E.2Cs and 1,877 B.E.2Ds and 2Es were produced for the War Office or on War Office Contracts, and 297 B.E.2Cs were produced for the Admiralty; 12 B.E.2C, built for the Admiralty, were transferred to the War Office, and 17 B.E.2Cs produced for the War Office were transferred to the Admiralty; 22 B.E.2Es, built for the War Office were also transferred to the Admiralty. Thus the revised figures, indicating aircraft actually delivered to the RFC and RNAS, were

Vickers, 135 (Nos 952-963 [Cs for RNAS, but transferred to RFC], 1075-1098 [Cs for RNAS], 1748-1779 [Cs for RFC], 4710-4731 [Cs for RFC], 5717-5441 [Cs for RFC], 9456-9475 [Cs for RFC but transferred to RNAS]). Blackburn, 111 Cs for RNAS (Nos 964-975, 1123-1146, 3999, 8606-8629 and 9951-10000). Hewlett & Blondeau, 42, all Cs for RNAS (Nos 976-987, 1189-1194 and 8410-8433). Martinsyde, 12, Cs for RNAS (Nos 988-999). Beardmore, 49 Cs for RNAS, (Nos 1099-1122, 8326-8337 and 8488-8500). Grahame-White, 36 Cs for RNAS (Nos 1147-1170 and 8293-8304). Eastbourne, 12 Cs for RNAS (Nos 1183-1188 and 8404-8409). British & Colonial, 1,156 (Nos 1652-1747 [Cs for RFC], 4070-4219 [Cs for RFC], 5730-5879 [Ds for RFC], 7058-7257 [Ds and Es for RFC], A2733-A2982 [Es for RFC], A8626-A8725 [Es for RFC, but 7 transferred to RNAS], and B4401-B4600 [Es for RFC]). Armstrong, Whitworth, 50 Cs for RFC (Nos 1780-2029). Daimler, 100 Cs for RFC (Nos 2030-2129). Wolseley, 120 Cs for RFC (Nos 2470-2569 and 5384-5403) and 120 Es for RFC (A3049-A3168). Ruston, Proctor, 200 (Nos 2670-2769 [Cs for RFC] and 6228-6327 [Ds and Es for RFC, some transferred to RNAS]). Weir, 300 Cs for RFC, some transferred to RNAS (Nos 4300-4599). Boulton & Paul, 50 Cs for RFC (Nos 5201-5250). Barclay, Curle, 150 Es for RFC (A1261-A1310 [4 transferred to RNAS] and C7001-C7100). Napier & Miller, 150 Es for RFC (A1311-A1360 [4 transferred to RNAS] and C7101-C7200). Denny, 150 Es for RFC (A1361-A1410 [4 transferred to RNAS] and C6901-C1700). Vulcan, 300 (Nos 6728-6827 [Ds and Es for RFC], A1792-A1891 [Es for RFC, but 3 transferred to RNAS] and B3651-B3750 [Es for RFC]). British Caudron, 50 Cs for RFC (B6151-B6200). Manufacturers not known: Nos 2570-2669, 100 Cs for RFC; Nos 7321-7345, 25 Cs for RFC; and B8829, an E for the RFC. Rebuilds for the RFC: No 1 (Southern) ARD, A376, B702, B707, B719 and B728 (all Cs); B705 (D); B723, B724 and B790 (all Es). No 3 (Western) ARD, F4096 and F4160 (Es). Note: 25 B.E.2Cs with 150hp Hispano-Suiza engines (N5770-N5794) ordered for the RNAS from Robey & Co, were cancelled.)

Summary of Service: B.E.2Cs served on Nos 2, 4, 5, 6, 7, 8, 9, 10, 12, 13, 15, 16, 21 and 46 Squadrons, RFC, on the Western Front; with No 7 Squadron, RNAS, and No 26 Squadron, RFC, in East Africa; with Nos 14 and 17 Squadrons, RFC, in Palestine; with No 67 (Australian) Squadron in Mesopotamia; with Nos 31 and 114 Squadrons, RFC, in India; and with Nos 2 and 3 Wings, RNAS, in the Aegean. B.E.2Cs also served on numerous home training stations and home-based training squadrons. B.E.2Ds served with No. 2, 4, 5, 6, 7, 8, 9, 10, 12, 13, 15, 16 and 42 Squadrons on the Western Front. B.E.2Es served with Nos. 2, 4, 5, 6, 7, 8, 9, 10, 12, 13, 15, 16, 21, 32, 42, 52, 53 and 100 Squadrons, RFC, on the Western Front, and with most of the B.E.2C-equipped Squadrons overseas, recorded above under the B.E.2C.

			Total
RFC	1,251 B.E.2Cs	1,855 B.E.2Ds and 2Es	3,106
RNAS	302 B.E.2Cs	22 B.E.2Es	324
Totals	1,553 B.E.2Cs	1,877 B.E.2Ds and 2Es	3,430

Left: *B.E.2D, No 2559, at Farnborough in 1916, experimentally fitted with a 150hp Hispano-Suiza engine.* (Photo: Royal Aircraft Factory, Neg No 1968 dated 13th December 1916)

Below: *A standard B.E.2E with 90hp R.A.F. 1A engine driving a four-blade propeller. The distinguishing feature of this version was the much extended upper wing with kingposts above the interplane struts. Ailerons were provided on upper and lower wings.* (Photo: A J Jackson Collection)

tice, whenever aircraft were available, to provide escorts for the vulnerable B.E.s. Efforts were made to fit defensive armament, but this simply served to reduce their performance still more. Because the B.E.2 was only flown as a single-seater when carrying bombs, the bombers were usually fitted with a single, spigot-mounted Lewis gun behind the pilot's cockpit to fire aft! The B.E.2C's normal bomb load was usually a pair of 112lb or up to eight 20lb Hales bombs.

With a raid by two aircraft of No 4 Squadron on Cambrai airfield on 19/20 February 1916, the B.E.2Cs began operating increasingly at night, and during the preparations for the Battle of the Somme in June and July that year fairly large formations of B.E.s carried out setpiece attacks on important targets behind the German lines; on one occasion about 30 aircraft from Nos 8 and 12 Squadrons dropped 57 112lb bombs on a key railway junction.

As the 90hp R.A.F. 1A engine became available in sufficient numbers it was adopted as standard in the B.E.2C, replacing the Renault, and this engine was retained in the other two variants, the B.E.2D with dual controls, and the B.E.2E which reached the RFC in France during the Battle of the Somme, No 34 Squadron bringing with it a full complement from England on the 15th. The B.E.2E featured a new single-bay wing-structure and with a substantial upper wing overhang.

Although the B.E.2C, 2D and 2E continued in service on the Western Front throughout much of 1917, their use as bombers declined after the autumn of 1916 owing to their vulnerability to ground fire and enemy fighters, and their inability to carry a worthwhile bomb load.

B.E.2s also served in smaller num-

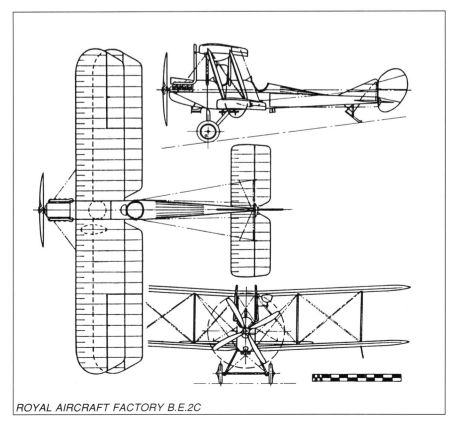

ROYAL AIRCRAFT FACTORY B.E.2C

bers with the RNAS, beginning with three B.E.2As taken to France by Wg-Cdr Charles Rumney Samson's Wing in August 1914. One of these aircraft, No 50, survived two year's service, accompanying Samson to the Dardanelles in 1915. Some naval B.E.2Cs which served during that ill-fated campaign with No 3 Wing, RNAS, were employed as bombers, a few being flown as single-seaters with the front cockpit faired over; others carried a rack for three light bombs directly beneath the engine.

B.E.2Cs also served in the bombing and reconniassance rôles in German East Africa, Egypt, Palestine, Macedonia and on the North-West Frontier of India.

Royal Aircraft Factory B.E.8

The Royal Aircraft Factory's B.E.8 was a rotary-engined derivative of the B.E.2, and probably flew in prototype form early in 1913. Powered by the 80hp Gnome engine, it differed from the contemporary B.E.2 in possessing heavily staggered wings, although early production examples retained wing warping, and the prototype had no fin. The fuselage was somewhat deeper than that of the B.E.2 in order to accommodate the engine within the nose contours, the rounded nose cowling being open in the lower segment to assist engine cooling.

As limited production got underway in 1914 a small triangular fin was added and fuselage top decking was fitted between the cockpits; the undercarriage was of the twin wheel-and-skid type, and most aircraft were fitted with four-blade propellers.

On the outbreak of war a single B.E.8 accompanied No 3 Squadron to France on 13 August 1914 but suffered a fatal crash three days later. Half a dozen further B.E.8s (known as 'Bloaters' in the RFC on account of their bulbous noses) were issued to Squadrons in France by the end of the year and, like the B.E.2s, began bombing attacks in March 1915. Four aircraft of No 1 Squadron, flown by Capt Edgar Rainey Ludlow-Hewitt (later Air Chief Marshal Sir Edgar, KCB, CMG, DSO, MC, RAF), Lieut Eustace Osborne Grenfell (later

B.E.8, No 625, at the Royal Aircraft Factory shortly after the outbreak of war; many RFC aircraft were at this time given a makeshift camouflage paint scheme, as can be seen on this aircraft. (Photo: Royal Aircraft Factory, Neg No 561, dated 16 August 1914)

Gp Capt, MC, DFC, AFC, RAF), Lieut Oswald Mansell Moullin and Lieut V A Barrington-Kennett, bombed railway targets at Douai on the 12th.

The B.E.8A, of which 42 were built by Vickers and the Coventry Ordnance Works, also powered by the 80hp Gnome, introduced wings similar to those of the B.E.2C with double-acting ailerons on upper and lower surfaces; later aircraft also featured the B.E.2C's tail unit with enlarged fin. One experimental B.E.8A was tested with the 120hp R.A.F.2 nine-cylinder radial engine.

Type: Single-engine, two-seat, two-bay biplane field reconnaissance aircraft, later flown in the light tactical bombing rôle.

Manufacturers: The Royal Aircraft Factory, Farnborough, Hants. B.E.8. The British & Colonial Aeroplane Co Ltd, Filton, Bristol; Vickers Ltd (Aviation Department), Knightsbridge, London SW. B.E.8A. The Coventry Ordnance Works Ltd, Coventry.

Powerplant: 80hp Gnome air-cooled rotary engine. Experimental. 120hp R.A.F.2.

Dimensions: Span, 39ft 6in (B.E.8A, 37ft 8½in); length, 27ft 3in.

Performance: B.E.8. Max speed, 70 mph at sea level; climb to 3,000ft, 10 min 30 sec.

Armament: No standard gun installation. One 100lb bomb could be carried.

Prototype: Prototype was probably No. 365.

Production: Completion of at least 27 B.E.8s (between No 373 and 740) has been confirmed, and 42 B.E.8As, Nos 2133-2174.

Summary of Service: Small numbers of B.E.8s and 8As served with Nos 1, 2, 3, 5, 6 and 9 Squadrons, RFC in France between September 1914 and November 1915. First used as a bomber in March 1915. B.E.8s and 8As were flown at the Central Flying School, Upavon, and one B.E.8 was flown by No 3 Flight, RNAS, Westgate, in July 1915.

Short Bomber

It was Commodore Murray Fraser Sueter who, more than any other, championed the cause of naval aviation as the modern extension of the Royal Navy's traditional task of attacking enemy ships at sea no less than in their ports. As Director of Admiralty Air Department since 1911, he had been instrumental in the creation of the Naval Wing, and shortly afterwards the Royal Naval Air Service. And once the marine aeroplane had proved itself potentially capable of lifting useful loads, be they in the form of additional crew members or fuel, he used his influence to accelerate the development of the torpedo-carrying seaplane.

As has been related, suitable targets for the airborne torpedo were seldom

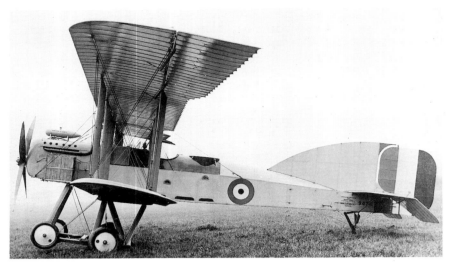

No 9476 was the first 250hp Rolls-Royce-powered Short bomber to be completed by Mann, Egerton & Co of Norwich, before the drastic steps had been taken at Shorts to lengthen the type's fuselage; indeed this aeroplane was probably never flown with the short fuselage shown here, and after modification it became one of the aircraft transferred to the RFC in mid-1916. (Photo: A J Jackson Collection).

presented in the early months of the War in circumstances that could be exploited, and Sueter, pointing to the relatively high power of these torpedo-çarriers, directed the Admiralty's attention to the development of the bomb-carrying seaplane. Indeed, the War was not four months old when Sueter began toying with the idea of developing a really large, long-range aeroplane capable of delivering a heavy load of large bombs — even though such weapons did not then exist. He saw this delivery of high explosive against enemy ports and shore establishments as the natural extension of the heavy naval gun, without exposing the capital ship to the inshore dangers presented by submarine and mine. Unfortunately such a very large load-carrying aeroplane was not yet fully practical in the United Kingdom owing to the lack of adequately powerful engines. Instead, it seemed logical to modify an existing floatplane as a landplane and develop this as a stopgap bomber and, not surprisingly, the choice fell on Short Bros to undertake such work.

By the time the first Short 184 seaplane was completed, early in 1915, a landplane derivative was already well advanced (as No 3706). This prototype was generally referred to as the Type 184 landplane, and retained the equal-span, three-bay wings of the Type 184

seaplane. These, however, soon underwent extensive redesign as two-bay wings, the lower wings being shortened considerably and the outer pairs of interplane struts discarded; to support the large upper wing overhang, cable-bracing using kingposts was adopted. This wing design, with ailerons on the upper wing only, was to feature on production Bombers.

The fuselage of 3706 was little changed from that of a standard Type 184, complete with 225hp Sunbeam engine driving two-blade propeller. A sturdy but cumbersome four-wheel undercarriage was fitted with band-brakes on the rear pair of mainwheels. Perhaps the most grotesque feature was the positioning of the observer/gunner who, occupying the front cockpit, was required to climb on to the upper decking of the fuselage in order to man his Lewis gun, which was provided with a pillar mounting on top of the upper wing.

With the wings extended to span 84 feet, 3706 proved capable of lifting its intended bomb load of nine 65lb bombs, its two-man crew and sufficient fuel for about four hours' flight. Handling in the

air, however, was quite unacceptable, the aircraft being wholly unstable in pitch and yaw, and it became obvious that this shortcoming could only be overcome by substantially increasing the tail moment with a much lengthened rear fuselage, a remedy opposed by Horace Short, bearing in mind that the first production machines had been completed (but not yet flown) and that such a modification would demand substantial restressing of the fuselage. By a simple subterfuge, Ronald Kemp (Shorts' chief pilot) and Wg-Cdr Arthur Longmore, on a visit to the works, undertook the necessary modification to the first production aircraft during a stage-managed absence of the chief designer, by the simple expedient of sawing through the longerons immediately aft of the rear cockpit and inserting an 8ft 6in long, parallel-section fuselage extension. On his return, an angry Horace Short checked the stressing calculations and reluctantly agreed that the proposed modification was suitable for introduction in production aircraft.

By then, however, production orders had been placed, not only with Shorts but with sub-contractors, and a number of aircraft had already been completed to the original drawings, but remained unaccepted owing to the instability problems. The aircraft, therefore, had to

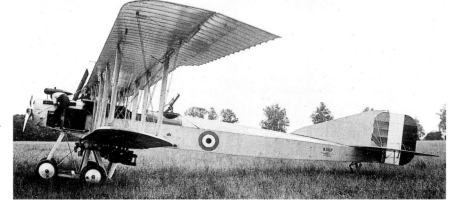

Second of the Sunbeam production batch of bombers, 9357, powered by the 225hp Sunbeam engine. With lengthened fuselage, this aircraft features a fin with straight leading edge. After acceptance, 9357 served with No 5 Wing, RNAS, at Dunkerque. (Photo: via J M Bruce)

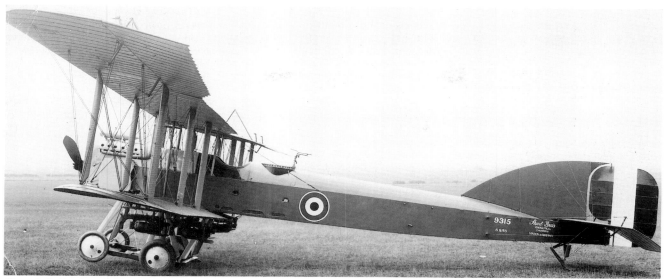

Short-built Bomber, 9315, was the tenth Sunbeam-powered production aircraft, shown here with its load of eight 65lb bombs for acceptance tests before delivery. This was one of the 15 aircraft destined to be handed over to the RFC at the time of the Somme battles of July 1916. (Photo: A J Jackson Collection)

undergo modification. While those produced by Shorts and the Sunbeam Motor Car Company retained the 225hp Sunbeam engines, the aircraft ordered from Mann, Egerton & Co, Parnall & Sons, Bristol and the Phoenix Dynamo Company were all destined to be allocated the new 250hp Rolls-Royce I (soon to be named the Eagle I).

These changes from the existing Type 184 fuselage served to delay acceptance of the Short bomber until well into 1916, by which time the first Handley Page O/100 twin-engine heavy bomber had flown, and plans had been laid to put this very large bomber into production for the RNAS. Therefore there was no question of extending production of the Short bomber, and Sunbeam-powered Short-built aircraft began delivery to the RNAS in mid-1916. In the meantime the cockpits had reverted to the customary arrangement of the observer/gunner occupying the rear cockpit, this being provided with the conventional gun ring. The Service aircraft proved capable of lifting a load of eight 112lb bombs although, in the interests of a worthwhile range, 65lb bombs were usually carried instead.

At about the time that the Shorts were being accepted by the RNAS, the RFC, suffering disastrous losses during the terrible summer battles on the Western Front, appealed to the Admiralty for the transfer of as many aircraft as could be spared, and a total of 15 Short bombers was accordingly delivered to the RFC. This had the effect of seriously delaying delivery of the bombers to the RNAS'

3rd Wing. In the meantime, other aircraft were delivered to No 7 (Naval) Squadron, 5th Wing, RNAS, and on 15 November 1916 four Shorts attacked the submarine base at Zeebrugge at night, dropping a total of thirty-two 65lb bombs. With the arrival of much heavier bombs that winter, the 5th Wing's Shorts were able to mount raids against Zeebrugge on four successive nights in April 1917 using 520lb light case bombs (each containing 340lb of Amatol).

The simultaneous issue of these much heavier bombs and delivery of the first Handley Page O/100s, combined with the onset of German daylight bombing raids by aeroplanes over Eng-

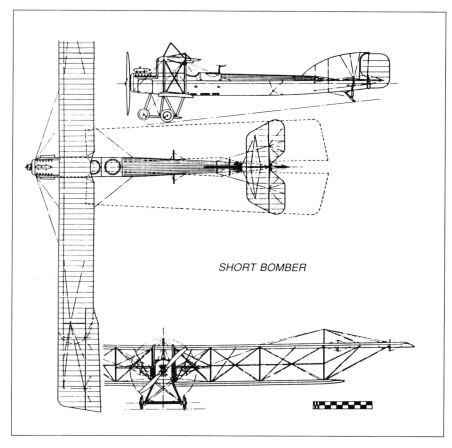

SHORT BOMBER

land, prompted the Admiralty to concentrate on operations by the new twin-engine heavy bombers; after all, the Short bombers had never been regarded as the mainstay of any strategic bomber offensive, but merely as an interim measure. Unfortunately the Short took an unconscionable time to enter service, and when eventually it did so it was already something of an anachronism, with the inevitable result that most, if not all, had been withdrawn from operational flying by mid-1917. It is not even certain that any of the aircraft so generously handed over by the Admiralty to the War Office in 1916 were ever put to any operational use.

Type: Single-engine, two-seat, three-bay biplane naval landplane bomber.
Manufacturers: Short Brothers, Rochester, Kent; Mann, Egerton & Co Ltd, Prince of Wales Road, Norwich, Norfolk; Parnall & Sons Ltd, Eastville, Bristol; The Phoenix Dynamo Manufacturing Co Ltd, Bradford; The Sunbeam Motor Car Co Ltd, Wolverhampton.
Powerplant: One 225hp Sunbeam; one 250hp Rolls-Royce (Eagle).
Dimensions: Span, 84ft 0in; length, 45ft 0in; height, 15ft 0in; wing area 870 sq ft.
Weights: Tare, 5,000lb; all-up, 6,800lb.
Performance: Rolls-Royce. Max speed, 77 mph at 6,500ft; climb to 10,000ft, 45 min; absolute ceiling, 10,600ft; endurance, 6 hr. Sunbeam. Max speed, 72 mph at 6,500ft.
Armament: One 0.303in Lewis machine gun with Scarff ring on rear cockpit. Maximum bomb load, eight 112lb bombs on underwing racks; usual load, eight 65lb bombs.
Prototypes: One, No 3706, first flown in mid-1915.
Production: A total of 83 Short Bombers (excluding prototype) was built. Short, 35 (Nos 9306-9340); Sunbeam, 15 (Nos 9356-9370); Mann, Egerton, 20 (Nos 9476-9495); Parnall, 6 (Nos 9771-9776); Phoenix, 7 (Nos 9831-9836 and A3932). 15 aircraft transferred to the RFC: Nos 9315, 9319, 9320, 9325, 9476-9479, 9482-9485, 9487, 9488 and A3932.
Summary of Service: Short Bombers served with 3rd Wing, RNAS, at Luxeuil, and with No 7 (Naval) Squadron, 5th Wing, RNAS, at Coudekerque.

Wight Admiralty Type 840

The appearance of the 225hp Sunbeam engine encouraged not only Short Bros to embark on their successful Type 184, but also the East Cowes company of J Samuel White, whose chief designer, Howard T Wright, recognised that an engine of this power made possible a torpedo-carrying seaplane, capable of realising Admiralty demands for a worthwhile range as well as a relatively heavy warload. The ensuing design was the Admiralty Type 840, so designated from the serial number of an example in the first production batch ordered, Nos 831-840.

The Type 840 was an almost exact contemporary of the Short 184 and, despite featuring four-bay wings, possessed a closely comparable performance. Moreover, on account of much longer, three-step main floats, the Wight seaplane could dispense with a tail float. The 14in torpedo was held by crutches on the rear three inter-float ties, and would have been partly submerged when the aircraft was resting on the water.

Although the Short was probably recognised from the outset as being the superior aircraft, the Admiralty clearly felt Wright's design worthy of production orders, and 52 examples (from at total of 68 ordered) came to be built, though none ever joined an operational unit of the RNAS, serving instead at various naval ports, perhaps occasionally performing coastal patrols.

Just as the Short 184 came to provide

The landplane bomber version of the Wight Admiralty Type 840, of which only one example is believed to have been completed. (Photo: GSL/JMB Collection)

the basis of a landplane bomber, which was built in numbers and reached operational service (see Short Bomber above), Whites produced a landplane version of their Type 840, retaining the four-bay wings. Small changes were made to the tail unit, the tailplane being raised to top of the fuselage. A much simpler twin mainwheel undercarriage replaced the floats, incorporating a small, forward-rigged wheel to avoid the possibility of grounding the propeller during landing. Unlike the Short, the Wight landplane inherited a long slim fuselage, and one is perhaps able to conjecture that handling of this version would have been superior to that of the original Short 184 landplane. Bomb load would probably have been of the order of eight 65lb bombs in place of the seaplane's 810lb torpedo. It has been suggested that at some time in its life a 275hp Rolls-Royce engine might have been fitted, but as far as is known only one example of the landplane was completed.

Type: Single-engine, two-seat, four-bay biplane torpedo-bomber seaplane.
Manufacturers: J Samuel White & Co, East Cowes, Isle of Wight; William Beardmore & Co Ltd, Dalmuir, Dumbartonshire; Portholme Aerodrome Ltd, Huntingdon.
Powerplant: One 225hp Sunbeam eight-cylinder, water-cooled, in-line engine driving two-blade propeller.
Dimensions: Span, 61ft; length, 41ft; wing area, 568 sq ft.
Weights: Tare, 3,408lb; all-up (with 810lb torpedo), 4,810lb.
Performance (without torpedo): Max speed, 81 mph at sea level; max endurance, 7 hr.
Armament: Either one 810lb 14in torpedo or equivalent weight of bombs; no provision for gun armament.
Production: A total of 68 Type 840s was ordered, of which 52 were built. White, 24 (Nos 831-840, 1300-1319 and 1351-1354); Beardmore, 25 (Nos 1400-1411 and 9021-9033); Portholme, 3 (Nos 8281-8283). The remainder were delivered as spares (Nos 8284-8292 and 9034-9040).
Summary of Service: Wight Type 840s served at a number of RNAS Seaplane Stations, including Felixstowe, Scapa Flow and Gibraltar.

Armstrong, Whitworth F.K.2 and F.K.3

The old-established engineering company of Sir W G Armstrong, Whitworth & Co Ltd had tentatively entered the aircraft industry in 1910 with the rebuilding of a crashed Farman, and two years later began manufacturing ABC engines to the design of Granville Bradshaw. Expansion and diversification in the aircraft business followed in 1913 with airship manufacture at Selby in Yorkshire, and the production of aeroplanes at Gosforth, Newcastle-upon-Tyne. The latter business commenced with the acquisition of the services of the Dutchman, Frederick Koolhoven, as aeroplane designer.

Early work included War Office contracts for the manufacture of B.E.2As, 2Bs and 2Cs, delivery of which began in 1914, and it was during the production of these aircraft that Koolhoven in March 1915 devised means by which the B.E.2C's structure might be simplified for ease of manufacture. The new design was tendered to the War Office and met with general approval, this leading to the raising of a small exploratory production contract for seven trials aircraft, designated the F.K.2, in August that year. Koolhoven's proposals were vindicated and rewarded by contracts for fairly large-scale production — by the standards of the time — although the War Office maintained a stipulation that the production F.K.3 should not compete seriously with the Government Factory's B.E.2C, a policy that would in due course contribute to a serious breakdown in relations between the commercial aircraft manufacturers and the Service authorities.

The F.K.2 differed principally in almost completely eliminating welded joints and complex metal components in the airframe, and featured greater dihedral on the upper wing than on the B.E.2C. The prototype, probably first flown in September or October 1915 by Norman Pratt, was powered by the 70hp Renault, but subsequent aircraft were fitted with 90hp R.A.F.1A engines. A generally popular and ingenious feature was the oleo-sprung undercarriage, the vertical shock absorbers being set into the sides of the fuselage. The cockpit arrangement of the trials F.K.2s followed that of the B.E.2C in that the pilot

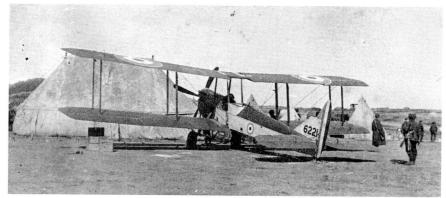

Rare photograph of an AW-built F.K.3, No 6221, serving with No 47 Squadron at Salonika. (Photo: GSL/JMB Collection, photo dated February 1917)

Type: Single-engine, two-seat, two-bay tractor biplane for ground support.

Manufacturers: Sir W G Armstrong, Whitworth & Co., Ltd, Gosforth, Newcastle-upon Tyne; Hewlett & Blondeau, Ltd., Oak Road, Leagrave, Luton, Beds.

Powerplant: One 90hp R.A.F.1A or one 105hp R.A.F.1B in-line engine driving four-blade propeller. Some aircraft were fitted temporarily with the 120hp Beardmore engine in 1916.

Structure: All-wood wire-braced construction with dual flying controls and oleo-sprung wheels-and-skid undercarriage.

Dimensions: Span, 40ft 0⅝in; length, 29ft 0in; height, 11ft 10¾in; wing area, 442 sq ft.

Weights (R.A.F.1A engine): Tare, 1,386lb; all-up, 2,056lb.

Performance (R.A.F.1A engine): Max speed, 97 mph at sea level; climb to 5,000ft, 19 min; service ceiling, 12,000ft; endurance, 3 hr.

Armament: One Lewis gun on pillar mounting at the rear of the cockpit; however, when carrying bombs, neither observer nor gun could be carried. Bomb load, one 112lb or one 100lb bomb, or up to six 16lb anti-personnel bombs on external racks.

Prototypes: Seven F.K.2 trials aircraft ordered in April 1915, Nos. 5328-5334, built by Armstrong, Whitworth; first flight by Norman Spratt, late summer 1915.

Production: Total F.K.3s built, 493, excluding the above trials aircraft: Armstrong, Whitworth, 143 (Nos 5504-5553, 5614, 6186-6227, A8091-8140); Hewlett & Blondeau, 350 (A1461-A1510 and B9501-B9800).

Summary of RFC Service: F.K.3s served operationally with No. 47 Squadron, RFC, in Macedonia, and with No. 35 (Reserve) Squadron, RFC, Northolt; served also with No. 31 (Training) Squadron, Schools of Aerial Gunnery, etc.

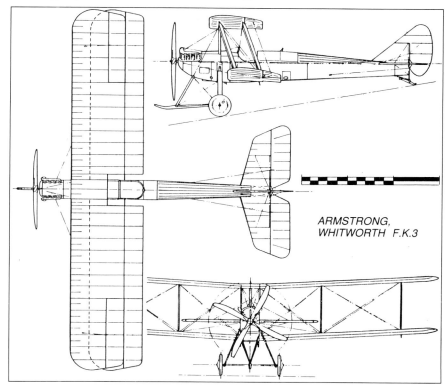

ARMSTRONG, WHITWORTH F.K.3

A late-production Hewlett & Blondeau-built F.K.3, B9554, probably in service with a home-based training unit. Note the oleo strut for the undercarriage incorporated into the side of the fuselage. (Photo: Real Photographs Co, Neg No 649)

occupied the rear position, with the gunner in front; however, owing to the difficulty the gunner experienced in aiming and firing his gun, all subsequent production F.K.3s featured these cockpits reversed, enabling the gunner/observer to provide a more effective defence to the rear.

A single 100lb or 112lb bomb could be carried beneath the fuselage, although this precluded the carrying of the gunner owing to the limited engine power available. Alternatively, up to six 16lb anti-personnel bombs could be attached to underwing racks.

It is said that a temporary shortage of R.A.F.1A engines led to the fitting of the larger and heavier 120hp Beardmore engine in a number of F.K.3s early in 1916, but this was not considered satisfactory owing largely to a deterioration in handling qualities, and the aircraft reverted to standard when availability of the R.A.F. engine was restored.

Despite returning a slightly better performance than the R.A.F. B.E.2C,

the F.K.3 did not see any active service on the Western Front, being delivered instead to No 47 Squadron at Beverley in Yorkshire in March 1916, and accompanying it to Salonika in September that year. Local field reconnaissance work gave place to frequent bombing attacks by the F.K.3s (dubbed 'Little Acks' by the RFC to distinguish them from the later, larger F.K.8s), particularly against Hudova, while based at Janes.

Nevertheless, the F.K.3 production built up too late for the type's serious consideration for widespread service, and most aircraft were delivered to training units at home, being found to be sufficiently tractable for instruction purposes. By the date of the Armistice none remained with No 47 Squadron, most of its F.K.3s surviving in Palestine and Egypt, while 53 examples were on charge with home training units.

Blackburn T.B.

Although only tenuously qualifying for inclusion in this work as a bomber, the Blackburn T.B. was the third seaplane with twin fuselages to be built to an Admiralty requirement, in this instance as an anti-Zeppelin interceptor 'bomber', to be armed with canisters of Ranken incendiary darts which, it was proposed, would be dropped on enemy airships from above to ignite their gas envelopes.

The Blackburn Aeroplane and Motor Company at Leeds, under its founder Robert Blackburn, had been engaged in building aeroplanes since 1909, and had attracted the Admiralty's attention with several of its prewar aircraft, leading to a close association with the Royal Navy that was to survive for over half a century. Expressing a favourable opinion of the high degree of workmanship that enamated from Blackburn's shops, the Admiralty placed an order for R.A.F. B.E.2Cs in May 1914, and in due course 111 examples were completed for both the RNAS and the RFC.

The first appearance by German

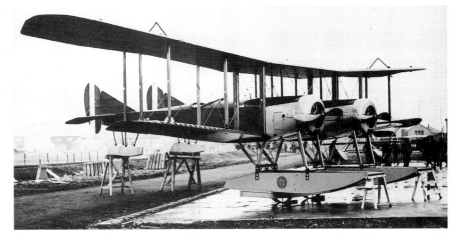

The ninth and last T.B. built, No 1517 with Clerget engines, at the Isle of Grain (just visible in the right background is a Port Victoria seaplane. Note the T.B.'s unmistakable B.E.2C fins and rudders. (Photo: Blackburn & General Aircraft Ltd., Neg No D.931)

bombing airships over England during the winter of 1914-15 prompted the Admiralty to issue a requirement for a dart-armed, two-seat aeroplane capable of long endurance and an ability to reach an altitude of at least 12,000 feet while carrying a minimum of three Ranken dart canisters (each loaded with 24 one-pound darts).

Coinciding with these events was the arrival in Britain of the American John

W Smith, bringing with him his design drawings of a ten-cylinder air-cooled radial engine. According to Smith this engine developed 150hp with an installed weight of only 380lb, and possessed an exceptionally low specific fuel consumption. Such characteristics recommended this engine for use in Blackburn's proposed anti-airship aircraft and, an order for nine T.B.s (Twin Blackburns) was placed in about March 1915,

Smith Static engines being specified.

The T.B. featured twin wire-braced, fabric-covered wooden box-girder fuselages, each with a tractor engine at the front, joined together with a 10ft parallel-chord wing centresection; the outer wings were of three bays rigged without stagger and with ailerons on the upper wings only; construction was of spruce spars and ribs, the considerable upper wing overhang being braced using kingposts. The twin fins and rudders were adapted from Blackburn's production B.E.2C components, and beneath each fuselage was mounted a short main float and a tail float. Each fuselage accommodated a crew member, the pilot on one side (with all flying and engine controls) and the observer on the other.

Although early bench testing of the Smith engine seemed to confirm its designer's performance figures, resulting in a production order being placed with Heenan and Froude Ltd at Worcester, flight trials proved less than satisfactory, and it was found necessary to turn to an alternative powerplant of equivalent interrelated weight and specific fuel consumption, the choice falling on the 100hp Gnome *monosoupape*, an excellent engine but clearly unequal to the performance demands.

The inability of the Gnome-powered T.B.s to come close to the required performance, in particular their inability to climb above 8,000 feet with the three dart canisters, was only one of several reasons that the aircraft did not gain acceptance for operational use; more serious were the shortcomings evident in handling in the air, aileron control being badly affected by wing flexing, to some extent due to inadequate bracing of the centresection. With no more than two-thirds of the intended power available, and then at a markedly higher specific fuel consumption, it was necessary to limit the weapon load to two canisters in order to carry sufficient fuel for four hours' flying, but even this was regarded as academic if the aircraft had little chance of even reaching the altitude of attacking airships, let alone climbing above them to deliver the darts. Nor does it appear to have occurred to the

aircraft designer that the necessary hand-signalling between the two crew members, situated ten feet apart, was likely to be unreliable to say the least during the hours of darkness — when the German airships most frequently operated.

Although the ninth and final T.B. to be completed was powered by 110hp Clerget engines, the performance was only just discernably improved. Several aircraft, including the Clerget-T.B., underwent trials at RNAS Isle of Grain during 1916, but it was clear that the

whole idea of attempting to attack approaching airships with bomber-type aeroplanes, with little speed margin and poor manœuvrability, was badly flawed, especially when it was shown that the German airships could achieve far greater rates of climb *at high altitude* when danger presented itself, simply by jettisoning ballast. Indeed, the T.B.s proved a blind alley, and little was heard of them after 1916, and only four aircraft served for a short time at RNAS Killingholme before being broken up.

Type: Twin-engine, two-seat, two-bay biplane anti-airship bomber with twin fuselages and central wing-bay.
Manufacturer: The Blackburn Aeroplane and Motor Co Ltd, Leeds, Yorkshire.
Powerplant: Two 100hp Gnome *monosoupape*; two 110hp Clerget 9b.
Dimensions: Span, 60ft 6in; length, 36ft 6in; height, 13ft 6in; wing area, 585 sq ft.
Weights: Tare, 2,310lb; all-up, 3,500lb.
Performance (Gnome): Max speed, 86 mph; climb to 5,000ft, 12 min; endurance, 4 hr.
Armament: Intended to be three canisters each with 24 one-pound Ranken darts.
Production: Nine aircraft, Nos 1509-1517. No 1509 first flown in August 1915 by J W Seddon. No 1517 powered by Clerget engines.
Service: Four aircraft saw limited service at RNAS Killingholme in 1917.

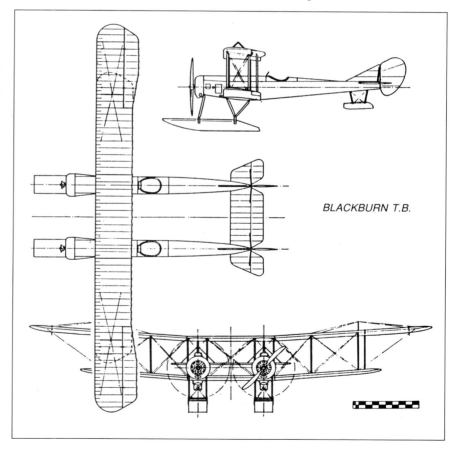

BLACKBURN T.B.

Handley Page
H.P.11 O/100

The manner in which Britain's air forces acquired their first truly successful heavy bomber was both a masterpiece of individual enterprise and an assembly of technical knowledge and experience of

epic proportions, comparable by the standards of the time with those that characterised the Royal Air Force's acquisition of the Avro Lancaster almost a quarter century later. Size alone had

not deterred other British manufacturers, such as J Samuel White, from venturing into the realms of very large aeroplanes, but none could compare with the sheer muscle of Handley Page's extraordinary O/100, whose prototype was first flown in under one year from the issue of its original specification.

Origins of the O/100 lay in an urgent message from that familiar naval officer, Charles Rumney Samson in Flanders, who pleaded with the Admiralty to send 'a bloody paralyser' with which to bomb the Germans to a standstill in their advance on Antwerp in December 1914. Implicit in this call was the need for very large aeroplanes, capable of laying a carpet of heavy bombs in the path of an advancing army, an extension of air power hitherto undreamed-of by the British War Office, but seized on at the Admiralty Air Department by Murray Sueter, the influential and energetic exponent of naval air power. Already, in line with advice by his technical adviser, Harris Booth, Sueter had placed an order for a very large bomber, the Wight Twin (see page 25), and Harris Booth's own design, the A.D.1000, was also under construction at East Cowes. Neither of these huge aeroplanes would prove successful.

Sueter, knowing that Frederick Handley Page seemed instinctively to 'think big', having embarked on a pre-war design of a proposed transatlantic aircraft, the L/200, summoned him and his designer, George Rudolph Volkert, to the Admiralty to discuss the naval requirement for a heavy bomber. As a sequence to this discussion, Volkert prepared project drawings for a twin-engine land-based bomber, designated the Type O, with a wing span of 114 feet. Further discussion, however, disclosed certain mandatory limitations on the aircraft's overall size, necessitating folding wings, yet on 28 December 1914 the final specification was agreed and issued, and an order for four prototypes was placed.

The aircraft called for was required to be powered by a pair of 150hp Sunbeam engines with 200 gallons of fuel, was to be capable of carrying six 100lb bombs and a bombsight, of climbing to 3,000 feet in 10 minutes and to have a crew of two. Armour protection from small arms fire was to be provided for crew, engines and fuel tanks, and a single Lee-Enfield rifle would suffice for self-protection. The aircraft was to be capable of storage within a 70-foot-square building, and a top speed of 65 mph at sea level was demanded; a wing loading of 5 lb/sq ft was not to be exceeded at all-up weight.

When one considers the capabilities of the aircraft of the time, this was indeed a demanding specification; after all, the 100lb bomb was only just entering production, and the call for armour and folding wings imposed the need for an extremely robust but relatively light airframe.

Design and component manufacture began immediately as Handley Page's Cricklewood factory worked round the clock, seven days a week. In the interests of low structural weight, Volkert favoured parallel-chord, straight-edged wings of unequal span, the upper wing being of 100 feet span, the lower of 70 feet (necessary for ground clearance when folded). The wings were of R.A.F.6 section, being built up on two rectangular-section spruce spars, spindled to I-section between strut attachments. Ailerons were fitted to the upper wings only, being horn-balanced outboard of the wing tips and extending aft of the wing trailing edge. Closely-spaced spruce wing ribs, reinforced longitudinally with oak tongues, imparted considerable torsional stiffness.

The fuselage was of rectangular section, the upper longerons being horizontal and the lower longerons providing taper upwards towards the tail. Built in three sections, the fuselage structure featured joint and strut attachments of mild steel, folded round the components and brazed together. An example of the careful attention paid to detail was provided by the deliberate choice of stranded cabling for internal bracing, being of the type capable of being spliced by any naval artificer.

The engines and fuel tanks were housed in armoured nacelles mounted at the centre of the wing gap, as close to the fuselage as the 11-foot propellers allowed. The radiators were mounted vertically atop the nacelles.

The two-man crew was located in a cabin in the short fuselage nose, enclosed by a deep V-shaped Triplex windscreen with transparent Cellon roof and side panels. The cockpit floor and sides up to the sills were of 10- and 14-gauge manganese-steel armour.

Every structural component was manufactured in duplicate so that a representative item could be tested to destruction in order to confirm stressing calculations, and a model of the complete aircraft underwent tunnel tests at the National Physical Laboratory.

Work had only been underway for a couple of months when Rolls-Royce announced that its new Mark II 250hp twelve-cylinder, water-cooled engine would be ready in time for the prototype's first flight and, on account of its much improved power/weight ratio, this engine was substituted for the Sunbeam.

In place of the a rotary bomb dispenser, originally intended to be incorporated in the centre fuselage with a load of eight bombs, it was decided to suspend the bombs vertically by nose rings, a change that allowed no fewer than sixteen 112lb HERL (High Explosive, Royal Laboratory) Mark I bombs to be stowed in the space formerly occupied by the rotary dispenser. Such an increase in bomb load was made possible by the 60 per cent greater power available from the new Rolls-Royce II engines.

Manufacture of the first prototype Handley Page O/100 (an arbitrary designation that simply referred to the aircraft's wing span) was completed in November 1915, and final assembly took place in the requisitioned factory at Kingsbury. After being towed along the Edgware Road at night with its wings folded, No 1455 was ready at Hendon on 17 December for its maiden flight. Taken aloft that afternoon by Lt-Cdr John Tremayne Babington (one of the naval Avro 504 pilots who had taken part in the attack on Friedrichshafen on 21 November 1914, see page 21) accompanied by Lt-Cdr Ernest W Stedman (later Air Vice-Marshal, CB OBE), the big aeroplane successfully rose above the grass for a short distance before landing and coming to a stop within the boundary of the field.

During the course of further testing it was found necessary to relocate the radiators to the sides of the nacelles and remove the cockpit enclosure and armour, modifications that reduced the aircraft's weight by some 500 pounds. Some tail oscillation resulted in extensive strengthening both of the rear fuselage and and rear attachments of the wings to the fuselage.

The second prototype, No 1456, was first flown early in April 1916 by an American, Clifford B Prodger, and soon proved itself capable of exceeding all the performance requirements demanded. On 7 May this aircraft was formally accepted by the RNAS. The third aircraft, 1457, featured a much lengthened nose to maintain cg position without ballast for the reduced cockpit weight, and a third crew position for a midships gunner.

The fourth prototype, 1458, was the first to carry gun armament, being equipped with a Lewis gun and Scarff ring in the extreme nose, a pair of pillar mountings for Lewis gun on the midships dorsal position, and a ventral quadrant mounting for a Lewis gun to fire aft beneath the tail. No 1458 was also the first O/100 to be powered by the new 320hp Rolls-Royce Eagle III engines.

In due course, production orders for a total of 42 aircraft were placed, of which 34 were powered by Rolls-Royce Eagle IIs or IVs (Nos 1458-1466, 3115, 3116 and 3118-3141); No 3117 was fitted with a succession of ex-perimental engines which included the R.A.F.3A and Sunbeam Cossack in conventional nacelles, and four 200hp Hispano-Suiza engines mounted in tandem in the two nacelles.

The majority of the initial batch of production aircraft was delivered to RNAS Manston in 1916 for pilot train-

Type: Twin-engine, four-crew, three-bay biplane heavy bomber.
Manufacturer: Handley Page Ltd, Cricklewood, London.
Powerplant: Production aircraft. Two 250hp Rolls-Royce Mk II (260hp Eagle II) twelve-cylinder, water-cooled engines driving four-blade propellers; also two 320hp Sunbeam Cossack engines. Experimental aircraft. Two 260hp Fiat A.12bis; and four (two tractor, two pusher) 200hp Hispano-Suiza engines; two Fiat A.12bis engines; two R.A.F.3A engines.
Structure: All-wood, ply- and fabric-covered; two-spar folding wings.
Dimensions: Span, 100ft 0in; length, 62ft 10¼in; height, 22ft 0in; wing area, 1,648 sq ft.
Weights: Tare, 8,000lb; all-up, 14,000lb.
Performance: Max speed, 76 mph at sea level; climb to 5,000ft, 19 min 40 sec; service ceiling, 8,700ft; endurance, 8hr.
Armament: Bomb load of up to sixteen 112lb bombs. Normal gun armament of two Lewis machine guns, one with Scarff ring on nose gunner's cockpit and one on pillar mounting on midships gunner's cockpit; some aircraft carried a Lewis gun fitted to fire rearwards through hatch under the centre fuselage.
Prototypes: Four, Nos 1455-1458; No 1455 first flown by Lt-Cdr J T Babington at Hendon on 17 December 1915.
Production: Total of 42, excluding prototypes, all built by Handley Page: Nos 1459-1466, 3115-3142 and B9446-B9451 (Cossack engines).
Summary of Service: O/100s served with Nos 7, 7A, 14 and 15 Squadrons, RNAS, in France for bombing operations over Belgium, these units later becoming Nos 207, 214 and 215 Squadrons, RAF. One O/100 served at the RNAS Station, Mudros, in the Aegean for bombing operations against Constantinople. O/100s also flew with the Handley Page Training Squadron at RNAS Manston, Kent.

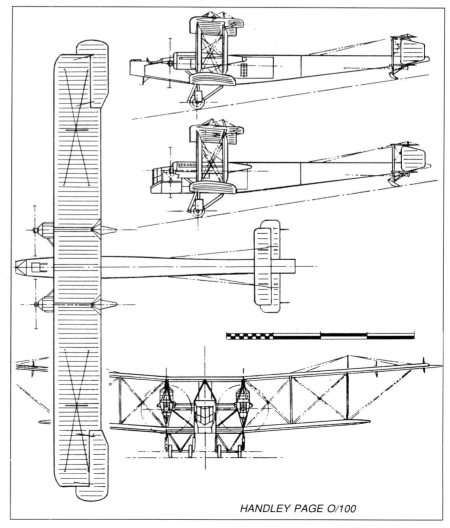

HANDLEY PAGE O/100

An elaborately camouflaged O/100 at Manston, an aerodrome used by the RNAS both as an O/100 crew training station and as a base for operational North Sea patrols. (Photo: via R C B Ashworth)

ing with the Handley Page Training Flight, prior to delivery to operational units, the first of which was simply referred to as the Handley Page Squadron and assigned to the RNAS' 3rd Wing at Luxeuil-les-Bain under the command of Sqn-Cdr John Babington. The first O/100 to arrive at Luxeuil was No 1459, and the first operational sortie flown by the Squadron was a raid by No 1460, flown by Babington against a railway junction near Metz on the night of 16/17 March 1917. Unfortunately, in the meantime Lt H C Vereker, the pilot of an O/100, No 1463, had become lost during its delivery flight to Luxeuil on 1 January, and had landed his aircraft intact on the German-held aerodrome at Chalandry, near Laon. The Germans subsequently flew the aircraft to Johannisthal where it was, however, to be destroyed in a crash before any detailed evaluation could be completed by the enemy.

The 3rd Wing was to be disbanded on 30 June 1917, and two O/100s, Nos 1459 and 1460, were transferred to the 5th Wing at Coudekerque for daylight bombing attacks on the U-boat bases at Bruges, Ostend and Zeebrugge. The first Squadron to be extensively equipped with O/100s was No 7 (Naval) Squadron, RNAS, which took over the remaining aircraft from Luxeuil and Manston. Four of these bombers attacked German destroyers in daylight on 25 April, sinking one and damaging another, but losing one of their number. This led to the suspension of daylight

attacks, and a change to night operations which included bombing raids on the heavily protected submarine pens in the Belgian ports. The 520lb Light Case and 550lb Heavy Case bombs had been specially developed for use against these targets, and the O/100 carried two such weapons.

In the meantime, Murray Sueter had left the Air Department and been posted to the Mediterranean. The Dardanelles campaign had reached stalemate, and Sueter requested that a Handley Page O/100, converted as a seaplane, should be sent out to Mudros for the purpose of bombing Constantinople (much of the route lay over water). Instead it was decided to despatch the standard O/100 No 3124 (hitherto intended for gun trials with a 6-pounder Davis gun in the nose) to Mudros and, flown by Sqn-Cdr Kenneth Savory DSC, this aircraft arrived on 8 June. After two attempts to reach Constantinople (each thwarted by headwinds), Savory finally succeeded and, on 9 July, dropped eight 112lb bombs on the German cruiser *Goeben*, four more on a steamer being used as a German headquarters, and two on the Turkish War Office. No 3124 landed safely back at Mudros after a flight of almost eight hours, an exploit for which Savory was awarded a Bar to his DSC.

The O/100 flew a number of other raids, but on 30 September it suffered engine failure and was ditched in the Gulf of Xeros; the pilot, Flt-Lt Jack Alcock (later of Atlantic crossing fame) and his crew were made prisoners of war.

The final production batch of six O/100s, B9446-B9451, was completed with Sunbeam Cossack engines, and was intended as an interim stage in the development of the Handley Page Type 12 O/400 bomber (see page 92). They did not, however, reach an operational unit. Numerous other experiments were conducted on O/100s, including the installation of Fiat A.12bis engines in No 3142, being the power unit stipulated in a production order from Russia; this aircraft crashed before completion of the trials, and the onset of the Revolution put an end to Russian participation in the War.

The mention above of the trials with a Davis 6-pounder recoilless gun in the nose of the O/100 requires further explanation. The trials were intiated by the Admiralty, who were becoming alarmed by increasing inshore activity by German submarines during the spring of 1917. A total of four O/100s, Nos 1459, 1461, 1462 and 3127 were fitted with these single-shot weapons in special mountings on the nose gunner's position. As the gun fired its shell the recoil force was dissipated by a rearwards-fired charge of fragmenting lead shot and grease which, it was intended,

The O/100, No 3124, arriving back at Mudros after one of its bombing sorties over the Eastern Mediterranean in the summer of 1917, flown by Sqn-Cdr Kenneth Savory DSC (Photo: Sqn-Cdr Savory, via A J Jackson Collection)

would pass over the aircraft's cockpit and upper wing. As the gun had to be fired at a considerably depressed angle of sight to avoid damage to the wing, it was extremely difficult to load and fire and, although three of the aircraft were delivered to the RNAS at Coudekerque in the autumn of 1917, the guns were scarcely used and were withdrawn from service early in 1918.

The O/100 bombers based in France with the RNAS continued to give excellent service during the second half of 1917, equipping Nos 7 and 7A Squadrons and dropping an impressive tonnage of bombs on all manner of targets behind the Western Front.

It was the increasing number of day and night raids by German bombers over south-east England during the latter half of 1917 that spurred the War Office to engage in strategic raiding of Germany at the earliest possible opportunity, and although requests for a transfer of naval O/100s to the RFC for this purpose fell on deaf ears, the considerable success achieved by these bombers encouraged the Government to sanction accelerated development and production of the improved Handley Page O/400, and it was to be this type that formed the heavy bombing element of the Royal Air Force's Independent Force, and the veteran O/100s began to be withdrawn from service in the spring of 1918.

Airco D.H.3 and 3A

The famous pioneer designer/pilot, Geoffrey de Havilland, who had for three and a half years designed and flown aircraft at Farnborough before the War, had left to join The Aircraft Manufacturing Company in June 1914, his first two designs in his new appointment being the Airco D.H.1 and 2 fighters.

His next design, undertaken with at least some recollection of the early project studies that had resulted in the Factory's F.E.4, was the D.H.3. Although somewhat smaller than the F.E.4, de Havilland's design was prompted by a firm belief that the Army would express a determination to acquire a bomber capable of delivering a worthwhile bomb load against German centres of war production remote from the Western Front.

Being aware of the restrictions on the size of aeroplanes favoured by the War Office, de Havilland decided on relatively short-span, folding wings of moderate chord, but employed two 120hp Beardmore engines, driving two-blade pusher propellers through short extension shafts in order to keep the engine mass close the aircraft's centre of gravity without having recourse to large cutouts in the wing trailing edges for propeller clearance.

The structure throughout was of wood, the slender fuselage being a Warren girder built of spruce, wire-braced internally, and ply-covered over the forward

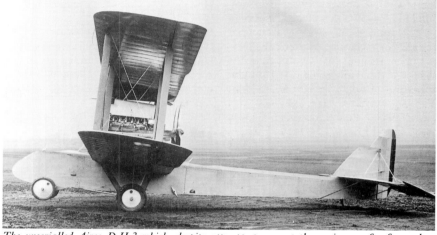
The unserialled Airco D.H.3 which, despite attempts to mount the engines as far forward as possible, still rested on its tailskid when not occupied by its crew. (Photo: Real Photographs Co, Neg No 1804)

half. The wings, rigged without stagger, carried generous, unbalanced ailerons on upper and lower surfaces and, like the rear fuselage and tail unit, were fabric-covered.

A wide-track undercarriage, with single mainwheels each side, was attached to the fuselage and the wings directly beneath the engine support struts, and was complemented by a bumper wheel on each side of the nose. The three-man crew comprised pilot, and nose and midships gunners

The first prototype D.H.3, not being built to a formal War Office contract, was not allocated a serial number, but was first flown by de Havilland, probably in late January or early February 1916. It demonstrated good handling qualities and a useful performance, and

No 7744, the Airco D.H.3A with 160hp Beardmore engines, whose increased weight more than cancelled the benefit of extra power and bestowed a slightly reduced performance compared with that of the D.H.3. (Photo: Imperial War Museum, Neg No Q67535)

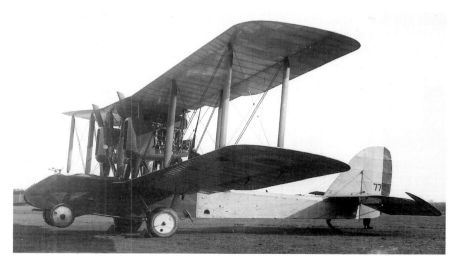

a production contract for 50 aircraft had already been placed by the War Office for an improved version, the D.H.3A, powered by 160hp Beardmore engines, driving four-blade pusher propellers without recourse to extension shafts.

By the time the second aircraft, No 7744, was flown, the acrimony, which had upset relations between the commercial aircraft manufacturers and the War Office over the alleged preferential regard held for the Factory's products, was beginning to influence decisions with regard to the issue of production contracts for 'privately' designed military aircraft. Consequently the contract for D.H.3As was cancelled; the quoted pretext was a shift in opinion at the War Office, that strategic bombing by aeroplanes was unlikely to influence the course of the War. In any case, opinions being expressed at the War Office were that large twin-engine bombers were impractical — this despite the fact that the Admiralty's much larger and heavier Handley Page O/100 prototype had recently flown successfully.

The decision to cancel the second D.H.3A prototype and the production order may now be seen to have been one of the most ill-advised ever taken by the War Office with regard to military aeroplanes. Before a further six months had elapsed, the Army in France was locked in a calamitous battle on the Somme, with no effective bombers with which to support the soldiers on the ground, and with rapidly mounting losses. Appealing to the Admiralty, the War Office obtained some Short Bombers from the RNAS production — but never used them.

In all likelihood, the first production D.H.3As could have being entering operational service by the end of the summer of 1916 and, carrying six 112lb bombs each, would have provided stimulating support for the Army at that critical time. Their presence in the front line would have demonstrated the feasibility of large bombers, and action to create an autonomous bombing force could have been initiated early in 1917; as it was, another year was to elapse

before such action was taken.

Although the D.H.3 and 3A were both scrapped without full flight trials being completed[1], they did provide de Havilland with the design basis of a later twin-engine bomber, the D.H.10 which, flown in March 1918, was still awaited

by the Service when the Armistice was signed (see page 106).

[1] It has been suggested that the D.H.3A prototype was simply the D.H.3 prototype rebuilt. However, it is known that at least one photograph exists showing both aircraft, apparently complete, standing together.

Type: Twin pusher-engine, three-seat, three-bay biplane light bomber.
Manufacturer: The Aircraft Manufacturing Co Ltd., Hendon, London NW9.
Powerplant: D.H.3. Two 120hp Beardmore six-cylinder, water-cooled, in-line engines driving two-blade pusher propellers. D.H.3A. Two 160hp Beardmore engines driving four-blade pusher propellers.
Structure: Wire-braced wooden structure, the forward section of the fuselage ply-covered, the remainder fabric-covered.
Dimensions: Span, 60ft 10in; length, 36ft 10in; height, 14ft 6in; wing area, 793 sq ft (D.H. 3A, 770 sq ft.)
Weights (D.H.3): Tare, 3,980lb; all-up, 5,810lb.
Performance (D.H.3): Max speed, 95 mph at sea level, 87 mph at 10,000ft; climb to 5,000ft, 16 min 12 sec; endurance, 8 hr.
Armament: Two 0.303in Lewis machine guns with pillar mountings on nose and midships gunners' cockpits; design provision for up to 680lb of bombs, probably planned as six 112lb bombs carried as three under each wing.
Prototypes: Two. The D.H.3 was first flown early in 1916 and apparently did not carry any serial number; the D.H. 3A carried No 7744. No production (50 aircraft, A5088-A5137, were ordered, but cancelled).

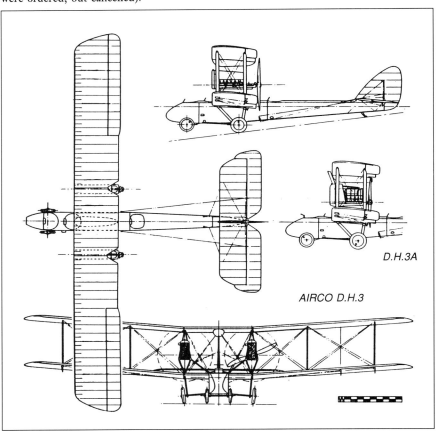

D.H.3A

AIRCO D.H.3

Sopwith 1½-Strutter Bomber

Design of the Sopwith 1½-Strutter probably began quite early in 1915 although, being in effect a private venture at the outset, manufacture of a prototype at Kingston was accorded less

urgency than to aeroplanes being prepared to specific Admiralty orders. As with most of the early Sopwith aircraft, delineation of design responsibility was nebulous, frequent informal discussions

A Sopwith-built 1½-Strutter N5504 a single-seat bomber destined for the RNAS. This aeroplane survived the War and was converted for private sporting use as G-EAVB. (Photo: Sopwith Aviation Co Ltd, Neg No S102)

on new designs being held between Thomas Sopwith himself, his works manager Fred Sigrist, and his chief pilot Harry Hawker, with R J Ashfield and Herbert Smith representing their respective design offices.

Being almost exclusively involved with Admiralty requirements, Sopwith would have been familiar with that Ministry's shift towards bombing aircraft during 1915 (away from purely torpedo-carrying seaplanes), yet no less aware of the Army's desperate shortage of effective light tactical bomb-carrying aeroplanes, and in particular such aeroplanes capable of defending themselves in the presence of German fighting scouts.

The 1½-Strutter (so called on account of the shortened inboard wing struts being attached to the upper longerons and not extending down to the lower wing spars) was therefore deliberately intended to attract both Admiralty and War Office orders for a self-defensible light bomber. Designed initially as a two-seater, it was provided with a Lewis gun on the rear cockpit and later a fixed, front Vickers gun, firing through the propeller, made possible by the Vickers and Scarff-Dibovski synchronizing gears. The former gear was preferred by the War Office, the latter by the Admiralty.

Structurally the 1½-Strutter was entirely conventional by Sopwith standards, that is to say it was of all-wood construction with ply and fabric covering; ailerons were fitted to upper and lower wings, which were of equal span. Early aircraft were fitted with the 110hp Clerget engine, but also came to be powered by the 130 and 135hp Clergets, and Le Rhône engines of similar power.

The aircraft featured two interesting innovations which served to demonstrate the efforts made to alleviate any handling difficulty that might arise when carrying and dropping bombs. These were a pair of rudimentary airbrakes set in the lower surfaces of the wing centre-section, and a variable-incidence tailplane, adjustable by a control wheel in the pilot's cockpit to compensate for variations in trim. The latter innovation was patented by Harry Hawker and, in 1920, when the Sopwith company went into liquidation, the patent rights were de-

Type: Single-engine, single- and two-seat, single-bay biplane light bomber.

Manufacturers: The Sopwith Aviation Co Ltd, Kingston-upon-Thames, Surrey; Mann, Egerton & Co Ltd, Prince of Wales Road, Norwich, Norfolk; Morgan & Co, Leighton Buzzard, Bedfordshire; Westland Aircraft Works, Yeovil, Somerset.

Powerplant: One 110hp Clerget 9Z or 130hp Clerget 9Bc nine-cylinder rotary engine driving two-blade propeller.

Dimensions: Span, 33ft 6in; length, 25ft 3in; height, 10ft 3in; wing area, 346 sq ft.

Weights (Clerget 9Z): Tare, 1,354lb; all-up (with four 56lb bombs), 2,362lb.

Performance (Clerget 9Z): Max speed, 104 mph at sea level; climb to 10,000ft, 26 min 55 sec; service ceiling, 12,500ft.

Armament: One synchronized 0.303in Vickers machine gun on nose decking; bomb load of four 65lb bombs or equivalent weight of lighter bombs carried internally in bay aft of the pilot's cockpit.

Production: No special bomber prototype. Of the total of 1,513 Sopwith 1½-Strutters recorded as having been ordered for the RFC and RNAS, 172 were built as single-seat bombers: Sopwith, 145 (Nos 9651, 9652, 9655, 9657, 9660, 9661, 9664, 9666-9673, 9700, 9704, 9707, 9711, 9714, 9715, 9718, 9720, 9723, 9724, 9727, 9729, 9732, 9733, 9736, 9738, 9741, 9742, 9745 and 9747; A6014 and A6015; N5088 and N5089; N5120-N5179; N5500-N5537 and N5550-N5559); Morgan, 2 (A6014 and A6015); Mann, Egerton, 20 (N5200-N5219); Westland, 5 (N5600-N5604).

Summary of Service: Sopwith 1½-Strutter single-seat bombers served with 3rd and 5th Wings, RNAS, in France, and with RNAS units in Italy (at Otranto), Macedonia and the Aegean, including 'F' Squadron which flew a number of bombing raids in the Smyrna area.

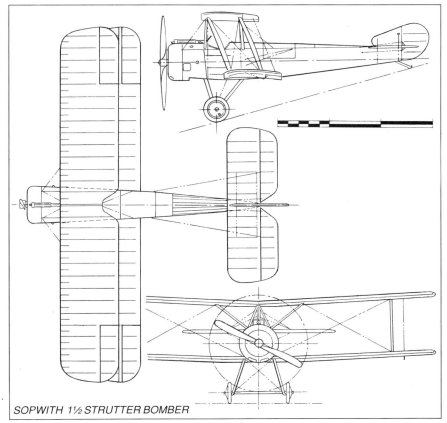

SOPWITH 1½ STRUTTER BOMBER

Sopwith 1½-Strutter single-seat bombers of the 3rd Wing, RNAS, probably at Luxeuil-les-Bains. The aircraft's bomb load was stowed in a compartment immediately aft of the pilot's cockpit, slightly aft of the centre of gravity, hence the assumed need for a variable-incidence tailplane. (Photo: GLS/JMB Collection)

termined in favour of the H G Hawker Engineering Company. (The variable-incidence tailplane was to be a feature of most Hawker aircraft produced between 1926 and 1935, as well as others)

The prototype, No 3686, was placed on an Admiralty contract, and probably first flew at the end of December 1915 or early the following month. It was followed by numerous production contracts — which were widely sub-contracted — from the Admiralty (where the aircraft was referred to as the Type 9700) and War Office, the majority of the former being for bombers, and the latter for fighters. The 50 naval aircraft of the first production order, built by Sopwith, were two-seaters, but it was quickly decided that, when carrying the normal bomb load (of up to four 65lb bombs in an internal fuselage bay), it was necessary to fly without the observer/gunner, with the result that all subsequent Admiralty orders for bombers required the rear cockpit to be deleted altogether, and faired over. The front gun was, however, retained. A total of 172 naval single-seat bombers was built by Sopwith, Westland, and Mann, Egerton.

It is perhaps worth recording here that it was Warrant Officer F W Scarff at the Admiralty Air Department who drew up the design of the front gun synchronizing gear from proposals made by a Russian, Lt-Cdr V V Dibovski, and that Scarff it was who also designed the gun mounting ring that was to carry his name in the RAF for a quarter century. Some 1½-Strutters were fitted with a Nieuport ring of French origin, but when two-seater naval aircraft were transferred to the RFC at the time of the great summer battles of 1916, General Trenchard ordered all his Service's 1½-Strutters to be converted to have Scarff rings, so superior were they found to be.

The arrival of the 'Strutter' bomber in the RNAS was intended to be central to the build-up of a bombing campaign by No 3 Wing, based at Luxeuil, but this plan was severely delayed when the Admiralty agreed to transfer more than 70 of these aircraft to the RFC to help make good the losses being suffered during the Somme battle of July.

Despite these delays, naval 1½-Strutters flew a number of outstanding bombing attacks during the summer of 1916, including raids on the airships stations at Evere, Berchem Ste Agathe and Cognelée, an ammunition dump at Lichtervelde and the shipyards at Hoboken, serving with Nos 5 and 8 (Naval) Squadrons.

Apart from anti-submarine coastal patrols, which 1½-Strutters flew as stop-gap equipment from such stations as Mullion, Pembroke and Prawle Point, the aircraft gave long service with the RNAS in the Mediterranean both as anti-submarine aircraft and bombers in Italy, Macedonia and the Aegean (probably sinking an enemy submarine with a 65lb delayed-action bomb on 17 September 1917).

The aircraft were also supplied to a number of Allied air forces, in most instances as two-seat fighters or reconnaissance aircraft, although France (where the 1½-Strutter was also licence-built by Lioré et Olivier and Hanriot) also received single-seat bombers.

Deployment of British Bomber Units, 1 January 1916

Royal Flying Corps

No 2 Squadron	R.A.F. B.E.2C	Auchel, France
No 9 Squadron	R.A.F. B.E.2C	Bertangles, France
No 12 Squadron	R.A.F. B.E.2C	St Omer, France
No 21 Squadron	R.A.F. R.E.7	Netheravon, Wiltshire

The above Squadrons, based in France, were not declared as specialist bomber units, being principally engaged in local 'corps reconnaissance' duties, but undertook occasional bombing raids.

Royal Naval Air Service (Naval detachments overseas)

HMS *Ark Royal*	Short Type 166	Salonika
HMS *Ben-my-Chree*	Short Type 184	Eastern Mediterranean
RNAS Detachment	Short Type 830	Mesopotamia

The above detachments undertook local bombing sorties in support of ground forces; a number of home-based units, though tasked with coastal patrol duties, frequently carried light bombs.

2. ACCEPTANCE OF THE PURPOSE-BUILT BOMBER

Passing references have already been made to the deteriorating relations between the War Office (and, to a lesser extent, the Admiralty) and the commercial aircraft industry in Britain. It might be thought that such acrimony was inevitable, bearing in mind the private manufacturers' statutory obligation to have their products evaluated, not so much by the Services themselves, but by the very government authorities who were vying to justify their own existence in the field of aircraft design and production. In the instance of military aeroplanes, designed and built for the RFC, there was growing suspicion in commercial industry that unfair plagiarism of ideas and innovations which, in peacetime would be protected by patent, was being freely exercised by the Royal Aircraft Factory to the potential detriment of commercial contracts.

This belief was probably overstated in some cases, but the apparently ill-judged and continuing award of production contracts for Factory-originated aircraft in preference to 'privately' designed aeroplanes had perpetuated the issue of a number of thoroughly inferior Factory aircraft to the RFC long after their effective lives had expired, to the obvious exclusion of superior products from the independent industry. This cavalier treatment was particularly obnoxious bearing in mind that private individuals had gone to considerable personal expense to expand their works and work forces in 1914 to concentrate on work for national defence, and were nevertheless subject to heavy taxation on any profit. (Moreover, after the Armis-tice of 1918, the Treasury imposed swingeing demands by taxation of so-called excess war profits, which not only took no account of the original private investment, but were themselves so excessive

that more than 60 per cent of the aircraft industry was forced into liquidation.)

The rumblings of discontent had been heard as early as mid-1915, emanating in part from the RFC itself, whose squadrons in the field on the Western Front found themselves without aircraft capable of adequately defending themselves from the fast-improving German fighting scouts, such as the Fokker monoplanes; word quickly spread that there was, as yet, nothing better in the pipeline for those hard-pressed squadrons. Obsolescent Factory-designed aeroplanes were being called on to carry bombs — impedimenta that rendered sitting ducks dead ducks. Taken in conjunction with the commercial manufacturers' feelings of unfair treatment, these distant rumblings broke in a storm of parliamentary outrage, to the discomfort of the Government which in due course caused official enquiries to be made into the rôle of the Factory in influencing the issue of contracts for the military, and into the process of evaluation of new aircraft and equipment.

Although the reports on these enquiries were largely inconclusive (public censure of the military in time of war might be deemed counter-productive), as was further campaigning by a Parliamentary pressure group of 'Air Enthusiasts' led by the vociferous Noel Pemberton Billing, a number of measures came into effect which, given time, certainly put the whole process of military procurement on a more open and logical basis. Among these was the es-

tablishment of the Society of British Aircraft Constructors (SBAC), whose purpose was to safeguard the interests of the private aircraft industry.

Henceforth the War Office and Admiralty would issue requirements by their respective air arms after discussions with all interested manufacturers, as well as their own research and design agencies, and specifications would be circulated to any manufacturer that expressed an interest in tendering a realistic design. Commercial and national secrecy would extend to all contractors, and competitive evaluation would be undertaken by Service establishments, to be set up for that purpose. Contract and sub-contracts would be let on the merits of efficiency, cost and timescale.

*   *   *

Unfortunately, with extensive production orders already in hand — the great majority, it should be said, involving obsolescent Factory aircraft — to have summarily cancelled them would have been to starve the Services not only of combat and attrition replacements, but of potential training aircraft.

The sensible alternative was adopted: to encourage commercial manufacturers, hitherto only employed in work on sub-contracted production of aircraft of Factory origin, to undertake original designs of their own, and submit them alongside those of the established manufacturers. This would have the effect of loosening the ties that had previously

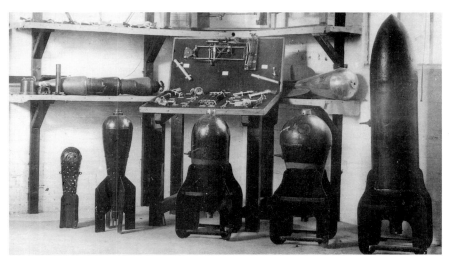

Some of the types of light bomb carried by bombers of the RFC during the First World War; from left to right, incendiary, 20lb, 100lb, 112lb and 230lb. (Photo: via Bruce Robertson)

existed between the government ministries and their respective 'favoured' contractors.

This far-reaching upheaval took place fairly leisurely. In the instance of bomber procurement — itself only slowly becoming regarded as a matter of urgency for the RFC — the process would gather momentum with an increase in the number of bomber requirements being evident in 1917 as the War Office came to realise the importance of strategic bombing, not to mention the increasing number of reliable British engines suitable for large aircraft (such as the Rolls-Royce Eagle and big Sunbeams) which were becoming available.

Two outstanding British aircraft exerted a remarkable influence on the growing awareness of the vital part capable of being played by the bomber, namely the big Handley Page O/100 and, at the other end of the scale, the Airco D.H.4. Unfortunately the structure of the RFC, as it existed in 1916-17, was inappropriate to accommodate an autonomous strategic bombing arm, organised as it was exclusively for the support of the Army in the field. Being, in effect, an integral Corps wholly within the command structure of the War Office, the RFC was staffed extensively by officers seconded from line regiments with little but rudimentary training in anything but the skill in piloting a small aeroplane in close combat. By the same criteria, it might be suggested that naval airmen were, by training and instinct, more suited to the vagaries of long-distance navigation and, by tradition, more receptive to the demands of strategic warfare.

Such a distinction was probably facile, yet after the amalgamation of the RFC and RNAS to form the Royal Air Force on 1 April 1918, the joining together of the former Services' bombing arms to form the Independent Force of strategic bomber squadrons came about smoothly, effectively and with surprising speed, even if the Army's initial contribution was largely composed of personnel from the 41st Wing, flying D.H.4 and F.E.2B light bombers, while the RNAS had subscribed a squadron of O/100s.

Progress in the development of the aerial bomb was spectacular during the last two years of the War, the heaviest weapon in service by the beginning of 1917 being the 550lb heavy case high explosive bomb, capable of being lifted by the O/100. By the end of the War, O/400s were delivering the 1,650lb SN bomb over German towns and cities, while the monster 3,360lb SN Major was being made ready for the Handley Page V/1500, an aircraft intended to reach Berlin from its base in Norfolk.

The fact that the Armistice was signed in time to prevent this bomber from performing its planned raid only served to sharpen speculation as to the heavy bomber's ultimate capabilities, and no doubt embroidered the philosophical outpourings from the rash of bomber strategists that proliferated once peace had been secured.

The 3,360lb SN Major bomb being displayed at the Crystal Palace shortly after the Armistice; it is not thought likely ever to have been flown on the V/1500. (Photo: via Bruce Robertson)

Aerial Bombs carried by RFC and RNAS Aircraft, 1914—1918

Nominal Weight	Type	Approx. Period	Remarks (Aircraft Compatible, etc.)	Nominal Weight	Type	Approx. Period	Remarks (Aircraft Compatible, etc.)
6.5 oz	Baby Incendiary	1916/18?	Aircraft not known.	112lb	HE RL	1915–c.1933	All aircraft classed as bombers; actual weapon weight varied from 96lb to 113lb according to explosive filling.
14.5lb	Carcass Incendiary	1917-1918	Possibly replaced by Thermite-filled weapon.				
16lb	HE RL	1915-1918	All close-support aircraft.	160lb	9.45in Trench Howitzer (Conv)	1917-1918	Carried by O/400 *inter alia.*
20lb	Hales	1914-1918	All close-support aircraft.				
20lb	Cooper	1915-	All close-support aircraft	180lb	HE RL Mk I	1917-1918	All aircraft classed as bombers.
20lb	CFS	1917?	Aircraft not known.	230lb	RFC	From 1916	Most RFC/RNAS/RAF bombers until 1935. Weapon weights
25lb	Cooper	1914-	All close-support aircraft.				were between 200lb and 230lb.
34lb	Thermalloy Incendiary	1916-1918?	Aircraft not known.	230lb	RNAS LC	From 1917	Hydrostatic fuze; anti-submarine.
40lb	Bourdillon Phosphorus	1916-1918	Bombers of RFC and RNAS	336lb	RAF (RAE)	1916-1918	Close-support aircraft (eg R.E.7)
				520lb	HE LC	From 1916	O/100, O/400, Vimy, etc.
50lb	HE RL	1916	All aircraft classed as bombers.	550lb	HE HC	From 1916	O/100, O/400, Vimy, etc.
65lb	HE RL (LC)	1916-1918	All close-support aircraft.	1,650lb	SN	1918-1919	O/400 and V/1500.
100lb	HE RL	1916-1918	All aircraft classed as bombers.	1,800lb	SN (Mod)	1918-1919	O/400.
100lb	Hales	1915	Close-support aircraft.	3,360lb	SN Major	1918-1919	V/1500.

Royal Aircraft Factory B.E.12

The growing clamour during the latter half of 1915 over the inferior aircraft being supplied to the RFC in France was focused principally on the Factory's B.E.2C, an aeroplane that had been applauded early in its Service life on account of its inherent stability in all three axes — a laudable quality for unopposed reconnaissance work but suicidal in the presence of enemy fighters. It was slow and simply incapable of evasive manœuvre and, when required to carry bombs, suffered enormous losses. Nor was the B.E.8's performance significantly better.

For months the Army remained deaf to calls for an enquiry into the administration of the Factory and the reasoning behind the continued letting of contracts for B.E.2 production. Moreover, during the early months of 1916, as a result of further Parliamentary charges by Noel Pemberton Billing, the Burbidge Committee's report was published, only to demonstrate steadfast support for the B.E.2C as an effective operational aeroplane. None of the report's authors was a close witness to events over the Western Front.

Discomfited by further charges in Parliament, the War Office halted production of the B.E.2C in mid-1916, although the aircraft continued in service for a further year. It had, however, been divulged that the Factory had already, in mid-1915, initiated action to further develop the B.E.2/B.E.8 formula, and a marginally improved aircraft, the B.E.12, was first flown in August that year.

Nevertheless, it was the War Office's clear intention to introduce a fighter aircraft into service (the Airco D.H.2), capable of meeting the German fighting scouts on equal terms, rather than to pursue fundamental changes in existing bombing and reconnaissance aircraft, believing that providing escorts for the established B.E.s would halt the rising losses being suffered.

Little urgency was therefore lent to the B.E.12's development. The prototype was a converted B.E.2C, No 1697, in which the front cockpit was deleted and a 140hp R.A.F.4A twelve-cylinder air-cooled in-line engine replaced the 90hp R.A.F.1A. No gun armament was

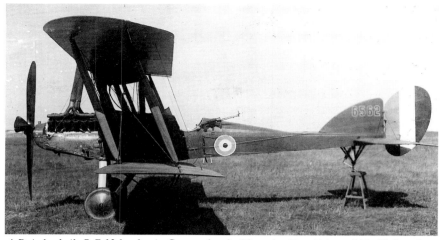

A Daimler-built B.E.12 bomber in German hands. Flown by Lieut Briggs of No 19 Squadron, RFC, from Fienvillers, No 6562 was forced down on 26 August 1916, the pilot being made prisoner. Note the pillar-mounted, rearward-firing Lewis gun aft of the cockpit. The front Vickers gun and underwing bomb racks for four 65lb bombs are not visible in this photo, taken at the German Adlershof aerodrome during evaluation. (Photo: GSL/JMB Collection).

provided initially (confirming that the new aircraft was conceived as yet another bomber/reconnaissance type, for which fighter escort would be available).

While No 1697 went to France during the autumn of 1915 for Service trials, production orders were placed with three Coventry-based manufacturers, Daimler also being contracted to produce the Factory's R.A.F.4A engine. Delays with the latter prevented completion of the first production B.E.12s until March 1916, and it was midsummer before examples were reaching the Squadrons in France, by which time the superior German scouts had been demonstrating their ability to evade the RFC's escorts to attack the reconnaissance machines.

As a result, the B.E.12s were provided with a single fixed, forward-firing Vickers gun on the side of the fuselage, but this was found to be virtually useless as the B.E. still lacked the manœuvrability to engage in any sort of dogfighting. By adopting the smaller tailplane of the B.E.2E, some improvement in handling was evident, but when a Lewis gun was also provided on a pillar mounting *behind the pilot's left shoulder*, the aircraft proved almost unmanageable and the gun incapable of being aimed. In August 1916, therefore, the aircraft was withdrawn from daylight reconnaissance duties and transferred almost exclusively to night bombing, a task which it continued to perform until February 1917.

Type: Single-engine, single-seat, two-bay biplane light reconnaissance/bomber.

Manufacturers: The Daimler Co Ltd, Coventry; The Standard Motor Co Ltd, Coventry; The Coventry Ordnance Works Ltd, Coventry.

Powerplant: One 140hp R.A.F.4A in-line engine driving four-blade propeller.

Dimensions: Span, 37ft 0in; length, 27ft 3in; height, 11ft 1½in; wing area, 371 sq ft.

Weights: Tare, 1,635lb; all-up, 2,352lb.

Performance: Max speed, 102 mph at sea level, 91 mph at 10,000ft; climb to 10,000ft, 33 min; service ceiling, 12,500ft; endurance, 3 hr.

Armament: Gun armament comprised one 0.303in Vickers machine gun on nose with Vickers mechanical interrupter gear, and occasionally one Lewis gun on pillar mounting aft of the cockpit on the port side; bomb load of up to two 112lb, four 65lb, sixteen 16lb or eight 20lb or 25lb bombs carried under the wings.

Prototype: No 1697 (a converted Bristol-built B.E.2C), first flown at Farnborough by Frank Goodden in August 1915.

Production: A total of about 400 B.E.12s was built but, by the time the aircraft began bombing operations, many had been lost in action while flown as fighting scouts. The following are known to have been built: Nos 6136-6185 (Standard Motors, 50, all built as B.E.12s); Nos 6478-6677 (Daimler, 200, all built as B.E.12s); A562-A611 (Coventry Ordnance, 50; six completed as B.E.12As); A4006-A4055 (Daimler, 50; three completed as B.E.12As); A6301-A6350 (Daimler, 50; three completed as B.E.12As); C3081-C3280 (Daimler, 200; mixed B.E.12s, B.E.12As and B.E.12Bs).

Summary of Service: B.E.12s served with Nos 10, 19 and 21 Squadrons on light bombing duties over the Western Front, and No 17 Squadron at Salonika.

In mid-1916 an attempt was made to improve the B.E.12's manoeuvrability by adopting the B.E.2E's single-bay wings of unequal span, this version — the B.E.12A — arriving on the Squadrons at the end of the year, but with little real evidence of improvement. (The B.E.12B, of late 1917, was an anti-Zeppelin fighter, powered by a 200hp Hispano-Suiza engine, and therefore lies outside the scope of this work.)

A few B.E.12s served with No 17 Squadron at Mikra Bay, near Salonika, from November 1916, being flown as fighters, bombers and reconnaissance aircraft, as opportunity dictated; and it was this Squadron's well-known pilot, Capt Gilbert Ware Murlis-Green (later Gp Capt, DSO, MC, RAF) who achieved the rare score of three enemy aircraft shot down while flying the B.E.12.

These operations only served to extend the original B.E.'s dismal service and anachronistic operational rôle. That B.E.s continued to be manufactured and flown on operations long after they had been shown to be disastrously outdated emphasised the War Office's wholly unjustified dependence on the products of the Royal Aircraft Factory.

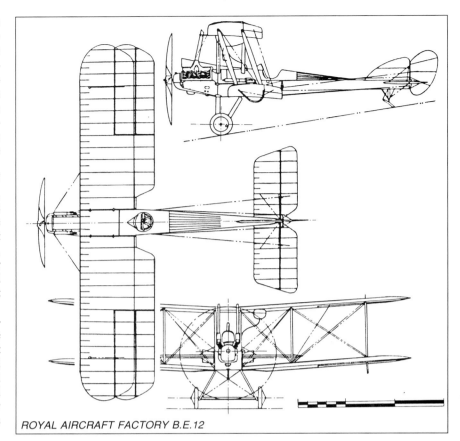

ROYAL AIRCRAFT FACTORY B.E.12

Grahame-White Type 18

Notwithstanding the work already in progress on the big Handley Page O/100 heavy bomber, the Admiralty issued a requirement in mid-1915 for a rather smaller, single-engine, land-based bomber, possessing a range of about 700 miles, capable of lifting 800lb of bombs with a crew of two and a speed of 80 mph. Shorts had been quickest to produce a contender to this requirement, and accordingly received production orders. However, both Grahame-White and J Samuel White also produced prototypes, although none of the three aircraft tendered fully satisfied the performance demands (see Short Bomber, page 37, and Wight Bomber, page 70).

Design of the big Grahame-White Type 18 occupied much of the summer and autumn of 1915 and centred on the choice of a single 285hp Sunbeam 12-cylinder water-cooled engine, the bear-

The sole Grahame-White Type 18 prototype, before covering. (Photo: A J Jackson Collection)

ers being extensions of the upper fuselage longerons. The wooden box girder, which constituted the fuselage primary structure, carried formers to fair the fuselage to oval section. The three-bay wings were built up on twin spruce spars with closely-spaced ribs and four pairs of interplane struts, the inboard pairs (which replaced conventional centresection struts) providing the rigidity required for the wing-folding attachments.

The wings, of parallel chord and equal span, featured ailerons on upper and lower surfaces, and the twin mainwheel undercarriage with V-struts and spreader bar was augmented by a small balancing nosewheel. Bomb racks, capable of supporting two 230lb or four 112lb bombs were attached under the lower wings immediately outboard of the fold axis. A large fuel tank was located forward of the pilot's cockpit, and the gunner/observer was evidently provided with a Lewis gun on what appears to be a ring mounting.

The Type 18 was probably completed in the spring or summer of 1916, by which time the Handley Page O/100 was confounding its critics by demonstrating the practicality of large bombing aeroplanes and, of the three bomber designs tendered, only the Short Bomber entered production, while the Wight Bomber was developed further by conversion into a floatplane, for which production orders were placed. By contrast,

work was evidently halted on the Grahame-White Type 18 soon after com-pletion, and no record of flight performance has been traced.

Type: Single-engine, two-seat, four-bay biplane naval bomber.
Manufacturer: The Grahame-White Aviation Co Ltd, Hendon, London NW9.
Powerplant: One 285hp Sunbeam Maori twelve-cylinder water-cooled in-line engine driving four-blade propeller.
Structure: All-wood, fabric-covered; two-spar folding wings.
Dimensions, Weights and Performance: Not known.
Armament: Single Lewis gun on observer's cockpit; details of bomb load speculative.
Prototype: Believed, one; details of first flight (probably in 1916) not known. No production.

Avro Type 519

The Avro Type 519 appears to have been a contemporary of the Grahame-White Type 18 (see above) and, like that aeroplane, very little is known about it. By a process of elimination, it seems certain that the Type 519 was intended as a possible bomber, and was evidently an attempt to adapt the Avro Type 510 'Round Britain' racing seaplane of 1914 for military consideration. (Although the 1914 race had been cancelled on the outbreak of war, the Admiralty had purchased the prototype and five further examples.)

The Type 519 retained the earlier aircraft's 150hp Sunbeam Nubian water-cooled engine as well as similar two-bay wings of unequal span. The fuselage was generally similar, but was faired to incorporate curved upper decking and raised headrest fairings aft of the cockpits. The wheel-and-skid undercarriage with oleo struts was reminiscent of that on the Avro 504. In order to meet naval storage requirements, provision was made to fold the wings.

The design drawings, prepared by Roy Chadwick and H E Broadsmith, met with interest at the Admiralty and War Office to the extent that Avro

The first Admiralty single-seat Type 519, No 8440, in Avro's new erecting shops at Hamble in May 1916. (Photo: via J M Bruce)

received orders for four aircraft — two single-seat Type 519s for the RNAS and two two-seat Type 519As for the RFC; the latter featured fixed wings and a plain V-strut undercarriage without the central skid.

All four aircraft are believed to have been delivered to Farnborough by May 1916 for trials, but it is said that they did not meet the Service strength requirements with the Nubian engine, and their ultimate fate is not known.

Type: Single-engine, single- and two-seat, two-bay biplane (probably intended as experimental bomber).
Manufacturer: A V Roe & Co Ltd, Miles Platting, Manchester.
Powerplant: One 150hp Sunbeam Nubian eight-cylinder, water-cooled, in-line engine driving two-blade propeller.
Dimensions: Span (Type 510), 63ft 0in.
Performance: Max speed, approx 76 mph at sea level.
Armament: No gun armament; provision for bomb load, unknown.
Prototypes: Four; two Type 519s for Admiralty, Nos 8440 and 8441, and two Type 519As for War Office, Nos 1614 and 1615.

Avro Type 523 Pike

Designed by Roy Chadwick to the Royal Aircraft Factory's Specification Type VII of 1915, the Avro Type 523 Pike represented a realistic approach to the War Office's demand for a night bomber,

although it must be said that the Army's attitude at that time towards the need for large bombing aircraft was less than enthusiastic, and was probably influenced more by a determination to keep abreast of the Admiralty's partisan assumption of the strategic bombing rôle.

The Pike was a fairly large three-bay biplane with equal-span wings, and with a crew of three, comprising pilot, and

nose and midships gunners. The handed 160hp Sunbeam Nubian engines were located at mid-gap with frontal car-type radiators and driving pusher propellers through extension shafts so as to clear the wing trailing edges. Ailerons were fitted to upper and lower wings. The bomb load was to be carried internally in the fuselage with horizontal tier stowage.

The Type 523 Pike with Nubian engines driving pusher propellers. (Photo: via J M Bruce)

The Type 523 was assembled at Avro's newly opened works at Hamble in Hampshire after manufacture at the Manchester factory early in 1916. Unfortunately, despite being designed to a Factory specification, neither the Admiralty nor War Office expressed tangible interest in the Pike, with superior bombers already ordered into production.

On the other hand the Avro company itself undertook further development, producing the Type 523A with 150hp Green engines driving tractor propellers, and later proposing the 523B with 200hp Sunbeams and the 523C with 190hp Rolls-Royce Falcon engines. Neither of the latter came to be built, but their design provided much experience in the evolution of the Type 529 and 533 Manchester bombers. Both the Type 523 and 523A continued to fly at Hamble until 1918

The Type 523 Pike gained small notoriety when, on one occasion during an early test flight the pilot, Fred Raynham, discovered that the cg was too far aft to permit throttling back to land. The situation was saved when R H Dobson (later Sir Roy, CBE, and Chairman of the Hawker Siddeley Group), who was occupying the midships gunner's cockpit, climbed out and made his way along the top of the fuselage to transfer his weight to the front gunner's position. With the cg restored to manageable limits, Raynham was able to throttle back without the danger of stalling.

Type: Twin-engine, three-crew, three-bay biplane day/night bomber.
Manufacturer: A. V. Roe and Co. Ltd., Miles Platting, Manchester.
Powerplant: Type 523. Two 160hp Sunbeam Nubian water-cooled, in-line engines driving handed two-blade pusher propellers. Type 523A. Two 150hp Green water-cooled, in-line engines driving unhanded two-blade tractor propellers.
Dimensions: Span, 60ft 0in; length, 39ft 1in; height, 11ft 8in; wing area, 815 sq ft.
Weights (Type 523): Tare, 4,000lb; all-up, 6,064lb.
Performance (Type 523): Max speed, 97 mph; climb to 10,000ft, 27 min; endurance, 7 hr.
Armament: Provision for single Lewis machine guns on nose and midships gunners' cockpits with Scarff rings. Internal, horizontal-tier stowage of two 100lb or 112lb bombs.

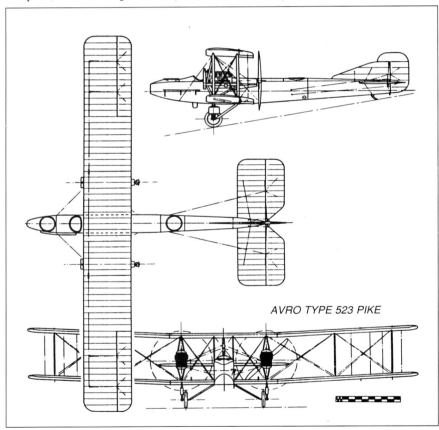

AVRO TYPE 523 PIKE

Blackburn GP

Designed by Bob Copley, who had been largely responsible for the earlier TB floatplane (see page 42), the Blackburn GP was a more orthodox attempt to interest the Admiralty in a large torpedo- and bomb-carrying seaplane to complement the Handley Page O/100 land-based heavy bomber, also destined for the RNAS. Design had started in the late autumn of 1915, and the first prototype, No 1415, was completed and first flown at RNAS Isle of Grain in July 1916 powered, like the Avro Type 523 (see above), by a pair of handed 150hp Sunbeam Nubian engines, but driving four-blade tractor propellers.

The GP featured a long, slim fuselage accommodating pilot and two gunners, one of the latter being charged with bomb aiming and provided with a bomb

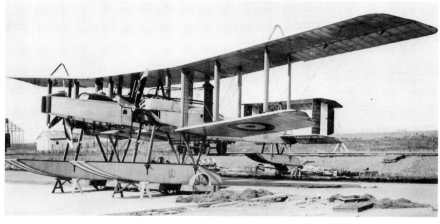

sight attached externally to the starboard side of the nose. Construction was largely of wood with metal joint fittings, the box girder structure carrying formers to provide rounded top decking. The wings, with considerable overhang, employed kingpost bracing and were of parallel chord, being rigged without stagger so as to simplify folding — a feature demanded in all large naval aeroplanes.

To facilitate the carriage of torpedo and bombs, the twin floats were independently mounted beneath the engine bearer struts without cross-members, and the weapon racks were attached to the fuselage and lower wing roots with provision to carry either a 1,100lb 18in torpedo or four 230lb bombs, the latter in tandem on parallel beams.

Fuel sufficient for eight hours' patrol was carried in tanks located aft of the engines in the long nacelles which were positioned on the upper surface of the lower wings.

A second prototype[1], No 1416, was also completed in 1916, and this differed from the first machine in numerous respects. Not least of these was the considerable airframe strengthening throughout in order to conform to Admiralty requirements which stipulated strength factors of 5 and 4 on front and rear trusses respectively, necessitating the use of heavier-gauge metal joint fittings. Power for 1416 was provided by a pair of 190hp Rolls-Royce Falcon engines whose nacelles were now located in mid-gap.

Both GPs underwent testing at the Isle of Grain, and the second aircraft participated in Service trials at RNAS Great Yarmouth early in 1917. However the GP failed to secure a production contract, presumably because the Short 184 had demonstrated continued reliability in the bomb-carrying patrol rôle at much less cost.

---

[1] For many years the second aircraft was referred to as the Blackburn SP. It seems likely however, as pointed out by J M Bruce, that no such designation existed, and possibly resulted from an error in, or misreading of, company documents.

Type: Twin-engine, three-crew, three-bay biplane long-range patrol bomber seaplane.
Manufacturer: The Blackburn Aeroplane and Motor Co Ltd, Leeds and Brough, Yorkshire.
Powerplant: Two 150hp Sunbeam Nubian or 190hp Rolls-Royce (Falcon) water-cooled in-line engines driving four-blade handed propellers.
Dimensions: Span, 74ft 10½in; length, 46ft 0in; height, 16ft 10in; wing area, 880 sq ft.
Weights (Rolls-Royce engines): Tare, 5,840lb; all-up, 8,600lb.
Performance (Rolls-Royce engines): Max speed, 97 mph at sea level; climb to 5,000ft, 10 min; ceiling, 11,000ft; endurance, 8 hr.
Armament: Two Lewis machine guns with Scarff rings on bow and midships gunners' positions. War load comprised either four 230lb bombs or one 18in Whitehead torpedo.
Prototypes: Two, Nos 1415 and 1416. No 1415 (GP) first flown at RNAS Isle of Grain in July 1916; No 1416 first flown at Brough late in 1916. No production.

Short Type 310

Despite the outstanding, if isolated success achieved by the torpedo-carrying Short 184s at the Dardanelles in August 1915, it was evident that in order for a single-engine aircraft to possess adequate performance while carrying the 1,100lb 18in torpedo (particularly in hot climates) it was necessary to acquire an engine of more than 300 horsepower, itself weighing scarcely more than the existing 250hp engines. The new Rolls-Royce twelve-cylinder water-cooled powerplant, soon to be named the Eagle, was already approaching the 300hp rating, but production engines were being earmarked for the Handley Page O/100.

At Sunbeam, however, Louis Coatalen was developing a 300hp engine, later named the Cossack, and it was for this engine that Horace and Oswald Short designed new seaplanes, the Type 310A

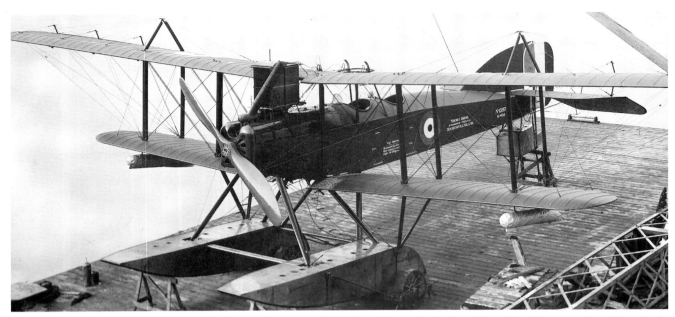

Short-built production Type 310-A4, N1397, showing the position of the observer's gun ring in the trailing edge of the upper wing. Note also the additional V-struts between the rear of the main floats and the wing beneath the inboard interplane struts. The beautifully executed inscription on the fuselage below the pilot's cockpit reads: 'Very Important: The Removable Rear Crossbar Must always be in Position Before the Wings are Folded'. (Photo: Short Bros Ltd.)

(torpedo-carrier) and the 310B (patrol scout)[1] — the former being accorded the highest priority owing to increased enemy naval activity in the Mediterranean early in 1916.

In contrast to the earlier Type 184, which carried its torpedo beneath arched float cross-members, the Type 310A incorporated torpedo crutches on the fuselage underside, thereby ensuring that the torpedo was always carried clear of the water. To provide additional float rigidity, a detachable cross-member interconnected the rear ends of the floats when a torpedo was not carried, and extra fixed raked struts gave adequate float rigidity when carrying the torpedo, while allowing the weapon unrestricted

---

[1]   Confusion has existed for many years with regard to the correct designation of the Type 310, resulting from the various systems of referring to the Short seaplanes. The term Type 310 was adopted to identify aircraft powered by the 310hp Sunbeam engine, this being the initial normal power. The rating was soon raised to 320hp (maximum), and eventually came to be regarded as the 'normal' rating. Strictly speaking the aircraft with these more powerful engines should have been referred to as Type 320s, and often were. However, the designation was never sanctioned, and Short's own designation, the Type 310-A4, came to be officially adopted.

View of a Type 310-A4 which well illustrates the wings' considerable overhang. Production aircraft reverted to two-blade propellers. (Photo: via R C Sturtivant)

fall when released. The front float cross-member was located forward of the torpedo in any case, and therefore remained fixed.

When carrying a torpedo, the Short 310A was invariably flown as a single-seater, the pilot occupying the rear cockpit so as to maintain the aircraft cg within acceptable limits. These crew dispositions were regarded as unsatisfactory as, occupying the front cockpit, the observer was so beset by interplane struts and upper wing that, without a gun mounting, the aircraft was defenceless. To overcome this, later aircraft featured a Lewis gun with Scarff ring level with the upper wing trailing edge; to man the gun, the observer was obliged to stand on his seat with most of his body exposed to the slipstream — but at least he possessed an excellent field of fire.

Two prototype Type 310As and two 310Bs had been ordered, and the first two, Nos 8317 and 8318, were first flown by Ronald Kemp in July and August 1916 respectively. (Of the two 310Bs ordered, only No 8319 was completed as such, No 8320 being converted to become an additional Type 310A during manufacture.)

Nos 8317 and 8318 were quickly despatched to RNAS Otranto in Italy for operational torpedo trials, but both aircraft broke up in the air following failures of their rear float attachment. This was rectified in production aircraft by moving the floats further apart, and an additional V-strut was added to brace the float to the lower wing on each side; these struts were disconnected and rotated downwards to allow the wings to be folded. With this modification in

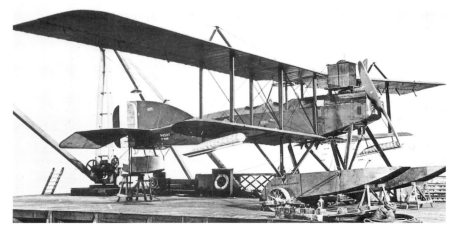

Short Type 310-A4, N1393, taxying with
an 18in torpedo. The pilot's forward field of
view must have been minimal. (Photo: via J M
Bruce)

place, the aircraft was termed the 310-
A4.

A total of 127 Type 310-A4s was built
by Short Bros and the Sunbeam Motor
Car Company, all carrying N-prefix
serial numbers. The first 54 production
machines were shipped to Otranto and
Malta during the spring of 1917.

Their first operation, however, ended
in failure before it even began, when six
310-A4s, having been towed on rafts to
Traste Bay, were destroyed by a sudden
storm which capsized all the craft
moments before the aircraft were due to
be disembarked for take off. Their task
had been to attack with torpedoes a
flotilla of enemy submarines, known to
be off Cattaro in the Adriatic. No such
target was ever again presented.

The Mediterranean-based seaplanes
were employed on long-range patrols,
made possible by their six-hour endurance when carrying a pair of 230lb
bombs. No submarine kill by a 310-A4
was ever confirmed, although the pilot
of a Kalafrana-based aircraft claimed to
have 'probably destroyed' a submarine
which had attacked a French warship off
Malta on 8 February 1918.

The production of torpedo-carrying
seaplanes was ended by the Admiralty
late in 1917 when it became evident
from trials aboard HMS Furious that year
that deck-landing aircraft could operate
with greater flexibility — a belief that
persisted for the remainder of the aerial
torpedo's history.

Nevertheless, no fewer than fifty
Short Type 310-A4s remained in service
with the RAF at the Armistice.

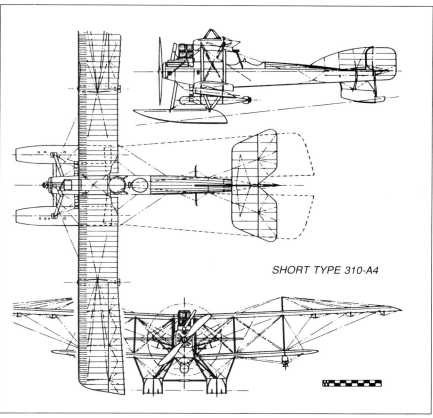

SHORT TYPE 310-A4

Type: Single-engine, single- or two-seat, two-bay biplane reconnaissance torpedo bomber seaplane.

Manufacturers: Short Bros, Rochester, Kent; The Sunbeam Motor
Car Co Ltd, Wolverhampton.

Powerplant: One 310hp (later 320hp) Sunbeam Cossack twelve-
cylinder, water-cooled, in-line engine.

Dimensions: Span, 75ft 0in; length, 49ft 9in; height, 17ft 6in; wing
area, 810 sq ft.

Weights (320hp Cossack): Tare, 4,933lb; all-up, 7,014lb (with 18in
torpedo).

Performance (18in torpedo; Cossack): Max speed, 72.5 mph at sea
level; climb to 2,000ft, 12 min; ceiling, 3,000ft; endurance, 2 hr.

Armament: One Lewis gun with Scarff ring on wing centresection
requiring observer to stand on front cockpit seat to fire gun. Bomb load

either one 1,000lb 18in Mk IX torpedo or two 230lb bombs. (Flown
as single-seater when carrying torpedo.)

Prototypes: Two, Nos 8317 and 8318. No 8317 first flown at
Rochester in July 1916, 8318 in August, both by Ronald Kemp.

Production: Total of 125 Short 310As built (excluding prototypes): Short, 75 (N1150-N1159, N1300-N1319, N1390-N1409
and N1480-N1504); Sunbeam, 50 (N1360-N1389 and N1690-
N1709).

Summary of Service: Short 310As served at RNAS Bembridge
(equipping No 253 Sqn, RAF, after August 1918); at RNAS
Otranto, Italy (equipping No 263 Sqn, RAF, after September
1918); at RNAS Mudros, Aegean (equipping No 266 Sqn, RAF,
after August 1918); at RNAS Kalafrana, Malta (equipping No 268
Sqn, RAF, after August 1918); and at RNAS Killingholme.

Royal Aircraft Factory R.E.8

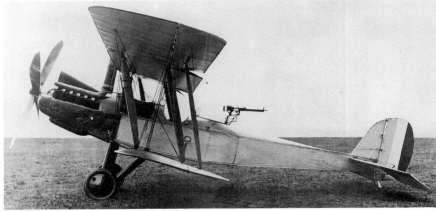

One of the two R.E.8 prototypes, either No 7996 or 7997. The aircraft was armed with a Lewis gun of the observer's cockpit, a feature that was criticised by the RFC when the type was first flown in France. (Photo: Imperial War Museum, Neg No Q57581)

Despite its designation, the Royal Aircraft Factory's R.E.8 was in no respect a development of the R.E.5 or R.E.7, and it is said to have carried that designation so as to avoid any obvious connotation with the discredited B.E. family — to which it was in fact closely related. It was unfortunate in acquiring ill-repute through flying accidents and combat casualties, and it has to be said that a very high proportion of these were more the result of poor pilot training that any specific fault in the design.

Design of the R.E.8 (inevitably dubbed the Harry Tate by the RFC, after a popular music hall comedian) started in the winter of 1915-16 in response to an RFC requirement for a reconnaissance aircraft capable of defending itself from German fighting scouts. The aircraft was of all-wood construction, a distinctive feature being the rear longerons, which appeared to slope upwards aft of the rear cockpit; this, combined with the large air scoop above the R.A.F.4A engine (a feature common to the B.E.12), bestowed on the R.E.8 a curious upward curving profile. The heavily staggered wings of unequal span and large overhang were reminiscent of those of the B.E.2E, and were probably adopted in the belief that this was the feature mainly responsible for the B.E.2E's apparent superiority over the despised 2C. The tailplane was also similar to that of the B.E.2E, and its incidence was adjustable by a handwheel in the pilot's cockpit. The most prominent difference between the two aircraft was the R.E.8's much smaller fin, and herein lay one of the causes of the handling difficulties experienced by fledgling pilots of the RFC.

In an effort to improve the observer/gunner's field of fire forward in level flight, the engine was mounted to provide a downward thrust line (ie tail-up in level flight); however, in the event of the aircraft stalling, the tail surfaces were so far above the propeller's slipstream as to be useless, and a spin frequently proved fatal. Moreover, the steeply sloping engine air scoop, forward of the front windscreen, produced an unfamiliar illusion when approaching to land that the aircraft was on the point of stalling and, on moving the stick forward instinctively, the pilot would either crash on undershooting or land too fast and crash on overshooting. In either instance there was a likelihood that the engine would be forced back and rupture the fuel tank, which was located immediately in front of the pilot. In these circumstances, fire was a not unnatural consequence, and the R.E.8 quickly earned a reputation as a 'flaming coffin' — indeed it was probably no more prone to fire than any other combat aircraft of the period.

Two prototype R.E.8s, No 7996 and 7997, were built, the first being flown by the Factory's chief pilot, Frank Goodden, on 17 June 1916. The second was quickly despatched to France for assessment by the Service's airmen. Being experienced pilots, they approached the new machine with caution, but soon recognised and accepted its idiosyncrasies, reporting very favourably on its performance; the one important requirement was that the observer's Lewis gun should be replaced by a belt-fed Vickers (this was not put into effect).

On the strength of this report (endorsed by Col H R M Brooke-Popham, later Air Chief Marshal Sir Robert, GCVO, KCB, CMG, DSO, AFC, RAF), the War Office immediately placed orders for no fewer than 1,475 R.E.8s, of which only 75 were to be built at the Royal Aircraft Factory; apart from 200 (which were intended to be produced by the British & Colonial Aeroplane Company, but which were cancelled), the remaining 1,200 were built by six commercial sub-contractors. Further substantial orders were to follow during the next eighteen months.

The first RFC Squadron to receive R.E.8s was No 52, which began converting from B.E.2Cs at Hounslow Heath in October 1916, and transferred to France the following February. However, owing to a spate of flying accidents and a consequent drop in morale on the Squadron, it was decided to revert to B.E.2Cs. In the meantime, No 34 Squadron gave up its B.E.12s at Alonville in January in favour of the R.E.8, and by April six

An early production R.E.8, A3433, built by The Siddeley-Deasy Motor Car Co Ltd, with the original small vertical tail surfaces. (Photo: via J M Bruce)

squadrons had been fully re-equipped in France.

There could have been no more unfortunate time for an aircraft to receive its baptism of fire than 'Bloody April', the worst single month of the War for the RFC in terms of combat casualties over the Western Front, and the ferocity of the air battles served to demonstrate just how unsuited for corps reconnaissance the R.E.8 was. For instance, on the 13th a formation of six aircraft from No 59 Squadron set out from Bellevue on a reconnaissance sortie, two of the aircraft being camera-equipped and escorted by the other four; the formation was also to have been covered by about a dozen genuine fighters, but these evidently failed to reach the area of reconnaissance. The R.E.8s were attacked by six German single-seat scouts, led by Manfred von Richthofen, which shot down every one of the British machines, ten of the twelve airmen being killed. The following month five further squadrons were re-equipped with R.E.8s, and by the end of the year no fewer than seventeen R.E.8 squadrons were in action over the Western Front, as well as four in Greece and the Middle East.

Of course there were those experienced pilots who mastered the R.E.8's handling difficulties, and not only survived the depredations of enemy fighters but gave good account of themselves in combat. And during the great battles of Messines and Ypres the R.E.8s of Nos 16 and 21 Squadrons achieved excellent results when assisting Allied gunners to silence enemy gun batteries.

On 6 September 1917 R.E.8s began night bombing attacks in support of the Ypres offensive, statistics showing that in the following 90 days a total of 260 such sorties were flown, during which 390 112lb and 65lb bombs were dropped. Thereafter the aircraft continued to divide their efforts between bombing and reconnaissance, although the greatest care had to be taken to ensure their close protection by fighters when operating by day.

R.E.8s were used on a number of occasions towards the end of the War to lay smokescreens in support of ground forces; on 8 August 1918 aircraft of Nos 5, 9 and 3 (Australian) Squadrons used 40lb phosphorus bombs to provide screens during the Amiens offensive, and in Palestine the following month No 113 Squadron's R.E.8s dropped smoke candles in support of Commonwealth infantry during the great Turkish re-

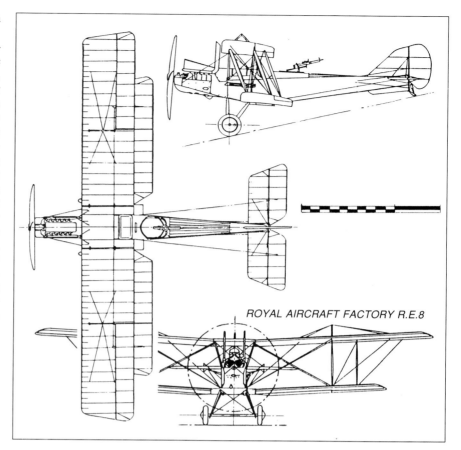

ROYAL AIRCRAFT FACTORY R.E.8

Type: Single-engine, two-seat, single-bay biplane corps reconnaissance bomber.

Manufacturers: The Royal Aircraft Factory, Farnborough, Hampshire; The Austin Motor Co (1914) Ltd, Northfield, Birmingham; The Coventry Ordnance Works Ltd, Coventry; The Daimler Co Ltd, Coventry; D Napier & Sons Ltd, Acton, London; The Siddeley-Deasy Motor Car Co Ltd, Park Side, Coventry; The Standard Motor Co Ltd, Coventry.

Powerplant: R.E.8 Production. 150hp R.A.F.4A. Experimental. 200hp R.A.F.4D; 150hp R.A.F.5. R.E.8A. 200hp Hispano-Suiza.

Dimensions: Span, 42ft 7in; length, 32ft 7½in; height, 11ft 4½in; wing area, 377.5 sq ft.

Weights: Tare, 1,803lb; all-up (two 112lb bombs), 2,869lb

Performance: (With two 112lb bombs). Max speed, 109 mph at sea level, 95 mph at 10,000ft; climb to 10,000ft, 39 min 50 sec; service ceiling, 11,000ft; endurance, 2¾ hr.

Armament: One synchronized 0.303in Vickers machine gun on port side of nose, and one Lewis gun with Scarff ring on rear cockpit. Bomb load usually two 112lb or four 65lb bombs.

Prototypes: Two, Nos 7996 and 7997; first flown at Farnborough by Frank Goodden on 17 June and 5 July 1916 respectively.

Production: A total of 4,180 R.E.8s and R.E.8As (excluding prototypes) was built. Royal Aircraft Factory, 75 (A66-A115 and A3506-A3530); Austin, 250 (A3169-A3268 and A4261-A4410); Siddeley-Deasy, 685 (A3405-A3504, A3681-A3830, B6451-B6625, B7681-B7730, E1151-E1250, F1553-F1602 and F3246-F3305); Daimler, 1,450 (A3531-A3680, A4161-A4260, B3401-B3450, B5001-B5150, C2231-C3030 and F3548-F3747); Napier, 400 (A3832-A3931, B2251-B2300, C4551-C4600, D4811-D4960 and E1101-E1150); Standard, 570 (A4411-A4560, A4564-A4663, D1501-D1600, D4661-D4810 and F1665-F1734); Coventry Ordnance Works, 750 (A4664-A4763, A6631-B6730, C5025-C5125, D6701-D6850 and E1-E300). In addition 49 R.E.8s underwent rebuilding, as follows: No 1 (Southern) Aircraft Repair Depot: B737, B738, B742, B765, B814, B821, B832, B836, B845, B853, B7808, B7893 and B7917; No 2 (Northern) ARD: B4048, B4069, B4105 and B4134; No 3 (Western) ARD, B8884, B8885, B8886, B8887, B8900, D4980 and D4998; contractors not known: F5879, F5897, F5902, F5909, F6016, F6018, F6044, F6049, F6050, F6277, H6843, H7018, H7022-H7027, H7033, H7038, H7042, H7055, H7057, H7262 and H7265.

Summary of Service: R.E.8s served with Nos 4, 5, 6, 7, 8, 9, 12, 13, 15, 16, 21, 52, 53, 59 and 69 Squadrons, RFC and RAF, on the Western Front; with No 6 Squadron, RAF, in Iraq after the War; with Nos 30 and 63 Squadrons in Mesopotamia; with Nos 34 and 42 Squadrons, RFC and RAF, on the Western Front and in Italy; with Nos 67, 113, 142, 144 and 208 Squadrons, RFC and RAF in Egypt and Palestine; and with Nos 37, 50, 89, 91, 106, 110 and 117 Squadrons in the United Kingdom and Ireland.

A mid-production standard Daimler-built R.E.8, C2670, with extended ventral fin and modified engine cowling; later the upper fin was considerably enlarged. (Photo: Imperial War Museum, Neg No 63818)

treat; shortly afterwards the Squadron dropped many 20lb fragmentation bombs when the Turks were caught in the open on the road to Amman.

However, for the sake of dropping small numbers of relatively light bombs, whether by day or night, such operations were seen to be a waste of resources, and it had been proposed to withdraw R.E.8s from front line duties as early as April 1918, replacing them with Bristol F.2B Fighters. This plan failed to materialise and the R.E.8 continued in operational service right up to the Armistice (when there were still 21 squadrons in the field), and for many months after. The last RAF squadron to give up its R.E.8s was No 208 in November 1920, then stationed at Ismailia in Egypt.

Despite its poor reputation both as a flying and fighting aeroplane, the R.E.8 underwent very little remedial treatment, due largely, it is said, to the gradual dispersion of the design staff at the Royal Aircraft Factory from the summer of 1917 onwards. The obvious lack of directional control attracted attention, and when minor increases in ventral fin and rudder area were seen to provide only marginal improvement, the upper fin area was almost doubled; yet, despite this modification being found to effect an almost complete remedy, it was very slow to be introduced in production aircraft.

Relatively early in its life the R.E.8 came to be used in a number of interesting experiments, although few were pursued as serious efforts to improve the aircraft in service. For instance, an R.E.8 was fitted with a 200hp R.A.F.4D engine with exhaust-driven turbo-supercharger and four-blade variable-pitch propeller of Factory design; the aircraft was easily distinguishable by its enormous air scoop (some three feet in diameter) above the engine. A variant, known as the R.E.8A, was produced by replacing the customary R.A.F.4A engine by a 200hp Hispano-Suiza; however, with the majority of these engines earmarked for the Factory's S.E.5 fighter, the R.E.8A was not built in quantity.

Armstrong, Whitworth F.K.7 and F.K.8

The rôle of corps reconnaissance must have been one of the least popular of the duties undertaken by RFC flying personnel during the First World War, and on account of the appalling casualties suffered by the B.E. aircraft over a period of two years, Service pilots tended to be extremely critical of the aeroplanes they were obliged to fly. This was particularly true of the B.E.s themselves, as well as the R.E.8 which was intended to replace them. Frederick Koolhoven, aircraft designer with Sir W G Armstrong, Whitworth Aircraft Ltd, having produced what he considered to be 'an improved version of the B.E.2C' with his F.K.3 (see page 41), went further with his bigger and more powerful F.K.8 — predictably known as the 'Big Ack'. As such, the latter was seen to be comparable with the Factory's R.E.8. In terms of performance it was found to be inferior, but this was more than balanced by it being fairly free of handling vices. Moreover, in contrast to the apparent unwillingness to effect improvements in the R.E.8 (for a number of possibly valid reasons), the makers of the F.K.8 went to some effort to improve the features that attracted criticism in their aeroplane.

Design of the F.K.8 was orthodox and incorporated the increased strength factors being recommended by the Factory on behalf of the War Office by 1916. Like its predecessor, it was a two-

An early production Armstrong, Whitworth-built F.K.8, A2725, displaying the triple V-strut undercarriage, long vertical radiator blocks, angular nose cowling and short engine exhaust manifold. (Photo: RAF Museum)

A late production F.K.8, built by Angus Sanderson, F7546, with compact radiators, long exhaust pipe, rounded nose contours and AW-designed plain-V undercarriage. (Photo: GSL/JMB Collection)

bay staggered biplane with ailerons on upper and lower, equal-span wings. Contrary to suggestions that persisted for years, the F.K.8 was powered from the outset by the 160hp Beardmore engine, a powerplant of approximately the same power/weight ratio as the R.E.8's 140hp R.A.F.4A. However the installation of the straight-six, water-cooled Beardmore was untidy, with angular cowling panels and large vertical radiator blocks attached to each side of the nose and angled inwards to meet at a point on the aircraft's centreline above the engine; the provision of cumbersome exhaust manifolds and the triple V-strut undercarriage with oleo struts on the sides of the fuselage all conspired to limit the F.K.8's speed performance. Indeed, the maximum speed of 95 mph at sea level was 5 mph below that considered essential for corps reconnaissance machines, and 8 mph slower than the R.E.8.

Despite these shortcomings, Koolhoven's aeroplane probably became more popular among its pilots, being straightforward and relatively simple to fly, as well as possessing a robust airframe capable of withstanding battle damage.

The prototype, F.K.7 A411, first flew in May 1916, and acceptance tests were flown at Upavon the following month. The first production orders were placed with Armstrong, Whitworth in August, and the first deliveries were made from Gosforth before the year's end, several aircraft joining No 55 Training Squadron at Lilbourne in December. The first examples to fly with a front-line squadron were delivered to No 35 Squadron, which took a full complement to St Omer in France on 25 January 1917. By

the end of that fateful April No 35 had been joined by No 2 Squadron, as demands for improvements in the aircraft were already being received by the manufacturers.

Apart from severely restricting the pilot's forward vision, the long, angled radiator honeycomb blocks were inefficient and were replaced by much smaller blocks attached lower on the sides of the nose. At about the same time the nose cowling was improved in shape, the angular panels giving place to a more rounded profile in side elevation. The crude engine exhaust manifold, whose efflux was found to distort the crew's field of vision through mirage effect, was eventually changed to a conventional pipe which extended aft of the cockpits.

The undercarriage was also criticised as unsatisfactory, and the RFC suggested using components of the Bristol Fighter's plain V-strut gear, a proposal adopted by No 1 Aircraft Depot, where several such conversions were undertaken — until stocks of the Bristol components ran out and resort was made to the use of B.E.2C parts! In due course Armstrong, Whitworth came up with its own improved plain-V design, still retaining the oleos located in the fuselage sides, but significantly improving the aircraft's performance.

The F.K.8 was ordered in large numbers. Oliver Tapper[1] suggests that the total production amounted to at least 1,652 aircraft, but explains that the exact number may never be known owing to the absence of differentiation between F.K.3s and F.K.8s in some contract

documents. Yet, despite this relatively large number of aircraft, the F.K.8 only served on a total of six squadrons in France, and three in the Balkans and Palestine. Three squadrons, based in the United Kingdom, flew the aircraft on home defence and training duties.

Like the R.E.8, the F.K.8 also undertook bombing raids on the Western Front, commencing in September 1917, and later in Macedonia. The aircraft was capable of carrying up to four 65lb bombs, but more frequently mounted six 40lb Bourdillon phosphorus weapons, especially when required to lay smokescreens in support of ground forces.

It was while the Big Acks were engaged in bombing operations that two pilots won Victoria Crosses. On 27 March 1918, while returning in the F.K.8 B5773 from a raid during the German offensive on the Western Front, 2/Lieut Alan A McLeod was attacked by a Fokker Dr I triplane, which was quickly shot down by his observer, Lt A W Hammond MC. They were then attacked by seven more Fokkers, of which four were shot down — two by McLeod with his front gun. Both crew members were badly wounded, the pilot being hit five times and severely burned when his fuel tank was set on fire. Despite great pain, McLeod climbed out on to the port wing but managed to retain his hold on the control column and, by sideslipping, kept the flames away from the cockpit as he crash landed in No Man's Land, where the two airmen were rescued by British troops. Both miraculously survived, although Hammond lost a leg; McLeod, who was only eighteen years of age, was awarded the Victoria Cross, and Hammond a Bar to his Military Cross.

[1] *Armstrong Whitworth Aircraft since 1913*, Oliver Tapper, Putnam, London, 1988, page 64.

During a period in the summer of 1918, when F.K.8s were taking part in trials with No 8 Squadron in co-operation with the Army's tanks on the Western Front, the second Victoria Cross was won by a Big Ack pilot. On 10 August, as Capt Ferdinand Maurice Felix West MC and Lt J A G Haslam (later Gp Capt, MC, DFC) were returning from a bombing raid on German gun batteries, their F.K.8 was attacked at low level by six enemy fighters. Despite being hit in both legs, one of which was almost severed, and scarcely conscious owing to excruciating pain and loss of blood, the 22-year-old pilot managed to land in the British lines, yet refused to be taken to hospital until he had passed his vital report to the local tank commander. West's Victoria Cross was gazetted three days before the Armistice, and this officer continued to serve in the RAF until his retirement in March 1946 as an Air Commodore.

The F.K.8 survived in service for a few months after the War, the last Squadron, No 150, being disbanded at Kirec in Greece on 18 September 1919.

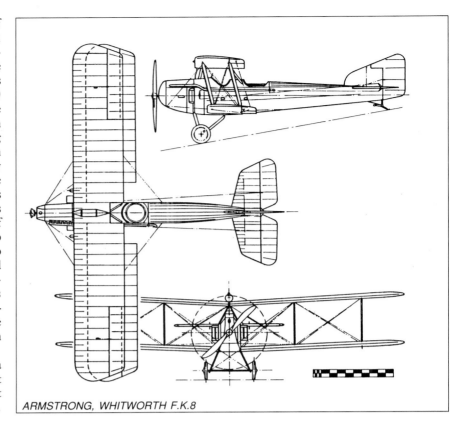

ARMSTRONG, WHITWORTH F.K.8

Type: Single-engine, two-seat, two-bay tractor biplane for ground support and short-range bombing.

Manufacturers: Sir W.G. Armstrong, Whitworth & Co, Ltd., Gosforth, Newcastle-upon-Type; Angus Sanderson & Co, Newcastle-upon-Tyne.

Powerplant: One 160hp Beardmore six-cylinder water-cooled in-line engine driving two-blade propeller. Experimental installations: 150hp R.A.F.4A and 150hp Lorraine Dietrich.

Structure: All-wood wire-braced construction with partial dual flying controls and oleo-sprung undercarriage.

Dimensions: Span, 43ft 6in; length, 31ft 0in; height, 10ft 11in; wing area, 540 sq ft.

Weights: Tare, 1,916lb; all-up, 2,811lb.

Performance: Max speed, 94 mph at sea level; climb to 5,000ft, 11 min; service ceiling, 13,000ft; endurance, 3 hr.

Armament: One forward-firing, synchronized 0.303in Vickers machine gun, and one Lewis or Vickers machine gun on Scarff ring on rear cockpit; provision for bomb load, normally comprising up to six 40lb, four 65lb or two 112lb bombs on underwing racks.

Prototype: One F.K.7 prototype, A411, first flown in May 1916.

Production: Total of 1,652 F.K.8s stated as being delivered to the RFC and RAF prior to 1st September 1918, including 210 probably in component form only. Armstrong, Whitworth, 650 (A2683-A2372, A9980-A9999, B201-B330, B3301-B3400, B5751-B5850 and C8401—C8650). Angus Sanderson, 600 (C3507-C3706, F7347-F7546 and H4425-H4624). 330 further aircraft were ordered (D5001-D5200, F616-F645 and H4625-H4724) but not all are known to have been completed, and their manufacturers have not been confirmed. Upwards of 40 aircraft were repaired and rebuilt, being re-allocated various isolated B, F, and H-prefixed numbers.

Summary of Service: F.K.8s served operationally with Nos 2, 10, 35, 55 and 82 Squadrons, RFC and RAF, and on tank co-operation trials with No 8 Squadron on the Western Front; with Nos 17, 47 and 150 Squadrons in Macedonia; and with No 142 Squadron in Palestine. They also served with Nos 31, 39 and 98 (Training) Squadrons, No 50 (Home Defence) Squadron, Schools of Army Co-operation, School of Photography, Air Observer and Air Gunnery Schools and other training units.

Air Department A.D.1 Navyplane

It is sometimes said that Harold Bolas, in effect deputy chief designer at the Admiralty's Air Department, saw part of his job as exerting a restraining influence on the wilder excesses of his immediate senior, Harris Booth. Yet it

should be remarked that, although most of Booth's own designs bordered on the grotesque, he was able to use his undoubted influence with the Board of Admiralty when it came to gaining official support for the designs of his subordinates (and he it was who strongly advised Murray Sueter to have such outstanding aeroplanes as the Handley Page O/100, and Sopwith 1½-Strutter, Pup and Camel adopted by the Admiralty when they were still

on the drawing board).

It fell to Harold Bolas to initiate the design early in 1916 of a reconnaissance/bombing seaplane, officially designated the A.D.1, but generally referred to as the Navyplane. As the Air Department's Experimental Construction Depot at Port Victoria, Isle of Grain, was not yet fully equipped to undertake the building of complete aeroplanes, the initial A.D.1 design was handed over to the Supermarine Avia-

The A.D.1 Navyplane, No 9095, at the Supermarine works in 1916 with Cdr John Seddon and Hubert Scott-Payne. The wings were rigged without stagger, but did not fold. (Photo: Author's Collection)

tion Works at Woolston, Southampton, for the detail design to be completed and construction of a prototype. Working in close collaboration with Bolas, Reginald Mitchell finished the necessary manufacturing drawings in an exceptionally short time, and the prototype, No 9095, was ready for testing by Cdr John Seddon in August.

The A.D.1 was a compact two-bay biplane whose two-man crew was accommodated in a finely-contoured lightweight monocoque nacelle located in the wing gap, the experimental air-cooled 150hp Smith Static radial engine driving a four-blade pusher propeller. Twin pontoon-type floats were braced to the nacelle and to the lower wings immediately below the inboard interplane struts. Twin fins and rudders were carried between two pairs of steel tubular tail booms, and the tailplane was mounted above the vertical surfaces. Twin tail floats, each with a water rudder, were attached beneath the lower pair of tail booms. The pilot occupied the rear cockpit, with the observer in the bow position. Two 100lb bombs were to be carried under the wing centresection.

The ten-cylinder Smith engine, brainchild of an American John W Smith, had evidently attracted the Admiralty's interest, and had shown promise during bench testing. A production order was placed with Heenan & Froude Ltd, but the engine never gave satisfactory performance in the few prototype aircraft in which it was flown.

Little more was heard of the A.D.1 until May 1917, when it re-appeared with by an A.R.1 engine, designed by W O Bentley. However, although this engine displayed much improved reliability, the A.D.1's performance remained below that demanded by the Admiralty, and six further aircraft originally ordered were not built.

Supermarine had made some efforts to continue development of an enlarged version of the A.D.1, called the Submarine Patrol Seaplane, powered by a 200hp engine, and submitted the design to the Air Board's Seaplane Specification N.3A. Although two prototypes were allotted the serial numbers N24 and N25, work on the project was

discontinued when it was decided that the veteran Short Type 184 adequately met the requirements and would continue in service. (In any case the Super-

marine aircraft would have been unable to lift the 1,100lb 18in torpedo, and did not possess folding wings — both requirements of N.3A.)

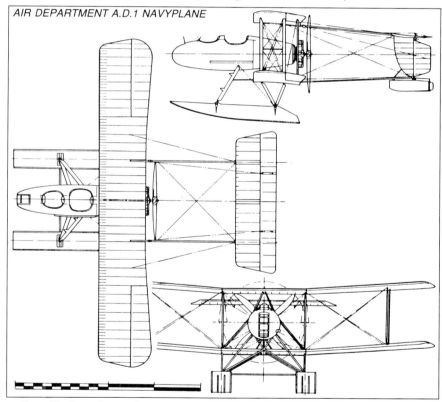

AIR DEPARTMENT A.D.1 NAVYPLANE

Type: Single pusher engine, two-seat, two-bay reconnaissance-bomber biplane with twin main-float undercarriage.

Manufacturer: The Supermarine Aviation Works Ltd, Woolston, Southampton, Hampshire, under the design leadership of Harold Bolas of the Air Department, Admiralty.

Powerplant: One 150hp Smith Static ten-cylinder, single-row, air-cooled radial engine driving four-blade pusher propeller; later replaced by a 150hp A.R.1 (Admiralty Rotary)

Dimensions: Span: 36ft 0in; length, 27ft 9in; height, 12ft 9in; wing area, 364 sq ft.

Weights (Smith Static engine): Tare, 2,100lb; all-up, 3,102lb.

Performance: Max speed, 75 mph at 2,000ft; endurance, 6 hr.

Armament: Provision for one 0.303in Lewis gun on rotatable mounting in nose of nacelle. Provision for bomb load, probably not exceeding 200lb.

Prototype: One, No. 9095, first flown with Smith Static engine by Lt-Cdr John Seddon RN, in August 1916. Second aircraft, No 9096, was cancelled, as was a batch of five aircraft, N1070-N1074.

Airco D.H.4

Captain Geoffrey de Havilland's superb D.H.4 has been called 'the Mosquito of the First World War', a by no means superficial observation for, implicit in the comparison was recognition of *classic* attributes, and all that is suggested by that much-bandied adjective — superiority of performance, efficient structure, good cost-efficiency and, probably most important of all, popularity among its aircrews. The comparison survives further examination; both were produced under the aegis of de Havilland, both were of predominantly wooden construction, both were designed as light bombers yet both were as fast as or faster than the best fighters of their respective periods of service. Equally significant was the fact that both aeroplanes were powered by Rolls-Royce engines (though not exclusively in the instance of the D.H.4), in each case the engines selected being themselves arguably the best powerplants extant in their respective ages.

When first conceived in 1915 by Geoffrey de Havilland at the Aircraft Manufacturing Company, the Airco D.H.4 was envisaged as being powered by the 160hp Beardmore, an engine which Maj Frank Bernard Halford had evolved from the 120hp version, without the penalty of a proportionate increase in power/weight ratio. However, having been favourably impressed by examination of the Hispano-Suiza engine's use of cast aluminium monobloc cylinders with screwed-in steel liners, Halford obtained the co-operation of Sir William Beardmore and Thomas Charles Willis Pullinger to design a new version of the Beardmore along similar lines and, in so doing, produced the 230hp BHP engine, achieving a 40 per cent increase in power

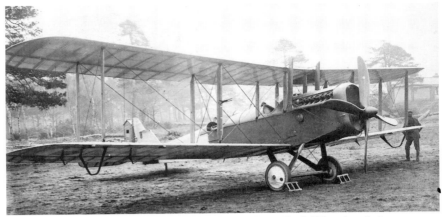

An early Airco-built D.H.4, A2152, with 250hp Rolls-Royce Eagle III engine, during assessment trials at the Royal Aircraft Factory, Farnborough. Note the considerable distance between the cockpits, one of the few features which drew criticism from the RFC. (Photo: Royal Aerospace Establishment)

at a power/weight increase of only 12 per cent. This achievement must be seen in retrospect as being one of the important landmarks in the development of British aero engines during the First World War.

This engine was therefore selected for the prototype D.H.4, No 3696, the prototype bench example of the new BHP being installed for flight trials which began in August 1916 at Hendon. The airframe was of all-wood construction, the fuselage being a wire-braced box-girder built in two sections; the forward, ply-covered portion was joined to the rear, fabric-covered component by steel fishplates immediately aft of the observer's rear cockpit.

The moderately staggered, parallel-chord, two-bay, fabric-covered wings featured upper and lower pairs of ailerons, and were built up on two spruce main spars, spindled out between the compression struts to economise in weight. The wooden, fabric-covered tail unit included a variable-incidence tailplane, and the horn-balance rudder was of the shape by then becoming characteristic of de Havilland's designs.

The undercarriage was of plain wooden V-strut configuration with the wheel axle attached to the strut apices by stout rubber cord binding. Early aircraft featured fairly short undercarriage struts, and there was some risk of damaging the big propeller if the tail was raised too high during take-off. Later, as engine power increased sharply and propellers were accordingly enlarged, the undercarriage V-struts were lengthened, and this design came to be adopted in production, no matter what engine was fitted.

The D.H.4's bomb load varied between four 100 or 112lb bombs and a pair of 230lb weapons, normally carried on racks under the lower wings but occasionally under the fuselage; there were occasions when eight 65lb bombs were carried, although these were considered to be a waste of limited resources when they could be carried by corps reconnaissance aircraft. In truth, the D.H.4 was the RFC's first truly effective, purpose-designed bomber and its operations tended to be confined to set-piece raids against targets behind the German lines.

For all the promise shown by the prototype BHP engine, its introduction into production was far from straightforward, and demanded extensive simplification and redesign. Indeed, these changes delayed the first production deliveries for almost a year. However, de

A D.H.4 with 230hp BHP, the engine intended for the first production aircraft but which did not materialise until mid-1917; note the engine's characteristic oval-shaped radiator and the lengthened undercarriage, introduced since the early production aircraft. (Photo: Imperial War Museum, Neg No H(AM) 90).

A Fiat-powered D.H.4 with bomb rack under the fuselage — possibly intended for a single 230lb bomb. Although the engine cowling contours appeared better than other D.H.4 installations, the overall effect was considerably greater drag owing to the exposed cylinders and the mounting of the radiator under the nose. (Photo: C H Barnes Collection)

Havilland was already aware that Rolls-Royce had successfully bench-run a promising vee-twelve, water-cooled engine as long ago as May 1915, but production examples of this had been earmarked for naval aircraft, not least the Handley Page O/100.

By the end of 1916, when the extent of modifications required by the BHP became known, the production rate of 250hp Rolls-Royce Mk III engines (now named the Eagle III) had reached the stage at which adequate quantities could be allocated to production D.H.4s. An initial order for fifty aircraft was therefore placed with Airco for urgent delivery to the RFC, and the first reached No 55 Squadron at Lilbourne, replacing F.K.8s, in January 1917, and was taken to its base at Fienvillers in France on 6 March. (No 55 Squadron continued to fly D.H.4s until January 1920.)

As further production contracts were raised with Airco, and sub-contracts placed with Westland, F W Berwick and Vulcan, No 55 Squadron remained the only operational RFC D.H.4-equipped unit during 'Bloody April' and in the Battle of Arras. The Squadron's first operational sortie was a bombing attack against Valenciennes railway station by six aircraft on 6 April. Possessing excellent performance and tractable handling qualities the D.H.4, unlike the R.E.8 and F.K.8, was usually able to make good its escape when confronted by enemy fighters, simply by using its superior climb and speed margin; it was, after all, primarily a bomber and was armed with no more than a single forward-firing Vickers gun and a Scarff-mounted Lewis in the rear.

If there was one criticism of the D.H.4, it was that the two cockpits were placed too far apart, the pilot being located well forward so as to possess a good field of view downwards over the lower wing leading edge, and the observer well aft to combine a wide field of view with an effective field of fire if attacked. It was therefore almost impossible for the two crew members to communicate, as the speaking tube between them was of little value in a dogfight.

The heavy losses suffered by so many other RFC squadrons during April 1917 lent further urgency to continue re-equipping and, during the following month, Nos 18 and 57 Squadrons received Airco-built D.H.4s, followed by No 25 Squadron in June. By the end of the year six squadrons were fully equipped with the aircraft.

Meanwhile, as development of the Rolls-Royce Eagle was continuing apace, much work was being done to examine alternative powerplants. The BHP eventually appeared in production form and joined the aircraft assembly lines, as did the Factory's 200hp R.A.F.3A — this version serving with No 18 Squadron in France and No 49 at home — and the 200hp Fiat. The last-named engine had been selected for a consignment of D.H.4s intended for supply to Russia in the late summer of 1917, but the Revolution intervened, taking that nation out of the War. As a result the Fiat D.H.4s were diverted to the Western Front. The other engine that came to be fitted in production D.H.4s was the 230hp Siddeley Puma, but none of these alternative engines could match the excellent 375hp Eagle VIII which, by the end of 1917, powered the majority of front-line D.H.4s.

*   *   *   *   *

From the outset the Admiralty expressed an interest in acquiring D.H.4s, with which to equip RNAS light bomber squadrons in France and elsewhere, and a total of about 90 is thought to have been built to naval requirements by Westland, the majority of them powered by Eagle and BHP engines; about 16 others, with Eagles and R.A.F.3As, were also transferred from War Office production.

The naval D.H.4s differed from the RFC version in being armed with a pair of front Vickers guns, and the observer's

A 230hp Siddeley Puma-powered D.H.4, probably with No 27 Squadron at its base at Ruisseauville in France during 1918, seen here carrying a pair of 112lb RL bombs under the wings. (Photo: GLS/JMB Collection)

An Eagle VIII-powered D.H.4, N5997, of No 202 Squadron at Bergues in 1918, wearing highly individual markings. This example was of the first Westland-built batch for the RNAS, having been completed before the decision was taken to raise the observer's gun ring. Note the forward Vickers guns. (Photo: C H Barnes Collection)

gun ring, instead of being recessed into the rear fuselage decking, was raised so as to be level with the top decking profile.

RNAS D.H.4s began equipping No 2 (Naval) Squadron at about the same time as the RFC squadrons began bombing raids in April 1917, and No 5 (Naval) Squadron also re-equipped during the summer of that year. In all, eight operational RNAS squadrons flew D.H.4s, of which four were based in Italy and the Aegean during 1918, their rôle being to mount long-range bombing attacks over the Balkans.

It may be a matter of interest to note that, although fewer D.H.4s were produced than the much inferior F.K.8 tactical reconnaissance bomber, the D.H. enjoyed far greater operational utilisation, yet actually began to decline in numbers with the RFC from the spring of 1918. This was principally on account of the hopes pinned on the D.H.9 (see page 83), a direct development of, and similar in most respects to the D.H.4.

At the time when an independent bombing force was being assembled, during the winter of 1917-18 when it was designated the 41st Wing of the RFC and commanded by Lt-Col Cyril Louis Norton Newall (later Marshal of the RAF Lord Newall GCB, OM, GCMG, CBE, AM), Maj-Gen Hugh Trenchard scornfully deprecated the use of such aircraft as the F.E.2B and D.H.4 as already being obsolescent. The widespread belief that the D.H.9 would constitute a significant advance over the D.H.4 prompted the War Office prematurely to initiate contracts for the D.H.9 before it became apparent that much work needed to be done before that aircraft was fully ready for service.

Thus it was that by mid-1918 there were still only nine RAF D.H.4 bomber squadrons in France (including four recently transferred from the former RNAS). Eight further squadrons, employed on home defence and training duties, were based in Britain.

Many D.H.4s came to be employed for experimental purposes, including use as test beds for other engines such as

Type: Single-engine, two-seat, two-bay biplane light bomber.
Manufacturers: The Aircraft Manufacturing Co Ltd, Hendon, London NW9; F W Berwick & Co Ltd, Park Royal, London NW10; Palladium Autocars Ltd, Putney, London SW15; Waring and Gillow Ltd, Hammersmith, London W6; Westland Aircraft Works, Yeovil, Somerset; Vulcan Motor and Engineering Co (1906) Ltd, Crossens, Southport, Lancashire. (Production of D.H.4B undertaken by five manufacturers in America.)
Powerplant: Prototype. One 230hp B.H.P. water-cooled in-line engine driving four-blade propeller. Production aircraft. 230hp B.H.P., 230hp Puma, 250-375hp Rolls-Royce Eagle (various versions), 200hp R.A.F. 3A and 260hp Fiat. Experimental installations included 300hp Renault 12Fe, 400hp Sunbeam Matabele and 353hp Rolls-Royce 'G'. American-built version with Liberty 12A engines.
Structure: Wire-braced wooden structure, fabric- and ply-covered; two spruce wing spars; wooden V-strut undercarriage with rubber cord-sprung wheel axle.
Dimensions: Span, 42ft 4⅝in; length (B.H.P. and Eagle engines), 30ft 8in; height, (Puma) 10ft 1in, (Eagle VIII) 11ft 0in; wing area, 434 sq ft.
Weights: Puma. Tare, 2,230lb; all-up, 3,344lb. Eagle VIII. Tare, 2,387lb; all-up, 3,472lb.
Performance: Puma. Max speed, 108 mph at sea level, 104 mph at 10,000ft; climb to 10,000ft, 14 min; service ceiling, 17,400ft; endurance, 4½ hr. Eagle VIII. Max speed, 143 mph at sea level, 133 mph at 10,000ft; climb to 10,000ft, 9 min; service ceiling, 22,000ft; endurance, 3¾ hr.
Armament: Max bomb load, 460lb, comprising combinations of 230lb or 112lb bombs on external racks. Gun armament comprised one synchronized forward-firing 0.303in Vickers machine gun on nose decking (two guns on some Westland-built aircraft); observer's cockpit fitted with either Scarff ring or pillar mounting(s) for either one or two Lewis machine guns.
Prototype: One, No 3696, first flown by Capt Geoffrey de Havilland at Hendon in August 1916.
Production: A total of 1,449 aircraft built in Britain for the RFC and RNAS: Airco, 960 (A2125-A2174, A7401-A8089, B1482, C4501-C4540, D8351-D8430, D9231-D9280 and F2633-F2732); Berwick, 100 (B2051-B2150); Vulcan, 100 (B5451-B5550); Westland, 167 (B3954-B3970, B9476-B9500, D1751-D1775, N5960-N6009 and N6380-N6429); Palladium, 100 (F5699-F5798); Waring and Gillow, 46 (H5894-H5939). Of the above total production, twelve were delivered into store and eventually reached the civil register, and twelve N-registered Westland-built aircraft were re-numbered in the B3954-B3970 batch. Some aircraft were also rebuilt during repair and re-allocated different numbers.)
Summary of RFC and RNAS Service: D.H.4s served with Nos 18, 25, 27, 49, 55 and 57 Squadrons, RFC and RAF on the Western Front; Nos 30 and 63 Squadrons, RFC and RAF, in Mesopotamia; Nos 223, 224, 226 and 227 Squadrons, RAF in the Aegean; and with the Russian contingent at Archangel. D.H.4s served with Nos 5, 6 and 11 Squadrons, RNAS (later Nos 205, 206 and 211 Squadrons, RAF) on the Western Front; Nos 2, 5 and 17 Squadrons, RNAS (later Nos 202, 205 and 217 Squadrons, RAF) on Coastal Patrol, based in Britain; and at RNAS Stations, Great Yarmouth, Port Victoria and Redcar (becoming Nos 212 and 273 Squadrons, RAF). D.H.4s also served on Nos 31 and 51 Training Squadrons, RFC, Air Observers' Schools, the Reconnaissance School at Farnborough and various armament schools.

Full production-standard naval Eagle-powered D.H.4, N6000, with flat rear fuselage decking and flush-mounted rear Scarff gun ring. The aircraft is armed with twin front Vickers guns and is shown carrying a fuselage-mounted 112lb RL bomb and eight wing-mounted light bombs. The repetition of the rudder flash on the elevators was unusual. (Photo: via J M Bruce)

the Eagle VI (in A7401), the 300hp Renault 12Fe (in A2148), the R.A.F.4D (A7864), and the 400hp Sunbeam Matabele (A8083); another D.H.4 was flown in 1919 with an experimental Rolls-Royce Type G engine.

And while the War Office (and later the new Air Ministry) decided to replace the D.H.4 with the D.H.9, the United States, having laid plans in May 1917 to adopt the former in large qualties, persisted with this intention, and eventually produced a total of 3,227 aircraft. The original contracts, placed with three large American manufacturers, were ulitmately increased to cover no fewer than 9,500 aircraft — even before the American engine, the 400hp Liberty 12, had been built and bench run.

The first flight by a D.H.4 with the Liberty was made on 29 October 1917, yet during the next twelve months 1,885 US-built examples had been shipped to France for use by the American Expeditionary Force. The D.H.4A, as it was designated, became the only British type built in the USA to give operational service during the War. There was to be an ironic twist of fortune when, after the Armistice, the widely criticised D.H.9 gave way to much-improved D.H.9As, many of which were to be fitted with the American Liberty 12 engine!

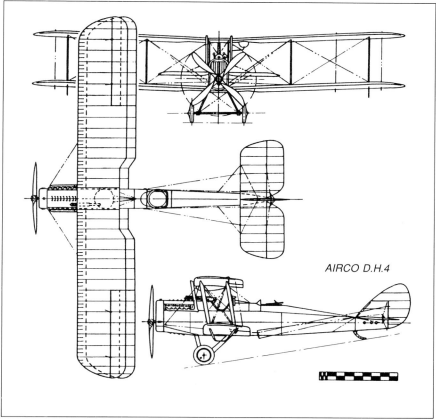

AIRCO D.H.4

Avro Type 528

Little is known of the Avro Type 528, a single-engine, three-bay biplane whose construction at Miles Platting is said to have followed immediately after the Type 523A Pike in the late summer of 1916. It was covered by Avro Works No 2350 and only one example was built; however, it has been suggested that two serial numbers, A316 and A317, allocated to A V Roe by the Admiralty, may have been allocated to this type, and that a second aircraft was planned, but cancelled.

The Avro Type 528, probably at Hamble. (Photo: RAF Museum, Ref No B554/13/3)

Powered by a 225hp Sunbeam driving a four-blade propeller, the Type 528

was designed as a bomber, its bombs being carried in two nacelles on the lower wing, inboard of the inner pair of interplane struts. Bearing in mind that the aircraft was in fact larger than the twin-engine Pike with 150hp Green engines, the bomb load must have been relatively small, and in no way comparable with that of the successful Short Type 184. The Avro aircraft also featured folding wings.

The Sunbeam engine installation, though itself neatly cowled, was compromised by the attachment of two large vertical radiators on either side of the front fuselage immediately forward of the pilot's cockpit, a location that must have severely restricted his view, further limited by the bomb containers on the lower wings.

Few details have survived of the aircraft, and the date of first flight — probably during the autumn of 1916 — is not known.

Type: Single-engine, two-seat, three-bay biplane experimental light bomber.
Manufacturer: A V Roe & Co Ltd., Miles Platting, Manchester, and Hamble, Hampshire.
Powerplant: One 225hp Sunbeam eight-cylinder water-cooled in-line engine driving four-blade propeller.
Dimensions: Span, approx 65ft.
Weights and Performance: No details traced.
Armament: Provision for a single 0.303in Lewis gun on rear cockpit; light bomb load carried in nacelles on lower wings.
Prototype: One only (serial number and first flight date not known)

Wight Bomber

Although superficially appearing to be in the same general category as the Avro Type 528 (described above), Howard Wright's Wight Bomber was obviously superior, due principally to the choice of a 275hp Rolls-Royce Eagle engine, the increased power available making possible the lifting of four 112lb bombs. Like the Avro aircraft, the Wight design possessed three-bay folding wings of about 65-foot span, but carried its bombs on conventional racks under the lower wings.

Single-acting ailerons were fitted to the upper wings only, and the large upper wing overhang was wire-braced using kingposts. The usual box-girder fuselage was of small cross-sectional area, and the tall undercarriage was of simple V-strut configuration.

The single Wight prototype was almost certainly ordered at about the same time as, and for comprison with, the Short Bomber, and was therefore at an immediate disadvantage owing to the latter's use of existing Short 184 com-

The Wight Bomber, N501; despite its greater power, the Eagle installation was little tidier than that of the Avro 528's Sunbeam. In other respects the Wight was an altogether superior aeroplane. (Photo: via J M Bruce)

ponents (being a direct development of that aircraft). Thus by the time the Wight Bomber first flew, late in 1916, the Short had already been ordered into production by several manufacturers. Nevertheless, while the Avro 528 was not considered worthwhile to develop further, successful development of the Wight resulted in production orders being placed by the Admiralty for a seaplane derivative (see page 78).

Type: Single-engine, two-seat, three-bay biplane naval bomber.
Manufacturer: J Samuel White & Co, East Cowes, Isle of Wight.
Powerplant: One 275hp Rolls-Royce Eagle II twelve-cylinder water-cooled in-line engine driving two-blade propeller.
Dimensions: Span, 65ft 6in; wing area, 715 sq ft.
Weights: Tare, 3,162lb; all-up, 5,166lb.
Performance: Max speed, 89 mph at sea level; climb to 10,000ft, 34 min.
Armament: One Lewis machine gun with Scarff ring on rear cockpit; bomb load, four 112lb bombs.
Prototype: One, N501, first flown in 1916. No production.

Dyott Bomber

George M Dyott gained his RAeC pilot's certificate on 11 August 1911 and almost immediately set off on a tour of North America, giving public demonstrations in a Deperdussin monoplane. On returning home he designed a small sporting monoplane, which he had built by Hewlett & Blondeau Ltd, and shortly before the War he designed a twin-engine biplane intended for exploration in Africa.

This aircraft attracted the Admiralty's attention as a potential naval bomber and Dyott was prevailed upon to adapt it for Service consideration. Once again manufacture was the subject of a contract with Helwett & Blondeau during the spring and summer of 1916, and the aircraft emerged as a well-proportioned biplane with parallel-chord, equal-span, four-bay wings outboard of the engines, which were located in the gap. Power was provided by a pair of 120hp Beardmore water-cooled engines without cowlings — the only engines available to a relatively unknown aircraft designer on the fringe of the aircraft industry, and clearly unequal to the task of providing adequate power for a fairly large bomber.

No fewer than five Lewis machine guns were carried, two being located to fire through ports in the sides of the nose; two spigot mounted on the front gunner's spacious cockpit and another

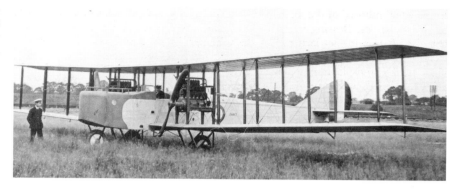

The first Dyott Bomber, No 3687, in the aircraft's initial configuration with uncowled Beardmore engines, probably photographed at RNAS Hendon in August 1916. (Photo: via J M Bruce)

on a gunner's position aft of the wings.

After initial flights at Chingford, Essex, in August 1916, the first aircraft, No 3687, was delivered for trials at Hendon, while efforts were made to improve the design of the engine installations by introducing fully-cowled nacelles with frontal radiators. The nose contours were improved by straightening the top line of the fuselage and eliminating the slope upwards to the pilot's windscreen.

No 3688 joined 3687 at Hendon at the beginning of September 1916. Both remained there until early October, when 3687 went to the Experimental Armament Depot on the Isle of Grain. After a period with the Design Flight at Eastchurch, No 3688 was transferred to Dunkerque for Service trials, but records suggest that it had been written off by March 1918.

In efforts to improve the Dyott, the first aircraft was later fitted with uncowled BHP engines (with their characteristic oval radiators), enlarged rudders and an improved front gun mounting. (Photo: Air Ministry, Neg No H1017)

Type: Twin-engine, three-crew, four-bay biplane naval bomber.
Manufacturer: Hewlett & Blondeau Ltd, Leagrave, Luton, Bedfordshire, to the design of George M Dyott.
Powerplant: Two 120hp Beardmore six-cylinder water-cooled in-line engines driving two-blade tractor propellers. Later fitted with 230hp BHP engines.
Dimensions (approx.): Span, 70ft; length, 50ft; height, 12ft; wing area, 800 sq ft.
Weight (approx.): All-up, 7,800lb.
Armament: Gun armament comprised five Lewis guns — four in the nose and one on midships gunner's cockpit. Details of intended bomb load not known.
Prototypes: Two, Nos 3687 and 3688. No 3687 was flown at Chingford in August 1916.

Mann, Egerton Type B

The motor car manufacturer Mann, Egerton & Co Ltd of Norwich had been one of the first companies to offer its services to build aircraft for the Admiralty after the outbreak of war in 1914, and had received a contract to produce twelve Short Type 184s in the spring of 1915. Later that year the Admiralty encouraged such sub-contractors to embark on designs of their own, believing that experience gained in building aeroplanes of other companies' design would bring fresh opinions on how best to improve the aircraft themselves as well as, for instance, simplifying their production. (It has already been recorded that the Armstrong, Whitworth F.K.3 was produced for the War Office as a development of the Factory's B.E.2C, structurally simplified in order to speed production.)

So it was with Mann, Egerton who, in collaboration with both Short Bros and the Admiralty, prepared the design (the Type B) of a modified version of the Type 184 seaplane, intended to make for simpler production as well as improved performance and handling. The new wings were of two-bay configuration with reduced lower wing span and much increased upper wing extensions, the large overhang being liberally wire-braced using tall kingposts; indeed the entire wing form was similar to that of the Short Bomber, production of which followed on after the Type B at Norwich. The float undercarriage, fuselage

The first Mann, Egerton Type B, No 9085, at Norwich in 1916. Note the very long, inversely-tapered ailerons fitted on the upper wings only. (Photo: via J M Bruce)

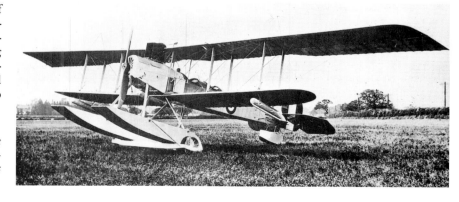

and tail unit were constructed with standard Type 184 components, but the 225hp Sunbeam engine was located several inches higher than in the Short aircraft, resulting in the upper fuselage line sloping downwards behind the radiator towards the pilot's cockpit. The outrigger floats were moved inboard beneath the lower wing tips (although it is difficult to understand what purpose they now served, being located so close to the main float gear).

The bomb load remained the same as that of the Type 184, although it is unlikely that the Mann, Egerton Type B

was ever required to carry a torpedo. A production order for ten Type Bs was completed at Norwich during 1916, and these entered service with the RNAS alongside the standard Type 184s. No suggestion, however, has been found that the Service appreciated any marked improvement in the modified seaplanes

and, apart from the company's indigenous H.1 and H.2 single-seat fighters and the Short Bombers (referred to above), Mann, Egerton reverted to sub-contracted production of other companies' designs (including the French Spad S.VII, and the Airco D.H.9, D.H.9A and D.H.10).

Type: Single-engine, two-seat, two-bay biplane patrol bomber seaplane.
Manufacturer: Mann, Egerton & Co Ltd, Prince of Wales Road, Norwich, Norfolk.
Powerplant: One 225hp Sunbeam water-cooled engine driving two-blade propeller.
Dimensions: Span, 70ft 0in; length, 40ft 7in.
Armament: One 0.303in Lewis machine gun in rear cockpit; provision to carry light bombs under the wings.
Production: Ten aircraft, Nos 9085-9094.

Royal Aircraft Factory F.E.2B Bomber

The venerable F.E.2 (Farman Experimental) was originally flown long before the War, and production examples of the first variant, the F.E.2A, were sent to France in January 1915 — the first British aeroplanes designed for air combat to reach the RFC. As such the F.E.2A was to shoulder much of the early responsibility for defence against the Fokker monoplane scouts over the Western Front, a brave but largely ineffective defence owing to the aircraft's deficiencies in performance and agility.

When British purpose-designed dog-fighters, beginning with the Airco D.H.2, began arriving in France, some of the pressure was removed from the F.E.2As and 2Bs — the latter with 120hp Beardmore engines — and the opportunity was taken to investigate the possi-

An early production F.E.2B, No 4962, probably built at the parent Factory with 120hp Beardmore engine and the cumbersome oleo undercarriage with nose wheel. (Photo: Real Photographs Co.)

bility of operating the F.E.2B at night, and No 6 Squadron flew a number of night patrols from Abeele, confirming that the aircraft was indeed suitable for night operations, provided that the outrigged nosewheel was removed; to begin with, however, the oleo struts were retained, until these were replaced by plain V-struts. Late production F.E.2Bs were powered by the 160hp

Beardmore, but this engine initially proved unpopular owing to unreliability.

By the spring of 1916 a new generation of German fighting scouts had started appearing over the Front, and new efforts were made to find a substantially more powerful engine for the F.E.2, and the choice fell upon the new 250hp Rolls-Royce, soon to be named the Eagle. The version thus powered, the F.E.2D, entered production in March and the first example to be despatched left for France on 30 June, only to be captured intact by the Germans later that day when its pilot landed at Lille in mistake for St Omer.

This aircraft had been intended for No 20 Squadron at Clairmarais, and subsequent deliveries were safely made during the following month, the Squadron being engaged in converting from

Standard production F.E.2B with plain V-strut undercarriage; the nose Lewis gun has not yet been fitted on this factory-fresh example. (Photo: Stuart Leslie)

the F.E.2B during the Battle of the Somme. No 57 Squadron, also flying the F.E.2D, arrived in France during December that year, and No 25 Squadron converted in March 1917.

By then, however, it was recognised that the slower F.E.2B was fatally vulnerable in daylight operations, and it was No 6 Squadron, drawing on its previous night flying experience, which flew the first significant night bombing sorties on the night of 16/17 November 1916, when four aircraft, each carrying three 100lb bombs, took off to attack targets of opportunity — and achieved notable success against enemy rail targets.

With a relatively large number of F.E.2B squadrons now in service (and a shortage of Rolls-Royce engines threatening early in 1917), the decision was taken to retain the 2B in service as a night bomber, a rôle it continued to perform for the remainder of the War. On the other hand, the F.E.2D (of which very few were ever flown with bombs) was withdrawn from front-line service before the end of 1917.

Results of the early night attacks by No 6 Squadron were examined closely by the War Office, and the first dedicated night bombing Squadron to be equipped with F.E.2Bs was No 100, which was formed at Hingham in Norfolk on 23 February 1917 and moved to France the following month, where it was placed under the direct command of RFC HQ. The aircraft flown by this Squadron featured the plain V-strut undercarriage, without oleos, as standard, for this configuration permitted the aircraft to carry a 230lb RL bomb, whereas the gear with oleos did not.

During the first week of July No 100 Squadron twice raided targets at Douai, location of a German fighter aerodrome and, during an attack on the night of the 7th/8th included a pair of newly-arrived F.E.2Bs each armed with a single Vickers one-pounder quick-firing gun. Although these guns, which continued to be used for about three months, were found to be quite effective so long as they continued firing, any stoppage that occurred could not be rectified in the air; there was also a danger that spent shell cases could foul the propeller. Aircraft armed with the one-pounder (also flown by No 102 Squadron) were distinguishable by the side-by-side disposition of the crew, the gunner being seated to the right of the pilot.

In August No 100 Squadron was heavily engaged during the battles of Messines and Ypres, dropping four-and-a-half tons of bombs in attacks on Mouveaux aerodrome and on railway targets at Comines, Courtrai, Menin and Roulers on the night of the 16th/17th.

This series of raids presaged a continuing bomber offensive that lasted through the autumn and winter, and was joined by the bomb-carrying F.E.2Bs of Nos 58, 83, 101, 102, 148 and 149 Squadrons although, with Trenchard's creation of

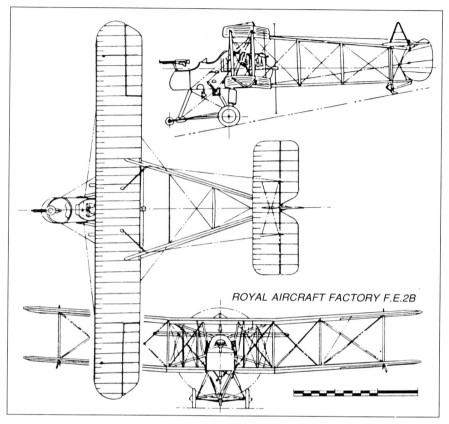

ROYAL AIRCRAFT FACTORY F.E.2B

Type: Single pusher engine, two-seat, three-bay biplane as employed as a night bomber.
Manufacturers: The Royal Aircraft Factory, Farnborough, Hampshire; Boulton & Paul Ltd, Norwich, Norfolk; Richard Garrett & Sons, Leiston, Suffolk; Ransome, Sims & Jefferies, Ipswich, Suffolk; G & J Weir, Cathcart, Glasgow.
Powerplant: F.E.2B as bomber. 120hp or 160hp Beardmore six-cylinder, water-cooled, in-line engine driving four-blade pusher propeller. F.E.2D. One 225hp Rolls-Royce (Eagle I).
Dimensions: Span, 47ft 9in; length, 32ft 3in; height, 12ft 7½in; wing area, 494 sq ft.
Weights (160hp Beardmore): Tare, 2,061lb; all-up, 3,037lb.
Performance (160hp Beardmore): Max speed, 91.5 mph at sea level, 76 mph at 10,000ft; climb to 10,000ft, 39 min 44 sec; service ceiling, 11,000ft.
Armament (as a bomber): Usually a single 0.303in Lewis machine gun, bracket-mounted on the front cockpit. 160hp Beardmore-powered night bombers could carry up to three 112lb bombs when flown as single-seaters, or one 230lb bomb when flown as two-seaters; combinations of smaller bombs were sometimes carried, equivalent to these bomb loads.
Production: Total number of F.E.2Bs converted or built and flown as bombers is not known (some sources give the total as about 860). The following figures refer to the entire new production of F.E.2Bs and F.E.2Ds (1,810 aircraft). Royal Aircraft Factory, 137 (Nos 6328-6377 [Bs], No 7995 [D], A1-A40 [Ds], A1932-A1966 [Ds], A5143-A5152 [Ds] and A8950 [B]); Boulton & Paul, 550 (Nos 5201-5250 [Bs], 6928-7027 [Bs], 7666-7715 [Bs], A6351-A6600 [Ds], B1851-B1900 [Ds] and A5438-A5487 [Bs]); Garrett, 60 (D3776-D3835 [Bs]); Ransome, Sims & Jefferies, 250 (B401-B500, C9786-C9835 and D9900-D9999, all Bs); Weir, 650 (Nos 4838-4937, A778-A877, A5500-A5649, A5650-A5799 and D9081-D9230, all Bs); constructors not known (probably R.A.F., Farnborough), 163 (Nos 4938-5000 and E7037-E7163, all Bs). Bomber conversions are known to have been made in almost all the above batches.
Summary of Service: F.E.2Bs operated regularly as night bombers with Nos 58, 83, 100, 101, 102, 148 and 149 Squadrons, RFC and RAF, and with No 3 Naval Wing, RNAS, in France. They were also flown by numerous other squadrons over the Western Front on short-range bombing-reconnaissance attacks.

A presentation F.E.2B, A5478, Gold Coast No 10, of No 22 Squadron, probably at Chipilly during 1917; it is shown carrying a single 230lb bomb under the nacelle and six 25lb fragmentation bombs under the wings — the maximum bomb load of the F.E.2B with a two-man crew. The tube extending down from the nose of the nacelle is a flare chute. (Photo: Stuart Leslie)

the 41st Wing for the strategic bombing of German industrial targets, No 100 Squadron, itself coming to be regarded as the spearhead of the RFC's night bombing effort, was transferred to the new force on 11 October 1917. Its first major attack with the Wing was flown on the 24th of that month, when fourteen F.E.2Bs accompanied nine naval Handley Page O/100s to bomb the Burbach factory near Saarbrüchen.

As early as January 1917 it had been assumed that, with the F.E.2B's approaching obsolescence, its value as a bomber would be shortlived, and for several months its production was allowed to run down, and would have ceased altogether by the end of that year had not No 100 Squadron's early successes suggested that the F.E.2B represented an economical, and by all accounts effective bombing weapon by

night. Therefore, as new squadrons were about to be formed and others transferred to the night bombing rôle, new orders were placed for F.E.2B production — so much so that as late as the third quarter of 1918 its production rate was still accelerating. Indeed, at the date of the Armistice, the venerable pusher bomber was still serving with six front-line squadrons, while a further six were training on the type in the United Kingdom.

That the F.E.2B was outdated long before the end of the War is undeniable, and it was quite fortuitous that the art of night fighting was still in its infancy, so that bombing by night could be, and was performed with some impunity by both

sides. Yet the old pusher aeroplane demonstrated a number of important attributes that recommended it for such operations: it possessed docile handling qualities and was straightforward to land at night, and with the engine located aft the crew was afforded an excellent field of view, unimpeded by exhaust flash. With generous wing area and ample power, it could lift a 230lb bomb or, perhaps surprisingly, as many as fourteen 25lb bombs[1] — the latter a most appropriate armoury for use against diffuse targets such as trains and other troop transport.

---

[1]   The actual weight of the Cooper '20-pounder' with fragmentation case.

Martinsyde G.102 Elephant

An almost exact contemporary of the Factory's F.E.2B in the bombing rôle, the single-seat Martinsyde G.102 was nevertheless of more modern concept and configuration, yet was possibly less popular among its pilots when used for night operations. Ironically, although both aeroplanes were powered by the 160hp Beardmore engine in their finite bombing configurations, and carried much the same bomb load, the Martinsyde was about ten per cent faster at all altitudes (being somewhat smaller and lighter), yet fewer than two hundred were built, and only fully equipped one front line bombing squadron in France.

The G.102 was a derivative of the G.100, a fighting scout of portly dimensions and powered by the 120hp Beardmore. It entered service at the end of 1915, before the appearance of reliable British front gun synchronizing gear. Thus during the Battle of the

A Martinsyde G.102, A6263, of No 27 Squadron. Being without synchronized front gun, the aircraft carried a Lewis gun on the top wing and another behind the pilot's left shoulder; these were usually retained when engaged in bombing operations. (Photo: Stuart Leslie)

Somme the G.100s, which equipped No 27 Squadron (commanded by Maj Sydney Smith, later Bt Col, DSO, MC), were generally outclassed in air combat and straightway became employed as light support bombers over the battlefield and immediately behind the German lines, being capable of carrying a pair of 112lb bombs or up to eight 25-pounders.

Like the F.E.2B, the Martinsyde was

then fitted with the 160hp Beardmore to improve its weight-lifting abilities, a remedy that increased its ground level speed (without bombs) from 93 to 103 mph, and enabled it to carry a maximum load of one 230lb bomb under the fuselage and four 25lb bombs under the wings, although more often it flew with two 112lb and four 25lb bombs, or four 65-pounders. This version was termed the G.102, quickly gaining the unofficial, but widely accepted name of Elephant, a name prepetuated in the device of the official Badge of No 27 Squadron.

Unlike the F.E.2B, the G.102 was little used as a night bomber for, despite possessing adequate range to attack targets well behind the enemy lines, it was not considered realistic for the pilot to navigate himself over long distances at night, nor for that matter to aim his bombs with any great accuracy. The G.102 therefore confined its bombing raids to daylight, being capable to a reasonable degree of defending itself against enemy fighters. Nevertheless No 27 Squadron flew many noteworthy raids, particularly during the Battles of Arras, Messines and Ypres.

Being thus confined to daylight bombing over short ranges, the Elephant was not chosen for inclusion in the 41st Wing's order of battle for strategic bombing during the winter of 1917-18, and was therefore replaced on No 27

Squadron by D.H.4s by November 1917.

Overseas, however, Elephants equipped Nos 14 and 67 (Australian) Squadrons in Palestine and Mesopotamia, as well as elements of Nos 30, 63 and 72 Squadrons, also based in Mesopotamia, between September 1916 and the end of the War, when they also were withdrawn from service.

Type: Single-engine, single-seat, two-bay biplane light support bomber.
Manufacturer: Martinsyde Ltd, Brooklands, Byfleet, Surrey.
Powerplant: One 160hp Beardmore water-cooled in-line engine driving two-blade propeller.
Dimensions: Span, 38ft 0in; length, 27ft 0in; height, 9ft 8in; wing area, 410 sq ft.
Weights: Tare, 1,793lb; all-up (with two 112lb bombs), 2,692lb.
Performance (with two 112lb bombs): Max speed, 96 mph at sea level, 92 mph at 10,000ft; climb to 5,000ft, 9 min 15 sec; service ceiling, 12,800ft; endurance, 3 hr.
Armament: One forward-firing 0.303in Lewis machine gun above the wing centresection and one Lewis gun on mounting behind the cockpit on the port side. Bomb load of either one 230lb and four 25lb bombs, two 112lb and four 25lb bombs, or four 65lb bombs on external racks under fuselage and wings.
Prototype: Identity of first aircraft with 160hp Beardmore engine not known.
Production: 171 G.102s built (A1561-A1610, A3935-A4004 and A6250-A6300). At least two aircraft, B864 and B865, formerly G.100s, rebuilt as G.102s by No 1 (Southern) Aircraft Repair Depot, South Farnborough, Hampshire.
Summary of Service: G.102s served with No 27 Squadron, RFC, over the Western Front, with Nos 14 and 67 (Australian) Squadrons in Palestine, and with elements of Nos 30, 63 and 72 Squadrons, RFC, in Mesopotamia. They also flew with the Central Flying School, Upavon, and with Nos 31, 39 and 51 (Training) Squadrons.

Beardmore W.B.I

Among the numerous commercial manufacturers contracted to build the Royal Aircraft Factory's B.E.2C was the Scottish shipbuilder, William Beardmore & Co Ltd of Dalmuir, its output of these aeroplanes being destined for the Admiralty whose Inspector of Naval Aircraft at the factory was Lieut George Tilghman Richards. This officer had, before the War, been engaged in aircraft design and, in 1916, was permitted to resign his Commission in order to take up the appointment of chief designer in Beardmore's aviation department, so as to enable the company to respond to the Admiralty's encouragement of commercial manufacturers to embark on the design of their own aircraft.

Richards' first aircraft, the W.B.I, was an imaginative, if not radical attempt to produce a naval bomber whose *modus operandi* was to attack in a long shallow glide in order to achieve tactical surprise. To this end, careful attention was paid to limiting drag, especially in the engine installation, and it is said that the gliding angle, with engine throttled back and at about half-fuel weight, was of the order of six degrees, made possible by large, high-aspect ratio three-bay wings and a wing loading of 5 lb/sq ft at this weight. Power was initially

Two views of the Beardmore W.B.I, N525, as originally powered by the 230hp BHP engine. (Photos: Imperial War Museum, Neg Nos Q67450 and Q67451)

provided by a 230hp BHP engine built by the Galloway Engineering Company, the radiators being of the vertical type, attached to the sides of the fuselage and extended upwards to converge beneath the upper wing.

Despite all the care taken to provide clean contours for the engine cowling,

the undercarriage was cumbersome, consisting of two pairs of mainwheels, each pair being provided with two small forewheels on struts extending forward, cross-braced and wire-braced to the lower wings.

It is thought that the heavily staggered wings were not made to fold owing to the interplane strut configuration and, because the mainwheels of the undercarriage were located well forward, the aircraft would have rested on its tailskid if the wings were folded. Ailerons were provided on upper and lower wings, interconnected by external cables.

The W.B.I was designed to carry six 112lb bombs, probably suspended from two parallel beams attached beneath the fuselage between the two mainwheel mounting structures. The bombs were to be aimed by the observer/gunner who, occupying the rear cockpit situated well aft, was provided with an aperture in the underside of the fuselage for sighting, and two large transparent panels in the sides.

The sole W.B.I, N525, was delivered to the RNAS at Cranwell on 6 June 1917

(though it was probably first flown rather earlier), but suffered damage in a landing accident while being flown by Wg-Cdr Richard Edmund Charles Peirse RN (later Air Chief Marshal Sir Richard, KCB, DSO, AFC, RAF, C-in-C, Bomber Command, during the Second World War). By the time of this accident the BHP engine had been replaced by a 240hp Sunbeam.

The aircraft, however, was not accepted by the Admiralty for production, principally because, by the time it was flown, the Handley Page O/100 heavy bomber was already being delivered to the Service; moreover, assuming the wings were not made to fold, the span of the W.B.I would not have conformed to the maximum naval hangar storage dimensions.

Type: Single-engine, two-seat, three-bay biplane long-range bomber.
Manufacturer: William Beardmore & Co Ltd, Dalmuir, Dunbartonshire.
Powerplant: One 230hp Beardmore; later one 240hp Sunbeam.
Dimensions: Span, 61ft 6in; length, 32ft 10in; height, 14ft 9in; wing area, 796 sq ft.
Weights (Beardmore): Tare, 3,410lb; all-up (with 660lb bomb load), 5,600lb.
Performance (Beardmore): Max speed, 91 mph at sea level; climb to 5,000ft, 26 min; endurance, 7¼ hr.
Armament: One 0.303in Lewis machine gun with ring mounting on rear cockpit; bomb load of six 110lb bombs.
Prototype: One, N525, probably first flown early in 1917. No production.

Fairey F.16-F.22 Campania

Formed in 1915 by Charles Richard Fairey (formerly chief engineer with Short Bros Ltd, Rochester, and later Sir Richard, Kt, MBE), Fairey Aviation Co Ltd was set on its path of aircraft manufacture by a production order for a dozen Short Type 827 seaplanes, aircraft whose configuration appears to have set a pattern for the majority of the company's own designs for several years to come. After an initial design, the F.2 — somewhat unrealistically termed a 'fighter', it being a large, gangling twin-engine aeroplane — Fairey turned his attention to producing a single-engine floatplane, drawing on his previous experience with Shorts, although the head of the design staff was F Duncanson. And in building this aeroplane, the Fairey F.16, the company embarked on a family of aircraft whose lineage could be traced through progressive deriva-

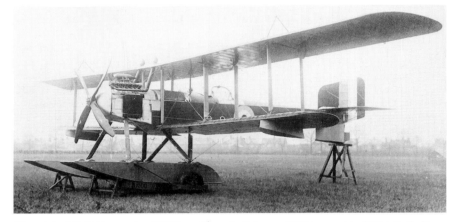

The original F.16 Campania, N1000, at Hayes in February 1917 powered by 250hp Rolls-Royce Mk IV, showing the slab radiators on the sides of the nose and the exhaust manifolds passing through the upper wing. (Photo: Fairey Aviation Co Ltd)

tives to the famous Fairey IIIF of 1926 (after which Duncanson left to join the Gloster Aircraft Company).

In the early days of floatplane operation from ships at sea the normal proce-

dure was to hoist the seaplanes outboard from their 'carrier' prior to take-off from the water, a time-consuming and dangerous process in enemy waters as the parent vessel was obliged to heave-to.

The most powerful of all Campania seaplanes were some of the later F.17s with 345hp Rolls-Royce Eagle VIIIs, as depicted by Fairey-built N2363 at the Isle of Grain on 10 December 1917 with a pair of 112lb bombs on the centreline beam. The engine demanded increased louvres in the nose panels. (Photo: Imperial War Museum, Neg No Q61696)

The prototype F.22, N1006, shown at Calshot late in 1917 with the Sunbeam Maori II driving a two-blade propeller and with the small frontal radiator fitted to the early production aircraft. (Photo: Imperial War Museum, Neg No Q 69382)

There were, moreover, frequent accidents when pilots attempted take-off from choppy seas. In an effort to circumvent this procedure, the Admiralty had purchased the ex-Cunard liner *Campania*, 20,000 tons, converted her to carry seaplanes and provided a 120-foot flight deck over the fo'c'sle, it being intended to fly the seaplanes off the deck, using a trolley chassis which separated from the floats as the aircraft left the deck. The first successful trolley launch was carried out by a Sopwith Schneider flown by Flt-Lt William Lawrie Welsh RN (later Air Marshal Sir William, KCB, DSC, AFC, RAF) on 6 August 1915.

It was immediately obvious that a much longer deck would be required if larger floatplanes were to be operated in this manner, and the *Campania* was extensively modified to have a 200-foot flight deck. The Fairey F.16 was therefore designed specifically to examine the possibility of operating from this ship, with dimensions tailored to match the size of her hatches, and the name Campania was bestowed on the aircraft and its direct developments.

Powered by a 250hp Rolls-Royce IV engine (later to become the 284hp Eagle IV), the F.16 was a well-proportioned two-bay, two-seat patrol aircraft. The folding wings, of unequal span, featured triangular kingpost structures to brace the outer sections of the upper wing, to which ailerons were fitted; small floats were located flush up to the undersurface of the bottom wing tips. The engine installation included radiator blocks attached to the sides of the nose, and the twin exhaust manifolds extended upwards through the upper wing.

The prototype F.16, N1000, was the first in an order for ten aircraft (N1000-N1009) placed with Fairey, and was flown by Sydney Pickles at Hamble on 16 February 1917; soon afterwards it underwent official trials at the Marine Aircraft Experimental Depot, Isle of Grain.

The following aircraft, N1001, termed the N.17, embodied numerous alterations, including the installation of a 275hp Rolls-Royce Mk V on longer engine bearers which enabled the twin exhaust stacks to incline upwards ahead of the wing; the cumbersome side radiators were discarded in favour of a more efficient frontal radiator. The chord of the ailerons was increased so that they now extended beyond the line of the wing trailing edge, and the kingposts were altered to rectangular structures, bestowing improved torsional rigidity on the outer wing sections. The wing floats were lowered by attaching them by short struts to provide better stability on the water, and the fin was enlarged by extending it forward some two feet. This version of the Campania returned a maximum sea level speed of 90 mph, an increase of 5 mph over that of the F.16, and was first flown on 3 June, again by Pickles.

The F.16 was probably not fitted with bomb racks, although the RNAS trials reports issued in July 1917 quote performance figures with military loads of up to 699lb, a likely ballast weight to make allowance for the rear Lewis gun and ammunition, as well as two 230lb bombs. For the purposes of maximum patrol endurance, however, the F.17 was capable of carrying over 1,000lb of fuel, and the normal bomb load would usually comprise four 100lb anti-submarine bombs mounted on a long beam suspended beneath the fuselage.

The finite Campania was designated

Late production Maori-powered F.22 Campania with the enlarged frontal radiator. (Photo: Imperial War Museum, Neg Ref H[AM]43)

the F.22 and was characterised by installation of the 260hp Sunbeam Maori II vee twelve-cylinder water-cooled engine, also with frontal radiator but with a large single exhaust stack well forward above the engine. This was a generally tidier installation than those of the Rolls-Royces although, in response to an Admiralty request, late production F.22s were fitted with larger radiators with adjustable shutters to cater for possible service in tropical climates. Resort to the Maori engine was made when it seemed likely that demands for the Rolls-Royce Eagle would exceed supply, and the Sunbeam was fitted in twenty-five F.22s (N2375-N2399), all produced by the parent company.

Thus, of the total of 62 Campanias completed, a total of 36 were F.17s and, of these, twelve were built by Barclay, Curle & Co Ltd of Whiteinch, Glasgow. According to availability, the F.17s were powered by several versions of the Eagle, including Marks IV, V and VII, and the 345hp Mark VIII; in the latter configuration the maximum all-up weight was increased to 5,986lb.

In service, Campanias joined HMS *Campania* in 1917, and in the following year were also embarked in two light carriers, HMS *Nairana* and *Pegasus*. In 1919 five F.17s (with two Sopwith Camel fighters) accompanied HMS *Nairana* with the British North Russian Expeditionary Force to Archangel.

The Maori-powered F.22s were confined mainly to operations from RNAS shore stations, including Bembridge, Calshot, Dundee, Portland, Rosyth and Scapa Flow, often serving alongside Short 184s. The Campania gained an excellent reputation in the RNAS and RAF, from various accounts being considered a pleasant aeroplane to fly on long patrol sorties, the Rolls-Royce engines being regarded as utterly reliable.

The last Campanias were declared obsolete and withdrawn from service with the RAF when the last squadrons were disbanded in 1919.

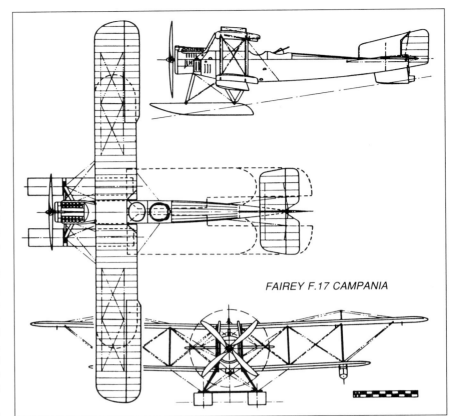

FAIREY F.17 CAMPANIA

Type: Single-engine, two-seat, two-bay biplane shipborne patrol bomber seaplane.
Manufacturers: The Fairey Aviation Co Ltd, Hayes, Middlesex; Barclay, Curle & Co Ltd, Whiteinch, Glasgow.
Powerplant: F.16. One 250hp Rolls-Royce Mk IV twelve-cylinder water-cooled in-line engine driving four-blade propeller. F.17. One 275hp Rolls-Royce Eagle V or 340hp Rolls-Royce Eagle VIII; F.22. 250hp Sunbeam Maori II driving two-blade propeller.
Structure: All-wood construction with fabric covering.
Dimensions: Span, 61ft 7½in; length, 43ft 3⅝in (F.16), 43ft 0⅝in (F.17 and F.22); height, 15ft 1in; wing area, 639.8 sq ft (F.16), 627.8 sq ft (F.17 and F.22).
Weights: F.16. Tare, 3,725lb; all-up (max load), 5,786lb. F.22 (Eagle VIII). Tare, 3,874lb; all-up, 5,986lb.
Performance: F.22 (Maori). Max speed, 85 mph at 2,000ft; climb to 5,000ft, 18 min; service ceiling, 6,000ft; endurance, 4½ hr.
Armament: Bomb load of up to six 112lb bombs carried externally under wings and fuselage. Single 0.303in Lewis machine gun with Scarff ring on rear cockpit.
Prototype: One, N1000 (F.16), first flown by Sydney Pickles at Hamble on 16 February 1917.
Production: Total of 61 built, excluding prototype. Fairey, 49 (N1001-N1009 and N2360-N2399); Barclay, Curle, 12 (N1840-N1851). 138 cancelled: Barclay, Curle, 38 (N1852-N1899); Frederick Sage/Sunbeam, 100 (N1890-N1959 and N2200-N2229).
Summary of Service: Campanias served aboard HMS *Campania, Pegasus* and *Nairana* (in the latter with the British North Russian Expeditionary Force during 1919), and with No 240 Squadron, RAF, at Calshot, and No 241 Squadron, RAF, at Portland, and at Bembridge, Dundee, Rosyth and Scapa Flow.

Wight Converted Seaplane

The intensification of submarine warfare by Germany during 1917, to a degree that threatened Britain's ability to sustain her population and ultimately to continue the War against the Central Powers, concentrated the minds at the Admiralty to pursue all possible measures to protect Allied shipping round the coasts of the British Isles. Among these measures was the urgent strengthening of RNAS patrols by seaplanes. As the Short 184 came to provide the backbone of this effort, newer aircraft, such as the Fairey Campanias (see above), were entering service in relatively small numbers. Another aircraft in this category was the Wight Converted Seaplane which, as its unimaginative title sug-

Left: *A standard Converted Seaplane, with Rolls-Royce Mk II engine, alighting off Bembridge in the Isle of Wight. Note the tall radiator block above the engine.* (Photo: via C H Barnes)

Below: *A Sunbeam Maori-powered Seaplane, No 9853. The installation of this engine was altogether neater than that of the Rolls-Royce.* (Photo: Imperial War Museum, Neg No MH2892)

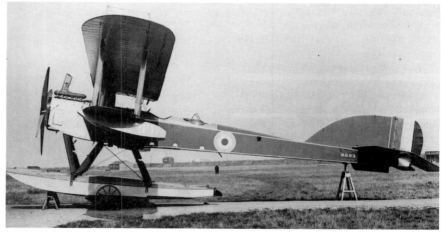

gests, was a development of the unre-warded Wight Bomber (see page 70).

As it happened, this transformation was remarkably successful, and 50 ex-amples were ordered, of which 37 came to be built. The design conversion was relatively straightforward, the seaplane retaining the basic wing and fuselage structure of the Bomber. Rectangular kingpost structures replaced the in-verted vees of the earlier aircraft, being found to provide better torsional stiff-ness for the wing extensions, and double-acting ailerons replaced the single-acting control surfaces of the Bomber.

The undercarriage consisted of a pair of boat-built, three-step floats which were of sufficient length to enable the aircraft to float tail-up, although a small buoyancy chamber was added under the rear fuselage. Small floats were also added to the lower wings directly below the outboard pair of interplane struts.

Most of the Wight Seaplanes were powered by the 275hp Rolls-Royce Mk II, and this was regarded as the standard powerplant; however the incipient short-age of Rolls-Royce engines encouraged Wight (as it had influenced Fairey with the F.22) to adopt the Sunbeam Maori as an alternative, and once again the employment of a frontal radiator re-sulted in a generally neater installation.

The normal bomb load carried by the Wight comprised four 100lb anti-sub-marine bombs, although its maximum fuel capacity limited its patrol endur-ance to little more than half that of the Fairey seaplanes.

Wight Converted Seaplanes entered service in 1917, flying coastal patrols from Calshot, Cherbourg and Portland — a grouping of Flights that was to become No 241 Squadron of the RAF in 1918. And it was a Wight Seaplane flown by Flt Sub-Lieut C S Mossop and Air Mechanic A E Ingledew which,

flying from Cherbourg on 18 August 1917, came upon the U-boat UB.32 in the English Channel, and sank it with a single direct hit from a 100lb

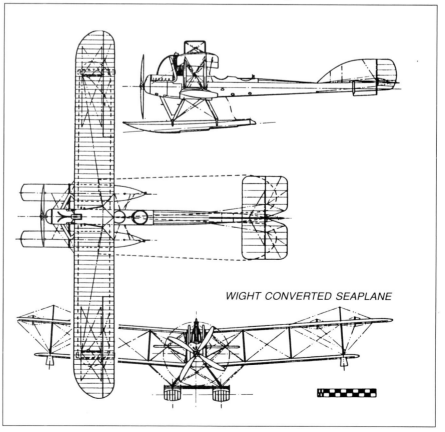

WIGHT CONVERTED SEAPLANE

bomb — the first submarine to succumb to direct air action by a British aircraft in the Channel.

Manufacture of the Wight Seaplane was abandoned when the company was persuaded to switch production to the Short 184. Only seven Converted Seaplanes were still on RAF charge at the time of the Armistice.

Type: Single-engine, two-seat, three-bay biplane, twin-float patrol bomber seaplane.
Manufacturer: J Samuel White & Co, East Cowes, Isle of Wight.
Powerplant: One 275 hp Rolls-Royce (322hp Eagle VI); one 265hp Sunbeam Maori.
Dimensions: Span, 65ft 6in; length, 44ft 8½in; height, 16ft 0in; wing area, 715 sq ft.
Weights: Tare, 3,578lb; all-up (with four 112lb bombs), 5,556lb.
Performance: Max speed, 84 mph at 2,000ft; climb to 6,500ft, 18 min 20 sec; service ceiling, 9,600ft; endurance, 3½ hr.

Armament: One 0.303in Lewis machine gun with Scarff ring on rear cockpit; bomb load of up to four 112lb bombs carried on under-fuselage racks.
Production: Total of 50 Converted Seaplanes ordered, all built by White: Nos 9841-9860, N1280-N1289 and N2180-N2199. Some sources suggest that Nos 9841-9850 were completed as landplanes, but were converted to floatplanes before delivery, and that N2195-N2199 were delivered into storage without engines.
Summary of Service: 'Converted' Seaplanes are known to have served at RNAS Stations, Calshot, Portland and Cherbourg.

Avro Type 529

A natural development of the Avro 523A Pike, the Type 529 retained the same basic configuration, being a slightly larger three-bay, twin-engine biplane with parallel-chord, unstaggered wings. Suitably impressed by the choice of more powerful engines and a potential ability to lift a worthwhile weight of bombs over a range of about 400 miles, the Admiralty ordered two prototypes in 1916, allocating the serials 3694 and 3695.

Powered by two 190hp Rolls-Royce Falcon engines, the first aircraft was flown at Hamble in April 1917, having been built entirely at Manchester. The engines, mounted at mid-gap, were uncowled and drove four-blade propellers, a single 140-gallon fuel tank being situated in the centre fuselage. The undercarriage was similar to that of the Pike, and ailerons were again fitted to both upper and lower wings.

The wings of the Type 529 were, on the insistance of the Admiralty, capable of being folded, a feature that dictated a considerable reduction in the tailplane

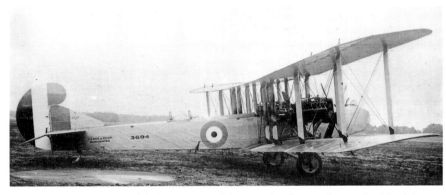

The Avro Type 529, No 3694. The presence of the control rocker arm low on the side of the rear fuselage discloses the provision of dual controls for the rear gunner, a provision that beggars a logical explanation. (Photo: Imperial War Museum, Neg No Q67447)

and elevator areas, and this adversely affected the already poor longitudinal control and stability. Directional control, however, was markedly improved by adopting an enlarged rudder (somewhat of the same shape as the Avro 504's famous 'comma' silhouette).

It is likely that the first aircraft was never intended for more than handling evaluation, and in this respect it was generally regarded as satisfactory in most respects, being capable of being flown straight and level on one engine; the elevator control was however

sharply criticised. With the large fuel tank in the fuselage, bombs were probably not capable of being carried.

The second aircraft, termed the Type 529A, was flown at Hamble in October 1917, and differed from the first in being powered by two 230hp Galloway-built BHP engines, completely cowled in nacelles located directly on the lower wings, driving two-blade handed propellers. Each nacelle accommodated a 60-gallon fuel tank for its engine, a small wind-driven pump supplying fuel to a 10-gallon gravity tank under the top wing above the engine.

Removal of the fuel to the nacelles allowed the centre fuselage between the wing spars to incorporate a bomb bay in which up to twenty 50lb HE RL bombs

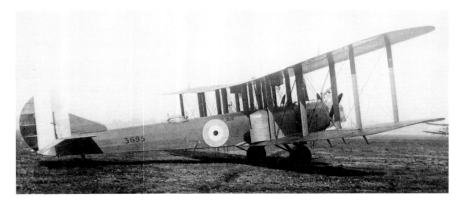

The Avro Type 529A. Just visible in this photograph is the chin fairing on the aircraft's nose enclosing a transparent hatch through which the front gunner, lying prone, aimed the bombs. Note the gravity fuel tanks under the upper wing. (Photo: G Kinsey)

could be stowed, suspended vertically from circumferential rings round their noses. However, owing to the arrangement of the stowage beams, it was not possible to carry fewer, heavier bombs.

The Type 529A carried a three-man crew comprising pilot, midships gunner and nose gunner, the last also being charged with bomb aiming; communications between him and the pilot was by means of a speaking tube. An unusual feature of the aircraft was the provision of dual controls in the midships gunner's cockpit.

There seems little doubt but that the Avro 529A was designed to perform a bombing rôle (that of a medium bomber over moderate ranges) whose requirement steadily disappeared with the approaching deliveries of the Handley Page O/400, an aircraft that promised to be so highly adaptable in terms of fuel and bomb load that the need for a relatively specialised bomber with the limited capabilities of the Avro 529 had become superfluous by the time the second example flew; accordingly it never progressed beyond the experimental stage.

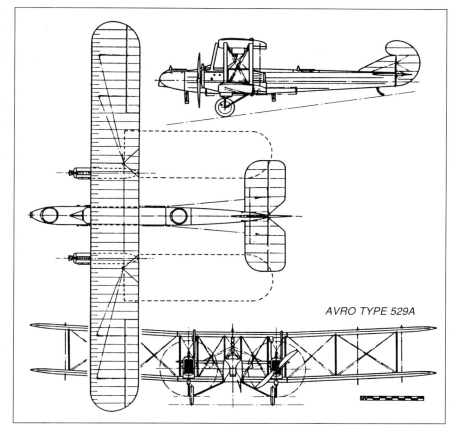

AVRO TYPE 529A

Type: Twin-engine, three-crew, three-bay biplane medium bomber.

Manufacturer: A. V. Roe & Co. Ltd., Clifton Street, Miles Platting, Manchester, and Hamble Aerodrome, Southampton, Hampshire.

Powerplant: Type 529. Two 190hp Rolls-Royce Falcon I water-cooled in-line engines driving handed four-blade tractor propellers. Type 529A. Two 230hp B.H.P. (Galloway-built) water-cooled in-line engines driving two-blade tractor propellers.

Structure: All-wood, wire-braced box-girder fuselage and two-spar, three-bay folding wings; dual controls in midships gunner's cockpit.

Dimensions: Type 529. Span, 63ft 0in (Type 529A, 64ft 1in); length, 39ft 8in; height, 13ft 0in; wing area, 922.5 sq ft (Type 529A, 910 sq ft).

Weights: Type 529. Tare, 4,736lb; all-up, 6,309lb. Type 529A. Tare, 4,361lb; all-up, 7,135lb.

Performance: Type 529. Max speed, 95 mph at sea level; climb to 10,000ft, 21 min 40 sec; service ceiling, 13,500ft; endurance, 5 hr. Type 529A. Max speed, 116 mph at sea level; climb to 10,000ft, 17 min 20 sec; service ceiling, 17,500ft; endurance, 5 hr.

Armament: Single 0.303in Lewis machine guns with Scarff rings on nose and midships gunners' cockpits. Type 529A could carry up to twenty 50lb bombs in mid-fuselage bay, suspended vertically (nose up).

Prototypes: One Type 529, No 3694, first flown at Hamble in April 1917. One Type 529A, No 3695, first flown in October 1917. No production. (Both prototypes stated to have crashed while on test at Martlesham Heath in 1918.)

Sopwith B.1

Although comprehensive records of the origins of this Sopwith aeroplane do not appear to have survived, it is known that early in October 1916 T O M Sopwith entered discussions with the Admiralty on the subject of two related proposals, one for a single-seat bomber and the other for a similar aircraft capable of carrying an 18in torpedo. The basis of the Sopwith proposals was the belief that both aircraft could be sufficiently small (spanning less than 40 feet) to

avoid the necessity for folding wings. When, however, the Admiralty issued its formal requirement for a single-seat torpedo-bomber, the demand for sufficient fuel for four hours' flying at full throttle indicated the need for larger wings to provide more lift. The greater span thus demanded wing folding and, in order to avoid fouling the tail surfaces, a longer fuselage.

Admiralty interest in the smaller bomber project proved to be little more than academic (as the D.H.4 promised to be adequate to meet foreseeable requirements), and Sopwith decided to pursue it as a private venture, and man-

aged to secure a licence (No 6) to go ahead with a prototype — as demanded by the 1917 regulations — basing the design on use of a 200hp Hispano-Suiza geared engine in an installation similar to that being used in the second Sopwith Hispano Triplane fighter.

Thus the B.1 bomber design was in effect a scaled down version of the T.1 torpedo aircraft (later to appear as the Cuckoo, see page 86), but there the relationship ended. The longer fuselage of the bomber was dictated, not by the span of the two-bay wings but by the inclusion of a bomb bay located in the fuselage aft of the cockpit, capable of

The first Sopwith B.1, still carrying the manufacturers' stencil on its fin, and apparently without a serial number on the white rectangle forward of the tailplane, having its compass swung — essential when loaded with bombs — with No 5 (Naval) Squadron, RNAS, at Petite Synthe on 16 May 1917. The unpainted rectangle immediately aft of the cockpit is the upper hatch of the bomb bay. Note the Lewis gun on the front fuselage decking, added during the Service trials. (Photo: Sqn Ldr C P O Bartlett DFC)

accommodating nine 50lb HE RL (amatol) bombs, stowed vertically and suspended by their nose rings (as in the Avro Type 529A, see page 80). However, further discussions with the Admiralty elicited the information that the RNAS in France was interesting in using the French 10kg 'liquid-anilite' bomb[1] as an alternative to the British HE RL, and in order to cater for twenty of these weapons the bomb suspension beams in the Sopwith were moved further apart by about two inches (without alteration to the overall dimensions of the bomb bay).

The B.1 prototype, believed to have been numbered X.6 (although no photographs have come to light showing this serial on the aircraft), was first flown at Brooklands early in April 1917 and underwent brief assessment at the Isle of Grain in the same month. During these trials the aircraft was loaded with twenty 10kg anilite bombs and, at an all-up weight of 2,945lb, returned a maximum speed of 118.5 mph at 10,000 feet.

Although this was regarded as an exceptionally good performance, the B.1 was criticised for its lack of longitudinal control, being found to be tail heavy while carrying the full bomb load, and nose heavy when flying light, a lack of trim that could not be fully countered, even with the adjustable tailplane at its limits of travel. The ailerons were also criticised, though probably owing to undue friction in the control circuits.

Nevertheless the Admiralty stepped in and purchased this aircraft and it was delivered to the RNAS 5th Wing at Dunkerque for Service trials, participating in raids by the naval squadrons flying from Petite Synthe and Coudekerque alongside their D.H.4s. During these operations the B.1 was armed with a single synchronized Lewis gun mounted above the engine.

On return to the United Kingdom, the engine (still Sopwith's property) was removed and returned to Kingston, while the airframe was delivered to the Admiralty's Experimental Construction Depot at Port Victoria. Here it was rebuilt as a two-seat naval reconnaissance aircraft; as such, and given the experimental naval serial number N50, it became the prototype of the Grain Griffin. Later, seven production examples were built by the ECD (N100-N106), powered by the 200hp Sunbeam

Arab; one aircraft, N101, was later fitted with a 230hp Bentley B.R.2 rotary engine.

At Brooklands, investigation into the control criticisms expressed by the naval pilots suggested that the complex control linkage in the elevator circuit, previously located within the fuselage structure, made necessary to clear the mounting beams in the bomb bay, was restricting the full movement of the control surfaces. A second aircraft[2] was therefore built with the elevator control cables and rocking arms located outside the fuselage, a much simpler circuit which appears to have cured the problem. It is not clear, however, whether changes were also made to the tailplane incidence controls, or to the aileron circuits.

This second aeroplane was also purchased by the Admiralty as B1496 and underwent further trials by Service pilots. However, no further interest appears to have been expressed in the project and the ultimate fate of this aircraft is not known.

---

[1] This bomb's explosive filling comprised petrol (the hydrocarbon element) and liquid nitric oxide in separate cells; after release from the aircraft, a small wind-driven vane ruptured the separating diaphragm, allowing the elements to mix and thus 'arming' the highly sensitive explosive compound. No impact detonator was therefore required.

[2] Despite a number of statements suggesting that more than two B.1 aircraft were completed by Sopwith, an examination of Works manifests in 1958 indicated fairly conclusively that only two complete sets of components were manufactured for airframe assembly, these two airframes always being referred to in Works records as 'No 6' and 'No 1496'.

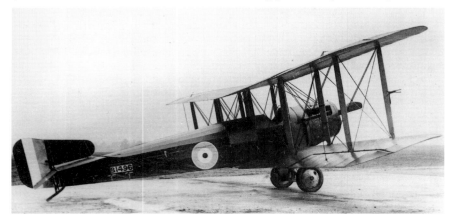

The second Sopwith B.1 bomber, B1496, in 1918, almost certainly at Martlesham Heath. The full Service camouflage makes it almost impossible to distinguish the external elevator control cables and rocking arms on the sides of the fuselage. It is thought likely that this B.1 only had provision to carry the twenty British 28lb HE RL bombs as the Martlesham trials report on B1496 referred to a war load of 560lb. (Photo: Imperial War Museum, Neg No Q67562)

Type: Single-engine, single-seat, two-bay biplane bomber.
Manufacturer: The Sopwith Aviation Co Ltd, Kingston-upon-Thames, Surrey.
Powerplant: One 200hp Hispano-Suiza eight-cylinder, water-cooled, in-line engine driving two-blade propeller.
Dimensions: Span, 38ft 6in; length, 27ft 0in; height, 9ft 6in; wing area, 460 sq ft.
Weights: Tare, 1,700lb; all-up (with max bomb load), 3,055lb.
Performance (with max bomb load): Max speed, 118.5 mph at 10,000ft; climb to 10,000ft, 15 min 30 sec; service ceiling, 19,000ft;

endurance, 3¾ hr.
Armament: Single, fixed, synchronized 0.303in Lewis machine gun located centrally on the nose decking (fitted only during Service trials in 1917); bomb load of twenty 25lb HE RL bombs, or twenty 10kg anilite bombs, carried in internal bomb cell immediately aft of the cockpit.
Prototypes: Two, the first being authorised under Licence No 6, and first flown early in April 1917. A second example, B1496, was probably first flown in January 1918. No production.

Sunbeam Bomber

A contemporary of the Sopwith B.1, and approximating to its general configuration and purpose, was the Sunbeam Bomber, designed and built in response to encouragement from the Admiralty by a company which had not only produced numerous aircraft on behalf of other manufacturers, notably Short Bros, but also an impressive range of aircraft engines of its own design.

For this reason the Admiralty appeared more generously disposed towards Sunbeam than Sopwith in this instance, ordering two prototypes of the former company's Bomber while declining to offer support for the Sopwith B.1. Unfortunately the Sunbeam aircraft proved a thoroughly inept design, and the Sunbeam engine chosen to power it, the 200hp Arab, was found to suffer from severe vibration which, for many months, defied rectification.

The Sunbeam Bomber was a single-seat, two-bay biplane which, despite spanning 42 feet, did not feature folding wings. The bomb load, amounting to no more than 332lb, was suspended from beneath the wings, and the 50-gallon fuel tank was located in the fuselage about the aeroplane's centre of gravity. The cockpit was therefore located well aft, some 13 feet from the nose of the aircraft, with a deplorable field of view for the pilot. His single synchronized Vickers machine gun was situated in the extreme nose and, being nine feet from

A view of the sole Sunbeam Bomber, N515, which well illustrates the aircraft's long nose decking forward of the cockpit. (Photo: A J Jackson Collection)

the cockpit, was of course inaccessible in the event of a gun stoppage.

At no time did the Admiralty suggest folding wings, nor would they have been possible as the upper wing possessed no centresection, the two halves meeting on the aircraft's centreline and being bolted to pyramidal cabane struts.

The first example, N515, was flown during the latter half of 1917 at Castle

Bromwich, but almost immediately encountered engine vibration which considerably delayed the Service trials; these eventually took place at Martlesham Heath in August 1918, and were only conducted to satisfy contractual obligations. The second aircraft was not completed, and N515 was not held on Air Ministry charge at the date of the Armistice.

Type: Single-engine, single-seat, two-bay biplane naval bomber.
Manufacturer: The Sunbeam Motor Car Co Ltd, Wolverhampton, Staffs.
Powerplant: One 200hp Sunbeam Arab eight-cylinder, water-cooled, in-line engine driving two-blade propeller.
Dimensions: Span, 42ft; length, 31ft 6in; height, 11ft; wing area, 466 sq ft.
Weights: Tare, 1,915lb; all-up (with three 100lb bombs), 2,952lb
Performance: Max speed, 112.5 mph at 6,500ft; climb to 10,000ft, 14 min 20 sec; service ceiling, 18,500ft; endurance, 4½ hr.
Armament: Single fixed synchronized 0.303in Vickers machine gun located over engine; bomb load said to comprise three 100lb bombs, carried externally.
Prototypes: One, N515 (second aircraft, N516, not built). First flown late in 1917 at Castle Bromwich.

Airco D.H.9

The unexpected appearance by German bombers over London on 13 June 1917 sparked an immediate reaction by the

Chief of the General Staff, Sir William Robertson, who forthrightly demanded a considerable and immediate increase in aircraft production — assumed to be fighters with which to bolster the air defences of the British Isles. Eight days later, however, this expansion of the air

services was qualified when it was decided to increase the number of RFC squadrons from 108 to 200, the majority of the new units to be equipped with bombers. The initial understanding of this was that Britain was planning retaliation by establishing a new bombing

C6051 was the first production D.H.9, and this view clearly shows the improved arrangement of the cockpits. The aircraft was powered by a Siddeley-built BHP engine with a short exhaust manifold; the engine radiator is shown in the retracted position. (Photo: A J Jackson Collection)

force with which to strike at German cities.

This was not to be — at least in the short term — and the only direct action taken at the time of the German daylight raids was to withdraw a single fighter squadron from France to an aerodrome in Kent.

The real significance of the decision announced on 21 June was the implicit recognition, by the relative success of the first German raid, of the bomber as a potentially decisive weapon of war, whether it was to be used against the enemy in the field or in his home. An immediate and significant increase in the production of long-range heavy bombers would have been beyond the conceivable capacity of British manufacturers. Instead, production orders were

immediately issued for 700 extra Airco D.H.4s, an aircraft that was beginning to appear in service and, with some reservations, was spoken of highly by the RFC.

On 23 July the Air Board was given preliminary details of an improved development of the D.H.4, to be termed the D.H.9, in which the shortcomings of that aeroplane would be overcome — while retaining 90 per cent of the original airframe. The principal alteration was to relocate the pilot further aft, so as to be closer to his observer/gunner, by moving the fuel tank forward from its former position between the two crew members to a position between the engine and the pilot. This change would at least be applauded by many D.H.4 crews and remove one weakness of the aircraft in combat.

The other major change was in the choice of the BHP engine, said at that time to be developing 300hp. Based on this power the D.H.9 was calculated to be capable of a speed of 112 mph at 10,000 feet, a performance considered adequate to match enemy fighters. With such a degree of commonality with the D.H.4, it was pointed out that factories already producing that aeroplane would lose only a few weeks' production when changing over to the D.H.9. As if to prove the point, Airco had converted a D.H.4, A7559, to become the prototype D.H.9, and this was flying by the end of July.

Unfortunately, yet again a new British engine, which had attracted considerable Government support and public funding, encountered serious difficulties when efforts were made to introduce it into production. The BHP engine had been selected for the D.H.9 as it was already scheduled for mass production, for which responsibility had been vested in the Siddeley-Deasy Motor Car Company, with 2,000 engines already

A standard production D.H.9, C6277, powered by a Siddeley Puma engine with exhaust pipe extending upwards to discharge over the top wing; this aircraft, possibly of No 99 Squadron, shows the radiator extended beneath the nose. (Photo: Stuart Leslie)

ordered. By July sufficient quantities of the engines' cast aluminium cylinder blocks were being delivered to enable Siddeley-Deasy to produce 100 complete engines each month — until it was discovered that 90 per cent of the blocks were defective. A quick assessment of the cause and rectification of the fault proved impossible, and the decision to de-rate production BHP engines to 230hp was taken on the assumption that lower engine stresses would prevent the fault from causing engine failure, and so as not to delay deliveries to the Service. The assumption was badly flawed.

The first deliveries were made in November 1917 to No 108 Squadron, the first of the squadrons newly formed to fly the D.H.9 and then stationed at Stonehenge. Owing to the inevitable trouble with its engines, this Squadron did not move to France until July the following year. No 103 Squadron took delivery of its D.H.9s at nearby Old Sarum in December, and moved to France five months later.

D.H.9s were delivered to Nos 98 and 99 Squadrons, RFC, and Nos 2, 6 and 11 (Naval) Squadrons, RNAS, all in France during the first four months of 1918, followed by No 27 Squadron, RFC, shortly afterwards. By June nine squadrons were flying D.H.9s over the Western Front, and thirteen others were working up on them in the United Kingdom. All this, despite the fact that Maj-Gen Hugh Trenchard had learned in November 1917 that the performance of the D.H.9 was inferior to that of the D.H.4, which it was intended to replace. And on 14 November Sir Douglas Haig, influenced by Trenchard's dissatisfaction, expressed the view that the D.H.9 would be wholly outclassed as a day bomber by June 1918.

In action the D.H.9 fared disastrously, combat loss figures being doubled by losses due to engine failures. For instance, between May and November 1918, Nos 99 and 104 Squadrons (flying with the VIII Brigade) between them flew 848 aircraft sorties in the course of 83 bombing raids; 123 aircraft were forced to return with engine trouble, 54 aircraft were lost to enemy action, and 94 were destroyed in accidents. In a raid by twelve D.H.9s of No 99 Squadron against Mainz on 31 July, three aircraft turned back with engine trouble and seven others were shot down by German fighters; only the leader, Capt A H Taylor and one other pilot brought their machines back to their aerodrome at Azelot. During another raid by 21 D.H.9s of Nos 27 and 98 Squadrons against Aulnoye on 1st October, no fewer than fifteen turned back with engine trouble; the remainder turned back as they were unable to defend themselves with such depleted numbers.

The increasing scale of D.H.9 service in the face of heavy losses on the Western Front was the outcome of political intransigence by politicians, and Staffs' determination to pursue a policy that was demonstrably wrong, being afraid of the consequences if they changed course.

No one denied that the D.H.9 could have been an excellent bombing aircraft had the right engine been decided upon in the first place. Various alternatives were tried, including the six-cylinder, in-line Fiat A-12, of which Sir William Weir, Controller of Aeronautical Supplies on the Air Board, had ordered 2,000 examples for delivery between January and June 1918, but only 100 Fiat D.H.9s were produced (by Short Bros). Other engines flown experimentally in the aircraft included a 290hp high compression version of the Siddeley Puma, and the 430hp Napier Lion (an aircraft which possessed a maximum speed of 144 mph at sea level without bombs). Another engine flown experimentally in the USA was the new Liberty 12, an engine that opened a new and more auspicious chapter in the history of the D.H.9, that of the D.H.9A (see page 102).

It transpired that most of the D.H.9 squadrons which were formed in Britain during the spring and summer of 1918 were not destined to go to France; instead the aircraft began assuming the duty of coastal patrol off the British coasts. In doing so, they took over from another Airco aircraft, the D.H.6. This biplane was designed at the outset as a trainer but, with the increasing toll of shipping being taken by German submarines in 1917, they were adapted to carry a single 100lb anti-submarine bomb, and equipped about 30 Flights distributed among a dozen coastal aerodromes. (In the Second World War, during the months when a German invasion threatened, a few de Havilland Tiger Moths were adapted to carry light bombs for 'anti-invasion' patrols off the coasts of Britain.)

D.H.9s gave valuable service in Palestine with sustained attacks on the retreating Turks during Allenby's offensive in the closing months of the War. Other D.H.9s, based in the Aegean, made attempts to bomb Constantinople,

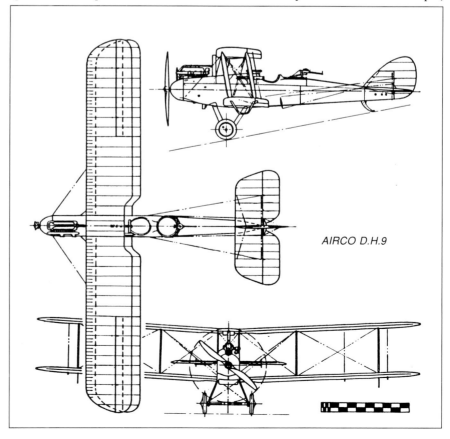

AIRCO D.H.9

flights which took the aircraft to the limit of their endurance — even when carrying locally-made extra fuel tanks. Limited bombing raids were flown by No 47 Squadron, based in Macedonia, including attacks on retreating Bulgarian troops during September 1918.

A total of 3,204 D.H.9s had been built by the end of 1918, of which 2,166 had been delivered to the RFC, RNAS and RAF. Production even continued into 1919, with most of the postwar examples being delivered into storage, and most of them scrapped without ever being flown. A few remained in service until 1920, but by then the D.H.9A was equipping the peacetime Service.

Type: Single-engine, two-seat, two-bay biplane light bomber.

Manufacturers: The Aircraft Manufacturing Co Ltd, Hendon, London NW9; The Alliance Aeroplane Co Ltd, Hammersmith, London W6; F W Berwick & Co Ltd, Park Royal, London NW10; Cubitt Ltd, Croydon, Surrey; Mann, Egerton & Co Ltd, Aircraft Works, Norwich, Norfolk; National Aircraft Factory No 1, Waddon, Surrey; National Aircraft Factory No 2, Heaton Chapel, Lancashire; Short Bros (Rochester and Bedford) Ltd, Rochester, Kent; The Vulcan Motor and Engineering Co (1906) Ltd, Crossens, Lancashire; Waring and Gillow Ltd, Hammersmith, London W6; G & J Weir Ltd, Cathcart, Glasgow; Westland Aircraft Works, Yeovil, Somerset; Whitehead Aircraft Co Ltd, Richmond, Surrey.

Powerplant: One 230hp Galloway Adriatic (BHP) six-cylinder in-line water-cooled engine driving two-blade wooden propeller; also 230hp Siddeley Puma (and 290hp high compression version), 230hp Fiat A-12; 430hp Napier Lion.

Structure: Wire-braced wooden structure, fabric- and ply-covered; two spruce wing spars, wooden V-strut undercarriage with rubber cord-sprung wheel axle.

Dimensions (Puma engine): Span, 42ft 4⅝in; length, 30ft 5in; height, 11ft 3½in; wing area, 434 sq ft.

Weights (Puma engine): Tare, 2,230lb; all-up (460lb bomb load), 3,790lb.

Performance (Puma engine): Max speed, 113 mph at sea level, 109.5 mph at 10,000ft; climb to 10,000ft, 18 min 30 sec; service ceiling, 15,500ft; endurance, 4½ hr.

Armament: Bomb load of up to 460lb, comprising combinations of 230lb and 112lb bombs on external racks. Gun armament comprised one synchronized 0.303in Vickers machine gun on nose decking, offset to port, and either one or two Lewis guns with Scarff ring on observer's cockpit.

Prototype: One, A7559 (a converted D.H.4), first flown by Capt Geoffrey de Havilland at Hendon in July 1917.

Production: Total number of D.H.9s ordered, 4,630; total number built, 4,091. Westland, 300 (B7581-B7680, D7201-D7300 and F1767-F1866); Vulcan, 100 (B9331-B9430); Weir, 400 (C1151-C1450 and D9800-D9899); Berwick, 180 (C2151-C2230 and D7301-D7400); Airco, 1,200 (C6051-C6121, C6123-C6349, D2876-D3275, E5435, E5436, E8857-E9056 and H9113-H9412); Cubitt, 500 (D451-D950); National Aircraft Factory No 2, 500 (D1001-D1500); Mann, Egerton, 100 (D1651-D1750); Short Bros, 100 (D2776-D2875); Waring and Gillow, 500 (D5551-D5850 [50 sub-contracted] and F1101-F1300); Whitehead, 100 (E601-E700); National Aircraft Factory No 1, 300 (F1-F300); Alliance, 350 (H5541-H5890). Of these 539 were cancelled, and approximately 800 were only partly completed or were delivered into storage from late-1918 onwards.

Summary of Service with RFC, RNAS and RAF: D.H.9s served with Nos 27, 49, 98, 99, 103, 104, 107, 108 and 110 Squadrons, RFC, on the Western Front; with Nos 17 and 47 Squadrons, RFC, in Macedonia; with No 105 Squadron, RAF, in Ireland; with Nos 117, 119, 120, 121, 122, 123, 124, 125, 126, 127, 128, 129, 130, 132 and 137 Squadrons, RFC and/or RAF, based in the United Kingdom; with Nos 55, 142 and 144 Squadron in the Middle East; with Nos 202, 206, 211 and 218 Squadron, RAF, ex-RNAS, on the Western Front; with Nos 212, 219, 233, 250, 254 and 273 Squadrons, RAF, home based on coastal patrol; with Nos 55 and 142 Squadrons, RAF, in the Middle East (postwar); No 221 Squadron in the Aegean, on anti-submarine patrol and bombing; No 223 Squadron in the Aegean as light bomber unit; Nos 224, 226 and 227 Squadrons, RAF, in the Mediterranean as light bomber units; with No 269 Squadron, RAF, based in Egypt for coastal patrol; and with No 186 (Training) Squadron.

Sopwith T.1 Cuckoo

As recorded on page 81, the single-seat Sopwith T.1 torpedo aircraft was the subject of a discussion between T O M Sopwith and Murray Sueter at the Admiralty at the beginning of October 1916. The fact that Sopwith took with him to the meeting project drawings of the aircraft suggests, though not conclusively, that the idea of a single-seat torpedo-carrying landplane originated at Kingston; it is, however, clear that the Admiralty tentatively suggested that either one or two torpedoes should be carried together with fuel for four hours' flying. Sopwith would have ruled out the two-torpedo capability in a single-engine aircraft small enough to be accommodated in any aircraft carrier likely

Early-standard Blackburn-built Sopwith Cuckoo I, N6971. (Photo: Sopwith Aviation Co Ltd.)

to be planned in the foreseeable future. This discussion was confirmed in an Admiralty memorandum, dated 9 October, requesting that the Sopwith company should go ahead with the aircraft, expressing the view that some sort of catapult would be made available to assist the heavily-laden aircraft into the

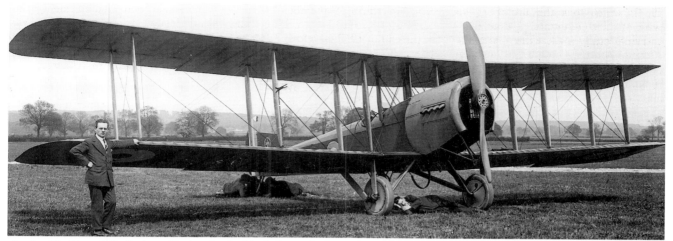

Another Blackburn-built Cuckoo, this time fitted with the large, fixed torpedo pistol-stop structure under the engine; on some later aircraft this could be folded to lie flat under the nose after dropping the weapon. (Photo: Blackburn & General Aircraft Ltd, Neg No A786)

air (an innovation that was possibly the brainchild of Murray Sueter himself).

With the posting of Commodore Sueter to the Mediterranean in January 1917, the Admiralty's interest in the project was temporarily shelved, but the following month Wg-Cdr Arthur Longmore, who was shown the half-completed T.1 prototype during a visit to Sopwith, suggested that the aircraft should be completed forthwith, and shortly afterwards arranged for a licence, No 6, to be issued for its manufacture. In the event, the prototype was made the subject of an Admiralty contract and the licence was transferred to the B.1 Bomber at Sopwith's suggestion as the two designs were interrelated, and the B.1 would be ready to fly first.

The prototype T.1, which probably flew first in June 1917, was powered by a 200hp Hispano-Suiza engine and underwent official trials at the Isle of Grain the following month, the performance report being dated 20 July. The three-bay, unstaggered wings spanned 46ft 9in and were made to fold on the plane of the inner pairs of interplane struts; these struts were constructed in halves along their length, the outboard halves being attached to the folding sections of the wings, and the inboard halves fixed so as to provide rigidity of wing structure. The undercarriage, attached to the fixed inboard wing section, comprised sturdy double-V struts.

Like the first B.1, the tail control cables were enclosed in the rear fuselage for much of their length but, as on the second B.1, the production T.1, named the Cuckoo, featured external tail control cables. The production aircraft were also fitted with a much lengthened

tailskid to allow greater ground clearance for the rear of the torpedo, which was slung below the fuselage between the split-axle mainwheels.

The first production order for 100 Cuckoos was placed on 16 August with the Fairfield Shipbuilding & Engineering Company of Glasgow (Sopwith being fully occupied with production of Camel fighters). Shortly afterwards Sir David Beatty, commanding the Grand Fleet (later Admiral of the Fleet Earl Beatty GCB, OM, GCVO, DSO, 1st Sea Lord) put

forward an ambitious plan for 200 Cuckoos to launch a torpedo offensive against the German Fleet in their harbours. Although this was not accepted as a realistic undertaking, an order was nevertheless placed for a further 50 Cuckoos with Pegler & Co Ltd of Doncaster.

Introducing the Cuckoo into production was beset about with problems and delays. The Royal Aircraft Factory was given priority for deliveries of the Hispano-Suiza engine for its S.E.5A

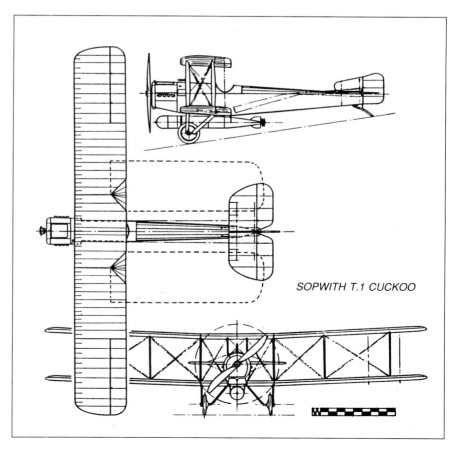

SOPWITH T.1 CUCKOO

fighter, and as a result the heavier 200hp Sunbeam Arab was selected as an alternative; this change occasioned extensive alterations to the Cuckoo's nose structure, and the engine was further delayed by unsatisfactory performance and reliability during development.

Moreover, neither of the original contractors possessed any significant knowledge of aircraft production, and both were very slow to set up their production lines. In February 1918, therefore, 230 further aircraft were ordered from the Blackburn Aeroplane & Motor Company, its first two Cuckoos being completed only two months later. (The first Fairfield-built Cuckoo was not delivered until September 1918, and the first of only 20 Pegler aircraft the next month.)

Fifty Blackburn-built Cuckoos had been completed by the end of August, and production was allowed to continue into 1919, by which time the company had built 162 aircraft in its factory at Sherburn-in-Elmet, Yorkshire. Early production examples were delivered for pilot training at East Fortune, East Lothian, with the Torpedo Aeroplane School, and in October began to equip No 185 Squadron, RAF, also at East Fortune. This Squadron began to embark in HMS *Furious* on the 19th of that month, but did not take part in any war operations before the Armistice, and was disbanded on 14 April 1919.

In July 1919 Cuckoos joined No 186 Squadron for naval co-operation duties at Gosport, remaining in service until April 1923 (this Squadron being renumbered No 210 on 1 February 1920).

An alternative to the Arab engine had been sought and a number of Cuckoos (all the Fairfield-built aircraft and about nine from the Blackburn production) were fitted with the 275hp Wolseley W.4A Viper, and became known as the Cuckoo Mk II; another aircraft, N7990, was flown experimentally with the 275hp Rolls-Royce Falcon III, but neither this nor the Viper gave any significant improvement in performance.

Once the Arab's early unreliability had been improved, the Cuckoo came to be generally liked by Service pilots, and its replacement by the Blackburn Dart in 1923-24 was more on account of a preference, then being expressed, for two-seat torpedo-bombers than any appreciable performance shortcoming in the Cuckoo.

Type: Single-engine, single-seat, three-bay biplane torpedo-carrier.
Manufacturers: The Sopwith Aviation Co Ltd, Kingston-upon-Thames, Surrey (prototype only); The Blackburn Aeroplane and Motor Co Ltd, Leeds, Yorkshire; Fairfield Shipbuilding and Engineering Co Ltd, Govan, Glasgow; Pegler & Co Ltd, Doncaster.
Powerplant: Prototype. 200hp Hispano Suiza. Production. 200hp Sunbeam Arab; 200hp Wolseley W4.A Viper. Experimental: 275hp Rolls-Royce Falcon III.
Dimensions (Arab engine): Span, 46ft 9in; length, 28ft 6in; height, 10ft 8in; wing area, 566 sq ft.
Weights (Arab engine): Tare, 2,199lb; all-up (with 18in torpedo), 3,883lb.
Performance (Arab engine): Max speed, 103.5 mph at 2,000ft; climb to 6,500ft, 15 min 40 sec; service ceiling, 12,100ft; endurance, 4 hr.
Armament: No gun armament nor provision to carry bombs. War load comprised one 18in Mark IX Whitehead torpedo weighing nominal 1,000lb.
Prototype: One, N74 (Sopwith-built), first flown in June or July 1917.
Production: A total of 350 production Cuckoos was ordered, of which 232 were built: Blackburn, 162 (N6900-N6920, N6950-N6999, N7150-N7199 and N7980-N8011; N8012-N8079 cancelled); Pegler, 20 (N6930-N6949); Fairfield, 50 (N7000-N7049; N7031-N7099 cancelled).
Summary of Service: Sopwith Cuckoos served with No 185 Squadron, RAF, at East Fortune from October 1918 to April 1919; with No 186 Squadron at Gosport from July 1919 to February 1920 (this became No 210 Squadron and continued to fly Cuckoos at Gosport until April 1923).

Fairey F.128 and Types IIIA-C

During the spring of 1917 F Duncanson completed the preliminary designs of two floatplanes to the Air Board's Specification N.2(A), which called for a single-engine seaplane with folding wings, capable of being flown from a carrier deck using the trolley-separation method. These two aircraft, the Fairey F.127 and F.128, became generally known by their serial numbers, N9 and N10.

The first, powered by a 200hp Rolls-Royce Falcon I engine, failed to meet the performance requirements laid down, but proved to be of exceptional value in tests carried out in the early development of aircraft catapults. First flown on 5 July 1917, N9 was a single-bay two-seat biplane with wings of unequal span,

Although the Fairey F.127 never carried bombs, it is known that for part of the catapult trials aboard HMS *Slinger it was ballasted for two 112lb weapons. (Photo: Fairey Aviation Co Ltd.)*

the top wing, with a 7ft 6in overhang on each side, being wire braced using kingposts. Wing flaps (the so-called camber-changing system patented by Fairey the previous year) were fitted over the full span of the lower wings.

Delivered to the Isle of Grain in June 1918, N9 was embarked in HMS *Slinger*, a converted mud-carrying vessel fitted with a 60ft-long compressed-air catapult built by Sir W G Armstrong, Whitworth Aircraft Ltd. Trials were completed by Lt-Col Harry Busteed (the first such launches in Britain by a seaplane at sea), before Fairey repurchased N7 from the Admiralty in 1919, fitted it with a 260hp Sunbeam Maori II, and later sold it to Norway.

Fairey F.128

Type: Single-engine, two-seat two-bay biplane shipborne twin-float seaplane.

Manufacturer: The Fairey Aviation Co Ltd, Hayes, Middlesex.

Admiralty Specification: N.2A

Powerplant: One 260hp Sunbeam Maori II twelve-cylinder, in-line engine.

Dimensions: Span, 46ft 2in; length, 36ft 0in; height, 11ft 10in; wing area, 476 sq ft.

Weights: Tare, 2,970lb; all-up, 4,159lb.

Performance: Max speed, 104 mph at sea level, 94.5 mph at 10,000ft; climb to 10,000ft, 23 min 30 sec; service ceiling, 14,000ft; endurance, 4½ hr.

Armament: One 0.303in Lewis gun on rear cockpit. Bomb load, two 112lb bombs.

Prototype: One, N10, first flown by Lt-Cdr Vincent Nicholl at the Isle of Grain on 14 September 1917.

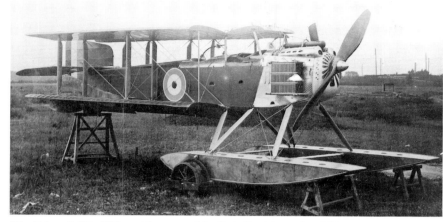

The Fairey F.128, N10, at Hayes as originally built with two-bay folding wings and Sunbeam Maori II engine with side-located radiators. (Photo: Fairey Aviation Co Ltd.)

The second floatplane, N10, powered at the outset by the Maori II engine, was flown by Lt-Col Vincent Nicholl at the Isle of Grain on 14 September 1917 and satisfied all N.2(A)'s performance and load requirements. It was a rather larger aircraft than N9, with equal-span two-bay wings, though the fuselage was identical to that of the single-bay aeroplane. Following successful trials as a seaplane, N10 was converted to landplane configuration to become the Fairey Series III prototype by substitution of the main floats and tail float with plain V-strut, cross-axle wheel undercarriage and tailskid. Trials were flown by RNAS pilots, including performance evaluation while carrying a pair of 112lb bombs. The Maori II engine was retained, but with frontal radiator, and in this form, re-termed the Fairey IIIA, the aircraft-was ordered into production to replace the obsolescent Sopwith 1½-Strutter with the RNAS. The first aircraft, N2850, was flown by Lt-Col G L P Henderson MC, AFC, on 6 June 1918 at Northolt.

Fifty Fairey IIIAs were ordered, of which fourteen featured plain wheel undercarriage and the remainder wheel-and-skid gear — a temporary recourse adopted on then-current deck-operating aircraft in an attempt to keep the aircraft straight during take-off and landing. As far as is known, none of these IIIAs ever reached a squadron, most of them being used either as trainers or for various trials, although a few may have joined the coastal mine-spotting patrols undertaken after the Armistice. Others are known to have been delivered into storage to await scrapping.

The first production seaplane variant of the basic Fairey III series was the IIIB, intended from the outset to be a bomber, as defined by Admiralty Specification N.2(B) which called for a bomb load of up to 600lb. To enable this weight to be carried, the wing area was increased from 542 to 616 sq ft, the upper wing being extended to give an overhang of some eight feet on each side. To compensate for the side area of the floats, both fin and rudder areas were

increased by about 25 per cent.

Sixty Fairey IIIBs were ordered, but fewer than thirty were built as such, many being completed as IIICs (see below). The first production IIIB to be flown made its maiden flight on 8 August 1918 at Hamble, and subsequent aircraft reached No 219 Squadron at Westgate in Kent the same month. Others joined No 230 Squadron at Felixstowe in October, and No 229 Squadron in Flanders during November. None took part in bombing operations before the Armistice, but subsequently flew mine-spotting patrols over the Thames Estuary with the coming of peace. Two were used to operate a naval mail service between Ostend and Harwich between February and May 1919. In January 1919 No 229 Squadron took

Fairey Type IIIA

Type: Single-engine, two-seat, two-bay biplane shipborne bomber.

Manufacturer: The Fairey Aviation Co Ltd, Hayes, Middlesex,

Admiralty Specification: N.2A

Powerplant: One 260hp Sunbeam Maori II twelve-cylinder in-line engine.

Dimensions: Span, 46ft 2in; length, 31ft 0in; height, 10ft 8in; wing area, 542 sq ft.

Weights: Tare, 2,532lb; all-up, 3,694lb.

Performance: Max speed, 109 mph at sea level; climb, 17 min 40 sec; service ceiling, 15,000ft; endurance, 4½ hr.

Armament: One 0.303in Lewis gun on rear cockpit Scarff ring.

Prototype: One, N10 (modified); first flown by Lt-Col G L P Henderson at Northolt on 6 June 1918.

Production: 50 aircraft: N2850-N2852 with wheels; N2853-N2862 with skids; N2863 with hydrofoils; N2864-N2888 with skids, and N2989-N2999 with wheels.

Service: A small number of Fairey IIIAs served with No 219 Squadron at Westgate.

The F.128, N10, modified as a landplane bomber and powered by the Maori II engine with frontal radiator, thus becoming the prototype Fairey IIIA. (Photo: Fairey Aviation Co Ltd.)

up residence at Great Yarmouth for spotting patrols off the Norfolk coast.

The Fairey IIIC's first flight acutally predated that of the IIIB, the aircraft being flown by Vincent Nicholl in July 1918. It was widely recognised as the best British seaplane produced during the War, an opinion that owed its expression to the excellent 375hp Rolls-Royce Eagle VIII engine, renowned for its great reliability. Retaining the float undercarriage, fuselage and tail unit of the IIIB, and the equal-span wings of the IIIA, the Fairey IIIC featured engine radiators on the sides of the fuselage, and was intended to combine the reconnaissance rôle of the IIIA with the bombing rôle of the IIIB. Its normal bomb load comprised either two 230lb or four 112lb bombs carried beneath the fuselage. Fairey IIICs were armed with a synchronized Vickers gun and a Lewis gun on the rear cockpit.

Production aircraft were delivered to Nos 229 and 230 Squadrons in November but were prevented from making any war flights against the Germans by the Armistice. However, in 1919, several Fairey IIICs were embarked in HMS *Pegasus* with the North Russian Expeditionary Force, making their base at Archangel. In June they carried out a bombing attack against four Russian warships and later attacked rail targets.

The last Fairey IIICs were withdrawn from service with the RAF at Kalafrana, Malta, in August 1923, where they had been serving with No 267 Squadron since December 1920.

Fairey Type IIIC

Type: Single-engine, two-seat, two-bay biplane bomber-reconnaissance seaplane.

Powerplant: One 375hp Rolls-Royce Eagle VIII twelve-cylinder water-cooled in-line engine driving two-blade propeller.

Dimensions: Span, 46ft 1in; length, 36ft 0in; height, 12ft 2in; wing area, 542 sq ft.

Weights: Tare, 3,392lb; all-up (with maximum bomb load), 5,039lb.

Performance: Max speed, 110.5 mph at sea level; climb to 10,000ft, 14 min 15 sec; service ceiling, 17,000ft; endurance (max fuel), 5 hr.

Armament: One synchronized 0.303in Vickers machine gun and one Lewis gun on rear cockpit; bomb load of up to 460lb.

Prototype: One, N2246; first Fairey IIIC to fly, N2255, flown by Vincent Nicholl at Hamble in July 1918.

Fairey Type IIIB

Type: Single-engine, two-seat, two-bay biplane bomber seaplane.
Manufacturer: The Fairey Aviation Co Ltd, Hayes, Middlesex.
Admiralty Specification: N.2B
Powerplant: One 260hp Sunbeam Maori II twelve-cylinder, water-cooled, in-line engine.
Dimensions: Span, 62ft 8¹⁵/₁₆in; length, 37ft 1in; height, 14ft 0in; wing area, 570 sq ft.
Weights: Tare, 3,258lb; all-up weight (with three 230lb bombs), 4,892lb.
Performance: Max speed, 97 mph at sea level, 90 mph at 10,000ft; climb to 10,000ft, 37 min 50 sec; service ceiling, 10,300ft; endurance, 4½ hr.
Armament: One 0.303in Lewis gun on rear cockpit; bomb load of up to three 230lb bombs.
Prototype: None. N2225 first flown by Vincent Nicholl at Hamble on 8 August 1918.
Production: 28 aircraft: N2225-N2232, N2234-N2245 and N2247-N2254.
Service: Fairey IIIBs served with Nos 219, 229 and 230 Squadrons, RAF.

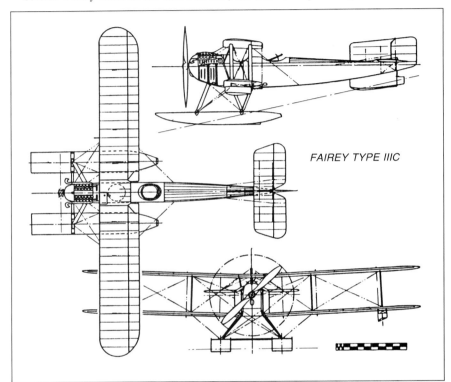

FAIREY TYPE IIIC

The first Fairey IIIC, N2246, was a factory conversion of a IIIB. (Photo: via R C B Ashworth)

Summary of Service: Fairey IIICs served with No 229 Squadron, RAF, at Great Yarmouth, No 230 Squadron at Felixstowe and No 267 at •Kalafrana, Malta (the latter until August 1923); they also served with the North Russian Expeditionary Force in 1919.

Sopwith 2B.2 Rhino

The Sopwith Rhino two-seat triplane bomber was a private venture, not intended to approximate to any official requirement, and therefore subject of a special licence (No 14) for the manufacture of two prototypes, X7 and X8. Designed during the late summer of 1917, the first aircraft was flown at Brooklands in October, powered by a 230hp BHP six-cylinder in-line water-cooled engine. The dominant feature, apart from the triplane wings, was the exceptionally deep fuselage, necessitated by the internal bomb bay beneath the pilot's cockpit, the bombs being loaded into a self-contained structure which was winched into the aircraft's bomb bay. The choice of the BHP engine, which was fully cowled, also resulted in a deep nose profile. The second Rhino was flown around the end of the year.

Although the engine was cooled by an orthodox water-circulation system, with radiators on the sides of the nose (each with an adjustable ramp shutter), a small frontal air intake was incorporated above the propeller shaft to provide additional cooling of the tandem cylinder blocks and exhaust manifold.

The single-bay wings, of generous area, were all fitted with ailerons and were rigged with slight stagger. The ailerons on both prototypes were originally horn-balanced, extending beyond the wing structure, but were later shortened to blend with the profile of the wing tips. The lower pairs of ailerons were interconnected by faired struts, and the upper pairs by cables.

Front gun armament comprised a single synchronized Vickers gun above the nose decking, and rear protection was afforded by a Lewis gun on the rear

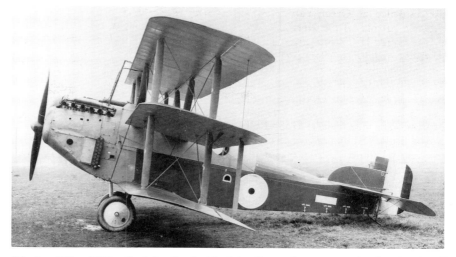

The first Rhino (X7), after being fitted with plain ailerons; it was not equipped with a Scarff ring on the rear cockpit. (Photo: Sopwith Aviation Co Ltd, Neg No 147 dated December 1917)

cockpit; on X7 the rear gun was pillar-mounted, and on X8 a Scarff ring was provided.   No bomb sight could be fitted, and downward view for the pilot (situated directly below the upper wing) was assisted by cutout panels in the roots of the centre and lower wings.

The undercarriage comprised plain steel tubular V-struts with bungee-bound cross-axle, the whole wheel structure giving an impression of being understressed.

Both Rhinos were officially tested at Martlesham Heath in February and March 1918, but returned somewhat pedestrian performance figures with and without bomb load, and the aircraft was not accepted for production.

Type: Single-engine, two-seat, single-bay triplane bomber
Manufacturer: The Sopwith Aviation Co Ltd, Kingston-upon-Thames, Surrey.
Powerplant: One 230hp Beardmore-Halford-Pullinger (BHP) six-cylinder, water-cooled, in-line engine driving two-blade propeller.
Dimensions:[1] Span, 41ft; length, 30ft 3in; height, 10ft 11in; wing area, 612 sq ft.
Weights:[2] Tare, 2,184lb; all-up (with four 112lb bombs), 3,590lb.
Performance (with four 112lb bombs)[2]: Max speed, 114 mph at sea level, 103 mph at 10,000ft; climb to 10,000ft, 24 min 50 sec; service ceiling, 12,000ft; endurance, 3¾ hr.
Armament: One synchronized 0.303in Vickers machine gun located centrally on nose decking, and one Lewis gun on rear cockpit (with Scarff ring on second aircraft); bomb load of up to four 112lb bombs or equivalent weight of smaller bombs carried in a detachable structure winched into internal bomb bay.
Prototypes: Two, X7 and X8, built under Licence No 14. X7 first flown in October 1917. No production.

[1] These figures are suspect, and a span of 33ft (sometimes quoted) is also believed to be incorrect; unfortunately no copies of the original Sopwith drawings appear to have survived, and Sopwith records themselves are inconsistent.
[2] Quoted from Martlesham Reports M.167A and B, dated February and March 1918.

Kennedy Giant

The product of a gifted young man, Chessborough J H Mackenzie-Kennedy, the Giant was of impressive proportions, but of doubtful structural integrity and badly underpowered. As an eighteen-year-old and with three pounds in his pocket, Kennedy had left England for Russia, convinced of aviation's future and, in particular, the potential of very large aeroplanes. In 1908 he completed the design of Russia's first aeroplane, and formed the Kennedy Aeronautic Company the following year. Becoming associated with Igor Sikorskii in 1911, he was involved in the design of the first Sikorskii four-engine biplanes before returning to England on the outbreak of war.

Kennedy discussed his ideas for very large aeroplanes with the War Office, by which he was promised support, and established his design office at 102 Cromwell Road, South Kensington, together with T W K Clarke, G C McClaughlin and E A Vessey.

The fruits of this encouragement were the Giant, whose manufacture was undertaken by the Gramophone Company Ltd and the Fairey Aviation Co Ltd, both of Hayes, Middlesex. Final assembly took place at Hendon but, owing to its great size, the aircraft had to be erected in the open. The four-bay, unstaggered wings spanned 142 feet; ailerons were fitted to the upper wings

The Kennedy Giant, No 2337, at Hendon in 1917. Mr J M Bruce is quoted as stating that it required two lorries and seventy men to move it, but even this effort broke the aircraft's back. It was repaired, but with the fuselage shortened by 10 feet, presumably in the form shown here. The Giant bears more than a superficial resemblance to the Sikorskii Il'ya Mouram'etz, the world's first four-engine aeroplane. (Photo: via J M Bruce)

only, their control rods extending along the top of the leading edge, and the wing overhang being braced by pairs of outraked struts. The four engines, mounted in tandem pairs in nacelles on the lower wings, were very early British-built examples of the Canton-Unné/Salmson Z9 nine-cylinder water-cooled radials, each of which was provided with a pair of large vertical radiators on the sides of the nacelles.

The fuselage, of singularly bizarre appearance, was of rectangular section over its entire length and tapered towards the tail only in plan. It provided fully-enclosed accommodation for the crew, the pilot being situated in the extreme nose, with individual compartmented cabins aft. The tail surfaces were clearly of inadequate area, the tiny rudder (later enlarged) being unbalanced and without a fixed fin. The undercarriage was an extraordinarily complicated struc-ture of multiple V-struts and skids. One is left to conjecture that the bomb load would have been suspended beneath the aeroplane, though exactly where it is difficult to imagine.

Supply of the Sunbeam engines, manufactured under licence by the Dudbridge Iron Works Ltd of Stroud, were afforded very low priority (and were not subject of official trials until May 1919). Early examples were rated at only 200hp and, with these, the Giant was made ready for flight at Hendon late in 1917. This power proved insufficient to gain true flight, and despite being taxied at full throttle downhill, the pilot, Lieut Frank Courtney, only managed to lift the mainwheels off the ground for a short hop — with the tailskid still dragging along the ground.

Although no further attempts were made to fly the Giant, Kennedy was not discouraged from designing a second, smaller version, and construction was underway at the works of John Dawson & Co Ltd, Newcastle-upon-Tyne, in 1920 when the venture was abandoned owing to financial failure.

Type: Four-engine (two tractor, two pusher), three-crew, four-bay biplane bomber.
Manufacturers: Fairey Aviation Co Ltd, and the Gramophone Co Ltd, both of Hayes, Middlesex, to the design of Kennedy Aeroplanes Ltd, South Kensington, London W.7
Powerplant: Four 200hp Canton-Unné Salmson Z9 nine-cylinder water-cooled radial engines driving two tractor and two pusher two-blade propellers.
Dimensions: Span, 142ft 0in; length, 80ft 0in; height, 23ft 6in.
Weight: Tare, 19,000lb.
Performance: No true flight achieved.
Prototype: One, No 2337. One partial flight made by Lieut Frank T Courtney late in 1917.

Handley Page H.P.12 O/400

The principal difference between the Handley Page O/100 (see page 43) and the O/400 lay in the choice of 360hp Rolls-Royce Eagle VIII engines in place of the Eagle II and IV. Final clearance to install Eagle VIIIs was, however, delayed pending finalisation of reports on the fuel system, and because Rolls-Royce was unable to meet delivery schedules with both left- and right-handed versions of the new engine, still assumed to be essential in large twin-engine aircraft to alleviate the control asymmetry caused by engine torque.

The reasons for and process leading to the introduction of the O/400 had evolved throughout much of 1917. It is true that the arrival in service of the

An early O/400, possibly one of the early 'hand-built' aircraft assembled at the Royal Aircraft Factory, showing the O/400's short engine nacelles. (Photo: A J Jackson Collection)

O/100 had betokened a marked increase in the strategic striking power of the RNAS, small though the initial effect of this power was seen to be. A total of 46 O/100s had been ordered and, although they had given good service, they were becoming short on performance by the standards of 1917 and their use of left-and right-handed engines had severely complicated maintenance and engine replacement.

A standard O/100 was therefore set aside during the summer of 1917 for the progressive development of an improved version, the period in which German bombers launched their short series of

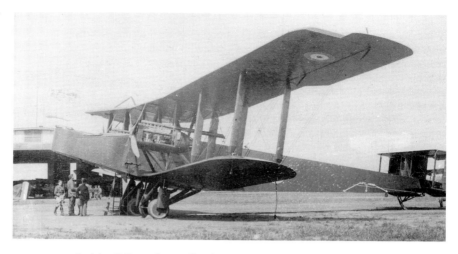

A standard Handley Page O/400 at Ternhill during 1918. (Photo: A T Dickinson, via P H T Green)

daylight attacks on south-east England and London. It has already been recounted how this sparked a premature decision, widely misinterpreted, to expand the RFC by the creation of many new light bomber squadrons (see pages 83-84). In September that year, however, the Germans switched to night raids, a militarily insignificant campaign by seldom more than a score of aircraft, but one that was to focus the Air Board's attention on the matter of increasing the British bombing capabilities against German towns and cities much further behind the Western Front. It was at this time, incidentally, that the first decisions were being taken that led to the development of the Handley Page V/1500 — a much larger bomber than the O/400 and one that was intended to be able to reach and bomb Berlin from the west. And it was in October that Maj-Gen Hugh Trenchard was ordered to begin assembling a dedicated bombing force, and established the 41st Wing with this rôle in mind. With numbers of O/100s now dwindling (and the majority of these being flown by the RNAS), there was increasing pressure to introduce the O/400 into production without delay.

The O/100, No 3138, was test flown, first with 320hp Rolls-Royce Eagle IVs and then with 275hp Sunbeam Maoris, and on the strength of preliminary reports of these trials an order for one hundred O/400s was placed with Handley Page. However, as the company's Cricklewood works could not tool up quickly to cope with this production, Handley Page-built components were immediately despatched to Farnborough so that the first twelve urgently-needed aircraft could be hand-built at the Royal Aircraft Factory.

It then emerged that the assumed benefit of handed engines was erroneous, and had in fact been the *cause* of directional instability in the O/100, and that the torque effects of two identical engines and propellers could be overcome by adjusting the incidence angle of the central fin of the O/400. Indeed, the benefit of handed propellers had originally been propounded by the Wright brothers, and blindly perpetuated by the Air Board's Technical Department. The

exposure of this fallacy immediately ended Rolls-Royce's difficulties and enabled the delivery schedule of single-type Eagle VIIIs to be met, albeit after some three months' delay had already been occasioned.

The other significant change introduced in the O/400 involved the fuel system. It will be recalled that fuel for the O/100's engines was carried in each engine nacelle; in the O/400 the nacelle tanks were replaced by two 130-gallon tanks located in the fuselage, enabling the nacelles to be significantly shortened. The nacelles also now incorporated large frontal radiators with horizontal shutters.

In the event the first hand-built O/400s from Farnborough were only a few weeks ahead of the Cricklewood aircraft, and it was April 1918 before the first aircraft reached the new Royal Air Force's squadrons. In that month Nos 207 and 215 Squadrons took delivery of their full complements at Netheravon, the former being issued with Farnborough-built O/400s, and the latter with Handley Page aircraft. Almost simultaneously No 216 began receiving its first aircraft at Cramaille in France.

By April 1918, as these squadrons began working up on their new bombers, the 41st Wing had increased in size to become the VIII Brigade. On 6 June the Independent Force officially came into being, and by the end of August comprised four day bombing squadrons, equipped or equipping with D.H.9s and D.H.9As, and four with O/400 night bombers (Nos 97, 115, 215 and 216 Squadrons). Elsewhere in France, Nos 100, 207 and 214 were also flying O/400s, temporarily but separately from the Independent Force.

Although the O/400's airframe was little changed from that of the O/100,

and the internal bomb load was the same (despite the presence of the fuel tanks in the fuselage), the new aircraft's greater power and improved specific fuel consumption enabled it to carry heavier bomb loads without fuel penalty. The increased power of the engines and reduced drag of the nacelles with their associated mounting struts brought an increase of 12 per cent in the cruising speed which, with the endurance remaining at about eight hours, resulted in a range increase of some 100 miles with the same bomb load.

Production of the 520lb light case and 550lb heavy case bombs had increased five-fold during 1917. When carrying three of these bombs internally in the O/400, it was also possible to load two 112lb bombs on external racks under the fuselage, and still carry full fuel. Another bomb which had been tested in 1917 was the 1,650lb SN but, using a heavy cast case, this large weapon was not available until July 1918; an improved version, the 1,800lb SN(Mod), specially tailored to the O/400 and, like the standard SN, normally carried on Gledhill slips under the fuselage, became available in August 1918.

The remaining naval O/100s continued to serve alongside the new O/400s and flew a number of outstanding raids, particularly against the submarine base at Zeebrugge, both before and after the famous amphibious raid of 22/23 April. On account of much strengthened gun defences, widely introduced as the result of increasing Allied bombing, new tactics were being evolved and, on No 214 Squadron, Capts Cecil Curtis Darley (later Air Cdre, CBE, AM, RAF) and T A Batchelor, using a special low-level bombsight, designed by the latter and tested at Cranwell, evolved a form of surprise attack against such heavily-defended targets as lock gates; this involved a steep glide approach to the target from 9,000 feet to 80 feet to release their 520lb bombs in a carefully sequenced pattern, eventually gaining excellent results, despite heavy anti-aircraft fire.

The first 1,650lb SN bomb was also dropped by No 214 Squadron when on the night of 24/25 July Sgt Dell attacked Middelkerke; the first such bomb dropped by a squadron of the Independent Force was delivered in September, and on the night of 21/22 October three SN bombs were dropped on Kaiserslautern.

It is perhaps interesting to note that, in contrast to the manner in which Bomber Command operated at night during the Second World War, the O/400 Squadrons based in France during the last five months of the Kaiser's War seldom attacked a single target with more than four or five aircraft, even though up to forty aircraft might be attacking targets elsewhere. In this way Trenchard believed that the largest number of targets would be attacked (and the Air Council had compiled a list of over 100 strategic targets to be bombed) but that the greatest disruption would be caused to the German war industry and transportation system with the minimum losses. To these targets were also added enemy bomber bases, and the damage caused among these substantially reduced enemy air support during the last great Allied advance during the final weeks of the War.

It is, moreover, often overlooked, when quoting the well-publicised bombing figures achieved by the Independent Force, which fielded around seventy O/400s during the last three months of the War, that at least forty other O/400s and O/100s were also flying bombing raids by non-attached squadrons.

During those last months, such were the relatively light losses among the O/400s that supply was outstripping wastage, and at any time sufficient spare aircraft were available to create two new squadrons at a moment's notice.

Of course the statistics and economics favouring the use of night bombers were incontestable. To deliver the same load of bombs carried by a single O/400, itself costing £9,600 and crewed by four men, would require five D.H.9As, together costing £16,000 and crewed by ten men, while the loss rate from all causes during the last five months of the War was almost four times higher among

the single-engine aircraft, capable of carrying nothing heavier than a couple of 230lb bombs. Such statistics were, not unnaturally, bound to shape the overall bombing philosophy of the Royal Air Force for the next half-century.

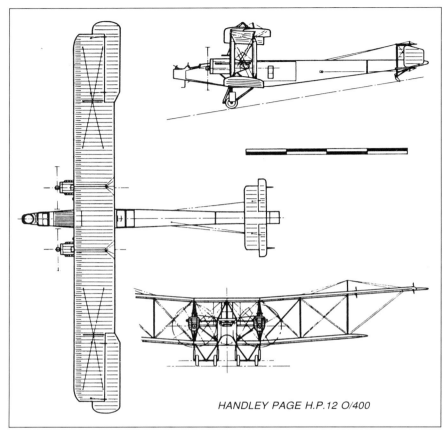

HANDLEY PAGE H.P.12 O/400

Type: Twin-engine, four/five crew, three-bay biplane heavy bomber.

Manufacturers: Handley Page Ltd, Cricklewood, London; The Birmingham Carriage Co, Birmingham; British Caudron Co Ltd, Cricklewood, London N.W.2; Clayton and Shuttleworth Ltd, Lincoln; The Metropolitan Waggon Co, Birmingham; National Aircraft Factory No 1, Waddon; and the Royal Aircraft Factory, Farnborough, Hants. (Also The Standard Aircraft Corporation, Elizabeth, New Jersey, USA).

Powerplant: Two 360hp Rolls-Royce Eagle VIII twelve-cylinder, water-cooled, in-line engines driving four-blade tractor propellers. 275hp Sunbeam Maori; 350hp Liberty 12-N.

Structure: All-wood box girder fuselage structure with spruce longerons. Twin wooden wing box spars with steel tubular engine nacelles; wings folded outboard of the engines.

Dimensions: Span, 100ft 0in; length, 62ft 10¼in; height, 22ft 0in; wing area, 1,648 sq ft.

Weights (Eagle VIII): Tare, 8,502lb; all-up (sixteen 112lb bombs), 13,360lb.

Performance (Eagle VIII): Max speed, 97.5 mph at sea level, 87 mph at 5,000ft; climb to 5,000ft, 23 min; service ceiling, 8,500ft.

Armament: Standard gun armament was five 0.303in Lewis guns, two double-yoked on nose Scarff ring, two on midships dorsal position with separate pillar mountings, and a single gun firing rearwards through ventral hatch. The bomb load could comprise one 1,650lb SN bomb, three 550lb, three 520lb, eight 250lb or sixteen 112lb bombs.

Production: A total of 554 O/400s was built: RAF (RAE), Farnborough, 24 (B8802-B8813 and C3487-C3498); Handley Page, 211(C9636-C9785, D8301-D8350 and F3748-F3758); Metropolitan Waggon, 100 (D4561-D4660); Birmingham Carriage, 102 (D5401-D5450, F301-F318 and J2242-J2275¹); Clayton & Shuttleworth, 46 (D9681-D9726); Standard, USA (assembled at NAF No 1), 70 (F5439-F5418). One other aircraft, J1934, was ordered from Harland & Wolff Ltd and delivered by Handley Page Ltd.

Summary of Service: O/400s served with Nos 58, 97, 100, 115, 207, 214, 215 and 216 Squadrons, RAF, with IX Brigade and VIII Brigade (the Independent Force) in France. A small number, possibly only one, served with No 144 Squadron in the Aegean in October 1918, and with No 70 Squadron in Egypt after the War. (No 134 Squadron was scheduled to receive O/400s at Ternhill in 1918, but it is believed that none was delivered before the Squadron disbanded on 4 July that year.)

¹ J2276-J2291 cancelled; J2265-J2275 delivered to No 1 Aircraft Acceptance Park for storage.

The Handley Page O/400 was the outstanding large bomber of the War. It was, however, recognised that its technology was fundamentally over three years old at the time of the Armistice and, within the limits of that technology, was not capable of further significant development, even though there had been trial installations of alternative powerplants, including a pair of American 350hp Liberty 12-N engines; this was followed by 70 sets of components being manufactured by The Standard Aircraft Corporation of New Jersey and shipped before the Armistice to Britain where they were assembled as Liberty-powered O/400s at the National Aircraft Factory, Waddon. The Vickers Vimy, with its ability to lift a 25 per cent greater bomb load at significantly lower production cost, was selected to remain in production to meet the needs of the peacetime RAF at home and overseas, while production of the O/400 was allowed to run out in 1919, the last remaining aircraft serving with No 216 Squadron in Egypt in October 1921.

The second Vickers Vimy prototype, B9953, powered by two 260hp Sunbeam Maori engines, and fitted with inversely-tapered, plain ailerons. This aircraft was to be destroyed in a crash within a month of arriving at Martlesham Heath for evaluation. (Photo: GSL/JMB Collection)

Vickers F.B.27 Vimy

It is perhaps reasonable to speculate that, had a Vickers Vimy, flown by Alcock and Brown, not been the first aeroplane to fly non-stop across the Atlantic, the aircraft might have remained relatively obscure in the annals of the Royal Air Force; it was, after all, too late to give service during the First World War and, in the first half-dozen years of peace thereafter, it served on only five home-based squadrons.

Following hard on the heels of the decision to increase substantially the number of light bomber squadrons in the RFC, the Air Board opened discussions to investigate the possibility of introducing new heavy bombers into service with which to extend the offensive against German targets well beyond the Western Front. It has been told how large orders were quickly placed with Handley Page to hasten deliveries of the O/400, an excellent aeroplane, yet one that — apart from the Eagle engines — was already a long-established design.

The basic proposals for new heavy bombers were discussed at the Air Board's meeting of 28 July 1917 and, in response to the subsequent memorandum sent to Handley Page and Vickers, both companies embarked on new designs, three prototypes of each being ordered. The Vickers company was approached as it was known that its chief designer, Reginald Kirshaw Pierson, was already working on the preliminary design of a heavy bomber intended to meet the requirements set out in Air Board Specification A.3(B), issued in April, calling for an aircraft able to carry a 3,000lb bomb load. In this he followed the general configuration of his previous F.B.7 and F.B.8 gun carriers (twin-engine biplanes), though of course the new bomber was to be much larger. The new requirements, in contrast to those of Specification A.3(B), placed less emphasis on bomb load and more on cruising speed and range, the former being reduced to around 2,200lb and the latter increased to 90 mph and 400 miles respectively; an earlier demand for folding wings was also waived.

Reflecting the urgency attached to the new aircraft, the first Vickers F.B.27 prototype, B9952, was flown by Gordon Bell at Joyce Green on 30 November, only four months after the requirement had been first discussed, but made possible by use of the company's established steel construction.

Power was provided by two geared 200hp Hispano-Suiza engines and, with these, B9952 was delivered to the Aeroplane Experimental Station at Martlesham Heath in January 1918 where, despite some trouble with the engines, at an all-up weight (ballasted for a bomb load of 2,200lb) it returned a sea-level maximum speed of 90 mph, thereby meeting the Specification's main requirements. This prototype featured horn-balanced ailerons on upper and lower wings, extending outboard of the square-tipped mainplane structure.

By then, however, all Hispano-Suiza engines were being allocated to production S.E.5A fighters, and the second Vickers prototype, B9953, was flown in April with a pair of 260hp Sunbeam Maori II engines, and delivered to Martlesham on the 25th. This aircraft featured inversely tapered ailerons, whose outer ends blended with the curved tips of the wings; it also introduced a ventral hatch through which a Lewis gun was mounted to fire, in addition to the upper gun positions in the nose and midships. B9953 was, however, to be destroyed in a crash in May.

At about this time the first aircraft was returned to Joyce Green, where the Hispano engines were replaced by a pair of 260hp Salmson 9Zm nine-cylinder water-cooled radials (though these engines never succeeded in producing

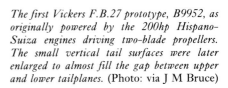

more than about 230hp, and gave constant trouble with the cooling system).

The last of the original Vimy prototypes, B9954, was fitted with 300hp Fiat A.12bis engines with octagonal frontal radiators, these having been scheduled to power the proposed 'Vimy Mark III' in production. Arriving at Martlesham on 15 August, this prototype demonstrated a maximum sea level speed of 98 mph while carrying 2,124lb of bombs. This aircraft, however, was also destroyed when, on 11 September, it crashed on take-off for a bombing test from Martlesham and its bombs exploded.

Meanwhile an initial production order for 150 Vimys had been raised with Vickers Ltd for production at the company's Crayford works, the engines being specified as the 230hp BHP, 400hp Fiat or the 400hp Liberty 12 — according to availability. In the event, only twelve of these aircraft were completed, and it is not known what engines were installed, although it is unlikely that any were fitted with Liberties as deliveries from America of these engines were temporarily halted in August.

With uncertainty surrounding the delivery of engines already flown in the Vimy, two further prototypes were ordered in August, it now being intended to fit 360hp Rolls-Royce Eagle VIII engines, whose production and

delivery was assured. The first of these aircraft, F9569, arrived at Martlesham on 11 October for brief Service trials, returning a maximum speed of 103 mph at sea level. The aircraft was fitted with a single 452-gallon fuel tank in the fuselage bomb bay, sufficient for an endurance of about eleven hours while carrying two 520lb bombs on external racks. This Vimy was then delivered to No 3 Aircraft Depot of the Independent Force in France, where it remained until after the Armistice. There is little doubt but that half-formed plans had existed for this aircraft to attempt a bombing raid on Berlin — involving a round flight of about 1,000 miles from the closest Independent Force aerodrome. Such a raid would have been marginally within F9569's capabilities.

The other new Vimy prototype, F9570, was destroyed by fire at Joyce Green before completion on 11 January 1919, but it is not known what engines were intended for this aircraft.

Production of the Vimy was severely reduced following the Armistice and, of the 776 then on order from Vickers and six other contractors, only 199 came to be built for the Royal Air Force, and contracted delivery dates were relaxed considerably owing to the postwar reductions in factory labour forces.

An order for 30 Fiat-powered Vimys (often referred to as Mark IIIs) was

placed with the Royal Aircraft Establishment, but delivery of engines was erratic and only twenty aircraft were completed. As far as is known, only Eagle-powered aircraft were delivered to the RAF, and these became officially known as Mark IVs, simply to differentiate from the possible future use of the American Liberty engines in later aircraft (bearing in mind that many D.H.9As were to be powered by this powerplant). 150 Liberty-Vimys were ordered from Westland Aircraft Works, that company having been given the resposibility of designing the Liberty installation in the D.H.9A, but the superiority of the Eagle VIII in the Vimy caused this contract to be changed to the Rolls-Royce engine in the Westland-built Vimys, and the number of aircraft reduced to 25.

The first three production Mark IVs (one aircraft each from Vickers, Clayton & Shuttleworth and Morgan) were delivered in February 1919. No home-based squadrons were yet scheduled to re-equip with Vimys and most of the early aircraft were shipped out to Egypt where they began to re-equip No 58 Squadron at Heliopolis in July that year, joining, and later replacing Handley Page O/400s.

Meanwhile, Vickers had begun the modifications to enable a Vimy to attempt an east-west non-stop crossing of the Atlantic, under conditions stipulated before the War for a prize of £10,000 offered by the *Daily Mail*. The thirteenth aircraft in the production line at Vickers' new factory at Weybridge was modified to carry 865 gallons of fuel and all military equipment was omitted. The aircraft was shipped out to Newfoundland and, crewed by Capt John Alcock (later Sir John, KBE) and Lieut Arthur Whitten-Brown (later Sir Arthur, KBE) took off near St John's on 14 June 1919, landing 16 hours 12 minutes later near

A standard Vimy IV, probably of fairly early vintage, with Eagle VIIIs. (Photo: via J M Bruce)

Clifden, Co Galway in Ireland, a distance flown of 1,890 miles.

The next long-distance Vimy was an aircraft prepared for the first aeroplane flight by Australians from Britain to Australia completed before the end of 1919, for which the Australian government was offering £A10,000. The flight was made by the two brothers, Capt Ross Smith and Lieut Keith Smith (later Sir Ross KBE and Sir Keith, KBE) of the Australian Air Force with crew members Sgts W H Shiers and J M Bennett. The flight was made between between Hounslow, Middlesex, and Darwin, Australia, and took place between 12 November and 10 December, a distance of 11,294 miles being covered in 135hr 55min elapsed flying time.

The third of the great trail-blazing flights by Vimys was an attempt to fly fròm England to Cape Town by Lieut-Col Pierre Van Ryneveld (later Gen Sir Pierre, KBE, CB, DSO, MC) and Maj Christopher Joseph Quintin Brand (later Air-Vice Marshal Sir Christopher, KBE, DSO, MC, DFC, RAF). Setting off from Brooklands on 4 February 1920, their aircraft, however, crashed south of Cairo with a leaking radiator, and another attempt was made in a second Vimy, whose flight also ended prematurely, this time at Bulawayo in Southern Rhodesia. They completed their journey in a D.H.9, to be awarded £5,000 each by the South African government.

At Heliopolis No 58 Squadron was renumbered No 70 in February 1920, this Squadron's rôle being that of bomber-transport, the Vimys being replaced by Vickers Vernon transports in November that year. The next Squadron to fly Vimys (including some of the aircraft just discarded by No 70) was No 45, re-formed at Helwan as a bomber unit on 1 April 1921. This Squadron was tasked with route-proving flights throughout the Middle East in preparation for the introduction of commercial air travel in the region.

The first home-based Vimy Squadron to be equipped was No 100, newly returned from Ireland to become a day bomber squadron flying a mixed complement of D.H.9As and Vimys at Spittlegate (Grantham), and continuing in this rôle until May 1924 when it was re-equipped with Fairey Fawns.

The next Squadron to receive the Vimy was No 216, at the time regarded as the RAF's premier bomber squadron, having flown O/400s with great distinction during the War, and later equipped with D.H.10s in Egypt. On receiving Vimys at Heliopolis in June 1922, the Squadron was declared a bomber-transport unit, dividing its efforts between practice bombing and carrying passengers (in some discomfort) and mail throughout the Middle East. No 216 Squadron continued to fly the Vimy until January 1926.

All the remaining four Vimy squadrons were home-based, No 7 re-forming at Bircham Newton in Norfolk with the aircraft on 1 June 1923, and continuing to fly them until April 1927. Most of the aircraft received on the Squadron from mid-1924 onwards were from a new production batch ordered in December 1923 (J7238-J7247). Nos 9 and 99 Squadrons, at Upavon and Netheravon respectively, began receiving Vimy IVs in April 1924, the former moving to Manston in the following month and the latter to Bircham Newton.

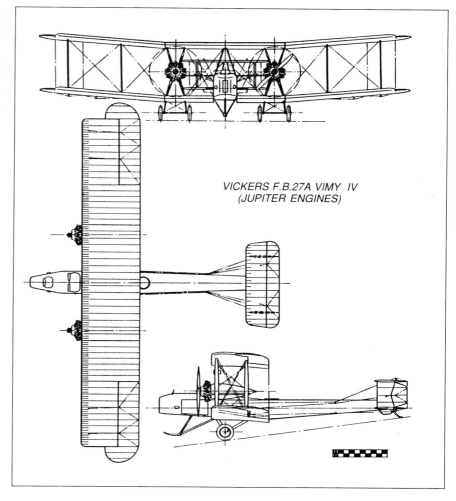

VICKERS F.B.27A VIMY IV
(JUPITER ENGINES)

Left: *A Morgan-built Vimy IV, FR3182, of No 216 Squadron flying from Heliopolis in late 1925 or early 1926; 'R' in the serial number denotes that the aircraft had been rebuilt (in this case by the Aircraft Depot at Aboukir).* (Photo: RAF Museum, Neg No P016931)

Below: *A Vimy IV of No 4 Flying Training School, probably flying from Heliopolis in 1926; most aircraft flying with this School were converted to provide dual controls, but also carried full bombing equipment for training purposes.* (Photo: via R C Sturtivant)

The last Squadron to receive Vimys was No 502 of the Special Reserve formed at Aldergrove on 15 May 1925, being declared a dedicated heavy bomber squadron and retaining these aircraft until July 1928.

Second-line duties performed by the Vimy included training, the type becoming the standard heavy bomber training aircraft during the early and mid-1920s. Many ex-squadron aircraft were converted with dual controls and issued to No 2 Flying Training School at Duxford and No 4 FTS in Egypt, and remained with these schools until the early 1930s. Others were used by the Parachute Training School at Henlow

and by the Night Flying Flight at Biggin Hill. Many of these aircraft were re-engined late in their lives with air-cooled

Bristol Jupiter and Armstrong Siddeley Jaguar radial engines when supplies of Eagle VIIIs became exhausted.

Type: Twin-engine, three-crew, three-bay biplane heavy bomber.

Specification: War Office (later RAF) Type V of 1917.

Manufacturers: Vickers Ltd (Aviation Department), Knightsbridge, London (manufacture at Bexley, Crayford and Weybridge); Clayton & Shuttleworth Ltd, Lincoln; Morgan & Co, Leighton Buzzard; Royal Aircraft Establishment, Farnborough, Hants; Westland Aircraft Works, Yeovil, Somerset. Production orders placed (but cancelled) with Boulton and Paul Ltd, Norwich; Ransomes, Sims and Jefferies, Ipswich, Suffolk; Kingsbury Aviation Co, Kingsbury; and The Metropolitan Wagon Co, Birmingham.

Powerplant: Prototypes. Two 200hp Hispano-Suiza, two 260hp Sunbeam Maori II, two 260hp Fiat A.12bis, two 400hp Liberty 12 and two 260hp Salmson 9Zm engines. Production. Two 260hp Fiat A.12bis, two 230hp B.H.P., and (Mk IV) two 360hp Rolls-Royce Eagle VIII engines.

Structure: Composite steel tube and wooden construction with ply and fabric covering.

Dimensions: Span, 67ft 2in; length, 43ft 6½in; height, 15ft 3in; wing area, 1,330 sq ft.

Weights (Mark IV): Tare, 7,101lb; all-up (with 1,650lb war load), 12,500lb.

Performance (Mark IV with bomb load): Max speed, 103 mph at sea level, 95 mph at 6,500ft; climb to 6,500ft, 33 min; service ceiling, 7,000ft.

Armament: One Lewis gun on nose gunner's cockpit with Scarff ring, and another amidships. Bomb load, carried internally and on wing racks, could comprise two 230lb and eighteen 112lb bombs (a total of 2,476lb).

Prototypes: Three, B9952-B9954; B9952 first flown on 30 November 1917 by Capt Gordon Bell. Other prototypes included F9569 (Mark IV prototype) and J6855 (ambulance prototype).

Production: A total of 776 Vimy bombers was ordered before the end of the First World War (excluding prototypes), of which 239 were built, all of them after the Armistice. Those built were: Vickers, 113 (F701-F712, F8596-F8645, F9146-F9195 and H9963); R.A.E., 10 (H651-H660); Clayton & Shuttleworth, 50 (F2996-F3045); Morgan, 41 (F3146-F3186); Westland, 25 (H5065-H5089). 30 Vimy bombers (all Mark IVs) and two ambulances were ordered after the War from Vickers, and all were built: J7143-J7144 (ambulances), J7238-J7247, J7440-J7454 and J7701-J7705.

Summary of Service: Vimy bombers served as follows: With No 7 Squadron at Bircham Newton from June 1923 to April 1927; with No 9 Squadron at Manston from April 1924 to June 1925; with No 24 Squadron at Kenley in 1925; with No 45 Squadron in Iraq from November 1921 to March 1922; with No 58 Squadron at Heliopolis from July 1919 to February 1920 and at Worthy Down from April 1924 to March 1925; with No 70 Squadron from February 1920 to November 1922 at Heliopolis, Egypt, and in Iraq; with No 99 Squadron at Netheravon and Bircham Newton from April to December 1924; with No 100 Squadron at Spittlegate from March 1922 to May 1924; with No 216 Squadron at Heliopolis, Egypt, from June 1922 to January 1926; and with No 502 Squadron of the Special Reserve at Aldergrove from June 1925 to July 1928. They also served with the Night Flying Flight, Biggin Hill, and with Nos 2 and 4 FTS.

Short N.2B

The first new seaplane produced by the Rochester manufacturers, Short Bros Ltd, after the death of Horace Short on 6 April 1917, was designed to Air Board Specification N.2B, and was therefore in direct competition with the Fairey III and the Wight Converted Seaplane.

Design of the Short N.2B was the responsibility of Francis Webber, under the supervision of Oswald Short, and the first aircraft appeared rather later than its rivals, the prototypes being based on use of the 260hp Sunbeam Maori I engine. As both the Fairey and Wight had been ordered into production with Rolls-Royce Eagles, Oswald sought permission to use the same engine but, owing to an anticipated shortage of these engines, his request was refused.

Eight prototype Short N.2Bs were ordered but only the first two were completed. The aircraft was a two-seat, two-bay folding biplane with prominent wing overhang, braced by outward-raked pairs of struts. The Maori was fully cowled with copious provision of cooling louvres and with a frontal radiator. The main floats were complemented by an outrigged tail float and wingtip floats, and the bomb load of two 230lb bombs was carried on side-by-side racks under the fuselage.

The first aircraft, N66, was launched at Rochester on 22 December 1917 and flown before the end of that month,

The first Short N.2B, N66, with wings folded and carrying two 230lb bombs, probably at the Isle of Grain in February 1918. (Photo: A J Jackson Collection)

being delivered for evaluation at the Isle of Grain on 2 February 1918. Here it was seen to possess no better performance than the established Short Type 184, and subsequent efforts to reduce drag, and therefore improve performance, achieved little benefit.

A second prototype, N67, was flown early in 1918 with shorter floats and a generally tidied-up engine cowling with fewer louvres, but it was obvious that, no matter what cosmetic treatment was

applied, the Maori engine did not impart adequate power, and work on the other prototypes was abandoned.

Rather later, in 1919, Oswald Short had a borrowed, low-compression Rolls-Royce Eagle installed in N67 but, although this imparted a small speed improvement, it was much too late to consider the aircraft in the context of Specification N.2B. N67 had its Maori reinstated at the end of that year and was taken on RAF charge in January 1920.

Type: Single-engine, two-seat, two-bay biplane, patrol bomber twin-float seaplane.
Air Board Specification: Type N.2B
Manufacturer: Short Brothers, Rochester, Kent.
Powerplant: One 260hp Sunbeam Maori I water-cooled in-line engine driving two-blade propeller.
Dimensions: Span, 55ft 2in; length, 40ft 2in; height, 13ft 9in; wing area, 678 sq ft.
Weights: Tare, 3,280lb; all-up, 4,911lb.
Performance: Max speed, 92 mph at sea level; climb to 6,500ft, 19 min 30 sec; service ceiling, 10,600ft.
Armament: One 0.303in Lewis machine gun with Scarff ring on rear cockpit; bomb load of two 230lb bombs on underfuselage racks.
Prototypes: Two, N66 and N67. N66 first flown in December 1917. No production. (Six other aircraft, N68-N73, cancelled.)

Blackburn R.T.1 Kangaroo

The Blackburn Kangaroo twin-engine maritime patrol bomber was a fairly large, but attractively proportioned biplane, developed directly from the G.P. seaplane (which had flown in 1916). Indeed, the Kangaroo's design had begun as a twin-float seaplane powered by a pair of Rolls-Royce Falcons, and around an ability to carry a 1,100lb torpedo, but this came to be changed when the Admiralty switched its preference to land-based patrol aircraft with long endurance when the German submarine activity intensified

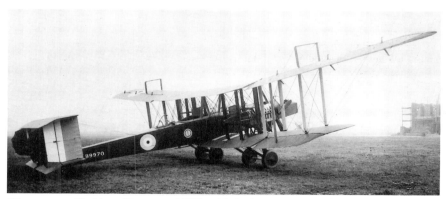

The prototype Blackburn Kangaroo, B9970, with slender nose profile and unsprung undercarriage struts. Note the enormous wing overhang. (Photo: via Stuart Leslie)

during 1917; there was probably more than a suggestion of influence in this preference as the Admiralty came to appreciate the value of the Handley Page

O/100s in this rôle, prior to their transfer to the night bombing duties.

As a result of this changed requirement (though the Blackburn aircraft was

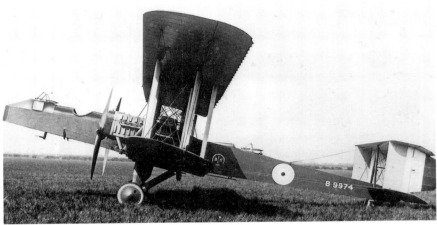

Delivered to the RAF in May 1918, Kangaroo B9974 displays all the modifications found necessary to overcome the Service's criticisms expressed during trials, including the modified nose gunner's cockpit and the oleo-sprung undercarriage. (Photo: Imperial War Museum, Neg No Q63799)

not conceived with any formal requirement in mind), the large pontoon floats were replaced by two pairs of mainwheels mounted beneath the engine nacelles. The latter, accommodating 250hp Rolls-Royce Falcon II twelve-cylinder, water-cooled engines with frontal radiators, were now raised above the lower wings. Rigged without stagger, the wings folded immediately outboard of the engines to give the aircraft a folded span of only 46 feet. Much of the G.P.'s primary structure was retained, although the curved fuselage decking aft of the wings was omitted, so that the fuselage possessed a rectangular and extremely slim cross-section.

Unusually for an aircraft with such large upper wing overhang, ailerons were fitted to upper and lower wings, and interconnected by a single vertical faired rod. Another innovation, which was not tested, was the use of double-action ailerons which, by operating a handwheel on the pilot's control column, could be lowered to act as landing flaps, while retaining their differential roll control.

The Kangaroo carried a crew of three, with pilot, nose and midships gunners — the nose gunner doubling as bomb aimer and being provided with an RNAS Mk IIA low-level bomb sight. As in the Avro Type 529, the midships gunner was inexplicably provided with limited dual controls, although in this instance these were confined to engine throttles and rudder bar, but with no engine switches nor control column!

Twenty Kangaroos were ordered by the Admiralty as N1720-N1739, but before the first was flown by the American Clifford E Prodger, probably late in December 1917, these were changed to B9970-B9989. The prototype, B9970, was delivered to the AES, Martlesham Heath, on 3 January 1918, where it was

flown in competitive evaluation with the Avro Type 529A.

The Kangaroo prototype was criticised as being very nose-heavy in the glide, while the rear fuselage lacked torsional rigidity — tending to twist when recovering from a steep turn. The fuselage was now so slender that it was only with considerable discomfort that the nose gunner could operate his Lewis gun, and the midship gunner's field of fire was severely restricted by the large tail surfaces.

It had been understood from the outset that about 50 Kangaroos would be required but, owing to an apparent misunderstanding, the number eventually authorized was no more than 20. This came about as the result of a belief in the War Office Technical Department that all the production aircraft then being worked on by Blackburn

were identical to the prototype, and instructions were passed to the company to halt production when these aircraft had been completed. In fact almost all the criticisms were satisfactorily remedied on the first two or three aircraft following the prototype — as was the prototype itself. The rear fuselage structure was considerably strengthened, and the front fuselage decking was built up to afford the front gunner better protection from the slipstream while manning his gun. The undercarriage of the prototype, comprising four pairs of plain V-struts without any shock-absorption, had collapsed during the AES trials; it was hurriedly re-designed to incorporate four faired oleo struts.

Nevertheless the order for 20 Kangaroos remained unchanged, and these aircraft completed delivery to the RAF between April and September 1918, first joining No 246 Squadron at Seaton Carew, Durham, in May that year. Although the aircraft could have been flown as a night bomber without difficulty, being able to carry up to 1,000lb of bombs, it was deemed more impor-

Type: Twin-engine, three-crew, four-bay biplane anti-submarine patrol bomber.
Manufacturer: The Blackburn Aeroplane and Motor Co Ltd, Olympia Works, Leeds, and Brough Aerodrome, East Yorks.
Powerplant: Two 250hp Rolls-Royce Falcon II (later 270hp Falcon III) twelve-cylinder water-cooled in-line engines driving four-blade tractor propellers.
Structure: Fabric- and ply-covered wire-braced wooden construction with forged metal joints and fittings.
Dimensions: Span, 74ft 10¼in (wings folded, 46ft 1in); length, 44ft 2in; height, 16ft 10in; wing area, 868 sq ft.
Weights: Tare, 5,284lb; all-up (with 920lb bomb load), 8,017lb.
Performance (with 460lb bomb load): Max speed, 100 mph at sea level, 86 mph at 10,000ft; climb to 10,000ft, 38 min 10 sec; service ceiling, 10,500ft; endurance, 8 hr.
Armament: Provision for single 0.303in Lewis machine guns with Scarff rings on nose and midships gunners' cockpits. Bomb load of up to four 230lb bombs carried internally, suspended vertically, nose-up; alternative lighter load carried externally. A single 520lb LC AS bomb could be carried nose-up internally, although it was usual for anti-submarine bombs to be carried externally for release from low altitude.
Prototype: One, B9970, first flown c.30 December 1917 by Clifford B Prodger at Brough, Yorks.
Production: Nineteen aircraft, B9971-B9989. (Four others, B8837-B8840, commenced construction during 1917-18, but only much later the first three were completed as trainers and civil registered G-EBMD, G-EBOM and G-EBPK)
Summary of RAF Service: Approximately ten aircraft flown by No 246 Squadron at Seaton Carew in 1918-19; subsequently served with No 1 Marine Observers' School and RAF Reserve School, Brough. (Suggestions that Kangaroos joined an operational RAF bomber squadron in Belgium have not been substantiated.)

tant to assume coastal anti-submarine duties. Carrying two RNAS 230lb LC anti-submarine bombs externally with hydrostatic fuzes, the Kangaroo possessed an endurance of eight hours, or a total patrol range of about 560 miles.

Alternatively, a standard 520lb LC bomb, hydrostatically fuzed, could be carried vertically in an internal bay, and it was one of these bombs, dropped by Kangaroo B9983, flown by Lieut Edmund Francis Waring (later Air Cdre, CBE, DFC, AFC, RAF) that crippled a German submarine, *UC.70*, on 28 August 1918 near Whitby, enabling it to be sunk by depth charges.

The Kangaroos continued to serve with No 246 Squadron until May 1919, by which time some were being transferred to No 1 Marine Observers' School at Aldbrough.

Eight aircraft were subsequently sold to commercial buyers and given civil registrations; one (G-EAMJ, ex-B9977) was even entered by Winston Churchill in the first King's Cup Race of 1922. Several Kangaroos were converted as cabin aircraft for passenger flying, and others were provided with full dual controls for flying training. Three of these are believed to have been part-completed aircraft, B8837-B8839, whose production by Blackburn had been halted by the War Office during the winter of 1917-18, but were later completed as G-EBMD, G-EBOM and G-EBPK; known as *Wilfred*, *Pip* and *Squeak* respectively, they were flown as trainers during the 1920s. All were eventually broken up in 1929.

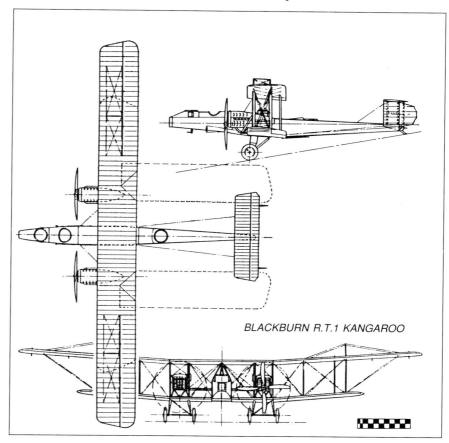

BLACKBURN R.T.1 KANGAROO

Deployment of British Bomber Squadrons, 1 January 1918

Royal Flying Corps		
Home Bases		
No 58 Squadron[1]	R.A.F. F.E.2B	Dover, Kent
No 98 Squadron[1]	Various	Old Sarum, Wiltshire
No 103 Squadron[1]	Airco D.H.9	Old Sarum, Wiltshire
No 104 Squadron[1]	Airco D.H.9	Andover, Hampshire
No 108 Squadron[1]	Airco D.H.9	Lake Down, Wiltshire
France		
No 18 Squadron	Airco D.H.4	Auchel
No 25 Squadron	Airco D.H.4	Boisdinghem
No 27 Squadron	Airco D.H.4	Serny
No 49 Squadron	Airco D.H.4	La Bellevue
No 55 Squadron	Airco D.H.4	Tantonville
No 57 Squadron	Airco D.H.4	Ste Marie Capelle
No 100 Squadron	R.A.F. F.E.2B/D	Ochey
No 101 Squadron	R.A.F. F.E.2B/D	Clairmarais
No 102 Squadron	R.A.F. F.E.2B/D	Treizennes

Royal Naval Air Service		
France		
No 5 (Naval) Squadron	Airco D.H.4	Petite Synthe
No 6 (Naval) Squadron[2]	Airco D.H.9	Petite Synthe
No 7 (Naval) Squadron	Handley Page O/100	Coudekerque
No 14 (Naval) Squadron	Handley Page O/100	Coudekerque
'A' Squadron, 41st Wing	Handley Page O/100	Ochey
Mediterranean		
'A' Squadron, RNAS	Airco D.H.4	Thasos, Aegean
'B' Squadron, RNAS	Airco D.H.4	Mitylene, Aegean
'C' Squadron, RNAS	Airco D.H.4	Mudros, Aegean
'D' Squadron, RNAS	Airco D.H.4	Stavros, Aegean
No 6 Wing, RNAS	Airco D.H.4	Southern Italy

[1]   Non-operational
[2]   Re-formed on this day

Airco D.H.9A

'Hyderabad No 7', F1000, one of the presentation D.H.9As of No 110 Squadron, the first squadron to fly the 'Nine-Ack' in action. (Photo: Air Ministry, Neg No H1561)

The original plans for the creation of a strategic bombing force in 1917 assumed the use of light day bombers capable, if not necessarily of being fully able to defend themselves, at least of being escorted by fighters, and a force of heavy night bombers. The appearance of the D.H.9, steadfastly favoured by ministers and boards remote from the fighting fronts, attracted bitter criticism from commanders in the field, who pointed to its lack of speed, agility and muscle, as well as its inevitable obsolescence by mid-1918.

Plans to introduce a new version, the D.H.9A, powered by the 375hp Rolls-Royce Eagle VIII, suffered a major setback when the Air Board allocated elsewhere the great majority of these, the best British engines being produced in quantity during the winter of 1917-18. As a result, attention was quickly focused on the new American Liberty 12 — for which extravagant steps had been announced towards mass production, and had first flown in a D.H.4 during October 1917 — and by the end of

January 1918 the Air Board had requested the supply of 3,000 examples.

Because the Aircraft Manufacturing Company was by then fully occupied with developing the D.H.10, responsibility for redesigning the D.H.9 to incorporate the American engine was vested in the Westland Aircraft Works, a manufacturer that had already built numerous D.H.4s and D.H.9s, and whose high quality of workmanship was something of a byword in aviation circles. New wings of almost 46 feet span, and with an area increased by 12 per cent, were designed, and the fuselage box-girder was strengthened by employing wire cross-bracing in place of the former ply partitions. Because no Liberty engine was yet available, a Westland-built D.H.9 underwent these airframe modifications and was fitted with an Eagle VIII together with a frontal radiator similar to that of the Liberty engine. The structure of the latter engine's installation was similar to that of the Rolls-Royce, and in due course, when production of the Eagle increased, the new D.H.9A with the British engine was

also built in small numbers (though the Liberty version came to be regarded as the standard machine). B7664 was first flown at Yeovil in March 1918 and underwent Service evaluation at the EAS the same month; the first Eagle-powered prototype had arrived at Martlesham towards the end of February.

The first Liberty 12 was received by Westland in March; indeed, production of the American engine began to lag behind schedule from the outset, and delivery of the 3,000 engines for Britain, intended to be completed by the end of July 1918, was suspended in August after no more than 1,050 had been shipped. The first Liberty-powered, British-built D.H.9A, C6122, was flown by Harry Hawker at Yeovil in April, and by the end of June 18 examples had been delivered to the RAF.

One of the early Liberty-D.H.9As was flown at Martlesham in July, enabling comparisons to be made with the Eagle aircraft. When carrying a pair of 230lb bombs — the normal load — there was little to choose between the two versions, although with the extra power of the Liberty the aircraft with this engine returned a service ceiling of 16,750 feet, compared with 14,000 feet with the Eagle. Endurance was also sig-

A Westland-built early-standard Liberty-powered D.H.9A, during performance trials at the Experimental Aircraft Station, Martlesham Heath, in 1918. Because Westland undertook all the early design work to install the American engine in the aircraft, it became regarded as the parent company. (Photo: Air Ministry, A & A E E, Neg No 315)

Originally flown by No 39 Squadron in the United Kingdom in 1923, this Whitehead-built D.H.9A was shipped to the Middle East in 1924 where it was fitted with an auxiliary radiator at the Hinaidi Aircraft Depot. It is seen here with No 84 Squadron flying from Shaibah in 1926, equipped for night flying and carrying a spare main wheel on the side of the front fuselage. (Photo: A J Jackson Collection)

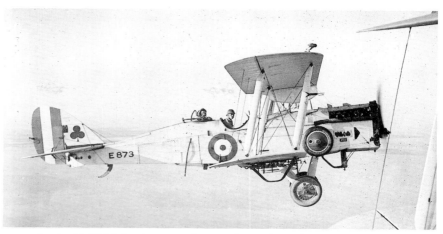

nificantly better. However, the Eagle D.H.9A demonstrated its ability to carry a maximum bomb load of 740 pounds.

Eight squadrons of the RAF received D.H.9As before the Armistice, of which four were light bomber units that took part in bombing operations, two did not become operational during the War, and two were engaged in anti-submarine patrols flying from Great Yarmouth in Norfolk.

The first Squadron to take deliveries was No 110 in July 1918, then stationed at Kenley with D.H.9s. The Squadron moved to France where it became part of the Independent Force at Bettoncourt on 1 September. All this unit's initial complement of D.H.9As ('Nine-Acks' in the current RAF parlance) were subscribed by HH the Nizam of Hyderabad, a gesture that gained lasting recognition when the Squadron was officially named No 110 (Hyderabad) Squadron. Unfortunately No 110 fared badly in the small number of operations flown before the Armistice and, in a daylight raid on Frankfurt on 21 October, 7 out of 13 aircraft despatched failed to return, and another returned early with engine trouble. During its two months in action the Squadron lost 17 D.H.9As to enemy action, and 28 others in accidents.

In August No 205 Squadron began re-equipping on its French aerodrome at Bovelles, followed by Nos 99 in September and 18 in October. Nos 25 and 120 Squadrons, though in the process of re-equipping with D.H.9As at the time of the Armistice, had no opportunity to fly them in action. Two Squadrons at Great Yarmouth, Nos 212 and 273, received their new machines in August and September and flew them on a number of anti-submarine patrols before the end of hostilities.

By the end of the War a total of 2,250 D.H.9As had been ordered from six manufacturers, the vast majority of them scheduled to be powered by Liberty 12s; by 31 December, 885 of these aircraft had been built. However, that month had brought about the cancellation of 520 aircraft, despite the decision taken

to retain the D.H.9A in the peacetime RAF; it is likely that the cancellation was brought about owing to the uncertainties surrounding the continued production of the Liberty 12 in America. Any fears of that production being terminated however, proved groundless, and the Americans were quick to recognise the excellence of their engine. On the other hand, with the Geddes Axe beginning to be imposed in Britain, there were other uncertainties concerning the likely size of the peacetime RAF, and the scale of appropriations likely to be voted in Parliament. (Bearing in mind this uncertainty, it is perhaps worth mentioning that the 375hp Eagle VIII was almost exactly one-third more expensive than the 400hp Liberty engine.)

Postwar Service

Paradoxically all the above squadrons disposed of their D.H.9As within eighteen months of the Armistice, all but one of them being disbanded; only No 25 Squadron survived, to become a fighter squadron on 1 February 1920, flying Sopwith Snipes.

Two other squadrons were equipped with D.H.9As for a short time immediately after the War. No 57 Squadron was given a few of the new aircraft with which to operate a temporary mail service between France and the United Kingdom before being disbanded in December 1919.

No 221 Squadron (formerly 'D' Squadron of the RNAS prior to the creation of the Royal Air Force) had been engaged in bombing duties in the Aegean with D.H.4s and 9s during 1918. On moving to Mudros in December that year, it was equipped with D.H.9As before embarking in HMS *Riviera* for southern Russia, setting up a temporary base at Baku on the shores of the Caspian. It then flew north to Petrovsk

whence it carried out bombing raids and armed reconnaissance over Astrakhan in support of 'White Russian' forces fighting the Bolsheviks. In September the RAF personnel were ordered home and the D.H.9As were handed over to the Russians. (The D.H.9A was also built in Russia as the R-1, being powered by M-5 engines — assumed to be copied from the Liberty.)

In due course the D.H.9A was confirmed as the RAF's principal light day bomber in the peacetime Service; between 1920 and 1931 it served on no fewer than 24 squadrons, nine of them in the Middle East and India. The early 1920s were the period of the RAF's fight for survival in the face of wrangling by the War Office and Admiralty, each determined to create its own air arm in place of the fledgling Service. Trenchard, as the first Chief of the Air Staff, saw in the light bomber (and implicitly the D.H.9A) the ideal instrument with which to exercise Britain's Mandate to supervise the restructuring of the Middle East, following the destruction of the Ottoman Empire.

Handicapped by a lack of established aerodromes throughout the theatre, which covered the vast area later defined as Palestine, Syria, Lebanon, Jordan and Iraq, the RAF was initially obliged to depend on stations in north-east Egypt and those at Baghdad and Basra, later establishing bases at Ramleh, Amman, Hinaidi, Kirkuk and Shaibah. To these were added countless desert landing grounds throughout the area at which aircraft could put down to refuel. During 1920 and 1921 five Squadrons, Nos 8, 30, 47, 55 and 84, all flying D.H.9As, were formed or re-formed at Suez, Helwan and Baghdad, retaining these aircraft almost throughout the 1920s.

Their duties were officially described as 'local security' but, as the months

One of the last Westland-built D.H.9As, produced to Specification 13/26, J8118 first flew in 1927 and was shipped to the Middle East where it served with Nos 8 and 45 Squadrons, being lost in an accident on 30 January 1928 in Egypt. (Photo; via H Horton)

passed, it became all too clear that self-preservation in an environment of harsh desert conditions was the concern uppermost in the minds of air- and groundcrews alike. The Liberty engine, not conceived to operate in ambient temperatures often well above 35°C, was provided with a larger tropical radiator in the nose plus an additional radiator under the nose, as well as additional water containers carried beneath the wings, lest the machine was forced down in the desert with an overheating engine. Landings in the desert or at one of the makeshift strips were also hard on the aircraft's wheels and tyres, so it became common practice for the 'Nine-Acks' to carry a spare wheel attached to the fuselage for such emergencies.

Not surprisingly, occasional bombing attacks were carried out against marauding or dissident tribesmen, and their rifles, though often fired at random, presented a threat to the slow and low-flying D.H.9As, whose Vickers and Lewis machine guns were used as a necessary deterrent. The bombs most frequently dispensed were 112-pounders of which, in a temperature of 38°C, the D.H. could scarcely carry more than one — when added to the impedimenta for survival.

Yet the D.H.9A performed its duties with admirable reliability, the Liberty engine being considered to be 'as good as any Rolls-Royce', while a single well-placed light bomb invariably served to satisfy the purpose of the Mandate.

In February 1927 No 8 Squadron moved with its D.H.9As to Aden, where an airstrip was established at Khormaksar, later to become an important RAF Station. A year afterwards the D.H.s were replaced by Fairey IIIFs, but No 8 was to remain at Aden until 1945.

The other overseas deployment of D.H.9As was in India, the first such aircraft arriving at Ambala with No 99 Squadron from France in June 1919. This squadron was disbanded on 1 April 1920 to become No 27 and, as such, moved to Risalpur near Peshawar in the North-West Frontier Province where it was to be joined by No 60 Squadron in April 1923, also with D.H.9As. This theatre and the Khyber Pass in particular, constantly wracked by the depredations of marauding Afghan tribesmen, was even more demanding than the deserts of the Middle East, and the Liberty's reliability was vital, simply

because the mountainous terrain rendered any forced landing out of the question.

At home, the D.H.9A served on Nos 11, 12, 35, 39, 100, 101 and 207 Squadrons, their principal stations being Bircham Newton in Norfolk, and Spittlegate, Grantham. The last front-line aircraft to serve with the regular Service in the United Kingdom were those of No 35 Squadron, replaced by Fairey IIIFs in January 1930.

The D.H.9A was notable in one other respect in being selected as the initial equipment of the Auxiliary Air Force, which came into being in September 1925. The first three Squadrons, Nos 600 (City of London), 602 (City of Glasgow) and 603 (City of Edinburgh), received their first aircraft in October that year at Northolt, Renfrew and Turnhouse respectively, all being declared light bomber units. In the years that followed they were to be joined by Nos 601, 604 and 605 Squadrons, and

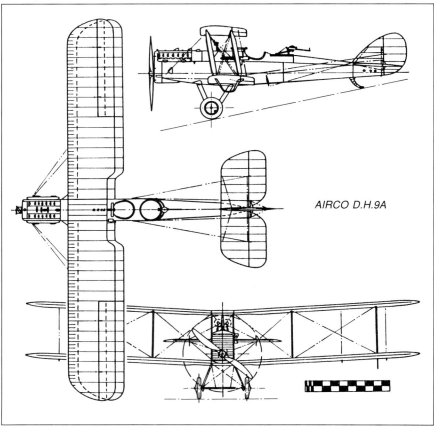

AIRCO D.H.9A

Right upper: *E8673 was a D.H.9A ordered from Airco during the War and completed in 1920; in 1923 it was shipped to India and was converted to a dual-control trainer before joining No 27 Squadron at Risalpur, in whose markings it is shown here.* Right lower: *First of the Westland-built Lion II-powered D.H.9As, J6957, at Martlesham Heath in 1923; note the elaborate oleo undercarriage fitted on this variant.* (Photo: via J M Bruce)

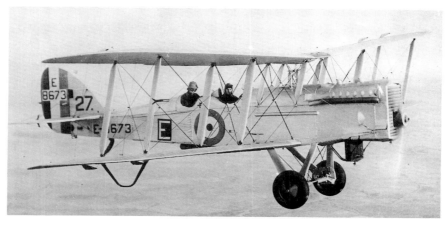

No 501 Squadron of the Special Reserve at Filton.

Although production of the D.H.9A, ordered under wartime contracts, had been allowed to run out in 1919, with many of the early production aeroplanes undergoing progressive modification and rebuilding in the course of the next seven years, new production contracts were found necessary in 1925 and 1926. To cater for slightly modified requirements, new contracts were issued to de Havilland, Westland, Short, Hawker, Parnall, Saunders and Blackburn — in some instances for work that was to provide a lifeline at a time when the aircraft industry was fighting for survival. Among the new aircraft produced under these contracts was a Westland-built batch of 35 D.H.9A (Dual Control) trainers, J8460-J8494. Another batch of aircraft, converted by Westlands during rebuilding, were six much-modified D.H.9As, J6957-J6962, powered by 465hp Napier Lion II engines — which bestowed a sea level maximum speed of 144 mph; only one of these Lion aircraft ever served with a Squadron when J6958 joined No 55 in February 1927 at Hinaidi, Iraq, for the personal use of Air Vice-Marshal Sir John Higgins KCB, KBE, DSO, AFC, Air Officer Commanding British Forces in Iraq.

Type: Single-engine, two-seat, two-bay biplane light bomber.

Manufacturers: Wartime. The Aircraft Manufacturing Co Ltd, Hendon, London NW9; F W Berwick & Co Ltd, Park Royal, London NW10; Mann, Egerton & Co Ltd, Aylsham Road, Norwich, Norfolk; The Vulcan Motor and Engineering Co (1906) Ltd, Crossen, Lancashire; Westland Aircraft Works, Yeovil, Somerset; Whitehead Aircraft Co Ltd, Richmond, Surrey. *Postwar.* The de Havilland Aircraft Co Ltd, Stag Lane, Edgware, Middlesex; The Blackburn Aeroplane and Motor Co Ltd, Leeds and Brough, Yorkshire; H G Hawker Engineering Co Ltd, Canbury Park Road, Kingston-upon-Thames, Surrey; George Parnall and Co Ltd, Coliseum Works, Bristol; S E Saunders Ltd, East Cowes, Isle of Wight; Short Bros (Rochester and Bedford) Ltd, Rochester, Kent; Westland Aircraft Works, Yeovil, Somerset.

Powerplant: One 400hp Liberty 12 twelve-cylinder, water-cooled, in-line engine; 375hp Rolls-Royce Eagle VIII; 465hp Napier Lion II.

Structure: Wire-braced wooden box structure in fuselage; forward section ply covered, rear fabric-covered. Laminated spruce wing spars.

Dimensions: Span, 45ft 11⅜in; length (Liberty 12 engine), 30ft 3in; height, 11ft 4in; wing area, 486.75 sq ft.

Weights (Liberty 12): Tare, 2,800lb; all-up (two 230lb bombs), 4,645lb.

Performance (Liberty 12, with two 230lb bombs): Max speed, 123 mph at sea level, 114.5 mph at 10,000ft; climb to 10,000ft, 15 min 45 sec; service ceiling, 16,750ft; endurance, 5¼ hr.

Armament: One synchronized 0.303in Vickers machine gun on port side of nose, with Constantinesco CC interrupter gear, and single or twin Lewis machine guns with Scarff ring on rear cockpit. Bomb load of 740lb carried on underwing and fuselage racks.

Prototypes: Three (all converted D.H.9s, two with Eagle engines and one with Liberty 12)

Production: Wartime orders for 2,250 aircraft, of which 1,730 were built, plus peacetime orders for 267 aircraft of which all were built; total production, 1,997. Aircraft built: Wartime production: Whitehead, 300 (E701-E1000); Airco, 575 (E8407-E8806 and H1-H175); Mann, Egerton, 150 (E9657-E9756 and J551-J600); Vulcan, 225 (E9857-E9956 and H3546-H3670); Westland, 350 (F951-F1101, F1603-F1652 and H3396-H3545); Berwick, 140 (F2733-F2872); Peacetime production: de Havilland, 45 (J7700, J7787-J7798, J7877-J7883 and J8129-J8153); Westland, 101 (J7799-J7819, J7855-J7866, J8096-J8128 and J8460-J8494); Short Bros, 37 (J7823-J7834, J7884-J7890 and J8154-J8171); Hawker, 30 (J7835-J7854 and J7867-J7876); Parnall, 18 (J8172-J8199); Saunders, 18 (J8190-J8207); Blackburn, 18 (J8208-J8225). In addition, 204 aircraft were rebuilt (unusually involving the assembly of stored components), all being allocated new serial numbers, by the following: Westland (66), Handley Page (21), de Havilland (18), Gloster (35), Hawker (39), and Packing Depot, Ascot (25).

Summary of Service: D.H.9As served with Nos 18, 99, 110 and 205 Squadrons, RAF, on the Western Front; with No 25 Squadron in Germany, 1919; with the following home-based light bomber Squadrons after the War, Nos 11, 12, 35, 57, 100, 101 and 207 Squadrons; with Nos 212 and 273 Squadrons, home based on coastal patrol duties; with No 3 Squadron, home-based for fleet co-operation; with No 24 (Communications) Squadron; and No 120 Squadron, home-based for mail services. D.H.9As served with the RAF overseas with No 8 (Iraq and Aden), 14 (Palestine), 27, 30, 39 and 60 (India), 45 (Egypt), 47 (Russia and Egypt), 55 and 84 (Iraq), and 221 (Russia). D.H.9As equipped No 501 Squadron of the Special Reserve, and Nos 600, 601, 602, 603, 604 and 605 Squadrons of the Auxiliary Air Force.

Airco D.H.10 Amiens

Originally commenced as the first D.H.10 prototype, C4283 was completed after the three true prototypes had flown, and became representative of the initial production version with Liberty 12 engines, and without the twin nosewheels. (Photo: via J M Bruce)

It has been said, possibly apocryphally, that while the German bombers were attacking London in daylight on 7 July 1917, the sole D.H.3 twin-engine bomber prototype was being burnt in a scrapyard at Hendon. True or false, it is ironic that it required the daylight raids on the British capital to persuade the Air Board to reconsider its ill-judged opinion that twin-engine bombers were impractical, a view that had brought development of the D.H.3 to a premature end eighteen months earlier.

By the end of July 1917 Air Board Specification A.2.b had been drafted, calling for a single- or twin-engine day bomber with a two-man crew, capable of carrying bombs and racks weighing 500lb at a height of at least 19,000 feet, with a maximum speed with this load at 15,000 feet of not less than 110 mph. Moreover, the Air Board's Technical Committee went a step further by expressing the view that the D.H.3, if fitted with two 200hp BHP engines, could meet this requirement, and straightway ordered a single prototype, C4283.

As work got underway on this aircraft, Geoffrey de Havilland started a radical redesign of the D.H.3, using 230hp Siddeley Puma engines in a slightly enlarged airframe, and on 18 October Airco was instructed to concentrate on this version, ordering three new prototypes, C8658-C8660, ten days later.

The first of the new prototypes, C8658, was flown at Hendon on 4 March 1918, cut-outs in the trailing edge of the upper wing being necessitated by the use of pusher propellers. This machine was delivered to Martlesham Heath on 7 April for evaluation, but failed by a substantial margin to meet the performance demands, being scarcely able to manage 90 mph at 15,000 feet with the stipulated bomb load.

This lack of performance had, however, been anticipated, and the second prototype, C8659, was flown on 20 April with 360hp Rolls-Royce Eagle VIIIs in tractor installations, becoming known as the Amiens Mark II — even though the Air Ministry explained that this version was unlikely to achieve production owing to heavy demand for this engine elsewhere. As with the D.H.9A, the Eagle installation was only undertaken to test the various airframe modifications introduced, not least those associated with the tractor engines. Indeed the Eagle installation was similar to that of the American 395hp Liberty 12 engine, selected for the finite production Amiens.

The prototype of this, the Amiens Mark III, C8660, was delivered to Martlesham Heath on 28 July, demonstrating a maximum sea level speed of about 120 mph while carrying four 230lb bombs — well in excess of the speed and load demanded. It failed, however, to meet the load-at-altitude requirements by a slender margin. This aircraft also had the twin nosewheels removed — relics of the old D.H.3 design.

Meanwhile work had resumed on the original prototype, C4283, now referred to as the fourth prototype as it was intended to represent the Amiens Mark III in its production guise. With raked wing tips and horn-balanced ailerons, and 405hp Liberty 12 high-compression engines, it exceeded all the speed, altitude and load requirements.

The first major alteration to production D.H.10s involved mounting the engine nacelles on the lower wings instead of at mid-gap and, following a favourable report from Martlesham, this modification was introduced into Mann, Egerton's production line at Norwich as the Amiens IIIa, of which 32 were produced. All production D.H.10s were covered by the Air Ministry's Specification Type VII, issued in April 1918.

The only other significant variant was the D.H.10C Amiens IIIc, powered by 375hp Eagle VIIIs, but this was no more than a shortlived insurance against discontinuation of Liberty production in America. As far as can be discovered only five examples were produced, all random installations in Airco's final production batch. Two of these, E5458 and E5550, were experimentally armed with

The first D.H.10A Amiens Mk IIIa, F1869, with Liberty engines mounted on the lower wings, and with larger mainwheels. It was delivered for trials at Martlesham Heath on 17 August 1918, and subsequently 32 examples were built by Mann, Egerton at Norwich. (Photo: de Havilland Aircraft Ltd., Neg No 9650)

Delivered to the RAF on 1 March 1919, F9421 was the first Mann, Egerton-built Amiens IIIa; most of these aircraft were issued to No 60 Squadron on the North-West Frontier. (Photo: Imperial War Museum, Neg No Q67976)

the 1½-pounder COW gun for trials at Ordfordness in 1920.

The general uncertainty of and delays in the delivery of Liberty engines during 1918 was the cause of the production of Amiens aircraft falling further and further behind schedule during the last six months of the War, and it had been planned to have the aircraft in service with eight squadrons of the Independent Force by the spring of 1919. A total of 1,291 D.H.10s was on order with seven companies by November 1918, but only eight had been delivered by that month. Post-Armistice cancellations then reduced to actual number built to just 258. More than 100 of these remained in store until the aircraft was declared obsolete in April 1923.

Postwar Service

In the event the D.H.10 only fully equipped Nos 97 (becoming No 60), 104 and 216 Squadrons, and none gave service as a bomber in the United Kingdom. Moreover, its Service life only spanned the period between November 1918 and April 1923.

First deliveries were made to No 104 Squadron in the first half of November 1918, then based at Maisoncelle in France, and it was with this unit that the Amiens flew its one and only wartime operation when on the day before the Armistice, F1867, flown by Capt Ewart Garland, joined a raid on Sarrebourg in Lorraine. No 104 gave up its aircraft in February 1919, returned to the United Kingdom and disbanded six months later.

In the meantime No 97 Squadron, hitherto equipped with Handley Page O/400s, had returned to England and began taking on a full complement of D.H.10s at Ford in January, the first two Airco-built examples, E5450 and E5456, arriving that month. In July the Squadron sailed for India, and between August and November took delivery of tropicalised D.H.10s, identified by taller radiators to provide extra cooling of the Libertys.

On 1 April 1920 No 97 Squadron was renumbered No 60 while at Lahore, and the new Squadron took charge of the D.H.10s, moving to Risalpur to provide support for the ground forces on the North-West Frontier.

That same month the Squadron's Amiens helped the army to suppress the Pathan revolt that marked the climax of the Third Afghan War, but another Pathan rising in November brought further air action when D.H.10s, in company with other RAF bombers, attacked bands of rebel tribesmen in the Tilli area. No 60 Squadron continued to fly its Amiens until April 1923 when they were replaced by D.H.9As.

The only other Squadron to be fully equipped with D.H.10s was No 216 at Abu Sueir in Egypt, which received its first Amiens in December 1919, with eight further machines arriving during the next six months. To begin with, the D.H.10s were flown by one Flight, charged with pioneering an air mail service between Cairo and Baghdad, while, until October 1921, the other Flight continued to fly O/400 heavy bombers. Owing to the low weight of mail payloads, No 216 Squadron simultaneously flew a 'taxi' service in the mail aircraft, adding a second cockpit behind that of the pilot. In June 1922, with the arrival of Vimys, the D.H.10s became

Type: Twin-engine, three-crew, three-bay biplane medium bomber.

Specification: Air Board (1917) Specification A.2.B

Manufacturers: The Aircraft Manufacturing Co Ltd, Hendon, London NW9; Birmingham Carriage Co, Birmingham; The Daimler Co Ltd, Coventry; Mann, Egerton & Co Ltd, Aylsham Road, Norwich, Norfolk; The Siddeley-Deasey Motor Car Co Ltd, Parkside, Coventry; National Aircraft Factory No 2, Stockport.

Powerplant: Mark I. Two 230hp BHP six-cylinder liquid-cooled in-line engines driving two-blade pusher propellers. Mark II. Two 360hp Rolls-Royce Eagle VIII twelve-cylinder liquid-cooled in-line engines driving two-blade tractor propellers. Mark III and IIIA. Two 400hp Liberty 12 engines. Mark IIIC. Two 375hp Rolls-Royce Eagle VIII engines.

Structure: All-wood, wire-braced box structure; forward fuselage ply-covered, rear fabric-covered. Twin laminated spruce wing spars with ash ribs and silver spruce interplane struts.

Dimensions (Mark IIIA): Span, 65ft 6in; length, 39ft 7⁷⁄₁₆in; height, 14ft 6in; wing area, 837.4 sq ft.

Weights (Mark IIIA): Tare, 5,750lb; all-up (with bomb load), 9,060lb

Performance (Mark IIIA): Max speed, 131 mph at sea level, 124 mph at 10,000ft; climb to 10,000ft, 11 min; service ceiling, 19,000ft; endurance, 6 hr.

Armament: Bomb load of up to 920lb (112lb and 230lb bombs or combinations) carried internally. Single- or double-yoked 0.303in Lewis machine guns with Scarff rings mounted on nose and midships gunners' cockpits.

Prototypes: Three, C8658-C8660. First aircraft, Mark I C8658, first flown by Capt Geoffrey de Havilland at Hendon on 4 March 1918. One other prototype, C4283, was converted to full Amiens III production standard.

Production: A total of 1,291 D.H.10s was ordered, but only 258 were built, as follows: Airco, 138 (E5437-E5558 and F1867-F1882, all D.H.10 Mark IIIs); Birmingham Carriage, 20 (E6037-E6056, all Mark IIIs); Siddeley-Deasey, 28 (E7837-E7864, all Mark IIIs); Daimler, 40 (E9057-E9096, all Mark IIIs); Mann, Egerton, 32 (F8421-F8452, all Mark IIIAs).

Summary of Service: D.H.10 Mark IIIs and IIIAs served with No 104 Squadron, RAF, in France between November 1918 and February 1919; with No 97 Squadron (renumbered No 60 Squadron on 1 April 1920) at Risalpur, India, between April 1919 and April 1923; and with No 216 Squadron at Abu Sueir and Heliopolis, Egypt, between December 1919 and June 1922. E5459 served with No 24 (Communications) Squadron at Kenley and London Colney in 1919; two D.H.10s flew bombing operations with No 27 Squadron in India in 1922; one (C8658) was evaulated as a heavy fighter with No 51 Squadron, and one operated a night mail service with No 120 Squadron between Hawkinge and Cologne in May 1919.

redundant as the Vickers aircraft could more efficiently perform passenger, mail and bombing duties on its own.

Amiens aircraft also served in small numbers with other Squadrons, including one (E5459) with No 24 at Kenley in the communications rôle, two with No 27 Squadron for bombing duties on the North-West Frontier late in 1922, one (the first prototype, C8658) with No 51 Squadron in Norfolk during 1918 for evaluation as a heavy fighter, and one with No 120 Squadron for an experimental night mail service between Hawkinge in Kent and Cologne during May 1919.

Another experimental Amiens was the Birmingham Carriage Company-built E6042, which underwent prolonged trials with various tail configurations, including twin fins and rudders; first delivered to the RAE at Farnborough on 25 October 1919, it was last flown on 8 July 1926.

A few Amiens trainers with dual controls were produced for No 6 Flying Training School at Manston, and at least one of these was flying in 1922.

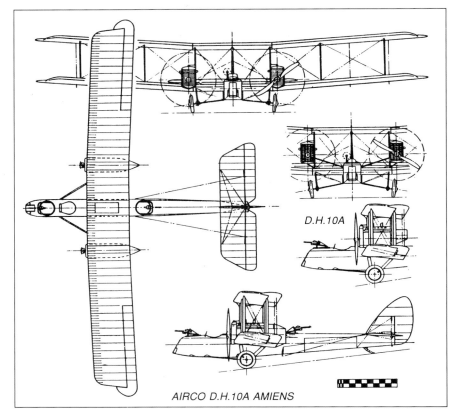

D.H.10A

AIRCO D.H.10A AMIENS

A standard Amiens Mk III, E6042, built by the Birmingham Carriage Company, was modified to have twin fins and rudders, and was delivered to the RAE at Farnborough in October 1919, continuing to fly until 1926 in what was probably a basic research programme into directional control and stability of twin-engine biplanes. (Photo: Royal Aerospace Establishment, Neg No MH3316)

Handley Page H.P.15 V/1500

Last of the very heavy bombers to enter production during the First World War, the Handley Page V/1500 was a further result of the German air attacks on England in 1917 and their influence on changing British strategic bombing policy. In this instance, implicit in the Air Board requirement was an ability to reach and bomb the German capital.

Drawing on the company's unmatched experience in building very large land-

plane bombers, Handley Page had already been engaged in the preliminary design of an aeroplane twice the weight of the O/400, to be powered by either two 600hp Rolls-Royce Condor or Siddeley-Deasy Tiger engines.

Known initially as the Type V, three prototypes (B9463-B9465) of the Handley Page aircraft were ordered under the Air Board's Specification A.3(b), but it soon became obvious that the provisions of the Specification would be greatly exceeded, and it was to be completely rewritten in April 1918 as RAF Type VII. By then, however, Henry Royce had informed Handley Page that the Condor was unlikely to be

available until 1919, and advised him to consider redesigning the aircraft to feature four 375hp Eagle VIIIs, and the official designation, V/1500, referred to the total engine power.

Owing to a lack of space immediately available at Cricklewood, design and manufacture of the prototype was transferred to Harland & Wolff Ltd at Belfast under the leadership of George Volkert, who took with him Francis Arcier and S T A ('Star') Richards; stressing was to be undertaken by Capt T M Wilson RN of the Admiralty.

Construction of the V/1500, a four-bay biplane spanning 126 feet, was entirely of wood, the fuselage being built

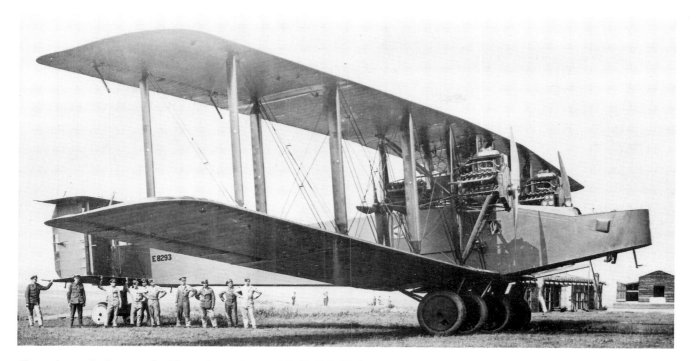

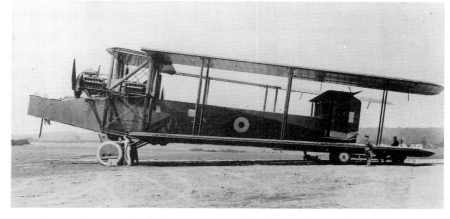

Two views of the second Alliance-built V/1500, F7135, of No 274 Squadron at Bircham Newton late in 1919. The lower wings possessed dihedral so as to provide adequate ground clearance when folded, although even then the tail needed to be supported on a trolley. It is said that the combined buoyancy provided by the four landing wheels was about two tons in the event that the aircraft was ditched in the sea. (Photo: Air Ministry)

in three sections. The nose, principally of silver spruce longerons and frames, was covered with ply; the centre section, containing the bomb bay (beneath a 1,000-gallon fuel tank), was entirely of spruce except for two massive ash cross-beams which supported the bomb load; the rear fuselage was built to form a box-girder of rolled-up laminated spruce sections and longerons, and incorporated a catwalk to the tail gunner's position in the extreme rear.

The wings, which folded immediately outboard of the engines, were rigged without stagger and were constructed about two silver spruce box main spars, the compression struts being either box-type or rolled-up laminated spruce structures. Ribs and ailerons were all of spruce. The upper wing was constructed in five sections, the centresection accommodating two gravity fuel tanks and four cooling water tanks. The lower wings were built in six sections.

The four Eagle engines were arranged in tandem pairs, mounted at mid-gap by steel tube V-struts attached to front and rear wing main spars. A single massive radiator, serving all four engines, was located on top of the centre fuselage, forward of the centresection wing struts. The two front engines drove two-blade propellers, and the rear pair four-blade propellers of smaller diameter; though all four engines were right-handed, the front and rear propellers were of course counter-rotating.

The biplane tail unit, with narrow gap, incorporated four balanced rudders, without fixed fins but with hinge rods attached to the front tailplane main spar.

The maximum bomb load of the V/1500 comprised thirty 250lb HE RL bombs or combinations of 550lb and 250lb bombs. The aircraft was also intended to be able to carry a single 3,360lb SN Major bomb, which was being developed specially for the V/1500 but was not ready for flight trials before the Armistice.

Manufacture of the first prototype, B9463, was an extraordinary feat of dedicated application and ingenuity and, as early as 27 January 1918, Harland & Wolff received an order for 20 production examples (E4304-E4323). Moreover, as an insurance against possible labour disputes — always a consideration in wartime conditions of food and coal shortages — another production contract for 20 V/1500s (E8287-E8306) was signed with William Beardmore & Co Ltd at Dalmuir.

The first flight by B9463 had been intended to take place in March at Crumlin (later named Aldergrove) but, owing to disputes and bad weather, it was decided to move the entire aircraft to Cricklewood, a feat completed by sea, road and rail by 12 April. Final assembly was achieved in nine days and on 22 May, flown by Capt Vernon E G Busby

Stated in some works to be a Cricklewood-built V/1500, this aircraft is of the finite production standard, with symmetric hexagonal frontal radiators and tailplanes with increased gap; note the two-blade tractor propellers and the four-blade pushers of reduced diameter. (Photo: via J M Bruce)

RAF, the prototype made a short straight hop over the grass at the new Clutterhouse Farm aerodrome.

On 8 June, however, on its thirteenth flight, B9463 crashed and was destroyed by fire, Busby and four passengers being killed; one other, Col Alec Ogilvie, survived, having been occupying the tail gunner's position. The total loss of the aircraft, and the impossibility of determining its cause, severely delayed further production. During its short life a number of modifications had been found necessary and had been introduced in B9463; engine cowlings had been fitted, and then removed; frontal radiators had replaced the large central unit; and a lack of directional stability had resulted in increased tailplane gap and the introduction of fixed fins, the rudders being unbalanced.

The V/1500 had consituted a major element in the plans to enlarge the Independent Force and, had the second and third prototypes joined in the flight programme as planned, in July, production machines would have probably fully equipped two, or even three squadrons before the end of the War. As it was, work on the remaining two prototypes was delayed — and they were eventually completed as J1935 and J1936, the former being flown on 3 August and the latter in October. Both these aircraft carried the full gun armament, with Scarff rings in nose and tail, as well as pillar mountings amidships — a possible total of six Lewis guns. J1936 also underwent trials at Orfordness with a three-inch mortar in the midships gunner's position, launching bombs aft over the tail.

Meanwhile, No 86 Wing, No 27 Group, of the Independent Force had been formed in great secrecy at Bircham Newton under Wg Cdr Redford Henry Mulock DSO* (later Air Cdre,

CBE, DSO*, RCAF) with Nos 166 and 167 Squadrons, these being the units intended to fly bombing raids over the heart of Germany. The two Squadrons received their first V/1500s in October and November 1918 respectively.

By the date of the Armistice, a total of seven V/1500s had been delivered to the RAF, comprising the first two built by Harland & Wolff, but assembled by Handley Page, three Handley Page aircraft and two Beardmore aircraft. The first of the latter had originally been delivered with 500hp Galloway Atlantic engines, but these were removed in favour of Eagle VIIIs following the Air Ministry's decision to abandon the Atlantic.

Two aircraft of No 166 Squadron were each bombed-up with four 250lb bombs on 9 November, ready to attack targets in Germany (the primary objective being Berlin), their pilots under orders to fly on to Czechoslovakia if they considered insufficient fuel remained for a safe return flight. Bad weather caused these sorties to be cancelled, but

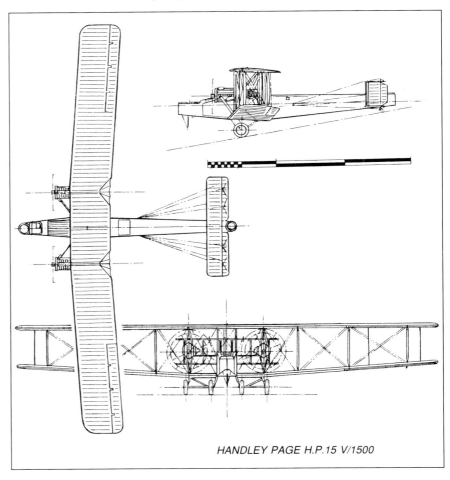

HANDLEY PAGE H.P.15 V/1500

the engines were ready for starting two days later when the Armistice was announced.

No records appear to have survived to indicate whether the bomb rack, designed to mount the heavy SN Major bomb, was ever completed, and it is believed that this weapon was never carried aloft. Nos 166 and 167 Squadrons were disbanded in March 1919, their aircraft and some of their crews being absorbed into No 274 Squadron at Bircham Newton (hitherto a coastal patrol unit flying Airco D.H.6s).

A total of 213 V/1500s had been ordered from five manufacturers, but post-Armistice cancellations caused the number completed to be reduced to 41, plus a further 22 unassembled aircraft delivered into storage as spares. One of the latter was eventually assembled and flown as J6573 with Napier Lion engines, although an entire Handley Page order for 50 Lion IB-powered aircraft was cancelled, as were 40 ordered from Grahame-White Aviation Ltd.

In the postwar months V/1500s made a number of notable flights. Following its weapon trials at Orfordness, J1936 — named HMA *Old Carthusian* — was prepared for a flight to India by way of Egypt during December 1918. Flown by Maj A S C MacLaren and Capt Robert Halley (later Gp Capt, DFC, AFC), with three sergeant crew members, and Brig-Gen Norman Duckworth Kerr MacEwen (later AVM, CMG, DSO, RAF) as passenger, the aircraft set out from Martlesham Heath on the 13th, and eventually force landed 35 miles from Karachi on 16 January 1919 with only the front two engines in operation. During its period in India J1936, having been repaired, was ordered north to Risalpur and, flown by Halley, carried out a daring raid on Kabul on 24 May, crossing and re-crossing the Pathan mountains.

Another V/1500, F7140 built by Alliance Aircraft Co Ltd, was shipped to Newfoundland in May 1919 for an attempt to become the first aeroplane to fly the Atlantic non-stop, to be flown by Sqn Ldr Herbert George Brackley DSO, DSC, and the 55-year-old Vice-Admiral Mark Edward Frederick Kerr CB, MVO, with Major Geoffrey Ingram Taylor and Major Tryggve Gran (a Norwegian who had been the first to fly the North Sea in 1914, crossing from Scotland to Norway in a Blériot). To accomplish the Atlantic crossing, Volkert had made provision for the V/1500 to carry a 2,000-gallon fuel tank — sufficient for well over 30 hours' endurance. However, owing to delays in assembling the Handley Page in Newfoundland, the Vickers Vimy of Alcock and Brown achieved the first successful Atlantic crossing, and the Handley Page's attempt was abandoned.

Instead, Frederick Handley Page instructed Brackley and Kerr to fly on to New York, a flight which began on 5 July and presaged a veritable odyssey in the New World that ended with a crash landing at Cleveland on 16 November.

Many of the postwar flights by V/1500s had been motivated by Frederick Handley Page's confidence in the future of large commercial airliners, and were intended to demonstrate his aircraft's considerable long-range potential. Ironically, they only served to show that the design of aircraft, considered adequate for wartime operations, left much to be desired — in particular with regard to reliability — when it came to persuading a fare-paying public that danger and discomfort were acceptable penalties. Much remained to be accomplished before commercial operators would find suitable airliners that were truly profitable, without recourse to government subsidy.

Type: Four-engine (two tractor, two pusher), eight- or nine-crew, four-bay biplane heavy bomber.

Air Board Specification: A.3(b)

Manufacturers: Handley Page Ltd, Cricklewood, London; William Beardmore & Co Ltd, Dalmuir, Dunbartonshire; Harland & Wolff Ltd, Belfast; Alliance Aircraft Ltd, Acton, London.

Powerplant: Four 375hp Rolls-Royce Eagle VIII twelve-cylinder, water-cooled, in-line engines (with two tractor and two pusher propellers); four 500hp Galloway Atlantic; four 450hp Napier Lion I.

Structure: Forward fuselage of ply-clad spruce construction; centre fuselage structure, with bomb-bay, built of spruce with cross members of ash; rear fuselage, incorporating catwalk to rear gun position, of spruce, cross-braced box girder construction. Twin silver spruce box-spars in wings, the top wing being built in five sections, the lower in six. The wings folded aft at the attachment points for the engine support struts.

Dimensions: Span, 126ft 0in; length, 64ft 0in; height, 23ft 0in; wing area, 2,800 sq ft.

Weights: Tare, 17,602lb; all-up (max), 30,000lb.

Performance: Max speed, 99 mph at sea level; climb to 10,000ft, 41 min 25 sec; service ceiling, 11,000ft; range, 1,300 miles; max endurance, 17 hrs.

Armament: Normal armament comprised twin 0.303in Lewis machine guns with Scarff ring on nose gunner's position, two Lewis guns on beam pillar mountings in the dorsal position, and a single Lewis gun on Scarff ring in the extreme tail. Maximum bomb load of thirty 250lb bombs, carried internally.

Prototypes: One, B9463, first flown by Capt Vernon E G Busby (accompanied by Jack Hathaway) on 22 May 1918 at Clutterhouse Farm aerodrome, Cricklewood, London. Aircraft manufactured by Harland & Wolff and assembled by Handley Page. Two other aircraft, B9464 and B9465, intended as prototypes, extensively modified and delivered later as J1935 and J1936 (see under Production below).

Production: Two aircraft, B9464 and B9465, manufactured by Harland & Wolff, assembled and delivered by Handley Page as J1935 and J1936. 20 aircraft ordered from Harland & Wolff (E4304-E4323; three aircraft, E4304-E4306, assembled and delivered by Handley Page; five aircraft, E4307-E4311, built and delivered by Harland & Wolff; twelve aircraft, E4312-E4323, delivered by Harland & Wolff as spares, one of which was later assembled and delivered as J6573). 50 aircraft ordered from Beardmore (E8287-E8306 and F8201-F8230; nine aircraft, E8287-E8295, assembled and delivered; eleven aircraft, E8296-E8306, delivered as spares; F8201-F8230 cancelled). 10 aircraft ordered from Alliance Aircraft Co, F7134-F7143, and all completed and delivered by Handley Page Ltd. 90 aircraft ordered from Handley Page, F8281-F8320 and J6523-J6572 (ten assembled and delivered, F8281-F8290; the remaining 80 aircraft cancelled). 40 aircraft ordered from Grahame-White Aviation Ltd (H4825-H4864), but all cancelled. A further order for 50 aircraft, F8231-F8280, was placed with an unknown contractor — possibly Handley Page — but cancelled. Summary, 210 aircraft ordered (excluding prototypes), 38 completed (excluding prototypes), assembled and delivered, 22 delivered in storage as spares (unassembled).

Summary of Service: Handley Page V/1500s served with No 166 Squadron, RAF, at Bircham Newton (between October 1918 and March 1919), with No 167 Squadron, RAF at Bircham Newton (between November 1918 and May 1919), and with No. 274 Squadron, RAF, at Bircham Newton (between June 1919 and January 1920). One aircraft, J1936, carried out bombing attack on Kabul, Afghanistan, operating independently, on 24 May 1919.

Short Shirl

The second Short Shirl, N111, at the Isle of Grain in July 1918; note the twin-wheel and skid undercarriage. (Photo: Imperial War Museum)

The path followed by the Sopwith Cuckoo into service as the Royal Air Force's first new single-seat landplane torpedo bomber, and the first torpedo aircraft designed from the outset for carrier operation, has been described on page 86.

If a significant shortcoming existed in the Cuckoo's concept it was that it was only able to carry the 1,086lb Mark IX torpedo, a weapon that was not thought capable of sinking any ship larger than a light — that is, unarmoured — cruiser. The Admiralty's decision to adopt landplane torpedo aircraft coincided with plans to complete two through-deck aircraft carriers in 1918, HMS *Argus* and *Eagle*.[1]

Air Board Specification N.1B of April 1917 covered a number of naval requirements in single-engine, single-seat aircraft, one of which was to be a torpedo carrier, intended in due course to replace the Cuckoo. The Specification outlining the requirements for the latter was amended several times, and in October 1917 called for the aircraft to be capable of carrying the Mark VIII torpedo, a 1,436lb weapon that possessed a warhead 50 per cent larger than that of the Mark IX. Both Short Bros and Blackburn submitted tenders, and each company was invited to build three prototypes

Little time was allowed before the first prototypes were required for preliminary Service evaluation, and both manufacturers made tremendous efforts to meet the deadline set for the end of April 1918. The Short aircraft, named the Shirl (N110-N112), was of simple configuration, owing much to Oswald Short's N.2B seaplane, but with the single cockpit situated in much the same position as the observer's cockpit in the earlier aircraft. As permitted in the Contracts, power was provided by the 375hp Rolls-Royce Eagle VIII driving a two-blade propeller and being neatly cowled with frontal radiator.

The broad-chord wings of equal span and with square tips were rigged without stagger, being foldable and with ailerons on upper and lower wings. An unusual requirement, partly occasioned by delays in the completion of HMS *Eagle*, was that the wheel landing gear was to be jettisonable so as to simplify ditching if the need arose, and flotation

gear was to be provided to increase the chances of salvaging the aircraft from the sea.

When first flown by John Parker at the Isle of Grain on 27 May 1918, the first Shirl, N110, was fitted with a simple two-wheel undercarriage with V-struts and cross-axle, this being necessary to meet the test deadline, and when the aircraft was delivered to Martlesham Heath a few days later it carried a dummy Mark VIII torpedo which of course could not have been released with such an undercarriage. During the early tests the aircraft was found to be severely tail-heavy, and this appeared to be rectified by introducing wings with sweepback when N110 returned to Rochester. At about this time the original undercarriage was replaced by twin-wheel units, each pair of wheels being provided with a skid and attached to the lower wing by a pair of V-struts, thereby eliminating the cross-axle. A large inflatable flotation bag could be carried within each undercarriage structure.

The second Shirl, N111, was delivered to Grain on 8 July and subsequently took part in torpedo dropping trials at East Fortune alongside the Blackburn Blackbird. It then went to Martlesham for Service performance and handling evaluation trials in August. In these, however, despite meeting the general performance and

load requirements, the Shirl attracted criticism on account of sluggish handling characteristics, lacking the manoeuvrability of the Cuckoo, particularly during evasive action after releasing its torpedo. It was also found that, while carrying the torpedo, the aircraft was still excessively tail-heavy, and that, after releasing the torpedo, it became nose-heavy.

The third Shirl, N112, did not fly until December 1918 when, with the War over, the urgency for a new torpedo aircraft had largely disappeared, and official interest in the Shirl (and the Blackburn Blackburd) gave place to further production orders for the established Sopwith Cuckoo.

---

[1] HMS *Argus*, 15,775 tons, had been begun in 1914 as a liner, *Conte Rosso*, for an Italian shipping company, but came to be launched in 1917 with a full-length flight deck, and was indeed completed in 1918. HMS *Eagle*, 22,600 tons, had been begun in 1913 as a dreadnought battleship, *Almirante Cochrane* for Chile; she was launched in 1918 but did not achieve full service with the Royal Navy until 1923. HMS *Furious*, 22,000 tons, the only other ship with a true flight deck, was eventually completed in 1917 with a flight deck forward of the superstructure (she had been laid down as a light battle cruiser in 1915); in 1917-18 an after deck was added, and between 1921 and 1925 she was fully converted to a flush-deck carrier).

Type: Single-engine, single-seat, two-bay biplane torpedo bomber.
Admiralty Specification: N.1B (later RAF Type XXII).
Manufacturer: Short Brothers, Rochester, Kent.
Powerplant: One 375hp Rolls-Royce Eagle VIII twelve-cylinder, water-cooled, in-line engine driving two-blade propeller.
Dimensions: Span, 52ft 0in; length, 35ft 0in; height, 13ft 3in; wing area, 791 sq ft.
Weights (360hp Eagle VIII): Tare, 3,319lb; all-up, 5,512lb (with torpedo).
Performance (360hp Eagle VIII; with torpedo): Max speed, 93 mph at 6,500ft; climb to 6,500ft, 17 min 30 sec; service ceiling, 10,000ft; endurance, 3¾ hr.
Armament: One 1,423lb 18in Mark VIII torpedo. No gun armament.
Prototypes: Three, N110-N112. N110 first flown at Grain by John Parker on 27 May 1918. No production.

Blackburn Blackburd

The incorrigible Harris Booth was nothing if not unorthodox in his approach to aircraft design, and in long retrospect it must be wondered at Robert Blackburn's wisdom in entrusting the design of his N.1B tender to someone whose previous essays could only be described as quaint, bordering on the grotesque.[1] After all, Blackburn had for several years been anxious to perpetuate a favoured working relationship with the Admiralty and, with orders for the Sopwith Cuckoo already in hand, it must have seemed encouraging that Blackburn should be asked to tender the design of a possible Cuckoo replacement.

If the Short Shirl appeared as a straightforward, conventional approach to the N.1B requirement, Booth's creation was little more than a vehicle in which he let his fertile imagination run riot. The Blackburd was a three-bay biplane whose wings, of almost equal span and of parallel chord without sweepback, were rigged without stagger. The fuselage consisted of a rectangular-section box of uniform depth from nose to tail, but built-up on four tapering spruce box longerons. Four long-span ailerons could be partially lowered to reduce take-off run and landing speed; however, not being double-acting when lowered, they thus deprived the pilot of all lateral control. The pilot's cockpit was situated only seven feet forward of the fin, with seventeen feet of fuselage forward of the windscreen; vision from the cockpit must have been minimal.

Perhaps the most extraordinary feature of the Blackburd was the manner in which the interplane, centresection and undercarriage steel tubular struts were faired to aerofoil section, using doped fabric on ply formers, linked together by wire and secured by metal clips to the steel tubes.

The hefty undercarriage comprised twin parallelogram structures of steel struts, pin-jointed together, each structure carrying a single wheel and a short steel skid built as a Warren truss. The wheels, with their cross-axle, had to be jettisoned prior to dropping the Mark VIII torpedo, so the pilot was obliged to make a deck landing on the skids when

The first Blackburd, N113. The pilot may just be seen to the left of the aft interplane strut, showing the great length of fuselage forward of the cockpit. (Photo: Blackburn Aircraft Ltd.)

operating from a carrier.

The first Blackburd, N113, was flown by R W Kenworthy in May 1918, and was delivered to Martlesham on 4 June for preliminary performance and handling trials. Here it was unfavourably received on account of longitudinal and directional instability, with excessive nose-heaviness in almost every flight regime, whether carrying the torpedo or not. Indeed, the rudder was virtually useless during landing — a fatal flaw in a deck-landing aeroplane. The aircraft crashed before the trials were completed.

N114, with an enlarged rudder and a deepened frontal radiator, was not flown until mid-August, and went immediately to East Fortune for torpedo trials. These were completed in November, but the subsequent handling trials were curtailed when the aeroplane was grounded pending an examination of the fuselage structure. It was never flown again, and was disposed of for spares.

The third Blackburd, N115, was

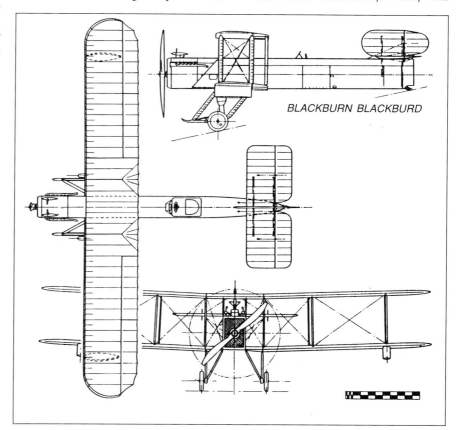

BLACKBURN BLACKBURD

---

[1]   The Blackburn G.P. seaplane had been designed by Bob Copley.

probably flown in November but, as with the Shirl, interest in the aircraft had waned. It was, however, delivered to the Gosport Development Squadron, and later flew trials aboard HMS *Argus* in the Mediterranean.

By inference, the Blackburd was rated as inferior to the Shirl, but there was irony in the fact that Blackburn was awarded a production contract to build 100 Shirls, only for this to be cancelled almost immediately — and replaced by an order for a further 100 Sopwith Cuckoos!

Type: Single-engine, single-seat, three-bay biplane shipborne torpedo-bomber.
Air Ministry Specification: N.1B (later Type XXII)
Manufacturer: The Blackburn Aeroplane and Motor Co Ltd, Olympia Works, Leeds.
Powerplant: One 350hp Rolls-Royce Eagle VIII 12-cylinder water-cooled in-line engine.
Structure: Composite wood and steel construction, comprising spruce-ply box longerons and wing spars, distanced and braced with steel tie rods.
Dimensions: Span, 52ft 5in (wings folded, 17ft 1in); length, 34ft 10in; height, 12ft 4½in; wing area, 684 sq ft.
Weights: Tare, 3,228lb; all-up (with torpedo), 5,700lb.
Performance (with torpedo): Max speed, 90.5 mph at 6,500ft; climb to 6,500ft, 16 min 15 sec; service ceiling, 11,000ft; endurance, 3 hr.
Armament: No gun armament. Provision for one 1,423lb Admiralty Type VIII torpedo, capable of being dropped only after jettisoning landing wheels and cross-axle.
Prototypes: Three, N113-N115. N113 first flown by R W Kenworthy at Brough at the end of May 1918. No production.

Bristol Types 24/25 Braemar

Capt Frank Barnwell, chief designer of the British & Colonial Aeroplane Company, submitted proposals for his B.1 heavy bomber to the War Office late in 1917, in which 'the performance estimates, based on the use of four 365hp Rolls-Royce Eagles, suggested that it would be capable of reaching Berlin with a small load of bombs. Because the project was not formally prepared to conform to a specific Air Board requirement, Barnwell was informed that Eagle engines would not be made available for the bomber; however, the War Office expressed sufficient interest in the aircraft to issue a contract, signed on 11 December 1917, for three prototypes (C4296-C4298).

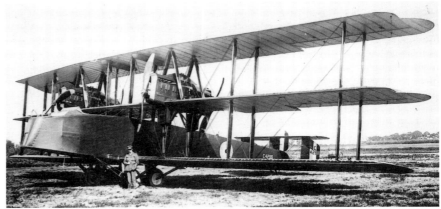

A view of the Braemar Mk I, C4296, powered by 230hp Siddeley Puma engines, which emphasises its great height and tiny undercarriage. (Photo: Imperial War Museum, Neg No Q67529)

The draft layout was delegated to Wilfrid T Reid for detail design. Nevertheless, despite its imposing bulk, the Bristol bomber was to be much smaller than the Handley Page V/1500. Obliged to use four 230hp Siddeley Puma engines the aircraft, which became the Type 24 Braemar, was probably doomed to obscurity from the outset as it scarcely represented any advance beyond the the Handley Page O/400. Moreover, owing to the company's lack of suitable manufacturing space, only one Braemar could be assembled at a time.

The Braemar Mk II, C4297, in flight near Bristol. Criticism levelled at the pilots' poor field of view was occasioned more by the side-by-side seating and the width of fuselage than by obstruction caused by the wings and engines. (Photo: A J Jackson Collection)

The aircraft was a three-bay, folding biplane with the engines in tandem in fully-cowled nacelles on the centre wing, each engine driving a right-handed two-blade propeller; unlike those of the V/1500, the tractor and pusher propellers were of the same diameter. The two upper wings were of equal span, and the lower slightly shorter, with horn-balanced ailerons fitted to the two upper wings. The fuselage, constructed almost entirely of spruce with wire bracing, was ply-covered except for the nose section. The crew comprised two pilots, a wireless operator, a flight engineer and two gunners (in the nose and amidships). The bomb load, intended to amount to six 250lb bombs, was carried in an internal fuselage bay. The four-wheel undercarriage featured pairs of tandem wheels, with a braking system, attached to mounting struts anchored to the lower fuselage longerons and the wing spars below the engines, this structure resulting in a very narrow track.

The first Braemar, C4296, was completed in August 1918 and flown by Fred Raynham on the 13th. The same pilot delivered the aircraft to Martlesham Heath exactly one month later. It was evaluated against the RAF Specification Type VIII which had been issued during its period of design and, with certain reservations, was considered to come close to the requirements, though it did not meet the load and endurance figures by fairly large margins. Some criticism was levelled at the flying controls, the ailerons being particularly heavy, and at the very poor field of vision from the pilots' cockpit. Doubt has been cast on a figure often quoted for this Braemar's maximum speed of 106 mph at a gross weight of 16,200lb, for the highest *corrected* speed achieved by the aircraft at Martlesham was 102 mph at a weight of about 13,000lb. C4296 was taken on RAF charge in May 1919, but was written off in a crash two months later.

From the outset it was obvious that the first prototype was underpowered and, once C4296 had left the factory, a second aircraft, the Type 25 Braemar II, C4297, powered by four 410hp Liberty 12A engines, was built, making its maiden flight on 18 February 1919. This aeroplane incorporated a number of improvements, including slight alterations to the nose profile to increase the pilots' field of view, and strengthening of wing tie rods; the undercarriage was also improved, though its narrow track remained unchanged. As far as is known the Braemar never carried its full intended bomb load, although in trials at Martlesham in 1919 C4297 recorded a speed of 122 mph at 5,600 feet while loaded with six 112lb bombs. This aircraft was to be destroyed in an accident when, taking off out of wind on 16 August 1921, it swung out of control and struck a building.

A third Braemar, C4298 (the Mark III), was flown in June 1919 but was almost immediately converted to a passenger-carrying aircraft and renamed the Type 26 Pullman. As such it was evaluated at Martlesham during September and October 1920, but its ultimate fate is not known.

Type: Four-engine, six-crew, three-bay triplane long-range heavy bomber.
Air Ministry Specification: RAF Type VIII.
Manufacturer: The British and Colonial Aeroplane Co Ltd., Filton, Bristol.
Powerplant: Mark I. Four 230hp Siddeley Puma six-cylinder water-cooled in-line engines, two driving two-blade tractor and two driving pusher propellers, and mounted in tandem in two nacelles mounted on the centre wing. Mark II. Four 410hp Lincoln-built Liberty 12A water-cooled in-line engines.
Structure: Wire-braced, all-wood structure, the fuselage ply-covered, and the two-spar, folding wings, fabric-covered.
Dimensions: Span, 81ft 8in; length, 51ft 6in; height, 20ft 8in; wing area, 1,905 sq ft.
Weights (Mark II): Tare, 10,650lb; all-up (max bomb load), 18,500lb.
Performance (Mark II): Max speed, 125 mph at sea level, 110 mph at 10,000ft; climb to 10,000ft, 17 min 40 sec; absolute ceiling, 17,000ft.
Armament: Five 0.303in Lewis machine guns: two on nose gunner's cockpit with Scarff ring; two guns with pillar mountings on midships gunner's cockpit; and single gun on Scarff ring in floor of fuselage amidships. Max bomb load, six 230lb bombs.
Prototypes: Three: C4296 (Mark I) and C4297 (Mark II); C4296 first flown by F P Raynham at Filton on 13 August 1918. No production. (Third aircraft, C4298, was converted to Bristol Type 26 Pullman commercial passenger aircraft, but not operated as such.)

Deployment of British Bomber Squadrons at the Armistice, 11 November 1918

Home Bases

Squadron	Aircraft	Base
No 120 Squadron	D.H.9A	Hawkinge, Kent
No 166 Squadron	Handley Page V/1500	Bircham Newton, Norfolk
No 167 Squadron[1]	Handley Page V/1500	Bircham Newton, Norfolk
No 219 Squardon[1]	D.H.9	Manston, Kent

France

Squadron	Aircraft	Base
No 6 Squadron[2]	R.E.8	Gondecourt
No 9 Squadron[2]	R.E.8	Premont
No 15 Squadron[2]	R.E.8	Selvigny
No 18 Squadron	D.H.9A	Le Brayelle
No 25 Squadron	D.H.4	La Brayelle
No 27 Squadron	D.H.9	Villers-lez-Cagnicourt
No 49 Squadron	D.H.9	Villers-lez-Cagnicourt
No 52 Squadron[2]	R.E.8	Aulnoye
No 55 Squadron	D.H.4	Azelot
No 57 Squadron	D.H.4	Bethencourt
No 58 Squadron	Handley Page O/400	Proven
No 83 Squadron	F.E.2B/D	Estrée-en-Chaussée
No 97 Squadron	Handley Page O/400	Xaffévillers
No 98 Squadron	D.H.9	Abscon
No 99 Squadron	D.H.9/9A	Azelot
No 100 Squadron	Handley Page O/400	St. Inglevert
No 101 Squadron	F.E.2B/D	Hancourt
No 102 Squadron	F.E.2B/D	Bevillers
No 103 Squadron	D.H.9	Ronchin
No 104 Squadron	D.H.9	Azelot
No 107 Squadron	D.H.9	Moislains
No 108 Squadron	D.H.9	Bisseghem
No 110 Squadron	D.H.9	Bettoncourt
No 115 Squadron	Handley Page O/400	Roville-sur-Chenes
No 148 Squadron	F.E.2B/D	Erre
No 149 Squadron	F.E.2B/D	Le Quesnoy
No 202 Squadron	D.H.4/9	Bergues
No 205 Squadron	D.H.4/9A	Moislains
No 206 Squadron	D.H.9	Linselles
No 207 Squadron	Handley Page O/400	Estrée-en-Chaussée
No 211 Squadron	D.H.9	Clairy
No 214 Squadron	Handley Page O/400	Chemy
No 215 Squadron	Handley Page O/400	Xaffévillers
No 216 Squadron	Handley Page O/400	Roville
No 218 Squadron	D.H.9	Reumont

Belgium		
No 38 Squadron	F.E.2B	Harlebeke
No 217 Squadron	D.H.4	Varssenaere

Italy and the Balkans		
No 34 Squadron[2]	R.E.8	Santa Luca, Italy
No 47 Squadron	D.H.9	Salonika, Greece
No 221 Squadron	D.H.9(AS)	Mudros, Aegean
No 223 Squadron	D.H.4/9	Stavros, Aegean

No 224 Squadron	D.H.9	Andrano, Italy
No 226 Squadron	D.H.9	Lemnos, Aegean
No 227 Squadron[1]	D.H.4/9	Taranto, Italy

The Middle East		
No 30 Squadron[2]	R.E.8	Kifri, Mesopotamia

[1] Not operational on this date
[2] Bombing not the Squadron's primary operational rôle

3. TRENCHARD'S PEACETIME BOMBERS

The ending of the First World War occurred with little more than a few weeks' indication of its imminence. At the date of the Armistice British heavy bombers were literally standing by to take off for a raid deep inside Germany — a raid of propaganda value, but a symbolic one for which, a year earlier, the British people had clamoured. Sir Hugh Trenchard, the architect of the Independent Force, was now Chief of the Air Staff, a position of theoretically equal influence to those of the First Sea Lord and Chief of the General Staff.

By November 1918 the Royal Air Force was, by a considerable margin, the most powerful air force in the world, and huge contracts were in hand for the production of all manner of aircraft by an industry already overtrading by conventional commercial criteria. To assist several manufacturers to invest in additional factory space, the Treasury had waived taxation on wartime profits, a dispensation that few captains of industry made allowance to repay sometime in the future. Unfortunately for them (and tens of thousands of employees in their factories) the nation at large was no longer tolerant of those it saw as wartime profiteers and, in an economic environment embracing unemployment and privations, the Treasury quickly imposed swingeing — and retrospective — taxes on what were formally declared as Excess Profits, wilfully ignoring the fact that those 'profits' had invariably been reinvested in manufacturing facilities and workforce training to accelerate the supply of weapons.

Coming at a time when the Air Ministry, now deprived of almost all appropriations for new equipment, summarily cancelled more than 92 per cent of all outstanding contracts, the effect on the industry was calamitous. Some companies ceased trading and disappeared forever (such as Martinsyde

and Grahame-White), and others went into liquidation so as to continue trading in changed circumstances (Sopwith, Airco and British & Colonial, which became Hawker, de Havilland and Bristol, respectively). It can be seen that the hardcore of 'professional' manufacturers, the very bedrock of the industry, were made to pay a disproportionate tax penalty when compared with those manufacturers who, as former members of other non-related industries, had exchanged faltering wartime commerce for the rich pickings from munitions contracts — without having to support costly design teams and research staffs of their own. After all, the profit on a fixed cost aeroplane was uniform no matter who built it, yet few, if any, of the 'shadow' contractors received tax demands against excess profits and, when the War was over, simply melted back to their former commercial industries.

In November 1918 the Air Ministry prepared a statement listing those aircraft, already in service, which were now selected to continue in peacetime service, together with designs, already tendered, selected to compete as prototypes of ultimate replacements.

In the field of bomber aircraft, the Airco D.H.9A was only just coming into service, and was expected to remain for several years, even though unstarted production contracts suffered cancellation; no replacement was therefore planned for the foreseeable future. The standard medium bomber, also only just reaching its first squadrons, was the Airco D.H.10 Amiens which, on account of a much smaller planned production, was scheduled for replacement during 1920-21, and contracts had been issued for prototypes of the likely contenders; these were the Boulton & Paul Bourges, Sopwith Cobham, Avro Type 533 Manchester, Airco D.H.11 Oxford and the Airco D.H.14 Okapi. Unfortu-

nately, all but the last-named of these prototypes were being designed around the ABC Dragonfly radial engine, which had attracted numerous aircraft designers' attention on account of its promised low power/weight ratio, but which was already showing signs of serious problems during development. As with many fighters, similarly conceived with this engine, none of the above bombers succeeded in reaching production owing to the Dragonfly engine being all but abandoned.

Neither of the two British heavy bombers, the O/400 already established in service and the V/1500 on the point of becoming fully operational, were strictly relevant in a Europe supposedly at peace. Existing stocks of the O/400 would be adequate to equip the handful of squadrons not immediately disbanded. And the V/1500, impressive in its wartime concept and well ahead in its field, was even more superfluous as the former Central Powers were disarmed. The coming of peace therefore brought swift cancellation of both these excellent bombers, save only those whose manufacture had already begun.

The other aircraft, euphemistically classed as a heavy bomber, was the Vickers Vimy. This admirable, but fairly pedestrian aeroplane in terms of warload and performance, would remain in service for much of the decade following the Great War, proving to be a useful aircraft in a number of rôles, and pointing the way to a new, utilitarian classification of Service aircraft, the bomber-transport.

Thus, as Europe settled into an era of uneasy peace, a state of international politics brought about by the Allies' inability to comprehend the hazards presented by the imposition of crippling reparations on Germany, Britain allowed her air force to wither to the brink of extinction. The strength of the RAF, measured in terms of manpower, number of combat-ready front-line aircraft, and operational flying stations at home and abroad (but excluding those of a temporary nature in continental Europe), fell by between 80 and 90 per cent inside two years. There were insufficient full-strength operational squadrons to meet the possible contingencies and responsibilities shouldered by an autonomous armed Service, particularly that of a nation whose essential trade routes criss-crossed the globe.

As the realities of peacetime reductions in the military dawned on the Service chiefs, Trenchard, who had assumed that the future of the Royal Air Force was assured, soon discovered that the admirals and generals had other ideas and, in order to secure their share of Service funding, were intent on carving out their own portions of the young Service. Fortunately there were adequate influential politicians who recalled the near-fatal results of maintaining separate military and naval air arms during the War. However, it was the intervention of fate which strengthened Trenchard's hand — himself always uneasy in the presence of politicians, and never a model of tact.

The dismantling of the former Ottoman Empire, following the defeat of Turkey, threatened to create an administrative vacuum in the Middle East, complicated by the Jewish claim to a sovereign state in Palestine. Indeed, a vast area, extending from the Levant to the Persian Gulf and from the Caspian Sea to the Arabian peninsula, was now without formally constituted governments and internationally agreed frontiers, yet the whole area — largely desert, often mountainous — was peopled by ancient tribes, many nomadic, and races in ill-defined kingdoms and sheikhdoms. And with the security of developing oilfields assuming major importance to the Western World, the League of Nations vested in Britain a Mandate to keep the peace throughout this huge region until such time that agreement could be reached for the creation of self-determining, independent States.

For some years the British Army had struggled with inadequate resources to limit the activities of warring tribal bands but was inevitably thwarted by the sheer distances involved in reaching a potential trouble spot. Trenchard's proposal, accepted through continuing frustration, was to employ aircraft such as the D.H.9A, sometimes dropping leaflets to warn the tribesmen to disperse or face attack from the air. In a remarkably short time a single squadron of light bombers was achieving results that had eluded the efforts of the ground forces, and at a fraction of the cost.

It was this successful and inexpensive use of aeroplanes in the Middle East that led the way to survival of the Royal Air Force, and very few aircrew members of the young Service did not serve at least one tour in that theatre during the years between the World Wars. Before long the RAF's larger aircraft, led by the Vimy and followed by purpose-designed troop transports, were being called on to move soldiers from one part of the Mandated territories to another, often at very short notice. By degrees the RAF was able to establish a network of bases from which to operate a growing number of squadrons newly established in the Middle East.

At home, the 'Ten Year Rule' was formulated by British politicians, as much as anything else on the pretext of avoiding the necessity for powerful armed Services. The idea was that the likelihood of a future conflict between nations would become discernible ten years in advance and allow diplomatic steps to be taken to avoid the outbreak of war. It was, in effect, a tentative step towards international disarmament which, had other nations followed suit, might well have had far-reaching results. Events were to demonstrate that diplomacy would only succeed if backed by strength of arms, and the Rule was soon shown to be quite superfluous as soon as a powerful and ruthlessly ambitious dictator emerged.

In some important respects the Rule played into the hands of the Air Ministry and, in particular, Trenchard. Though the Chief of Staff would most probably have vigorously denied being any man's disciple, least of all the Italian Emilio Douhet, Trenchard certainly believed that the heavy bomber was the Royal Air Force's *raison d'être*. All other operational duties should be subordinate to the rôle of the bomber as an offensive weapon, capable of attacking the social and economic structures of an enemy and destroying his will to wage war. He also believed that it was only necessary to equip a small number of bomber squadrons in the field, but at the same time keep the bomber at the forefront of technology by means of a constant stream of prototypes. Moreover, the research necessary to ensure this advance would become the responsibility of the privately-owned industry. Thus the bomber made slow technological progress within the funds available although, by implication, the interceptor fighter — the logical instrument with which to gain major advances, but one that Trenchard regarded as almost entirely unnecessary in his understanding of the Principles of War — was permitted to stagnate.

Thus the 1920s were the heyday of British bomber prototypes, as the number of aeroplane types described in this chapter well illustrates. Yet the most successful of all these aircraft, if measured by longevity and volume of production, was the Vickers Virginia heavy bomber, which remained in front-line service until the mid-1930s, and the Hawker Hart light bomber, whose widely distributed and considerable production contracts certainly enabled the aircraft industry to weather the Depression of the early 1930s. Yet neither of these bombers was significantly different *in concept* from the O/400 and D.H.9A of the Kaiser's War.

Trenchard certainly saved the Royal Air Force from extinction. He also patronised a number of greatly gifted senior officers, and ensured that they were set on the path to high rank and influence. In these respects he may justifiably be regarded as 'the father of the Royal Air Force'. In other respects, however, his blinkered infatuation with the big bomber blinded him to the correct balance of responsibilities in the real world.

Trenchard stepped down as CAS on the last day of December 1929, his place being taken by Air Marshal Sir John Salmond, KCB, CMG, CVO, DSO, a brilliant staff officer who had followed Trenchard in command of the RAF in the field during 1918-19, and most recently had been AOC-in-C, Air Defence of Great Britain; as such, he had become all too aware of the parlous state of Britain's fighter defences. Moreover, at the same time, the Ten Year Rule was being shown as inappropriate as signs of Fascism began appearing in Germany, Italy and Japan, nations that were being forced into international isolation. These danger signs were there for those who cared to look, and it was Salmond who set in train the revival of the Royal Air Force as a balanced Service. The problem was how to achieve this within the slender finances allowed by the Treasury. It was the big bomber that now took its turn to stand still.

Avro Type 533 Manchester

The culmination of A V Roe's dogged persistence in the development of a twin-engine medium bomber, and one that maintained the general configuration of the Type 523A and 529, the Type 533 might well have gained substantial production orders had it not been for the unfortunate choice of powerplant, the 320hp ABC Dragonfly I nine-cylinder air-cooled radial engine.

The Dragonfly had been designed by Granville Bradshaw in 1917, who claimed that it would develop 340hp at a weight of just over 600lb, and, with simplicity of production said to be an important attribute, was ordered in huge numbers in 1918 (amounting to no fewer then 11,050 engines from 13 manufacturers). Production got underway, and it was planned to have completed over 4,000 engines by mid-1919.

Production engines were soon giving trouble. Apart from being overweight, they failed to deliver the promised power and vibrated violently in flight, leading to component breakage and total failure after very few running hours. New pistons and cylinder heads were designed but, early in 1919, it was clear that the entire engine required redesign, the troubles being caused by dynamic imbalance and high-frequency torsional vibration, a phenomenon not understood in 1918.

Three prototypes of the Type 533 Manchester (F3492-F3494) were ordered from A V Roe on 15 May 1918, the Dragonfly I engine being scheduled to be fitted in all three. However, by the time the first airframe was taking shape, the company was warned that, owing to the problems then emerging, deliveries of the engine were being temporarily suspended. In order to proceed with flight trials as quickly as possible, 300hp high-compression Siddeley Puma engines were substituted, this aircraft being termed the Type 533A Manchester II, and first flown early in December 1918.

The new bomber, capable of carrying a bomb load of 880lb, incorporated a number of improvements over the Type 529, including a shorter, deeper fuselage, enlarged tail surfaces and bench-type aileron balances; these comprised small aerofoils located above and forward of the ailerons, so that depressing

The Avro Type 533 Manchester I, F3493, with the ill-fated Dragonfly I engines, the second prototype to fly. (Photo: The Royal Aeronautical Society)

the aileron increased the incidence angle of the small aerofoils, thereby providing a balancing moment. The Puma engines, being slightly lighter than the Dragonfly, bestowed an excellent performance, though slightly inferior to that expected with the latter, and the Manchester was found to be pleasant to

handle, and possessed of outstanding manoeuvrability. In due course the aircraft was looped, and proved to be entirely manageable in a spin.

The Dragonfly engines were delivered during December 1918 and were fitted in the second Manchester, F3493, which now became the Mark I, as being

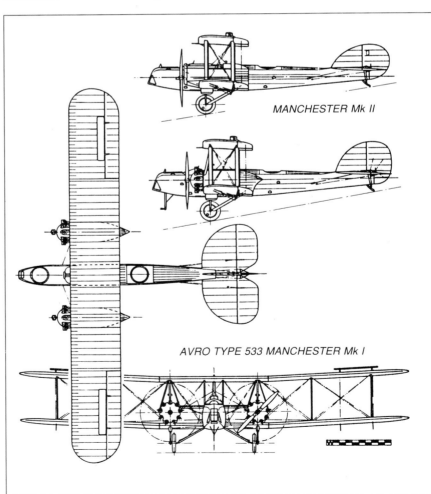

MANCHESTER Mk II

AVRO TYPE 533 MANCHESTER Mk I

the version intended for production. F3493 was first flown on 27 May 1919, and was delivered to Martlesham Heath in April for performance trials, exactly on schedule. In these trials it confirmed the expectations provided by the Puma-powered prototype, which had undergone evaluation the previous month, returning a speed of 112 mph at 10,000 ft while carrying full fuel and half the maximum bomb load. It was generally considered to handle better than the other twin-engine aircraft then being prepared for competition to decide on a replacement for the D.H.10 Amiens in service.

However, continuing trouble with the Dragonfly engine caused Roy Chadwick to consider the Liberty 12 engine as a possible alternative, and there is little doubt but that this powerplant would have resulted in a first-class medium bomber. In the event a pair of modified Dragonfly IA engines became available and these were fitted in the third

Manchester, F3494 (the Mark III). This was flown in about September or October 1919, and delivered to Martlesham Heath on 21 October, remaining there until September the following year.

In the meantime, in the absence of adequate Service funding, the Air Ministry had decided to abandon a replacement for the D.H.10, preferring to let it remain in service until, by natural wastage, the aircraft became extinct. With the grounding of the Dragonfly in September 1920, all flying of the Manchester also ended.

Type: Twin-engine, three-crew, three-bay biplane bomber.
Air Ministry Specifications: RAF Types IV, VI and VIII.
Manufacturer: A V Roe & Co Ltd, Hamble, Hampshire
Powerplant: Mark I. Two 320hp ABC Dragonfly I nine-cylinder, air-cooled, radial engines driving two-blade propellers. Mark II. Two 300hp Siddeley Puma high-compression in-line engines. Mark III. Scheduled for two 400hp Liberty 12 in-line engines, but flown with Dragonfly IA radials, and/or Lion in-line engines.
Dimensions: Span, 60ft 0in; length, 37ft 0in; height, 12ft 6in; wing area, 813 sq ft (Mark I), 817 sq ft (Mark II).
Weights: Mark I. Tare, 4,887lb; all-up, 7,390lb. Mark II. Tare, 4,574lb; all-up, 7,158lb.
Performance: Mark I. Max speed, 130 mph at sea level, 112 mph at 10,000ft; climb to 10,000ft, 14 min 20 sec; service ceiling, 19,000ft; endurance, 5¾ hr. Mark II. Max speed, 125 mph at sea level; climb to 10,000ft, 16 min 30 sec; service ceiling, 17,000ft; endurance, 3¾ hr.
Armament: Two 0.303in Lewis machine guns with Scarff rings on nose and midships gunners' positions. Bomb load of up to 880lb.
Prototypes: Three, F3492-F3494. First flight by F3492 in December 1918 at Hamble; F3493 first flown on 27 May 1919, and F3494 in about October 1919. No production.

Airco D.H.11 Oxford

It was perhaps to be expected that the manufacturers of the D.H.10 Amiens bomber should be invited to tender a design for an aircraft intended to replace that aircraft in service, and a Contract was signed with the Aircraft Manufacturing Company at Hendon for three prototypes (H5891-H5893) on 27 July 1918; all were required to be powered the 320hp ABC Dragonfly.

Like the Avro Manchester, the D.H.11 was a twin-tractor biplane with a crew of three, and was designed to carry its bomb load internally. It was, however, an entirely different design from its antecedent, the D.H.10, often being likened to an enlarged, twin-engine version of the D.H.9. Construction was entirely of wood with wings and rear fuselage fabric-covered, the fuselage nose being ply-clad. The unswept, unstaggered, parallel-chord wings were fitted with horn-balanced ailerons on upper and lower surfaces; the lower wing possessed dihedral of two degrees outboard of the engines, and the upper of four degrees from the roots, giving the illusion from some aspects that the top wing was swept forward. The engine nacelles were mounted directly on the

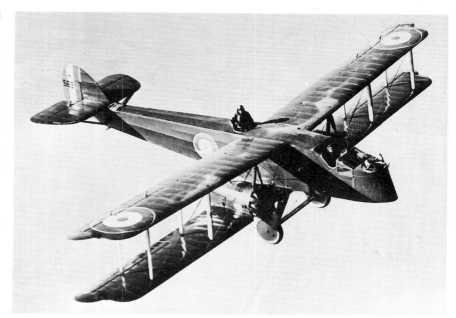

In-flight view of the D.H.11 Oxford, H5891, showing the excellent field of fire provided for the midships gunner. (Photo: Samson Clark, Ref No SCDH 9397)

upper surface of the lower wings.

The very deep fuselage occupied the entire wing gap, enabling the midships gunner to command an excellent all-round field of fire, while the pilot (occupying the left hand side of a very wide cockpit) and the nose gunner both enjoyed good fields of view.

It seems likely that difficulty arose with regard to locating the bomb bay,

owing to the type and disposition of the undercarriage fitted on the first prototype, as well as to the position of the aircraft's centre of gravity, a problem compounded by the fact that, when delivered, the engines were each found to be some 120lb heavier than previously notified — a discrepancy that required hurried recalculation of weight distribution. The undercarriage was of plain

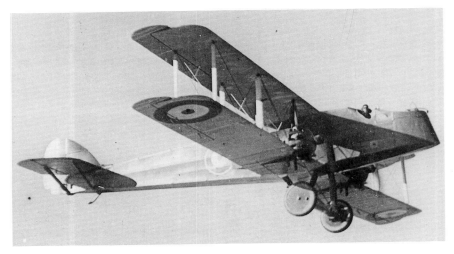

Another view of the D.H.11, illustrating the illusion given by the upper wing's dihedral that it was swept forward. Such was the width and depth of the fuselage that there was space for a catwalk between the pilot's cockpit and the midships gunner's position. (Photo: de Havilland Aircraft Ltd.)

V-strut design with wheel cross-axle, the upper ends of the struts being anchored to the fuselage at the junctions of the wing spars with the lower longerons. If, as seems likely, the bomb bay was to be located between the planes of the wing spars, so as to be close to the aircraft's centre of gravity, the bombs would have fouled the wheel cross-axle. This all suggests that the first prototype was not equipped with a bomb bay and that the undercarriage was no more than a jury structure, fitted temporarily pending design of a more robust split-axle type.

Being roughly a month behind the completion of the Avro Manchester, the first D.H.11 prototype, H5891, was able to make its maiden flight in January 1919 powered by the Dragonfly engines. From the outset the aircraft encountered handling problems associated primarily with longitudinal and directional control and stability, the aircraft being nose-heavy in most flight regimes. It was therefore returned to the factory in July for repositioning of the engines — and possibly the fitting of a divided-axle undercarriage. It is not clear from records that have been located whether the D.H.11 had visited Martlesham Heath for trials in the meantime.

In any case, owing to general dissatisfaction with the Dragonfly engine, the second and third prototypes had been cancelled on 30 June by the Air Ministry. The name Oxford had been officially bestowed on the D.H.11 during 1918 and, although this appears in Air Ministry documents of that time, it seems that the name was seldom used, particularly by the manufacturers, whose reports reflect an air of frustration with the design, not least when it also emerged that the engines were not only heavier

than expected, but incapable of producing the power promised.

Paradoxically, it is known that de Havilland undertook an alternative design of the D.H.11 to be powered by two 300hp high-compression Siddeley Puma engines in an Oxford Mk II, and these may have been intended for fitting in one of the uncompleted prototypes. In any case, this would have been abandoned when the Air Ministry dropped its plans to replace the D.H.10 Amiens.

Type: Twin-engine, three-seat, three-bay biplane medium bomber.
Air Ministry Specification: RAF Type IV, VI and VIII.
Manufacturer: The Aircraft Manufacturing Co Ltd, Hendon, London N.W.9
Powerplant: Two 320hp ABC Dragonfly I 9-cylinder air-cooled radial engines driving 2-blade tractor propellers.
Structure: All-wood airframe structure, ply- and fabric-covered.
Dimensions: Span, 60ft 2in; length, 45ft 2¾in; height, 13ft 6in; wing area, 719 sq ft.
Weights: Tare, 4,105lb; all-up (four 230lb bombs), 7,027lb.
Performance (with two 230lb bombs): Max speed, 123 mph at sea level, 116 mph at 10,000ft; climb to 10,000ft, 13 min 45 sec; service ceiling, 14,500ft; endurance, 3 hr.
Armament: Bomb load of up to four 230lb bombs carried internally. Gun armament comprised nose and midships 0.303in Lewis machine guns on Scarff rings.
Prototypes: One, H5891, first flown in January 1920; two others, H5892 and H5893, cancelled in 1919. No production.

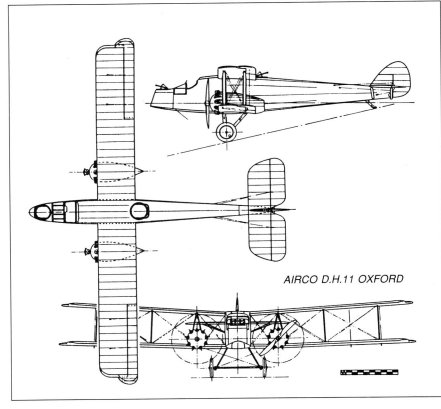

AIRCO D.H.11 OXFORD

Sopwith Cobham

Notable as being the only twin-engine Sopwith aeroplane ever built, the triplane Cobham's career was also bedevilled by its association with the ABC Dragonfly engines. Designed during the summer of 1918 to the Air Ministry Specification IV, as qualified in Specifications VI and VIII — by virtue of variations in range and bomb load (all three of which were amalgamated in the Department of Research Type 3 Specification) — the Cobham began building in September that year.

Although the aircraft was designed as a three-seat medium bomber, capable of carrying three 250lb bombs (stowed internally and suspended vertically), the greater part of the Cobham's life was preoccupied with attempts to come to terms with the thoroughly unreliable Dragonfly. The first of three prototypes ordered, H671, was completed at Brooklands in about December 1918 but, owing to delays in the delivery of the 320hp Dragonfly I engines, Herbert Smith (whose design the Cobham was) was instructed to make provision to install a pair of standard 240hp Puma engines, so as to begin flight trials as quickly as possible. H671 was therefore termed the Cobham Mark II, and was flown in about April 1919. It was, however, never destined to receive Dragonfly engines as, some time in 1919, it suffered an accident and was undergoing repair at about the time that the first modified Dragonfly IA engines were starting delivery. It was therefore fitted with high-compression Pumas and underwent performance trials with these at Martlesham Heath in March 1920, and in November that year was delivered to the RAE, Farnborough, where it was last flown on 27 January 1921.

Neither of the other two Cobhams was flown during 1919; these, termed Mark Is, were both powered by 360hp Dragonfly IAs with redesigned cylinders and pistons. H672 and H673 were

Cobham Mk I, H672, with Dragonfly IA engines; note the curious 'kinked' stagger on the upper and lower wings and the extended rudder. (Photo: Sopwith Aviation Co Ltd, Neg No 444)

first flown in January and February 1920 respectively but, with the Sopwith company beginning to suffer serious financial difficulty, they were taken on Air Ministry charge and delivered to Martlesham Heath in February. Recurring engine failures caused them to be forwarded on to Farnborough to await a decision on the future of the Dragonfly and, when its development was abandoned in September, the Cobham Is were struck off Air Ministry charge.

The Cobham's airframe design underwent fairly extensive change when it was discovered that the Dragonfly was substantially over the weight originally notified to Sopwith; compared with the original works drawings of the aircraft, the Mark I prototypes had their engines set some fifteen inches further aft, with the plane of the cylinder centreline in line with the centre wing's leading edge. Moreover, the Mark Is featured changes in wing stagger, the top wings being rigged with positive stagger, and no stagger on the bottom wings; the Puma-powered Mark II featured slight sweepback and back stagger on the top wing. The Mark I was also found to require increased rudder area, this being extended below the fuselage sternpost, with horn balances at each end. This modification was said to have been demanded by Harry Hawker who, having had to land a Cobham with one dead engine, found the aircraft almost unmanageable and entirely devoid of rudder control.

Type: Twin-engine, three-crew, three-bay triplane medium bomber.
Air Ministry Specification: RAF Types IV, VI and VIII.
Manufacturer: The Sopwith Aviation Co Ltd, Kingston-upon-Thames, Surrey.
Powerplant: Mark I. Two 360hp ABC Dragonfly IA nine-cylinder, air-cooled, radial engines driving two-blade propellers. Mark II. Two 240hp Siddeley Puma six-cylinder, water-cooled, in-line engines.
Structure: Wire-braced wooden box-girder fuselage with ply and fabric covering; two spruce wing spars and fabric-covered wings.
Dimensions: Span, 54ft; length, 38ft; height, 13ft. *Performance:* No records traced.
Armament: Single 0.303in Lewis machine guns in nose and midships positions with Scarff rings; bomb load, carried internally, said to be about 750lb.
Prototypes: Three, H671-H673. H671, the Puma-powered Mark II, first flown about April 1919; H672 first flown, January 1920; H673 first flown, February 1920. No production.

Boulton & Paul P.7 Bourges

No company toiled more persistently to secure the winner's production con-

tracts for a D.H.10 replacement than the Norwich-based manufacturer, Boulton & Paul Ltd; nor indeed came closer to success. And once all ties with the Dragonfly engine had been broken, leaving the designer free to exploit his own choice of powerplant, the resulting aeroplane, possessing undreamed-of

qualities of handling, performance and manœuvrability, set the company on the path to building medium bombers that served the Royal Air Force until 1937. Despite the cancellation of the D.H.10 replacement requirement (after ultimate failure of the Dragonfly), Boulton Paul's experience with the Bourges and its

Left: *The first Bourges, F2903, the Mark IIA, as it was originally flown, with Bentley B.R.2 rotary engines mounted in mid-gap and with plain ailerons and straight top wing.* (Photo: Boulton Paul Aircraft Ltd., Neg Ref 021).

Below: *The short-lived Bourges Mk IB, F2904, with lower wing-mounted Dragonfly engines, gull wing, dihedral tailplane and horn-balanced ailerons.* (Photo: Boulton Paul Aircraft Ltd., Neg Ref 04)

derivatives was rewarded by contracts for the Sidestrand, and later the Overstrand medium day bombers.

Following the design of several fighters which did not achieve production status, John North undertook the design of a twin-engine day bomber to the same Air Ministry requirement as the Manchester, Oxford and Cobham, attracted as usual by the promise held out by the ABC Dragonfly engine. Smaller and lighter than the Manchester and Oxford, but on a par with the Cobham, North's P.7 Bourges was delayed by late delivery of the ABC engines, and the company opted to commence flight trials in June 1919 with F2903 powered by 230hp Bentley B.R.2 rotary engines mounted in mid-gap, this aircraft being designated the P.7/1 Bourges Mark IIA with these engines. As originally flown, this Bourges featured plain ailerons on upper and lower wings.

Almost immediately, unmodified Dragonfly I engines became available and with these F2903, now termed the P.7/1 Bourges Mk IA, was delivered to Martlesham Heath for preliminary trials in July, returning a maximum speed of 123 mph at 6,500 feet while carrying full fuel and half bomb load, and now fitted with horn-balanced ailerons.

While F2903 was away at Martlesham, the second Bourges, F2904, made its maiden flight with Dragonfly engines mounted on the lower wings, but with gulled upper wings attached to the upper fuselage longerons and marked dihedral on the tailplane, resulting in a change to a new designation, the P.7/2 Bourges Mk IB (the B suffix referring to the gull wing). This aircraft, however, crashed in October and was written off. The gull wing was adopted as a means of improving the field of fire for the midships gunner (and also slightly reduced wing drag), and the dihedral tailplane was thought — probably with justification — to improve lateral stability while landing.

The third Bourges, P.7/3 F2905, was also originally a Mark IB with Dragonfly engines, and was probably first flown during the winter of 1919-20, but abject frustration with these engines prompted Boulton & Paul to revert to the much less powerful but infinitely more reliable B.R.2 rotaries, the aircraft becoming the Bourges Mk IIB with gull wing. It then underwent further transformation (on the manufacturers' own initiative) with a change to 450hp Napier Lion IIB engines, becoming the Bourges Mk IIIA — with straight upper wing — and making its first flight early in 1921. Soon after, it was given the gull wings as the Mk IIIB, and with these it demonstrated an excellent top speed of 130 mph at

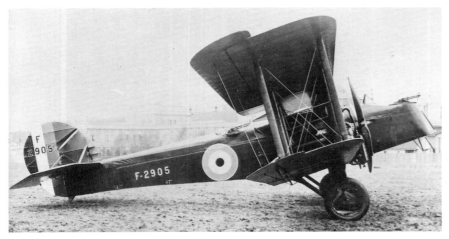

Two views of the third and final Bourges, F2905, in its Mark IIIA configuration with Napier Lion engines. Above: F2905, with the original Lion installation in the form it underwent performance trials at Martlesham Heath; note the transparent panels in the nose, used by the front gunner when acting as bomb aimer. Left: The aircraft at the RAE, Farnborough, during radiator development trials. The Bourges was unusual in having the upper wing extensively cut away to improve the midships gunner's field of fire. (Photos: Boulton Paul Aircraft Ltd, Neg Ref No 037, above; and A J Jackson Collection, left)

10,000 feet with full fuel and bomb load at Martlesham Heath in March that year. In this form the Bourges could be regarded as having reached a stage beyond any achieved by the other contenders for the Air Ministry's requirement for a D.H.10 replacement. By then the requirement had lapsed, and F2905 was delivered to the RAE, Farnborough, on 9 February 1922 for prolonged flight trials and development work on the Napier Lion's radiator, and these lasted until June 1924. There is little doubt that the results of work done during this period — which would have reached Boulton & Paul — were employed in formulating the Air Ministry's Specification 6/24, to which the Sidestrand was successfully tendered.

The outstanding manoeuvrability of the Bourges, of which mention was made above, was never more dramatically demonstrated than by Frank Courtney, who publicly rolled, looped and spun F2903 at the first Hendon Air Pageant in June 1920, a feat of handling wholly unimagined in a twin-engine bomber!

Type: Twin-engine, three-crew, three-bay biplane close-support light bomber.
Air Ministry Specifications: RAF Types IV, VI and VIII (later D of R Type 3).
Manufacturer: Boulton and Paul Ltd, Riverside, Norwich, Norfolk.
Powerplant: Mark I. Two 320hp ABC Dragonfly I nine-cylinder, air-cooled radial engines driving two-blade propellers. Mark II. Two 230hp Bentley B.R.2 rotary engines driving two-blade propellers. Mark III. Two 450hp Napier Lion IIB twelve-cylinder, water-cooled 'broad-arrow' in-line engines driving four-blade propellers.
Dimensions: Span (with horn-balanced ailerons), 57ft 4in; length, 37ft 0in; height, 12ft 0in; wing area, 738 sq ft.
Weights (Mark II): Tare, 3,820lb; all-up, 6,326lb.
Performance (Mark IIIB): Max speed, 130 mph at 10,000ft; climb to 10,000ft, 13 min 35 sec; service ceiling, 20,000ft; endurance, 9¼ hr.
Armament: Single 0.303in Lewis machine guns with Scarff ring mountings on nose and midships gunners' cockpits; provision for bomb load of up to four 230lb bombs.
Prototypes: Three, F2903-F2905. First recorded flight by F2903 at Norwich in June 1919; pilot believed to be Frank Courtney. No production.

Airco D.H.14 Okapi

Conceived as a successor to the Airco D.H.4, D.H.9 and D.H.9A, before the last-named had entered widespread service, the D.H.14 was ordered in prototype form a fortnight before the Armistice was signed when a far-reaching appraisal of the RAF's peacetime aircraft requirements was hurriedly conducted. The document produced (now in Public Record Office AIR/1/2423, dated 25 November 1918) lists the D.H.14 as being considered as future equipment and a possible replacement for the D.H.10 Amiens day bomber under the Air Ministry Technical Department's Specification VIII. In fact the manufacturer was at that time working to an amended version of Specification IVA, which had been superseded.

The apparent confusion arose because the likely performance of the D.H.14, particularly in range and bomb load, was not far short of that being demanded of the prototypes already ordered for competitive evaluation to become a potential D.H.10 replacement, a fact that had not escaped the Air Ministry's notice. Being powered by a single engine and with a two-man crew, it was likely that the unit cost of the D.H.14 would be significantly less than the twin-engine contenders. This consideration would become progressively more significant as the postwar cost-cutting began to take effect on the Services.

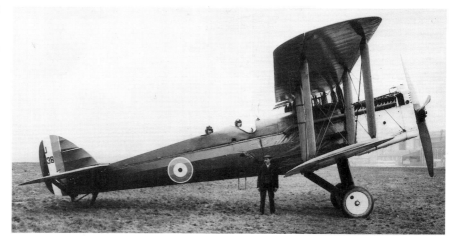

The first D.H.14 Okapi, J1938, with Condor I engine; this differed from previous Rolls-Royce engine in having four valves per cylinder. (Photo: Imperial War Museum, Neg No MH3554)

The D.H.14, named the Okapi, was a large aeroplane for a single-engine aircraft, its size being dictated by the big 600hp, 21.4-litre Rolls-Royce Condor engine selected, and the bomb and fuel loads envisaged. Superficially it was not unlike an enlarged Liberty-powered D.H.9A, the Condor being provided with a large rectangular frontal radiator. Construction of the three prototypes was of wood throughout, the bomb load of six 112lb bombs being accommodated

Type: Single-engine, two-seat, two-bay biplane medium bomber.
Air Ministry Specifications: D of R Type 4A (as amended); later RAF Type IX.
Manufacturer: The Aircraft Manufacturing Co Ltd, Hendon, London NW9.
Powerplant: One 525hp Rolls-Royce Condor I (later IA) V-twelve, water-cooled, in-line engine driving four-blade propeller. D.H.14A. 450hp Napier Lion.
Dimensions: Span, 50ft 5in; length, 33ft 11½in (D.H.14A, 37ft 7in); height, 14ft 0in; wing area, 617 sq ft.
Weights: Tare, 4,484lb; all-up (six 112lb bombs and full fuel), 7,074lb.
Performance (Condor I): Max speed, 126 mph at sea level, 122 mph at 10,000ft; endurance, 5 hr.
Armament: Provision to carry six 112lb bombs internally. Gun armament comprised one fixed, synchronized, 0.303in Vickers machine gun firing forward, and one Lewis gun with Scarff ring on observer's cockpit.
Prototypes: Two D.H.14s, J1938 (first flight, 29 or 30 September 1920) and J1939; J1940 (D.H.14A) first flown as G-EAPY on 4 December 1919. No production.

in the fuselage in two bays between the wing spars and beneath the pilot's cockpit.

Work on the Condor engine slowed down after the Armistice, and the first military D.H.14, J1938, was not flown until September 1920 at Stag Lane, having been taken over and completed by the new de Havilland Aircraft Company after the demise of Airco. (The third D.H.14, J1940, had been completed a year earlier and, as G-EAPY on the Civil Register, was powered by a 450hp Napier Lion engine. Flown by F S Cotton and W A Townsend in an attempt to fly to South Africa, it crashed in Italy on 4 February 1920. Repaired, and carrying its military serial, J1940, it was delivered to Martlesham Heath for comparative trials with the other, Condor-powered D.H.14 prototypes in April 1921.)

The Okapi J1938 paid its first visit to Martlesham in December 1920, the month in which the second Okapi was first flown. Both aircraft underwent a long series of flight trials, much of their time being spent contributing to the development of the Condor engine, expected to become one of the RAF's cornerstone powerplants in a few years' time. The initial version, the Mark I, although intended to produce 600hp, was derated for the Okapi trials at 525hp, until J1939 was fitted with a fully-rated Condor IA in November 1921. Both prototypes were written off early in 1922, J1938 hitting a tree and being destroyed by fire on 10 February, while J1939 was damaged beyond economic repair in an accident during April.

Nieuport London

Often erroneously referred to in the same context as the Amiens day bomber replacement contenders, the Nieuport London night bomber triplane was designed about entirely different parameters, with the emphasis on a relatively heavy bomb load at the expense of speed performance. Indeed the aircraft, despite its very modest dimensions, was much closer to the Vimy in respect of load carried.

Designed by Henry Folland for Nieuport (England) Ltd in 1918 — the company that became Nieuport and General Aircraft Co Ltd — with simplicity of manufacture an important aspect of production, the London possessed severe and austere lines, the only curved contours being the fin's leading edge and the engine nacelles. Construction was entirely of wood (cypress, deal and pine), the fuselage being covered by quarter-inch, tongued-and-grooved match-boarding; jointing was by means of nails, wooden pegs and dowels, and

The London, whose first prototype, H1740, is shown here in 1920, was a remarkably small aircraft for one that could carry 2,250lb of bombs. (Photo: Stuart Leslie)

the wings and tail surfaces were all fabric-covered. Yet the consummate skill with which Folland kept loads within the factors of this extremely simple structure enabled a bomb load of up to nine 250lb bombs to be carried. The wings, all of equal span and parallel chord, were rigged without stagger, and all carried horn-balanced ailerons (although it has been said that the upper two pairs were later removed without noticeably affecting the excellent lateral control). The undercarriage comprised two separate single-wheel structures carried directly below the engine nacelles with diagonal struts attached to the lower fuselage longerons. There was thus no impediment to the bomb stowage. The only obvious sign of Folland's hand in the London's design was the prominent ventral fin which had characterised the Royal Aircraft Factory S.E.5 and Nieuport Nighthawk fighters.

A total of six Nieuport London prototypes, H1740-H1745, was ordered on 13 July 1918, it being the original intention to power all these aeroplanes with the 320hp ABC Dragonfly. The last four

Being designed as a night bomber, no provision was made in the London for a midships gunner. The second aircraft, H1741, is believed to have only flown for about a month before its manufacturer went into liquidation, when it was delivered into store. (Photo: RAF Museum)

aircraft were, however, cancelled, on 16 December that year.

The first prototype, H1740, was flown at Acton on 13 April 1920, having been delayed for many months by the non-delivery of these engines, and at one time Folland had, with some reluctance, prepared alternative designs to install 290hp high-compression Siddeley Pumas in the second prototype (as the London Mark II). In the event, Dragonflies were delivered in time to enable both H1740 and H1741 to be fitted accordingly.

The second London made its maiden flight in July, but all development work on the aircraft was halted the following month when the Nieuport and General Company stopped trading. Both prototypes were taken on Air Ministry charge, H1740 already being at Martlesham

Heath and H1741 being sent to the Marine Aircraft Experimental Establishment at the Isle of Grain for storage; the latter was also to be delivered to

Martlesham in January 1921. With the grounding of the Dragonfly engine, it is unlikely that either of the Londons were actually flown after September 1920.

Type: Twin-engine, two-seat, two-bay triplane night bomber.
Air Ministry Specification: RAF Type VII.
Manufacturers: Nieuport (England) Ltd, later Nieuport and General Aircraft Co Ltd, Cricklewood, London NW.
Powerplant: Mark I. Two 320hp ABC Dragonfly I nine-cylinder, air-cooled radial engines driving two-blade propellers. Mark II (not built). 290hp Siddeley Puma engines
Structure: Wooden structure throughout (deal, pine and cypress); fuselage matchboard covered; wings and tail fabric-covered.
Dimensions: Span, 59ft 6in; length, 37ft 6in; height, 17ft 6in; wing area, 1,100 sq ft.
Performance: Max speed, 100 mph at sea level; climb to 10,000ft, 30 min; endurance, 4 hr.
Armament: Double-yoked 0.303in Lewis machine guns with Scarff ring on nose gunner's cockpit; bomb load of up to nine 250lb bombs, believed carried internally.
Prototypes: Two, H1740 and H1741. H1740 first flown at Acton on 13 April 1920 as Mark I with Dragonfly engines. H1741 first flown in July 1920. Four other aircraft, H1742-H1745, cancelled in December 1918. No production.

Grahame-White E.IV Ganymede

It is necessary here to return to 1918 to make brief mention of three other aircraft intended for consideration by the Air Ministry as very heavy long-range bombers, cast in a similar mould to that of the Bristol Braemar, but which, for various reasons of difficulty or misfortune, failed even to attract academic interest. Their manufacturers persevered mainly in the hope of recovering some of their losses suffered by contract cancellations at the end of the War or in an attempt to retain as much of their workforce as possible until better times arrived for the aircraft industry.

Indeed, if they possessed a common design weakness, it was on account of their designers allowing the basic configuration of their aircraft to be compromised by attention to relatively unimportant elements in the Air Ministry requirements. The companies were also probably misguided in attempting to achieve too much, by means of unjustified ingenuity, at a time when the design staffs should have sought to improve and combine the best of existing design configurations.

Chronologically, the first of these big bombers to be completed was the Grahame-White Ganymede, an aircraft originally intended to be powered by three 400hp Liberty 12 engines. It was a four-bay biplane with horn-balanced

Manhandling the Ganymede C3481 at Hendon early in 1919. The photo emphasises the size of the exhaust stacks above the engines, and also shows well the unusual configuration of the tail unit. (Photo: *Flight*, Neg No 173)

ailerons, two of the three engines driving tractor propellers and located at the front of twin fuselages attached to the lower wings, and the third engine driving a pusher propeller at the rear of a central nacelle, which also accommodated the pilots and front gunner; the latter was also the bomb aimer. Each engine was provided with a large rectangular radiator mounted above it.

Two midships gunners were also carried, in a mistaken belief that importance would be attached to a significant gun defence to the rear, whereas the Air Ministry seldom placed much emphasis on such a defence in night bombers. One gunner was located in each of the fuselages aft of the wing, and was provided

with a Scarff ring. The biplane tail unit featured three fins and rudders, the outer surfaces being situated at the rear of each fuselage, the large triangular fins extending forward of the sternposts to which the rudders were hinged; the tailplanes were mounted one below the rear of the fuselages and the other several inches clear of the top of the fins; horn-balanced elevators were hinged to each, and each fuselage was fitted with a sprung tailskid.

Uncertainty surrounding delivery of the Liberty engines in the late summer of 1918 resulted in recourse being made to three 270hp Sunbeam Maori engines, with the result that the Ganymede was inevitably underpowered, and it is doubtful whether the aircraft ever carried a bomb load. The Maoris were enclosed in square-section cowlings, neatly faired to the contours of large spinners fitted over the four-blade propellers; the overall effect was, however, marred by huge exhaust stacks extending upwards from the branch-manifolds to direct the exhaust gases over the upper wing — so as to pass well clear of the midships gunners. The undercarriage comprised four mainwheels arranged in separate pairs, one under each fuselage, and each with its own crossaxle. The wheel-mounting V-struts, incorporating oleos, were very short, and it is clear from photographs that the pilot would need to be very careful not to raise the tail too high during take-off, to avoid grounding the propellers.

Three prototypes of this fairly large bomber, C3481-C3483, were ordered, and C3481 was completed before the end of 1918, although it may not have been flown until early in 1919. In any event flight trials went ahead as it was particularly important that Grahame-White received the contracted payment when so many production contracts were being summarily cancelled — including the second and third Ganymedes.

Unfortunately C3481 suffered some damage in a forced landing when it dug its nose into soft ground. Either then, or shortly after, the Air Ministry notified Grahame-White that it would not be purchasing the Ganymede and, in an effort to recoup some of the financial loss, the company determined to examine the feasibility of modifying C3481 as a commercial aircraft, removing the centre engine altogether and rebuilding the nacelle as a long, glazed cabin capable of accommodating twelve passengers. The remaining Maoris were replaced by two 450hp Napier Lion engines, and the aircraft received its Certificate of Airworthiness on 12 September 1919, being re-registered G-EAMW — only to be destroyed by fire twelve months later.

Type: Three-engine (two tractor and one pusher), five-crew, four-bay biplane heavy night bomber.
Manufacturer: The Grahame-White Aviation Co Ltd, Hendon, London NW9.
Powerplant: Three 270hp Sunbeam Maori twelve-cylinder water-cooled engines (two tractor engines located at forward end of outboard fuselages, and one pusher engine at rear of central nacelle). Later two tractor 450hp Napier Lion engines (in commercial conversion).
Dimensions: Span, 89ft 3in; length, 49ft 9in; height, 16ft 0in; wing area, 1,660 sq ft.
Weights: Tare, 11,500lb; all-up, 16,000lb.
Performance: Max speed, 105 mph at sea level, 93 mph at 10,000ft; endurance, 9 hr.
Armament: Three 0.303in Lewis machine guns with Scarff rings, one in nose of central nacelle, and one amidships in each outboard fuselage; details of bomb load not recorded.
Prototype: C3481, first flown late in 1918 or early 1919. Two others, C3482 and C3983, ordered, but cancelled. No production.

Tarrant Tabor

Not only was the Tarrant Tabor six-engine triplane almost fifty per cent heavier than the Handley Page V/1500, but it was expected to be able to carry a ton greater bomb load about thirty per cent further. It was the product of highly competent engineers and an imaginative concept.

W G Tarrant Ltd was a well-known woodworking contractor at Byfleet, Surrey, which had supplied countless structural components to other aircraft manufacturers and had patented a method of constructing wing spars featuring wooden lattice webs. In 1917 W G Tarrant took this a stage further, securing a patent for lattice-braced circular girders for use in large aircraft fuselages. He was to be joined by Marcel Lobelle from the nearby company of Martinsyde, and by W H Barling from the Royal Aircraft Factory.

Together they produced the design of a very large four-engine biplane towards the end of 1917, intending that it should be powered by four 600hp Siddeley Tigers, arranged in tandem pairs at midgap. It soon became evident, however, that the Tiger would not be ready in the timespan of the aircraft and, in order to maintain a comparable power/weight

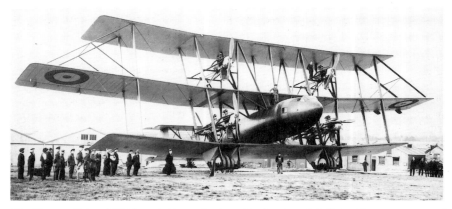

The Tarrant Tabor, F1765, probably on the day of its first intended flight. The arrangement of the six engines is clearly shown, the rear lower engines driving four-blade pusher propellers. Only the long-span central wing carried ailerons. (Photo: Imperial War Museum, Neg No MH3542)

ratio, Tarrant elected to fit six 450hp Napier Lions instead, at the same time adding an upper, third wing with the same dimensions and structure as those of the bottom wing, transferring the support for what became the central wing's large overhang to the top wing, the diagonal support struts now being stressed in tension instead of compression.

The additional Lion tractor engines were mounted directly above the lower pairs, the pairs of interplane struts to which the nacelles were braced being raked outwards towards their apices; additional diagonal centresection struts passed from the upper wing, through the central wing to meet on the aircraft's centreline below the fuselage and on the lower wing, thereby forming, in effect, the section of a huge Warren truss of great strength. It is assumed that the bomb load, amounting to the equivalent of about twenty 230lb HE RL bombs, would have been carried under the lower wing centresection, for the wing structure would thus have distributed the load to all the wings without compromising the cylindrical fuselage structure.

The fuselage was a finely-streamlined, cigar-shaped structure which carried a biplane tail unit, comprising two tailplanes, the lower of which incor-

A photo taken during the engine starting process for the Tabor, immediately before its ill-fated first flight attempt at Farnborough on 26 May 1919. Close examination of the original print discloses that the enormous gantry incorporated an engine-starting linkage to a clutch attachment at ground level, the vehicle presumably having been driven away after starting all the engines; it must therefore have been the largest Hucks starter ever built. The photo well illustrates the very considerable thrust moment of the upper engines about the undercarriage. (Photo: The Daily Mail)

porated a horn-balanced elevator, and the upper a trimming surface operated by handwheel in the pilot's cockpit. A second elevator was mounted in the tailplane gap.

The undercarriage comprised two suitably massive structures, each carrying three five-foot-diameter main wheels on their own common axle. With each wheel assembly being attached by struts directly beneath the engine mounting interplane struts, the landing loads were distributed directly between the three wings and, at the same time provided an uninterrupted wheel track of no less than 31ft 5in.

Such was the great overall height of the Tabor (37ft 3in compared, for instance, to 20ft 8in of the Bristol Braemar triplane bomber) that Tarrant arranged for its final assembly to be undertaken in the huge balloon shed at Farnborough, the finished aircraft being moved in and out sideways on a specially-constructed pair of railway tracks.

Prior to its first scheduled flight, the Tabor was examined and tunnel-tested by both the Royal Aircraft Establishment and the National Physical Laboratory. Unfortunately the reports by the two authorities conflicted, the RAE suggesting that the aircraft was excessively tail-heavy, and it is understood that representations were made to add 1,000lb of lead ballast in the nose, although this proposal was put forward by a third party. Tarrant disagreed with this recommendation and, on the instructions of Maj-Gen Henry Robert Moore Brooke-Popham, the Deputy Assistant QMG (later Air Chief Marshal Sir Robert, GCVO, KCB, CMG, DSO, AFC, RAF), the investigation reports were not to be divulged. It is therefore not known whether Tarrant and the pilots, detailed

to make the first flight, were aware that the ballast had been added on that occasion.

The aircraft was made ready for flight on 26 May 1919, the pilots being Capt F G Dunn AFC, RAF and Capt P T Rawlings DSC, accompanied by four crewmen. After completing the lengthy process of starting the six engines, which required the use of a large gantry, Dunn carried out a number of trial taxying runs before starting his take-off. After lifting the tail, he opened up the two upper engines, and the huge triplane was seen to tip on to its nose; the undercarriage collapsed, the aircraft reared up and came to rest tail-up, the nose being crushed. Both Dunn and Rawlings died shortly afterwards in hospital.

The subsequent investigation concluded that the direct cause of the accident was the sudden onset of increased thrust from the top pair of engines (whose thrust line was about 28 feet from the ground), which caused the aircraft to pitch on to its nose. It seems likely that, had the pilots been aware of

the heavy ballast added in the nose, they would have been much less inclined to apply so much extra power from the upper engines, bearing in mind that the overall weight of the aircraft was relatively light (without bombs and with only limited fuel).

Thus ended a courageous attempt to produce a very large bomber whose capabilities seemed likely to represent a marked advance beyond those of the V/1500. Whether such a radical attempt was justified, especially as there were important differences of opinion among the best specialist technical agencies in the country as to the stability of the aeroplane, it is impossible to decide. Certainly it was clearly not economical to further develop the Tabor as a six-engine, passenger-carrying commercial airliner, even if Tarrant had felt inclined to do so. Yet one is perhaps left with the impression that, with the top wing discarded, together with the two upper engines, a biplane might well have succeeded on the power produced by, say, four Rolls-Royce Condor engines.

Type: Six-engine, six-crew, three-bay triplane long-range heavy bomber.
Manufacturer: W G Tarrant Ltd, Byfleet, Surrey; aircraft assembled at the RAE, Farnborough.
Powerplant: Six 450hp Napier Lion twelve-cylinder, water-cooled, broad-arrow in-line engine (four tractor and two pusher) driving two-blade propellers.
Structure: All-wood throughout with Tarrant lattice-webbed circular fuselage frames, covered overall with 2mm or 4mm ply.
Dimensions: Span, 131ft 3in; length, 73ft 2in; height, 37ft 3in; wing area, 4,950 sq ft.
Weights: Tare, 24,750lb; all-up (with 5,130lb war load), 44,672lb.
Performance (estimated): Max speed, over 110 mph; climb to 10,000ft, 33 min 30 sec; service ceiling, 13,000 ft; endurance, 12 hr.
Armament: No gun armament on prototype; bomb load equivalent to about twenty 230lb HE RL bombs.
Prototype: One, F1765 (second aircraft, F1766, cancelled); F1765 crashed on take-off for first flight on 26 May 1919 at Farnborough, killing the two pilots, Capt F G Dunn and Capt P T Rawlings. No production.

Siddeley Sinaia

Despite its design being started early in 1918, the Siddeley Sinaia[1] was not flown until mid-1921. It was designed under the leadership of John Lloyd, who had joined the Siddeley Deasy company from the Royal Aircraft Factory in 1917. However, company and official records appear to be contradictory as to the intended rôle and classification of the aircraft, the manufacturers tending to refer to it as a 'heavy day bomber', while the very few references to it in official documents suggest it was intended to be a night bomber.

The Sinaia was not formally tendered to any Air Board or Air Ministry requirement and only superficially conformed to the RAF Type XI Specification. It is likely that Siddeley Deasy was deliberately vague in its description of the aircraft's intended rôle, but was primarily anxious to secure an Air Ministry order for prototypes in which the new 500hp Siddeley Tiger engines could be flown. By the time it became evident that the Air Ministry regarded heavy defensive armament as largely superfluous in night bombers, Lloyd had finalised the basic configuration of the Sinaia, and a wide defensive field of fire appeared to dictate the entire design configuration, rather than being subordinated to it.

A provisional Contract was signed for four prototypes on 12 February, but the delivery schedule was put back and the Contract amended on 22 June that year, it being realised that the Tiger engine would not be ready for flight for at least a year. Because the aircraft had not been tendered to a formal requirement, licences had to be obtained to build the prototypes in order to obtain the materials needed, the four aircraft being allocated the serial numbers X21-X24. A start was made on building the first prototype at the end of 1918 but, with the coming of peace, work came to a virtual standstill as much of the workforce was laid off.

Design and development of the Tiger engine suffered from reduced financing

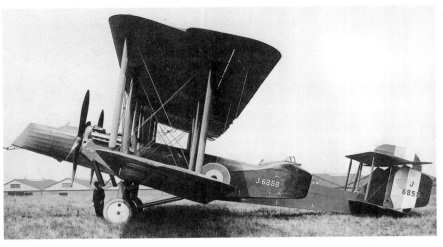

J6858 at Farnborough in 1921. It can be seen that the Sinaia was rigged with slight wing stagger, and wing-folding with this rigging was unusual at the time, although Short Bros had patented a working system some six years earlier. (Photo: via J M Bruce)

with the arrival of peace. Designed under the direction of S D Heron (also recruited from Farnborough), the Tiger was a Vee-twelve water-cooled in-line engine, consisting of two slightly-improved Puma cylinder blocks attached to a single crankcase.

As if to compound the lack of progress on the aircraft and engines, Siddeley Deasy was purchased early in 1919 by Armstrong Whitworth (following a proposal by John Davenport Siddeley, later Lord Kenilworth), the company's engine department becoming Armstrong Siddeley Motors Ltd in 1921. The new company seems to have remained unconvinced of a future for the Sinaia, but evidently agreed to continue work on it, if only to provide a vehicle in which to fly the Tiger engine. (The third and fourth prototypes were cancelled on 7 March 1921).

The Sinaia was an equal-span biplane with horn-balanced ailerons on upper and lower wings, the two engines being mounted in nacelles on the lower wings. Each nacelle extended about ten feet aft of the trailing edge to mount a gunner's cockpit at the rear, together with a raised Scarff ring to provide a field of fire

above the upper wing; this would have placed the gunner fully at the mercy of the engine's slipstream and rendered accurate aiming of his Lewis gun almost impossible.

The biplane tail unit comprised short-span tailplanes, the lower of which was fitted with a conventional elevator; a trimming surface was attached to the upper tailplane. Three rudders were fitted, that in the centre being hinged to a small fixed fin which extended above the upper tailplane.

The wings were designed to fold, but it is difficult to see how this was accomplished without supporting the fuselage almost horizontally so as to allow ground clearance of the wing tips. (In any case, by 1919, the Air Ministry was no longer determined on wing-folding in any but the very large bombers; moreover, in the flight trials of the Sinaia, it was found that the wing fold hinges were inadquate to withstand flight loads, and partial failure occurred.)

The components of the first prototype, J6858 (formerly X21), were despatched to Farnborough early in 1921 for assembly at the RAE and, despite constant trouble with the hith-

---

[1] Various sources have referred to the Sinaia as the Type 103. No authoritative explanation has been traced for this nomenclature; it may have been a Works No, or simply the third of a series of Siddeley Deasy aircraft beginning at No 101, the earlier designs being the R.T.1 reconnaissance two-seater and the S.R.2 Siskin fighter.

Type: Twin-engine, four-crew, three-bay biplane heavy/medium bomber.
Air Ministry Specification: Approximated to RAF Type XI
Manufacturer: The Siddeley Deasy Motor Car Co Ltd, Parkside, Coventry.
Powerplant: Two 480hp Siddeley Tiger twelve-cylinder, water-cooled, in-line engines driving four-blade tractor propellers.
Dimensions: Span, 86ft 10in; wing area, 1,823 sq ft.
Weight: All-up, 16,000lb.
Performance: No details have been traced.
Armament: Three single 0.303in Lewis machine guns mounted in fuselage nose and at the rear of each engine nacelle on Scarff rings. Intended bomb load not known.
Prototypes: Four ordered and licensed as X21 to X24. Only two commenced manufacture, J6858 and J6859. J6858 first flown by Capt Frank T Courtney on 25 June 1921. J6859 not assembled, and no production.

erto unflown Tiger engine, the aircraft was flown by Capt Frank Courtney on 25 June that year. The subsequent flight trials were dogged by engine unreliability and structural faults. Examination disclosed evidence of inadequate stressing, sub-standard materials and generally poor workmanship. The RAE report recommended much redesign, and

said that the aircraft should be rebuilt.

As the aircraft had attracted no significant interest at the Air Ministry, and Armstrong Siddeley was unwilling to waste any more time and money on the Tiger engine, J6858 was grounded permanently in October 1921. The second machine, J6859, had also been sent to Farnborough for assembly, but in the

event the components were simply used as spares for J6858.

Although there had been tentative proposals to consider fitting 500hp Beardmore Atlantic or 600hp Rolls-Royce Condor engines as alternatives to the Tigers, nothing tangible was accomplished in these respects, and the Sinaia lapsed into well merited obscurity.

Airco D.H.15 Gazelle

The sole Galloway Atlantic-powered Airco D.H.15 Gazelle, J1937. (Photo: via J M Bruce)

Although intended from the outset as an experimental test bed for the big Galloway Atlantic engine, the Airco D.H.15 (named the Gazelle, in line with the current practice of naming all military aeroplanes) was ordered by the Air Ministry on 7 September 1918. The single prototype, J1937, was a standard D.H.9A airframe with local structural modifications to accommodate the new engine, and retained all the standard D.H.9A's armament, including provision to carry its bomb load — presumably so that a realistic performance comparison could be made with the standard aeroplane, as well as other variants.

The Galloway Atlantic was evolved in much the same manner as the Siddeley Tiger, except that two standard cast-iron BHP cylinder blocks were brought together on a common crankcase. Drive to the two-blade propeller was without reduction gear, and a large rectangular frontal radiator, similar to that of the Liberty 12, was provided. Two other features readily distinguished the Gazelle. The long, almost horizontal exhaust pipe on each side of the fuselage extended as far aft as the gunner's cockpit, while the pair of front centre-

section wing struts were rigged almost vertically, whereas previously they had been raked forward.

J1937 was completed in July 1919, and was eventually delivered to Martlesham Heath for performance trials the following May. Compared with the standard Liberty-powered D.H.9A's

maximum speed of about 114 mph at 10,000 feet (without bomb load), the Gazelle achieved 133 mph under the same load conditions; it also displayed a 10 per cent all-round performance superiority over the 450hp Napier Lion-powered version of the D.H.9A.

Type: Single-engine, two-seat, two-bay biplane experimental light bomber.
Manufacturer: The Aircraft Manufacturing Co Ltd, Hendon, London NW9.
Powerplant: One 500hp (BHP) Galloway Atlantic twelve-cylinder water-cooled in-line engine driving two-blade propeller.
Dimensions: Span, 45ft 11⅜in; length, 29ft 11ft; wing area, 486.73 sq ft.
Weights: Tare, 2,312lb; all-up, 4,773lb.
Performance: Max speed, 139 mph at sea level, 133 mph at 10,000ft; climb to 10,000ft, 8 min 12 sec; service ceiling, 20,000ft.
Armament: One forward-firing synchronized 0.303in Vickers machine gun on nose, and one Lewis gun with Scarff ring on observer's cockpit; provision to carry 460lb bomb load.
Prototype: One, J7936, flown in July 1919. No production.

Deployment of British Bomber Squadrons — 1 January 1920

Home Bases

No 55 Sqn.[1]	D.H.4	Shotwick, Cheshire
No 219 Sqn.[2]	D.H.9	Manston, Kent
No 274 Sqn.	Handley Page V/1500	Bircham Newton, Norfolk

India

No 97 Sqn.	D.H.10	Lahore
No 99 Sqn.	D.H.9A	Ambala

Egypt

No 58 Sqn.	Vimy/H.P. O/400	Heliopolis
No 214 Sqn.	Handley Page O/400	Abu Sueir
No 216 Sqn.	D.H.10/H.P. O/400	Abu Sueir

[1] Cadre only
[2] Bombing not the Squadron's primary rôle

Blackburn T.1 Swift

The final year of the War had brought a sharpened awareness of the potential value of the carrier-borne torpedo aeroplane, evidenced by the commissioning of one aircraft carrier (HMS *Furious*) with flight decks forward and aft of the superstructure, and launching of two flush-deck carriers (HMS *Argus* and *Eagle*). These three carriers would be joined by HMS *Hermes* (12,900 tons) in 1923, the world's first ship to be designed from the outset as a flush-deck carrier; she also introduced the convention of placing the superstructure on the starboard side of the flight deck — a feature of aircraft carriers that survives all over the world seventy years later.

That last year of the War had also witnessed the introduction of the Sopwith Cuckoo into service, as well as the failure by the Blackburn Blackburd and Short Shirl to gain acceptance as the Cuckoo's ultimate replacement. The Air Ministry re-issued the Specification (as Type XXII) at the beginning of 1920 hoping that, with the growing reliability of more powerful engines, such as the 450hp Napier Lion, a new contender — capable of delivering the all-important Mark VIII torpedo — would be forthcoming.

In the event, only the Blackburn company essayed a prototype as a private venture, designed by Maj Frank Arnold Bumpus, and this aircraft, the T.1 Swift, was sufficiently complete to be exhibited at the Olympia Aero Show of July 1920. It was a fairly big aeroplane, which at the same time gave an

The Blackburn Swift at Martlesham Heath after being fitted with the enlarged rudder and small fin. (Photo: Real Photographs Co.)

impression of compact efficiency. A single-seat, two-bay, staggered biplane, it was indeed powered by the Lion, and the Mark VIII torpedo was duly accommodated between the components of a split-axle undercarriage.

The achieve the strength to withstand the shock loads imposed by deck landing, Bumpus sought to produce an immensely strong, rigid central structure of steel tube comprising the front fuselage, to which the entire powerplant was bolted, the upper wing centresection containing the 15-gallon gravity fuel tank, the lower stub wings with the undercarriage anchorages, the torpedo attachments, the main 66-gallon fuel tank, and the cockpit.

The fuselage structure was of steel tube throughout, but the two-spar wings were of fabric-covered wooden construction. A statutory feature, now required to be included in all single-engine Service aeroplanes following a

spate of fatal flying accidents, was the inclusion of a fireproof bulkhead between the engine and fuel tank. The wings folded about hinges located at the rear outer corners of the upper wing centresection, and at the rear of the stub wings, resulting in a folded width of only 17ft 6in so as to fit the deck lifts on the new aircraft carriers.

The first Swift, N139, was flown by R W Kenworthy at Brough about two months after the Olympia show, the aircraft narrowly escaping destruction on its maiden flight when, immediately after take-off, it assumed a steep nose-up attitude which the pilot was unable to correct with the stick pushed fully forward. Realising that the aircraft's cg was well outside its design limits, Kenworthy managed to make a wide circuit of his aerodrome and, by using the throttle as the elevator, he landed safely. The fault was easily resolved by introducing slight sweepback on the wings.

After pre-delivery trials at Brough, N139 was flown to Martlesham Heath on 23 December for full performance trials with the Mark VIII and IX torpedoes, in the course of which the directional control came in for criticism so that an enlarged rudder was fitted to a smaller fin. By 20 April 1921 the Swift had negotiated its tests satisfactorily.

After fitting arrester claws to the stub wheel axles[1] N139 was delivered to the Gosport Development Squadron on 9 May, and subsequently made its first

A Blackburn Swift, one of those destined for export to Spain, dropping a torpedo during the course of pre-delivery trials. (Photo: Blackburn & General Aircraft Ltd, Neg No D533)

deck landings on HMS *Argus* in the hands of the Canadian pilot, Gerald Boyce.

A new Specification, 3/20 (in fact little more than a rewrite of the earlier requirement), had resulted in the next three Swifts being slightly modified in the light of the Martlesham Heath trials. These three prototypes, and the subsequent production aircraft, were renamed the T.2 Dart, and are described on page 133.

Meanwhile, the ability of the Swift N139 to carry either the Mark VIII or IX torpedoes, or alternatively a load of bombs, had attracted attention abroad and, as it was to be the Dart and not the Swift that was selected for production by the Air Ministry, Blackburn was permitted to service the small export orders for the Swift that followed, among them two aircraft sold to the United States for evaluation.

---

[1] The early deck arrester cables on British and American carriers were stretched lengthways along the flight deck about 18 inches above the surface. The claws on the aircraft's undercarriage engaged the cables so that the resulting friction slowed the aircraft to a standstill.

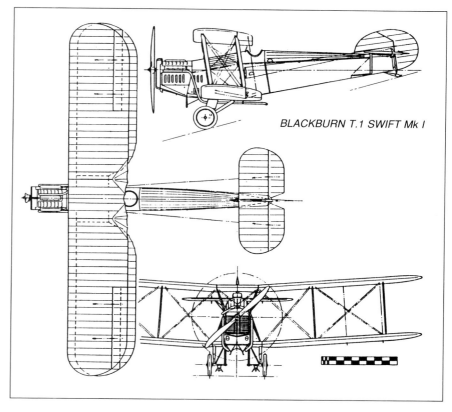

BLACKBURN T.1 SWIFT Mk I

Type: Single-engine, single-seat, two-bay shipborne biplane torpedo bomber.

Air Ministry Specification: Type XXII as re-issued in 1920.

Manufacturer: The Blackburn Aeroplane and Motor Co Ltd, Olympia Works, Leeds, and Brough Aerodrome, East Yorks.

Powerplant: One 450hp Napier Lion IB twelve-cylinder, water-cooled in-line engine driving two-blade propeller.

Structure: Tubular steel fuselage structure and folding wooden wings. Divided-axle undercarriage.

Dimensions: Span, 48ft 6in; length, 35ft 6in; height, 12ft 3in; wing area, 720 sq ft.

Weights: Tare, 3,550lb; all-up (with torpedo), 6,300lb.

Performance: Max speed, 106 mph at sea level; service ceiling, 15,000ft; max range, 350 miles.

Armament: Equipped to carry one 1,423lb Mark VIII or one 1,086lb Mark IX torpedo, or up to four 230lb bombs; no gun armament.

Prototype: One, N139, first flown by R W Kenworthy at Brough in about September 1920 (also civil registered as G-EAVN, but probably did not carry the letters). No production (although two examples were shipped to the USA for evaluation, two to Japan and three to Spain).

Fairey Type IIID

Justifiably encouraged by the promise held out by the earlier Lion-powered Fairey IIIC, and realising thereby that the expanding air arm of the Royal Navy would continue to see a need for shipborne aircraft, complementary to torpedo-carriers such as the Cuckoo and its replacement, Richard Fairey determined to advance the potential of this aircraft by use of new versions of the Lion engine which were expected to become available soon after the end of the War.

Although initially embarked on as a private venture, the natural development of the IIIC was conceived primarily as a seaplane, the Air Ministry being

satisfied, for the time being at least, with the trolley system of launching floatplanes from the decks of carriers. In the course of discussions at the Air Ministry's R and D Department early in 1920 Duncanson, in charge of Fairey's design staff, learned of the experience gained during the IIIC's service in north Russia, in particular the difficulties encountered under operational conditions of replacing damaged engines, and that future naval specifications would likely require the whole powerplant, together with its bearers and cowlings, to be quickly removable with the least possible manpower and equipment.

In view of the much reduced peacetime defence expenditure, it was clear that the Air Ministry would be looking to standardise on a single naval dual-rôle aircraft capable of performing medium-

range fleet and coastal reconnaissance and fleet spotting, at the same time capable of carrying a light bomb load. In the short term the deck trolley would continue in use, but as this always required the aircraft to alight on the sea afterwards, it was suggested that an interchangeable wheel and float undercarriage would ultimately be required.

Duncanson quickly prepared a design, in effect a modified Type IIIC, incorporating a third cockpit and an improved wing camber-changing system. The Eagle VIII was retained as an expedient while efforts were made to suit the Napier Lion II for self-contained installation and removal purposes. Fairey was awarded a contract for no fewer than fifty seaplanes in the late spring of 1920 (a large order by the standards of the time — Fairey having

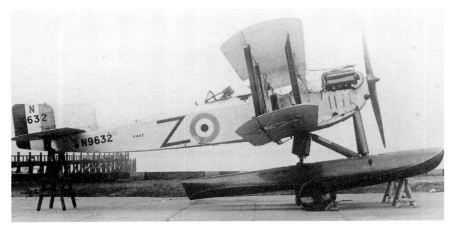

One of the early Fairey IIIDs, N9632, of the third production batch which were fitted with Eagle VIII engines while awaiting the Lion IIB. After receiving its Lion, N9632 was flown with boat-built metal floats and steel wings; it is shown here at the MAEE, Felixstowe, and the 'Z' on the fuselage probably denotes this 'shore station'. These long floats enabled the tail and wingtip floats to be discarded; note the oleo-pneumatic rear float strut. (Photo: Imperial War Museum, Neg No MH2939)

only built about 20 aircraft in the whole of 1919).

The first aircraft, regarded as the prototype IIID, N9450, was largely 'hand-built', as were the next four or five examples, and was first flown by Vincent Nicholl at Hamble in August. However, the speed with which Fairey undertook this work was hardly matched by the Air Ministry, and service evaluation of one sort or another occupied much of 1921.

A landplane version was flown in August that year, also by Nicholl. The undercarriage of this IIID was exceptionally neat and efficient, being designed to cater for the greater rate of descent in deck landings. The structure comprised a pair of cross-braced V-struts attached beneath the nose of the aircraft with radius rods hinged at their apices to which was attached the cross-axle with mainwheels; each wheel was provided with an oleopneumatic leg which picked up on the lower fuselage longerons at the same attachment point of the central float mounting when otherwise fitted. On later aircraft the wheel and float undercarriages were designed to be easily interchangeable.

Production of the IIID did not get

underway fully until 1922, when the Air Ministry Specification 38/22 was finalised, and it was July 1924 before the first deliveries were made to the recently created Fleet Air Arm. In the meantime six Eagle-powered IIIDs had been delivered to the Australian Air Force (prefixed Royal on 31 March 1923) during 1921-22, and in the latter year the first of eleven aircraft were produced for Portugal.

After the first batch of 50 Eagle-powered IIIDs had been completed, 12 seaplanes were ordered with Lion II engines, followed by 12 with Lion IIBs, although the first six of the latter batch first appeared with Eagle VIIIs — these being replaced later by Lion IIBs; the third aircraft, after receiving its Lion engine, was experimentally fitted with steel wings and boat-built metal floats for trials at Felixstowe.

After 62 further Lion IIB seaplanes had been completed in 1924, the Fairey IIID Mark II was introduced in 1925, 36 being built with interchangeable wheel/float undercarriages and 465hp Napier Lion Vs. The final version, the IIID Mark III, of which 35 were produced, was similar to the Mark II but featured the Lion VA engine.

The first IIIDs to reach an opera-

tional Fleet Air Arm unit were delivered to No 441 Flight in July 1924 for service aboard HMS *Argus*, replacing Parnall Panthers; early Eagle-powered aircraft were soon replaced by Lion IIB aircraft. This and the next unit, No 442, were the longest serving carrier-based IIID Flights, the latter in HMS *Hermes*, and spent much of their service in the Far East.

Until the end of 1926, by which time five Flights had equipped with Fairey IIIDs, all had been serving in the Fleet bomber-reconnaissance rôle. In January 1927, however, the rôle changed as IIIDs joined No 422 (Fleet Spotter) Flight in HMS *Argus*, being employed primarily in gunnery spotting for other warships of the Fleet. The last operational Fairey IIIDs with the Fleet Air Arm were disposed of by No 444 Flight in September 1931, having served almost continuously aboard HM Seaplane Carrier *Vindictive*. One other Flight, No 481, which had taken on several IIID Mark IIIs at Kalafrana, Malta, in January 1929 for seaplane maritime reconnaissance, later became No 202 Squadron of the RAF, but gave up its aircraft in September 1930. Some of these then equipped the Malta Base Flight, the last IIID, S1107, being disposed of in March 1932.

The Fairey IIID had joined the RAF in 1925 at the time the first Mark IIs and IIIs were completed. In November that year the Cape Flight was formed at Hendon under the command of Wg Cdr Conway Walter Heath Pulford (later Air Vice-Marshal, OBE, AFC) for the purpose

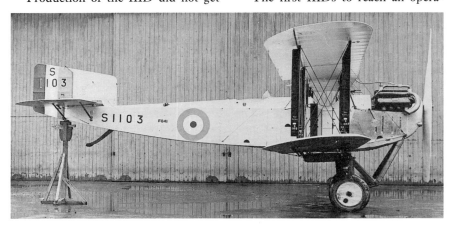

S1103 was one of the specially-prepared Fairey IIID Mark IIIs which took part in the famous Cape Flight of 1926, its wheel undercarriage being interchangeable with floats; these long-distance aircraft were not equipped with a Scarff ring on the rear cockpit, a small windscreen being fitted instead. (Photo: Fairey Aviation Co Ltd.)

of making a flight to Cape Town to show the flag, and providing the Service with long distance flying experience. Seven aircraft were allocated to the Cape Flight but, in the event, only four (S1102-S1105) took part. Flying with wheel undercarriages, the IIID Mark IIIs took off from Hendon on 1 March 1926, flying out via Egypt, Sudan, Kenya and Southern Rhodesia; after setting off to return home from Cape Town, the four aircraft called at Pretoria for eleven days while their engines were overhauled. They called in at Aboukir in Egypt to exchange their wheel undercarriages for floats for the final stages, arriving at Lee-on-Solent on 21 June. The 13,900-mile flight had been accomplished with scarcely any trouble, replacements being confined to a wheel, two propellers and a magneto.

This fine performance was wholly characteristic of the Fairey IIID's entire service. Very few were lost in accidents, and the aircraft was much liked by its pilots and crews.

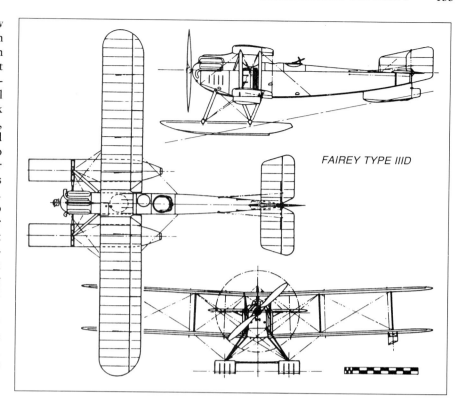

FAIREY TYPE IIID

Type: Single-engine, three-seat, two-bay, land- or carrier-based bomber/spotter/reconnaissance landplane or twin-float seaplane.

Air Ministry Specification: 38/22

Manufacturer: Fairey Aviation Co Ltd, Hayes, Middlesex, and Hamble, Hampshire.

Powerplant: Early aircraft. One 365hp Rolls-Royce Eagle VIII 12-cylinder Vee water-cooled in-line engine or 450hp Napier Lion II 12-cylinder broad-arrow water-cooled in-line engine. Later aircraft. Eagle IX (Civil conversions) and Lion IIB, V and VA.

Dimensions: Span, 46ft 1in (folded, 13ft 0in); length, 31ft 5in (seaplane, 36ft 1in); height, 12ft 0in (seaplane, 13ft 0in); wing area, 500 sq ft.

Weights: Landplane. Tare, 3,430lb; all-up, 5,050lb. Seaplane. Tare, 3,990lb; all-up, 5,050lb.

Performance: Landplane (Lion IIB). Max speed, 120 mph at sea level; climb to 5,000ft, 4 min 50 sec; normal range, 550 miles. Seaplane (Lion IIB). Max speed, 117 mph at sea level; climb to 10,000ft, 12 min 30 sec; normal range, 530 miles.

Armament: One forward-firing synchronized 0.303in Vickers machine gun on nose, and one 0.303in Lewis gun with Scarff ring on rear cockpit. Normal bomb load, up to four 112lb bombs.

Prototype: One, N9450, first flown as seaplane by Vincent Nicholl at Hamble in August 1920.

Production: Total of 207 Fairey IIIDs (including prototype) produced for the Fleet Air Arm: 50 (N9450-N9499) powered by Eagle VIII. 12 (N9567-N9578) powered by Lion II. 12 (N9630-N9641), first six with Eagle VIII, and later Lion IIB; remainder with Lion IIB from new. 62 (N9730-N9791) with Lion IIB. 36 (S1000-S1035) Mark II with interchangeable wheel/float undercarriage; Lion V. 35 (S1074-S1108 Mark III with interchangeable undercarriage, Lion VA; some long-range aircraft.

Summary of Service: Fairey IIIDs served with No 441 Flt aboard HMS *Hermes*, *Eagle* and *Argus* between July 1924 and May 1929; No 442 Flt, mostly in the Far East aboard HMS *Hermes* between October 1924 and October 1930; No 440 Flt between January 1925 and October 1927 (aboard HMS *Hermes* from September 1926); No 444 Flt aboard HM Seaplane Carrier *Vindictive* between January 1925 and September 1931; No 443 Flt between August 1925 and May 1928 (one section with HMS *Argus* in Far East); No 422 Flt (Fleet Spotter) aboard HMS *Argus* between January 1927 and May 1928; and No 481 Flt (later No 202 Sqn, RAF) at Kalafrana, Malta, between January 1929 and September 1930.

Blackburn T.2 Dart

At about the time that the first Blackburn Swift, N139, was successfully negotiating its early Service trials, the Air Ministry issued an amended production Specification, 3/20, largely based on the Blackburn prototype, and, although the other three Swift prototypes were by then in their early stages of construction, it was agreed that these

should be subjects of a new contract for adaptation and evaluation as likely 'production prototypes'. The three aircraft, N140-N142, had already undergone a number of design improvements at Blackburn's expense in the light of early flight trials with N139 with a view to offering the Swift for export, and this clearly gave the company a head start over any other manufacturer that might be inclined to tender to Specification 3/20.

The first machine, N140, now named

the Blackburn T.2 Dart, was powered by a Napier Lion IIB with a new radiator installation replacing the established 'frontal' type. The latter, highly efficient when maximum cooling was required, with shutters fully opened at low forward speeds, imposed considerable drag with the shutters partially closed. Much work was being done, both at the RAE and elsewhere, to arrive at a compromise solution which offered less drag at speeds which produced higher cooling air mass flow through partly

The seventh production Dart, N9542, powered by the Lion IIB, at Brough carrying the Mark VIII torpedo. (Photo: Blackburn Aircraft Ltd, Neg No A-2)

closed shutters. Blackburn, in collaboration with D Napier & Sons, had evolved such an installation whereby the radiator was inclined beneath the engine inside a faired compartment, with a series of 'roller blind' shutters which, when closed or partially closed, presented relatively smooth contours to the external air flow round the nose of the aircraft. Although of extremely ugly appearance, the new nose profile certainly reduced radiator drag spectacularly, and became a common feature of numerous single-engine aircraft in the early 1920s.

This 'chin' radiator was the most obvious feature that distinguished the T.2 Dart from the Swift N139. Others included the sweepback on the wings (found necessary in N139 after its first flight), and a shortening of the wing span by almost three feet. The new vertical tail surfaces, already tidied up for the export Swifts, also reappeared in the Dart.

The three Dart prototypes were first flown in October 1921, and January and February 1922 respectively, all being delivered to Martlesham Heath within days of their maiden flights. The last aircraft featured a simple stick-type control column in an effort to discard the time-honoured, but unwieldy aileron wheel, but when flown in comparison it was found that aileron stick forces were still far too heavy and the wheel control survived (until the introduction of differential trimming tabs some years later).

There is no doubt but that the considerable work already done by the time the Dart was flown in competitive evaluation with the Handley Page Hanley (see below), also designed to 3/20, placed the Blackburn aeroplane in an almost unassailable position, bearing in mind that the Air Ministry was, by that time, impatient to place production contracts for a torpedo bomber to replace the aging Cuckoo, which was expected to become extinct within a year. That is not to say that the Hanley did not run the Dart to a close verdict but, featuring the old frontal radiator, it returned a significantly poorer speed performance and, despite employing leading-edge slats, could not match the Dart's extraordinary landing speed of 38 mph — achieved with a wing loading in landing configu-

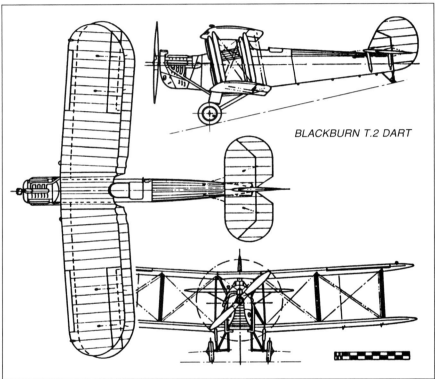

BLACKBURN T.2 DART

Type: Single-engine, single-seat, two-bay carrier-borne torpedo-bomber biplane.
Air Ministry Specification: 3/20
Manufacturer: The Blackburn Aeroplane & Motor Co Ltd., Leeds and Brough, Yorkshire.
Powerplant: One 450hp Napier Lion IIB (or 465hp Lion V) twelve-cylinder, water-cooled, broad-arrow, in-line engine driving two-blade propeller.
Dimensions: Span, 45ft 5¾in (folded, 17ft 6in); length, 35ft 4½in (40ft 2½in with floats); height, 12ft 11 in (17ft 0in with floats); wing area, 654 sq ft.
Weight: Tare, 3,599lb; all-up (with Mk VIII torpedo), 6,383lb.
Performance (with Mk VIII torpedo): Max speed, 107 mph at 1,000ft; initial rate of climb, 575 ft/min; service ceiling, 10,200ft; normal range, 300 miles.
Armament: One Mk VIII or IX 18in torpedo, or one 520lb bomb; no gun armament.
Prototypes: Three, N140-N142. N140 first flown in October 1921.
Production: Total of 114 built (excluding prototypes): 26 (N9536-N9561), 10 (N9620-N9629), 10 (N9687-N9696), 10 (N9714-N9723), 32 (9792-N9823), 10 (N9990-N9999), 6 (S1115-S1120), and 10 (S1129-S1138).
Summary of Service: Blackburn Darts served with No 460 (Fleet Torpedo) Flight, HMS *Eagle*, between April 1923 and November 1930; No 461 (Fleet Torpedo) Flt, HMS *Furious*, between April 1923 and January 1930; No 462 (Fleet Torpedo) Flt, HMS *Furious*, between May 1924 and March 1919; and Nos 463 and 464 (Fleet Torpedo Bomber) Flts, HMS *Courageous*, between September 1927 and April 1933, and then with Nos 810 (Fleet Torpedo Bomber) Squadron from April 1933 until November 1934.

ration of less that 6 lb/sq ft. (It was perhaps ironic that, in 1928, when Darts were being returned for refurbishing after some years in service, Handley Page leading-edge slats were fitted.)

Three days after the Dart was declared the winner, N142 was delivered to the Gosport Development Squadron in March, and a production order for 26 aircraft signed simultaneously. By simply diverting three export Swifts, suitably modified as Darts to Air Ministry requirements, the first production aircraft were delivered within two months, and completed their Service proving trials before the end of the year, enabling the newly formed No 460 (Fleet Torpedo) Flight, aboard HMS *Eagle*, and 461 (Fleet Torpedo) Flight, aboard HMS *Furious*, each to take delivery of six aircraft in April 1923. These two Flights replaced the RAF's No 210 Squadron, hitherto flying the Sopwith Cuckoo, and one year later, on 1 April 1924, the Fleet Air Arm formally came into being.

Two further production batches were ordered in 1923, enabling a third Dart Flight, No 462, to be equipped, embarking in HMS *Furious* in May 1924. A total of 42 Darts was ordered that year, the last 32 being powered by more powerful Lion V engines. And it was in one of these, N9804, that on 1 July 1926 Flt Lt (later Air Cdre, CB, AFC) George Harold Boyce of No 462 Flight made the first night landing on a carrier, *Furious*, at sea — a practice that was to become commonplace within four years.

The same year Darts, which had always possessed the capability, underwent Service trials to carry a 520lb bomb as an alternative to the Mark VIII torpedo. The need to do so had not previously arisen as the Fairey IIID was usually available in the aircraft carriers then in commission, and was able to deliver 112lb bombs — the heaviest stocked in the ships.

The last 16 Darts with interchangeable wheel or float undercarriages, ordered in 1926 and also powered by 465hp Lion Vs, were to be reclassified as torpedo-bombers and as such provided the equipment of the last two Dart Flights to be formed, Nos 463 and 464 (Torpedo-Bomber), in September 1927, embarking in the new aircraft carrier HMS *Courageous* (26,500 tons) when she commissioned on 21 February 1928. The carrier's first aircraft launch was marred when a Dart, being flown off for

Malta on 11 June, struck the ship's superstructure and fell into the sea, killing the pilot.

The Dart, like its contemporaries, the Fairey IIID and the Fairey Flycatcher fleet fighter, was extremely popular in service, and contributed immeasurably to those salad days of naval flying between the World Wars. None possessed what could be called scintillating performance in terms of speed or climb, yet all were outstanding when operating under difficult deck conditions, and performed their allotted fleet tasks with ease and efficiency. It has been said that each, performing its own class of fleet duty, was a 'pilot's aeroplane'. Darts served for over eleven years, the last being retired from No 810 Squadron (which in April 1933 was formed from Nos 463 and 464 Flights) at Gosport in November 1934, being replaced by Blackburn Baffins.

Handley Page H.P.19 Hanley

Immediately attracted by the torpedo-carrier Specification 3/20, when it was formally issued in 1920, Frederick Handley Page believed such an aircraft represented the ideal type of vehicle to benefit from his high-lift wing leading-edge slat system, the patent rights for which were shared with a German engineer, Gustav Victor Lachmann. This made possible increased controlla-

bility at low speeds — of considerable importance not only during deck landing but during the delivery of a torpedo.

Handley Page's chief designer, George Volkert, accordingly prepared a preliminary design tender, the H.P.19, to this Specification in the late summer of 1920, this attracting a contract for three prototypes, N143-N145. Volkert at this point, however, left Handley Page to join the British Air Mission to Japan, the final design of the H.P.19 becoming the responsibility of 'Star' Richards, the new chief designer.

The aircraft, named the Hanley, was similar in general configuration to the

Blackburn Swift, being powered by a 450hp Napier Lion IIB, with large frontal radiator, and divided-structure undercarriage. However, instead of providing a midships structural nucleus of great strength, as in the Swift, Richards chose a three-bay wing cellule, with the wing fold immediately outboard of the inner interplane struts, and the main undercarriage attachment points directly below the front struts. Full-span leading-edge slats were fitted on upper and lower wings, as were plain ailerons.

The first Hanley, N143, was flown at Cricklewood by Capt Arthur S Wilcockson on 3 January 1922, follow-

The third Hanley prototype, N145 (the so-called Mark III), carrying the Mark VIII torpedo. Note the full-span leading-edge wing slats. Despite its many shortcomings, the Hanley looked a thoroughly purposeful aeroplane, but disclosed a lack of understanding of the highly specialised requirements of naval aeroplanes. (Photo: Handley Page Ltd.)

ed by N144 and N145 during the next eleven weeks. N143 reached Martlesham Heath on 11 March, just five days *after* the Blackburn Dart had been declared the successful 3/20 contender, and two days after a production contract had been awarded to Blackburn.

Nevertheless, N143 commenced initial performance trials, only to suffer damage to the lower wing and undercarriage during April; it was returned to Cricklewood for repair. N144 had been extensively damaged on 17 March when it somersaulted during a landing, leaving N145 to continue the trials.

Comparison with the Blackburn aircraft showed the Hanley to be inferior not only in most aspects of performance but, more seriously, in low speed handling. Furthermore, the view from the cockpit was generally poor — a damning indictment of a deck-landing aeroplane.

N143 was rebuilt with a number of cosmetic alterations to the airframe in efforts to reduce drag, wasting effort — when time was important — on such minor modifications as placing the ele-

vator control cables inside the rear fuselage, while no attempt was made to eliminate the hugh frontal radiator. The aircraft was redesignated the Hanley Mark II and re-submitted to Martlesham in April and, although it now came closer to matching the Dart's performance, its handling was still criticised, this time in respect of the high nose-up attitude adopted by the aircraft with the wing slots open, again a dangerous feature of a deck-landing aeroplane.

There was just time to re-submit N145 for Service trials under Specification 32/22, issued to seek an improved

replacement for the Dart in two or three years' time but, even though some aspects of the Hanley's ground handling had been improved, the Dart was still regarded as generally superior and, as has already been recorded, continued to be ordered in quantity for the next three years — and survived in service until 1934.

Although Handley Page probably possessed unmatched experience in the aerodynamics associated with wing slats, the particular characteristics of the deck-landing aeroplane had been found to demand considerable further research, while in other areas, attention to detail design in the Hanley showed the aircraft in a poor light when assessed by the Service. And, despite shortage of work in his factory, Frederick Handley Page was unable to obtain permission to offer the Hanley for export.

Type: Single-engine, single-seat, three-bay biplane torpedo-carrying biplane.
Air Ministry Specifications: 3/20 and 32/22
Manufacturer: Handley Page Ltd, Cricklewood, London.
Powerplant: One 450hp Napier Lion IIB twelve-cylinder, water-cooled, broad-arrow, in-line engine driving two-blade propeller.
Dimensions: Span, 46ft 0in; length, 33ft 4in; wing area, 562 sq ft.
Weight: All-up (with Mark VIII torpedo), 6,444lb.
Performance (Mark III): Max speed, 116 mph at sea level; landing speed, 55 mph.
Armament: One Mark VIII 18in torpedo; no gun armament and no provision to carry bombs.
Prototypes: Three, N143-N145. N143 flown by Capt Arthur Wilcockson at Cricklewood on 3 January 1922. No production.

Avro Type 549 Aldershot

By mid-1920, with the future of the Dragonfly engine in doubt and obvious difficulties being experienced in ensuring a replacement for the D.H.10 medium bomber, the Air Ministry hit on the idea of seeking a single-engine aircraft, capable of operating both as a medium and heavy bomber, powered by the Rolls-Royce Condor, expected to

deliver some 600hp. At that time the heaviest bomb extant was the 1,800lb SN weapon and the initial idea was that the new aircraft should carry one such weapon externally, and that a range of 500 miles should be sought.

However, by the time Specification 2/20, effectively a rewrite of the D of R Requirement Type IVB, was promulgated in November 1920, the decision had been taken not to continue production of the SN bomb, and with stocks almost exhausted, the bomb load was specified as being four 550lb weapons, carried externally. Both Chadwick, at

A V Roe, and de Havilland had pointed to the difficulty of loading these weapons into an internal bomb compartment in a single-engine aircraft, bearing in mind that these bombs were usually suspended vertically nose-up, and the load requirement was changed yet again to comprise eight 250lb bombs, carried internally. A crew of between three and five members was recommended, depending on the feasibility of combining in-flight duties.

Both the above companies tendered design proposals, A V Roe securing a contract for two prototypes, J6852 and

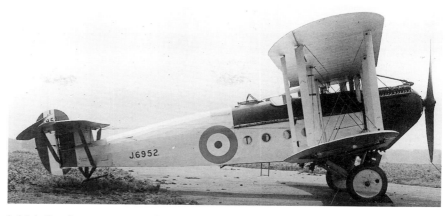

The Avro Aldershot III, J6952, the first such aircraft delivered to No 99 Squadron, after being sent to Martlesham Heath to complete the Service trials in 1924. It was later fitted with experimental metal wings. (Photo: Air Ministry, A&AEE, Neg No 4199)

J6853, on 2 December 1920. The Type 549 (shortly named the Aldershot) was to be the first Avro to make extensive use of metal construction, the primary fuselage structure being of steel, with a crew compartment and secondary structure of birch ply. The unstaggered wings were built on two spruce mainspars and Warren girder ribs and steel drag struts and faired interplane struts. The wings were initially unswept and were made to fold immediately outboard of the inner interplane struts. 'Park-bench' balanced ailerons on the upper wings were interconnected by cable to unbalanced ailerons on the lower wings.

Provision was made for a four-man crew, the pilot occupying a two-seat cockpit with dual controls, the seat on the starboard side being occupied when necessary by the navigator. The latter, when engaged in bomb aiming, occupied a seat at the forward end of the cabin (which was provided with four large circular windows on each side). A single synchronized Vickers machine gun was provided for on the nose of the aircraft, but was seldom fitted, and Lewis guns were mounted in a ventral position and on a Scarff ring on the midships gunner's cockpit immediately behind the pilot. Crew access was by an external ladder on the port side of the fuselage, and thence by a ladder inside the cabin. Forward of the cabin was located the bomb bay, above which was the 210-gallon fuel tank. A fire-proof bulkhead separated the engine from the fuel tank bay.

The prototype originally featured separate undercarriage assemblies, each a braced V-strut structure carrying a single large wheel, sprung with bungee straps. Production aircraft were fitted with an improved and strengthened structure comprising pairs of pyramidal V-struts, an oleo leg containing multiple rubber pads to absorb the landing shock, and a divided swing-axle for each wheel.

J6852, with an overall length of about 39 feet and a long dorsal fin, was first flown early in October 1921 at Hamble by H J L ('Bert') Hinkler, Avro's chief test pilot, and was delivered to Martlesham Heath on 2 January 1922 for

initial Service assessment. It was evidently found to be seriously lacking in directional control and, in the course of tunnel tests (possibly at Farnborough) it was discovered that airflow separation over the rear of the short fuselage rendered the rudder almost useless. After the dorsal fin was shortened to no more than a tiny surface occupying the space between the fuselage and the high-set tailplane, and was found to be of no benefit, the fuselage was rebuilt, extended by some five feet — drastic major surgery that was found to rectify the trouble.

In this form, J6852 appeared at the RAF Display at Hendon on 24 June 1922 and, flown by Fg Off Charles Edwin Horrex, won the Handicap Race at a speed of 116 mph. In July the second aircraft, J6853, was flown with many of the modifications introduced in J6852.

The eventual ability of the prototype to satisfy the A & AEE led to production orders for three Type 549s (J6942-J6944) and twelve Type 549B Aldershot Mark IIIs (J6945-J6956) being signed on 26 January 1923 — although it is not known how the two versions differed. Continuing radiator and other trials at Farnborough and Martlesham Heath led to a number of alterations, including the introduction of strut-interconnection between upper and lower ailerons

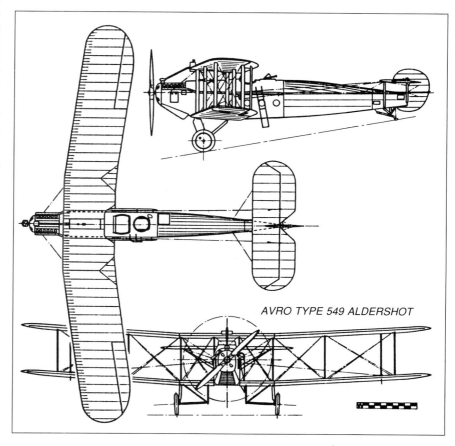

AVRO TYPE 549 ALDERSHOT

The original Aldershot prototype, J6852, towards the end of its eventful life, being flown in 1927 with the 850hp Beardmore Typhoon slow-revving engine whose long exhaust pipes can be seen extending below it; note that the four-wheel undercarriage, fitted while previously flying with the Napier Cub, has been removed and replaced by the standard Aldershot two-wheel undercarriage. (Photo: A J Jackson Collection)

(the 'park-benches' being removed), these modifications delaying the first Service delivery until 2 June 1924, when J6952 was taken on charge by No 99 (Bomber) Squadron at Bircham Newton. After a month's flying, this aircraft was sent to Martlesham to take over further Service trials, but four further Aldershots were delivered to No 99 Squadron in July, and seven in August.

Equipping only this one Squadron, Aldershots gave reliable, if undramatic service for less than two years, not one aircraft being lost during this period. The greater part of their activities was confined to night flying, punctuated by the occasional daylight air exercise. With the introduction of the Handley Page Hyderabad, the eleven Aldershots were disposed of to the Home Aircraft Depot in April 1926. One of the Squadron aircraft was flown temporarily by the Night Flying Flight at Biggin Hill.

Meanwhile the first prototype, J6852, had embarked on an interesting career as an engine test vehicle, beginning in December 1922. On return to Hamble it had been fitted with one of the six prototype 1,000hp Napier Cub engines purchased by the Air Ministry at a price of £10,000 each. This 16-cylinder, X-type, water-cooled in-line engine weighed 2,450lb driving a four-blade propeller, and required the Aldershot (termed the Mark II) to be extensively strengthened, the modifications including the introduction of four mainwheels, each pair with its own axle and two oleo struts. It was first flown on 15 December 1922.

Flight trials with this engine contin-

ued with Napiers and the RAE until J6852 returned to Hamble at the end of 1924, when it became the turn of another large experimental engine to be flight tested, this time the extraordinary 850hp Beardmore Typhoon inverted six-cylinder, water-cooled, in-line, slow-revving engine, the Aldershot now becoming the Type 549C Mark IV. Not flown until 10 January 1927 the aeroplane remained at Hamble for five months before being delivered to Farnborough for the remainder of that year.

Another trial installation that should be mentioned was one of considerable importance to A V Roe involving the fitting of metal wings to the Aldershot III, J6952, after its brief stay with No 99 Squadron and completion of Service trials at Martlesham in July 1924. The wings themselves were introduced in March 1925 (the aircraft being termed the Type 549M), and J6952 underwent prolonged tests at Farnborough until mid-1927, the various reports issued by the RAE being of great value to Chadwick's design staff in their evolution of subsequent all-metal aircraft.

Although the Aldershot gave unblemished service with but a single squadron, the Air Ministry had already lost faith in the potential of large single-engine bombers even before the Avro aircraft had joined that squadron, most Establishment authorities favouring at least two engines, principally on account of operational flexibility and safety.

Type: Single-engine, four-crew, three-bay biplane night medium/heavy bomber.
Air Ministry Specification: 2/20 (previously D of R Type IVB)
Manufacturer: A V Roe & Co Ltd, Manchester, and Hamble, Hampshire.
Powerplant: Prototypes. One 550hp Condor IB. Production (Mk III). One 650hp Rolls-Royce Condor III twelve-cylinder, water-cooled, in-line engine driving two-blade propeller. Experimental: 1,000hp Napier Cub sixteen-cylinder engine; 850hp Beardmore Typhoon inverted six-cylinder engine.
Structure: Metal fuselage primary structure with plywood cabin, and wooden wings and tail with steel tubular fittings. Folding wings.
Dimensions: Span, 68ft 0in; length, 45ft 0in; height, 15ft 3in; wing area, 1,064 sq ft.
Weights: (Mark III). Tare, 6,310lb; all-up, 10,950lb.
Performance: Max speed, 110 mph at sea level; ceiling, 14,500ft; normal range, 625 miles.
Armament: Bomb load, either up to four 520lb bombs carried externally or eight 250lb bombs carried internally; gun armament of one 0.303in synchronized Vickers machine gun on fuselage forward of cockpit; one 0.303in Lewis gun with Scarff ring on dorsal midships gunner's cockpit, and one Lewis gun mounted in ventral gunner's position.
Prototypes: Two, J6852 and J6953. J6852 first flown by H J L Hinkler at Hamble early in October 1921.
Production: Total of fifteen Aldershots were built: 3 Type 549 Aldershots, J6942-J6944, and 12 Type 549B Aldershot IIIs, J6945-J6956.
Summary of Service: Aldershots served with No 99 (Bomber) Squadron at Bircham Newton, Norfolk, from June 1924 until April 1926. One aircraft flew trials with the Night Flying Flight during 1925.

---

de Havilland D.H.27 Derby

Also designed to Air Ministry Specification 2/20, which had brought forth the

Avro Aldershot, the single-engine D.H.27 medium/heavy bomber was the new de Havilland company's first essay in military aeroplanes (though not the first aircraft ordered by the Air Ministry — the D.H.29 Doncaster long-range research aircraft had been ordered on 7 March 1921).

The D.H.27 Derby, of which two prototypes, J6894 and J6895, came to be built, was the subject of a contract signed on 23 May 1921 and, like the Aldershot, was to be powered by a Rolls-Royce Condor. There, however, any similarity to the Avro aircraft ended. Construction of the Derby was of wood throughout, the long rectangular-section fuselage being a plywood-covered spruce box girder. The fabric-covered, two-bay, parallel-chord wings were each built on two spruce main spars, being made to fold immediately outboard of the inner interplane struts. There were no centresection wing struts, the wing centresection being attached to a large streamlined cabane superstructure containing the 212-gallon fuel tank.

Locating this fuel tank outside the confines of the fuselage did not, however, permit the bomb load to be accommodated internally, and the crew cabin occupied the interior of the fuselage from immediately aft of the engine bulkhead to a point about eight feet aft of the wings, and the midships gunner, situated well aft, gained access to the cabin through a hatch in its rear frame. The three-man crew therefore comprised pilot, navigator (who could also occupy the right-hand seat in the pilot's cockpit, located beneath the upper wing leading edge), and a single gunner. As far as is known, there was no provision for front or ventral guns.

The Derby's structural weight was a good deal greater than that of the Aldershot (by about 800 pounds), reflecting the use of wood throughout, and the proposed bomb load of four 520lb bombs would have reduced the aircraft's performance disproportionately. The undercarriage was suitably sturdy with separated swing-axle units, each with a large oleo leg and V-struts supporting a single wheel.

The first prototype, J6894, was flown at Stag Lane on 13 October 1922, a year after the first Aldershot. It spent four months at Martlesham Heath after delivery for acceptance trials on 9 November. A brief return to Stag Lane in April 1923 was followed by delivery to Grain for loading tests, but in January 1924 it was broken up for spares at Farnborough.

J6895 was first flown on 22 March 1923, only to be placed in storage at Northolt two months later, and moved on to Kenley the following January. A tentative proposal was made to flight test the 850hp Beardmore Typhoon engine in this Derby but, as the Aldershot was considered more suitable, J6895 was written off Air Ministry charge in March 1924.

In comparison with the Avro aircraft,

Type: Single-engine, three-crew, two-bay biplane medium/heavy bomber.
Air Ministry Specification: 2/20
Manufacturer: The de Havilland Aircraft Co Ltd, Stag Lane Aerodrome, Edgware, Middlesex
Powerplant: One 650hp Rolls-Royce Condor III 12-cylinder, water-cooled, in-line engine driving four-blade propeller.
Structure: Wooden construction throughout, with folding wings.
Dimensions: Span, 64ft 6in; length, 47ft 4in; height, 16ft 10in; wing area, 1,120 sq ft.
Weights: Tare, 6,737lb; all-up, 11,545lb.
Performance: Max speed, 105 mph at sea level; ceiling, 12,800ft; normal range, 550 miles.
Armament: Bomb load of up to four 550lb bombs carried externally; gun armament of one 0.303in Lewis gun with Scarff ring on midships gunner's cockpit.
Prototypes: Two, J6894 and J6895, first flown at Stag Lane on 13 October 1922 and 22 March 1923 respectively. No production.

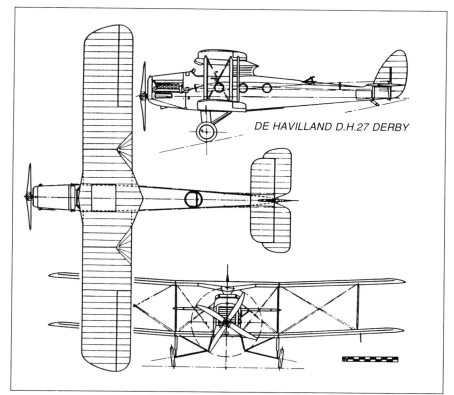

DE HAVILLAND D.H.27 DERBY

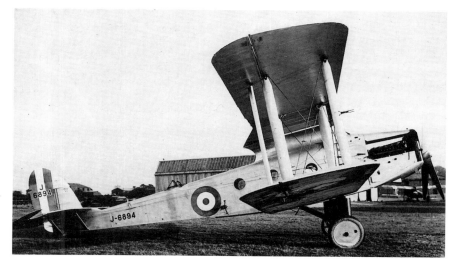

The first de Havilland D.H.27 Derby, J6894, at Stag Lane, probably at about the time of its first flight. Obscured by the front wing struts is the pilot's cockpit, close behind the engine. (Photo: The de Havilland Aircraft Co Ltd, Neg Ref No 9375)

the Derby was logically a non-starter. The Condor III clearly developed sufficient power to enable an aircraft of its size to lift a worthwhile warload yet, with a structure weight some 800lb greater, the aircraft would be labouring, and such design deficiencies as inferior defensive gun armament, external bomb carriage and reliance on wooden construction throughout, clearly placed the D.H.27 at a severe disadvantage. Unfortunately no comparative handling reports have been traced, so no comment can be passed on this aspect. Suffice to remark that, characteristic of the Derby's somewhat dated design approach was the retention of a large frontal radiator — a relic that could have been discarded, bearing in mind that the Aldershot, with its improved 'chin' radiator, had flown a whole year earlier.

Boulton & Paul P.15 Bolton

Determined to pursue the apparently successful formula of his Bourges twin-engine light bomber, John North took what was seen as an important step for his company in designing an all-metal derivative; this design, the P.15 Bolton, attracted sufficient interest at the Air Ministry to earn a contract for a single experimental prototype, J6584, on 7 July 1920 under requirements set out in Specification 4/20, apparently formulated around North's proposals.

At the time this prototype was approaching completion, the Boulton & Paul Bourges F2905, with Napier Lion engines, was at Farnborough taking part in a trials programme to investigate the optimum radiator configuration for this engine, and early indications suggested that a relatively small radiator would suffice provided that unrestricted airflow was allowed to pass through its matrices, even though this would probably impose a drag penalty. North, therefore, in selecting these engines once more for the Bolton, decided to dispense with most of the upper nacelle panels and continue with the lower wing installation, and to provide smaller radiators.

The fuselage was of steel tubular construction, a box girder being fabric-covered over most of its length, but with ply and light alloy panels providing upper decking sections over the front half. The wings were of orthodox two-spar configuration, the upper wing being of considerably greater chord than the lower. North produced a curious vertical tail design, the deep rudder with horn balance being hinged to a fin that extended above and below the fuselage. Forward of the fin was a narrow hinged

The Bolton, while achieving little in the advance of bomber design, set its manufacturer firmly on the path of metal aircraft manufacture. (Photo: Boulton Paul Aircraft Ltd, Ref No 027)

trimming surface, adjustable by a handwheel in the pilot's cockpit. Unlike the majority of such tabs, the Bolton's tail trimmer operated independently of the rudder.

The other curious feature (by then an anachronism) of the Bolton was the inclusion of a forward, central landing wheel carried by a structure extending forward from the bottom of the oleo legs. It must be assumed that this was primarily intended to prevent the aircraft from nosing over during landing, though it may have been considered necessary when landing with the cg position at its forward limit. In any case it is likely to have interfered with the positioning of the bomb load although, despite being allowed for in the Specification, a war load was not uppermost in the designer's mind.

J6584 was first flown in November 1922 and delivered to Martlesham Heath the following month for preliminary handling assessment. It seems likely, however, that the Bolton's directional trimming system did not meet with approval, for the aircraft was returned to Norwich in June 1923 where entirely new vertical surfaces were fitted, an enlarged fin replacing the former fin and trimming surface. Little is known of J6584's subsequent life, except that it returned to the A & AEE in May 1924 for performance trials, remaining there until June the next year.

Type: Twin-engine, three-crew, three-bay experimental bomber biplane.
Air Ministry Specification: 4/20
Manufacturer: Boulton and Paul Ltd, Riverside, Norwich, Norfolk.
Powerplant: Two 450hp Napier Lion II twelve-cylinder water-cooled in-line engines driving four-blade propellers.
Structure: All-metal. Steel-tubular box-girder fuselage, with fabric, ply and sheet metal covering.
Dimensions: Span, 62ft 6in.
Weight: All-up, 9,500lb.
Performance: Records not traced.
Armament: Intended provision for up to four 230lb bombs; two Lewis guns with Scarff rings on nose and midships gunners' cockpits.
Prototype: One, J6584, first flown at Norwich in November 1922. No production.

Vickers Types 57 to 139 Virginia

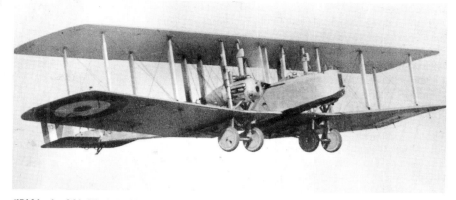

J7131, the fifth Virginia III, with No 7 Squadron during Service Trials at Bircham Newton in 1924. After serving as a Mark VII and as the prototype Mk IX, it finally served as a Mark X, making its last flight on 20 May 1940. (Photo: RAF Museum, Neg No P003282)

To many who have recollections of the Royal Air Force between the World Wars, the majestic Virginia[1] epitomised the British heavy bomber, seemingly destined to remain in service for ever. Indeed, the fact that the prototype first flew in 1922 and the last example was withdrawn from Bomber Command's first line squadrons in February 1938 was not only a tribute to the aeroplane's extraordinary adaptability in a period of accelerating technological advance but also an ironic commentary upon successive Air Staffs' vacillating attitudes towards the heavy bomber. As will be shown, the Virginia underwent continuous development — and improvement — between 1923 and 1929 during the patronage of Sir Hugh Trenchard, but thereafter it remained scarcely altered as the Air Staff turned its attention to other classes of operational aircraft, not least the interceptor fighter. Yet during Trenchard's tenure of high office only 76 Virginias were ordered for production, and just three squadrons were equipped with the aircraft. The onset of the Depression brought about reduced expenditure on new aircraft, so that the progressive modification (often involving extensive rebuilding) seemed a convenient expedient and, as a result, 52 of the veteran bombers were rebuilt and reintroduced into service, equipping a total of ten squadrons during the mid- and late-1930s

Nor was the Virginia particularly outstanding in any respect at any time, being extremely slow, often excessively tiring to fly and, only in its ultimate form capable of carrying a bomb load of 3,000 pounds at a speed of 81 mph. At no time during its period of service could it reach a target more than 50 miles inside Germany, carrying anything but the smallest bomb load from its bases in England. Yet this was the aircraft which, a dozen years after its maiden flight, was to become one of the RAF's principal heavy bombers during the years of 're-armament' against a fast-expanding,

[1] Contrary to speculation widely expressed elsewhere, the name Virginia was selected by Vickers in reference to the small town of Virginia Water, half a dozen miles from the Weybridge factory, and the home of several members of the Vickers management.

modern *Luftwaffe*.

Designed under the leadership of Reginald Kirshaw Pierson[2] to the Air Ministry's D of R Type 4A Specification, which set out the parameters of a Vickers Vimy replacement, the Vickers Type 57 Virginia was, in effect, a Vimy

[2] Later appointed CBE, 'Rex' Pierson (1891-1948) was Vickers' chief designer from 1917 until 1948, being one of the very few long-serving and widely respected senior aircraft designers who was also a qualified pilot, having been awarded the RAeC Pilot's Certificate No 660 on 24 October 1913 at Brooklands on a Vickers monoplane.

with enlarged wings and powered by a pair of 450hp Napier Lion engines. Fundamental to the official Requirement was an ability to carry a pair of 550lb RL bombs over a distance of 1,200 miles at a speed of 95 mph at a height of 10,000 feet. (This performance was, however, never to be achieved by the Virginia.)

There is little doubt that the origins of this Specification (later rewritten as 1/21) lay in the epic long-distance flights made by the Vimy during 1919 which so dramatically demonstrated the potential of this aircraft and which, if provided

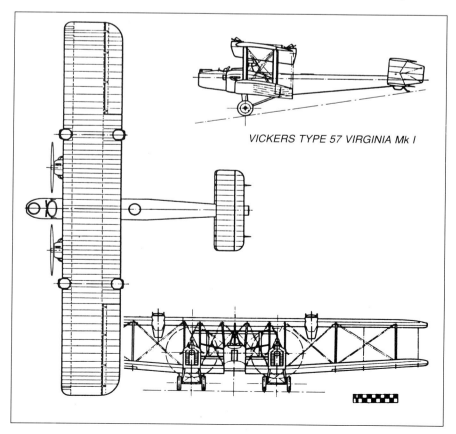

VICKERS TYPE 57 VIRGINIA Mk I

with greater power and lift, could be transformed into an excellent long-range heavy bomber by the time that Treasury appropriations for the Services were able to bear the cost of its production.

A draft order for two prototypes of Pierson's aircraft, J6856 and J6857, was sent to Vickers in January 1921 and signed on 17 March, these two aeroplanes costing £13,250 each (of which £4,100 were for its two Lion engines). The first was flown by Capt Stan Cockerell AFC, Vickers' chief test pilot, at Brooklands on 24 November 1922, followed by the second in July the next year.

Retrospectively referred to as the Virginia Mark I and Mark II, these two prototypes were built predominantly of wood, the wings being parallel chord without sweepback or stagger, only the lower wing being rigged with dihedral outboard of the engines. After J6856's maiden flight, Cockerell complained that the rudders provided scarcely any directional control at all so that, before the next flights, these were considerably lengthened, to extend well aft of the elevators, but they now proved almost impossible to move, so heavy were the flight loads. Despite these problems, as well as persistent vibration of the starboard engine, the aircraft successfully negotiated its manufacturers' trials and full-load tests. As originally installed, the two Lion engines were fully cowled in flat-sided nacelles and large frontal radiators with adjustable shutters, and these were probably largely responsible for the disappointing returns recording the initial performance measurements; after all, there were several large bombers of wartime vintage easily capable of matching the early Virginia's top speed of 97 mph without warload. Nor, for that matter, was the bomb load, comprising nine 112lb bombs, even comparable with the loads being carried by the so-called medium bombers of the day.

As no provision had been made for rear defence, Vickers was asked to design gunners' cockpits in the upper wing in order to provide protection in the upper hemisphere, and in June 1923 J6856 re-appeared with two large nacelles built into the underside of the upper wing, each incorporating a gunner's cockpit at the forward and rear end, each provided with a Scarff ring, a modification that added 1,033lb to the aircraft's tare weight. These gunner's stations were referred to as 'fighting

tops', and were inaccessible from the fuselage; the gunner's position in the nose of the fuselage was also without access to and from the pilot's cockpit.

The second prototype, J6857, first appeared with Lion II engines raised about 18 inches clear of the top surface of the lower wings, being now much more efficiently cowled in circular-section nacelles with semi-circular, shuttered Lamblin-type radiators situated between the undercarriage oleo legs below the wings. The nose of the aircraft was lengthened by about two feet in order to allow more leg-room for the nose gunner lying prone while aiming the bombs; even so, one of the 112lb bombs had to be discarded. To relieve the pilot of the tiring effort needed to fly the aircraft, the rear fuselage was hinged so that, by means of a handwheel in his cockpit, the pilot could alter the angle of incidence of the entire tail unit as a means of trimming the aircraft to fly straight and level with the minimum effort.

Martlesham and Service trials with the 'fighting tops' continued but, while the A & AEE expressed general satisfaction, it was felt that the nacelles imposed a significant drag penalty, and it was thought likely that in squadron service the gunners would comment adversely on their complete isolation, particularly at night. Vickers was therefore instructed

to produce single-cockpit fairings extending aft of the wing trailing edge, with access through a circular aperture in the upper wing centresection, and a 'crawlway' with handrails outboard to the nacelles.

The first production aircraft to be ordered were two fitted with dual controls, J6992 and J6993, being defined in Specification 1/21, a contract having been signed on 23 October 1922, even before the first prototype had flown. These two aircraft were first flown in April 1924, the first being delivered to No 7 (Bomber) Squadron at Bircham Newton the next month for exhaustive Service trials. These, and the next four, J7129-J7132 (ordered on 10 July 1923, but without dual controls) were designated Type 79 Virginia Mk IIIs, and all had been completed by July 1924. (On 28 June J6993 had made its public debut, appearing as 'No 7' in the New Types Park at the annual Hendon Display.)

By the end of July, one Flight of No 7 Squadron had received five Virginia IIIs, and these were joined by the Mk II, J6857, in September, having completed night trials with the Night Flying Flight, and for the next seven months this Squadron completed the bomber's main Service Trials. Although these trials were not completed until May 1925, all

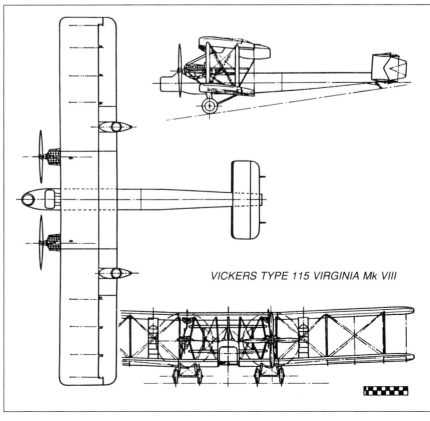

VICKERS TYPE 115 VIRGINIA Mk VIII

J7130 was one of the original Virginia IIIs before being progressively modified as a Mark VII and, as shown here, a Mark X, experimentally fitted with a pair of 622hp Bristol Pegasus IIM3 radial engines in 1933. This was the Virginia which later took part in air defence trials to establish the nature of a large aircraft's signal return on early coastal radar screens in 1936 while on the strength of the A & AEE at Martlesham Heath. (Photo: Air Ministry, RTP Neg No 7373C)

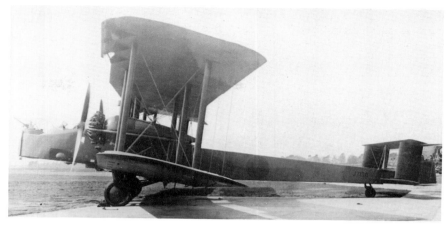

the early indications were that, despite its disappointing performance, the Virginia was a sturdy and reliable aeroplane, and in December 1924 it was decided to go ahead with deliveries for operational duties.

Just how sturdy the bomber was, had already been demonstrated when J6857, after less than a month with No 7 Squadron suffered an engine failure in flight and, while attempting a forced landing at Bishop's Stortford, the pilot hit a tree on the approach and crashed. The aircraft was repaired and was flying again within a year. (Records show that, between 1924 and 1930, the 76 Virginias manufactured during that period — Mks I to IX — between them suffered 81 flying accidents, but in 53 instances the aircraft were salvaged, repaired or rebuilt, and returned to flying duties.)

A pair of Virginias, J7274 and J7275, referred to as Type 99 Mk IVs and ordered in March 1924, differed from the Mark III in being equipped with external bomb racks to enable a pair of 230lb RL bombs to be carried, in addition to the internal 112-pounders. They were also fitted with improved night flying equipment. The former Virginia featured an additional, central rudder in a further effort to improve the directional control. After being reported on favourably by Vickers' newly-appointed 16-stone chief test pilot, Flt Lt E R C ('Tiny') Scholefield, J7274 was delivered for brief Service trials with No 9 Squadron at Manston in September.

It was probably these various Service trials that have led to conflicting accounts as to the first operational Virginia squadron. No 58 (Bomber) Squadron was the first to receive a full complement of Virginias, thirteen aircraft being received by March 1925 — when the last of the Squadron's Vimys was flown away. At about this time command of the Squadron passed to a 33-year-old Squadron Leader, Arthur Travers Harris — later Marshal of the Royal Air Force Sir Arthur, BT, GCB, OBE, AFC, and C-in-C Bomber Command from 1942-45.

One of his flight commanders at that time was Flt Lt Robert Henry Magnus Spencer Saundby (later Air Marshal Sir Robert, KCB, KBE, MC, DFC, AFC, and Senior Air Staff Officer at Bomber Command, and Sir Arthur Harris' Deputy during the Second World War.)

No 58 Squadron was equipped with Type 100 Virginia Mk Vs, a version that introduced the central rudder into production and was produced to a revised Specification, 12/24 — which embraced all Virginias built during the next five years. It was finished overall in the newly-standardised Nivo dark green dope scheme and carried 'low visibility' roundels as a gesture to night camouflage. Production of the 22 Mark Vs was contracted in 1924, sufficient to bring No 9 Squadron up to full strength during 1925 as the second Virginia unit after completion of the Service trials.

Production continued uninterrupted at Weybridge as the Type 108 Virginia VI followed the Mark V, a total of 25 being built in two batches and completed before the end of 1925. To these were added six of the former Mark Vs, now modified to Mark VI standard. These 31 aircraft commenced delivery to all three squadrons (Nos 7, 9 and 58) so that, for the first time all could be said to be flying a standard version. The distinguishing feature of the Mark VI was a change in the wing dihedral rigging, introduced to counter criticism of the wing folding process, equal dihedral of two and a half degrees being provided on both upper and lower wings.

It was during this period, as the squadrons began flying realistic exercises over long cross-country routes, often under simulated attack by RAF interceptor fighters, and making practice bombing flights over the coastal ranges, that serious and orchestrated criticism of the Virginia's handling

qualities gained currency. In practice, the aircraft could *not* be flown hands-off with anything but the lightest load. The trimming tail proved useless in compensating for different throttle settings — as would be required during formation flying — while laterally the Virginia proved over-stable, demanding constant and coarse use of the ailerons in any but the calmest weather conditions. Directionally the aircraft tended to 'hunt' continuously, for which no adequate trimming device had been provided. Thus to merely keep the bomber on an even keel imposed an enormous physical workload on the pilot, while giving the other crew members a thoroughly uncomfortable ride. Night flying was therefore somewhat hazardous for the less experienced pilot.

To overcome these complaints, which had resulted from numerous weight and cg alterations (principally caused by the tail-hinge, a newly introduced downward-firing Lewis gun and the increased bomb load), the Type 112 Mark VII Virginia incorporated wings that were swept back six degrees to reposition the cg at 0.332 mean chord, thereby greatly improving the longitudical stability. Frise ailerons, also introduced, rectified the lateral stability and control.

While these remedies transformed the Virginia, and were universally welcomed on the squadrons when Mark VIIs arrived early in 1927, the Royal Aircraft Establishment began experimenting with the first automatic pilot designed for a large aircraft in J7424 (this being joined during the next six years by J7131, J7275, J7434 and J7551; see table at the end of this entry. By the time the Virginia X was entering production an exceptionally reliable three-channel autopilot was being manufactured.)

While Virginia VIIs were being issued

An early Virginia X, J7711 (formerly a Mk VI, VII and IX), serving with No 9 (Bomber) Squadron at Manston in 1930. Note the prominent automatic wing slats which automatically closed at an airspeed above 85 mph. This aircraft was fitted with Chrysler wheel brakes, and features light bomb racks under the nose. (Photo: Vickers Ltd.)

to No 7 Squadron, which moved from Bircham Newton to Worthy Down on 7 April, command of the Squadron passed to a 33-year old Squadron Leader, Charles Frederick Algernon Portal (later Marshal of the Royal Air Force Viscount Portal of Hungerford, KG, GCB, OM, DSO, MC, and Chief of the Air Staff from 1940 until 1946), and it was under this officer's leadership that No 7 won the first annual Laurence Minot trophy — awarded for the best individual crew performance (pilot and bomb aimer). In both 1927 and 1928 Portal's name was inscribed on the trophy, and No 7 Squadron ultimately took the prize seven times between 1927 and 1935 (and shared it with No 58 Squadron in 1934). In every instance the winners were flying Virginias.

One of the aircraft being flown by No 7 Squadron in 1927 was the original prototype, J6856, now converted to Mark VII standard, but still retaining the two-position 'fighting tops'. By then, however, the scheme had attracted almost universal dislike, and it was probably Portal's report, expressing his objections, that finally brought about its end.

Between its appearance as a Mark III and as a Mark VII, J6856 had undergone one other 'conversion'. This had been effected during 1925 when, powered by 650hp Rolls-Royce Condor III engines (and still equipped with 'fighting tops'), it had been intended as the prototype of a new version, the Virginia VIII, and featured a dihedral tailplane, this being intended to alleviate the Virginia's then-characteristic 'hunting' tendencies; in fact, this innovation proved wholly ineffective. The search for an alternative powerplant to the venerable Lion involved several engines, other than the Condor, and included the Bristol Jupiter and Pegasus and Armstrong Siddeley Jaguar, all of which were flown in various Virginias; in the

event, the Air Ministry opted to retain the Lion, albeit in more powerful form. The Mark VIII Virginia did not enter production.

The penultimate version of the bomber was the Type 128 Mark IX, introduced following the final demise of the 'fighting tops'. Air exercises had emphasised the vulnerability of the Virginia to fighter attack from above and the rear, accentuated by the bomber's ponderous rate of movement to such an extent that there was scarcely a British fighter in service during the late 1920s that did not possess a speed margin over the Virginia of at least 50 mph at all heights up to 10,000 feet — the Virginia's effective ceiling with a bomb load.

Concerned that the addition of a new gun position in the extreme tail would accentuate the Virginia's critical longitudinal instability, particularly with respect to stall recovery, Vickers had been reluctant to suggest adding a tail gunner; in any case, the Air Ministry had not hitherto favoured tail gun positions in bombers owing to the obvious discomfort suffered by their occupants. However, the RAE was beginning to work to improve the heating of crew members' clothing (trials in which Virginia J7131 would later participate), so that Vickers set about a major re-design of the bomber to introduce the tail gunner's station.

J7131, formerly a Mark III and in 1927 appearing as a Mark VII, was selected as the prototype Mark IX. The entire tail unit was changed to include longer tailplanes with partially balanced elevators, and the fins and rudders set further apart. To balance the weight of the rear gunner, cockpit, Scarff ring, Lewis gun and ammunition, the fuselage nose was lengthened by some three feet, and the wireless bay moved forward. Other refinements included the introduction of wheel brakes, Palmer, Chrys-

ler, Dunlop and Ferodo systems all being evaluated; attempts were made to reduced the noise in the cockpits, and at one time a Virginia was flown with a cockpit canopy — though this was not adopted in production. Considerable work was done with automatic wing slots, although a fully satisfactory design was not achieved until 1930, so most Virginias had to await their next visit to the factory for their periodic upgrading or rebuilding before the modification could be introduced retrospectively.

1927 also saw the draft issue of a new heavy bomber Specification, this time intended to attract designs for an aircraft to replace both the Vickers Virginia and the Handley Page Hinaidi, probably as soon as 1932. This Specification, B.19/27, attracted more than a dozen design tenders, including an improved version of the Virginia itself (powered by Bristol Pegasus engines). Such, however, was the rapid advance made in fighter design from 1930 onwards, that the bomber Specification was re-written several times and it became obvious that only an entirely new aircraft would suffice.

The delay encouraged Vickers to submit a radical redesign of the basic Virginia, embodying metal construction throughout, a project that had been studied at Vickers since early 1927 when J7439 (then a newly-rebuilt Mark VII, having been flown into the sea in fog off the Kent coast on 7 April 1925, while with No 9 Squdron, and salvaged) was fitted with a set of metal wings; other aircraft, notably J7717, had also been given similar wings, as well as other metal components. It was about the time that J7439 was first flown in August 1927 that the Air Ministry announced that it was proposing to run down the woodworking trades in the RAF, and that within six years it was intended to have replaced all wooden operational aircraft with those of all-metal construction. J7439, with its metal wings and wooden fuselage, underwent trials with No 58 Squadron during 1928, and later that year Vickers received a contract to build a total of 50 new Virginias employing entirely metal airframes, as well as no fewer than seven contracts to convert all surviving Virginias to this standard (ultimately involving no fewer than 52 veterans).

As the new version, the Type 139 Mark X, would be powered by the new Lion VB, and eventually the Lion XI engines, it is difficult to see how re-building the old Virginias, often adding the rear gun position but always replac-ing the entire fuselage and wings, would bring about any financial saving, bearing in mind that the aircraft had to be completely dismantled in the first place.

The first production all-metal Vir-ginia Xs were completed in 1930, and among the first squadrons scheduled to receive the new bombers were No 500 (County of Kent) and No 502 (Ulster) Squadrons of the Special Reserve, sta-tioned at Manston and Aldergrove re-spectively. All the established regular Virginia squadrons had re-equipped by the end of 1931, and in the continuing absence of a new bomber fulfilling the requirements of B.19/27, Mark Xs began to equip other regular squadrons, begin-ning with No 10 (Bomber) Squadron at Boscombe Down in September 1932.

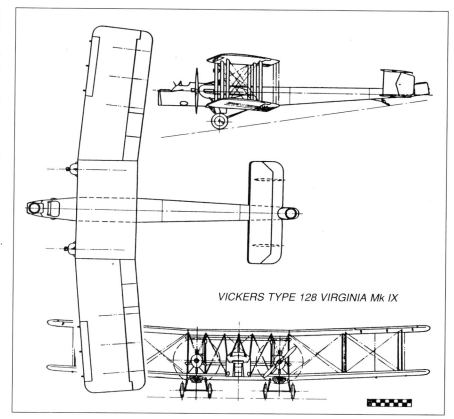

VICKERS TYPE 128 VIRGINIA Mk IX

Type: Twin-engine, four/seven crew, three-bay biplane long-range day/night bomber.

Air Ministry Specifications: D or R Type 4B (later 2/20), 1/21, 28/23, 12/24 and 5/31

Manufacturer: Vickers (Aviation) Ltd, Weybridge, Surrey

Powerplant: Prototypes. Two 468hp Napier Lion IAZ and II twelve-cylinder, water-cooled, in-line engines driving two-blade propellers. Mks III, IV, V, VII and IX. 450hp Lion II, 468hp Lion II and 486hp Lion II. Mks VII and IX. 520hp Lion V. Mk X. 580hp Lion VB and 590hp Lion XIA. Experimental. 650hp Rolls-Royce Condor III, 620hp Bristol Pegasus IIM3; Bristol Jupiter IX; Arm-strong Siddeley Jaguar; Gnome Rhône Jupiter VIII.

Structure: Marks I-IX. All-wooden construction (although numerous aircraft of various Marks were re-built with some metal structural components). Mk X. All-metal.

Dimensions: Span, 86ft 6in (Mk X, 87ft 8in); length, 50ft 7in (Mk X, 52ft 3in); height, 17ft 3in (Mks I and II), 16ft 11in (Mk VII), 18ft 2in (Mk X); wing area, 2,166 sq ft (Mk X, 2,178 sq ft).

Weights: Tare, 9,243lb (Mk X, 9,650lb); All-up, 16,750lb (Mk VII, 16,500; Mk X, 17,600lb).

Performance: (All figures without bomb load). Mks I-III. Maxi-mum speed, 97 mph at sea level; climb to 5,000ft, 12 min 30 sec; service ceiling, 8,700ft; range, 1,000 miles. Mk VII. Max speed, 104 mph at 2,000ft; climb to 5,000ft, 12 min 30 sec; service ceiling, 8,800ft; range, 980 miles. Mk X. Max speed, 108 mph at 5,000 ft; climb to 5,000ft, 10 min; service ceiling, 13,800ft; range, 985 miles.

Armament: Mk I. Bomb load, 1,008lb (nine 112lb bombs stowed internally); gun armament, five Lewis guns mounted singly on Scarff rings in nose and on four 'fighting tops' positions. Mk X. Bomb load, up to 3,000lb (nine 112lb bombs internally, and various combinations of 550lb, 250lb, 112lb and 20lb bombs externally under wings and fuselage) and up to three Lewis guns in nose and tail positions.

Prototypes: Two, J6856 (Mk I) and J6857 (Mk II). J6856 first flown at Brooklands on 24 November 1922 by Capt S Cockerell AFC (both aircraft later progressively modified to Mk Xs); prototypes of other Marks were modified from production aircraft.

Production: Total of 124 aircraft built as new (excluding proto-types). 6 Mk IIIs (J6992-J6993 and J7129-J7132; 4 ultimately con-verted to Mk Xs); 2 Mk IVs (J7274-J7275; 1 converted to Mk X); 22 Mk Vs (J7418-J7439; 15 converted to Mk X); 25 Mk VIs (J7558-J7567 and J7706-J7720; 15 converted to Mk X); 11 Mk VIIs (J8236-J8241 and J8326-J8330; 7 converted to Mk X); 8 Mk IXs (J8907-J8914; 6 converted to Mk X); 50 Mk X (K2321-J2339 and K2650-K2680). Note: Many of the above conversions were made to intermediate Marks before the aircraft ultimately became Mk Xs.

Summary of Service: Virginias served with No 7 (Bomber) Squadron from April 1927 until June 1935 (at Worthy Down with Mks I, VIII and X); No 9 (Bomber) Squadron from January 1925 until May 1936 (at Manston, Boscombe Down, Andover and Aldergrove with Mks V, VI, VII, VIII, IX and X); No 10 (Bomber) Squadron from September 1932 until November 1934 (at Boscombe Down with Mk X); No 51 (Bomber) Squadron from March 1937 until February 1938 (at Boscombe Down with Mk X); No 58 (Bomber) Squadron from December 1924 until December 1937 (at Worthy Down, Upper Heyford, Driffield and Boscombe Down with Mks V, VII, IX and X); No 75 (Bomber) Squadron from March until September 1937 (at Driffield with Mk X); No 214 (Bomber) Squadron from September 1935 until January 1937 (at Boscombe Down, Andover and Scampton with Mk X); No 215 (Bomber) Squadron from October 1935 until November 1937 (at Worthy Down, Upper Heyford and Driffield with Mk X); No 500 (County of Kent) Squadron, SR and AAF, from March 1931 until January 1936 with Mk X); and with No 502 (Ulster) Squadron, SR and AAF, from December 1931 until October 1935 (at Aldergrove with Mk X). Virginias also served with the Parachute Test Unit, Henlow (later No 13 MU), and with Nos 15 and 22 (Testing) Squadrons of the A & AEE, Martlesham Heath. The last recorded Virginia in service was J7434 which crashed at Henlow on 4 September 1941; it had been taken on charge by No 9 Squadron on 9 February 1925 as a Mk V, later being modified to Mks VII and X, and serving in turn with Nos 7, 58, 502 and 214 Squadrons and with the Parachute Testing Unit; its span of service was therefore 16 years and 7 months — believed to be the longest of any Virginia.

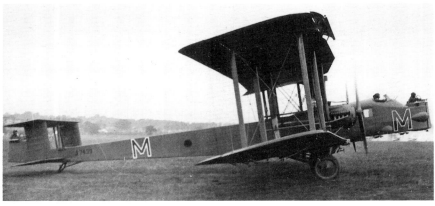

The original metal-wing Virginia, J7439, after having been brought up to full Mark X production standard, seen here with No 9 Squadron at Hendon in 1932. Its final service was with No 215 Squadron during 1936-37. (Photo: RAF Museum, Neg No P007432)

Early standard Virginia Xs continued to be powered by Lion VBs but, from late in 1930, aircraft were increasingly being fitted with Lion XIs of 590hp. Nevertheless, despite this significant increase in power, the Virginia X still struggled to exceed 100mph when carrying bombs, and even when being flown light could only just manage 110mph. The fact that the aircraft still continued to equip new Squadrons in the mid-1930s (No 214 in September 1935, No 215 in October 1935, and Nos 51 and 75 in March 1937) must be attributed to the old biplane's flaccid but forgiving flying qualities, arguably the best sort of aeroplane with which to introduce young fledgling airmen to the rigours of flying a heavy aeroplane over long distances. By the time the RAF were taking positive steps to regain some measure of the strength and authority squandered during the 1930s, the Virginia had become a much safer and less tiring aeroplane to fly; indeed, it well merited the sobriquet of workhorse in its later days, undertaking the most unlikely tasks that were but a pointer to the future of aviation. For instance, two Virginias were employed at the RAE for catapult launching, a scheme hatched in the belief that heavily-laden bombers would ultimately need to be catapulted if they were to become airborne within the confines of the aerodromes of limited area. Another Virginia was fitted with additional fuel tanks to act as a flying tanker for the early experiments being conducted with in-flight refuelling of other aircraft in 1934-35. And in 1936 J7130 was flown in secret trials to discover the nature of signals provided

by a large aeroplane on a cathode-ray oscilloscope — the beginning of radar.

Finally, mention should be made of the service given by the Virginia to the Parachute Testing Unit at Henlow, for the sight of three aircraft plodding across the sky at the prewar Hendon displays, as airmen allowed themselves to be dragged from platforms by their billowing parachutes, remain one of the indelible memories of those far-off years. Indeed, shortly before the Second World War, when No 13 Maintenance Unit assumed the duties of the PDU, the Virginias continued to perform this unsung chore.

It would be convenient when chronicling the fortunes of an aeroplane whose working life spanned almost the entire interwar period, to have been able to point to a steady advance in bomber design philosophy depicted by the Virginia. Though this was far from being the case, as the successive milestones were passed elsewhere, particularly in the United States of America, the old Vickers biplane contributed vastly to the research and development that lay behind that advance.

Summary of Flight Research performed in Virginia aircraft, 1923-1939

Nature of trials	Aircraft first employed and date	Nature of trials	Aircraft first employed and date
Single wing gun position	J6856, 1923	Wing slots	J6857 (super auto-slots, 1929); J6856 (plain slots, 1930)
'Fighting tops'	J6856, 1923-1927		
Parachute exits and platforms	J7717, 1925; J6992, 1926	Magnetic bomb-release gear	J7717, 1929
Cockpit/nav light generators	J7129, 1926	Enclosed cockpit canopy	J7720, 1929
Four-blade propellers	J7130, 1926	Cockpit silencing	J7720, 1929
Auto-pilot	J7424 and J7434 (RAE auto-pilot, 1926-27); J7131, J7275, J7551 (3-channel auto-pilot, 1931-33)	Catapult launching trials	J8236, J8326 (RAE, 1930-33)
		Roller-blind radiator shutters	J8238, 1930
		Crew intercom.	J7274, 1931-32
Metal wings	J7439, 1927-29; J7717, 1928-29	Tailwheels (various)	J7558, 1931
Wheel brakes	J6856, J6857, J7436, J7566 (Chrysler brakes, 1928-30); J8236 (Palmer brakes, 1929); J7558 (Ferodo brakes)	Heated crew clothing	J7131, 1933
		Airframe anti-icing	J7708, 1933-34
		In-flight refuelling	J7275, 1934-35
Landing lights	J8241 (Davis lamp, 1929); J7131, J7422, J8238, (RAE lamps, 1931-34)	Radar reflection trials	J7130, 1936
		Air defence trials	J7130, 1939

Vickers Types 71 to 126 Vixen I to VI

While the Virginia's long programme of production and development provided Vickers with a steady flow of work for many years, the company was by no means idle in other areas of military

aircraft development, not least the single-engine close-support fighter/reconnaissance/bomber which might, in due course, be considered as a replacement for the D.H.9A and Bristol F.2B Fighter.

The Vickers Type 71 Vixen, G–EBEC, shortly after being entered on the Civil Register, at Martlesham Heath after the first minor modifications had been made. (Photo: C F Andrews Collection)

As both these aeroplanes were expected to continue in service for the foreseeable future, no official Specification had been considered for a replacement so that, after informal discussion with the Air Ministry's Directorate of Research, Pierson drew up his own, selecting the low-compression ·450hp Napier Lion I as the powerplant.

The resulting Type 71 embodied a steel tubular fuselage structure and wooden single-bay wings, the fuselage being sheet-metal, ply and fabric covered. For an aeroplane that spanned only 40 feet, the Lion engine seemed relatively large and powerful and, despite use of a huge frontal radiator, the Type 71 Vixen I returned an excellent maximum speed of 137 mph with full warload at 10,000 feet. It was first flown, without any identifying registration markings, in February 1923 by Capt Tommy Broome, and shortly afterwards underwent performance tests at Martlesham Heath. A number of modifications followed before the Vixen I was issued with a Certificate of Airworthiness and entered on the Civil Register as G–EBEC — this despite having provision for two synchronized Vickers guns, a Lewis gun on the rear cockpit and a bomb load of two 230lb bombs.

Although the Vixen did not attract any orders from the Air Ministry, interest abounded overseas, with enquiries from Australia, Chile, Denmark, Greece, Peru, Portugal, Russia and Serbia, of which Portugal and Chile placed orders. Vickers also undertook a complete re-build of the Type 71 to produce the Type 87 Mark II (still registered G–EBEC) which was flown at Brooklands on 13 August 1923. While at Martlesham in this form, G–EBEC was flown by Flt Lt Augustus Henry Orlebar AFC (later of Schneider Trophy fame) who reported on the aircraft in sufficiently favourable terms to enable Vickers to secure a contract for six development aircraft to an official Specification, 45/23 (see Vickers Venture, page 154).

A new Vixen prototype, the Type 91 Mark III, was produced as G–EBIP, being flown both as a land- and floatplane, featuring a lengthened fuselage and revised engine installation to improve

the pilot's field of view, rounded wing tips and slight dihedral on the upper wing. At the same time the 468hp Lion II engine was introduced.

The Vixen V, of which 18 examples were built for Chile, was based on the Mark III but featured a high-compression Lion V engine as well as the addition of two service fuel tanks above the upper wing centresection.

Meanwhile the Vixen G–EBEC had been fitted with a 650hp Rolls-Royce Condor III direct-drive engine, to become the Vixen IV interceptor fighter, and this aircraft was submitted for evaluation under Specification 26/27, this time as the Mark VI, reverting to a bomb-carrying general purpose aircraft,

in competition with the Bristol Beaver (page 173), Fairey Ferret (page 174), D.H.65 Hound (page 186), Gloster Goral (page 187), Westland Wapiti (page 188), and Vickers Valiant (page 191). The winner was to be the Westland Wapiti, powered by a 420hp Bristol Jupiter, the verdict on the Vixen VI being that its Condor engine was too heavy and too powerful — a clear indication that speed performance was of secondary importance.

Vickers gained valuable experience, not to mention a profitable trade overseas, with the Vixen and its immediate derivatives, even if the path of the light general purpose bomber proved to be a blind alley for the company. The exp-

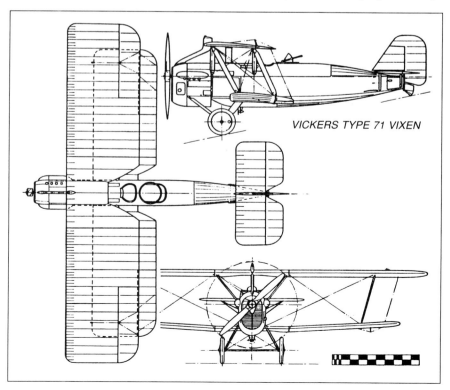

VICKERS TYPE 71 VIXEN

erience did, however, demonstrate the Air Ministry's involuntary philosophy of the 1920s, that encouraging a company to persevere with a promising project was motivated, not by the likelihood of an ultimate production contract, but by the fact that it was a means by which technological advances might be made at the expense of privately-owned manufacturers so long as the Treasury was forced to keep a tight rein on publicly-funded research. Fortunately Vickers was a company of such financial stature that such a seemingly heavy burden could be shouldered; others were less fortunate in this respect.

Type: Single-engine, two-seat, single-bay light general purpose biplane bomber.
Manufacturer: Vickers (Aviation) Ltd, Weybridge, Surrey.
Powerplant: Vixen I. One 450hp low-compression Napier Lion I twelve-cylinder water-cooled in-line engine driving two-blade propeller. Vixen VI. 650hp Rolls-Royce Condor.
Structure: Steel-tube fuselage, fabric, ply and aluminium sheet covered; wooden wings.
Dimensions: Span, 40ft 0in (Mk VI, 44ft 0in); length, 29ft 0in; height, 13ft 0in (Mk VI, 12ft 0in); wing area, 526 sq ft (Mk VI, 590 sq ft).
Weights: Mk I. Tare, 3,098lb; all-up, 4,720lb. Mk VI. Tare, 3,320lb; all-up 5,080lb.
Performance (with full military load): Mk I. Max speed 137 mph at 10,000ft; climb to 10,000ft, 10 min 30 sec; service ceiling, 19,400ft. Mk VI. Max speed, 126mph at 10,000ft; climb to 15,000ft, 25 min; range 764 miles.
Armament: Bomb load, up to 500lb; one or two forward-firing synchronized 0.303in Vickers machine guns, and one Lewis gun with Scarff ring on rear cockpit.
Prototypes: Two, G-EBEC and G-EBIP. G-EBEC flown in February 1923 by Capt Broome as Type 71 Mk I, later modified as Type 87 Mk II, Type 105 Mk IV and Type 126 Mk VI. G-EBIP flown as Type 91 Mk III. No production for Air Ministry.

Fairey Fawn

Designed by F Duncanson, the Fairey Fawn was structurally a direct descendant from the Pintail reconnaissance fighter seaplane and was, like the Vickers Vixen described above, a light day bomber intended to replace the D.H.9A, although it was well into 1922 before an Air Ministry Specification, 5/21, setting out this requirement, was issued in draft form.

Of primarily wooden construction, three prototypes, J6907-J6909, were ordered on 25 October 1921, the first of which was flown by Vincent Nicholl on 8 March 1923. This aeroplane retained the short fuselage of the Pintail, as well as its auxiliary fins beneath the tailplane, and was powered initially by a 450hp Napier Lion II twelve-cylinder broad-arrow engine with slab radiators on the fuselage sides. Unlike the Pintail, however, the Fawn featured an upper wing raised above the fuselage so as to provide improved forward view for the pilot. Armament comprised a single synchronized Vickers gun on the port side of the nose decking and a Lewis gun on the rear cockpit; provision was made to carry a pair of 230lb or four 112lb bombs under the lower wings. The second aircraft, J6908, flown at about the same time, featured a lengthened fuselage, and the auxiliary fins were deleted. Both these aircraft were delivered to Martlesham Heath within a few weeks of their maiden flights for contractor's trials (although J6908 crashed about three months later). The third prototype, J6909, also with lengthened fuse-

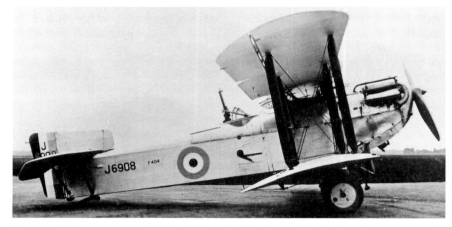

The second Fawn prototype, J6908, with lengthened fuselage, during its Service assessment trials at Martlesham Heath in the spring of 1923; the aircraft was scheduled to attend the Hendon Display on 30 June that year, but hit a tree stump and overturned during a take-off two days earlier. (Photo: The Fairey Aviation Co Ltd.)

lage, was flown in September, but appears to have remained at Northolt for flight trials with the manufacturers until 1925.

A further pair of prototypes, J6990 and J6991, had been ordered on 13 January 1923, and were flown before the end of the year. Being built to a slightly altered production Specification, 20/23, J6990 was delivered to No 11 Squadron in February 1924 for abbreviated Service trials and assessment.

An alarming spate of flying accidents among D.H.9As during the winter of 1922-23, as well as an unexpected increase in the shipment of these aircraft overseas, had lent some urgency to the provision of new light bomber aircraft, and it was in 1923 that the Air Ministry notified Fairey that it was likely that the Fawn would be required to supersede all squadron D.H.9As based in the United Kingdom, expected to comprise the

aircraft of Nos 11, 12, 39, 100 and 101 Squadrons. In the event, however, No 39 Squadron was posted to the Middle East, and No 101 was expected to become a medium or heavy bomber unit during the next two or three years. It was therefore decided that 50 aircraft would suffice to equip the other three Squadrons, and a contract for this number, J7182-J7231, was signed with Fairey on 31 August 1923.

The first two of these aircraft were completed as Mark Is, but the full production Mark IIs began flying almost simultaneously. No 12 (Bomber) Squadron took over its first Fawn IIs at Northolt in March and moved to Andover the same month, followed the next month by No 11 (Bomber) Squadron at Bircham Newton which, in turn, moved to Netheravon at the end of May. By the end of that month almost all the first production batch had flown, and the

third and last regular Squadron, No 100, began re-equipping at Bircham Newton.

Apart from five Fawn IIs which suffered accidents during 1924 (of which all but one were later repaired), most of the spare aircraft, while being held as reserves, were allocated to experimental flying, the RAE using three aircraft for short-range R/T development. Another, J7215, was set aside to be fitted with a 520hp Napier Lion VI with exhaust-driven turbo-supercharger driving an adjustable-pitch two-blade propeller; this became the prototype Fawn Mk IV and was first flown at Farnborough on 12 March 1925. It it unlikely that all Fawn IVs featured supercharged engines.

Early in 1925, a revised Specification (1/25) was issued covering the Fawn Mark III, to be powered by the 468hp Lion V, and an order for 12 such aircraft (J7768-J7779) was signed in March that year, it being intended that these should be distributed as replacements among the three Squadrons. The first aircraft (as well as J7773 and J7774) were completed as Lion VI-powered Fawn IVs, the last two being issued to No 12 Squadron in March 1926. A final production batch of 8 aircraft, J7978-J7985, was ordered in March 1926; once again, two of these aircraft, J7980 and J7981, were completed as Mark IVs and issued to No 12 Squadron.

The Fawn was withdrawn from the three regular squadrons in December 1926, being replaced by the Hawker Horsley or, in the case of No 12 Squadron, by the Fairey Fox. However, already one of the new Special Reserve Squadrons, No 503 at Waddington, had been formed in October that year and had received its first Fawns, while in September 1927 No 603 (City of Edinburgh) Squadron of the Auxiliary Air

A Fairey Fawn II, J7210, of No 12 (Bomber) Squadron in 1925. It has already been remarked that the Royal Air Force was not particularly concerned with high speed in its light bombers during the 1920s and, with aircraft of the Fawn's appearance, it would have been superfluous to engage in cosmetic drag reduction, and the external, overwing fuel tanks did nothing to enhance the aircraft's looks; even the starting crank handle is left in situ on the side of the cowling. (Photo: A J Jackson Collection)

Force at Turnhouse, was issued with Fawn IIIs and IVs. The last of these were withdrawn in 1929.

From many accounts the Fawn was not a popular aircraft, and pilots expressed a preference for the older but more reliable D.H.9A; its performance was no better and its bomb load was similar. Owing to temporary Air Ministry safety requirements, Fawns were required to carry their fuel in tanks situated above the top wing, a position that was psychologically uncomfortable for the crew in the event that the aircraft overturned when landing, and the pilot's field of view was severely restricted

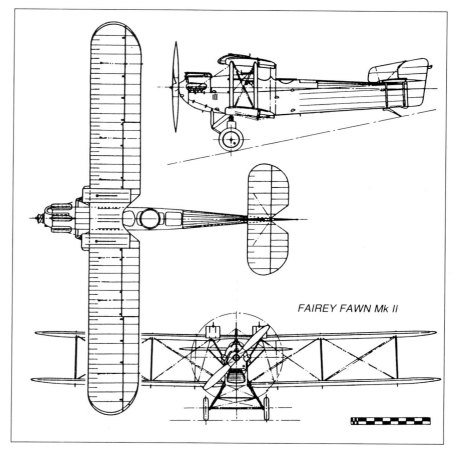

FAIREY FAWN Mk II

Fairey Fawn II, J7214/ '2' of No 100 (Bomber) Squadron, during a visit to Cranwell, probably during 1925. (Photo: RAF Museum, Neg No P003633)

by the big Lion engine — especially during landing.

It seems that Richard Fairey himself was a critic of the Fawn and is on record as having expressed frustration that the Air Ministry would, throughout the early 1920s, only sanction production of light bombers powered by what he regarded as a thoroughly unsuitable engine.

Type: Single-engine, two-seat, two-bay light day bomber biplane.
Air Ministry Specifications: 5/21, 20/23 and 1/25
Manufacturer: The Fairey Aviation Co Ltd, Hayes, Middlesex.
Powerplant: Mk I and II. One 450hp Napier Lion II 12-cylinder, water-cooled, broad-arrow in-line engine driving two-blade propeller. Mk III. 468hp Napier Lion V. Mk IV. 520hp Napier Lion VI (some with exhaust-driven turbo-superchargers).
Dimensions (Fawn III): Span, 49ft 11in; length, 32ft 1in; height, 11ft 11in; wing area, 550 sq ft.
Weights: Tare, 3,481lb; all-up, 5,834lb.
Performance: Max speed, 114 mph at sea level; climb to 5,000ft, 6 min 30 sec; service ceiling, 13,850ft; range 650 miles.
Armament: One synchronized 0.303in Vickers gun on the nose and either one or two Lewis guns with Scarff ring on rear cockpit; bomb load of either two 230lb or four 112lb bombs carried under the wings.
Prototypes: Five, J6907-J6909, and J6990 and J6991. J6907 first flown on 8 March 1923 by Vincent Nicholl at Northolt.
Production: A total of 70 Fawns was built (excluding the above prototypes): J7182-J7231 (Mks I and II; J7215 was prototype Mk IV); J7768-J7779 (Mks III and IV) and J7978-J7985 (Mks III and IV).
Summary of Service: Fairey Fawns served on Nos 11, 12 and 100 (Bomber) Squadrons between March 1924 and December 1926, and with No 503 (County of Lincoln) Squadron of the Special Reserve and No 602 (City of Glasgow) Squadron, Auxiliary Air Force, between October 1926 and December 1929. Several aircraft also served with No 1 Flying Training School in July 1924 and the Parachute Testing Section of the Home Aircraft Depot during 1926-27.

de Havilland D.H.42A and B Dingo

Developed from the de Havilland D.H.42 Dormouse reconnaissance fighter, J7005, which had been designed to Specification 22/22 and first flown on 25 July 1923, the D.H.42A Dingo represented a move towards what was becoming known as the army co-operation rôle, namely battlefield reconnaissance and close-support bombing capabilities. The latter element of these army co-operation duties constituted the principal difference from the former 'corps reconnaissance' rôle (and, incidentally, was a subtle expression of the autonomous nature of the RAF when compared with the former Army-related RFC).

Designed to Specification 8/24 for an army co-operation aircraft, the D.H.42A

Dingo I, J7006, was first flown on 24 March 1924. Powered by a 410hp Bristol Jupiter III, it was of all-wood construction, and its configuration was clearly influenced by the D.H.9A — which it was designed to replace. As with other single-engine military aircraft of that period, the fuel was contained in two tanks located on top of the upper wings, and efforts were made to concentrate all items of significant weight close around the aircraft's cg. The pilot's cockpit was directly beneath the upper wing centre-section, necessitating a large wing cutout for access and upward view, with the gunner's cockpit close behind. The bomb load, usually comprising four 112lb

bombs, was carried beneath the lower wings.

Dingo J7006 attended acceptance trials at Martlesham Heath during April and May 1924, and commenced brief Service trials with No 41 Squadron at Northolt; these were abruptly ended on 5 June when the aircraft broke up in the air and crashed, being burnt out.

A second prototype, the D.H.42B Dingo II, of all-steel construction, was built, being powered by a 436hp Bristol Jupiter IV (although it had at one time been intended to use the heavier Armstrong Siddeley Jaguar engine), this aeroplane being first flown in September 1924. Several minor improvements

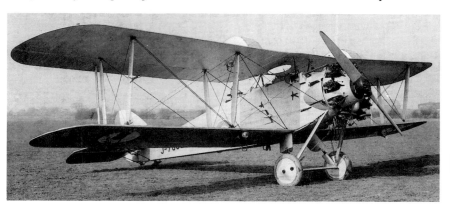

The short-lived D.H.42A Dingo I, J7006, at Stag Lane at the time of its first flight in March 1924; the location of the fuel tanks on the upper wings was never popular among Service pilots. (Photo: A J Jackson Collection)

J7007, the Dingo II, at the RAE, Farnborough, in 1926. Note the circular cutout in the upper wing for access to the pilot's cockpit, and the message pick-up gear under the rear fuselage. (Photo: Imperial War Museum, Neg No MH3318)

were incorporated in the Dingo II, as a result of increasing service experience with the D.H.9A and Bristol F.2B in the Middle East, not least of these being a rudimentary message pick-up device under the rear fuselage (a feature that was to become commonplace on all army co-operation aircraft); the capacity of the wing fuel tanks was increased from 60 to 81 gallons.

After trials at Martlesham Heath, the Dingo II was delivered to the RAE in 1926, where it ended its days. It had never attracted much interest simply because it represented scarcely any advance on the aircraft it was intended to replace.

Type: Single-engine, two-seat, two-bay army co-operation biplane.
Air Ministry Specification: 8/24
Manufacturer: The de Havilland Aircraft Co Ltd, Stag Lane, Edgware, Middlesex.
Powerplant: One 410hp (436hp) Bristol Jupiter III (IV) 9-cylinder air-cooled radial engine.
Dimensions: Span, 41ft 6in; length, 28ft 3in; wing area, 398 sq ft.
Weights: Mk I. Tare, 2,346lb; all-up, 3,700lb. Mk II. Tare, 2,780lb; all-up, 4,038lb.
Performance: Max speed, 127 mph at sea level (Mk II, 128 mph); ceiling, 17,500ft.
Armament: Two forward-firing synchronized 0.303in Vickers machine guns on nose decking and one Lewis gun with Scarff ring on rear cockpit; bomb load, up to 460lb.
Prototypes: Two. Dingo I, J7006, first flown on 12 March 1924; Mk II, J7007, first flown in September 1924. (D.H.42 Dormouse, J7005, first flown on 25 July 1923.) No production.

Boulton & Paul
P.25 Bugle

Clearly the Directorate of Research wished to encourage John North in his development work on highly manoeuvrable medium bombers, and his P.15 Bolton had been flying for less than a month when a new contract was signed with Boulton and Paul Ltd on 19 December 1922 for a new, rather lighter aircraft, the P.25 Bugle, to be powered by a pair of the new Bristol Jupiter radial engines.

Of predominantly steel construction, the first two Bugle Mark Is were three-crew, three-bay biplanes whose engines were situated in mid-gap with hinged, circular steel tubular mounting frames. The fuel tanks were located in the underside of the upper wing centresection. The split-unit undercarriage incorporated sturdy oleo struts, the tailskid also being oleo-sprung. The bomb load, of up to six 112lb or three 230lb bombs, was carried externally under the fuselage.

The first of two prototypes ordered initially, J6984, was flown in about August 1923, and was evaluated at Martlesham Heath against Specification 30/22, drawn up around North's pro-

The first two Bugle I prototypes, J6984 (above) and J6985 (below). The clean engine installation of the Jupiter radials is apparent in these views. (Photos: via Alec Brew)

posals. To begin with, it was flown with a pair of 400hp Jupiter IIs but, early the next year when 425hp Jupiter IVs became available, both J6984 and the second aircraft were fitted with these engines.

In the meantime, three further Bugle Is, J7235, J7259 and J7260, had been

ordered, these examples being completed with full military equipment, and the first — a four-crew aircraft — underwent Service trials with No 58 (Bomber) Squadron, beginning on 25 March 1925. These were conducted, not so much in the context of a possible production order, but as a means of learning how the aircraft would behave under operational conditions. This Bugle also attended the Hendon Display on 27 June that year, giving a public demonstration of its outstanding agility, which included a loop.

A final order for two modified P.25A Bugle Mark IIs, J7266 and J7267, had been signed in February 1924, these four-seaters being given the extra power of a pair of 450hp Napier Lions, mounted on the lower wings; the fuel tanks were moved from their former wing positions to a location inside the fuselage amidships. Both of these aircraft spent much of their lives with the test Squadrons (Nos 15 and 22) of the A & AEE at Martlesham Heath.

By the time the last Bugle (J7260) was

struck off RAF charge in 1929, Boulton and Paul's persistence with its family of twin-engine bombers had been rewarded

when, in 1927, the P.29 Sidestrand (see page 180) had been ordered into production.

Type: Twin-engine, three/four-crew, three-bay biplane experimental medium day bomber.
Air Ministry Specification: 30/22 (amended several times).
Manufacturer: Boulton and Paul Ltd, Riverside, Norwich, Norfolk.
Powerplant: Mark I. Two 400hp Bristol Jupiter II or 425hp Jupiter IV nine-cylinder air-cooled radial engines. Mark II. Two 450hp Napier Lion II twelve-cylinder water-cooled, in-line engines.
Structure: Predominantly steel tubular construction throughout.
Dimensions: Span, 65ft 0½in.
Weights: Tare, 5,079lb; all-up, 8,110lb (Mk II, 8,914lb).
Performance: Max speed, 120 mph at sea level.
Armament: Bomb load of up to about 690lb carried externally; gun armament of two Lewis machine guns with Scarff rings on nose and midships positions.
Prototypes: Five Mark Is, J6984, J6985, J7235, J7259 and J7260; J6984 first flown in about August 1924. Two Mark IIs, J7266 and J7267; J7266 first flown on 6 March 1925. No production.

Handley Page H.P.24 Hyderabad

Following the Armistice, with the disbanding of O/400 squadrons, as well as the disposal of other surplus aircraft, some of these machines were converted for commercial use, either as O/7 or O/10 passenger aircraft or O/11 freighters. In due course George Volkert embarked on the design of an airliner derivative series, beginning with the H.P.16 (W.8). And when the Air Min-

Two views of a standard Hyderabad, J7745, showing well the low-set nose gunner's cockpit and the ventral gun position. This aircraft underwent extensive modification to become the prototype H.P.33 Hinaidi. (Photos: A J Jackson Collection)

istry issued Specifications DoR Nos 4, 9 and 12 for a long-range night bomber, coastal defence torpedo-bomber and a troop transport respectively, Volkert tendered designs, all of which were based on the W.8 airliner.

DoR Specification No 4 was rewritten several times, and reappeared in 1922 as Specification 31/22, setting

down the requirements for a Vimy replacement and, as the W.8 passenger aircraft had by then entered commercial service, 'Star' Richards (who had temporarily taken over as chief designer) and C D Holland produced the design of an aircraft, the W.8D, adapted to carry a crew of four and a bomb load of two 550lb or four 112lb bombs. (Richards

Hyderabad J8806/'O' of No 99 (Bomber) Squadron during a visit to Cranwell in 1929, displaying the angular vertical tail surfaces which were introduced part-way through the aircraft's production; this aircraft was one of those powered by Napier Lion VA engines. (Photo: RAF Museum, Neg No P013825)

also produced drawings of a 'Middle East bomber transport', the W.9 to Specification 41/22, powered by three Siddeley Jaguar engines, capable of lifting a single 550lb bomb, but this was not proceeded with.)

The W.8D design met with the Air Ministry's qualified approval, and a single prototype, J6994, was ordered on 13 January 1923, to be powered by a pair of 450hp Napier Lion II engines. Under the company designation H.P.24, the new bomber retained many of its commercial predecessor's features, its unsightly single fin and rudder, as well as its three-bay wings and four paired mainwheel undercarriage, each pair of wheels with its own cross-axle. The crew comprised two pilots in tandem, a front gunner/bomb aimer and a midships gunner; both dorsal and ventral midships gun positions were prvided. The nose gunner's Scarff ring was located below the line of the pilots' coaming so as not to impair their field of view.

The W.8D was flown in October 1923 by Arthur Wilcockson, and was delivered the same month to Martlesham Heath, remaining there for five months while it underwent comparative assessment with the early production Virginia III J6993.[1]

A production Specification, 15/24, was drawn up and a contract for fifteen aircraft (J7738-J7752), now named the Hyderabad, awarded to Handley Page. A number of domestic problems within the company stood in the way of completing this production order quickly, and it was December 1925 before the first production aircraft was flown. J7738 was taken on charge by No 99 (Bomber) Squadron at Bircham Newton that month, and was followed by eleven

others during the next six months.

For two years No 99 Squadron remained the sole Hyderabad unit, during

that time losing four aircraft in flying accidents. In anticipation of a continuing high rate of attrition, therefore, a

Type: Twin-engine, four-crew, three-bay biplane medium/heavy night bomber.
Air Ministry Specifications: 21/22, 15/24, 18/26 and 15/27.
Manufacturer: Handley Page Ltd, Cricklewood, London NW2
Powerplant: Two 450hp Napier Lion II or 500hp Lion V or VA twelve-cylinder water-cooled in-line engines driving two- or four-blade propellers.
Structure: All-wood construction with ply and fabric covering.
Dimensions: Span, 75ft 0in; length, 59ft 2in; height, 16ft 9in; wing area, 1,471 sq ft.
Weights: Tare, 8,910lb; all-up, 13,590lb.
Performance: Max speed, 109 mph at sea level (full fuel, no bomb load); service ceiling, 14,000ft; range, 500 miles.
Armament: Single 0.303in Lewis machine guns in nose, midships dorsal and midships ventral positions; bomb load of up to 1,100lb carried externally.
Prototype: One, J6994, first flown by Arthur Wilcockson in October 1923.
Production: A total of 44 Hyderabads was built. 15 with Lion IIs, J7738-J7752; 19 with Lion VAs, J8317-J8324 and J8805-J8815; and 10 with Lion Vs, J9031, J9032, J9034-J9036 and J9293-J9297. (J9033 was completed as a Hinaidi.)
Summary of Service: Hyderabads served with No 10 (Bomber) Squadron between January 1928 and March 1931; with No 99 (Bomber) Squadron between December 1925 and January 1931; with No 502 (Ulster) Squadron, SR, between July 1928 and December 1931; and with No 503 (County of Lincoln) Squadron, SR, between 1929 and 1933.

---

[1] It has been recorded by the late C H Barnes (*Handley Page Aircraft since 1907*, Putnam, London, 2nd Edition, page 186) that J6994 returned a 'considerably better performance with the same military load'. It should be pointed out, however, that the Virginia was a rather larger aeroplane, capable of lifting a much heavier bomb load over almost twice the W.8D's range, with the same engine power.

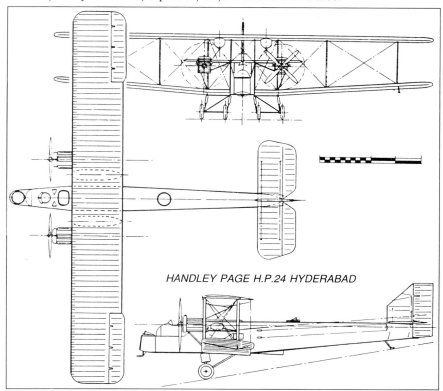

HANDLEY PAGE H.P.24 HYDERABAD

second production order for eight aircraft, powered by 500hp Lion VA engines driving four-blade propellers, was placed in 1926. The first of these, J8317, was badly damaged in an accident during October near Leeds almost as soon as it arrived on the Squadron!

As plans were laid to equip a second regular Squadron, No 10, when it reformed at Upper Heyford in January 1928, a new contract for eleven Lion VA-powered Hyderabads, J8805-J8815, to Specification 15/27 was signed. At the same time earlier aircraft underwent reconditioning by rotation, some being given the higher-powered Lions. In January 1928 No 10 (Bomber) Squadron duly received its first six aircraft as the Air Ministry announced that the Hyderabad bomber squadron establishment would henceforth be reduced to two flights, each of four aircraft. One of this production batch, J8813, was held back by the manufacturers for the first five months of 1928 for flight trials of the patented Handley Page wing slats, but remained the only Hyderabad to be so equipped.

With the repair and conditioning programme underway by mid-1928, and two final production orders totalling eleven aircraft, it was considered that there were adequate Hyderabads to re-equip two of the Special Reserve Squadrons, Nos 502 and 503. In July that year the two regular squadrons were instructed to hand over their oldest aircraft to No 502 (Ulster) Squadron at Aldergrove, where they replaced Vimys, and in 1929 it was the turn of No 503 (County of Lincoln) Squadron at Waddington, this Squadron receiving brand-new aircraft of the final production batch.

The Hyderabad was declared obsolete in December 1931 (except for a small number of reconditioned and re-engined examples which continued to fly with No 503 Squadron until 1933). By then, however, an improved development, the H.P.33 Hinaidi (see page 198) had entered service, its prototype having been evolved by modification of Hyderabad J7745.

The Hyderabad must have been something of a disappointment to its manufacturer. It was never, despite its official classification as a heavy bomber, considered anything but pedestrian in terms of performance and load-carrying; its accident rate was high, though it must be said that few of the aircraft losses were attributable to mechanical failure, with a result that the Service was constantly pressing for a quicker turn-around of reconditioned and repaired machines. A detailed examination of records between 1926 and 1931 shows that, notwithstanding the establishment order mentioned above, the average unit strength during this period was slightly under seven aircraft, and that between January 1928 and December 1931 there was no time when at least ten aircraft were not grounded.

Vickers Type 94 Venture

Following the receipt of Flt Lt Orlebar's complimentary flight report on the Vickers Type 87 Vixen II in February 1924 (see page 147), the Directorate of Research awarded a contract for six army co-operation development aircraft to the terms of Specification 45/23.

These aircraft were intended to combine the latest features of the Vixen series, including the lengthened fuselage of the Mark III, as well as its underslung nose radiator (as distinct from the Vixen I's frontal type). A small bomb load, of up to four 112lb bombs, would be carried on underwing racks.

All six aircraft, J7277-J7282, named the Venture, were built simultaneously and the first was flown at Brooklands on 3 June, the others following on during the next six weeks. J7277 was delivered to Martlesham Heath for manufacturer's tests on 17 June, during which a maximum speed of 135 mph at sea level was recorded. Its handling was said to be 'docile', but the aircraft evidently failed to impress the A & AEE, whose report criticised it for its poor longitudinal stability, the pilot's lack of view and its long landing run; the aircraft was also

One of the Vickers Ventures, said to be J7277; the tripod structure aft of the rear cockpit was probably associated with stability trials at the RAE. (Photo: A J Jackson Collection)

considered to be too large. For an aircraft intended for 'army co-operation' and its likely use of relatively small landing grounds, these criticisms compromised any possibility of a production order. Although J7277 appeared in the New Types Park at the Hendon Display on 28 June and subsequently underwent short Service trials with No 4 Squadron at Farnborough in January 1925, this Venture, and those that followed, were destined to spend their lives at Mar-

Type: Single-engine, two-seat, single-bay biplane light reconnaissance bomber.
Air Ministry Specification: 45/23.
Manufacturer: Vickers (Aviation) Ltd, Weybridge, Surrey.
Powerplant: One 450hp Napier Lion I twelve-cylinder water-cooled in-line engine driving two-blade propeller.
Dimensions: Span, 40ft 0in; length, 32ft 0in; height, 13ft 3in; wing area, 526 sq ft.
Weights: Tare, 3,140lb; all-up, 4,890lb.
Performance: Max speed, 129 mph at 10,000ft; service ceiling, 19,200ft.
Armament: Two synchronized 0.303in Vickers machine guns and one Lewis gun with Scarff ring; provision to carry up to four 112lb bombs on underwing racks.
Prototypes: Six development aircraft built, J7277-J7282; J7277 first flown at Brooklands on 3 June 1924. No production.

tlesham and the RAE flying a long series of stability trials.

Without extensive modifications, for which funds were not available, the Venture's longitudinal stability problems proved insuperable and J7277, the longest-lived of the six examples, was finally struck off charge as incurable in January 1933.

Blackburn T.4 Cubaroo

The manner in which air power had threatened to influence the course of the war at sea, whether in anti-submarine or coastal patrol activities, or indeed in the use of torpedoes against large warships, certainly brought influence to bear on postwar aircraft requirements, not only with regard to carrier-borne aeroplanes but also to land-based torpedo and bomb carrying aircraft. For several years the Air Ministry considered the likelihood of launching the naval 21in torpedo — which weighed over 2,000lb — from the air.

By 1922 the Directorate of Research was ready to formulate a Requirement for a fairly large, folding-wing aircraft capable of lifting either this torpedo or a similar weight of bombs over a range of some 800 miles. While the 600hp Rolls-Royce Condor was already becoming available, another very large engine, the 16-cylinder 1,000hp Napier Cub was not far off. Six examples of the latter engine had been ordered.

Both A V Roe and Blackburn submitted designs to the Specification, 16/22 (previously D or R Type 9), namely the Avro Type 556 and the Blackburn T.4 — each a huge biplane powered by a single Cub engine. Chadwick withdrew his Type 556, but Maj F A Bumpus persevered with his design and was rewarded with a contract for two prototypes. (Chadwick returned to Specification 16/22 with the Avro Type 557, with twin Condor engines, and also won an order for two aircraft; see Avro Type 557 Ava, page 156).

Spanning 88 feet, the Blackburn T.4, named the Cubaroo, may have been the largest single-engine military aircraft in the world at that time. Of mostly steel and duralumin construction, it featured folding two-bay wings with a four-wheel undercarriage, arranged in two pairs, each pair with its own axle. The fuselage, no less than 11 feet deep at its forward end, occupied almost the entire depth of the wing gap, but tapered sharply in side elevation towards the

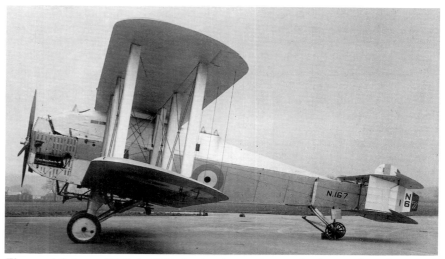

The second Cubaroo, N167, in 1925, showing the torpedo mounting beam and crutches, as well as the Leitner-Watts variable-pitch propeller. The wheeled object under the tail skid was a ground handling dolly. (Photo: Blackburn Aircraft Ltd, Neg No A-422-G)

rear. The generous proportions of the front fuselage were dictated largely by the big Cub engine (which weighed over a ton, excluding radiators), yet it was neatly and almost entirely enclosed in cowling panels — although these were extensively pierced with cooling louvres.

The crew comprised pilot and navigator, seated side-by-side forward of the wings and over the rear of the engine, a bomb aimer/gunner in a cabin aft of the engine (with provision for two Lewis

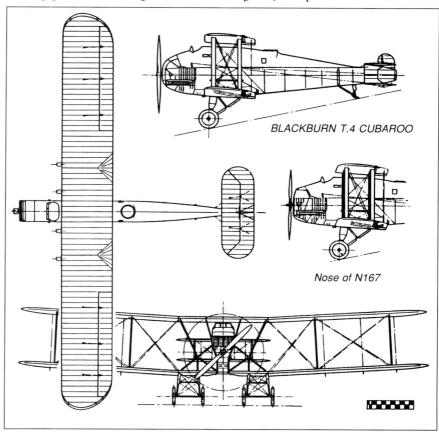

BLACKBURN T.4 CUBAROO

Nose of N167

guns to fire aft through hatches close to the trailing edges of the lower wings, and a midships gunner with Scarff ring aft of the upper wing. The aircraft featured a biplane tail unit with very small twin fins and rudders and a large central rudder; both tailplanes had variable incidence, adjustable by the pilot.

The torpedo, or alternative bomb load, was carried below the fuselage between the two undercarriage structures and, at a maximum all-up weight of 19,000lb (including some 400 gallons of fuel), the Cubaroo was an impressive aeroplane by any standards. The first prototype, N166, was flown in conditions of considerable secrecy during the summer of 1924 by Flt Lt Paul Ward Spencer Bulman MC, AFC (later Gp Capt, CBE, one of the most respected Farnborough experimental pilots of his day, and for twenty years chief test pilot of the H G Hawker Engineering Company).

Bulman reported that the Cubaroo and engine behaved impeccably (having already flown the Avro Aldershot experimentally fitted with the Cub engine), and was no more tiring to fly than a D.H.9A. The two-blade propeller used initially was then replaced by a three-blade metal, adjustable-pitch

Leitner-Watts propeller, and the aircraft delivered to Martlesham Heath for contractor's trials. After further brief trials at Brough, N166 was sent to the RAE at Farnborough on 2 February 1925 for further engines trials but was written off after its undercarriage collapsed, damaging the aeroplane irreparably.

The second Cubaroo, N167, was flown in 1925 and differed from the first aircraft principally in having a flat, almost vertical frontal radiator. This aeroplane flew with the Leitner-Watts variable-pitch propeller from the outset,

and was shown at the 1925 Hendon Display as New Type No 6.

It was at about this time that support for the Cub engine came to an end. Air Ministry interest shifted away from very large single-engine bombers, and the idea of launching the 21in torpedo from aircraft was abandoned. N167 was accordingly allocated to trial installation of other engines and, in 1927, was flown with the little-known 1,100hp Beardmore Simoon, a low-revving, inverted eight-cylinder water-cooled in-line engine developed from the six-cylinder Beardmore Typhoon.

Type: Single-engine, four-crew, two-bay biplane long-range torpedo bomber.
Air Ministry Specification: 16/22 (previously D of R Type 9).
Manufacturer: The Blackburn Aeroplane and Motor Co Ltd, Leeds and Brough, Yorkshire.
Powerplant: One 1,000hp Napier Cub sixteen-cylinder X-type water-cooled in-line engine driving either a two-blade wooden fixed-pitch, or a three-blade metal variable-pitch Leitner-Watts propeller. N167 experimentally flown with 1,100hp Beardmore Simoon engine.
Structure: Steel and duralumin tubular construction with ply and fabric covering.
Dimensions: Span, 88ft 0in; length, 54ft 0in; height, 19ft 4in.
Weights: Tare, 9,632lb; all-up (maximum), 19,020lb.
Performance: Max speed, 115 mph at sea level; absolute ceiling, 11,800ft; max range, 1,800 miles (no warload, and not confirmed on test).
Armament: Either one 21in naval torpedo or four 550lb bombs carried externally; three Lewis guns in midships gunner's cockpit and in midships beam hatches.
Prototypes: Two, N166 and N167; N166 first flown by Flt Lt P W S Bulman at Brough, probably in the late summer of 1924. No production.

Avro Type 557 Ava

Of even greater proportions than the Blackburn Cubaroo, the Avro Type 557 Ava represented Roy Chadwick's interpretation of the 16/22 Specification for a 21-inch torpedo carrier although, following his withdrawal of the Type 556 Napier Cub-powered design, he adopted two 650hp Rolls-Royce Condor III engines instead. Whether these 'second thoughts' were voluntary or enforced by the use of all available Cub engines elsewhere is not known. On the other hand, the change to Condors may have been requested by the Air Ministry on the pretext of securing a twin-engine prototype with which to make comparisons with the radical Cub-powered Cubaroo. At all events, the power and

wing loadings of the two aircraft were not dissimilar.[1]

Like the Blackburn aircraft, design, construction and preliminary flight testing of the Avro went ahead in great secrecy, principally on account of the

[1]	Power loading* bhp/lb	Wing loading* lb/sq ft
Blackburn		
Cubaroo	0.053	10.51
Avro Ava	0.063	9.21
	* As tested	

sensitivity attaching to the Air Ministry's decision to pursue the air-dropped Whitehead 21in torpedo — a matter that is said to have been anathema in the councils of admiralty (the 21-inch weapon being thought capable of sinking the largest warship extant).

Two prototype Type 557s (N171 and N172) were ordered. They were well-proportioned, three-bay, folding-wing biplanes, their uncowled Condors being located at mid-gap with radiators imme-

The second Avro Ava prototype, N172, of all-metal construction, distinguishable from the first aircraft in having square-cut wing tips. It is shown here carrying the 21-inch Whitehead torpedo. (Photo: P T Capon, Ref No 634)

diately above in the underside of the upper wing. Divided undercarriage structures each mounted a pair of mainwheels, each pair with its own cross-axle. The first aircraft was of all-wood construction with fabric covering. The five-man crew comprised two pilots seated side-by-side with dual controls in a spacious and lofty cockpit well forward in the nose, nose and midships gunners, and a navigator/bomb aimer in a long cabin which extended from the nose to about nine feet aft of the wings. The biplane empennage featured wide-span tailplanes with twin fins and characteristic Avro 'comma'-shaped horn-balanced rudders. The 20-foot-long torpedo (or equivalent bomb load) was carried beneath the fuselage on external racks.

N171 is believed to have been completed and flown in mid-1924 although it was not displayed in public for two years, first appearing at the Hendon Display on 3 July 1926 as New Type No 14. By that time, however, the Air Ministry had abandoned its plans to adopt the 21in torpedo, and the original *raison d'être* of the Ava had evaporated.

Nevertheless, A V Roe was encouraged to continue construction of the second Ava prototype, N172, whose structure was all-metal. It was evident from the aircraft about to enter production elsewhere that the Air Ministry favoured a universal move towards metal construction, and Chadwick had taken part in discussions with the Directorate of Technical Development that left him in no doubt that an all-metal heavy bomber was about to become the subject of a major Air Ministry requirement.

N172, the Ava Mark II, was flown at Hamble on 22 April 1927 and appeared at the Hendon Display on 3 July, being mainly distinguishable by its square wing tips. By the time the new heavy bomber Specification, B.19/27, was issued on 17 August, official interest in the Condor engine had waned (the

Bristol Orion being favoured) and certain other fundamental limitations were being imposed — not least on the overall size of the aircraft. Yet, although an extensively altered design was hurriedly tendered by A V Roe, to join more than a dozen from other hopeful manufacturers, it soon became clear

that the Air Ministry was now in a powerful position to look beyond the generation of bombers whose technology had been firmly rooted in the early 1920s. No one could foresee that a further eight years would elapse before a true break with that tradition would materialise.

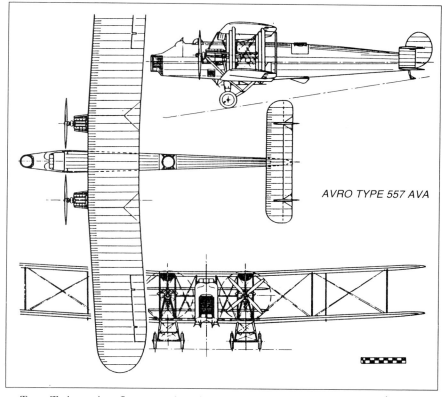

AVRO TYPE 557 AVA

Type: Twin-engine, five-crew, three-bay biplane long-range torpedo/night bomber.
Air Ministry Specification: 16/22
Manufacturer: A V Roe & Co Ltd, Manchester and Hamble, Hampshire.
Powerplant: Two 650hp Rolls-Royce Condor III twelve-cylinder water-cooled in-line engines driving four-blade propellers.
Structure: Mark I, all-wood. Mark II, predominantly metal. Both fabric-covered.
Dimensions: Span, 96ft 10in (Mk II, 95ft 4in); length, 58ft 3in; height, 19ft 7¾in; wing area, 2,163 sq ft.
Weights: Mark I. Tare, 12,760lb; all-up, 19,920lb. Mark II. Tare, 13,304lb; all-up, 20,465lb.
Performance: Records not traced.
Armament: Either one 21in Whitehead torpedo or up to four 550lb bombs carried externally; gun armament of three single Lewis guns in nose, midships dorsal and midships ventral positions.
Prototypes: Two, N171 and N172. N171 (Mk I) believed to have flown in mid-1924, and N172 (Mk II) on 22 April 1927. No production.

Handley Page
H.P.25 Hendon

A direct development of the single-seat H.P.19 Hanley, the two-seat H.P.25

Hendon was tendered to Air Ministry Specification 37/22 during the autumn of 1923, this requirement seeking a number of naval research aircraft, embracing the rôles of carrier-borne torpedo bomber and fleet reconnaissance aircraft[1]. The Hendon torpedo bomber earned a contract for six proto-

types, N9274-N9279, a generosity that reflected the Air Ministry's determination to acquire plenty of test aircraft in advance of a Blackburn Dart-replacement, whose Specification was already in the early stages of preparation and would probably call for a gun-armed two-seater.

The third Hendon Mk I, N9727, after being fitted with sweptback wings; the exhaust pipes were arranged so as to warm the rear of the torpedo, when fitted. This aircraft was successively modified to Mark II and III standard and was the aircraft which, carrying a torpedo, landed on HMS Furious *without use of arrester gear in 1925. (Photo: Handley Page Ltd.)*

The Hendon retained the Hanley III's Lion IIB, but with modified exhaust system; the fuselage was lengthened and the rudder enlarged. Full-span leading edge slats were fitted to the folding wings, and the inner pairs of interplane struts were omitted, while the divided undercarriage structures were revised, the swing-struts being moved aft of the wheels. In contrast to the single-seater, which was unarmed, the Hendon featured both a synchronized Vickers front gun and a Lewis gun on the rear cockpit.

The first aircraft, N9274, was flown by Arthur Wilcockson at Cricklewood on 7 July 1924, and delivered to Martlesham Heath the next month for contract trials. In the course of these flights the aircraft was found to be tail-heavy when carrying the torpedo, a characteristic which was corrected by introducing five degrees of sweepback to the wings outboard of the fold line; this modification was, in time, included on all the Hendons, either before or after their first flights. The remaining five aircraft were all flying by early September, being flown by Wilcockson, Gordon Olley and Capt Walter L Rogers (the

last-named a commercial pilot of Handley Page Air Transport Ltd).

These aircraft then embarked on a long series of flight trials with the object of examining the effects of various leading edge slat/slot designs, evolved under the direction of George Volkert after his return to Handley Page early in 1924. The Hendon Mark II (as N9724, N9725 and N9727 became when modified) was fitted with vertical-motion slats, and the Hendon Mark III (N9727) was modified

to feature interlinked slotted flaps, slats and ailerons; In October 1925 this aircraft was successfully landed on the carrier HMS *Furious*, without the use of arrester gear and while carrying a Mark VIII torpedo.

Although this experimental work provided a mass of research data of use in design for flying at low airspeeds, the invention of the automatic slat shortly afterwards, of essentially simple operation, rendered the Hendons redundant.

Type: Single-engine, two-seat, two-bay biplane experimental carrier-borne torpedo bomber.

Air Ministry Specification: 37/22

Manufacturer: Handley Page Ltd, Cricklewood, London,

Powerplant: One 450hp Napier Lion IIB twelve-cylinder water-cooled in-line engine driving two-blade propeller.

Dimensions: Span, 46ft 0in; length, 34ft 6in; wing area, 562 sq ft.

Weight: Max all-up, 6,970lb.

Performance: Max speed, 110 mph at 2,000ft; landing speed, 55 mph; service ceiling, 9,500ft.

Armament: One forward-firing synchronized 0.303in Vickers machine gun and one Lewis gun with Scarff ring on rear cockpit; one Mark VIII torpedo or two 230lb bombs carried externally.

Prototype: Six, N9724-N9729. N9724 first flown at Cricklewood on 7 July 1924 by Arthur Wilcockson. No production.

---

[1] C H Barnes relates how the Hendon's design tender documents were accidentally left in a London underground train, a lapse which earned Handley Page a severe reprimand from the Air Ministry as being a gross breach of the Official Secrets Act.

Handley Page H.P.28 Handcross

Specification 26/23, issued in late 1923, set out the Air Ministry's requirements for a single-engine day bomber powered by the 650hp Rolls-Royce Condor III. The Specification was amended several times during the next two years but, as originally promulgated, called for a maximum speed of 120 mph at 10,000

feet, a crew of up to three, and a bomb load of at least one 550lb bomb; a landing speed of not more than 55 mph was also stipulated. Preference was expressed for metal construction and, if wooden prototypes were ordered, any production order subsequently placed would require metal construction.

Schemed and tendered by 'Star' Richards for Handley Page, the H.P.28 Handcross[1] was a fairly large, three-bay biplane of wooden construction (conforming to newly introduced increased strength requirements) with a fully-

cowled Condor and frontal radiator, a big 15-foot diameter two-blade, hollow-steel, Leitner-Watts propeller with ground-adjustable pitch being employed. The pilot's cockpit was located directly beneath the upper wing, between pairs of inwards-raked cabane struts, the fuel

---

[1] At the time the Handcross was referred to as the C.7 — part of the manufacturer's arcane system of nomenclature. It was George Volkert who introduced the retrospective 'H.P.' system later in the 1920s, a system that survived until the final days of the company in the 1960s.

being carried in gravity tanks projecting above and below the upper wings on either side.

The divided undercarriage structures provided a wheel track of 13ft 6in, the single 550lb bomb being recessed into the port side of a ventral fuselage fairing which also contained the bomb aimer's station, this crew member lying prone beneath the pilot's cockpit. Gun armament comprised a single forward-firing Vickers gun on the starboard side of the nose decking, a Lewis gun on a Scarff ring amidships and another firing aft through a ventral hatch. A crew of three was provided for, but this was later reduced to two, the rear gunner being required to double as bomb aimer. There was no requirement for folding wings, and bomb carriers could also be attached under the lower wings; perhaps surprisingly, wing slats were not fitted on this Handley Page aircraft, presumably on account of the fairly generous landing speed requirement.

Three prototypes, J7498-J7500, were ordered on 1 March 1924, the first being flown by Capt Hubert Stanford Broad MBE, AFC, at Cricklewood on 6 March that year, before being delivered to No 22 Squadron, commanded by Sqn Ldr Tom Harry England, at Martlesham Heath. The other two prototypes were flown during the next two months, J7500 being of all-metal construction.

Trouble was experienced with the wing fuel tanks, these being found to cause airflow separation and buffeting at high angles of attack, especially during landing. This was remedied by repositioning the tanks entirely below the wings. Engine overheating was also experienced during ground running and

The third, all-metal, Handcross, J7500, showing the enlarged and repositioned underwing fuel tanks, and the cooling air exit vents cut in the sides of the cowling. The ventral gun hatch has been faired over, having been found to be unusable. (Photo: Handley Page Ltd, Neg No 132)

taxying, despite the use of controllable frontal shutters. Large circular vent holes, capable of being blanked off selectively, were therefore cut in the sides of the cowling.

Other criticisms were levelled at the engine exhaust system, which gave rise to suspicion that carbon monoxide could enter the cockpit, and at the design of the ventral crew fairing, which was found to be so draughty that the gunner's stations were said to be unusable.

By the time J7498 underwent Service trials with No 11 Squadron at Netheravon in August 1925, these problems were of academic importance only. The Specification had undergone considerable change; the bomb load demanded had been doubled, at some expense of

range requirements, and the maximum speed, which the Handcross had failed to satisfy in any case, was increased to 120 mph at 12,000 feet.

Thus, although the Handley Page aircraft underwent periodic performance trials at Martlesham Heath, they were allocated to general research testing, J7500 spending much of its life with the RAE at Farnborough. The last Handcross, J7499, was struck off charge in 1929. By then the Hawker Horsley (see page 161), the successful contender to Specification 26/23, had entered service, largely on account of its ability to double as a torpedo bomber — subject of a separate Requirement, but being considered in parallel to 26/23 by the Air Ministry.

Type: Single-engine, two/three-crew, three-bay biplane day bomber.
Air Ministry Specification: 26/23
Manufacturer: Handley Page Ltd, Cricklewood, London.
Powerplant: One 650hp Rolls-Royce Condor III twelve-cylinder, water-cooled in-line engine driving 15ft-diameter Leitner-Watts hollow-steel two-blade propeller.
Structure: First two aircraft of spruce construction; third aircraft of metal construction.
Dimensions: Span, 60ft; length, 40ft; wing area, 788 sq ft.
Weights: Tare, 5,215lb; all-up, 75,00lb.
Performance: Max speed, 106 mph at 10,000ft; 120 mph at 2,000ft; ceiling, 19,250ft; range, 500 miles.
Armament: Bomb load of one 550lb bomb recessed into underside of fuselage, or two 230lb bombs carried under the lower wings. One synchronized 0.303in Vickers machine gun in starboard side of nose decking, one Lewis gun with Scarff ring in midships dorsal position and one Lewis gun in ventral hatch.
Prototypes: Three, J7498-J7500. J7498 first flown by Capt Hubert Broad at Cricklewood on 6 December 1924. No production.

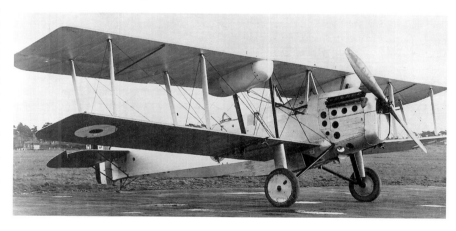

Bristol Type 90 Berkeley

Also designed to the day bomber Specification 26/23, the Bristol Type 90 Berkeley was largely the work of Wilfrid

T Reid and Clifford Wilfrid Tinson (the latter recently arrived from A V Roe & Co Ltd) under the direction of Capt Frank Barnwell. Like the Handley Page Handcross, described above, it was a three-bay biplane, powered by a 650hp Condor III and capable of carrying a single 550lb bomb under the fuselage or two smaller bombs under the lower

wings. However, the rear gunner occupied a bomb aiming station on the floor of the fuselage aft of the central bomb carrier in a large cabin which extended from the engine bulkhead to a fuselage frame nine feet aft of the wings. The pilot occupied a cockpit with an excellent field of view forward of the upper wing, whose centresection chord was

Left: *The first, all-wooden Berkeley, J7403, at Filton, with a wooden two-blade Watts propeller, probably at about the time of its first flight as no bomb racks have yet been fitted. (Photo: RAF Museum, Neg No P0013980)*

Below: *J7405, the Berkeley which introduced a metal wing. It is fitted with the Leitner-Watts hollow-steel variable-pitch propeller and the radiator block has been divested of its cowling panels on the pretext of improved cooling; note also that fuselage and wing bomb racks are carried. (Photo: C H Barnes Collection)*

reduced by cutouts in the leading and trailing edges, this section accommodating the fuel tanks.

Three prototypes, J7406-J7408, were ordered in April 1924 and construction of these went ahead fairly quickly until November, when, as J7406 approached completion, new stress levels and more stringent spruce grading were ordered by the RAE, requiring the fuselage longerons to be removed and replaced, thus delaying the aircraft's first flight, made by Flt Lt Cyril Frank Uwins AFC, RAFO, on 5 March 1925 — three months after the Handcross.

Arriving at Martlesham at the end of the month, J7406 was assessed as being somewhat better than the Handcross, both in the air and on the ground, although one may conjecture that benefit had been gained after learning of the criticisms levelled at the Handley Page aeroplane. For instance, it was perhaps significant that the cowling panels round the frontal radiator block were removed on the second and third Berkeleys — a more drastic remedy for engine overheating than that adopted by Handley Page — although no evidence can be found that the Berkeley ever suffered from overheating to the same extent.

The second aircraft was not flown until 24 November 1925, by which time J7406 had completed its Service trials with No 11 (Bomber) Squadron, this despite the fact that Bristol had been informed that no production order would be placed for the aircraft. The final

Berkeley, introducing metal wings, was flown on 11 February 1926, delivered to Martlesham in June and then flown to Catterick on 12 November that year for a series of experiments involving long-range short-wave wireless equipment. It was ultimately delivered to Farnborough where it underwent various trial programmes until July 1928.

The Berkeley proved to be a sound design, albeit unimaginative and representing no significant advance; nor was it compatible with the carrying of a torpedo owing to difficulty in reconciling the aircraft's centre of gravity. Thus in this respect, if in no others, it was at a disadvantage when compared with the very adaptable Horsley.

Type: Single-engine, two-seat, three-bay biplane day bomber.
Air Ministry Specification: 26/23
Manufacturer: The Bristol Aeroplane Co Ltd, Filton, Bristol.
Powerplant: One 650hp Rolls-Royce Condor III twelve-cylinder, water-cooled in-line engine driving two-blade wooden Watts, or two-blade hollow-steel Leitner-Watts propeller.
Structure: First two aircraft of all-wood construction, and third aircraft with metal wings.
Dimensions: Span, 57ft 11in; length, 47ft 6in; height, 14ft 4in; wing area, 985 sq ft.
Weights: Tare, 5,200lb; all-up, 8,128lb.
Performance: Max speed, 120 mph at 2,000 ft; service ceiling, 17,900ft; range, 860 miles.
Armament: Bomb load of one 550lb or two 230lb bombs; one synchronized 0.303in Vickers machine gun on port side of nose, one Lewis gun with Scarff ring on rear cockpit and another firing aft in a ventral hatch.
Prototypes: Three, J7403-J7405; J7403 first flown on 5 March 1925 by Flt Lt Cyril Uwins at Filton. No production.

Deployment of British Bomber Squadrons — 1 January 1925

Royal Air Force
Home Bases

No. 7 Sqn. (H)	Vickers Vimy	Bircham Newton, Norfolk
No. 9 Sqn. (H)	Vickers Vimy	Manston, Kent
No. 11 Sqn. (L)	Fairey Fawn III	Netheravon, Wiltshire
No. 12 Sqn. (L)	Fairey Fawn II/III	Andover, Hampshire
No. 39 Sqn. (L)	de Havilland D.H.9A	Spittlegate, Lincs
No. 58 Sqn. (H)	Vickers Vimy and Virginia	Worthy Down, Hampshire
No. 99 Sqn. (M)	Avro Aldershot	Bircham Newton, Norfolk
No. 100 Sqn. (L)	Fairey Fawn	Spittlegate, Lincs.
No. 207 Sqn. (L)	de Havilland D.H.9A	Eastchurch, Kent

Middle East

No. 8 Sqn. (L)	de Havilland D.H.9A	Basra, Iraq
No. 30 Sqn. (L)	de Havilland D.H.9A	Kirkuk, Iraq
No. 45 Sqn. (BT)	Vickers Vernon	Hinaidi, Iraq
No. 47 Sqn. (L)	de Havilland D.H.9A	Helwan, Egypt
No. 55 Sqn. (L)	de Havilland D.H.9A	Hinaidi, Iraq
No. 70 Sqn. (BT)	Vickers Vernon	Hinaidi, Iraq
No. 84 Sqn. (L)	de Havilland D.H.9A	Shaibah, Iraq
No. 216 Sqn. (H)	Vickers Vimy	Heliopolis, Egypt

India

No. 27 Sqn. (L)	de Havilland D.H.9A	Risalpur
No. 60 Sqn. (L)	de Havilland D.H.9A	Risalpur

Fleet Air Arm

No. 460 Flt.	Blackburn Dart	HMS *Eagle*
No. 461 Flt.	Blackburn Dart	HMS *Furious*
No. 462 Flt.	Blackburn Dart	HMS *Furious*

(H) — Heavy bomber; (M) — Medium bomber; (L) — Light bomber; (BT) — Bomber Transport.

Note: Blackburn Darts were classified as Fleet Torpedo aircraft but were adaptable to carry a bomb load. From 1st January 1930 all Fleet Air Arm Flights from Nos 460 to 466 were reclassified as Fleet Torpedo Bomber Flights.

Hawker Horsley

Regarded by observers at the time as an outsider in the Air Ministry's competition to obtain a new day bomber, the H G Hawker Engineering Company possessed no first-hand experience in the design and building of bomber aircraft when it tendered to Specification 26/23 what was an entirely orthodox design by Wilfred George Carter employing a well-proven formula embodying a broad-chord high-lift upper wing and a reduced-span, narrow-chord, low-drag lower wing.

This tender was accepted by the Air Ministry in February 1924, but with certain reservations as the Hawker company was not yet prepared to disclose any plans to introduce manufacture of metal airframes in its Kingston factory, and it was mandatory that any production order resulting from the prototype competition would require the aircraft to be of metal construction.

The apparent indecision by Hawker in fact concealed disagreement among the management, Carter expressing an opinion that it would not be possible, within the timescale demanded, to produce a relatively large aeroplane (implicit in the requirements) in metal, bearing in mind that almost all the Kingston workforce would have to be

The first all-wood 26/23 Horsley prototype, J7511, with radiators on the sides of the fuselage amidships; it also featured no sweepback on the wings and a deep rudder; note the plain 3-strut undercarriage that was, in a moment of lèse-majesté, *to suffer failure with its designer aboard.* (Photo: Sydney Camm Collection)

retrained. Fred Sigrist, the Works Manager, accepted that all-metal military aeroplanes were 'just around the corner', and, himself a master welder by trade, was able to point to his own small experimental metal working department. He it was who undertook to handle the manufacture of a metal aeroplane, provided that this could be allowed to progress by stages. Thomas Sopwith, the chairman, was asked to discover whether the Air Ministry would accept a wooden prototype (without prejudice) for competitive evaluation and, if Hawker was declared the winner, would be

prepared to accept a mixed first batch of wooden and metal aircraft.

Partly as a result of this disagreement, Carter left Hawker in 1924 to join Short Bros at Rochester (to engage in the design of the Crusader racing seaplane of predominantly wooden construction). His place as chief designer at Kingston was taken by Sydney Camm, a young man whose sole previous design experience was in wooden aircraft. Yet Camm possessed a number of rare talents, not least his extraordinary attention to detail, and it was probably this trait that transformed the Horsley from medioc-

A pair of Horsley IIs of No 504 (County of Nottingham) Squadron, flying from Hucknall in 1929; by then wing slats had become standard on the aircraft, seen here fitted with wing racks for four 230lb bombs. (Photo: GSL/JMB Collection)

rity to superiority in its particular field. His other much admired philosophy — which he propounded throughout his long, illustrious career, and which many of his peers applauded but all too few emulated — was that 'the pilot is the vital element of an aeroplane, the starting point in its design, and about whom it must be designed.'

A single prototype, J7511, was ordered in about June 1924 and was nearing completion when it was slightly damaged in an accident (whose nature is not known). When first flown by Flt Lt P W S ('George') Bulman in about March 1925, the aircraft, named the Horsley after Thomas Sopwith's home, Horsley Towers, and powered by a 650hp Condor III driving a 13ft 4in diameter Watts wooden propeller, featured a closely-cowled engine with vertical radiator blocks attached to the sides of the fuselage just forward of the pilot's cockpit. The wings were staggered, two-bay structures, ailerons being fitted in the upper wings only, the outboard pairs of interplane struts diverging outwards, and the inboard struts being of sturdy 'N' configuration. The fuel tanks were located in the deep upper wing centre-section, and the divided main undercarriage structures comprised simple V-struts and vertical oleo legs.

The two-man crew occupied cockpits immediately aft of the wings, being arranged in close tandem. Provision was made to mount racks for one 550lb bomb under the fuselage and for two 230lb bombs under the wings; the former was later strengthened to enable a 1,000lb bomb to be carried.

Bulman applauded the Horsley's handling qualities but encountered some engine overheating while taxying, and also suggested a change to a finer-pitch propeller. The side radiators were abandoned in favour of an external 'chin' installation with shutter exit, this proving successful as well as being 60lb lighter. It is not known whether this modification had been included when J7511 arrived at Martlesham on 4 May to undergo the contractor's performance trials with No 22 Squadron. After a brief return to Brooklands, it joined No 11 (Bomber) Squadron at the end of July for Service trials, returning home once more the next month when, following a tyre burst, the undercarriage collapsed (the pilot being Bulman and his passen-

ger Camm himself — the only occasion on which he ever flew in one of his aeroplanes).

This accident prompted Camm to introduce an improved undercarriage with V strut-mounted swing struts aft of the wheels, this gear being incorporated in the second prototype, J7721, which was flown by Bulman on 6 December at the start of intensive flight trials at Brooklands. This aircraft featured 'hand-built' metal wings of considerably higher strength factors, an attribute that caused the Horsley to be delivered to Farnborough for a short series of assessment flights. J7721 attended the 1926 Hendon Display as New Type No 13, by which time the Horsley had been declared the winner of the Specification 26/23 contest, and a production order for 40 aircraft placed — to conform to a new Specification, 22/25. In an unusual annex to the contract, the Air Ministry stipulated that ten aircraft (including both Mk I wooden aircraft as well as some Mk II part-metal aircraft) were to be completed by the end of 1926, and that all forty aircraft should be complete and ready for delivery by the end of 1927. The original prototype, J7511, was withdrawn from the type trials and allocated for engine testing, being flown with Condor IIIA and IIIB, Eagle VIII, Rolls-Royce H-10 and 580hp Napier Lion V during the next three years.

Conversion to metal production at Kingston progressed more quickly than expected, with the result that aircraft with airframes partly constructed of metal (referred to as Mark IIs) began emerging from the factory alongside all-wood aircraft (Mark Is) as early as August 1926, and on the 30th No 100 (Bomber) Squadron took delivery of its first aircraft, and reached its established strength of twelve by the end of the year — when the last of its Fawns was flown

A fine in-flight view of a Horsley II bomber, J8615, adapted to carry the 18-inch torpedo, and shown here flying near Portsmouth (note the warship just to the right of the aircraft's propeller) with the Gosport-based Torpedo Development Flight in 1931. (Photo: Flight, Neg No 12310)

Horsley J8620 fitted with an Armstrong Siddeley Leopard II radial engine, during performance evaluation at Martlesham Heath in 1930 with torpedo. The aircraft was found to be impossible to spin with the wing slots open, so they were temporarily fixed in the closed position. (Photo: Air Ministry, A & AEE)

away, four months ahead of schedule. In January 1927 No 11 (Bomber) Squadron, commanded by Wg Cdr J H A Landon DSO, AFC, at Netheravon began replacing its Fawns with Horsleys.

The aircraft was generally liked in service, and its ground-adjustable variable-incidence tailplane was much appreciated in view of the wide range of bomb loads carried on exercises and practice sorties. By mid-1927 aircraft of a second production batch (25 Mark IIs, J8597-J8621) were beginning to arrive on No 11 Squadron with 665hp Condor IIIA engines.

It was the Horsley's excellent load-carrying ability that recommended it for an attempt on the world long-distance record, and a specially prepared aircraft of this production batch, J8607, was modified to carry a total of 1,100 gallons of fuel in additional wing and fuel tanks; the cockpits were moved aft by eighteen inches to allow space for the latter, and the undercarriage was strengthened to permit a maximum take-off weight increased from less than 9,000lb to over 14,000lb.

This aircraft was delivered to a specially-formed Long Range Flight early in May, and on the 20th Flt Lt Charles Roderick Carr (later Air Marshal Sir Roderick, KBE, CB, DFC, AFC), accompanied by Flt Lt L E M Gillman, took off from Cranwell in an attempt to reach India non-stop. The aircraft was, however, forced down in the Persian Gulf following fuel starvation, having successfully established a new world record of 3,420 miles, but one that stood for only a few hours before Charles Lindbergh landed at Paris after his famous Atlantic crossing on 22 May (a flight of 3,590 miles).

Carr and Gillman made two further attempts to reach India in a second, similar Horsley, J8608, on 16 June and 2 August, but both failed; the first ended no further than Martlesham Heath where the greatly overloaded aeroplane was landed safely after an oil leak developed, while the second was terminated by a forced landing in the Danube.

One other regular RAF squadron flew Horsleys when No 33 (Bomber) Squad-

ron re-formed on 1 March 1929 at Netheravon with a mixed complement of Mark Is and IIs, although this came to be regarded as no more than a training deployment when it was announced that No 33 was to become the RAF's first Hawker Hart light bomber squadron the following year.

Horsley Mark IIs provided the initial equipment of No 504 (County of Nottingham) Squadron of the Special Reserve when it began flying the aircraft at Hucknall on 3 September 1929; these Horsleys remained in service with the Squadron until February 1934. During the Squadron's annual summer camp on 7 August 1933, one of its aeroplanes, J8025, accidentally landed on top of No 25 (Fighter) Squadron's hangar at Hawkinge and set fire to the building, destroying six Hawker Fury fighters

inside. The Horsley's crew escaped unhurt.

Coastal Torpedo Bomber

Prompted by the issue of a Specification, 24/25, for a coastal defence torpedo bomber, Hawker modified a Horsley II, J8006, to carry a 2,069lb 18in torpedo in August 1926, and this was received sufficiently well when sent for performance evaluation at Martlesham Heath that month for the Air Ministry to issue a new Specification, 17/27, for a production torpedo bomber version of the Horsley. This coincided with the first flight of the first all-metal example, J8932, in May 1927, and equipped to carry the torpedo this aeroplane paid a brief visit to the A & AEE before the end of that year.

As a result, orders totalling 48 all-

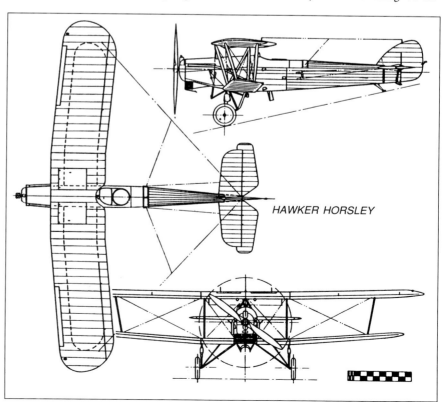

HAWKER HORSLEY

The second Dantorp, '202', for Denmark, shown here at the MAEE, Felixstowe, with twin-float undercarriage and torpedo; the floats were mounted as separate structures without inter-bracing, thereby permitting the launching of a torpedo. (Photo: Air Ministry, MAEE)

metal Horsley torpedo bombers were placed with Hawker, the first, S1236, being delivered to Martlesham for full performance and torpedo trials in July 1928. The following month two aircraft, S1237 and S1239, were issued to the Coastal Defence Torpedo Flight at Donibristle. On 1 October this unit was redesignated No 36 (Torpedo Bomber) Squadron, taking on a complement of eleven Horsley Mk II torpedo aircraft. (The designation Mark III for the torpedo aircraft was never officially sanctioned, though sometimes incorrectly used.)

A deteriorating military situation in the Far East in 1930 led to the decision to strengthen the defences of Singapore, and No 36 Squadron received new Horsleys, powered by Condor IIIBs and prepared for tropical operation. Leaving behind its initial issue of Horsleys, No 36 Squadron sailed for Seletar, Singapore, its new aeroplanes being shipped out aboard ss *City of Barcelona* from Birkenhead. It continued to fly Horsleys until July 1935 when these aircraft were replaced by Vickers Vildebeests.

No 36 Squadron's duties and aircraft at Donibristle were taken over by No 100 Squadron, redesignated a Torpedo Bomber unit in November 1930. This Squadron was also shipped out to Seletar in December 1933, although by then it had received Vildebeests.

Various efforts were made to modernise the Horsley, especially in the torpedo bomber rôle, these being concerned with introducing new engines, of which the Armstrong Siddeley Leopard 14-cylinder air-cooled radial had seemed the most promising. Several versions of this engine (see data table) were flown in J8620 and assessed by the A & AEE, but it was generally disliked and found unacceptable; another unsuccessful engine, flown in the all-metal J8932, was the 810hp Rolls-Royce H-10, but this also found little favour owing to constant ice accretion in the carburettor.

The first aircraft of the final all-metal Horsley production batch, S1436, which had been retained in the United Kingdom, was allocated to Rolls-Royce in 1935 for that company's programme to develop the P.V.12 engine, shortly to become the famous Merlin, and was fitted with a succession of variants, of which the Merlin Mark X made its first flight on 7 September 1937, this 1,145hp engine eventually being chosen to power the Whitley V and Halifax heavy bombers. A second Horsley, J8611, joined S1436 in 1935 for flight work on the Merlin and continued until 1938.

Mention should be made of two other aspects of Horsley operations. Trials as a floatplane with the MAEE began in October 1929 with S1247 and were continued by J8612 in August 1933, leading to interest being expressed by Denmark and the export of two aircraft (named the Dantorp and powered by Leopard II engines) with interchangeable wheel and float undercarriages to that country.

Finally, as a result of the use of an early Horsley I (J7995) by No 25 (Fighter) Squadron as a makeshift target tug in 1927, two or three further target towing conversions (with wind-driven winches on the port side of the fuselage) were made among the all-metal aircraft, and at least one, S1452, was shipped out to Singapore in February 1932 for use by No 36 (Torpedo Bomber) Squadron.

Type: Single-engine, two-seat, two-bay biplane day bomber and land-based torpedo bomber.

Air Ministry Specifications: 26/23. 22/25 and 23/25.

Manufacturer: The H G Hawker Engineering Co Ltd, Kingston-upon-Thames, Surrey.

Powerplant: Production. One 650hp Rolls-Royce Condor III 12-cylinder, water-cooled in-line engine driving two-blade wooden Watts propeller; 665hp Condor IIIA and IIIB. Experimental. 460hp Rolls-Royce Eagle VIII; 810hp Rolls-Royce H-10; 480hp Condor (compression-ignition); Rolls-Royce Buzzard III; 1,025hp Rolls-Royce Merlin C, E, F, G, Mk II and Mk X; 765hp Armstrong Siddeley Leopard I (800hp Mk II and IIIA, and 805hp Mk III); Junkers Jumo IV.

Construction: Mark I, all-wood; Mk II, composite or all-metal.

Dimensions: Span, 56ft 5¾in; length, 38ft 4½in; height, 14ft 1in; wing area, 693 sq ft.

Weights: Tare, 5,360lb; all-up, 8,230lb.

Performance: Max speed, 126 mph at 3,200ft; climb to 10,000ft, 12 min 50 sec; service ceiling, 18,450ft; range, 900 miles (normal).

Armament: One synchronized 0.303in Vickers machine gun in nose, one Lewis gun with Scarff ring on rear cockpit and another firing aft through ventral hatch. Bomb load of up to one 1,000lb or two 550lb bombs or equivalent weight; torpedo bomber carried an 18in torpedo.

Prototypes: Three, J7511 (wood); J7721 (part-metal); J8932 (all-metal). J8006 (a production Mark II became the torpedo bomber prototype). J7511 was first flown in about March 1925 by Flt Lt P W S Bulman at Brooklands.

Production: A total of 113 production Horsleys was built. 10 Mark Is (J7987-J7996); 55 Mark II bombers (J7997-J8026 and J8597-J8621); and 48 Mark II torpedo bombers (S1236-S1247, S1436-S1453 and S1597-S1614). The torpedo bombers were sometimes referred to as Mark IIIs but this was not an official designation.

Summary of Service: Hawker Horsley day bombers served with Nos 11, 33 and 100 (Bomber) Squadrons, and No 504 (County of Nottingham) Squadron, AAF, and as torpedo bombers with No 36 and 100 (Torpedo Bomber) Squadrons. Horsleys also served in small numbers with the Anti-Aircraft Co-operation Flight, No 25 (Fighter) Squadron (as a target tug), the RAF College, Cranwell, and No 1 Flying Training School.

Westland Yeovil

Arthur Davenport's approach to Specification 26/23 was orthodox, his Yeovil biplane being of much the same general configuration as the other three design tenders, although it was certainly surprising that the Westland aircraft was almost entirely of wooden construction, bearing in mind that the company already possessed plenty of experience in building metal airframes and that the Air Ministry was making it all too clear that an uncompromising switch to metal was required.

After receipt by Westland of the Specification details in August 1923, design began three months later after the decision was taken to aim for the smallest possible airframe compatible with the preferred Condor engine and the minimum permissible bomb load — yet the resulting design was little different in size and weight from the other contestants.

In the event, Westland joined Handley Page and Bristol in being awarded a contract for three prototypes, J7508-J7510, in March 1925, and manufacture began the next month.

The fuselage was constructed in three sections; only the nose section, comprising the engine mounting and cowlings were of metal, being steel tube and aluminium sheet respectively. The centre and rear sections were built up on four spruce longerons and spruce struts to form a box-girder with wire cross-bracing, and fabric and ply covering. The wings were entirely of wood, being constructed about a pair of ash box spars; even the interplane struts were of solid wood, shaped to aerofoil section.

The undercarriage employed vertical oleo struts with rear radius rods attached to the lower longerons and wing spars by means of four V-struts with a transverse spreader bar between the wheels, the latter demanding that the bomb be carried somewhat further aft than was usual in order to avoid fouling the undercarriage. This weight aft required the pilot's and gunner's cockpits to be positioned well forward, so much so that the former was located directly below the upper mainplane so that, despite provision of a large wing cutout, the view from the front cockpit was severely impaired.

The engine installation employed the familiar frontal radiator, but this was

The first Yeovil, J7508, probably at Andover shortly after its maiden flight. Just visible are the streamlined over-wing fuel tanks, while the rear bomb slip, almost directly below the gunner's cockpit, indicates the aft location of the bomb. (Photo: Real Photographs Co)

fully cowled with frontal shutters, thus demanding generous provision of cooling air exit louvres on the side panels.

An innovative feature was the manner in which the fuel was accommodated in the upper wings, a pair of wide but shallow tanks being shaped to provide a deep aerofoil section proud of the upper surface, thereby probably imparting an appreciable element of additional lift.

The first prototype, J7508, was flown by freelance pilot Frank Courtney at Yeovil's small airfield on 3 April 1925, and transferred to Andover's larger field the same day, whence much of the subsequent flying was performed by Laurence Openshaw, Westland's recently appointed pilot. Later the same month

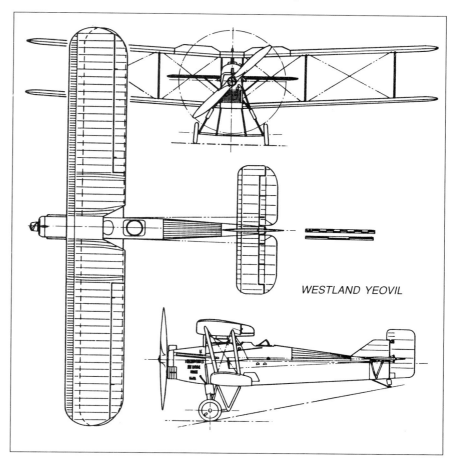

WESTLAND YEOVIL

the aircraft was delivered to Martlesham Heath for acceptance trials by No 22 Squadron of the A & AEE; the performance trials were completed in July.

The Yeovil was the last of the 26/23 contenders to undergo evaluation and attracted a good deal of criticism. The undercarriage was considered to be unnecessarily complex without being particularly robust, apart from making difficult the loading of the bomb under the fuselage. A lack of directional control came in for much adverse comment, particularly at the lower speeds, and the view from the pilot's cockpit was deemed to be the worst of all four aircraft being considered.

The second Yeovil appeared late in 1925 with a much taller rudder, but was otherwise little changed from the first machine. The third aircraft, believed to have incorporated an all-metal fuselage, but retaining the wooden wings, was flown in 1926, long after the competition had been decided in favour of the Hawker Horsley. Therefore, as bomb-

carrying was no longer relevant, J7510 featured a plain V-strut undercarriage, retaining the oleo struts but adopting a cross-axle. The flat over-wing fuel tanks were discarded and replaced by long, streamlined and ribbed containers which now contributed more drag and no lift, and probably further reduced the pilot's field of view. The vertical tail surfaces had been redesigned with an enlarged

fin, while the rudder reverted to its original size.

Allocated to general research flying, J7510 underwent trials to compare the performance of the ground-adjustable Leitner-Watts and Hele-Shaw Beacham propellers. J7509 attended the 1926 Hendon Display as a 'New Type', and was the last of the three Yeovils to remain flying in 1928.

Type: Single-engine, two-seat, two-bay biplane day bomber.
Air Ministry Specification: 26/23
Manufacturer: Westland Aircraft Works Ltd, Yeovil, Somerset.
Powerplant: One 650hp Rolls-Royce Condor III 12-cylinder water-cooled, in-line engine driving two-blade wooden Watts propeller.
Structure: Composite wood and metal construction.
Dimensions: Span, 59ft 6in; length, 36ft 10in; height, 14ft 3in; wing area, 813 sq ft.
Weights: Tare, 5,191lb; all-up, 8,121lb (with one 520lb bomb).
Performance: Max speed, 123 mph at 6,500ft; climb to 10,000ft, 12 min 24 sec; service ceiling, 17,700ft; range, 640 miles.
Armament: One synchronized 0.303in Vickers machine gun on nose decking and one Lewis gun with Scarff ring on rear cockpit; provision for one Lewis gun firing through ventral hatch. Bomb load, one 550lb bomb carried externally under fuselage.
Prototypes: Three, J7508-J7510; J7508 first flown by Frank Courtney at Yeovil on 3 April 1925, No production.

Fairey Fox

The Fairey test pilot, Norman Macmillan, poses with the first production Fox Mark I, J7941. Just visible is the surface-type radiator in the upper wing centresection. The Felix engine installation was distinguishable by its lower propeller shaft line. (Photo: Flight, Neg No 3853)

It will have been evident in describing the concept and selection of British bombers during the early 1920s — particularly the single-engine day bombers — that in almost every instance the various Air Ministry Specifications had been beset by restrictions based on inadequate research and prior consultation. Examples of this had been provided by such paradoxes as those afforded by fuel location, defensive arma-

ment, crew positions and duties, engine cooling requirements and many others. In the matter of fuel location, the demands made for wing tanks had originated following a number of accidents in which pilots had perished when fuselage tanks had caught fire. Fireproof bulkheads had become mandatory to protect the tank from the effects of an engine fire, until the requirement was changed to the provision of wing tanks, despite

their proximity to the pilot and crew. No thought had been given to demanding a fireproof bulkhead *between a fuselage tank and the pilot.*

Nor, for that matter, had due consideration been afforded to the commonsense of the aircraft designer himself — at a time when the Air Ministry was obliged to rely to a considerable extent on the ingenuity of the aircraft industry. Matters had come to a head when the

The attractive lines of the Fox are apparent in this view of the second of four Mark IAs, J9026, being flown by a No 12 Squadron pilot in May 1929. The Kestrel's small retractable radiator is shown in the extended position just forward of the undercarriage oleo legs. This particular aeroplane continued to fly with the RAE until July 1934. (Photo: *Flight*, Neg No 6870)

Fairey Fawn had been accepted for service in the RAF, an aircraft that possessed an overall performance about five per cent *lower* than the aircraft it was intended to replace, while its normal bomb load remained exactly the same. (During the first three years of service almost one third of the Fawns in the first production batch of 50 aircraft suffered flying accidents, involving the loss of 17 crew lives[1].)

When first conceived, Specification 26/23 (whose contenders are described in the four preceding entries) was not so much primarily concerned with seeking to improve the design of day bombers but to acquire an all-metal aircraft, and resulted in a largely wooden aeroplane being selected as the successful contender on its weight-lifting ability — a strange criterion for a 'light' day bomber!

It was therefore little wonder that it was Richard Fairey, himself somewhat critical of the Fawn for its implicit lack of ingenuity, who threw convention to the winds and embarked on a private venture in an attempt to break the stalemate brought on by ill-judged caution.

This process of independent thought had started when Fairey witnessed the victory by an American Curtiss R-3 racing seaplane, powered by a Curtiss D-12 engine, in the Schneider Trophy race on 28 September 1923 — about a month after the issue of Specification 26/23. Impressed by the low frontal area of the engine's installation, using surface

radiators, Fairey set about acquiring an example of the D-12 (it was not to be licence-built in Britain, but 50 engines, named the Felix, were imported), and on 20 April 1924 Marcel Lobelle (design) and P A Ralli (aerodynamics) began work on a new light bomber, to be named the Fox, in which minimum overall size, simplification of sytems, and low frontal area and reduction of drag were to be paramount.

With single-bay, sharply-staggered wings spanning only 33ft 6in, the new prototype possessed an exceptionally clean engine installation, its two radiators being of the surface type, located flush with the underside of the inboard ends of the main upper wing panels. The 75-gallon fuel tank was placed inside the fuselage with fireproof bulkheads fore and aft. Apart from steel tubular components in the engine mounting, centre fuselage and undercarriage structure, the aircraft was constructed of wood. On production aircraft, the forward-firing Vickers gun was 'buried' in the fuselage side and fired through a long blast channel ex-

tending forward beside the engine, and the rear Lewis gun was provided with a special Fairey low-drag mounting. A simple V-strut undercarriage with cross-axle was fitted as the bomb load (either two 230lb of four 112lb bombs) was carried beneath the lower wings.

Without the constant supervision and inspection by Ministry specialists, the private venture Fox was completed in slightly under six months, and was first flown by Norman Macmillan at Hendon on 3 January 1925. This flight disclosed the inadequacy of the wing radiators when the engine water boiled after only eight minutes in the air, and eventually a single radiator in the upper wing centresection was linked with a retractable radiator (without the need for shutters) immediately forward of the undercarriage; this system proved entirely satisfactory, without substantially increasing the overall drag.

Further minor adjustments and modifications were made to the unnumbered prototype before Macmillan was required to give a flying demonstration before Sir Hugh Trenchard, the

[1]   Six crashes in flight (following mechanical failure), five crashes while landing (four involving aircraft overturning), three in-flight collisions) and two fires in the air (both caused by engines overheating.)

The Fox IA, J9026, during performance trials with No 22 Squadron of the A & AEE at Martlesham Heath, shown here carrying a pair of 250lb bombs and with the radiator retracted. The Kestrel I engine was usually flown with a Fairey Reed propeller — in essence a licence-built version of the original American Curtiss-Reed. (Photo: Air Ministry, A & AEE)

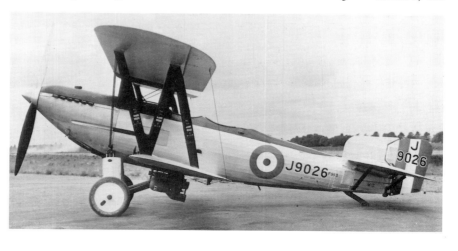

Chief of the Air Staff, and a number of other RAF officers.[1] Following a conversation between the CAS and Macmillan, in which the latter extolled the simplicity of flying the Fox, Trenchard informed Richard Fairey that he had decided to 'order a squadron of Foxes'.

A production Specification, 21/25, was hurriedly prepared and a contract for 18 Fox Mark Is, J7941-J7958, was issued in June 1925, the first of which was flown by Macmillan on 10 December that year. It was in effect a 'hand-built' prototype, as the private venture aircraft was not to be taken on Air Ministry charge (as J9515) until 1928.

This anonymous prototype first visited Martlesham in August 1925 for performance measurements while carrying two 230lb bombs, returning a maximum speed of 156 mph at 6,500 feet at a take-off weight of 4,018lb, and a service ceiling of 17,000 feet, a performance that was greeted with astonishment and admiration at the Establishment, bearing in mind the relatively low power available. Shortly after these tests the aircraft's wing span was increased to 37ft 6in, this serving to reduce the take-

off run by about 20 per cent, and increase the service ceiling to 19,350 feet. This increase in span was incorporated in the production Foxes.

The first Foxes reached No 12 (Bomber) Squadron, commanded by Sqn Ldr Alexander Grey, MC, at Andover on 16 June 1926, a total of four being delivered that month. Two of these, however, J7942 and J7944, were involved in an air collision at 1,000 feet near Andover on the 26th of the next month, the former eventually being rebuilt but the latter written off; both crews escaped unhurt. Four more new aircraft were delivered in July, one in August and six in September.

No 12 Squadron was the only operational unit ever to fly the Fox, and

continued to do so until January 1931. With their top speed of over 150 mph between ground level and 10,000 feet they were the fastest bomber in the RAF. And at the latter height there was no RAF fighter capable of matching their performance, a situation that remained in being until mid-1929, when Bristol Bulldogs reached No 3 (Fighter) Squadron with a top speed of 174 mph at 10,000 feet. So as to achieve a modicum of training benefit from the annual defence exercises, No 12 Squadron was ordered not to fly its Foxes faster than 140 mph at any height in order that the fighter squadrons might at least have some chance of catching the light bombers; even so, they seldom did.

No 12 Squadron suffered further attrition, and five more Felix-powered Fox Is, J8423-J8427, were ordered in 1927. Between 1926 and 1930 five aircraft were destroyed in accidents, and five others were sufficiently badly damaged to warrant complete rebuild-

---

[1] These included Air Vice-Marshal Sir Tom Ince Webb-Brown CB, CMG (recently Air Council Member for Supply and Research), Air Vice-Marshal Sir Geoffrey Salmond KCB, KCMG, DSO (Director General of Supply and Research at the Air Ministry), Air Cdre Felton Vesey Holt, CMG, DSO (Senior Air Staff Officer, Air Defence of Great Britain), Sqn Ldr William Sholto Douglas (later Lord Douglas of Kirtleside), and Sqn Ldr Alexander Grey, MC, Commanding Officer of No 12 (Bomber) Sqauadron (later Air Vice-Marshal, CB, MC). The presence of the last-named officer is interesting, and suggests that Trenchard had already decided to order the Fox into production before he attended the demonstration.

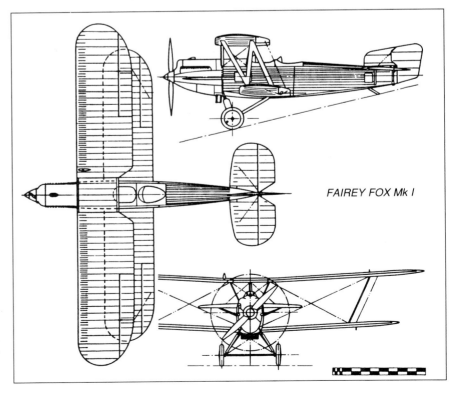

FAIREY FOX Mk I

ing, these losses making it impossible at times for the Squadron to maintain its established strength of twelve aircraft.

The problem was alleviated with the development of the Fox IA, powered by Rolls-Royce's new 490hp F.XIIA engine (which became the Kestrel IIA). The first engine to be cleared for flight, an F.XI (Kestrel I) was flown in J9026 by Macmillan on 29 August 1927, and the four Fox IAs reached No 12 Squadron late in 1928 and early 1929.

Foxes were employed in a variety of guises, including dual-control trainer and target tug. J9026 was also used in 1930 to test the Kestrel IIIA steam-cooled engined, with a large steam condenser fitted on the upper wing centresection. This engine, later to become the Rolls-Royce Goshawk, was written into a number of Air Ministry Specifications in the early 1930s, but failed to live up to its early promise.

The appearance of the Fox in 1925 certainly achieved what Richard Fairey had intended, and probably quickened the pace of new engine development in Britain — apart from demonstrating in dramatic fashion the way ahead in fighter and light bomber design. The manner in which he brought this course to the notice of the Air Ministry was undoubt-edly interpreted as an implied criticism (as it certainly was) of the over-cautious processes in aircraft development and acquisition, particularly as it involved the use of a foreign engine — perhaps justifiable anathema in times of economic restriction — which was demon-strably several years in advance of any-thing being manufactured in Britain.

Trenchard, who steadfastly held himself aloof from technical matters, judged the Fox by what he saw and heard, and his precipitate acceptance of the aircraft was an implicit criticism of his own technical departments. As a result, Fairey came to be regarded, quite unjustifiably, as a maverick industrialist — an attitude plain to recognise for a decade to come as successive aircraft, which were worthy of serious examina-tion, suffered summary dismissal or thinly disguised insouciance.

Type: Single-engine, two-seat, single-bay biplane light day bomber.

Air Ministry Specifications: Mark I. 21/25 and 17/30. Mark IA. 11/27.

Manufacturer: The Fairey Aviation Co Ltd, Hayes, Middlesex.

Powerplant: Mark I. One 430hp Curtiss Felix twelve-cylinder water-cooled in-line engine driving two-blade fixed-pitch metal propeller. Mark IA. One Rolls-Royce F.XIIA (Kestrel IIA) twelve-cylinder water-cooled in-line engine driving two-blade wooden propeller.

Structure: Composite wood and metal construction, fabric-covered.

Dimensions: Span, 37ft 8in (prototype, 33ft 6in); length, 28ft 3in; height, 10ft 8in; wing area, 324 sq ft.

Weights: Mark I. Tare, 2,609lb; all-up, 4,170lb. Mark IA. Tare, 3,075lb; all-up, 4,170lb.

Performance: Mark I. Max speed, 156 mph at 6,500ft; 150mph at 10,000ft; climb to 15,000ft, 21 min 30 sec; service ceiling, 19,300ft; range, 480 miles. Mark IA. Max speed, 160 mph at sea level.

Armament: One forward-firing synchronized 0.303in Vickers machine gun on port side of front fuselage; one Lewis gun in rear cockpit. Bomb load of either two 250lb or 230lb bombs, or four 112lb bombs carried beneath the lower wings.

Prototype: One, originally unregistered, but later J9515, first flown on 3 January 1925 by Norman Macmillan at Hendon. (One Fox IIM, J9834, first flown, 25 October 1929.)

Production: A total of 23 Fox Is and 4 Fox IAs was built. Mark I, J7941-J7958 and J8423-J8427; Mark IA, J9025-J9028.

Summary of Service: Foxes served with No 12 (Bomber) Squadron at Andover between June 1926 and January 1931.

Armstrong Whitworth Atlas

The Armstrong Whitworth Atlas, de-signed under the leadership of John Lloyd, newly appointed chief designer at Parkside, Coventry, was one of a trio of related aircraft, the others being the Ajax and Aries. All three were pro-claimed to be 'army co-operation' ma-chines, with greater or lesser connota-tions with a light bombing rôle. An attempt to qualify this bombing capabil-ity by examination of contemporary records and correspondence has failed to produce anything but conflicting refer-ences — a company policy that may have been deliberate owing to differing opin-ions within the Air Ministry as to exactly what an army co-operation aircraft was required to be. Reference to the Ajax as a 'bomber' has not been confirmed by any record of the aircraft being tested with anything heavier than eight 20lb

An Atlas I, J8800, of the first production batch, before the introduction of wing slats. These early aircraft featured a large fin and rudder, the former being removed after it was discovered that the aircraft could not be sideslipped. The aircraft shown here later served with Nos 13 and 26 (Army Co-operation) Squadrons. (Photo: The Aeroplane)

bombs. The Atlas, designed for a broader capability, was capable of carrying four 112lb bombs, a reconnaissance camera and two guns, and often did so when serving in the army co-operation rôle. In the event, only four examples — at most — of the Ajax, and one of the Aries, were produced, whereas no fewer than 478 Atlases were built, of which 446 were for the RAF (including 175 dual control trainers).

The last of the 'corps reconnaissance' Specifications, 8/24 and 30/24, had been issed in 1924, to which the Bristol

A late standard Atlas, J9537, with its message pick-up hook lowered during a demonstration, apparently at Farnborough. Note the ultimate rudder shape, absence of fin and the prominent wing slat bracket fairings. (Photo: Flight, Neg No 8838)

Boarhound and Vickers Vespa (see page 173) had been designed. Neither of these requirements was found to be satisfactory as they took little account of the conditions of service in the Middle East, implicit in the Specifications being an aim to replace the Bristol F.2B Fighter and D.H.9A. Nevertheless, Lloyd used these requirements as the original bases of his Atlas design, which began late in 1924, and which was to be influenced by the issue of one of the first army co-operation Specifications, 20/25.

The airframe of the prototype comprised a steel tubular, fabric-covered fuselage, and wooden, fabric-covered wings with ailerons on the top surfaces only; power was provided by a 400hp Armstrong Siddeley Jaguar IV fourteen-cylinder two-row radial, while operational equipment carried included an aerial camera, short-range wireless, a message pick-up hook under the rear fuselage and provision for a 460lb bomb load. The aircraft was built as a private venture and, registered G-EBLK, was first flown at Whitley on 10 May 1925. It was delivered to Martlesham Heath for competitive evaluation against the requirements originally set out in 30/24, vying with the Boarhound, Vespa and D.H.56 Hyena (the Short Chamois was a late, unsuccessful contender), and was recommended for production and RAF service. In surpassing the other aircraft in almost all aspects of performance and handling, the Atlas drew flattering opinions of Lloyd's design.

As first tested, the Atlas prototype's wooden wings, of RAF 15 section, were unswept and this feature was thought to have prompted one important criticism that *was* levelled at the aircraft's handling, that it could not be sideslipped steeply. In efforts to rectify this, the rudder travel was increased and wing sweepback introduced in conjunction

with small changes in wing incidence and dihedral. New metal wings (of RAF 28 section) were fitted in 1927 and the prototype resubmitted to the A & AEE. However, the former control sensitivity had disappeared and the Atlas prototype (now carrying the military serial J8675) came in for sharp criticism, being found to display vicious wing drop at the stall so that wheeling the aircraft on to the ground with plenty of speed was recommended for landing in order to avoid the wing drop before touchdown.

An initial production batch of 37 aircraft had already been ordered in 1927, many of these being delivered to No 13 (Army Co-operation) Squadron at Andover and to one Flight of No 26 (Army Co-operation) Squadron when it

re-formed at Catterick on 11 October that year. Others were taken on charge at the School of Army Co-operation at Old Sarum in February 1928.

During the first nine months of service, Atlases suffered eleven accidents during take-off and landing, almost all following stalls, although only two had fatal results. Nevertheless the accidents spurred efforts to solve the handling problems at low speeds, and Lloyd realised that this could best be remedied by introducing wing slats. J8794 accordingly joined the prototype in trials with automatic slats and with sweepback increased to six degrees. Tested once more at Martlesham, the Atlas received a much more encouraging verdict, and won a new production order for 49 aircraft of the improved version, including the automatic slats and powered by the 450hp Jaguar IVC. Meanwhile J8794 underwent continuing trials, at one time being flown by the Central Flying School with ailerons on both upper and lower wings (this was not adopted in RAF

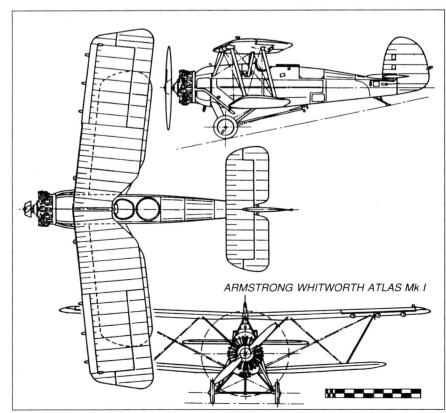

ARMSTRONG WHITWORTH ATLAS Mk I

Atlases but featured in aircraft supplied to Canada).

Nos 2 and 4 (Army Co-operation) Squadrons received the new versions in December and October 1929 at Manston and Farnborough respectively, while further orders totalling 171 aircraft kept the production line working until 1933, and enabled No 26 Squadron to be brought up to the normal two-Flight strength. Atlases were shipped overseas for the first time early in 1930 when the Bristol F.2Bs on No 208 Squadron at Heliopolis in Egypt were discarded in favour of the new aircraft, which remained in service with this Squadron until supplanted by Hawker Audaxes in August 1935. The last to equip with Atlases was No 16 (Army Co-operation) Squadron at Old Sarum in January 1931.

In service the Atlas, without in any way possessing a sparkling performance, did the job it was designed for and was popular. Once the wing slats had been introduced, the aircraft was tractable at low speeds, particularly in gusty weather near the ground, whether being used to observe ground troop movements or to pick up messages. During its overall period of service, accidents were relatively few, and this must be attributed to the introduction of an Atlas dual control trainer, of which 175 examples were produced. These were introduced with No 1 Flying Training School at Netheravon on 12 December 1928, and afterwards with Nos 3 and 5 Flying Training Schools.

A Mark II version was pursued by Armstrong Whitworth, powered by a 535hp Armstrong Siddeley Panther II and, after it had been rejected by the RAF in favour of the Hawker Audax, this variant was promoted overseas but with only limited success (14 examples being supplied to China).

Type: Single-engine, two-seat, single-bay army co-operation biplane with light bombing capability.

Specifications: 8/24, 20/25 and 33/26 (8/31 for trainer).

Manufacturer: Sir W G Armstrong Whitworth Aircraft Ltd, Parkside and Whitley, Coventry.

Powerplant: Prototype. One 400-hp Armstrong Siddeley Jaguar IV 14-cylinder air-cooled two-row radial engine. Production. 450hp Jaguar IVC.

Structure: Production aircraft were of all-metal construction with fabric covering.

Dimensions: Span, 39ft 6½in; length, 28ft 6½in; height, 10ft 6in; wing area, 391 sq ft.

Weights: Tare, 2,550lb; all-up, 4,020lb.

Performance: Max speed, 142 mph at sea level, 134 mph at 10,000ft; climb to 5,000ft, 5 min 30 sec; service ceiling, 16,800ft; range, 400 miles.

Armament: One forward-firing synchronized 0.303in Vickers machine gun in nose decking and one Lewis gun with Scarff ring on rear cockpit; provision to carry up to four 112lb bombs under lower wings.

Prototype: One, G-EBLK (later J8675), first flown at Whitley on 10 May 1925.

Production: A total of 271 Atlases was built for the RAF in the army co-operation rôle: J8777-J8801, J9039-J9050, J9516-J9564, J9951-K1037, K1113, K1114, and K1507-K1602. (175 Atlas Trainers were built: J9435-J9477, K1172-K1197, K1454-K1506 and K2514-K2566).

Summary of RAF Service: Atlases served in the army co-operation rôle with Nos 2, 4, 13, 16, 26 and 208 Squadrons, and with the School of Army Co-operation, Old Sarum; and as trainers with Nos 1, 3 and 5 Flying Training Schools at Netheravon, Spittlegate and Sealand respectively, and at the Royal Air Force College, Cranwell.

Above: *J9516 was the first production aircraft fully modified to the final production standard with 450hp Jaguar IVC, wing slats, and six-degree wing sweepback. The aircraft is seen here during trials at Martlesham Heath with cowled engine. It spent the last three years of its life at the RAE, and was last flown on 1 December 1933.* (Photo: Air Ministry, A & AEE)

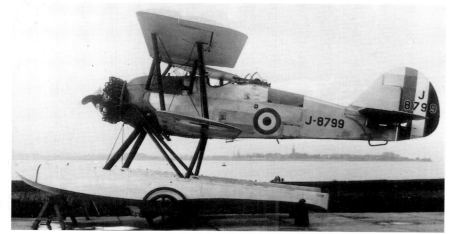

Left: *This early Atlas, J8799 (without wing slats, but with fin), was converted for trials as a floatplane, and is seen here at the MAEE, Felixstowe, early in 1931. This and another example, J9998, served as seaplane trainers with the High Speed Flight for the final Schneider Trophy race, held later that year.* (Photo: Air Ministry, MAEE)

de Havilland D.H.56 Hyena

Hyena J7780 at Stag Lane, as first flown with the partially-cowled Jaguar III engine; note the control rocker arm and pushrod forward of the tailplane. (Photo: A J Jackson Collection)

A direct development of the all-metal de Havilland Dingo (see page 150), the D.H.56 Hyena was designed to Specification 30/24 and was powered by a 385hp Jaguar III engine. Of similar size and weight to the Armstrong Whitworth Atlas, it was therefore at a disadvantage from the outset in being underpowered, a fact that was evident when the first prototype flew on 17 May 1925.

The Hyena retained the wing arrangement of the Dingo, with reduced chord and span on the lower wings and splayed-out interplane struts but, in an effort to reduce control circuit backlash, pushrods were introduced in the aileron and elevator controls. Ailerons were fitted in both upper and lower wings. Owing to partial relaxation of fuel tank requirements, the fuel was now contained in a single fuselage tank behind a fireproof bulkhead. In order to limit the drag produced by the radial engine, the crankcase was closely cowled, leaving only the cylinder heads exposed.

The first Hyena was delivered to Martlesham Heath on 24 November 1925 for initial assessment under Specification 30/24, during which its handling qualities were generally applauded, although its performance fell significantly short of the requirements. However, part way through the trials, 30/24 was shelved and 20/25 substituted.

The aircraft was shown to the public at Hendon (as New Type No 10) on 3 July 1926, but suffered engine failure during its display and had to force land. It was returned to Stag Lane where it was fitted with a Jaguar IV — which, according to contemporary records, appears to have been consistently down on power, producing only marginally more than the earlier engine. The crankcase cowling was now omitted.

J7780 underwent Service trials with No 4 (Army Co-operation) Squadron, commanded by Sqn Ldr John Cotesworth Slessor (later Marshal of the Royal Air Force Sir John, GCB, DSO, MC) at Farnborough, but it was considered to be difficult to fly with any steadiness and accuracy close to the ground, principally owing to the poor field of vision from the cockpit. It returned to Martlesham Heath for a final assessment in December 1926 in comparison with the Atlas (by then ordered into production, but still suffering from directional control problems), but the earlier verdict was upheld.

The second prototype, J7781, was flown on 29 June 1926, apparently with a better Jaguar IV engine. It had not been considered worthwhile to introduce any significant modifications to overcome the criticisms previously expressed, and the new engine gave only a slight improvement in performance. The aircraft was therefore transferred to the RAE for general research, remaining at Farnborough until May 1928.

Type: Single-engine, two-seat, two-bay experimental army co-operation biplane.
Air Ministry Specifications: 30/24 and 20/25.
Manufacturer: The de Havilland Aircraft Co Ltd, Stag Lane, Middlesex.
Powerplant: One 385hp or 394hp Armstrong Siddeley Jaguar III or IV 14-cylinder air-cooled two-row radial engine.
Dimensions: Span, 43ft 0in; length, 29ft 9in; height, 10ft 9in; wing area, 425.25 sq ft.
Weights: Tare, 2,399lb; all-up, 4,200lb.
Performance: Max speed, 126 mph at 6,500ft; climb to 10,000ft, 13 min 24 sec; service ceiling, 19,230ft.
Armament: One synchronized 0.303in Vickers machine gun in port side of fuselage and one Lewis gun with Scarff ring on rear cockpit. Four light bombs carried under port wing.
Prototypes: Two J7780 and J7781; J7780 first flown on 17 May 1925. No production.

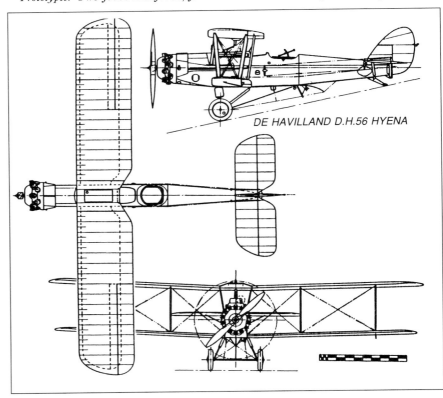

DE HAVILLAND D.H.56 HYENA

Bristol Type 93 Boarhound

The Bristol Type 93 Boarhound I, G-EBLG, at Filton about the time of its first flight in 1925; note the small vertical tail surfaces. (Photo: The Bristol Aeroplane Co Ltd, Neg No 465)

Designed by Frannk Barnwell as a private venture to the corps reconnaissance Specification 8/24, the Bristol Type 93 was motivated by encouragement from the Air Ministry, who suggested that the aircraft selected to replace the Bristol F.2B Fighter would need to be ordered in sufficient numbers to equip four squadrons. Despite some preference being expressed for the Napier Lion engine (of which several hundred were held in storage), Barnwell chose to employ the 425hp Bristol Jupiter IV with variable timing.

The Type 93 Boarhound featured a portly fuselage with ample space for a reconnaissance camera and wireless set but, inexplicably, no provision was made for a message pick-up hook. As the aircraft, being a private venture, was liable for a commercial certificate of airworthiness, it was necessary to place the fuel tanks in the wings, occupying almost the entire width of the upper centresection but without altering the aerofoil section. The wings were of equal span, the lower pair being of reduced chord. The fairly small, balanced rudder was without a dorsal fin, but a tiny ventral fin was fitted forward of the lower extension of the sternpost. It was intended that provision for a light bomb load would follow later.

Registered G-EBLG, the Boarhound was first flown by Cyril Uwins at Filton on 8 June 1925 and was submitted for evaluation by the A & AEE on 10 August. The aircraft was found to be lacking in performance at low altitude, the variable timing gear only serving to maintain power at high altitude — wholly superfluous in a corps reconnaissance/army co-operation aeroplane.

With the 8/24 competition being declared void and replaced by Specification 20/25 (and later by 33/26), G-EBLG was returned to Filton for a change of engine to the higher-compression 450hp Jupiter VI. It was again flown to Martlesham in about June 1926, where brief performance measurements recorded a speed of 128 mph at 6,500 feet, before being passed to the School of Army Co-operation at Old Sarum for Service trials.

The main criticisms of the Boarhound, fairly widely expressed, were lateral instability and a lack of control crispness, said to be caused by control circuit backlash; both were faults that ruled the aircraft out of contention in the army co-operation rôle.

A second aircraft, the Type 93A Beaver, was a general purpose aeroplane and a close derivative of the Boarhound and, as another private venture, was intended to compete for consideration as a D.H.9A replacement. However, with use of the Lion engine now mandatory, Barnwell's Jupiter-powered Beaver was a non-starter.

Finally, a pair of Boarhound Mark IIs, the Type 93B, were prepared as reconnaissance fighters and sold to Mexico in January 1928, all bombing accoutrements having been removed.

Type: Single-engine, two-seat, two-bay, experimental army co-operation biplane.
Air Ministry Specifications: 8/24 and 20/25.
Manufacturer: The Bristol Aeroplane Co Ltd, Filton, Bristol.
Powerplant: One 400hp (or 450hp) Bristol Jupiter IV or VI nine-cylinder single-row air-cooled radial engine.
Structure: All-steel construction with aluminium and fabric covering.
Dimensions: Span, 44ft 9in; length, 31ft 6in; height, 11ft 8in; wing area, 464 sq ft.
Weights: Tare, 2,565lb; all-up, 4,026lb (without bomb load).
Performance: Max speed, 128 mph at 6,500ft; climb to 10,000ft, 10 min 38 sec; service ceiling, 23,600ft (without bomb load).
Armament: One synchronized 0.303in Vickers machine gun in port side of fuselage and one Lewis gun with Scarff ring on rear cockpit. Bomb load said to be two 112lb bombs.
Prototypes: One Type 93, G-EBLG (first flown by Cyril Uwins at Filton); one Type 93A, G-EBQF, and two Type 93Bs for Mexico. No production.

Vickers Type 113 Vespa

Pierson's Type 113 Vespa constituted a curious and highly individualistic interpretation of the 30/24 corps reconnaissance requirement, so much so that, if subtlety was a keynote of the design, it was lost on the Service evaluation authorities.

Like the Atlas and Boarhound, the Vespa was designed as a private venture, being registered G-EBLD and first flown by E R C Scholefield in September 1925. With long wooden wings of unequal span and chord, whose area was 53 per cent greater than the wings of the Atlas, the Vespa possessed a relatively short, slim fuselage that proved just capable of accommodating the mandatory reconnaissance camera and wireless set without placing them too far from the aircraft's cg; for the same reason the pilot and observer/gunner were located

The Vickers Vespa I, G-EBLD, at Brooklands about the time of its first flight. The coaming of the pilot's cockpit may just be seen above the large gun fairing on the side of the fuselage. The base line of the rudder was later raised to the lower line of the fuselage and the horn balance at the top of the rudder was reduced. (Photo: Vickers (Aviation) Ltd)

well forward, the former almost directly beneath the mid-chord line of the upper wing, necessitating a large trailing-edge cutout and a semi-circular aperture between the centresection spars.

Moreover, in a manner reminiscent of the Bristol F.2B Fighter, the fuselage was located clear of the lower wing at mid-gap, so that there was little space between the upper wing and fuselage decking, a feature that was said to provide an excellent field of view upwards! However, because the wings were heavily staggered, a fairly good view of the ground was obtained forward of the lower wings.

Although the Vespa was evidently stressed to carry a light bomb load, the intended disposition cannot be ascertained from surviving factory drawings.

G-EBLD was flown to Martlesham Heath for preliminary Type testing in February 1926, having been fitted with mass-balanced ailerons since its first flight. Its performance was, however, rated as poor, with a top speed of no more than 126 mph at 6,500 feet. View of the ground while low flying and during landing was criticised, although

handling qualities were regarded as 'just acceptable'. Directional control during landing demanded coarse use of rudder, this being thought to be due to over-balancing. The Jupiter IV engine was also found to be down by some 20hp on the manufacturer's figures

Unfortunately G-EBLD was extensively damaged in a crash landing following engine failure (a Jupiter VI had just been fitted) while preparing for the Hendon Display in June, Scholefield only just managing to avert a total loss

of the prototype.

The aircraft was rebuilt as the Vespa Mark II, now fitted with metal wings with fabric covering. It was, however, clear that the Air Ministry was not interested in purchasing the aircraft, and no production order ensued. Notwithstanding, Vickers managed to interest a military mission from Bolivia, to which country six Vespa IIIs were supplied in 1928; other versions were sold for service with the Irish Army Air Corps. And it was the original prototype that, after progressive modification, and flown by Cyril Uwins, established a new world altitude record of 43,976 feet on 16 September 1932.

Type: Single-engine, two-seat, two-bay experimental army co-operation biplane.
Air Ministry Specifications: 8/24 and 20/25
Manufacturer: Vickers (Aviation) Ltd, Weybridge, Surrey.
Powerplant: One 400hp (or 420hp) Bristol Jupiter IV (or VI) nine-cylinder single-row air-cooled radial engine.
Structure: Initially steel fuselage and wooden wings, and later with steel wings, fabric-covered.
Dimensions: Span, 50ft 0in; length, 31ft 3in; height, 10ft 3in; wing area, 561 sq ft.
Weights: Tare, 2,468lb; all-up, 3,925lb.
Performance: Max speed, 126 mph at 6,500ft; climb to 10,000ft, 11 min 48 sec; service ceiling, 20,300ft.
Armament: One synchronized 0.303-in Vickers machine gun faired into port side of fuselage and one Lewis gun with Scarff ring on rear cockpit. Bomb load, probably up to about 260lb, but disposition not known.
Prototype: One built to Air Ministry requirements, G-EBLD, first flown by Flt Lt E R C Scholefield in September 1925 at Brooklands. No production for the RAF.

Fairey Ferret

While the RAF's commitment to support surface forces on the land had continued with the search for an aircraft to replace the wartime D.H.9A and Bristol F.2B in service at home and overseas, the need continued to provide aircraft to support the fleet at sea. Both

The Jaguar-powered Ferret I three-seat naval reconnaissance aircraft, N190, during evaluation at Martlesham Heath under the terms of Specification 37/22. (Photo: Air Ministry, RTP)

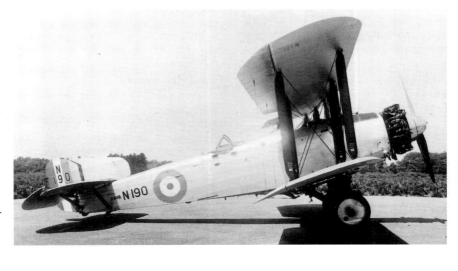

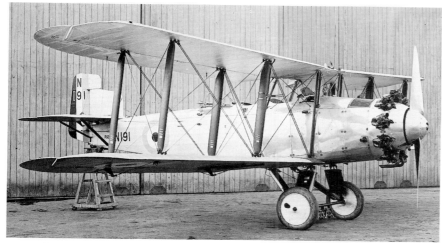

categories of aircraft had much in common, in effect being regarded as 'general purpose' machines; central to their rôles was what was loosely termed reconnaissance, be it visual or photographic. However, whereas the aircraft committed to supporting the land forces were relatively straightforward in design, with little in the way of impedimenta to influence their configuration, the aircraft for the fleet had to meet stringent demands, not least being a mandatory limit on their size, in order to fit within the dimensions of carrier lifts; they had to be able to operate from a small deck area and withstand the loads imposed by deck landing, and had to meet flotation requirements against the possibility of an involuntary alighting on the water. To these demands were being added the interchangeability of wheel and float undercarriage, and the airframe strength needed to withstand being catapult launched from a warship at sea.

It was not surprising, therefore, that companies such as Blackburn and Fairey had gained the experience in, and a reputation for, the provision of such specialised 'naval' aircraft. The latter company had continued to produce a series of aeroplanes in the famous Type III family, which reached the IIID in 1920 and continued for some years thereafter.

The next aircraft in this category from Fairey, though not strictly in the Type III series, was an obvious derivative in the general fleet reconnaissance class, and commenced design in 1923 to Specification 37/22. The Fairey Ferret was of all-metal construction with sheet aluminium covering the front fuselage, the remainder of the airframe being fabric-covered. It was somewhat smaller than the IIID, spanning some seven feet less, and was about 25 per cent lighter.

Three prototypes were ordered, N190-N192. The first, built as a three-seater and powered by a 400hp Armstrong Siddeley Jaguar IV fourteen-cylinder radial engine, was first flown by Norman Macmillan at Northolt on 5 June 1925. Unlike the IIID, its wheel was of the oleo V-strut type, while the wings, with ailerons on upper and lower surfaces, featured stagger and sweepback; the fin and rudder profile remained much the same as that on previous Fairey aircraft.

Ferret N190 was evaluated by the A & AEE soon after its first flight, in competition with the Hawker Hedgehog and Blackburn Airedale under the requirement of 37/22 (and appeared to be superior to them). However, part way through the competition, the Air Ministry withdrew the requirements as a new Specification (22/26) was being formulated, its demands clearly exceeding the abilities of the three aircraft then under test.

The second Ferret, N191, also a three-seater, differed from the first in being having a Bristol Jupiter IV nine-cylinder radial, but was nearing completion when 37/22 was withdrawn. The aircraft was taken on Air Ministry charge,

and was later transferred to the MAEE at Felixstowe for experimental work — being flown as an amphibian with wheel-and-float undercarriage.

There was time to alter the design of the third Ferret, however, and this aeroplane was completed as a two-seater in the RAF's general purpose category. Like N191, the aircraft featured a Jupiter engine (now a 482hp Mk VI), and was prepared to meet requirements set out by the Air Ministry early in 1926. As first drafted under the reference 12/26, these called for a 'general purpose' aircraft — the first time the term had been employed officially — and attracted eleven design tenders.

It is necessary here to explain that Specification 12/26 was temporarily withdrawn in mid-1927 when the Air Ministry learned of the considerable advances in aircraft performance likely to be gained with the introduction of the new Rolls-Royce F.XI and F.XII Falcon-derivative (later to become the Kestrel). Early project drawings and performance estimates of the Hawker Hart, designed by Sydney Camm, suggested that 12/26 was better suited to a new light bomber for the RAF, and the

Specification was changed accordingly and reissued in August 1927 — but without change of title. There were therefore two competitions, ostensibly governed by 12/26, one held in 1927 for general purpose aircraft, and one in 1928 for light bombers.

The third Ferret, N192, in its category as a general purpose entry, was competing against the Bristol Beaver, de Havilland D.H.9J Stag, D.H.65 Hound, Fairey IIIF (in two- and three-seat versions), Gloster Goral, Vickers Vixen VI and Valiant, and Westland Wapiti. By the time the final stages of the trials were reached, in May 1927, all but the Ferret, Fairey IIIF two-seater, Westland Wapiti and Vickers Valiant had been eliminated, and had not the Ferret been dogged by engine and propeller trouble, it is likely that it would have been declared the outright winner. As it was, the Wapiti was ordered into production, and IIIFs, already in production for naval work, were also diverted for RAF general purpose duties.

There is no doubt but that the Ferret III possessed an excellent performance, and was well liked by the Service pilots, but the company had the consolation of winning further orders for its IIIF. It is worth emphasising the significance of the dilemma facing the Air Ministry, in its decision to withdraw Specification 12/26, by pointing out that whereas the Wapiti, as a general purpose aeroplane carrying four 112lb bombs, possessed a top speed of 126 mph at 6,500 feet, the Kestrel-engine Hart light bomber, with the same load and at the same height, had a maximum speed of 176 mph. Both were supreme in their respective categories.

(The other contenders to 12/26, where applicable to bomb-carrying duties, are described on page 186 *et seq*; the accompanying data table refers to the Ferret Mark III, the only version flown with bombs.)

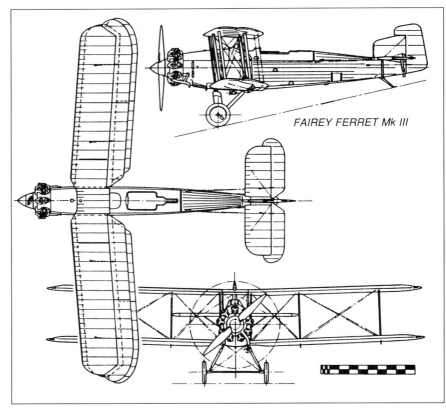

FAIREY FERRET Mk III

Type: Single-engine, two-seat, two-bay general purpose biplane.
Air Ministry Specification: 12/26 (first two prototypes to 37/22)
Manufacturer: The Fairey Aviation Co Ltd, Hayes, Middlesex.
Powerplant: One 482hp Bristol Jupiter VI nine-cylinder two-row air-cooled radial engine driving two-blade metal Fairey propeller.
Structure: All-metal construction with metal sheet and fabric covering.
Dimensions: Span, 40ft 7in (15ft folded); length, 29ft 6in; height, 10ft 3in; wing area, 380 sq ft.
Weights: Tare, 2,583lb; all-up, 4,179lb (or at overload, 4,765lb, including bombs, spare wheel, emergency bedding and desert equipment).
Performance: Max speed, 135 mph at 10,000ft; time to 10,000ft, 13 min 20 sec.
Armament: One synchronized 0.303in Vickers machine gun in nose and one Lewis gun with Fairey low-drag mounting in rear cockpit; bomb load, up to 460lb.
Prototypes. Three, N190-N192 (Marks I-III respectively). N190 first flown by Norman Macmillan on 5 June 1925 at Northolt. No production.

Blackburn T.3 Velos

The Velos was a two-seat development of the Blackburn T.2 Dart, which it closely resembled, and was designed by Maj F A Bumpus in 1925 to a Greek Navy requirement for a coastal defence seaplane with torpedo dropping, bombing, reconnaissance and training capabilities. It was to be primarily a floatplane but was to be easily converted to operate with a wheel undercarriage. It was to be wired for night flying and had to have

A Velos seaplane with torpedo, probably in Phaleron Bay. (Photo: A J Jackson Collection)

electric intercom between the pilot and observer/gunner.

Powered by a 450hp Napier Lion V, the first Velos was probably flown early in October 1925, this and a second example being demonstrated to a group of guests at Brough on the 28th by Flt Lt Norman Hargreave Woodhead DSC.

After two further Velos aircraft were built for Greece at Leeds, production started at the National Aircraft Factory at Old Phaleron, near Athens, completed by the Blackburn company, which had secured a contract to run it, using local labour. The first Greek-built Velos was flown on 28 March 1926 by Colonel the Master of Sempill[1].

When operating as a torpedo carrier, the Velos was flown as a single-seater, but for bombing duties it was crewed by pilot and observer/gunner. The torpedo crutches were replaced by a beam with four racks for 230lb bombs; sighting was through a slot close to the starboard side of the fuselage.

Several Brough-built Velos seaplanes were later entered on the British Civil Register from 1928 onwards for use by the RAF Reserve School at Brough, but when Reserve seaplane training ended in 1929 the aircraft were converted to landplanes, only to be sold for scrap in 1932.

[1] Later 19th Baron Cdr William Sempill AFC. In January 1926 he was asked by the Greek Government to report on the reorganization of the Greek Naval Air Service. He had previously retained the ranks of Colonel and Commander on transfer to the Royal Air Force from both the RFC and RNAS in which he had been commissioned. He had also directed the creation and organization of the Imperial Japanese Naval Air Service in the early 1920s.

Type: Single-engine, two-seat, two-bay biplane torpedo bomber seaplane/landplane.
Manufacturer: The Blackburn Aeroplane and Motor Co Ltd, Leeds and Brough, Yorkshire.
Powerplant: One 450hp Napier Lion V 12-cylinder water-cooled broad-arrow in-line engine driving two-blade propeller.
Dimensions: Span, 48ft 6in; length, 35ft 6in; height, 12ft 3in; wing area, 654 sq ft.
Weights: Tare, 3,890lb (floatplane, 4,520lb); all-up, 6,200lb (floatplane, 6,830lb).
Performance: Max speed, 107 mph (floatplane, 101 mph) at sea level; service ceiling, 14,100ft (floatplane, 9,700ft); range, 360 miles (floatplane, 300 miles).
Armament: One Lewis gun with Scarff ring on rear cockpit; either one 2,000lb 18in torpedo or four 230lb bombs.
Prototype: One for Greece, first flown in about October 1925; no military examples built for the RAF.

Fairey Type IIIF

The longest serving member of the famous Fairey III series of naval biplanes, the IIIF was built in larger numbers than any other British operational aircraft between the end of the First World War and the mid-1930s, with the exception of the Hawker Hart variants. It was, in effect a 'tidied-up' derviative of the IIID, the first ten production examples having actually started life in the factory as IIIDs.

The aircraft was designed to Specification 19/24, which called for a fleet reconnaissance aircraft after the failure of 37/22 to produce a satisfactory contender. Two prototypes, N198 and N225, were ordered for evaluation in 1926-27. The first, built with a composite wood and metal fuselage and wooden wings, was flown by Norman Macmillan on 19 March 1926 as a three-seat landplane, but shortly afterwards was flown to Hamble to be fitted with Fairey metal floats and tested at the MAEE. After gaining a satisfactory verdict as a seaplane, it was returned to landplane guise and delivered to Martlesham Heath for official type testing in the autumn of that year. It attracted favourable comment, particularly for its slow, docile landing behaviour, made possible by use of the Fairey camber-changing flaps. As an expedient Fairey was asked to complete

Two Fairey IIIF Mark Is (the nearest S1181) transferred from the Fleet Air Arm to No 45 (General Purpose) Squadron, RAF, seen at Kano, Nigeria, during a long-distance flight from Cairo on 5 November 1927. (Photo: JMB/GLS Collection)

the last ten Type IIIDs, then under construction at Hayes, to a standard similar to that of N198, most of these aircraft being transferred immediately to the RAF and shipped out to Aboukir, Egypt, for theatre trials with Nos 5 and 60 Squadrons, these trials being successfully completed in April 1927.

Meanwhile it was announced that competitive evaluation of aeroplanes designed to a new Specification, outlining the requirements for a new class of 'General Purpose' aircraft, was now scheduled to commence in the summer of 1927. As explained on page 175, the Specification 12/26 had been divided into two requirements, the first for a general purpose aircraft and the second for a light bomber, both for the RAF.

Fairey was already entering the Ferret for the former and, prompted by the success of the IIIF in its various trials for the Navy, now decided to enter both a two- and three-seat version of the IIIF for the RAF's requirement. Although none of the Fairey entries was declared the outright winner, it was clear that, despite being narrowly defeated, the IIIF could be made ready for production and delivery before the winning Westland Wapiti.

A production contract for 25 Fairey

A composite Fairey IIIF Mark II seaplane, S1251, of No 440 (Fleet Spotter Reconnaissance) Flight, probably flying from HMS *Hermes; these seaplanes were hoisted outboard for take-off from the water; when flying from capital ships and cruisers, they were launched by catapult.* (Photo: JMB/GSL Collection)

IIIF Mark IV C/M (GP)s was therefore quickly signed, and the first example was completed and tested at Martlesham in September 1927; all were delivered and in service by the end of 1928 — the majority of them with No 8 (General Purpose) Squadron at Aden and No 207 (Bomber) Squadron at Eastchurch.

It has, however, been fairly widely stated elsewhere that, while Fairey IIIFs entered first-line service with the RAF in 1927, those delivered to the Fleet Air Arm languished in store for a year before entering service. In fact the first RAF unit, the Cape Flight (a non-operational formation which existed to train crews for long-distance flights from Cairo to Cape Town and return each year) received six of the first ex-Fleet Air Arm aircraft, designated Type IIIF Mark I (Interim), during the early part of 1927, while theatre trials were still being completed. The first Fleet Air Arm deliveries were made to No 443 (Composite) Flight in May 1927 for active deployment aboard HMS *Furious*, and later as a Catapult Flight aboard ships of the 2nd, 6th and 8th Cruiser Squadrons. Indeed, by the time the RAF Type IIIF Mark IVs reached the first front-line Squadron, No 47 (General Purpose) at Khartoum in December 1927, Fleet Air Arm IIIFs had been serving with Nos 440, 445 and 446 (Fleet Spotter Reconnaissance) Flights aboard HMS *Argus* and *Courageous* for several months.

It should be explained that, apart from 61 Fleet Air Arm IIIF Mark Is and IIIs, which were transferred to the RAF, all RAF aircraft were of the Mark IV type, of which the sub-variant 'C/M' was of composite metal and wood construction, 'M/A' was all-metal, and the IIIF Mark IVB (to Specification 3/31) was strengthened to permit catapulting. Seventeen RAF aircraft were fitted with dual controls (denoted by 'DC').

The Fleet Air Arm variants com-prised Mark I (Lion VA, metal fuselage and wooden wings), Mark II (Lion XIA and strengthened airframe), Mark IIIM (Lion XIA, all-metal) and Mark IIIB (Lion XIA and further strengthened to permit catapulting, to Specification 12/29).

It is a paradox that the production of the IIIF gained its initial impetus as a result of being highly commended in the 12/26 competition to select a new General Purpose aircraft for the RAF, and that by far the widest use of the IIIF was by the Fleet Air Arm. By the beginning of 1930, RAF Squadrons flying the IIIF were No 35 (Bomber) and No 207 (Bomber) in the United Kingdom, and No 14 (General Purpose), No 45 (General Purpose) and No 47 (General Purpose) Squadrons in the Middle East. In the Fleet Air Arm they equipped seven Fleet Spotter Reconnaissance Flights embarked in HM Carriers *Argus, Courageous, Eagle, Furious, Glorious* and *Hermes*. And whereas the IIIFs were phased out of service in the RAF in 1935, they continued with first-line Fleet Air Arm Squadrons until 1936, but continued to serve in a number of second-line duties until 1941. Indeed, at least one IIIF was still serving as a target tug at Kai Tak, Hong Kong, when the colony was seized by the Japanese at the end of that year.

In their heyday Fairey IIIF catapult seaplanes had served as gunnery spotters in HM Battleship *Valiant*, HM Battle Cruiser *Hood* and the cruisers HMS *Dorsetshire, Exeter, Norfolk* and *York*.

As already stated, the Cape Flight received IIIF Mark Is in 1927, the

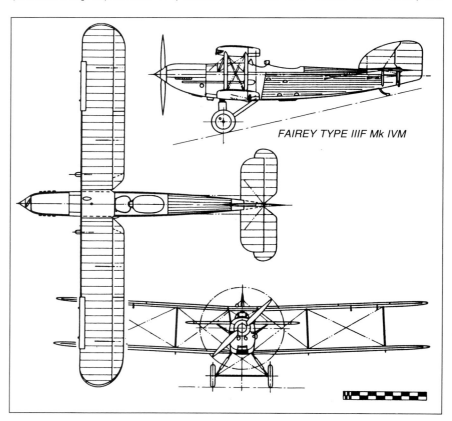

FAIREY TYPE IIIF Mk IVM

J9150 was a IIIF Mark IV C/M (GP) but was allocated to the Bristol Aeroplane Company for installation of a 520hp Jupiter VIII, with which it was first flown on 2 July 1928; it was then returned to Fairey to be fitted with floats (one of the few aircraft on RAF contracts to be so fitted.) It was then delivered to the MAEE at Felixstowe in October 1929. (Photo: The Fairey Aviation Co Ltd, Neg No 3936)

journey to Cape Town that year being led by the legendary Air Cdre Charles Rumney Samson CMG, DSO, AFC (then SASO, Middle East), his second-in-command being Sqn Ldr (later Gp Capt) Reginald Stuart Maxwell, MC, DFC, AFC. The years between 1926 and 1934 were notable for long-distance route-proving flights, or flag-showing tours by RAF aircraft, and many were those that served with distinction during the Second World War who had featured among the pioneer flights by Fairey IIIFs as relatively junior officers.

Not surprisingly, the Fairey IIIF lent itself admirably to the trial installation of new and experimental engines, these being listed in the accompanying data table; some of these engines had been specified by overseas purchasers of the IIIF, including Argentina, Canada, Chile, Egypt, Greece, Ireland, New Zealand and Russia.

Sixty-seven IIIFs were subsequently converted to Fairey Gordons under Specification 18/30 (see page 222), and three aircraft were modified as Fairey

Type: Single-engine, two/three-seat, two-bay general purpose/fleet reconnaissance float/wheel biplane with bombing capability.

Air Ministry Specifications: 19/24, 36/26, 37/26, 12/27, 12/29 and 3/31.

Manufacturer: The Fairey Aviation Co Ltd, Hayes, Middlesex.

Powerplant: One 440-455hp Napier Lion VA, XA, XI or XIA 12-cylinder broad-arrow water-cooled in-line engine driving two-blade propeller. Experimental. 460hp Armstrong Siddeley Jaguar VI/VIS; 525hp Armstrong Siddeley Panther IIA; 520hp Bristol Jupiter VIII; 450hp Lorraine Ed12; Napier Culverin (Junkers-Jumo V-205C); 500hp Rolls-Royce Kestrel II (and 480hp Kestrel IIA/IIS).

Structure: Originally composite wood-and-metal fuselage and wooden wings; then all-metal fuselage and wooden wings; ultimately all-metal fuselage and wings.

Dimensions: Span, 45ft 9in (folded 14ft 3in); length, 34ft 0in (Mk III landplane), 36ft 9in (Mk IV); height, 12ft 9in (Mk III landplane), 14ft 2in (Mk IV); wing area, 439 sq ft.

Weights: Mk IV. Tare, 3,855lb; all-up, 6,014lb.

Performance: Max speed, 136 mph at sea level (Mk III landplane), 130 mph (Mk III seaplane), 120 mph (Mk IV at 10,000ft); climb to 5,000ft, 6 min (Mk IV); range, 400 miles (Mk IV with bombs), 1,520 miles (Mk IV with max fuel, no bombs).

Armament: One synchronized 0.303in Vickers machine gun in port side of nose and one Lewis gun with Fairey low-drag mounting in rear cockpit; bomb load of up to 500lb.

Prototypes: Two naval prototypes, N196 and N225; N196 first flown by Norman Macmillan at Northolt on 19 March 1926.

Summary of Production: A total of 243 Fairey IIIF Mark IVs was ordered for the RAF and 352 Fairey IIIF Marks I, II and III for the FAA. **RAF.** J9053-J9057 (25 Mk IV C/M(GP); 3 converted to Gordon); J9132-J9174 (43 Mk IV C/M (GP); 8 converted to Gordon); J9637-J9681 (45 Mk IV M/A; 12 converted to Gordon); J9784-J9831 (48 Mk IV M/A; 23 converted to Gordon); K1115-K1121 (7 Mk IV M/A; 1 converted to Gordon); K1158-K1121 (13 Mk IV M/A (GP); 11 converted to Gordon); K1697-K1720 (24 Mk IVB (GP); 1 completed as Gordon and 4 converted to Gordon); K1721-K1728 (8 Mk IVB; all completed as Gordon); K1749-K1778 (30 Mk IVB; 20 completed as Gordon). **FAA.** S1139-S1148 (10 IIIF, all converted from IIID on production line); S1168-S1207 (40 Mk I; 5 converted to Gordon); S1208-S1227 and S1250-S1262 (33 Mk II); S1303-S1356 and S1370-S1408 (93 Mk III); S1454-S1463 (10 Mk III DC); S1474-S1552 and S1779-S1865 (166 Mk IIIB; incl 11 DC). Of the above aircraft ordered for the FAA, 38 IIIFs and IIIF Mk Is, and 25 Mk IIIs were transferred to the RAF. The actual number of production Fairey IIIFs delivered to the RAF and FAA was thus 566, and of these 67 were later rebuilt as or converted to Gordons.

Summary of RAF and FAA Service: **RAF.** Fairey IIIF Mk IVs served with No 6 (Bomber) Sqn, Target Towing Flt, at Ramleh, 1934; No 8 (General Reconnaissance) Sqn at Khormaksar, 1928-29; No 14 (General Purpose) Sqn at Ramleh and Amman, 1929-32; No 24 (Communications) Sqn at Northolt, c.1932; No 35 (Bomber) Sqn at Bircham Newton, 1929-32; No 45 (General Purpose) Sqn at Helwan, 1929-35; No 47 (General Purpose) Sqn at Khartoum, 1927-33; No 55 (General Purpose) Sqn, Target Towing Flt at Hinaidi, 1931; No 202 (Flying Boat) Sqn at Kalafrana, Malta, 1930-35; No 203 (Flying Boat) Sqn at Basra, Iraq, 1929; and No 207 (Bomber) Sqn at Eastchurch and Bircham Newton, 1927-32. They also served with Nos 1, 2 and 4 Flying Training Schools; the Central Flying School; Armament Practice Station, Sutton Bridge; Armament and Gunnery School; and No 2 Anti-Aircraft Co-operation Unit. **FAA.** Fairey IIIFs served with No 406 (Catapult) Flt, 4th Cruiser Sqn, 1935-36; No 421 (Fleet Spotter) Flt aboard HMS *Furious*, 1929; No 440 (Fleet Reconnaissance) Flt aboard HMS *Hermes*, 1927-33; No 441 (Fleet Reconnaissance) Flt aboard HMS *Glorious*, 1929-33; No 442 (Fleet Reconnaissance) Flt aboard HMS *Furious*; No 443 (Catapult) Flt with 2nd, 6th and 8th Cruiser Sqns, 1927-36; No 444 (Catapult) Flt with 1st and 2nd Battle Sqns and 1st Cruiser Sqn, 1931-36; No 445 (Fleet Spotter Reconnaissance) Flt aboard HMS *Courageous*, 1927-33; No 446 (Fleet Spotter Reconnaissance) Flt aboard HMS *Courageous*, 1927-33; No 447 (Fleet Spotter Reconnaissance) Flt aboard HMS *Glorious* and with 1st Battle Sqn, 1929-36; No 448 (Fleet Spotter Reconnaissance) Flt aboard HMS *Eagle* and *Glorious*, 1929-33; No 449 (Fleet Spotter Reconnaissance) Flt aboard HMS *Courageous*, 1931-33; No 450 (Fleet Spotter Reconnaissance) Flt aboard HMS *Courageous*, 1930-33; No 460 (Fleet Torpedo Bomber) Flt aboard HMS *Glorious*, 1932-33; No 820 (Fleet Spotter Reconnaissance) Sqn aboard HMS *Furious* and *Glorious*, 1933-34; No 821 (Fleet Spotter Reconnaissance) Sqn aboard HMS *Courageous*, 1933; No 822 (Fleet Spotter Reconnaissance) Sqn aboard HMS *Furious*, 1933-36; No 823 (Fleet Spotter Reconnaissance) aboard HMS *Glorious*, 1933-34; No 824 (Fleet Spotter Reconnaissance) Sqn aboard HMS *Eagle*, 1933-34; and No 825 (Fleet Spotter Reconnaissance) Sqn aboard HMS *Eagle* and *Glorious*. Fairey IIIFs served ashore at RN Air Stations Aboukir, Amriya, Catfoss, Donibristle, Gosport, Hal Far, Kai Tak, Lee-on-Solent, Leuchars, Manston, Netheravon and many others. Last Fairey IIIFs in service as target tugs in 1941.

Queens — radio-controlled gunnery targets equipped with auto-pilots. The first two, launched from HMS *Valiant*, crashed without a shot being fired; the third, however, was duly shot down off Malta by the gunners of HMS *Shropshire* after 20 minutes' expenditure of ammunition!

J9154 was rebuilt as an all-metal IIIF Mark V and fitted with a 460hp Jaguar VI, as seen here; this was later replaced by a 525hp Panther IIA to produce the Fairey Gordon prototype. (Photo: A J Jackson Collection)

Boulton & Paul P.29 Sidestrand

The first 9/24 Sidestrand prototype, J7938, at Mousehold in 1926; the Jupiter VI engines are fitted with small diameter propellers; this aircraft had slightly curved wing tips and had not been fitted with the Flettner servo-tab on the rudder. (Photo: Boulton & Paul Ltd, Neg No 3088)

The failure by Boulton and Paul Ltd to gain production contracts for any of John North's family of twin-engine bombers reflected the Air Ministry's indecision as to whether any worthwhile advantage of a twin-engine over a single-engine aircraft existed, rather than any significant shortcomings in his designs. The general requirement for a twin-engine day bomber was therefore left on the table while North continued to receive encouragement to pursue development of his successful formula. Specification 9/24 was issued for a rather larger and more powerful aircraft — now uncompromisingly of all-metal construction — to be powered by Napier Lion engines.

Two prototypes, J7938 and J7939, were ordered early in 1925, the engine requirement being altered to Bristol Jupiter VIs. North introduced a new structure in the fuselage of his design,

the P.29 Sidestrand, whereby stainless steel strip was drawn to semi-tubular form, with one edge reversed and wrapped around a bead, providing a fabricated structure of great strength at no significant weight penalty. The fuselage was of improved aerodynamic shape, although the wings remained angular with square wing tips and parallel chord. The vertical tail surfaces remained generous in area, the rudder incorporating a prominent balance. A bomb load of either two 520lb or four 250lb bombs

was to be carried externally under the fuselage.

Sqn Ldr C A Rae flew J7938 for the first time in about March 1926 at Mousehold aerodrome on the outskirts of Norwich, and evidently expressed satisfaction with the aircraft, as it was sent to Martlesham Heath later that month for initial manufacturer's tests by Service pilots.

Several minor modifications were made from time to time at Norwich during that summer before J7938 was delivered to the RAF for brief preliminary Service trials, after which it underwent extended type performance trials at the A & AEE. All pilots appear to have agreed that the aircraft lacked the manœuvrability they had come to expect from North's designs, though the Sidestrand was exceptionally stable in

J9176 was the first production Sidestrand Mk II; only partly visible in this photograph is the Flettner servo-tab aft of the rudder. After various trials at Martlesham Heath, this aircraft was converted to a Mark III and served on No 101 (Bomber) Squadron from June 1930 until July 1935. (Photo: via R C B Ashworth)

Boulton & Paul Sidestrand Mk III, J9177/ 'C', of No 101 (Bomber) Squadron, after conversion from Mark II; the 550hp Jupiter VIIIF engines are fitted with enlarged propellers, and the square-tipped wings are equipped with leading-edge slats. Despite being classified as a day bomber, this aircraft is fully equipped for night flying, probably at Bicester. (Photo: via R C Sturtivant)

all three axes, considered to be essential for a successful bomber. However, the aileron control was sluggish and the rudder unacceptably heavy.

Meanwhile the second prototype, J7939, had flown in June 1926 and appeared at the 1927 Hendon Display on 2 July as New Type No 8. Both aircraft were then re-engined with direct-drive Jupiter VIs to become Sidestrand Mark IIs; there followed a long series of trials to correct the directional control problem, the eventual outcome being the introduction of a large Flettner servo-balance tab mounted well aft of the rudder. (J7938 was shown at the 1928 Hendon Display as New Type No 13.)

The Sidestrand was ordered into limited production, with six Mark II aircraft being contracted in 1927; the first of these, J9176, was subjected to full armament trials with No 15 Squadron and performance trials with No 22 Squadron at the A & AEE beginning in February 1928. Handling was considered acceptable, although engine over-heating was frequently experienced. The first Sidestrands entered service with No 101 (Bomber) Squadron — the only operational unit to fly the aircraft — in March 1929 (replacing D.H.9As), with the delivery of J9176-J9179 to Bircham Newton that month.

In service the Sidestrand II was initially criticised on account of severe engine vibration, and it was decided to modify the aircraft by changing to the more powerful, geared 550hp Jupiter VIIIF, this being set down in Specification 10/29, to which the next nine aircraft were completed as Sidestrand Mark IIIs (of which eight were supplied to No 101 Squadron).

During the years 1930-32 three Sidestrands (J9180, J9767 and J9769)

were written off in accidents — none as a result of aircraft or engine failure — and these were replaced by a last production order for three aircraft (K1992-K1994) placed in 1933. (However, at no time after August 1931 was No 101 Squadron able to operate with more than ten aircraft, a figure which dropped to eight by January 1934.)

No 101 (Bomber) Squadron continued to fly Sidestrands until July 1936, having moved to Andover in October 1929 and to Bicester in December 1934;

during the last eighteen months of their service they flew alongside the improved Boulton Paul P.75 Overstrand (see page 254).

Continuing development of the Sidestrand had centred on two examples, J9186 and J9770, the former being re-engined with Jupiter XFs and XFBMs, known as Mark IIIS, and then with the Bristol Pegasus as the proposed Sidestrand Mark V with a power-operated nose gun turret. The Sidestrand V was renamed the Overstrand.

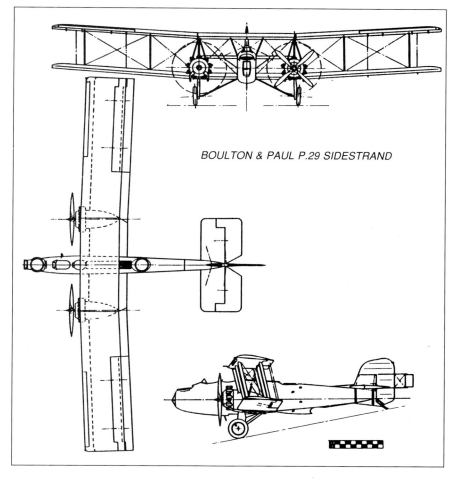

BOULTON & PAUL P.29 SIDESTRAND

Type: Twin-engine, three/four-crew, three-bay biplane medium day bomber.

Air Ministry Specifications: 9/24 and 10/29.

Manufacturer: Boulton & Paul Ltd, Riverside, Norwich, Norfolk.

Powerplant: Prototypes and Mark II. Two 425hp Bristol Jupiter VI 9-cylinder air-cooled radial engines driving 2-blade propellers. Mark III. 460hp Jupiter VIIIF. Experimental. 575hp Jupiter XFB and XFBM; 555hp Pegasus IM3; 580hp Pegasus IIM3; 720hp Pegasus IV.

Structure: All-metal with ply and fabric covering.

Dimensions: Mark III. Span, 71ft 11in; length, 46ft 0in; height, 14ft 9½in; wing area, 979.5 sq ft.

Weights: Mark III. Tare, 6,370lb; all-up, 10,200lb.

Performance: Mark III with bomb load. Max speed, 139 mph at 6,500ft; climb to 6,500ft, 6 min 42 sec; service ceiling, 20,800ft; range, 520 miles.

Armament: Gun armament of three Lewis guns in nose, midships dorsal and ventral positions; bomb load of up to 1,040lb (two 520lb bombs carried externally).

Prototypes: Two, J7938 and J7939. J7938 first flown by Sqn Ldr C A Rae in about March 1926 at Mousehold, Norwich.

Production: A total of 18 Sidestrands (excluding prototypes) was built: J9176-J9181 (Mk II, five converted to Mk III); J9185-J9189 (Mk III), J9767-J9770 (Mk III), and K1992-K9114 (replacements).

Summary of Service: Sidestrands served with No 101 (Bomber) Squadron at Bircham Newton, Andover and Bicester between March 1929 and July 1936.

Blackburn T.5 Ripon

With the benefit of hindsight, the Blackburn Ripon can be seen to have established the configuration of the British carrier-borne torpedo bomber that was to remain in being until the arrival of the Bristol Beaufort in service in 1939 — but also continued in service with the Fleet Air Arm as the Fairey Swordfish throughout much of the Second World War.

The Ripon was designed to Specification 21/23, which was intended to set down the requirement for a replacement of the Dart single-seat torpedo carrier, itself cast in the same operational mould as the wartime Sopwith Cuckoo. As originally drafted, 21/23 called for a maximum range of 900 miles or an endurance of 12 hours when operating in the fleet reconnaissance rôle, requirements which rendered a single-seater out of the question. In the parallel attack rôles the aircraft was to be capable of carrying either an 18in torpedo, three 520lb or six 230lb bombs. The require-

The first Ripon I prototype, N203, in its original configuration with the Lion V's cylinder banks uncowled and the coolant header tank above them. (Photo: Air Ministry, RTP)

ment for a very long range was soon relaxed considerably, but the necessity for a two-man crew persisted.

Three prototypes were tendered for testing, the Blackburn T.5 Ripon, Handley Page Harrow and the private venture Avro Buffalo (page 185). Two Blackburn prototypes were built, N203 being flown as a landplane on 17 April 1926 at Brough by 'George' Bulman, by

then chief test pilot of the H G Hawker Engineering Company, and N204 as a seaplane on 26 August that year by Flt Lt N H Woodhead DSC.

The Ripon was a single-bay, equal-span biplane of composite wood and metal construction, powered by a 467hp Napier Lion V with chin radiator and roller-blind shutters; the lower wing featured considerable anhedral on the section extending about two feet from the roots, and a 155-gallon fuel tank was located between fireproof bulkheads in the fuselage.

The fourth pre-production Ripon II, S1268; this was the second floatplane sent to the MAEE at Felixstowe and is shown with an 18in torpedo being carried. Note the radiators on the sides of the fuselage, and the interconnected wing slats and ailerons. (Photo: Air Ministry, MAEE, Neg No MH 2824)

Originally a pre-production Ripon II, S1270 was brought up to full Mark IIC standard and is seen here in the markings of No 462 (Fleet Torpedo Bomber) Flight. The swastika marking on the wheel cover was a flight insignia. The photograph well illustrates the great improvement achieved in the engine installation. (Photo: Air Ministry, A & AEE)

As N203 was flown to Martlesham Heath for preliminary tests in October 1926 in competition with the other two contenders, N204 underwent floatplane trials at Felixstowe. At the A & AEE none of the three landplanes was adjudged satisfactory, and a second phase of trials was scheduled to begin in May 1927. The Ripon had been found to be prone to severe yawing tendencies due to an over-balanced rudder, and the aileron control was heavy and sluggish, while its performance was well below that stipulated.

In preparation for the second trials, the engine installation was changed and cleaned up, and the new twin radiators moved to the sides of the nose; the rudder was enlarged and the wings provided with increased sweepback, alterations which evidently transformed the Ripon for, when a new prototype, N231, was delivered to Martlesham Heath it was declared the outright winner, the Establishment pilots reporting light and pleasant controls and a performance, bestowed by a 570hp Lion X engine, significantly better than the Avro and Handley Page contenders.

An unusual step was taken when a development batch of eight aircraft, termed Mark IIs S1265-S1272, was ordered, a valuable expedient that enabled Blackburn to investigate further improvements which would not delay the prototypes as they underwent all manner of routine testing and evaluation. For instance, the last of these aircraft, S1272, featured a 570hp Lion XIA in an entirely new nose design, an enlarged rear cockpit, interconnected wing slats and ailerons and a wholly new tail unit. This was designated the Ripon Mark III, though it did not enter production. In due course, having completed their trials, six of these pre-production Ripons joined Nos 462 (Fleet Torpedo Bomber) Flight aboard HMS *Furious* in January 1929 and No 461 Flight aboard HMS *Glorious* in the Mediterranean in December that year.

The first 13 production Mark IIs, S1357-S1369, were built in 1929 and delivered during January and February 1930. Meanwhile a new production Specification, 2/29, brought the Ripon up to current Fleet Air Arm operational standard, and the Mark IIA introduced duralumin wing ribs, a forward-firing Vickers gun and a Fairey high-speed mounting for the Lewis gun; catapult spools were fitted and a transparent bomb-aiming panel incorporated in the underside of the fuselage. A total of 40 Mark IIAs was delivered between July 1930 and May 1931, enabling the older Mark IIs on Nos 461 and 462 Flights to

Above: *The first production Ripon IIA, S1424, with torpedo at Martlesham Heath for performance and handling evaluation, probably in about mid-1930.* (Photo: Air Ministry, RTP)

Right: *Scarcely recognisable as a Ripon was S1272 in the Mark III guise. When first flown the aircraft was criticised on account of poor field of view from the cockpit resulting from a deepened nose with humped decking; as shown here, the nose decking line was lowered and the wing gap increased. This version had a top speed of 128 mph at 5,000 feet while carrying the torpedo.* (Photo: via R C B Ashworth)

be returned to Brough to be modernised, and No 460 Flight to replace its Darts. The latter unit embarked temporarily in HMS *Eagle* with five Ripon IIAs to attend the British Empire Exhibition at Buenos Aires in March 1931.

The final production version of the Ripon for the Fleet Air Arm was the Mark IIC, introduced to Specification 13/31, in which all-metal wings replaced the former composite structures; increased wing sweepback was also included. Production of 30 new Mark IICs followed the IIBs on the production line and continued until March 1932 (although the last four, K2884-K2887, were manufactured between January 1933 and January 1934 as spares, and delivered to storage at Cardington).

The Mark IIC equipped Nos 465 and 466 Flights during 1931, but in April 1933, with the re-organisation of the Fleet Air Arm, by which time all surviving Ripon IIs and IIAs had been rebuilt as IICs, 36 aircraft were distributed between the new Fleet Torpedo Bomber Squadrons, Nos 810, commanded by Cdr Edmund Walter Anstice, embarked in HMS *Courageous*, No 811, commanded by Sqn Ldr Thomas Arthur Warne-Browne (later Air Marshal Sir Thomas, KBE, CB, DSC) embarked in HMS *Furious*, and No 812, commanded by Flt Lt Frederick Edward Vernon (later Air Cdre, CB, OBE) embarked in HMS *Glorious*. The last Ripons in service were those of No 811 Squadron, which were replaced by Blackburn Baffins when

HMS *Furious* put in to Malta that month.

The Ripon was seldom flown as a seaplane in service, various examples being converted temporarily for trials with the MAEE at Felixstowe. Much of the experimental work at Brough was related to Finland's wish to build the Ripon under licence, and a single example of an *ad hoc* version, the Ripon IIF (F=Finland), with Bristol

Jupiter, was produced at Brough as a pattern aircraft for that country, followed by 25 at the Finnish National Aircraft Factory; these were flown with a variety of in-line and radial engines (see accompanying data table). Finnish Ripons survived well into the Second World War, being flown in action during the Winter and Continuation Wars.

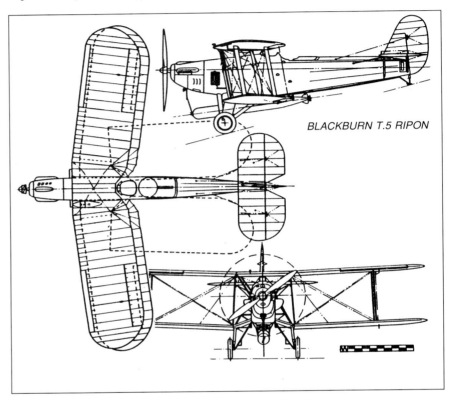

BLACKBURN T.5 RIPON

Type: Single-engine, two-seat, single-bay, fleet reconnaissance/torpedo bomber, wheel/float biplane.

Air Ministry Specifications: 21/23, 2/29 and 13/31.

Manufacturer: The Blackburn Aeroplane & Motor Co Ltd, Leeds and Brough, Yorkshire.

Powerplant: Prototypes: One 467hp Napier Lion V 12-cylinder water-cooled, broad-arrow, in-line engine driving two-blade propeller. Production. 570hp Napier Lion X, XI and XIA. Experimental (and Finnish aircraft). 535hp Armstrong Siddeley Panther IIA; 650hp Armstrong Siddeley Tiger I; 530hp Bristol Jupiter VIII; 580hp Bristol Pegasus IIM.3; 525hp BMW 132.A; 480hp Gnome-Rhône Jupiter VI; 600hp Hispano-Suiza 12 Nbr; 525hp Pratt & Whitney Hornet B; 525hp Wright Cyclone R-1750.

Structure: Composite wood and metal construction; later all-metal construction (Mk IIC).

Dimensions: Mark IIC Landplane. Span, 44ft 10in (17ft 10in folded); length, 36ft 9in; height, 12ft 10in; wing area, 683 sq ft.

Weights: Mark IIC Landplane. Tare, 4,132lb; all-up, 7,282lb.

Performance: Mark IIC Landplane with torpedo/bomb load. Max speed, 111 mph at sea level; climb to 6,500ft, 15 min 30 sec; service ceiling, 10,000ft; range, 410 miles.

Armament: One Lewis gun with Scarff ring on rear cockpit. Either one 18in torpedo or up to three 520lb or six 230lb bombs. Mark IIA

introduced forward-firing Vickers machine gun.

Prototypes: Two Mk Is, N203 and N204; N203 first flown by Flt Lt P W S Bulman at Brough on 17 April 1926; one Mk II prototype, N231; and one Mk III prototype, S1272.

Production: Excluding the above four prototypes, a total of 90 Ripons was built to Air Ministry orders. Mk IIs, 20 (S1265-S1271 and S1357-S1369); Mk IIAs, 40 (S1424-S1432, S1465-S1473 and S1553-S1574); Mk IICs, 30 (S1649-S1674 and K2884-K2887). Many early aircraft were converted to Mk IICs. (One additional example was built by Blackburn for Finland, where 25 further aircraft were produced under licence.)

Summary of Service with Fleet Air Arm: Ripons served with the following Fleet Torpedo Bomber Flights: No 460 Flight from November 1930 to November 1932 aboard HMS *Glorious*, No 461 Flight from December 1929 to April 1933 aboard HMS *Glorious*, No 462 Flight from February 1929 to April 1933 aboard HMS *Furious*, No 465 Flight from March 1931 to April 1933 aboard HMS *Furious*, and No 466 Flight from April 1931 to April 1933 aboard HMS *Furious*. They also served with the following Torpedo Bomber Squadrons: No 810 Squadron from April 1933 to November 1934 aboard HMS *Courageous*, No 811 Squadron from April 1933 to January 1935 aboard HMS *Furious*, and with No 812 Squadron from April 1933 to January 1934 aboard HMS *Glorious*.

Handley Page H.P.31 Harrow

The H.P.31 Harrow, N205, in its Mark II form, flying at Cricklewood. The clean installation of the Lion engine with its side radiators may be appreciated, although the view from the cockpit during torpedo dropping was said to be poor. (Photo: Handley Page Ltd.)

Of the same general configuration as the H.P.25 Hendon torpedo carrier and H.P.28 Handcross bomber, Harold Boultbee's Type E (later designated the H.P.31 Harrow) was tendered to Specification 21/23 on 21 August 1925, and was rewarded with a contract for two prototypes, N205 and N206, for evaluation late the following year.

The first Harrow emerged as a two-bay, equal-span biplane without stagger, and with 4½ degrees dihedral on the upper wings, the lower wings being flat. Power was provided by a 470hp Lion VA with a large frontal radiator with shutters. Leading-edge slats were fitted, the outboard pairs being interconnected with the ailerons on the upper wings, the inboard pairs to the flaps.

First flown by Hubert Broad on 24 April 1926, and later taken over by Arthur Wilcockson, N205 underwent carrier trials aboard HMS *Furious* before being delivered to Martlesham Heath for preliminary assessment in August; unfortunately, however, it was badly damaged in a heavy landing soon after arrival. It was returned to Cricklewood for rebuilding, and N206 was sent to Martlesham Heath in its place for the competitive evaluation with the Blackburn Ripon and Avro Buffalo. Because none of the contenders was regarded as satisfactory (the Harrow suffering recurring engine cooling trouble), the three manufacturers were asked to undertake numerous modifications — the majority relatively minor — before resubmitting their entries in 1927 for re-evaluation.

In the meantime N205 was rebuilt with a Lion XI and an uncowled chin radiator, but continued to be dogged by engine overheating; a Lion XIA was therefore fitted, as the Ripon's successful side radiators were examined.

Both N205 and N206 suffered a succession of mechanical failures, but Handley Page was encouraged to persevere although, unlike Blackburn, it was not to be awarded a contract for a third prototype. Instead, Handley Page decided to introduce a much altered Harrow Mark II by rebuilding N205 with a Lion XIA in a cowling similar to that of

the Ripon with side-mounted radiators. The lower wing was rigged with the same dihedral as that on the upper wing.

In the final trials of 1927, though with handling much improved, the Harrow was considered to be inferior to the Ripon, returning a disappointing speed and climb performance, particularly when loaded with torpedo.

N205 suffered damage to the tail in 1928 during seaplane trials at Felixstowe and was eventually scrapped, N206 having been dismantled a year earlier.

Type: Single-engine, two-seat, two-bay, fleet reconnaissance/torpedo bomber, wheel/float biplane.

Air Ministry Specification: 21/23

Manufacturer: Handley Page Ltd, Cricklewood, London.

Powerplant: One 470hp Napier Lion V 12-cylinder, broad-arrow, water-cooled in-line engine driving two-blade propeller; also 530hp Lion XA and 550hp Lion XIA.

Dimensions: Mark I. Span, 44ft 0in; length, 33ft 9in; wing area, 563 sq ft.

Weights: Mark I. Tare, 4,403lb; all-up (with torpedo), 7,140lb.

Performance: Mark I with torpedo. Max speed, 106 mph at 3,000ft; climb to 6,500ft, 18 min 45 sec; service ceiling, 8,700ft; range, 440 miles.

Armament: Provision for single Lewis gun with Scarff ring on rear cockpit; either one 18in torpedo or three 520lb bombs.

Prototypes: Two, N205 and N206; N205 first flown by Hubert Broad at Cricklewood on 24 April 1926; no production.

Avro Type 571/572 Buffalo

Originally designed as a private venture to succeed the Avro Type 555 Bison (a deck-landing sea reconnaissance/fleet spotter), the Type 571 Buffalo was submitted to the requirement set out in

Specification 21/23 for a fleet torpedo bomber, but the Air Ministry declined to order a prototype. Nevertheless, Avro opted to build an aircraft at private expense, and applied to enter the competitive trials at Martlesham Heath.

Flown at Hamble during 1926 this aircraft, registered G-EBNW, was of mixed construction, the folding wing structure comprising spruce spars with spruce and duralumin ribs and tubular

steel drag struts. Ailerons were fitted to the lower wings only, and the divided undercarriage incorporated long-travel oleos with rubber shock absorbers. Power was provided by a cleanly-cowled Napier Lion VA engine with a small radiator beneath the nose.

G-EBNW was flown to Martlesham Heath in October 1926 for the 12/23 competition but was deemed to possess such poor handling qualities that no

The Type 571 Buffalo Mk I, G-EBNW, as it first appeared, with rounded wing planform and ailerons on the lower wings only and no wing slats. It was the largest and heaviest of the three contenders to Specification 21/23, the fuselage being sufficiently deep to include a cabin beneath the crew's cockpits, evidenced by the circular transparent panel directly beneath the pilot's cockpit. As far as is known no performance figures were ever recorded for the aircraft carrying either torpedoes or bombs. (Photo: A V Roe & Co Ltd.)

performance figures were formally recorded, the aileron control being singled out for special criticism.

No result of the competition was announced and Avro decided to replace the engine with a Lion XIA and to fit entirely new wings of more rectangular planform, built on an all-metal structure. The aircraft returned to Martlesham Heath in May 1927 where its handling was provisionally assessed as much improved. However, the Buffalo suffered undercarriage collapse and was once again returned to the manufacturer for repair, the wings being changed to include leading-edge slats interconnected with Frise ailerons on all four wings.

By the time G-EBNW, now referred to as the Type 572 Buffalo Mark II, arrived at the A & AEE for the third

time, the Ripon had been declared the competition winner. The Avro aircraft, however, must have acquired acceptable handling qualities, for the Air Ministry purchased the aircraft which, now

numbered N239 as an experimental naval aeroplane, was fitted with a pair of duralumin floats at Hamble and delivered to Felixstowe for general seaplane trials with the MAEE.

Type: Single-engine, two-seat, single-bay fleet torpedo bomber wheel/float biplane.
Air Ministry Specification: Private venture to 21/23.
Manufacturer: A V Roe & Co Ltd, Manchester, and Hamble, Hampshire.
Powerplant: One 450hp Napier Lion VA 12-cylinder, broad-arrow, water-cooled, in-line engine driving two-blade propeller; 530hp Napier Lion XIA.
Structure: Composite metal and wood construction.
Dimension: Mk I. Span, 46ft 0in; length, 36ft 0in; height, 13ft 9in; wing area, 684 sq ft.
Weights: Mk I. Tare, 4,233lb; all-up (with torpedo), 7,430lb.
Performance: Mk I (without warload). Max speed, 135 mph at sea level; service ceiling, 11,800ft; range, 620 miles.
Armament: One synchronized 0.303in Vickers machine gun on side of fuselage and twin-yoked Lewis guns with Scarff ring on rear cockpit; one 18-inch Mark VIII torpedo or three 520lb bombs.
Prototype: One, G-EBNW (later N239), first flown in 1926 at Hamble. No production.

---

de Havilland D.H.65 Hound

It will be recalled that, when describing the events that resulted in the Fairey IIIF being short-listed for selection in the heavily-subscribed competition under the terms of Specification 12/26 in its general purpose category (see pages 176-177), a number of aircraft failed to reach or negotiate the final competitive stage under Specification 26/27; they included the D.H.65 Hound and Gloster Goral.

Clearly recognisable as a D.H.9A derivative, the Hound, seen here with the Napier Lion XA geared engine, was little more than an exercise in exploiting the additional power available from this engine, and demonstrated little understanding of advancing military requirements. (Photo: A J Jackson Collection)

The de Havilland D.H.65 Hound, produced as a private venture, was a determined effort to demonstrate that, given a free hand, an aircraft designer could achieve high performance and still meet the principal requirements set out in an Air Ministry Specification. Unfortunately, in doing so, de Havilland failed to understand the wider considerations

with which the Air Ministry was burdened, not least the *necessity* to progress towards all-metal manufacture of military aeroplanes, a fact made abundantly clear in Specification 12/26.

The Hound was of all-wood construction, and retained wings, tail and fuselage very similar to those of the D.H.9A which it was intended to re-

place. The principal difference of course lay in the use of a Lion engine, in this instance a direct-drive 530hp Lion VIII.

Carrying the civil registration G-EBNJ, the Hound was flown at Stag Lane by Hubert Broad on 17 November 1926. The direct-drive engine was then replaced by a geared 540hp Lion XA and the rudder enlarged before the aeroplane, now termed the D.H.65A, was sent to Martlesham Heath for the competition.

In the performance tests the Hound returned the best overall figures of all the contenders, demonstrating a maximum speed of 163 mph at sea level and climbing to 10,000 feet in 6 min 28 sec. (without warload), a performance considered to have been achieved by a slim fuselage constructed in wood — which in turn compromised the stowage of mandatory equipment. The aircraft proved difficult to land with precision, leading to doubts that it would be suitable for operating from small landing strips. Unlike other manufacturers who also depended to some degree on wooden construction, de Havilland gave no indication that it would be prepared to offer an all-metal prototype.

Failing to achieve short-listing at Martlesham, the Hound was flown by Broad on 26 April 1928 to establish a number of speed-with-load world records, this in all likelihood being a gesture to underline de Havilland's belief that the Air Ministry's judgement in the 12/26 Specification had been flawed.

The D.H.65A did not achieve a production contract, although G-EBNJ was purchased by the Air Ministry and numbered J9127. It returned to Martlesham for further trials, unrelated to 12/26, on 11 September 1928. However, a routine inspection of the airframe ten days later disclosed that the wood in the rear fuselage had deteriorated beyond economical repair, and the aircraft was grounded.

A second prototype had been proposed, but this was cancelled. Ironically, a derivative of the D.H.65 was built to an Australian government specification for composite wood and metal construction, termed the D.H.65J Hound II. Powered by a Bristol Jupiter VIIIF, this aeroplane underwent limited trials at Martlesham late in 1928, but its performance was much inferior to that of the earlier aircraft.

Type: Single-engine, two-seat, two-bay experimental general purpose biplane.
Air Ministry Specification: Private venture to 12/26.
Manufacturer: The de Havilland Aircraft Co Ltd, Stag Lane, Edgware, Middlesex.
Powerplant: One 530hp Napier Lion VIII 12-cylinder, broad-arrow, water-cooled in-line engine driving two-blade propeller. Also 540hp Lion XA and XI.
Structure: All-wood construction.
Dimensions: Span, 45ft 0in; length, 11ft 6in; height, 11ft 6in; wing area, 461.5 sq ft.
Weights: D.H.65A. Tare, 2,981lb; all-up, 4,934lb.
Performance: D.H.65A. Max speed, 153 mph at 6,500ft; climb to 10,000ft, 8 min 48 sec; absolute ceiling, 21,500ft.
Armament: Provision for one synchronized 0.303in Vickers machine gun on the side of the fuselage and one Lewis gun with Scarff ring on rear cockpit; provision to carry up to two 230lb bombs.
Prototype: One, G-EBNJ (later J9127), first flown by Capt H S Broad at Stag Lane on 17 November 1926. Second prototype, G-EBNK cancelled. No production.

Gloster G.22 Goral

The Gloucestershire Aircraft Company's tender to Specification 26/27 for a general purpose aircraft to replace the age-old D.H.9A was another design employing that aircraft's wings, of which several hundreds of surplus sets remained unused.

The G.22 Goral was designed under the direction of Henry Folland by Capt S J Waters (who had, with Folland, been largely responsible for the design of the F.E.4 at the Royal Aircraft Factory early in the First World War), and the prototype, J8673 ordered by the Air Ministry, was first flown on 8 February 1927 with a 420hp Bristol Jupiter V radial engine, and within a month was delivered to No 22 Squadron of the A & AEE at Martlesham Heath for preliminary testing. The unattractive aircraft was soon back at Hucclecote for some cosmetic treatment, but to little avail. It simply failed to find favour with any of the pilots who flew it.

When it returned to Martlesham for the competition, J8673 had been fitted

The Goral, J8673, at Hucclecote in 1927; the bulky Jupiter radial engine was fairly neatly cowled with crankcase panels which left only the cylinders exposed. (Photo: C H Barnes Collection)

with a 492hp Bristol Jupiter VI, which bestowed a maximum speed of 129 mph at 5,000 feet, and a climb to 10,000 feet in no less than 17 min 5 sec while carrying desert equipment. It was said to be unpleasant to fly, and the slim fuse-

Type: Single-engine, two-seat, two-bay general purpose biplane.
Air Ministry Specification: 26/27
Manufacturer: The Gloucestershire Aircraft Co Ltd, Hucclecote, Gloucester.
Powerpant: One 420hp Bristol Jupiter V nine-cylinder air-cooled radial engine driving two-blade propeller. Also 425hp Jupiter VIA.
Structure: All-metal construction with fabric covering.
Dimensions: Span, 46ft 7in; length, 31ft 6in; height, 11ft 4in; wing area, 494 sq ft.
Weights: Jupiter VIA. Tare, 2,943lb; all-up, 5,005lb.
Performance: Jupiter VIA. Max speed, 129 mph at 5,000ft; climb to 10,000ft, 17 min 5 sec; range, 750 miles (without warload).
Armament: One synchronized 0.303in Vickers machine gun on nose decking and one Lewis gun on rear cockpit; bomb load of up to two 230lb bombs.
Prototype: One, J8673, first flown at Hucclecote on 8 February 1927. No production.

lage was only just capable of accommodating the mandatory military equipment, but with difficult access. The Goral was, therefore, one of the first to be eliminated. The manufacturer, however, gained financial benefit from the contest when the Westland Wapiti was declared the winner, for Gloster was awarded a sub-contract to manufacture 525 sets of all-metal Wapiti wings.

The company also sought to interest foreign governments in the Goral, and presented J8673 for performance testing at Martlesham Heath with a 480hp Jupiter VIIIF in February 1929, but, despite some evidence of interest by an Argentine purchasing mission in January 1931, no order was placed.

Westland Wapiti

From the earliest days of the Wapiti's trials periods at Martlesham Heath the aircraft appeared favourite to become the eventual winner of the general purpose competition to Specification 26/27. The prototype seemed capable of meeting the performance and equipment requirements, it employed D.H.9A wings (superficially modified) and any criticism of its handling qualities were relatively minor when compared with the majority of the other competitors.

Designed under the direction of Arthur Davenport, who enjoyed the benefit of having undertaken the development and production of the D.H.9A for more than half-a-dozen years, the Wapiti featured a twelve-inch deeper and almost six-inch wider fuselage, built in three sections; the nose and centre components were of steel and duralumin tubular steel with fluted, removable aluminium panels and plywood decking; the rear fuselage was a wooden structure with fabric covering. The D.H.9A wing cellule was retained, but rigged with increased stagger so that, with the cockpits located further aft, the field of view was considerably improved. The oleo-pneumatic cross-axle undercarriage, later equipped with wheelbrakes, allowed good

Wapiti Mk I J9102 in standard production configuration. Later it was to be employed in engine research, among those fitted being the Bristol Phoenix diesel. (Photo: A J Jackson Collection)

control on the ground and more positive spot landing in confined spaces. The maximum bomb load comprised four 112lb bombs, carried under the wings, and up to six 20lb bombs on light racks under the centre fuselage.

When first flown by Laurence Openshaw at Yeovil on 7 March 1927, the prototype, J8495, featured a 420hp Jupiter VI engine somewhat crudely cowled with crankcase panels which did not extend as far forward as the front exhaust collector ring. More important, Openshaw reported that the rudder had proved almost entirely ineffective — probably being shielded by the bulkier

fuselage; this was temporarily improved after fitting a much taller and angular rudder than the D.H.9A's component used initially.

Five days after its first flight, J8495 was flown to Martlesham Heath where it underwent brief manufacturer's tests before being accepted for Service trials with No 12 (Bomber) Squadron at Andover, starting on 3 June. Later that month it returned to Martlesham for the 26/27 competitive evaluation. In comparison with the other six aircraft on which reports were made, the Wapiti was rated as the best in take-off distance and landing speed, third in climb performance and ceiling and fourth in speed performance. Where, however, it was regarded as by far the most superior was in the stowage and accessibility of military equipment — which included oxygen, wireless, camera, emergency food and drinking water, tools and spares (not forgetting the spare wheel and tyre) — this being a clear indication of Westland's first-hand experience with

Another Wapiti I, J9084, at Martlesham Heath with 112lb bombs under the wings during bombing trials in 1931; this aeroplane, apart from being tested with floats (see photo opposite) had already served with No 60 Squadron in India. (Photo: Air Ministry, A & AEE)

the veteran D.H.9As serving in the Middle East and India.

Both the Vickers Valiant and Fairey Ferret were also rated highly, but they were eliminated as neither used D.H.9A components, and the Valiant was some 30 per cent more expensive. Thus, although some further trials were required to assess recommended modifications, the Wapiti was declared the winner in October 1927, and a preliminary production order for 25 aircraft (Mark Is, J9078-J9102) was placed with Westland.

Meanwhile the Wapiti's tail had undergone complete redesign to arrive at its finite and characteristic shape, the large horn-balanced rudder blending in a smooth convex curve with the fin. Handley Page slats were fitted to the upper wings, and the Jupiter VI crankcase cowling was improved to reduce drag. Seventeen of the Mark Is were delivered to the Packing Depot at Ascot for shipment to India and Egypt, being distributed between Nos 11 and 34 (General Purpose) Squadrons at Risalpur, India, No 39 Squadron at Hinaidi, and No 84 Squadron at Shaibah, Iraq. J9095 and J9096 were specially prepared as VIP aircraft for delivery to No 24 (Communications) Squadron at Northolt,

the former for use by HRH Edward, Prince of Wales. Most of the remaining aircraft were retained in the United Kingdom for trials purposes. For instance, J9094 was tested with floats at the MAEE, Felixstowe (as were at least seven later aircraft), and J9102 was flown with various Bristol Phoenix diesel engines and shown at the 1933 Hendon Display (as New Type No 11). Two of the aircraft sent overseas, J9082 and J9083, were completed as dual control trainers to assist the squadrons in India to convert to the Wapiti.

From early experience with the Wapiti in service, it soon became clear that the aircraft represented an excellent replacement for both the D.H.9A and Bristol F.2B Fighter. A new standard of tropical equipment fit was drawn up in Specification 12/30, and this was to be included in the main production version, the Wapiti Mark IIA. As a preliminary step, however, eleven pre-production examples, J9237-J9247, were built as Mark IIs, two of which (J9238 and

J9247) became full-standard Mark IIA prototypes. Only four of these aircraft served with a Squadron (No 84), the remainder being used for test purposes, including J9237 which underwent cold weather trials with a ski undercarriage in Canada between 1930 and 1932. Later still, J9247 became the prototype Wapiti Mark VIII with a 550hp Armstrong Siddeley Panther IIA engine.

Production of the Wapiti IIA got underway when the first 35 examples, J9380-J9414, were completed between October 1928 and February 1929, aircraft of this batch reaching Nos 11 (Risalpur), 30 (Hinaidi), 39 (Risalpur) and 84 (Shaibah) Squadrons during 1929. The aircraft featured all-metal rear fuselages and wings, the latter being manufactured by the Steel Wing Company, a wholly-owned subsidiary of the Gloster Aircraft Company. Power was provided by 550hp Jupiter VIII engines.

Hitherto, all Wapiti squadrons had previously been flying either Hawker Horsleys or D.H.9As. The first former

---

Type: Single-engine, two-seat, two-bay general purpose biplane.

Air Ministry Specifications: 26/27, 1/29, 12/30 and 17/31.

Manufacturer: Westland Aircraft Works, Yeovil, Somerset.

Powerplant: Prototype. One 420hp Bristol Jupiter VI nine-cylinder air-cooled radial engine driving two-blade propeller. Production. 420hp Jupiter VI; 550hp Jupiter VIII and VIIIF. Experimental. 560hp Jupiter VIIIS; Jupiter IXF; 565hp Jupiter XFA; 490hp Armstrong Siddeley Jaguar VI; 550hp Panther IIA; 400hp Bristol Phoenix I (diesel); 460hp Phoenix II; 590hp Draco I (diesel).

Structure: Early aircraft of composite metal and wood construction; later all-metal. Metal and fabric covering.

Dimensions: Mark IIA. Span, 46ft 5in; length, 31ft 8in; height, 13ft 0in; wing area, 488 sq ft.

Weights: Mark IIA. Tare, 3,810lb; all-up, 5,410lb.

Performance: Mark IIA fully equipped with warload. Max speed, 129 mph at 6,500ft; climb to 10,000ft, 15 min; service ceiling, 18,800ft; range, 360 miles.

Armament: One synchronized 0.303in Vickers machine gun on port side of fuselage and one Lewis gun with Scarff ring on rear cockpit; bomb load, up to 580lb.

Prototype: One, J8495, first flown by Laurence Openshaw at Yeovil on 7 March 1927.

Production: A total of 516 Wapitis was built to Air Ministry orders (excluding the above prototype). Mark I, 25: J9078-J9102; Mark II, 11: J9237-J9247; Mark IIA, 429: J9380-J9414, J9481-J9514, J9592-J9636, J9708-J9724, J9835-J9871, K1122-K1157, K1254-K1309, K1316-K1415, K2252-K2320; Mark V, 35: J9725-J9759; Mark VI, 16: K2236-K2251. J9247 became prototype Mark IIA. A total of 18 of the above were delivered to Canada and 6 to Australia, and 45 were converted to Westland Wallaces.

Summary of Service with Royal Air Force and Auxiliary Air Force: Wapitis served with Nos 5, 11, 20, 27, 28, 31, 39 and 60 (General Purpose) Squadrons in India between February 1929 and October 1940, with Nos 30, 55 and 84 Squadrons in the Middle East between July 1928 and March 1937, and with Nos 11 (Bomber) and 24 (Communications) Squadrons in the United Kingdom between October 1928 and about 1934. Wapitis served with the following Auxiliary Air Force Squadrons in the United Kingdom; Nos 501, 502, 503, 600, 601, 602, 603, 604, 605, 607 and 608 Squadrons between July 1929 and about January 1937. Wapitis also served in small numbers with Flying Training Schools, the School of Army Co-operation, No 1 (later No 22) Army Co-operation Unit, No 3 (Fighter) Squadron, etc. Many were transferred to the Indian Air Force from RAF stocks in India.

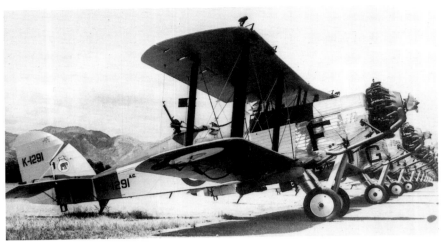

Line-up of No 27 (General Purpose) Squadron Wapiti IIAs in 1933 at Kohat, south of Peshawar and only forty miles from the Khyber Pass. The nearest aircraft, K1291, is loaded with a pair of high fineness ratio 250lb bombs under the wings and four 20lb bombs under the fuselage, the maximum bomb load normally carried by the Wapiti in service. Note the slats and navigation lights on the upper wing. (Photo: via M W Payne)

Bristol Fighter Squadron to re-equip with Wapitis was No 31 at Quetta, India, in February 1931, and by the end of that year nine squadrons were flying the Westland aircraft.

Moreover, a new 'home-standard' had been drawn up in Specification 1/29 to enable Wapitis to serve with squadrons of the Special Reserve and Auxiliary Air Force. The first, No 602 (City of Glasgow) Squadron at Renfrew gave up its Fairey Fawns and received its first Wapitis in July 1929, followed by the former D.H.9A Squadrons, Nos 600 (City of London) and 601 (County of London) at Hendon in August and November that year. Nos 501, 603, 604 and 605 followed suit during the next three years, and Nos 607 and 608 rather later.

The Wapiti Mark III, powered by the 480hp Armstrong Siddeley Jaguar VI geared radial, was a version developed specially for South Africa in 1929, of which four were built by Westland and twenty-five under licence by the SAAF Workshops at Roberts Heights, Pretoria. Little is known of the Wapiti IV, or whether it was ever built; incorporating a fuselage lengthened by two feet and powered by a 650hp Hispano Suiza 12Nbis engine, it was designed to meet a Spanish Air Ministry requirement. One example, according to contemporary records, may have been delivered to China in about 1931.

The Wapiti V, on the other hand, was built in quantity for the RAF, being intended as an army co-operation variant with message pick-up hook, the extended fuselage of the Mark IV and powered by a 600hp Jupiter VIIIFA engine (the 'F' in the engine's nomenclature denoting forged cylinder heads). Thirty-five Mark Vs (J9725-J9759) were built, small numbers being delivered to

Nos 5, 11, 20, 27, 28, 31 and 60 Squadrons overseas. The last Mark Vs continued in service with No 5 Squadron until June 1940 at Lahore, and with No 27 Squadron until October the same year at Risalpur, when they were replaced by Hawker Harts (India).

The final version to serve with the RAF was the Wapiti Mark VI dual control trainer to Specification 17/31, of which sixteen (K2236-K2251) were produced in 1932-33, powered by the Jupiter IXF; these were 'home service'

aircraft of which examples were delivered to Nos 501, 601, 602, 607 and 608 Squadrons of the Auxiliary Air Force for conversion and operational training.

The Wapiti VII was a single aeroplane developed from the Mark V to become the Westland P.V.6 and ultimately, carrying the military serial K3488, the Westland Wallace prototype (see page 231). The Wapiti VIII was the designation of four further Panther IIA-powered aircraft supplied to China in 1932.

Although, as stated above, several

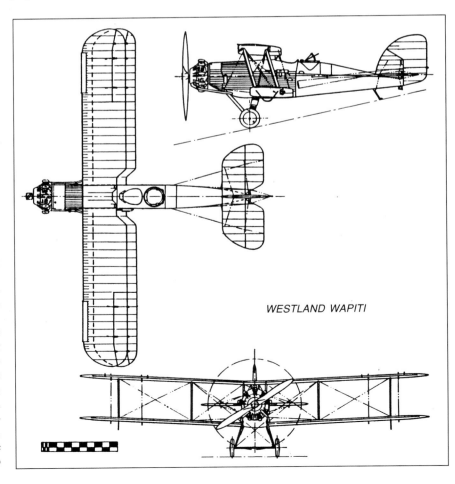

WESTLAND WAPITI

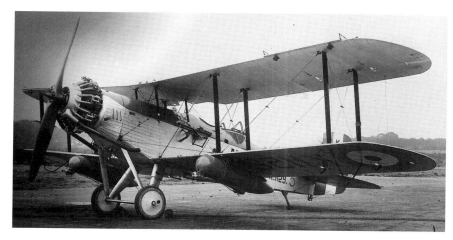

Left: *A mid-production Wapiti IIA, K1129, during long-range trials at the A & AEE, Martlesham Heath, in September 1930. The aircraft is shown fitted with a pair of under-wing fuel tanks with wind-driven pumps; although provision was made for a message pick-up hook, in-service Wapitis were seldom so equipped.* (Photo: The Bristol Aeroplane Co Ltd, Neg No 17519)

Below: *Wapiti IIB J9405 of No 30 (General Purpose) Squadron, based at Hinaidi, Iraq, being flown by the squadron commander, Sqn Ldr (later Gp Capt) P Murgatroyd in 1929. Note the bomb racks under the wings and fuselage, and removal of the wheel covers.* (Photo: JMB/GSL Collection)

squadrons continued to fly Wapitis throughout the 1930s, the extraordinarily harsh operating conditions in the Middle East and India — particularly on the North-West Frontier — contributed to a very high number of accidents, and the Aircraft Depots at Drigh Road, India, and Hinaidi, Iraq, were seldom without dozens of aircraft under repair. For this reason, with production of new Wapiti IIAs being discontinued in 1932, Nos 11 and 39 Squadrons exchanged their aircraft for the Hawker Hart (India), beginning as early as December 1931.

Vickers Type 131 Valiant

The unregistered Vickers Valiant at Martlesham Heath in 1927, fitted with metal propeller and carrying a pair of 112lb bombs. (Photo: Air Ministry, A & AEE)

Although Vickers (Aviation) Ltd had not been fortunate enough to have any of its light bomber essays accepted by the RAF during the early 1920s, a number of them had been sold to foreign governments, notably the Vixen, whose wooden wing structure had suffered badly in the extreme heat of northern Chile. In 1926 this had prompted the company to design a new version, the Vixen VII, with metal construction throughout (to be renamed the Vivid, see page 197). A parallel design was produced of an all-metal general purpose aircraft for the RAF, motivated by the requirement which was eventually set out in Specification 26/27.

Rex Pierson, however, set his face against the use of D.H.9A wings, as 'recommended' by the Air Ministry, with the result that no contract was placed to purchase a prototype. Instead, the company decided to produce a proto-

type as a private venture and applied to enter the 26/27 competion.

The Vickers Type 131 Valiant was powered by a 492hp Bristol Jupiter VI which, in its initial flight configuration-drove a Fairey Reed metal propeller. However, during the early manufacturer's tests at Martlesham, the metal propeller and its spinner suffered a number of failures following blade flutter, and E R C Scholefield recommended a change to the customary wooden propeller. The Valiant featured relatively broad-chord wings of gener-

ous area, with ailerons on upper and lower planes. The front fuselage was of deep section and, although the pilot's field of view forward and downwards was considered to be poor, the gunner's field of fire was fairly good.

When the Valiant attended the competition, during the latter half of 1927, the pilots at Martlesham Heath were very complimentary regarding its handling qualities, rating it second only to the Wapiti in this respect, but worst in climb and ceiling; and the positioning of the front gun came in for criticism.

Nevertheless, the Valiant was short-listed to the final three — probably on account of its predominantly metal structure — and was sent to a number of RAF stations and squadrons to obtain reactions from line pilots and enigneering officers. Surviving reports suggest that criticism was fairly widely voiced about the positioning of equipment.

Moreover, without even a token effort made to employ D.H.9A components, the Valiant was probably compromised from the outset. The Air Ministry made no offer to purchase the prototype, and the aircraft, registered G-EBVM in January 1928, was shipped out to Chile for demonstration purposes, but no order resulted.

Type: Single-engine, two-seat, single-bay experimental general purpose biplane.
Air Ministry Specification: Private venture to 26/27.
Manufacturer: Vickers (Aviation) Ltd, Weybridge, Surrey.
Powerplant: One 492hp Bristol Jupiter VI nine-cylinder air-cooled radial engine driving two-blade propeller.
Structure: All-metal construction.
Dimensions: Span, 45ft 7in; length, 34ft 0in; height, 13ft 0in; wing area, 590 sq ft.
Weights: Tare, 2,896lb; all-up, 5,105lb.
Performance: Max speed, 129 mph at 6,500ft; climb to 10,000ft, 17 min 12 sec; service ceiling, 16,400ft.
Armament: One synchronized 0.303in Vickers machine gun on port side of fuselage and one Lewis gun with Scarff ring on rear cockpit. Bomb load of up to four 112lb bombs.
Prototype: One, later G-EBVM, probably first flown early in 1927. No production.

Short S.3b Chamois

Among the prototypes submitted in 1923 to Corps Reconnaissance Specifications 19/21 and 8/22, alongside the Hawker Duiker and Armstrong Whitworth Wolf (not within the scope of this work), was the Short S.3 Springbok I, an all-metal aircraft in which the Air Ministry expressed considerable interest at that time.

Unfortunately the Springbok J6975 crashed, killing its pilot, and none of the aircraft submitted succeeded in meeting the requirements. Nevertheless, the Short aircraft had shown sufficient promise for the Air Ministry to order three further examples as Springbok Mark IIs (J7295-J7297), and the first of these was modified by Short with the object of submitting it to a new Army Co-operation Specification, 30/24, intended to redefine a Bristol Fighter replacement. The modifications to J7295 included replacing the former two-bay wings with a single-bay cellule and moving the fuel tanks to the wings.

In its new guise, renamed the Short S.3b Chamois, J7295 was flown with a 425hp Jupiter IV by John Lankester Parker at Lympne, Kent, on 14 March 1927, and delivered for contractor's trials at Martlesham Heath on 27 April — already long after the 30/24 competion had been completed. It was at once realised that the Chamois was severely underpowered and, although it was shown at the Hendon Display on 2 July 1927 (as New Type No 3), it was much too late to be considered for production, the Armstrong Whitworth Atlas having long since been declared the winner and ordered into production (see page 169).

In any case, the Chamois was thoroughly disliked by the pilots at Martlesham Heath, who found it excessively noisy (the monocoque fuselage being said to act as a 'kettle drum') and lacking in directional control. The view from the pilot's cockpit also earned harsh criticism, although the aircraft was deemed to be fairly easily maintained owing to its metal structure. Not surprisingly, therefore, J7295 was scrapped fairly soon afterwards.

Type: Single-engine, two-seat, single-bay experimental army co-operation biplane.
Air Ministry Specification: 30/24
Manufacturer: Short Bros Ltd, Rochester, Kent.
Powerplant: One 425hp Bristol Jupiter nine-cylinder air-cooled radial engine.
Structure: Metal construction with semi-monocoque fuselage and fabric-covered wings.
Dimensions: Span, 45ft 1in; length, 30ft 1in; wing area, 440 sq ft.
Weights: Tare, 2,720lb; all-up, as tested, 4,210 lb.
Performance: Max speed, 116 mph at 6,500ft; climb to 10,000ft, 17 min 6 sec; service ceiling, 14,600ft.
Armament: One Lewis gun with Scarff ring on rear cockpit; bomb load of up to four 112lb bombs. (Provision for synchronized forward-firing Vickers machine gun, but not fitted.)
Prototype: One, J7295 (formerly Springbok), first flown by John Lankester Parker at Lympne on 14 March 1927. No production.

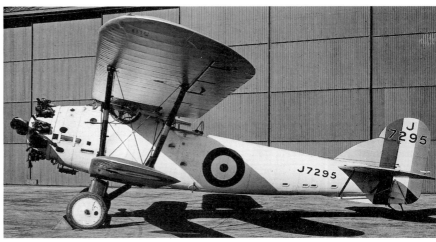

A photograph taken at Lympne of the Short Chamois, J7295, dated 12 March 1927 (but almost certainly taken three days earlier), shortly before its first flight. The aeroplane was unquestionably of clean design, especially in the engine installation, but the location of the pilot's cockpit so close under the upper wing necessitated a large circular cut-out in its centresection — entirely superfluous as a means to provide a good field of view of the ground (essential in an army co-operation aircraft). (Photo: Short Bros Ltd)

Hawker Harrier

Specification 23/25 set out requirements for a Horsley bomber replacement, while a second, 24/25, called for a new coastal defence torpedo bomber. The former brought forth four contenders, the Hawker Harrier, Gloster Goring, Westland Witch and Handley Page Hare, and the latter produced the Blackburn Beagle and Vickers Vildebeest. It was soon realised, however, that any aircraft which satisfied the 24/25 torpedo-carrying requirements would almost certainly meet or surpass the Horsley replacement specification. Therefore, in order to give manufacturers the opportunity to study both requirements, the Air Ministry announced that a single competition would be held, beginning in January 1929.

First of the new prototypes to fly was Sydney Camm's Harrier, J8325, powered by a geared 583hp Bristol Jupiter VIII, taken aloft on its maiden flight by 'George ' Bulman early in February 1927, in its initial configuration equipped as a bomber to Specification 23/25. Embodying new 'dumb-bell' spars comprising two rolled hexagonal steel booms joined on their flanges by a steel web (patented jointed by Fred Sigrist and Roy Chaplin, the latter Camm's newly-appointed deputy), the Harrier was an exceptionally strong aeroplane with a divided, levered-suspension undercarriage that enabled two 500lb bombs to be carried beneath the fuselage as an alternative to a load of four 250lb bombs to be mounted under the wings.

J8325 visited Martlesham in November 1927 for contractor's trials, during which the Harrier proved just able to meet the bomber requirement and was declared to handle satisfactorily. However, the A & AEE pointed out that its bomb load, while meeting the Specification, was inferior to that of the Horsley, and that it was then unlikely that the Air Ministry would persist with a requirement for a Horsley replacement in view of the Sidestrand's ability to perform the 'medium' bomber rôle.

The Harrier was therefore returned to Brooklands and restressing undertaken to enable the 2,800lb torpedo to be carried between the undercarriage units.

The Harrier at Filton with a 870hp Bristol Hydra engine driving a three-blade propeller in the early 1930s. (Photo: Author's Collection)

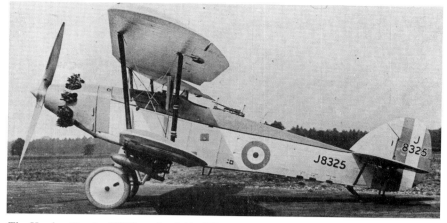

The Hawker Harrier J8325 at the A & AEE carrying a pair of 250lb bombs during the combined evaluation under Specifications 23/25 and 24/25. (Photo: Air Ministry, A & AEE)

It returned to Martlesham Heath in January 1929 for the torpedo bomber competition, but now proved to be so underpowered that it was incapable of taking off with the torpedo, gunner *and* full fuel load; indeed, most of the torpedo-carrying flight trials were carried out at half fuel weight and without even ballast for the second crew member. Moreover, pilots admitted that on occasion they had to apply emergency throttle to avoid accidents on take-off. The aircraft was also criticised for the poor view from the cockpit.

By October that year it was clear that nothing short of installing a much more powerful engine would enable the Harrier to meet the 24/25 requirements, while the Vickers Vildebeest, Blackburn Beagle and Handley Page Hare were short-listed for further competition after being re-engined with Jupiter XF engines.

After being flown at Martlesham during August 1929 to decide whether J8325 was suitable for use by the Home Aircraft Depot for parachute testing — which it was not — the aircraft was leased to Bristol for engine testing, being flown with the 870hp Hydra and 495hp Orion experimental engines, continuing in this capacity for several years.

Type: Single-engine, two-seat, single-bay coastal defence torpedo bomber biplane.
Air Ministry Specifications: 23/25 and 24/25
Manufacturer: The H G Hawker Engineering Co Ltd, Kingston-upon-Thames, Surrey.
Powerplant: One 583hp Bristol Jupiter nine-cylinder air-cooled geared radial engine. Experimental. 870hp Brstol Hydra; 495hp Bristol Orion.
Structure: All-metal construction with ply and fabric covering.
Dimensions: Span, 46ft 3in; length, 29ft 7in; height, 13ft 4in; wing area, 496.8 sq ft.
Weights: Tare, 3,278lb; all up, bombs, 5,656lb; torpedo, 7,179lb.
Performance: Bombs. Max speed, 135 mph at 6,500lb; climb to 10,000ft, 18 min 30 sec; service ceiling, 20,000ft. Torpedo. Max speed, 126 mph at 6,500ft; climb to 10,000ft, 29 min 15 sec; service ceiling, 10,500ft.
Armament: One synchronized Vickers machine gun in nose decking and one Lewis gun with Scarff ring on rear cockpit; either 1,000lb of bombs or one 2,800lb Mark VIII torpedo.
Prototype: One, J8325, flown by Flt Lt P W S Bulman at Brooklands in February 1927.

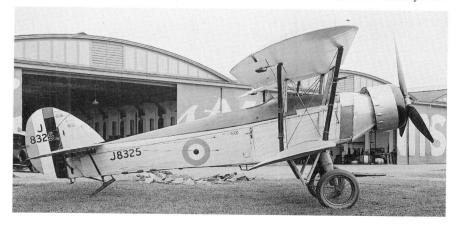

Gloster G.25 Goring

Rather smaller and lighter than the Hawker Harrier, the Gloster Goring was similarly designed to the two Specifications 23/25 and 24/25 by Capt S J Waters under Henry Folland's supervision in 1926, and first flew in March 1927. It was constructed almost entirely of wood, with steel joints, the longerons being of ash and the struts of spruce. The shorter-span lower wings were of inverted gull configuration, while ailerons were fitted to the upper planes only; the latter were of thick, high-lift section, enabling the two 75-gallon fuel tanks to be located within the aerofoil section.

The prototype, J8674, built as a private venture, was purchased by the Air Ministry on completion and first arrived at Martlesham Heath for contractor's trials in April, after which it was fitted with a 425hp Jupiter VI and a pair of floats for short trials as a seaplane at Felixstowe, being first flown in this form on 7 May. During the following month it reverted to landplane form and commenced evaluation with No 22 Squadron of the A & AEE in July, powered by a Jupiter VIII.

Unfortunately the undercarriage was no match for the poor surface at Martlesham that year, and suffered three failures during the eight months the aircraft spent with the A & AEE, and because of its failure to carry a torpedo (owing to the stop-gap use of a cross-axle undercarriage), J8674 could not be considered a valid contender in the 24/25 competition, which began in January 1929.

J8674 returned to Hucclecote in September 1929, when it was again fitted with floats for a longer visit to Felix-stowe, the rudder being enlarged

The Goring, J8674, with Jupiter VI engine at Martlesham Heath, carrying the New Type No 6 which it wore at the Hendon Display on 2 July 1927. (Photo: Air Ministry, A & AEE)

to compensate for the side area of the floats. In 1931 the Goring underwent flotation trials at Calshot before being allocated for engine test bed work. The opportunity was taken to fit improved tail surfaces (an enlarged rudder and shortened dorsal fin). Between May 1933 and January 1935 the aeroplane was flown with a variety of Bristol radial engines (see accompanying data table).

Type: Single-engine, two-seat, single-bay coastal defence torpedo-bomber biplane.
Air Ministry Specifications: Private venture to 23/25 and 24/25.
Manufacturer: Gloster Aircraft Co Ltd, Cheltenham and Hucclecote, Gloucester.
Powerplant: One 425hp Bristol Jupiter VI nine-cylinder air-cooled direct-drive radial engine. Experimental. 460hp Jupiter VIII; 745hp Mercury VIIA; 570hp Pegasus II; 670hp Perseus IIL.
Structure: Predominantly wooden structure; also tested with duralumin floats.
Dimensions: (Landplane). Span, 42ft 0in; length, 30ft 0in; height, 11ft 6in; wing area, 450 sq ft.
Weights: (Landplane). Tare, 2,914lb; all-up, 5,374lb.
Performance: (Landplane with bombs). Max speed, 136 mph at 4,000ft; climb to 10,000ft, 13 min; service ceiling, 16,500ft.
Armament: One synchronized 0.303in Vickers machine gun in nose and one Lewis gun with Scarff ring on rear cockpit; bomb load of up to 690lb.
Prototype: One, J8674, first flown in March 1927. No production.

The Goring during one of its visits to the MAEE, Felixstowe, as a floatplane, seen here carrying a pair of 112lb bombs. Note the enlarged rudder. The inverted gull-wing roots on the lower wings are visible. (Photo: Flight, Neg No 5814)

Westland Witch

Arthur Davenport's Witch parasol monoplane was a courageous and, for its

day, radical approach to day bomber development, but one that was compromised by the problem posed by undercarriage rigidity without recourse to the cross-axle layout.

Construction was of composite wood

and metal, the wing — built in two halves and joined on the centreline, and attached to the fuselage by a pair of inverted-V cabane struts — being constructed about two spruce box spars with spruce ribs and steel-tube struts.

The fuselage was built up using duralumin tube, with steel tube at high stress points, the joints using riveted flitch plates. The divided-type undercarriage was necessary owing to Davenport's decision to incorporate an internal bomb bay in the fuselage, and comprised a multiplicity of underwing and V-struts outrigged from the upper and lower longerons; the front wheel struts incorporated oleo shock absorbers.

A single prototype, J8596, was purchased by the Air Ministry, this being powered by a 425hp Jupiter VI. Specification 23/25 had suggested the use of a Bristol Orion engine — in effect a turbo-supercharged Jupiter VI — but owing to difficulties in manufacturing high-performance turbine wheels and achieving gas-tight volute casings, this engine was not available in the time frame.

J8596 was first flown by Louis Paget at Andover on 30 January 1928, and was delivered to No 22 Squadron at the A & AEE for performance trials, attracting favourable comments on the aeroplane's steadiness while bombing. It returned a creditable maximum speed but the landing speed, at 62 mph, was regarded as being on the high side. Moreover, the undercarriage proved unequal to its task, and numerous failures occurred, and struts were distorted during several landings. The Witch was eliminated as the result of these design shortcomings.

The Westland Witch in its original Jupiter VI-powered Mark I configuration at Martlesham Heath in 1928. The need to distribute landing loads to wings spars and fuselage main structure demanded a wealth of struts. (Photo: Air Ministry, RTP, Neg No 1241)

It was not designed to carry a torpedo, and was therefore not entered for the 24/25 competition in 1929, although it returned (in a Mark II guise) to Martlesham Heath in August that year for performance trials with a 555hp Jupiter VIIIF engine. Thereafter it was taken on charge by the Parachute Testing Section of the Home Aircraft Depot at Henlow until 1931.

Type: Single-engine, two-seat parasol-wing monoplane day bomber.
Air Ministry Specification: 23/25
Manufacturer: Westland Aircraft Works, Yeovil, Somerset.
Powerplant: Mark I. One 420hp Bristol Jupiter VI nine-cylinder air-cooled direct-drive radial engine. Mark II. 480hp Jupiter VIIIF geared engine.
Structure: Composite wood and metal construction with metal, ply and fabric covering.
Dimensions: Span, 61ft 0in; length, 37ft 8in; height, 11ft 6in; wing area, 534 sq ft.
Weights: Tare, 3,380lb; all-up, 6,050lb.
Performance: Max speed, 138 mph at 6,500ft; climb to 6,500ft, 14 min 12 sec; service ceiling, 19,000ft.
Armament: One synchronized 0.303in Vickers machine gun in fuselage decking and one Lewis gun with Scarff ring on rear cockpit. Bomb load of up to 520lb carried internally.
Prototype: One, J8596, first flown on 30 January 1928 by Louis Paget. No production.

Handley Page H.P.34 Hare

Handley Page attached much importance to the H.P.34 Hare in its attempt to secure a production contract under Specification 23/25 for a Horsley bomber replacement. A completely new design by Harold Boultbee, it was intended for a Bristol Orion turbo-supercharged engine, but in the event the Orion was not ready in time and recourse was made to a 450hp Gnome-Rhône Jupiter.

A single prototype, J8622, was ordered by the Air Ministry and first flown by Sqn Ldr Tom Harry England RAF(Rtd) on 24 February 1928. The aircraft suffered several mishaps (including a collapsed undercarriage) before being delivered to Martlesham Heath for manufacturer's trials in June, by

The H.P.34 Hare, J8622, in its ultimate Jupiter-powered form with split-axle undercarriage for torpedo installation and short wing slats, at Martlesham Heath in 1929 with a pair of 230lb bombs under the lower wings. (Photo: Air Ministry, A & AEE)

which time a Jupiter VIII had been substituted and the rudder horn balance reduced. These early trials showed that the rudder was largely ineffective at low speed and that, as maximum speed was approached, both the aileron and elevator controls became progressively too heavy.

By the end of August the fuselage had been lengthened by two feet, and a new, enlarged tailplane and elevator fitted. Shortly afterwards, a smaller fin and high aspect ratio rudder were introduced, as was an entirely new upper wing with full-span leading-edge slats. In this configuration the Hare was found to be capable of being flown hands-off at all speeds.

At this point England suggested to Volkert that, if a split undercarriage was incorporated, the Hare would likely satisfy the parallel torpedo bomber requirements set out in Specification 24/25. With provision for the additional equipment and all-up weight increased to 6,960lb, the Hare's entry to the forthcoming competition was accepted.

After a further undercarriage collapse, resulting in extensive damage to the Hare, the prototype was completely rebuilt in three weeks. Modifications included a lengthened undercarriage of split-axle type, torpedo crutches, provision for a wider range of wing bomb racks, flotation gear, short wing slats and new Palmer wheel brakes. Further tests at Stag Lane (where a larger airfield was available) led to J8622 being delivered —

somewhat late — for the 24/25 competition on 10 June 1929, in which it was flown principally by Fg Off (later Gp Capt) Frank Maynard Denny and Flt Lt (later Gp Capt) Stuart Douglas Culley DSO.

By that time, however, the appearance of the Hawker Hart light bomber had caused the Air Ministry to lose interest in a Horsley replacement. In the torpedo competition, the Hare was short-listed alongside the Vickers Vildebeest, subject to a change to the Armstrong

Siddeley Panther engine. This was not quickly achieved in the Hare, which did not fly until 21 September 1930, when England was able to make a short flight before the engine overheated (the Vildebeest had flown with a Panther the previous month). A Townend ring was fitted on J8622, but the aircraft failed to reach Martlesham until June the following year, by which time the Vildebeest had been ordered into production.

The Hare was eventually struck off RAF charge in May 1932.

Type: Single-engine, two-seat, single-bay biplane torpedo/day bomber.
Specifications: 23/25 and 24/25.
Manufacturer: Handley Page Ltd, Cricklewood, London.
Powerplant: One 450hp Gnome-Rhône Jupiter nine-cylinder air-cooled radial engine driving two- or four-blade propeller. Also 485hp Jupiter VIII, 525hp Jupiter XF and 525hp Armstrong Siddeley Panther II.
Structure: Composite wood and metal construction. Aluminium, ply and fabric covering.
Dimensions: Span, 50ft 0in; length, 32ft 2in; wing area, 454 sq ft.
Weights: Tare, 3,270lb; all-up (with bombs), 5,742lb.
Performance (with bombs): Max speed 139 mph at 6,500ft; climb to 6,500ft, 17 min 50 sec; service ceiling, 16,500ft.
Armament: One synchronized 0.303in Vickers machine gun in nose and one Lewis gun with Scarff ring on rear cockpit; either two 550lb bombs or one 18in Mk VIII torpedo.
Prototype: One, J8622, first flown by Sqn Ldr T H England on 29 February 1928 at Cricklewood. No production.

Blackburn
B.T.1 Beagle

The Blackburn Beagle was designed by George Edward Petty to the Air Ministry Specification 23/25 as a Horsley bomber replacement, as well as to 24/25, issued for the coastal torpedo bombing rôle. A single prototype, N236, was ordered in December 1926, and once more the delay in overcoming difficulties with the intended Bristol Orion powerplant caused it to be replaced in the design by a Jupiter VIII.

First flown at Brough on 18 February 1928 by 'George' Bulman, the B.T.1 Beagle was of composite wood and steel tubular construction, the non-folding, staggered wings being built on two spruce spars with aluminium compression struts and steel tie rods. Frise ailerons were fitted on upper and lower wings, and wingtip leading-edge slats on the upper surfaces. A divided undercarriage, including oleo and V-struts, was featured from the outset so that, unlike some of the other two-Specification contenders, there was no need for significant airframe adaptation to meet

The Blackburn Beagle, N236, at the Aeroplane & Armament Experimental Establishment during its 1931 visit with a Jupiter XF engine, which had by then been declared unsuitable for the torpedo rôle. (Photo: Air Ministry, A & AEE)

each operational requirement.

Early flight trials showed the rudder to be substantially overbalanced, and the front of the horn balance was reduced before the Beagle underwent manufacturer's contract trials at Brough in the hands of a Martlesham pilot. Some engine overheating was experienced, and this was remedied by reducing the crankcase cowling diameter so that more of the cylinder profile was exposed to the airstream.

The Beagle remained at Brough for several other minor modifications to be made (principally in the two cockpits and the bomb aiming position), and was then delivered in July to Martlesham Heath for the competitive evaluation. However, like some of the other competitors, the Beagle suffered several wheel and tailskid failures at Martlesham in 1929 and, although generally liked by the pilots for its handling qualities, it was severely criticised on account of what the Establishment considered to be avoidable design flaws.

Because the aircraft received favourable performance and handling reports, the Beagle was nevertheless short-listed for further evaluation with the Jupiter XF (and subject to improvements being made in the undercarriage design), along with the Vildebeest and Handley Page Hare.

N236 eventually returned to Martlesham Heath for evaluation with the Jupiter XF on 19 March 1931. Unfortunately the Jupiter XF had since been declared unsuitable for torpedo bomber aircraft, and the other two remaining contenders had already been submitted with Panther engines. No quantifiable verdict appears to have been made on

the Beagle, and performance figures were of academic importance anyway, as the Vildebeest had long since been declared the winner. The Blackburn aircraft was last recorded as having flown on 3 October 1932.

Type: Single-engine, two-seat, single-bay biplane torpedo/day bomber.
Air Ministry Specifications: 23/25 and 24/25.
Manufacturer: The Blackburn Aeroplane & Motor Co Ltd, Leeds and Brough, Yorkshire.
Powerplant: One 526hp Bristol Jupiter VIIIF nine-cylinder air-cooled radial engine driving two-blade propeller; also 590hp Jupiter XF.
Structure: Composite wood and metal construction. Split-axle undercarriage.
Dimensions: Span, 45ft 6in; length, 33ft 1in; height, 11ft 9in; wing area, 569 sq ft.
Weights: With bombs. Tare, 3,739lb; all-up, 6,047lb. With torpedo. Tare, 3,770lb; all-up, 7,445lb.
Performance: With bombs. Max speed, 130 mph at 5,000ft; climb to 6,500ft, 16 min 45 sec; service ceiling, 15,800ft. With torpedo. Max speed, 124 mph at 5,000ft; climb to 6,500ft, 25 min 30 sec; service ceiling, 11,200ft.
Armament: One synchronized 0.303in Vickers machine gun on port side of nose and one Lewis gun with Scarff ring on rear cockpit. Either two 550lb bombs or one 2,000lb 18in Mk VIII torpedo.
Prototype: One, N236, first flown by Flt Lt P W.S. Bulman on 18 February 1928 at Brough. No production.

Vickers Types 130/146 Vivid

Although not submitted to Specification 23/25, the Vickers Vivid was at one time being considered in this context, being in some respects capable of meeting the requirement. However it would not have been accepted for formal competitive evaluation, being unlikely to carry the bomb load demanded, and owing to its perpetuation of the Napier Lion .

The Type 131 was the outcome of a plan to produce an all-metal Mark VII version of the Vixen V that had met with some success in Chile, and was being built at about the time that the all-metal Valiant was being sent to that country for demonstration.

The Vivid, as the metal Vixen VII came to be named, was completed with a wheel undercarriage and underwent brief trials as a private venture and registered G-EBPY. It was then converted to a seaplane with a pair of Short floats with oleo-pneumatic mounting structure, and underwent trials at Hamble before being sent to Felixstowe for Service evaluation in May 1928; by then the aircraft had been re-engined with a 540hp Napier Lion XI, and in this form it was termed the Type 146.

There was, however, now no requirement outstanding by the RAF for a general purpose landplane, even though

The Vickers Type 146 Vivid G-EBPY at Martlesham in 1929 with split-axle wheel undercarriage and Napier Lion XI engine. (Photo: *Flight*, Neg No 10242)

the aircraft had, in some of its trials, been ballasted for four 112lb bombs; nor was the Vivid capable of carrying a torpedo as a floatplane. And when no further interest was expressed by Chile, G-EBPY was returned to landplane configuration and flown to Bucharest by Scholefield in September 1928 to participate in competitive trials to select a

general purpose aeroplane for Romania, but without success.

G-EBPY was therefore sold in 1931 to J R Chaplin who, with Capt Neville Stack as pilot, made a number of record flights between European capitals, and also an attempt on the England—Australia record. It was destroyed by fire at Chelmsford in 1932.

Type: Single-engine, two-seat, single-bay experimental general purpose float/landplane.
Manufacturer: Vickers (Aviation) Ltd, Weybridge, Surrey.
Powerplant: One 490hp Napier Lion VA (also 540hp Lion XI) twelve-cylinder water-cooled broad-arrow in-line engine driving two-blade propeller.
Dimensions: Span, 45ft 1in; length, 32ft 0in; wing area, 588 sq ft.
Performance: Max speed, 135 mph at 5,000ft; climb to 10,000ft, 14 min 30 sec.
Armament: One synchronized 0.303in Vickers machine gun on port side of nose and one Lewis gun with Scarff ring on rear cockpit; bomb load of up to four 112lb bombs.
Prototype: One, G-EBPY, first flown by E R C Scholefield on 27 June 1927. No production.

Handley Page
H.P.33/36 Hinaidi

The appearance of the Hinaidi night bomber represented the realisation of two significant policies espoused by the Air Ministry since early 1925, namely a move away from wooden-structured first-line aeroplanes in the RAF (and an inevitable run-down of the woodworking trades among the Service's technical personnel), and discontinuation of support for the generation of relatively inefficient powerplants exemplified by the Napier Lion broad-arrow engine in favour of the lighter air-cooled radial.

Yet despite lip service paid by some aircraft manufacturers in support of these policies, the transfer to all-metal construction was slow and tentative, reflecting a lack of confidence among designers, many of whom had been weaned on a diet of ash, spruce, mahogany, elm and all the other exotic timbers that behaved differently in varying conditions of temperature and humidity, and which demanded meticulous grading to perform in anything approaching a predictable manner.

Handley Page was no stranger to metal construction, even though the company's very large bombers — the O/100, 0/400 and V/1500 — had employed a preponderance of timber structures. Such construction had dominated in the Hyderabad, even

The first prototype Hinaidi, J7745, originally converted from a Hyderabad, but seen here at Peshawar after its purchase by the Indian government. It has been stripped of its Nivo night camouflage and doped silver overall. (Photo: Air Ministry, Neg No H1087)

though rigidity had been achieved by use of steel tube bracing. And it was Frederick Handley Page himself who, seeing the writing on the wall, suggested early in 1927 a progressive move towards an all-metal version of the Hyderabad as a means of extending the Service life of a bomber which otherwise faced early retirement with the planned elimination of woodworking trades in the Service. This suggestion was readily accepted by the Air Ministry, provided that the transition coincided with the proposed change of powerplant to the Bristol Jupiter in place of the Lion engine, with which the Service was becoming increasingly disenchanted.

Already, in 1926, a Hyderabad, J7745 allocated for test purposes, was being converted to take a pair of French-built 500hp Gnome-Rhône Jupiter IXA radials. This aircraft of course retained the

basic wooden airframe but when it was displayed at the Hendon Display of 1927 it had been rechristened the Hinaidi, and was indeed a 'New Type'.

J7745 underwent Service trials with No 15 Squadron, then commanded by Sqn Ldr P C Sherren MC, at Martlesham Heath, and the subsequent report recorded in glowing terms the aeroplane's excellent manœuvrability and stability, returning a maximum speed at full load of 110 mph at 6,500 feet. A major criticism, and one that would dog the Hinaidi for several years, was of excessive vibration and noise, thought to have been caused by the four-blade propellers. The aircraft was then delivered to Cricklewood for Bristol-made Jupiter VIIIs to be installed.

While the factory began to make preparations for metal production, Handley Page was instructed to go

The first production Hinaidi I to fly was J9033, originally ordered as a Hyderabad but completed as a Hinaidi and first flown on 11 April 1928; it later served with No 99 (Bomber) Squadron at Upper Heyford in 1930. Note the bomb racks under the wings. (Photo: Handley Page Ltd)

ahead with six wooden Hinaidi Mark Is, these being the last aircraft ordered as Hyderabads but completed with Jupiter VIIIs. Four others were either completed as Hinaidis or converted from existing Hyderabads.

Meanwhile the original prototype, J7745, had been purchased by the Indian government on 13 February 1928, and this underwent tropical trials in India and Egypt during that year, spending some of that time flying from the hot-and-high aerodromes at Kohat and Ar-awali in the North West Frontier Province and, incidentally, withstanding the harsh climatic conditions extremely well. In February 1929 the aircraft was employed in the evacuation of civilians from the British Embassy at Kabul, following the rebellion against King Amanullah of Afghanistan, making eight flights to and from the Afghan capital in severe winter conditions. J7745 was also used as the personal transport of Sir Philip Sassoon Bt (later GBE, CMG), Under-Secretary of State for Air, during his tour of RAF stations in India. The old aeroplane was eventually scrapped in 1934.

The tropical trials referred to above were conducted largely to examine the behaviour of the Jupiter engines rather than with any thought of deploying the Hinaidi in the Middle East. Indeed, Air Staff notices of 1928 make it clear that the aircraft was intended to equip no more than two bomber squadrons, both of them based in England.

Following the sale of J7745 to India, the Air Ministry ordered a replacement Hinaidi Mk I prototype, J9030, this being intended for performance and handling comparisons with the forthcoming all-metal H.P.36 Hinaidi Mark IIs, the prototype of which, J9478, was designed to Specification 14/28 and first flown on 8 February 1929. The aircraft underwent trials with wing slats at the A & AEE but they were not adopted in production.

The first Hinaidi to reach a line bomber squadron was the Mark I, J9036, one of the converted Hyderabads, which spent seven months with No 99 (Bomber) Squadron at Upper Heyford in Oxfordshire for squadron trials between September 1928 and March 1929. Service entry proper did not start until October that year, when two production Mark Is, J9298 and J9303, were delivered to the same Squadron.

Although Handley Page had been warned to tool up for all-metal Hinaidi

production many months earlier, the Air Ministry delayed giving the go-ahead owing to a number of unresolved problems, not least a report from No 99

Squadron that its aircraft were very nose heavy, a malady that was already under investigation at Martlesham Heath; with some apparent reluctance, Handley Page

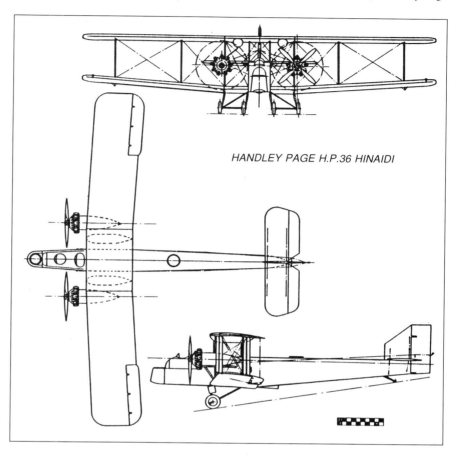

HANDLEY PAGE H.P.36 HINAIDI

Type: Twin-engine, four-crew, three-bay biplane night medium bomber.
Air Ministry Specifications: 14/28 and B.13/29
Manufacturer: Handley Page Ltd, Cricklewood, London
Powerplant: Prototype. Two 506hp Gnome-Rhône Jupiter IXAF nine-cylinder air-cooled radial engines driving four-blade propellers. Production: 450hp Bristol Jupiter VIII geared engines. Experimental. 545hp Jupiter VIIIF.
Structure: Mark I, predominantly wood; Mark II, all-metal.
Dimensions: Span, 75ft 0in; length, 59ft 3in; height, 17ft 4in; wing area, 1,471 sq ft.
Weights: Mark II. Tare, 8,040lb; all-up, 14,500lb.
Performance: Mark II. Max speed, 115 mph at 6,500ft; climb to 6,500ft, 11 min 50 sec; service ceiling, 14,750ft; range (half bomb load), 840 miles.
Armament: Single Lewis guns in nose and midships dorsal positions with Scarff rings, and in ventral midships position. Maximum bomb load of two 520lb and four 112lb bombs carried externally under fuselage and wings. Four 20lb 'sighter' bombs.
Prototypes: Three. J7745 (previously Hyderabad, converted to Hinaidi Mk I prototype, first flown by Sqn Ldr T H England at Martlesham Heath on 26 March 1927); J9030 (scratch-built Hinaidi Mk I prototype); J9478 (all-metal Hinaidi Mk II prototype, first flown by Maj J L Cordes at Cricklewood on 8 February 1929).
Production: Excluding the above three prototypes, a total of 43 Hinaidis was delivered to the RAF. These comprised 6 new-build Mark Is, J9298-J9303 (of which J9301-J9303 featured experimental metal fuselages); four Mark Is, originally ordered as Hyderabads (J9031 rebuilt as Hinaidi Mk I, J9032 and J9036, converted to Hinaidi Mk Is, and J9033 manufactured as Hinaidi Mk I); and 33 all-metal Hinaidi Mk IIs, K1063-K1078 and K1909-K1925.
Summary of Service: Hinaidis served with No 10 (Bomber) Squadron, joining Hyderabads at Upper Heyford in December 1930 and remaining in service until September 1932; with No 99 (Bomber) Squadron, also joining Hyderabads at Upper Heyford, from October 1929 until March 1934; and with No 503 (County of Lincoln) Squadron, Special Reserve, replacing Hyderabads in 1933 at Waddington, and remaining in service until October 1935.

agreed to introduce 5 degrees of sweepback on the outer wings, a remedy that cured the problem.

A feeling at Handley Page arose that delivery of Jupiter VIII engines might be delayed and, by way of insurance, an Armstrong Siddeley Jaguar-powered Hinaidi Mark III was planned; in the event it was not found necessary.

In due course the production Mark II Specification, 13/29, was released to Handley Page together with an order for sixteen aircraft (K1063-K1078). Most of these aircraft were delivered to No 99 (Bomber) Squadron, replacing the Squadron's old Hyderabads during the last six months of the year, and continuing to serve at Upper Heyford until

March 1934, when they were replaced in turn in favour of Handley Page's next bomber, the aptly-named Heyford.

The other regular line squadron to receive Hinaidis was No 10 (Bomber) Squadron, also at Upper Heyford. A second production order for 17 Mark IIs had been placed early in 1930, and most of these were delivered to this Squadron, starting in December that year.

The decision to re-equip No 10 Squadron relatively soon was prompted

by the need to introduce Hinaidis into service with No 503 (County of Lincoln) Squadron at Waddington in Lincolnshire, as the availability of Hyderabads was diminishing rapidly by 1933. No 10 Squadron therefore gave up its Hinaidis in September 1932 and converted to Vickers Virginia Is, passing its Hinaidis on to No 503, with whom they remained until October 1935, when the Squadron was reclassified as a light day bomber squadron of the Auxiliary Air Force.

Vickers Types 132/286 Vildebeest

The winner of the coastal defence aircraft competition under the terms of Specification 24/25 was the Vickers Vildebeest; by inference, therefore, it would have satisfied the day bomber requirement for a Horsley replacement (23/25) had the Air Ministry not suspended its demands in the meantime.

A single prototype, N230, the Vickers Type 132, was ordered and permission was given for a 460hp Jupiter VIII geared engine to be used in place of the recommended Orion and, flown by Scholefield, the aircraft made its maiden flight in April 1928. Of all-metal construction, the Type 132, later to be named Vildebeest, featured single-bay, rectangular planform unstaggered wings with tip slats, and ailerons fitted to upper and lower planes. A robust, divided-axle undercarriage with oleo main strut enabled landing loads to be distributed between upper and lower fuselage longerons and both wing spars. An important feature, whose benefit was not lost on the evaluation pilots at Martlesham Heath, was the locating of the pilot's cockpit directly below the *leading* edge of the upper wing, thereby

The Vildebeest prototype, N230, during loading trials at Martlesham Heath in 1929, with four 112lb bombs under the wings. The photograph emphasises the excellent positioning of the pilot's cockpit. (Photo: Air Ministry, A & AEE, Neg No 1217)

providing a superlative view forward for torpedo delivery.

N230 underwent contractor's trials at Weybridge in September, flown by a Martlesham pilot who gave a favourable verdict and recommended its acceptance for entry in the 24/25 competition. As previously recorded, the Vildebeest, Blackburn Beagle and Handley Page Hare were shortlisted to go forward for re-evaluation with the Jupiter XF engine.

Vickers, however, had already en-

countered unacceptable vibration with the Jupiter VIII and, as an insurance against the Jupiter XF also proving unsatisfactory (as indeed it did), decided to build a second prototype as a private venture, powered in due course by a geared Armstrong Siddeley Panther IIA radial. This aircraft, flying under 'B conditions' as O-1, was flown in August 1930 and, after a fairly abbreviated assessment at the A & AEE, beginning on the 22nd, the Vildebeest was finally confirmed as the winning 24/25 contender,

beating the Hare by a narrow margin.

The Establishment reported that the two prototypes handled easily and were pleasant to fly, although both aircraft suffered a number of engine failures. In the search for a suitable engine in the production Vildebeest, the second prototype was fitted in January 1931 with the 600hp Jupiter XFBM, which introduced the use of a mineral-based lubricant, and this was found to alleviate the vibration and cooling problems hitherto encountered. The engine was renamed the Pegasus IM3 and selected for the first production order for nine Vildebeest Mark Is (Vickers Type 244), ordered to Specification 22/31 in 1931, the first of which was flown on 5 September 1932. Of this batch, five were delivered to No 100 (Torpedo Bomber) Squadron at Donibristle, Fife, during October and November, replacing Hawker Horsleys — this Squadron being

tasked with the coastal defence of the Firth of Forth.

Other Vildebeest Is were employed in a wide range of trials, including S1715 which underwent Service trials as a night bomber with No 7 (Bomber) Squadron; it was later to become the Vickers Type 266 Vincent prototype. A second batch of 13 Mark Is, K2810-K2822, included an aircraft tested with a float undercarriage, K2816, and another, K2819, flown with the 635hp

Pegasus IIM3 and a Curtiss variable-pitch propeller.

Production continued with 30 Vildebeest IIs (Type 258), K2916-K2945, which introduced the Pegasus IIM3 into production, with deliveries to No 100 Squadron starting on 21 July 1933, this being the only Squadron equipped with this version. On 7 December No 100 left the United Kingdom and sailed for the Far East, making its base at Seletar, Singapore, as evidence of the British government's policy of strengthening the defences of the strategically-located naval base against a background of growing Japanese military influence in that theatre.

The most widely used version of the Vildebeest was the Mark III, produced to Specification 15/34, which introduced provision for a third crew member in an enlarged rear cockpit. A total of 162 was built, of which twelve with folding wings were produced to an order for the New Zealand Permanent Air Force (these being joined by 28 aircraft transferred from RAF stocks in the Far East). Two aircraft, K4157

One of the relatively small number of Vildebeest Mark IVs built only three years before the outbreak of the Second World War. K6408 was the first production example to fly and underwent trials at Martlesham Heath in 1937. This version's neatly cowled Perseus VIII engine, driving a variable-pitch propeller, increased the overall length of the aircraft by 12 inches. The faired tailwheel was introduced in production Vildebeests beginning about 1935, and was a retrospective modification on earlier surviving examples. K6408 later served with the Development Flight at Gosport. (Photo: RAF Museum, Neg No P009204)

and K4163, joined a Mark I, K2813, with the Gosport-based Torpedo Development Flight in a long series of trials to evolve new torpedo-dropping patterns — procedures which were brought to a peak of efficiency during the last years before the Second World War.

Deliveries of Mark IIIs to the RAF began in February 1935, these being sent straight to the packing depots for shipment to the Far East where they replaced the Mark IIs of No 100 Squadron and equipped No 36 (Torpedo Bomber) Squadron, also at Seletar, replacing the old Hawker Horsleys. At home, No 22 Squadron at Donibristle began deliveries of Mark IIIs in May 1935, and in October that year was detached to Hal Far, Malta, during the Abyssinian crisis lest the Italians threatened hostilities against the island's naval base, returning to Scotland the following August.

The Vildebeest IV, of which only 18 were produced, introduced the 825hp Bristol Perseus VIII sleeve-valve engine. They were delivered between March and November 1937, and were shared between Nos 22 and 42 Squadrons in the United Kingdom; both were still flying the biplanes during the first year of the War.

In the Far East, the Vildebeest was still serving with the two Singapore-based squadrons when the Japanese invaded Malaya in December 1941. No 36 Squadron, commanded by Sqn Ldr R F C Markham, had a flight detached to Gong Kedah in Kelantan when the Japanese landed on the coast less than ten miles away; at dawn on the 8th the Vildebeests went into action with torpedoes against an enemy cruiser off the landing beaches, but failed to score hits owing to heavy rain cutting visibility.

When the invaders reached the airfield on the following day, the Vildebeests were withdrawn south to Kuantan, and later to Seletar. During the defence of the island base, No 36 and 100 suffered further casualties, so the two squadrons combined to operate together. When the Japanese landed 150 miles up the coast from Singapore on 26 January 1942, a dozen Vildebeests led by No 100's CO, Sqn Ldr Ian Terence Byathan Rowland, escorted by Hurricane and Buffalo fighters, carried out a forlorn bombing attack but lost five of their number, including the squadron commander. Later that evening all available aircraft of No 36 Squadron, including the spares and reserves taken out of storage, attempted

to dive-bomb the Japanese landing ships but were set on by Japanese fighters which shot down eight Vildebeests, including that flown by Markham.

The ten surviving Vildebeests were withdrawn to airfields in Java and on 28 February launched their last and most successful attack, when nine aircraft attacked a Japanese convoy found north of Rembang and claimed eight ships sunk by bombs and torpedoes; alas, yet another squadron commander, Sqn Ldr John Trevor Wilkins, the new CO of No 36 Squadron, was killed. On the morning of 6 March the crews of the last two biplanes were ordered to escape to Burma, but both crashed in Sumatra and were lost.

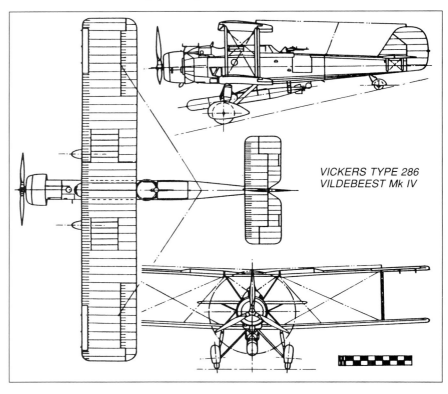

VICKERS TYPE 286
VILDEBEEST Mk IV

Type: Single-engine, two-seat, single-bay biplane coastal defence torpedo bomber.

Air Ministry Specifications: 24/25, 22/31 and 15/34.

Manufacturer: Vickers (Aviation) Ltd, Weybridge, Surrey.

Powerplant: Prototypes. One 460hp Bristol Jupiter VIII, XF, XIF and XFBM; Hispano-Suiza 12Lbr; Armstrong Siddeley Panther IIA. Production: 600hp Bristol Pegasus IM3; 635hp Pegasus IIM3; 825hp Bristol Perseus VIII.

Structure: All-metal construction, dural, ply and fabric covering.

Dimensions: Span, 49ft 0in; length, 36ft 8in (Mark IV, 37ft 8in); height, 14ft 8in; wing area, 728 sq ft.

Weights: Mark I. Tare, 4,229lb; all-up, 8,100lb; Mark IV. Tare, 4,724lb; all-up, 8,500lb.

Performance: Mark I. Max speed, 140 mph at 10,000ft; climb to 5,000ft, 7 min 30 sec; ceiling, 19,000ft; range (max) 1,250 miles. Mark IV. Max speed, 156 mph at 5,000ft; climb to 5,000ft, 6 min; ceiling, 19,000ft; range (max), 1,625 miles.

Prototypes: Two, N230/G-ABGE (first flown by E R C Scholefield in April 1928) and O-1/G-ABJK (flown in August 1930).

Production: A total of 220 Vildebeests was built for the RAF. Mark I (Type 244), 22: S1707-S1715 and K2810-K2822 (one later sold to New Zealand); Mark II (Type 258), 30: K2916-K2945; Mark III (Type 267), 150: K4105-K4188, K4588-K4614 and K6369-K6407 (15 later sold to New Zealand); Mark IV (Type 286), 18: K6408-K6414 and K8078-K8088 (12 later sold to New Zealand). In addition 12 Mark IIIs were built for New Zealand (as NZ101-NZ112), and 25 Type 245 aircraft were licence-built in Spain in addition to one built by Vickers. Total built (including two prototypes), 260.

Summary of RAF Service: Vildebeests served with No 22 (Torpedo Bomber) Squadron at Donibristle, Hal Far and Thorney Island between May 1934 and February 1940 (Mks I, III and IV); No 36 (Torpedo Bomber) Squadron at Seletar and airfields in Java between July 1935 and March 1942 (Mk IIIs); No 42 (Torpedo Bomber) Squadron at Donibristle, Thorney Island and Bircham Newton between December 1937 and April 1940 (Mk IIIs and IVs); with No 100 (Torpedo Bomber) Squadron at Donibristle and Seletar between October 1932 and February 1942 (Mks II, III and IV); and No 273 Squadron at China Bay, Ceylon, between August 1939 and March 1942 (Mk III). They also served with the Experimental (Torpedo) Development Flight, Gosport, No 7 Squadron in 1933 (for General Purpose Service Trials), and No 84 Squadron at Shaibah in 1933 for tropical trials.

Armstrong Whitworth Ajax

Relatively little is known of the early life of the Ajax, whose design was undertaken in parallel with that of the Atlas, and Oliver Tapper conjectures[1] that it was probably flown in mid-1925 as G-EBLM — a private venture intended to meet Specification 20/25. Powered at that time by a 385hp Jaguar II engine, the aircraft is more likely to have originated within the terms of Specification 30/24 (for which the RAF selected the Atlas), but underwent some modifications to suit the 1925 requirements after its first flight.

At all events, the Ajax was not submitted for formal evaluation at Martlesham Heath, but remained with the manufacturer for about two years before any further serious attempt was made to modernise it with Frise ailerons and wingtip slats; later in 1927 the aircraft was rebuilt as the so-called Ajax Mark II with a 550hp Armstrong Siddeley Panther II, with which it returned a maximum speed of 158 mph at sea level; it was purchased by the Air Ministry and allotted the serial number J9128.

In the meantime, however, the Air Ministry had ordered two Ajax Is, J8802 and J8803, for Service trials. J8803 underwent normal Service trials with No 4 (Army Co-operation) Squadron at Farnborough before being shipped out to India for tropical trials with No 27

The Ajax II, J9128, with wingtip slats. (Photo: Imperial War Museum, Neg No MH3300)

Squadron at Risalpur in October 1927, but crashed three months later. J8802 was therefore sent out to No 5 Squadron, also at Risalpur, to continue the trials between April and October 1928.

By 1928 the Atlas was well established in RAF service and, as the Ajax offered no worthwhile advantage, its develop-ment was accordingly discontinued. The Mark II, J9128, was allocated for experimental work and spent several months with the RAE, reverting to the Jaguar II engine in 1929.

[1] *Armstrong Whitworth Aircraft since 1913*, Putnam, 1988, p.153)

Type: Single-engine, two-seat, single-bay army co-operation/general purpose biplane.

Air Ministry Specifications: Private venture to Specifications 30/24 and 20/25.

Manufacturer: Sir W G Armstrong Whitworth Aircraft Ltd, Parkside and Whitley, Coventry.

Powerplant: One 385hp Armstrong Siddeley Jaguar II 14-cylinder air-cooled two-row radial engine; also 550hp Panther II.

Dimensions: Span, 39ft 6in; length, 28ft 3in; wing area, 392 sq ft.

Weights: Tare, 2,240lb; all-up, 3,700lb.

Performance: (Jaguar II). Max speed, 140 mph at sea level; climb to 5,000ft, 7 min; service ceiling, 19,700ft; range, 350 miles.

Armament: One Lewis gun on rear cockpit; bomb load of up to four 112lb bombs.

Prototype: Three. J8802 and J8803 (Mk Is, probably first flown in 1927), and J9128 (formerly G-EBLM, flown in 1925, and modified to Mk II and flown as such on 26 January 1928). No production.

Hawker Hart

Sydney Camm's Hawker Hart must be counted as the outstanding British light bomber of the interwar period. It was made possible by the advent of the best engine of its day, the Rolls-Royce F.XI Kestrel, development of a sound and simple metal structured airframe, painstaking attention to design detail and a hitherto unmatched empathy between the designer and his chief test pilot. Indeed, the Hart appeared on the scene at just the right moment — when the Air Ministry was looking for a light bomber with high performance. The fact that the Hart was also easily adaptable as a two-seat fighter, army co-operation aircraft, fleet reconnaissance fighter (with floats, if necessary) and operational trainer, earned the H G Hawker Engineering Company very large production contracts over a period of ten years; extensive sub-contracts with seven other major manufacturers undoubtedly prevented the demise of the British aircraft industry in the face of the Depression in the early 1930s. Such was its escape from extinction that, in 1935, the industry was well able to meet demands by the Air Ministry faced with expanding the Royal Air Force prior to the Second World War.

It was in 1926 that Camm was made aware of the new Rolls-Royce F.XI (formerly the Falcon Mk XI), but at that time he had no suitable aeroplane in which it could be flown, and it fell to the Fairey Aviation Company to engage in flight testing F.XI No 1 when Norman Macmillan took the first Fox Mark IA aloft on 29 August 1927.[1]

The F.XI differed from its predecessors in having its banks of cylinders cast

Mother of them all. The Hart prototype, J9052, at Martlesham Heath during its first visit in 1928. Note the absence of wing slats and the provision for an anti-spin parachute, evidenced by the taped panel forward of the fin. (Photo: Air Ministry, A & AEE Neg No 6086)

as a single block, instead of individual cylinder barrels and jackets being bolted separately to the crankcase, resulting in a worthwhile saving in weight. Unfortunately the engine encountered a number of connecting-rod failures which were thought to be due to lubrication starvation, and delays followed until it was discovered that the rod cap bolts were being over-tightened during assembly, causing the white-metal bearing shells to seize. The simple remedy was to introduce torque spanners during assembly.

Meanwhile, designed to Specification 12/26 as a light bomber, the Hart

---

[1] There was intense rivalry between Hawker and Fairey during 1926-27 to win the light bomber competition, and a wealth of anecdote is on record telling of efforts to breach the opposing company's security precautions — what would be considered in latter-day parlance as actionable industrial espionage. It is most unlikely that such efforts would have gained managerial sanction, but one cannot but assume that a blind eye was invariably turned. It was certainly a case of six of one and half-a-dozen of the other.

prototype was beginning to take shape in the shops in Canbury Park Road, Kingston-upon-Thames. The original drawings, tendered to the Air Ministry in December 1926, showed an aircraft with split-axle undercarriage with pneumatic shock-absorbers and a gravity fuel system. By the time a mock-up had been constructed in April 1927 a cross-axle undercarriage with Vickers oleo-pneumatic struts had been substituted, a pump-fed fuel system introduced and a wooden model of the F.XI engine supplied by Rolls-Royce. The original I-type interplane struts had been replaced by stronger and lighter N-struts. A single prototype, J9052, was ordered in July and this was first flown by 'George' Bulman in June the following year at Brooklands.

Of remarkably simple metal construction, the Hart was a single-bay biplane, employing the patented Sigrist/Chaplin dumb-bell steel wing spars with ailerons on the upper wing only, but not fitted with wing slats. The fuselage comprised a simple steel tubular box girder faired to oval section with secondary wooden formers, with sheet duralumin panels covering the structure as far aft as the cockpits, the remainder being fabric-covered. The engine, without exhaust

The ill-fated private venture Hart with a pair of 250lb bombs and Panther engine with double Townend ring during its visit to the A & AEE in 1931. The fact that it failed to recover from a spin, when no trouble had been experienced in this respect with any other Harts, suggested that the airflow behind the radial engine installation rendered the rudder relatively ineffective. The pilot, however, baled out safely. (Photo: Air Ministry, A & AEE)

Armstrong Whitworth-built Hart SEDB K4471 of No 6 Squadron at Ramleh, Palestine, in 1937 with tropical breather louvres on the engine cowling. It was one of many later transferred to the South African Air Force. Note the light bombs on the underwing racks. (Photo: Author's Collection)

manifolds, drove a fixed-pitch wooden two-blade Watts propeller.

After painstaking flight trials by Bulman, who set about 'fine tuning' the prototype in close collaboration with Camm's design staff, J9052 was delivered to Martlesham on 8 September 1928 powered by an early flight example of the Rolls-Royce F.XIB rated at 531bhp at 2,250 rpm and provided with a small retractable radiator under the nose. Its fellow competitors were the private venture Jupiter VIII-powered de Havilland Hound (see page 186) which had been purchased by the Air Ministry, the Fairey Fox II (also powered by an F.XIB engine), and the Avro Antelope (see page 208). Preliminary trials with the Establishment's No 22 Squadron were followed by a brief return to Brooklands for small alterations to the gunner's cockpit, and then Service trials with Nos 12 and 100 (Bomber) Squadrons. The initial reports from the A & AEE showed the Hart to be clear favourite to win the competition, with pilots enthusing about the beautifully harmonized controls and excellent performance, J9052 returning a maximum speed of 176 mph at 6,500 feet, and a climb to 10,000 feet in 7 min 37 sec with a load of two 250lb bombs. Without wingtip slats the landing speed was 61 mph (a figure soon reduced to 47 mph when slats were introduced). On return to Martlesham Heath in 1929, J9052 was dived vertically from 16,000 to 2,000 feet, reaching a true airspeed of 328 mph!

Not surprisingly, the Hart was de-

clared the winner of the 12/26 competition by the Air Staff in April 1929, considerable importance being attached to the aeroplane's simple construction and maintenance. Within a month Hawker had received a preliminary production order for 15 aircraft (J9933-J9947) to be powered by the 525hp Kestrel IB (formerly the F.XIB), 12 of these being delivered to No 33 (Bomber) Squadron at Eastchurch, commanded by Sqn Ldr John Joseph Breen OBE (later Air Marshal, CB, OBE). The first aircraft, J9935 and J9937, arrived on the Squadron on 25 February 1930.

The other three aircraft of this first batch had interesting histories. J9933 underwent trials with a supercharged Kestrel IIS engine to become the prototype Hart Fighter (later to be named the Demon) and continued to fly until 1938; J9946 was completed with dual controls and was thus, in effect, the prototype Hart Trainer; and J9947 was shipped out to India in March 1930, joining No 39 (Bomber) Squadron at Risalpur for tropical trials, thereby laying the groundwork for the Hart (India).

Encouraged by first reports from the early Service trials, Sopwith authorised the manufacture of four privately-funded Harts, which Sigrist, Camm and Bulman believed could be put to good use to

accelerate the development of new engine installations, and demonstrate to foreign governments the excellence of the basic aeroplane. The first, G-ABMR, became a Kestrel development and demonstration aircraft during the following eight years, being fitted with a dozen versions of the engine (and survives to this day); the second, G-ABTN, was adapted to accommodate various Bristol Jupiter and Pegasus radial engines before it was lost in the English Channel in 1932. The third special Hart, suggested by Rolls-Royce to test a new version of the Kestrel V which employed evaporative cooling (later to become the Goshawk), was fitted with steam condensers along the entire upper wing leading edge; it was also fitted with a cockpit canopy to protect the pilot from water blowing off from the condensers, and was purchased by the Air Ministry as K1102 for further testing of the cooling system. The last aircraft, powered by an Armstrong Siddeley Panther, was designed as a private venture tender to the light bomber Specification 20/30, remaining the property of Hawker after its first flight in 1931, but was lost at Martlesham Heath in October that year when it failed to recover from a spin before gaining its C of A. (This aircraft had been dived at a true airspeed of 340 mph!)

Officially termed the Hart Single-Engine Day Bomber (SEDB), the Kestrel IB-powered version continued in production with an order for 32 aircraft, placed in 1930, enabling No 12 (Bomber)

Hawker Hart (India), K2119 of No 39 Squadron flying over the inhospitable terrain of the North-West Frontier Province. This aircraft was later transferred to the Indian Air Force and served with No 1 (Indian) Service Flying Training School. It met its end when it was blown away in a dust storm at Ambala on 25 May 1942. (Photo: RAF Museum, Neg No P009763)

Squadron to re-equip, commanded by Sqn Ldr Donald Fasken Stevenson DSO, MC (later Air Vice-Marshal, CB, CBE, DSO, MC) at Andover. No 33 Squadron passed its early Harts to No 57 (Bomber) Squadron at Netheravon, and received new aircraft. By the end of 1932 six home-based squadrons were flying Hart SEDBs.

Following the trials with J9947 by No 39 Squadron in India, Hawker had received a contract for 50 specially prepared Hart (India) aircraft to Specification 9/31, their Kestrel IB engines provided with breather louvres in the cowlings as well as additional water stowage and supply container racks. The first aircraft of the batch underwent trials at Martlesham Heath with this paraphernalia in addition to two 230lb bombs, returning a maximum speed of 164 mph at 5,000 feet and a climb to 10,000 feet in 10 min 24 sec. Harts (India) served on Nos 11 and 39 Squadrons at Risalpur until 1939, as well as No 1 (Indian) Service Flying Training School at Ambala until 1944.

Beginning in 1932, sub-contracts were let to other manufacturers, Vickers (Aviation) receiving an initial contract for 65 aircraft, followed by 24 to be built by Sir W G Armstrong Whitworth. A total of 720 Harts was built by these two companies and Gloster Aircraft Co, which undertook production later of a new variant, the Hart (Special) — a tropicalised version, usually powered by a derated Kestrel X engine and often fitted with low-pressure tyres for service in the deserts of the Middle East.

In February 1933 No 601 (County of London) Squadron became the first of twelve Auxiliary Air Force squadrons to equip with Hart SEDBs during the next four years, reclassified as light day bomber squadrons. By September 1936 no fewer

than 209 Harts were held on charge by the Auxiliary Air Force.

In service, the Hart bomber was much liked by pilots, being easily trimmed to fly hands-off, forgiving of rough handling, and fast enough in its early days to outpace contemporary interceptors during defence exercises. Only when the RAF's fighter squadrons began equipping with Hawker Furies and Demons was any realistic defence possible against the Hart day bombers. Indeed, Nos 25 and 43 Squadrons, equipped with the nimble Fury fighters, used Harts as trainers!

During the Abyssinian crisis of 1935-36, two home-based Hart Squadrons, Nos 33 and 142, re-equipped with Harts (Special), shipped out to Egypt to join the defence of the Suez Canal, while No

45 Squadron gave up its Fairey IIIFs to deploy an detachment of newly-delivered Harts (Special) to Nairobi to contribute an element of air power to cover British interests in East Africa.

As the improved Hind light bomber began to reach the RAF late in 1935, Harts were released for training duties during the Expansion period, and the accompanying data table provides an indication of the extent to which the Hart was used as a trainer. Nevertheless, No 33 Squadron continued to fly the Hart bomber until 1938, while in the Middle East it served in the front line until 1940, and in India Harts replaced Wapitis on Nos 5 and 27 Squadrons at the beginning of the Second World War and remained in service until 1941.

As Harts were phased out of service from 1937 onwards it was decided to ship them out to the South African Air Force after refurbishing. A total of 222 aircraft was shipped from Britain and the Middle East, a stream that continued until 1941; not all arrived, however, as it is known that at least three ships, carrying Harts, were torpedoed during 1941. Other ex-RAF aircraft were sup-

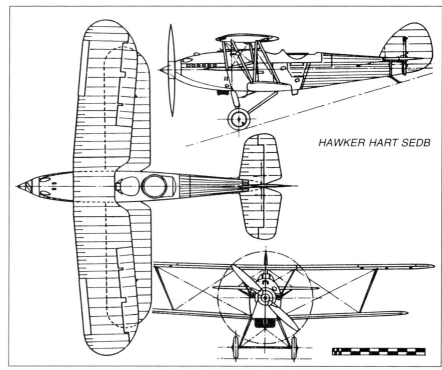

HAWKER HART SEDB

K3036 was one two Harts used as test beds for the Rolls-Royce P.V.12 (later to become famous as the Merlin). Its radiator was located amidships, as on Camm's equally famous Hurricane fighter. (Photo: Author's Collection)

plied to the Southern Rhodesian Air Force and the Royal Egyptian Air Force.

Despite numerous demonstrations by the Hawker pilots ('George' Bulman was joined by Philip Edward Gerald Sayer in 1930, and by Flt Lt Philip Gadesden Lucas RAFO in 1931), few Harts were exported. Eight were sold to Estonia in 1932 with interchangeable wheel and float undercarriages, and four were sold as pattern aircraft to Sweden, powered by Bristol Pegasus engines,

prior to a licence being negotiated for the production of 42 further aircraft at the Swedish State Aircraft Factory at Trollhättan during 1935-36. The fruits

of the Hawker pilots' demonstrations were to be gained in numerous orders for the Hart derivatives, the Osprey, Audax and Hind.

Type: Single-engine, two-seat, single-bay light day bomber biplane.

Air Ministry Specifications: 12/26, 9/29, 15/30, 20/30, 9/31, 8/32, 12/33 and 8/35.

Manufacturers: The H G Hawker Engineering Co Ltd (from 1933, Hawker Aircraft Ltd), Kingston-upon-Thames and Brooklands, Surrey; Sir W G Armstrong Whitworth Aircraft Ltd, Coventry; The Gloster Aircraft Co Ltd, Hucclecote, Gloucester; Vickers (Aviation) Ltd, Weybridge, Surrey.

Powerplant: Prototype: One 531hp Rolls-Royce F.XIB 12-cylinder water-cooled in-line engine driving two-blade Watts wooden propeller. Production. 525hp Kestrel IB; 510hp Kestrel XDR. Experimental. 530hp Kestrel IS, 510hp Kestrel IIB, 525hp Kestrel IIS, 525hp Kestrel IIIS, 510hp Kestrel IIIMS; 640hp Kestrel V; 695hp Kestrel VIS; 550hp Kestrel XFP; 695hp Kestrel XVI. 450hp Bristol Jupiter XFAM, 580hp Pegasus IM2, 690hp Pegasus IIIMS; 600hp Mercury VI, 840hp Mercury VIII, 890hp Mercury XI; 890hp Perseus. 780hp Halford-Napier Dagger I, 805hp Dagger II and III. Hispano-Suiza 12Xbrs; 720hp Lorraine Petrel Hfrs. 980hp Rolls-Royce PV.12, 1,025hp Rolls-Royce Merlin 'C' and 'D'.

Structure: All-metal with sheet aluminium and fabric covering.

Dimensions: SEDB. Span, 37ft 3in; length, 29ft 4in; height, 10ft 5in; wing area, 349.5 sq ft.

Weights: SEDB. Tare, 2,530lb; all-up, 4,596lb.

Performance: SEDB. Max speed, 185 mph at 13,000ft; climb to 10,000ft, 8 min 30 sec; service ceiling, 22,800ft; range, 430 miles.

Armament: One synchronized 0.303in Vickers machine gun in port side of front fuselage and one Lewis gun with Scarff ring on rear cockpit. Bomb load of up to two 250lb or 230lb bombs or four 112lb bombs, carried under the wings.

Prototype: One, J9052, first flown by Flt Lt P W S Bulman in June 1928 at Brooklands.

Production: A total of 992 Harts was built (including the six prototypes and experimental aircraft, J9052, K1102, K2915, G-ABMR, G-ABTN and the unmarked Panther PV aircraft). These comprised: J9933-J9947 (15 Hawker-built SEDB); K1416-K1447 (32 Hawker-built SEDB; one later to SAAF); K2083-K2132 (50 Hawker-built Hart [India]); K2424-K2473 (50 Hawker-built SEDB; 9 later to SAAF); K2474 and K2475 (2 Hawker-built Trainers); K2966-K3030 (65 Vickers-built SEDB; 18 later to SAAF and one to SRAF); K3031-K3054 (24 AWA-built SEDB; 2 later to SAAF); K3146-K3158 (13 Hawker-built Trainers; 2 later to SAAF); K3743-K3763 (21 Hawker-built Trainers; 7 later to SAAF); K3808-K3854 (47 Vickers-built SEDB; 22 later to SAAF; 4 to Royal Egyptian Air Force); K3855-K3904 (50 AWA-built SEDB; 10 later to SAAF; 2 to SRAF); K3921 and K3922 (2 Hawker-built Hart [India]); K3955-K3972 (18 AWA-built SEDB; 6 later to SAAF and one to Royal

Egyptian Air Force); K4297 and K4298 (2 Hawker-built Hart [Communications]); K4407-K4436 (30 Gloster-built Hart [Special]; one later to SAAF); K4437-K4495 (59 AWA-built SEDB; 40 later to SAAF; 5 to Royal Egyptian Air Force); K4751-K4770 (20 Hawker-built Trainers; 5 later to SAAF); K4886-K5052 (167 AWA-built Trainers; 27 to SAAF; 3 to Royal Egyptian Air Force; one to Fleet Air Arm in 1941); K5784-K5797 (114 Vickers-built Trainers; 35 to SAAF; 3 to Fleet Air Arm in 1941); K6415-K6550 (146 AWA-built Trainers; 38 to SAAF; one to Royal Egyptian Air Force; one to Fleet Air Arm in 1941); K8627-K8631 (5 Hawker-built Hart [India]). Also included in the above total were 8 Harts built for Estonia and 4 for Sweden, and 42 Harts licence-built in Sweden. The above total does not include 6 Hart Fighters, later named Demons. It does, however, include the Osprey (J9052), Demon (J9933), Audax (K1438) and Hardy (K3013) prototypes as these were originally built as Harts.

Summary of RAF Service: Harts SEDB served with the following: No 12 (Bomber) Squadron at Andover from January 1931; with No 15 (Bomber) Squadron at Abingdon from June 1934 until March 1936; with No 18 (Bomber) Squadron at Upper Heyford from November 1931 until May 1936; with No 33 (Bomber) Squadron at Eastchurch, Bicester and Upper Heyford from February 1930; with No 57 (Bomber) Squadron at Netheravon and Upper Heyford from October 1931 until May 1936; with No 142 Squadron at Andover from June 1934, and with Nos 500, 501, 503, 600, 601, 602, 603, 604, 605, 609, 610 and 611 Squadrons, Auxiliary Air Force, between February 1933 and December 1938. Harts (India) served with No 5 Squadron at Lahore, India, from June 1940 until February 1941, with No 11 Squadron at Risalpur, India, from February 1932 until July 1939, with No 27 Squadron at Risalpur, India, from October 1939 until October 1940, and with No 39 Squadron at Risalpur, India, from November 1931 until July 1939. Harts (Special) served with No 6 Squadron in Palestine and Egypt from October 1935 until March 1938, with No 12 Squadron at Aden in 1936, with No 17 Squadron at Kenley from October 1935 until March 1936, with No 33 Squadron in Egypt from October 1935 until March 1938, with No 40 Squadron at Abingdon from November 1935 until March 1936, with No 45 Squadron at Nairobi, Kenya, from September 1935 until January 1936, with No 142 Squadron in Egypt from October 1935 until January 1937 and with No 235 Squadron at Nairobi, Kenya, from June until September 1940. Among the many units with which Harts served were the Flying Training Schools, No 1 (Leuchars), 2 (Brize Norton), 3 (Grantham), 4 (Egypt), 5 (Sealand), 6 (Netheravon), 7 (Peterborough), 8 (Montrose), 9 (Thornaby), 10 (Ternhill) and 11 (Wittering), and Nos 1, 2, 3, 4, 5, 6, 7, 8, 9, 10, 13, 15, 16, 19, 20, 21, 25, 29 and 46 Elementary and Reserve Flying Training Schools. Harts served on Nos 24, 173 and 510 (Communications) Squadrons as well as at the Royal Air Force College, Cranwell.

Avro Type 604 Antelope

J9183, the Avro Antelope, probably at Hamble in 1928, showing the two-blade Fairey metal propeller and the low-drag Avro gun ring on the rear cockpit. (Photo: A J Jackson Collection)

A measure of the superiority of the Hawker Hart may be gained from the belief that its two opponents in the 12/26 competition, the Fairey Fox II and the Avro Type 604 Antelope, were among the most advanced two-seat military biplanes of their day, yet both were comprehensively eclipsed by Sydney Camm's masterpiece.

The Avro design was tendered to the Air Ministry in about August 1927, and a single prototype, J9183, was ordered, subject to satisfactory inspection of a mock-up prior to commencement of manufacture. The Type 604 was a single-bay, staggered biplane, each half of the upper mainplane being joined on the aircraft's centreline above a pair of inverted-V cabane struts. Frise ailerons were fitted on upper wings only, being interconnected with wingtip slats. The fuselage comprised a box-girder of L-section duralumin strip with stainless steel joint fittings; the engine bearers were of welded tubular steel. As in the Hart, the rear gunner took up a prone position in the bottom of the fuselage for bomb-aiming. A variable-incidence tailplane was fitted.

The engine installation was an anachronism in that the valve rocker boxes were left uncowled, and a chin radiator with shutters was fitted; tail control cables were left exposed. For an aircraft whose high performance requirements were explicit, the Antelope was an untidy aeroplane with precious little attention paid to detail design.

The aircraft was probably flown in July 1928 with a pre-production 480hp Rolls-Royce F.XIB engine driving a metal two-blade Fairey propeller, but during the following month the F.XIB was replaced by a production-standard engine, and on 13 September it arrived at Martlesham Heath for manufacturer's

trials and performance measurements by No 22 Squadron[1].

For the remainder of the year the Antelope underwent Service trials alongside the Hart with Nos 12 and 100 (Bomber) Squadrons and, although the pilots considered that the Avro met the speed and climb requirements, and was pleasant to handle, its landing speed was high (at 64 mph) — despite the use of wing slats. These opinions were endorsed when J9183 returned to the A &

[1] A J Jackson (*Avro Aircraft since 1908*, Putnam, page 254) suggests that the Antelope was first flown in November 1928, but Tim Mason (*British Flight Testing: Martlesham Heath 1920-1939*, Putnam, page 68) records the arrival of J9183 at the A & AEE on 13 September that year. Rolls-Royce records, moreover, indicate that 'a second F.XI engine was delivered to Avro in August *following erratic flight behaviour by the first*'.

AEE for the competitive evaluation stage, although the aircraft finally lost the contest on the grounds of poor structural design, the use of non-standard metal fittings being without justification, while lack of accessibility for maintenance also came in for criticism. Its spinning characteristics were markedly inferior to those of the Hart prototype.

Being on Air Ministry charge, the Antelope was allocated to experimental engine/propeller trials at the RAE, being returned to Avro to incorporate dual controls. Between August 1930 and September 1933 it was flown with a supercharged Kestrel IIS driving a variable-pitch Hele-Shaw-Beacham propeller. The nose cowling was cleaned up and the radiator moved to the rear of the engine bay.

Type: Single-engine, two-seat, single-bay light day bomber biplane.
Air Ministry Specification: 12/26
Manufacturer: A V Roe & Co Ltd, Manchester and Hamble, Hampshire.
Powerplant: One 480hp Rolls-Royce F.XIB 12-cylinder water-cooled in-line engine driving 2-blade Fairey metal propeller; also 525hp Kestrel IB and 477hp Kestrel IS.
Structure: All-metal construction with duralumin sheet and fabric covering.
Dimensions: Span, 36ft 10in; length, 31ft 2in; height, 10ft 9in; wing area, 377 sq ft.
Weights: F.XIB engine. Tare, 2,859lb; all-up, 4,538lb.
Performance: F.XIB engine. Max speed, 171 mph at 6,500ft; climb to 10,000ft, 8 min 9 sec; service ceiling, 20,700ft; range, 520 miles.
Armament: One 0.303in Vickers machine gun in port side of nose, and one Lewis gun with Avro low-drag gun ring on rear cockpit; bomb load of up to two 250lb bombs.
Prototype: One, J9183, probably first flown in July 1928 at Hamble (see text). No production.

Deployment of British Bomber Squadrons — 1 January 1930

Royal Air Force Home Bases					
No 7 Sqn (H)	Vickers Virginia	Worthy Down, Hampshire	No 35 Sqn (L)	Fairey IIIF	Bircham Newton, Norfolk
			No 36 Sqn (M)	Hawker Horsley I	Donibristle, Fife
No 9 Sqn (H)	Vickers Virginia VII	Manston, Kent	No 58 Sqn (H)	Vickers Virginia VII	Worthy Down, Hampshire
No 10 Sqn (H)	Handley Page Hyderabad	Upper Heyford, Oxon	No 99 Sqn (H)	Handley Page Hyderabad/Hinaidi	Upper Heyford, Oxon
No 12 Sqn (L)	Fairey Fox I/IA	Andover, Hampshire			
No 33 Sqn (M)	Hawker Horsley II	Eastchurch, Kent	No 100 Sqn (M)	Hawker Horsley II/III	Bicester, Oxon

Royal Air Force, Home Bases (contd.)
No 101 Sqn (M) Boulton & Paul Sidestrand Andover, Hampshire
No 207 Sqn (L) Fairey IIIF   Bircham Newton,
                                            Norfolk

Middle East
No 8 Sqn (L) Fairey IIIF   Khormaksar, Aden
No 14 Sqn (L) Fairey IIIF   Ramleh, Palestine
No 30 Sqn (L) Westland Wapiti IIA   Mosul, Iraq
No 45 Sqn (L) Fairey IIIF   Helwan, Egypt
No 47 Sqn (L) Fairey IIIF   Khartoum, Sudan
No 55 Sqn (L) de Havilland D.H.9A   Hinaidi, Iraq
No 84 Sqn (L) de Havilland D.H.9A   Shaibah, Iraq

India
No 11 Sqn (L) Westland Wapiti IIA   Risalpur
No 27 Sqn (L) Westland Wapiti IIA   Kohat
No 39 Sqn (L) Westland Wapiti IIA   Risalpur
No 60 Sqn (L) de Havilland D.H.9A   Kohat

Auxiliary Air Force and Special Reserve
No 502 Sqn (H) Handley Page Hyderabad Aldergrove, Ulster

No 503 Sqn (H) Handley Page Hyderabad Waddington, Lincs.
No 504 Sqn (M) Hawker Horsley II   Hucknall, Derbyshire
No 600 Sqn (L) Westland Wapiti IIA   Hendon, Middlesex
No 601 Sqn (L) de Havilland D.H.9A/   Hendon, Middlesex
                 Westland Wapiti IIA
No 602 Sqn (L) Westland Wapiti IIA   Renfrew,
                                            Renfrewshire
No 603 Sqn (L) de Havilland D.H.9A   Turnhouse,
                                            Midlothian
No 605 Sqn (L) de Havilland D.H.9A   Castle Bromwich,
                                            Warwickshire

Fleet Air Arm
No 460 Flt (TB) Blackburn Dart   HMS *Eagle*
No 461 Flt (TB) Blackburn Dart/Ripon II HMS *Furious*
No 462 Flt (TB) Blackburn Ripon II   HMS *Furious*
No 463 Flt (TB) Blackburn Dart   HMS *Courageous*
No 464 Flt (TB) Blackburn Dart   HMS *Courageous*

H—Heavy bomber; M—Medium bomber; L—Light bomber; TB—Torpedo bomber; SRU—Special Reserve Unit.

4. BOMBERS IN THE DOLDRUMS

The succession of Air Chief Marshal Sir John Salmond as Chief of the Air Staff on 1 January 1930 marked the end of an era for the Royal Air Force, the nature of which was never to be repeated. Trenchard had built for the Service a firm foundation of autonomy and self-sufficiency in specialist personnel. It has been shown in the previous chapter that the bomber had been the favoured weapon, with a relatively large number of prototypes ordered and built, while the fighter defences of Britain had progressed little, as had the performance of their aeroplanes.

Trenchard, the archetypal 'bomber disciple', had had his way, and such money made available for research and development had, by and large, been spent — some would say squandered — on these bomber prototypes, with precious little to show for it.

Salmond, though not overtly a 'fighter man', had from 1925 until 1929 been Air Officer Commanding-in-Chief, Air Defence of Great Britain, and had experienced at first hand a succession of fighters that, for all their agile antics at Hendon each year, were little better than those that had fought over the Western Front in 1918, and certainly no better armed. He was therefore determined to end this state of affairs. It was also decided that the appointment of Chief of the Air Staff should never again

be held by one man for more than about three or four years.

The seeds of the Depression had already been sown when Trenchard left the Air Ministry, and if Salmond had any ideas of introducing radical demands for new fighters, and purchasing expensive prototypes, other aircraft development would have to be held in abeyance for the time being.

After all, one could point to the satisfactory outcome of the recent light bomber competition, with the acceptance of the Hart light bomber, the first production batch of which was almost ready to join a line squadron. The 'medium' day bomber was a somewhat nebulus category, which no one could honestly reconcile as being a vital element in the RAF's peacetime armoury (especially with Service appropriations at an all-time low in real terms). Nevertheless, only one squadron was equipped with the Sidestrand, and production was held at a level no more than necessary to offset attrition.

And if one questioned the ability of the Vickers Virginia, Handley Page Hyderabad and Hinaidi to reach any conceivable target in continental Europe, drop a bomb bigger than 500lb *and* survive ground or air defences while flying at 84 mph at 10,000 feet, it could be pointed out that two 'cornerstone' Requirements for new heavy bombers

had been issued over two years previously, for which half a dozen prototypes had been ordered.

The Air Ministry had tried all it knew to persuade the aircraft industry to tender designs of all-metal aircraft — both bombers and fighters — for half a decade, yet it was the industry itself that had been unwilling or unable to comply fully with this dictate, companies producing composite wood-and-metal prototypes accompanied by undertakings to change to all-metal construction if the tender was accepted for production. It was now no longer a matter of the industry calling the Air Ministry's bluff; the RAF was already disestablishing the woodworking trades. Vickers, for one, was hard at work rebuilding in metal almost every Virginia extant.

And it is worth mentioning here that one very large all-metal aeroplane, ordered by the Air Ministry as long ago as 1923, had flown in 1928 but, contrary to public reports issued at the time, it was *not* a bomber (and therefore not conventionally eligible for this work, though it is the subject of an appendix). This was the Beardmore Inflexible, a massive aeroplane powered by three 600hp engines. It handled remarkably well in the air but, to be realistic, only confirmed that a large all-metal aeroplane — and a monoplane at that — could be built and that it could fly, but it made no provision for a bomb load. Had there been the slightest suggestion that a bomber version was envisaged, every bomber airfield in Britain would have had to undergo considerable enlargement, not to mention revised hangarage. However, the Inflexible had already made its last flight before Sir John Salmond came to the helm.

The first of the two bomber Requirements referred to above, B.19/27, attracted design tenders from Vickers, Fairey, Handley Page, Hawker, Avro and Bristol, prototypes being ordered from the first three of these manufacturers (although the unbuilt Avro Type 613 was allotted a serial number, suggesting that at one time a contract was under consideration). The second Specification, B.22/27, brought forth design tenders from Boulton and Paul and de Havilland for even larger bombers, and prototypes of these had been ordered.

Until these heavy bomber prototypes could be evaluated by the Service establishments and squadrons there appeared to be no immediate need to issue further bomber requirements and, owing to the adaptability of the Hart, other categories, such as army co-operation and general purpose aircraft (the latter satisfactorily filled by the Wapiti) could be ignored.

Ironically, neither B.19/27 nor B.22/27 succeeded in producing a significant advance in bomber design. B.22/27 was abandoned when neither of the two three-engine prototypes impressed the Air Ministry or the A & AEE. B.19/27, however, produced two 'winners', the Handley Page Heyford and the Fairey Hendon. The former was a twin-engine biplane of singular appearance but possessed a mediocre performance; it was also found to display a number of aggravating design blemishes whose rectification delayed entry into service. The latter, a large twin-engine monoplane with a very thick wing, paltry bomb load and pedestrian performance, was ready for service so late that it had long been overtaken by more imaginative aeroplanes, and joined only one squadron — in November 1936!

By 1932, with neither heavy bomber Specification on the table about to produce any significant advance (heavy bomber performance having increased by about ten per cent in eight years), the Air Ministry decided to issue a new Specification for what, at the time, were

referred to as night heavy bombers but which, by the time they reached the Service, were realistically no more than medium bombers. This Specification, B.9/32, proved to be the long-awaited catalyst of bomber advance, producing in due course the Handley Page Hampden and the Vickers Wellington. Neither of these monoplanes flew until 1936 — well into the period of RAF expansion — and they are therefore described in Chapter 5.

The performance demanded by B.9/32 demonstrated the Air Ministry's determination to introduce monoplanes into the RAF, even though the process was likely to occupy at least five or six years. The Hendon monoplane to Specification B.19/27 had first flown in November 1930, but had crashed soon after, and although it was to gain the distinction of becoming the RAF's first monoplane bomber, it was evident that the path being followed by the Fairey Aviation Company into the monoplane era was a cul-de-sac.

Much more promising was the design philosphy adopted by Vickers (Aviation) Ltd, a company fortunate in having re-acquired, in 1930, the services of Barnes Neville Wallis, a gifted engineer who was appointed head of the structures department at Weybridge. When in 1931 the Air Ministry issued a Specification (G.4/31) for an eventual Wapiti replacement in the general purpose category, Vickers tendered two designs, one a biplane and the other a monoplane. In these the airframe employed the fruits of Wallis' original lines of thought, namely the elimination of what he saw as the redundant secondary structure, by designing a lattice structure of primary members only — the geodetic principle. From the monoplane, tendered to G.4/31, it was but a short step to the Wellesley bomber, an aeroplane of exceptional range and certainly one of the outstanding British aircraft produced during the period.

If the Wellesley itself did not give widespread service in the RAF (though it was to establish a world distance record later, and fought with some distinction in East Africa early in the Second World War), it enabled Vickers to cut its teeth on the geodetic airframe that was to become the trademark of the Wellington, Warwick and Windsor bombers.

The long gestation period occupied in

introducing the first monoplane bombers into service was in part due to the expense of their development being borne by private industry. The result was that the bomber squadrons of the RAF had to continue making do with biplanes rather longer than, say, the United States Army Air Corps, which began taking deliveries of its first Martin B-10 twin-engine, all-metal monoplane bombers in June 1934. Capable of carrying a 2,260lb bomb load, the B-10 had a top speed of 207 mph (almost precisely the same speed of the RAF's best interceptor fighter, the Hawker Fury, and rather better than any fighters in the USAAC).

The early 1930s were therefore a period of marking time in the RAF. Even so, the number of bomber squadrons increased from 23 at the beginning of 1930 to 32 on 1 January 1935, made possible by the one significant technological advance — the widespread adoption of the excellent Rolls-Royce Kestrel, an engine of undreamed-of reliability. In terms of armament, the bomber still relied largely on the venerable drum-fed Lewis gun as well as the First World War-vintage 112lb and 230lb bombs, although the thick-cased 250lb weapons, of much improved shape, were being introduced throughout the squadrons.

And what of the men of the bomber squadrons? For fifty years the RAF assumed that the instinctive traits of fighter and bomber pilots were as chalk and cheese, the one individualistic, the other calculating in leadership, and on this basis of selection it became the Service convention that 'once a bomber man, always a bomber man'. Air Ministry records showed that, at the beginning of 1930, 339 pilots (officers and NCOs) and 517 aircrew (officers, NCOs and other ranks) were on the strength of the 23 regular squadrons at home and overseas. The majority of the pilots were 'career' officers, most of the squadron commanders being veterans of the First World War; many of the flight commanders were among the earliest of Trenchard's Cranwell officer cadets. The former would have reached group captain or higher ranks by the start of the Second World War; the latter would lead squadrons of the new monoplane bombers on raids over Germany, having served their apprenticeship among the struts and wires of Hart, Sidestrand and Virginia biplanes.

Vickers B.19/27 Types 150/195/255

Early in 1927 information reached Vickers (Aviation) Ltd that the Air Ministry was preparing a new night bomber Requirement, intended to replace the Virginia and Handley Page Hyderabad. Rex Pierson's staff was already preparing the design of an aeroplane with exactly that objective in mind so that, with the tacit aim of either pre-empting the new Specification or achieving certain relaxations in favour of the Vickers project, this design was submitted to the Air Ministry 'for comment'.

It is not known whether or to what extent Vickers' proposal influenced the Air Ministry's deliberations, but on 17 August that year the terms of Specification B.19/27 were distributed among the major manufacturers, including Vickers, Avro, Bristol, Fairey, Handley Page and Hawker. Briefly, the requirements were as follows:

1. Twin engines and metal airframe structure throughout.
2. A maximum speed of 120 mph at 10,000 feet with full load.
3. A service ceiling of 17,000 feet with full war load.
4. A range of 920 miles at 115 mph at 10,000 feet.
5. A maximum bomb load of not less than 2,200lb.
6. A landing speed of not more than 55 mph without bomb load.
7. Full-load take-off run not exceeding 200 yards.
8. Three defensive gun positions with Lewis guns.
(9. Two Bristol Orion engines were recommended, but this suggestion was soon dropped.)

In due course three prototypes were ordered from Vickers, Handley Page and Fairey, though not without lengthy discussions with each manufacturer beforehand. In the case of the Vickers Type 150, consideration was given to the Bristol Jupiter VIII and Mercury II as possible alternatives, but the Air Ministry eventually agreed to accept Rolls-Royce F.XIV engines, and a prototype, J9131, was ordered in 1928 and first flown by Maurice ('Mutt') Summers at Brooklands on 30 November 1929.

As initially flown, the unequal-span, two-bay biplane featured ailerons, three

The Vickers Type 150, J9131, at the A & AEE in 1932 after being fitted with Kestrel III engines and wheel spats, and modified with wing sweepback reduced to seven degrees and dihedral to two degrees. (Photo: Air Ministry, A & AEE)

degrees of dihedral and twelve degrees of sweepback on both upper and lower wings, and wingtip slats on the upper mainplanes. Twin unfinned rudders and biplane elevators without tailplanes were fitted, all surfaces being of narrow chord and high aspect ratio. Unusual for the time was the inclusion of a tailwheel. The aircraft was first delivered to Martlesham Heath for contractor's trials in March 1930, and appeared as New Type No 7 at the Hendon Display on 29 June that year.

On 28 August J9131 was delivered to No 15 Squadron at the A & AEE for armament testing, but the aircraft met with almost universal dislike, displaying quite unacceptable lateral instability, a constant rolling and yawing motion

(much later referred to as Dutch roll); heaviness of rudder and elevator controls was ascribed to the unbalanced tail surfaces — a criticism vigorously discounted by Vickers. No 15 Squadron pilots condemned the aircraft as being wholly unacceptable for night bombing and instrument flying.

After less than two months at Martlesham Heath, J9131 crashed while taking off on 9 October when both engines cut, the aircraft being extensively damaged; after investigation, the failure was deemed to have resulted from contaminated fuel. The aircraft was returned to Weybridge for rebuilding, during which much modification was undertaken.

The engines were replaced by Kestrel

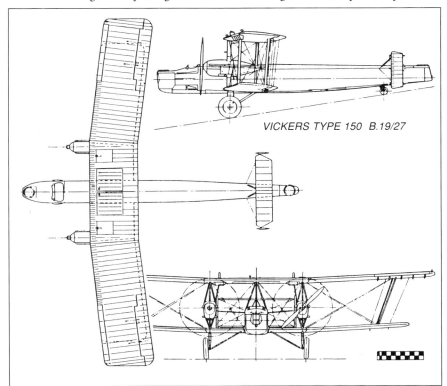

VICKERS TYPE 150 B.19/27

IIIs (the steam-cooled production version of the F.XIV), fuselage torsional rigidity was increased by stronger internal wire bracing, and lateral instability was alleviated by increasing the wing dihedral to 3½ degrees. Wheel fairings were also added at this time. In an effort to avoid an association with the former unpopular configuration, the name Vanox was bestowed by Vickers — a name not accepted by the Air Ministry, to whom the aeroplane belonged and who continued to refer to it as the Vickers B.19/27. In this form, J9131 was first flown in May 1931 and returned to Martlesham Heath the following month when it again attracted adverse criticism on account of persistent lateral instability, now acknowledged by Vickers to be attributable to excessive wing sweepback.

As a winner of the B.19/27 competition had still not been announced (the Fairey entrant having crashed in 1930 and that of Handley Page having to contend with numerous minor modifications), Vickers decided to persevere with J9131, reducing the wing sweepback to

seven degrees; and when Rolls-Royce announced that further lengthy development would be needed for the steam-cooled engines, Vickers obtained permission to substitute a pair of 622hp Bristol Pegasus IM3 radials.

When these and other extensive alterations had been completed in May 1932, J9131 (now referred to as the Type 195) returned to the A & AEE on 2 June, and went on to Service trials with No 9 (Bomber) Squadron in September. Although the aircraft now met all the performance and handling requirements, it continued to encounter numerous

minor criticisms on matters such as crew discomfort, poor cockpit layout and difficulty in bombing-up.

By the time these had been rectified, and Vickers (intending to further improve the aircraft's performance) had fitted new, three-bay wings, it was too late: both the Heyford and Hendon had won the prized production contracts.

The Vickers B.19/27, Type 255 in its ultimate configuration, was eventually allocated to the RAE for in-flight refuelling trials, which continued until 1937, and it was flown on 7 January 1938 for the last time.

Type: Twin-engine, four-crew, two-bay night bomber biplane.
Air Ministry Specification: B.19/27
Manufacturer: Vickers (Aviation) Ltd, Weybridge, Surrey.
Powerplant: Two 480hp Rolls-Royce F.XIV twelve-cylinder, evaporative-cooled in-line engines; also 525hp Kestrel III, and 622hp Bristol Pegasus IM3.
Structure: All-metal construction throughout.
Dimensions: Span, 76ft 6in; length, 60ft 6in; height, 19ft 3in; wing area, 1,367 sq ft.
Weights: Type 150. Tare, 10,435lb; all-up, 16,170lb.
Performance: Type 150. Max speed, 125 mph at 11,000ft; climb to 6,500ft, 19 min 45 sec; range, 920 miles. Type 195. Max speed, 135 mph at 5,000ft; climb to 6,500ft, 7 min 29 sec.
Armament: Two Lewis guns in nose and tail positions; bomb load of up to 2,200lb.
Prototype: One, J9131, first flown by M Summers at Brooklands on 30 November 1929. No production.

The prototype Heyford, J9130, at the time of the 1932 RAF Display at Hendon, carrying the New Type No 12. Just visible are the extended exhaust pipes, deemed necessary for night flying. Production aircraft featured angular, rather than rounded, rear ends to the engine nacelles. (Photo: Ministry of Defence Neg No H735)

Handley Page H.P.38/50 Heyford

The second of three prototype bombers ordered under the terms of Specification B.19/27, issued by Air Cdre John Adrian Chamier CB, CMG, DSO, OBE, Director of

Technical Development at the Air Ministry in August 1927[1], was the Handley Page H.P.38. This aeroplane, of all-metal construction, embodied a slim fuselage structure of steel tubular components and wings employing steel spars manufactured by the Steel Wing

[1] Air Commodore Chamier was to retire from the Royal Air Force in 1928.

Co Ltd of Gloucester. The nose, accommodating the pilots and front gunner, was a metal monocoque structure.

Early in the project stage, Handley Page had evaluated alternative configurations including the conventional location of engines and fuselage mounted directly on the lower wing but, because this presented problems of restricted fields of fire for the midships gunner,

The first production Heyford I, K3489, at Radlett on 25 November 1933, showing its 'ram's horn' exhaust pipes. Later this aeroplane was flown with an experimental Steiger (General Aircraft Ltd) nose turret. (Photo: *Flight*, Neg No 13661)

George Volkert and Harold Boultbee decided on a radical configuration — attaching the fuselage and engines to the undersurfaces of the upper wing. This allowed an unrestricted upper surface of the upper wing and, by accommodating the bomb load inside the centresection of the lower wing, provided maximum lift for minimum drag. The choice of engines fell upon Rolls-Royce F.XIVs.

The 'high fuselage' layout allowed the nose and midships dorsal gunners an excellent field of fire, while defence against attack from below was provided by a Lewis gunner situated in a retractable 'dustbin' suspended from a Scarff ring amidships, an expedient also made possible by the height of the fuselage when on the ground. It was also thought at the time that the positioning of the bomb cells in the lower wing would facilitate the loading of bombs; however, because the landing wheel suspension was integral with the lower front spar, the bomb cell doors were so close to the ground that Service armourers later complained bitterly when they had to lie in soaking grass as they lifted the bombs into place.

The H.P.38 prototype, J9130, made its first flight at Handley Page's new factory aerodrome at Radlett, near St Albans, on 12 June 1930 in the hands of Maj James Lucas Brome Hope Cordes. In the month that followed, numerous modifications were made, including installing larger radiators to cure engine overheating, strengthening the tailwheel (which had collapsed), stiffening the nose monocoque, fitting revised rudders and rearranging the cockpit layout.

As the Vickers B.19/27 had been flying for about six months already, there was some urgency to deliver J9130 to Martlesham Heath without delay; indeed, it seemed that the H.P.38 was in danger of being eliminated by default when, providentially for Handley Page, the Vickers prototype crashed and suffered serious damage, causing the Air Ministry to postpone the competition until February 1931. Then the Fairey B.19/27 monoplane contender also crashed, resulting in the trial being put back still further.

It now proved possible to address a number of other areas of criticism that had arisen in J9130, not least of which were the cramped crew stations. The rudder area was increased by 25 per cent, thereby enabling the aircraft, not only to maintain height on one engine, but to turn against a dead engine.

The Handley Page arrived at Martlesham on 3 October 1931 and was generally well received; further minor modifications were made to the pilot's rudder pedals, while lengthened exhaust pipes extended over the upper wing to reduce glare while flying at night. J9130 was sent to No 10 (Bomber) Squadron at Boscombe Down for Service trials on 1 April and the five pilots who flew the aircraft were unanimous in their approval. Handley Page became confident that its new bomber was heading for victory, and began preliminary design adaptation for production.

The first potentially serious misfortune befell J9130 when, on 10 June 1932, while being demonstrated before Sir Geoffrey Salmond at Upper Heyford, a

Type: Twin-engine, four-crew, two-bay biplane night bomber biplane.
Air Ministry Specifications: B.19/27 (prototype), B.23/32 (Mark I), B.28/34 (Mark II) and B.27/35 (Mark III).
Manufacturer: Handley Page Ltd, Radlett, Hertfordshire.
Powerplant: Two 575hp Rolls-Royce Kestrel IIIS twelve-cylinder supercharged in-line engines driving two-blade propellers; also 640hp Kestrel VI (Mks II and III).
Structure: All-metal construction throughout.
Dimensions: Span, 75ft 0in; length, 58ft 0in; height, 17ft 6in; wing area, 1,470 sq ft.
Weights: Mark I. Tare, 9,200lb; all-up, 15,534lb. Mark III. Tare, 10,200lb; all-up (max), 17,176lb.
Performance: Mark III. Max speed, 154 mph at 10,000ft; climb to 6,500ft, 9 min; service ceiling, 19,100ft; range, 930 miles.
Armament: Single Lewis guns in nose and midships dorsal positions, and in ventral retractable 'dustbin'. Normal bomb load of up to ten 250lb bombs (maximum fourteen).
Prototype: One, J9130, first flown by Capt J L B H Cordes at Radlett on 12 June 1930.
Production: A total of 124 Heyfords (excluding prototype) was built. Mark I, 15: K3489-K3503; Mark IA, 23: K4021-K4043; Mark II, 16: K4863-K4878; Mark III, 70: K5180-K5199 and K6857-K6906. Some aircraft modified to later versions after completion.
Summary of Service: Heyfords served with the following Squadrons of the RAF: No 99 (Bomber) Squadron from November 1933 until October 1938 at Upper Heyford and Mildenhall (all Marks); No 10 (Bomber) Squadron from August 1934 until June 1937 at Boscombe Down and Dishforth (Marks IA and III); No 7 (Bomber) Squadron from April 1935 until April 1938 at Worthy Down and Finningley (Marks II and III); No 38 (Bomber) Squadron from September 1935 until June 1937 at Mildenhall and Marham (Marks I, IA and III); No 97 (Bomber) Squadron from September 1935 until February 1939 at Catfoss and Leconfield (all Marks); No 102 (Bomber) Squadron from October 1935 until October 1938 at Worthy Down and Driffield (Marks II and III); No 9 (Bomber) Squadron from March 1936 until February 1939 at Aldergrove and Stradishall (Mark IIIs); No 78 (Bomber) Squadron from November 1936 until October 1937 at Boscombe Down and Dishforth (Marks II and III); No 166 (Bomber) Squadron from November 1936 until September 1939 at Boscombe Down and Leconfield (Marks II and III); No 149 (Bomber) Squadron from April 1937 until March 1939 at Mildenhall (all Marks); No 148 (Bomber) Squadron from November 1938 until March 1939 at Stradishall (Mark IIIs); and temporarily with No 58 (Bomber) Squadron at Linton-on-Ouse in April 1939. Heyfords also served with No 3 Air Observers' School at Aldergrove, No 4 Air Observers' School (No 4 Bombing & Gunnery School) at West Freugh and the Ferry Pilots' Pool.

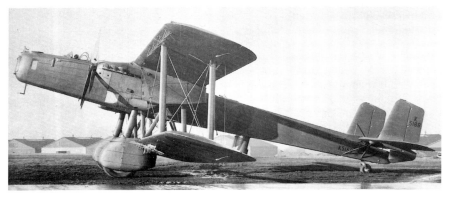

K5188 was a standard Heyford III, seen here with 'dustbin' gun position extended and additional bomb carriers outboard of the wheel spats. Flown by Fg Off John Edwin Campbell Gascoigne Flemyng Gyll-Murray, it was one of the Heyfords to survive No 102 (Bomber) Squadron's disastrous encounter with severe icing conditions on 12 December 1936, making a successful forced landing near York. Four other aircraft were less fortunate. (Photo: Imperial War Museum, Neg No MH3331)

fatigue failure occurred in the lower wing centresection front spar while taxiing, causing the starboard undercarriage to collapse; the damage was, however, quickly repaired and the aeroplane attended the Hendon Display on 25 June (as New Type No 12).

The H.P.38 was duly declared the winner of the B.19/27 competition but, at that moment, the Geneva Disarmament Conference (under the auspices of the League of Nations) — then agonising over a proposal to outlaw all aerial bombing — was thrown into disarray, first by the emergence of the Nazi party as the strongest element in the German *Reichstag*, and then by the League's refusal to recognise the Japanese-inspired puppet state of Manchukuo. Handley Page initially only received an Instruction to Proceed with five production aircraft, now named the Heyford. It was not until March 1933 that a full Contract for fifteen aircraft (H.P.50, K3489-K3503) to Specification B.23/32 was raised.

Meanwhile, the prototype Heyford had been lost in an accident while undergoing armament trials with No 10 (Bomber) Squadron on 8 July 1932, so the first of the production aircraft was assembled by hand in order to speed its completion to test the various alterations required by the production Specification. (K3489 was later used to test a Steiger nose turret, but this did not enter production.)

The first Squadron to equip with Heyford Is was No 99 (Bomber) Squadron at Upper Heyford, Oxfordshire, commanded by Wg Cdr (later Gp Capt) Francis John Linnell OBE, whose deliveries began in November 1933.

A second production order was placed for 23 Heyfords, these aircraft being fitted with two-piece, four-blade propellers and engine-driven electric generators in place of the former wind-driven units. Termed Mark IAs, these aircraft equipped the next Heyford Squadron, No 10, commanded by Wg Cdr (later Gp Capt) Charles Beauvois Dallison DFC at Boscombe Down.

The final aircraft of the first production batch, K3503, had been retained at Radlett as efforts were made to increase the Heyford's performance, alternative engines such as the Bristol Pegasus III and Armstrong Siddeley Tiger being considered. No decision was immediately forthcoming from the Air Ministry, and a third alternative, the Kestrel VI, was selected (as this engine had successfully passed its type test in March 1934). K3503 was accordingly completed with these engines for flight trials, while a similarly powered Mark IA, K4209, was set aside as the prototype Heyford Mark II, of which 16 production examples were ordered to Specification B.29/34, most of these equipping the third Heyford Squadron, No 7 at Worthy Down, in April 1935. This version returned a maximum speed of 154 mph at 6,500 feet, as well as being capable of lifting a maximum bomb load of 3,500lb in exceptional circumstances (comprising fourteen 250lb bombs, six of them on external underwing racks).

In an effort to improve the Heyford's Service appeal yet further, so as to secure a worthwhile proportion of the bomber orders likely to be placed to fuel the RAF's expansion plans, well underway by 1936, the prototype Heyford II, K4029, was fitted with an enclosed cockpit canopy and given a raised upper

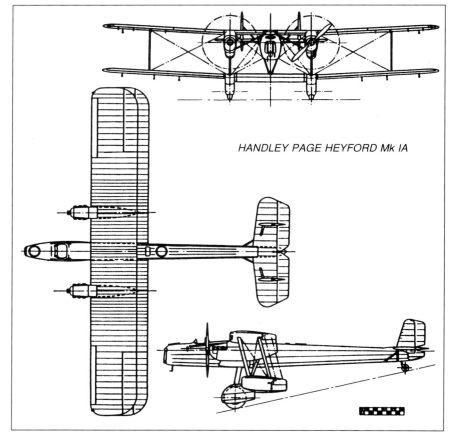

HANDLEY PAGE HEYFORD Mk IA

fuselage line in order to provide a degree of protection from the slipstream for the dorsal gunner. However, it was made clear that the Heyford's production rate must be increased as soon as possible, and such cosmetic alterations could not be justified. Accordingly the final version, the Mark III, featured relatively few modifications, these being confined to the engine installation; the steam-cooled Kestrel VIs were provided with improved wing-located steam condensers as well as rubber-seated engine bearers.

A total of 70 Heyford IIIs was built and, by the end of 1936 — when the RAF's new Bomber Command had been in existence for some six months — nine squadrons were equipped with this, the last biplane heavy bomber to join the RAF. Ironically, one of the first squadrons to begin to dispose of its Heyfords (No 38) was also the only squadron to be equipped with the Fairey B.19/27 Hendon monoplane. Yet it was on the Heyford that so many regular officer pilots, who were to bear the brunt of Bomber Command's raids in the first eighteen months of the War, had served their first tours. Their periodic exercises had become progressively more realistic and demanding, their mock attacks being flown over longer distances, sometimes against targets in France, often in unfavourable weather. On 19 February 1936 No 10 (Bomber) Squadron suffered its first flying fatalities since being reformed in 1928 with Hyderabads, when two Heyfords crashed at night, one in the Channel, while returning from a 'raid' over France; both pilots survived, but six crewmen died. And on 12 December the same year disaster struck No 102 Squadron, seven of whose Heyfords encountered severe icing over the Midlands; two pilots made successful forced landings and one brought his aircraft back to his base at Finningley, but four aircraft crashed and were destroyed, and three crew members were killed.

Even though the Heyford did not constitute the bridge between the old and the new technology, it was by circumstance the aircraft in which a generation of bomber pilots were brought face to face with the reality of a likely European war.

Summary of Flight Research performed by Heyford aircraft

K3503, K4029	Trials with enclosed cockpits
K3489	Steiger nose turret
K3503	Trojan nose turret
K5184	Atcherley in-flight refuelling system
K5184	Catapult-assisted take-off (RAE)
K6902	Signal echoes on ground radar (1935-36)
K6902	First airborne radar transmitter/receiver, 1937
K4029, K5184	First assault glider towing trials (Hotspur), 1940

Fairey B.19/27 Hendon

Although the Fairey design tender to the B.19/27 night bomber Specification was the only monoplane offered, it was a logical, not to say courageous attempt to break the mould of large bomber design. Logical, for it was designed by a team led by D L Hollis Williams and P A Ralli, who had been responsible for the design and stressing of the famous Fairey long-range cantilever monoplanes, one of which was to establish for Britain a new world distance record in February 1933.

The bomber design featured a low-set cantilever wing centresection built integrally with the fuselage. The two main spars of the exceptionally deep wing, of fairly high maximum lift/drag ratio, comprised upper and lower booms of square-section tube fabricated from steel strip, with sheet steel webs on the inboard sections giving place to a

The Fairey B.19/27 prototype, K1695, before its untimely accident; at this stage no attempt had been made to complete the midships and tail gunners' positions and the aircraft was still powered by Bristol Jupiter engines. (Photo: The Bristol Aeroplane Co Ltd, Neg No 17582)

Warren girder towards the tips.

The fuselage, of almost parallel section nose to tail in plan and side elevation from, was built in three sections, the two forward sections being rectangular Warren box girders, changing to triangular Warren-girder towards the tail, the entire airframe being fabric-covered. The 525hp Bristol Jupiter XF engine nacelles, located at the outer extremities of the rectangular wing centresection, surmounted large undercarriage trouser fairings, with a single diagonal bracing strut from wheel centre to front wing spar.

The tailplane, with slight dihedral, was mounted low on the rear fuselage, the twin fins being braced to the fuselage by two pairs of V-struts on each side.

Gunners' positions were provided in nose, midships and extreme tail locations, and there was a corrugated-aluminium catwalk along the entire length of the fuselage, but no ventral gun position. The main bomb bay was located in the centre fuselage section, large enough to accommodate a single example of the new 1,000lb bomb; further cells in the wing centresection could accommodate smaller bombs or addi-

The first of 14 production Hendons, K5085. The washout on the outer wings gave an illusion of elliptical planform. The domed cupola was introduced not only to shield the nose gunner but to eliminate the blast of icy air which swept through the fuselage. (Photo: A J Jackson Collection)

tional fuel tanks. The pilot's cockpit, offset to port to allow space for the catwalk, was enclosed (on production aircraft) by a multi-panel transparent canopy. A wireless operator/navigator's station was located forward of the main wing spar, and was provided with windows on either side of the fuselage.

Some delay resulted from the Air Ministry's scepticism of the practicality of the design, but after provisional endorsement of the design by the RAE (as well as Richard Fairey's undertaking to bear much of a prototype's cost), a single prototype, K1695, was ordered in 1928, and construction began immediately at Fairey's factory at Hayes; it was not, however, until January 1930 that a decision on the wing section was reached (following tunnel tests at Farnborough). On this account, K1695 was not completed until November that year, some months after the Vickers and Handley Page B.19/27 prototypes had flown. K1695 was first flown by Norman Macmillan at Harmondsworth on 25 November — the last Fairey prototype to be test flown by that famous pilot.

As already recorded, both of the other contenders encountered problems which caused the competitive evaluation to be delayed by some nine months, and it was while the Vickers and Handley Page prototypes were undergoing modification that, on 15 March 1931, the Fairey bomber also crashed, and was extensively damaged. As no Service report had by then been made, the Fairey tender was eliminated from the competition, and in due course the Heyford was declared the winner.

Nevertheless, determined to persevere, Richard Fairey gave instructions for K1695 to be rebuilt (largely at his expense), incorporating numerous changes in the design. The Jupiters were replaced by 480hp Rolls-Royce Kestrel IIIS engines, the pilot's canopy was temporarily discarded, the tailplane dihedral eliminated, and the wing section was modified to incorporate prominent washout towards the tips to delay tip-stall. In this form, K1695 was flown by Chris

Staniland in November 1931, and on 18 May 1932 arrived at Martlesham Heath. Contractor's trials, performance assessment and armament trials were followed by Service trials with No 10 (Bomber) Squadron, suggesting that the Air Ministry was, by 1933, beginning to regard the Fairey bomber with more favour — on account of its performance superiority over the Heyford rather than as a stepping stone from biplane to monoplane *per se*. Its performance was,

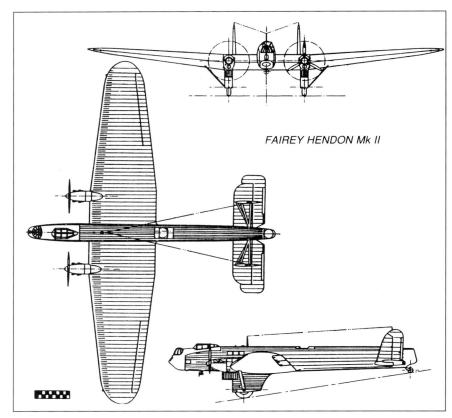

FAIREY HENDON Mk II

after all, inferior to that being demanded in a new Specification, B.9/32.

A tentative production order was therefore raised during the spring of 1934 for 14 Fairey bombers, to be named the Hendon Mark II, and a new Specification, B.20/34, covering a change to Kestrel VIs and other small alterations, was issued. These aircraft would suffice to equip a single squadron and establish a production line should delays occur in introducing the new generation of heavy bomber monoplanes, intended to begin service in 1938 or sooner.

Built at Heaton Chapel, Stockport, the first Hendon IIs reached No 38 (Bomber) Squadron, commanded by Sqn Ldr (later Gp Capt) Stanley Miles Park at Mildenhall in November 1936, by which time the Whitley, Wellington and Hampden bomber prototypes had all flown and were showing great promise. A small batch of four further Hen-

dons (K5768-K5771), intended as possible attrition replacements, was therefore cancelled, as was a much bigger order for 58 aircraft (K6555-K6612).

The Hendon IIs remained in service with No 38 Squadron only until Janu-

ary 1939, when most were struck off Air Ministry charge and scrapped. Four aircraft were, however, delivered as ground instruction machines to No 1 Electrical and Wireless School at Cranwell.

Type: Twin-engine, five-crew, low-wing night bomber monoplane.
Air Ministry Specifications: B.19/27 (prototype); B.20/34 (production).
Manufacturer: The Fairey Aviation Co Ltd, Stockport, Cheshire.
Powerplant: Prototype. Two 525hp Bristol Jupiter XF air-cooled radial engines driving two-blade propellers; later Kestrel IIIS. Production. Two 600hp Rolls-Royce Kestrel VI twelve-cylinder water-cooled in-line engines driving three-blade propellers.
Structure: All-metal construction throughout, fabric-covered.
Dimensions: Span, 101ft 9in; length, 60ft 9in; height, 18ft 8in; wing area, 1,146 sq ft.
Performance: Mark II. Max speed, 152 mph at 15,000ft; climb to 6,500ft, 9 min 12 sec; service ceiling, 21,400ft; range, 1,360 miles.
Armament: Single Lewis guns in nose, midships dorsal and tail positions; bomb load, maximum of 1,660lb, including one 1,000lb bomb.
Prototype: One, K1695, first flown by Norman Macmillan at Harmondsworth on 25 November 1930.
Production: Fourteen Hendon IIs were built, K5085-K5098.
Summary of Service: Hendon IIs served with No 38 (Bomber) Squadron at Mildenhall and Marham from November 1936 until January 1939.

Blackburn 3MR4

The Blackburn company's pre-eminent reputation for the design of torpedo-carrying aircraft encouraged the Japanese manufacturer Mitsubishi to request the British firm to produce a design for a new carrier-borne, long-range torpedo bomber with which to enter a 1927 competition held by the Imperial Japanese Navy to decide on an aircraft to replace its Mitsubishi B1M1 attack bombers.

In due course Maj F A Bumpus tendered a design, the Blackburn T.7B, which was in effect an enlarged Ripon, but incorporating a number of features of the Beagle. Powered by a 625hp Hipano-Suiza 12Lbr twelve-cylinder water-cooled engine, the design was finalised by George Edward Petty and submitted with a licence agreement to Mitsubishi on 29 May 1928.

The design was declared the winner by the Japanese Government and a prototype, referred to as the 3MR4, was ordered from Blackburn; this was first flown by 'Dasher' Blake at Brough on 28 December 1929.

Constructed of steel tube, the 3MR4 featured two-bay, high aspect ratio, narrow-gap, staggered, folding wings (the lower wing being of marginally greater span than the upper), and a three-seat fuselage built in three sections. Aluminium sheet panels covered

The Blackburn-built 3MR4 prototype in Japanese markings after delivery to Japan, with a pair of 250lb bombs. Note the Handley Page wingtip slats. (Photo: Blackburn Aircraft Ltd)

the forward fuselage, and fabric the rear section, containing flotation bags. The pilot was armed with a single Vickers front gun, and the rear gunner with a pair of Lewis guns. The war load comprised either a 2,000lb torpedo and reduced fuel, or a pair of 250lb bombs (aimed by use of a high-altitude bomb sight) for long-distance operations.

Production of two variants of the

3MR4 was undertaken in Japan, the B2M1 carrier-borne attack bomber of 1932, and the B2M2 short range bomber capable of carrying 1,764lb of bombs. Both versions served aboard the Japanese carriers *Akagi*, *Kaga* and *Ryujo* between 1934 and 1937, and total Japanese production amounted to 205. The accompanying data refer to the Blackburn T.7B prototype.

Type: Single-engine, three-seat, two-bay carrier-borne attack bomber biplane for Japan.
Manufacturer: The Blackburn Aeroplane and Motor Co Ltd, Leeds, Yorkshire.
Powerplant: One 625hp Hispano-Suiza Type 51-12Lbr 12-cylinder in-line engine.
Dimensions: Span, 49ft 3½in; length, 33ft 3in; height, 12ft 5in; wing area, 592 sq ft.
Weights: (Torpedo bomber) Tare, 3,896lb; all-up, 7,966lb.
Performance: (Torpedo bomber) Max speed, 132 mph at sea level; service ceiling, 11,500ft; range, 390 miles.
Armament: One synchronized 0.303in Vickers machine gun and two Lewis guns; either one 2,000lb torpedo or two 250lb bombs.
Prototype: One (unmarked), first flown by A M Blake at Brough on 28 December 1929. No British production.

Armstrong Whitworth A.W.17 Aries

The Aries, J9037, at Martlesham Heath, showing the Warren-truss interplane struts and the very long-span ailerons. (Photo: Air Ministry, A & AEE)

As Armstrong Whitworth approached the end of Atlas production, without any recent army co-operation aircraft requirement being issued, it seemed appropriate for the company to capitalise on the success of the earlier aircraft with an improved version drawing on the wealth of experience gained.

Design went ahead in 1929 and an order for a single prototype, J9037, previously held in abeyance for several years, was finally confirmed that year, the aircraft flying on 5 March 1930.

Emphasis in the new design by John Lloyd was on improving the Atlas' low speed handling and increasing accessibility to the equipment needed for the army co-operation rôle. The upper wing was increased in span, and the Handley Page slats were interconnected with the ailerons; the majority of the wing lift and drag bracing wires were omitted, being replaced by a pair of diagonal interplane struts forming a Warren truss — thereby considerably reducing the rigging time during maintenance.

To improve accessibility to the fuselage interior, removable aluminium panels were provided as far as a point about two feet aft of the gunner's cockpit, though these were found to be troublesome and later changed back to fabric panels.

The Aries was flown to Martlesham on 8 April for preliminary trials, but the Service was non-committal largely, it was thought, as a result of Hawker Engineering having submitted a proposal to adapt the much-favoured Hart for army co-operation duties.

The A.W.17 Aries returned to Martlesham Heath for evaluation by No 22 Squadron in November 1931 and for comparison with the prototype Hawker Audax, but was rejected on the grounds that it did not represent any worthwhile advance on the Atlas. It ended its days at Farnborough in 1933, having been fitted with a Jaguar VIC engine.

Type: Single-engine, two-seat, single-bay experimental army co-operation biplane.
Manufacturer: Sir W G Armstrong Whitworth Aircraft Ltd, Coventry.
Powerplant: One 460hp Armstrong Siddeley Jaguar IV 14-cylinder air-cooled radial engine driving two-blade propeller. Also Jaguar IVC.
Dimensions: Span, 42ft 0in; length, 28ft 4in; height, 10ft 11in; wing area, 399.4 sq ft.
Weight: All-up, 4,350lb.
Performance: Records not traced.
Armament: One synchronized 0.303in Vickers gun and one Lewis gun on rear cockpit.
Prototype: One, J9037, first flown on 5 April 1930. No production.

Bristol Type 118

The Bristol Type 118, carring RAF markings and the serial K2873, showing the deep front fuselage which permitted a prone bomb-aiming position for the observer; note the aircraft's single-piece four-blade propeller. (Photo: Real Photographs Co.)

Another designer to advocate a private venture aircraft as a replacement for long-established general purpose types, Frank Barnwell began the design of his Bristol Type 118 in 1929 more to meet the likely requirements of potential customers overseas than of the RAF. It was accordingly a fairly orthodox and straightforward aeroplane intended for a wide range of military duties which included bombing, army co-operation, photo reconnaissance and casualty evacuation. Construction was of steel throughout, with round tubular and strip Warren girder fuselage structure, and two-spar, unequal-span, staggered wings with N-type interplane struts. Power was provided by a 590hp Bristol Jupiter XFA radial engine.

Perhaps the one unusual feature of this aircraft, as well as the related Type 120 (see page 244), was the depth of the front fuselage, so designed to provide a station for the observer/gunner, lying prone, when engaged in bomb aiming, enabling him to see forward as well as vertically down; alternatively, the same space could be employed to accommodate a stretcher casualty (with another under the detachable top decking of the rear fuselage.)

First flown as G-ABEZ by Cyril Uwins at Filton on 21 January 1931, the Type 118 underwent flight trials at the factory during the following summer (carrying the B conditions marking R-3) before being delivered to Martlesham at the end of October with the military serial number K2873.

After being well received by pilots of the A & AEE, the aircraft (now termed the Type 118A) was leased by the Air Ministry for type trials of the Bristol Mercury V radial, including tropical trials in Iraq, remaining in the Middle East for much of 1932 and 1933.

It then returned to Filton, where it remained in store until April 1935 when it was re-engined once more, this time as a flight test bed with an 820hp Bristol

Pegasus PE-5SM two-speed supercharged prototype radial engine (later the Pegasus XVIII in the Handley Page Hampden and Vickers Wellington).

Type: Single-engine, two-seat, single-bay experimental general purpose biplane.
Manufacturer: The Bristol Aeroplane Co Ltd, Filton, Bristol.
Powerplant: Type 118. One 590hp Bristol Jupiter XFA radial. Type 118A. One 600hp Mercury V; one 820hp Pegasus PE-5SM.
Dimensions: Span, 40ft 8in; length, 34ft 0in; height, 12ft 0in; wing area, 376 sq ft.
Weights: Tare, 3,632lb; all-up, 5,200lb.
Performance: Max speed, 165 mph at 5,000ft; service ceiling, 25,600ft.
Armament: One synchronized 0.303in Vickers gun in port side of front fuselage and one Lewis gun on rear cockpit; bomb load of two 250lb or four 112lb bombs.
Prototype: One, G-ABEZ (later R-3 and K2873), first flown by Cyril Uwins at Filton on 22 January 1931. No production.

Hawker Audax

The RAF's standard army co-operation aircraft, the Armstrong Whitworth Atlas (page 169), had been in service for only two years when the Air Ministry's Directorate of Technical Development (DTD) was instructed to begin a fundamental analysis of the rôle of the aeroplane in support of ground forces, a rôle which embraced an extremely diverse spectrum of demands, ranging from the support of a Western-style mobile army, requiring constant short-range reconnaissance with a likelihood of air opposition, to the equally demanding task of policing huge tracts of treacherous terrain over which potentially hostile but ill-armed marauders imposed their will over otherwise tractable populations.

The postwar generation of 'corps reconnaissance' aircraft, followed by the army co-operation Atlas, had produced a fairly clear understanding of the problems involved, particularly in the Middle East (in support of Britain's mandate, following the break-up of the Ottoman Empire) as well as in the North-West Frontier Province of India. The Atlas had enabled procedural understanding to be gained both in the RAF and among the ground forces but, was, however, relatively slow (attracting criticism when prompt action in policing duties was important), and its obsolescent 14-cylinder Jaguar engine left much to be desired in matters of reliability and maintenance — and not only overseas.

At the time of these deliberations, during a meeting between Sir John Salmond and T O M Sopwith in May 1930 (held principally to discuss the need to speed up a fighter adaptation of the Hart bomber), Sopwith mentioned

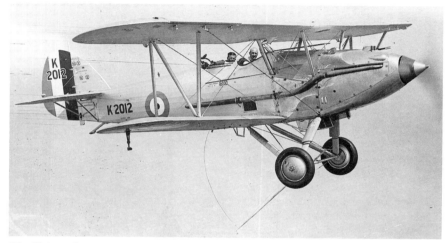

The 18th production Hawker Audax, K2012, in flight with Hawker's chief test pilot, easily identifiable as 'George' Bulman, at the controls early in 1932. The aircraft later served with No 13 (Army Co-operation) Squadron and the School of Army Co-operation. Note the message hook extended for the benefit of the photographer. (Photo: H G Hawker Engineering Co Ltd.)

that Camm was also working on an army co-operation version of the Hart that would, he believed, be a worthwhile advance on the Atlas.

Salmond himself was not particularly anxious to become personally involved in advocating such a project, but a couple of months later Hawker was asked to forward its proposals to the DTD as a new requirement was about to be formulated for an ultimate replacement for the Atlas. Referred to in Hawker records at the time as the 'AC-Hart', the new design retained the unsupercharged Kestrel I engine, and showed that all the war load and equipment embodied in the latest Atlas requirements could be accommodated, and that a performance of 170 mph at 2,500 feet and a range of 540 miles could be achieved. Perhaps most important was the justifiable assurance that the Hart's handling qualities, applauded by the pilots at Martlesham Heath, would be undiminished. There is no doubt that

these proposals formed the basis of the new Specification, 7/31, issued in the spring of 1931[1].

An early production Hart, K1438, had been set aside for mock-up installations to be made of equipment and confirmation of centre of gravity location, and in due course authority was granted to treat this aircraft as the prototype 7/31 aircraft, wireless, desert equipment, water

---

[1] It is worth mentioning that, in September 1930, Air Vice-Marshal Hugh Caswall Tremenheere Dowding, CB, CMG, had been appointed Air Member for Supply and Research; this officer, later to become the revered leader of Fighter Command during the Battle of Britain, fought ten years later, not only possessed first-hand knowledge of Britain's fighter deficiencies, having also commanded Air Defence of Great Britain (in succession to Salmond), but had served in the Middle East, and shortly afterwards had been sent out to Palestine by Trenchard to report, *inter alia*, on the development of air policing tactics in the theatre.

Identifiable in this photo are Audax (India) K4840/BF-Z (no hook, Gloster-built) and H5561/BF-F (with hook, Avro-built) of No 18 Squadron flying with night equipment from Ambala over the Karakoram late in 1938; the normal bomb load of the Audax in India was two 112lb and two 25lb bombs, as well as the Vickers and Lewis guns. The aircraft of this squadron were being painted in 'post-Munich' camouflage. (Photo: via Robert Chalmers)

stowage, and message pick-up hook all being fitted and tested at Brooklands. Some weight increase was offset by elimination of the Hart's bomb aiming station in the lower fuselage. Even before K1438 was due at Martlesham Heath for contractor's trials and performance measurement, Hawker had received a production contract for 40 aircraft, to be named the Audax.

Early interest by the Air Ministry in the Audax was divided between service at home with the regular army co-operation squadrons — five of them — and with three in India. The first production orders, totalling 200 aircraft, placed over three years (the last 26 ordered from The Gloster Aircraft Company), began delivery to No 4 (Army Co-operation) Squadron at Farnborough, followed by Nos 13, 26, 16 and 2 Squadrons, in that order, over the next three years, as well as the Schools of Army Co-operation and Photography.

The speed with which K1438 (and the first production Audax, K1994) negotiated their trials at the A & AEE, as well as the Serivce trials with No 4 Squadron, bore testimony to the popularity of the Hart in RAF service, added to which the Audax introduced powerful wheel brakes, enabling it to operate into rather smaller fields that its bomber sire.

For service in India, a special variant, simply referred to as the Audax (India), was introduced, all the paraphernalia found necessary during twelve years' service by the D.H.9A and Bristol F.2B Fighter (excepting the spare wheel) being accommodated without difficulty. The first examples reached No 20 Squadron at Peshawar in December 1935, and Audaxes subsequently flew with Nos 5,

28 and 146 Squadron, remaining in operational service until July 1942. Many other Audax (India) aircraft were supplied to the Indian Air Force from 1939 onwards, serving until 1944. No 208 Squadron, at Heliopolis, received spe-

cially tropicalised Audaxes in August 1935.

Only one Auxiliary Air Force Squadron, No 615 (County of Surrey) was declared for army co-operation duties at Kenley; this unit was equipped with late production aircraft in November 1937, although they were replaced by Hawker Hectors (see page 280) after only 18 weeks.

The great majority of Audaxes, however, played an important rôle in the RAF's expansion programme as light bomber trainers between 1936 and 1939,

Type: Single-engine, two-seat, single-bay army co-operation biplane.
Air Ministry Specifications: 7/31, 9/34, 19/34 and 34/34.
Manufacturers: H G Hawker Engineering Co Ltd, and Hawker Aircraft Ltd, Kingston and Brooklands, Surrey; A V Roe & Co, Ltd, Manchester; The Bristol Aeroplane Co Ltd, Filton, Bristol; The Gloster Aircraft Co Ltd, Hucclecote, Gloucester; Westland Aircraft Ltd, Yeovil, Somerset.
Powerplant: One 530hp Rolls-Royce Kestrel I 12-cylinder, water-cooled, in-line engine driving Watts 2-blade wooden propeller. Also Rolls-Royce Kestrel IIS and V, Bristol Pegasus IIM2 and Pegasus VIP, Pratt & Whitney Hornet S2B (with 3-blade Hamilton propeller).
Structure: All-metal primary structure with duralumin sheet and fabric covering.
Dimensions: Span, 37 ft 3in; length, 29ft 7in; height, 10ft 5in; wing area, 348 sq ft.
Weights: Tare, 2,938lb; all-up, 4,386lb.
Performance: Max speed, 170 mph at 2,400ft; climb to 10,000ft, 8 min 40 sec; service ceiling, 21,500ft; range, 560 miles.
Armament: One synchronized 0.303in Vickers machine gun in port side of nose and one Lewis gun on rear cockpit; maximum bomb load of either two 250lb or four 112lb bombs.
Prototype: One, K1438 (formerly early production Hart SEDB, modified), first flown by Flt Lt P W S Bulman at Brooklands in about August 1931.
Production: A total of 755 Audaxes was built, of which 653 were built to Air Ministry contracts; these comprised K1994-K2034, K3055-K3145 and K3679-K3721 (174 Hawker-built Audax I); K4381-K4406 (26 Gloster-built Audax I); K4838-K4862 (25 Gloster-built Audax [India]); K5120-K5176 and K7307-K7568 (219 Avro-built Audax I); K5561-K5585 (25 Avro-built Audax [India]); K5201-K5256 and K7469-K7553 (141 Bristol-built Audax I); K5586-K5603 and K8311-K8335 (43 Westland-built Audax I; the latter batch was sub-contracted from Avro). In addition, 102 other Audaxes were exported on foreign orders from Persia, Iraq and Egypt.
Summary of Service: Hawker Audaxes served with the following Army Co-operation Squadrons: No 2 (Manston, from Sept 1934), No 4 (Farnborough, from Dec 1931), No 13 (Netheravon, from July 1932), No 16 (Old Sarum, from Dec 1933), No 26 (Catterick, from July 1933); No 208 (Heliopolis, Egypt, from Aug 1935); No 237 (Nairobi, Kenya, from April 1940); and No 615, AAF (Kenley, from Nov 1937). Audax (India) served with No 5 Squadron (Risalpur, India, from Feb 1941), No 20 (Peshawar, India, from Dec 1935), and No 146 (Risalpur, India, from Oct 1941). Audax Is served as light bombing trainers with the following Bomber Squadrons: Nos 61, 63, 77, 105, 114, 144, 148, 211 and 226 Squadrons. They also flew with Nos 24, 173 and 267 (Communications) Squadrons. Audaxes served at the Central Flying School, the RAF College, Cranwell, the School of Army Co-operation, the School of Photography, Radio Schools, Glider Operational Training Units, numerous Flying Training Schools, Elementary & Reserve Flying Training Schools, etc. Several Audaxes were transferred to Admiralty charge in 1941 for service as trainers with No 780 Squadron, Fleet Air Arm, at Lee-on-Solent.

nine squadrons — many of them later becoming heavy bomber squadrons and serving with great distinction in the War — between them taking delivery of some 200 aircraft as initial equipment, pending the arrival of such aircraft as the Blenheim, Whitley, Wellington and Hampden. More than 250 other Audaxes, often fitted with dual controls, served with the Flying Training Schools, the Royal Air Force College, Cranwell, and the Central Flying School.

Audaxes were exported in small numbers to overseas air forces in 1935-36, the largest customer being Iraq, which ordered 34 aircraft powered by Bristol Pegasus radial engines, while Persia took delivery of 26 similarly-powered aircraft. It is interesting to record that during the Iraqi uprising under Raschid Ali in 1941, the Iraqi Air Force was still equipped with Pegasus-Audax bombers, while at Habbaniya, then home of the RAF's No 4 Flying

Training School, Audax trainers were pressed into combat service as bombers, flying from the base which was, for a short time, under heavy artillery bombardment by the Iraqi guns. Several of the Persian Audaxes were still flying after the Second World War.

Audaxes also equipped the Royal Egyptian Air Force, the South African Air Force and the Straits Settlements Volunteer Air Force (the latter aircraft being termed the Audax [Singapore]).

Westland P.V.3

No doubt influenced, if not necessarily impressed, by the adaptability of the Hawker Hart to meet a multiplicity of operational rôles, Arthur Davenport believed that his own Wapiti might still gain selection by the RAF as an Atlas-replacement in the army co-operation rôle. The uncompromising attitude by the Air Ministry, however, towards wooden aircraft — particularly in the tropics — forced the decision to switch to a metal airframe.

As it was already clear that a Hart derivative stood an odds-on chance of gaining a short-term production contract for the army co-operation rôle, the Air Ministry declined to support a Westland tender, with the result that the company was obliged to bear the cost of producing a new all-metal prototype, the P.V.3. As an insurance against failure to satisfy the army co-operation requirement, the P.V.3 incorporated an entirely new, wide-track, split-axle undercarriage to enable it to carry a torpedo, for it was known that the Admiralty was developing a lightweight torpedo and might, in due course, consider a well-tried aircraft appropriate.

Still retaining the aerodynamically untidy, uncowled Bristol Jupiter XFA radial engine (on the grounds of cost and availability), the P.V.3, carrying the B Conditions marking P3 and fitted with wheel spats, was first flown by Louis Paget in February 1931. It was rushed to Martlesham Heath the following month for performance assessment, but almost immediately the Admiralty halted the development of the new torpedo.

Westland therefore made great efforts during 1931 to optimise the P.V.3 for the army co-operation rôle (removing

The Westland P.V.3 after undergoing conversion as G-ACAZ for the Houston-financed Everest flights of April 1933; note the cabin windows aft of the pilot's cockpit and the Townend ring encircling the Pegasus engine. (Photo: *Flight*, Neg No 12602)

the wheel spats and fitting wing bomb racks and message pick-up hook), and the aircraft returned to the A & AEE for Service evaluation with full military loads in the autumn of that year, prior to an Air Ministry decision whether to confirm the Hart/Audax for general service in India and the Middle East. The P.V.3's Frise ailerons contributed to its generally pleasant handling characteristics, although it was suspected that the untidy engine installation caused

poor airflow over the tailplane and elevator, so that coarse use of elevator was necessary in the final stages of landing, although the Bendix wheelbrakes enabled the aircraft to operate into small airfields with little difficulty. Retention of the Jupiter XFA supercharged engine was unfortunate, as it had already been discarded by the Air Ministry in this rôle. The Westland aeroplane thus failed to gain the A & AEE's recommendation for Service adoption.

Type: Single-engine, two-seat, two-bay experimental army co-operation biplane.

Manufacturer: Westland Aircraft Ltd, Yeovil, Somerset.

Powerplant: As Military Prototype. One 575hp Bristol Jupiter XFA nine-cylinder, air-cooled, supercharged radial engine driving two-blade propeller. As G-ACAZ. One 630hp Bristol Pegasus IS3.

Structure: All-metal construction with duralumin sheet and fabric covering. Two-spar folding wings.

Dimensions: Span, 46ft 6in (folded, 20ft 4in); length, 34ft 2in; height, 11ft 8in; wing area, 500 sq ft.

Weights: Military Prototype. Tare, 3,963lb; all-up, 5,614lb.

Performance: Military Prototype. Max speed, 155 mph at 13,000ft; climb to 10,000ft, 9 min 29 sec; service ceiling, 23,300ft.

Armament: One synchronized 0.303in Vickers machine gun and one Lewis Mk III gun on No 7 Scarff ring on rear cockpit; bomb load of up to two 550lb bombs carried under lower wings.

Prototype: One, P3 (later G-ACAZ and then K4048), first flown by Louis Paget in February 1931. No production.

At Yeovil the P.V.3 remained idle for several months until, in November 1932, it was selected (in company with the P.V.6 Wallace prototype) for use by the 1933 Houston Mount Everest Flying Expedition team, for an attempt to fly over the world's highest mountain. Two major changes were made to suit the aircraft for the undertaking, a change to a 630hp Pegasus IS3 supercharged engine, and replacement of the rear cockpit by an enclosed cabin. In due course the P.V.3, now carrying the civil registration G-ACAZ, was shipped out to India with the Wallace G-ACBR. Flying G-ACAZ from Purnea in Bihar,

Sqn Ldr Lord Clydesdale set out on the 150-mile flight with Lieut Col Stewart Blacker on 19 April 1933 to photograph the summit of Everest.[1]

Once home at Yeovil, G-ACAZ was bought by the Air Ministry in November 1933 and converted to a standard approaching that of a Wallace, with the serial number K4048. It was shown at the 1934 RAF Display at Hendon, underwent various trials with the RAE and, before being employed as a test bed with various Bristol radial engines, flew with No 501 (County of Gloucester) Squadron, Auxiliary Air Force, at Filton. It was ultimately struck off Air

Ministry charge on 30 March 1939, but its ultimate fate is unknown.

[1] Less often remembered, and little publicised at the time, was the fact that a flight by G-ACAZ on 3 April 1933, ever since commemorated as the 'first flight over Everest', brought back photographs of another summit, that of Makalu, 27,790 feet, about ten miles from Everest, evidence of the great difficulty in identifying mountain peaks from the air. The first photographically authenticated flight over Everest was that made on 19 April, and the photographs, much trumpeted in the world Press, on 24 April under the banner headline 'Nature's Last Terrestrial Secret Revealed', did not reveal *Everest's* secrets, being those taken on the 3rd!

Fairey Gordon

The Gordon and Seal had originally been designated the Fairey IIIF Mark V and VI respectively, but were newly named when the aged Napier Lion XIA of the IIIF Mark IV was discarded in favour of thr 525hp Armstrong Siddeley Panther IIA two-row radial engine.

Specification 18/30, prepared around Fairey's proposal to switch to the Panther, reflected the lower installed weight of the radial engine, for roughly the same power and with rather better specific fuel consumption, resulting in an improvement of about 10 per cent in air mileage per gallon. The all-metal airframe of the Type IIIF Mk IVMA was generally tidied up, and the numerous minor improvements were embodied in K1697 while on the production line, this aircraft then being designated the prototype Gordon, and first flown as such by Chris Staniland at Fairey's Harmondsworth aerodrome on 3 March 1931.

K1697 confirmed a generally improved performance, including a take-off ground distance reduced by 15 per cent at a given weight, and a service

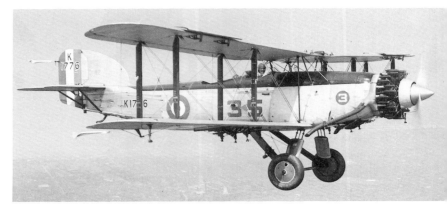

A Gordon I, K1776, of No 35 (Bomber) Squadron; this aircraft, formerly a IIIF Mk IVB, crashed in the Sudan on 27 January 1936. (Photo: *Flight*, Neg No 13335)

ceiling increased by almost 10 per cent. A brief series of performance measurements, which were completed by A & AEE pilots by the end of March, led to negotiation of a new-build contract for 28 Gordons, K1721-K1748, the first eight of which, previously scheduled as IIIF Mk IVBs, would be completed to the same standard as K1697.

The first 12 production aircraft completed were furnished as bomber aircraft (with prone bomb aimer's position) for home service, and were delivered in April direct to No 40 (Bomber)

Squadron at Upper Heyford under the command of Sqn Ldr Malcolm Lincoln Taylor AFC (later Air Vice-Marshal, CBE, AFC); the following 14 Gordons were delivered to the Packing Depot at Ascot for shipment to the Middle East, where they joined No 6 (General Purpose) Squadron in June at Ramleh, Palestine, then commanded by Sqn Ldr John Patrick Coleman AFC (later Air Cdre, CB, AFC), replacing veteran Bristol F.2B Fighters.

A rather larger production order, for 47 Gordons, placed with Fairey at the end of 1931, enabled a second home-based bomber squadron, No 35 at Bircham Newton, to dispose of its Fairey IIIFs in July 1932, as well as bringing the

An early Gordon I, K1740, during seaplane trials with the Marine Aircraft Experimental Establishment at Felixstowe; the numeral '40' on the fuselage is evidence of its previous use by No 40 (Bomber) Squadron. Tropical trials were flown from the waters of the Nile. It was struck off Air Ministry charge in 1939. (Photo: Air Ministry, MAEE, Neg No MH 3014)

A pair of No 47 Squadron Gordons at Khartoum, their engines seeming not to disturb the equanimity of the Sudan Defence Force camels; the aircraft in the foreground, KR1730, is carrying store containers under the wings and is fitted with low pressure tyres. The general arrangement drawing below illustrates the revised tail unit introduced on the Gordon II. (Photo: via R C Sturtivant)

first two Squadrons up to established strength. A second General Purpose Squadron, No 14 at Ramleh, also discarded Fairey IIIFs in favour of Gordons during 1932. The first five Gordons, including two with dual controls, reached No 4 Flying Training School in the Middle East at the end of that year.

The last and largest order for 87 Gordons followed immediately on the heels of the previous batch, deliveries being made between May 1932 and January 1933, particularly to No 207 (Bomber) Squadron at Bircham Newton, starting in September 1932.

No 47 (General Purpose) Squadron, based at Khartoum on the Nile, flew Gordons longer than any other, establishing a routine by which one Flight would operate its aircraft with floats from the waters of the Nile and along the river and the Red Sea coast in concert with the Sudan Defence Force to combat the flourishing slavery and smuggling trades in the area. All the Gordons supplied to No 47 Squadron had the facility of interchangeable wheel/float undercarriage.

Meanwhile a Gordon, K1731, had undergone trials with underwing 75-gallon fuel tanks, intended principally to enable aircraft of No 47 Squadron to undertake much longer patrols; the tanks, however, were not introduced into service as the all-up weight of the Gordon, thus equipped, was well beyond the safe take-off limits in the tropics.

With the onset of Italy's treacherous campaign in Abyssinia in 1935, two of the home-based Gordon Squadrons, Nos 35 and 207, were dispatched to Ed Damer in the Sudan to reinforce No 47;

and at about this time a fighter Squadron, No 29 near Cairo, used a small number of Gordons for night patrols, lest the Italian navy should attempt any offensive action in the Canal Zone.

Further south, No 45 (General Purpose) Squadron sent a detachment to Nairobi, Kenya, equipped with Gordons and, eventually, this formed the nucleus of a new Squadron, No 223, also at Nairobi.

An improved version, the Gordon Mark II, prepared to Specification 14/33, introduced a redesigned fin and rudder (the latter with horn balance), a revised rear fuselage and Frise ailerons. At the same time, low pressure tyres were provided for all Gordons serving in the Middle East — a most welcome provision. Only 24 Gordon IIs were, however, produced, and all but one were shipped to the Middle East in 1934. Thirteen of them were shipped to the Royal New Zealand Air Force in May 1939, as well as Mark Is from earlier batches.

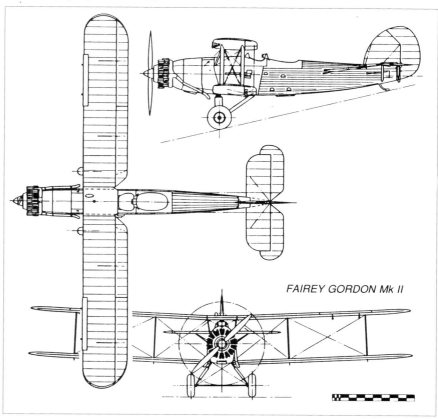

FAIREY GORDON Mk II

Although the Gordon had only recently been removed from front-line service when war broke out in September 1939, about 40 examples remained with second-line units, engaged in target towing and communications duties until around mid-1941. It had been a popular aeroplane in service and, despite a poor reputation said to attach to the Panther engine, returned one of the RAF's best serviceability records in the Middle East during the 1930s.

Type: Single-engine, two-seat, two-bay biplane general purpose/day bomber.

Air Ministry Specifications: 18/30 and 14/33.

Manufacturer: The Fairey Aviation Co Ltd, Hayes, Middlesex.

Powerplant: One 525hp Armstrong Siddeley Panther IIA 14-cylinder air-cooled two-row radial engine driving 2-blade propeller.

Dimensions: Span, 45ft 9in; length, 36ft 9in; height, 14ft 2in; wing area, 438 sq ft.

Weights: Tare, 3,891lb; all-up, 5,809lb.

Performance: Max speed, 140 mph at 6,500ft; climb to 10,000ft, 12 min 55 sec; service ceiling, 17,100ft; range, 560 miles.

Armament: One synchronized 0.303in Vickers machine gun mounted on the port side of the centre fuselage, and one Lewis gun with Fairey low-drag mounting on rear cockpit. Short-range bomb load of up to two 250lb bombs (usually two 230lb or four 112lb bombs).

Prototype: One, K1697 (originally Fairey IIIF Mk IVMA, converted to IIIF Mark V, then renamed Gordon), first flown by C S Staniland on 3 March 1931 at Harmondsworth.

Production: A total of 162 Gordon Mark Is was built (to Specification 18/30): K1721-K1748 (28, of which the first 8 were converted from IIIF Mk IVB during production); K2603-K2649 (47, of which 2 were supplied to the RNZAF); K2683-K2769 (87, of which 2 were supplied the RNZAF, and 3 to the Royal Egyptian Air Force); 24 Gordon Mark IIs built to Specification 14/33, K3986-K4009 (of which 13 were supplied to the RNZAF). In addition a further 79 Fairey IIIFs were converted to Gordons, between S1178 and S1203, between J9062 and J9828 and between K1159 and K1778.

Summary of RAF Service: Gordons served with No 40 (Bomber) Sqn from April 1931 until November 1935 at Upper Heyford and Abingdon; No 6 (General Purpose) Sqn from June 1931 until November 1935 at Ramleh, Palestine; No 35 (Bomber) Sqn from July 1932 until August 1937 at Bircham Newton and in the Sudan; No 14 (General Purpose) Sqn from September 1932 until June 1938 at Ramleh, Palestine; No 207 (Bomber) Sqn from September 1932 until August 1937 at Bircham Newton and in the Sudan; No 47 (General Purpose) Sqn from January 1933 until June 1939 at Khartoum, Sudan; No 45 (General Purpose) Sqn from January until December 1936 at Nairobi, Kenya; No 29 (Fighter) Sqn from March until August 1936 at Amriya, Egypt; and one Flight of No 223 (General Purpose) Sqn from December 1936 until February 1937 at Nairobi, Kenya. Gordons also served with Nos 3 and 8 Armament Training Camps, Nos 1, 4 and 8 Flying Training Schools, No 1 Air Observers' School and No 1 Anti-Aircraft Co-operation Unit.

The fifth production Seal, K3481, of No 821 (Fleet Spotter Reconnaissance) Squadron from HMS Courageous. This aeroplane continued in service until May 1939. (Photo: A J Jackson Collection)

Fairey Seal

Although the Air Ministry raised a Specification (12/29) covering the Fairey IIIF Mark VI *before* that of the Mark V (the Gordon), it was not until 27 November 1931 that a prototype was flown, when Christopher Staniland took a converted IIIF, S1325, aloft — this Panther IIA-powered three-seater for the Fleet Air Arm being named the Seal.

However, as production got underway with the Gordon, further work was required on the Seal to satisfy Specification 12/29 fully. The prototype, fitted with floats, was flown by Staniland at Hamble on 29 September 1932. Indeed, preoccupation with pro-duction of the Gordon I resulted in the Seal's Service standard of preparation moving in advance of the Gordon II, with the result that a fairly late production Seal (K3577) became the Gordon II prototype.

The first production order was placed for 11 Seals early in 1932, these featuring Frise ailerons, a fin of increased aspect ratio and an A-frame arrester hook under the rear fuselage (the latter

A mid-production Seal, K3577, experimentally powered by a Panther VI engine in long-chord cowling; although continuing to be referred to as a Seal, this aeroplane was employed as the prototype Gordon Mark II, even though the engine installation remained experimental. (Photo: The Fairey Aviation Co Ltd.)

becoming commonplace as the Royal Navy's carriers introduced the transverse system of arrester cables), and a tailwheel replaced the long-established skid. All these features predated their introduction in the Gordon (which, of course, was not fitted with the deck arrester hook).

The first four production Seals were flown before the end of November 1932 and were delivered to No 444 (Fleet Reconnaissance Catapult) Flight before the end of the year, and were shortly embarked in ships of the 2nd Battle Squadron in home waters.

The first Squadron to fly Seals aboard a carrier was No 821 (Spotter Reconnaissance), commanded temporarily by Flt Lt (Lt, RN) Richard Anthony Peyton RAF at Gosport in April 1933. The following month, command of the Squadron was assumed by Sqn Ldr B E Harrison AFC, RAF, as it embarked in HMS *Courageous*. For two years the carrier remained in home waters, but in August 1935 she joined the Mediterranean Fleet for the duration of the Abyssinian crisis, sailing frequently between Malta and Alexandria.

HMS *Courageous* embarked a second Seal Squadron, No 820, for six months in 1934, commanded at the outset by Lt Cdr (Sqn Ldr) Anthony Paul Colthurst, but succeeded by Lt Cdr (later Rear Admiral, CB) Matthew Sausse Slattery in August that year. The Seals were, however, replaced by Blackburn Shark torpedo bombers in December.

Seals eventually equipped eight Fleet Air Arm Squadrons, although at no time were they serving simultaneously with more than four. Only with No 824 Squadron were they deployed east of Suez when, on 6 January 1935, they arrived at Hong Kong in HMS *Hermes*. For the next three years this carrier remained on the China Station but, in

April 1937, while at Seletar, Singapore, the Seals were exchanged for Swordfish.

During their service with the carriers HMS *Courageous, Eagle, Furious* and *Glorious*, the Seals seldom flew with floats, but occasionally took part in fleet exercises, attacking makeshift targets with 112lb bombs. No 824 was the last carrier-borne Squadron to fly Seals, the aircraft thereafter equipping No 701 Catapult Squadron at Kalafrana, Malta;

fitted with floats, they were sometimes hoisted aboard the battleships HMS *Barham, Malaya* and *Valiant* with the Mediterranean Fleet.

The last Seals in service were those of No 782 Squadron, commanded by Lt Cdr A Goodfellow RNVR, its rôle being, in effect, a communications unit serving the outlying naval air stations in northern Scotland, the Orkneys, Shetlands and Northern Ireland.

Type: Single-engine, three-seat, two-bay biplane fleet spotter/reconnaissance bomber.
Air Ministry Specifications: 12/29 and 24/32
Manufacturer: The Fairey Aviation Co Ltd, Hayes, Middlesex.
Powerplant: One 525hp Armstrong Siddeley Panther IIA 14-cylinder, air-cooled, two-row radial engine driving 2-blade Fairey metal propeller; also Panther IIIA and VI, Bristol Pegasus IIIM3, and Napier Lion XI.
Dimensions: Span, 45ft 9in; length, 33ft 8in (seaplane, 35ft 4in); height, 12ft 9in (seaplane, 14ft 4in); wing area, 443.5 sq ft.
Weights: All-up, 6,000lb (seaplane, 6,400lb).
Performance: Landplane. Max speed, 138 mph; climb to 5,000ft, 5 min 20 sec; service ceiling, 17,000ft; range, 480 miles. Seaplane. Max speed, 129 mph; service ceiling, 13,900ft; range, 440 miles.
Armament: One synchronized 0.303in Vickers machine gun on port side of fuselage and one Lewis gun on Fairey mounting in rear cockpit. Bomb load of up to two 250lb bombs.
Prototype: One, S1325 (previously a Fairey IIIF Mk IIIB), first flown as a Seal landplane by C S Staniland at Harmondsworth on 11 September 1930, and as a seaplane at Hamble on 29 September 1932.
Production: A total of 91 Seals was built for the Fleet Air Arm: K3477-K3487, K3514-K3545, K3575-K3579, K4201-K4225 and K4779-K4796. (In addition six were sold to Peru, four to Latvia, two to Chile and one to Argentina).
Summary of Service with the Fleet Air Arm: Seals served with No 444 (Fleet Reconnaissance Catapult) Flight with the 2nd Battle Squadron between December 1932 and December 1933; No 821 (Fleet Spotter Reconnaissance) Sqn aboard HMS *Courageous* between April 1933 and March 1936; No 820 (Fleet Spotter Reconnaissance) Sqn aboard HMS *Courageous* between June and December 1934; No 824 (Fleet Spotter Reconnaissance) Sqn aboard HMS *Eagle* between October 1934 and April 1937; No 823 (Fleet Spotter Reconnaissance) Sqn aboard HMS *Glorious* between December 1934 and December 1936; No 822 (Fleet Spotter Reconnaissance) Sqn aboard HMS *Furious* between June and November 1936; No 701 (Catapult) Sqn at Kalafrana, Malta, between November 1936 and February 1938; No 702 (Catapult) Sqn at Mount Batten between February 1937 and October 1938; No 753 (Training) Sqn at Lee-on-Solent during 1939; and No 782 (Armament Training) Sqn at Donibristle from December 1940 to January 1941.

de Havilland D.H.72 B.22/27 Canberra

The heavy bomber Specification B.19/27 was still in rough draft form when work began on a more optimistic requirement, to be spelt out in Specification B.22/27. Determined not to be

sidetracked by consideration of new engines of high-cost development, which were beginning to proliferate during 1927-29, the Air Ministry opted to state a starting point preference for three

The D.H.72, J9184, shown fitted with its bomb racks beneath the centre fuselage. As far as is known, the name Canberra was not officially recognised by the Air Ministry. (Photo: The de Havilland Aircraft Co Ltd.)

tail controls impossibly heavy.

The engines originally selected for the prototype, J9184, ordered in the autumn of 1927 — Jupiter VIs — were replaced, first by 595hp Jupiter XFS engines, and later by Jupiter XIS engines.

As the aircraft spanned 95 feet, it was necessary to incorporate wing folding and, to support an aeroplane that would weigh over 20,000lb all-up, a four-wheel undercarriage was included, each pair of wheels being provided with two oleo legs and a cross-axle beneath the two lower engines.

Such was the heavy weather being made at Stag Lane, the Air Ministry agreed that J9184 should be moved to the Gloster Aircraft Company's factory at Brockworth; with it went George Carter who, under Henry Folland's direction, steered the huge aeroplane through final assembly and preparation for first flight.

This flight was made at Brockworth on 27 July 1931. All appears to have gone fairly satisfactorily, and J9184 paid a short visit to Farnborough for a cursory structural inspection before being delivered to Martlesham Heath on 24 Nov-

Jupiter engines but, at the same time, demanded defensive gun positions in the nose and tail of the fuselage — and, by considering such design minutiae, dictated the basic aircraft configuration; some would say that it compromised the entire Requirement.

Several tenders to this Specification were received late in 1927, and these suggested that designers were experiencing difficulty in equating performance demands with load and airframe strength requirements. As a result, the Specification underwent a number of amendments which were thought likely to favour certain companies' particular forte in large aircraft design, and all but two tenders were withdrawn. They were, perhaps surprisingly, the de Havilland D.H.72 and the Boulton and Paul P.32.

Handicapped by a relative lack of experience in metal construction in large aircraft, design and assembly of the prototype de Havilland D.H.72 seemed to take an unconscionable age, the aircraft appearing to be little more than a scaled-up version of the company's wooden D.H.66 Hercules three-engine airliner. Even the name, Canberra, sel-

ected provisionally by de Havilland, seemed to connote an extension to the series of predominantly Empire cities after which D.H.66s were named.[1]

However, as if to compound the difficulties at Stag Lane, because of the stated need to include a nose gunner's cockpit, it was necessary to incorporate the centre engine in the upper wing centresection, a location that introduced a number of complications, not least in balancing the longitudinal and directional stability and control qualities of the aircraft. To have perpetuated the biplane empennage with triple fins and rudders might well have rendered the

[1] City of Delhi, City of Perth, City of Adelaide, City of Cape Town, City of Jodhpur and City of Karachi, to mention the most apt.

Type: Three-engine, four-crew, three-bay biplane heavy night bomber.
Air Ministry Specification: B.22/27
Manufacturers: Manufacture initiated by de Havilland Aircraft Co Ltd, Stag Lane, Edgware, Middlesex; completed by Gloster Aircraft Co Ltd, Hucclecote, Gloucester.
Powerplant: Three 595hp Bristol Jupiter XFS (later Jupiter XIS) radial engines.
Dimensions: Span, 95ft 0in. All-up Weight: 21,462lb.
Performance: No record traced.
Armament: Provision made for single Lewis machine guns on nose and tail gunners' positions with Scarff rings. Bomb load said to be ten 250lb bombs carried on external racks under the fuselage.
Prototype: One, J9184, first flown on 27 July 1931 at Brockworth. No production.

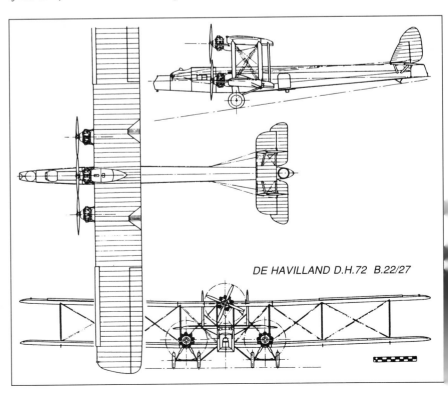

DE HAVILLAND D.H.72 B.22/27

ember for full-load trials with No 22 Squadron.

No full trial report appears to have been compiled at the A & AEE as it was

Boulton & Paul P.32

John North's P.32 design to Specification B.22/27 was probably favoured with an Air Ministry prototype contract, late in 1927, on account of the high regard in which his twin-engine Sidestrand medium bomber was held by RAF pilots, for it was made clear in the P.32 design proposal that it was closely related to the earlier aircraft.

Like the D.H.72, the third Jupiter engine was located on the upper wing centresection, the wings being, like those of the Sidestrand, square-tipped; the four-wheel undercarriage comprised what were, in effect, four Sidestrand wheel structures, with handed struts and an oleo leg for each wheel. The fuselage profile was clearly derived from that of the earlier bomber but the tail unit comprised large twin fins and rudders, each with Flettner tabs. Unlike the D.H.72, the P.32 was provided with a tailwheel.

In order to allow adequate ground clearance for loading bombs under the fuselage without increasing the height and weight of the undercarriage, the lower wing sections inboard of the engines were provided with marked anhedral.

The prototype, J9950, is believed to have first flown in January 1931 at Norwich, but suffered severe engine overheating, causing the Jupiter XF engines to be replaced by Jupiter XFBMs, provided with Townend rings and driving two-piece four-blade propellers.

It is believed that the aircraft was re-assembled at Martlesham Heath during

becoming apparent that Air Ministry interest in very large bombing aeroplanes was waning (to some extent influenced by the attitudes currently

the summer of 1931 and first flown there in its modified form on 23 October 1931. It underwent full load tests with No 22 Squadron of the A & AEE during the winter, but was thoroughly disliked by every pilot who flew it. The flying controls were found to be exceptionally heavy in all three axes; the elevator response was considered to be dangerously sluggish, particularly when landing with the upper engine throttled. Great care was needed, in the event of overshooting, not to open the centre engine throttle too far or too fast as the nose-down trim change would almost certainly be beyond the pilot's ability to control. The Flettner tabs, much appreciated on the Sidestrand, were found on the P.32 to demand coarse adjustment to correct the smallest trim changes. The cockpit was said to be cramped and poorly laid out, the pilot being provided with a shatter-prone plate-glass windscreen!

The unfavourable reception of the P.32 was of academic importance for,

being expressed at the Geneva Disarmament Conference), and in September 1932 the Requirement was formally withdrawn.

as already mentioned, Specification B.22/27 was withdrawn later in 1932. The aircraft was nevertheless shown at the 1932 Hendon Display, and continued flying at the RAE until 1934, much of the time being spent investigating the effects of the Flettner tabs.

Type: Three-engine, four-crew, three-bay biplane night heavy bomber.
Air Ministry Specification: B.22/27.
Manufacturer: Boulton & Paul Ltd, Riverside, Norwich, Norfolk.
Powerplant: Three 555hp Bristol Jupiter XF 9-cylinder radial engines; later changed to 575hp Jupiter XFBM engines.
Dimensions: Span, 100ft; length, 69ft.
Weight: All-up, 22,800lb.
Performance: No record traced.
Armament: Provision for single Lewis guns with Scarff rings on nose, midships and tail gunners' positions; bomb load reported to have been up to nine 250lb bombs.
Prototype: One, J9950, said to have been flown by Flt Lt C A Rae in January 1931 at Mousehold, Norwich. No production.

Two views of the P.32, showing the complex levered-suspension undercarriage, the anhedral on the lower wing centresection, engine Townend rings, Flettner tabs and wingtip slats. (Photos: via R C B Ashworth (upper) and Boulton Paul Aircraft Ltd, Neg No 017, via Alec Brew)

Vickers Type 163

Rex Pierson's Type 163 was, in many respects, an outstanding aeroplane, completed too late for consideration in the context of the heavy bomber Specification B.19/27, designed to meet the new bomber transport Specification C.16/28, but eliminated owing to an Air Ministry misunderstanding of engine performance figures, and not entered for the heavy bomber Specification B.22/27 — all of whose performance and load requirements the Type 163 showed itself capable of exceeding. Unfortunately, failure to gain official support placed Vickers under a considerable financial burden that was fortunately shortlived when the Air Ministry changed direction in its future bomber requirements, and lost interest in both B.22/27 and C.16/28.

Vickers' Type 150 was just starting construction towards the end of 1928 under the design terms of B.19/27 when the Air Ministry's DTD invited several manufacturers to tender to a new Specification, C.16/28, for what was termed a 'bomber transport'. Like so many Requirements being formulated in the late-1920s, the initial draft was couched in fairly general terms, and invited manufacturers' comments so that more specific design parameters might be included in a formal Specification. What, however, was immediately clear was that the aircraft now being sought was not intended to emulate the rôle being performed by the Handley Page Clive and Vickers Victoria (as the Requirement suggested), that is to say the movement of soldiers by aircraft which, in a secondary rôle, could be used to drop bombs.

The Air Ministry had in mind an aircraft capable of carrying thirty fully-armed troops or *an equal weight of bombs* — a bomb load of not less than 6,000lb, very much in excess of that carried by any previous British bomber. Clearly the bomb load accommodation would determine the power and configuration of the aircraft and, in couching the Specification in these terms, the Air Ministry had inadvertently created an entirely new category of heavy bomber. It required little expertise to understand that 6,000lb of human beings required very different accommodation from that required by 6,000lb of bombs, unless the bomb load could be racked in a dual-purpose cabin/bomb bay. By good for-

The private venture Vickers Type 163, O-2, as it appeared at the 1932 Hendon Display carrying the New Type No 11 on the fuselage. It had appeared at the previous year's display, but without the huge wheel spats. Note the very small tail surfaces. (Photo: Vickers (Aviation) Ltd.)

tune or by clever reasoning, this dual-rôle capability requirement was to be demanded in numerous heavy bomber Specifications during the coming decade, and thereby dominated the design of almost every RAF heavy bomber of the Second World War, even though the secondary troop-carrying rôle was to reappear in very different circumstances from those envisaged in 1928. Thus, despite its superficial classification as a transport Specification, C.16/28 was primarily a bomber requirement in every respect but in name.

Rex Pierson submitted his observations on the Specification early in 1929, pointing out that an aircraft required to carry 6,000lb of bombs at 10,000 feet required much more power than the 1,700hp available from three of the preferred engines mentioned in the Specification; as a result of these comments, the Specification was altered to allow four engines, and relaxed to reduce the statutory bomb load to 3,000lb.

Because of delays resulting from these changes in the bomber transport Specification, Vickers decided to go ahead with the Type 163, intending that it should be entered as a private venture to B.19/27, as well as a *de facto* entry under C.16/28. However, when calculating the design performance of the Type 163, Rex Pierson's staff used engine performance figures achieved during the type test of the Rolls-Royce F.XIV

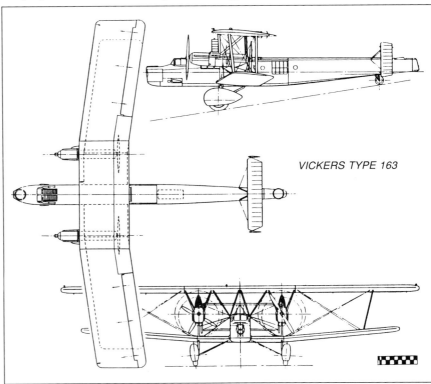

VICKERS TYPE 163

engines; these proved rather better than the design figures supplied to the Air Ministry by Rolls-Royce. The DTD therefore severely reduced the Vickers figures, believing them to be over-optimistic, and the Air Ministry accordingly informed Vickers that the Type 163 prototype would not be purchased.

Not being a contracted prototype, the Vickers 163 did not qualify to receive production Rolls-Royce Kestrel IIIS engines, but eventually Vickers managed to secure four of the earlier F.XIVs. Bearing in mind the failure by the Type 163 to gain evaluation, it is perhaps strange that efforts were not made to seek A & AEE assessment under Specification B.19/27 but, following the first flight of 'O-2' (made at Brooklands on 12 January 1931 by 'Mutt' Summers, with John Radcliffe as observer), the aircraft suffered repeated engine overheating, forcing a decision to revert to the steam condenser system used on the Type 150, which necessitated

lengthy modification to the Type 163.

Thus it was that the Type 163 did not arrive at Martlesham until 15 February 1932 for full-load tests with No 22 Squadron. In the course of these the Service pilots expressed dissatisfaction with the directional control, as they had on the Type 150. One can only conjecture that to have embarked on expensive redesign of the whole tail unit would

have imposed an unjustifiably high cost, particularly when it was rumoured that the Air Ministry was losing interest in pursuing further large biplanes. As it was, at a time of industrial depression, Vickers could be thankful that at least the expenditure on the Type 163 would be offset by continuing work on rebuilding Virginia biplane bombers for several years to come.

Type: Four-engine, four-crew, two-bay biplane heavy night bomber transport.

Air Ministry Specifications: Private venture to B.19/27 and C.16/28.

Manufacturer: Vickers (Aviation) Ltd, Weybridge, Surrey.

Powerplant: Four 480hp Rolls-Royce F.XIVS (later Kestrel IIIS) 12-cylinder evaporatively-cooled, supercharged in-line engines mounted in tandem pairs, the front engines driving 2-blade propellers and the rear driving 4-blade propellers of reduced diameter.

Dimensions: Span, 90ft 0in; length, 66ft 9in; height, 22ft 4in; wing area, 1,918 sq ft.

Weight: All-up, 25,700lb.

Performance: Max speed, 160 mph at 6,500ft; climb to 10,000ft, 18 min 15 sec; service ceiling, 25,200ft; range, 1,150 miles at 140 mph.

Armament: Single Lewis guns in nose and tail gunners' position; bomb load of up to twelve 250lb bombs recessed into underside of fuselage, and four 20lb sighting bombs. (Provision also made to accommodate 10 fully-armed troops as alternative to bomb load.)

Prototype: One, given B Conditions marking O-2, first flown on 12 January 1931 by Capt J Summers (with John Radcliffe as observer) at Brooklands. No production.

Gloster TC.33

Although the Gloster Aircraft Company was, throughout its long life, best known for its fighters, which included such famous aeroplanes as the Grebe, Gamecock, Gladiator, Meteor and Javelin, it also produced a number of other interesting aircraft, not least of which was the very big TC.33 bomber transport prototype, designed to Specification C.16/28, which was fortunate enough to attract an Air Ministry order.

Unlike Rex Pierson at Vickers, Henry Folland at Gloster chose to interpret the Requirement as being primarily for a transport, which might also perform a bombing rôle. Nevertheless, with the start of design work delayed until 1930, it was possible to exploit the Specification's relaxation by adopting the four-engine configuration and, having an Air Ministry order, Gloster was able to obtain production Kestrel IIIS engines, two of which were installed in the front of nacelles located at mid-wing gap; Kestrel IIS engines drove pusher propellers at the rear.

The TC.33 was an equal-span, two-bay biplane with pronounced anhedral on the inboard sections of the lower wing so as to maintain a generous gap and at the same time allow an unre-

J9832 at Martlesham Heath with its Hendon New Type No 6 on the nose. The condensers for the front Kestrel IIIS were mounted above the engine; the radiators for the rear Kestrel IIS were located beneath the nacelle. (Photo: Air Ministry, A & AEE, Neg Ref 7288C)

stricted cabin by passing the spars over the top. Accommodation was provided for only ten troops.

Despite its size and weight, the aircraft possessed single mainwheels on either side, mounted directly below each engine, with separate oleo structures to permit easy access to a large freight hatch in the underside of the front fuselage. A biplane tail unit with twin fins and rudders was included. It is said that provision was made for a 3,580lb bomb load on under-fuselage racks, but no record has been located to show that this load was ever carried.

The prototype, J9832, was first flown

by Capt Howard Saint on 23 February 1932, and the aircraft appeared at that year's Hendon Display as New Type No 6. A long period of trials followed at Martlesham Heath from October 1932 until September 1933, and these confirmed the opinion that, although the aircraft satisfied almost all the demands of the relaxed Specification, it was simply too big and unwieldy for Service use. By 1933, moreover, the RAF was changing course in its heavy bomber demands, and a new troop-carrier Specification, C.26/31, was on the table, as the Service began to come to terms with the approach of the monoplane era.

Type: Four-engine, four/five-crew, two-bay biplane heavy night bomber transport.

Air Ministry Specification: C.16/28.

Manufacturer: The Gloster Aircraft Co Ltd, Hucclecote, Gloucester.

Powerplant: Two 580hp Rolls-Royce Kestrel IIIS 12-cylinder tractor engines and two 580hp Kestrel IIS pusher engines arranged in tandem pairs in wing-gap nacelles and driving two-blade propellers.

Dimensions: Span, 95ft 1in; length, 80ft 0in; height, 25ft 8in; wing area, 2,493 sq ft.

Weights: Tare, 19,063lb; all-up, 29,004lb.

Performance: Max speed, 141 mph at 13,000ft; climb to 6,500ft, 16 min 26 sec; service ceiling, 19,100ft.

Armament: Single Lewis guns in nose and tail positions; max bomb load, 3,580lb, comprising fourteen 250lb and four 20lb bombs; alternative accommodation for ten fully-armed troops or military freight.

Prototype: One, J9832, first flown by Capt Howard Saint at Brockworth on 23 February 1932. No production.

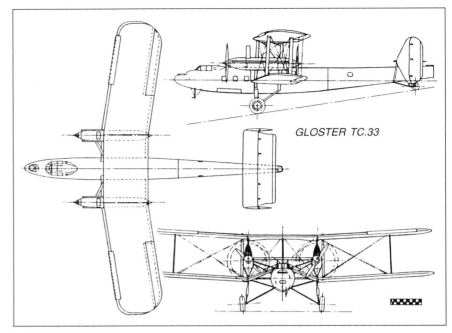

GLOSTER TC.33

Handley Page H.P.43

It would have been almost unthinkable for Frederick Handley Page's company to decline to tender a design to Specification C.16/28 and, like Folland at Gloster, George Volkert chose to give the troop transport element of this Requirement almost exclusive emphasis, rather than that of the heavy bomber.

It so happened that Volkert and Boultbee had been engaged in the preliminary design of a large four-engine airliner for Imperial Airways — later to gain lasting fame as the H.P.42 Hannibal Series. Anxious not to attract complex problems associated with tandem engines which, in their solution, would have added to the cost of spares and maintenance in commercial operation[1], Volkert opted to arrange the engines as tractors on the leading edge of the upper and lower wings in a compact co-planar group. The interplane struts were arranged to form a large Warren truss, with the engine nacelles located at its

---

[1] It was, by the mid-1920s, fully understood that the power required from front and rear engines in a tandem pair differed considerably, this being achieved by a number of alternative expedients, such as the use of different engine types, use of two- and four-blade propellers, and propellers of different diameter.

The Handley Page H.P.43, J9833, at Radlett. The integrally-stepped pilot's cabin enclosure was relatively uncommon among military aircraft of the period. (Photo: Flight, Neg No 5395)

inboard apices, thereby distributing thrust, drag, lift and landing stresses to the wing and fuselage structures with the minimum possible weight penalty.

This arrangement was selected for Handley Page's C.16/28 design tender, the H.P.43, although, with only three engines included in the design, the overall dimensions and weights were generally scaled down by about ten per cent. It was said to have been capable of carrying 30 'fully-armed' troops, but this is extremely improbable on the power available from the three early Pegasus IM3 radials. It is also thought most unlikely that more than token bomb loads were ever carried on test, or that the bomb load exceeded 3,000lb.

The prototype, J9833, purchased eventually by the Air Ministry for £41,250, was first flown at Radlett by Major Cordes on 21 June 1932. Despite efforts to get the aeroplane ready for the Hendon Display, a week later, Cordes expressed considerable disappointment with the H.P.43's handling, and it was not shown at Hendon until 1933. It was flown by Martlesham pilots, but no formal report was raised as Handley Page had formally applied to the Air Ministry to convert this aircraft to a monoplane and tender it to the new Specification C.26/31 as the H.P.51.

Nevertheless, the Service pilots were agreed that, for all its graceful appearance, the H.P.43 was grossly underpowered, and that its controls were sluggish and badly harmonised. In its biplane configuration, it certainly fell far short of the requirements set out in C.16/28.

Yet for all its inauspicious conception, the H.P.43's later transformation into the monoplane H.P.51 represented the opening of an exceptionally prolific and succesful chapter in Handley Page's history.

Type: Three-engine, four-crew, two-bay biplane heavy night bomber transport.
Air Ministry Specification: C.16/28.
Manufacturer: Handley Page Ltd, Cricklewood, London, and Radlett, Herts.
Powerplant: Three 580hp Bristol Pegasus IM3 nine-cylinder air-cooled radial engines driving two-piece, four-blade propellers.
Dimensions: Span, 114ft 0in; length, 75ft 9in. *Weight:* All-up, 22,500lb.
Performance: Max speed, 116 mph at 6,500ft; max range, 1,200 miles.
Armament: Single Lewis guns with No 12 Scarff rings on nose and tail positions; bomb load said to be up to twelve 250lb bombs; probably never carried.
Prototype: One, J9833, first flown by Major J L B H Cordes at Radlett on 21 June 1932. No production.

Westland P.V.6 and Wallace

The Westland Wallace was a product of the Depression in the early 1930s. With the Wapiti still in production and no Requirement issued for an eventual replacement, Arthur Davenport set to work in 1930 to incorporate limited improvements in the earlier aircraft, his object being to create an all-purpose aeroplane as a private venture at a time when standardisation would be attractive to the Air Ministry, particularly if existing Wapitis could be modified at no significant expense.

One of the Wapiti Mark V airframes, G-AAWA, was selected as the new prototype, being temporarily referred to as the Wapiti VII. The cross-axle undercarriage was discarded in favour of divided units with differential brakes and wheel spats added. The engine was changed to a 550hp Pegasus IIM3 with a Townend ring and, in due course, new formers were introduced in the forward half of the fuselage to increase its width and improve its aerodynamic shape.

By the summer of 1931 so many other modifications had been made (including revised tail surfaces and improved Frise

The Westland P.V.6 during Service assessment at Martlesham Heath in 1932. The tailwheel was one obvious advance on the Wapiti, though wheel spats, commonplace on aeroplanes of the 1930s, were not popular among servicing personnel. (Photo: Westland Aircraft Ltd.)

ailerons) that the aircraft was re-termed the P.V.6. It was first flown by Harald Penrose at Yeovil on 31 October that year and an application was entered by Westland for the Air Ministry to accept the aeroplane for assessment by the A & AEE — an application which appears to have been accepted with some reluctance. Nevertheless, there could be no denying that the P.V.6 represented a significant improvement on the Wapiti IIA, returning a maximum speed about 20 mph higher, and possessing pleasant though still rather heavy controls; the new Dunlop differential brakes were

especially appreciated. However, it was inevitable that comparisons would be drawn with the Hawker Hart and Audax.

Notwithstanding the Hawker aeroplanes' demonstrated superiority (having been safely dived at 240 mph, for instance, compared with the P.V.6's maximum of 210 mph), the Air Ministry awarded a 'consolation' production contract for eight aircraft, to be named the Wallace and to conform to a new Specification, 19/32.

The P.V.6 was re-engined, first with a 655hp Pegasus IV, and shortly afterwards with a 587hp Pegasus IM3. At the same time, as an interim step, twelve early Wapiti IIAs were returned to Yeovil for conversion to Wallace Mark I (19/32) standard. It was, however, made clear by the Air Ministry that the Wallace would not equip first-

Converted from Wapiti IIA, K1362, this Wallace I, K3672, wears the markings of No 501 (City of Bristol) Squadron in 1934. It later served with Nos 2 and 3 Armament Training Camps and No 3 Bombing & Gunnery School, being destroyed in a flying accident on 4 March 1940. (Photo: A J Jackson Collection)

The original P.V.6, modified as the G.31/35 Wallace Mark II prototype, K3488, during trials with underwing bombs and the distinguishing enclosed cockpits; the lines on the centre and rear fuselage sides were zip-fastners in the fabric, giving access to structure and equipment. (Photo: Westland Aircraft Ltd.)

line squadrons, nor would it be deployed overseas, and the first deliveries were duly made in January 1933 to No 501 (City of Bristol) Squadron of the Special Reserve at Filton, commanded by Sqn Ldr William Elliot DFC (later Air Chief Marshal Sir William, GCVO, KCB, KBE, DFC*).

No further new-build Wallace Mark Is were ordered, and three further Special Reserve Squadrons received converted Wapitis. Indeed, by the summer of 1934 it seemed likely that the Air Ministry would not order any further Wapiti conversions. (The P.V.6 had, in the meantime, been selected to accompany the P.V.3 to India for the Everest flights, see page 222).

With the deterioration of the political situation in Europe, *vis-à-vis* the onset of German rearmament and the plans to set in train considerable expansion of the Royal Air Force, the Wallace was one of a number of aircraft types selected for use as bombing and gunnery trainers, as well as trainers for air observers and for anti-aircraft co-operation. Specification G.31/35 was raised to cover an improved Wallace Mark II, to be powered by the 665hp Pegasus IV engine, the crew being provided with enclosed cockpits. The prototype of this version was none other than the aged P.V.6, now returned from India and at last dignified by the allocation of a military serial, K3488.

A total of 107 Wallace IIs was ordered, with replacement deliveries to the Special Reserve Squadrons beginning on 31 December 1935; the accompanying table indicates the wide range of training units subsequently equipped with Wallaces during the Expansion period — the Air Observers' School formed at North Coates, Lincolnshire, in 1938, at one time possessing on charge no fewer than 36 Wallaces. Some aircraft were fitted with wind-driven target winches for drogue towing with Bombing and Gunnery Schools and the AACU at Biggin Hill. A Wallace, flown as an experimental tanker, gave a demonstration of in-flight refuelling of a Hawker Hart during the 1935 Hendon Display.

The Wallace showed itself to be a sound if somewhat pedestrian aeroplane, conceived at a time of defence austerity, yet conveniently available for accelerated production when a sturdy, reliable and vice-free aircraft was needed quickly. The old biplane, whose origins dated back to the Wapiti's maiden flight in 1927 — complete with its mandatory D.H.9A components — continued to give valuable, albeit unglamorous, service until 1943.

Type: Single-engine, two-seat, two-bay general purpose biplane.
Air Ministry Specifications: 19/32, 7/33, 9/33 and G.31/35 (Mk II).
Manufacturer: Westland Aircraft Works Ltd, Yeovil, Somerset.
Powerplant: Mark I. One 550hp Bristol Pegasus II 9-cylinder air-cooled geared, radial engine driving 2-blade wooden propeller. Mark II. 665hp Bristol Pegasus IV geared and supercharged engine.
Dimensions: Span, 46ft 5in; length, 34ft 2in; height, 11ft 6in; wing span, 488 sq ft.
Weights: Mark I. Tare, 3,792lb; all-up, 5,635lb. Mark II. Tare, 3,867lb; all-up, 5,792lb.
Performance: Max speed, 158 mph at 15,000ft; climb to 10,000ft, 8 min 45 sec; service ceiling, 22,200ft.
Armament: One synchronized 0.303in Vickers machine gun in the port side of the fuselage, and one Lewis gun with Scarff ring or low-drag mounting on the rear cockpit. Bomb load of up to 580lb, comprising combinations of 250lb, 200lb or lighter bombs.
Prototype: One, G-AAWA/P6, formerly referred to as the Wapiti Mk VII and P.V.6, first flown by Harald Penrose at Yeovil on 31 October 1931.
Production: A total of eight new Wallace Mark Is was built, K3906-K3913; in addition, 58 Wallace Is were produced by conversion of Wapiti IIAs and VI, being allocated new serial numbers: K3462-K3573, K3664-K3677, K4010, K4012-K4020, K4337-K4345, K5071-K5082 and K5116 (the latter formerly the civil Wallace G-ACJU). 107 new Wallace Mark IIs: K4346-K4348, K6012-K6086 and K8674-K8702.
Summary of Service: Wallaces served with No 501 (City of Bristol), 502 (Ulster), 503 (County of Lincoln) and 504 (County of Nottingham) Squadron, Special Reserve, between January 1933 and May 1937; they also served at the Royal Air Force College, Cranwell, and with Anti-Aircraft Co-operation Units, Air Armament Schools, Air Observers' Schools, Armament Training Camps and Station, Bombing and Gunnery Schools, Electrical and Wireless Schools, and Ground Defence Gunners' Schools.

Blackburn B-3 (M.1/30)

Specification M.1/30 was issued by the Director of Technical Development,

Air Cdre Felton Vesey Holt, CMG, DSO, on 22 March 1930, setting out the requirement for an aircraft to replace the Lion-powered Blackburn Ripon torpedo bomber, and capable of operating from the new carriers, HMS *Glorious* and *Courageous*. The Specification superseded another, M.5/28, which had made

demands that were impossible to meet, bearing in mind the design preferences expressed and the general level of knowledge of the strength characteristics of light alloy structures.

These opinions had been reached independently by the design staffs at both Blackburn and Handley Page, with

The second B-3, K3591, intended for Specification M.1/30A, although the monocoque construction suggests that Blackburn had set its sights rather further ahead. (Photo: Air Ministry A & AEE, Neg 7295C dated May 1933)

the result that M.5/28 was replaced by M.1/30, in which the maximum all-up weight was relaxed very slightly; at the same time, the Air Ministry expressed a preference for either the Rolls-Royce Buzzard in-line or Armstrong Siddeley Leopard radial engine. Performance requirements were exceptionally demanding, including a maximum speed of not less than 130kt (150 mph) at 4,000ft, a landing speed of not more than 55kt (63 mph), and an operating endurance of 7½ hours while carrying a war load of 2,874lb. The latter included a bomb load of 2,200lb as an alternative to a 1,900lb Mark VIII torpedo. The all-up weight limit of 9,300lb was now immutable, as this represented the load limit of the carrier deck lifts.

Single prototypes were ordered from Blackburn (B-3), Handley Page (H.P.46) and Vickers (Type 207). The first flown was the Blackburn B-3, this being closely related to the company's design essay for M.5/28. It was a deceptively large aircraft with a wing span only six inches less than the maximum stipulated of 50 feet. The powerplant was the officially-preferred Rolls-Royce Buzzard IIIM, its exceptionally clean installation being achieved by the use of divided radiators located under the lower wing roots; the engine drove a very large two-blade propeller of 15 feet diameter. The torpedo mounting demanded a split-axle undercarriage, and this incorporated Blackburn oleo-pneumatic main legs and bracing V-struts anchored to the lower fuselage longerons. Alternative heavy-load bomb racks under the lower wings could carry four 550lb bombs. The folding wings carried almost full-span ailerons which could be lowered for use as landing flaps.

The prototype, S1640, was first flown by 'Dasher' Blake at Brough on 8 March 1932, but the pilot evidently expressed

general dissatisfaction with the aircraft's handling as it paid only a couple of very brief visits to Martlesham Heath during 1932 before being presented for performance tests in January 1933. However, S1640 crashed and was destroyed on 30 June that year after the Buzzard cut on take-off.

In the meantime both the other M.1/30 contenders had met with misfortune, and neither reached Martlesham for evaluation. Some of the performance demands made in M.1/30 had been further relaxed (the service ceiling, already reduced from 20,000 to 16,000 feet, was now reduced to 14,000) and the requirements reissued as M.1/30A.

Blackburn had therefore, at private expense, built a new aircraft with a metal monocoque fuselage but of almost

indentical dimensions, but when this was offered for assessment at Martlesham Heath in 1933 the Service pilots were wholly unimpressed, finding that the machine was still incapable of reaching anything like the height required; it failed to reach the required maximum speed by 10 mph and — more critically — was too heavy by 1,000lb for the carrier lifts. They also complained that the cockpit was cold and cramped, while the aircraft's general handling was sluggish and tiring. (Vickers offered a modified Vildebeest to this Specification, but, as it was powered by a Pegasus and not by one of the prescribed engines, it was not considered.)

Specification M.1/30A was therefore also withdrawn, re-written once more, and re-issued later in 1933 as S.15/33.

Type: Single-engine, two-seat, single-bay biplane ship-borne torpedo bomber.
Air Ministry Specification: M.1/30 and M.1/30A.
Manufacturer: The Blackburn Aeroplane and Motor Co Ltd, Brough, Yorkshire.
Powerplant: One 825hp Rolls-Royce Buzzard IIIMS 12-cylinder, water-cooled, super-charged, in-line engine driving a 15ft diameter 2-blade wooden propeller.
Dimensions: M.1/30A. Span, 49ft 6in (folded, 18ft 7in); length, 39ft 10in; height, 14ft 7in; wing area, 651 sq ft.
Weights: M.1/30A. Tare, 6,138lb; all-up, 10,393lb.
Performance: M.1/30A. Max speed, 142 mph at sea level; climb to 6,500ft, 20 min; service ceiling, 9,150ft.
Armament: One synchronized 0.303in Vickers Mk II machine gun in the port side of the nose, and one Lewis Mk III gun on rear cockpit. Bomb load of up to four 550lb, 520lb or 500lb bombs, or one 1,900lb Mk VIII or X 18in torpedo.
Prototypes: Two, S1640 (M.1/30), first flown by Flt Lt A M Blake at Brough on 8 March 1932, and K3591 (M.1/30A), first flown by Flt Lt Blake on 24 February 1933. No production.

Handley Page
H.P.46 (M.1/30)

Like Blackburn, Handley Page had prepared a design tender to Specification M.5/28, but this had been criticised by the DTD on the grounds that crew field of view during a torpedo attack would have been inadequate; the tender

had been withdrawn and the Specification followed suit. Handley Page was, however, invited to tender to Specification M.1/30, which was in some respects similar to the previous requirement but omitted some of the conten-

One of a small number of amateur snapshots taken of the H.P.46 at Radlett in 1934 (the only known surviving photographs), in its red primer paint and without its wheel fairings fitted. (Photo: B Cornthwaite)

tious demands — such as wheel/float interchangeability and catapulting facility. Nevertheless, with engines such as the Buzzard and Leopard now being recommended in M.1/30, it was clear that the previous Handley Page aircraft was much too small. Gustav Lachmann was therefore given the task of producing an entirely new design tender.

Lachmann's approach was certainly radical in its attempt to achieve the necessary very low airframe structure weight as a percentage of the all-up weight. Innovations included combining internally-sprung landing wheel mountings with a sharply anhedralled inboard lower wing section, integral fuel tanks being incorporated in these wings sections — these expedients being said to save almost 200lb in airframe weight. Unfortunately, the Air Ministry introduced restrictions on such novelties owing to the cost involved in proving their reliability and safety.

Nevertheless, without seriously compromising the airframe strength, which implied a high constant value because major items of mass such as powerplant, fuel for a given minimum range, war load, maximum wing span, folded span and maximum all-up weight, were all statutorily defined, it was becoming clear that the Specification could not, at the current level of technology, be met. This was a fault created almost entirely by the DTD, through its lack of consultation both with the aircraft industry and its own research establishments.

The H.P.46 was therefore never anything but a compromised design for, when it was weighed prior to its first flight, its all-up weight was found to be 10,438lb, or more than 1,000lb above the permissible maximum. It was decided, therefore, to go ahead with flight trials without carrying warload, if only to assess the aircraft's handling qualities. Accordingly, Tom Harry England took S1642 aloft at Radlett on 25 October 1932 — or rather performed a short straight 'hop', as it was all too obvious that the aircraft was in no safe condition to fly. Indeed, such was the long list of snags and design faults compiled following this and a second flight that England

refused to fly the aircraft again until all had been rectified. Apart from difficulty in co-ordinating the wing slot opening with the drooping ailerons — a matter with which Handley Page, of all companies, should have coped without difficulty — England found that the tail controls had four inches of play due to cable whip, a sure prescription for tail flutter. No alternative could be found but to make an entirely new tail unit.

By mid-summer of 1933 the Air Ministry had lost patience with the

various contenders to M.1/30, and the H.P.46 had not even visited Martlesham Heath, having only logged 75 minutes' flying time in the course of eight flights. The Air Ministry had no intention of accepting it on charge as it had not proved itself able to meet the Requirement.

The aircraft was ultimately disposed of to the RAE in 1935, by which time it had cost Handley Page over £36,000 and had spent just five hours in the air with nothing but problems to show for them.

Type: Single-engine, two-seat, single-bay biplane carrier-borne torpedo bomber.
Air Ministry Specification: M.1/30
Manufacturer: Handley Page Ltd, Cricklewood, London, and Radlett, Hertfordshire.
Powerplant: One 825hp Rolls-Royce Buzzard IIIS 12-cylinder water-cooled supercharged in-line engine driving 2-blade propeller.
Dimensions: Span, 50ft 0in; length, 39ft 5in; wing area, 656 sq ft.
Weights: Tare, 6,250lb; all-up (estimated full load), 10,600lb.
Performance: Max speed (design estimate), 140 mph at 12,000ft.
Armament: Provision for synchronized 0.303in Vickers Mk II front gun and one Lewis gun on rear cockpit. Designed for one 1,460lb Mark X torpedo or up to 2,200lb of bombs.
Prototype: One, S1642, first flown by T H England at Radlett on 25 October 1932.

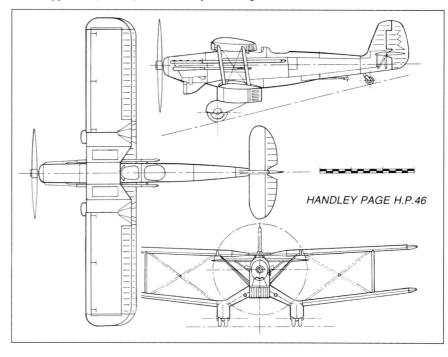

HANDLEY PAGE H.P.46

Vickers Type 207 (M.1/30)

It was ironic that, while the other manufacturers found Specification M.1/30 impossible to satisfy and failed to make any significant contribution to the progress of aircraft design in their efforts to succeed, Vickers (Aviation) Ltd emerged with the design of an aeroplane which, although unable to meet the requirements, represented a significant advance in airframe design technology; indeed, not only did the manner in which it met its end cause the structural textbooks to be rewritten, but it set the company on a long and profitable path of aircraft design.

Following the decision by the British government to discontinue the development and manufacture of airships (after the tragedy involving the loss of the R.101), the designer of Vickers' R.100, Barnes Neville Wallis, was moved to Weybridge to become Rex Pierson's chief structural designer in the aeroplane department. Applying his wealth of experience in light-alloy structures, Wallis took a hand in the company's design tender to M.1/30, employing typical airship rib design in the wings, not least in the main spars (these comprising duralumin tubular booms with Warren girder webs using lightened diagonal channels).

The performance and loads demanded in the M.1/30 requirements resulted in large aeroplanes being tendered, and this applied not least to Vickers' Type 207, which has been described as a 'typically big-boned beast', powered as it was by the obligatory Buzzard III engine. Yet of the three designs tendered, that from Wallis' drawing board possessed the lightest airframe structure by a margin of over 500lb, while still apparently conforming to adequate strength factors. Certainly all the evidence showed that the *airframe component* assemblies were exceptionally strong.

Of single-bay configuration, the biplane's unstaggered wings were built to fold, and featured wingtip slats and steel tubular interplane struts with large-section fairings. The customary split-axle undercarriage was included to allow carriage of a torpedo, although engine cooling difficulties — once Vickers had decided to abandon the Buzzard's steam-cooling system — arose from the use of

a large radiator between the undercarriage legs, which temporarily prevented a torpedo from being carried. The pilot's cockpit was located well forward under the leading edge of the upper wing (imparting an excellent field of view forward), while the gunner's cockpit was nine feet further aft.

'Mutt' Summers first flew the prototype, S1461, at Brooklands on 11 January 1933, and flying continued for much of that year, a number of alterations being found necessary, including the introduction of two degrees of dihedral on the upper wing to improve lateral stability. The engine exhaust system also gave trouble, and tests were carried out with pipes of different lengths; the radiator fairing underwent some changes, both in shape and position, to enable the torpedo to be carried.

The upshot of these delays was that the Type 207 was too late for consideration in the context of M.1/30, the Air Ministry having decided to introduce an entirely new Specification. However, Vickers still had to submit the prototype for contractors' trials for the contract terms to be satisfied. As the aircraft was carrying out its final check flights prior to delivery to Martlesham Heath, disaster occurred during a check dive with

torpedo on 23 November 1933. At a speed of about 230 mph in a 45-degree dive the aeroplane began to break up. Both Summers and his observer, John Radcliffe, escaped by parachute — the latter recalling afterwards that he had seen the fuselage, wings and tail each falling as separate structures, though with the fabric being ripped away.

In subsequent investigations it was deduced that while, in effect, Wallis' structural assemblies appeared to have been correctly stressed, some of the sub-assembly joints, particularly those between the wings and fuselage, had failed under abnormal loads caused by wing flexing. In writing new fuselage strength requirements, the RAE was itself invalidating the terms of M.1/30.

Whether or not Wallis was aware that existing design parameters were already suspect is not known; however, by the time the Type 207 met its end (almost certainly performing well outside the planned flight envelope), Wallis' next aircraft was already flying with a structural innovation, the geodetic principle, that was to impart considerable strength without undue weight penalty, initially to the fuselage structure and later to an aeroplane's wings and tail.

The Vickers M.1/30 S1641 immediately before its first flight, at Brooklands on 11 January 1933. Note the compromising position of the Buzzard's radiator. (Photo: Author's Collection)

Type: Single-engine, two-seat, single-bay biplane carrier-borne torpedo bomber.
Air Ministry Specification: M.1/30.
Manufacturer: Vickers (Aviation) Ltd, Weybridge, Surrey.
Powerplant: One 825hp Rolls-Royce Buzzard IIIMS 12-cylinder water-cooled in-line engine driving 2-blade propeller.
Structure: Steel and duralumin construction with aluminium and fabric covering.
Dimensions: Span, 49ft 8in; length, 43ft 7in; height, 14ft 5in; wing area, 720 sq ft.
Weights: Tare, 5,120lb; all-up, 9,670lb.
Performance: Max speed, 159 mph at 4,000ft; climb to 6,500ft, 9 min 10 sec; service ceiling, 16,100ft.
Armament: One synchronized 0.303in Vickers machine gun in nose decking, offset to port, and one Lewis gun on rear cockpit; one 1,800lb 18in torpedo or up to 2,200lb of bombs comprising, for example, four 550lb bombs.
Prototype: One, S1641, first flown by Joseph ('Mutt') Summers with John Radcliffe at Brooklands on 11 January 1933. No production.

Gloster FS.36 and TSR.38

As the effects of constraints on government defence expenditure began to influence the Air Ministry's plans for new aircraft procurement, there was increasing interest in what would become known half a century later as 'multi-rôle' aircraft. Although there was a habit of referring to such aircraft as General Purpose types, there was a subtle difference between them and the 'Jacks of All Trades' conceived during the 1920s, and epitomised by the Westland Wapiti. The new categories — one for the Royal Navy, the other for the land-based Royal Air Force, which would be beckoned by the DTD throughout the early 1930s — were intended to embrace duties ranging through bombing (including dive bombing), torpedo delivery, reconnaissance up to medium ranges, army co-operation and, in the case of naval aircraft, the ability to operate with float and wheel undercarriage and be suitable for catapult operations.

For the Fleet Air Arm, Specification S.9/30 called for a three-seat torpedo bomber/fleet spotter/reconnaissance aircraft with folding wings and deck-landing gear, and later incorporated some of the less contentious features of the abortive M.1/30 requirements. The new Requirement attracted design tenders from Hawker (an enlarged three-seat, Panther-powered derivative of the Osprey), Avro (the Type 632 project with an Armstrong Siddeley Tiger radial engine), Gloster (the FS.36) and an undesignated Fairey design. The first two of these were not accepted, but single prototypes of the Gloster and

The Gloster FS.36, S1705, with water-cooled Kestrel engine at Brockworth before its second visit to Martlesham Heath as the TSR.38. (Photo: Gloster Aircraft Co Ltd.)

Fairey designs were ordered as S1705 and S1706 respectively.

As a relative stranger in the specialised area of naval aircraft, Gloster tendered to S.9/30 a design that certainly merited being regarded as a serious and worthwhile effort which, had it not been pitted against an efficient, compact and highly adaptable opponent from Fairey (which, incidentally, was in a better financial position to support a second, private venture, prototype as well), might easily have achieved production status. The Specification certainly demanded an intimate knowledge of carrier operation, with emphasis on strong undercarriage and airframe and particular attention to structural resistance to salt water corrosion.

Because of the enforced reduction of Gloster's staff and labour force in the early 1930s, progress with the FS.36 was slow, and the prototype was not flown until April 1932. In its initial configuration S1705 was powered by a 600hp Rolls-Royce Kestrel IIMS supercharged, water-cooled engine with conventional

radiators under anhedralled inboard lower wing sections.

By the time S1705 paid its first visit to Martlesham Heath for contractor's trials, however, Specification S.9/30 was being withdrawn to make way for a new set of requirements. Nevertheless, the Gloster aeroplane attracted promising opinions, albeit with reservations, and its performance with the early Kestrel compared favourably with that of the Fairey S.9/30, which was even slower reaching Martlesham Heath (though, as will be shown, delays with the Fairey prototype were occasioned by a decision to 'leapfrog' the original Specification).

Realising that the new Specification, S.15/33, would almost certainly make increased demands on the S.9/30 prototypes, Gloster set about remedying the A & AEE's criticisms — principally concerned with poor control response at low speeds and inefficient wheel brakes. When, however, the new requirements materialised (towards the end of 1933), it was seen that the Air Ministry was now expressing preference for the new Goshawk III steam-cooled engine, despite continuing difficulties in developing an efficient, finite condenser. S1705, redesignated the TSR.38, was accordingly fitted with the new engine but, owing to the need to replace the underwing radiators by full-span wing leading edge condensers, the version ultimately selected by Gloster was the 690hp

The Goshawk VIII-powered TSR.38 at Martlesham Heath in 1934, during its eventual full Service assessment trials, with an 18in torpedo. As far as is known, it was never tested with float undercarriage — unlike the Fairey S.9/30. (Photo: Air Ministry, A & AEE, Neg No 8016C)

Goshawk VIII. Unfortunately, the necessity for this type of condenser meant that the wingtip slats had now to be omitted, and this led to further deterioration of the aeroplane's low-speed handling qualities.

Nevertheless, mostly unaware of the successful progress being made by the Fairey contender, Gloster delivered S1705 for dummy deck landing trials at Gosport prior to its joining HMS *Courageous* for carrier trials in August 1934. It then revisited Martlesham Heath for full evaluation in the context of S.15/33, Report No M.653 dated June 1935 suggesting that it was now markedly inferior to Fairey's latest private venture prototype, by then named the TSR.II — and well on the way to becoming the immortal Swordfish.

Fortunately, Gloster's survival was

no longer in doubt, this famous company having been rescued in 1933-34 by T O M Sopwith of Hawker Aircraft Ltd with amalgamation to provide the foundation of the new Hawker Siddeley Group. Already the factory was filling up with work on Hart variants and its own Gauntlet fighters.

Type: Single-engine, three-crew, single-bay torpedo bomber/fleet spotter/reconnaissance biplane.
Air Ministry Specifications: S.9/30 and S.15/33.
Manufacturer: The Gloster Aircraft Co Ltd, Hucclecote, Gloucester.
Powerplant: FS.36. One 600hp Rolls-Royce Kestrel IIMS 12-cylinder water-cooled supercharged in-line engine driving Watts wooden 2-blade propeller. TSR.38. One 690hp Rolls-Royce Goshawk VIII 12-cylinder evaporatively-cooled supercharged engine.
Structure: Steel and duralumin construction throughout; some salt-vulnerable components manufactured in stainless steel and anodized aluminium.
Dimensions: Span, 46ft 0in (folded, 17ft 9in); length, 37ft 4½in; height, 11ft 6in; wing area (TSR.38), 611sq ft.
Weights: Tare, 4,340lb; all-up, 7,100lb (8,038lb with torpedo).
Performance: TSR.38. Max speed, 145 mph at sea level (with torpedo); climb to 10,000ft, 14 min 15 sec (with torpedo); service ceiling, 20,000ft (without torpedo).
Armament: One synchronized 0.303in Vickers machine gun on port side of nose, and one Lewis gun on rear cockpit; either one 18in Mk VIII torpedo or up to 1,700lb of bombs.
Prototype: One, S1705, first flown at Brockworth in April 1932, probably by Howard Saint. No production.

Fairey S.9/30 and TSR.I

A cynic might be forgiven for observing that the British aircraft industry only ever produced a truly classic aeroplane by accident. Such an observation would, however, be to gainsay the many examples of brilliant application and logical development, yet it cannot be denied that some of the aeroplanes that gave the most outstanding service came into being without the benefit of long and costly evolution along conventional paths of development — often as the result of a privately sponsored divergence from the 'official' formula. The Hawker Hart, the de Havilland Mosquito, the Bristol Blenheim, the Hawker Siddeley Harrier — even the Hawker Hurricane and

The Fairey S.9/30, S1706, probably at about the time of its first flight; just visible as dark patches are the steam condensers under the upper wing centresection; the long exhaust pipes were soon replaced by 'ram's horn' exhaust manifolds. (Photo: The Fairey Aviation Co Ltd.)

Supermarine Spitfire — all owed much to a particular stroke of genius that pre-empted, or at least accelerated, the logical train of thought emanating

from the orthodox civil servant.

Thus it was that, when Fairey's design tender to S.9/30 was accepted and a prototype ordered, its design team was already looking beyond the immediate requirement. As with the Gloster prototype, work on the Fairey aircraft, S1706, proceeded slowly, and it was not until 22 February 1934 that it was flown by Chris Staniland at Harmondsworth aerodrome.

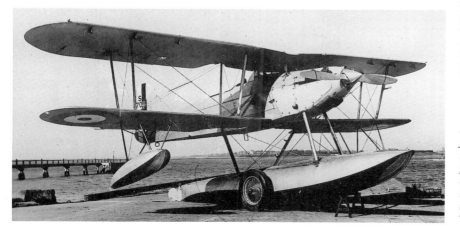

S1706 during trials with a single, central float at the Marine Aircraft Experimental Establishment, Felixstowe, whose pilots expressed good opinions of the water handling characteristics of this float arrangement, but were less complimentary regarding its effects on the aircraft's handling in the air. (Photo: The Fairey Aviation Co Ltd.)

The private venture Fairey TSR.I after the decision had been taken to bring it up to a standard that might enable it to be tendered to Specification S.15/33; the earlier Panther engine had been replaced by a Pegasus in a Townend ring, and a deck arrester hook was fitted (but the addition of wheel spats was somewhat superfluous). It was probably in this configuration that the aeroplane, carrying a torpedo, was lost on 11 September 1933 following Staniland's inability to recover from a flat spin. The aircraft was never allocated a military serial number. (Photo: The Fairey Aviation Co Ltd.)

Of course, by the time this flight took place, its official Requirement had been abandoned in favour of S.15/33, and its visit to Martlesham Heath was of little more than academic importance. Though outwardly of two-bay biplane configuration, S1706 was, technically, of single-bay layout, the inboard interplane struts being intended merely to provide centresection rigidity for wing folding. Power was provided by a derated Kestrel IIMS employing evaporative cooling with surface-type steam condensers in the underside of the upper wing centresection. The structure was predominantly of stainless-steel strip and tube, the fuselage being built in four sections.

After return from the A & AEE, S1706 was converted to a seaplane, with a large central main float and small outrigged balancing floats under the lower wings, for trials at the MAEE, Felixstowe, alongside the similarly-equipped Hawker Osprey, S1700.

Meanwhile Fairey had, in 1932, been engaged in designing a torpedo/spotter/reconnaissance aircraft for the Greek Navy and, although no Greek order was placed, a privately-financed prototype was built, powered by a 625hp Panther VI radial engine and flown by Staniland on 21 March 1933. The engine was then replaced by a 635hp Bristol Pegasus IIM radial with Townend ring and, now termed the TSR Mk I, the aircraft was flown on 10 July that year. Flights were made with and without wheel spats, and stressed for deck landing with arrester hook, and tests continued at Harmondsworth to discover whether the aircraft might be officially assessed by the A & AEE as a likely contender to Specification S.15/33, then just issued.

All appeared to be progressing satisfactorily when, on 11 September, during spinning trials while carrying a torpedo, the TSR.I failed to recover

from a flat spin. Although Staniland escaped (after 14 turns), the aircraft was destroyed.

Despite this setback, previous flight reports suggested that, despite the use of an engine not officially favoured in the

Type: Single-engine, three-seat, single-bay (see text) torpedo/spotter/reconnaissance experimental biplane with wheel or float undercarriage.

Air Ministry Specifications: S.9/30 and private venture (TSR.I) to S.15/33.

Manufacturer: The Fairey Aviation Co Ltd, Hayes, Middlesex.

Powerplant: S.9/30. One 525hp Rolls-Royce Kestrel IIMS 12-cylinder evaporatively-cooled, in-line engine driving 2-blade metal fixed-pitch Fairey propeller. TSR.I. One 625hp Armstrong Siddeley Panther VI 14-cylinder air-cooled radial; 635hp Bristol Pegasus IIM 9-cylinder air-cooled radial engine driving 2-blade wooden propeller.

Structure: Predominantly stainless-steel strip and tubular construction with light-alloy panels and fabric covering.

Dimensions: S.9/30 landplane. Span, 46ft 0in (folded, 17ft 10in); length, 34ft 1in; height, 14ft 0in; wing area, 442 sq ft.

Weight: S.9/30 landplane (no torpedo). All-up, 5,740lb.

Performance: S.9/30 landplane (no torpedo). Max speed, 147 mph at sea level; climb to 5,000ft, 5 min 30 sec.

Armament: Provision for Lewis gun on rear cockpit; either one 1,800lb Mk VIII torpedo (landplane only) or up to 1,200lb of bombs.

Prototypes: One S.9/30 prototype, S1706, flown as landplane by C S Staniland on 22 February 1934; one TSR.I prototype, flown by Staniland on 21 March 1933. No production.

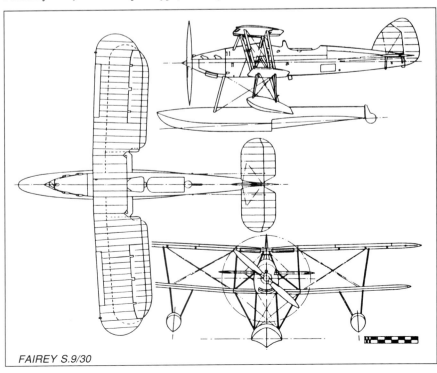

FAIREY S.9/30

Specification[1], the TSR.I was clearly capable of meeting the latest requirements so that, with a number of alterations to the airframe (including strakes forward of the fin to assist spin recovery), construction of a second prototype was commenced. This aircraft, also a private venture and known as the TSR

Mk II (see page 281), made its maiden flight on 17 April 1934, less than two months after the original S.9/30 had

[1] By the time Fairey's new prototype came under serious scrutiny by the DTD, the entire evaporative-cooling programme was in the melting pot, and the successful development of the Rolls-Royce Merlin

first flown. The TSR.II was to become better known as the Fairey Swordfish prototype.

rendered the supposed benefits of 'steam cooling' superfluous. All development work on the steam-cooled Kestrel and Goshawk was halted late in 1935.

Blackburn Baffin

The Blackburn Ripon, which had first flown in 1926 and entered Fleet Air Arm Service in 1930 was, by 1933, in urgent need of replacement, featuring as it did the outdated Napier Lion and partial wooden construction. A Ripon replacement, however, assuming it to be another two-seater and a 'single-rôle' fleet torpedo bomber, was not relevant to the Specifications M.1/30 and S.9/30 (the latter calling for a three-seat 'multi-rôle' aircraft). In any case Blackburn had anticipated the need for such an aircraft, powered by the newly favoured air-cooled radial engines, with the construction of two private venture Ripon Mark V prototypes; these aeroplanes were registered as B-4, powered by a 650hp fourteen-cylinder Armstrong Siddeley Tiger I, and B-5 with a nine-cylinder 545hp Bristol Pegasus I.MS.

Both prototypes attracted Air Ministry interest but, believing the Tiger engine to need further development, accepted the Pegasus-powered machine as the basis of a short-term Ripon replacement, confirming its decision when Major Frank Bumpus stated that conversion of existing Ripon II airframes to accommodate the Pegasus radial could be achieved at a unit cost of £1,090 (excluding the engine's cost, but including complete overhaul and re-

The prototype Baffin, B-5, termed the Ripon V, at Brough after its Martlesham trials, fitted with Townend ring and Blackburn bomb racks. (Photo: Real Photographs Co.)

placement of any defective component). This version, initially referred to as the T.5J Ripon V, was first flown by A M Blake on 30 September 1932; when, however, two pre-production examples, K3589 and K3590, were ordered and a new Specification, 4/33, issued to cover the performance required, the name Baffin was selected.

Aircraft B-5 underwent performance, handling and armament trials at Martlesham Heath, beginning in January 1933. The only significant criticism arose from the obscuring of some instruments owing to the cramped cockpit (this fault being largely remedied in 1935 by the introduction of an articulated control column).

With three Squadrons of Ripons in

service, the normal scale of production Baffin requirements would have been about 55-60 aircraft and, to meet these, contracts for a total of 24 newly-built aircraft and 38 Ripon IIA conversions were placed with Blackburn. However, during the late summer of 1935 trouble was being experienced with the Tiger engines in the Blackburn Sharks of No 820 Squadron (Lt Cdr Robert Godmond Poole), which was about to sail for the Canal Zone at the beginning of the Abyssinian crisis, and it was decided to send Baffins with the Squadron instead. This, and the expected increase in the number of Fleet Air Arm Squadrons during the Expansion period, resulted in a further 26 Ripons (this time Mk IICs) being converted to Baffins.

The first Fleet Air Arm Squadron to be equipped with Baffins was No 812 at Hal Far, Malta, commanded by Sqn Ldr (later Gp Capt) Bruce Bernard Caswell, in January 1934; before the end of that month they had joined HMS *Glorious* with the Mediterranean Fleet, but when that carrier returned home for

A Baffin, S1671, of No 811 Squadron, Fleet Air Arm, normally embarked in HMS Furious, at Gosport in 1935 being loaded with a torpedo. (Photo: Flight, Neg No 15376)

Three Baffins of 'A' Torpedo Development Flight, stationed at Gosport in the mid-1930s; the nearest aircraft, S1562, was the Baffin which crashed on the French liner Normandie *on 22 June 1936. (Photo: Imperial War Museum, Neg No MH27)*

refit the Squadron transferred to HMS *Furious*. No 812 continued to fly Baffins until December 1936, when most of them were destroyed in the tornado which struck Malta and demolished their hangar; the opportunity was then taken to re-equip the Squadron with Fairey Swordfish.

Although the Baffin possessed a performance only marginally better than that of the Ripon, the Air Ministry issued a supplementary Specification, 17/34, to cover an improved version powered by the new Pegasus II.M3, but only three examples, termed T.8As, were built — and all were shipped out to No 812 Squadron in the Mediterranean.

The second Baffin Squadron was No 810 (Sqn Ldr George Harold Boyce AFC, later Air Cdre, CB, AFC), equipped in July 1934, followed by No 811 in January 1935 (Lt Cdr Frederick William Howard Clarke).

By the time the first Baffins were joining No 812 Squadron in January 1934, the Blackburn Shark prototype had been flying for more than four months and, as this had already been accepted for production, the Baffin quickly became regarded as no more than stop-gap equipment. As it was, it served for over three years and, by the time it was being withdrawn from service, the Fairey Swordfish was coming on stream, so that it was the Shark itself that performed the Fleet Air Arm's

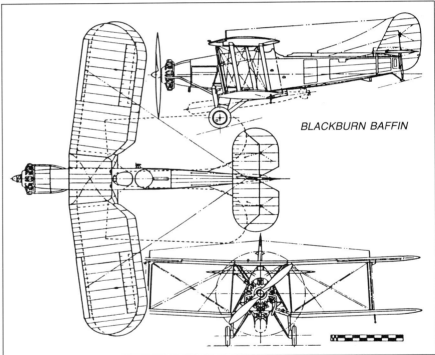

BLACKBURN BAFFIN

Type: Single-engine, two-seat, single-bay biplane carrier-borne torpedo bomber.

Air Ministry Specifications: 4/33 and 17/34

Manufacturer: The Blackburn Aeroplane and Motor Co Ltd, Brough, Yorkshire.

Powerplant: T.8. One 565hp Bristol Pegasus I.M3 9-cylinder air-cooled radial engine driving 2-blade propeller. T.8A. One 580hp Pegasus II.M3.

Structure: Predominantly steel tubular construction, but with wooden, tie rod-braced rear fuselage structure.

Dimensions: Span, 44ft 10in (folded, 17ft 10in); length, 38ft 3¾in; height, 12ft 10in; wing area, 683 sq ft.

Weights: T.8. Tare, 3,184lb; all-up (with torpedo), 7,610lb.

Performance: T.8. Max speed, 136 mph at 6,500ft; service ceiling, 15,000ft; normal range, 490 miles.

Armament: One synchronized 0.303in Vickers machine gun in nose and one Lewis gun with Fairey low-drag mounting in rear cockpit; one 1,800lb 18in Mk VIII or X torpedo or 1,600lb of bombs.

Prototype: One (formerly termed Ripon Mk V), B-5, first

flown by A M Blake at Brough on 30 September 1932.

Production: A total of 97 Baffins was produced, of which 29 were newly built, and 68 were converted from Ripons: K3589 and K3590 (2 newly-built pre-production); K2884-K2887 (4 converted from Ripon IIC); K3546-K3559, K4071-K4080 and K4776-K4778 (27 newly built Baffins, of which the last three were T.8As); between S1266 and S1574 (38 converted from Ripon IIAs) and between S1469 and S1674 (26 converted from Ripon IICs). Of the above aircraft, 29 Baffins were supplied to the Royal New Zealand Air Force.

Summary of Fleet Air Arm Service: Baffins served with No 812 Squadron from January 1934 until December 1936 mainly embarked in HMS *Glorious* and *Eagle* in the Mediterranean; with No 810 Squadron from July 1934 until April 1937 mainly embarked in HMS *Courageous* in home waters and the Mediterranean; with No 811 Squadron from January 1935 until November 1936 embarked in HMS *Furious* in home waters; and with No 820 Squadron from August 1935 until February 1936 embarked in HMS *Courageous* in the Mediterranean. They also flew with 'A' Flight (Torpedo Development), Gosport, and 'C' Flight, Hal Far, Malta.

stop-gap torpedo bomber rôle.

Stocks of Baffins were held at Hal Far as replacements after accidents at sea with the Mediterranean Fleet. At home, torpedo development and training was carried out by Gosport's 'A' Flight, one of whose Baffins, S1562, during an over-enthusiastic and illicit welcome to the French liner *Normandie* on 22 June 1936, struck one of the ship's derricks and crashed on her deck.

The withdrawal of the Baffin from squadron service by the late spring of 1937 coincided with a decision by the New Zealand government to raise a number of Territorial coastal defence squadrons, and that country agreed to purchase a number of the surplus Baffins. In due course 29 were shipped out to equip the Wellington, Auckland and Christchurch Territorial Squadrons, and some of them continued to serve well into the Second World War.

Blackburn T.9 Shark

Despite the relatively large number of Blackburn Sharks built (237 for the Fleet Air Arm) between 1934 and 1938, the aircraft gave very little front-line operational service, being an almost exact contemporary of the Baffin, just described. The fundamental difference between the two aircraft, despite their common ancestry, was that the Baffin perpetuated the specialist torpedo bomber rôle as a two-seater, whereas the Shark (being tendered to Specification S.15/33 in the first place) was a three-seat multi-rôle torpedo bomber/fleet spotter/reconnaissance aircraft. In the latter naval 'general purpose' category, it was not particularly efficient nor popular, and it was quickly replaced by the Fairey Swordfish.

Thus, with so many surplus Sharks, principally Mark IIs and IIIs, it was inevitable that the aircraft should be relegated to a whole host of second-line support duties.

The origins of the Shark lay in the first of two private venture Blackburn Ripon Vs, B-4, powered by a 650hp Armstrong Siddeley Tiger Mk I radial engine. This was a fourteen-cylinder air-cooled radial developed in 1930-32 in an attempt to capitalise on the success of the earlier Panther, it being intended

The prototype Shark, B-6, with uncowled Tiger radial engine early in the flight trials at Brough in the summer of 1933; lines of unpainted filler emphasise the Alclad panels on the rear fuselage. (Photo: Hawker Siddeley Aviation Ltd, Neg Ref A951)

to introduce a two-speed supercharger in its later marks. High hopes were pinned on the engine but, despite continued development during the 1930s, the Tiger suffered from all manner of problems, particularly when propeller gearing was introduced, and after an initial burst of enthusiasm by the Air Ministry, attracted by sanguine promises of relatively high power potential, it came to be relegated to a stop-gap status; much of its development flying was therefore undertaken in hack aeroplanes of only limited value and at commercial expense.

The Ripon V, B-4, did not attract a purchase contract, but Blackburn was encouraged to submit a further private venture prototype to the nebulous S.15/33 requirement. This aircraft, al-

lotted the B Conditions marking B-6, was therefore to compete against the Gloster TSR.38 and Fairey TSR.I, and was initially termed the Blackburn TSR. It was roughly the same size as the Baffin, and was powered by the first production version of the Tiger, the 700hp geared Mark IV. It inherited the Blackburn M.1/30A's compartmented fuselage, covered with Alclad to provide buoyancy should the aircraft be forced down on to the sea. A high structural content of stainless steel components provided corrosion resistance, the tubular wingspar booms being manufactured in the material by Boulton and Paul Ltd. The interplane strut arrangement formed a 'semi-Warren girder' with a single-bay cellule lower wing and a two-bay upper wing, providing considerable strength to enable the full underwing bomb load to be carried — even with the wings folded in a carrier's below-deck hangar. Frise ailerons were fitted to upper and lower wings, and provision was made for interchangeable wheel and float under-carriage.

Prototype B-6 was flown by Blake at Brough on 24 August 1933, and he delivered it to Martlesham Heath for

The fourth production Shark Mk.I, K4352, probably at Gosport in the markings of No 820 Squadron and HMS Courageous in 1935. (Photo: via R C Sturtivant)

In-flight view of another Shark I, K4357. After being replaced on No 820 Squadron, this aircraft went on to serve with 'A' and 'C' Flights at Gosport, but when the Shark was declared obsolete in September 1937 K4357 was simultaneously declared 'flying time expired' and became a ground instruction machine, 990M. (Photo: Air Ministry, Neg No H54)

performance trials on 6 November that year. As this was a private venture tender at that time, and not bound under contract by the statutory provisions of S.15/33, these trials were not the subject of a formal Establishment report. However, the A & AEE was sufficiently impressed with B-6 to recommend it for carrier trials, these being successfully negotiated early in 1934. They were in turn followed by Air Ministry purchase of the prototype, which was then serialled K4295, and the issue of a contract for 16 aircraft, named the T.9 Shark, in August that year. In due course K4295 underwent floatplane trials with the MAEE, Felixstowe.

Most of the first batch of Shark Is were delivered to No 820 Squadron at Gosport, commanded by Lt Cdr Matthew Sausse Slattery, beginning in December 1934, replacing Fairey IIIFs and Seals and embarking in HMS *Courageous* the following month.

While manufacture of these Mark Is occupied the first half of 1935, Blackburn was asked to go ahead with the development of an improved version, the T.9A Shark II, to be powered by the 760hp Tiger VI and carrying additional internal tankage for 33 gallons of fuel with provision also to carry a 150-gallon overload tank which increased the range from 792 to 1,130 miles when not carrying a torpedo; alternatively, the Shark II could be flown as a two-seat bomber carrying a 500lb bomb load over a range of 900 miles (although there is no evidence that there was a Service requirement for this rôle). Specification S.13/35 was raised to cover the new version, and three pre-production examples, K4880-K4882, were ordered (the first being flown on 16 November 1935). As an insurance against delays with the Tiger VI engine, K4882 was

flown with an 840hp Bristol Pegasus IX nine-cylinder radial, thereby incidentally becoming the prototype Shark III (see below).

Intended as the definitive production version, 53 Shark IIs were ordered in September 1935, followed by a further 70 in January 1936. These began replacing Seals with No 821 Squadron (Sqn Ldr Herbert Nind Hampton DFC) at Gosport in March 1936, embarking in HMS *Courageous* on 13 July that year.

In July 1936 Shark II seaplanes joined No 705 (Catapult) Squadron, com-

manded by Lt Cdr Douglas William Mackendrick, to be embarked in the battleships HMS *Repulse* and *Warspite* for fleet spotter/reconnaissance duties only, but full TSR Sharks joined Nos 822 and 823 Squadrons in November that year, and No 810 Squadron the following April.

By then, however, it had become clear that recurring troubles with the inadequately developed Tiger engine would prevent the Shark from gaining the unqualified confidence of the Fleet Air Arm, particularly at sea. The expected significant increase in engine power had not yet materialised and if, indeed, the Bristol Pegasus proved to be superior (as was suggested by flight trials of the pre-production Shark II, K4882), the Fairey

Type: Single-engine, three-crew, single/two-bay biplane torpedo/spotter/reconnaissance shipborne aircraft with wheel or float undercarriage.

Air Ministry Specifications: S.15/33, S.12/34, S.13/35 and 19/36.

Manufacturers: The Blackburn Aeroplane and Motor Co Ltd (Blackburn Aircraft Ltd from April 1936), Brough, Yorkshire, and Dumbarton, Dunbartonshire; Boeing Aircraft of Canada Ltd, Vancouver, BC, Canada.

Powerplant: B-6 and Mark I. One 700hp Armstrong Siddeley Tiger IV 14-cylinder air-cooled geared radial engine driving 2-blade propeller. Mark II One 760hp Tiger VI. Mark IIA. One 760hp Tiger VIC. Mark III. One 800hp Bristol Pegasus 9-cylinder radial or 840hp Pegasus IX. 760hp Tiger VI.

Structure: Stainless steel and light alloy throughout with Alclad and fabric covering..

Dimensions: Span, 46ft 0in (folded, 15ft 0in); length, 35ft 3in (seaplane, 38ft 5in); height, 12ft 1in (seaplane, 14ft 3in); wing area, 489 sq ft.

Weights: Mark II landplane. Tare, 4,039lb; all-up, with torpedo, 8,111lb.

Performance: Mark II landplane with torpedo. Max speed, 150 mph at 6,500ft; climb to 6,500ft, 7 min 6 sec; service ceiling, 15,600ft; normal range, 625 miles.

Armament: One synchronized 0.303in Vickers machine gun in nose decking and one Vickers-Berthier gas-operated machine gun in rear cockpit. Either one Mark VIII or X 18in torpedo carried under the fuselage or up to four 500lb bombs carried under the wings.

Prototype: One, B-6 (later K4295), first flown by A M Blake at Brough on 24 August 1933.

Production: A total of 269 Sharks was built (excluding prototype), of which 237 were for the Fleet Air Arm and Royal Air Force. Mark I, 16: K4349-K4364; Mark II, 126: K4880-K4882, K5607-K5659 and K8450-K8519; Mark III, 95: K8891-K8935 and L2337-L2386. In addition, six Mark IIAs were exported to Portugal, and seven Mark IIs and two Mark IIIs to Canada. 17 Mark IIIs were built by Boeing in Canada.

Summary of Service: Sharks served with the following operational Squadrons of the Fleet Air Arm between December 1934 and September 1937: Nos 810, 820, 821, 822 and 823 Squadrons aboard HM Carriers *Courageous*, *Furious* and *Glorious*; and with the following second-line Squadrons between July 1936 and October 1943: Nos 701, 705 (aboard HMS *Repulse* and *Warspite*), 750, 753, 755, 757, 758, 767, 774, 780 and 785. They also served with the School of Naval Co-operation, Gosport; Air Observers' School, Trinidad; Seaplane Training Squadron, Calshot; No 2 Anti-Aircraft Co-operation Unit, Gosport; No 4 AACU, Seletar, Singapore; No 269 Squadron, RAF, Bircham Newton (for target towing); also several torpedo training units, etc.

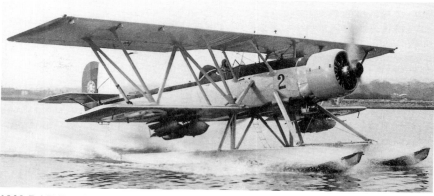

Second of the Shark IIAs scheduled for delivery to Portugal in January 1936, but delayed until March; the photograph was probably taken on 3 March when, flown from the Humber at Brough by Blake, the aircraft was demonstrated to the Press and to members of the Portuguese Naval Air Mission. The bombs appear to comprise one 230- and one 112-pounder under the starboard wing, and three 112lb bombs under the port. (Photo: The Aeroplane, Neg No 1015)

Swordfish — then beginning to enter service with the Fleet Air Arm — should re-equip *all* TSR squadrons of the Fleet Air Arm and become the Royal Navy's standard torpedo bomber. Bearing in mind that the Swordfish was an almost wholly viceless aeroplane with docile deck landing qualities, and that its Pegasus engine was some 40 per cent cheaper than the troublesome Tiger, it was logical that the Shark be taken out of front line service as soon as possible and replaced by the Fairey aeroplane. It was accordingly withdrawn from the carrier squadrons and declared obsolete in September 1937. Ironically, as the urgency increased to introduce the Tiger engine into the new Whitley bomber, greater efforts were made to improve the engine's reliability, and by the end of

1938 RAF Bomber Command declared itself satisfied with the engine's dependability. Further irony was provided by the fact that it was a Shark engine test bed, L2379, that undertook a considerable share of the flight test development of the 880hp Tiger IX engine with Armstrong Siddeley in 1938.

A new version of the Shark, the Mark III had, however, begun delivery to No 810 Squadron (Sqn Ldr Harry Manner Mellor MVO) in April 1937, these aircraft being fitted with a long glazed canopy over all three cockpits. The suddenness with which the decision was taken to withdraw the Shark from operational service may be judged by the fact that an order for 95 Shark IIIs was placed in January 1937, and that only five months

later brand new aircraft were being delivered into store pending a decision on their future. Late production aircraft were being completed at Blackburn's newly opened factory at Dumbarton in Scotland throughout 1937.

Between then and 1940 Shark IIIs (the majority of earlier versions having been modified to the final production standard) were employed in all manner of second-line duties, principally target-towing, being fitted with wind-driven winches on the port side of the rear fuselage. About 20 such aircraft were shipped out to No 4 Anti-Aircraft Co-operation Unit at Seletar, Singapore, during 1938 and 1939, and most of them were still in service at the time of the Japanese invasion of Malaya; during the last days before the fall of Singapore, four Shark target tugs were hurriedly fitted with bomb racks and flown from Batu Pahat as bombers against approaching Japanese columns on 3 January 1942. It is believed that none survived.

In addition to the second-line squadrons with which Sharks flew (see accompanying table), Gosport-based aircraft were employed at night during the Dunkirk evacuation of May-June 1940 to tow lighted flares between the North Foreland and the Schelde estuary in an attempt to illuminate enemy E-boats.

Six Shark IIA seaplanes had been exported to Portugal early in 1936, three of them being fitted with torpedo equipment, and all were capable of carrying underwing bomb racks. Seven Shark IIs were supplied to Canada in 1936 for service with No 6 (Torpedo Bomber) Squadron of the RCAF; these were followed by two Mark IIIs supplied as pattern aircraft to Boeing Aircraft of Canada to assist in preparations to built the aircraft under licence; however, only 17 Shark IIIs were produced in Canada.

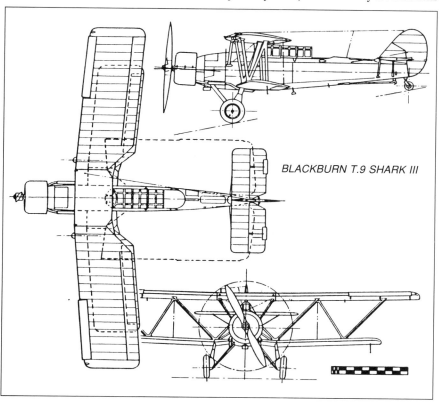

BLACKBURN T.9 SHARK III

Bristol Type 120 (G.4/31)

The circular 'porthole' in the fuselage forward of the undercarriage oleo leg is evidence of the Type 120's cabin beneath the pilot's cockpit, serving both as the space for a casualty stretcher and bomb aimer's position; entry to the rear cockpit was through the hinged triangular hatch covered by the R-6 markings. (Photo: The Bristol Aeroplane Co Ltd, Neg No. 995 dated April 1932)

The Bristol Aeroplane Company was singularly unfortunate in its efforts to produce a general purpose aircraft that was acceptable to the Air Ministry as a replacement for the long-serving Bristol F.2B and D.H.9A, and the more recent Westland Wapiti and Fairey Gordon. Frank Barnwell had produced the private venture Type 118 (see page 218), but although he had sought to include a wide range of capabilities the Air Ministry's reaction had been lukewarm (partly due to the Air Staff's preoccupation with fighter aircraft at the time), preferring to hire it for hot climate engine trials in Iraq during 1932.

A second, similar private venture prototype was authorised at Bristol in 1931, when it became apparent that a new General Purpose Specification was about to be issued, in all likelihood based on the company's own proposals. When the Specification, G.4/31, was first issued in July that year, it seemed that the new prototype, the Bristol Type 120, would at least be within reach of the performance being demanded. The Requirement called for an aircraft suitable for operation both in tropical and temperate climates, capable of light bombing by day and night with a station for a prone bomb aimer, of performing army co-operation duties, of dive bombing, of reconnaissance and of casualty evacuation. It had to be able to carry 500lb of bombs up to 20,000 feet or a 1,000lb bomb at 12,000 feet; maximum speed was required to be not less than 165 mph at 6,500 feet.

It was decided to go ahead with the Type 120 without delay, fitting a 600hp Mercury V engine so as to get the aeroplane into the air as soon as possible, well ahead of its likely rivals. Unfortunately, in October 1932, the Air Ministry chose to make a fundamental change in the Specification by introducing the joint coastal reconnaissance and torpedo bombing rôle, thereby effectively putting paid to any chance the Type 120 might have had of meeting the Requirement (and, incidentally, making the Specification virtually impossible to meet in all respects without considerable ingenuity and development costs, the very policy indeed of the Air Ministry at that time, while offering in return the rewards of very large production contracts for the successful contender). A significant feature of G.4/31 was that the Air Ministry's DTD had stated no preference for either a biplane or a monoplane.

Bristol had, perhaps ill-advisedly, included in the Type 120 an innovative feature, a rudimentary 'turret' cupola on the rear gunner's position, said to enable the gun to be fired when flying at the aircraft's maximum speed. Yet this feature served only to cause the aircraft to be placed on the secret list, a distinct disadvantage for the manufacturers of a private venture aircraft.

Nevertheless, the Type 120 flew for the first time at Filton on 29 January 1932, and Bristol was afforded the opportunity to submit the aeroplane for evaluation by the A & AEE, not in the context of Specification G.4/31 (as it was fully accepted that its inability to meet the torpedo bombing rôle disqualified it from the competition), but to examine the effects of a 'turret' on the handling qualities and performance of a relatively small aeroplane. Indeed, it was on account of this quite superfluous feature that the Air Ministry agreed to purchase the Type 120 in March 1933, allotting the serial number K3587, although the Bristol Aeroplane Company's involvement in the G.4/31 requirement resulted in a substantial financial loss. The aeroplane was finally struck off Air Ministry charge in January 1938, probably without ever having carried a bomb.

Type: Single-engine, two-seat, single-bay general purpose biplane.

Air Ministry Specification: Private venture to G.4/31.

Manufacturer: The Bristol Aeroplane Co Ltd, Filton, Bristol.

Powerplant: One 600hp Bristol Mercury V 9-cylinder air-cooled radial engine driving 2-blade propeller; also 650hp Bristol Pegasus IM.3 radial.

Dimensions: Span, 40ft 8in; length, 34ft 0in; height, 12ft 0in; wing area, 376 sq ft.

Weights: Tare, 3,632lb; all-up, 5,200lb.

Performance: (Pegasus engine). Max speed, 173 mph at 6,500ft; service ceiling, 25,500ft.

Armament: One synchronized 0.303in Vickers machine gun in upper port side of nose and one Lewis gun with Scarff ring on rear cockpit under rotating transparent cupola; bomb load of up to four 230lb bombs; no torpedo-carrying capability.

Prototype: One (originally marked R-6, but later allotted K3587), first flown at Filton on 29 January 1932. No production.

Westland PV.7 (G.4/31)

The first to fly of the eight G.4/31 prototypes whose design began after the Specification had been altered in October 1931 to include the torpedo bombing and coastal reconnaissance rôles, the private venture Westland PV.7 was one of only two contenders to feature monoplane configuration. The wing was located at the shoulders of the deep fuselage, the pilot's cockpit being situ-

Only a fortnight before its loss following wing failure, the PV.7 displays its front cockpit canopy and segmented side panels. (Photo: Westland Aircraft Works, dated 10 August 1934)

ated in line with the wing leading edge above a cabin whose purpose was to accommodate a casualty stretcher (when operating in the casualty-evacuation rôle) or the gunner/bomb aimer lying prone. Each wheel of the wide-track, split-axle undercarriage was mounted at the apices of tripodal struts, the vertical member of each incorporating an oleo-pneumatic shock absorber. Parallel, broad-chord underwing struts terminated at their inboard extremities with near-horizontal transverse struts which located the upper ends of the oleo members.

While the pilot's cockpit was initially uncovered, the second crew member normally occupied a midships ventral position immediately aft of the wings, being provided with a segmented transparent canopy which could be folded forward to enable the gunner to operate his gun at all speeds. A castoring tailwheel was fitted, as were Handley Page wing-tip slats and Westland-patented trailing-edge split flaps, the latter also being used as dive brakes. Power was provided by a 722hp Bristol Pegasus III.M3 radial engine encircled by a Townend ring.

Harald Penrose first flew P-7 on 30 October 1932 and, as subsequent investigation of the flight envelope progressed, a number of important modifications were found necessary, not least the torsional strengthening of the wings, which were removed so that additional triangulated tubular members could be added between the spars; and to provide the pilot with better protection from the fierce slipstream, the front cockpit was enclosed by a canopy with segmented side members. The rudder was found to be considerably over-balanced, and this was replaced by a constant-chord surface with much reduced mass balance.

The Westland aircraft began its Service evaluation at the A & AEE in July 1934, but on 25 August Penrose, who was visiting Martlesham, was asked to carry out a diving test with the cg moved well aft of its normal position. During the course of this flight, during a dive from 14,000 feet and at a true speed of about 220kt, the port wing broke away, taking the entire tail unit with it. With some difficulty Penrose managed to escape through the side windows, and landed safely by parachute. In the ensuing investigation it was deduced that the

wing parted company following the failure of one of the main underwing bracing struts (almost certainly as the result of damage caused on a previous occasion when a landing wheel was lost prior to a landing, the shock received when the oleo leg dug into the

ground possibly causing an unseen crack in the wing strut.)

The PV.7 was not insured at the time of the accident and, as Westland could not afford to build a second prototype, the company was obliged to withdraw from the G.4/31 contest.

Type: Single-engine, two-seat, shoulder-wing general purpose monoplane.
Air Ministry Specification: G.4/31.
Manufacturer: Westland Aircraft Works Ltd, Yeovil, Somerset.
Powerplant: One 722hp Bristol Pegasus IIIM.3 9-cylinder air-cooled radial engine.
Dimensions: Span, 60ft 3in; length, 38ft 8in; height, 12ft 0in; wing area (gross), 537 sq ft.
Weights: Tare, 4,820lb; all-up (with torpedo), 8,660lb.
Performance: Max speed, 168 mph at 5,000ft; climb to 10,000ft, 8 min 24 sec.
Armament: One synchronized 0.303in Vickers machine gun in port side of nose, and one Lewis gun with Scarff ring on rear cockpit. Max bomb load of up to two 500lb bombs or one 18in torpedo.
Prototype: One, P-7, first flown by Harald Penrose on 30 October 1933. No production.

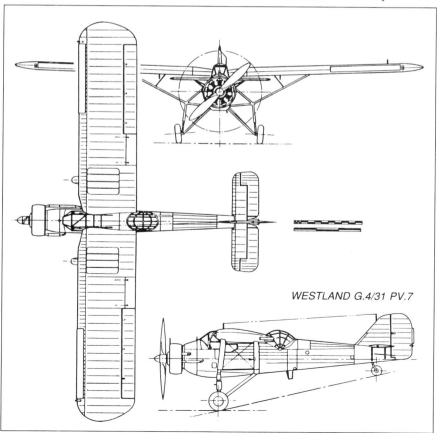

WESTLAND G.4/31 PV.7

Handley Page H.P.47 (G.4/31)

K2773 at Martlesham Heath during the G.4/31 competition in 1935, carrying a pair of 250lb GP bombs, and with wing slots fully open. (Photo: Air Ministry, A & AEENeg No 8177C)

It is quite likely that, of all the aircraft designers whose companies tendered designs to Specification G.4/31, only three were fully convinced that its requirements could only be met in all respects by a monoplane; they were Arthur Davenport of Westland, Gustav Lachmann of Handley Page, and Barnes Neville Wallis, the Head of Structures at Vickers. Davenport's braced shoulder-wing PV.7 suffered a structural failure when the aircraft was flying at or near the outer limits of its flight envelope; and it will be shown that Vickers was not ready to submit a monoplane prototype within the required timescale, but produced a biplane which, though unorthodox in several respects, came close enough to meeting most of the requirements to earn its manufacturer a production contract. The contract was then changed to cover the monoplane, the prototype of which flew no less than four years after the Specification was issued and was scarcely relevant to the original requirement. This was the cause of much ill feeling among other companies which had been encouraged to invest fairly large sums of private money in prototypes, few of which were ultimately purchased by the Air Ministry. Some of these companies faced bankruptcy, but were reprieved as huge production contracts and sub-contracts were awarded during the Expansion years.

The H.P.47 was unquestionably advanced for its time (unlike the Westland PV.7, it was a cantilever, low-wing monoplane). In referring to the correspondence and records relating to the H.P.47, one cannot fail to be impressed by the obvious integrity and professionalism of the Handley Page company, in particular of Lachmann himself. In contrast to other companies, which sought to have difficult requirements waived, or simply submitted prototypes which did not meet them (the excuse in some instances being that the engine — usually the Tiger — did not fulfil its manufacturer's forecast performance or reliability), Handley Page displayed uncommon determination to meet the Specification in full *and within the desired timescale*. It was mere coincidence that the only two monoplanes that flew within the 'mandatory' timescale were

the only two monoplanes tendered.

Lachmann's cantilever wing of high aspect ratio employed a stressed-skin torsion box comprising the leading edge and single main spar, and an auxiliary rear spar to which the ailerons and flaps were hinged. The entire wing centresection was metal skinned to accommodate the fuel tanks, thereby leaving the front and centre semi-monocoque fuselage free to incorporate a remarkably spacious cabin. The pilot's cockpit was situated well forward, providing excellent all-round view, particularly downwards over the wing leading edge. Three sitting casualties or two stretcher cases could be carried in the cabin, access to which was from the rear cockpit. The latter, the rear gunner's position, was stepped down below the top line of the centre fuselage, thereby affording protection from the slipstream as well as very wide arcs of fire. Aft of the wing full monocoque structure was used for the rear fuselage of oval, reduced cross-section; this boom structure carried the cantilever empennage. The horizontal tail surfaces comprised an adjustable-incidence tailplane and a single-piece

elevator with variable gearing. Sections of the fuselage, fin and rudder were skinned with corrugated light-alloy sheet.

The wings incorporated ailerons and full-span flaps, as well as full-span leading-edge slats, the inboard sections of the latter being linked to the flaps. A very wide track, divided-axle undercarriage featured vertical long-stroke oleos attached to the front of the torsion box, and two diagonal bracing struts jointed to the main and auxiliary wing spars. The mainwheels were spatted, as was the oleo-sprung tailwheel.

The wide, clear space between with mainwheel structures enabled the entire range of alternative loads to be carried close to the aircraft's c.g., unlike any of the other G.4/31 prototypes, that is to say a single 1,500lb AP, 1,000lb GP, two 550-, 500- or 450lb GP bombs, four 250lb GP or AS or 112lb GP bombs, or K-Type, Mk VIII* or X torpedo. Provision was also made to fit a twin-float undercarriage as an alternative to the wheel gear.

A single prototype, K2773, was ordered at a cost of £9,270 and this was

Type: Single-engine, two-seat, low-wing general purpose cantilever monoplane.
Air Ministry Specification: G.4/31
Manufacturer: Handley Page Ltd, Cricklewood, London, and Radlett, Hertfordshire.
Powerplant: One 660hp Bristol Pegasus III.M3 9-cylinder air-cooled supercharged radial engine driving 2-blade wooden propeller.
Structure: All-metal monocoque and semi-monocoque fuselage with light-alloy sheet covering. Wings constructed on stressed-skin torsion-box and auxiliary rear spar with metal sheet covering and flush-riveting; fabric-covered control surfaces.
Dimensions: Span, 58ft 0in; length, 37ft 7½in; wing area, 438 sq ft.
Weights: Tare, 5,362lb; all-up, 9,244lb (max, with torpedo), 7,708lb (as bomber).
Performance: Max speed, 161 mph at 5,000ft; climb to 10,000ft, 9 min 53 sec; service ceiling, 19,900ft; range (as bomber), 550 miles.
Armament: One synchronized 0.303in Vickers machine gun in port side of front fuselage and one Lewis gun with low-drag mounting on rear cockpit. Bomb load comprised either one 1,500lb AP, 1,000lb GP, two 500lb or 450lb, or four 250lb bombs, or one 18in K-Type, Mark VIII* or X torpedo.
Prototype: One, K2773, first flown by Sqn Ldr T H England at Radlett on 27 November 1933. No production.

first flown by Sqn Ldr Tom Harry England on 27 November 1933, and also by J L B H Cordes on the same day. (The airframe had been virtually complete since mid-June but the Pegasus I.M3 engine had not been delivered, and the results of model spinning tests at the RAE had taken two months to analyse.)

The Handley Page pilots both reported a number of unsatisfactory handling qualities and design deficiencies, ranging from heavy elevator control and soft undercarriage oleos to unequal wheelbrakes and a cockpit hood that was too stiff to slide.

A Pegasus III.M3 with an improved Townend ring, with the exhaust collector ring integral with its leading edge, was fitted. The sliding cockpit hood was discarded altogether.

After several postponements of the official trials had been announced, the H.P.47 was finally assessed at Martlesham Heath in April 1935, the majority of its flying being undertaken by Flight Lieutenants Neil Hope Bilney (later Air Vice-Marshal, CB, CBE), Terrance Howard Carr (later Gp Capt, DFC, AFC) and Charles Edwin Horrex (later Gp Capt, AFC*). As the PV.7 had already crashed, and the Vickers monoplane was nowhere near ready, the H.P.47 was the only monoplane tested. The Service pilots were fairly critical of its low-speed handling qualities, in particular the longitudinal instability, and control column vibration. The Air Ministry's

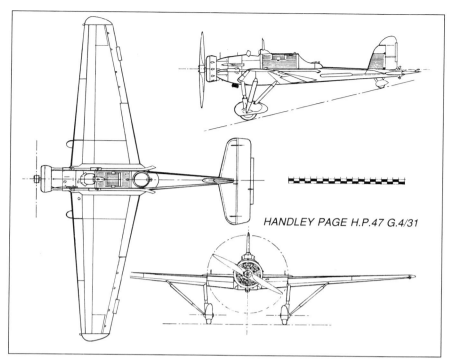

HANDLEY PAGE H.P.47 G.4/31

verdict placed the Handley Page second behind the Vickers Type 253, but ahead of the Blackburn B-7.

That Handley Page was unfortunate not to win the competition cannot be denied, especially as the Vickers Type 253 itself was not to be produced in quantity. Yet when the H.P.47 was submitted for the competition, its manufacturers were aware that modifications would be necessary in any production version. Lachmann had already

planned to enlarge the tailboom cross-section, increase the monocoque skin gauge, and replace all the corrugated skinning by heavier-gauge smooth panels. Other improvements would certainly have been made in production aircraft but, truth to tell, by 1935 the Air Ministry had lost interest in the general purpose aeroplane and, when the Vickers 'G.4/31 monoplane' was ordered into production as the Wellesley, it was termed a medium bomber!

An in-flight view of the H.P.47, showing the rear fuselage and tail to good advantage; the pilot's sliding hood had by this time been discarded. The bright sections of the exhaust pipe are heating muffs for cabin warm air pipes, just visible. (Photo: The Aeroplane, Neg No 6107)

Armstrong Whitworth A.W.19 (G.4/31)

The A.W.19 at Martlesham Heath in 1935 for the G.4/31 competition. (Photo: Air Ministry)

Smaller and lighter than the Westland PV.7 monoplane, the private venture Armstrong Whitworth A.W.19 was, however, designed to carry the heavier K-type torpedo of 2,000lb and, although a biplane, was to some extent conceived along similar lines, the G.4/31 requirements being interpreted with much the same emphasis. The pilot's cockpit was, for instance, placed high in the front fuselage above a spacious cabin. To provide a good field of vision, the upper wing was attached to the shoulders of the fuselage and, to provide plenty of ground clearance for the propeller and allow space to load the torpedo while limiting the length of the undercarriage, the lower wings were gulled.

Not only were established Armstrong Whitworth structural practices retained, but choice also fell on an Armstrong Siddeley engine, the Tiger IV supercharged fourteen-cylinder radial. Provision for alternative equipment was made according to the aircraft's immediate tasks, including flotation bags for oversea duties (although, unlike the Handley Page, no provision was made for interchangeable float undercarriage), a stressed attachment point for a message pick-up hook for army co-operation duties, a prone bomb-aiming position for the level bombing rôles, and so on.

Alan Colin Campbell Orde AFC (later CBE, AFC), Armstrong Whitworth's chief test pilot, took the A.W.19 aloft for its maiden flight on 26 February 1934, and the aircraft was duly delivered to Martlesham Heath on 6 April, bearing its A-3 B Conditions marking, for preliminary performance trials. With a slightly more reliable Tiger VI, the aircraft attracted favourable comments from the Service pilots on its performance and general design, despite persistent overheating of the engine.

By the date of the official G.4/31 competitive evaluation in 1935, however, the biplane configuration was beginning to appear dated, and the ingenuity of, for instance, Lachmann's Handley Page, tended to consign the traditionalist designs to the sidelines. Moreover, the Air Ministry was no longer seeking aircraft that were, in effect, maids of all work but masters of none. By the standards of 1932, the

A.W.19 might have been considered an efficient machine, capable of assuming the duties of the Wapiti and Gordon; by 1935, as Germany began to build a modern air force, the RAF needed specialist aeroplanes, and as financing quickly became available to support those manufacturers which had borne the costs of research and development

during the lean years, preference was increasingly expressed for designs that displayed the fruits of this enterprise.

The A.W.19 prototype was purchased by the Air Ministry late in 1935, given the military serial K5606, and promptly relegated to the flight development of the recalcitrant Tiger engine. It was struck off charge on 28 June 1940.

Type: Single-engine, two/three-crew, single-bay general purpose biplane.
Air Ministry Specification: G.4/31
Manufacturer: Sir W G Armstrong Whitworth Aircraft Ltd., Coventry.
Powerplant: One 706hp Armstrong Siddeley Tiger IV 14-cylinder air-cooled, supercharged radial engine driving 2-blade propeller. Later Tiger VI and VII.
Dimensions: Span, 49ft 8in; length, 42ft 2in. *Weights:* Tare, 4,749lb; all-up, 8,871lb.
Performance: (Bomber load). Max speed, 150 mph at 6,500ft; climb to 10,000ft, 9 min 56 sec; service ceiling, 15,400ft.
Armament: One synchronized 0.303in Vickers machine gun in nose decking, offset to starboard, and one Lewis gun with Scarff ring on rear cockpit. Bomb load of either one 1,000lb or two 500lb bombs, or one 2,000lb Type K 18in torpedo.
Prototype: One, A-3 (later K5606), first flown by A C Campbell Orde on 26 February 1934. No production.

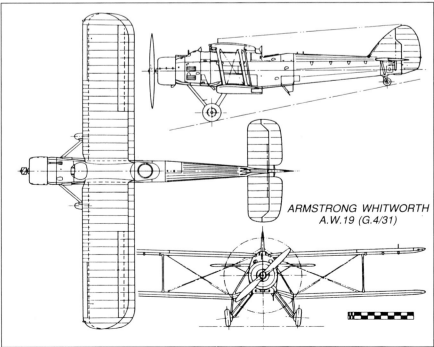

ARMSTRONG WHITWORTH
A.W.19 (G.4/31)

Fairey G.4/31

Such were the large production contracts likely to be issued for the successful entrant to the proposed G.4/31 competition that the Fairey Aviation Company was tempted into preparing two design tenders, a biplane and a monoplane — both private ventures. Both designs were accepted for entry, and manufacture of both began. Such, however, was the radical nature of the monoplane, with the need for lengthy tunnel testing, that it became obvious that a prototype monoplane would be nowhere near completion by the proposed competition date, and Fairey persuaded the Air Ministry to transfer the purchase contract to the biplane.

The Fairey G.4/31 biplane was a portly and, when it first appeared, untidy aeroplane with uncowled Pegasus II.MS radial engine. The vertical tail surfaces were angular and, probably reflecting some embarrassment at the loss of the Fairey TSR.I following its inability to recover from a flat spin, longitudinal strakes were included on the rear fuselage immediately forward of the tailplane. Like most of the G.4/31 prototypes, the Fairey featured a spacious cabin in the forward fuselage, being entered by a passageway on the starboard side from the rear cockpit or through a fairly large door on that side of the fuselage. The pilot's cockpit was offset to port, with generous cut-outs in the wing trailing edges to provide adequate fields of view for the pilot. The second crew member could take up a prone position in the cabin for bomb aiming.

When first flown by Chris Staniland on 29 March 1934, the big biplane was powered by a 635hp Bristol Pegasus engine, but this proved to be inadequate to approach the performance demanded and, with some reluctance, it was decided to fit the much heavier and more powerful 750hp Tiger IV radial, even though this engine was widely known to be still thoroughly unreliable and, as yet, underdeveloped. The opportunity was also taken to tidy up the aeroplane. Wheel spats were added and the vertical tail surfaces were reshaped into a more rounded profile, a small ventral fin, previously fitted, being deleted. The Tiger engine was enclosed in a long-chord cowling and, before the aircraft was delivered to Martlesham,

The Fairey G.4/31 in its tidied-up form, albeit with the Tiger engine. Just visible is the cabin access door immediately aft of the numeral '12'. (Photo: The Fairey Aviation Co Ltd).

the former wooden propeller was replaced by a Fairey metal type.

The cleaned-up version, known unofficially as the Mark II, and now covered

Type: Single-engine, two/three-crew, single-bay general purpose biplane.
Air Ministry Specification: G.4/31
Manufacturer: The Fairey Aviation Co Ltd, Hayes, Middlesex.
Powerplant: Fitted initially with one 635hp Bristol Pegasus II.M3 9-cylinder air-cooled radial engine driving 2-blade wooden propeller; later with 750hp Armstrong Siddeley Tiger IV (and VI) 14-cylinder radial engines.
Structure: Stainless-steel and duralumin structure with fabric covering.
Dimensions: Span, 53ft 0in; length, 40ft 10in; height, 15ft 8in; wing area, 658 sq ft.
Weights: Tare, 6,987lb; all-up (bomber), 8,790lb.
Performance: Bomber. Max speed, 157 mph at 6,500ft; climb to 5,000ft, 7 min 12 sec; service ceiling, 23,200ft.
Armament: One free-firing Lewis machine gun in the port lower wing (with one 97-round drum), and one Lewis gun with low-drag Fairey mounting in rear cockpit; bomb load of one 1,000lb or three 500lb bombs, or a Mark VIII or Type-K torpedo.
Prototype: One (originally with B Conditions marking F-1, later K3905), first flown by C S Staniland at Harmondsworth on 29 March 1934. No production.

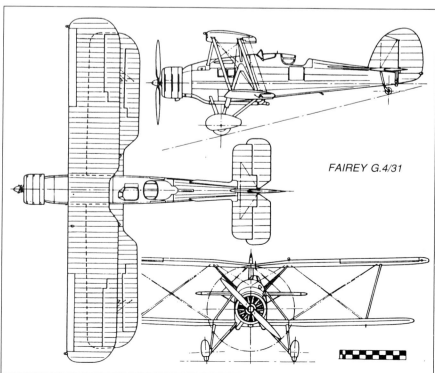

FAIREY G.4/31

by an Air Ministry purchase contract, was first flown by Staniland on 22 June 1934, but straightway the Tiger's refractory behaviour made itself known, with scarcely a single flight not being prematurely terminated by chronic overheating of the engine. Nevertheless, with this serious shortcoming notified to the Air Ministry in advance, K3905 was delivered to the A & AEE at the end of 1934 for performance trials. These proved to be quite impossible to complete, and it is believed that no report was issued so that, early in 1935, the aircraft was returned to its manufacturer and eventually withdrawn from further evaluation under the terms of G.4/31. It subsequently joined other surplus aircraft on Air Ministry charge in the Tiger engine development programme at the Royal Aircraft Establishment.

Parnall G.4/31

George Parnall's company at Yate, formerly in south Gloucestershire, was the smallest manufacturer to enter a tender for the G.4/31 competition to decide on a Wapiti and Gordon replacement, and had suffered a succession of disappointments in its previous efforts to attract production contracts (and sub-contracts) from the Air Ministry. The long-serving chief designer, Harold Bolas, had left the company in 1929, his place being taken by H V Clarke who, at the end of 1931, began work on the Parnall tender to G.4/31.

The design contained in this tender, though of unusual appearance, was by most accounts a most creditable effort and, had it not been so long in manufacture, might well have been awarded a small consolation contract for research purposes, if nothing better. As it was, it attracted sufficient interest at the DTD to warrant a prototype being ordered and paid for, so that George Parnall would not to have to bear the cost of failure.

The aircraft, K2772, was first flown at Yate by Capt Howard Saint during the winter of 1934-35[1], and was a large two-bay biplane with gulled upper wing — yet another expedient adopted to afford the pilot a good field of view; his cockpit was located immediately forward of the carry-

Adoption of the gulled upper wing (difficult to appreciate in this view) may have invited directional stability problems with Parnall's G.4/31 prototype, particularly with its relatively short fuselage, requiring drastic alterations to the tail surfaces. (Photo: A J Jackson Collection)

through members of the front wing spar. A much smaller cabin than in other G.4/31 prototypes was situated beneath the pilot's cockpit with access through a door on the port side of the fuselage immediately aft of the front Vickers gun.

Perhaps the strangest feature of the aircraft was the extraordinary shape of the vertical tail surfaces, the angular rudder possessing a large horn balance extending forward over a pentagonal fin; a ventral fin included an integral fairing over the tailwheel. The tail profile suggests that some fairly drastic cosmetics were called for following tunnel testing.

K2772 may have encountered handling problems during its early flight trials, but the reason for it not being delivered to Martlesham Heath until 1936 — long after the G.4/31 competition had been completed — is not known. No report of trials appears to have survived and, being on Air Ministry charge, it remained at Martlesham Heath; here, and at the RAE, K2772 participated in various undisclosed armament trials, until its pilot was obliged to make a forced landing on 9 March 1937; and it was to be irreparably damaged during recovery.

[1]   The date of K2772's maiden flight has not been established beyond doubt. Kenneth Wixey (*Parnall Aircraft since 1914*, Putnam, 1990, page 197) states simply '1935'. However, correspondence between George Parnall Ltd and the DTD, held in the PRO files under AIR2, suggests that the first flight may have taken place as early as October 1934, a suggestion borne out by various secondary sources, but not capable of verification owing to a break in administrative records when Parnall Aircraft Ltd was formed following the sale of George Parnall & Co in 1935.

Type: Single-engine, two-seat, two-bay general purpose biplane.
Air Ministry Specification: G.4/31
Manufacturer: George Parnall & Co, Yate, Gloucestershire.
Powerplant: One 630hp Bristol Pegasus IM3 9-cylinder air-cooled radial engine.
Dimensions: Span, 57ft 0in; length, 35ft 9in; height, 15ft 0in; wing area, 687 sq ft.
Weight: All-up (without bombs or torpedo), 6,800lb.
Performance: Max speed, approx 165 mph at 5,000ft without warload.
Armament: One synchronized 0.303in Vickers machine gun on port side of nose, and one Lewis gun on rear cockpit; bomb load of up to 1,500lb of bombs or one Mk VIII 18in torpedo.
Prototype: One, K2772, first flown by Capt Howard Saint during the winter of 1934-35 at Yate. No production.

Blackburn B-7 (G.4/31)

Most obvious differences between Blackburn's G.4/31 prototype and the Shark I were the broad-chord wings and removal of the arrester hook. (Photo: Blackburn Aircraft Ltd, Neg No 11371S)

As the original G.4/31 requirements underwent changes between October 1931 and December 1934, two other manufacturers entered the list of contenders with private venture adaptations of aircraft already in production for the RAF and Fleet Air Arm. These were the Blackburn Aeroplane and Motor Company and Hawker Aircraft Ltd.

With the addition of torpedo bombing and coastal reconnaissance rôles to the range of 'general purpose' duties listed in the Requirement in October 1931, it seemed logical that the Shark, with its torpedo-carrying capabilities, could be adapted to perform most of the other duties and thereby stood an outside chance of earning further production orders.

Employing something like 80 per cent of the Shark I's standard airframe, as well as the Tiger IV engine, a special prototype, referred to as the B-7, was introduced into the Shark I production line early in 1934. As folding wings were not required, fixed wings of similar span but increased chord were fitted, thereby obtaining the increased wing area and lift needed to lift the large K-type torpedo. The necessary modifications to the electrical system were made to include navigation lights for night bombing. The all-up weight was increased from the 8,050lb of the torpedo-

carrying Shark I to the 8,338lb of the similarly-loaded G.4/31 prototype. This was first flown by A M Blake on 28 November 1934, and the same pilot began the manufacturer's trials on 5 January 1935 before delivering the B-7 to Martlesham on 28 May for the official G.4/31 competition.

By then, however, the torpedo bomber rôle had been withdrawn from the Requirement and, as the Blackburn B-7 had never aspired to meet the dive-

bombing and casualty evacuation requirements, its attendance at the eventual competition was entirely meaningless, even though it was placed third in the final results.

Possibly on account of very low investment by Blackburn in preparation of the B-7 prototype and the fact that it failed to meet almost every performance demand, the Air Ministry declined to purchase the aircraft, and it was returned to Brough and scrapped.

Type: Single-engine, two/three-crew, single/two-bay general purpose biplane.
Air Ministry Specification: Private venture to G.4/31.
Manufacturer: The Blackburn Aeroplane and Motor Co Ltd, Brough, Yorkshire.
Powerplant: One 700hp Armstrong Siddeley Tiger IV radial driving 2-blade propeller.
Dimensions: Span, 46ft 0in; length, 35ft 4⅝in; height, 12ft 9in.
Weight: Torpedo bomber rôle. All-up, 8,338lb.
Performance: Torpedo bomber rôle. Max speed, 145 mph at 6,500ft; service ceiling, 10,500ft; range, 475 miles.
Armament: One synchronized 0.303in Vickers machine gun and one Lewis gun on rear cockpit; bomb load of one 1,000lb or two 500lb bombs, or one 1,800lb K-type 18in torpedo.
Prototype: One (B Conditions marking B-7), first flown by A M Blake at Brough on 28 November 1934. No production.

Hawker P.V.4 (G.4/31)

Hawker's late decision to enter the G.4/31 contest was prompted by reports circulating the aircraft industry in 1933 suggesting that, in view of the seemingly impossible task of producing an aircraft capable of performing all the operational rôles listed by the Air Ministry, the requirement would either have to be divided into two disparate

parts for different aircraft or omit at least two of the rôles.

As none of the aircraft being prepared (in some secrecy) was said to be suitable

for both dive bombing *and* torpedo launching, Sopwith suggested to Camm that, in view of the excellent handling qualities of the Hart in steep dives (a

The P.V.4, carring bombs, at about the time of its first appearance at Martlesham Heath, while still powered by the 690hp Pegasus radial engine. (Photo: via R C B Ashworth)

feature of the aircraft particularly commented upon at Martlesham Heath), it might be worthwhile to prepare a variant of the new Hind bomber (page 259) — itself intended as a Hart successor — for the eventual G.4/31 competition, which was not likely to be held much before the end of 1934.

Drawing on the company's experience in producing Hart variants with radial engines, principally for overseas customers, Camm's design staff accordingly produced a Hind variant, with most of that aeroplane's intended modifications, such as a tailwheel, night flying instrumentation and lights, and a strengthened airframe, as well as G.4/31's favoured Pegasus III radial engine.

The prototype (built alongside the company's other PV aircraft, the P.V.3 fighter to Specification F.7/30 — another imaginative but equally abortive venture) was first flown by 'George' Bulman at Brooklands on 6 December 1934, wearing the B Conditions marking IPV4). However, before being flown to Martlesham Heath in the spring of 1935, it was fitted with the latest 800hp Pegasus X engine, purchased at Sopwith's personal expense.

In the trials that followed, the P.V.4 was found to be the only contestant wholly suitable for dive bombing; being fitted with a cross-axle undercarriage, it was not able to carry a torpedo. Nor did it meet the bomb load requirements for level bombing. Strangely, the final report on the competition stated that the Hawker aeroplane 'was not fast enough' for the level bombing rôles — yet its performance was quoted as being superior to all the other contenders by a significant margin! It was also criticised for not possessing adequate gun armament, despite mounting the stipulated Vickers and Lewis guns and more ammunition that most of the other aircraft.

After the trials had been completed, IPV4 was purchased by the Air Ministry as K6926 for type testing of various new engines, including the Bristol Perseus and Taurus sleeve-valve radials. It was struck off charge on 29 March 1939.

Type: Single-engine, two-seat, single-bay general purpose biplane.
Air Ministry Specification: Private venture to G.4/31.
Manufacturer: Hawker Aircraft Ltd, Kingston-upon-Thames and Brooklands, Surrey.
Powerplant: One 690hp Bristol Pegasus IIIM.3 9-cylinder air-cooled radial engine driving 2-blade Watts wooden propeller. Also 820hp Pegasus X, Perseus and Taurus sleeve-valve radial engines.
Dimensions: Span, 40ft 0in; length, 29ft 10in; height, 11ft 10in; wing area, 348 sq ft.
Weights: Tare, 3,728lb; all-up, 6,650lb.
Performance: Max speed, 183 mph at 6,600ft; climb to 10,000ft, 6 min 45 sec; service ceiling, 23,700ft; range, 460 miles.
Armament: One synchronized 0.303in Vickers Mk III machine gun in port side of nose, and one Lewis gun with Somers mounting in rear cockpit. Bomb load of up to two 250lb bombs.
Prototype: One (IPV4, later K6926), first flown by P W S Bulman at Brooklands on 6 December 1934. No production.

Vickers Type 253 (G.4/31)

Mention has already been made of the events that led to, and followed, the declaration of the Vickers Type 253 as the winner of the G.4/31 competition in 1935, a decision that fuelled a good deal of ill feeling among other manufacturers. Much correspondence was generated among the principal parties, and only if this is examined in the broadest context can a clear idea be gained of the train of events.

There is no doubt but that the original issue of Specification G.4/31 was welcomed by the Vickers company, especially as Barnes Wallis was already cutting his teeth on the design of an aircraft (the M.1/30) using structural techniques familiar to him from his work in airship design. However eager that great engineer was to extend other, more radical techniques to aeroplane design, it had to be accepted that no flight experience had yet been gained, nor would expensive research aircraft be ordered during the period of the Depression. It now seemed likely that if a prototype designed to G.4/31 could

The Vickers Type 253, K2771, at Martlesham Heath at the time of the G.4/31 competition, with a pair of 250lb bombs; at some time in the aircraft's life a sliding canopy over the pilot's cockpit was fitted. (Photo: Air Ministry, RTP Neg No 8174C)

be ordered from Vickers by the Air Ministry, it would represent a convenient vehicle in which to apply the new structural principles.

In the event, Rex Pierson offered three design tenders, of which an outwardly orthodox biplane, the Type 253, was selected and a prototype, K2771, contracted. One of the other designs offered, the Type 246, was a low-wing monoplane with very high aspect ratio wings; this was the design favoured by Wallis, as it lent itself most readily to the expression of his own structural concepts.

In being instructed to concentrate on the Type 253 biplane, in the short term at least, Wallis was able to apply his advanced structural theories by stages, in this instance employing his geodetic structure in the fuselage only. In geographical terms the geodetic principle, when applied to the globe, is referred to as a great circle — the shortest distance between two points. Wallis' structural application was to wrap light alloy members in a spiral around conventional longerons, and by doubling the spiral, but in contra-direction, the system produced an almost fail-safe structure

The root sections of both upper and lower wings of the Vickers G.4/31 were swept foward, but only the lower wings were gulled, a configuration that gives rise to a curious optical illusion in this view of the aircraft. (Photo: Air Ministry RTP, Neg No 8174B)

with the greatest possible weight economy: if one of the spirals is in compression, the contra-spiral is in tension.

Such a Specification as G.4/31 offered an opportunity to demonstrate an aeroplane with a very broad range of structural demands, and both Pierson and Wallis decided to exploit the prototype's potential to the full, probably with the idea that it constituted a halfway stage to a fully geodetic monoplane. (It may be remarked here that Wallis was, in 1933-34, also undertaking preliminary design drawings of a geodetic-structured twin-engine bomber to Specification B.9/32, that would materialise as the Wellington bomber, see page 292).

It is quite possible that some at Vickers subscribed to the fairly common belief that no outright winner of the G.4/31 contest would be declared. Nevertheless, it was important that Vickers should be able to demonstrate the Type 253's superiority over the other contestants, and considerable play was made of the efficiency of the fuselage structure (even though the wings remained of Vickers' conventional two-spar structure with close-pitch Warren-girder ribs).

In configuration the aeroplane was a large two-bay biplane with gulled lower wings, and upper wings attached at the fuselage shoulders. The pilot's cockpit was located immediately forward of the upper wing leading edge, above and ahead of a spacious cabin (whose long side windows disclosed the diagonal geodetic members as lattice frames). A robust split-axle undercarriage allowed the torpedo and bomb load to be carried inboard of the wheels, and therefore close to the aircraft's centre of gravity.

'Mutt' Summers first flew K2771 at Brooklands on 6 August 1934, a 635hp Bristol Pegasus IIM.3 engine being fitted at this stage. To avoid unexpected handling qualities in this prototype, Pierson had elected to retain the familiar RAF 15 wing section, and the manufacturer's trials went ahead with relatively little difficulty and few surprises. Partway through the trials, Vickers was handed a bonus when the Air Ministry withdrew the casualty evacuation, tor-

pedo carrying and army co-operation rôles from the Requirement, which enabled Summers to concentrate on the flying qualities associated with day and night level bombing.

By the time K2771 was first deliver-

ed to Martlesham Heath in April 1935 it was clear that the Vickers aeroplane stood a good chance of being declared the winner, assuming that the Air Ministry was sufficiently interested in a result. The Westland PV.7 had

---

Type: Single-engine, two-seat, two-bay general purpose biplane.

Air Ministry Specification: G.4/31.

Manufacturer: Vickers (Aviation) Ltd, Weybridge, Surrey.

Powerplant: One 635hp Bristol Pegasus IIM.3 9-cylinder air-cooled radial engine driving 2-blade wooden propeller. Later 680hp Pegasus IIIM.3.

Structure: Fuselage of lightweight longeron primary structure wrapped with geodetic left- and right-handed spiral members, and conventional two-spar wings with Warren-girder spar webs and inter-spar ribs. Wing of Raf 15 section.

Dimensions: Span, 52ft 7in; length, 37ft 0in; height, 12ft 6in; wing area, 579 sq ft.

Weights: Tare, 4,365lb; all-up, 8,350lb.

Performance: Max speed, 161 mph at 4,500ft; climb to 10,000ft, 8 min 30 sec; service ceiling, 21,700ft.

Prototype: One, K2771, first flown by Joseph ('Mutt') Summers at Brooklands on 6 August 1934. No production.

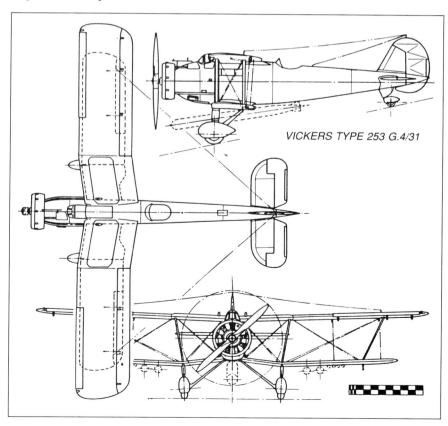

VICKERS TYPE 253 G.4/31

crashed many months earlier, the Blackburn B-7 failed to meet the performance demands by a wide margin, the Hawker aircraft was no more than a dive bomber, and some doubt existed about the structural integrity of the Handley Page entry. The Fairey and Armstrong Whitworth aircraft were handicapped by use of Tiger engines which still demanded plenty of development, while the Parnall contender was still not ready for assessment by the Service.

Moreover, the Air Ministry was well aware that Vickers had gone ahead with the construction of the monoplane Type 246 prototype as a private venture, although no application had been made for its inclusion in the G.4/31 competition (on the grounds that it could not be made ready in time).

The announcement that the Type 253 was the winner was, under these circumstances, a foregone conclusion, although the background lobbying was scarcely suspected by the other manufacturers. By August, the month in which the Type 246 monoplane first flew, a contract for 150 Type 253 biplanes had been placed with Vickers.

Vickers immediately embarked on a series of comparative flight trials with their two prototypes at Brooklands. Such was the obvious superiority of the monoplane (whose fuselage was almost identical to that of the biplane, but was married to a geodetic-style wing) that, following representations by Vickers' chairman, Sir Robert McLean Kt, the Air Ministry agreed to cancel its biplane order, substituting a contract for 90 monoplanes. In efforts to appease the other manufacturers, who had had to contend with constant prevarication by the Air Ministry and repeated alterations to the Specification, the Air Ministry sought to justify its verdict by pointing to the industry's inability to meet the multi-rôle requirement as being the reason for abbreviating the Specification, and that, being left with only the bombing rôle to consider, the Vickers aeroplane was adjudged to be the best available aircraft in this category. Indeed, henceforth, the rôle of General Purpose aircraft was not recognised by the RAF, and when the Vickers Type 246 was described as a 'medium bomber', it was selected for production in that category (see page 273).

The Type 253, by 1936 redundant as an operational prototype, was relegated to engine testing, and joined the growing number of such aircraft being assembled at Filton to assist in the development of the new Bristol radial engines.

Boulton Paul P.75 Overstrand

Just as Specification G.4/31 signalled the end of the biplane era in the General Purpose category, so the long saga of Boulton and Paul medium bomber biplanes closed with the Sidestrand Mark V — renamed the Overstrand in 1934.

The Sidestrand had first flown in 1926 and joined only one Squadron, No 101, at Bircham Newton in 1928, moving to Andover the following year. One of the late production Sidestrands, J9186, had been set aside for general development work in 1929, being fitted with a succession of Jupiter radial engines in various cowlings and Townend rings.

Because No 101 Squadron was unique in being equipped with what was termed a 'medium bomber', the matter of replacing its old Sidestrands posed something of a dilemma for the Air Ministry. It appears that no one was prepared to state categorically that there was no place in the RAF's armoury for a day bomber that could scarcely reach any target in continental Europe from its base in England. It might have been thought conceivable that No 101 Squadron could perform a useful rôle in the Middle East, but it was never sent there. On the other hand, the Air

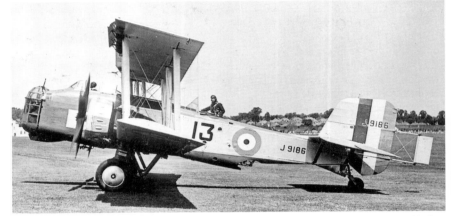

The first Overstrand, J9186, wearing its New Type No 13 at the Hendon Display on 30 June 1934; the front gunner has swung his turret fully to port to prevent the airstream penetrating the gun slot and sweeping aft through the fuselage. (Photo: via J M Bruce)

Staff — after the departure of Trenchard — was not willing to authorise development of an entirely new medium bomber in the short term (owing to severe financial constraints), and because it was intended to introduce modern monoplane bombers into service in the longer term.

When, early in 1933, John North suggested introducing the 550hp Bristol Pegasus into the Sidestrand, in place of its obsolescent Jupiters, he could point to likely worthwhile and cost-effective improvements in performance, load and range, provided that no additional alterations to the airframe were found necessary, other than in the engine nacelles. He also suggested modifying all surviving Sidestrands in service. As this effectively meant taking No 101 Squadron 'out of the line' while its veteran bombers underwent modification, the Air Ministry sanctioned the conversion of only three Sidestrands immediately, while acknowledging the likelihood of a new production order the following year.

The Air Ministry therefore raised a Specification, 29/33, covering the preparation of a prototype, J9186, and two other conversions of J9185 and J9187, all Mark III Sidestrands. J9186 had only just completed brief performance trials with No 22 Squadron of the A & AEE,

Sometimes referred to as the second Overstrand prototype, K9770 was more correctly the pre-production trials aircraft. It is shown here at Martlesham Heath during armament tests, carrying a pair of 250lb and eight 20lb bombs. The pilot's cockpit enclosure, front turret details and the nonagonal Townend rings — peculiar to the Overstrand — are clearly visible. This machine was at one time used in flight refuelling trials. (Photo: Air Ministry, A & AEE Neg No 5799)

fitted with Jupiter XFBM engines, and now returned to Norwich in early April 1933 where work got underway immediately to install the new Pegasus engines.

This work, however, threatened to disrupt a continuing programme of trial installations, planned by the DTD for J9186, and the Air Ministry decided that this should go ahead while the engine change was being instituted. Thus it was that when, probably sometime in August that year, Sqn Ldr C A Rae first flew the Sidestrand V prototype, it not only featured the Pegasus engines but also a new nose turret, hydraulically rotated and mounting a single Lewis machine gun. (As far as can be discovered, this was the first time a power-operated gun turret was flown in a British bomber.)

The obvious improvement gained by the change to the more powerful Pegasus engines, now enclosed in specially developed, nonagonal Townend rings with integral leading-edge exhaust collector manifolds, encouraged North to introduce a whole host of other modifications (also previously scheduled for *ad hoc* trial installation), including improved balancing of the tail controls — while retaining the Flettner tab — and a stronger undercarriage with levered suspension, the latter now essential on account of a 50 per cent greater bomb load. Apart from the introduction of the prominent new nose gun turret, slipstream protection for the other crew members included a sliding canopy for the pilot, as well as cockpit heating, and a shield for the midships dorsal gunner. An autopilot was also introduced.

After a visit in February 1934 by J9186 to No 101 Squadron (then com-

manded by Sqn Ldr Eric Bourne Coulter Betts DSC, AFC, later Air Vice-Marshal, CBE, DSC, AFC) for Service trials, the Air Ministry confirmed its order for a total of 24 production aircraft, and announced that the name Overstrand had been selected.

The Overstrand, like the Sidestrand before it, was only intended to equip No 101 Squadron, and 18 of the first batch of 19 aircraft were delivered to Bicester between September 1935 and January 1936, progressively replacing the

Sidestrands on a one-for-one basis. (The one aircraft not delivered to No 101 Squadron was K4552, which was issued to the Air Armament School at Eastchurch for the purpose of training nose-turret gunners for the Squadron.)

The aircraft was generally very popular among the Squadron crew members, it being a new experience to fly an aircraft in which so much attention had been given to crew comfort. The Squadron also found that, with such equipment as the autopilot, bombing results

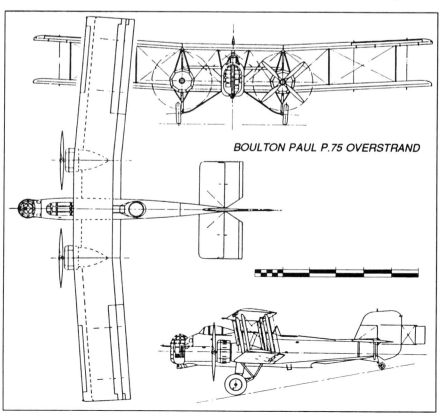

BOULTON PAUL P.75 OVERSTRAND

Standard Overstrand K4561/U of No 101 (Bomber) Squadron; just visible is the midships dorsal gunner, perched high in his gun ring but well protected from the slipstream by his raised windscreen. Unlike the RAF's night bombers between the Wars, the day bombers were doped silver overall. (Photo: RAF Museum)

improved on training exercises, while the gunnery accuracy by the nose gunners increased spectacularly.

Of course, the Sidestrand quickly became an anachronism as monoplane bombers began entering service all over Europe. Yet No 101 Squadron played a minor part in the RAF's expansion scheme when, in January 1937, it lent four of its aircraft and four crews to provide the nucleus of the newly formed No 144 Squadron (Sqn Ldr C W L Trusk, AFC); the aircraft, however, were retained for only a month before Ansons were delivered in preparation for Blenheim day bombers.

It was No 101 Squadron's turn to begin disposing of its biplanes in June 1938, with the arrival of Blenheim monoplanes. The Overstrands were then delivered to aircrew training units — Air Observers' Schools and No 10 Bombing & Gunnery School — and a few soldiered on into the war years, the last aircraft to be struck off charge being

K8176 at the Army Co-operation Development Unit on 30 May 1941. With

the passing of the Overstrand came the end of a chapter, not only in the history of the RAF, but in the splendid enterprise of a small company whose chief designer, John North, had steadfastly held to a belief for more than a dozen years that his particular formula represented the best in the middle ground of bomber design.

Type: Twin engine, five-crew, three-bay biplane medium day bomber.
Air Ministry Specifications: 29/33 and 23/34.
Manufacturer: Boulton Paul Aircraft Ltd, Riverside and Mousehold, Norwich, Norfolk.
Powerplant: Prototype. Two 555hp Bristol Pegasus IM.3 9-cylinder air-cooled radial engines driving 4-blade propellers. Production. 580hp Bristol Pegasus IIM.3. Experimental. 720hp Bristol Pegasus IV engines.
Dimensions: Span, 72ft 0in; length, 46ft 0in; height, 15ft 6in; wing area, 980 sq ft.
Weights: Tare, 7,936lb; all-up, 11,923 lb.
Performance: Max speed, 148 mph at 6,500ft; climb to 6,500ft, 5 min 24 sec; service ceiling, 21,300ft; range, 545 miles.
Armament: Single Lewis guns in hydraulically-operated nose turret, and with ring mountings in midships dorsal and ventral positions; bomb load of up to three 500lb GP bombs or six 250 lb GP bombs over short distances.
Prototype: One, J9186 (a converted Sidestrand III), first flown by Sqn Ldr C A Rae at Mousehold with Pegasus IM.3 engines, and limited modifications, in August 1933.
Production: Apart from the prototype, J9186 (above), two Sidestrand IIIs, J9185 and J9186, were converted to Overstrands; a total of 24 new Overstrands was built: K4546-K4564 and K8173-K8177.
Summary of Service: Overstrands served with No 101 (Bomber) Squadron at Bicester from January 1935 until August 1938 (and temporarily with No 144 Squadron, formed out of No 101 Squadron, during January 1937 at Bicester). They also served with Nos 2 and 10 Air Observers' School (the latter becoming No 10 Bombing & Gunnery School), the Air Armament School, the Central Landing School and the Army Co-operation Development Unit.

Vickers Type 266 Vincent

The issue by the Air Ministry of Specification G.4/31 for a general purpose aeroplane, with its all-embracing demands covering half-a-dozen rôles, had prompted Rex Pierson in 1931 to undertake as a private venture the conversion of the Vildebeest coastal defence tor-

pedo bomber to the traditional general purpose rôle as performed by RAF aircraft in the Middle East, that is to say a ground support light bomber. The one

failing expressed by the squadrons in the aircraft they had flown for a dozen years had been their lack of range — an obvious shortcoming in a region of

A Vincent at Brooklands, showing the large ventral fuel tank and attachment points for the underwing bomb racks. This aircraft is not fitted with the customary message pick-up hook, nor the front Vickers gun. (Photo: The Aeroplane, Neg No 6162)

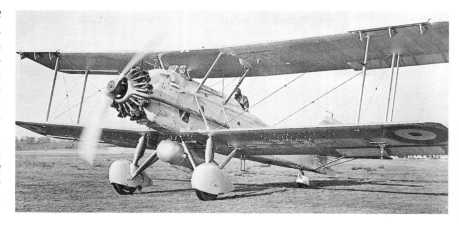

Bereft of wheel spats and Townend ring, this Vincent, K4712, bears the code letters of No 8 Squadron and camouflage applied at about the time of the start of the Second World War. The message pick-up hook, aft of the ventral fuel tank, suggests that it may have been engaged in collaboration with British forces in Italian Somaliland. (Photo: via R C B Ashworth)

harsh terrain where landing grounds were few and far between.

By deleting the Vildebeest's torpedo gear and making provision for an additional 100-gallon fuel tank under the fuselage, the aircraft's range was extended to well over 1,000 miles; being a relatively large aircraft, the Vildebeest was perfectly capable of accommodating the equipment being called for in the army co-operation demands of G.4/31, and Pierson included provision for a bomb load of up to 1,056lb, desert survival equipment, a message pick-up hook and a wireless set.

The Air Ministry accepted Pierson's proposals in principle, and sanctioned the conversion (during production) of a Vildebeest Mark I, S1714, adopting the Pegasus IIM.3 engine of the Mark III. This aeroplane was first flown on 24 November 1932, and less than a month later was shipped to Egypt to begin Service trials; these took the form of a tour of all RAF stations in the Middle East and East Africa for brief assessment by the general purpose squadrons in the theatre.

On successful negotiation of these trials, the aircraft returned to the United Kingdom and the Air Ministry prepared Specification 21/33 around Pierson's design, instructing Vickers to deliver S1714 to Martlesham Heath for assessment and handling trials. Later in 1933 a contract was issued for 51 production examples, K4105-K4155, and in the following year the name Vincent was announced.

The first production Vincent was retained in the United Kingdom, shuttling between Brooklands, Martlesham and Farnborough on numerous trials until 1940, when it was retired, but all the other aircraft were shipped to the Middle East, first joining in January 1935 No 84 Squadron, appropriately commanded by Sqn Ldr Stanley Flamant Vincent AFC at Shaibah, Iraq, an officer with unsurpassed experience in the Middle East and the RAF's responsibilities under the British mandate.

Three months later, Vincents began

equipping No 8 Squadron (Sqn Ldr Hugh Stanley Porter Walmseley MC, DFC, later Air Marshal Sir Hugh, KCB, KCIE, CBE, MC, DFC) at Kormaksar, Aden, this Squadron retaining the Vickers aeroplanes until March 1942. These two Squadrons between them took delivery of 46 aircraft.

Meanwhile, orders totalling 100 further Vincents had been placed, and these began delivery in September 1935, without exception being delivered to the Middle East where they first joined No 45 Squadron at Nairobi, Kenya, in December that year during the Abyssinian crisis, followed by Nos 207 and 47 Squadrons in the Sudan in 1936.

By the outbreak of the Second World War, Vincents had been replaced on all

but Nos 8 and 47 Squadrons, although a new Squadron, No 244, was formed at Shaibah with Vincents in November 1940; indeed, the latter Squadron was called into action to bomb units of the Iraqi Army (using 250-pounders) during the rebellion under Raschid Ali, which threatened the RAF base at Habbaniya in May 1941.

The Vincents of No 8 Squadron undertook various tasks at Aden early in the Second World War, being flown on bombing attacks against the Italians in the Horn of Africa and flying coastal and anti-submarine patrols over the Red Sea and its southern approaches. The Vincents usually carried the big ventral fuel tank and a token bomb load under the wings. An exception to this was on

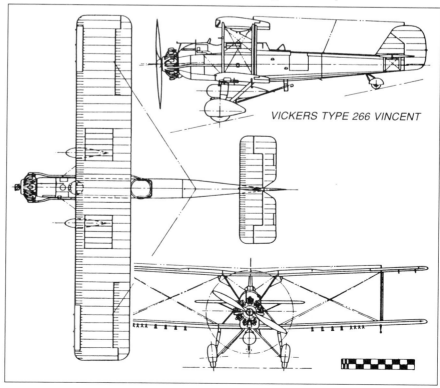

VICKERS TYPE 266 VINCENT

the occasion, during the defence of Aden, when the brand-new Italian submarine *Galileo Galilei* was found on the surface close to the port, its crew being encouraged to surrender their vessel after an Aden-based Vincent dropped a 250lb depth charge nearby.

An unusual task undertaken by Vincents in the Middle East was with the Anti-Locust Flight (Persia), three aircraft being detached to assist in operations against this pest, which posed the greatest threat to that nation's precarious agriculture.

The last squadron Vincents were those of No 244 Squadron, finally replaced by Blenheims at Sharjah in January 1943. A total of 22 Vincents (taken from surplus RAF stocks in the Middle East) was supplied to New Zealand, as well as four to Iraq.

Type: Single-engine, three-crew, single-bay general purpose biplane.
Air Ministry Specification: 21/33
Manufacturer: Vickers (Aviation) Ltd, Weybridge, Surrey.
Powerplant: One 635hp Bristol Pegasus IIM.3 9-cylinder air-cooled radial engine driving 2-blade propeller.
Structure: Steel tubular fuselage and tail structure; steel tubular wing spar booms and light alloy tubular wing ribs; fabric covered.
Dimensions: Span, 49ft 0in; length, 36ft 8in; height, 17ft 9in; wing area, 728 sq ft.
Weights: Tare, 4,229lb; all-up, 8,100lb.
Performance: Max speed, 142 mph at 5,000ft; ceiling, 19,000ft; normal range, 625 miles; maximum range, 1,250 miles.
Armament: One 0.303in synchronized Vickers Mk II machine gun in nose, offset to port, and one Lewis gun on rear cockpit; bomb load of up to eight 112lb and eight 20lb bombs.
Prototype: One, S1714 (a converted Vildebeest I), first flown as such on 24 November 1932 at Brooklands.

Production: A total of 197 Vincents was built: K4105-K4155 (of which four were supplied to New Zealand and one to Iraq); K4615-K4619 (one to New Zealand); K4656-K4750 (17 to New Zealand and three to Iraq); K4883-K4885; and K6326-K6368. Only one Vincent (K4105) was retained in the United Kingdom.
Summary of Service: Vincents served in the Middle East and East Africa as follows: No 84 Squadron from January 1935 until June 1939 at Shaibah, Iraq; No 8 Squadron from April 1935 until March 1942 at Khormaksar, Aden; No 45 Squadron from November 1935 until December 1937 at Nairobi, Kenya, and in Egypt; No 207 Squadron from April until August 1936 at Gabeit, Sudan; No 47 Squadron from July 1936 until July 1940 at Khartoum, Sudan; No 55 Squadron from February 1937 until May 1939 at Hinaidi and Habbaniya, Iraq; No 223 Squadron from February 1937 until June 1938 at Nairobi, Kenya; and No 244 Squadron from November 1940 until January 1943 at Shaibah, Iraq, and Sharjah, Oman. Vincents also served with the Communications Flights at Heliopolis and Aden; Station Flight, Khormaksar; and the Anti-Locust Flight (Persia).

Hawker Hardy

At roughly the same time that the Air Ministry took the decision to order the Vickers Type 266 into production as a medium-range general purpose aircraft for service in the Middle East, the need for an aircraft of rather more limited capabilities was expressed. No 30 Squadron, flying Wapitis in northern Iraq, would be due for new aircraft within two years, the range and load requirements being substantially less than called for in the Type 266 Vincent.

The Hawker Audax had already shown itself to be a suitable variant of the Hart in the army co-operation rôle, and Camm now submitted a tender in reply to Specification G.23/33, adapting the Hart for general purpose duties in the harsh desert conditions of the Middle East. As well as the Audax's message pick-up hook, the aircraft was to feature provision to carry up to 500lb of store containers (or a similar weight of bombs), ground pyrotechnics, an emergency tent, bedding, food and drinking water (wireless not being required); low-pressure 'doughnut' tyres were to be fitted to facilitate landings on rough desert strips. The normal range, with standard desert equipment and supply/bomb load, was to be 380 miles and, to meet engine cooling requirements, the Kestrel en-

K5919, one of the last Hardys to be built, during trials at the A & AEE in 1936; note the 250lb bombs, low-pressure tyres and enlarged Potts oil cooler. (Photo: Air Ministry, A & AEE)

gine was provided with a slightly enlarged coolant radiator, a 13-element Potts oil cooler and, in due course, pierced cowling panels to assist crankcase cooling.

A standard, Vickers-built Hart, K3013, was delivered to Brooklands and brought up to the 'desert GP' standard, being first flown by Philip Edward Gerald ('Gerry') Sayer on 7 September 1934. By then, however, a preliminary production order had been placed under sub-contract with the Gloster Aircraft Company for 21 aircraft, this manufacturer having recently been purchased by T O M Sopwith to form, with Hawker, the nucleus of the Hawker Siddeley

Group. 'Gerry' Sayer was also to move to Gloster.

The first production aircraft, named the Hardy, were completed in October, and the entire batch was shipped out to the Middle East, reaching No 30 Squadron the following April. This Squadron, commanded by Sqn Ldr Arthur Leonard Fiddament DFC (later Air Vice-Marshal, CB, CBE, DFC), was tasked with policing local tribes that might, under the excuse of domestic disagreements, threaten the safety of the fast-growing northern oilfield installations.

Elsewhere, civil unrest was increasing in the Middle East and, by 1936, the RAF was required to strengthen its

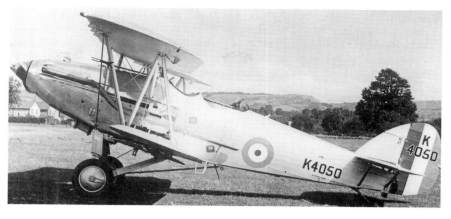

K4050, the first Gloster-built Hawker Hardy, at the Hucclecote airfield. With its message pick-up hook, it is scarcely distinguishable from a standard Hawker Audax. (Photo: Flight, Neg No 233)

presence in Palestine in its attempts to maintain the fragile peace between Arabs and Jews. No 6 Squadron had flown Harts since 1935 but, in 1937, expressed the need to re-equip with a more suitable aircraft. New contracts had been placed for 26 Hardys, but in the meantime No 30 Squadron's aeroplanes were transferred in January 1938 to No 6 (commanded by Sqn Ldr E R C Hobson DFC), No 30 receiving the first Bristol Blenheims to arrive in the Middle East.

No 6 Squadron continued to fly the Hardys until April 1940 when they were handed on to yet another Squadron, No 237, newly re-formed at Nairobi in Kenya as an intended precaution against mischief by potential Axis forces in Italian East Africa.

After Italy's entry into the War on 10 June 1940, it was not long before her colonial forces began to threaten the shipping route through the Red Sea. In the subsequent campaign, No 237 Squadron moved to the Sudan to support the ground forces in their advance to occupy Eritrea and Northern Ethiopia. The Italian air force reacted fairly energetically, at least one of the old biplanes being shot down in combat, and another four were lost in a raid on their airstrip at Goz Regeb on 12 December 1940.

The last Hardys were withdrawn from No 237 Squadron in April 1941, and either scrapped or handed over to the Southern Rhodesian Air Force.

Type: Single-engine, two-seat, single-bay general purpose biplane.

Air Ministry Specification: G.23/33

Manufacturer: The Gloster Aircraft Co Ltd, Hucclecote, Gloucester.

Powerplant: One 530hp Rolls-Royce Kestrel IB 12-cylinder water-cooled in-line engine driving 2-blade wooden propeller; some later aircraft with 580hp Kestrel X engines.

Dimensions: Span, 37ft 3in; length, 29ft 7in; height, 10ft 7in; wing area, 348 sq ft.

Weights: Tare, 3,195lb; all-up, 5,005lb.

Performance: Max speed, 161 mph at sea level; climb to 10,000ft, 10 min 12 sec; service ceiling, 17,000ft; range 380 miles.

Armament: One synchronized 0.303in Vickers machine gun in port side of front fuselage and one Lewis gun with ring mounting on rear cockpit. Bomb load or supplies up to 500lb, carried under wings.

Prototype: One, K3013 (a Vickers-built Hawker Hart, modified by Hawker Aircraft Ltd), first flown by P E G Sayer at Brooklands on 7 September 1934.

Production: Three production contracts, totalling 47 aircraft: K4050-K4070, K4306-K4321 and K5914-K5923. Four ex-RAF aircraft transferred to Southern Rhodesian Air Force in 1940.

Summary of Service: The Hardy served in turn with No 30 Squadron from April 1935 until January 1938 at Mosul and Habbaniya, Iraq; with No 6 Squadron from January 1938 until April 1940 at Ramleh, Palestine; and with No 237 Squadron from April 1940 until April 1941 at Nairobi and Umtala, Kenya, and Gordon's Tree and Barentu, Sudan. They also served with the Middle East Training Unit and Reserve Pool (TURP), the Hinaidi Communications Flight, and the Communications Flight, Summit, Sudan, in 1941.

Hawker Hind

The Hind day bomber equipped more RAF squadrons and training units than any other aeroplane during peacetime in the Service's history. This came about on account of being ordered into and remaining in production throughout the first two years of the Expansion period before the Second World War. Employing essentially the same production facilities and an almost identical airframe as the Hart light bomber, it required no significant workforce retraining at the two Hawker factories (at Kingston and Brooklands), and the necessary supply of Rolls-Royce Kestrel engines was already well established.

Bearing in mind the popularity and

A standard production Hind bomber at Brooklands early in 1937; K6689 served with No 34 (Bomber) Squadron at Lympne in Kent, but was written off when it collided with a tree during a forced landing on 6 December that year. (Photo: Author's Collection)

reputation for dependability already achieved by the Hart and Audax, the

Hind was a logical choice as the aircraft on which the pilots and gunner/observ-

Hind K5523 of No 103 (Bomber) Squadron at Odiham in 1937; this aircraft features the newly-introduced 'ram's horn' exhaust manifolds, intended to reduce exhaust glare during night flying. It was not a popular expedient owing to the tendency of the manifolds to explode, but after some development their reliability improved to an acceptable standard. The aircraft shown here was one of those supplied to New Zealand in 1940. (Photo: RAF Museum, Neg No P020983)

ers of the host of new bomber squadrons could cut their teeth. With extraordinary foresight, Thomas Sopwith began the process of making factory space available in anticipation of large production orders, negotiating the distribution of sub-contracts throughout the aircraft industry of outstanding orders for Harts, Demons, Audaxes, Hardys and Fury fighters; in so doing, as is now well appreciated, he thus played a leading rôle in ensuring the survival of numerous companies which had experienced lean times in the early 1930s, so that when the call came three or four years hence, to accelerate production of the big British bombers, their manufacturers already possessed the necessarily skilled factory manpower to meet the challenge.

Indeed, it took Hawker only two years to produce all 527 Hinds for the RAF, before switching to production of the vital Hurricane fighter in 1937 (of which, it may be remarked, Hawker produced about the same number in the two years remaining before the War).

The Hind was in no sense a modern aeroplane (its fabric-covered, tubular Warren-girder primary fuselage structure having originated with the Hart prototype in 1927-28) and, despite its official classification as a light day bomber, few people doubted that this was a

thinly-veiled euphemism for an operational trainer; moreover, its capabilities in this rôle were ideal. Later, as one by one, the fledgling bomber squadrons received their new monoplane Blenheims, Battles, Whitleys, Wellingtons and Hampdens, the Hind underwent swift transmutation to an undisguised training aeroplane with dual flying controls, this version becoming in 1938 the aeroplane in which the increasing flow of new RAF Volunteer Reserve pilots advanced from the *ab initio* Tiger Moth trainers towards the new generation of monoplane bombers. Indeed, there were very few bomber pilots serving in the front line squadrons of Bomber Command at the outbreak of war in September 1939 who had not flown Hinds at some point in their service since 1936.

The fact that this relatively undistinguished light bomber had come to play such a vital rôle in Bomber Command's preparation for a likely war, and that it was conceived and built by a company that was much better known for its fighter aircraft, may be explained by the bleak outlook facing manufacturers in

the early 1930s. The Hawker Hart, and its early derivatives, were almost alone in enjoying a glut of orders, and Camm had, in June 1931, suggested undertaking a 'rolling programme' of development on a specimen aircraft ('without bothering to fly the aeroplane unless, or until asked to do so' — his own words). Sopwith took this proposal to the DTD and suggested setting aside a Hart airframe on which design improvements might be included so that, if the need arose, a prototype would be available 'off the hook'.

The Hart airframe, not yet covered by Air Ministry contract, was duly set aside at the end of 1931, purchased on deferred payment and given the serial K2915. However, such was the uncertainty surrounding the RAF's short-term bomber requirements (and, indeed, the Air Ministry's ability to pay for them), that Hawker found it convenient to employ K2915, in its partly completed state, to make trial installations in it of the various modifications and variations of the design called for by potential overseas customers for the Hart.

Early in 1934, however, Camm put forward a proposal for a general purpose variant of the Hart, to be powered by the forthcoming Rolls-Royce P.V.12 (for

One of the last Hinds to be built, L7193 is shown flying at dusk in the markings of No 18 (Bomber) Squadron during 1938. Like so many Hinds, this aeroplane had a crowded life spanning only two years, during which it also served on Nos 21, 503 and 616 Squadrons, and as a trainer with No 19 E & RFTS and No 3 FTS, before coming to grief during a forced landing at Waverton, Cheshire, while flying with No 10 FTS on 30 October 1939. (Photo: RAF Museum, Neg No P104053)

which its manufacturers had asked for a Hart and two Horsleys to be modified as test beds).

It is clear that the Air Ministry was less than impressed by Camm's proposal, and restated that the purpose of K2915 was to provide a prototype of a new Hart light bomber variant at short notice, and promptly issued a new general purpose Specification, G.7/34, calling for a prototype light day and night bomber to be powered by the Kestrel V. The implication was that K2915 should now be flown as that prototype. It was accordingly flown with this engine on 12 September 1934.

Although not obviously much different from the Hart, K2915 had undergone considerable internal improvement, particularly in the provision of a much improved prone bomb aiming position in the lower fuselage, enabling the gunner/observer to adopt his bombing position more easily, and with better means of communicating with the pilot and of bomb selection and fuzing. A 640hp Kestrel V was fitted, as was a tailwheel in place of the Hart's skid, and the rear gun ring tilted and lowered to afford better protection for the gunner from slipstream buffeting.

After K2915 had been reported on favourably by the A & AEE, an initial order for 20 Hinds was placed early in 1935, and these were delivered in December and January that winter.

In contradiction to the accepted practice of re-equipping a single squadron immediately, the Air Ministry decided to distribute the first Hinds among several squadrons almost simultaneously, and progressively bring them up to a unit establishment as new pilots completed their *ab initio* training. As Hawker quickly received a new order for 193 aircraft, four Squadrons were each provided with four Hinds, the first two, Nos 34 at Bircham Newton and No 104 at Abingdon in January, being followed

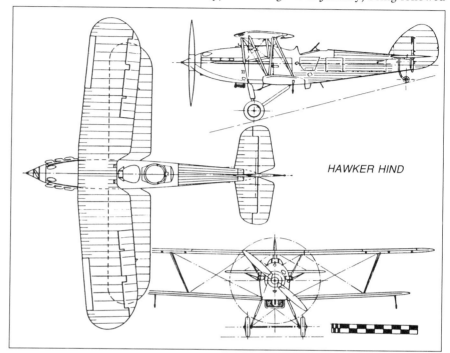

HAWKER HIND

Type: Single-engine, two-seat, single-bay light day bomber biplane.

Air Ministry Specifications: 25/31, G.7/34, 11/35 and 13/37.

Manufacturer: Hawker Aircraft Ltd, Kingston-upon-Thames and Brooklands, Surrey.

Powerplant: Standard bomber. One 640hp Rolls-Royce Kestrel V 12-cylinder, water-cooled, in-line engine driving 2-blade Watts wooden propeller. Standard trainer. 599hp Kestrel VDR. Export aircraft. Rolls-Royce Kestrel XVI, Gnome-Rhône K-9 Mistral, Bristol Mercury VIII and IX.

Dimensions: Span, 37ft 3in; length, 29ft 3in; height, 10ft 7in; wing area, 348 sq ft.

Weights: Standard bomber. Tare, 3,195lb; all-up, 4,657lb.

Performance: Standard bomber. Max speed, 185 mph at 15,500ft; climb to 10,000ft, 8 min 6 sec; service ceiling, 26,400ft.

Armament: One synchronized 0.303in Vickers Mk III or V machine gun in port side of forward fuselage, and bomber version mounted a Lewis gun with No 15 ring on rear cockpit. Bomb load of up to 510lb on underwing racks.

Prototype: One, K2915, first flown by Flt Lt P W S Bulman on 12 September 1934 at Brooklands.

Production: A total of 527 Hinds was built under Air Ministry contracts: K4635-K4655 (9 later converted to trainers, 2 supplied to Kenya and 2 to New Zealand); K5368-K5560 (47 later converted to trainers, 46 to South Africa, 24 to New Zealand, 3 to Afghanistan, 3 to Eire and 1 to Kenya); K6613-K6856 (47 later converted to trainers, 66 to South Africa, 44 to New Zealand, 6 to Afghanistan, 2 to Eire and unknown number to Indian Air Force); and L7174-L7243 (17 converted to trainers and L7224-L7243 built as trainers; 9 to South Africa, 7 to New Zealand and 3 to Afghanistan). Approximately 30 of those shipped to South Africa and New Zealand were lost at sea in transit. In addition to the Air Ministry contracts, 35

Mercury VIII-powered Hinds were built for Persia, 8 new Hinds for Afghanistan, 4 for Portugal, 3 for Yugoslavia, 3 for Latvia and one for Switzerland. Total Hind production, 581, excluding prototype.

Summary of RAF Service: Between January 1936 and December 1939, Hinds served with the following Bomber Squadrons: Nos 12, 15, 18, 21, 34, 40, 44, 49, 50, 52, 57, 62, 63, 82, 83, 88, 90, 98, 103, 104, 106, 107, 108, 110, 113, 114, 139, 142, 185, 211, 218, 500, 501, 502, 503, 504, 602, 603, 605, 609, 610, 611, 613, 614 and 616; and with Nos 24 and 267 (Communications) Squadrons. They also served with the following Flying Training Schools, Nos 1, 2, 3, 4, 5, 6, 8, 9, 10, 11, 12, 14, 15, 16 and 29; with the following Elementary Flying Training Schools, Nos 1, 3, 7, 8 and 22; with the following Elementary & Reserve Flying Training Schools, Nos 1, 3, 4, 5, 6, 7, 8, 9, 11, 12, 13, 14, 15, 16, 18, 19, 20, 21, 22, 23, 24, 25, 26, 27, 28, 29, 30, 31, 32, 33, 34, 35, 38, 39, 40, 42, 43, 44, 45, 46, 47, 50, 56 and 60. Hinds served at the Royal Air Force College, Cranwell, and the following units: No 2 Air Observers School, No 10 Bombing & Gunnery School, No 1 Parachute Flying Unit, Nos 1, 2 and 4 Glider Towing Schools, No 1 Ferry Pilots Pool, Nos 2 and 4 Armament Training Camps, No 2 Photographic Reconnaissance Unit, Nos 7 and 20 (Pilots) Advanced Flying Units, No 7 Armament Training Station, No 54 Repair & Servicing Unit, No 70 Operational Training Unit, Nos 101 and 102 Glider Operational Training Units, the Glider Towing Squadron, the Glider Instructors School, the Glider Pilots Exercise Unit, the Training Unit and Reserve Pool (Middle East), the Special Duties Flight, the Western Desert Communications Flight and the Levant Communications Flight. Hinds were used by the Air Transport Auxiliary as air taxis, and by the Station Flights at Abingdon, Andover, Catterick, Duxford, Grantham, Heliopolis, Hucknall, Northolt and Yeadon. They also equipped the Oxford University Air Squadron, Cambridge University Air Squadron and the University of London Air Squadron.

by Nos 49 and 98 in February (also at Bircham Newton and Abingdon respectively). Some idea of the haste with which these deployments were made may be judged by the fact that a Flight Lieutenant was given command of No 49 Squadron, and on No 104 Squadron the Australian CO, Sqn Ldr J E Hewitt, reported that he was short of pilots, groundcrews and equipment for several months after receiving his aircraft.

With the formation of Bomber Command in the summer of 1936, the process of equipping two of its three Groups with Hinds gradually settled down, so that by the end of that year there were no fewer than 18 Squadrons thus equipped. One of these, No 602 at Abbotsinch (commanded by Sqn Ldr the Marquess of Douglas and Clydesdale AAF, MP), being the first Auxiliary Air Force Squadron with Hinds.

A further 18 Squadrons followed in 1937 as Hawker completed production contracts for 314 Hinds. Eight more squadrons re-equipped in 1938, but already the new monoplane bombers were entering service.

Apart from a final contract covering twenty Hinds (L7224–L7243), completed from the outset as trainers, 120 former bombers were taken out of service and delivered to General Aircraft Ltd for conversion to dual control, the bomb aiming position being stripped of all armament wiring and the gun ring being removed; Specification 13/37 was issued by the Air Ministry to cover this standard of preparation. These Hind Trainers were distributed among the Flying Training Schools, EFTS and E & RFTS, as well as the Royal Air Force College, Cranwell (which at one time had 58 such aircraft on charge).

Other Hind bombers, not required for pilot training, were flown by bomber Station Flights and by numerous armament training units. Early in the War, Hinds were widely used for light glider training, and became a common sight in many parts of the country with a General Aircraft Hotspur glider in tow. As can be seen in the accompanying table, Hinds served in second-line duties with the RAF in the Middle East, as well as with the South African Air Force and the Royal New Zealand Air Force.

At least three Hinds survive to this day, the Shuttleworth Collection maintaining one in flying condition. The other two are on display at the Royal Air Force Museum, Hendon, and the National Air Museum, Ottawa, Canada. All were formerly flown by the Afghan Air Force, and were presented the the museums for renovation and display.

Deployment of British Bomber Squadrons — 1 January 1935

Royal Air Force
Home Bases

No 7 Sqn (H)	Vickers Virginia X	Worthy Down, Hampshire
No 9 Sqn (H)	Vickers Virginia X	Boscombe Down, Wiltshire
No 10 Sqn (H)	Handley Page Heyford IA	Boscombe Down, Wiltshire
No 12 Sqn (L)	Hawker Hart	Andover, Hampshire
No 15 Sqn (L)	Hawker Hart	Abingdon, Berkshire
No 18 Sqn (L)	Hawker Hart	Upper Heyford, Oxon
No 22 Sqn (TB)	Vickers Vildebeest I	Donibristle, Fife
No 33 Sqn (L)	Hawker Hart	Upper Heyford, Oxon
No 35 Sqn (L)	Fairey Gordon	Bircham Newton, Norfolk
No 40 Sqn (L)	Fairey Gordon	Abingdon, Berkshire
No 57 Sqn (L)	Hawker Hart	Upper Heyford, Oxon
No 58 Sqn (H)	Vickers Virginia X	Worthy Down, Hampshire
No 99 Sqn (H)	Handley Page Heyford	Mildenhall, Suffolk
No 101 Sqn (M)	Boulton Paul Overstrand/Sidestrand	Bicester, Oxon
No 207 Sqn (L)	Fairey Gordon	Bircham Newton, Norfolk

Middle East

No 8 Sqn (L)	Fairey IIIF	Khormaksar, Aden
No 14 Sqn (L)	Fairey Gordon	Ramleh, Palestine
No 30 Sqn (L)	Westland Wapiti IIA	Mosul, Iraq
No 45 Sqn (L)	Fairey IIIF	Helwan, Egypt
No 46 Sqn (L)	Fairey Gordon	Khartoum, Sudan
No 55 Sqn (L)	Westland Wapiti IIA	Hinaidi, Iraq
No 84 Sqn (L)	Westland Wapiti IIA/ Vickers Vincent	Shaibah, Iraq

India and the Far East

No 5 Sqn (L)	Westland Wapiti IIA	Quetta, India
No 11 Sqn (L)	Hawker Hart	Risalpur, India
No 20 Sqn (L)	Westland Wapiti IIA	Peshawar, India
No 27 Sqn (L)	Westland Wapiti IIA	Kohat, India
No 28 Sqn (L)	Westland Wapiti IIA	Ambala, India
No 31 Sqn (L)	Westland Wapiti IIA	Quetta, India
No 36 Sqn (TB)	Hawker Horsley III	Seletar, Singapore
No 39 Sqn (L)	Hawker Hart	Risalpur, India
No 60 Sqn (L)	Westland Wapiti IIA	Kohat, India
No 100 Sqn (TB)	Vickers Vildebeest II/III	Seletar, Singapore

Auxiliary Air Force

No 500 Sqn (H) SRU	Vickers Virginia X	Manston, Kent
No 501 Sqn (L) SRU	Westland Wallace	Filton, Bristol
No 502 Sqn (H) SRU	Vickers Virginia X	Aldergrove, Ulster
No 503 Sqn (H) SRU	Handley Page Hinaidi	Waddington, Lincs
No 504 Sqn (L) SRU	Westland Wallace	Hucknall, Derbyshire
No 600 Sqn (L) AAF	Hawker Hart	Hendon, Middlesex
No 601 Sqn (L) AAF	Hawker Hart	Hendon, Middlesex
No 602 Sqn (L) AAF	Hawker Hart	Abbotsinch, Renfrewshire
No 603 Sqn (L) AAF	Hawker Hart	Turnhouse, Midlothian
No 604 Sqn (L) AAF	Hawker Hart	Hendon, Middlesex
No 605 Sqn (L) AAF	Hawker Hart	Castle Bromwich, Warks
No 607 Sqn (L) AAF	Westland Wapiti IIA	Usworth, Co Durham
No 608 Sqn (L) AAF	Westland Wapiti IIA	Thornaby, Yorkshire

Fleet Air Arm

No 810 Sqn (TB)	Blackburn Baffin	Gosport, Hampshire
No 811 Sqn (TB)	Blackburn Baffin/ Ripon IIC	Gosport, Hampshire
No 812 Sqn (TB)	Blackburn Baffin	Hal Far, Malta
No 820 Sqn (TB)	Blackburn Shark	HMS *Courageous*

H—Heavy bomber; M—Medium bomber; L—Light bomber; TB—Torpedo bomber; SRU—Special Reserve Unit; AAF—Auxiliary Air Force

5. MONOPLANES DURING THE YEARS OF EXPANSION

By the summer of 1934 reliable intelligence had reached Britain that Germany, having stamped out of the Geneva Disarmament Conference the previous year, was well advanced with plans to create a military air force. Although the details of those plans were the subject of somewhat wild speculation by various ministers of the Crown, it soon required no more than common sense to realise that Hitler and the Nazi Party were embarked on a course to gain military domination of Europe, no matter what the pacifists might prefer to believe.

Once the reality of the German plans became evident to the British Air Staff, and the true strength of the Royal Air Force was being questioned in Parliament, figures relating to the number of 'operational aircraft' available were being quoted — without any qualification — in the House of Commons, and were therefore accepted as relating to aircraft of a quality at least adequate to meet on equal terms any that Germany might be producing, bearing in mind that it was generally believed that German aircraft manufacturers had had no experience in producing military aeroplanes for more than a dozen years and, being without an air force, no military airmen had been trained for a similar period.

The lesson, of course, that stood to be learned from the mistakes of the mid-1930s, was that a totalitarian state can achieve a rate and efficiency of military resurgence and expansion far in excess of that achievable by democratically accountable states. Germany was assisted on its course by the dereliction of the League of Nations in its failure to discover and monitor the covert activities of numerous dedicated military figures who had successfully sought to keep in being the structure of a military machine throughout the 1920s and early 1930s.

By contrast, reference to the table opposite will disclose that, on 1 January 1935:

1. Not one monoplane bomber was yet in service with the Royal Air Force.
2. Among the heavy bombers in service, none was of a design less than five years old, and most were nearer twelve.
3. The one and only medium day bomber squadron was part-equipped with a 'new' aircraft, the Overstrand, that was fundamentally some *eight* years old.
4. None of the light bomber and general purpose squadrons was flying aircraft whose design was less than six years old.

Much more significant, perhaps, is the fact that no British bomber in service on this date could reach the nearest point in Germany, drop a bomb larger than a 500-pounder, and return to its base in the United Kingdom.

This was the concealed legacy of the Trenchard era, a period in which all semblance of balanced forces within the RAF disappeared. The bomber had been allowed to swallow almost all the available finance available for aircraft development and production, and the fighter had been largely ignored. To be more precise, the Virginia heavy bomber was little more than a white elephant, not significantly different in capabilities from the Handley Page O/400 of the Kaiser's War, and this aeroplane was expected to remain as the RAF's princi-

pal heavy bomber at least until 1936, sharing the responsibility with the almost equally ponderous Heyford. In the realm of fighters, the brightly polished, nimble Hawker Fury was armed with exactly the same two, unreliable Vickers machine guns that gave the Camel its hump in 1917.

Japanese defection from the Geneva Disarmament Conference in March 1933, followed by that of Germany seven months later, prompted all the restraints to be lifted by the Air Ministry, and the planned orders for prototypes of the new generation of monoplane bombers were confirmed.

It has been shown in the previous chapter that efforts failed to acquire the so-called 'General Purpose' aeroplane for the Royal Air Force largely because the Specification, G.4/31, was too demanding for the aircraft industry to undertake the necessary research under private funding, but also because the subsequent dilution of the demands of the Specification produced aircraft little better than those already in service. Instead, as if to be seen to have rescued something from the most costly design competition hitherto staged, the Air Ministry (knowing full well that a monoplane derivative was nearing completion) selected the Vickers biplane tender for production, and with indecent haste went on to change the contract to embrace the Wellesley monoplane — an aircraft which never underwent competitive evaluation. As if to emphasise the demise of the General

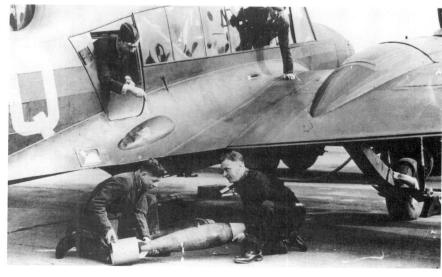

So familiar for the training rôle in which it was to serve for more than a dozen years in the Royal Air Force, the Avro Anson is frequently forgotten as a coastal reconnaissance aeroplane in the late 1930s. In this picture, taken at about the outbreak of the War, armourers are shown manhandling a 100lb anti-submarine bomb on to the racks. Four such weapons could be carried. (Photo: via A Stamper)

Purpose category, the Wellesley was euphemistically termed a medium bomber. A 'long range light bomber' would have been more accurate. It will be shown that the Wellesley was superfluous in the successive expansion plans in that it possessed no conceivable place in the Service's order of battle in a European war.

By the middle of the 1930s the parameters had been set for the RAF's Expansion Programme. In July 1934 the National Government (composed mainly of Conservatives) had proposed increasing the RAF's strength by 41 squadrons, despite dogmatic opposition by the Labour and Liberal parties[1].

Be that as it may, just as the aircraft manufacturers (Hawker and Supermarine) were being actively and effec-

---

[1] Politicians of the day bandied, and many historians ever since have quoted, arbitrary numbers of squadrons in service, or planned, on or by certain dates. None of those figures bore the slightest resemblance to reality. In the case of the bomber squadrons, the 'Parliamentary figures' were those of the Air Ministry, based on an outdated Unit Establishment figure (UE) of 12 aircraft at first line strength, plus 50 per cent reserve. These were revised upwards and downwards no fewer than eight times between 1933 and 1939. For instance, between 1936 and 1939, new squadrons were frequently 'formed' by one squadron shedding a Flight to form the nucleus of another; in 1936 the Air Ministry represented that this constituted the *de facto* addition of a new squadron — despite the fact that *both* squadrons remained well below the UE (both in aircraft and personnel), often for at least a year. It has also been shown that, for almost two years, most of the new Hind light bomber squadrons were little more than training units, and certainly in no sense could they be regarded as 'first-line' squadrons. Furthermore, in quoting figures for planned or actual bomber production, no indication was given that, included in those figures, were many hundreds of Hawker Hinds, all being assumed to be bombers — whereas at least half were trainers.

This false picture may have been painted as part of a planned propaganda scenario, but the figures *were* believed, and were probably broadcast in Parliament in good faith. The results were at best embarrassing; they could have been, and almost were disastrous when war became reality. When it was necessary, under treaty obligations, to provide bombers (and fighters) overseas, it was with considerable risk and difficulty that the RAF contrived to do so. The despatch of Fairey Battle light bombers to France was a flagrant penalty of inaccurate classification of aircraft, if not the continuous misquotation of inflated bomber squadron strengths.

tively encouraged to produce modern monoplane fighter prototypes, the Hurricane and Spitfire, during 1934 and 1935, so Vickers, Handley Page, Armstrong Whitworth and Bristol were hard at work on the first generation of twin-engine monoplane bombers. To this list were soon added, with less success, the names of Fairey and Hawker, for their attempts to produce single-engine light bomber monoplanes (to become the Battle and Henley respectively).

However, before the famous early wartime trio of medium and heavy bombers (classified as such by the standards of the time) were to appear — the Whitley, Wellington and Hampden — an assortment of monoplanes appeared, most of which were destined to enter limited production and service. If they served no better purpose, they certainly subsidized the growth and training of both the Royal Air Force and the aircraft industry. To these should be added the Fairey Hendon monoplane, whose origins lay in a 1927 Specification but which was eventually rewarded by a token consolation order in the mid-1930s; see page 215.

Apart from the Anson, the 'faithful Annie' to countless airmen of the Second World War, which originally carried bombs in the coastal reconnaissance rôle before becoming a long-lived aircrew trainer the world over, the RAF was fortunate to be handed on a plate what would become a cornerstone of its armoury in the first three years of the Second World War, for the Bristol Blenheim was second only to the Hawker Hurricane in the number of war theatres in which it flew and fought.

In the process of settling upon heavy bombers for the new Bomber Com-

mand, created on 14 July 1936 at Uxbridge under the command of Air Chief Marshal Sir John Steel KCB, KBE, CMG (later GCB, KBE, CMG), there had been for some years a requirement expressed in successive Specifications for all heavy bombers to be able to carry soldiers as an alternative to a load of bombs. This had originated in a belief that, if the British forces charged with policing the Mandate in the Middle East needed reinforcement at short notice, heavy bombers would be flown out from Britain, each with a complement of soldiers on board. Although this circumstance never arose, the provision 'As an alternative to the bomb load, a complement of troops is required to be carried if necessary' continued in vogue. At the same time, purpose-designed troop-carrying aeroplanes were required, in a secondary rôle, to be able to carry a bomb load in place of troops. Thus came into being the category of Bomber Transport, of which the Bristol Bombay and Handley Page Harrow were perhaps the best known.

However, the secondary troop-carrying requirement also originally persisted in the Specification B.3/34, which in turn was related to the earlier Specification C.26/31 for a troop carrier. B.3/34 brought forth the Whitley heavy bomber, whose design always made allowance for the possibility of being called on to carry troops — a possibility that became

Among the lighter bombs most frequently carried by the RAF in the Second World War was the 500lb HE GP. The bombs seen here, manufactured in 1936, are being tail-fuzed for operations over the Western Desert, probably in about 1941. (Photo: via Bruce Robertson)

reality in the Second World War. And the original draft Specifications which were to give rise to the famous Halifax, Manchester and Stirling heavy bombers were all designed with a secondary troop-carrying rôle in mind. All were to be called upon to carry troops in the evenings of their lives (the Manchester having undergone transformation into the Lancaster in the meantime)[2].

Perhaps not surprisingly, those first three classic twin-engine bombers, the Whitley, Wellington and Hampden, were long in gestation, all being first flown within a period of less than three weeks in June 1936, each in its own concept breaking new ground in technology. All served with great distinction during the Second World War, though only the Wellington continued in production (and in first-line service) until 1945. These were the aircraft the Air Ministry had planned as the equipment with which Bomber Command would undergo expansion. Only as the three prototypes flew and demonstrated the practicality of their innovative designs did the Air Ministry issue the Specifications that would bring to reality the first true heavy bombers referred to above.

[2] It is interesting to recall here that in Germany a similar dualling of the transport and bomber rôles had taken place — but with a subtle difference. The internationally-acceptable passenger- or mail-carrying Junkers Ju 52/3m, Junkers Ju 86, Heinkel He 111 and Dornier Do 17, originally conceived ostensibly for commercial work, were all either quickly adaptable as bombers or developed as such after the emergence of the *Luftwaffe* in the mid-1930s. They were first shown in their true colours during the Spanish Civil War.

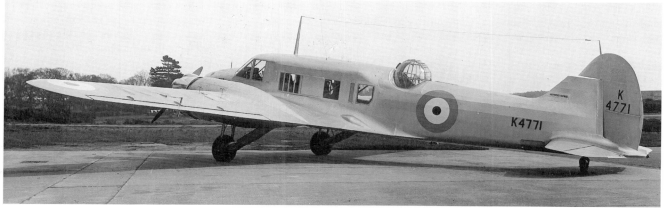

Avro Type 652A Anson

Distinguishable as the Avro Type 652A prototype by its square cabin windows, helmeted engine cowlings and horn-balanced rudder, K4771 was almost unique in carrying its military serial number on the upper *surfaces of the wing, presumably a commercial habit its manufacturers found difficult to break.* (Photo: Air Ministry, RTP Neg No 8159D)

The monoplane was relatively late appearing in service with the Royal Air Force, progress along this path having been slowed by an age-old Air Staff prejudice which had effectively originated during the months before the First World War. That is not to say there had been no half-hearted attempts to encourage the aircraft industry to come up with monoplane prototypes with which to demonstrate their superiority, strength and safety in such a manner as to render in-service aircraft obsolete. Most of the British designers had periodically tried their hand at 'paper' monoplanes, but without Air Ministry backing they were not commercially viable and remained on the drawing boards. Several externally-braced monoplanes had been built and attended evaluation at Martlesham, but, like the Schneider Trophy seaplanes, with their cat's cradle of struts and wires, they simply were not suitable for Service use; and when R J Mitchell first tried his hand at a cantilever monoplane, he was the first to admit that it needed a great deal more research before realistic Service fighters and bombers could be evolved. Unfortunately, such were the continuing financial restrictions that the Air Ministry was not willing to fund that research.

On the other hand, there were growing signs that the commercial airlines were likely to offer substantial rewards for the development of efficient load-carrying monoplanes. The Dutch manufacturer Fokker had, for some years, been in the European forefront with efficient high-wing, cantilever monoplanes with two, three and four engines and, since the late 'twenties, A V Roe & Co had possessed a licence to build the Fokker F.VIIIB/3m, an eight-passenger, three-engine aircraft with a high cantilever wing. This was a thick, ply-covered wooden structure (something that the Air Ministry had refused to countenance in its insistence on all-metal Service aeroplanes), set above a fuselage of welded steel covered with fabric. Avro's little 'airliner', the Type 618, varied in detail from the Fokker on account of differing British airworthiness requirements, and fourteen examples were built.

As the influence of American high performance commercial monoplanes reached Europe in the early 1930s, Imperial Airways handed Avro a specification for a small long-range twin-engine, low-wing charter passenger monoplane, reflecting the current American formula. The design prepared by Roy Chadwick, the Type 652, employed the proven construction of the Type 618, simply moving the wooden wing to the bottom of the fuselage and discarding the centre engine. With two 270hp Armstrong Siddeley Cheetah V engines driving Fairey Reed metal propellers, the four-passenger aeroplane was expected to have a range of 600 miles and cruise at 150 mph.

While the Type 652 for Imperial Airways was still on the drawing board in 1934, the Air Ministry invited Avro to tender for a twin-engine coastal patrol

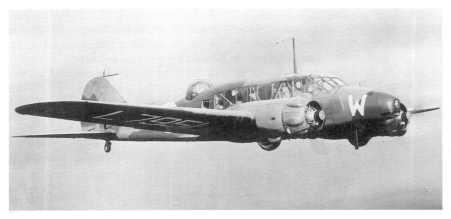

Although equipped for bombing training, this Anson I, L7951, served in turn with No 7 E & RFTS, No 3 Civil Air Navigation School and No 5 Air Observers Navigation School at the beginning of the Second World War before being shipped out to the South African Air Force in September 1940. (Photo: *The Aeroplane*, Neg No 1286)

aircraft whose specification was so close to the Type 652 that Chadwick was able to meet the requirement simply by using slightly more powerful Cheetah VIs; provision was made to carry a light bomb load and a single Lewis gun in a midships dorsal gun turret.

Despite the wooden wing, the Air Ministry accepted this design, the Avro Type 652A, issued a Specification, G.18/35, and ordered a prototype. Meanwhile, another contender had also met with qualified approval and a militarised version of the de Havilland D.H.89 Dragon Rapide twin-engine biplane, the D.H.89M, was also ordered, the two aircraft being allotted the serial numbers K4771 and K4772 respectively.

The prototype 652A, K4771, made its maiden flight on 24 March 1935 with S A ('Bill') Thorn at the controls; apart from the provision for military equipment, this aeroplane differed externally from its civil counterparts — which had flown a couple of months earlier — in having three large square windows on each side of the cabin in place of round windows, helmeted instead of smooth engine cowlings and the cabin entry door on the starboard rather than port side of the fuselage. K4771 featured a horn-balanced rudder, but this was changed later to mass balancing. What, however, constituted the most notable innovation was the introduction of a retractable undercarriage — the first such refinement to appear on an operational RAF aeroplane. Retraction of the

mainwheels into the engine nacelles was by means of a manually-operated winch handle that required no fewer than 140 turns by a second crew member.

The Type 652A and D.H.89M prototypes underwent evaluation at Martlesham Heath during 1935, the latter failing to impress the Service pilots on account of its inferior performance and a suspicion that the airframe was too fragile for operational flying. (de Havilland managed to sell several examples of the D.H.89M to foreign customers.)

The Avro aircraft attracted several criticisms, of which the heavy rudder control was potentially the most serious. The change to mass balance cured this and, apart from the manual undercarriage retraction, which continued to exercise occupants of the aeroplane for many years, the aircraft, now named the Anson, was soon declared acceptable, and an immediate production order for 174 aircraft was placed before the end of 1935. This was considered adequate to equip nine squadrons, each at a UE of 18 aircraft, including reserves.

This programme went ahead exactly to schedule, the first Squadron, No 48 at Manston, receiving its quota of Ansons in March 1936. This General Reconnaissance Squadron, commanded by Sqn Ldr Thomas Audley Langford-Sainsbury DFC AFC (later Air Vice-Marshal, CB, OBE,

DFC, AFC**)[1], undertook much of the navigation training of future Anson crew members for the first eighteen months, at one time holding no fewer than 49 aircraft on charge. After this period, during which it was attached to the School of Navigation, the Squadron settled down to routine coastal reconnaissance duties. However, from mid-1938 it also flew numerous sorties to simulate approaching German bombers to assist in developing the British coastal radar chain and interception techniques. By mid-1937 twelve Squadrons were equipped with the Anson, of which Nos 51, 58, 61, 75, 144 and 215 were either well-established or newly-formed bomber units. These Squadrons employed the Anson as a bomber trainer, principally for long-distance (*sic*) navigation exercises, often carrying out night bombing over the increasing number of bombing ranges throughout Britain.

Five of the other Squadrons, all General and Coastal Reconnaissance units (Nos 206, 220, 224, 233 and 269), performed a massed flypast at the Hendon

---

[1] Tom Langford-Sainsbury had formerly been a test pilot at Martlesham Heath for six years, during which time he experienced more than his fair share of 'incidents' in the course of his flying, on one occasion involuntarily performing a terminal velocity dive in a Virginia. He was only the third RAF officer to be awarded a second bar to the AFC (on 11 May 1937), one of the two earlier recipients being that redoubtable test pilot Flt Lt (later Gp Capt) P W S ('George') Bulman, whose second bar had been awarded as long ago as 3 June 1922. There being no appropriate gallantry award for test pilots in those days (until the institution of the George Medal in September 1940), the AFC was, and still is, awarded for this often hazardous work.

Anson I, N4877, delivered to No 3 Ferry Pilots' Pool in 1939 with bomb gear removed, spent most of the War years with the Air Transport Auxiliary as a taxi for ferry pilots. It was eventually sold by the Air Ministry in 1950 but failed to obtain a Certificate of Airworthiness as there was no guarantee that the glue in the wooden wings was safe any longer. (Photo: R W Cranham)

Display of 26 June 1937 — almost certainly the largest assembly of monoplanes yet seen in Britain. The aircraft represented the nucleus of the newly-created Coastal Command and, by 1939, the number of squadrons engaged in coastal reconnaissance and anti-submarine patrol work had increased to eleven, including four (Nos 500, 502, 608 and 612) of the Auxiliary Air Force. The normal bomb load for their duties comprised a pair of 100lb anti-submarine bombs and up to eight flares or smoke floats.

With the arrival of the first American Lockheed Hudsons in Britain[2], the Anson appeared noticeably obsolescent, and slowly disappeared from operational use. Nevertheless, Ansons went to war with some panache, No 500 Squadron attacking a U-boat (which escaped) on 5 September 1939. Later that month a Dornier Do 18 flying boat was claimed shot down by an Anson of No 269 Squadron. It is also recorded that Anson crews claimed the destruction of a number of German fighters (and at least one German minelaying seaplane), these successes being rather unkindly attributed to the enemy pilot's confusion engen-

[2] 250 Hudsons had been ordered in 1938, but only No 224 Squadron was thus equipped at the outbreak of war. By the standards of its day it was a very efficient aeroplane, possessing twice the Anson's range and being capable of carrying five times the bomb load. It was also 60 mph faster.

dered by the Anson's very slow speed.

Large production contracts were placed for Anson trainers from 1938 onwards, and it is beyond the scope of this work to dwell on the enormous contribution these aeroplanes made to the training of thousands of Allied airmen at home and overseas during the Second World War.

The accompanying table therefore only refers to the bomb-carrying Anson Mark Is which primarily served on operational squadrons before and early in the War. Suffice it to say that the last and 8,138th production Anson built in Britain, was delivered to the RAF in May 1952.

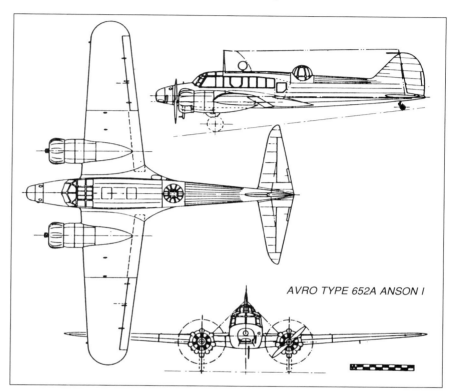

AVRO TYPE 652A ANSON I

Type: Twin-engine, three-crew, low-wing general reconnaissance monoplane.

Air Ministry Specification: G.18/35

Manufacturer: A V Roe & Co Ltd, Newton Heath, Manchester, and Woodford, Cheshire.

Powerplant: Type 652A prototype. Two 290hp Armstrong Siddeley Cheetah VI 7-cylinder air-cooled radial engines driving 2-blade propellers. Anson Mark I. 335hp Cheetah IX.

Structure: Welded-steel tubular fuselage construction with wooden formers and fabric covering; wooden wings and tail unit.

Dimensions: Span, 56ft 6in; length, 42ft 3in; height, 13ft 1in; wing area, 410 sq ft.

Weights: Tare, 5,375lb; all-up, 8,000lb.

Performance: Max speed, 188 mph at 7,000ft; climb to 6,500ft, 6 min 15 sec; service ceiling, 19,500ft; range, 725 miles.

Armament: One fixed forward-firing 0.303in Vickers (later Browning or Bren) machine gun and one Lewis or Vickers K gas-operated machine gun in midships dorsal turret. Bomb load, two 100lb AS bombs and up to eight 20lb bombs or smoke floats.

Prototype: One, K4771, first flown by S A Thorn on 24 March 1935; production prototype, K6152, first flown by Geoffrey Tyson at Woodford on 31 December 1935.

Production: Bomb-carrying Anson Is, engaged in the General and Coastal Reconnaissance rôles and on bombing training with otherwise operational squadrons, were delivered from the first 1,335 production aircraft of the first five production batches: 174 (K6152-K6325, delivered between March 1936 and April 1937; less 12 supplied to RAAF); 143 (K8703-K8845, delivered between April and September 1937; less 26 to RAAF, 4 to Finland and one to Estonia);

28 (L7046-L7073, delivered between October and December 1937; 98 (between L7903 and L9165, N1330-N1339, delivered between March and September 1938, less 17 to RAAF); and 850 (between N4856 and N9999, delivered between October 1938 and September 1939; less 6 to Turkey). A total of 11,020 Ansons of all types was built, of which 8,138 were produced in the United Kingdom and 2,882 in Canada; of this total 7,032 were Anson Mark Is, not all of which were able or adaptable to carry bombs.

Summary of Service: (In the Coastal and General Reconnaissance rôles, and as bombing trainers, 1936-1941). Anson Is served with the following General and Coastal Reconnaissance Squadrons: Nos 206, 217, 220, 224, 233, 269, 320 (Dutch), 321 (Dutch), 500, 502, 608 and 612 Squadrons. Anson Is served as bomb-carrying trainers with the following Bomber Squadrons: No 7 (March 1939 to May 1940), No 35 (July 1939 to April 1940), No 44 (February to June 1939), No 51 (March 1937 to February 1938), No 52 (February 1939 to April 1940), No 58 (February to December 1937), No 61 (March 1937 to January 1938), No 63 (March 1939 to April 1940), No 75 (March 1937 to October 1939), No 76 (May 1939 to April 1940), No 97 (February 1939 to April 1940), No 104 (September 1939 to April 1940), No 106 (May to September 1939), No 108 (May 1939 to April 1940), No 144 (January to December 1937), No 148 (April 1939 to April 1940), No 207 (July 1939 to April 1940), and No 215 (February 1937 to April 1940). Ansons also served with numerous training units, but in most instances the bomb-carrying equipment had been removed. Later in the War, early Ansons, still carrying bomb gear, were employed in the Air/Sea Rescue rôle (with Nos 251, 275, 276, 278, 280, 281 and 282 Squadrons), and with No 516 Squadron for Combined Operations training.

Bristol Type 142/149 Blenheim I and IV

If the Avro Anson constituted a modest advance in cantilever monoplane design, and at the same time satisfied the demands of an important operational duty during the period of RAF expansion, another aeroplane of more dramatic potential was approaching completion at the time the Anson prototype made its first flight. The Bristol Blenheim was unquestionably a very advanced light bomber when it was designed, and was certainly comparable with any new aircraft at the same stage of development elsewhere in the world.

Such, however, was the necessity to settle quickly on a suitable standard of preparation and attain accelerated production, that the Blenheim Mark I was no more than an adequate aeroplane by the time it reached the first squadrons in 1937, and undeniably obsolete (by the standards of the major air forces of Europe) by the outbreak of war.

Limited improvements had been incorporated, and the Mark IV (the famous 'long-nose' Blenheim) remained the RAF's standard light bomber for the first two years of the War and, like its illustrious fighter contemporary, the Hawker Hurricane, fought on almost every front in conditions of repeated military setback and retreat. Yet this was the aeroplane which spearheaded the fightback after the dark days of almost continuous defeat and, with that qualifying criterion, the Blenheim and its crews earned the accolade of immortality.

At about the same time that Roy Chadwick was relocating the Avro 618's wing low on the fuselage of his new Type 652, Frank Barnwell had been comparing the results and characteristics of two aircraft designs with exactly

K7033 was the first production Blenheim I and, in the absence of a true prototype, it served in this capacity. The propeller spinners gave no noticeable benefit and were discarded on subsequent aircraft. (Photo: Author's Collection)

the same fuselages and with identical wings, one placed at the high, the other at the low position, the findings being much the same as those arrived at in the USA. When Lord Rothermere, proprietor of the *Daily Mail*, learned of the capabilities of such aircraft as the Douglas DC-1, he stated his wish to purchase a British six-passenger twin-engine 'executive' aeroplane with a top speed of 240 mph. This proposal, while obviously most attractive to the Bristol company from a commercial aspect, was also seen as likely to cause some embarrassment at the Air Ministry, the company's most important customer, as the RAF had at the time no *fighter* capable of matching that speed.

Nevertheless, when approached in April 1934 by Bristol, who suggested a parallel light bomber design powered by Mercury engines and with a maximum speed of 280 mph, the Air Ministry gladly, though inscrutably, gave its approval for Rothermere's aircraft to go ahead. The Bristol company was not party to DTD discussions elsewhere which would, in less than two years'

time, result in the appearance of the Hurricane and Spitfire.

As a result of Bristol's meeting with the Air Ministry, Rothermere ordered from the company the Type 142 at a cost of £18,500, provided it was flown by June 1935. Bristols also went ahead with a private venture version, the Type 143, powered by their new 500hp Aquila radial engines.

The first flight of the 650hp Mercury VIS2-powered Type 142 took place at Filton on 12 April 1935 with fixed-pitch four-blade wooden propellers. Two months later it was delivered to Martlesham Heath for airworthiness acceptance trials during which, now fitted with three-blade, two-position, Hamilton Standard propellers, it duly returned a maximum speed of 280 mph at 16,500 feet.

At this point the Air Ministry sat up and took note. The Type 142 was already demonstrating a speed some 40 mph faster than the declared winner of the important F.7/30 competition, the private venture Gloster Gladiator biplane, now ordered into production — and the DTD promptly issued a new light bomber Specification, B.28/35, calling for an aircraft with a performance similar to that of Lord Rothermere's aeroplane.

Motivated by recognition of the Air Ministry's task of expanding and strengthening the Royal Air Force,

K7040 was one of the initial deliveries of Blenheim Is to No 114 (Bomber) Squadron at Wyton, the first to fly the new monoplanes in March 1937. (Photo: Real Photographs Co.)

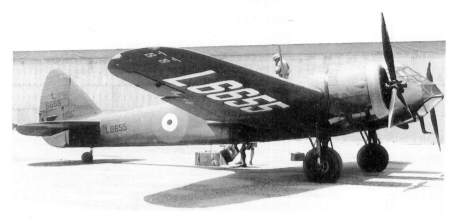

Rothermere — always a staunch and outspoken advocate of Britain's air superiority — named the Type 142 *Britain First* and offered it to the nation, an offer immediately accepted by the Air Ministry. As the 142 remained at Martlesham Heath for full Service assessment (being allocated the serial K7557), Barnwell now formally tendered the military version, the Type 142M; this differed principally in that the wing was re-located at the mid-position in order to allow the inclusion of a bomb bay below the wing spars; it was also powered by 840hp Bristol Mercury VIII engines. So impressed were the RAF pilots with K7557 at the A & AEE that the Air Ministry placed an immediate order for 150 production examples 'off the drawing board', together with an Instruction to Proceed with long-lead items for a further 450 aircraft. (It is perhaps interesting to note that this order was placed some nine months before the first Hurricane order — also for 600 aircraft).

After several mishaps while at Martlesham during 1935 and 1936, K7557

underwent trials at the RAE, and continued to fly until 1942, when it was grounded and became a ground instruction machine at No 10 S of TT.

The first production Type 142M, K7033, named the Blenheim, made its first flight on 25 June 1936, this aircraft being employed as the production prototype, and reaching Boscombe Down on 27 October 1936, despite only being ballasted for military equipment. The first Service deliveries were made to No 114 (Bomber) Squadron, commanded by Sqn Ldr Hugh Hamilton Brookes (later Air Vice-Marshal, CB, CBE, DFC) at Wyton on 10 March 1937, the event being marred when the first Blenheim to land was totally wrecked after the pilot evidently applied the brakes too harshly, causing the aeroplane to overturn and

break its back. No 90 (Bomber) Squadron at Bicester followed suit in May, and Nos 44, 139 and 144 Squadrons by the end of the year.

With Blenheim production accelerating early in 1938, Hawker Hinds began to be withdrawn from operational squadrons during the last eighteen months before the War, being replaced by Blenheims — often following a short spell with Ansons to provide twin-engine training. By the time of the Munich crisis in September 1938, Blenheim I bombers had reached Nos 21, 34, 44, 57, 61, 62, 82, 90, 101, 104, 107, 108, 110, 114, 139 and 144 Squadrons, distributed between Nos 1, 2 and 5 Groups of Bomber Command at home. The first deliveries had also been made overseas, Blenheim Is replacing Hawker Hardys on No 30 Squadron at Habbaniya, Iraq, in July 1938.

By early 1938, however, it was becoming evident that the Blenheim I was already obsolescent. Despite its much advertised maximum speed of 280 mph, it proved unable to exceed 215 mph at 10,000 feet when carrying its complement of four 250lb bombs and full fuel and, with only one rotatable defensive gun, was obviously extremely vulnerable to the new generation of single-seat interceptor fighters, particularly the new

An early Blenheim IV of No 139 (Bomber) Squadron at Betheniville, France, during January 1940. Later Blenheims introduced a pair of Browning machine guns in an undernose fairing, firing aft for tail protection. (Photo: via Derek James)

German Messerschmitt Bf 109, which had already publicly demonstrated a maximum speed of well over 300 mph. (On 11 November 1937 the experimental Bf 109V13, powered by a DB601 engine, had established a new world speed record at 379 mph). This unpalatable conclusion was confirmed during the RAF defence exercise of August 1939, when the pilots of No 111 (Fighter) Squadron's Hurricanes claimed to have 'run rings round' every Blenheim they encountered.

Fortunately, events at Filton had occurred that served to alleviate what might easily have been a disaster for Bomber Command early in the War. Despite its heavy commitment to maintaining a high delivery rate of Blenheim Is to the RAF, the Bristol company had been permitted to undertake sales of the aircraft to certain 'politically reliable' nations overseas, and limited numbers of Blenheims were sold to Finland, Turkey and Yugoslavia, all of whom had held discussions with the company with a view to obtaining versions of the Blenheim capable of improved speed and range performance. It was, however, partly as a result of discussions with a Canadian technical delegation in 1936, which had expressed interest in a longer-range Blenheim, that Barnwell approached the DTD with his Type 149, featuring fuel tanks in the outer wing sections, a strengthened undercarriage and a lengthened nose to provide an improved wireless operator's/bomb aiming position.

The Air Ministry issued a new Specification, 11/36, for this version, renamed the Bolingbroke, and approved its production with the proviso that it

should not be at the expense of, nor delay production of, the Blenheim. The prototype Bolingbroke, K7072 (a modified Blenheim I) was flown by Cyril Uwins on 24 September 1937, this aircraft featuring nose glazing similar to that on the Mark I Blenheim, but extending forward by some three feet. Uwins, however, reported that he found a windscreen some six feet from the pilot's eyes disconcerting, an opinion shared by other Service pilots. Various alterations were made, but it was not until the late spring of 1938 that K7072 appeared with the characteristic asym-

metric 'scalloped' nose shape of the 'long-nose' Blenheim; the pilot was provided with a conventional stepped windscreen aft of a glazed nose, recessed on the port side; the navigator's station was thus located below the pilot's line of sight.

K7072 underwent trials at Martlesham Heath in July 1938, now being referred to as the prototype Blenheim IV (the name Bolingbroke being retained only for aircraft built in Canada for the RCAF), and production of this version commenced with L4823, partway through Bristol's third Blenheim production batch. Early aircraft were completed without the outer-wing fuel tanks, and when these tanks were installed the aircraft was sometimes referred to as the Mark IVL (L=Long-range), although Service charge lists and unit strengths, as well as production records, made no differentiation, and the designation remained unofficial.

With no alternative long-range light bomber capable of achieving large-scale production in the immediate future, the Blenheim IV was quickly adopted to

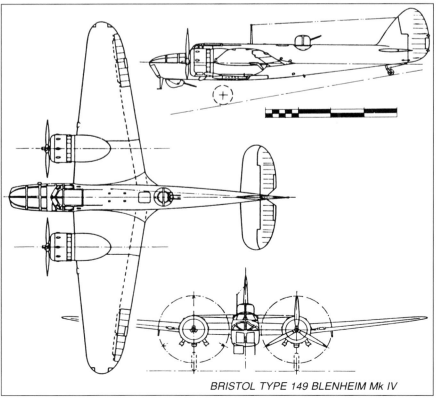

BRISTOL TYPE 149 BLENHEIM Mk IV

replace the Mark I, a decision that coincided with the opening up of Blenheim production at the new Rootes Securities 'shadow' factory at Speke, Liverpool. After its completion of 250 Blenheim Is this assembly line switched to the Mark IV, no fewer than 2,230 such aeroplanes being produced here in the next two years.

Blenheim IV bombers began delivery to No 53 (Bomber) Squadron at Odiham in January 1939, and by the end of that year the unit had been joined by 14 others, as the Mark I was withdrawn from front-line squadrons at home. The first RAF aircraft to fly over Germany during the Second World War was Bristol-built Blenheim IV N6215 of No 139 (Bomber) Squadron, flown on 3 September by Fg Off Andrew Macpherson on an armed reconnaissance over

German warships in the Schillig Roads off Wilhelmshaven. The next day, five Blenheim IVs of No 110 Squadron and five of No 107 set out from Wattisham to attack German warships in the Heligoland Bight, led by Flt Ltd Kenneth Christopher Doran of No 110. The aircraft each carried two 500lb semi armour-piercing bombs, and the two squadrons made their way out independently. Doran's formation attacked the German pocket-battleship *Sheer*, lying off Wilhelmshaven, and scored three or four direct hits but, owing to the low level at which the attacks were carried out, the bombs failed to explode as their eleven-second delay fuses had insufficient time to work off their safety devices. The ship was out of action for no more than five weeks. The Blenheims of No 107 Squadron, as well as five

others from No 139 Squadron, failed to acheive any damage. Five Wattisham-based Blenheims failed to return.

Unfortunately, the early wartime daylight raids, not only by the Blenheims but also by the heavier Hampdens and Wellingtons, all provided a painful lesson for the RAF: that unescorted bombers with a performance and armament inadequate to face a dedicated, professional and well-equipped enemy air defence system would inevitably suffer unsustainable casualties. The only remedy available to the Air Staff under these circumstances, distasteful though it was, was to abandon the daylight raids, at least until the balance of air superiority could be wrested from the German *Luftwaffe*.

While the home-based Blenheim squadrons were digesting the unpalat-

---

Type: Twin-engine, three-crew, mid-wing monoplane light bomber.

Air Ministry Specifications: B.28/35, 11/36, 33/36, 34/36, 2/37 and 10/37.

Manufacturers: The Bristol Aeroplane Co Ltd, Filton, Bristol; A V Roe & Co Ltd, Chadderton, Lancashire; Rootes Securities Ltd, Speke, Liverpool, Lancashire.

Powerplant: Prototype. Two 650hp Bristol Mercury VI S.2 9-cylinder air-cooled radial engines driving 3- or 4-blade propellers. Mark I. 840hp Bristol Mercury VIII. Mark IV. 920hp Bristol Mercury XV. Experimental. 920hp Mercury XX; 850hp Wright Cyclone G3B; 750hp Pratt & Whitney Twin Wasp Jr SB4G.

Structure: All-metal construction with sheet light-alloy skin; fabric-covered control surfaces.

Dimensions: Span, 56ft 4in; length (Mk I), 39ft 9in; (Mk IV), 42ft 7in; height, 9ft 10in; wing area, 469 sq ft.

Weight: Mk I. Tare, 8,100lb; all-up, 12,500lb. Mk IV. Tare, 9,790lb; all-up, 13,500lb.

Performance: Mk I. Max speed, 260 mph at 15,000ft; climb to 6,500ft, 3 min 40 sec; service ceiling, 28,000ft; range, 1,050 miles. Mk IV. Max speed, 266 mph at 11,000ft; climb to 6,500ft, 4 min 10 sec; service ceiling, 22,500ft; range, 1,450 miles (Mk IVL).

Armament: Mark I. One fixed forward-firing 0.303in Vickers Mk V (later Browning) machine gun in port wing, and one Vickers K gas-operated machine gun in dorsal Bristol Mk I, II or III turret. Bomb load of up to four 250lb bombs carried internally. Mark IV. One fixed 0.303in Browning gun in port wing; twin Browning guns, remotely aimed and fired, in Frazer-Nash undernose mounting, firing aft, and twin Browning guns in Midships Bristol Mk IV turret. Bomb load of up to four 250lb GP bombs carried internally and up to 320lb of light bombs carried externally.

Prototype: One militarised commercial prototype (*Britain First*, K7557) first flown at Filton on 12 April 1935. Mark I prototype, K7033 (1st production aircraft), first flown on 25 June 1936. Mark IV prototype, K7072 (originally a modified Mark I, named Bolingbroke), first flown on 24 September 1937.

Summary of Production: A total of 4,430 Blenheims was built in the United Kingdom, including the aircraft above (K7033 and K7072); these comprised 1,134 Mark Is (Bristol, 634; Avro, 250; and Rootes, 250) and 3,296 Mark IVs (Bristol, 316; Avro, 750; and Rootes, 2,230): K7033-K7182 and L1097-L1546 (Bristol, 600 aircraft, all Mk Is. 5 supllied to Turkey); L4817-L4934 (Bristol, 34 Mk Is and 84 Mk IVs; one Mk I and 3 Mk IVs to Turkey); L6594-L6843 (Avro; all Mk Is; 19 to Romania and 19 to Yugoslavia); between L8362 and L9044 (Rootes, 380 aircraft; between L8362 and L8731, 250 Mk Is; and between L8732 and L9044, 130 Mk IVs. 2

to Greece, 21 to Romania and 3 to Finland); between L9170 and L9482 (Rootes, 220 aircraft, all Mk IVs. 14 to Finland, 2 to Portugal); between N6140 and N6242 (Bristol, 100 aircraft, all Mk IVs); between P4825 and P4927 (Bristol, 70 aircraft, all Mk IVs. 6 to Greece, 18 to Canada); between P6885 and P6961 (Bristol, 62 aircraft, all Mk IVs. 6 to Greece); R2770-R2799 (Avro, 30 aircraft, all Mk IVs. 3 to Portugal); between R3590 and R3919 (Rootes, 250 aircraft, all Mk IVs. 2 to Portugal, 1 to Free French Forces); between T1793 and T2444 (Rootes, 400 aircraft, all Mk IVs. 7 to Free French Forces, 1 to Turkey, 2 to Portugal); between V5370 and V6529 (Rootes, 600 aircraft, all Mk IVs. 6 to Portugal); between Z5721 and Z6445 (Avro, 420 aircraft, all Mk IVs. 3 to Free French Forces, 6 to Portugal); between Z7271 and Z7992 (Rootes, 430 aircraft, all Mk IVs. 4 to Free French Forces, 1 to Portugal and 1 to Turkey); between Z9533 and Z9836 (Avro, 200 aircraft, all Mk IVs). 5 other aircraft, AE449-AE553, were ordered as replacements but not completed. Overseas manufacture included 45 Mk Is and 10 Mk IVs built in Finland, 16 Mk I built in Yugoslavia and 506 Bolingbrokes built in Canada.

Summary of RAF Service: Blenheim Mk Is served as light bombers or in associated rôles in the United Kingdom between March 1937 and April 1941 with the following Squadrons: Nos 18, 21, 44, 57, 61, 82, 90, 101, 104, 107, 108, 110, 114, 139, 144 and 252; of these, Nos 18 and 57 were detached to France in 1939-1940; they served in the Middle East between 1938 and March 1942 with the following Squadrons: Nos 8, 11, 39, 45, 55, 84, 113, 203, 211 and 223; they served with Nos 20 and 60 Squadrons in India between June 1939 and December 1941, and in Malaya and Singapore between July 1938 and January 1942 with Nos 11, 34, 39, 60 and 62 Squadrons. Blenheim Mk IV bombers served in the United Kingdom between January 1939 and August 1943 with the following Squadrons: Nos, 13, 15, 18, 21, 35, 40, 53, 57, 59, 82, 86, 88, 90, 101, 104, 105, 107, 108, 110, 114, 139, 140, 143, 212, 218, 226, 252, 608 and 614; in France between November 1939 and May 1940 with Nos 18, 53, 57, 59, 114, 139 and 212 Squadrons; in the Mediterranean and the Middle East between March 1940 and November 1943 with Nos 6, 8, 11, 14, 18, 21, 39, 45, 52, 55, 82, 84, 105, 107, 113, 162, 173, 203, 211 and 244 Squadrons; and in India, Ceylon, Burma, Malaya, Singapore and the East Indies between November 1941 and September 1943 with Nos 11, 34, 45, 60, 84 and 211 Squadron. Apart from Blenheim fighters (converted from bombers) serving with 24 fighter squadrons of Fighter and Coastal Command, Blenheim Is and IVs also served with numerous second-line and training units in the United Kingdom, Mediterranean, Middle East, India and the Far East theatres between 1937 and 1945.

able results of the early attacks, the RAF was discharging its undertaking to France by despatching squadrons of Hurricane fighters and Battle light bombers to France with the Air Component and the Advanced Air Striking Force, in defence and support of the British Expeditionary Force. In due course four Blenheim bomber Squadrons were also deployed (Nos 18 and 53, initially with Blenheim Is and later with Mk IVs with the Air Component, and Nos 114 and 139, sent out in December 1939 with Mk IVs to join the AASF), as well as No 59 Squadron, whose Blenheims were employed on night reconnaissance over the front occupied by the BEF.

All of these squadrons were heavily engaged when the German offensive in the West opened on 10 May 1940. When possible, the short-range raids flown against tactical targets were provided with escorts, but the heavy casualties suffered by the Blenheims were more the result of German bombing attacks on their French airfields than of air combat. Nos 114 and 139 lost almost all their aircraft before being withdrawn to Britain to re-equip and train new crews.

While the Blenheim IVs now took over almost all the light bombing duties of the home-based RAF during and following the Dunkirk evacuation (the Fairey Battle squadrons having been decimated during the Battle of France,

and their aircraft discredited), the Blenheim I was assuming a growing importance with the RAF in the Middle and Far East. Thus, by 10 June 1940, when Italy joined Nazi Germany in the War, there were six Blenheim bomber squadrons in the Middle East (Nos 45, 55, 113 and 211 in Egypt, No 8 at Aden and No 84 at Shaibah). Only No 113 was equipped with Blenheim IVs.

After Italy's entry into the War the Blenheims, constituting the most modern light bombers available in the Mediterranean, were widely employed, participating in the abortive Greek campaign as Nos 84 and 211 Squadrons re-equipped with Blenheim IVs early in 1941. The airfields on the island of Malta were frequently used as bases for Blenheims, sent either from the Western Desert or the United Kingdom to mount attacks against the Italian airfields in Sicily and Libya. Among those squadrons that flew out to Malta in July 1941 from Britain was No 105, commanded by Wg Cdr Hughie Idwal Edwards VC, DFC (later Air Cdre, VC, CBE, DSO, DFC, ADC). Edwards, an Australian, had on the 4th of that month won the Victoria Cross when he led a low-level daylight bombing attack by Blenheim IVs of Nos 105 and 107 Squadrons from Swanton Morley against the German city of Bremen. Despite the handicap of paralysis of the lower leg, resulting from an

earlier flying accident, Edwards attacked the German port from below 100 feet, dodging a balloon barrage while doing so and being heavily hit by the considerable gun defences. Of twelve Blenheims despatched, only five returned.

The Blenheims in the Middle East suffered relatively light casualties as long as the Italian *Regia Aeronautica* was the only opponent. However, when the *Luftwaffe* appeared in the theatre early in 1941, the remaining Blenheim Is were withdrawn and many despatched to the Far East. The Blenheim IVs, escorted whenever possible by Hurricane or Tomahawk fighters, continued in action until well into 1943 as the opposing armies advanced and retreated back and forth across the Western Desert — being eventually replaced by aircraft such as the Blenheim V (see page 349).

In South-East Asia, Blenheim Is had been serving since August 1939 when No 39 Squadron moved from India to Tengah at Singapore, leaving behind its Harts to convert to the twin-engine bombers; it was joined the next month by No 62 Squadron, also with Blenheims, fresh from Britain.

When Japan attacked Malaya on 7/8 December 1941, Nos 34 and 60 Squadrons were at Tengah, the former with Mark IVs, the latter still with Mark Is. No 62 Squadron was based on the Malayan mainland with Blenheim Is at

A late-production Rootes-built Blenheim Mk IV, V6083, carrying the code letters of No 13 OTU. The Bristol Mk IV midships turret, fully raised, mounts a pair of Browning guns, as does the undernose mounting. The aircraft features a modified wing leading edge with balloon cable cutters and an extended root fillet, and may have been undergoing trials with this equipment. (Photo: The Bristol Aeroplane Co Ltd, Neg No T142M/282)

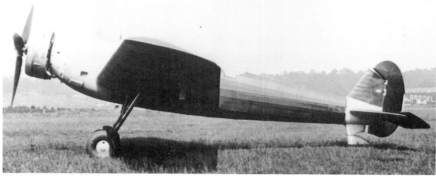

Alor Star but, on the first day of the Japanese invasion, moved to Butterworth. (No 39 Squadron had been transferred to the Middle East.)

Confronted by modern Japanese fighters, the Blenheims again suffered very heavy casualties and, despite many desperate attempts to stem the enemy's advance, the tiny force of British bombers (which also included a number of Lockheed Hudsons) was eventually forced to seek bases on Sumatra and

Java, where they were joined by the Blenheim IVs of Nos 84 and 211 Squadrons, hurriedly sent by sea from Egypt. Inevitably, heavily outnumbered and handicapped by the lack of co-ordinated control, the Blenheims were either destroyed or rendered incapable of flying, and the personnel of all five Squadrons were evacuated to India.

During the early stages of the long-drawn-out campaign in Burma, Blenheim IVs of Nos 11, 34, 45, 60

and 84 Squadrons were employed in frequent raids on the Japanese forces advancing northwards through the jungle, as well as their bases in the south of the country, until aircraft such as the Hurricane IIC fighter-bomber — more able to defend themselves against enemy fighters — arrived to take over the tactical bombing rôle. The last Blenheims flown in action were those of No 60 Squadron, based at Yelahanka, India, in August 1943.

Vickers Type 246/281 Wellesley

It will be recalled that, following the evaluation of the surviving contenders in the G.4/31 competition and despite a steady evaporation of Air Ministry interest in the 'general purpose' rôle, Vickers (Aviation) Ltd had been awarded a contract for 150 examples of its Type 253 biplane. Within a matter of weeks this had been cancelled and replaced by a production order for a monoplane, the Vickers Type 246, already built in prototype form as a private venture.

Indeed, the company had sanctioned the design and manufacture of the Type 246 as long ago as 1932, it being Dr Barnes Wallis' intention to extend the geodetic principle to the entire airframe structure (whereas the less radical Type 253 biplane only featured geodetics in the fuselage).

Employing a fuselage similar in many respects to that of the biplane, the Type 246 featured a cantilever, two-spar wing of exceptionally high aspect ratio, conventional ribs and riblets being replaced by diagonally orientated geodetic members. Equally radical (though by no means unique) was the wide-track manually-operated retractable undercarriage. Powered by a Pegasus IIIM3 radial engine in a narrow-chord Bristol-Townend ring, the aeroplane was too late for attendance at the G.4/31 evaluation, being first flown by 'Mutt'

The short-lived Vickers Type 246, O-9, which crashed only a month after its first flight. The photographic foreshortening of this picture exaggerates the wing chord, and gives little idea of the Wellesley's very high aspect ratio. (Photo: Vickers (Aviation) Ltd)

Summers on 19 June 1935. Unfortunately this prototype suffered serious wing damage in a landing accident on 23 July, following malfunctioning during retraction at take-off, the port wheel gear penetrating the wing structure.

Nevertheless, on the strength of the performance figures obtained during the short period of flight trials, the Air Ministry was persuaded to amend the Type 253 production contract, substituting the manufacture of 96 examples of the monoplane Type 246. This amended contract was signed on 10 September that year, and was accompanied by the issue of a new Specification, B.22/35. At the same time the damaged prototype 246 was purchased by the Air Ministry, and Vickers was instructed to

repair it, incorporating any improvements agreed with the DTD. The new bomber was to be named the Wellesley.

In fact the rebuilt prototype, now styled the Type 281 and allotted the serial K7556, featured numerous improvements, including an hydraulically-retracting undercarriage, enclosed cockpits, a Pegasus X engine and a more angular fin. The aircraft underwent full performance trials during the summer of 1936 at Martlesham Heath, returning figures that were considerably in advance of any achieved during the G.4/31 competition.

Consideration had been given to the accommodation of the 2,000lb bomb load in a fuselage bay, but it was thought unwise for the time being, given the

An early standard production Wellesley, K7729, which was allocated to a life of trials at Martlesham Heath and Farnborough; it was destroyed in a crash near Farnham on 5 October 1938. Like most in-service Wellesleys it was fitted with a 3-blade Hamilton Standard 2-pitch propeller. (Photo: RAF Museum)

The very long range development Wellesley, K7717, still carrying No 148 (Bomber) Squadron markings, and displaying the long-chord cowling for its high-compression Pegasus XXII engine. All military equipment was removed in the interests of saving weight to make way for maximum fuel. (Photo: Flight, Neg No 7805)

current lack of knowledge about the strength penalties incurred by interrupting the geodetics. Instead, two large streamlined bomb panniers were to be carried under the wings. At the A & AEE, K7556 returned a top speed of 202 mph at 8,000 feet, a climb to 10,000 feet in 9 min 30 sec, and a service ceiling of 26,200 feet.

The first production aircraft, K7713, was flown by Summers on 30 January 1937, and soon afterwards Fg Off Jeffrey Kindersley Quill RAFO, of Vickers' flight test staff, completed the Type Tests at the A & AEE. The Wellesley was cleared for delivery to No 7 (Bomber) Squadron (Wg Cdr Frank Ormond Soden) at Finningley in April, but almost immediately one of its Flights was detached to form No 76 Squadron, also at Finningley under the command of Wg Cdr Strang Graham MC (later Air Cdre, MC, GM), who was, in turn quickly succeeded by Sqn Ldr Edward John George (later Gp Capt, OBE). No 7 Squadron was not destined to keep the Wellesley, and all the initial deliveries were taken over by No 76. By the end of the year this Squadron had been joined by Nos 35, 77, 148 and 207, all flying Wellesleys in Bomber Command, while the first aircraft sent overseas (K7773-K7786) were shipped to Egypt, where they joined No 45 (General Purpose) Squadron at Helwan in November 1937, commanded by Sqn Ldr (later Gp Capt) Noel Vivian Moreton.

Although the introduction of the Wellesley into service brought forth a bomber of much improved performance, replacing Fairey Gordons and Hawker Audaxes, it was soon obvious that it was not fast enough nor adequately armed to survive combat with the new German fighters, and it was decided instead to redeploy the bomber to the Middle East, where its long range would be of considerable value and it

would, at worst, only meet the Italian Air Force in the event of war.

No further home-based Squadrons were therefore equipped with Wellesleys, although No 76 continued to fly them until they were replaced by Handley Page Hampdens in April 1939. As they were withdrawn at home, and production ran out in May 1938, they were shipped out to Aboukir for distribution to Nos 14, 47 and 223 Squadrons.

Meanwhile, the exceptional long-range potential of the Wellesley (confirmed when Vickers showed that it would be possible for the aircraft to carry more than 1,200 gallons of fuel), led to the decision to establish a special unit to prepare for an attempt on the world distance record, and in January 1938 the

Long Range Development Unit came into being at Upper Heyford under the command of Wg Cdr Oswald Robert Gayford DFC, AFC.[1] A modified Wellesley, K7717, had undergone trials with strengthened wings and undercarriage, a high-compression Pegasus XXII specially prepared to run on 100-octane fuel, a long-chord cowling and a smaller supercharger, preparing the way for long-distance flights, and in due course five similar Wellesleys, adapted to accommodate three-man crews, L2637, L2638, L2639, L2680 and L2681, were delivered to the LRDU. On 5 November 1938 three of these, flown by Sqn Ldr Richard Kellett (later Air Cdre, OBE, DFC, AFC) in L2638, Flt Lt Henry

[1] As a Squadron Leader in February 1933, Gayford had established a world long-distance record of 5,410 miles for Britain, flying with Flt Lt Gilbert Edward Nicholetts AFC from Cranwell to Walvis Bay in South Africa in the special Fairey Long-Range Monoplane, K1991.

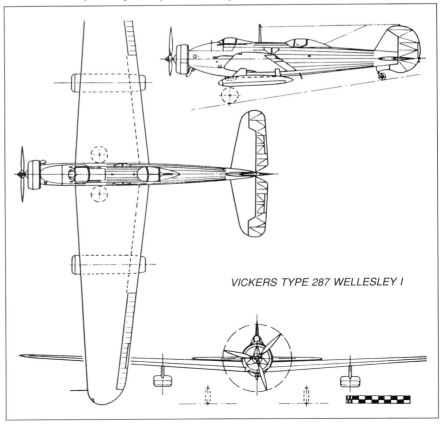

VICKERS TYPE 287 WELLESLEY I

A pair of No 14 Squadron Wellesleys flying from Amman over the inhospitable terrain of Jordan early in the War; the nearest aircraft, L2697, went on to serve with No 47 Squadron, but was lost on operations in September 1940. The fairing over the tail-wheel, a feature of early aircraft, was discarded by Middle East Squadrons. (Photo: Real Photographs Co.)

Algernon Vickers Logan in L2639, and Flt Lt Andrew Nicholson Combe (later Gp Capt, AFC) in L2680, took off from Ismailia in Egypt and set course for Australia. Forty-eight hours later Kellett and Combe landed at Darwin, having established a new world record of 7,157.7 miles; Logan, with insufficient fuel remaining to cross the Timor Sea, had landed at Kupang, Timor, to refuel.

After Italy's entry into the War in June 1940, the Wellesley squadrons in the Middle East were extensively used during the campaign in Italian East Africa which began the same month. Flying from airfields in the Sudan, Nos 14 and 47 carried out a number of successful raids on the airfield at Massawa, the former Squadron on one occasion destroying 780 tons of the enemy's fuel in the port. No 223 Squadron, which Air Chief Marshal Sir Arthur Longmore GCB, DSO, commanding the Royal Air Force in the Middle East, moved from the Sudan to Aden at the beginning of the campaign, flew a number of outstanding long distance raids, bombing the military airfields around Addis Ababa. The Squadron most heavily engaged during the campaign, No 47, lost six aircraft shot down and seven others destroyed in Italian raids on its forward base at Gedaref in the Sudan; eight others, damaged by enemy action, crashed on landing.

After the successful conclusion of the campaign in Eritrea, most of the surviv-ing Wellesleys were withdrawn from front-line service and issued to various second-line units, including Nos 70 and 71 OTU. The longest serving Wellesley unit, No 47 Squadron, continued to fly Wellesleys in Egypt until March 1943, although they had been joined by Bristol Beauforts the previous year.

Type: Single-engine, two-seat, low/mid-wing monoplane general purpose medium bomber.

Air Ministry Specifications: G.4/31 and B.22/35.

Manufacturer: Vickers (Aviation) Ltd, Weybridge, Surrey.

Powerplant: Prototype. One 680hp Bristol Pegasus IIIM3 9-cylinder air-cooled radial engine driving 3-blade Fairey Reed propeller. Later Pegasus X. Mark I. One 925hp Bristol Pegasus XX. Distance Record aircraft. Pegasus XXII.

Structure: Geodetic construction throughout, with fabric covering.

Dimensions: Span, 74ft 7in; length, 39ft 3in; height, 12ft 4in; wing area, 630 sq ft.

Weights: Tare, 6,812lb; all-up, 11,128lb.

Performance: Max speed, 222 mph at 15,000ft; climb to 10,000ft, 10 min 50 sec; service ceiling, 26,100ft; normal range, 1,100 miles (Record Distance, 7,162 miles).

Armament: One synchronized 0.303in Vickers Mk V machine gun firing forward, and one Vickers K gas-operated machine gun in rear cockpit. Maximum bomb load of 2,000lb carried in underwing containers.

Prototype: One (private venture, 0-9, later K7556), first flown by Joseph ('Mutt') Summers at Brooklands on 19 June 1935.

Production: A total of 176 Wellesleys was built (excluding prototype): K7713-K7791 (79), K8520-K8536 (17) and L2637-L2716 (80); delivered between 4 March 1937 and 30 May 1938.

Summary of Service: Wellesleys served with the following Bomber Squadrons in the United Kingdom: No 7 at Finningley in April 1937; No 35 at Cottesmore between July 1937 and June 1938; No 76 at Finningley between April 1937 and April 1939; No 77 at Honington between November 1937 and November 1938; No 148 at Scampton and Stradishall between June 1937 and November 1938; and No 207 at Worthy Down between August 1937 and April 1938. They served in the Middle East with Nos 14, 45 and 47 Squadrons, and with Nos 45, 47 and 223 Squadrons in Kenya between November 1937 and March 1943. In second-line rôles they served with Nos 117 and 267 Squadrons in the Communications rôle in the Middle East and with several communications flights between 1940 and 1942; other units included the Long Range Development Unit, the Air Torpedo Development Unit, Nos 70 and 71 OTUs (Middle East), the Pilots Reserve and Reinforcement Pool (ME), and Training Unit and Reserve Pool (ME).

Handley Page H.P.51

Just as the 'portmanteau' Specification, G.4/31, had sought a multi-rôle aircraft — a necessity born of privation — so Specification C.26/31 sought a dual-rôle bomber transport, or, more accurately, a transport capable of carrying bombs as an alternative to troops. However, unlike G.4/31, the three prototypes submitted to C.26/31, all supported by Air Ministry purchase, were all to lead with varying deviation to aeroplanes built in quantity for RAF service.

The Handley Page H.P.51, an ingenious adaptation of a former biplane prototype, progressed almost directly to the Harrow heavy bomber, but thence to uninterrupted transport work. The Bristol Type 130, with scarcely any significant alteration, entered production and joined the RAF as a transport which, in the most unlikely circumstances came to be used as a night bomber. The Armstrong Whitworth A.W.23, after an undistinguished appearance as a transport, underwent extensive surgery to be transmogrified into one of the most austere collections of straight lines ever to fly in the RAF; the Whitley was, nevertheless, the Service's first modern heavy bomber and one that carried Bomber Command into the

Complete with its Bristol Pegasus III engines, four-blade propellers and enlarged tailplane and elevator, the H.P.51 J9833 poses at the RAE, Farnborough in 1937. Note the underfuselage bomb racks. (Photo: Royal Aerospace Establishment, Neg No 21677)

Second World War. It was, moreover, to be employed as a troop transport during the War. As will become evident, the Air Ministry found it difficult to break with the tradition that all heavy bombers should possess a secondary ability to carry trrops.

After the failure by Specification C.16/28 to produce a satisfactory bomber transport, the Handley Page H.P.43, J9833, seemed destined to become something of a white elephant, as the Air Ministry expressed reluctance to purchase the prototype (which had been built under contract). In April 1932, however, C.26/32 was issued, calling for a twin-engine bomber transport monoplane capable of carrying up to 24 fully-armed soldiers, three aero-engines each weighing 1,000lb, ten stretcher casualties with four attendants, or up to eight 250lb GP bombs and eight 20lb sighting bombs. Soon afterwards the Air Ministry was persuaded to honour its commitment to purchase the H.P.43 prototype.

Drawing on his monoplane experience with the H.P.47 (G.4/31) and receiving favourable strength test reports on its wing spar from the RAE, Lachmann embarked on scaling up the H.P.47 wing to span 90 feet, this being appropriate to match the fuselage of the otherwise redundant three-engine H.P.43 biplane. The Air Ministry accepted the proposal to convert the H.P.43 for contention in the C.26/31 competition, but when Handley Page asked if the two remaining Tiger engines might be replaced by 750hp Bristol Pegasus III engines (the engines favoured in the new Specification), the Air Ministry declined to meet their cost.

The H.P.51 was first flown by Major Cordes at Radlett on 8 May 1935, the

Handley Page pilot reporting favourably on the aircraft's handling qualities in general terms, but complaining that, as anticipated, the elevator control was poor when flying at low speed with the slotted flaps extended. In the interests of cost-limiting, Frederick Handley Page had vetoed the fitting of a revised tail unit (the company being considerably out of pocket on the H.P.43, notwithstanding the Air Ministry's purchase).

As reports reached Handley Page that results of the C.26/31 competition were a foregone conclusion in favour of the Bristol Type 130, permission was obtained to withdraw the H.P.51 from the contest in order to concentrate on a developed version (the H.P.54) which might attract production orders for an aircraft that seemed likely to satisfy a slightly different requirement then being discussed.

Once freed of the constraints of C.26/31, Handley Page was allowed to incorporate a modified tail unit in J9833 (which Lachmann had already surreptitiously designed), and the Tigers were replaced by Pegasus IIIs. As told later (see page 301), the H.P.54 *was* accepted

for production as the Harrow bomber.

In January 1937 J9833 visited the A & AEE for short performance and handling tests, several flights being made with a bomb load suspended from the external fuselage racks. It was then transferred to the Air Ministry's experimental charge at the RAE, and was used for a host of trials, including troop carrying exercises on Salisbury Plain, in-flight refuelling as a tanker (with Flight Refuelling Ltd), and blind landing trials in 1938. It was even-tually struck off charge in mid-1940.

Ironically, it transpired somewhat later that in 1934, long before J9833 was flown in monoplane guise, the Air Staff had decided to adopt the Bristol Type 130 for production before the prototype had flown, only requiring confirmation that the aeroplane did indeed satisfy the requirements of C.26/31. This tends to confirm suggestions that there existed abrasive relations between Handley Page and the Air Ministry at this time — not relieved by the cavalier treatment which Frederick Handley Page considered he had received in the ultimate verdict on the G.4/31 competition.

Type: Twin-engine, five-crew, high-wing cantilever monoplane bomber transport.
Air Ministry Specification: C.26/31
Manufacturer: Handley Page Ltd, Cricklewood, London NW 2, and Radlett, Herts.
Powerplant: Two 700hp Armstrong Siddeley Tiger IV 14-cylinder air-cooled radial engines driving 2-blade wooden propellers; later two 750hp Bristol Pegasus III 9-cylinder radial engines driving 2-piece 4-blade propellers.
Dimensions: Span, 90ft 0in; length, 78ft 4in; wing area, 1,170 sq ft.
Weights: (Approx) Tare, 12,000lb; all-up, 18,000lb.
Performance: Max speed, 188 mph at 6,500ft; normal range, 950 miles.
Armament: Nose and tail gun positions with provision to mount single Vickers K gas-operated machine guns. Provision to carry up to eight 250lb GP bombs and eight 20lb sighting/practice bombs.
Prototype: One, J9833 (formerly the H.P.43, modified as twin-engine monoplane), first flown by J L B H Cordes at Radlett on 8 May 1935. No immediate production, but see Handley Page H.P.54 Harrow, page 301.

The prototype Bristol Type 130 K9583 at Filton, displaying its New Type No 9 for the 1936 Hendon RAF Display. (Photo: The Bristol Aeroplane Co Ltd, Neg No T130/26)

Bristol Type 130 (C.26/31) Bombay

In the mid-1920s Frank Barnwell had designed a radical all-metal twin-engine monoplane fighter, the Bristol Type 95 Bagshot, with a semi-cantilever wing built on a conventional two-spar structure. At the outset of flight trials evidence came to light of potentially disastrous torsional flexing of the wings, leading to aileron reversal, with the result that the aircraft came to be confined to structural research into this phenomenon.

Stemming directly from this work, the structural research department at Filton, under Harold John Pollard, developed a cantilever wing structure of great torsional strength, employing multiple spars and ribs with high-tensile steel flanges having sheet webs and pressed Alclad ribs, to which was riveted Alclad skin, together with a stressed-skin fuselage. When Specification C.26/31 was received, Barnwell tendered his Type 130 employing these structures. The twin-engine aircraft was of high-wing configuration with twin inset fins and rudders on a high-set tailplane. Power was provided by two 750hp Bristol Pegasus III radial engines driving two-blade propellers. The tender was accepted in March 1933, and a prototype ordered. Construction of this went ahead slowly, as Barnwell required every component and joint to undergo stress tests as the design progressed.

Obviously impressed by the Bristol design team's painstaking approach to structural integrity, not to mention the realistic performance forecasts in line with the Requirement, the Air Ministry began discussions with Bristol to make alternative plans for the likely production of the Type 130, as it was clear that it was too large an aeroplane to be produced in any quantity at the Filton factory.

The prototype, K3583, was flown by Cyril Uwins on 23 June 1935, and was delivered to Martlesham Heath before the end of the year, where it was commented upon very favourably, although the tail controls were considered to be too heavy — attributed to excessive friction in the circuits. Other criticisms related to minor layout faults which could be simply rectified. With regard to armament, the gun positions were as yet of a makeshift nature, it being intended to introduce Bristol hydraulically-operated single-gun cupolas in the nose and tail. In an exercise to discover the Type 130's maximum bomb load, it was found possible to load no fewer than 168 twenty-pound bombs into the cabin (presumably to be dropped by hand from the side door), in addition to the eight statutory 250lb bombs carried on external under-fuselage racks. (There is no record of a Bombay being flown with a 5,360lb bomb load.)

Confirmation that the Bristol Type 130 met the specification requirements was the signal awaited by the Air Ministry to issue a production contract and Specification 47/36. An order for 80 aircraft named Bombay (the name Bedford had been suggested, but was refused), was placed with the new company Short and Harland Ltd at Belfast, formed by Short Brothers Ltd and Harland & Wolff Ltd who operated a new Government-owned 'shadow factory' on Queen's Island. The prototype returned to Filton for various development trials, but was written off after a forced landing at Chigwell, Essex, on 4 February 1939.

The complex wing structure delayed production at Belfast, and it was not until April 1939 that the first aircraft were ready for delivery to the RAF. The Bombay had been intended solely for use in the Middle East, and the first Squadron to receive them, in October 1939, was No 216 (Bomber Transport) Squadron, commanded at Heliopolis by Wg Cdr George Cecil Gardiner DSO,

The first production Bombay L5808 at Belfast with Pegasus XXII engines with three-blade Rotol propellers, and bomb racks fitted. Note that the wheel spats have been discarded; such impedimenta would have given untold trouble in the Western Desert. (Photo: Air Ministry, RTP, Neg No 10138 dated April 1939)

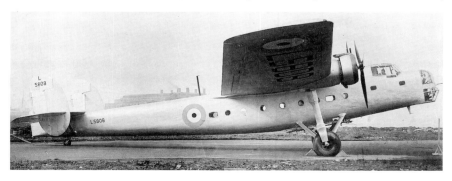

A Bombay of No 216 (Bomber Transport) Squadron, L5857/C. This, the last Bombay of the production batch, was one of the the aircraft of the Squadron destroyed in an enemy raid against Kufra airstrip on 25 September 1942, shortly before the Battle of Alamein. (Photo: Air Ministry, Neg No CM786)

DFC. It soon became necessary, however, to hold a number of Bombays in Britain for urgent transport duties, particularly with No 271 Squadron which, on 1 May 1940, was formed out of No 1680 Flight at Doncaster to operate transport aircraft (including Handley Page Harrows and impressed airliners) to and from France. And it was one of this Squadron's Bombays, L5813, while delivering pilots, groundcrews and Hurricane spares to No 501 Squadron on 11 May (the day following the start of the *Blitzkrieg*), that stalled and crashed on the approach to Betheniville, killing three pilots and injuring five others.

In the event, only No 216 Squadron was operationally equipped with the Bombay (the last thirty production aircraft being cancelled). Indeed, of the 50 aircraft built, no fewer than 39 served on this Squadron at one time or another. From the outset the Squadron was ordered to be ready to undertake bombing operations in the event that Italy should enter the War, while continuing to perform its customary transport duties, retaining its ancient Valentias alongside the Bombays.

It was early in the war with Italy that 216 Squadron's Bombays were called into action to fly a series of night

bombing raids on Benghazi, each carrying its full quota of 250lb bombs, while crew members dropped other makeshift

explosives from the cabin door. Only one aircraft was lost in these raids (L5816 on 19 October 1940).

A more tragic loss involved L5814, shot down by Messerschmitt Bf 109Fs of *Jagdgeschwader 27* over the Western Desert on 7 August 1942. Flown by 19-year-old Sgt H G James (later Sqn Ldr,

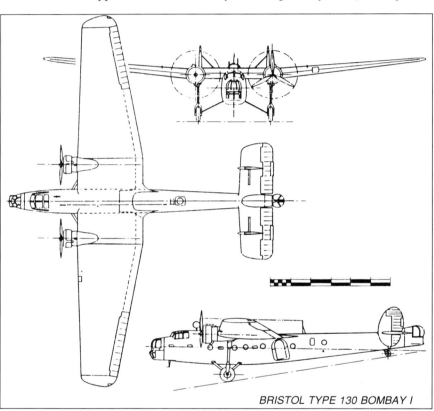

BRISTOL TYPE 130 BOMBAY I

Type: Twin-engine, four-crew, high-wing cantilever monoplane bomber transport.

Air Ministry Specifications: C.26/31 and 47/36

Manufacturers: Prototype. The Bristol Aeroplane Co Ltd, Filton, Bristol. Production. Short & Harland Ltd, Belfast.

Powerplant: Type 130. Two 750hp Bristol Pegasus IIIM3 9-cylinder air-cooled radial engines driving 2-blade wooden propellers. Production. Two 1,010hp Pegasus 32 engines with 3-blade Rotol variable-pitch propellers.

Structure: All-metal fuselage structure with Alclad stressed-skin, and cantilever wing with multi-cellular, seven-spar construction with high-tensile steel flanges and sheet webs with Alclad sheet covering.

Dimensions: Span, 95ft 9in; length, 69ft 3in; height, 19ft 11in; wing area, 1,340 sq ft.

Weights: Tare, 13,800lb; all-up, 20,180 lb.

Performance: Max speed 192 mph at 6,500ft; service ceiling, 24,850ft; normal range, 880 miles; overload-fuel range, 2,230 miles.

Armament: Single 0.303in Vickers K gas-operated machine

guns in hydraulically-operated Bristol B.II and B.III nose and tail turrets; bomb load of up to 2,160 lb carried on underfuselage racks.

Prototype: One Type 130 prototype, K3583, first flown by Cyril Uwins at Filton on 23 June 1940.

Production: 50 Bombays were built, L5808-L5857, and delivered to the RAF between April 1939 and June 1940. (30 others, L5858-L5887, were cancelled.)

Summary of RAF Service: Bombays served as night bombers and transports with No 216 (Bomber Transport) Squadron in Egypt and the Western Desert from October 1939 until June 1943; with No 271 (Transport) Squadron at Doncaster during May and June 1940; and with No 117 (Communications) Squadron at Khartoum. They also served in single figures with the Central Flying School, the Iraq Communications Flight, the Khartoum Communications Flight, the Overseas Aircraft Delivery Flight, the Airborne Forces Experimental Establishment, the Ferry Training Unit, the Air Ambulance Unit, No 10 FTS and No 15 OTU.

AFC*, DFM), the Bombay was carrying Lieut-Gen W H E Gott and his staff officers forward to assume command of the Eighth Army, when the enemy fighters intercepted the transport and forced it down, and then set about destroying it as it stood in the desert. Gott and all the other officers were killed; James alone was later found alive, still in his cockpit. As is well known, Gott's death led to the appointment instead of General Bernard Montgomery to command the Eighth Army.

No 216 Squadron continued to fly Bombays until June 1943, being constantly called on to move personnel and urgent supplies around North Africa, as well as, on occasion, evacuating casualties from the front line. Several other aircraft fell to enemy fighters and flak, and three Bombays were destroyed in an enemy raid on the airstrip at Kufra on 25 September 1942.

The last few surviving Bombays were struck off charge in the Middle East when the aircraft was finally declared obsolete on 31 August 1944.

Armstrong Whitworth A.W.23 (C.26/31)

An early in-flight view of the A.W.23, with undercarriage extended; the length of the cabin may be judged by the extent of the windows. (Photo: The Aeroplane, Neg No 342)

The third of the twin-engine monoplanes tendered to Specification C.26/31 for a 24-troop bomber transport was John Lloyd's A.W.23, a low-wing aeroplane powered by a pair of Armstrong Siddeley Tiger VI radial engines. In the annals of its manufacturer it broke new ground in two respects: it was the first to feature a retractable undercarriage, and it employed an entirely new wing structure, comprising a massive box-spar with light-alloy corrugated webs, the channels being arranged spanwise and vertically; this structure proved immensely strong, but resulted in a very deep aerofoil section with high drag.

Interpreting the Specification with overriding emphasis upon the troop-carrying rôle, Lloyd provided a cabin 40 ft long, 7ft high and 7ft 6in wide — an exceptionally generous volume for 24 soldiers, but allowing space provision for internal bomb racks beneath the cabin floor. So as not to interrupt the wing box structure, the undercarriage retracted forward into the engine nacelles, a system that did not provide for geometric wheels-down ground lock, and necessitated an engine-driven hydraulic lock — an unfortunate choice, as would later become evident.

Campbell Orde flew the prototype, K3585, on 4 June 1935, and before the end of the month it appeared at the Hendon Display. The choice of Tiger engines also proved unwise (albeit a company policy), and served to delay the aircraft's delivery to Martlesham Heath until late in 1936, and then only for take-off and landing measurements. By then, not only had the Bombay been adjudged the C.26/31 winner, but it was entering production.

The Tiger engines gave constant trouble, there being seven occasions of failure during the twelve months following K3585's first flight. On 9 March 1936 the port engine failed soon after take-off and, as this was the engine that powered the hydraulic undercarriage lock, the gear collapsed on landing.

By then, however, Lloyd had produced a dedicated bomber design to Specification B.3/34, employing the wings and tail of the A.W.23 (with little alteration), but introducing an entirely new fuselage, tailored for ease of production and the carriage of bombs. The prototype had flown, and production — which would ultimately total over 1,800 Whitley bombers — had already been ordered (see page 288).

Type: Twin-engine, four-crew, low-wing cantilever monoplane bomber transport.
Air Ministry Specification: C.26/31
Manufacturer: Sir W G Armstrong Whitworth Aircraft Ltd, Whitley, Coventry.
Powerplant: Two 810hp Armstrong Siddeley Tiger VI 14-cylinder air-cooled radial engines driving 4-blade single-piece wooden propellers, later 3-blade 2-pitch propellers.
Structure: Fuselage of braced steel tubular construction, fabric-covered; wing built up on single light-alloy box spar structure with sheet metal webs corrugated vertically and spanwise, with sheet-metal covered nose ribs. Fabric-covered control surfaces.
Dimensions: Span, 88ft 0in; length, 80ft 9in; height, 19ft 6in; wing area, 1,308 sq ft.
Weight: All-up, 24,100lb.
Performance: Max speed, 162 mph (TAS) at 6,500ft; climb to 10,000ft, 10 min 50 sec; service ceiling, 18,100ft; range, 790 miles (estimated).
Armament: Provision to mount single machine guns in nose and tail turrets, and to carry eight 250lb GP bombs internally.
Prototype: One, K3585, first flown by A C Campbell Orde on 4 June 1935. No production.

Hawker Hartbees

The intention, stated in 1934 by the South African government, to expand its air force to 250 aircraft within four years, led to negotiations between Oswald Pirow, the South African Defence Minister, and the British government to adopt a version of the Hawker Audax for close support and light bombing duties.

The fourth and final pattern Hartbees built by Hawker at Brooklands in 1935. Most of these aircraft, when they served in East Africa in 1940, acquired 'doughnut' low-pressure tyres to provide a bigger footprint on sandy desert airstrips. Note the deep tropical radiator. (Photo: Hawker Aircraft Ltd, Neg No 30/14K)

Hawker was accordingly authorised to build four pattern examples, named the Hartbees[1], and subsequently agreed licence production of the aircraft at the Roberts Heights factory of the SAAF Depot at Pretoria.

Two versions of the Hartbees were produced, a 'light' aircraft with dual controls and provision to carry up to eight 20lb bombs, and an armoured version capable of carrying two 250lb GP bombs under the wings. Power was to be provided by the 600hp Rolls-Royce Kestrel V engine with an enlarged tropical radiator; this was later found to be inadequate when flown in the tropics and, on Rolls-Royce's advice, additional louvres were cut in the nose panels to provide improved crankcase cooling.

The first two aircraft (SAAF Nos 801 and 803) were flown on 28 June 1935 by Philip Lucas, and shipped out to South Africa later that year, and production of 65 licence-built examples got underway in 1936, the first being flown early the next year.

The armoured Hartbees served with two squadrons at Waterkloof, these being sent north to Kenya as Nos 11 and 12 (Light Bomber) Squadrons in 1940 to serve alongside the RAF for defence against the Italian colonial forces being strengthened in East Africa. On 11 June, the day following Italy's entry into the War, 25 aircraft of these two Squadrons flew pre-emptive bombing attacks against the Italians at Royale on the Kenyan border with Ethiopia, and on Banda Hill nearby.

Later, two further Hartbees units, Nos 40 and 41 (Army Co-operation) Squadrons of the SAAF, were also sent to East Africa, but by 1941 most had been withdrawn from first-line duties; at least one Hartbees served with the RAF at Habbaniya in April that year.

---

[1] Sometimes referred to as the Hartbeest, although not in any British official documents traced.

Type: Single-engine, two-seat, single-bay biplane ground support light bomber.
Air Ministry Specification: 22/34 (on behalf of South African government)
Manufacturer: Hawker Aircraft Ltd, Kingston-upon-Thames and Brooklands, Surrey.
Powerplant: One 600hp Rolls-Royce Kestrel V 12-cylinder water-cooled in-line engine driving 2-blade wooden propeller.
Dimensions: Span, 37ft 3in; length, 29ft 7in; height, 10ft 5in; wing area, 348 sq ft.
Weights: Tare, 3,150lb; all-up (armoured version), 4,970lb.
Performance: Max speed, 176 mph at 6,000ft; climb to 10,000ft, 8 min 30 sec; service ceiling, 22,000ft; range, 370 miles.
Armament: One forward-firing synchronized 0.303in Vickers Mk III machine gun, and one Lewis gun on rear cockpit; bomb load of up to 500lb.
Prototype: One (SAAF No 801), first flown by P G Lucas on 28 June 1935 at Brooklands.
Production: Four pattern aircraft built by Hawker; 65 aircraft built in South Africa.

Hawker Hector

Last of the large family of Hawker Hart variants, the Hector was alone in that family in being designed from the outset for an engine other than the Rolls-Royce Kestrel. It was intended as a stopgap replacement for the Audax until the winner of a new army co-operation Specification (A.39/34) could enter service, possibly in 1938.

Following flight trials by the Hart test bed K2434, powered by a Napier Dagger 24-cylinder, air-cooled upright-H in-line engine, Specification 14/35 was drawn up to include this engine, in its more reliable Mark III version, in the Audax replacement. With very large orders being placed for the Hind light

The first Westland-built Hawker Hector K8090 at Yeovil, carrying a pair of supply containers under the wings. (Photo: Westland Aircraft Ltd, Neg No 3366)

bombers, not to mention the likely heavy orders for the forthcoming Hurricane and Spitfire fighters (then still only just being built in prototype form), pressure on Rolls-Royce to meet the demands for Kestrel and Merlin engines would certainly occupy that manufacturer's immediate factory facilities to the utmost.

Experience with the Dagger-Hart had, however, shown that the greater weight of the engine brought the Hart's cg so close to its safe limit that if it was to be required to carry the same warload as the Audax the simplest method of restoring a safe cg range was to adopt an unswept upper wing. This was done by introducing the Fury's outer wing sections, scaled up by about a quarter, and attaching them to the Hart's existing rectangular centresection.

Hawker Aircraft Ltd built the Hector prototype, K3719, and it was flown by Bulman at Brooklands on 14 February 1936, it being intended that A V Roe should undertake subsequent production for the RAF. This company, however, was now faced with accelerating production of the Anson, and Westland Aircraft Ltd seemed the logical alternative (having also built Audaxes and appearing to be the front runner for the A.39/34 production contract).

The first production Hectors were delivered in May 1937 to Nos 4 and 13 (Army Co-operation) Squadrons, commanded respectively by Wg Cdr Gerald Hamilton Loughnan and Sqn Ldr, later Air Cdre, Selwyn Harmer Cecil Gray at Odiham, and by the end of the year production of all 178 aircraft on order had been completed. All six Regular army co-operation squadrons had been re-equipped with Hectors in that time,

as well as Nos 612, 614 and 615 Squadrons of the Auxiliary Air Force.

By September 1939 all the Regular squadrons had disposed of their biplanes in favour of either the new Lysander monoplane or of Blenheim light bombers. The remaining Hector squadrons of the AAF were not deployed to France with the Air Component or the AASF, and by the beginning of the Battle of France in May 1940 only No 613 (City of Manchester) Squadron was still flying Hectors at Odiham, although the first of its Lysanders had started to arrive. Such was the desperate situation in which the remnants of the BEF found themselves during the evacuation of Dunkirk and in other pockets of resistance that No 613 flew a number of ground support sorties over the French coast, mounting a dive bombing attack with 250lb bombs on 26 May and following up with supply-dropping sorties on the next day. When one aircraft, K8118, was apparently hit by flak and crashed attempting to get home, it was decided to withdraw the old biplanes from operational work.

Thereafter for several years Hectors were widely used in the United Kingdom as glider tugs for the Hotspur training glider, the powerful Dagger engine being found to be less prone to overheating that the Kestrel of the Audax, while others continued to serve as trainers, particularly at the School of Army Co-operation.

Type: Single-engine, two-seat, single-bay army co-operation biplane.
Air Ministry Specification: 14/35
Manufacturers: Prototype. Hawker Aircraft Ltd, Kingston-upon-Thames and Brooklands, Surrey. Production: Westland Aircraft Ltd, Yeovil, Somerset.
Powerplant: One 805hp Napier Dagger IIIMS 24-cylinder air-cooled H-type in-line engine driving 2-blade Watts wooden propeller.
Dimensions: Span, 36ft 11½in; length, 29ft 9¾in; height, 10ft 5in; wing area, 346 sq ft.
Weights: Tare, 3,389lb; all-up, 4,910lb.
Performance: Max speed, 187 mph at 6,500ft; climb to 10,000ft, 5 min 40 sec; service ceiling, 24,000ft; range, 300 miles.
Armament: One synchronized 0.303in Vickers Mk V machine gun in port side of front fuselage, and one Lewis gun with Hawker mounting on rear cockpit. Bomb load of two 230lb or four 112lb bombs, or lighter bombs, supply containers, etc.
Prototype: One, K3719, flown by Flt Lt P W S Bulman on 14 February 1936 at Brooklands.
Production: A total of 178 Hectors was built by Westland, K8090-K8167 and K9687-K9786, these being delivered to the RAF between February and December 1937.
Summary of Service: Hectors served with the following Regular Army Co-operation Squadrons, Nos 2, 4, 13, 26, 53 and 59, between May 1937 and September 1939, and with the Army Co-operation Squadrons of the Auxiliary Air Force, Nos 602, 612, 613, 614 and 615, between November 1937 and June 1940. They also served as glider tug trainers with No 296 Squadron and many other glider training units, the Royal Air Force College, Cranwell, the Central Flying School, the School of Army Co-operation, Schools of Photography, Anti-Aircraft Co-operation Units, Aircraft Gun Mounting Establishment, etc.

Fairey TSR.II and Swordfish

It is a matter of history that the Fairey Swordfish biplane, while serving with the Fleet Air Arm throughout the Second World War, claimed the destruction of a greater tonnage of enemy shipping than any other Allied aircraft. Despite the anachronism of being obsolescent almost from the date of its entry into

service with the Fleet Air Arm in mid-1936, this extraordinary feat of arms may be explained by the fact that it was

the *only* fully operational torpedo and bomb-carrying aircraft available in adequate numbers to equip every aircraft

The Fairey TSR.II, K4190, after being rebuilt with dual controls following its accident in February 1935. This aeroplane was generally regarded as the true Swordfish prototype. (Photo: A J Jackson Collection)

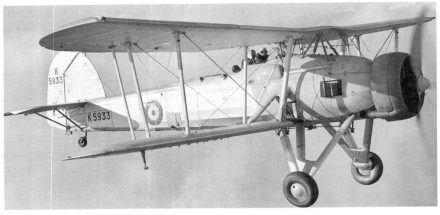

The third pre-production Swordfish, K5662, during floatplane trials with the Marine Aircraft Experimental Establishment, Felixstowe, shown here carrying a torpedo. A fairly large number of Swordfish seaplanes gave service with the Fleet Air Arm. (Photo: Air Ministry RTP, Neg No 8795C)

carrier in the Royal Navy from the beginning of the War and, as the necessity arose, was thrown into action against enemy warships — surface and submarine — whatever the likely defences might amount to. Fortunately, over the wastes of the Atlantic the enemy could seldom mount any air opposition; in European waters, from the coasts of Norway to the confines of the Mediterranean, it was a different story, and casualties were often extremely heavy.

It will be recalled that Fairey had, in 1933, produced a promising private venture, the TSR.I (see page 238), originally intended for the Greek Navy, but that the aircraft was lost in September that year, having failed to recover from a spin. At about this time the Air Ministry issued a more advanced Specification, S.15/33 (replacing S.9/30), and Marcel Lobelle's design staff produced an improved version of the TSR.I with an additional rear fuselage bay and with longitudinal fuselage strakes immediately forward of the tailplane, the longer fuselage being compensated for by sweeping back the upper wing by 4 degrees.

This aircraft, the TSR.II K4190, was first flown by Chris Staniland on 17 April 1934, and straightway underwent contractor's, catapult and deck-landing trials before being fitted with twin floats and flown by Staniland at Hamble on 10 November. It suffered damage in an accident in February 1935, but by then it had provided sufficient flight information to enable Lobelle to undertake the necessary modifications to satisfy the demands of S.15/33.

K4190 had undergone handling assessment at Martlesham Heath, beginning in June 1934, but had still attracted some criticism for its slow spin recovery and longitudinal instability in dives with the cg at its aft limit. These shortcomings were largely corrected by increasing the range of elevator movement, and it was also found that, when fitted with the heavier Fairey Reed metal propeller, in place of the two-blade wooden type, the aircraft's behaviour at the stall and in a spin was noticeably improved.

The effect of these changes satisfied the Service authorities by the end of 1934, and the following May Fairey was awarded a contract for three development aircraft (K5660-K5662) and 86 production examples, to be named the Swordfish. The third of the development trio was set aside for extended trials as a floatplane.

As the other two pre-production aeroplanes underwent handling and torpedo trials, the first full-standard Swordfish Mk Is were completed at Hayes and started delivery to the Mediterranean in July; there they joined No 705 (Catapult) Flight — later a 'full' Squadron — commanded by Lt-Cdr Douglas William Mackendrick RN at Kalafrana, Malta; equipped as floatplanes, these were held for use by the Battle Cruiser Squadron. Simultaneously, wheel-equipped torpedo bombers were delivered to No 825 Squadron (Lt-Cdr Henry Austin Traill RN) at Hal Far, Malta, replacing Fairey IIIFs, and shortly afterwards embarked in the fleet carrier, HMS *Glorious*. This Squadron was also to be one of the last to give up its Swordfish in 1945.

Other Squadrons to be equipped with Swordfish from the first production batch were No 822 (Lt-Cdr Aylmer Maurice Rundle RN) in August 1936 at Southampton, and No 823 (Lt-Cdr Godfrey Christopher Dickins RN) in November at Hal Far.

Further contracts were placed and, by the outbreak of war, Fairey was nearing the end of its seventh production batch. By the time this was complete the company had built a total of 692 Swordfish, all Mark Is, and twelve operational Squadrons had taken delivery of the aircraft. At that stage it was intended to switch production to the Fairey Albacore to the exclusion of the Swordfish but, as will be told (see page 321), the new aircraft failed to live up to expectations and, while Fairey did indeed discontinue Swordfish production, a new factory was opened by Blackburn Aircraft Ltd at Sherburn-in-Elmet, near Selby in Yorkshire, to undertake further production of the older aircraft. There was therefore a nine-month delay in deliveries, which did not start from the new factory until the end of 1940.

Meanwhile, Swordfish had been in frequent action, with outstanding suc-

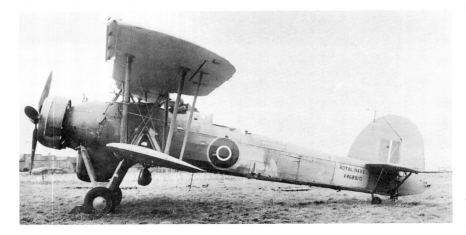

This, the eighth Swordfish I built, K5933, served all its life with No 825 Squadron — the first to fly the torpedo aeroplane — but was lost in an air collision near Alexandria on 30 January 1939. (Photo: via J M Bruce)

cess. In the first Battle of Narvik, during the Norwegian campaign, the battleship HMS *Warspite*, 31,000 tons, launched her Swordfish seaplane (flown by Petty Officer F C Rice, with Lt-Cdr W L M Brown RN as observer) to spot for her main armament as she sailed into Ofot Fjord on 13 April 1940. So effective was the work done by the aircraft's crew that the battleship sank six enemy destroyers, while the Swordfish itself dropped bombs to help in the destruction of a seventh, before going on to dive-bomb a German submarine (the *U-64*) on the surface in the fjord, sinking it with a direct hit.

This was perhaps a small beginning but, with Italy taking sides with Germany in the War on 10 June, the Swordfish's main operations moved to the Mediterranean with a vengeance. A minor bombing raid by nine aircraft of No 767 Training Squadron, temporarily detached to the south of France, against Genoa on 19 June, was followed by bombing attacks against targets in Sicily by Malta-based aircraft, and torpedo attacks by No 813 Squadron Swordfish on Italian ships at Bomba Bay on the Libyan coast on 5 July which sank a destroyer and a depot ship and damaged two supply ships.

The climax to the 1940 operations involved nineteen Swordfish of Nos 813, 815, 819 and 824 Squadrons flying in two waves from HMS *Illustrious* on 11 November against the Italian fleet in Taranto harbour. Led by Lt-Cdr K Williamson RN of No 815 Squadron and Lt-Cdr J W Hale RN of No 819, the Swordfish attacked in two waves, dropping flares and attacking an oil storage depot with bombs while eleven torpedo aircraft went for the ships. The new battleship *Littorio* and two older *Giulio Cesare* battleships were sunk in the attack that did much to restore the balance of sea power in the Mediterranean. The only casualty was Williamson's aircraft, shot down by flak, although the crew was taken prisoner.

The oldest-established Swordfish Squadron, No 825, in May 1941 commanded by Lt-Cdr Eugene Esmonde, was involved in the successful destruction of the German battleship *Bismarck*, at large in the Atlantic. In a dusk attack on the enemy warship on 24 May, nine aircraft, led by Esmonde from HMS *Victorious*, secured a torpedo hit, prompting the German captain to alter course, causing the shadowing ships to lose contact. She was located once more on

26 May, and that afternoon fifteen Swordfish of Nos 810 and 818 Squadrons, led by Lt-Cdr T P Coode of No 818, launched from HMS *Ark Royal* and, in a diving attack through cloud scored at least two torpedo hits, damaging the battleship's steering and causing her to execute a complete circle before heaving-to to attempt repairs. The following day the battleships HMS *King George V* and HMS *Rodney* closed and engaged *Bismarck* with their main armament before the heavy cruiser HMS *Dorsetshire* delivered the *coup de grace* with torpedoes.

Nine months later there occurred the most famous of all the Swordfish's epic actions, and certainly its most gallant failure. The escape from Brest on 12 February 1942 by the German warships,

Scharnhorst, Gneisenau and *Prinz Eugen*, and their subsequent dash eastwards up the Channel through the Dover Strait prompted concerted, if belated efforts to attack the ships before they reached the relative safety of their home ports in Germany. Among those efforts was an attack by six torpedo-carrying Swordfish of No 825 Squadron — still reforming after the loss of HMS *Ark Royal* in the Mediterranean on 13 November

A Swordfish II, V4689/G, undergoing trials at the Aeroplane and Armament Experimental Establishment, Boscombe Down, with ASV radar under the nose and a Leigh Light under the starboard wing. As far as is known, the latter equipment was not used by the Swordfish on operations. (Photo: The Bristol Aeroplane Co Ltd, Neg No 16293)

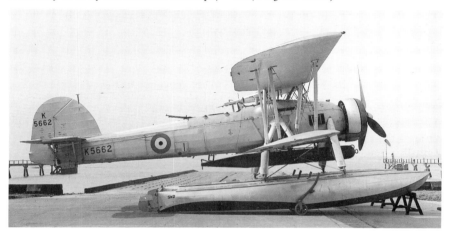

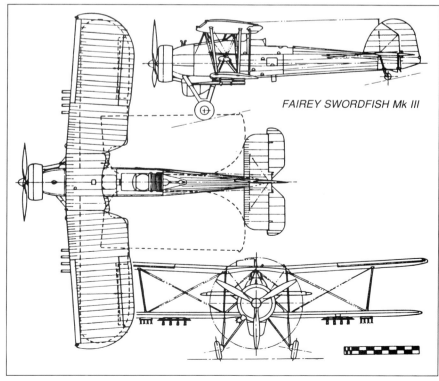

FAIREY SWORDFISH Mk III

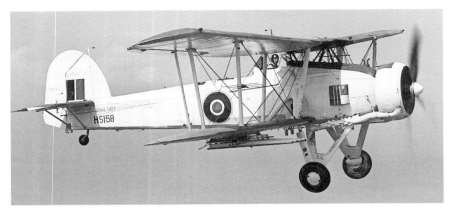

A fairly late production Swordfish II, HS158, fitted with torpedo crutches, underwing rocket rails and light bomb racks, as well as flame-damping exhaust manifolds. It was said of the Swordfish that it could be pulled round in a tight climbing turn at an indicated speed of 55 knots without danger of stalling. (Photo: Hawker Siddeley Aviation Ltd (Brough), Neg No E719)

1941. Flying from Manston, and having missed their rendezvous with escorting fighters, the biplanes, led by Lt-Cdr Esmonde once more, set course to the east to attack the German ships, now known to be heavily escorted by destroyers and E-boats and accompanied by a veritable umbrella of fighters. As they attacked from beneath a 700-foot cloudbase and with little over a mile visibility, the Swordfish succumbed one by one to the deadly barrage of flak and to the prowling Focke-Wulf fighters. All were shot down, and only five of the eighteen crew members were rescued from the sea. Esmonde himself died in Swordfish II W5984, being later awarded a posthumous Victoria Cross.

The Swordfish Mk II had been introduced into production by Blackburn in mid-1941, and it was to become the major variant. It differed from the earlier aircraft in featuring a strengthened lower wing with metal skinning on the undersurface, which enabled the aircraft to launch rocket projectiles; up to eight of these 60lb weapons could be carried by the Swordfish — which had pioneered their use during trials at the A & AEE at Boscombe Down in 1941. Later the Swordfish II came to be powered by the 750hp Pegasus 30 engines, as was the Swordfish III, of which Blackburn produced 320 examples.

By the time of the Channel Dash, the Battle of the Atlantic had moved into a new phase, with the introduction of escort carriers and merchant aircraft carriers (MACships). Owing to the loss of three fleet carriers in the early months of the War, the Royal Navy could no longer spare the use of such valuable ships to cover each of the many merchant convoys on the high seas at any given time, and had therefore introduced converted merchant ships, each

with a relatively small flight deck. Each ship could just manage to accommodate a flight of Swordfish, and sometimes perhaps one or two Sea Hurricane fighters. Usually equipped with air-to-surface radar (ASV) Mark X in a bulbous fairing in place of a torpedo, armed with rocket projectiles or depth bombs, and

occasionally fitted with rocket-assisted take-off gear to help the aircraft off the small flight decks, Swordfish accompanied the great majority of convoys sailing to and from Britain during the last four years of the War. In such a capacity, the aircraft constituted one of the vital weapons in the Royal Navy's arsenal to counter the German submarine — the one realistic means at Hitler's disposal that could so easily have brought Britain to her knees in the critical mid-War years.

Type: Single-engine, three-crew, two-bay biplane torpedo-bomber-reconnaissance land- or seaplane.

Air Ministry Specification: S.15/33

Manufacturers: The Fairey Aviation Co Ltd, Hayes, Middlesex; Blackburn Aircraft Ltd, Sherburn-in-Elmet, Yorkshire.

Powerplant: TSR.II, Swordfish Mk I and some Mk IIs. One 690hp Bristol Pegasus IIIM3 9-cylinder air-cooled radial engine usually driving 3-blade Fairey Reed metal propeller. Remainder of Mk IIs and Mk III. 750hp Pegasus 30.

Structure: Steel tubular fuselage structure, mainly fabric-covered; twin steel-strip built-up wing spars with steel drag struts and duralumin ribs. Folding wings.

Dimensions: Swordfish III landplane. Span, 45ft 6in (folded, 17ft 3in); length, 35ft 8in; height, 12ft 4in; wing area, 607 sq ft.

Weights: Swordfish III torpedo bomber. Tare, 4,110lb; all-up, 7,580lb.

Performance: Swordfish III torpedo bomber. Max speed, 139 mph at 4,750ft; climb to 5,000ft, 10 min; normal range with torpedo, 550 miles.

Armament: One synchronized 0.303in Vickers Mk V machine gun on starboard side of nose and one Vickers or Lewis gun with Fairey mounting in rear cockpit. One 1,610lb 18in torpedo, one 1,500lb sea mine or 1,500lb of bombs or depth charges, or up to eight 60lb rocket projectiles on underwing rails.

Prototype: One TSR.II, K4190, first flown by C S Staniland on 17 April 1934; first pre-production Swordfish, K5660, flown on 31 December 1935.

Production: Fairey built a total of 692 Swordfish Mk Is: K5660-K5662 (3), K5926-K6011 (86), K8346-K8449 (104), K8860-K8886 (27), L2717-L2866 (150), between L7632 and L7701 (62), between L9714 and L9785 (60) and between P3991 and P4279 (200). Blackburn built 300 Mk Is: between V4411 and V4719; 1,080 Mk IIs: between W5836 and W5995 (100), between DK670 and DK792 (100), between HS154 and HS678 (400), between LS151 and LS461 (250), and between NE858 and NF250 (230); and 320 Mk IIIs: between NF251 and NF414 (120), and between NR857 and NS 171 (200). Total built, 2,392.

Summary of Service: Swordfish served with the following operational Squadrons of the Fleet Air Arm: Nos 810, 811, 812, 813, 814, 815, 816, 818, 819, 820, 821, 822, 823, 824, 825, 826, 828, 829, 830, 833, 834, 835, 836, 837, 838, 840, 841, 842, 860 and 886; and with the following second-line Squadrons: Nos 700, 700W, 701, 702, 703, 705, 707, 710, 722, 726, 727, 728, 730, 731, 733, 735, 737, 739, 740, 741, 742, 743, 744, 745, 747, 753, 756, 759, 763, 764, 765, 766, 767, 768, 769, 770, 771, 772, 773, 774, 775, 776, 777, 778, 779, 780, 781, 782, 783, 785, 786, 787, 787Y, 787Z, 788, 789, 791, 794, 796 and 797. They served at sea aboard the fleet carriers HMS *Argus, Ark Royal, Courageous, Eagle, Furious, Glorious, Hermes, Illustrious, Indefatigable* and *Victorious,* and aboard the MACships and escort carriers HMS *Activity, Archer, Attacker, Avenger, Battler, Biter, Campania, Chaser, Dasher, Fencer, Hunter, Nairana, Rapana, Stalker, Striker, Tracker* and *Vindex.* They also served with No 119 Squadron, RAF, in Belgium in 1945, and No 202 Squadron, RAF, at Gibraltar between September 1940 and June 1941.

Fairey Battle

If the Fairey Swordfish gave long and honourable service, the operational life-span of the company's Battle light bomber was mercifully short. That is not to say that, by the standards existing at the time of its design and prototype order, it did not appear to be a thoroughly efficient aeroplane with a performance much in line with that of its contemporaries in other air forces. Yet, by the time it reached squadron service in 1937, fighters with a speed advantage of around 100 mph were already entering production. The fault in the Battle's concept lay in a lack of understanding of modern air tactics over the battlefield, especially when it emerged (a year before the Battle prototype flew) that the whole concept of the newly emerging *Luftwaffe* was the close support of the *Wehrmacht* in the field. With fighters like the Messerschmitt Bf 109 showing their paces during the Spanish Civil War, the Battle was already dangerously out of date two years before it was called on to support the British Army attempting to withstand the storm of *Blitzkrieg* in France.

Air Ministry Specification P.27/32, initially issued in August 1932, but not finalised until the following April, was unequivocal in its demands for an aircraft, required to be in service by 1936 to replace the Hart, to be able to carry a bomb load of not less than 1,000 pounds over a range of 1,000 miles at a speed of not less than 200 miles per hour. None of these requirements was radical yet, taken in combination, they were daunting. The speed target was, after all, roughly the same as the maximum attainable by the RAF's best in-service fighter, the Hawker Fury.

The Specification attracted designs from Armstrong Whitworth, Bristol, Fairey, Gloster, Hawker and Westland, but only those of Armstrong Whitworth and Fairey were deemed sufficiently realistic to attract prototype orders. At Fairey, Marcel Lobelle had been unable

The Fairey Battle prototype, K4303, in 1936 with the Merlin G engine, Fairey Reed fixed-pitch propeller and the original canopy design. (Photo: The Fairey Aviation Co Ltd)

to tender more than an overall scheme in 1933 as Rolls-Royce did not finalise the geometric data for installation of their new P.V.12 engine (the prototype Merlin) until the spring of 1934; nevertheless, the engine manufacturers were confident in their power and weight figures, enabling Lobelle to embark on the strength calculations of his airframe structure, which would be unrelated to any previous Fairey design. The cantilever wing, constructed in five sections, accommodated not only the undercarriage retraction cells but also the bomb traps, each wing containing bays for two 250lb GP bombs; the wing centresection was built integrally with the fuselage which, aft of the pilot's cockpit, was of semi-monocoque construction.

The pilot's cockpit was situated well forward and in line with the wing leading edge, while the wireless/air gunner occupied a cockpit some ten feet further aft, the intervening space being enclosed by a long transparent canopy; the bomb aimer/observer occupied a station in the centre fuselage, his prone aiming position being situated below and behind the pilot. This design was shown to the DTD in May and, on 11 June, a contract was awarded to Fairey

for a prototype.

An early Merlin C flight engine was delivered to Fairey in November 1935 for ground running and system functioning tests, but by the time Staniland first flew the Fairey P.27/32 prototype, K4303, on 10 March 1936 it is believed that a 970hp Merlin G had been delivered. This was the engine with which the aeroplane, now named the Battle, visited Martlesham Heath in July, where it was generally well-liked and returned a maximum speed of 258 mph; the normal range was calculated as 980 miles. The aircraft was dived to 308 mph and was reported to be pleasant to handle, although the rudder was considered heavy at low speeds. The wing of the prototype possessed no dihedral, but production wings were given four degrees. The bomb stowage was not popular as there was no means of visually checking that bombs, once loaded, were secure.

There can be little doubt but that the Air Staff had been impressed with the Battle at an early stage of the prototype's construction and a production Specification had been issued long before its first flight. An order for 155 aircraft was signed in September 1935 — thereby

No 63 (Bomber) Squadron was the first to be equipped with the Battle light bomber; the aircraft shown here, K7650, was one of the aircraft of the first production batch still powered by the troublesome Merlin I; compare the canopy design with that of the prototype shown above. K7650 was relegated to become a ground instruction airframe as early as April 1940. (Photo: Real Photographs Co.)

ensuring that 200 Merlin engines would be made available ahead of engines for the Hawker Hurricane and Supermarine Spitfire fighters.

Unfortunately, because the rocker-box design of the early Merlins proved to be unsuitable for the Hurricane and Spitfire, Rolls-Royce's preoccupation with engines for the Fairey Battle delayed the introduction of the improved Merlin II, and caused Hurricane production to be set back by almost six months.

The first production Battles were delivered to No 63 (Bomber) Squadron at Upwood in May 1937. Apart from the first aircraft, K7558 (which, having also been built at Hayes, took over the work as prototype in May), the remaining Battles of the firsxt batch were to be produced at Fairey's Heaton Chapel factory at Stockport. In August, No 105 (Bomber) Squadron at Harwell became the second to be equipped with the new light bomber, and by the end of the year five Squadrons had converted.

The Merlin Is in the early Battles of the first production batch gave considerable trouble in service and, after 136 aircraft had been built, engine production at Derby switched to the Merlin II — a step that further aggravated production of the Hurricane, completion of whose airframes soon outpaced the supply of Merlins and led to some aggressive correspondence between the DTD, Hawker, Fairey and Rolls-Royce. By March 1938, however, following intervention by Air Chief Marshal Sir Hugh Dowding, with Hurricane production gaining pace and the second production batch of Battles about to start delivery, the production rate of Merlin IIs had reached about 50 engines per month, and within three months would more than double.

By the outbreak of war in September 1939, fifteen Regular bomber squadrons at home bases were flying Battles in the light bomber rôle. The British War Plan involved the despatch of fighters and light bombers to France in support of the British Expeditionary Force and, on the day before war was declared, the Battles of Nos 12, 15, 40, 88, 103, 142, 150, 218 and 226 Squadrons left their stations in England and flew to France to provide the light bombing element of the Advanced Air Striking Force (No 105 Squadron following on 3 September).

With relatively little activity on the front facing Germany, the Battle squad-rons were seldom involved in combat and, whenever the weather permitted, training continued with local exercises as well as occasional reconnaissance sorties over the forward areas. At the end of the year, Nos 15 and 40 Squadrons con-

Type: Single-engine, three-crew, low-wing monoplane light bomber.
Air Ministry Specifications: P.27/32, P.25/35 and P.32/36
Manufacturers: The Fairey Aviation Co Ltd, Stockport, Lancashire; Austin Motor Co Ltd, Longbridge, Birmingham.
Powerplant: One 1,030hp Rolls-Royce Merlin I 12-cylinder liquid-cooled in-line supercharged engine driving three-blade de Havilland 2-pitch propeller; also Merlin II, III and V.
Structure: Front fuselage of metal sheet-covered built-up steel tubular frame; fuselage aft of semi-monocoque construction over metal hoop frames and Z-section stringers. Two-spar wings with girder spars inboard and flanged beams outboard.
Dimensions: Span, 54ft 0in; length, 42ft 4in; height, 15ft 6in; wing area, 433 sq ft.
Weights: Tare, 6,647lb; all-up, 10,792lb.
Performance: Max speed, 257 mph at 15,000ft; 210 mph at sea level; climb to 10,000ft, 8 min 24 sec; service ceiling, 23,500ft; range at 200 mph, 1,000 miles.
Armament: One free-firing 0.303in Browning machine gun in starboard wing and one Vickers K gas-operated machine gun with Fairey mounting in rear cockpit. Normal bomb load of four 250lb GP bombs carried in wing cells; provision occasionally made to carry two additional 250lb bombs on external racks.
Prototype: One, K4303, first flown by C S Staniland on 10 March 1936.
Production: A total of 2,200 Battles was built, excluding prototype. Fairey, 1,171: K7558-K7112 (155; last 19 with Merlin II), K9176-K9220 (45), K9221-K9486 (266), between N2020 and N2258 (189, including 29 to Turkey), between P2155 and P2369 (150), between P5288 and P5294 (50), between P6480 and P6769 (200, including 100 trainers), and between R7356 and R7480 (100); 16 additional Fairey-built aircraft were supplied to Belgium. Austin, 1,029: L4935-L5797 (863; the last 804 with Merlin III), between R3922 and R4054 (100) and between V1201 and V1280 (66, all target tugs). A total of 739 Battles from the above RAF aircraft was shipped to Canada, and 364 to Australia.
Summary of Service: Battles were delivered to the following bomber Squadrons before the outbreak of war in 1939: Nos 12, 15, 35, 40, 52, 63, 88, 98, 103, 105, 106, 142, 150, 185, 207, 218 and 226; of these, Nos 12, 15, 40, 88, 98, 103, 105, 142, 150, 218 and 226 were deployed to France with the AASF during 1939-40. Battles also served with the following Polish light bomber squadrons with the RAF during 1940: Nos 300, 301, 304 and 305. They served in the shipping protection rôle with No 234 Squadron, and as fighter and light bomber trainers with the following Squadrons between September 1939 and November 1940: Nos 141, 235, 242, 245, 253, 266, and 616 Squadrons.

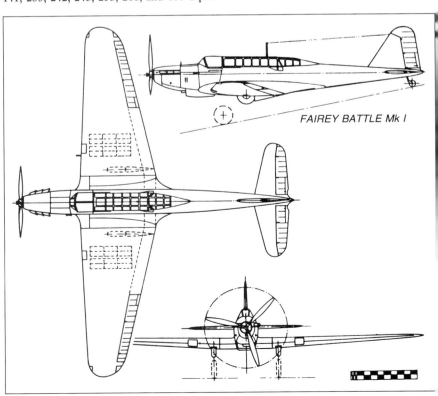

FAIREY BATTLE Mk I

verted to Blenheim IVs, but on 16 April 1940 another Battle Squadron, No 98, left Finningley for France.

When the great attack burst against France and the Low Countries on 10 May, the BEF was ordered forward into Belgium in an attempt to stem the German advance, the defence lines being bounded by a succession of rivers and canals. In the confusion that followed, several of the key bridges were left intact and captured, allowing the German armour to cut the defences in a number of places, and these bridges were among the vital targets which the Battle squadrons were ordered to bomb.

From the outset, the *Luftwaffe* enjoyed air superiority so that, with RAF fighters being called on to meet numerous enemy air attacks, not least those on their own bases, there were many occasions when the Battles went out on raids without fighter escort; not surprisingly, casualties among the light bombers increased rapidly.

The attack on the Meuse bridge at Maastricht on 12 May by five Battles of No 12 Squadron has become legendary.

Led by Fg Off Donald Edward Garland, with Sergeant Thomas Gray as his observer, the five crews — all volunteers — set out from Amifontaine with orders to destroy the bridge at any cost. In the face of intense flak, already deployed by the advancing enemy, the five Battles attacked and achieved at least one direct hit, emerging from the inferno severely damaged but intact; at that moment a formation of Bf 109s (which had been held at bay by a flight of Hurricanes) caught the Battles as they turned for home, shooting down four, including the aircraft of Fg Off Garland. The surviving bomber landed at Amifontaine with a dead gunner.

Important though this bridge was, its damage scarcely checked the German advance, yet the desperate efforts made by No 12 Squadron were characteristic of the actions of the Battle squadrons during the Battle of France. Both Garland and Gray were awarded posthumous Victoria Crosses — the first to be won by the Royal Air Force during the Second World War.

As the Battle of France approached

its inevitable conclusion, the remains of the nine Battle squadrons were withdrawn to Britain to re-equip and train new crews. Yet it was already plain to see that, no matter how skilled and courageous its crews might be, the Battle had no place in skies dominated by the German air force. Nor, apart from the Blenheim, was any other light bomber available to take its place. Indeed, the day of the lightly-armed single-engine day bomber, with a performance inferior to that of defending fighters, was at an end. Not too long afterwards the fighter-bomber would be introduced as Hurricanes and Spitfires — carrying only half the bomb load of the Battle, but well able to defend themselves — assumed the rôle of tactical support aircraft.

As the Battles were quickly withdrawn from squadron service, they were relegated to all manner of second-line duties, in pilot training and target-towing rôles. Ironically, the last first-line Squadron to discard its Battles was No 98 (in July 1941), the Squadron that had arrived in France less than a month before the great German attack.

Armstrong Whitworth A.W.29 (P.27/32)

John Lloyd's tender to Specification P.27/32 was the second design accepted by the Air Ministry for prototype purchase, being allotted the serial K4299. Bearing in mind that it was to be powered by the still-unreliable Armstrong Siddeley Tiger radial, one may surmise that it was selected from a number of nondescript tenders in order to provide competition for the Fairey tender, or even as insurance against the Rolls-Royce P.V.12 (selected by Lobelle) encountering delays in reaching production.

The A.W.29 was similar in general configuration to the Fairey aircraft, employing a semi-monocoque rear fuselage and a fabricated metal wing, though Lloyd chose to use a scaled-down version of the large box-spar that had featured in the twin-engine A.W.23 bomber transport. Like Lobelle's design, the undercarriage retracted rearwards into the wing, leaving the wheels partly exposed when retracted, and the

The Armstrong Whitworth A.W.29, K4299, photographed during its relatively short flying life, showing the cockpit and dorsal turret arrangement; entry to the cabin was by the hatch immediately forward of the turret. (Photo: Hawker Siddeley Aviation Ltd, Neg No M.90)

four 250lb bombs would be stowed in wing cells outboard of the undercarriage.

However, although the all-up weight was considerably less than that of the Fairey design, the lower power and greater drag of the Tiger installation — not to mention the drag of the exceptionally thick wing — resulted in a performance far below that demanded in the Specification.

Preoccupation with the Whitley heavy bomber's development, and preparation

for its production, delayed completion of the A.W.29, and it was not until 6 December 1936 that K4299 was flown by Charles Keir Turner Hughes (who had just been appointed chief test pilot after Alan Campbell Orde's retirement). By then the Fairey Battle prototype had been flying for nine months, and the first production aircraft were nearing completion.

Shortly afterwards, K4299 suffered a wheels-up forced landing following failure of the Tiger engine, and the aircraft was not delivered to Martlesham Heath for official trials. It was not repaired, and was ultimately scrapped in August 1940.

Type: Single-engine, two-seat, mid-wing monoplane light bomber.

Air Ministry Specification: P.27/32

Manufacturer: Sir W G Armstrong Whitworth Aircraft Ltd, Coventry.

Powerplant: One 920hp Armstrong Siddeley Tiger VIII 14-cylinder, air-cooled radial engine driving 3-blade 2-position Hamilton Standard propeller.

Structure: Metal monocoque fuselage aft of cockpit; alloy sheet-covered front fuselage of steel tubular construction. Wing built on large alloy-webbed box-spar with nose riblets light-alloy covered.

Dimensions: Span, 49ft 0in; length, 43ft 10in; height, 13ft 3in; wing area, 458 sq ft.

Weight: All-up, 9,000lb

Performance: Max speed, 225 mph at 15,000ft, 187 mph at sea level; climb to 10,000ft, 11 min; service ceiling, 21,000ft; range (estimated), 685 miles.

Armament: One synchronized, forward-firing 0.303in Vickers machine gun and one Lewis gun in dorsal manually-operated

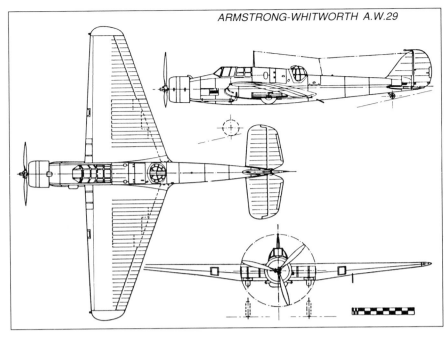

ARMSTRONG-WHITWORTH A.W.29

Armstrong Whitworth turret. Provision for bomb load of four 250lb GP bombs carried internally in wing cells.

Prototype: One, K4299, first flown by C K Turner Hughes on 6 December 1936. No production.

Armstrong Whitworth A.W.38 Whitley

The A.W.38 Whitley prototype, K4586, was John Lloyd's first military aeroplane employing stressed-skin construction. (Photo: P H T Green Collection)

It would be difficult to overestimate the importance of John Lloyd's Whitley in the history of the British heavy bomber. It was, after all, the first truly modern heavy bomber to enter squadron service with the newly-constituted Bomber Command in 1937, and was the first to embark on widespread night operations over Germany during the Second World War, being capable of carrying a much greater bomb load than its contemporary, the Vickers Wellington. Its relatively low operating speed was not regarded as a significant handicap in the early months of the War, owing to the absence of a dedicated night fighter defence over Germany but, with the growing British bomber offensive late in

1941, and the increasing number of four-engine bombers reaching the squadrons, the Whitley was honourably retired, while the Wellington — capable of carrying the important 4,000lb bomb, which the Whitley could not, owing to the small cross-section of its main bomb bay — remained in service for several further years.

Confident that his A.W.23 design re-

presented the best possible approach to the bomber transport formula, Lloyd went ahead with a related design of a heavy bomber (in which troop-carrying was relegated to a minor, alternative rôle) more than a year before the A.W.23's maiden flight. The A.W.38 was tendered to Air Ministry Specification B.3/34, which had been drafted around Lloyd's proposals, and two prototypes were ordered — despite the manufacturer's persistence in selecting the much-maligned Tiger radials.

The Whitley prototype, K4586, during grass airfield suitability trials in 1937 at the RAE, fitted with a massive, fixed jury undercarriage; the cross-girder could be loaded with steel plates to increase the aircraft's weight (Photo: RAE, Neg No 2316 dated 22 December 1937)

This Whitley I, K7208, completed without nose and tail gun turrets, was set aside for flight testing of the Merlin IV installation scheduled for the Whitley IV. (Photo: Sir W G Armstrong Whitworth Aircraft Ltd).

The A.W.38 featured the large single-box wingspar of the A.W.23 (as well as the impressive A.W.27 Ensign airliner) but, reflecting the stated urgency of adopting new aircraft capable of rapid production, introduced a monocoque fuselage of severely austere appearance, being of almost parallel straight outline in plan and elevation, to avoid the complexity of double-curvature skin panels. Owing to Lloyd's comparative lack of knowledge of the effect of flaps on the handling characteristics of a large, heavy monoplane, he arranged the wing-to-fuselage junction with considerable wing incidence, this feature imparting to the bomber a characteristic nose-down flying attitude when in level flight at speed. The sturdy undercarriage retracted forward and upwards into the engine nacelles, leaving the wheels partly exposed with the object of cushioning the aircraft and reducing damage in a wheels-up landing. The five-man crew comprised pilot, navigator, nose gunner/bomb aimer, observer/wireless operator and rear gunner, the latter manning a manually-operated Armstrong Whitworth tail turret mounting four Browning machine guns.

The first prototype A.W.38, K4586, was flown by Alan Colin Campbell Orde on 17 March 1936, and attended the Hendon Display on 27 June. Such was the urgent need to replace the biplane heavy bombers, still soldiering on in the RAF, that the new monoplane had already been ordered into production — on the assurance by Armstrong Siddeley that the Tiger engine had achieved a much improved level of reliability. K4586, powered by 795hp Tiger IX engines, was followed by the second prototype, K4587, which flew on 24 February 1937 with the more powerful Tiger VIIIs. Both aircraft, and the 34 aircraft of the first production batch (now named the Whitley Mark I) flew without wing dihedral but, following

some criticism at the A & AEE, this was introduced retrospectively and for the remainder of the Whitley's production.

Twelve of the first Whitley Is were delivered to No 10 (Bomber) Squadron, commanded by Sqn Ldr James Clement Foden AFC (later Gp Capt, CBE, AFC) at Dishforth in March 1937, and this unit was followed in July by No 78 (Bomber) Squadron, under Wg Cdr Matthew Brown Frew DSO, MC, AFC (later Air Vice-Marshal Sir Matthew, CB, DSO*, MC*, AFC), also at Dishforth; the third of the Squadrons equipped with Whitley Is was No 58 at Boscombe Down in October, commanded by Sqn Ldr (later Gp Capt) John Potter. On all three Squadrons the Whitleys replaced Heyford biplanes.

The original order for Whitleys, signed in 1935, had been for 160 aircraft but, after manufacture of the first 34 had started, the Whitley Mark II had been introduced with Tiger VIII engines, the first version that could be regarded as passably reliable; 46 Mark IIs were built, and the remaining 80 aircraft, Mark IIIs which retained the Tiger VIIIs, were distinguishable principally with regard to improvements in armament. The Armstrong Whitworth nose turret was replaced by a power-operated Nash and Thompson type, and the tail turret was supplemented by a retractable midships ventral 'dustbin' mounting a pair of Browning machine guns. Supplies of turrets for the early Whitleys failed to keep pace with aircraft manufacture, and, for many months the squadrons possessed a fairly significant proportion

of aircraft with no defensive guns at all, and the nose and tail turret positions faired over. The other improvements introduced in the Mark III involved the internal rearrangement of the fuselage bomb bay and the wing bomb cells, which allowed for stowage of four 1,000-pounders.

By the outbreak of war, almost all the Whitley Is and IIs had been withdrawn from operational status on the heavy bomber squadrons, of which seven were then equipped with either Mk IIIs or IVs. Nos 51, 58, 97 and 102 Squadrons were still flying the Tiger-powered Mark IIIs, No 10 was flying the Mark IV, and Mark Vs were just starting to arrive on Nos 77 and 78 Squadrons. The two latter versions introduced the Rolls-Royce Merlin, the Whitley IV powered by 1,030hp Merlin IVs and the Whitley V by 1,145hp Merlin Xs. (In fact the more powerful Merlin became available before production of the Mark IV ran out, and the last seven aircraft of the batch — with Merlin Xs — were termed Whitley IVAs.

A total of 1,445 Whitley Vs was built, becoming the definitive version and eventually equipping fifteen squadrons, although by no means all of these were engaged in bombing operations. The Whitley's war began somewhat prosaically, as it was the Chamberlain Government's policy to resist the temptation to bomb German territory for fear of prompting reprisal attacks on British towns and cities. Instead, Bomber Command was instructed to shower the enemy's cities with leaflets whose sub-

A Whitley II, K7244/ LT-G of No 7 (Bomber) Squadron, at Finningley shortly before the War. Note the curved leading edge of the fins, a feature that characterised the early Whitleys. This aircraft crashed in February 1941 while serving with No 9 Bombing and Gunnery School. (Photo: via RAF Finningley)

An Whitley IV N1532, probably on a routine production flight with its manufacturers before delivery to the RAF. Note the straight fin leading edges. (Photo: Real Photographs Co, Neg No 1041)

ject matter was intended to express the folly of Hitler's aggression against Poland. This task accordingly fell almost exclusively to the Whitleys of No 4 Group, Bomber Command, and continued well into 1940. Losses through enemy action were fairly light, and the sole benefit to the crews involved was to provide useful training in long-range night navigation. Many of these leaflet 'raids' were carried out over very long distances, Whitleys of No 77 Squadron on occasion flying as far as Warsaw. On one such night sortie, a Whitley pilot[1], becoming lost on the return journey but believing he was safely over France, landed the big bomber, N1387, to establish his whereabouts. Disillusioned when his crew spotted German troops approaching on bicycles, the pilot quickly regained his cockpit and managed to take off, under rifle fire, and eventually landed at a French airfield.

After the resignation of Neville Chamberlain and his replacement by Winston Churchill as prime minister (coinciding, on 10 May 1940, with the start of the German invasion of the Low Countries) the leaflets were replaced by bombs, although Bomber Command was still

[1]   Flt Lt Brian Stirling Tomlin RAF.

restricted to attacks against targets close behind the German frontier in the West. The first bombs were dropped on the German mainland when, on the night of 10/11 May, Whitley Vs of Nos 77 and 102 Squadrons, flying from Driffield, attacked rail communications in Germany close to the border with Holland, a round flight of some 750 miles. A more enterprising attack was undertaken on the night of 11/12 June — only 24 hours after Italy had entered the War — when 36 Whitleys from Nos 10, 51, 58, 77 and 102 Squadrons (all of No 4 Group), set out on the long flight to attack Genoa and Turin. Refuelling in the Channel Islands, the aircraft began the long 1,400-mile haul to cross the Alps, but bad weather and engine failures through icing prevented all but thirteen of the raiders from reaching and bombing their targets.

Of greater political significance was the raid, mounted on 25/26 August, at the height of the Battle of Britain, by 14 Whitleys of Nos 51 and 78 Squadrons, flying from Dishforth, which joined Wellingtons and Hampdens in the RAF's first bombing attack on Berlin. Bombing was, however, scattered, and it has been estimated that less than 15 per cent of the bombs dropped (none heavier than

1,000lb) fell within the boundaries of the German capital.

It is believed that the longest bombing raid flown by Whitleys was that against the Skoda works at Plzen in Czechoslovakia on 27/28 October 1940, a raid fraught with danger as much of the 1,480-mile flight had to be made over Germany in daylight.

The best-known Whitley pilot was undoubtedly Leonard Cheshire who, as a Flight Lieutenant on No 102 Squadron and pilot of Whitley P5005/N during a raid against Cologne on 12/13 November 1940, received a direct hit from flak which ignited a flare and severely damaged the monocoque of the rear fuselage. Nevertheless, he continued on to bomb the target before bringing the badly crippled Whitley home to base. The immediate award of the DSO was but the first of a series of gallantry awards that would culminate in the Victoria Cross. Other Whitley pilots whose names would later become famous in the great bomber offensive ahead were Donald Bennett, later to command the Pathfinder Force, and James Brian Tait, who would be awarded no fewer than four DSOs, and would command No 617 Squadron.

Whitleys continued to accompany Bomber Command raids throughout 1941 but, as the delivery of the four-engine Stirlings, Halifaxes and Lancasters steadily increased, so the Whitley squadrons received new aircraft. Their last bombing operation was against the port of Ostend on the night of 29-30 April 1942 (although a number of

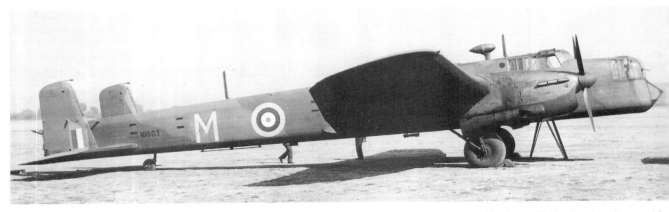

A full-standard Whitley V bomber, N1503/M, serving with No 19 Operational Training Unit, probably during 1940; the aircraft was withdrawn from flying duties in April the following year to become a ground instruction machine. (Photo: via Derek James)

Whitley VII Z9138/ WL-R of No 612 (County of Aberdeen) Squadron, serving in the anti-submarine rôle; the wartime censor has obliterated the dorsal ASV masts and underwing arrays. It was said that the Whitley was the only aircraft to adopt a nose-down attitude for take-off! (Photo: Air Ministry, Neg No C5250)

Whitleys from Operational Training Units took part in the first of the '1,000-bomber' raids, that against Cologne on the night of 30/31 May that year).

Indeed, the long range of the Whitley recommended its use by Coastal Command in the anti-submarine/coastal reconnaissance rôle, a task that had been carried out by Nos 502 and 612 Squadrons with that Command since October 1940. No 502 in particular was notable in pioneering the use of ASV radar, and achieved the distinction of being the first to locate and destroy a German submarine using this equipment, sinking *U-206* in the Bay of Biscay on 30 November 1941.

Early maritime reconnaissance work was carried out using makeshift Whitley Vs, but a specialist version, the Mark VII, was introduced into the production line owing to demand. This version retained the Merlin Xs of the Whitley V but carried a fuel load increased to 1,100 gallons with additional tanks in the forward bomb bay and in the rear fuselage. Central to the Whitley VII's

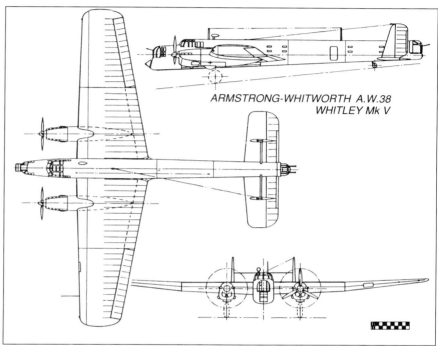

ARMSTRONG-WHITWORTH A.W.38
WHITLEY Mk V

Type: Twin-engine, five-crew, mid-wing monoplane night heavy bomber.

Air Ministry Specifications: B.3/34 and B.21/35.

Manufacturer: Sir W G Armstrong Whitworth Aircraft Ltd, Baginton, Coventry.

Powerplant: 1st prototype and Mk I. Two 795hp Armstrong Siddeley Tiger IX 14-cylinder air-cooled radial engines driving 3-blade 2-position DH propellers. 2nd prototype, Mks II and III. 845hp Tiger VIII. Mk IV. Two 1,030hp Rolls-Royce Merlin IV 12-cylinder liquid-cooled two-stage supercharged in-line engines. Mk V. 1,145hp Merlin X. Experimental: 1,500hp Armstrong Siddeley Deerhound 21-cylinder, 3-row air-cooled radial engine.

Structure: Wing built on light-alloy box-spar with steel flanges, light alloy-covered; fabric-covered aft of spar. Fuselage of light-alloy sheet stressed skin. Undercarriage retracted forward into engine nacelles.

Dimensions: Span, 84ft 0in; length, 69ft 3in (Mk V, 70ft 6in); height, 15ft 0in; wing area, 1,137 sq ft.

Weights: Mks II and III. Tare, 15,475lb; all-up, 22,990lb. Mk V. Tare, 19,350lb; all-up, 33,500lb.

Performance: Mks II and III. Max speed, 209 mph at 16,400ft; climb to 15,000ft, 23 min 30 sec; service ceiling, 23,000ft; normal range, 1,315 miles. Mk V. Max speed, 230 mph at 16,400ft; climb to 15,000ft, 16 min; service ceiling, 26,000ft; range, 1,500 miles.

Armament: Mk V. One 0.303in Browning machine gun in nose Nash and Thompson power-operated turret, and four Browning guns in tail Nash and Thompson turret. Max bomb load of 7,000lb (typically four 1,000lb bombs in fuselage and three 500lb bombs in inboard wing cells on each side).

Prototypes: Two, K4586, first flown by A Campbell Orde on 17 March 1936, and K4857, first flown by C Turner Hughes on 24 February 1937.

Production: Excluding the above prototypes, a total of 1,811 Whitleys was built: Mk I, 34 (K7183-K7216); Mk II, 46 (K7217-K7262); Mk III, 80 (K8936-K9015); Mk IV, 33 (K9016-K9048); Mk IV, 7 (K9049-K9055); Mk V, 1,445 (147 between N1345 and N1528; 164 between P4930 and P5115; 150 between T1430 and T4339; 486 between Z6461 and Z9516; 50, AD665-AD714; 229 between BD189 and BD693; 79 between EB282 and EB410; and 140 between LA763 and LA951); Mk VII, 166 (64 in the above Z-serial batch, 71 in BD-serial batch, 21 in EB-serial batch, and 10 in LA-serial batch).

Summary of Service: Whitleys served with the following heavy bomber Squadrons: No 7 (Mks II & III, from March 1938 to May 1939), No 10 (Mks I, IV & V, from March 1937 to December 1941), No 51 (Mks II, III, IV & V, from February 1938 to December 1942), No 58 (Mks I, II, III, V & VII, from October 1937 to December 1942), No 77 (Mks III & V, from November 1938 to May 1942, then to maritime reconnaissance); No 78 (Mks I, IV & V from July 1937 to March 1942), No 97 (Mk II & III, from February 1939 to April 1940), and No 102 (Mks III & V, from October 1939 to February 1942). They also served with other first-line Squadrons: Nos 53, 502 and 612 (maritime reconnaissance), No 109 (wireless intelligence), Nos 138 and 161 (Special Duties), No 166 (bomber operational training) and Nos 295, 296, 297 and 298 (airborne forces and glider training). Whitleys flew with numerous other units including Nos 7 and 9 BGS, Nos 7 and 8 AGS, Nos 8 and 10 AOS, Nos 10,19, 24 and 81 OTUs, BATS, CFS, EFCS, PTS, SDU, CLS, HGCU and BOAC.

rôle was the inclusion of ASV Mark II long-range radar, identified by masts along the top of the fuselage and aerial arrays beneath the outer wing leading edges. A sixth crew member was carried as radar operator. The usual weapon load of the Whitley VII was six depth charges.

Another important job undertaken by redundant Whitley bombers were those associated with the new British airborne forces, many aircraft being equipped to tow the General Aircraft Horsa troop-carrying glider. Apart from their use by many glider and airborne forces training units, Whitleys took part in the two pio-

neering operations by the airborne forces, the first, Operation Colossus, involving Whitley Vs of Nos 51 and 78 Squadrons flying from Malta with paratroops to attack the viaduct at Tragino in southern Italy. Although this attack failed in its purpose, the second, flown by Whitleys of No 51 Squadron, was a resounding success. On 27/28 February 1942 these aircraft dropped parachute troops on the German radar installation at Bruneval on the Channel coast, an accompanying technician being under orders to obtain details of the German equipment. After this task had been successfully completed, the soldiers destroyed the instal-

lation and were withdrawn by sea.

Space only permits mention of two others of the multifarious duties undertaken by Whitleys, the wireless intelligence gathering by the aircraft of No 109 Squadron, which accompanied bombing raids to discover the frequencies in use by the German communications network and defence system; and the often perilous work performed with the two Special Duties Squadrons, Nos 138 and 166, dropping agents into enemy-occupied Europe, and maintaining contact with, and dropping supplies to the various resistance groups operating in German occupied countries.

Vickers Types 271/638 Wellington

The Vickers B.9/32, K4049, with its New Type No 7 for the 1936 Hendon Display; the aircraft bore little resemblance to the Wellington and, in order to save design time, the fin profile was 'borrowed' from the Supermarine Stranraer flying boat. (Photo: *The Aeroplane* Neg No 6717)

At the time that Specification B.9/32 was being drafted at the Air Ministry early in 1932, the Geneva Conference on Disarmament, to which Britain was party, was seeking to impose a tare-weight limit of 6,500 pounds on all bombers, an imposition that would eliminate the 'heavy' bomber altogether, and prevent the RAF from acquiring any aeroplane capable of reaching beyond the North Sea or Channel with a bomb load. As world events were already showing unmistakable signs of pre-empting any such restriction, and as the Disarmament Conference itself disintegrated, the bomber Specification was revised repeatedly to permit progressively increased tare weights, while both Rex Pierson at Vickers and Gustav Lachmann at Handley Page tendered designs for twin-engine bombers, the Type 271 and H.P.52 respectively.

As originally proposed, the Vickers aircraft possessed a tare weight of 6,300lb but, as Pierson and Lachmann sought, successfully, to have the Air Ministry's

age-old cost-limiting insistence on a relationship between engine power and tare weight abolished, so the weight restriction was also effectively omitted altogether.

However, with the successful development of Wallis' geodetic structure, it appeared possible to improve greatly the performance and load-carrying potential of the Type 271 within a lightweight airframe, and still employ two of the most powerful engines then available. Moreover, structural tests of the Wellesley's airframe disclosed its extraordinary strength factor of 11, compared with the traditionally mandatory figure of 6. Faced with these figures, the Air

Ministry placed an order for a single prototype of the Type 271, as Pierson continued working on a more refined development, optimised for production.

The prototype B.9/32, K4049, was first flown by 'Mutt' Summers on 15 June 1936, and was displayed at Hendon at the end of that month with the name Crecy, this being changed to Wellington three months later. In its original guise the Type 271, with a tare weight of 11,508lb, was powered by two 915hp Bristol Pegasus X engines and, at an all-up weight of 21,000lb, demonstrated a maximum speed of 245 mph; its maximum range was calculated as 3,200 miles, representing an extraordinary technological advance, and one that placed the Wellington in the forefront of bomber design.

Meanwhile, Pierson's new design, the Type 284, enlarged to the maximum

The second production Wellington I, L4213, with Vickers nose and tail turrets, and Pegasus XVIII engines; this aeroplane spent most of its life at Martlesham Heath and was not fitted with the dustbin ventral gun position. (Photo: Vickers-Armstrongs Ltd)

Left: *Wellington III X3595/AA-K of No 75 (New Zealand) Squadron, the squadron in which Sergeant James Allen Ward* VC *served.* (Photo: RAF Museum, Neg No P012018)

Below: *Another Wellington III, this time X3763/KW-E of No 425 (Alouette) Squadron, RCAF. The starboard beam gun position may be seen immediately forward of the fuselage roundel.* (Photo: RAF Museum)

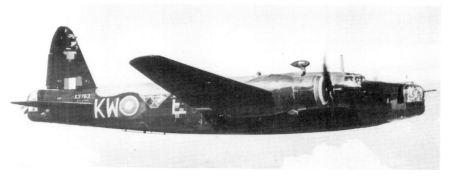

permissible wing span (determined by the door width of current Service hangars), was tendered to a new Specification, B.1/35, intended to replace B.9/32 in the light of the removal of tare weight restrictions. It was intended as the logical production configuration of his Type 271, exploiting engines of greatly increased power then being designed at Rolls-Royce and Napier. Indeed, the Type 284 Warwick has for long been represented as the ultimate *replacement* for the Wellington — which never really qualified for its classification as a heavy bomber. In reality, owing to the urgency afforded to the RAF's expansion needs, the production Wellington was to be a scaled-down Warwick, its limiting factor being the delay in finalising the installation details of the new power-operated Frazer-Nash nose and tail gun turrets (which the Warwick featured from the start, see page 327).

The first production Wellington Mk I, the Type 290, powered initially by 915hp Pegasus X engines, appeared on 23 December 1937 with the first flight of L4212, the first of a batch of 180 aircraft ordered in 1935 and defined in Specification 29/36. This aeroplane effectively became the true Wellington prototype, the old B.9/32 having been quite unrepresentative of the aircraft now destined for the Service. In any case, K4049 had been severely criticised at the A & AEE for a large number of design shortcomings and examples of shoddy workmanship before being destroyed in an accident on 19 April 1937. The majority of the earlier aircraft's faults had been rectified in L4212, and this aeroplane underwent extensive testing, not least that associated with its gun armament and bomb load — both increased threefold over that of the Heyford.

Wellington Is, powered by 1,000hp Pegasus XVIII engines, were first delivered in October 1938 to No 99 (Bomber) Squadron, commanded by Wg Cdr (later Air Cdre) Henry Edward Walker MC,

DFC, at Mildenhall, where they replaced Heyfords, and the following month to No 38 (Bomber) Squadron, led by Wg Cdr Ernest Spencer Goodwin AFC (later Air Vice-Marshal, CB, OBE, AFC*) at Marham, replacing Hendons.

At the outbreak of war, eight operational Squadrons (Nos 9, 37, 38, 99, 115, 149, 214 and 215) had received Wellingtons; these constituted the battle strength of No 3 Group, based in East Anglia with headquarters at Mildenhall under Air Vice-Marshal John Eustace Arthur Baldwin, CB, DSO, OBE (later Air Marshal Sir John, KBE, CB, DSO). Most of these squadrons had been declared operational by day, but none yet by night, and it was to Nos 9 and 149 Squadrons, flying from Honington and Mildenhall respectively, that on 4 September 1939 fell the task of mounting the Wellington's first daylight raid against German warships at Brunsbüttel. Of the 14 aircraft sent out, two (L4275 and L4292) failed to return.

The aircraft flown on these early operations were still the initial production Wellington Is with the Vickers nose and tail turrets, and the unpopular, retractable 'dustbin' turret, all mounting pairs of Browning machine guns. Despite constant representations by No 3 Group to Bomber Command that these very rudimentary gun turrets were quite inadequate to provide realistic defence against enemy fighters, the Wellington I equipped all the Squad-

rons noted above, as well as No 214 and 215, held in reserve at Methwold and Bassingbourne, and No 75 (Bomber) Squadron, engaged in training crews for the Group.

The supply of Frazer-Nash turrets was accordingly speeded up, and the next Wellington variant, the Mark IA, began reaching the squadrons soon after the early disappointing raids. To quell the lingering doubts as to the Wellington's ability to defend itself, the next raid, on 3 December, was launched by 24 Wellingtons of Nos 38, 115 and 149 Squadrons against German warships at Heligoland, but this proved inconclusive as no enemy fighters were encountered, and the bombers bombed through cloud, without achieving anything. Bomber Command mistakenly interpreted this as demonstrating the Wellington's ability to penetrate enemy defences in daylight and escape without loss, and No 99 Squadron was ordered on 14 December to fly 12 Wellington IAs (fitted with Frazer-Nash turrets in nose, tail and ventral positions) against German warships in the Schillig Roads. Flying in at low level, the bombers met heavy flak and intercepting fighters; three Wellingtons were shot down, two collided and a sixth crashed on landing.

Still not convinced that the bombers could not take care of themselves, Bomber Command on 18 December ordered 24 Wellingtons, this time from Nos 9, 37 and 149 Squadron, to attack the German

The prototype Wellington IV, R1220, with Pratt & Whitney Twin Wasp engines; converted from a Mark IC immediately after completion at Chester, it was flown to Weybridge but crashed nearby at Addlestone soon after arrival. (Photo: Vickers Ltd, Neg Ref No 5062F)

warships. Again the German pilots, now aware that the Wellington was incapable of defending itself from high beam attacks (owing to the nose and tail guns being unable to traverse through 180 degrees), took an even heavier toll, shooting down nine Wellingtons; three ditched in the sea and three, all badly damaged, forced landed away from base on return.

The loss of 21 Wellingtons from 36 despatched in two raids, not to mention the loss of almost one hundred airmen killed, wounded or missing, without apparently inflicting the slightest damage on their targets, finally demonstrated to the Air Staff the utter futility of mounting daylight raids by unescorted bombers in conditions of enemy air superiority, and these attacks were discontinued immediately.

The abandoning of daylight bombing without escort focused attention on night training, and during the first four months of 1940 the Wellington squadrons began to join in the leaflet-dropping sorties over Germany alongside the Whitleys. Once the restriction on bombing German territory was lifted, the Wellingtons provided the early spearhead of the slowly increasing bombing attacks over Europe, although during 1940 these seldom involved more than about fifty aircraft on any single night.

Once the necessity of defending the Wellington from enemy fighters largely disappeared (for the German night fighter force (*sic*) depended in 1940 almost exclusively on the pilot's eyesight to spot British bombers, and interceptions were rare), the aircraft proved popular among its crews, being generally reliable and sturdy, the geodetic structure proving capable of withstanding extensive damage before major failure. The aircraft's ability to carry its maximum bomb load was only marginal in the Mk IA, but with the arrival of the IC in 1940 (of which no fewer than 2,685 were built by all three Vickers factories at Weybridge, Chester and Blackpool), the vari-

ous armament anomalies which had arisen in the rush to increase production were eliminated; the first step was to discard the ventral dustbin turret (which,

when retracted into the fuselage, prevented access to the rear gunner) and substitute a manually-traversing machine gun in a beam hatch on each side of the rear fuselage. The other important modification involved the tidying up of the bomb bay to enable two 2,000lb

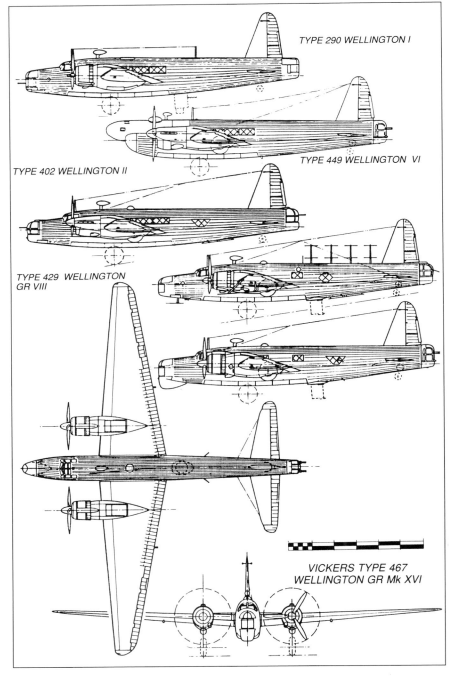

TYPE 290 WELLINGTON I

TYPE 449 WELLINGTON VI

TYPE 402 WELLINGTON II

TYPE 429 WELLINGTON GR VIII

VICKERS TYPE 467 WELLINGTON GR Mk XVI

AP and two 250lb GP bombs to be carried, this load becoming the most frequent used over ranges up to 1,500 miles (in particular against enemy warships in French Atlantic ports during 1940-41).

It was in a Wellington IC of No 75 (New Zealand) Squadron that an extraordinary example of gallantry earned the Wellington's only award of the Victoria Cross. Returning from a night raid on Münster on 7 July 1941, Wellington L7818 (captained by Sqn Ldr Reuben Pears Widdowson, a Canadian) was attacked and severely damaged by a Messerschmitt Bf 110 night fighter. The starboard engine was damaged and the hydraulic system put out of action. When a fire broke out close to the damaged engine, the second pilot, Sgt James Allen Ward, a New Zealander, climbed out of the astro hatch with a dinghy rope around his waist, clutching part of the cockpit canopy. Kicking holes in the fabric wing covering to obtain purchase, he reached the fire, and despite the vicious slipstream, pushed the canopy section into the hole made by the fire in an attempt to stifle the blaze. The slipstream, however, blew the canopy out of the hole and away into the night. Without anything further he could do to extinguish the fire, Ward managed to return to the astro hatch and climb back into the Wellington. In due course the fire burned itself out, and the pilot was able to bring the crippled bomber home. Ward had, however, probably prevented the fire from spreading at a time when the blaze was at its fiercest, and almost certainly saved the Wellington and its crew from being lost. He was to be killed in action only ten weeks later.

While deliveries of Wellington ICs were continuing, the Wellington Mk II began arriving in service, a total of 410 being built at Weybridge. Powered by the 1,145hp Rolls-Royce Merlin X, the

---

Type: Twin-engine, six-crew, mid-wing monoplane long-range night heavy/medium bomber.

Air Ministry Specifications: B.9/32, 29/36, B.23/39 and 17/40 (for Mk VI)

Manufacturer: Vickers-Armstrongs Ltd, Weybridge, Surrey; Chester, Cheshire; and Blackpool, Lancashire.

Powerplant: Prototype: Two 915hp Bristol Pegasus X radial engines. Mk I. 1,000hp Pegasus XVIII. Mk II. 1,145hp Rolls-Royce Merlin X in-line engines. Mk III. 1,500hp Bristol Hercules sleeve-valve radial engines. Mk V. Hercules VIII. Mk VI. 1,600hp Merlin 60. Mk VIII. 1,050hp Pegasus XVIII. Mk X. 1,675hp Hercules VI/XVI.

Structure: All-metal geodetic construction throughout with fabric covering.

Dimensions: Span, 86ft 2in (prototype, 86ft 0in); length, 64ft 7in (prototype, 61ft 3in; Mk VI, 61ft 9in); height, 17ft 5in; wing area, 840 sq ft.

Weights: Prototype: Tare, 18,000lb; all-up, 24,850lb. Mk IC. Tare, 18,556lb; all-up, 28,500lb. Mk X. Tare, 22,474lb; all-up, 36,500lb.

Performance: Prototype. Max speed, 245 mph at 15,000ft; service ceiling, 21,600ft; range, 3,200 miles. Mk IC. Max speed, 235 mph at 15,500ft; service ceiling, 18,000ft. Mk III. Max speed, 255 mph at 12,500ft; service ceiling, 18,000ft; range with 1,500lb bomb load, 2,200 miles; with 4,500lb bomb load, 1,540 miles.

Armament: Mk IC. Two 0.303in Browning machine guns in nose and tail power-operated turrets, and two manually-operated guns in beam positions. Max bomb load, 4,500lb. Mk III. Two Browning machine guns in nose turret, four in tail turret, and two manually-operated guns in beam positions. Max bomb load, 4,500lb.

Prototype: One (to Spec B.9/32), K4049, first flown by Joseph ('Mutt') Summers at Brooklands on 15 June 1936. (First production aircraft to Spec 29/36, L4212, first flown by Summers on 23 December 1937.)

Production: A total of 11,460 Wellingtons was built, excluding the above prototype. **Weybridge, 2,514:** Between L4212 and L4391 (175 Mk I); between N2865 and N3019 (120 Mk IA); between P5215 and P9300 (50 Mk IA, 50 Mk IC); R2699-R2703 (5 Mk I); between R3150 and R3299 (97 Mk IC, 1 Mk II, 2 Mk V); between T2458 and T3000 (293 Mk IC, 1 Mk II, 6 Mk VIII); between W5352 and W5815 (74 Mk IC, 199 Mk II, 1 Mk V, 19 Mk VIA, 27 Mk VIII); between Z8328 and Z9114 (200 Mk II, 229 Mk IC, 21 Mk VIII); between AD589 and AD653 (50 Mk IC); between BB455 and BB516 (43 Mk IC, 7 Mk VIII); between DR471 and DR528 (9 Mk VIA, 35 Mk VIG); ES980-ES995 (16 Mk IC); between HF828 and HF922 (62 Mk IC, 22 Mk VIII); between HX364 and HX786 (124 Mk IC, 176 Mk VIII); between LA964 and LB251 (16 Mk IC, 134 Mk VIII); and between MP502 and MS825 (105 Mk XI, 50 Mk XII, 42 Mk XIII, 53 Mk XIV). **Chester, 5,540:** Between L7770 and L7899 (3 Mk I, 17 Mk IA, 80 Mk IC); between N2735 and N2854 (100 Mk IC); between R1000 and R1806 (525 Mk IC, 25 Mk IV); between X9600 and Z1751 (378 Mk IC, 137 Mk III, 195 Mk IV); between BJ581 and BK564 (600 Mk III); between DV411 and DV953 (415 Mk IC); between HD942 and HF606 (85 Mk IC, 1 Mk III, 789 Mk X, 8 Mk XII, 241 Mk XIV); between LN157 and LR210 (1,380 Mk X); between NA710 and NB139 (263 Mk X); and between NB767 and NC234 (300 Mk XIV). **Blackpool, 3,406:** Between X3160 and X4003 (50 Mk IC, 450 Mk III); between DF542 and DF743 (145 Mk III, 5 Mk X); between HF609 and HF816 (123 Mk III, 27 Mk X, 3 Mk XI); between HZ102 and JA645 (62 Mk III, 301 Mk X, 72 Mk XI, 415 Mk XIII); between ME870 and MF742 (299 Mk X, 297 Mk XIII, 4 Mk XIV); MS470-MS496 (27 Mk X); between NV414 and ND133 (296 Mk X, 90 Mk XIII, 84 Mk XIV, 30 Mk XVIII); between PF820 and PG422 (208 Mk X, 162 Mk XIV, 30 Mk XVIII); and between RP312 and RP590 (206 Mk X, 20 Mk XVIII). **Totals built:** Mk I, 185; Mk IA, 183; Mk IC, 2,684; Mk II, 401; Mk III, 1,519; Mk IV, 220; Mk V, 3; Mk VI, 64; Mk VIII, 395; Mk X, 3,803; Mk XI, 180; Mk XII, 58; Mk XIII, 844; Mk XIV, 841; and Mk XVIII, 80.

Summary of RAF Service: Wellingtons served with the following Squadrons: No 8 (Mk XIII), No 9 (Mk I), No 12 (Mks II and III), No 14 (Mk XIV), No 15 (Mk I), No 24 (Mk XVI), No 36 (Mks I, VIII, X, XI, XII, XIII and XIV), No 37 (Mks I, III and X), No 38 (Mks I, III, VIII, X, XI, XIII and XIV), No 40 (Mks I, III and X), No 57 (Mks I, II and III), No 69 (Mks I, VIII and XIII), No 70 (Mks I, III and X), No 75 (Mks I, II and III), No 93 (Mk I), No 99 (Mks I, III, X and XVI), No 101, Mk I and III), No 103 (Mk I), No 104 (Mks II and X), No 108 (Mk I), No 109 (Mk I), No 115 (Mks I and III), No 142 (Mks II, III, IV and X), No 148 (Mks I and II), No 149 (Mk I), No 150 (Mks I, III and X), No 156 (Mks I and III), No 158 (Mk II), No 162 (Mks I, III and X), No 166 (Mks III and X), No 172 (Mks VIII, XII and XIV), No 179 (Mks VIII and XIV), No 192 (Mks I, III and X), No 196 (Mk X); No 199 (Mks III and X), No 203 (Mk XIII), No 214 (Mks I and II), No 215 (Mks I and X), No 221 (Mks I, VIII, XI and XIII), No 232 (Mk XVI), No 242 (Mk XVI), No 244 (Mk XIII), No 281 (Mk XIV), No 294 (Mks XI and XIII), No 300 (Polish), (Mks I, III, IV and X), No 301 (Polish), (Mks I and IV), No 304 (Polish), (Mks I, X, XIII and XIV), No 305 (Polish), (Mks I, II, IV and X), No 311 (Czech), (Mk I), No 405 (Canadian), (Mk II), No 419 (Canadian), (Mks I and III), No 420 (Canadian), (Mks III and X), No 424 (Canadian), (Mks III and X), No 425 (Canadian), (Mks III and X), No 426 (Canadian), (Mks III and X), No 427 (Canadian), (Mks III and X), No 428 (Canadian), (Mks III and X), No 429 (Canadian), (Mks III and X), No 431 (Canadian), (Mk X), No 432 (Canadian), (Mk X), No 458 (Australian), (Mk IV), No 460 (Australian), (Mks III and X), No 524, (Mk XIII), No 544 (Mk IV), No 547 (Mks VIII and XI), No 612 (Mks VIII and X), and No 621 (Mk XIII). Apart from very many other second line units of the RAF, notably 25 Operational Training Units, Wellingtons also served with Nos 716 (Mk XI), 728 (Mk XIV), 736 (Mk XI), 758 (Mk XI), 762 (Mk X), 765 (Mks X and XI), and 783 (Mks I and II) Squadrons of the Fleet Air Arm.

Left: *The prototype Vickers Type 431 Wellington VI high altitude bomber, W5795, probably at Boscombe Down; it later underwent development trials with Rolls-Royce Ltd and Rotol Ltd.* (Photo: Real Photographs Co.)

Below: *Unlike the prototype, this production Wellington VI, DR484, was not fitted with the tail gun turret, and was painted with sky blue undersides.* (Photo: Ministry of Aircraft Production, RTP)

Mark IIs first reached No 12 (Bomber) Squadron in October 1940, replacing its Battles at Binbrook; the next month they replaced the Battles on No 142 (Bomber) Squadron, also at Binbrook. This version, perhaps rather surprisingly, was less popular than the radial engine versions, but went on to equip eight squadrons.

The next version, the Wellington III powered by the 14-cylinder sleeve-valve Hercules XI of 1,500hp, appeared early in 1941. Most important, however, this version brought with it the ability to accommodate the 4,000lb HC parachute bomb — the heaviest yet carried by a British bomber (a distinction it shared with the Avro Manchester). This bomb was to become Bomber Command's most-used blast weapon; with barometric fuses set to detonate the bomb just before ground impact, the blast swept buildings away rather than dissipating the explosive force in a crater.

The first prototype Wellington III, L4251, had first flown on 19 May 1939, and this mark was intended to become Bomber Command's standard 'heavy' bomber until the arrival of Stirlings and Halifaxes. The Hercules III, however, proved disappointing, and the first production aircraft with Hercules XIs did not fly until January 1941 (by which time both the Stirling and Halifax had reached their first squadrons).

The Wellington III went on to equip a total of 17 Squadrons, including a number in the Middle East, and integral with the Mark III's standard of prepara-

tion was provision for tropicalisation, such as extra fuel tanks for the long distances flown in the Middle East, and provision for air filters over engine air intakes.

And so the Wellington versions proliferated, a fact that was to to appear anomalous for, in August 1940, it had been announced by the Air Staff that the RAF's strategic bomber force was to become equipped exclusively with four-engine aircraft as soon as possible — an aim that was not to be achieved for another three years owing to the survival of the Wellington.

The heavy demand for Pegasus, Hercules and Merlin engines had been anticipated at the beginning of the War, and the choice of an American alternative fell upon the Pratt & Whitney Twin Wasp. This engine therefore powered the next version of the Wellington, the Mark IV, of which 220 were produced at Chester, serving principally with the Polish Squadrons, Nos 300, 301 and

305, but also with Nos 142, 458, 460 and 544.

The Marks V and VI were high altitude variants which featured a pressure cabin in the nose, carried on a specially adapted geodetic structure and producing an entirely new nose profile. Designed to Specification B.23/39 and 17/40, the Mark V was powered by Hercules VIIIs with exhaust-driven superchargers, but only three examples were built (R3298, R3299 and W5796). The Mark VI was powered by Merlins, mostly 1,600hp Merlin 60s with two-speed, two-stage superchargers. Sixty-four were produced, but none saw operational service, although two (DR481 and DR485) flew with No 109 Squadron for a short period.

The only other version of the Wellington to fly with Bomber Command was the Mark X, no fewer than 3,803 aircraft of this type being produced. It was introduced into service with the improved Hercules XVIII engines late in 1942, and subsequently served with 29 squadrons during the last 30 months of the War, notably in the Middle East with Nos 37, 38, 40, 70, 104, 142, 150,

A Weybridge-built Wellington GR.XII, MP684, destined for Coastal Command. Powered by Hercules XVIs, it carried ASV Mk III in the chin fairing and a Leigh Light (shown retracted here) aft of the weapons bay. A shadow across the fuselage roundel discloses that the beam guns are fitted. (Photo: Vickers-Armstrongs Ltd, Neg No 5087-H)

The Wellington II, L4250, during trials with a dorsal 40mm gun. The installation was exceptionally complex and heavy, demanding a metal stressed-skin centre fuselage. L4250 was later flown with a dorsal turret mounting four 0.50in heavy machine guns. (Photo: Vickers Ltd)

420, 424 and 425 Squadrons, and in the Far East with Nos 99 and 215 Squadrons. At the end of the War, with hundreds of surplus Mark Xs available, conversions were undertaken to provide trainers for the peacetime RAF, and many of these survived in service until the 1950s.

Apart from Bomber Command, RAF Coastal Command was the other major destination of Wellingtons during the War, their long range being ideally suited to land-based maritime patrol and anti-submarine operations. However, the origins of maritime work by Wellingtons lay in January 1940, when a number of Mark Is were converted for the work of exploding German magnetic sea mines, 48-foot diameter hoops being attached at the nose and under the wings and rear fuselage. The hoop was in reality a magnetic coil carrying electrical power from a 35kW generator carried in the fuselage. These aircraft were termed Type 418 and 419 DWI Wellingtons (the initials denoting Directional Wireless Installation — a deliberately confusing designation). Most DWI Wellingtons were used in the Mediterranean theatre.

Later Coastal Command squadrons received Pegasus XVIII-powered Wellington GR Mk VIIIs, carrying ASV Mk II (and some with early Leigh Lights); Hercules-powered Wellington XIs and XIIs with ASV Mk III under the nose, retractable Leigh Lights in the rear fuselage and provision to carry two 18in torpedoes; the Wellington Mk XIII

with Hercules XVII and equipped with ASV Mk II; and the Wellington XIV, with Leigh Light, also powered by Hercules XVIIs. Two other variants were the Marks XVII and XVIII trainers, converted from earlier versions to provide 'classroom' training for Mosquito night fighter radar operators.

Transport Command employed two versions of the Wellington, the Marks XV and XVI, these being converted from redundant Mark ICs by sealing the bomb doors and fitting half a dozen rudimentary seats in the 'cabin'. A more specialised troop transport, the Type 437 Wellington IX, could carry 18 fully-equipped troops over a maximum range of 2,200 miles.

Space prevents more than passing mention of some of the multitude of experiments involving Wellingtons. Armament trials involved the mounting of a 40mm Vickers gun in a rotatable dorsal installation in Wellington II L4250 (this aeroplane being fitted at one time with twin fins and rudders); another Mk II, Z8416, was fitted with a forward-firing 40mm gun. A Wellington VIII (converted from a Mark IC), T2977, was modified to feature a Helmore Turbin-lite (a wide-beam searchlight) in the nose for consideration as an alternative to the Leigh Light.

As would be expected, the Welling-

ton came in for its share of engine test bed work, and apart from numerous non-standard variants of the Pegasus, Hercules and Merlin, more radical installations included early examples of the Rolls-Royce-Whittle W.2B/23 and Rover-built W.2B turbojet engines in the tails of Wellingtons W5389 and W5518, this flying beginning as early as July 1942. Much later, in 1948, a Wellington X, LN715, was use to test Rolls-Royce Dart turboprops destined for the Vickers Viscount airliner.

The Wellington was certainly one of aviation's classic designs; moreover, as with any truly great aeroplane, it was available when it was needed. Perhaps more important, by reason of its radical geodetic construction, it advanced aviation technology by demonstrating the practicality of a relatively sophisticated structure, and one that — in spite of predictions by the pundits to the contrary — proved capable of assembly by semi-skilled labour forces. The geodetic system was, of course, rendered obsolescent by metal monocoque almost before the Wellington entered service, yet the fact that more Wellingtons were built than any other multi-engine British bomber is surely ample testimony to the correct interpretation of Britain's needs in the mid-1930s.

Fairey Seafox

Specification S.11/32 was intended to complement S.9/30, and later S.15/33, by expressing the terms of a requirement for a shipborne reconnaissance seaplane capable of being carried aboard the smaller cruisers of the Royal Navy, to undertake short-range sea surveillance and gunnery spotting. It was also required to carry two 100lb anti-sub-

marine bombs. Alighting speed was not to exceed 46kt.

Fairey submitted two designs, one powered by a 500hp Bristol Aquila radial engine, the other by the 395hp Napier Rapier 16-cylinder upright-H air-cooled in-line engine. The latter version was selected and two prototypes were ordered.

The airframe was all-metal, the wings being fabric-covered and the fuselage an Alclad-covered monocoque structure. The wings were made to fold for ship-

board stowage, and the pilot's cockpit was open, though the observer was provided with a canopy (which hinged upwards at the rear to allow free movement of his Lewis gun). The specified bomb load was carried under the lower wings, but no optical means of bomb aiming was provided.

The first prototype Seafox flew on 27 May 1936 and at once showed itself to be underpowered, while the alighting speed of 50kt was substantially above that required. The MAEE at Felix-

The second Seafox prototype, K4305, during trials at the MAEE, Felixstowe, carrying 100lb anti-submarine bombs under the wings; this aircraft was also flown as a landplane. The Seafox was originally known as the Trout, but the name was not officially accepted. (Photo: Air Ministry, MAEE, Neg No 1303.)

stowe, however, eventually issued a report generally applauding the Seafox for its handling in the air and on the water. A preliminary production order for 49 aircraft had been placed in January 1936, and the first production example was flown on 23 April 1937.

The Seafox first joined No 714 (Catapult) Flight for service aboard the cruisers of the 4th Cruiser Squadron on the East Indies Station, namely HMS *Norfolk*, 9,950 tons, HMS *Emerald* and *Enterprise*, both 7,550 tons, and, during the next two years went on to join ships of the 3rd Cruiser Squadron in the Mediterranean, as well as being embarked in the armed merchant cruisers of the Northern Patrol.

The Seafox gained fame for the part played by the aircraft, launched by the light cruiser HMS *Ajax* on 13 December 1939, during the Battle of the River Plate. The pilot of this aircraft (the only one aboard the three British cruisers involved that could be launched after the aircraft aboard HMS *Exeter* had been damaged), Lieut Edward Duncan Goodenough Lewin RN, with Lieut R E N Kearney RN as his observer, spotted for the guns of the three cruisers throughout the action, and later witnessed and

reported the scuttling of the German pocket battleship *Admiral Graf Spee* on 18 December.[1]

Seafoxes also equipped No 754 Training Squadron, which was formed at Lee-on-Solent in May 1939, under the

command of another Fleet Air Arm pilot who was to achieve lasting fame, Lt-Cdr Eugene Esmonde VC, DSO.

---

[1]   Lieutenant Lewin (later Capt, CB, CBE, DSO, DSC*) was awarded the DSC for his part in the Battle, the first award of the DSC to a Fleet Air Arm pilot in the Second World War. Lewin later commanded No 808 Squadron, FAA, as well as HMS *Glory* (in Korean waters, 1952) and HMS *Eagle*, 1955. After retiring from the Royal Navy, he became Joint Managing Director, Blackburn Aircraft Ltd, in 1960 at the time the Buccaneer strike aircraft was approaching service with the Fleet Air Arm.

Type: Single-engine, two-seat, two-bay biplane twin-float shipborne reconnaissance seaplane.

Air Ministry Specification: S.11/32.

Manufacturer: The Fairey Aviation Co Ltd, Hamble, Hampshire.

Powerplant: One 395hp Napier Rapier VI 16-cylinder upright H-type air-cooled in-line engine.

Dimensions: Span, 40ft 0in; length, 33ft 5in; height, 12ft 2in; wing area, 434 sq ft.

Weights: Tare, 3,805lb; all-up, 5,420lb.

Performance: Max speed, 124 mph at 5,860ft; climb to 5,000ft, 15 min 30 sec; service ceiling, 9,700ft; range, 440 miles.

Armament: One Lewis gun with Fairey mounting on rear cockpit. Bomb load of up to 360lb (comprising two 100lb AS bombs and eight 20lb bombs).

Prototypes: Two, K5304 (first flown by C S Staniland at Hamble on 27 May 1936) and K5305 (first flown as landplane on 5 November 1936).

Production: Excluding the above prototypes, production totalled 64 Seafoxes: K8569-K8617 and L4519-L4533.

Summary of Service: Seafoxes served with the following Fleet Air Arm Catapult Flights: No 700 (from January 1940 to September 1942 at Hatston), 702 (from December 1940 until July 1943 aboard HM Armed Merchant Cruisers *Alcantara*, *Asturias*, *Canton* and *Queen of Bermuda*), 703 (from July until November 1942 aboard HM Armed Merchant Cruiser *Pretoria Castle*), 713 (from June 1937 until July 1938 aboard HM Cruisers *Arethusa*, *Galatea* and *Penelope*), 714 (from June 1937 until July 1938 aboard HM Cruisers *Emerald* and *Gloucester*), 716 (from October 1937 until January 1940 aboard HM Cruiser *Neptune*), and 718 (from August 1937 until January 1940 aboard, *inter alia*, HM Cruiser *Ajax*); and with Nos 754 Training Squadron, No 764 Squadron, No 765 Squadron (Seaplane Training School, Lee-on-Solent) and No 773 Squadron (Fleet Requirements Unit at Bermuda).

Westland Lysander

It was no secret among leading British aircraft designers in 1934 that the Air Ministry had for some months been giving considerable thought to acquiring an advanced army co-operation aircraft to replace the Hawker Audax, which was already effectively a seven year old design which had been ordered into production at a time when commonality with the Hart bomber was of paramount

importance. It was not of the same level of technology as the new generation of fighters and bombers under consideration at home and abroad, and was therefore irrelevant in the context of a possible European war. And although the Hector had not yet appeared as a stopgap, it would have no bearing on the new Specification, as any improvement it might represent over the Audax would be minimal.

The demands of the new Specification, A.39/34 (issued in April 1935), were, however, probably more rhetori-

cal than realistic, calling for a monoplane with a maximum speed of 260 mph, and a landing speed of not more than 50 mph and a bomb load of 500lb. Central to the demands were excellent low-speed handling qualities, excellent fields of view for the crew and an ability to operate from very restricted spaces. It had to be armed with two forward-firing machine guns and was to be able to carry out diving attacks with guns and bombs.

The Specification attracted design tenders from Bristol (the Type 148), Avro (the Type 670), Hawker (a bi-

The first Lysander prototype, K6127, at Yeovil. The small transparent panel below the fin was to enable a visual check to be made as to whether ballast weights were in place. (Photo: Westland Aircraft Ltd, Neg No 10093 dated 26 November 1936)

plane), and Westland (the P.8). The Hawker tender was rejected out of hand, and the Avro design was not pursued beyond a preliminary scheme, but prototypes were ordered of both the Bristol 148 and the Westland P.8.

The Bristol aeroplanes K6551 and K6552 were wholly conventional, being low-wing monoplanes, but met neither the maximum nor minimum speed requirements and were uncomfortable to fly at low speed. They were also very slow being completed, and the first only arrived at Martlesham Heath nearly two years after the first Westland prototype had flown; and then the first aircraft suffered damage when its retractable undercarriage failed.

By contrast, Arthur Davenport's P.8, which had been schemed as a high-wing monoplane even before the issue of A.39/34, passed through detail design stage in less than six months and was first flown by Harald Penrose on 15 June 1936 at Boscombe Down. The fuselage was of established Westland girder construction, with the engine mounting plate attached to the four longerons, metal panels covering the front section, and fabric the rear.

The high aspect ratio wings were the key to the aircraft's excellent low-speed performance and handling, being both flapped and slatted, built up on a single spar, and with reverse taper in chord and thickness to a point at semi-span where the bracing V-struts were attached to the wings. The fixed undercarriage was completely spatted and faired, employing an exceptionally strong extruded, arched cantilever strut. Bombs would be carried on stub winglets attached outboard of the wheel spats.

There is no doubting that the DTD was impressed with the P.8's ingenuity and potential, as the first production batch of 66 Mercury XII-powered air-

craft was ordered before K6127 had even flown, and a second batch of 78 Perseus XII-powered examples was ordered before the second prototype was flown in December the same year. The name Lysander had been selected and K6127 attended the 1936 Hendon Display as New Type No 6.

First production deliveries of the Lysander were made to No 16 (Army Co-operation) Squadron, commanded by Sqn Ldr (later Gp Capt) Thomas Humble at Old Sarum in June 1938. No 2 (AC) Squadron, based at Hawkinge, Kent, followed in September, being one of those commanded by Army officers, also holding rank in the RAF; in this instance No 2 was commanded by Capt (temporary Sqn Ldr) Andrew James Wray Geddes, RA.[1]

At the outbreak of war one year later, the number of Lysander Squadrons had increased to six, based in the United Kingdom, and one in the Middle East (No 208 Squadron at Qasaba, Egypt); No 6 Squadron, at Ramleh, Palestine, was receiving Lysanders within a fortnight.

It was part of the War Plan to send army co-operation aircraft with the Air Component of the BEF to France, and during the first week in October 1939 Nos 2, 4, 13, and 26 (AC) Squadrons flew out to French airfields in the

---

[1] In fact Geddes also held a Regular Commision in the Royal Air Force, retiring in 1954 as an Air Cdre, CBE, DSO.

British sector. No 16 (AC) Squadron followed on 14 April 1940. Much of the 'Phoney War' period during the winter of 1939-40 was spent by the Lysander squadrons exercising with the ground forces and generally reconnoitring the area in front of the BEF (though without penetrating Belgian airspace).

This seemingly unreal situation altered rapidly and drastically after the German attack opened on 10 May 1940, with all the army co-operation squadrons heavily committed. The Lysanders were seldom employed to bomb the advancing Germans, their task being simply to report on the progress of the advance itself. They were frequently found and attacked by enemy fighters, and suffered accordingly. Records show that of the 91 Lysanders in France (80 with the five Squadrons and 11 with the Air Component Pool) on 10 May, and 22 subsequently sent out as replacements, losses amounted to 62 aircraft, including those destroyed on the ground, and 17 others were written off as beyond economical repair after they had been flown back to the United Kingdom. Nos 13 and 26 Squadrons suffered the heaviest losses — 23 pilots and observers and 35 aircraft between them, all in the space of one month.

These heavy losses did not reflect any significant failing in the Lysander in performing its allotted task, but rather — once again — a failure by the Air Ministry to understand the value placed

A Lysander II, N1256/LX-M of No 225 Squadron; this unit initially flew the Lysanders on army co-operation exercises during 1939 and early 1940; later they were flown on anti-invasion patrols along the Channel coast and on air-sea rescue duties. Note the bomb racks under the stub winglets and rear fuselage. (Photo: Via Derek James)

by the Germans on the presence of fighter aircraft over the battlefield, and the great majority of Lysanders lost (discounting those destroyed by the RAF on the ground during evacuation) were shot down by enemy fighters.[2]

Apart from the Middle East (and to a lesser extent India and Burma), where the Lysander continued to perform army co-operation duties in the traditional manner, the end of the Battle of France accelerated radical changes in the means of supporting ground forces from the air. Instead, the Lysander in the United Kingdom began to undertake semi-operational rôles which exploited its excellent slow-flying and small-field operating qualities, duties such as air-sea rescue (searching for and signalling the position of ditched airmen by means of smoke floats) and coastal patrols — on the look-out for the possible landing of enemy agents. In particular, the exacting demands of the Special Duties Squadrons, Nos 138 and 161 in the United Kingdom, No 148 in the Balkans and No 357 in Burma, with their supremely hazardous work in supplying arms to resistance forces in enemy-occupied territory, and even landing to drop or bring out members of those forces, were met by the Lysander, an aeroplane that could take off and clear 50 feet in 300 yards.

2 The Germans possessed an army co-operation aircraft of very similar performance to the Lysander, the Henschel Hs 126. By comparison with the Lysander, records show that approximately 300 Hs 126s were deployed during the Battle of France, of which about 70 were shot down — just nine of them by RAF Hurricane fighters.

Yet, in the Mediterranean and North Africa from 1940 until May 1942 Nos 6, 208 and 237 *were* Army Co-operation Squadrons in the traditional sense until the arrival of the dedicated fighter-bomber, the anti-tank fighter and the camera-equipped reconnaissance fighter, a process that continued to evolve up to the present day. Lysanders participated in the Greek campaign of 1940-41, in Syria in 1941 and in the Western Desert until 1942.

When these three squadrons were re-equipped, the army co-operation aeroplane's 'trade mark', the message pick-up hook, disappeared from the RAF's inventory, and on 1 June 1943 Army Co-operation Command itself was disbanded.

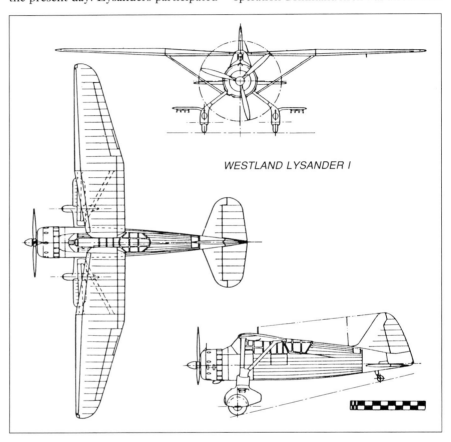

WESTLAND LYSANDER I

Type: Single-engine, two-seat, high-wing multi-rôle army co-operation/ground support monoplane.

Air Ministry Specifications: A.39/34 and A.36/36.

Manufacturers: Westland Aircraft Ltd, Yeovil, Somerset, and Westland (Doncaster) Ltd, Yorkshire; National Steel Car Corporation Ltd, Malton, Ontario, Canada.

Powerplant: Mk I. One 890hp Bristol Mercury XII 9-cylinder, air-cooled, supercharged radial engine driving 3-blade variable-pitch propeller. Mk II. 905hp Bristol Perseus XII. Mk III. 870hp Bristol Mercury XX or 30.

Structure: All-metal construction; front fuselage light-alloy covered; centre and rear fuselage, tail and wings, fabric-covered.

Dimensions: Span, 50ft 0in; length, 30ft 6in; height, 14ft 6in; wing area, 260 sq ft.

Weights: Mk III. Tare, 4,365lb; all-up, 6,330lb (Mk IIIA overload, 10,000lb).

Performance: Mk III. Max speed, 212 mph at 5,000ft; climb to 10,000ft, 8 min; service ceiling, 21,500ft; range, 420 miles.

Armament: Two free-firing 0.303in Browning machine guns in wheel-spats, and one or two Lewis guns in rear cockpit. Bomb load of up to two 250lb HE, four 112lb GP bombs or eight 20lb bombs carried on stub winglets; four 20lb bombs carried under the fuselage.

Prototypes: Two, K6127 and K6128, first flown by Harald Penrose on 15 June and 11 December 1936 respectively.

Production: Excluding the above prototypes, a total of 1,650 Lysanders was built: Mark Is: 169 (L4673-L4738, P1665-P1699 and between R2572 and R2652); Mark IIs: 442 (L4739-L4816, L6847-L6888, between N1200 and N1320, P1711-P1745, between P9015 and P9199, and between R1987 and R2047; 36 for Turkey and 6 for Eire); Mk IIIs: 367 (between R8991 and T1771, and, built by Westland (Doncaster), between W6939 and W6960); Mk IIIAs: 447 (between V9280 and V9750, and target tugs between V9751 and V9906). In addition, 75 Mk IIs and 150 Mk IIIs were built in Canada.

Summary of Service with RAF: Lysanders served with the following army co-operation and tactical reconnaissance Squadrons in the UK: Nos 2, 4, 13, 16, 26, 225, 231, 239, 268, 309 (Polish), 400 (Canadian), 613 and 614; of these, Nos 2, 4, 13, 16 and 26 Squadrons served in France during 1939-40. They served with Nos 6, 208 and 237 Squadrons on tactical reconnaissance duties in the Middle East, and with Nos 20 and 28 in India and Burma. They served on Special Duties with Nos 138 and 161 Squadrons in the UK, with No 148 in the Balkans and No 357 in India and Burma. They flew coastal patrols and air-sea rescue duties with Nos 241, 275, 276, 277 and 278 Squadrons, communications duties with Nos 173 and 267 Squadrons, with combined operations forces with No 516 Squadron, on Anti-Aircraft Co-operation duties with Nos 285, 287, 288, 289, 598 and 695 Squadrons, and for gun and radar calibration with No 116 Squadron.

Handley Page H.P.54 Harrow

The H.P.54 was a direct derivative of the single H.P.51 high-wing bomber transport, itself a monoplane conversion of the H.P.43 three-engine biplane, and although this might be reason enough to brush aside the Harrow as little more than a makeshift oddity, it still gave sterling service for more than eight years. It was selected for production, it is true, as interim equipment for five heavy bomber squadrons during the RAF's expansion period, but *central to its Requirement* was an ability to revert to the transport rôle once that short-term service as a bomber had ended, a rôle which it filled with seldom-remembered efficiency until the last month of the Second World War.

A production order for 100 H.P.54s was placed in 1935, when Lachmann's design was still no more than an optimised scheme evolved purely with speedy production in mind, a scheme produced as the result of examining American series production methods. Specification 29/35 was drawn up to cover the inclusion of gun turrets in nose, tail and amidships, and a bomb load of 3,000lb, carried internally beneath the cabin floor. To accommodate the required complement of troops when used in the transport rôle, and enable the c.g. to remain within acceptable limits when dropping bombs, the nose was lengthened by just over four feet; among the ingenious features introduced was a system of cabin heating — by steam boilers heated by engine exhaust— but this was not considered the most endearing feature of the Harrow.

The first Harrow prototype, K6933, without the gun turrets fitted. This aeroplane was to be written off after being damaged in the German raid on Ford of 18 August 1940, while flying with Flight Refuelling Ltd. (Photo: Real Photographs Co)

Delays in the delivery of the nose and tail turrets did not prevent Major Cordes from flying the first prototype Harrow, K6933 (the first aircraft of the production batch) on 10 October 1936; this aircraft was then delivered to Martlesham Heath on 30 November, being joined by the Mark II prototype, K6934, in January 1937, powered by Pegasus XX engines and fully-equipped with gun turrets. The Harrows' careers at the A & AEE were eventful and memorable for those who flew in them. The gunners' positions were cramped and exceedingly cold and, following one long-distance test, the tail gunner was taken ill with the effects of bad ventilation of his turret; on another occasion, unknown to the pilot, the starboard elevator spar failed during an involuntary dive at 250 mph; the failure made itself known on a subsequent flight when the aircraft became unmanageable in a dive, and a safe landing was only accomplished with the whole crew crowded into the nose, and the pilot rounding out entirely by use of the elevator trimmer.

All 100 Harrows were completed during 1937, No 214 (Bomber) Squadron being the first to take deliveries on 12 April that year at Feltwell. Within a fortnight this Squadron had shed its 'B' Flight, and this became No 38 (Bomber) Squadron, also equipped with Harrows. All five Squadrons scheduled to receive the bomber had re-equipped with Harrow IIs before the end of the year, the initial Mark I deliveries being redistributed between Nos 8 and 9 Air Observers' Schools.

Despite continuing attempts to improve the cabin and turret heating systems, the Harrow quickly acquired a lasting reputation as a very cold and draughty aeroplane, largely on account of the turret design, and in this respect the early aircraft, which were completed without turrets, were the most popular.

By the end of 1939 the Harrow had disappeared from all five Squadrons, in each instance having been replaced by Wellingtons. It was, however, to enjoy a new lease of life when, towards the end of April 1940, No 1680 (Transport) Flight at Doncaster received a Harrow (K7032) which had previously served with No 215 Squadron. As it had been decided that almost all Bristol Bombays should be shipped to the Middle East, No 1680 Flight was enlarged to become a Squadron, No 271, on 1 May and equipped initially with 13 Harrows. It

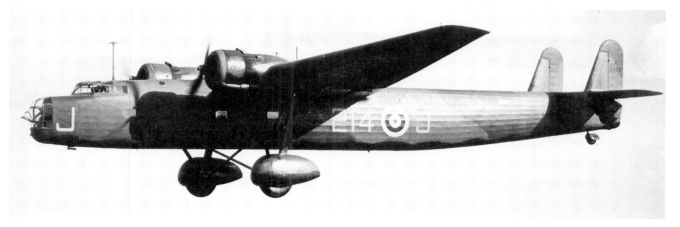

A Harrow II, K6988/J of No 214 (Bomber) Squadron, in 1938; it later served with No 271 (Transport) Squadron. (Photo: The Aeroplane)

eventually became a Dakota squadron with the airborne forces in January 1944, but continued to operate one flight of Harrow Transports until the end of the War.

From time to time No 271 flew the Harrows between England and Gibraltar — under the circumstances a somewhat risky undertaking owing to the Harrow's low cruising speed — however, only two aircraft were lost while flying this route. Shortly after the Normandy landings No 271's Harrows were converted for air ambulance duties, and most of these were parked on Brussels-Evere airfield on New Year's Day, 1945, when Joseph Priller led 60 Messerschmitt Bf 109G and Focke-Wulf Fw 190D fighter-bombers in an attack on the base as part of the German Operation *Bodenplatte*; seven Harrows were destroyed as well as a dozen Dakotas. This left only five surviving aircraft with which to equip the Squadron, and these were struck off charge on 25 May 1945.

One other operational duty was performed by Harrows, although not involving conventional bombing operations. Following trials by No 420 Flight, No 93 Squadron was formed under the command of Wg Cdr John Wood Homer with six Harrows based at Middle Wallop in December 1940, at the height of the German night *Blitz* against Britain, their rôle (in Operation 'Mutton') being to tow Long Aerial Mines (codenamed 'Pandora') into the path of enemy bombers, having been directed into position by ground radar controllers. Astonishingly, this unorthodox tactic — seldom involving more than one or two Harrows on any one night — brought about the confirmed destruction of six German bombers before the bombing campaign petered out in May 1941.

Type: Twin-engine, four/five-crew, high-wing monoplane bomber transport.
Air Ministry Specification: 29/35
Manufacturer: Handley Page Ltd, Cricklewood, London, and Radlett, Hertfordshire.
Powerplant: Mk I. Two 830hp Bristol Pegasus X 9-cylinder air-cooled radial engines. Mk II. 920hp Pegasus XX.
Dimensions: Span, 88ft 5in; length, 82ft 2in; height, 19ft 5in; wing area, 1,090 sq ft.
Weights: Tare, 13,600lb; all-up, 23,000lb.
Performance: Max speed, 197 mph at 11,000ft; climb to 6,500ft, 8 min 10 sec; service ceiling, 22,800ft; normal range, 1,260 miles.
Armament: Single 0.303in Vickers or Lewis machine guns in Hubbard-Frazer-Nash nose turret and dorsal cupola, and twin Vickers K machine guns in Hubbard-Frazer-Nash tail turret. Bomb load of up to six 500lb bombs carried internally; as transport or ambulance, ability to accommodate 20 fully-armed troops or 12 stretcher cases.
Prototypes: Two, Mk I, K6933, and Mk II, K6934; K6933 first flown by Maj J L B H Cordes on 10 October 1936 at Radlett.
Production: Excluding the above prototypes, 98 Harrows were built; Mk Is, K6935-K6952 (18); Mk IIs, K6953-K7032 (80).
Summary of Service: Harrows served with Nos 37, 75, 115, 214 and 215 (Bomber) Squadrons, all in the United Kingdom, between April 1937 and December 1939, with No 93 Squadron (previously No 420 Flight) on air defence operations from December 1940 until June 1941 at Middle Wallop, and with No 271 (Transport) Squadron from May 1940 until May 1945. They also served with Nos 2, 4, 7, 8, 9 and 10 AOS, Nos 7, 8, 9 and 10 BGS, No 1 AAS, No 8 AGS and No 42 OTU, as well as Flight Refuelling Ltd. Harrows served with No 782 Squadron, Fleet Air Arm, from June 1941 until July 1943, based at Donibristle.

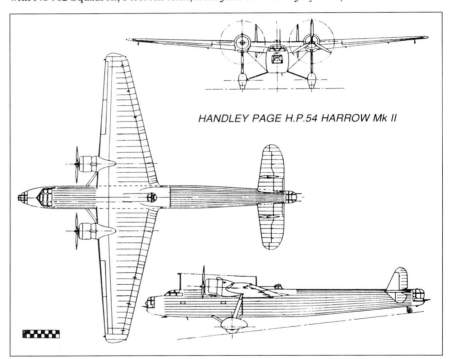

HANDLEY PAGE H.P.54 HARROW Mk II

Handley Page H.P.52 Hampden/Hereford

Third of the famous trio of medium and heavy bombers with which Bomber Command opened its modest assault on Germany towards the end of the first year of the War, the Handley Page Hampden, being much smaller and lighter than the Wellington and Whitley,

was more agile and never realistically rated any classification but that of a medium bomber — and only then when carrying reduced fuel.

Like the Wellington, the H.P.52 was originally designed to Specification B.9/32, and was therefore similarly handicapped by the limit on bomber weight, imposed through the Geneva Disarmament Conference by the League of Nations.

During this period of uncertainty, Lachmann began scheming a mono-

plane design employing twin engines, metal monocoque construction throughout with fabric-covered control surfaces, and retractable undercarriage — this being, in his opinion, the configuration likely to be favoured for an Overstrand replacement.

As originally issued, B.9/32 specified a maximum wing span of 70 feet, and it is likely that this dimension dominated Lachmann's entire configuration, and continued to do so even after the limitation had been waived. His H.P.52 was

Left: *The H.P.52 prototype, K4240, at Radlett in its 1936 Hendon guise, bearing the New Type No 8 and with the nose and dorsal gun position obscured by light-alloy panels* (Photo: The Aeroplane, Neg No 797)

Below: *The H.P.53 prototype, L7271, with the makeshift nose and dorsal outlines, and after being fitted with the Napier Dagger engines which were to be the cause of so much trouble.*(Photo: Short and Harland Ltd)

tendered in December 1933 with the choice of three alternative engines, the Bristol Aquila and the Bristol Mercury IV and VI, with all-up weight estimates ranging between 10,100 and 11,450lb, and speeds between 208 and 230 mph, depending on the engines selected. The design featured a straight-tapered wing set at mid-position on a deep, narrow and flat-sided fuselage, the tail unit having twin fins and rudders carried on a very slender rear fuselage boom. The undercarriage was to retract into the engine nacelles.

In the event, the single prototype ordered, K4240, was to be powered by the new Pegasus PE.5-SM (which, in production, became the Pegasus XVIII), these 1,000hp engines increasing the aircraft's tare weight considerably. At much the same time (March 1935) Handley Page was approached by the Swedish government to design a twin-engine, twin-float torpedo bomber, intending that it should be powered by Swedish-built Pegasus II radials. This design was to become the H.P.53 but, such were the uncertainties with regard to details of the armament available to the Swedes, not to mention the increasing pressure by the Air Ministry on Handley Page to fly a prototype of the H.P.52 as soon as possible, that the H.P.53 remained about one year behind the Hampden, despite almost 90 per cent of the structure being common to both aircraft.

The H.P.52, named Hampden — after much disagreement between the ministry and manufacturer — was first flown by Cordes at Radlett on 21 June

1936. The aeroplane was planned to make its public debut at the Hendon Air Display at the end of that month and, so that prying eyes should not be able to see that its interior was indeed entirely devoid of military equipment, other than essential cockpit furnishing, controls and instruments, the transparent nose panels were replaced by aluminium sheet.

If the Swedes were uncertain as to their armament requirements, the Air Ministry was equally so. The Hampden's fuselage was so narrow that no 'proprietary' gun mounting could be tailored to fit the gunners' stations. Indeed, the pilot's cockpit was no wider than that of a fighter. The lack of equipment in the Hampden prototype did not prevent it from visiting Martlesham Heath within a fortnight of its first flight for a brief handling assessment and, like the Wel-

lington, it was criticised for heavy elevator control, poor means of communication between crew and lack of heating. On its second visit the wing had been given slightly increased dihedral, a two-piece elevator had been fitted and the wing slats made operable and, following general acceptance of these improvements at the A & AEE, it was possible to decide on the standard of production preparation, although the matter of gun installation had yet to be resolved.

As production got underway at Handley Page, with an order for 500 aircraft to Specification 30/36, a contract was raised with the English Electric Company at Preston to tool up for an initial batch of 75 Hampdens.

In the meantime, the Swedish negotiations had run into problems, partly on account of the difficulty in agreeing the armament installation and other equip-

A carefully staged photograph of Hampdens of No 49 (Bomber) Squadron at Scampton, probably in 1940, showing 1,000lb and 500lb GP bombs. Visible on the nearest aircraft, P1333, is the fixed Browning machine gun with bead-sight foward of the pilot's windscreen. (Photo: via Derek James)

The Hereford never flew a bombing sortie with Bomber Command. The aircraft shown here, L6056, only ever served with No 16 OTU and No 5 Bombing and Gunnery School. (Photo: Handley Page Ltd, Neg No A271)

ment. A compromise was reached as the Swedish government agreed to accept a production Hampden instead of the Pegasus-powered prototype, and then to use it for trial installations in Sweden. The H.P.53 was therefore taken on charge by the Air Ministry as L7271 and first flown at Radlett with Pegasus XX engines on 1 July 1937. It was subsequently flown to Sydenham and transferred to Short & Harland Ltd, Belfast, that company being awarded a contract to develop a Napier Dagger-powered version, for which it was to be awarded a production contract to produce 150 aircraft. The original H.P.53 was re-engined with Daggers and first flown by Harold L Piper on 6 October 1938. Persistent overheating of the air-cooled Daggers, however, caused the aircraft to be grounded in August 1939, by which time the first production aircraft, now named the Hereford, had flown.[1]

The first production Hampdens for the RAF were completed in August 1938, twelve aircraft being delivered to No 49 (Bomber) Squadron at Scampton the following month. Two other Scampton-based Squadrons, Nos 83 and 50, followed suit in November and December respectively. During the last eight months of peace seven further squadrons converted to the new medium bomber, although only Nos 44 and 61 (in addition to the original three) were declared operational; Nos 7, 76, 106, 144

---

[1] The Hampden supplied to Sweden was the fifth in the production line at Radlett, being powered by Pegasus XXIV engines, and was flown out of Heston by a *Flygvapnet* pilot on 24 September 1938. It was to remain flying longer than any other Hampden, being finally retired on 17 November 1947, having been used by SAAB as an electronics test bed with the civil registration SE-APD.

and 185 were tasked with crew training.

From the first day of the War Hampdens flew operational sorties, with armed reconnaissance flights over the North Sea and off the German ports — on the look-out for units of the German Navy. Soon the Squadrons began the tiresome and little publicised task of sowing minefields off the enemy coasts, the Hampden being able to carry two 1,500lb parachute sea mines. In later months freshman crews on the operational squadrons would fly these 'gardening' sorties as their initiation to bombing raids.

In May 1940 the Hampdens of No 5 Group began bombing operations over German territory as aircraft from Nos 44, 49, 50, 61 and 144 Squadrons joined 18 Whitleys in an attack on rail targets at München Gladbach on the night of the 11th/12th. Four nights later the Hampdens were part of a 99-strong force sent against oil and steel targets in the Ruhr.

Among the Hampden pilots who took part in those early raids was a certain Fg Off Guy Penrose Gibson of No 83 Squadron, based at Scampton, and to him fell the job of delivering the first 2,000lb SAP bomb to be dropped by a Bomber Command aircraft when, on 1/2 July, he attacked the German battleship *Scharnhorst* at Kiel. Unfortunately, during his first five diving attacks the bomb failed to release, and on the sixth attempt the bomb fell off prematurely and landed in the centre of the town.

It was the pilot of a No 49 Squadron Hampden (L4403), Flt Lt Roderick Alastair Brook Learoyd, who was to win the first of two Victoria Crosses awarded to members of Hampden crews, for his part in a hazardous low-level attack on the heavily-defended Dortmund-Ems canal on the night of 12/13 August 1940. In the face of intense flak, he dropped his bombs from a height of 150 feet, his aircraft being repeatedly hit and losing larges pieces of the wings. He managed to return to base, but waited until dawn before risking a landing so as not to endanger his crew further. (Learoyd went on to command No 49 Squadron.)

A month later, on the night of 15/16 September, during a bombing attack on invasion barges assembling at Antwerp, Hampden P1355 of No 83 Squadron suffered a direct hit from flak which started a fire in the bomb bay, as well as puncturing the fuel tanks. Without knowing the fate of the rear gunner, the wireless operator, Sergeant John Hannah, made his way aft in order to reach the two fire extinguishers. Finding that the gunner had been forced to bale out, Hannah set to with the extinguishers, suffering severe burns while doing so as the floor of the cabin had started to melt. After the extinguishers were exhausted, he went on to beat at the flames with his log book. As the pilot struggled to bring the crippled bomber home, Hannah's efforts succeeded and the fire eventually went out. The young sergeant was obliged to leave the Service on account of his burns, but the award of his Victoria Cross was gazetted on 1 October 1940.

Hampdens continued to accompany

AE436/PL-J was an early Hampden torpedo bomber conversion of No 144 (Bomber) Squadron; it was to be lost on 4 September 1942 when it flew into a mountain near Kvikkjokk in northern Sweden while flying from Scotland to Vaenga in Russia for the protection of the North Cape convoys. (Photo: RAF Museum, Neg No P0105921)

Bomber Command's growing night raids against Germany, even though their bomb loads were relatively light; they were frequently sent against German warship targets in the French Atlantic ports, being able to carry a pair of the 2,000lb SAP bombs over these short ranges[2]. Indeed, the Hampden's final raid with the Command was flown by the Canadian No 408 Squadron against naval targets at Wilhelmshaven on the night of 14/15 September 1942.

This was not the final chapter in the Hampden's operational career. Quite apart from the Swedish interest in its potential as a torpedo bomber, Handley Page had tendered a torpedo-carrying variant of the Hampden to Specification M.15/35, but this was declined in favour of the Bristol Type 152 Beaufort. Yet it always seemed that a 'short' 18in torpedo could be accommodated in the H.P.52's bomb bay, and a design was submitted for modifications to omit the central bomb doors and to fix the outer flaps, thereby enabling the Mark XII

torpedo to be carried, its lower segment being only slightly proud of the under-fuselage line. Four Hampdens started

trials with the Torpedo Development Unit at Gosport in May 1942, and performance tests confirmed that with two

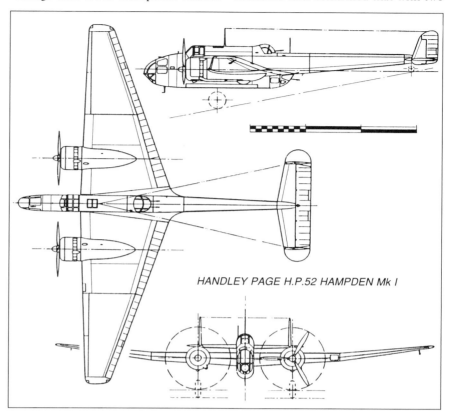

HANDLEY PAGE H.P.52 HAMPDEN Mk I

[2] During a raid on Brest no fewer than three direct hits were scored on the battleship *Gneisenau* with 2,000lb bombs but, as was so often the experience with these weapons, the fuses evidently shattered on impact and the bombs passed straight through the ship's bilges without exploding.

Type: Twin-engine, four-crew, mid-wing monoplane medium bomber and torpedo bomber.

Air Ministry Specifications: Hampden. B.9/32 (prototype) and 30/36 (production). Hereford, 44/36.

Manufacturers: Hampden. Handley Page Ltd, Cricklewood, London, and Radlett, Hertfordshire; English Electric Co Ltd, Preston, Lancashire; Canadian Association Aircraft Ltd, Quebec and Ontario. Hereford. Short & Harland Ltd, Belfast.

Powerplant: Hampden. Two 1,000hp Bristol Pegasus XVIII 9-cylinder air-cooled radial engines. Hereford. Two 1,000hp Napier Dagger VIII 16-cylinder upright H-type air-cooled in-line engines.

Construction: All-metal monocoque construction; fabric-covered control surfaces.

Dimensions: Span, 69ft 2in; length, 53ft 7in; height, 14ft 11 in; wing area, 688 sq ft.

Weights: Tare, 11,780lb; all-up, 18,576lb. (torpedo bomber, 23,500lb)

Performance: Max speed, 254 mph at 13,800ft; service ceiling, 19,000ft; range, 1,885 miles with 2,000lb bomb load, or 1,200 miles with 4,000lb bomb load. Torpedo bomber. Range, 1,960 miles with one Mk XII 18in torpedo.

Armament: Single 0.303in Vickers K gas-operated machine gun in nose, dorsal and ventral positions; dorsal position later modified with Rose mounting with twin Vickers K guns. One fixed, forward-firing Browning machine gun. Bomb load comprising eight 500lb GP or two 2,000lb AP bombs. Torpedo bomber carried one Mk XII 18in torpedo in fuselage and two 500lb GP bombs under wings.

Prototypes: One H.P.52 Hampden prototype, K4240, first flown by Maj J L B H Cordes on 21 June 1936 at Radlett. One H.P.53 prototype, L7271, first flown on 1 July 1937 (with Pegasus engines).

Production: Total production of the Hampden amounted to 1,451 aircraft. Handley Page, 500: L4032-L4211 (180) and between P1145 and P4418 (320). English Electric, 770: Between P2062 and P2145

(75), between X2893 and X3145 (150), between AD719 and AE442 (425), and between AT109 and AT260 (120). CAA, 180: Between P5298 and P5436, and between AJ988 and AN167. Short & Harland built 150 Herefords, L6002-L6101, and between N9055 and N9106. Eleven Herefords were converted to Hampdens after delivery to the RAF. One Hampden, inserted into the first production batch, between L4035 and L4036, was supplied to Sweden in September 1938, where it was designated the P.5 by the *Flygvapnet*.

Summary of Service: Hampdens served as medium bombers with the following Bomber Squadrons: No 44, from February 1939 to December 1941 at Waddington; No 49, from September 1938 to April 1942 at Scampton; No 50, from December 1938 to May 1942 at Scampton; No 61, from February 1939 to October 1942 at Hemswell; No 83, from November 1938 to January 1942 at Scampton; No 408 (Canadian), from July 1941 to September 1942 at Syerston and Balderton; No 420 (Canadian), from December 1941 to August 1942 at Waddington; and with No 455 (Australian), from July 1941 to April 1942 at Swinderby. They also served temporarily as stand-in bombers with Nos 97 (at Coningsby) and 207 Squadron (at Waddington) during July and August 1941. They served as bomber trainers with Nos 76, 106 and 185 Squadrons, the latter with Herefords as well, and with No 144 Squadron in the training, bombing and mining rôles from March 1939 at various stations, and in north Russia. Hampdens were used for weather reconnaissance by Nos 517, 519 and 521 Squadrons between August and December 1943 (formerly Nos 1404, 1406 and 1401 (Met) Flights at St Eval, Wick and Docking respectively), and in the torpedo bombing rôle by No 415 (Canadian) Squadron, and No 489 (New Zealand) Squadron, between August 1941 and November 1943. Hampdens also flew with Nos 5, 14, 16 and 25 OTUs, Nos 5 and 10 BGS, No 5 AOS, No 1 TTU, CFS, CGS, and TDU; Herefords flew with Nos 14 and 16 OTUs, No 1 AAS, No 5 AOS, No 5 BGS and CGS.

500lb bombs under the wings in addition to the torpedo, the Hampden could carry sufficient fuel for a 1,960-mile range at a take-off weight of 23,500lb. In due course Nos 144, 415 (Canadian) and 489 (New Zealand) Squadrons were equipped with the Hampden TB Mk I. No 144 Squadron took these aircraft to north Russia to cover the arrival of the North Cape convoys.

After these torpedo-carrying Hampdens had been replaced by the torpedo Beaufighter, they were given a less aggressive rôle, that of weather reconnaissance, being issued to Nos 1401, 1404 and 1406 (Met) Flights, which subsequently became Nos 517, 519 and 521 Squadrons, their purpose being to collect weather data over the Western Approaches.

A proposed version of the Hampden reached no further than prototype stage. As an insurance against failure of the supply of Pegasus engines, the choice of an alternative fell upon the Americna Wright Cyclone, and a trial installation in X3115 was followed by tests at the A & AEE, but the need never arose to put this, the Hampden Mark II, into production.

Fairey P.4/34

With the benefit of early discussions between Maj G P Bulman of the DRD, Sydney Camm of Hawker Aircraft Ltd and Reginald Mitchell of Supermarine, the Air Ministry was, in 1934, able to set out the parameters for a new light bomber intended ultimately to replace the P.27/32, which would enter service as the Fairey Battle. Three designs were tendered to the new Specification, P.4/34, which was issued on 12 November 1934, but that from Gloster (a derivative of an unsuccessful bid to P.27/32) was withdrawn at the suggestion of T O M Sopwith. The remaining two designs, from Fairey and Hawker, were accepted for prototype orders, the latter eventually being selected for production — though for a rôle very different from that originally anticipated.

Lobelle's tender to P.4/34 was broadly based on his successful Battle design, reducing the overall dimensions and improving the undercarriage by arranging it to retract inwards, thereby increasing its track substantially. The two crew members still occupied well-separated cockpits, though under a much tidier canopy. The fuselage, however, being too slender and with the wings set low, was unable to accommodate the 500lb bomb load required, which had therefore to be carried on external racks.

The first Fairey prototype, delayed on account of changes to the Merlin I engine, was flown by Staniland on 13 January 1937 but, despite being stressed for dive bombing, returned a disappointing performance little better than that of the Battle, and attracted criticism

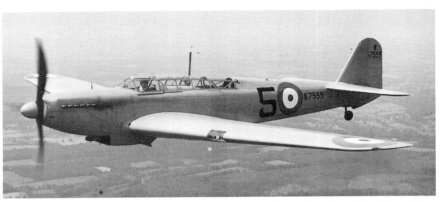

The second Fairey P.4/34, K7555, before its modifications to bring it into line with the fleet fighter Specification O.8/38. The inability to carry its bomb load internally probably compromised any chance of meeting the light bomber requirement. (Photo: The Fairey Aviation Co Ltd)

on a number of counts. These included excessively heavy rudder control and a shallow ground angle, resulting from the long fuselage and short undercarriage, which made likely the tail striking the ground first during landing.

It was, moreover, apparent that the Air Ministry had become disenchanted with the dive-bombing rôle and, although the Hawker Henley was adjudged the successful P.4/34 contender, the production contract was altered to cover target-towing duties instead.

Therefore, when Fairey learned that a new Specification, calling for a two-seat

monoplane fleet fighter, was being prepared, the second P.4/34 prototype, K7555, which had first flown on 19 April 1937, underwent a number of improvements in March 1938 (including reduction of the wing span and raising the tailplane by eight inches), and when tendered to the new Specification, O.8/38, it effectively became the aerodymanic prototype of the Fairey Fulmar fleet fighter.

The first Fairey P.4/34 was taken on charge at the RAE in May 1937, and was eventually grounded to become an instructional airframe.

Type: Single-engine, two-seat, low-wing monoplane light bomber.
Air Ministry Specification: P.4/34
Manufacturer: The Fairey Aviation Co Ltd, Hayes, Middlesex.
Powerplant: One 1,030hp Rolls-Royce Merlin I (later II) 12-cylinder liquid-cooled in-line supercharged engine.
Dimensions: Span, 47ft 4½in; length, 40ft 0in; height, 14ft 1in.
Weights: Tare, 6,405lb; all-up, 8,787lb.
Performance: Max speed, 283 mph at 15,000ft; service ceiling, 26,600ft; range, 920 miles.
Armament: Provision for one forward-firing Browning machine gun; bomb load comprised two 250lb GP bombs carried externally.
Prototypes: Two, K5099 and K7555; K5099 first flown by C S Staniland on 13 June 1937. No production.

Hawker Henley

Hawker's tender to Specification P.4/34 was in keeping with that company's policy of submitting designs closely derived from an existing project to

which the Air Ministry was already committed. In the event that its P.4/34 proposal came to be accepted for production, it was intended from the outset

The first Henley prototype, K5115, at Brooklands about the time of its first flight; just visible are the doors of the small bomb bay. The curious wheel D-doors, first fitted on the Hurricane, were shortly to be discarded as unnecessary. (Photo: Author's Collection).

that its manufacture should be undertaken at T O M Sopwith's recently acquired Gloster Aircraft factory.

Although the tendered scheme was accepted for prototype purchase, it was not until well into 1935 that design work got underway owing to preoccupation with the Hurricane. The P.4/34 in fact differed considerably from the fighter, only components of the outer wings, undercarriage and tailplane being common to both aircraft. The new dive bomber featured an entirely new fuselage with tandem cockpits, the Merlin engine's radiator moved forward to the chin position, and a deepened centre section incorporating a small bomb bay capable of enclosing two 250lb GP bombs. Because of this bay, the undercarriage imposed an entirely new wing centresection; and to cater for the deeper nose, the tail area had to be increased. Like the early production Hurricanes, the wings were fabric-covered.

The first prototype, K5115, now named the Henley, made its maiden flight with a Merlin 'F' (a pre-production Mark I) on 10 March 1937, and this was followed by a second aircraft, K7554, flown by Philip Gaddesden Lucas on 26 May 1938, the long delay being occasioned by the Air Ministry's decision to abandon the dive-bombing rôle.[1]

A production order under Specification 42/36 for 350 dive-bombers had been placed with Gloster, and preparations had gone ahead for this work. However, after a brief flying programme at Brooklands, K7554 was delivered to Hucclecote for work to begin on con-

verting this aeroplane for the humble task of towing gunnery targets. Company records show that in this form K7554 came to be known as the Henley Mark II, and therefore the production version was officially referred to as the Mark III, powered by the Merlin II.

As can be seen from the accompanying table, Henley target tugs were widely used by training units throughout the War, despite the order being reduced to 200 aircraft to make way for Hurricane production at Hucclecote.

There was even a shortlived return to the light bomber theme in 1940 when, with the threat of invasion at its most acute, a production Henley, L3276,

underwent trials at Boscombe Down as a 'last ditch' bomber, being fitted with underwing racks for two 112lb and eight 20lb Mk I bombs (the bomb bay in this aeroplane having been made redundant). The Ministry of Aircraft Production prepared a programme to withdraw 150 Henleys from the training units for bomber conversion at short notice by No 5 Maintenance Unit. Fortunately the need never arose.

Not being required for dive-bomber conversion, the first prototype, K5115, was taken over by Rolls-Royce Ltd and gave good service as an engine test bed, being flown with early versions of the Vulture and Griffon engines.

---

[1] Recent research has disclosed that a major factor influencing the Air Ministry's decision to abandon work on dive-bombers in 1937-38 stemmed from the lack of constant-speed propellers. Engine over-speeding in dives was, of course, a well-known phenomenon but, with the arrival of powerful engines in high-performance aircraft, serious damage would likely ensue, with disastrous results. The Hele-Shaw-Beacham patents were being introduced in the new Rotol constant-speed propellers, but these would not be available in numbers until 1940 — when all would be needed by Hurricanes.

Type: Single-engine, two-seat, mid-wing monoplane dive-bomber, served as target tug.
Air Ministry Specifications: P.4/34, 42/36.
Manufacturers: Prototypes. Hawker Aircraft Ltd, Kingston-upon-Thames, Surrey. Production: Gloster Aircraft Co Ltd, Hucclecote, Gloucester.
Powerplant: One 1,030hp Rolls-Royce Merlin II 12-cylinder liquid-ccoled in-line engine. Experimental test bed: 1,760hp Rolls-Royce Vulture I; 1,680hp Rolls-Royce Griffon II.
Dimensions: Span, 47ft 10½in; length, 36ft 5in; height, 14ft 7½in; wing area, 342 sq ft.
Weights: Tare, 6,010lb; all-up, 8,484lb.
Performance: As bomber. Max speed, 294 mph at 15,000ft; service ceiling, 27,200ft; range with 500lb bomb load, 940 miles.
Armament: One free-firing 0.303in Vickers gun in starboard wing and a single Lewis or Vickers K machine gun in rear cockpit. Bomb load of two 250lb bombs carried internally in fuselage, with provision to carry eight 20lb Mk I bombs externally under the outer wings.
Prototypes: Two, K5115 and K7554; K5114 first flown on 10 March 1937 by P G Lucas. K7554 first flown on 26 May 1938.
Production: A total of 200 Henleys was built by Gloster, L3243-L3442.
Summary of Service: Henleys served with the following Squadrons (usually as target tugs), Nos 264, 291, 587, 595, 631, 639 and 695, with No 1489 Flight, and Nos 1600-1628 Flights, with No 1 AACU, GRU, Nos 3, 5, 8 and 9 ATS, Nos 4, 5, 7 and 8 BGS, No 1 AAS, No 10 AOS and No 10 AGS.

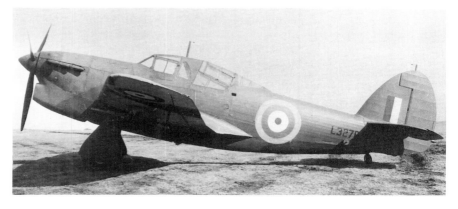

Henley L3276 undergoing trials as a light bomber at the A & AEE during the War; removal of the target winch required ballast weights to be carried aft, just visible below the serial number. (Photo: Air Ministry, A & AEE/RTP)

Blackburn Skua

During 1932 and 1933 the Air Ministry's DRD was considering scanty intelligence information emanating from the Far East that indicated the growing use by the Japanese of carrier-based attack aeroplanes. Their limited, though much trumpeted, success sowed the seeds of ambition in the mind of Admiralty for broadening the rôle of the fleet carrier — then regarded largely as a ship whose duties were almost entirely integral with those of the fleet at sea, its principal weapon being the air-launched torpedo. The aerial bomb was only carried as an alternative to the torpedo, and was wholly subordinate to that weapon.

Specification O.27/34 was therefore conceived as what, in America, came to be known as the attack bomber, an aircraft possessing a fairly high performance, capable of delivering a sizeable armour-piercing bomb, and at the same time able to defend itself against enemy naval fighters. Implicit in the requirement was a fighter-sized monoplane with folding wings, with a speed of 250 mph, and carrying an observer for oversea navigation. It was anticipated that operations against enemy ships would be by the diving attack, although there was as yet no place for this in the naval flying training syllabus.

Five design tenders were received, from Hawker, Boulton Paul, Vickers (Type 280), Avro (Type 666) and Blackburn. Only the last-named, designed by George Edward Petty as the D.B.1 (=first dive bomber design), was accepted for prototype purchase, K5178 and K5179 being ordered in April 1935.

Correspondence between the Air Ministry and Blackburn discloses an extraordinary lack of clarity as to exactly what the primary rôle of the aircraft was intended to be, an uncertainty that appeared to be resolved when, in the late summer of 1936, all reference to a fleet fighter rôle was discontinued.

Petty's design, though later regarded as entirely orthodox, was the first British shipborne cantilever monoplane, the first with multi-purpose flaps, a retractable undercarriage and a variable-pitch propeller. With its Alclad construction and skinning with flush riveting, it was, for a naval aeroplane, extremely clean aerodynamically, despite its radial engine and long cockpit enclosure with scarcely-raked windscreen. The wing folding was

An early Skua II, L2883, showing the Zap flaps in the diving position; this aircraft was one of the first to be delivered to an operational unit and served with No 803 Squadron from January 1939, joining HMS Ark Royal *on 3 April that year. It was also the first production aircraft to be delivered with the arrester hook fitted.* (Photo: via J M Bruce)

ingenious (a manual operation) in that it allowed for all four Browning machine guns to be mounted in the folding section, together with the undercarriage, when retracted, and the modified Zap flaps; the latter were provided to reduce the take-off run, steepen the landing approach and act as air brakes during diving attacks.

The first prototype was flown by 'Dasher' Blake on 9 February 1937 and delivered for preliminary assessment by the A & AEE prior to its attendance at the Hendon Display on 26 June. The name Skua was bestowed in August. It returned to Martlesham Heath for handling, performance and armament trials. In respect of the latter, the crutch-sling which threw the 500lb bomb clear when dropped in a dive was found to operate without any trouble. Only relatively minor criticisms were expressed and these were easily rectified, the aircraft being said to be simple and pleasant to fly. The second prototype featured turned-up wingtips to improve the spinning qualities, and wing slats, but the latter were not considered necessary, and were omitted from produc-

tion aircraft. The production Skua, produced to Specification 25/36, was termed the Mark II on account of its change of powerplant from the poppet-valve Mercury IX to the sleeve-valve Perseus XII, the nose of the aircraft being lengthened by about 30 inches.

The previous confusion with regard to the Skua's operational rôle appeared to be compounded when, early in 1938, the Air Ministry announced that the aircraft would replace the Nimrod and, eventually, the Sea Gladiator fleet fighters. Indeed, all four operational squadrons of the Fleet Air Arm with which the Skua served were fleet fighter units.

The first to receive the new monoplanes was No 800 Squadron (Lt-Cdr Geoffrey Napier Torry RN) at Worthy Down in October 1938, being embarked in HMS *Ark Royal* on 11 January 1939, followed by No 803 (Lt-Cdr Brian Harold Maule Kendall RN) in December 1938, also at Worthy Down.

The Skua was in action soon after the outbreak of war when aircraft of No 803 Squadron, flying from HMS *Ark Royal*, attacked the German submarine *U-30* in the North-West Approaches — two aircraft being lost in the action. On the 28th of that month, nine of this Squadron's aircraft attacked, and Lieut Bruce Straton McEwen RN shot down, a Dornier Do 18 flying boat over the North Sea, the first German aeroplane to be shot down by any British aircraft during the Second World War.

Undoubtedly the most famous success achieved by the Skua was the dive-bombing attack by 16 aircraft of Nos 800 and 803 Squadron at Bergen during the Norwegian campaign. Led by Capt Richard Thomas Partridge RM, the newly-appointed CO of No 800 Squadron, and Lieut William Paulet Lucy RN of No 803 Squadron, the aircraft took off from Hatston in the Orkneys for the 330-mile night flight across the North Sea to carry out a dawn attack on 10 April 1940 on the German light cruiser *Königsberg* lying damaged in Bergen harbour, sinking her with three direct hits with 500lb SAP bombs. Shortly afterwards the Skuas of No 800 Squadron shot down five Heinkel He 111 bombers, but in an abortive attack on the German battleship *Scharnhorst* on 6 June by aircraft of Nos 800 and 803 Squadrons, flying from HMS *Ark Royal*, eight Skuas were shot down, including that of No 800's CO, who was taken prisoner.

It was becoming all too evident that, in spite of fine achievements by Skua crews, the dive bomber was of doubtful value in the face of heavy ground and air defences — a lesson well learned by the *Luftwaffe* about two months later.

Indeed, the paradoxical attitude to the Skua's rôle with the Royal Navy had been resolved as early as the summer of 1939, with the decision to withdraw the aircraft from carrier operations as soon as the Fairey Fulmar could be brought into service as a fleet fighter. Moreover, from mid-August 1939 no operational Skua was delivered, the last fifty aircraft on order being completed as target tugs; almost all of these equipped No 2 Anti-Aircraft Co-operation Unit at Gosport, Eastchurch and Donibristle. The last Skuas in operational service with the Fleet Air Arm were withdrawn from service with No 801 Squadron in May 1941.

Skua II L2887/A7F of No 803 Squadron, flying from HMS Ark Royal *in 1939, shown carrying a 100lb anti-submarine bomb under the port wing. (Photo: RAF Museum, Neg No P002307)*

Type: Single-engine, two-seat, low-wing monoplane carrier-borne fleet fighter/dive-bomber.

Air Ministry Specifications: O.27/34 and 25/36.

Manufacturer: Blackburn Aircraft Ltd, Brough, East Yorkshire.

Powerplant: Prototypes. One 840hp Bristol Mercury IX 9-cylinder air-cooled poppet-valve radial engine. Production. One 890hp Bristol Perseus 9-cylinder air-cooled sleeve-valve radial engine.

Structure: Flush-riveted Alclad construction throughout with fabric-covered control surfaces; outwards-retracting undercarriage and folding wings.

Dimensions: Span, 46ft 2in (folded, 15ft 6in); length, 35ft 7in (first prototype, 33ft 2¼in); height, 12ft 6in; wing area, 319 sq ft.

Weights: Dive-bomber. Tare, 5,496lb; all-up, 8,228lb.

Performance: Max speed, 225 mph at 6,500ft; service ceiling, 19,100ft; range, 680 miles.

Armament: Four wing-mounted 0.303in Browning Mk II machine guns and one Lewis Mk IIIE gun in rear cockpit. Bomb load of one 500lb SAP bomb carried semi-recessed into underside of fuselage and eight light bombs on underwing racks.

Prototypes: Two, K5178 and K5179; K5178 first flown by Flt Lt A M Blake at Brough on 9 February 1937; K5179 flown on 4 May 1938.

Production: A total of 190 Skua Mk IIs was built: L2867-L3056.

Summary of Service with Fleet Air Arm: Skuas served with Nos 800 Squadron from October 1938 to April 1941; with No 801 Squadron from March 1939 to May 1941; with No 803 Squadron from December 1938 to October 1940; and with No 806 Squadron from February 1940 to July 1940. They also served in second line duties with Nos 757, 758, 759, 760, 767, 769, 770, 771, 772, 774, 776, 778, 779, 780, 782, 787, 788, 789, 791, 792, 794 and 797 Squadrons. They also served in the RAF with No 2 AACU.

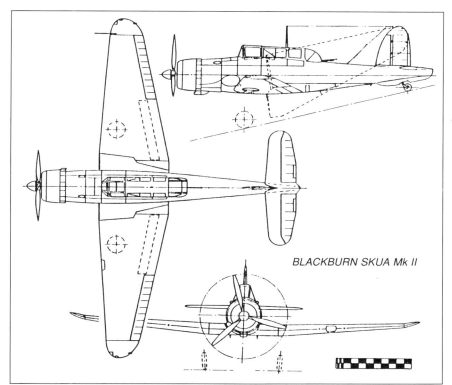

BLACKBURN SKUA Mk II

Deployment of British Bomber Squadrons — 1 January 1938

Royal Air Force
Home Bases

No 7 Sqn (H)	Handley Page	
	Heyford II/III	Finningley, Yorks
No 9 Sqn (H)	Handley Page	
	Heyford III	Scampton, Lincs
No 10 Sqn (H)	A W Whitley I	Dishforth, Yorkshire
No 12 Sqn (L)	Hawker Hind	Andover, Hants
No 15 Sqn (L)	Hawker Hind	Abingdon, Berks
No 18 Sqn (L)	Hawker Hind	Upper Heyford, Oxon
No 21 Sqn (L)	Hawker Hind	Lympne, Kent
No 34 Sqn (L)	Hawker Hind	Lympne, Kent
No 35 Sqn (M)	Vickers Wellesley	Worthy Down, Hants
No 37 Sqn (H)	Handley Page	
	Harrow II	Feltwell, Norfolk
No 38 Sqn (H)	Fairey Hendon	Marham, Norfolk
No 40 Sqn (L)	Hawker Hind	Abingdon, Berks
No 42 Sqn (TB)	Vickers	
	Vildebeest III	Donibristle, Fife
No 44 Sqn (L)	Bristol Blenheim I	Waddington, Lincs
No 49 Sqn (L)	Hawker Hind	Worthy Down, Hants
No 50 Sqn (L)	Hawker Hind	Waddington, Lincs
No 51 Sqn (H)	Vickers Virginia X	Boscombe Down, Wilts
No 52 Sqn (L)	Fairey Battle	Upwood, Hunts
No 57 Sqn (L)	Hawker Hind	Upper Heyford, Oxon
No 58 Sqn (H)	A W. Whitley II	Boscombe Down, Wilts
No 61 Sqn (L)	Bristol Blenheim[1]	Hemswell, Lincs
No 62 Sqn (L)	Hawker Hind	Cranfield, Beds
No 63 Sqn (L)	Fairey Battle	Upwood, Hunts
No 75 Sqn (H)	Handley Page	
	Harrow I/II	Driffield, Yorks
No 76 Sqn (M)	Vickers Wellesley	Finningley, Yorks
No 77 Sqn (M)	Vickers Wellesley	Honington, Suffolk
No 78 Sqn (H)	A W Whitley I	Dishforth, Yorks
No 82 Sqn (L)	Hawker Hind	Cranfield, Beds
No 83 Sqn (L)	Hawker Hind	Turnhouse, Midlothian
No 88 Sqn (L)	Fairey Battle	Boscombe Down, Wilts
No 90 Sqn (L)	Bristol Blenheim I	Bicester, Oxon
No 97 Sqn (H)	Handley Page	
	Heyford II/III	Leconfield, Yorks
No 98 Sqn (L)	Hawker Hind	Hucknall, Derbyshire
No 99 Sqn (H)	Handley Page	
	Heyford II/III	Mildenhall, Suffolk
No 101 Sqn (M)	Boulton Paul	
	Overstrand	Bicester, Oxon
No 102 Sqn (H)	Handley Page	
	Heyford II/III	Honington, Suffolk
No 103 Sqn (L)	Hawker Hind	Usworth, Co Durham
No 104 Sqn (L)	Hawker Hind	Hucknall, Derbyshire
No 105 Sqn (L)	Fairey Battle	Harwell, Berks
No 107 Sqn (L)	Hawker Hind	Harwell, Berks
No 108 Sqn (L)	Hawker Hind	Cranfield, Beds
No 110 Sqn (L)	Hawker Hind/	
	Bristol Blenheim I	Waddington, Lincs
No 113 Sqn (L)	Hawker Hind	Spittlegate, Lincs
No 114 Sqn (L)	Bristol Blenheim I	Wyton, Hunts
No 115 Sqn (H)	Handley Page	
	Harrow	Marham, Norfolk
No 139 Sqn (L)	Bristol Blenheim I	Wyton, Hunts
No 142 Sqn (L)	Hawker Hind	Andover, Hants
No 144 Sqn (L)	Bristol Blenheim I	Hemswell, Lincs
No 148 Sqn (M)	Vickers Wellesley	Scampton, Lincs

No 149 Sqn (H)	Handley Page	
	Heyford II	Mildenhall, Suffolk
No 166 Sqn (H)	Handley Page	
	Heyford III	Leconfield, Yorks
No 207 Sqn (M)	Vickers Wellesley	Worthy Down, Hants
No 211 Sqn (L)	Hawker Hind	Spittlegate, Lincs
No 214 Sqn (H)	Handley Page	
	Harrow II	Feltwell, Norfolk
No 215 Sqn (H)	Handley Page	
	Harrow II	Driffield, Yorks
No 218 Sqn (L)	Hawker Hind/	
	Fairey Battle	Upper Heyford, Oxon
No 226 Sqn (L)	Fairey Battle	Harwell, Berks

Africa and the Middle East

No 8 Sqn (L)	Vickers Vincent	Khormaksar, Aden
No 14 Sqn (L)	Fairey Gordon	Ramleh, Palestine
No 30 Sqn (L)	Bristol Blenheim I	Habbaniya, Iraq
No 33 Sqn (L)	Hawker Hart	Ismailia, Egypt
No 45 Sqn (M)	Westland Wellesley	Helwan, Egypt
No 47 Sqn (L)	Fairey Gordon	Khartoum, Sudan
No 55 Sqn (L)	Vickers Vincent	Hinaidi, Iraq
No 84 Sqn (L)	Vickers Vincent	Shaibah, Iraq
No 223 Sqn (L)	Vickers Vincent	Nairobi, Kenya

India and the Far East

No 5 Sqn (L)	Westland Wapiti IIA	Miramshah, India
No 11 Sqn (L)	Hawker Hart	Risalpur, India
No 27 Sqn (L)	Westland Wapiti IIA	Kohat, India
No 31 Sqn (L)	Westland Wapiti IIA	Drigh Road, India
No 36 Sqn (TB)	Vickers	
	Vildebeest III	Seletar, Singapore
No 39 Sqn (L)	Hawker Hart	Risalpur, India
No 60 Sqn (L)	Westland Wapiti IIA	Kohat, India

Auxiliary Air Force

No 500 Sqn (L)	Hawker Hind	Manston, Kent
No 501 Sqn (L)	Hawker Hart	Filton, Bristol
No 502 Sqn (L)	Hawker Hind	Aldergrove, Ulster
No 503 Sqn (L)	Hawker Hart	Waddington, Lincs
No 504 Sqn (L)	Hawker Hind	Hucknall, Derbyshire
No 602 Sqn (L)	Hawker Hind	Abbotsinch,
		Renfrewshire
No 603 Sqn (L)	Hawker Hart	Turnhouse, Midlothian
No 605 Sqn (L)	Hawker Hind	Castle Bromwich, Warks
No 609 Sqn (L)	Hawker Hind	Yeadon, Yorks
No 610 Sqn (L)	Hawker Hart	Hooton Park, Cheshire
No 611 Sqn (L)	Hawker Hart	Speke, Lancs

Fleet Air Arm

No 810 Sqn (TB)	Fairey Swordfish I	Gosport, Hants
No 811 Sqn (TB)	Fairey Swordfish I	Gosport, Hants
No 812 Sqn (TB)	Fairey Swordfish I	Hal Far, Malta
No 813 Sqn (TB)	Fairey Swordfish I	Kai Tak, Hong Kong
No 820 Sqn (TB)	Fairey Swordfish I	Eastleigh, Hants
No 821 Sqn (TB)	Fairey Swordfish I	Eastleigh, Hants
No 822 Sqn (TB)	Fairey Swordfish I	Gosport, Hants
No 823 Sqn (TB)	Fairey Swordfish I	Hal Far, Malta
No 824 Sqn (TB)	Fairey Swordfish I	Kai Tak, Hong Kong
No 825 Sqn (TB)	Fairey Swordfish I	Eastleigh, Hants

[1] Squadron also equipped with Hawker Audax army co-operation aircraft

6. THE BOMBER AS A DECISIVE INFLUENCE IN WAR

When Britain declared war on 3 September 1939 no one but the blindest optimist was surprised. Yet, despite all the gloomy political signals that had flashed across Europe for six years and the stupendous efforts made by her industries and armed Services, Great Britain was not wholly prepared to fight a modern, mechanised war.

The Royal Air Force had been transformed during those six years, Bomber Command in particular gaining the means to reach any part of Germany, albeit with relatively small loads of light bombs. A new generation of heavy bombers had been conceived, the like of which did not exist elsewhere in Europe[1], and much larger bombs were on the way. The largest bomb in operational use by the RAF in 1939 was the 1,000-pounder, a weapon that could be carried by the Wellington, Whitley and Hampden, although the 500lb GP bomb was more commonly carried when Bomber Command first started raiding German towns

[1] As early as 1935 Germany had embarked on the development of four-engine heavy bombers, in particular the Dornier Do 19 and Junkers Ju 90, intending that these should equip a strategic bombing force, advocated by Generals Walther Wever and Erhard Milch, the German Chief of Staff and Secretary of State for Air respectively. This force was conceived as being able to reach and attack any target in Europe from bases in Germany. With the death of Wever in 1936, the proposed strategic bombing force was abandoned, as were its intended heavy bombers (development of the Ju 90 only continuing in the transport rôle).

and cities in May 1940. Paradoxically, it was a Beaufort torpedo bomber of Coastal Command that dropped the first 2,000lb SAP 'long' bomb against a German warship off the Frisian Islands on 7 May that year.

The first of Bomber Command's four-engine heavy bombers, the Short Stirling, had flown in full-size prototype form on 14 May 1939, and the Handley Page Halifax followed suit on 25 October that year. The third of the new heavy bombers, the twin-engine Avro Manchester, had flown on 25 July 1939 and, despite being somewhat smaller than its two contemporaries, was the only one of the trio capable of carrying the next large bomb, the 4,000lb 'blockbuster', a high-capacity blast bomb dropped by

parachute; this weapon was not ready for operational use until the spring of 1941. Ironically, it was first dropped by Wellingtons, and was to be the principal blast weapon delivered by Bomber Command during the Second World War.

One other four-engine heavy bomber had been ordered before the War. Two prototypes of the Supermarine Type 317, originally conceived by the late Reginald Mitchell to Specification B.12/36, were in an advanced state of construction when they were severely damaged in a German bombing attack on the Supermarine works at Itchen on 26 September 1940. Their loss, and the advanced production of the Stirling, prompted the Air Ministry to abandon

Above: *Armourers loading a 1,000lb GP bomb on a Wellington, being checked by an armament warrant officer. Beyond, on the ground awaiting winching-up, is a pair of 500-pounders. These bombs were standard load components of the Wellington during 1940 and 1941.* (Photo: via Bruce Robertson)

Left: *A 2,000lb SAP 'long' bomb awaiting loading into a Wellington IC of No 149 Squadron at Mildenhall in 1941; Wellingtons dropped 235 of these bombs, all in 1941 and mostly against enemy ships in port. A fairly high percentage of direct hits was obtained with this bomb, but the fuse was unreliable in early operations.* (Photo: via Bruce Robertson)

Awaiting its 4,000lb HC bomb, this Lancaster III is shown with its load of Small Bomb Carriers (each containing up to 235 four-pound incendiaries. During the War Bomber Command aircraft dropped over 80 million of these small bombs, of which almost 50 million were carried by the Lancaster. (Photo: RAF Museum, Neg No P018568)

the Supermarine bomber and to concentrate on Spitfire production. (Despite sanguine expectations of the Type 317, it is unlikely that the aircraft would have achieved full production and service until at least 1943, by which time its capabilities would have been somewhat pedestrian, and scarcely better than those of the Stirling.)

Stirlings and Halifaxes reached their first squadrons during the second half of 1940 — the former at the height of the Battle of Britain. Although both of these aircraft appeared to represent a considerable potential in the build-up of bombing effort against Germany, it would be almost a year before either would make any significant contribution. Both displayed operational weaknesses, the Halifax being noticeably underpowered, and the Stirling incapable of carrying any bomb larger than the 2,000-pounder (although its maximum bomb load over

short distances — 14,000lb — was certainly impressive).

In theory, the Vulture-powered Manchester was also able to carry a 14,000lb bomb load, and with the important difference that this would include the new 4,000lb HC bomb. Unfortunately, owing to the urgency to develop and manufacture very large numbers of Rolls-Royce Merlin engines, the Vulture was starved of essential development effort during 1937-39 with the result that, when the first production Manchesters reached the RAF late in 1940, much work remained to be done to improve its reliability.

Although the Manchester went on to serve with Bomber Command for eighteen months, its manufacturers had undertaken the design of a private venture derivative, powered by four Merlins, more than a year before the War, and this design was effectively complete

before the Manchester even started trials at the A & AEE. Only when the Ministry of Aircraft Production suggested that A V Roe should switch to production of the Halifax after completion of the current batch of 200 Manchesters did the company formally submit the four-Merlin version of the Manchester as the logical alternative — pointing to the generally inferior load-carrying and performance qualities of the Halifax, as well as the ease with which the four-Merlin Manchester could be introduced into the existing production lines.

This course was adopted. The four-Merlin Avro Lancaster prototype was completed in only four months from contract, and from the outset gave promise of becoming an outstanding heavy bomber, with considerable development potential, particularly on account of its likely ability to accommodate new and heavier weapons.[2]

The saga of the Lancaster bomber was unmatched by any other British aeroplane. The speed with which it

[2]   The widely-held belief, prevalent for many years during and after the War, that the Lancaster only came into being *after* the Vulture was seen to be unreliable in service, has been shown to be wholly incorrect, stemming largely from wartime mythology. In this Author's book *The Avro Lancaster* (Aston, 1989) full documentary evidence is reproduced to indicate that the Air Ministry was fully aware of the four-Merlin Manchester's design progress a year before the War. Indeed, authority to proceed with the Lancaster prototype was given before the Manchester even reached its first squadron. Chadwick had been quick to realise that the Merlin X was unsuitable for a heavy bomber, and opted instead for the new Merlin XX — then planned for the Beaufighter night fighter. Only when it became all too obvious that the Halifax was not suitably powered (and would be re-engined with the Hercules radial) did both the MAP and Air Ministry press for the introduction of the Lancaster as quickly as possible.

A Lancaster of No 101 (Bomber) Squadron releases its 4,000lb bomb and a load of 30lb incendiaries over Duisberg on 14 October 1944. The two prominent dorsal aerial masts identify this aircraft as carrying the ECM equipment codenamed Airborne Cigar, equipment that was peculiar to No 101 Squadron. (Photo: P H T Green Collection)

achieved full production was evidence of extraordinary feats of organisation and single-minded application as hundreds of large and small (some very small) factories contributed components to a handful of main production lines. As the less muscular Whitleys and Hampdens were phased out of Bomber Command, the Lancaster arrived at a rapidly increasing rate until it equipped no fewer than 52 heavy bomber squadrons in 1945 — comprising more than 1,300 aircraft. No fewer than 7,000 of these heavy bombers were manufactured in little over four years, involving a total labour force of some 1,500,000 men and women.

It was the very adaptability of the Lancaster to accommodate special weapons, characterised by radical shape, size, weight, performance or method of delivery, that placed the aircraft in a class of its own. This all stemmed from the aeroplane's ability to carry the Capital Ship Bomb and the 8,000lb HC weapon, and there opened up an entirely new vista of bombing operations: a radical philosophy of creating special weapons for particular targets, delivered by expert crews on specially-established squadrons. Such a policy ran counter to the traditions of the RAF and gave rise initially to considerable scepticism, not least in the great bomber commander-in-chief, Sir Arthur Harris. But this early reluctance to identify and assemble the most talented and courageous crews into élite units evaporated with the successful introduction of the 8,000lb HC bomb (only capable of being delivered by the Lancaster), and the improved bombing efficiency that accompanied the creation of the Pathfinder Force, the evolution of the 'bomber stream', the improving efficiency of electronic countermeasures, radar bombing and navigation aids, and the establishment of No 100 (Bomber Support)

Group in Bomber Command.

By the end of the War Bomber Command could, at will and at short notice, launch more than one thousand four-engine heavy bombers in a single night against targets anywhere in Germany — in contrast to the specially-contrived '1,000-bomber raids' of May and June 1942, in which a high proportion of the participating aircraft were twin-engine bombers, some of them 'borrowed' from training units and Coastal Command to make up the magic total. The ultimate weapon, in terms of weight and its ability to penetrate hardened targets, was the 22,000lb Grand Slam deep penetration bomb, again carried exclusively by the Lancaster against Germany.

In other aspects of bombing aircraft, the immortal Mosquito was conceived as a reconnaissance aircraft and light bomber without gun armament, which relied entirely upon its own very high speed to escape interception, and ultimately proved able to deliver a 4,000lb HC bomb to the German capital. The aircraft, in its light bomber and fighter-bomber guises, proved almost immune from interception, and as a result Mosquito squadrons were on numerous occasions selected to make set-piece attacks on high-priority targets, such as the Amiens prison, and the Gestapo headquarters at The Hague, Aarhus, Oslo and Copenhagen. Mosquitos also played an important rôle in the Pathfinder Force, and, employing the very accurate Oboe radar, were increasingly used to mark targets for the benefit of the Main Force, often dropping their markers through thick cloud.

The climax of Bomber Command's bombing campaign was reached on 12 March 1945 when 1,107 Lancasters, Halifaxes and Mosquitos were launched against Dortmund, dropping 4,851 tons of bombs, the heaviest tonnage ever

dropped by the Command in a single day.

At sea, torpedo bombing duties were shared by the Beauforts, Beaufighters, Hampdens and Wellingtons of the RAF, and Swordfish, Albacores and Barracudas of the Fleet Air Arm, the aged Swordfish biplane topping the score of enemy shipping tonnage sunk. In 1944 the American Grumman Avenger torpedo bomber also joined the Fleet Air Arm.

In the maritime reconnaissance rôle, the Vickers Warwick — originally conceived in the mid-1930s as a heavy bomber — was just too late to give operational service, although it served with air-sea rescue squadrons from 1943 onwards. With the arrival in Bomber Command of the Halifax and Lancaster, squadrons of these aircraft were from time to time transferred to Coastal Command, 'on loan' for patrols in the Western Approaches, for convoy escort duties and search patrols over the Bay of Biscay on the look-out for German blockade runners. However, as Sir Arthur Harris strove to build up the striking power of his bomber force, the Lancasters' absence from Bomber Command was shortlived.

In conclusion, it is perhaps of interest to observe that, of a total of 31 awards of the Victoria Cross to British and Commonwealth airmen during the Second World War, 22 were made to pilots and members of British bomber crews[3], and of these, ten Crosses were won by those of Lancasters[4]; such was the measure of dominance gained by that remarkable aeroplane.

---

[3] One other VC was awarded to Sqn Ldr Leonard Henry Trent, DFC RNZAF, pilot of an American Lockheed Ventura bomber with the RAF.
[4] The Victoria Cross awarded to Wg Cdr Geoffrey Leonard Cheshire DSO, DFC, was in respect of repeated acts of gallantry while flying Whitleys and Halifaxes, as well as Lancasters.

Short Stirling

Bearing in mind the early date of its conception both in terms of the drafting of requirements and the manner in which Arthur Gouge (Shorts' chief designer, later Sir Arthur, Kt) interpreted them, the Short Stirling was one of aviation's technological pacemakers.

It was all the more remarkable because the Specification later imposed a wing span limitation of 100 feet — this being stated to be the maximum door width of current RAF hangars[1] — yet the Stirling could lift a bomb load of 14,000lb over a range of 500 miles. As with other Specifications issued early in 1936, B.12/36 reflected the British government's apprehension at the accelerating rate of German rearmament, and the Air

Ministry emphasised the need to avoid untried structures and concentrate on viceless handling qualities to facilitate

---

[1] A thorough search among design drawings of all Service hangars in use during the 1930s has disclosed none in which the door width was 100 feet. The most widely-used hangars on bomber stations of this period were the Type Cs of 152 feet overall width and a maximum door aperture of 126 feet with overlapping panels. They had almost universally replaced the Type As, which had a maximum door aperture of 88 feet.

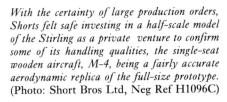

With the certainty of large production orders, Shorts felt safe investing in a half-scale model of the Stirling as a private venture to confirm some of its handling qualities, the single-seat wooden aircraft, M-4, being a fairly accurate aerodynamic replica of the full-size prototype. (Photo: Short Bros Ltd, Neg Ref H1096C)

pilot training. However, the persistent requirement for the aircraft to be able to carry 24 fully-armed troops as an alternative to its bomb load seems, to say the least, an anachronism.

Specification B.12/36 attracted eleven designs from five manufacturers, and from these the proposals from Supermarine (the Type 317) and Short were selected for prototype purchase, Gouge's intention to adapt his promising wing structure of the C-Class flying boats standing the design in good stead as its properties had already been established in tunnel tests, together with Gouge's own patented wing flaps. The DTD had been expressing concern that, with aircraft weights increasing rapidly, the ability to operate bombers out of grass airfields was becoming questionable within the accepted safety limits. Experiments were underway using catapult launching (referred to somewhat quaintly as 'frictionless take-off'), experiments which were to fascinate the RAE, if no one else, for years to come. Gouge believed that such assisted take-off was quite unnecessary when large-area flaps, such as his own, were incorporated in the aircraft's wing.

Nevertheless, Gouge felt it would be wise to confirm the handling qualities of his aircraft, particularly in the take-off and landing regimes, remembering that this was Short's first experience with a retractable undercarriage, and to confirm his forecast of the aircraft's behaviour using the large Gouge flaps. Accordingly a half-scale prototype, the Short S.31, of all-wood construction and powered by 90hp Pobjoy Niagara

seven-cylinder engines, was quickly built, and flown by John Lankester Parker on 19 September 1938. Brief handling flights were made by Martlesham pilots, who expressed the opinion that the full-size aircraft might still possess excessive take-off and landing runs, prompting Gouge to increase the on-ground attitude angle by lengthening the undercarriage, and incorporating a higher chassis in the production line — then taking shape at Rochester (an order for 100 Stirlings having already been received some months earlier).

The first full-size prototype, L7600, was flown by Parker on 13 May 1939 but, during the landing, one wheelbrake seized, slewing the aircraft violently and causing the long undercarriage to collapse, the Stirling being irreparably damaged.

An improved undercarriage design was incorporated in the second prototype, which was successfully flown on 3 December 1939 — although an engine cut on take-off. Meanwhile, a production order for a second batch of Stirlings had been placed with Short & Harland Ltd at Belfast.

First to receive the four-engine heavy bomber was No 7 (Bomber) Squadron, which re-formed at Leeming in Yorkshire on 1 August 1940 under the command of Wg Cdr (later Gp Capt) Paul Ivor Harris DFC, at the height of the Battle of Britain. Although no attempt by the *Luftwaffe* succeeded in reaching the Stirlings' new base, its factories were less fortunate, Rochester being heavily raided on 9 August, when six of the bombers were destroyed, and the Belfast

works suffering the same fate six days later, when five more were lost.

Conversion on to the Stirling was a slow task, as countless problems arose, the majority relatively small but, as one might expect with an aircraft so utterly different from the familiar and much smaller Wellingtons and Whitleys, demanding unfamiliar remedies. One of the faults discovered was that the ventral turret hydraulic retraction circuit tended to leak, thereby allowing the turret to inch down and strike the ground while the aircraft was taxiing. The unpopular turret was removed and replaced by beam guns in the short term, but both were then discarded altogether, the mid-upper turret being found adequate for beam defence.

It was not until the night of 10/11 February 1941 that No 7 Squadron flew its first operational sorties, joining a raid on oil storage tanks at Rotterdam. Only two other Squadrons converted to Stirlings during 1941, despite the fact that by the end of that year the first 200 aircraft had been delivered to the Service by the factories. It was, however, during the winter of 1941/42 that Bomber Command began expressing its frustration at the Stirling's operational limitations, caused principally by the aircraft being underpowered, pointing to the aircraft's inability to carry the 4,000lb HC bomb. The bomber had been of considerable value against short-range targets, particularly in 1941 when so many attacks were launched against German ships in French ports, notably Brest, and the 2,000lb SAP bombs carried by the Stirlings were thought to have caused worthwhile damage, if not to the ships then to the dock facilities. When, however, the Stirlings were ordered off against more distant targets, such as the German capital and the north Italian ports and cities, the big aircraft was limited to just seven 500lb bombs and, when flying

The first, short-lived, full-size Stirling prototype, L7600, photographed before its first — and last — flight on 14 May 1939. Dorsal and ventral gun turrets were not fitted. (Photo: Short Bros Ltd.)

N3641/MG-D was one of the first Stirling Is to be delivered to No 7 (Bomber) Squadron at Leeming in August 1940; the small protrusion beneath the fuselage (below the code letter M) indicates the position of the retracted ventral gun turret. As far as is known, this aeroplane never flew an operational sortie, being passed on to Nos 1607 and 1651 Conversion Flights early in 1941. (Photo: Air Ministry)

to Italy, the fuel load was so great that the Stirling Mark I could scarcely climb over the Alps.

It was following an attack by Stirlings of No 149 (Bomber) Squadron on the Fiat works at Turin in November 1942 that an Australian pilot, F/Sgt Rawdon Hume Middleton, captain of BF372, won the Victoria Cross for his selfless courage. Stricken with wounds and blinded in one eye when his aircraft was repeatedly hit by flak over the distant target, Middleton and his second pilot managed to coax the Stirling back over the Alps but, as they approached the English coast, Middleton realised that only five minutes' fuel remained. He insisted on staying at the controls long enough to enable his crew to bale out safely, and five members escaped before the bomber crashed. Middleton and two others, who remained behind to assist him, were killed. The pilot was awarded the Victoria Cross posthumously.

By coincidence, it was during another raid on Turin on 12 August 1943 that the Stirling's other Victoria Cross, also posthumous, was won, this time by a F/Sgt of No 218 Squadron, Arthur Louis Aaron, DFM. His aircraft was severely damaged by a night fighter over Italy, three engines being hit, and one of them put out of action. The navigator was killed and Aaron was struck by a bullet

which shattered his jaw and tore away part of his face; he was also hit in the lung and in one arm. Rather than attempt the return across the Alps Aaron, using signs, urged the bomb aimer to take control and set course for North Africa. With notes, scribbled with his uninjured hand, Aaron assisted the bomb aimer to fly the crippled Stirling across the Mediterranean and, five hours later, the airfield at Bone was sighted. After the crew had had to restrain the wounded pilot from attempting to regain his place in the cockpit, the bomb aimer succeeded in making a safe, wheels-up landing. Nine hours later Aaron died of his wounds.

The introduction into squadron service of the Stirling III early in 1943 went some way towards appeasing the aircraft's critics, the small additional power increment sufficing to increase the normal bombing altitude to around 14,000 feet — still somewhat below that of the Halifax and Lancaster, a handicap that imposed a need to structure each bomber stream very carefully if the Stirlings were not to attract enemy fighters on account of their prominence.

A measure of this vulnerability may be judged by the fact that, of the first 84

Stirling IIIs delivered to sqaudrons between February and May 1943, no fewer than 54 had been shot down during bombing operations within five months of arrival in service, and a further 13 had been lost in crashes resulting from combat damage. Such a sustained rate of attrition, involving a single type of aircraft, was unprecedented in Bomber Command's order of battle, representing a loss of 416 men on nine squadrons. Such a rate, relating to all of the Command's heavy bombers, would however become commonplace during the Battle of Berlin during the winter of 1943-44, as the German night defences got the measure of the British bombing tactics.

The reality of the situation was that the Stirling, on account of its long, narrow fuselage bomb bay (and its small wing bomb cells) was unable to carry a bomb load that made its inclusion in the bomber stream worthwhile, a criticism that was, to a lesser extent, being levelled at the Halifax as the Lancaster came to dominate the order of battle. The latter was able to carry twice the Stirling's bomb load over any but the shortest distances, and was at least 40 mph faster at an operating altitude about

A late-standard Stirling I Series III, R9302/ LS-Z of No 15 (Bomber) Squadron, at West Freugh in 1942. This aircraft survived a number of operational sorties, and was passed on to Conversion Units. It was finally written off on 14 January 1945, the day the order was issued to prepare all surviving Stirling bombers for scrapping. (Photo: via R M Burrows)

4,000 feet higher; and it could carry a wide mix of blast, penetration, demolition and incendiary weapons.

In 1943, therefore, the Stirling squadrons began to assume an increasing share of other duties, removed from the Main Force. The pioneer Stirling Squadron, No 7, had been one of the first to fly with No 8 Group, Air Vice-Marshal Donald Bennett's Pathfinder Force, which came into being in August 1942, but, handicapped by poor performance, its Stirlings were replaced by Lancasters in July 1943.

Increasingly, Stirlings were employed in minelaying (the long, slender sea mines being suited to the aircraft's bomb bay), a task hitherto undertaken as an initiation operation by freshmen crews prior to their embarking on bombing raids. No 199 Squadron were given Stirlings in July 1943, their crews tasked with the increasingly important rôle of electronic countermeasures, a rôle that did not necessarily require flying within the bomber stream.

With the approaching Allied invasion of Europe, a new version of the Stirling, the Mark IV, tailored to the requirements of the airborne forces squadrons, appeared during the summer of 1943 with the first flights of the prototypes,

EF506 (a glider tug) and LJ512 (a paratroop transport). In due course the Mark IV served with eleven squadrons in the airborne assault rôles during and after the Normandy landings of June 1944, towing the Horsa and Hamilcar heavy assault gliders and dropping para-

troops and their supplies as Allied forces advanced through Europe during the last nine months of the War.

The Stirling's last bombing operation was flown by No 149 Squadron against Le Havre on 8 September 1944, characteristically a very short range raid that

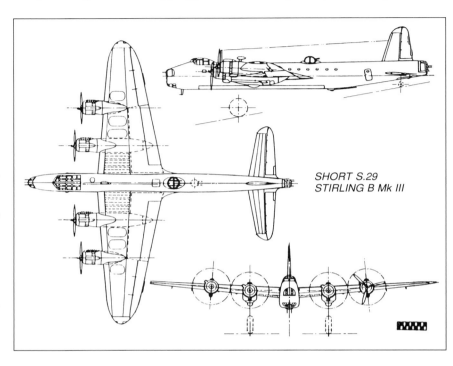

SHORT S.29
STIRLING B Mk III

Type: Four-engine, seven/eight-crew, mid-wing monoplane heavy bomber.

Air Ministry Specifications: B.12/36 (C.18/43 for commercial derivative)

Manufacturers: Short Bros Ltd, Rochester, Kent; Short & Harland Ltd, Belfast; Austin Motors Ltd, Longbridge, Birmingham.

Powerplant: Prototypes. Half-size, four 90/115hp Pobjoy Niagara III/IV 7-cylinder air-cooled radial engines; full-size, four 1,400hp Bristol Hercules II 14-cylinder air-cooled sleeve-valve radial engines. Mk I Series III. 1,590hp Hercules XI. Mk III. 1,650hp Hercules XVI.

Structure: Four-section fuselage of bolted-up frames and continuous stringers, light-alloy sheet-clad with flush riveting. Two-spar wings with lattice-braced ribs providing cells for fuel tanks within the spar-trusses, with flush-riveted light-alloy covering. Gouge-type trailing-edge flaps.

Dimensions: Span, 99ft 1in; length, 87ft 3in; height, 22ft 9in; wing area, 1,460 sq ft.

Weights: Mk III. Tare, 43,200lb; all-up, maximum, 70,000lb.

Performance: Mk III. Max speed, 270 mph at 14,500ft; range, 2,010 miles with 3,500lb bomb load, 590 miles with 14,000lb bomb load.

Armament: Mk III. Nose FN.5 turret with twin 0.303in Browning machine guns, dorsal FN.50 turret with twin Browning guns, and rear FN.20A turret with four Browning guns. Max bomb load, 14,000lb, comprising seven 2,000lb SAP bombs in the fuselage bay; alternatively, twenty-one 500lb bombs in fuselage bay and six 500lb bombs in wing cells.

Prototypes: Half-size prototype (M-4) first flown by J L Parker at Rochester on 19 September 1938. Two full-size bomber prototypes, L7600 and L7605; L7600 first flown by Parker on 14 May 1939 (but crashed); L7606 first flown, 3 December 1939.

Production: Excluding the above prototypes, a total of 2,369

Stirlings was built. Short Bros, 436: Mk Is, 250 (100 between N3635 and N3769, but N3645 and N3647-N3651 destroyed in enemy raid, and replaced by DJ972-DJ977; 100 between R9141 and R9290, and 50 between EF327 and EF400); Mk IIIs, 186 (174 between LJ440 and LJ670, and 12, PW255-PW266). Short & Harland, 1,313: Mk Is, 266 (100 between N6000 and N6129, but N6025 and N6025-N6028 destroyed in enemy raid, and not replaced; 50 between R9295 and R9358; and 116 between BF309 and BF454); Mk IIIs, 444 (84 between BF455 and BF580, and 360 between EE871 and EF323 and between EF401 and EF518); Mk IVs, 443 (360 between LJ810 and LK370; 13, PK225-PK237; and 70 between PW384 and PW464); Mk Vs, 160 between PJ878 and PK186. Austin, 620: Mk Is, 191 (150 between W7426 and W7639, and 41 between BK592 and BK647); Mk IIIs, 429 (109 between BK648 and BK818, 120 between EH875 and EJ127, and 200 between LK375 and LK624, of which 34 were converted to Mk IVs).

Summary of Service: Stirling Is and IIIs served with the following Bomber Squadrons: No 7 from August 1940 to July 1943, No 15 from April 1941 to december 1943, No 75 from October 1942 to April 1944, No 90 from December 1942 to June 1944, No 149 from November 1941 to September 1944, No 214 from April 1942 to January 1944, No 218 from January 1942 to August 1944, Nos 622 and 623 both from August 1943 to December 1943. They served with No 161 Squadron on Special Duties from September 1944 until June 1945 at Tempsford, with No 171 from September 1944 to January 1945 and No 199 from July 1943 to March 1945 in the ECM and Bomber Support rôles, and with Nos 196 from July 1943 to February 1944, and No 620 between June and November 1943 in airborne forces (support) rôles. Stirlings flew with No 513 Squadron at Chedburgh during October and November 1943, but did not become operational. They also served with Nos 1651, 1653, 1657, 1659, 1660 and 1665 Conversion Units, No 1521 BATF, BDU, NTU(PFF), and the TFU.

encountered no enemy fighter opposition and did not involve launching a bomber stream.

The big bomber never attracted much popularity among its crews, being regarded as the most vulnerable of Bomber Command's four-engine wartime bomber trio. It represented something of an operational millstone for Sir Arthur Harris when he inherited the Command's leadership in 1942, being the product — in many respects imaginative and far-sighted — of tactical thought more than half a decade before the great air assault on Germany began. But then, who could have conceived in 1936 that there would ever come a time when the Royal Air Force would be called upon to launch a thousand heavy bombers simultaneously against a German city? That the Stirling was not perfectly equipped to participate in such an attack was the measure of an age unaware that *la guerre totale* was at hand.

Bristol Type 152 Beaufort

Although the Vickers Vildebeest biplane torpedo bomber had only reached the RAF in 1933, the urgency to modernise the Service's front-line aircraft spurred the Air Staff to issue Specification M.15/35, setting out the requirements for a high-performance twin-engine monoplane capable of carrying an 18in torpedo internally, and possessing a maximum speed of 260 mph at 5,000ft and a range of not less than 1,200 miles; a crew of four was mandatory. A parallel requirement, set out in Specification G.24/35, called for a general reconnaissance bomber, and Bristol proposed a version of the Blenheim, later to be named the Bolingbroke, but this reached no further than the prototype stage, although the name was perpetuated in the Canadian-built Blenheims.

Frank Barnwell, who first studied Specification M.15/35 in September 1935, believed that, with no more than local modifications, an aircraft also based largely on his Type 142M Blenheim could meet the requirements, and submitted his Type 150 project design to the Air Ministry two months later. This retained the Blenheim's principal airframe structure, simply moving the pilot's cockpit forward by about four feet and the midships turret slightly aft to compensate for increased forward weight. By discarding the navigator's

An early view of the Beaufort prototype, L4441, at Filton, showing the original curved transparent front panels. The aircraft first flew with apron-type wheel doors, but after modification of the engine nacelles these were replaced by side-folding doors, not yet shown fitted in this photograph. (Photo: The Bristol Aeroplane Co Ltd, Neg No T152/35.)

station it proved possible to accommodate the torpedo, fully enclosed on the aircraft's centre of gravity. Bristol Perseus VI engines of 900hp were specified, these being considered adequate to meet the performance demanded.

The Air Ministry justifiably, however, refused to countenance the absence of a navigator, bearing in mind the long range demanded of the aircraft. When it was shown that to accommodate both torpedo and navigation station amidships would require an altogether larger fuselage, assuming the former to be above the wing carry-through structure and the latter below, the Air Ministry accepted that the torpedo could be partly exposed.

By raising the pilot's cockpit and placing the navigator immediately behind him, both crew members would still possess good fields of view; the upper decking of the fuselage was therefore raised between the pilot's cockpit and the dorsal turret to provide a much deeper centre section.

Despite this larger fuselage, the extra crew station and stronger weapon beams in the torpedo bay, the tare weight was kept fairly close to that of the Blenheim by increased use of light alloy in the airframe structure, replacing most of the former high-tensile steel components. Nevertheless, it was decided that Perseus engines would be inadequate, and the Air Ministry sanctioned a change to the new Taurus, also a sleeve-valve engine — even though it had yet to achieve production status and certification.

Without ordering a prototype, the Air Ministry in 1936 accepted the revised tender, the Type 152, issued a production Specification, 10/36, and placed a production order for 78 aircraft, the name Beaufort being selected in December. It was intended that Bristol's home factory at Filton should begin building the new torpedo bomber as soon as the Blenheim could be transferred to the new 'shadow' factories.

An early Beaufort I, L9878/MW-R of No 217 (Torpedo Bomber) Squadron. (Photo: via R C Sturtivant)

Scarcely anything is known of this Beaufort variant, L4456, modified as an experimental transport, shown here at Boscombe Down. It did not survive beyond the prototype stage. (Photo: Air Ministry, A & AEE, Neg No 842C)

In the event, the absence of a prototype almost certainly proved a mistake for, apart from slowing the initial production — owing to the need to incorporate numerous modifications in early aircraft already taking shape — it tended to foster an attitude of improvisation and compromise. Added to this, the Taurus proved to be yet another of those engines that suffered the penalties of abbreviated development in the late 1930s simply because airframe production was running ahead of engine availability.

The first aircraft, L4441, which made its maiden flight on 15 October 1938[1], therefore had to take the place of a conventional prototype while the following aircraft on the line awaited the Service's acceptance that the Beaufort did indeed meet its requirements.

By the time L4441 was flown to Martlesham Heath concern centred more on the Taurus engines than on the aircraft's performance and handling. The stalling speed in the landing configuration, at 70 mph, was higher than the pilots were used to, but it was the Taurus' dangerously high cylinder temperatures that confirmed Bristol's intention to substitute Taurus VIs in the production line.

The first unit to be selected to recieve Beauforts was No 22 (Torpedo Bomber) Squadron of No 16 Group, Coastal Command, commanded by Wg Cdr Francis Percival Don OBE at Thorney Island, and L4441 was delivered to this Squadron in November 1939 to enable pilots to gain some experience and give their comments on the aircraft before the first true production aeroplanes arrived two months later. Among the criticisms levelled at the Beaufort was the dislike of the curved transparent panels in the bomb aimer's station, and these were replaced by optically flat panels in the seventh and subsequent aircraft.

No 22 Squadron was tasked with introducing the Beaufort into service, being required to report on the best engine handling procedures as a result of experience during operational sorties. This proved to be an exceptionally hazardous undertaking and merely served to confirm that the Taurus was far from ready for operational use. When, in May 1940, the Squadron was ordered to commence minelaying off the Dutch coast, flying from North Coates, no fewer than five aircraft were lost though engine failure, and four others to enemy fighters. The loss of the commanding officer, who died in a crash while returning from a mining sortie, established that, owing to a fault in an hydraulic relief valve, the engines' sleeves were locking-up. After three further failures all of No 22 Squadron's early Beauforts were grounded pending modifications to their engines. It is believed that, on 7 May, a No 22 Squadron Beaufort was the first RAF aircraft to drop the new 2,000lb SAP bomb, attacking an enemy cruiser anchored off Norderney. The bomb missed, and the identity of the pilot is not known.

In the meantime, No 42 (Torpedo Bomber) Squadron had received Taurus XII-powered Beauforts in April. Nine aircraft of this Squadron attacked the German battleship *Scharnhorst* with bombs as she sailed south in the North Sea, but without scoring any hits and losing three of their number to the warship's heavy flak defences. Fleet Air

---

Type: Twin-engine, four-crew, mid-wing bomber and torpedo bomber monoplane.

Air Ministry Specifications: M.15/35, G.24/35 and 10/36

Manufacturers: The Bristol Aeroplane Co Ltd, Filton, Bristol, and Banwell, Somerset. Beaufort Division, DAP, Mascot, New South Wales, and Fishermen's Bend, Victoria, Australia.

Powerplant: Mark I. Two 1,130hp Bristol Taurus VI, XII or XVI 14-cylinder air-cooled sleeve-valve radial engines. Mark II. Pratt & Whitney Twin Wasp S3C4G radial engines. Australian-built Marks V, VI, VII, VIII and IX. Twin Wasp S3C4G and S1C3G.

Structure: All-metal construction, as in Blenheim I and IV, but employing light-alloy forgings and extrusions in place of high-tensile steel plates and angles.

Dimensions: Span, 57ft 10in; length, 44ft 3in; height, 12ft 5in; wing area, 503 sq ft.

Weights: Mark I. Tare, 13,100lb; all-up, 21,230lb.

Performance: Mark I. Max speed, 260 mph at 5,000ft; service ceiling, 16,500ft; range, 1,600 miles.

Armament: Standard armament of two 0.303in Vickers K machine guns in nose, and two in midships dorsal turret; some aircraft armed with one rearwards-firing machine gun in fairing under nose, and single beam machine guns. Bomb load of up to 1,500lb (exceptionally, one 2,000lb SAP bomb), one 1,500lb sea mine, or one 1,605lb 18in torpedo.

Prototype: One, L4441 (first production aircraft), first flown on 15 October 1938.

Production: Total Beaufort production amounted to 2,130 aircraft, including 1,430 by Bristol and 700 in Australia. Bristol, Mark Is, 1,015: L4441-L4518 (78), between L9790 and N1186 (272), between W6467 and W6543 (66), X8916-X8939 (24), between AW187 and AW243 (45), between DD945 and DE126 (60), between DW802 and DX157 (200), between EK969 and EL141 (50), between JM431 and JM593, and between LR885 and LS128 (109); Mark II torpedo bombers, 166: Between AW244 and AW384 (105), between DD870 and DD944 (60), and LS129 (1); Mark II Trainers, 249: LS130-LS149 (20), and between ML430 and ML722 (229).

Summary of Service: Beauforts served with the following Torpedo Bomber Squadrons: No 22 from January 1940 to June 1944 (in the UK until February 1942, then in Ceylon); No 39 from August 1941 to June 1943 (in the Mediterranean); No 42 from April 1940 to February 1943 (in the UK until June 1942, then in India and Ceylon); No 47 from July 1942 to June 1943 (in the Mediterranean); No 48 from May until November 1940 (in the UK); No 86 from June 1941 to July 1942 in the UK; and with No 217 from May 1940 until August 1944 (in the UK until May 1942, then in Ceylon). Beauforts also served with Nos 2, 3, 5, 9, 51, 54 and 132 OTUs, Nos 1, 301 and 302 FTUs, Nos 1 and 2 TTU, No 1 OADU, No 5 METS, TDU, TFU and CCDU. They also served with Nos 728, 733, 762, 788 and 798 Squadrons of the Fleet Air Arm.

---

[1] Less than three months earlier, Capt Frank Barnwell had been killed in a flying accident.

Arm Swordfish torpedo aircraft were no more successful.

As Bristol struggled to rectify the various faults in the Taurus, the Squadrons were constantly handicapped by temporary grounding orders or with the necessity to return their aircraft to Filton. On 25 September three of No 22 Squadron's aircraft were among five Beauforts destroyed in a German raid on the Bristol works.

Two other Squadrons, Nos 217 and 48, were issued with Beauforts in mid-1940, and conversion to the new aircraft was severely hampered by flying restrictions imposed during modifications to their engines. As a result of the limitations being placed on the RAF's principal torpedo bomber (remembering that Britain was facing the likelihood of an invasion across the Channel), Bristol was instructed to commence converting a fairly large proportion of aircraft on the production line to include dual controls and, as these aircraft were completed they began distribution among the squadrons and operational training units as a means of affording new pilots training in engine handling under supervision.

It was a No 22 Squadron Beaufort, captained by Fg Off Kenneth Campbell RAFVR, that scored a vital torpedo hit on the battleship *Gneisenau*, anchored in Brest harbour on 6 April 1941. Of four pilots despatched, Campbell was the only one to spot the enemy warship, and dived to low level amidst a veritable storm of flak to release his torpedo seconds before his Beaufort was blown to pieces. The *Gneisenau* was hurriedly moved into dry dock where, on the night of 10th/11th, she was hit by three 2,000lb bombs which, although they did not explode, prevented her from sailing for almost a year. Campbell was awarded a posthumous Victoria Cross.

Frustrated by the apparently insoluble problems of the Taurus engine, the Air Ministry opted to purchase American Pratt & Whitney Twin Wasp engines for the Beaufort Mark II, and these began delivery to No 217 Squadron in December 1941. By then, however, the Taurus XVI, being fitted in the Beaufort I, was proving to be reliable, and the aircraft were beginning to achieve notable successes, particularly in the Channel, so much so that the Germans were forced to provide greatly strengthened defences for their coastal shipping, both by the use of flak ships and of fighters, and in this combat environment the Beaufort was seen to lack adequate speed and manoeuvrability to penetrate such defences successfully. With the introduction of the torpedo-carrying Beaufighter, the home-based Beaufort Squadrons, Nos 22, 42 and 217, were redeployed to Ceylon for operations against the Japanese. Two other Squadrons, Nos 39 and 47, flew Beauforts in the Mediterranean with considerable success.

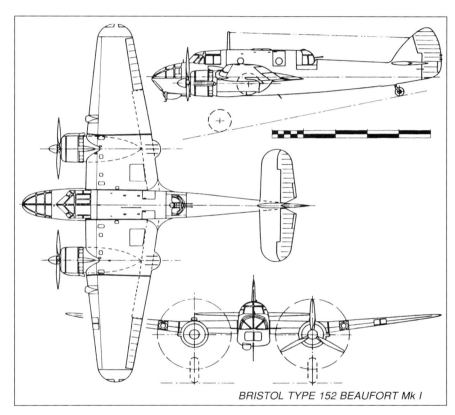

BRISTOL TYPE 152 BEAUFORT Mk I

Blackburn Botha

With its reputation for having produced torpedo bombers for the Services for more than fifteen years, it was no surprise that Blackburn tendered a design to Specification M.15/35 in competition with the Bristol Type 152 Beaufort. And like the Beaufort, the Blackburn B-26 was ordered into production 'off the drawing board' and without recourse to a prototype.

It was, however, to be a high-wing monoplane, powered by Bristol Perseus X engines, attempts to obtain the Taurus having failed. In the event this was fortunate, as the Blackburn aircraft, whatever other problems it faced later,

The first Botha, L6104, at Martlesham. Just visible is the inset elevator originally fitted, soon to be replaced. (Photo: RAF Museum, Neg No P006162)

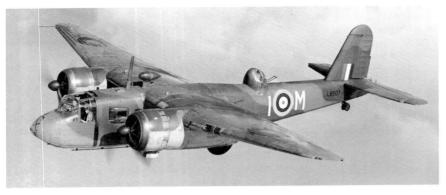

A Dumbarton-built Botha, L6507, of No 3 School of General Reconnaissance, stationed at Squire's Gate. The navigator's bulged side window was necessary as the engine nacelles almost completely obscured his field of view. This aircraft was one of many Bothas scrapped in July 1943 when the aircraft was declared obsolete. (Photo: Flight, Neg No 18136S)

escaped all the trials and tribulations experienced by the Beaufort with its engines. Nevertheless, as the aircraft's weight inexorably increased during its design stage, the Perseus was seen as likely to produce inadequate power. A proposed Botha Mark II, powered by the big Bristol Hercules engines, was not accepted by the Air Ministry as these were all scheduled for the Bristol Beaufighter.

The first Botha, L6104, was flown on 28 December 1938 at Brough by Flt Lt Henry Bailey RAFO, who had been appointed Blackburn's chief test pilot after the death of 'Dasher' Blake the previous year. As originally flown (and assessed at Martlesham Heath in 1939), L6104 was severely criticised on numerous counts, the most serious being a lack of longitudinal control and stability, a fault that was only partially cured by increasing the tailplane area and introducing large elevator horn balances. The Botha's stalling speed was even higher than that of the Beaufort (at 82 mph with wheels and flaps down), petrol and exhaust fumes were found to enter the cockpit, and rotating the midships turret caused rudder buffet.[1]

By the time the A & AEE's highly critical report on L6104 was rendered to the Air Ministry, the Botha was already in production, with an order for 242 aircraft in hand at Brough and a new Blackburn factory at Dumbarton about to come on stream.

The first production Bothas were de-

livered to No 1 OTU at Silloth in May 1940 and the following month to No 608 (North Riding) Squadron at Thornaby, the Anson pilots of the latter being sent to the OTU for a Botha conversion course.

No 608 Squadron remained the only operational unit to fly the Botha, and this solely on account of the desperate urgency to patrol Britain's coasts during that fateful first year of the War. North Sea patrols by the Squadron began on 10 August 1940 and continued only until 6 November, during which time 309 uneventful sorties were flown by the 32 aircraft delivered to the Squadron, two aircraft being lost in accidents.

Elsewhere the Botha suffered heavily. Of the 478 aircraft flown by training units between May 1940 and July 1943 no fewer than 169 were written off as the result of accidents, including 24 aircraft

ditched in the sea following engine failure.

The aeroplane was thoroughly disliked, principally on account of the lack of power, even after the introduction of the slightly more powerful Perseus XA engines. Minor modifications were made, such as improved side windows for the navigator, the introduction of a jettisonable main entrance door, and an improved undercarriage up-lock mechanism. There is no record of Bothas ever carrying torpedoes in service, the normal load carried by No 608 Squadron during patrols comprising either 100lb AS or 250lb GP bombs.

After withdrawal of the aircraft from No 608 Squadron, the Botha's wartime rôle was confined to training, apart from a small number used for communications duties with No 24 Squadron, and Nos 301 and 304 (Polish) Squadrons. Many aircraft never even left storage at the Maintenance Units before being scrapped in 1943.

---

[1] Almost every British aircraft which introduced power-operated gun turrets in the nose, dorsal and tail positions during the period 1937-40, particularly the F.N.7 dorsal turret which featured in the Botha, Stirling, Manchester and Sunderland, suffered airflow turbulence and aircraft yawing when the turrets were rotated. This was a phenomenon which should surely have been anticipated by designers and aerodynamicists, bearing in mind that most turrets were of asymmetric profile, or were asymmetric to the line of flight when rotated.

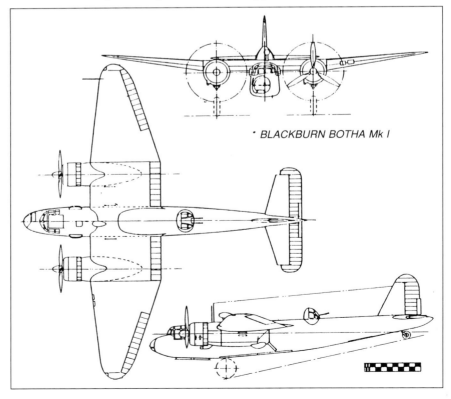

BLACKBURN BOTHA Mk I

Type: Twin-engine, four-crew, high-wing monoplane general reconnaissance aircraft and torpedo bomber.

Air Ministry Specifications: M.15/35 and 10/36.

Manufacturer: The Blackburn Aircraft Co Ltd, Brough, East Yorkshire, and Dumbarton, Dunbartonshire.

Powerplant: Two 880hp Bristol Perseus X (or 930hp Perseus XA) 14-cylinder air-cooled, sleeve-valve radial engines.

Structure: Alclad stressed-skin construction, with fabric-covered control surfaces.

Dimensions: Span, 59ft 0in; length, 51ft 0in; height, 14ft 7½in; wing area, 518 sq ft.

Weights: (Perseus XA) Tare, 12,036lb; all-up, 18,450lb.

Performance: (Perseus XA). Max speed, 220 mph at 15,000ft; service ceiling, 18,400ft; range, 1,270 miles.

Armament: One fixed forward-firing 0.303in Vickers Mk V machine gun and two Lewis Mk III guns in power-operated dorsal turret. Bomb load of up to 2,000lb of bombs, or one Mk XII or Mk XIV 18in torpedo.

Prototype: None; first aircraft, L6104, flown by Flt Lt H Bailey RAFO, on 28 December 1938.

Production: A total of 580 Bothas was built (including L6104 above). Blackburn, Brough, 380: L6104-L6345 (242) and between W5017 and W5169 (138); Blackburn, Dumbarton, 200: L6347-L6546.

Summary of Service: Bothas served with No 608 (North Riding) Squadron, AAF, at Thornaby from May until November 1940. They also flew with No 1 OTU, No 3 SGR, Nos 2 and 8 BGS, No 3 AONS, Nos 2,4 and 10 AOS, Nos 3, 4 and 8 AGS, Nos 3 and 6 PAFU, No 3 RDFS, and with No 770 Squadron of the Fleet Air Arm.

Fairey Albacore

At a time when it was becoming increasingly obvious that the biplane's life as a combat aeroplane was drawing to a close, the Air Ministry had, in 1936, committed itself to replacing the land-based Vildebeest torpedo bomber with a twin-engine monoplane, although whether this would be the Bristol Beaufort or Blackburn Botha, or both, remained to be decided. Whether a replacement for the Fairey Swordfish (which only reached its first Fleet Air Arm squadron in July that year) would be a biplane or monoplane would become clear from tenders to Specification S.41/36, which left the choice to the aircraft designer.

The Fairey Aviation Company tendered both biplane and monoplane designs, but neither manufacturer nor Service were yet confident that it was realistic to operate a carrier-based monoplane which would, by the nature of its load and required performance, possess a high wing loading, especially as the Fairey monoplane design was expected to have a landing speed of some 72 mph with wheels and flaps down. The biplane design was therefore selected and a contract for 100 aircraft, named Albacore, was placed in May 1937.

The aircraft was effectively little more than a 'modernised' Swordfish with true single-bay wings which folded on a hinge-line almost flush with the fuselage side. The crew was now fully enclosed by a long, transparent canopy, the pilot being located forward of the upper wing. The fixed undercarriage had been tidied up, its long-stroke oleo strut being faired to aerofoil section, two small bracing struts sufficing to provide the necessary

The second Albacore prototype, L7075, fitted with wheel spats as a trial installation; they were not adopted. The wing flaps/airbrakes are shown partly lowered, and the object on the rear fuselage decking is a test parachute for spinning trials. (Photo: The Fairey Aviation Co Ltd)

stability — although the aircraft later acquired a reputation for a somewhat soggy feel during taxying. Power was to be provided by the Taurus sleeve-valve radial engine, expected to develop more than 1,000hp. Hydraulically-operated flaps on the lower wings would be used both for landing and as airbrakes during diving attacks. Cosmetic efforts were made to improve the crew's comfort and efficiency, including cabin heating and a screen wiper for the pilot.

The first Albacore, L7074, was flown by Fg Off Foster Hickman Dixon RAFO on 12 December 1938 and was received favourably during a brief assessment at Martlesham Heath in May 1939, though the rudder control was mentioned as being too heavy. When, however, an early production aircraft underwent more searching handling trials, an entirely different verdict was expressed; although the rudder control had been improved by mass balancing, the ailerons and elevator were now said to be heavy and sluggish; the pilot's cockpit was found to be much too hot for comfort, while the rear cockpit was very draughty. The only real improvement over the Swordfish was stated to be the excellent field of view for the pilot.

Although it was not intended that the Albacore should operate with floats, L7074 underwent trials as a seaplane, but was not found to be satisfactory.

Despite the A & AEE's criticisms, this intended Swordfish replacement reached its first operational Fleet Air Arm Squadron, No 826, which was formed at Ford on 15 March 1940. Against a background of persistent engine cooling problems with the Taurus II, this Squadron first went into action during the Dunkirk evacuation, led by its third commanding officer in two months, Lt-Cdr Wilfrid Henry Saunt DSC, RN, attacking E-boats off Zeebrugge and road and rail targets behind the advancing German forces in Belgium. Their bomb loads were usually six 250lb bombs on each aircraft.

In June the second Albacore Squadron, No 829, was also formed at Ford under Lt-Cdr Owen Sandbach Stevinson RN, this unit taking part in bombing attacks on Brest in October (losing its CO on the 9th).

These two Squadrons embarked in

Left: *Albacore L7075 in production configuration with wheel spats removed. Under the wings can be seen six racks for 250lb bombs, and, just visible, the crutches for a torpedo. The field of view from the pilot's cockpit can well be appreciated.* (Photo: A J Jackson Collection)

Below: *Albacore T9132/4L of No 826 Squadron carrying a torpedo, possibly at Mersa Matruh, Egypt, in 1941. These aircraft, flying from strips in the Western Desert, were frequently flown against coastal shipping bringing supplies to the enemy's forward ports.* (Photo: via R C Sturtivant)

HMS *Formidable* on 15 November to escort a convoy to Egypt, via Cape Town, thereby beginning a year of strenuous operations against the Italians which included participation in the Battle of Matapan late in March 1941. Although an Albacore of No 829 Squadron obtained a torpedo hit on the battleship *Vittorio Veneto*, it was to lose another CO, this time Lt-Cdr John Dalyell-Stead RN being shot down and killed.

Although troubles with the Taurus engine had been overcome by early 1941, at least to the point at which the failure rate was no worse than that of the Pegasus in the Swordfish, the Albacore was still regarded as inferior to the earlier aircraft, principally on account of its lack of agility, as much in its deck operation as in a torpedo attack. The controls, never significantly improved despite the early trials reports, were too heavy to enable a pilot to take effective evasive action when, having dropped his torpedo, he was subjected to intense flak. Several Squadrons, among them No 829 — which had suffered extremely heavy casualties — were re-equipped with Swordfish, whose production continued after that of the Albacore was halted in 1943.

With eight squadrons equipped with the Albacore by mid-1941, it was to be expected that it would become involved in naval operations in support of efforts to sail convoys round the North Cape to Russian ports. The first such involvement occurred on 30 July, when Albacores of No 817 (Lt-Cdr D Sanderson RN), flying from HMS *Furious* attacked the port of Petsamo, recently captured by the Germans. Their pilots, however, found the port empty of shipping and opposition was only slight. An attack on the same day by Albacores of No 827 Squadron (Lt-Cdr J A Stewart-Moore RN) from HMS *Victorious* on nearby Kirkenes in Norway encountered heavy flak and air opposition, losing six of its

ten aircraft without inflicting any significant damage; a Junkers Ju 87 was shot down by an Albacore using its front gun!

By March 1942 the number of Albacore squadrons had risen to eight, and on the 9th of that month No 817 Squadron (Lt-Cdr Peter Goldthorpe

Sugden RN) and No 832 Squadron (Lt-Cdr William John Lucas RN), flying from HMS *Victorious*, attacked with torpedoes the German battleship *Tirpitz* off northern Norway, but obtained no hits. Later that year, on 17 November, an 817 Squadron Albacore attacked and sank the U-boat *U-517* in the North

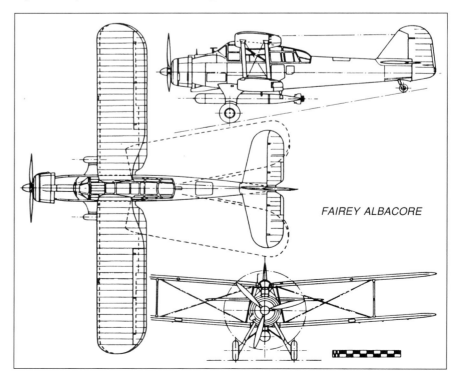

FAIREY ALBACORE

Atlantic; four days earlier, *U-331* had been sunk by an Albacore of No 820 Squadron while supporting the Torch landings in North Africa.

Albacores served in the Western Desert during periods when their carriers were in port, attacking enemy supply ports in Libya and providing cover for Allied coastal convoys. Other tasks carried out, notably by Nos 821 and 826 Squadrons, included support for the ground forces, often dropping flares over the night battles. Several successful attacks were launched against enemy convoys attempting to supply the Axis forces in Tunisia and Libya; later, in support of the invasion of Sicily, Nos 821, 826 and 828 Squadrons, based on Malta, were employed in mining and anti-submarine patrols in the central Mediterranean.

By the end of 1943 the Albacore had been withdrawn from operational duties with the Fleet Air Arm, although No 415 Squadron, RCAF, flew Albacores on anti-shipping sorties over the North

Sea from November 1943 until July 1944, having assumed this rôle when

No 841 Squadron of the Fleet Air Arm was disbanded.

Type: Single-engine, three-crew, single-bay biplane carrier-borne torpedo bomber.
Air Ministry Specification: S.41/36
Manufacturer: The Fairey Aviation Co Ltd, Hayes, Middlesex.
Powerplant: One 1,065hp Bristol Taurus II (later 1,130hp Taurus XII) 14-cylinder sleeve-valve air-cooled radial engine driving 3-blade propeller.
Dimensions: Span, 50ft 0in; length, 39ft 10in; height, 14ft 2in; wing area, 623 sq ft.
Weights: Tare, 7,250lb; all-up (with torpedo), 10,460lb.
Performance: Max speed, 161 mph at 4,500ft; climb to 6,000ft, 8 min; service ceiling, 20,700ft; range (with torpedo), 710 miles.
Armament: One 0.303in machine gun in upper starboard wing, and one or two Vickers K machine guns in rear cockpit; bomb load of up to four 500lb bombs carried under wings, or one 1,600lb Mk XIIA 18in torpedo.
Prototypes: Two, L7074 and L7075; L7074 first flown by Flt Lt F H Dixon RAFO at Harmondsworth on 12 December 1938.
Production: A total of 800 Albacores (including the above prototypes) was built: L7074-L7173 (100); between N4152 and N4425 (200); between T9131 and T9246 (100); between X8940 and X9290 (250); and between BF584 and BF777 (150).
Summary of Service: Albacores served with the following operational Squadrons of the Fleet Air Arm, Nos 810, 815, 817, 818, 820, 821, 822, 823, 826, 827, 828, 829, 830, 831, 832 and 841; and with the following second-line Squadrons: Nos 700, 733, 747, 750, 753, 754, 756, 763, 766, 767, 768, 769, 771, 774, 775, 778, 781, 782, 783, 785, 786, 787, 788, 789, 791, 793, 796, 797 and 799. Afloat, they served aboard the Fleet Carriers HMS *Argus, Ark Royal, Formidable, Furious, Illustrious, Indomitable* and *Victorious*. They also served with No 119 Squadron, RAF, and No 415 Squadron, RCAF, at Manston.

Avro Type 679 Manchester

It is unlikely that any Air Ministry Specification had even been prepared with such attention to detail or as the result of such extensive consultation before the issue of Specification P.13/36 in November 1936. The prefix 'P', the same as used in some recent light dive bomber Specifications, might have been thought to disguise the true nature of the aircraft, but this was not the case, as one of the original cornerstones of the requirement was that the aircraft would be a medium *dive* bomber whose *modus operandi* would be to deliver its bombs in a 30-degree dive so as to remain over the target for the shortest possible time. The other principal requirements may be summarised as follows:
1. That the aircraft should be capable of operating anywhere in the world.
2. That alternative range performance and bomb load combinations should be exploitable without modification to the airframe, fuel tankage or bomb bay.
3. That the aircraft should possess a high cruising speed to limit the time spent over enemy territory.
4. That all-round defence should be provided by nose and tail turrets with a

The first Manchester prototype, L7246, in August 1939, shortly after its first flight. It displays the short-span wings and tailplane, originally fitted, and the absence of gun turrets. (Photo: RAF Museum, Neg No P005200)

special crew member whose task would be to direct the defensive fire.
5. That as an alternative to the bombing rôle the aircraft should be suitable for use as a troop carrier, with only limited factory modification.

The aircraft was required to carry a maximum bomb load of not less than 8,000lb, including provision to carry two 18in torpedoes as an alternative to bombs, with fuel for a range of 2,000 miles, take-off in this configuration being assisted by a ground catapult system (then being investigated at the RAE, Farnborough). A cruising speed of 275mph at 15,000 feet at two-thirds power was specified. The new Rolls-Royce 24-cylinder X-type engine, then under development, was also manda-

tory, the manufacturuer predicting a take-off power of 1,700hp 'at a better power-weight ratio than the latest Merlin 12-cylinder engine'.

A V Roe & Co Ltd and Handley Page Ltd (as well as four other companies) tendered designs, and the Avro Type 679 and Handley Page H.P.56 were ordered in prototype form, being required for flight not later than January 1939. As will be told later (see page 329), Handley Page argued successfully for relaxation of some of the requirements, such as exclusion of the torpedo-carrying ability, before seeking, again successfully, to adopt a four-engine configuration).

Roy Chadwick at Avro, on the other hand, persevered to meet the original

The fully-armed second Manchester prototype, L7247. In efforts to improve the longitudinal control, the aircraft was flown with 'park-bench' elevator trim tabs, shown here; the eventual remedy involved increasing the tailplane span. Apart from these tabs, the aircraft represented the early production standard. (Photo: Air Ministry)

terms and, in so doing, produced a truly outstanding aeroplane. Indeed, in meeting the exacting bomb and torpedo demands, his design was dominated by the provision of an exceptionally large and unobstructed bomb bay, which was dictated by the torpedoes' length of 18ft 3in.

From the outset Chadwick was sceptical about Rolls-Royce's ability to direct sufficient time and effort to the development of the radical new X-type engine owing to the overriding necessity to introduce the Merlin engine into large-scale production. The X-type engine, later to be named the Vulture, comprised, in effect, two 12-cylinder Peregrine V-12 engines, one placed erect above the other, which was inverted, all 24 pistons driving a single crankshaft of great complexity and with fiendishly elaborate lubrication demands.

His fears proved to be justified when reports from Derby indicated that bench testing and early test bed flight trials had shown just how much more work needed to be done on the lubrication and cooling systems. Accordingly, while the Type 679 twin-Vulture bomber went ahead, Chadwick began drawing up alternative powerplant proposals, based on the new 24-cylinder Napier side-canted H-type sleeve-valve engine, later to become the 2,200hp Sabre, the proposed Bristol 18-cylinder radial (later named the Centaurus) and on a four-Merlin version, the Type 683, whose design began late in 1938.

The first Type 679 prototype, now named the Manchester, fell behind schedule, largely on account of at least four changes in engine installation geometry notified by Rolls-Royce during the second half of 1938, the last of which required some modification to the front wing spar in order the maintain the position of the aircraft's centre of gravity. Nevertheless the first flight by L7246 was conducted by Capt H A ('Sam') Brown at Ringway on 25 July 1939 and, apart from high engine temperatures, passed off without major trouble, although both directional stability and longitudinal control were unsatisfactory. Brown also reported that the take-off run was inordinately long , despite the fact that no gun turrets had yet been fitted, and little other military equipment was installed. These views were endorsed when the aircraft visited Boscombe Down (the A & AEE's new location after the outbreak of war).

Major alterations were made in the second prototype, L7247, which was flown on 26 May 1940. The outer wing sections were enlarged, increasing the span from 80ft 2in on the first aircraft to 90ft 1in. A small, crude-looking dorsal fin was also added to the rear fuselage, and engines of slightly increased power were fitted. Brown was still not satisfied, although the take-off run was much reduced.

By then a total of no fewer than 1,200 Manchesters were on order, with the first 20 aircraft taking shape at

Newton Heath, Manchester, and a second production line being laid down at nearby Trafford Park, where Metropolitan-Vickers Ltd had also received large orders.

Work on the Vulture was now continuing more slowly, the heavy RAF fighter losses in France creating heavy demands on Merlin production. At the same time, design work was still continuing on the four-Merlin version of the Manchester, and tunnel tests had indicated the benefit of a much-enlarged tailplane, and it was decided to introduce this in the Manchester production line, beginning on the 20th aircraft.

The first production Manchester Mk I, L7276, was delivered to Boscombe Down on 5 August 1940 with Vulture II engines, provisionally rated at 1,820hp for take-off, fitted with the large central fin, and with only two guns in the rear turret. Adverse criticism was still made of the poor longitudinal control, and it was decided to dispense with the fire-control crew member, referred to as the Master Gunner, as the aircraft now accommodated a second pilot. Doubt was also expressed about the need to retain the ventral turret, provided the rear turret had its four guns reinstated. It should be pointed out that it was then intended to introduce the F.N.7 two-gun dorsal turret in the Manchester (as fitted in the Stirling and Botha).

Nevertheless, with engines de-rated to 1,760hp and at a temporary take-off weight restricted to 52,000lb, the Manchester was cleared for squadron service. The first Squadron, No 207 (Bomber) Squadron, commanded by Sqn Ldr Noel Challis Hyde at Waddington, received its first aircraft on 10 November.

Thus began an ordeal which was probably unique in RAF history. It had

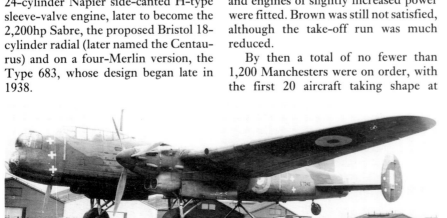

After completion of its prototype trials, the first Manchester, L7246, was delivered to the RAE to participate in the catapult trials for assisted take-off at high all-up weight. This project, conceived from the outset specifically for the Manchester, occupied the RAE for several years, but was never adopted. The aircraft is seen here on its special launching trolley. (Photo: Royal Aerospace Establishment)

The first Manchester, L7279, delivered to No 207 (Bomber) Squadron on 6 November 1940. Just visible is the lower surface of the retracted ventral 'dustbin' turret almost immediately below the fuselage roundel. This aeroplane survived until October 1943, when it was struck off RAF charge. (Photo: Author's Collection)

become fairly common practice for the first operational squadron to undertake intensive flying of a new aircraft type in order to subject it to the extreme rigours of in-service operations, thereby enabling training and operating procedures to be established for later squadrons. This task was given to No 207 Squadron, which received aircraft whose engines clearly still needed much work done to achieve the necessary operational reliability Added to this was the introduction of an entirely new bombing tactic, that of the diving approach to the target by an aeroplane which, contrary to the original Specification's classification of the Manchester as a medium bomber, was very much a *heavy* bomber. This extremely hazardous task for No 207 Squadron, in combat conditions, continued for over a year, accompanied by high losses owing to engine failure and increasingly determined German defences. Squadron aircraft were frequently grounded at short notice for modifications to be made, trials were ordered, and changes introduced in attack tactics — all imposing tremendous pressures on, and unsettling the pilots and crews. It was undoubtedly this Squadron's ordeal that gave rise to, and perpetuated, the Manchester's appalling reputation, whereas the fault lay almost wholly in engine unreliability, stemming directly from the impossibility of giving more attention to development of the Vulture before the War.

No 207's first bombing operation was

launched on the night of 24/25 February 1941, when six early production Manchesters set out with light bomb loads of 500lb SAP bombs to attack a *Hipper*-class cruiser at Brest (this despite the fact that these bombs would not penetrate the deck of such a ship). All aircraft returned, although one Manchester crashed on landing — without injury to the crew. Two nights later five Manchesters joined a raid on Cologne, this time carrying 1,000lb and 500lb GP bombs.

A second Manchester Squadron, No 97, commanded by Sqn Ldr Denys Finlay Balsdon, was formed on 25 February, also at Waddington, the CO and his flight commanders all having previously undergone conversion training with No 207 Squadron.

No 207 continued to join Bomber Command raids, and occasionally had to contend with a new hazard, when on 3/4 March, soon after take-off for a raid on Brest, a Manchester was shot down by a German intruder with the loss of all but one crew member. During that month No 207 Squadron was able to dispose of almost all of its early Manchesters and received instead aircraft fitted with the F.N.7 dorsal turret (and omitting the ventral 'dustbin'). These aircraft were also equipped to carry the 2,000lb SAP bomb which was soon to become the standard weapon dropped

against the French port of Brest; Manchesters normally carried three of these weapons.

Twelve Manchesters (eight from No 207 and four from No 97) took part in a raid on Kiel on 8/9 April, and it was from this raid that Wd Cdr Hyde (newly promoted) failed to return. Four days later all 40 Manchesters in the two squadrons were grounded so that the Vultures' crankshaft bearings could be replaced, as it had been discovered that repeated overheating of the engines had caused the oil to lose its viscosity in less than one-fifth of the time considered normal. The opportunity was taken to introduce the necessary minor equipment modifications to allow the aircraft to carry the 4,000lb HC bomb, and on 8/9 May a 207 Squadron Manchester dropped one of these bombs in a raid on Berlin.

By the end of May, figures showed that in four months of operations the two squadrons had flown 112 bombing sorties, of which 23 had been aborted for one reason or another; 14 aircraft had been lost (including three on training flights), 6 of them following mechanical failure. 49 pilots and crew members had been killed. These figures were not considered to be unduly heavy, given that No 207 Squadron was operating under extremely difficult circumstances, and Bomber Command took

The ninth production Manchester I, L7284 (without dorsal turret), in the markings of No 207 (Bomber) Squadron. It took part in the Squadron's first operation, the raid on Brest of 24/25 February 1941, captained by Fg Off P R Burton-Gyles DFC. (Photo: Author's Collection)

The ultimate version of the Manchester was the Mark IA with Lancaster-style wide tailplane and no central fin; this view of a No 207 Squadron aircraft illustrates the asymmetric profile of the F.N.7 dorsal turret which caused airflow instability when rotated. (Photo: Real Photographs Co)

the decision to relax some of the operating restrictions at the beginning of August, by which time a third Squadron, No 61, had received its first Manchester. This aircraft, L7388, is believed to have been the first example of a new version, the Mark IA, which discarded the central fin but introduced much taller outrigged fins and rudders (by then fitted as standard on the Lancaster, shortly to appear in service). These, as well as the wide-span tailplane, bestowed much improved handling qualities on the aircraft and, taken in conjunction with apparent solutions of the Vulture's problems, encouraged the formation of further Manchester squadrons. Records show that losses of Manchesters caused by mechanical failure had dropped to a rate no higher than those of the Stirling and Halifax. It was at this time that modifications were made to enable the Manchester to carry its full designed bomb load of 14,000lb, although there is no record of a load greater than 10,350lb ever being carried on operations, owing to the effect that the greater load would have had on the aircraft's bombing height.

By the late summer of 1941, therefore, Manchesters were frequently operating at 14,000 feet, often with a bomb load of 8,000lb, including a 4,000-pounder and mixed 1,000lb and 500lb GP bombs. Raids were resumed on Brest in December, as the Admiralty was convinced that the German warships *Scharnhorst*, *Gneisenau* and *Prinz Eugen*, which had been under repair in the port, were almost ready to break out. A night raid on the 17th/18th by 101 bombers failed to inflict any damage on the ships, and so was followed by a daylight attack by 41 bombers, including nine Manchesters of No 97 Squadron, on the following day. Led by the aircraft of the squadron commander, these bombers carried out the customary diving attack from about 10,000 feet, releasing their 2,000lb SAP bombs at about 5,000 feet, while the other bombers continued their

level runs above. Unfortunately the Manchesters were attacked by enemy fighters and came under heavy ground fire over the target; one aircraft was shot down, and the CO's aircraft was badly damaged, and crashed at base, the entire crew being killed. None of the German ships was seriously damaged, although one of the Manchesters' 2,000-pounders hit the lock gates of the dock in which the *Scharnhorst* was berthed, preventing the ship from being moved for a month.

By 12 February 1942, the date on which the German ships escaped from Brest, eastwards up the English Channel, four Manchester squadrons were operational, and eleven crews from Nos 61, 83 and 207 Squadron attemped to find and bomb the ships in conditions of low cloud. Although several near misses were reported, no damage was done and, despite being attacked by some German fighters, all the Manchesters returned safely.

A fortnight later, in an attack on Kiel,

the *Gneisenau* was struck and badly damaged by two 2,000lb SAP bombs. As Manchesters dropped eight such bombs in this raid, it will never be known which aircraft scored these important hits.

In March 1942 No 207 Squadron was relieved of its long and difficult task, exchanging its Manchesters for Lancasters. The eighth and final Squadron to be equipped with the Manchester, No 49, kept its aircraft for little over a month before it, too, made this change. By the end of June the Manchester had been withdrawn from operational use. Its last bombing raid was carried out on the night of 25/26 June, when a single aircraft of No 83 Squadron accompanied a raid on Bremen.

A Manchester pilot, Fg Off Leslie Thomas Manser RAFVR of No 50 Squadron, had won a posthumous Victoria Cross, awarded for great gallantry during the first 1,000-bomber raid on Cologne on the night of 30 May 1942. He

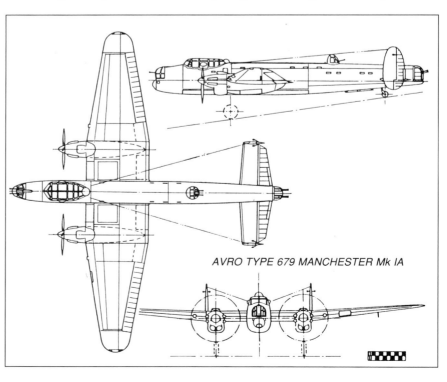

AVRO TYPE 679 MANCHESTER Mk IA

had just completed his bombing run at 7,000 feet when the aircraft was heavily damaged by flak. When the port engine caught fire, Manser ordered the crew to bale out, and, remaining at the controls, he held the crippled bomber level as his colleagues escaped safely. They witnessed the Manchester crash in flames, taking the pilot with it.

These early Manchester operations have been described in some detail as the conduct of these raids had a significant bearing on the manner in which Bomber Command was slowly developing its tactics in attacking targets on the Continent. They also explain some of the tribulations experienced by the Command which conspired to delay the build-up of a powerful bombing force that would begin to take shape under the leadership of Sir Arthur Harris later in 1942. In this respect, the efforts and sacrifices by No 207 Squadron should not be under-rated.

Type: Twin-engine, seven-crew, mid-wing monoplane night heavy bomber.
Air Ministry Specifications: P.13/36 and 19/37.
Manufacturers: A V Roe & Co Ltd, Newton Heath, Manchester, and Woodford, Cheshire; Metropolitan-Vickers Ltd, Trafford Park, Manchester.
Powerplant: Two 1,760hp Rolls-Royce Vulture I 24-cylinder X-type liquid-cooled, in-line engines driving 3-blade variable-pitch propellers.
Structure: All-metal semi-monocoque fuselage and two-spar, flush-riveted wing.
Dimensions: Span, 90ft 0in; length, 68ft 10in; height, 19ft 6in; wing area, 1,131 sq ft.
Weights: Tare, 26,760lb; all-up, 56,100lb (later, 59,750lb).
Performance: Max speed, 265 mph at 17,000ft; service ceiling, 19,200ft; max range, 1,630 miles with 8,100lb bomb load, 1,200 miles with 10,360lb bomb load.
Armament: Two 0.303in Browning machine guns in Fraser Nash nose and dorsal turrets (and retractable ventral turret on early aircraft), and four Browning guns in tail turret. Maximum bomb load carried, 10,350lb (later raised to 14,000lb, but never carried).
Prototypes: Two, L7246 (first flown by Capt H A Brown on 25 July 1939) and L7247.
Production: A total of 200 production Manchesters was built. Avro, 156, between L7276 and L7526 (L7517 destroyed at factory); Metro-Vick, 44, between R5768 and R5841.
Summary of Service: Manchesters served with the following Bomber Squadrons (listed chronologically in order of first deliveries): No 207 from November 1940 to March 1942 at Waddington and Bottesford; No 97 from February 1941 to January 1942 at Waddington and Coningsby; No 61 from July 1941 to June 1942 at North Luffenham and Syerston; No 83 from July 1941 to June 1942 at Scampton; No 106 from February to June 1942 at Coningsby; No 50 from March to June 1942 at Skellingthorpe and Swinderby; and No 49 from May to June 1942 at Scampton. Manchesters also served with No 25 OTU, Nos 1654, 1656, 1660, 1661 and 1668 CUs, Nos 3, 4, 6, 8 and 10 AGS, No 1 AAS, No 5 LFS, Nos 408 and 420 (Canadian) Squadrons*, No 44 (Bomber) Squadron Conversion Flight, No 4 AOS, No 1485 Flt, TDU and AFEE. * For training purposes.

Vickers Types 284/468 Warwick

The Vickers Warwick was originally conceived as a heavy bomber to complement the smaller Wellington medium bomber, with which it had much in common, not least being the use of a geodetic airframe structure. It was unfortunate in ultimately being given the Rolls-Royce Vulture engine, as it has been shown in the previous pages that this suffered under-development and therefore proved to be a failure within the necessary timescale.

Specification B.1/35, to which the Vickers Type 284 was tendered, called for a modest performance that included the ability to carry 2,000lb of bombs over a distance of 2,000 miles at a

The first B.1/35 Warwick prototype, K8178, powered by Rolls-Royce Vulture I engines, at Brooklands shortly before the outbreak of war in 1939. (Photo: Vickers-Armstrongs Ltd.)

cruising speed of not less than 195 mph at 15,000 feet. The wing span was not to exceed 100 feet, and provision for in-flight refuelling was to be considered.

Vickers' first tender to B.1/35 included the use of Bristol Hercules engines, with which the aircraft was expected to exceed the Specification by a substantial margin. By the time this

tender was examined by the Air Ministry, however, much more advanced requirements were being considered (which would result in aircraft such as the Stirling, Manchester and Halifax heavy bombers) and therefore Vickers proposed alternative designs employing the new Rolls-Royce 24-cylinder X-type engine (the Vulture) or the Napier 24-cylinder canted-H engine (the Sabre). The Air Ministry therefore considered the Vickers proposals in the context of Specification P.13/36 (to which the Avro Manchester had been tendered),

The second Warwick prototype, L9704, powered by early Bristol Centaurus engines, before this aircraft was fitted with the dorsal turret. The Warwick's close relationship with the Wellington is clearly apparent. (Photo: Vickers-Armstrongs Ltd)

Left: *The first of 16 production Warwick B Mk IIs, BV214, with Double Wasp engines, at Brooklands in 1943 complete with nose, dorsal, ventral and tail turrets.* (Photo: Vickers-Armstrongs Ltd)

Below: *The Type 468 Warwick fitted with gun barbettes in the rear of the engine nacelles as part of the programme to evolve the rear defence armament for the four-engine Vickers Windsor bomber.* (Photo: Vickers-Armstrongs Ltd)

and Vickers was accordingly awarded a contract for two prototypes under Specification B.1/35, but amended to cover one aircraft with Vulture engines and the other with Sabres.

The first Warwick prototype, K8178, was flown by 'Mutt' Summers at Brooklands on 13 August 1939, powered by Vultures, but trials with these engines were of limited value owing to limitations being imposed in the light of the current lubrication problems. Attention then switched to the second aircraft and the choice of engines, as plans for the Sabre installation had been abandoned when it was decided to allocate all available production to fighters (the Hawker Typhoon). The decision was therefore taken to fit two of the new Bristol Centaurus 18-cylinder sleeve-valve radials in the second prototype B.1/35, L9704, the Vickers Type 401), which Summers first flew on 5 April 1940.

It was evident by 1940 that production of the B.1/35 was unlikely to occur in the near future on account of production plans already in place for the Stirling and Halifax, and, as development of the Centaurus engine was as yet only in its early stages, any development of the Vickers heavy bomber would have to centre on yet another choice of engine. Therefore L9704 underwent conversion for installation of the American Pratt & Whitney Double Wasp R-2800-S1C4G, becoming the Vickers Type 422, this work being completed and the aircraft flown in July 1941.

Meanwhile, on 28 December 1940, Vickers had received a production contract for 250 Warwick bombers, provisionally planned as being 150 Mark Is with Pratt & Whitney Double Wasp engines and 100 Mark IIs with Bristol Centaurus engines. The desultory delivery of the American engines, however, resulted in these plans being changed repeatedly, and instead of a total of 400 engines being received, only about 80 arrived. Only 16 Mark I bombers were

therefore completed, and all were used for experimental purposes. By the time the first production Mark I Warwick was completed and flown, on 19 April

1942, the need for a twin-engine heavy bomber had long since disappeared, and the Wellington was performing the long-range medium bomber rôle perfectly

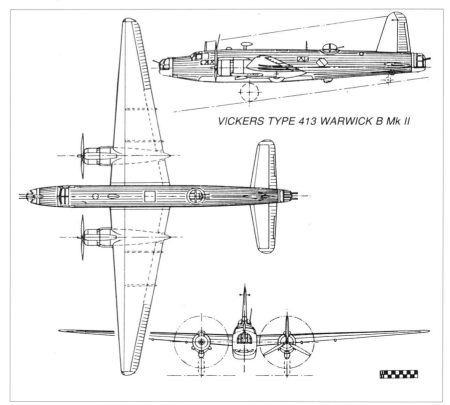

VICKERS TYPE 413 WARWICK B Mk II

adequately in service. Other Mark I airframes were therefore completed as transports, 14 being allocated to BOAC as G-AGEX to G-AGFK, and others, termed C Mk Is, entered service with RAF Transport Command. Only one Centaurus-powered Mark II bomber was built, this being BV216, a converted Mark I.

The second B.1/35 prototype, L9704, joined a test programme as the Type 468 to evolve a system of remotely-operated, rearwards-firing guns for the Windsor heavy bomber (see page 352). Mounted in barbettes in the rear of the Warwick's engine nacelles, these guns were sighted, controlled and fired by a gunner situated in the position normally occupied by the rear turret.

Warwicks underwent continuous development, once delivery of the Bristol Centaurus engine finally achieved reliability late in 1943, even though any ambitions to assume the bombing rôle

had evaporated. Airframes, still on the production line, were selected and completed for air-sea rescue, general reconnaissance, transport and meteorological reconnaissance duties. In all, 845

Warwicks were built, of which not one ever reached a bomber squadron. The accompanying data table refers to the Warwick B.II prototype, except where stated otherwise.

Type: Twin-engine, six/seven-crew, mid-wing monoplane heavy bomber.
Air Ministry Specification: B.1/35
Manufacturer: Vickers-Armstrongs Ltd., Weybridge, Surrey.
Powerplant: Two 2,000hp Bristol Centaurus IV (later Centaurus VIII) 18-cylinder air-cooled sleeve-valve radial engines driving 3-blade variable-pitch propellers. (Mark I bombers powered by 1,850hp Pratt & Whitney Double Wasp R-2800-S1A4-G radial engines.)
Structure: All-metal geodetic construction with fabric covering.
Dimensions: Span, 96ft 8½in; length, 70ft 0in; height, 18ft 6in; wing area, 1,019 sq ft.
Weights: Tare, 29,174lb; all-up, 47,500lb.
Performance: Max speed, 290 mph at 20,000ft; service ceiling, 28,200 ft; range, 2,075 miles with 2,000lb bomb load, or 1,150 miles with 8,000lb bomb load.
Armament: Twin machine guns in power-operated nose, dorsal and ventral turrets, and four in tail turret. Maximum bomb load of 8,000lb of bombs, or two 18in torpedoes.
Prototype: One, BV216 (a converted Mk I), first flown in July 1943. (Two original B.1/35 prototypes, K8178 (Vulture engines, first flown on 13 August 1939), and L9704 (Centaurus engines, first flown on 5 April 1940).
Production: The only production Warwick bombers built were 16 Mark Is: BV214, BV215, BV217-BV222, BV224, BV228-BV230, BV291, BV293, BV295 and BV296. None served with an operational unit.

Handley Page H.P.56/71 Halifax

The Handley Page Halifax was the second of the RAF's great four-engine heavy bombers of the Second World War to enter service, after the Short Stirling, and was second only to the Avro Lancaster in terms of numbers built and the extent of its employment by the RAF. It gave magnificent service during the mid-War years but, in performance and load-carrying ability, it was seriously handicapped by a number of design decisions taken early in its development, decisions that so fundamentally compromised the aeroplane's structure that no viable remedy was possible once the production lines had been established. In defending those decisions, one should emphasise that the likelihood of RAF bombers being called upon to carry weapons of weights greater than 4,000lb could not possibly have been foreseen in 1937, and the choice of the 'wrong' Merlin engines was made at a time when that version was the only one on offer. (By the time the Lancaster had reached the point at which a decision had to be taken with regard to its engines — mid-1939 — the Merlin XX was the obvious choice, and indeed this

The first Halifax prototype, L7244, at Boscombe Down. Note the leading-edge slats, and the absence of gun turrets. (Photo: Air Ministry, Neg No MH4861)

engine was to be introduced into the Halifax soon afterwards.)

When Specification P.13/36 reached Handley Page in November 1936, Volkert was inclined to tender a development of his H.P.55 design (previously intended to replace the Harrow, and eventually successful as the Hampden), but this was ruled out by the bomb load and range requirements, as well as that strange legacy of a bygone age, the secondary troop-carrying rôle, which imposed the need for a much larger fuselage cross-section.

The H.P.56 design, tendered in March 1937, was very much in keeping with the configuration imagined by the Air Staff, being powered by a pair of Rolls-Royce Vultures; the wing centre-section was a thick structure in which

roughly one-third of the bomb load was stowed, and, of rectangular outline in plan, carried large-chord landing flaps/ airbrakes; leading-edge slats were to be fitted on the outer wings.

Early doubts as to the manufacturers' ability to develop the Vulture — doubts that were to be entirely justified in due course — together with Volkert's preference for the use of four of the new Merlin engines (in which Frederick Handley Page supported him) led to permission being given to abandon the twin-Vulture design and, in 1937, to accept in its place a tender, the H.P.57, with four Merlin Xs, the engines currently being introduced into the Whitley IV's design. It might be argued that in so reducing the demand for the Vulture engine to a single bomber project, this

The first production Halifax Mk I, L9485, during armament trials at the A & AEE; it is fitted with the Boulton-Paul turrets. The transparent hatch in the rear fuselage suggests that provision has been made for the beam guns. (Photo: RAF Museum, Neg No P006828)

decision itself reduced the need for work priority on the Vulture, the very circumstance that delayed the achievement of that engine's reliability; if this argument is taken further, who is to say whether the Halifax or, for that matter, the Lancaster would have been in service when they were, or even that they would ever have appeared?

Volkert and Handley Page went on to question the need to carry the two torpedoes, as demanded in P.13/36, and the practicality of the proposed dive-bombing tactic, pointing to the severe structural penalties these requirements imposed. The Air Staff, now fairly confident of obtaining a modern, land-based torpedo bomber (the Beaufort or Botha), agreed to delete the torpedo load demand and, now that the four-engine configuration had been accepted, concurred that the traditional level bombing technique was more appropriate. When,

however, Volkert attempted to persuade the Air Ministry to relax the limitation on wing span in the interests of take-off performance, it was explained that plans had been made to install two catapult tracks on all heavy bomber airfields, and limiting the size and weight of the new heavy bombers made it unnecessary to enlarge the bomber airfields, an exceptionally expensive undertaking in peacetime. (It appears that by the end of 1938, the proposed catapult launching of heavy bombers was losing favour with the Air Staff, and that the hangar-door width limitation had been waived. See page 313, footnote. No such wing span limit was imposed in Specification B.1/39, issued to define the requirements for the next generation of heavy bombers.)

The Handley Page design progressed along lines rather different from those of the Stirling. The fuselage was about 17 feet shorter and, in order to provide

adequate tail area, twin fins and rudders, whose outline clearly owed something to the Harrow, were provided. The fuselage was also much deeper than that of the Stirling, the secondary troop-carrying requirement probably dictating this. The choice of in-line engines also enabled the nacelles to be set lower on the wing, thereby permitting a shorter undercarriage; nevertheless, so as to provide the strength necessary to support unprecedented landing loads Messier produced massive cast magnesium portal arch structures on which to mount the main wheels.

Freed of the necessity to cater for 18-foot-long torpedoes, Volkert was able to provide additional structural rigidity in the centre fuselage by extending the frames lower in the structure, although this had the effect of compartmenting the bomb bay, but this was not — at the time — considered a handicap, as the largest bomb then envisaged was the 'long' 2,000lb SAP bomb, expected to be in service early in 1940.

By the time the first Halifax prototype was completed at Cricklewood,

BB324/ZA-X was a Halifax Mk II Series 1 (Special) of No 10 (Bomber) Squadron, with nose and dorsal turrets removed in the interests of slightly improved speed. This aircraft was lost during a raid on Mulheim on 22/23 June 1943. (Photo: The Aeroplane)

A Halifax Mk II Series 2, HR758, with Merlin XX engines in Lancaster-style nacelles (in this instance with the inboard nacelles extended behind the wing trailing edge). Just visible is the low-profile four-gun Boulton Paul dorsal turret. (Photo: via R C B Ashworth)

early in September 1939, no decision had been reached on the gun turrets to be adopted in production aircraft, as the Nash & Thompson factory was already overloaded, and Boulton Paul was heavily pre-occupied with the four-gun turret required for the Defiant fighter.

The prototype, L7244, was taken by road to Bicester, near Oxford, for final assembly , being flown at that airfield by Maj Cordes on 25 October. It was followed by the fully-equipped and armed prototype, L7245, the decision having been taken to fit the Boulton Paul Type C turret in the nose, with two Browning guns, and a Type E four-gun turret in the tail. Neither of these turrets could traverse adequately to counter beam attacks, and dorsal and ventral turrets were also planned; in the meantime pairs of manually-traversing guns, firing through a hatch in each side of the rear fuselage, were provided. The crew of the early Halifax Is was variously six or seven men, the navigator also being required to man the front turret as well as aim the bombs. The Halifax, like the Stirling, also included a flight engineer in its crew.

The first production aircraft, L9485, was flown on 11 October 1940, being allocated for trials at Boscombe Down. The second aircraft was also delivered to Boscombe Down, to be used for familiarisation by the crews of the first operational unit, No 35 (Bomber) Squadron, who assembled there under the command of Acting Wg Cdr Raymond William Pennington Collings AFC (later Gp Capt, DSO, AFC).

The Squadron moved to its permanent station at Linton-on-Ouse on 5 December, taking charge of eighteen Halifax Is, L9487-L9504. The first six crews were declared night operational on 1 March, and on the night of 10th/

11th of that month joined a raid on Le Havre, one of the Halifaxes, L9489, being shot down over Normandy, Surrey, by an RAF night fighter. (The Squadron had suffered an earlier loss when, on 13 January, L9487 caught fire in the air, and crashed in Yorkshire.)

No 35 Squadron was provided with nine further Halifaxes during March in order to create a 'C' Flight which, when declared operational by night, became the nucleus of a second Halifax Squadron, No 76, which formed at Linton on 1 May and then moved to Middleton St George on 4 June.

These two Squadrons took an increasing part in the night raids over Europe. Losses were running at a sustainable rate, and the Air Staff felt encouraged to return to daylight raids in the belief that, with ten guns per aircraft, the Halifaxes should be well able to withstand attacks by enemy fighter interceptors. In the first such attack by six No 35 Squadron Halifaxes against Kiel in daylight on 30 June, two aircraft were shot down. When 15 aircraft from both Squadrons attacked the *Scharnhorst* at La Pallice in daylight on 24 July, five more were shot down. On the credit side, however, the Halifaxes scored five hits with 2,000lb AP bombs on the German battleship, although two failed to explode. With 3,000 tons of floodwater inside her, she was hurriedly sailed to Brest and docked for extensive repairs. However, with losses running at

one-third of the aircraft despatched in two raids, the Air Staff called another halt to daylight raids by heavy bombers.

Bombing operations by the Halifax were characteristic of Bomber Command's early bomber offensive of 1941. As yet there were still too few squadrons of true heavy bombers to impose a threat to Germany's ability to wage war. Added to this, there appeared to be no concerted strategy to use the avialable bombing force for strategic purposes. It was, moreover, about to become painfully clear that navigation and bombing accuracy by the British crews left much to be desired.

By the end of 1941 five Halifax squadrons had been equipped, and all were operational in Bomber Command by the time that Sir Arthur Harris was appointed its commander-in-chief. The improved H.P.59 Halifax Mark II, with Merlin XX engines, was in service and, resulting from the small increase in power, bombing from a slightly greater height, although the bomb load remained the same. With Bomber Command pressing for a higher rate of production, Handley Page had pointed to the excellent Messier undercarriage as being the one item of the airframe that nevertheless slowed the Halifax's rate of production, and the H.P.63 Halifax Mark V introduced an entirely new levered-suspension undercarriage, produced by George Dowty, and in due course 904 examples of this version were

Halifax III HX238, with the new 'D'-fins and powered by Hercules radials, during radar trials with H2S radome under the rear fuselage and, just visible beyond the base of the rudder, the automatic gun-laying radar known as 'Village Inn'. Aircraft of this standard flew operations during the final year of the War. (Photo: Real Photographs Co)

'O-Oscar', LW119/QB-O, an H2S-equipped Halifax B Mk III of No 424 (Tiger) Squadron, RCAF, at Skipton-on-Swale, Yorkshire , on 13 November 1944. As well as the 'Popeye' motif, the aircraft displays a tally of 57 raid symbols on the nose. (Photo: via R C Sturtivant)

built by Rootes and Fairey Aviation.

It was, however, the next version that came to be most widely used, namely the H.P.61 Halifax Mark III. This marked the change from the Rolls-Royce Merlin to the Bristol Hercules radial engine. The creation of the bomber stream tactic as a means of putting the largest number of aircraft over a target accurately and for the shortest possible time — with less risk of collision — had focused attention of the Halifax's inability to carry a worthwhile bomb load over a long distance at a cruising speed and height that ensured it remained within the protection provided by a compact bomber stream. The increase of 22 per cent in engine power and the small extension of the wingtips was certainly rewarded by an immediate and perceptible drop in the aircraft's operational casualty rate — which, during the Battles of the Ruhr and of Hamburg, had been running at a rate of just over 5.5 per cent, said by Bomber Command statisticians as being unsustainable.

Yet this small improvement in the Halifax's casualty rate was to count for little when Harris ordered his Command to open an all-out assault on the German capital during the darkest nights of the winter of 1943-44. His belief was that Bomber Command had the muscle to beat Berlin into rubble and thereby force Nazi Germany into submission. He had, however, badly underestimated the growing strength of the German night fighter force.

By the end of 1943 the Halifax was outnumbered by the Lancaster by a fairly large margin, equipping 20 Main Force bomber squadrons. Of these, half were in No 6 (Canadian) Group, based on airfields in Yorkshire; this deployment of the less capable bombers was

unfortunate as it placed a greater strain on the crews, who had further to fly before they even joined the bomber stream, and a longer return journey after having perhaps suffered crew casualties and battle damage.

The raid launched by Bomber Command against Nuremburg, which heralded an end to the Battle of Berlin on the night of 30/31 March 1944, emphasised the plight of the Halifax crews dramatically; out of 212 Halifaxes despatched on that raid against a target in southern Germany, 36 failed to return (nearly 17 per cent), of which 23 were shot down by enemy night fighters, six by flak, and seven were lost in accidents. This represented a loss 30 per cent heavier than the Lancasters, of which 569 had been despatched.

It was during this raid that a posthumous Victoria Cross was won by a 23-year-old Halifax captain, Plt Off Cyril Joe Barton RAFVR, of No 578 Squadron.

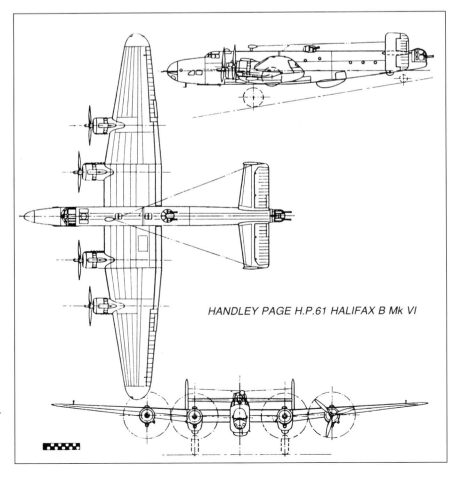

HANDLEY PAGE H.P.61 HALIFAX B Mk VI

When still 70 miles away from the target, his Halifax, LK797, was attacked by an enemy night fighter which put the hydraulic system out of action, thereby preventing the gun turrets from operating; the intercom was also put out of action and, following a misunderstanding of orders, the navigator, bomb aimer and wireless operator baled out. Nevertheless, Barton flew on to the target, navigating visually, and released the bombs himself. With a faltering engine, no navigator and two fuel tanks ruptured, he set course for base which lay some 600 miles away. On reaching the English coast he ordered the three remaining crew members to bale out, but the aircraft was by now too low for safety. The crew therefore took up crash positions as Barton attempted a landing on the one remaining engine. The Halifax stalled and crashed; Barton was killed, but his crew members survived.

The raid came at the peak of Halifax strength in Bomber Command, as most squadrons converted on to Lancasters soon afterwards; some remained in Bomber Command, performing special tasks — not necessarily less hazardous than operating in the bomber stream,

---

Type: Four-engine, six/seven-crew, mid-wing monoplane night heavy bomber, glider tug and airborne forces transport, and maritime reconnaissance aircraft.

Air Ministry Specifications: P.13/36 and 32/37.

Manufacturers: Handley Page Ltd, Cricklewood, London, and Radlett, Herts; English Electric Co Ltd, Preston, Lancs; Rootes Securities Ltd, Speke, Liverpool, Lancs; The Fairey Aviation Co Ltd, Stockport, Lancs; London Aircraft Production Group Ltd, Leavesden.

Powerplant: Mk.I. Four 1,145hp Rolls-Royce Merlin X 12-cylinder liquid-cooled, supercharged in-line engines driving 3-blade variable-pitch propellers. Mks II and V. 1,280hp Merlin XX. Mk III and VII. Four 1,650hp Bristol Hercules XVI 14-cylinder air-cooled sleeve-valve supercharged radial engines. Mk VI. 1,800hp Hercules 100.

Structure: All-metal stressed-skin construction with fabric-covered control surfaces.

Dimensions: Early production aircraft. Span, 98ft 10in; length, 70ft 1in; height, 20ft 9in; wing area, 1,250 sq ft. Later production aircraft. Span, 104ft 2in; length, 71ft 7in; height, 20ft 9in; wing area, 1,275 sq ft.

Weights: Mk I. Tare, 36,000lb; all-up, 60,000lb. Mk III. Tare, 38,240lb; all-up, 65,000lb. Mk VI. Tare, 38,900lb; all-up, 68,000lb.

Performance: Mk I. Max speed, 280 mph at 16,500ft; service ceiling, 19,100ft; range with 2,500lb bomb load, 3,000 miles; with 8,000lb bomb load, 1,060 miles. Mk III. Max speed, 282 mph at 13,500ft; service ceiling with 8,000lb bomb load, 18,600ft; range with max bomb load, 1,030 miles.

Armament: Mk III. Gun armament of single hand-held Vickers K gas-operated machine gun in nose, and four 0.303in Browning machine guns in each of Boulton Paul power-operated dorsal and tail turrets; some early aircraft were armed with single 0.5in Browning machine gun in ventral mounting. Bomb load up to 13,000lb (over very short ranges, seldom carried); normal loads comprised either four 2,000lb SAP or eight 1,000lb GP bombs or, occasionally, one 4,000lb HC and six 500lb GP bombs or four SBCs.

Prototypes: Two, L7244 and L7245. L7244 first flown on 25 October 1939 by Maj J L B H Cordes at Bicester, Oxon; L7245 first flown by Cordes on 17 August 1940 by Cordes at Radlett, Herts.

Production: A total of 6,135 Halifaxes was built, comprising 2 prototypes, 84 Mark Is, 1,937 Mark IIs, 2,132 Mark IIIs, 904 Mark Vs, 456 Mark IVs, 375 Mark VIIs, 100 Mark VIIIs and 145 Mark IXs. **Handley Page,** 1,562 comprising 84 Mk Is between L9485 and L9608; 615 Mk IIs: L9609-L9624, between R9363 and R9540, between W7650 and W7939, between HR654 and HR988, and between HX147 and HX225; 326 Mk IIIs: between HX226 and HX357, and between LV771 and LW195; 132 Mk VIs: between NP716 and NP927 and between PP165 and PP216; 15 B Mk VIIs: LW196-LW210; 145 A Mk VIIs: between NP681 and NP820, between PP339 and PP389, RT753-RT757 and TW774-TW796; 100 Mk VIIIs: between PP217 and PP338; 145 Mk IXs: between RT758 and RT938. **English Electric,** 2,145 comprising 860 Mk IIs: between V9976 and W1276; 940 Mk IIIs: between LW346 and LW724, between MZ500 and MZ934, between NP930 and NR290, and between RG345 and RG446; 325 Mk VIs: between RG480 and RG879 and ST974-ST818; 12 B Mk VIIs: RG447-RG458; and 8 A

Mk VIIs: RG472-RG479. **London Aircraft Production,** 710 comprising 450 Mk IIs: between BB189 and BB446, and between JN882 and JP338; and 260 Mk IIIs: between MZ282 and MZ495, and between PN365 and PN460. **Rootes Securities,** 1,070 comprising 12 Mk IIs: DG219-DG230 (one aircraft, DG223, crashed and was destroyed before delivery to the RAF); 280 Mk IIIs, between LL543 and LL615, and between MZ945 and NA310; 658 Mk V: between DG231 and DG424, between EB127 and EB276, and between LK890 and LL642; and 120 A Mk VII: between NA311 and NA468. Fairey Aviation, 662 comprising 326 Mk III: between LK747 and LK887, between NA492 and NA704, and PN167-PN208; 246 Mk Vs: between DJ980 and DK271, and between LK626 and LK746; and 90 B Mk VIIs: between PN223 and PN344.

Summary of Service: Halifax heavy bombers served with the following Squadrons in RAF Bomber Command: No 10 (Mks II,III, December 1941 to August 1945), No 35 (Mks I, II, III, November 1940 to March 1944), No 51 (Mks II, III, November 1942 to June 1945), No 76 (Mks I, II, III, V, VI, May 1941 to August 1945), No 77 (Mks II, III, V, VI, October 1942 to August 1945), No 78 (Mks II, III, VI, March 1942 to April 1945); No 102 (Mks II, III, VI, December 1941 to September 1945), No 103 (Mk II, July to November 1942), No 158 (Mks II, III, VI, June 1942 to July 1945), No 346 (French) (Mks V, III, VI, May 1944 to November 1945), No 347 (French) (Mks V, III, VI, June 1944 to November 1945), No 405 (RCAF) (Mk II, April 1942 to September 1943), No 408 (RCAF) (Mks V, II, III, VII between October 1942 and May 1945), No 415 (RCAF) (Mks III, VII, July 1944 to May 1945), No 419 (RCAF) (Mk II, November 1942 to April 1944), No 420 (RCAF) (Mk III, December 1943 to May 1945), No 424 (RCAF) (Mk III, December 1943 to January 1945), No 425 (RCAF) (Mk III, December 1943 to June 1945), No 426 (RCAF) (Mk III, VII, April 1944 to May 1945), No 427 (RCAF) (Mks V, III, May 1943 to March 1945), No 428 (RCAF) (Mks V, II, June 1943 to June 1944), No 429 (RCAF) (Mks II, V, III, August 1943 to March 1945), No 431 (RCAF) (Mks V, III, July 1943 to October 1944), No 432 (RCAF) (Mks III, VII, February 1944 to May 1945), No 433 (RCAF) (Mk III, November 1943 to February 1945), No 434 (RCAF) (Mks V, III, June 1943 to December 1944), No 460 (RAAF) (Mk II, August to October 1942), No 462 (RAAF) (Mks II, III, September 1942 to September 1945), No 466 (RAAF) (Mks II, III, September 1943 to May 1945), No 578 (Mk III, January 1944 to April 1945), No 614 (Mk II, March 1944 to March 1945), and No 640 (Mks III, VI, January 1944 to May 1945). Halifaxes served with the following Bomber Squadrons in the Mediterranean Theatre: No 148 (Mks II, V, May to September 1943) and No 178 (Mk II, May to September 1943). Halifaxes served with the following Special Duties Squadrons: Nos 138, 161, 301 (Polish), and No 640. They served with the following Airborne Forces and Transport Squadrons: Nos 47, 96, 113, 187, 190, 246, 295, 296, 297, 298, 304 (Polish), 620 and 644. They served with Nos 192 and 199 RCM Squadrons, Nos 202, 224, 517, 518, 519 and 521 (Weather Reconnaissance) Squadrons, as well as Nos 58 and 502 General Reconnaissance Squadrons in Coastal Command, and Halifax IIIs flew with No 171 (Bomber Support) Squadron. Among the numerous other training and trials units on which Halifaxes served were Nos 1651, 1652, 1658, 1659, 1662, 1666 and 1674 CUs, Nos 1427, 1445, 1473 and 1474 Flights, AFEE, No 1 OTU, TFU and No 1 OADU.

Right: *Halifax V DG235 during trials with Rolls-Royce Ltd to develop improved low-glare exhaust manifolds. The Dowty levered-suspension undercarriage, introduced in the Mark V, can just be discerned.* (Photo: RAF Museum, Neg No P006833)

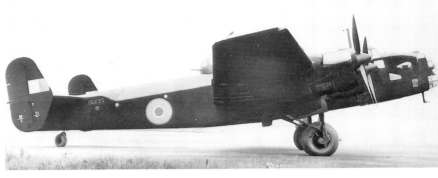

Below: *A late-wartime version of the Halifax bomber was the Mark VI with 1,800hp Hercules 100 engines. RG867/L8-H, with H₂S radar and 0.5in tail guns, served with the French No 347 (Tunisie) Squadron at Elvington in 1945.* (Photo: A J Jackson Collection).

and in many respects no less important. Such tasks included electronic counter-measures and bomber support away from the Main Force. And not all Halifax bomber squadrons disappeared; at the end of the War in Europe, Nos 10, 51, 76, 102, 158 and 640 Squadrons retained their Halifax Mks III, VI and VIIs until mid-1945.

Halifaxes also entered an entirely new field of warfare, alongside the Stirling (also retired from the Main Force),

when No 298 Squadron became an Airborne Forces Squadron, taking delivery of Halifax IIIs specially modified to tow the General Aircraft Horsa assault glider, as well as carrying parachute troops and other airborne forces. Later this and other Halifax squadrons would tow the very large Hamilcar assault gliders during the invasion of northern Europe in 1944 and 1945. At the end of the War many Halifaxes underwent modification to reappear as

C Mk VIII transports and A Mk IXs, assuming the rôle of the hundreds of Douglas C-47s that had been loaned to Britain by America, but which then had to be returned.

Yet it was the Halifaxes of Coastal Command that survived in service longest. Having equipped General Reconnaissance Squadrons of that Command (such as Nos 58 and 502 Squadrons) since the winter of 1942-43, they assumed the weather reconnaissance rôle with Nos 202, 517, 518, 519 and 521 Squadrons in 1943, and continued flying with No 224 Squadron at Gibraltar until March 1952.

In its originally intended rôle, that of delivering bombs against Germany, the Halifax had an impressive record. It flew a total of 82,773 operational sorties, and delivered 224,207 tons of bombs against its targets; it dropped over 13,000 of the 'long' 2,000lb bombs, but only 467 of the 4,000lb HC 'blockbusters' (compared with more than 64,000 dropped by the Lancaster).

Deployment of British Bomber Squadrons — 1 January 1940

Royal Air Force
Home Bases

Squadron	Aircraft	Base
No 7 Sqn (M)	Handley Page Hampden I	Finningley, Yorks
No 9 Sqn (H)	Vickers Wellington I	Honnington, Suffolk
No 10 Sqn (H)	A W Whitley IV	Dishforth, Yorks
No 15 Sqn (L)	Bristol Blenheim IV	Wyton, Hunts
No 21 Sqn (L)	Bristol Blenheim IV	Watton, Norfolk
No 22 Sqn (TB)	Bristol Beaufort I	Thorney Island, Hants
No 35 Sqn (L)	Bristol Blenheim IV	Bassingbourne, Cambs
No 37 Sqn (H)	Vickers Wellington IA	Feltwell, Norfolk
No 38 Sqn (H)	Vickers Wellington IA	Marham, Norfolk
No 40 Sqn (L)	Bristol Blenheim IV	Wyton, Hunts
No 42 Sqn (TB)	Vickers Vildebeest IV	Bircham Newton, Norfolk
No 44 Sqn (M)	Handley Page Hampden I	Waddington, Lincs
No 49 Sqn (M)	Handley Page Hampden I	Scampton, Lincs
No 50 Sqn (M)	Handley Page Hampden I	Waddington, Lincs
No 51 Sqn (H)	A W Whitley IV	Dishforth, Yorkshire
No 58 Sqn (H)	A W Whitley III	Boscombe Down, Wilts
No 61 Sqn (M)	Handley Page Hampden I	Hemswell, Lincs
No 63 Sqn (L)	Fairey Battle	Benson, Oxon
No 75 Sqn (H)	Vickers Wellington I	Harwell, Berkshire
No 76 Sqn (M)	Handley Page Hampden I	Upper Heyford, Oxon
No 77 Sqn (H)	A W Whitley V	Driffield, Yorkshire
No 78 Sqn (H)	A W Whitley IV/IVA	Linton-on-Ouse, Yorks
No 82 Sqn (L)	Bristol Blenheim IV	Watton, Norfolk
No 83 Sqn (M)	Handley Page Hampden I	Scampton, Lincs
No 90 Sqn (L)	Bristol Blenheim I	Upwood, Hunts
No 97 Sqn (H)	A W Whitley II/III	Abingdon, Berkshire
No 98 Sqn (L)	Fairey Battle	Hucknall, Derbyshire
No 99 Sqn (H)	Vickers Wellington IA	Newmarket, Suffolk
No 101 Sqn (L)	Bristol Blenheim IV	West Raynham, Norfolk
No 102 Sqn (H)	A W Whitley III/V	Driffield, Yorks
No 104 Sqn (L)	Bristol Blenheim I	Bicester, Oxon
No 106 Sqn (M)	Handley Page Hampden I	Finningley, Yorks
No 107 Sqn (L)	Bristol Blenheim IV	Wattisham, Suffolk
No 108 Sqn (L)	Bristol Blenheim IV	Bicester, Oxon

Royal Air Force, Home Bases (contd)
No 110 Sqn (L) Bristol Blenheim IV   Wattisham, Suffolk
No 115 Sqn (H) Vickers Wellington IA   Marham, Norfolk
No 144 Sqn (M) Handley Page Hampden I Hemswell, Lincs
No 148 Sqn (H) Vickers Wellington I   Harwell, Berkshire
No 149 Sqn (H) Vickers Wellington IA   Mildenhall, Suffolk
No 166 Sqn (H) A W Whitley I/III   Abingdon, Berkshire
No 207 Sqn (L) Fairey Battle   Cranfield, Beds
No 214 Sqn (H) Vickers Wellington IA   Methwold, Norfolk
No 215 Sqn (H) Vickers Wellington IA   Bassingbourne, Cambs

France
No 12 Sqn (L) Fairey Battle   Amifontaine
No 18 Sqn (L) Bristol Blenheim I   Meharicourt
No 53 Sqn (L) Bristol Blenheim IV   Poix
No 57 Sqn (L) Bristol Blenheim I   Rosières-en-Santerre
No 59 Sqn (BR) Bristol Blenheim IV   Poix
No 88 Sqn (L) Fairey Battle   Mourmelon
No 103 Sqn (L) Fairey Battle   Plivot
No 105 Sqn (L) Fairey Battle   Villeneuve-les-Vertus
No 114 Sqn (L) Bristol Blenheim IV   Condé-Vraux
No 139 Sqn (L) Bristol Blenheim IV   Betheniville
No 142 Sqn (L) Fairey Battle   Berry-au-Bac
No 150 Sqn (L) Fairey Battle   Ecury-sur-Coole
No 218 Sqn (L) Fairey Battle   Auberive-sur-Suippes
No 226 Sqn (L) Fairey Battle   Reims/Champagne

Middle East
No 8 Sqn (L) Bristol Blenheim I   Khormaksar, Aden
No 14 Sqn (M) Vickers Wellesley   Amman, Jordan
No 45 Sqn (L) Bristol Blenheim I   Fuka, Egypt
No 47 Sqn (L) Vickers Vincent   Khartoum, Sudan
No 55 Sqn (L) Bristol Blenheim I   Ismailia, Egypt
No 84 Sqn (L) Bristol Blenheim I   Shaibah, Iraq

No 113 Sqn (L) Bristol Blenheim I   Heliopolis, Egypt
No 211 Sqn (L) Bristol Blenheim I   El Daba, Egypt
No 223 Sqn (M) Vickers Wellesley   Summit, Sudan

India and the Far East
No 5 Sqn (L)   Westland Wapiti IIA   Fort Sandeman, India
No 11 Sqn (L) Bristol Blenheim I   Kallang, Singapore
No 34 Sqn (L) Bristol Blenheim I   Tengah, Singapore
No 36 Sqn (TB) Vickers Vildebeest III   Seletar, Singapore
No 39 Sqn (L) Bristol Blenheim I   Kallang, Singapore
No 60 Sqn (L) Bristol Blenheim I   Ambala, India
No 62 Sqn (L) Bristol Blenheim I   Tengah, Singapore
No 100 Sqn (TB) Vickers Vildebeest III   Seletar, Singapore

Fleet Air Arm
No 800 Sqn (FDB) Blackburn Skua II   HMS Ark Royal
No 801 Sqn (FDB) Blackburn Skua II   Hatston, Orkney
No 810 Sqn (TB) Fairey Swordfish I   HMS Ark Royal
No 812 Sqn (TB) Fairey Swordfish I   HMS Glorious
No 813 Sqn (TB) Fairey Swordfish I   HMS Eagle
No 814 Sqn (TB) Fairey Swordfish I   HMS Hermes
No 815 Sqn (TB) Fairey Swordfish I   Worthy Down, Hants
No 816 Sqn (TB) Fairey Swordfish I   Campbeltown, Argyllshire
No 818 Sqn (TB) Fairey Swordfish I   HMS Furious
No 820 Sqn (TB) Fairey Swordfish I   HMS Ark Royal
No 821 Sqn (TB) Fairey Swordfish I   HMS Ark Royal
No 823 Sqn (TB) Fairey Swordfish I   HMS Glorious
No 824 Sqn (TB) Fairey Swordfish I   HMS Eagle
No 825 Sqn (TB) Fairey Swordfish I   HMS Glorious

H—Heavy Bomber; M—Medium Bomber; L—Light Bomber; TB—Torpedo Bomber; BR—Bomber Reconnaissance; FDB—Fighter Dive Bomber.

Note: There were no Auxiliary Air Force Bomber Squadrons on this date.

Armstrong Whitworth A.W.41 Albemarle

Despite carrying prototype markings, P1362 was the first production Albemarle B Mk I. The Albemarle's characteristic transparent panels in the rear fuselage were relics of the original requirement to carry a fire-controller in that position. (Photo: Air Ministry, RTP)

Generally regarded as an unwanted foster child by the aircraft industry, the Albemarle was originally designed under the direction of Frank Barnwell at Bristol as the Type 155 to Specification P.9/38 as a fast medium bomber, capable of carrying 4,000lb of bombs which would be delivered in a 30-degree dive, its gun defence being co-ordinated by a fire-controller located in the aircraft's tail (similar requirements having been called for in the original Avro Manchester specification). Power was to be provided by a pair of Bristol Taurus, and armament was to comprise two 20mm cannon in a Bristol B.VI dorsal turret and two in a B.VII ventral turret. Its Lockheed nosewheel undercarriage was the first to be accepted for produc-

tion on a British military aircraft.

The Air Ministry soon amended the Specification by insisting that high-grade aluminium-alloy components should be excluded from the structure, and that welded-steel tube should be employed, together with unstressed plywood covering, thereby exploiting the semi-skilled light engineering and woodworking industries that abounded in Britain. These demands were contained in Specification B.17/38.

After the death of Barnwell, and Bristol's receipt of large Beaufort and Beaufighter orders, T O M Sopwith accepted responsibility for the Type 155 and directed that it should become the responsibility of John Lloyd at Sir W G Armstrong Whitworth Aircraft Ltd, and Specification B.18/38 was raised to cover this transfer, and also included the addition of reconnaissance to the aircraft's rôle. Shortly afterwards Lloyd was informed that the dive delivery, and

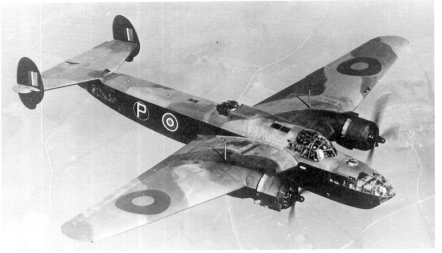

V1599, shown here, was the last of the Albemarle Mark I bombers to be produced, and later became the prototype of the Special Transport version. The four-gun dorsal turret, shown here, would be removed and a transparent fairing substituted. The shape of the transparent nose is reminiscent of the Blenheim/Beaufort design and was a legacy of Frank Barnwell's original design. The occupants of the Albemarle's nose found it fairly spacious but extremely noisy and badly laid out. (Photo: Real Photographs Co, Neg No 3894)

the need for a fire-controller, were being deleted from the Specification. By then, mid-1939, the Taurus engine allocation had been diverted elsewhere, and the Rolls-Royce Merlin X — chosen as an alternative — had been allocated to the Whitley and Halifax. The much heavier sleeve-valve Hercules was ultimately specified.

The Air Ministry was still optimistic that the new bomber would prove to be important in the process of building up the strength of Bomber Command, and had placed a production order for 200 aircraft, including two prototypes. With Whitley production being stepped up and filling the Armstrong Whitworth factory, Sopwith therefore arranged for the two prototypes to be assembled by Air Service Training Ltd (another member of the Hawker Siddeley Group) at Hamble, Hampshire, while a new company, A W Hawkesley Ltd — a name contracted from Armstrong Whitworth/Hawker Siddeley — was established in the No 2 shadow factory at Brockworth, Gloucester, to undertake production of the bomber, now named the Albemarle.

Although the first Albemarle prototype, P1360, was flown initially by Flt Lt Charles Keir Turner Hughes RAFO, Armstrong Whitworth's chief test pilot, at Hamble on 20 March 1940, subsequent flight testing continued at the Baginton factory; production aircraft were flown by John Grierson and other Gloster pilots at Brockworth. Early flights indicated that acceleration during take-off was inadequate to raise the nose-wheel soon enough to unstick in a reasonable distance, and the wing span was soon increased by about ten feet to provide the necessary lift.

With the first de Havilland Mosquito fast light bombers and reconnaissance

aircraft approaching completion, interest in the Albemarle waned during the autumn of 1940. Its performance was by no means scintillating and, when engine overheating proved difficult to overcome, the Hercules full-throttle time limit was reduced, thereby preventing the aircraft from attaining its former maximum speed before the cylinder-head temperatures reached dangerous levels.

At the end of 1940 the Air Ministry decided to abandon production of the Albemarle bomber after 40 aircraft had been completed. None of these ever served operationally. Instead, produc-

tion was concentrated on transport and glider towing versions, the Marks II, V and VI.

In these respects the aircraft may be said to have had a useful operational career, being employed to tow the Horsa troop-carrying glider and to lift small groups of specialist paratroops, as well as acting as pathfinders for major airborne landings. Albemarles took part in the invasion of Sicily on 9/10 July 1943, the Normandy landings on 6 June 1944, and the ill-fated Arnhem airborne landings on 17 September that year.

In an attempt to overcome the Albemarle's performance deficiencies, American Wright Double Cyclone

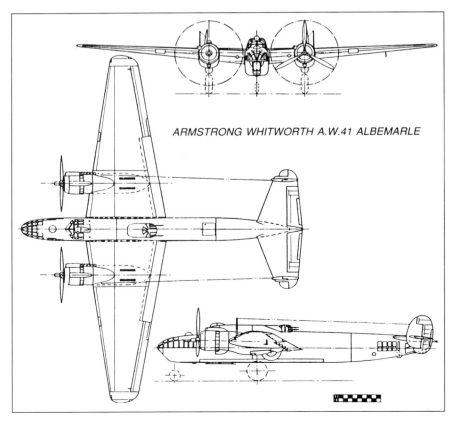

ARMSTRONG WHITWORTH A.W.41 ALBEMARLE

engines were fitted in two aircraft, but they were never adopted in production. The supply of aluminium alloys was never threatened during the War, and the aircraft did not play a major part in the airborne landing operations. Ten examples were shipped to Russia, but it is not known whether all reached their destination.

Type: Twin-engine, six/seven-crew, mid-wing monoplane reconnaissance medium bomber (later transport and glider tug).
Air Ministry Specifications: P.9/38, B.17/38 and B.18/38.
Manufacturers: Prototype manufacture. Sir W G Armstrong Whitworth Aircraft Ltd. Prototype assembly. Air Service Training Ltd, Hamble. Production. A W Hawksley Ltd, Brockworth, Glos.
Powerplant: Two 1,590hp Bristol Hercules XI 14-cylinder air-cooled sleeve-valve radial engines driving 3-blade DH Hydromatic propellers.
Structure: Steel primary structure with unstressed plywood covering.
Dimensions: Span, 77ft 0in (initially approx 67ft); length, 59ft 11in; height, 15ft 7in; wing area, 803.5 sq ft.
Weight: Bomber. All-up, 36,500lb.
Performance: Bomber. Max speed, 265 mph at 10,500ft; service ceiling, 18,000ft; range, 1,300 miles at 170 mph.

Armament: Four 0.303in Browning machine guns in Boulton Paul dorsal turret, and two in retractable ventral turret. Proposed bomb load, 4,000lb, comprising two 2,000lb AP or four 1,000lb GP bombs.
Prototypes: Two, P1360 and P1361; P1360 first flown by C Turner-Hughes at Hamble on 20 March 1940.
Production: 42 Albemarle B Mk I bombers, P1362-P1401 and V1598-V1599, were built (V1599 became transport prototype) Subsequent production amounted to 78 ST Mark Is, 80 GT Mark Is, 99 ST Mark IIs, one GT Mark II, one Mark IV, 49 GT Mark VI, 133 ST Mark VI, and 117 GT Mark VI. (ST= Special Transport, GT=Glider Tug). Total production, excluding two original prototypes, 600.
Summary of Service: No Albemarles served in the bomber rôle. Transports and glider tugs served on Nos 161, 295, 296, 297, 511 and 570 Squadrons.

de Havilland D.H.98 Mosquito Bombers

Apart from the overriding necessity to introduce the Hurricane and Spitfire into service with Fighter Command in large numbers and as quickly as possible, an important matter that was attracting the Air Staff's attention in 1938 was the disagreeable fact that the new Blenheim light bomber was already obsolete, and would require replacing fairly soon by an aircraft with a markedly improved performance.

Specification P.9/38 represented an early attempt to define a tactical medium bomber whose diving attack was intended to limit the time spent in the target area — a tacit admission that in daylight the bomber would be extremely vulnerable in the presence of the new Messerschmitt Bf 109B that was already showing its paces in Spain.

The de Havilland company, meanwhile, was examining the feasibility of extending their recently-acquired expertise in the manufacture of all-wood high-performance aircraft into the military field. The Albatross airliner, though not entirely free of problems (principally on account of its large size), featured a fuselage which incorporated laminations of cedar ply, sandwiching a thick layer of balsa wood; these were cemented together under pressure on a retractable jig which enabled the entire fuselage monocoque shell to be removed in one piece. The wing, spanning over

The first Mosquito prototype, carrying the marking E-0234, almost certainly at Salisbury Hall before its first flight. This was in effect an aerodynamic prototype and was not equipped according to any of its intended military rôles. The short engine nacelles, seen here, were to be extended beyond the wing trailing edge. (Photo: The de Havilland Aircraft Co Ltd, Neg No 475F)

one hundred feet, was also built as a single component on a load-bearing box spar using two planks of spruce applied diagonally.

When, in 1938, de Havilland submitted a proposal to the Air Ministry for a much smaller, unarmed bomber employing this form of construction, and depending on its own high speed to escape interception, it failed to spark the slightest enthusiasm — this despite that fact that one of the cornerstones of the medium bomber Specification B.17/38, which superseded P.9/38, was the demand that the aircraft should make the greatest possible use of wood in its airframe. It was, however, the idea of an unarmed bomber entering enemy airspace that was anathema to the traditionalists of the Air Staff, and caused the proposal to be turned down in October of that year.

Nothing further appeared to be accomplished until 29 December 1939. Then, as the result of behind-the-scenes lobbying by Air Marshal Sir Wilfrid Freeman KCB, DSO, MC (later Air Chief Marshal, GCB, DSO, MC), Air Council Member for Research and Development since 1936, de Havilland was instructed to go ahead with the detail design of a light bomber capable of carrying a 1,000lb bomb load over a distance of 1,500 miles. It was, moreover, to be equally suitable for production in parallel as a fighter or unarmed photo reconnaissance aircraft. A Specification, B.1/40, was drawn up and, on 1 March 1940, a contract was raised to cover the manufacture of 50 aircraft.

Designed under the leadership of Ronald Eric Bishop, and built in great secrecy at Salisbury Hall, London Colney, Hertfordshire (the location of the

An early Mosquito B Mk IX LR495 under test at Hatfield with 500lb bombs under the wings. The Merlin 70-series engines in the Marks IX and XVI were characterised by small chin air intakes. Almost all the Mosquito B Mark IXs served in the pathfinder rôle, and when replaced in No 8 (Pathfinder) Group by the Mark XVI, were modified to include the bulged bomb bay. (Photo: The de Havilland Aircraft Co Ltd, Neg No 967A dated 9 April 1943)

Mosquito Museum to this day), the prototype Mosquito was first flown by Geoffrey de Havilland Jnr on 25 November 1940. It was entirely of wooden construction, the fuselage being built in two halves in cedar ply and balsa laminations so as to enable the control circuits, wiring and system piping to be installed before mating the port and starboard halves. The single-piece stressed-skin wing was constructed around ten fuel tanks and the leading-edge radiators, and mounted a pair of 1,250hp Merlin 21 engines in low-drag nacelles. The pilot and navigator were accommodated side-by-side in a cockpit in the fuselage nose, and the bomb-bay was located amidships beneath the wing spars. No gun armament was carried.

Three prototypes were built, the first (flown initially as E-0234, but later as W4050) being a bomber, followed by the night fighter W4052, and the photo reconnaissance prototype W4051. The first production bomber version, the B Mark IV, was flown in prototype form as W4072 on 8 September 1941, this version joining its first Bomber Command Squadron, No 105, at Swanton Morley, Norfolk, in November 1941.

It was perhaps something of a paradox that, having been conceived primarily as a bomber, production of purely bomber versions of the Mosquito only accounted for about a quarter of the total number built, and these bombers only served on 18 squadrons out of a total of no fewer than 78 which flew the Mosquito.

No 105 Squadron remained the only Mosquito bomber squadron for more than nine months, flying its first operational sorties early in the morning of 31 May 1942, when four aircraft (among them W4072) carried out a high-level raid on the city of Cologne, the target of the previous night's first 1,000-bomber raid. The Squadron thereafter joined Bomber Command's night offensive as a component of the Main Force. Occa-

Type: Twin-engine, two-seat, mid-wing monoplane bomber.

Air Ministry Specification: B.1/40

Manufacturers: The de Havilland Aircraft Co Ltd, Hatfield, Herts; de Havilland Aircraft of Canada Ltd, Toronto, Canada.

Powerplant: Mark I, IV and VI. Two 1,460hp Rolls-Royce Merlin 21, 23 or 25 12-cylinder liquid-cooled supercharged in-line engines driving 3-blade DH variable-pitch propellers. B Mark IX and XVI. 1,680hp Merlin 72 and 73 or 1,710hp Merlin 76 and 77. B Mk 25. 1,620hp Packard Merlin 225. B Mk 35. 1,690hp Merlin 113 and 114.

Structure: All-wood cantilever monoplane employing cedar ply laminate sandwiching a layer of balsa.

Dimensions: Span, 54ft 2in; length, 40ft 6in; height, 12ft 6in; wing area, 454 sq ft.

Weights: Mark IV. Tare, 13,400lb; all-up, 21,462lb. Mark IX. Tare, 14,570lb; all-up, 22,780lb. B Mark 35. Tare, 14,635lb; all-up, 23,000lb.

Performance: Mark IV. Max speed, 380 mph at 17,000ft; service ceiling, 29,100ft; range (normal), 2,040 miles. Mark IX. Max speed, 408 mph at 24,000ft; service ceiling, 34,000ft; range (normal), 2,100 miles. Mark XVI. Max speed, 415 mph at 28,000ft; service ceiling, 37,000ft; range with 4,000lb bomb, 1,485 miles; B Mark 35. Max speed, 415 mph at 28,000ft; service ceiling, 42,000ft; range (maximum), 1,955 miles.

Armament: Apart from the Mark VI fighter-bombers, Mosquito bombers carried no gun armament. Bomb loads: Mark IV maximum, four 500lb bombs carried internally; Mark VI fighter-bomber, two 500lb bombs carried internally and two under the wings; Marks IX and XVI carried a maximum bomb load of one 4,000lb HC bomb internally and, if fuel was not carried in external tanks, two 500lb bombs under the wings. B Mark 35. Four 500lb bombs normally carried internally.

Prototypes. First Mosquito prototype, W4050, first flown by Geoffrey de Havilland Jnr on 25 November 1940; first Mosquito Mark IV bomber prototype, W4072, first flown on 8 September 1941.

Production: Out of a total of 7,781 Mosquitos built, 1,690 were completed as unarmed bombers, 1,020 by de Havilland at Hatfield and 670 in Canada. These comprised 296 Mark IVs, between DK284 and DK339, and between DZ311 and DZ652; 25 Mark VII (Canadian), KB300-KB324; 24 Mark IX bombers, between LR477 and LR513, and ML921-ML924; 432 Mark XVI bombers, between ML896 and MM226, MP469, between PF379 and PF619, and between RV295 and RV363;[1] 245 Mark XX (Canadian) bombers, between KB100 and KB369; 400 Mark 25 (Canadian) bombers, KA930-KA999 and KB370-KB699; and 271 Mark 35 bombers, RS699-RS723, RV364-RV367, between TA617 and TA724, between TH977 and TJ158, between TK591 and TK656, VP178-VP202 and VR792-VR806.

Summary of Service: Mosquito B IVs served with the following Squadrons in the bombing and pathfinder rôles, Nos 105, 109 and 139, and the Squadrons of the LNSF, Nos 627 and 692; they also served with No 192 Squadron in the RCM and Bomber Support rôles. Mosquito B IXs served in the pathfinder rôle with Nos 105, 109 and 139 Squadrons. Mosquito B XVIs served with the following Squadrons in the light bombing rôle, Nos 4, 14 (postwar), 98 (postwar), and 180 (postwar). They flew with the following Squadrons in the pathfinder rôle and with the LNSF, Nos 105, 109, 128, 139, 163 (postwar), 608 and 627; they also flew with No 502 Squadron, RAuxAF, after the War in the light bomber rôle. After the War Mosquito B Mark 35s equipped Nos 14 and 98 (Bomber) Squadrons in Germany, and Nos 109 and 139 (Bomber) Squadrons in the United Kingdom between December 1947 and November 1953.

---

[1] Numerous sources (presumably quoting each other) have stated that 'about 1,200' Mosquito XVI bombers were built. It has proved impossible to confirm such a figure after examining company records and the individual history cards; if such a figure was correct, almost every other production figure for Mosquitos, quoted here and elsewhere, would be suspect, and it must be assumed that the figure of 1,200 has mistakenly included a large number of other versions.

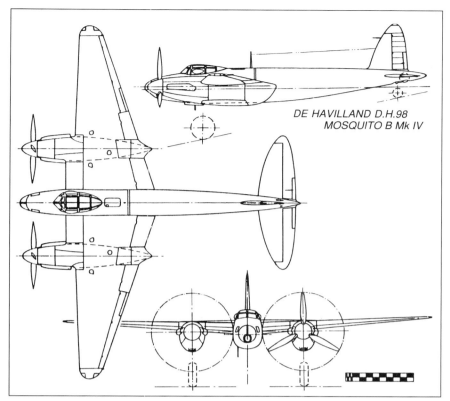

DE HAVILLAND D.H.98
MOSQUITO B Mk IV

broadcasting station three days later, and the Zeiss optical factory and Schott glass works at Jena on 27 May.

The Jena attack was the last daylight raid by Mosquito bombers (apart from equally spectacular attacks by Mark VI fighter-bombers) as both Nos 105 and 139 Squadrons were transferred from No 2 Group to No 8 Pathfinder Group. In July 1943 re-equipping with the Mosquito B Mark IX began, this version being powered by 1,680hp Merlin 72s and capable of carrying six 500lb bombs, including two under the wings. With a service ceiling, at half-fuel weight, of over 34,000 feet, these early pathfinder Mosquitos flew ahead of the bomber stream to mark the turning points on the journey to the target, Oboe being used increasingly.

Relatively few Mark IXs were built (most of their production being confined to the long-range photo reconnaissance version) before the next and most potent Mosquito appeared, the B Mark XVI. In all, 429 of these were produced, equipping 16 Squadrons, of which five were pathfinder units. The relatively small production for so many squadrons was a telling indication of the low rate of attrition enjoyed by this version. The Mark XVI differed from the Mark IX in having a pressurised cabin, enabling it to operate at 40,000 feet, a height at which it was effectively immune from enemy fighter interceptors. Powered by 1,710hp Merlin 76 and 77 engines, the Mark XVI also introduced bulged bomb doors which enabled it to carry a 4,000lb HC bomb and, with two 50gal auxiliary fuel tanks under the wings, could deliver this blast weapon all the way to Berlin — and release it from above 30,000 feet. This bomb bay modification was also made retrospectively to most of the Mark IXs and a few Mark IVs.

It is extraordinary testimony to the Mosquito bomber's capabilities that, during its pathfinder service, the aircraft dropped some 15,000 tons of bombs,

sionally, however, it was called on to carry out setpiece daylight attacks against pinpoint targets, the first of these being the Gestapo headquarters in Oslo, attacked at very low level on 25 September 1942.

In August 1942 the second bomber squadron was re-equipped with Mosquitos, although No 109 Squadron was not strictly a line unit, being primarily involved in the development of radar and other electronic warfare equipment. On the night of 20/21 December 1942 the Squadron first used the blind bombing radar, Oboe, in an individual raid on the Lutterade power station in Holland. This extremely accurate radar, introduced by No 109 Squadron into general use during 1943, was to bestow a devastating effect on the great bombing raids of 1944-45.

After the Mosquito IV bomber, the Mark VI fighter-bomber was introduced into squadron service in 1943, although being directly developed from the Mark II night fighter intruder, as well as retaining its full fighter armament of four 20mm Hispano cannon and four Browning machine guns, this version is

strictly outside the theme of this book. It should, nevertheless, be stated that in addition to its gun armament the Mark VI was capable of carrying a total of 1,500lb of bombs (comprising two 250lb bombs in a shortened bomb bay and two 500lb bombs under the wings). This version equipped a total of 44 squadrons.

No 139 (Bomber) Squadron at Marham converted to Mosquito IVs in October 1942, although it had flown some operational sorties using aircraft borrowed from No 105 in the previous month. Time and again during the following months these two Squadrons captured the nation's headlines with more than one hundred spectacular attacks on individual targets, singled out for demolition, including the Burmeister and Wain diesel engine works at Copenhagen on 27 January 1943, Berlin's main

DZ594 was one of a small number of Mosquito B Mark IVs modified to feature the bulged bomb bay for the 4,000lb HC bomb; it later served on No 627 Squadron with the Light Night Striking Force at the end of the War. (Photo: The de Havilland Aircraft Co Ltd.)

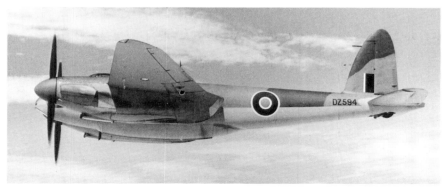

including 347 1,000lb and 16,632 250lb target indicators, totals that were only exceeded by the Lancaster and, apart from the Lancaster, more than were dropped by all other pathfinder aircraft combined. Mosquito bombers of Bomber Command flew a total of 28,639 operational sorties in three years, during which time they never equipped more than fifteen squadrons simultaneously, yet dropped a total of 26,867 tons of bombs — exceeded only by the Lancaster, Halifax, Wellington and, marginally, by the Stirling.

During the final years of the War Mosquito XVIs joined the Light Night Striking Force (LNSF) of No 100 (Bomber Support) Group, whose task was to divert enemy defences from Bomber Command's huge bomber streams in their final concentrated assault on the German homeland. Heavy electronic interference with enemy radar and radio, spoof raids and other diversionary activities were flown, not least the regular visits to Berlin by Mosquitos delivering the big blast bombs.

Mosquito production in Canada amounted to 670 bombers, in addition to 464 of other versions. The bombers comprised 25 Mark VIIs with Packard-built Merlin 31s, 245 Mark XXs with Packard Merlin 31s or 33s, and 400 Mark 25s with Packard Merlin 225s. The Mosquito Mark 25s arrived in Britain late in the War, but served on three squadrons of the LNSF and four with the Pathfinder Force during 1944 and 1945.

After the War, the Mosquito bomber remained in service alongside the night fighter and photo reconnaissance versions. A new bomber, the B Mark 35 powered by Merlin 113s and 114s, entered service with No 14 Squadron in Germany in December 1947, and was followed by No 98 Squadron, also based in Germany, and Nos 109 and 139 stationed in Britain. The last Mosquito bombers in service with Bomber Command were those of No 139 Squadron, which were finally replaced by Canberra jet bombers in November 1953.

By way of demonstrating the special place occupied by the Mosquito in the annals of the bomber, it is pertinent to quote figures issued after the defeat of the German flying bomb assault on Britain in 1944, when all types of Allied bombers were directed against the launch sites of those unpleasant weapons — hardened targets and often heavily defended. Mosquito forces averaged one launch site destroyed for every 39.8 tons of bombs dropped; the equivalent tonnages dropped by the American B-17 Fortress, B-26 Marauder and B-25 Mitchell to achieve the same destruction were 165.4 tons, 182 tons, and 219 tons respectively.

The Canberra (a light bomber in postwar terms), which assumed the Mosquito's bombing rôle in Bomber Command in the early 1950s, perpetuated exactly the same tactical philosophy that had so amply justified Air Marshal Sir Wilfrid Freeman's belief in the fast, unarmed bomber in 1939.

Fairey Barracuda

Designed to Specification S.24/37 by Marcel Lobelle as an intended replacement for the Albacore biplane torpedo aircraft, the Barracuda not only achieved this aim without ever carrying a torpedo in anger, but also succeeded in reintroducing the dive-bombing tactic to Fleet Air Arm operations.

The design was a continuation of the familiar Fairey Battle-Fulmar-Firefly formula, with pilot located well forward and the gunner well aft, and with a long transparent superstructure extending between the cockpits. A third crew member, however, dictated the provision of a cabin beneath the wing spars.

Tenders to Specification S.24/37 were received from Blackburn, Hawker, Westland, Fairey and Supermarine, but prototypes were ordered from only the two last-named companies. It soon transpired that Admiralty interest centred more on the dive-bombing tactic than the torpedo attack (an attitude that came to be justified as suitable torpedo targets decreased steadily in the last two years of the War). Lobelle therefore took the opportunity to fit large Fairey-Youngman flaps — large adjustable aerofoils attached to the wing trailing edge but

The first Barracuda prototype, P1767, with the low-set tailplane originally fitted; the equipment pack on the rear fuselage is a test anti-spin parachute. (Photo: Air Ministry)

below and aft of it; these could be used to increase lift for take-off, allow a steeper and slower approach to landing and, when set at a negative angle of incidence, allow a rapid rate of descent in a dive, while limiting the airspeed.

On account of the shoulder wing position, the undercarriage was hinged at the base of the fuselage and retracted outwards and up into the wing roots.

An early setback occurred when the proposed engine, the 1,200hp Rolls-Royce Exe 24-cylinder X-type pressure-air-cooled sleeve-valve engine, was abandoned late in 1939, and delays followed with the necessity to reposition the wing to cater for the lighter but more powerful Merlin 30.

It was not until 7 December 1940 that the prototype, P1767, was first flown by Staniland, this machine featuring a tailplane conventionally located at the base of the fin. Early diving trials, however, with the Youngman flaps set at the negative diving angle, gave rise to severe buffeting of the tail surfaces and loss of elevator control owing to a breakdown of the airflow aft of the big flaps. The remedy was to raise the tailplane about four feet up the fin, and this configuration was adopted henceforth.

The very wide range of external stores (apart from the 18in torpedo specified), which had to be cleared through the experimental establishments, included two types of sea mine, depth charges,

Right: *A Barracuda II flying with a torpedo, the one naval weapon not delivered by this aircraft despite being demanded in Specification S.24/37. This flying view illustrates the 'level-flight' position of the Fairey-Youngman flaps.* (Photo: A J Jackson Collection)

Below: *MX907 was the last of 700 Barracuda Mark IIs built by Blackburn. Note the ASV Mk IIN aerial array on the wing, and the Fairey-Youngman flaps, shown here in their diving position.* (Photo: G S Leslie)

500lb AP and GP bombs and 1,000lb HE bombs. However, deliveries began to the Fleet Air Arm in the early autumn of 1942 of Barracuda Mark Is, of which only 30 were produced, and these joined No 831 Squadron, commanded by Lt-Cdr Andrew Gurney Leatham RN, at Crail, Fife, in December.

Production then switched to the Barracuda Mark II, powered by the Merlin 32. Orders for this version had been placed with Blackburn, Boulton Paul and Westland, and production accelerated fairly quickly, and ten further operational squadrons being equipped with Barracudas during 1943.

It was a force of Barracudas that severely crippled the battleship *Tirpitz* in a highly successful dive bombing attack on 3 April 1944. The ship had spent the previous winter in Kaafjord in northern Norway, undergoing repairs following the famous attack by Royal Navy midget submarines, and was expected to be ready for sea very soon.

A carrier task force was accordingly assembled and set sail for the northern waters, comprising the fleet carriers HMS *Furious* (with No 831 Barracuda Squadron embarked, now with Mark IIs) and HMS *Victorious* (Nos 827, 829 and 830 Squadrons, all with Mark IIs), and four escort carriers, HMS *Emperor*, *Fencer*, *Pursuer* and *Searcher* with 80 Wildcat,

Seafire, Corsair and Hellcat naval fighters. The dive bombers attacked in two waves, scoring between 10 and 15 direct hits with 500lb SAP and 1,000lb HE bombs and, although there was never much chance of sinking the big ship with such bombs, the damage to superstructure and below decks must have been considerable, for it prevented her from putting to sea during the summer. Some

further damage was inflicted in following attacks by Barracudas, but none matched the success of that first raid. It was a fitting vindication of the Admiralty's return to dive bombing. (The *Tirpitz* was finally sunk by RAF Lancasters, dropping 12,000lb DP bombs, on 12 November 1944.)

Meanwhile the first Barracudas were making ready for service further afield. No 810 Squadron had taken delivery of Mark IIs in March 1943, and sailed in HMS *Illustrious* for the Mediterranean to support the landings at Salerno early in September. Two months later the carrier, now also joined by No 847 Squadron, sailed for Ceylon, the Barracuda Squadrons constituting the 21st TBR Wing. Although much of their work was confined to anti-shipping patrols (on one occasion searching in vain for three Japanese cruisers at large in the Indian Ocean), they were called on to launch a dive bombing attack on oil storage tanks and docks at Sabang in northern Sumatra in 1944.

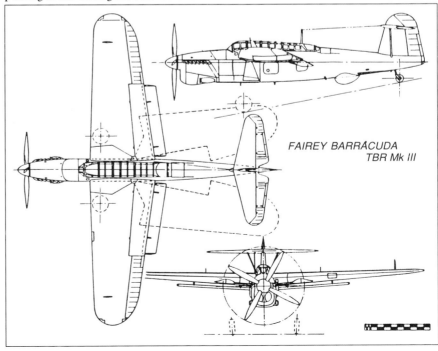

FAIREY BARRACUDA
TBR Mk III

RK558/325/LP, a Barracuda V of No 783 Squadron at Lee-on-Solent in the radar training rôle in 1948; note the radome on the wing leading edge and the retention of store racks under the fuselage. (Photo: via R C Sturtivant)

For the ship-search rôle, the Barracuda was equipped with ASV Mk IIN, whose yagi array aerials were mounted on the upper surface of the outer wings. However, a new version of the Barracuda, the Mark III, was first flown in 1943, this being intended for anti-submarine operations with depth charges and equipped with ASV Mk X; this was an altogether better, centimetric radar employing a scanner enclosed in a radome under the rear fuselage.

Barracuda IIIs began appearing at the end of 1944, but equipped no more than five Squadrons, Nos 810, 815, 821, 822 and 860. Only No 821 was embarked for operations in hostile waters, flying from various escort carriers to lay mines off the Norwegian coast during the last months of the War; each aircraft carried a single 1,500lb mine on the under-fuselage torpedo crutches.

The final version of the Barracuda, powered by a Rolls-Royce Griffon, was an entirely revised design, intended for the Far East. It was not, however, ready for delivery before the War in the Pacific ended, and none served on an operational squadron. The prototype, P9976, termed the Mark IV, was a converted Mark II powered by a Griffon VII and first flown on 16 November 1944. Production Mark Vs, with 2,020hp Griffon 37s, carried only two crew members, pilot and navigator/radar operator, and had an entirely new wing with increased span and square tips. The fin and rudder were progressively enlarged, first by extending the fin forward and later by enlarging both fin and rudder by extending them upwards. Only 30 Mark Vs were built, although some earlier Mark IIs and IIIs were converted.

Several interesting experiments were performed on Barracudas, including the mounting of an airborne lifeboat under the fuselage, this installation being conceived for use during convoy escort duties, when it proved hazardous for ships to stop to rescue survivors from

torpedoed merchantmen. (Thousands of such men perished from exposure in the icy seas through which the North Cape convoys sailed.)

Even more radical were experiments by the AFEE to carry paratroops in underwing containers. A two-man container was carried under each wing of Barracuda II P9795, the occupants being 'released' through trap doors operated by the pilot. Neither this, nor the lifeboat project, reached service.

As previously stated, the Barracuda's service did not include torpedo operations, principally owing to diminishing opportunities in European waters during the last two years of the War. For such operations in the Far East, the Fleet Air Arm increasingly depended on the excellent Grumman Avenger.

Barracudas were withdrawn from the Fleet Air Arm in July 1946, when No 827 Squadron was disbanded. However, No 815 Squadron, which had been disbanded and had given up its Mark IIIs in January 1946, was re-formed, again with Barracuda IIIs, at Eglinton on 1 December 1947, and continued to fly them until May 1953 — occasionally embarking in the fleet carriers HMS *Illustrious*, *Implacable* and *Indomitable*.

Type: Single-engine, three-crew, shoulder-wing monoplane carrier-borne dive-bomber/torpedo bomber.

Air Ministry Specification: S.24/37

Manufacturers: The Fairey Aviation Co Ltd, Hayes, Middlesex, and Heaton Chapel, Stockport; Blackburn Aircraft Ltd, Brough, Yorks; Boulton Paul Aircraft Ltd, Wolverhampton; Westland Aircraft Ltd, Yeovil, Somerset.

Powerplant: Prototypes and Mark I. One 1,300hp Rolls-Royce Merlin 30 12-cylinder liquid-cooled in-line engine driving 3-blade propeller. Marks II and III. 1,640hp Merlin 32 driving 4-blade propeller. Mark V. 2,020hp Rolls-Royce Griffon driving 4-blade propeller.

Structure: All-metal stressed-skin construction with fabric-covered control surfaces.

Dimensions: Mks I-III. Span, 49ft 2in (17ft 9in folded); length, 39ft 9in; height, 15ft 2in; wing area, 405 sq ft: Mk V. Span, 53ft 0in (18ft 5½in folded); length, 41ft 7in; height, 17ft 3in; wing area, 435 sq ft.

Weights: Mark III. Tare, 9,407lb; max all-up, 14,100lb. Mark V. Tare 11,430lb; max all-up, 16,000lb.

Performance: Mark III. Max speed, 239 mph at 1,750ft; climb to 5,000ft, 4 min 30 sec; service ceiling, 20,000ft; range with 1,500lb bomb load, 700 miles. Mark V. Max speed, 253 mph at 10,000ft; climb to 10,000ft, 8 min 36 sec; service ceiling, 24,000ft; range with 2,000lb bomb load, 600 miles.

Armament: Gun armament of two Vickers K machine guns in the rear cockpit. The Mark V possessed a single forward-firing Browning gun, but no rear gun. Provision for one 1,572lb torpedo, but seldom carried. Bomb load of up to 2,000lb, comprising 500 and 1,000lb bombs.

Prototypes: Two, P1767 and P1770; P1767 first flown by C S Staniland on 7 December 1940 at Harmondsworth.

Production: A total of 2,600 Barracudas was built (excluding prototypes). **Fairey,** 1,190: Mk Is, 25 (P9642-P9666); Mk IIs, 675 (between P9667 and P9986; between DT813 and DT887; and between LS464 and LS974); Mk IIIs, 460 (between PM682 and PN164; and between RK328 and RK523); Mk Vs, 30 (between RK530 and RK574), **Blackburn,** Mk IIs, 700 (between BV660 and BV981; between MD612 and MD807; and between MX535 and MX907). **Boulton Paul,** 692: Mk IIs, 300 (between DP855 and DR335); Mk IIIs, 392 (between MD811 and ME293; and between RJ759 and RJ966). **Westland,** 18: Mk Is, 5 (DN625-DN629); Mk IIs, 13 (DN630-DN642).

Summary of Fleet Air Arm Service: Barracudas served with the following operational Squadrons: Nos. 810, 812, 814, 815, 816, 817, 818, 820, 821, 822, 823, 824, 825, 826, 827, 828, 829, 830, 831, 837, 841, 847 and 860, between December 1942 and July 1946; and with the following second-line Squadrons: Nos 700, 703, 706, 707, 710, 711, 713, 714, 716, 717, 719, 731, 733, 735, 736, 737, 744, 747, 750, 753, 756, 764, 767, 768, 769, 774, 778, 780, 781, 783, 785, 786, 787, 796, 797, 798 and 799. Barracudas served aboard HM Fleet Carriers *Formidable, Furious, Illustrious, Implacable, Indefatigable, Indomitable* and *Victorious*; HM Light Fleet Carriers *Colossus, Glory, Venerable, Vengeance* and *Unicorn*; and aboard HM Escort Carriers *Atheling, Battler, Campania, Nairana, Puncher, Searcher, Thane* and *Trumpeter*.

Avro Type 683 Lancaster

Veteran Lancaster B.I W4113 was originally delivered to No 49 Squadron in August 1942, and took part in raids on Düsseldorf, Osnabrück, Flensburg, Kassel, Saarbrüchen, Duisberg (twice), Frankfurt, Bremen, Wilhelmshaven, Wismar, Aachen, Kiel, Cologne, Genoa (three times), Hamburg (twice), Stuttgart, Turin and Mannheim. It joined No 156 Squadron early in 1943 and later served with Nos 1661 and 1668 Conversion Units, and is shown here in the markings of No 5 Lancaster Finishing School. (Photo: Imperial War Museum, Neg No CH11933)

The unequivocal announcement by Lord Portal at the end of August 1940 of the Air Staff's determination to re-equip the RAF's strategic bombing force with four-engine aircraft exclusively as quickly as possible may have had the ring of propaganda about it, made as it was at the height of the Battle of Britain and at the low tide of Britain's fortunes. Yet with the Short Stirling just arriving on its first squadron, and the Halifax only three months away, it was a not unrealistic aim to express. The speed with which it was achieved was unquestionably one of the major factors contributing to Allied victory in the Second World War.

Behind the scenes, the question of how long the Air Ministry would continue to order the Manchester was being addressed for, as yet, this twin-engine heavy bomber promised to be every bit as good as the Halifax and Stirling, carrying a heavier bomb load than one, faster and higher than the other.

There was, however, the matter of the

high cost of the Vulture engine which had yet to achieve its full-service type test, while its continuing development was certainly occupying a disproportionate amount of labour. The immediate option was to complete those Manchesters whose manufacture had been started, and then to dismantle the production lines at Avro and Metropolitan-Vickers; certain officials at the Ministry of Aircraft Production wished then to introduce Halifax production into those factories, a course of action that caused

considerable offence to Chadwick and the Hawker Siddeley Group directors. They had, after all, kept the Air Ministry and Ministry of Aircraft Production fully informed of the design and development progress of the Manchester III — the four-Merlin Manchester — which had been under development for about two years, and which promised substantial improvements over the Vulture-powered version. It had been explained that, with span increased to 'about 100 feet and with Merlin XXs', the perform-

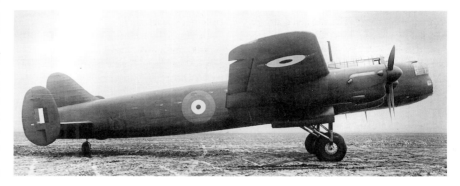

Above: *The first Lancaster prototype, BT308, as originally flown, with Manchester tail unit and undercarriage, and Merlin Xs, although the latter are enclosed in Merlin XX cowlings. (Photo: Rolls-Royce Ltd, Neg No WP5097)*

Left: *The second Lancaster prototype, DG595, at near-production standard, with dorsal and ventral gun turrets and Merlin XX engines. (Photo: RAF Museum, Neg No P009361)*

L7529 was the third production Lancaster I, originally laid down as a Manchester. It never served operationally but underwent glider towing trials, and then flew trials with the Capital Ship Bomb for which the bomb bay was enlarged. It is shown at Farnborough, still with the enlarged bomb bay, and with arrester hook under the rear fuselage during trials with a runway arrester cable system. (Photo: MoD (PF) Ref No 6040)

ance and bomb load would be superior to that of the Halifax, and that the Merlin-Manchester could be introduced into the existing Manchester production lines with scarcely any interruption in deliveries. (Chadwick was always highly critical of the Halifax, pointing to the ill-judged choice of the Merlin X and the fundamental restriction in its bomb bay design, which in turn limited the size of bomb that could be carried; indeed the Halifax could not carry anything larger than the 4,000lb HC bomb — which could be accommodated by both the Manchester and Wellington.)

Avro's arguments in favour of introducing the four-Merlin Manchester III into production were quickly accepted after W S Farren (later Sir William, CB, MBE), Director of Technical Development at the MAP, wrote to the Air Ministry on 4 September 1940, recommending that two prototypes should be ordered forthwith.[1]

The Contract to produce the first prototype was signed on 7 September 1940, and covering Minutes indicated it should be completed and flown within four months and that the greatest pos-

sible use be made of existing Manchester I components and jigs. It was also pointed out that four Merlin Xs would be made available to begin with, but that Merlin XXs would be delivered as soon as supply allowed.

Within the space of three weeks all necessary manufacturing drawings were prepared, and the first Manchester III prototype, BT308, now renamed the Lancaster, was first flown at Woodford on 9 January 1941 by Capt H A ('Sam') Brown. Allowing for the fact that a Manchester's wing centresection, undercarriage, fuselage and tail (complete with central fin), had been used in this prototype, as well as the unsatisfactory Merlin Xs, the early pilots' reports were very encouraging. It was, however, after the Manchester Mk IA's tall fins (without central surface), Merlin XXs and a new undercarriage with greatly enlarged wheels had been flown on the second prototype, DG595, on 13 May 1941, that the full potential of the Lancaster came to be realised. This aeroplane was delivered to Boscombe Down on 16 August for Service and full-load trials.

In accordance with the original proposals made by Farren in September 1940, the unqualified approval of the two prototypes by the A & AEE was followed by an instruction to introduce Lancasters into the Avro production line at Newton Heath after the 157th Manchester airframe had been completed, and the remaining 43 aircraft of

this Contract were completed as Lancasters, the first production Mark I being flown on 31 October 1941. These aircraft carried two-gun power-operated turrets in the nose, dorsal and ventral midships positions, and a four-gun turret in the tail. The maximum bomb load, carried over short ranges was 14,000lb, comprising either fourteen 1,000lb bombs, one 4,000lb HC and a mix of 1,000lb and 500lb bombs, and small bomb carriers containing incendiary bombs.

Into Squadron Service

The first Lancasters were issued to No 44 (Rhodesia) Squadron, commanded by Wg Cdr Roderick Alastair Brook Learoyd VC (Acting Commanding Officer, Sqn Ldr John Dering Nettleton) at Waddington on 24 December 1941, and within a week was fully equipped. This Squadron was quickly followed by No 97 (Bomber) Squadron at Coningsby, commanded by Wg Cdr John Henry Kynoch DFC.

The first Lancaster bombing operation was carried out by No 44 Squadron, whose aircraft joined a raid on Essen by Bomber Command on the night of 10/11 March 1942. And the first Lancaster to be lost on operations was an aircraft captained by F/Sgt Lyster Warren-Smith of No 44 Squadron, which failed to return from a mining operation with its eight-man crew.

It was, however, to be with a spectacular low-level daylight raid by twelve aircraft from both Nos 44 and 97 Squadrons on Augsburg that the Lancaster first seized the newspaper headlines.

---

[1] This, and other relevant correspondence under Ref. SB.8416, is held at the Public Record Office in AVIA15/590. It discloses beyond debate that the decision to go ahead with the Lancaster (then known as the Four-Merlin Manchester III) both in prototype and production form was taken several months before the Vulture engine showed signs that considerable development was required before it could be cleared for unrestricted Service use. See under Avro Manchester, page 324. This is in direct conflict with the long-held belief that the Lancaster came into being only because the Manchester failed to meet Service requirements.

Hercules-powered, AWA-built Lancaster II DS771. It served on Nos 408 and 426 (Canadian) Squadrons before being lost in a raid on Stuttgart on 15/16 March 1944. (Photo: A V Roe & Co Ltd, Neg No A/9/1/219)

No 617 Squadron's Lancaster I (Special), PB996/ YZ-C, releasing a 22,000lb Grand Slam Deep Penetration bomb. This aeroplane dropped four such bombs against the Arnsburg viaduct, the Nienburg bridge, the Bremen bridge and the Farge U-boat pens, all in the last fortnight of March 1945. (Photo: RAF Museum, Neg No P022483)

Against unexpectedly fierce German fighter opposition, the two Squadrons battled their way south-east across enemy-occupied Europe to the town of Augsburg, near Munich, to bomb the MAN diesel engine factory. Eight aircraft survived the long flight out and, of the thirty-two 1,000lb bombs dropped, seventeen hit the factory and twelve exploded, causing severe damage to the important machine shops. A further three Lancasters were shot down, and Nettleton's aircraft, leading No 44 Squadron's formation, was its only survivor. The Squadron Leader was awarded the Victoria Cross, the first of ten such awards to captains and crew members of Lancasters during the Second World War.

Although the build-up of Lancaster Squadrons during 1942 was slow (with a total of seventeen receiving their new aircraft by the end of the year), the aircraft represented the muscle of Bomber Command's growing night offensive against Germany, being the only aircraft capable of carrying any bomb larger than the 4,000lb HC weapon (also capable of being carried by the Wellington). One of the new Lancaster Squadrons was No 106 (formerly a Manchester squadron), commanded by a young man who was to stamp his extraordinary qualities of leadership on every operation in which he flew; his name was Wg Cdr Guy Penrose Gibson, DFC (later VC, DSO*, DFC*).

No 106 Squadron, by the quality of leadership and training, soon came in for more than its share of 'difficult' operations, and one of these was an attack on Gdynia on the night of 27/28 August when three Lancasters, led by Gibson, carried out a raid against German warships, which were believed to include the aircraft carrier *Graf Zeppelin* and the battlecruiser *Gneisenau*. The aircraft were loaded with special weapons weighing

about 5,000lb and referred to as Capital Ship Bombs, designed to penetrate any known warship armour before detonating and blowing a carbon-steel disc through the bottom of the ship. Unfortunately visibility over the target prevented the crews from sighting the enemy ships, and the two bombs dropped fell on Gdynia's dock area. Soon afterwards No 106 Squadron was pioneering bombing operations with a new weapon, the 8,000lb High Capacity bomb, carrying the weapon high over the Alps against targets in northern Italy.

The matter of apparently selecting a single Squadron to undertake special operations against key targets, using specialised weapons, was beginning to occupy the minds of the Air Staff, not to mention those of Bomber Command. Already (in August 1942) a new Pathfinder Group, No 8, had been created in an attempt to improve the bombing accuracy of Bomber Command, and this attained an element of élitism that was not always fully appreciated by other line squadrons.

Certainly the selection of No 106 Squadron to perform special bombing operations was instrumental in establishing strongly-held opinions in the minds of men like Sir Arthur Harris, and this became all-too apparent when No 617 Squadron was formed with

Lancasters to attack the German dams in May 1943. Indeed, it is frequently overlooked that, not only was Gibson given command of the Squadron, but he also selected every available ex-106 Squadron aircraft captain. In doing so, and in succeeding in breaching two of the five dams attacked with Barnes Wallis' special 'Upkeep' mines in May 1943, he set a pattern of operations that survived until the end of the War, and was not emulated by any other Air Force, Allied or enemy. The list of No 617 Squadron's commanding officers included some of the greatest names in the history of Bomber Command, not forgetting the greatest of them all, Gp Capt Geoffrey Leonard Cheshire, VC, OM, DSO**, DFC*.

That pattern was based firmly on the capabilities of the Lancaster alone, simply on account of the aircraft's unmatched weight-lifting capabilities. Just as No 106 Squadron had pioneered operations with the CSB and 8,000lb HC bomb, so No 617 became the first to carry the 12,000lb HC, the 12,000lb Tallboy (deep penetration) and the awesome 22,000lb Grand Slam (deep penetration) bombs.

It is of course impossible to list the thousands of raids in which Lancasters took such a leading part, except to record that they flew in all three of the

Victory-built Canadian Lancaster Mark X, FM148, at the Winterisation Experimental Establishment in Canada during 1946-47. Some RCAF Lancasters were not retired until the 1960s. (Photo: via Douglas Garton)

Left: To increase the range of the Lancaster for operations in the Far East, HK541 (shown here) and SW244 were modified to carry 1,500 gallons of extra fuel in saddle tanks, and flown out to India for trials with No 1577 (Special Duties) Flight in 1944. (Photo: Air Ministry, A & AEE)

Below: Lancaster B VII NX791 of No 617 Squadron at Digri, India, during 1945. Note the Rose tail turret. (Photo: via A S Thomas)

famous '1,000-bomber' raids of 1942 as well as the many raids that consititued the three great Bomber Battles of 1943, the Battle of the Ruhr, the Battle of Hamburg (when they first dropped the ECM device known as Window to obliterate the German radar defences) and the great Battle of Berlin. The last came to an end with the infamous raid on Nuremburg on the night of 30/31 March 1944, when over 100 British bombers were lost out of a total of 772 heavy bombers sent out. Of slightly less than 7,000 Lancasters delivered during the Second World War, no fewer than 3,345 were lost on operations, involving the loss of 21,751 crew members, killed or missing in action.

Technically, the Lancaster underwent very little development and significant modification throughout the War. The Mark I was the most numerous, followed closely by the Mark III (externally almost indistinguishable from the Mark I, but powered by American Packard-built Rolls-Royce Merlin 28 engines). Fast increasing demand for the Merlin engine in 1941 had prompted preparation of a third prototype, DT810, with Bristol Hercules VI sleeve-valve radial engines, and this was first flown on 26 November that year. Production of this version, the Mark II, was undertaken by Sir W G Armstrong Whitworth Aircraft Ltd at Coventry, which produced a total of 300 examples. (The majority of these Lancasters served with No 115 Squadron, RAF, and squadrons of the RCAF which flew alongside the RAF during the War.) By the end of the

War most of the Canadian heavy bomber squadrons had converted on to the Lancaster Mark X, of which 430 were produced by Victory Aircraft Ltd, Malton, Ontario, Canada (these aircraft powered by Packard Merlin engines).

Not surprisingly, the Lancaster topped almost every table of bombing statistics provided by Bomber Command between 1939 and 1945, perhaps the most impressive being the fact that, of the total of 955,044 tons of bombs dropped by the Command during the whole War, no less than 608,612 tons, or almost two-thirds, were dropped by the Lancaster in the last three years alone.

Minor variants included the Lancaster Mark VI, powered by Merlin 85s or 102s in annular cowlings and driving four-blade propellers, of which a small number was built, and the Lancaster VII which featured two 0.50in Browning guns in a Glenn Martin dorsal turret.

Almost all the Hercules-powered Lancaster IIs featured bulged bomb bays, originally developed to enable the 8,000lb HC bomb to be carried, and

when production of this weapon was cut back somewhat, it was decided to retain the bulged doors as they faired into the ventral turret, which was also a favoured feature of the Canadian Lancaster Squadrons. In this respect, it is perhaps interesting to record that one of the most deadly weapons employed by German night fighters in the last eighteen months of the War was the upward-firing heavy-calibre gun battery, enabling the fighter to attack, unseen, from beneath. Countless Lancasters and Halifaxes were lost to this German armament (known as *Schräge Musik*, or jazz) before the tactic was discovered; no doubt, the retention of the Lancaster's ventral guns might have reduced their losses.

In fact, very few Lancasters carried the ventral guns; instead, most were fitted with the large H₂S airborne radar scanner, used principally to begin with by PathfinderLancasters and Halifaxes, to assist in marking the route to be followed by the bomber stream, and then marking the aiming point at the target. Eventually, almost all Squadron Lancasters of Bomber Command were equipped with H₂S. Many others carried passive and active radar with which to defend themselves against the German night fighter defences.

The Empire Air Armament School's Lancaster Thor, with H₂S Mk IIIG, AGLT rear guns, Mk XIV bombsight, Loran, Rebecca and Gee Mk III, on the eve of its tour of the Far East in March 1946, during which it visited the Empire Air Armament School, RAAF. (Photo: R Grantham-Hill, DFC).

Left: *TX911 was one of a number of postwar Lancaster engine test beds, shown here with Armstrong Siddeley Python axial-flow turbo-props in the outboard engine positions.* (Photo: Armstrong Siddeley Motors Ltd, Neg No XA1812)

Below: *As part of wide-ranging bomber defence system trials, Lancaster LL780/G was fitted with twin 20mm Hispano cannon barbettes above and below the rear fuselage, with a remote control position and gun-laying radar in the extreme tail.* (Photo: via F G Swanborough)

Postwar Service

The end of the War was followed by a rapid run-down of Bomber Command, with almost all the Dominion and European Squadrons returning home or being disbanded in Britain.

It had, however, been intended to deploy a fairly large force of heavy bombers to the Far East, beginning with a number of Lancaster squadrons equipped with AWA-built B Mk I (FE) aircraft, and followed eventually by the Lancaster IV and V (later to become the much larger Lincoln B 1 and B 2, see page 355).

Although several Lancaster squadrons were deployed to India and Burma (including No 617 Squadron), their main areas of activity were elsewhere. No 35 (Bomber) Squadron took its white-painted Lancaster B I (FE)s to the USA in July-August 1946 on a goodwill tour; No 82 Squadron used a number of specially modified photo-reconnaissance Lancaster Is to complete an enormous aerial survey of West, Central and East Africa between 1946 and 1952. Other squadrons were based in Palestine to control the flood of Jewish immigrants from Europe, seeking to establish their own state.

With the return of so many American aircraft leased from the USA during the War, the Lancaster underwent superficial development to undertake the maritime reconnaissance rôle with Coastal Command, being termed either the MR or GR Mark 3; another version was the ASR Mk 3, equipped to carry a large airborne lifeboat for air-sea rescue operations.

Not surprisingly, with so many Lancasters becoming 'surplus to requirements' after the War, they were employed in countless trials and for trial installations, including test beds for

(Continued on page 349)

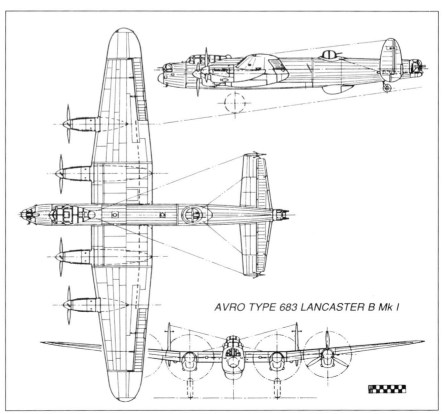

AVRO TYPE 683 LANCASTER B Mk I

Type: Four-engine, seven/eight-crew, mid-wing monoplane heavy night bomber.

Manufacturers: A V Roe & Co Ltd., Manchester, Woodford, Cheshire, and Yeadon, Yorks; Sir W G Armstrong Whitworth Aircraft Ltd, Coventry and Bitteswell; Metropolitan-Vickers Ltd, Manchester; The Austin Motor Co Ltd, Longbridge, Birmingham; Vickers-Armstrongs Ltd., Chester and Castle Bromwich; Victory Aircraft Ltd, Malton, Ontario, Canada.

Powerplant: Four 1,460hp Rolls-Royce Merlin XX, 22, 28, 38 or 224, 12-cylinder liquid-cooled, supercharged in-line engines driving 3-blade DH variable-pitch, constant-speed propellers; also 1,650hp Bristol Hercules VI 14-cylinder air-cooled two-row radial engines. Test beds fitted with Rolls-Royce Merlin 24s, 65s, 85s and 600s and Dart turboprops; Metrovick F.2/1 and F.2/4A Beryl turbojets; Armstrong Siddeley ASX and Adder turbojets, and Mamba and Python turboprops; Avro Canada Orenda and Swedish Dovern turbojets.

Structure: Light-alloy monocoque fuselage built in five sections; wing built in five sections (centre, outer and wing tips) about two mainspars of extruded Hiduminium booms and Alclad webs; entire airframe metal covered.

Dimensions: Span, 102ft 0in; length, 69ft 6in; height, 20ft 4in; wing area, 1,297 sq ft.

Weights: Tare, 36,457lb; all-up, with normal max bomb load, 68,000lb; with 22,000lb bomb, 72,000lb.

Performance: Mark III (normal max bomb load), max speed, 287 mph at 11,500ft; cruising speed, 210 mph at 12,000ft; climb to 20,000ft, 41 min 40 sec; service ceiling, 24,500ft (without bomb load); range with 14,000lb bomb load, 1,660 miles; range with 22,000lb bomb, 1,040 miles.

Armament: Gun armament comprised two 0.303in Browning machine guns in nose turret, two in dorsal turret, and four in the tail turret; some aircraft also armed with two guns firing downwards from ventral gun position. Bomb loads: (a) Special aircraft. Either one 22,000lb, one 12,000lb deep penetration bombs, one 9,500lb Upkeep pre-rotated 'bouncing' mine, one 5,490lb Type T 45in or one 5,300lb Type T 38in capital ship bomb. (b) Standard aircraft: One 8,000lb blast (HC) bomb and up to 6,000lb of smaller bombs; up to 14,000lb normal bomb load comprising one 4,000lb HC bomb and combinations of 2,000lb AP, 2,000lb GP, 1,000lb MC or GP, 500lb MC or GP, 250lb SAP, GP, MC, incendiary, sea mines or bombs, and/or up to 14 Small Bomb Carriers (SBCs) carrying a total of 3,400 four-pound incendiary bombs.

Prototypes: Three, BT308, DG595 and DT810 (Mark II). BT308 (originally Manchester III), first flown by Capt H A Brown on 9 January 1941,

Summary of Production: A total of 7,373 Lancasters was built. Avro, 3,669: L7527–L7584, between R5482 and R5763, W4102 and W4384, ED303 and ED202, JA672 and JB748, LM301 and LM756, ME295 and ME551, ND324 and NE181, PA964 and PD139, RE115 and RE226, SW319 and SW377, and TX263 and TW273. Armstrong Whitworth, 1,329: Between DS601 and DS852, LL617 and LM296, NF906 and NG503, RF120 and RF326, SW283–SW316 and between TW647 and TW911. Austin, 330: Between NN694 and NN816, NX548 and NX794 and RT670-RT699. Vickers-Armstrongs, 535: Between HK535 and HK806, PA158 and PA509, PP663 and PP792. Metrovick, 1,080: Between R5842 and R5917, between W4761 and W5012, DV155 and DV407, ME554 and ME868, PD198 and PD444, RA500 and RA806, SW243-SW279 and TW915-TW929. Victory, Canada, 430: FM100-FM229 and KB700-KB999. This total comprised 3,424 Mark Is, 300 Mark IIs, 3,039 Mark IIIs, 180 Mark VIIs and 430 Mark Xs. Numerous Lancaster Is were subsequently modified as Mark IIIs and some *vice versa.*

Summary of RAF Service: Lancasters served with the following Bomber Squadrons (listed chronologically by first deliveries): No 44 from December 1941 at Waddington; No 97 from January 1942 at Coningsby; No 207 from March 1942 at Bottesford; No 83 from April 1942 at Coningsby; No 106 from April 1942 at Coningsby; No 50 from May 1942 at Skellingthorpe; No 61 from May 1942 at Syer-

ston; No 49 from July 1942 at Scampton; No 109 from August 1942 at Wyton; No 9 from August 1942 at Waddington; No 57 from September 1942 at Scampton; No 460 (Australian) from October 1942 at Breighton; No 101 from October 1942 at Holme-on-Spalding Moor; No 103 from November 1942 at Elsham Wolds; No 12 from November 1942 at Wickenby; No 467 (Australian) from November 1942 at Scampton; No 156 from December 1942 at Warboys; No 100 from December 1942 at Grimsby; No 115 from March 1943 at East Wretham; No 617 from March 1943 at Scampton; No 619 from April 1943 at Woodhall Spa; No 7 from May 1943 at Oakington; No 426 (Canadian) from June 1943 at Linton-on-Ouse; No 405 (Canadian) from August 1943 at Gransden Lodge; No 408 (Canadian) from August 1943 at Linton-on-Ouse; No 116 from September 1943 at Kirmington; No 514 from September 1943 at Foulsham; No 625 from October 1943 at Kelstern; No 550 from October 1943 at Grimsby; No 432 (Canadian) from October 1943; No 463 (Australian) from November 1943 at Waddington; No 626 from November 1943 at Wickenby; No 576 from November 1943 at Elsham Wolds; No 630 from December 1943 at East Kirkby; No 622 from December 1943 at Mildenhall; No 15 from December 1943 at Mildenhall; No 419 (Canadian) from March 1944 at Middleton St George; No 35 from March 1944 at Graveley; No 635 from March 1944 at Downham Market; No 75 (New Zealand) from March 1944 at Mepal; No 582 from April 1944 at Little Staughton; No 300 (Polish) from April 1944 at Faldingworth; No 90 from June 1944 at Tuddenham; No 428 (Canadian) from June 1944 at Middleton St George; No 149 from August 1944 at Methwold; No 218 from September 1944 at Methwold; No 195 from October 1944 at Witchford; No 186 from October 1944 at Tuddenham; No 153 from October 1944 at Kirmington; No 227 from October 1944 at Bardney; No 170 from October 1944 at Kelstern; No 189 from October 1944 at Bardney; No 431 (Canadian) from October 1944 at Croft; No 150 from November 1944 at Fiskerton; No 434 (Canadian) from December 1944 at Croft; No 424 (Canadian) from January 1945 at Skipton-on-Swale; No 433 (Canadian) from January 1945 at Skipton-on-Swale; No 427 (Canadian) from March 1945 at Leeming; No 138 from March 1945 at Tuddenham; No 429 (Canadian) from March 1945 at Leeming; No 420 (Canadian) from April 1945 at Tholthorpe. *Post-War.* No 425 (Canadian) from May 1945 at Tholthorpe; No 279 (ASR) from September 1945 at Beccles; No 104 from November 1945 at Abu Sueir, Egypt; No 178 from November 1945 at Fayid, Egypt; No 214 from November 1945 at Fayid, Egypt; No 40 from January 1946 at Shallufa, Egypt; No 179 (ASR) from February 1946 at St Eval; No 37 from April 1946 at Fayid, Egypt; No 70 from April 1946 at Fayid, Egypt; No 621 (ASR) from April 1946 at Aqir, Palestine; No 541 (Photo Reconnaissance) from June 1946 at Benson; No 210 (Maritime Reconnaissance) from June 1946 at St Eval; No 38 (Maritime Reconnaissance) from July 1946 at Luqa, Malta; No 160 (General Reconnaissance) from August 1946 at Leuchars; No 18 (General Reconnaissance) from September 1946 at Ein Shemer, Palestine; No 82 (Photo Reconnaissance) from October 1946 at Benson; No 224 (General Reconnaissance) from October 1946 at St Eval; No 120 (General Reconnaissance) from November 1946 at Leuchars; No 148 (Bomber) from November 1946 at Upwood; No 203 (Maritime Reconnaissance) from May 1947 at St Eval; and No 683 (Photo Reconnaissance) from November 1950 at Fayid, Egypt. Lancasters also served with Nos 1651, 1653, 1654, 1656, 1657, 1659, 1660, 1661, 1662, 1664, 1666, 1667, 1668 and 1669 Conversion Units and Nos 1678 and 1679 Heavy Conversion Flights, Nos 1, 3, 5 and 6 Lancaster Finishing Schools, No 6 OTU, Nos 230 and 236 OCUs, No 1323 (Automatic Gun-Laying Training) Flight, No 1348 (Air-Sea Rescue) Flight, No 1384 Heavy Transport Flight, No 1577 (Special Duties) Flight, Nos 1 and 16 Ferry Units, the Empire Test Pilots' School, Navigation Training Unit, Torpedo Development Unit, Bombing Development Unit, Electronic Countermeasures Development Unit, Central Flying School, Central Gunnery School, Central Gunnery School, Radio Warfare Establishment, Empire Air Armament School, RAF Flying College, Joint Anti-Submarine Warfare School, etc, etc.

(Continued from page 347)

engines, guns and all manner of other equipment. Some of the early turbojet and turboprop engines were flown, not only in the normal wing position, but also in the fuselage nose, bomb bay and fuselage tail; Lancasters were used in flight refuelling trials, gust alleviation tests, engine icing investigation, remotely-fired gun armament trials, and trials with laminar-flow aerofoil sections at the College of Aeronautics. Lancasters were exported to France, Sweden, Egypt and Argentina, some of these serving for a further decade.

Half a century after the Second World War, only two Lancasters survive in flying condition — one in Britain, the other in Canada — living testimony to the Royal Air Force's part in the heaviest and most prolonged aerial bombardment ever undertaken by one nation against another.

The magnificently restored and maintained Lancaster B I PA474 of the Battle of Britain Memorial Flight in the early 1980s. Converted in the late 1940s to a PR Mk I, it served with No 82 Squadron before being taken over by Flight Refuelling Ltd in August 1952. Now christened 'City of Lincoln', in recognition of the large number of wartime bomber squadrons based in Lincolnshire, PA474 continues to attend flying displays, although its annual flying time is severely restricted owing to its age and previous extensive service. (Photo Brian Lowe, via R C Sturtivant)

Bristol Type 160D Blenheim V

The Bristol Type 160 Blenheim Mark V was a belated and wholly unsuccessful attempt to develop a version of that aircraft that might stand a chance of survival in the presence of modern enemy fighters. Testimony to this ineptitude and wasted effort lies in the disastrous losses suffered in North Africa following the Torch landings of November 1942.

Designed to Specification B.6/40, issued at a time when Blenheim IV squadrons of the AASF in France were bearing heavy losses, the Type 160 was the outcome of a proposal by Bristol for a close-support light bomber, with alternative rôles as a low-level fighter or trainer. The company proposed a direct development of the Blenheim IV, sug-

gesting that it should powered by 950hp Bristol Mercury XVI engines and feature a battery of four fixed Browning guns in the nose. The Air Ministry accepted the proposal but, when it became evident that prototypes would not be flown before 1941, decided to add the medium-level bombing rôle to the requirements, thereby simply perpetuating the Blenheim IV's normal function.

Two prototypes, AD657 and AD661, were built by Bristol and flown at Filton, the first on 24 February 1941. These were termed Type 149CS (=Close Support) Bisleys, but the name was dropped in favour of the Blenheim VB (=Bomber) when production was taken over exclusively by the Rootes Securities factories at Speke and Stoke-on-Trent. The nose battery was abandoned

and replaced by a bomb-aiming position, offset to port in the nose; on the starboard underside of the nose was added an FN.54 mounting for two rearward-firing Browning machine guns — tacit realisation that the new Blenheim was no faster than the old.

The first true production aircraft, powered by 850hp Mercury 25s, reached No 139 Squadron of Bomber Command at Horsham St Faith in June 1942 but, in view of its dismal capabilities, was not flown operationally with that Squadron (which in September was given Mosquitos). Instead, production continued with the tropicalised Mark VD (=Desert) which were issued to those squadrons scheduled to operate in North Africa, following the planned Torch landings on the Algerian coast in November that year.

DJ402 was the first Blenheim V completed by Rootes Securities, and served as a prototype, although it was strictly a production aircraft. (Photo: Imperial War Museum, Neg No E(MoS) 1231.

This Blenheim VD BA491 at Fayid, Egypt, in 1942, served with a lesser-known Squadron, No 162, in the Western Desert until March 1944. (Photo: RAF Museum, Neg No 015184)

As some aircraft were shipped to India and Aden, others duly equipped Nos 13, 18, 114 and 614 Squadrons which, after staging through Gibraltar, landed at Blida in Algeria. Once the Axis air forces had redeployed to counter the Allied threat in the central Mediterranean, the Blenheims quickly showed just how vulnerable they were, whether they operated at medium altitude or at low level. With a normal bomb load of no more than four 250lb bombs, they could scarcely better 220 mph at low level, and fell easy prey to the cannon-armed Messerschmitt Bf 109Fs and Gs, and Focke-Wulf Fw 190As, soon to appear. Two of the Blenheim VD Squadrons, Nos 13 and 18, between them lost 55 aircraft in the six weeks following the Torch landings.

The most memorable and disastrous action was fought on 4 December as nine Blenheim VDs of No 18 Squadron set out from Souk-el-Arba, without fighter escort, to attack the German-held landing ground at Chouigui in Tunisia. As they neared their target they were set on by a *Gruppe* of Bf 109s and, in a savage, one-sided fight that lasted all the way back to the Allied lines, every one of the Blenheims was shot down, the aircraft flown by the squadron commander, Wg Cdr Hugh Gordon Malcolm, being the last to fall; none of the Squadron's

bombs hit the enemy landing ground. Malcolm was awarded a posthumous Victoria Cross for his gallant leadership.

So complete was this defeat of No 18 Squadron that it was decided to confine the Blenheims to night operations. Unfortunately, only about a quarter of the crews had been fully trained for night operations, and self-inflicted losses merely added to the former battle casualties. On 6 January 1943 Gp Capt Laurence Frank Sinclair GC, DSO (later

Air Vice-Marshal Sir Laurence, GC, KCB, CBE, DSO*), commanding the Blenheim Wing, declared that, out of 59 aircraft and crews, only 12 were available for operations — and those only on moonlit nights.

With such a dismal record, the Blenheim V was withdrawn from operations, except those on which heavy fighter escort could be provided. Even so, the Blenheim VD did not finally disappear from the order of battle until early 1944.

Although some Blenheim VDs were also supplied to the South African Air Force, flying in the Mediterranean theatre, most RAF aircraft were employed in the training rôle.

Type: Twin-engine, three-crew, mid-wing monoplane close-support light bomber.
Air Ministry Specification: B.6/40.
Manufacturer: Rootes Securities Ltd, Speke and Stoke-on-Trent.
Powerplant: Two 840hp Bristol Mercury 25 or 30 9-cylinder air-cooled radial engines driving 3-blade variable-pitch propeller.
Dimensions: Span, 56ft 1in; length, 43ft 11in; height, 12ft 10in; wing area, 469 sq ft.
Weights: Tare, 11,000lb; all-up, 17,000lb.
Performance: Max speed, 252 mph at 10,000ft; service ceiling, 29,800ft; max range, 1,480 miles.
Armament: Two 0.303in Browning machine guns in FN.54 rear defence mounting under nose, and two in dorsal Bristol B.X turret; normal bomb load of four 250lb bombs.
Prototypes: Four, Type 149CS Bisley, AD657 and AD661; AD657 first flown on 24 February 1941; and DJ702 and DJ707 served as Speke-built Type 160 prototypes.
Production: 940 Type 160 Blenheim Vs were built: Between AZ861 and BB184 (780); and between EH310 and EH517 (160).
Summary of Service: Blenheim Vs served with No 139 (Bomber) Squadron in the United Kingdom from June to October 1942; with Nos 13, 18, 114, and 614 Squadrons during and after the Torch landings, and in Algeria and Tuinisia until March 1944; with No 162 Squadron in the Western Desert; with Nos 34, 42 and 113 Squadrons in India; with No 8 Squadron at Aden from September 1942 until January 1944, and with No 244 Squadron at Sharjah, Oman, from October 1942 until April 1944. Among the large number of training and other second-line units, Blenheim Vs served with Nos 13, 17, 42, 51, 54, 60, 63, 70, 72, 75, 79, 132 and 152 OTUs; some were supplied to the SAAF, and to Turkey.

Bristol Type 163 Buckingham

If the Blenheim Mark V failed in its purpose of advancing the capabilities of the Mark IV, it was because it continued to depend on the same outmoded engines, and was restricted by an airframe already half a decade old. The Bristol Type 163 failed even to reach squadron service, but for two very different rea-

sons: its concept, though an advance on that of the Blenheim, was already outmoded by that of the Mosquito; and its engines — like so many other British engines that came into being in the late 1930s — were not yet sufficiently reliable to survive the rigours of operational demands. In short, the Bristol Buckingham was simply not in the same league as the Mosquito, and was about two years behind it.

Following previous work on an earlier Specification, B.7/40, for a two-seat light bomber development of the

Beaufighter, and preliminary work on a subsequent three-seat derivative of this to the terms of Specification B.2/41 (the Bristol Type 162, unofficially named the Beaumont), Bristol found that both designs overreached the capabilities of the Hercules engines originally stipulated.

The company therefore revised its initial B.2/41 design to include the new 18-cylinder sleeve-valve Centaurus radial, and succeeded in persuading the Air Staff to consider the new tender. The new design, the Type 163, materi-

Left: *The fully-armed, second Buckingham I prototype, DX255; because of the installation of the nose gun battery, the bomb aiming station was at the forward end of the ventral 'bath' fairing.* (Photo: The Bristol Aeroplane Co Ltd, Neg No T163/292)

Below: *Production Buckingham B Mark I, KV335; note the dorsal four-gun turret and the nose battery. Although the maximum speed demanded in the Specification was relaxed, the aircraft still fell short of the requirements.* (Photo: Ministry of Supply, Neg No 6846)

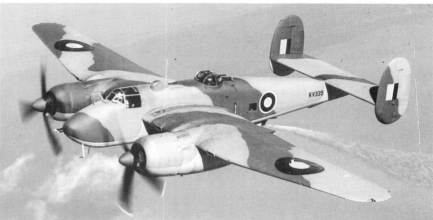

alised as a much larger, heavier and more powerful twin-engine bomber than was originally envisaged but, with two 2,400hp engines, it was expected to come close to the requirements set out in B.2/41. This called for a maximum speed of 370 mph, a range of 1,000 miles while carrying a 2,000lb bomb load, and a maximum bomb load of not less than 4,000lb, that might comprise a single 4,000lb HC bomb. A full gun armament totalling eight machine guns was also defined in detail. (It ought to be emphasised here that this Specification was issued before full prototype trials on the new Mosquito bomber had been carried out, and before any suggestion had been made that the Mosquito could carry the 4,000lb 'blockbuster'. B.2/41 attracted a number of design tenders from the aircraft industry, including one from Hawker Aircraft Ltd, to be powered by a pair of 2,300hp Napier Sabres. Only the Bristol Type 163 came to be produced.)

The Type 163 owed little or nothing to the Blenheim, Beaufort or Beaufighter, being considerably larger, and about 80 per cent heavier than the last-named. The big Centaurus radials were mounted on underslung nacelles, and the tail unit comprised twin outrigged fins and rudders. It was hoped to have a prototype flying by February 1942 but, during the summer of 1941, the Air Ministry changed its bomb load and range requirements, while Bristol argued to be allowed to include its own gun turrets in place of the Boulton Paul types specified. Moreover the Centaurus was proving recalcitrant in development, crankshaft lubrication and oil cooling problems defying all remedies attempted. When Air Ministry Research and Development staff inspected the mock-up in October 1941, it was demonstrated that a three-man crew would not suffice to perform the duties demanded, and a change of design to accommodate a four-man crew was authorised.

This all conspired to delay the start of prototype building but, on 16 March 1942, Bristol received a contract for four prototypes and 400 production aircraft; a new Specification, replacing B.2/41, was issued ('Buckingham I/P.1'), easing the maximum speed demand to 355 mph, accepting the installation of Bristol gun turrets and defining the tasks of a four-man crew; on the 'debit side', the bomb load of 2,000lb was now required to be carried over a range increased to 1,600 miles.

The first prototype, DX249, was flown by Cyril Uwins at Filton on 4 February 1943, five days after Bomber Command Mosquitos had made their first daylight raid on Berlin. This prototype was without armament and bomb aimer's ventral 'bath' fairing, and its Centaurus IV engines were de-rated to 2,100hp. The remaining three prototypes were, however, fully equipped and their engines were rated to give full power at 18,500 feet.

It was already obvious that the Buckingham was about two years too late for the European War, and could not contribute anything that existing aircraft could not do. Production was reduced to 300 aircraft, and Bristol was instructed to prepare tropicalisation modifications

Type: Twin-engine, four-crew, mid-wing monoplane medium day bomber.

Air Ministry Specifications: B.2/41 (later modified by Buckingham I/P.1).

Manufacturer: The Bristol Aeroplane Co Ltd, Filton, Bristol.

Powerplant: Prototypes: Two 2,360hp Bristol Centaurus IV 18-cylinder air-cooled sleeve-valve radial engines driving 4-blade propellers. B Mark I. 2,400hp Centaurus VII or XI engines.

Dimensions: Span, 71ft 10in; length, 46ft 10in; height, 17ft 7in; wing area, 708 sq ft.

Weights: Tare, 24,042lb; all-up, 38,050lb.

Performance: Max speed, 330 mph at 12,000ft; service ceiling, 25,000ft; range, 2,200 miles.

Armament: Four fixed forward-firing 0.303in Browning machine guns in nose, four in a Bristol B.XII dorsal turret, and two in a B.XIII ventral turret. Bomb load of up to 4,000lb, comprising two 2,000lb SAP bombs or four 1,000lb GP bombs.

Prototypes: Four, DX249, DX255, DX259 and DX266; DX249 first flown by C F Uwins at Filton on 4 February 1943.

Production: Apart from the above four prototypes, 119 Mark Is were built, between KV301 and KV479. Of these, 54 (between KV301 and KV365) were completed as bombers and delivered into RAF storage; 65 (between KV366 and KV479) were completed as four-passenger courier transports, and the original bombers were later returned to Filton for similar conversion. No bomber entered operational service with an RAF squadron.

in case the Buckingham should be required for service in the Far East.

The first production Buckingham B Mark I, KV301, was flown on 12 February 1944, powered by Centaurus VII engines (the first version to be regarded as adequately reliable for operational use and rated to give maximum power at about 12,500 feet). Production of the Buckingham was further delayed when flight trials disclosed inadequate directional and longitudinal control with one engine stopped. A hurried series of tests

was followed by the introduction of an enlarged rectangular tailplane and modified vertical tail surfaces. Production was resumed in May 1944, and by the end of that year 54 Mark I bombers had been delivered into RAF store (at a cost stated to be slightly over £3m).

At this point Bristol was instructed to halt all further production of the Buckingham bomber, and to complete the 65 aircraft already on the assembly line as fast courier transports, omitting all armament, installing additional fuel tanks

and making provision for four passengers. In due course most, if not all, the redundant bombers were returned to Filton for conversion in similar fashion, the courier version being redesignated the C Mark I. With a genuine range of slightly over 3,000 miles, a few of these transports served with the Transport Command Development Unit, flying between the United Kingdom and the Mediterranean and Middle East immediately after the end of the War in Europe.

Vickers Types 447/483 Windsor

The second Windsor prototype, Type 457 DW512, with Rolls-Royce Merlin 85s in annular cowlings. The unique four-unit undercarriage is clearly shown. (Photo: Real Photographs Co)

With its long history of producing large bombers for the RAF, second only to that of Handley Page, it was almost inevitable that Vickers should contemplate submitting a design for a four-engine development of the Warwick, the more so when it became clear that the Warwick itself had been pre-empted by the Stirling and Halifax heavy bombers. However, Rex Pierson's first essay for a four-engine heavy bomber monoplane, submitted to Specification B.12/36, failed to attract a prototype order, principally because his choice of a large-span wing of high aspect ratio exceeded by a substantial margin the hangar-door limitation of 100 feet — then still in being (see page 313, footnote). This was followed by a second unsuccessful tender to Specification B.1/39, in which no such span limitation was expressed.

When Specification B.5/41 was issued, calling for a four-engine, high altitude bomber, with pressure cabin and capable of a speed of 345 mph at 31,000 feet, Pierson submitted a new design, the Type 433, based on the Warwick but retaining the high-aspect-

ratio, elliptical wing of his B.12/36 tender. This design was accepted and two prototypes, DW506 and DW512, were ordered, to be powered by Rolls-Royce Merlin 60 engines with two-stage, two-speed superchargers and named the Windsor. Considerable detail design work was completed on these prototypes before Specification B.5/41 was withdrawn, and replaced by B.3/42 which deleted the demand for a pressure cabin. The new design was designated the Type 447.

Geodetic construction was to be employed throughout, and it was not long before the undercarriage was changed to incorporate four separate mainwheel units, each retracting into one of the engine nacelles. This was

considered necessary owing to the considerable wing span and weight outboard of the inner nacelles into which the former two-wheel undercarriage retracted.[1]

Hitherto, B.3/42 had specified the use of conventional nose, midships and tail gun turrets, these being featured in the Vickers Type 447 design. Operational experience gained by the RAF and USAAF daylight raids had, however, demonstrated all too painfully that the 0.303in and 0.5in machine guns on their heavy bombers constituted inadequate defence against German intercep-

---

[1] No such expedient was deemed necessary in the larger and much heavier Avro Lincoln, which had a wing aspect ratio about 11 per cent greater than that of the Windsor, suggesting that, contrary to Dr Barnes Wallis' earlier assertions, the geodetic structure was perhaps, weight-for-weight, less strong than a conventional spar and rib structure with metal stressed skin.

The Type 480 Windsor prototype, NK136, with the nacelle gun barbettes and fire controller's station in the tail, showing the aircraft's characteristic high-aspect-ratio fin and rudder. This view emphasises the Windsor's family resemblance to the Wellington/Warwick design. (Photo: Ministry of Aircraft Production)

An in-flight view of the third Windsor, NK136, showing well the elliptical wing planform. Without considerable alteration to the nose contours, it is difficult to see how defensive front guns could have been mounted in an orthodox turret. (Photo, Vickers Ltd)

tors armed with 20mm cannon and even heavier weapons. The Air Ministry, whose armament research had for years included investigation of large-calibre gun defence for bombers, therefore decided on 15 February 1943 to call for the Windsor to carry a remotely-controlled armament of four 20mm cannon, mounted in pairs in the rear of the outboard engine nacelles so as to cover the aircraft's entire rear hemisphere; sighting, control and firing of the guns would be the responsibility of a fire control crew member, using automatic gun-laying radar situated in the tail of the aircraft.

The first prototype Type 447, DW506, made its maiden flight at Farnborough on 23 October 1943 in the hands of 'Mutt' Summers. No armament or bomb gear was included and the take-off weight was limited to 46,000lb, initial speed measurements returning 302 mph at 25,000 feet.

The second Windsor, DW512, termed Type 457, with Merlin 85 engines in annular cowlings, made its first flight from Wisley on 15 February 1944, but only shortly afterwards, on 2 March, the first aircraft was badly damaged in a forced landing and was subsequently broken up for component testing.

The third aircraft, the Type 461 NK136, was flown on 11 July 1944 and, like the two previous prototypes, was initially unarmed. Diving trials with DW512 had disclosed ballooning of the wing fabric and, in an attempt to avoid this, a wire-backed, heavyweight fabric was introduced in NK136, the penalty being a reduction by 25 mph in the maximum speed.

Meanwhile, however, the second Warwick prototype, L9704, had been fitted with the nacelle-mounted barbettes for a series of tests (with 0.5in guns) and as these progressed satisfactorily, Windsor NK136 underwent conversion early in 1945 to Type 480.

A total of five prototypes and 300 production Windsors had been ordered in 1943, but the above three aircraft were the only examples completed before the War ended. The fourth aircraft, Type 471 NN670, almost completed when the entire Windsor programme was can-

celled, was to have become the first pre-production prototype with Merlin 100s, and the later Windsor B Mark Is were to have been powered by Rolls-Royce Griffons. The proposed Windsor II, planned to be powered by four 3,020shp

Type: Four-engine, six/seven-crew, mid-wing monoplane long-range heavy bomber.
Air Ministry Specifications: B.5/41 and B.3/42.
Manufacturer: Vickers-Armstrongs Ltd, Weybridge, Surrey.
Powerplant: 1st Prototype. Four 1,560hp Rolls-Royce Merlin 61 (later Merlin 65) 12-cylinder liquid-cooled in-line engines with 2-stage, 2-speed superchargers, driving 4-blade constant-speed propellers. 2nd Prototype. 1,750hp Merlin 85s. Proposed B Mark I production. 1,850hp Merlin 100s. B Mark II. Four 3,020shp Rolls-Royce RB.39 Clyde turboprops.
Structure: Geodetic construction throughout with reinforced fabric covering. Four separate undercarriage units.
Dimensions: Span, 117ft 2in; length, 76ft 10in; height, 23ft 0in; wing area, 1,248 sq ft.
Weights: First prototype. Tare, 38,606lb; all-up, 54,000lb.
Performance: Max speed, 317 mph at 23,000ft; operating ceiling, 27,250ft; typical range, 2,890 miles with 8,000lb bomb load.
Armament: Four 20mm cannon mounted in pairs in remotely-controlled barbettes in the rear of the outboard engine nacelles, covering the rear hemisphere. Maximum bomb load proposed as being approximately 15,000lb.
Prototypes: Three flown, DW506 (first flown, 23 October 1943), DW512 (first flown, 15 February 1944) and NK136 (first flown, 11 July 1944). All production cancelled.

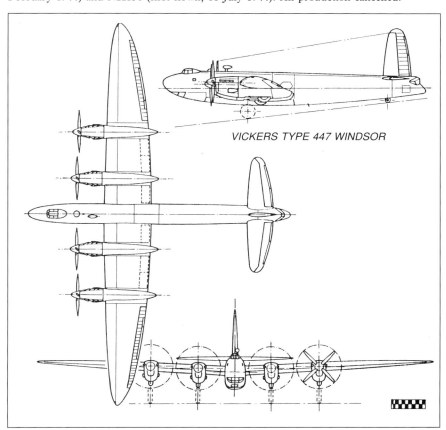

VICKERS TYPE 447 WINDSOR

Rolls-Royce Clyde axial-flow turboprops, was to have had a maximum range of 4,000 miles.

In some respects the Vickers Windsor was an advanced concept; it was certainly a courageous and imaginative project. The fact that the whole programme was ended after only three,

relatively unrepresentative, prototypes had flown, left scores of pertinent questions unanswered, and to have considered introducing the aircraft into service much before the end of the 1940s was optimistic indeed. The wisdom of employing fabric covering on a modern, high-performance, high-altitude bomber

in hot, humid conditions has been doubted ever since. Defence in the aircraft's forward hemisphere had not been addressed at the time of cancellation. More disturbing was the fact that performance forecasts by the Vickers design staff had already repeatedly been shown to be somewhat over-optimistic.

Supermarine
Type 322 (S.24/37)

Designed to the same Specification, S.24/37, as that for which the Fairey Barracuda was the successful contender, the Supermarine Type 322 merits brief inclusion in this work largely on account of the ingenious manner in which Joseph Smith, Supermarine's chief designer, approached what was, after all, an extremely demanding requirement.

As previously shown, S.24/37 defined a three-crew, carrier-borne aircraft capable of dive and torpedo bombing and featuring folding wings. This combination of attack tactics emphasised the importance of providing the pilot with the best possible view over the nose, both in the dive and in the approach to deck landing, that is to say at low speed.

It is not known whether, in choosing to incorporate a variable-incidence wing in his tender to S.24/37, Smith ever believed his design could successfully compete against the Barracuda, with its Fairey-Youngman flaps, or whether he saw the Specification as an opportunity to explore the complexities of the incidence-changing mechanism (whose screw-jacks acted on the rear wing spar), full-span leading-edge automatic slats and full-span trailing-edge landing flaps, all combined within folding wings. Certainly the resulting aeroplane, with a

Widely known by its nickname 'Dumbo', the Type 322's austere appearance was accentuated by the inclusion of a fixed undercarriage. (Photo: Vickers Ltd)

maximum lift coefficient of 3.9, did eventually come close to meeting the torpedo/dive bomber requirements, even though the two Type 322 prototypes only flew after the Barracuda had entered service. (He was, moreover, to extend this combination of lift-enhancing devices in his Seagull amphibian flying boat, designed to Specification S.12/40.)

After the Rolls-Royce Exe 24-cylinder X-type air-cooled sleeve-valve engine, originally selected for the Type 322, had been abandoned at the outbreak of war, the choice fell on the Merlin, and manufacture of the two prototypes went ahead with this engine, R1810 with a Merlin 30 and R1815 with a Merlin 32. The former was first flown in February 1943 — much too late to be considered for production — and it is doubtful whether either aircraft was ever flown with bombs or torpedo, R1810 being

delivered to the RAE for a number of applied research programmes scarcely connected with a military rôle.

Type: Single-engine, three-crew, shoulder-wing monoplane experimental shipborne torpedo/dive bomber.

Air Ministry Specification: S.24/37.

Manufacturer: Supermarine Division of Vickers-Armstrongs Ltd, Southampton.

Powerplant: 1st aircraft. One 1,300hp Rolls-Royce Merlin 30 12-cylinder liquid-cooled in-line engine driving 3-blade propeller. 2nd aircraft. 1,645hp Merlin 32.

Dimensions: Span, 50ft; length, 40ft; height, 14ft 2in; wing area, 319.5 sq ft.

Weights: Tare, 9,175lb; all-up, 12,000lb.

Performance: Max speed, 279 mph at 4,000ft; max range, 825 miles.

Armament: Provision for one Browning gun in one wing and one in the rear cockpit (never fitted). Bomb load of up to 1,500lb or one 18in torpedo (probably never carried).

Prototypes: Two, R1810 (first flown in February 1943) and R1815. No production.

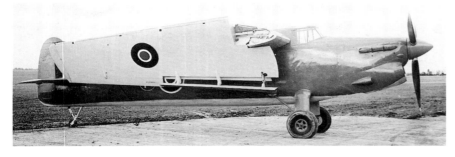

As no vertical movement of the front spar within the Type 322's fuselage was possible, wing incidence was varied by attaching the screw-jacks to the rear spar. To achieve wing folding, the inboard sections of the trailing-edge flaps had to be extended to the position shown here. It is assumed that the long tailwheel leg was necessary to provide ground clearance to mount a torpedo. (Photo: via E B Morgan)

Avro Type 694 Lincoln

The fully-equipped third Lincoln prototype, PW392, late in its life at Cranfield in September 1960; the underfuselage scanner was for H₂S Mark III. (Photo: via George Jenks)

If anyone on the Air Staff needed to be told, the first year of the Pacific War, following the Japanese attack on Pearl Harbor, had demonstrated the two elements of air power that set it apart from a European war, elements that successive British governments had steadfastly ignored ever since the threat of Japanese imperialism in the Far East had become reality ten years earlier. These were the essential rôles of the aircraft carrier and the very-long-range bomber.

In neither respect had the British and Commonwealth orders of battle included anything approaching adequate equipment, a situation that was becoming less and less relevant in the short term as the Japanese imperial perimeter quickly expanded, inexorably depriving the Allies of more and more potential naval and bomber bases from which to strike the Japanese homeland.

Any participation by the Royal Air Force in very-long-range aerial bombing could only realistically be achieved in the relatively short term by acquiring the Consolidated B-24 Liberator, and then only when the American aircraft industry could provide adequate numbers of this bomber beyond those needed by the USAAF in Europe and the Pacific theatres; this was not expected to occur before the end of 1944 (and could not, in any case, be accommodated by the RAF itself before that date owing to the necessary training effort and logistics required to introduce an American heavy bomber into service remote from the United Kingdom, and with the RAF's European priorities). And, it should be remembered, the Liberator could contribute only very small bomb loads when flown over its greatest range.

Late in 1942, therefore, the Air Ministry began discussions with Chadwick to explore the possibility of greatly extending the range of the Lancaster, without sacrificing its bomb-carrying ability when operated over shorter ranges. It was obviously essential to retain as much as possible of the Lancaster's structure, crew stations and general handling characteristics so as to use the existing production, training and operational facilities in the interests of speedy introduction into service, preferably early in 1945. (It was inevitable that parallel discussions should take place with other manufacturers, and several proposals were advanced by Handley Page, Bristol and Vickers for long-range heavy bombers at this time, but in each case the essential urgency to introduce the aircraft into service was entirely overlooked, and had therefore to be dismissed out of hand; not one of the dozen or so projected aircraft could possibly have reached operational service before the end of the 1940s.)

Chadwick's design staff began work on the Avro Type 694 Lancaster Mark IV in December 1942, the proposed design retaining 80 per cent of the earlier aircraft's structure, including the front and centre fuselage sections and the entire wing centresection. The outer wing sections were enlarged by about 10 per cent and the rear fuselage lengthened by 13 per cent, the extra space thereby provided being used to accommodate additional fuel. Power was to be provided by 1,750hp Merlin engines with two-stage, two-speed superchargers, and a much sturdier undercarriage was to be provided to support the greatly increased operating weight.

Meanwhile, Specification B.14/43 had been prepared around Chadwick's proposals, and an order for three prototypes and 80 production aircraft was placed with Avro (to be shared with Metropolitan-Vickers when that company's existing Lancaster orders had been completed). Unfortunately, plans to introduce the Lancaster IV into production were set back owing to the need to increase current Lancaster I and III production during the winter of 1943-44, to make good the sharply increased Bomber Command casualties suffered in the Battle of Berlin, and the subsequent decision to replace the Halifax by the Lancaster as quickly as possible.

The first Type 694 prototype, PW925, now named the Lincoln, was flown by 'Sam' Brown on 9 June 1944. This was primarily an aerodynamic test aircraft intended to provide confirmation of drag calculations and range predictions. The aircraft was powered by Merlin 85 engines in annular cowlings; no nose turret was fitted, and a dummy H₂S scanner fairing was fitted below the rear fuselage. Flight trials with PW925 confirmed that, with a maximum take-off fuel load of 3,580gal (compared with the Lancaster's 2,145gal), the Lincoln would possess a maximum range of 4,450 miles with a 3,000lb bomb load, or 1,470 miles with a 14,000lb bomb load. In the matter of speed and ceiling, the Lincoln fell well below the demands of Specification

One of the last Lincoln B Mk 2s built by Metrovick, RA722, fitted with the much-enlarged H₂S scanner with 'double-bubble' radome. The front pair of 0.5in Browning machine guns (when fitted) were remotely aimed and fired by the bomb aimer. (Photo: Stephen Peltz)

An Armstrong Whitworth-built Lincoln B Mark 2, SX986/SR-A of No 101 (Bomber) Squadron, flying over Cleethorpes, Lincolnshire, in about 1950; this aircraft was later converted to a Mark 4, being fitted with British-made Merlin 85s. (Photo: P H T Green Collection)

B.14/43 (which had assumed the use of either Griffon or Centaurus engines; the former was not yet ready for bomber application, and the production of the latter was largely earmarked for Tempest fighters).

In the event the Lincoln did not give operational service at all during the Second World War, either in Europe or the Far East. The first RAF Squadron to take delivery of Mark 1s, for Service trials, was No 57 (Bomber) Squadron at East Kirkby in August 1945, this Squadron being disbanded in November and its number being taken over by a Flight from No 103 (Bomber) Squadron at Elsham Wolds on the 26th. No 44 (Bomber) Squadron was the only other to convert to Lincoln 1s during 1945.

By the time these first two Squadrons were receiving their Lincoln Mk 1s, production orders totalled 2,800 aircraft, placed with the former Lancaster manufacturers. The Mark 1 was discontinued after the original 80 aircraft had been completed, production being switched to the Mark 2, powered by Packard-built Merlin 68, 68A and 300 engines, and this version replaced the earlier aircraft on Nos 44 and 57 Squadrons in 1946, and equipped Nos 9, 12, 50, 61, 83, 97, 100, 101 and 617 Squadrons the same year (all in the United Kingdom). The redundant Mark 1s were then issued to a Lincoln Operational Conversion Unit, No 230, at Lindholme in 1947, and were employed to train crews being posted to three new Squadrons, Nos 15, 90 and 138.

As the decision was taken to withdraw Lancasters from Bomber Command, and to settle on a peacetime level of 20 Lincoln heavy bomber squadrons, the production orders were drastically reduced by cancellation, and planned production in Canada by Victory Aircraft Ltd, Malton, Ontario, was terminated after only one Lincoln had been completed. Production by Austin and Vickers-Armstrongs was cancelled outright.

The descent of the Iron Curtain, and the onset of the Cold War in 1948, focused concern as to the length of useful service likely to be enjoyed by the Lincoln among major air forces about to be dominated by jet fighters. For the Royal Air Force a new generation of turbojet-powered heavy bombers was being examined, and a new jet light bomber prototype (the Canberra) had been ordered. Moreover, the entire bombing philosophy associated with the advent of nuclear weapons had an obvious bearing on the Lincoln's value in a possible war against the Soviet Union (as yet without an operational nuclear weapon) and, in view of its obvious

Above: *Lincoln SX925 after conversion to B Mark 4; some of these aircraft, flown by squadrons of RAF Signals Command, carried no armament, yet were frequently loaded with bulky, heavy and exceptionally powerful electronic jamming equipment, much to the embarrassment of RAF ground radar operators during defence exercises in the 1950s. (Photo: A J Jackson Collection)*

Left: *Representative of a dozen Lincolns employed as engine test beds was RF403, fitted with a pair of Armstrong Siddeley Python turboprops in the outer engine location and driving eight-blade Rotol contraprops. On other test beds engines were fitted in the nose or bomb bay. (Photo: P H T Green Collection)*

vulnerability when matched against the new Russian MiG-15 jet fighter, no plans were laid to deploy atomic bombs with Lincoln squadrons, it being assumed that, by the time such weapons became available to the RAF, the new jet heavy bombers would be in service. It therefore seemed likely that the Lincoln would remain in first-line service only until the mid-1950s.

Thus the aircraft came to assume a more mundane rôle status within Bomber Command's responsibilities, and no sooner had the Lincoln achieved its planned deployment of 20 squadrons in January 1950 than plans were finalised to introduce the American Boeing B-29 Superfortress into Bomber Command as its replacement, plans that were accelerated with the onset of the Korean War that year. The B-29 (named Washington in RAF service) first reached No 115 (Bomber) Squadron in August 1950, and ultimately equipped nine squadrons during the early half of that decade.

Meanwhile, Lincolns had been deployed to Singapore in March that year as No 57 (Bomber) Squadron joined the Commonwealth forces in Malaya in their efforts to contain the communist terrorist activities in that country. Relieved by No 100 (Bomber) Squadron in June, the Lincoln crews were called forward by the ground forces operating in the jungle to saturate a defined area with 1,000-pounders. Little or nothing could be seen of the terrorists from the air, and the only value of such bombing was its effect in preventing the communists from creating permanent guerrilla-dominated areas from which it would

prove difficult to clear them. Soon afterwards, Australian-built Lincoln Mark 30s of the RAAF also deployed to Tengah (and later to Butterworth) to continue these operations.

In November 1953 a similar task fell to Nos 49, 61, 100 and 214 (Bomber) Squadrons which were deployed in rotation to Kenya to deal with Kikuyu tribal dissidents on the rampage in the African jungle during the former Col-

ony's move towards independence within the British Commonwealth.

As the Washingtons in service with Bomber Command proved to be less than satisfactory, owing largely to prolonged unserviceability of aircraft (exacerbated by wholly inadequate spares procurement), the Lincoln was proving useful in a number of operational fields — apart from providing fairly easy 'targets' for Fighter Command's Meteor

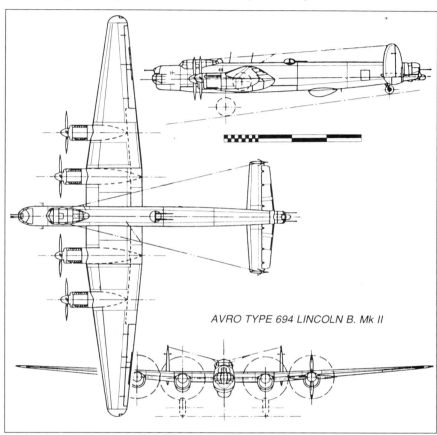

AVRO TYPE 694 LINCOLN B. Mk II

Type: Four-engine, seven/eight-crew, mid-wing heavy bomber.
Air Ministry Specification: B.14/43.
Manufacturers: A V Roe & Co Ltd, Middleton, Manchester, Woodford, Cheshire, and Yeadon, Yorks; Metropolitan-Vickers Ltd, Manchester; Sir W G Armstrong Whitworth Aircraft Co Ltd, Whitley, Coventry; Victory Aircraft Ltd, Ontario, Canada; Australian Government Factory, Fishermen's Bend, Melbourne, Australia.
Powerplant: Four 1,750hp Rolls-Royce Merlin, 66, 68, 85, 102 or 300 12-cylinder liquid-cooled supercharged in-line engines driving 4-blade propellers. Experimental. Bristol Phoebus turbojet, Bristol Theseus 11 and 21and Proteus turboprop; Napier Naiad and Nomad turboprop; Armstrong Siddeley Python turboprop; Rolls-Royce Derwent turbojet; Rolls-Royce Tyne turboprop.
Dimensions: Span, 120ft 0in; length, 78ft 3½in; height, 17ft 3½in; wing area, 1,421 sq ft.
Weights: B Mk 2. Tare, 44,148lb; all-up, 82,000lb.
Performance: B Mk 2. Max speed, 297 mph at 15,400ft; operating ceiling, 22,100ft; operational range, 4,450 miles with 3,000lb bomb load, 1,470 miles with 14,000lb bomb load.
Armament: Two 0.50in Browning machine guns in Boulton Paul nose and tail turrets, and two 20mm Hispano cannon in Bristol Type 17 Mk II dorsal turret; maximum normal bomb load, fourteen 1,000lb bombs or, exceptionally, one 22,000lb DP bomb.

Prototypes: Three, PW925, PW929 and PW932; PW925 first flown by Capt H A Brown on 9 June 1944 at Ringway.
Production: Lincoln production totalled 3 prototypes and 583 production aircraft. The latter comprised 80 Mark 1s, 449 Mark 2s and 54 Australian Mark 30s. Mark 1s: Avro, 52 (between RE227 and RE288, SS713 and SS714); Metrovick, 28 (RA628-RA655). Mark 2s: Avro, 116 (between RE289 and RE424, and SS715-SS718); Metrovick, 52 (between RA656 and RA724). Armstrong Whitworth, 299 (between RF329 and RF577, between SX923 and SX993, and between WD122 and WD149) plus 18 supplied to Argentina. Australian Government Factory, 54 (Nos A73-1 to A73-54). 60 B Mk 2s between SX923 and SX993 (listed above) were converted to B Mark 4s after delivery to RAF.
Summary of Service: Lincolns served with the following RAF Squadrons between August 1945 and May 1963: Nos 7, 9, 12, 15, 35, 44, 49, 50, 57, 58, 61, 83, 90, 97, 100, 101, 115, 116, 138, 148, 149, 151, 192, 199, 207, 214, 527 and 617. They also served with No 230 OCU, No 1426 Flight, Aden, Central Bomber Establishment, Air-Sea Warfare Development Unit, Bomber Command Instructor's School, Radio Warfare Establishment, Empire Air Armament School, Central Gunnery School, Empire Test Pilots' School, Radar Reconnaissance Flight, Radar Bombing School, etc.

and Vampire jet fighters in defence exercises — not least in the operational development of advanced H₂S radar for blind bombing, in particular H₂S Mark IIIG and Mk IVA (the latter distinguishable by the enlarged 'double-bubble' radome under the rear fuselage). The considerable operational experience gained in the use of this equipment, as well as advanced ECM developed by Nos 116, 192, 199 and 527 (Countermeasures) Squadrons of Signals Command during the 1950s, served to place the RAF at the forefront of ECM technology, a position of world leadership it enjoyed for almost a decade during the early years of the V-Force.

The last Lincolns in operational service were the radar development aircraft of No 151 Squadron, which were disposed of in May 1963.

Bristol Type 164 Brigand

The Bristol Type 164 Brigand was one of a trio of related designs, originated by Leslie George Frise, which were intended to exploit the unexpectedly dramatic success of the makeshift adaptation of the Beaufighter as a torpedo strike fighter in the mid-War years. The other two aircraft were the Type 163 Buckingham bomber (see page 350) and the Type 166 Buckmaster trainer. Ironically, when Frise proposed a twin-Centaurus torpedo strike fighter, capable of carrying two torpedoes, in response to Specification S.7/42, the Air Ministry showed greater interest in an alternative suggestion by Clifford Wilfrid Tinson, Bristol's Assistant Chief Project Engineer, who favoured a single-torpedo aircraft powered by Hercules XVII engines and with a smaller, slimmer fuselage than the Buckingham. The previous Specification was reissued as H.7/42 with the single torpedo capability, but now calling for a trainer variant. However, when further performance calculations showed that the Hercules engines would not be adequate to meet the 330 mph low-level speed requirement, it was decided to revert to the Centaurus.

Moreover, the new requirement for side-by-side seating of a pilot trainer, implicit in the Specification, would have compromised Tinson's slim fuselage design, and Bristol was able to persuade

The first Brigand torpedo fighter prototype, MX988, as originally fitted with Centaurus VII engines in long-chord tapered cowlings. (Photo: Ministry of Supply, RTP)

the Air Ministry to regard the trainer version entirely separately (with the result that the trainer requirement was redefined in a new Specification, T.13/43). Detail design of the Type 164 therefore went ahead, with a fuselage having a cross-section little greater than that of the Beaufighter, with a single-seat pilot's cockpit, the other two crew members being situated close behind, under a single transparent canopy.

Four Type 164 prototypes, named the Brigand, were ordered on 11 March 1943, the first, MX988, being flown by Uwins on 27 October 1944. All four aircraft were powered initially by Centaurus VII engines, but these were replaced by Mark XVIIs, and by Centaurus 57s with water-methanol injection in the 80 production aircraft then on order.

The Brigand was an attractive, purposeful-looking design, combining wings, engine installation and tail unit similar to those of the Buckingham, but with the smaller, slimmer fuselage. Attitudes,

however, towards the large, land-based torpedo strike fighter underwent a profound change during the last eighteen months of the War, the rôle of torpedo attack being seen as the sole responsibility of the Fleet Air Arm as carrier-borne aircraft, such as the Blackburn Firebrand single-engine strike fighter, came to be conceived. Thus, although eleven early production Brigand TF Mk 1s were delivered to Coastal Command Maintenance Units in 1946 (some of these being passed on to the Air/Sea Weapons Development Unit), the planned re-equipping of Nos 36 and 42 Squadrons did not take place.

Instead, production at Filton was halted temporarily and a revised standard of preparation issued, it being intended to ship the aircraft — fully tropicalised — to Burma and Malaya, where they would take over the rôle of light bomber from the Mosquito VI (whose wooden structure had been found to be unsuitable for prolonged service in the hot, humid climate).

The first production Brigand TF Mk 1, RH742, carrying a torpedo and underwing 60lb rocket projectiles. The twin Browning gun dorsal armament was omitted in the bomber conversion. Note the Fairey-Youngman 'bellows-operated' airbrakes under the wings; these were operated by a venturi in the wing leading edge. (Photo: The Bristol Aeroplane Co Ltd, Neg No T164/139)

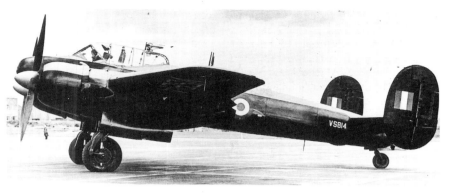

VS814 was a late production Brigand B.1, shown here in standard Bomber Command night paint scheme; the aircraft was later converted to a T Mk 4, and then to a T Mk 5, both aircrew trainer versions flown by Operational Conversion Units. (Photo: via R C B Ashworth)

Although the former Brigand TF.1s were returned to Filton for conversion to light bombers, difficulties were encountered in clearing the Centaurus engines for service in the tropics, while the fundamental change in the Brigand's operational rôle demanded all manner of weapon clearance trials at Boscombe Down, and it was not until 1948 that production deliveries restarted to the RAF, followed by brief Service trials with No 84 Squadron at Habbaniya, Iraq, which began in February 1949.

These trials passed off fairly smoothly, and No 84 Squadron went on to equip with a full complement of Brigands as No 8 Squadron at Khormaksar, Aden, also started converting in July that year.

Meanwhile, increasing activity by communist terrorists in the Malayan jungles had caused the British administration to declare a state of emergency in the area. Definition of the RAF's contribution to the anti-terrorist campaign (Operation Firedog) resulted in re-equipping No 45 Squadron with Brigands in November 1949, and the transfer of No 84 Squadron from the Middle East to Tengah, Singapore, this becoming the base for all Brigand operations over the Malayan jungle.

The Bristol aeroplane proved to be a popular aircraft with the pilots and crews, affording an excellent field of view of the ground; without having to contend with air opposition, the crews could concentrate on searching for and attacking the guerrilla forces with bombs, rockets and cannon. Ground fire was almost entirely confined to small arms, from which casualties and aircraft damage were very light. On the rare occasions of undercarriage or engine damage, the Brigand's sturdy airframe proved entirely adequate in protecting the crew in the event of a forced landing.

However, the Centaurus proved something of a liability owing to complex servicing demands, and when de Havilland Hornets, with their familiar Rolls-Royce Merlin engines, began arriving in the area, it was decided to begin phasing out the Brigand, a process completed in February 1953, both at Singapore and with No 8 Squadron at Aden.

Type: Twin-engine, three-crew, mid-wing monoplane light bomber.
Air Ministry Specification: H.7/42.
Manufacturer: The Bristol Aeroplane Co Ltd, Filton, Bristol.
Powerplant: Two 2,470hp Bristol Centaurus 57 18-cylinder air-cooled, sleeve-valve, radial engine with water-methanol injection and driving 4-blade Rotol propellers.
Dimensions: Span, 72ft 4in; length, 46ft 5in; height, 17ft 6in; wing area, 718 sq ft.
Weights: As bomber: Tare, 25,600lb; all-up, 39,000lb.
Performance: Max speed, 358 mph at 14,600ft; service ceiling, 26,000ft; normal range, 2,000 miles (2,800 miles with drop tanks).
Armament: Four forward-firing 20mm Hispano Mk 5 cannon; external underwing racks for four 500lb or two 1,000lb bombs, or two 500lb bombs and eight 60lb rocket projectiles.
Prototypes: Four, MX988, MX991, MX994 and TX374. (MX988 first flown by Cyril Uwins on 4 December 1944).
Production: A total of 143 Brigands was built (excluding the above prototypes); these comprised 118 Mark 1s: Between RH742 and RH852, between VS828 and VS877, WA560 and WB236. 16 Met Mark 3s: VS812-VS827. 9 Mark 4s: WA561-WA569. Numerous Mark 1s were subsequently converted to Met Mark 3s, T Mark 4s and 5s.
Summary of Service: Early Brigand Mark 1s were completed as torpedo fighter/bombers and allocated to Nos 36 and 42 (Torpedo Bomber) Squadrons, but not taken on charge. Brigand B Mark 1s served with No 8 Squadron at Khormaksar, Aden, from July 1949 to February 1953; with No 45 Squadron at Tengah, Singapore, from November 1949 to February 1952; and with No 84 Squadron at Habbaniya, Iraq, from February 1949 to April 1950, and at Tengah, Singapore, from April 1950 to February 1953. Other Brigand units included No 1301 (Met) Flight, Nos 228 and 238 Operational Conversion Units.

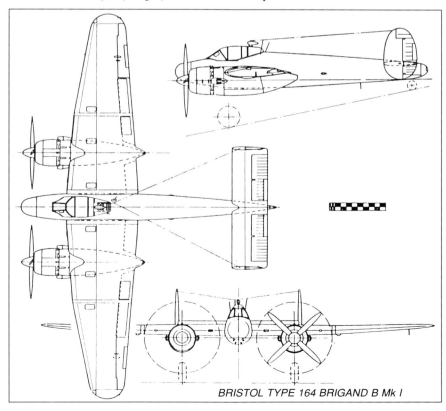

BRISTOL TYPE 164 BRIGAND B Mk I

Deployment of British Bomber Squadrons — 1 January 1944

(At the Height of the Battle of Berlin)

Royal Air Force
Home Bases

Squadron	Aircraft	Base
No 7 Sqn (HPF)	Avro Lancaster I/III	Oakington, Cambs
No 9 Sqn (H)	Avro Lancaster I/III	Bardney, Lincs
No 10 Sqn (H)	Handley Page Halifax II	Melbourne, Yorks
No 12 Sqn (H)	Avro Lancaster I/III	Wickenby, Lincs
No 15 Sqn (H)	Avro Lancaster I/III	Mildenhall, Suffolk
No 21 Sqn (L)	D.H. Mosquito VI	Hunsdon, Herts
No 35 Sqn (HPF)	H.P. Halifax II/III	Graveley, Hunts
No 44 Sqn (H)	Avro Lancaster I/III	Dunholme Lodge, Lincs
No 49 Sqn (H)	Avro Lancaster I/III	Fiskerton, Lincs
No 50 Sqn (H)	Avro Lancaster I/III	Skellingthorpe, Lincs
No 51 Sqn (H)	H.P. Halifax II/III	Snaith/Yorkshire
No 57 Sqn (H)	Avro Lancaster I/III	East Kirkby, Lincs
No 58 Sqn (H)[1]	H.P. Halifax II	St David's, Pembrokeshire
No 61 Sqn (H)	Avro Lancaster I/III	Skellingthorpe, Lincs
No 75 Sqn (H)	Short Stirling III	Mepal, Cambs
No 76 Sqn (H)	H.P. Halifax V	Holme-in-Spalding Moor, Yorks
No 77 Sqn (H)	H.P. Halifax II	Elvington, Yorks
No 78 Sqn (H)	H.P. Halifax II/III	Breighton, Yorks
No 83 Sqn (HPF)	Avro Lancaster I/III	Wyton, Hunts
No 88 Sqn (L)	(Douglas Boston III/IIIA)	Blackbushe, Hants
No 90 Sqn (H)	Short Stirling III	Tuddenham, Suffolk
No 97 Sqn (HPF)	Avro Lancaster I/III	Bourn, Cambs
No 98 Sqn (M)	(North American Mitchell II)	Dunsfold, Surrey
No 100 Sqn (H)	Avro Lancaster I/III	Grimsby, Lincs
No 101 Sqn (H)	Avro Lancaster I/III	Ludford Magna, Lincs
No 102 Sqn (H)	H.P. Halifax II	Pocklington, Yorks
No 103 Sqn (H)	Avro Lancaster I/III	Elsham Wolds, Lincs
No 105 Sqn (LPF)	D.H. Mosquito IX	Marham, Norfolk
No 106 Sqn (H)	Avro Lancaster I/III	Metheringham, Lincs
No 107 Sqn (L)	(Douglas Boston IIIA)	Blackbushe, Hants
No 109 Sqn (LPF)	D.H. Mosquito IX	Marham, Norfolk
No 139 Sqn (LPF)	D.H. Mosquito IX	Wyton, Hunts
No 149 Sqn (H)	Short Stirling III	Lakenheath, Suffolk
No 156 Sqn (HPF)	Avro Lancaster I/III	Warboys, Hunts
No 158 Sqn (H)	H.P. Halifax II/III	Lissett, Yorks
No 166 Sqn (H)	Avro Lancaster I/III	Spilsby, Lincs
No 180 Sqn (M)	(North American Mitchell II)	Dunsfold, Surrey
No 199 Sqn (H)[2]	Short Stirling III	Lakenheath, Suffolk
No 207 Sqn (H)	Avro Lancaster I/III	Spilsby, Lincs
No 214 Sqn (H)	Short Stirling III	Downham Market, Norfolk
No 218 Sqn (H)	Short Stirling III	Downham Market, Norfolk
No 226 Sqn (M)	(North American Mitchell II)	Swanton Morley, Norfolk
No 300 Sqn (M)	Vickers Wellington X	Ingham, Lincs
No 320 Sqn (M)	(North American Mitchell II)	Lasham, Hants
No 342 Sqn (L)	(Douglas Boston IIIA)	Blackbushe, Hants
No 405 Sqn (RCAF)[3] (HPF)	Avro Lancaster I/III	Gransden Lodge, Beds
No 408 Sqn (RCAF)[3] (H)	Avro Lancaster II	Linton-on-Ouse, Yorks
No 415 Sqn (RCAF)[3] (TB)	Vickers Wellington/ Fairey Albacore I	Various airfields in UK.
No 419 Sqn (RCAF)[3] (H)	H.P. Halifax II	Middleton St George, Co Durham
No 420 Sqn (RCAF)[3] (H)	H.P. Halifax III	Tholthorpe, Yorks
No 424 Sqn (RCAF)[3] (H)	H.P. Halifax III	Skipton-on-Swale, Yorks
No 425 Sqn (RCAF)[3] (H)	H.P. Halifax III	Tholthorpe, Yorks
No 426 Sqn (RCAF)[3] (H)	Avro Lancaster II	Linton-on-Ouse, Yorks
No 427 Sqn (RCAF)[3] (H)	H.P. Halifax V	Leeming, Yorks
No 428 Sqn (RCAF)[3] (H)	H.P Halifax II/V	Middleton St George, Co Durham
No 429 Sqn (RCAF)[3] (H)	H.P. Halifax II/V	Leeming, Yorks
No 431 Sqn (RCAF)[3] (H)	H.P. Halifax V	Croft, Co Durham
No 432 Sqn (RCAF)[3] (H)	Avro Lancaster II	East Moor, Yorks
No 433 Sqn (RCAF)[3] (H)	H.P. Halifax III	Skipton-on-Swale, Yorks
No 434 Sqn (RCAF)[3] (H)	H.P. Halifax V	Croft, Co Durham
No 460 Sqn (RAAF)[3] (H)	Avro Lancaster I/III	Binbrook, Lincs
No 463 Sqn (RAAF)[3] (H)	Avro Lancaster I/III	Waddington, Lincs
No 466 Sqn (RAAF)[3] (H)	H.P. Halifax III	Leconfield, Yorks
No 467 Sqn (RAAF)[3] (H)	Avro Lancaster I/III	Waddington, Lincs
No 487 Sqn (RNZAF)[3] (L)	D.H. Mosquito VI	Hunsdon, Herts
No 514 Sqn (H)	Avro Lancaster II	Waterbeach, Cambs
No 550 Sqn (H)	Avro Lancaster I/III	Grimsby, Lincs
No 576 Sqn (H)	Avro Lancaster I/III	Elsham Wolds, Lincs
No 617 Sqn (H)	Avro Lancaster I/III	Coningsby, Lincs
No 618 Sqn (L)[2]	D.H. Mosquito IV	Skitten, Caithness
No 619 Sqn (H)	Avro Lancaster I/III	Woodhall Spa, Lincs
No 622 Sqn (H)	Avro Lancaster I/III	Mildenhall, Suffolk
No 625 Sqn (H)	Avro Lancaster I/III	Kelstern, Lincs
No 626 Sqn (H)	Avro Lancaster I/III	Wickenby, Lincs
No 627 Sqn (LPF)	D.H. Mosquito IV	Oakington, Cambs
No 630 Sqn (H)	Avro Lancaster I/III	East Kirkby, Lincs
No 692 Sqn (LPF)	D.H. Mosquito IV	Graveley, Hunts

Mediterranean and North Africa

Squadron	Aircraft	Base
No 14 Sqn (M)	(Martin Marauder I)	Blida, Algeria
No 18 Sqn (L)	(Douglas Boston III/IIIA)	Foggia No 1, Italy
No 37 Sqn (M)	Vickers Wellington X	Tortorella, Italy
No 40 Sqn (M)	Vickers Wellington X	Foggia Main, Italy
No 52 Sqn (L)	(Martin Baltimore IV)	Borizzo, Sicily
No 55 Sqn (L)	(Martin Baltimore IV/V)	Foggia No. 1, Italy
No 70 Sqn (M)	Vickers Wellington X	Cerignola, Italy
No 104 Sqn (M)	Vickers Wellington X	Foggia Main, Italy
No 114 Sqn (L)	(Douglas Boston III/IIIA)	Perugia, Italy
No 142 Sqn (M)	Vickers Wellington X	Cerignola, Italy
No 150 Sqn (M)	Vickers Wellington X	Cerignola No 3, Italy
No 178 Sqn (H)	(Consolidated Liberator VI)	Terria, Libya
No 223 Sqn (L)	(Martin Baltimore IV)	Celone, Italy
No 458 Sqn (RAAF)[3] (TB)	Vickers Wellington	Various Mediterranean bases
No 462 Sqn (RAAF)[3] (H)	H.P. Halifax II	Terria, Libya
No 624 Sqn (H)[4]	H.P. Halifax II/V	Blida, Algeria

India and Ceylon

Squadron	Aircraft	Base
No 22 Sqn (TB)	Bristol Beaufort II	Vavuniya, Ceylon
No 45 Sqn (DB)	(Vultee Vengeance II)	Kumbhirgram, India
No 82 Sqn (DB)	(Vultee Vengeance III)	Dohazari, India
No 84 Sqn (DB)	(Vultee Vengeance III)	Marharajpur, India
No 99 Sqn (M)	Vickers Wellington X	Jessore, India
No 110 Sqn (DB)	(Vultee Vengeance III)	Kumbhirgram, India
No 159 Sqn (H)	(Consolidated Liberator III)	Digri, India
No 160 Sqn (H)	(Consolidated Liberator (III/V)	Sigiriya, India
No 215 Sqn (M)	Vickers Wellington X	Jessore, India
No 355 Sqn (H)	(Consolidated Liberator III)	Salbani, India

Fleet Air Arm

Squadron	Aircraft	Base
No 810 Sqn (TB)	Fairey Barracuda II	HMS *Illustrious*
No 811 Sqn (TB)	Fairey Swordfish II	Stretton, Cheshire
No 813 Sqn (TB)	Fairey Swordfish II	Dunino, Fife
No 815 Sqn (TB)	Fairey Barracuda II	Tain, Ross and Cromarty
No 816 Sqn (TB)	Fairey Swordfish II	Donibristle, Fife

Fleet Air Arm (Continued)

No 817 Sqn (TB)	Fairey Barracuda II	Lee-on-Solent, Hants
No 818 Sqn (TB)	Fairey Swordfish II	HMS *Unicorn*
No 819 Sqn (TB)	Fairey Swordfish II	Sydenham, Co Down
No 820 Sqn (TB)	Fairey Barracuda II	Lee-on-Solent, Hants
No 822 Sqn (TB)	Fairey Barracuda II	Tain, Ross and Cromarty
No 823 Sqn (TB)	Fairey Barracuda II	Fearn, Ross and Cromarty
No 824 Sqn (TB)	Fairey Swordfish II	HMS *Striker*
No 825 Sqn (TB)	Fairey Swordfish I/II	HMS *Vindex*
No 826 Sqn (TB)	Fairey Barracuda II	Lee-on-Solent, Hants
No 827 Sqn (TB)	Fairey Barracuda II	HMS *Furious*
No 829 Sqn (TB)	Fairey Barracuda II	Tain, Ross and Cromarty
No 830 Sqn (TB)	Fairey Barracuda II	HMS *Furious*
No 831 Sqn (TB)	Fairey Barracuda II	Machrihanish, Argyllshire
No 832 Sqn (TB)	(Grumman Avenger I)	Machrihanish, Argyllshire
No 833 Sqn (TB)	Fairey Swordfish II	Maydown, Londonderry
No 834 Sqn (TB)[5]	Fairey Swordfish II	HMS *Battler*
No 835 Sqn (TB)[5]	Fairey Swordfish II	HMS *Nairana*
No 836 Sqn (TB)	Fairey Swordfish II	Maydown, Londonderry
No 838 Sqn (TB)	Fairey Swordfish II	HMS *Nairana*
No 842 Sqn (TB)[6]	Fairey Swordfish II	HMS *Fencer*
No 845 Sqn (TB)	(Grumman Avenger I)	Hatston, Orkney
No 846 Sqn (TB)[7]	(Grumman Avenger I)	Machrihanish, Argyllshire
No 847 Sqn (TB)	Fairey Barracuda II	HMS *Illustrious*

No 848 Sqn (TB)	(Grumman Avenger I)	Gosport, Hants
No 849 Sqn (TB)	(Grumman Avenger I)	Grimsetter, Orkney
No 850 Sqn (TB)	(Grumman Avenger I)	Sea Island, Canada
No 851 Sqn (TB)	(Grumman Avenger I)	*En route* to HMS *Shah*
No 853 Sqn (TB)	(Grumman Avenger I)	Hatston, Orkney
No 854 Sqn (TB)	(Grumman Avenger II)	Squantum, USA
No 860 Sqn (RNethN)(TB)[8]	Fairey Swordfish II	Maydown, Londonderry

[1] Squadron not operating in the bomber role on this date.
[2] Squadron non-operational on this date.
[3] Squadron operational within the Royal Air Force Order of Battle.
[4] Squadron's bombing rôle secondary to Special Duties.
[5] Squadron also operating Sea Hurricane fighters.
[6] Squadron also operating Seafire fighters.
[7] Squadron also operating Wildcat fighters.
[8] Squadron operating with the Royal Navy.

H—Heavy Bomber; M—Medium Bomber; L—Light Bomber; HPF—Pathfinder Heavy Bomber; MPF—Pathfinder Medium Bomber; LPF—Pathfinder Light Bomber; DB—Dive Bomber; TB—Torpedo Bomber.

Note: American bombers (such as the Lockheed Hudson, Boeing Fortress and Consolidated Liberator), employed by the RAF squadrons on maritime reconnaissance duties, are not included above.

7. THE COLD WAR BOMBERS

Royal Air Force Bomber Command attained its zenith in size and power shortly before the end of the War in Europe, its order of battle in April 1945 comprising 1,850 heavy bombers immediately available for operations, as well as 265 light bombers and 260 bomber support aircraft, distributed between 97 squadrons; in the Mediterranean, the RAF fielded 6 squadrons of Liberator heavy bombers (*sic*) and 7 of Boston, Baltimore and Marauder medium and light bombers, and in South-East Asia 5 squadrons of Liberators and 4 of Mosquito light bombers.

With the coming of peace, despite an aura of thinly-veiled distrust of Russian ambitions both in Europe and the Far East, the newly-elected Atlee administration pursued a policy of stringent military cutback, rendered fairly straightforward by the natural process of demobilisation of manpower with the coming of peace. In the Royal Air Force 60 per cent of the operational squadrons were disbanded within two years, and over 70 per cent of the second-line support flying units and stations closed down.

All production contracts on which work had not yet started were either drastically reduced or simply cancelled outright. Almost every American aircraft previously supplied to the RAF under the wartime Lend-Lease Act was returned to the United States.

In Bomber Command, the Halifax — still equipping 13 squadrons (of which all but two were Canadian, Australian or 'Free' French) — was to be confined to transport duties, while introduction of the Lincoln was to go ahead, though at a much reduced rate. The peacetime strength of Bomber Command's heavy bomber force was to be limited to 20 squadrons, it being intended to achieve this level by January 1950, replacing the Lancaster exclusively with the Lincoln.

The early promise shown by RAF Meteor jet fighters, as well as evidence provided by captured German jet bombers at the end of the War, encouraged the Air Staff to lay plans for the ultimate replacement of the Lincoln and Mosquito by jet bombers, although, with government financing of aviation research cut by 86 per cent in FY 1946-47, it was impossible to achieve any significant technological advance in the short term. It would be ten years before the jet-powered 'heavy' bombers arrived in

Of all the RAF bombers of the Cold War period the English Electric Canberra served longest, its underlying technology dating from the late 1940s. Here armourers are seen handling the pair of 1,000lb bomb triplets which constituted the aircraft's normal warload. (Photo: Ministry of Defence)

service with the Royal Air Force.

The knock-on effect of reduced defence expenditure had an immediate effect on the British aircraft industry, the manufacturers being obliged to reduce their work force — including the all-important design and research staffs, whose highly specialised experience had been accumulated over many years — by well over half. The pathetic inability of successive government Chancellors of any political hue, and their Treasury civil servants, to appreciate the lasting damage caused by rote-inspired 'remedies' has, over the second half of the twentieth century, repeatedly contrived to emasculate the nation's ability to defend itself and to fulfil its international obligations.

The vacuum created in the aeronautical research field by the socialist administration in 1946-47 cost British industry dearly, and its lead in aircraft and aero engines, enjoyed at the end of the War, had completely evaporated within a year, as the United States assumed the status of a major world power, and continued its technical and industrial advance to sustain that status. The first four-engine American jet bomber prototype, later to serve with the USAF, the North American XB-45, made its maiden flight on 17 March 1947 and showed itself capable of a Mach 0.77 performance. Before that year was out, the six-jet, swept-wing, Mach 0.82 Boeing XB-47 had also flown. Both aircraft were designed to carry bomb loads of up to 20,000lb. Both would be in service in the early 1950s.

The traditional British heavy bomber manufacturers, Handley Page, A V Roe, Vickers and Short, essayed to take the RAF into the big jet bomber era. Yet it was a fifth manufacturer, the English Electric company — which had produced large numbers of Handley Page Hampdens and Halifaxes during the War, but none of its own design — which came up with a successful twin-turbojet light bomber, an aircraft that was to serve with the Royal Air Force for more than 40 years. The Canberra was essentially an extremely primitive aeroplane, albeit efficient in its simplicity, with thick, unswept, low-aspect-ratio wings, a small pressure cabin and (initially) entirely manual controls.

Yet for all its lack of sophistication and its subsonic performance, the Canberra proved a difficult exercise target for RAF Meteors and Vampires when it entered service with Bomber Command's

No 101 Squadron early in 1951. And it was to be Canberras that were deployed to Germany (with the RAF's Second Tactical Air Force) in the early years of NATO — in a purely tactical rôle, for their range with six 1,000lb bombs was quite inadequate to reach far behind the Iron Curtain. Moreover, the radar blind-bombing system that was originally central to the Canberra's operational concept never materialised.

Thus, at the beginning of the Cold War, which was signalled by the Russian blockade of Berlin in 1948, and the more serious, communist inspired invasion of South Korea two years later, Britain was unable to contribute any RAF component to the United Nations air forces. And as the USAF faced aircraft of Soviet origin in Korea, RAF Lincoln heavy bombers were deployed against communist jungle terrorists in Malaya, and two years later against Kikuyu tribesmen in Kenya. That was the legacy of Treasury parsimony inspired by Britain's first postwar government.

It was, nevertheless, the outbreak of war in Korea that demonstrated to the Air Staff, if not to the politically bankrupt Labour government, the folly of a new 'ten-year rule'. Russia would inevitably emerge as a nuclear power, and her air force would reach parity with the

American Strategic Air Command in global striking power within the foreseeable future. Recognising that Bomber Command had nothing capable of matching the Boeing B-50 in striking power (the Lincoln being unable to reach the Soviet Union from any RAF base, and return), the British government opted to purchase 87 obsolete B-29s and B-29As from America as interim equipment for Bomber Command, these aircraft eventually serving with nine squadrons between August 1950 and April 1954 (although the countermeasures Squadron, No 192, continued to fly them until February 1958).

On paper the B-29s (named Washington B.1s in RAF service) lent a flicker of respectability to Bomber Command's potential striking power, but in reality the five-year-old veterans proved disappointing and expensive in RAF service, the relatively small scale of spares purchased proving wholly inadequate to enable the squadrons to achieve an average serviceability higher than 40 per cent. Needless to say, no one ever seriously suggested that Washingtons should take their turn in Kenya — the logistics would have been enormous.

Returning to the Air Staff's long-term plans for a peacetime bomber force, initiated almost as soon as the

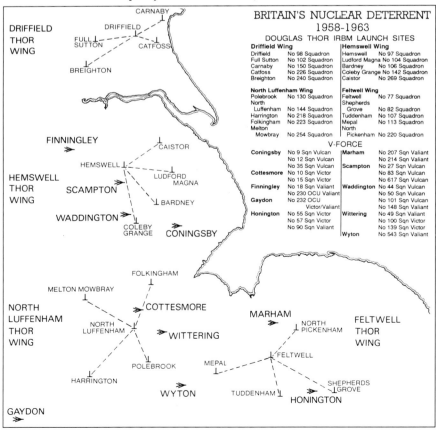

BRITAIN'S NUCLEAR DETERRENT
1958-1963
DOUGLAS THOR IRBM LAUNCH SITES

Driffield Wing		Hemswell Wing	
Driffield	No 98 Squadron	Hemswell	No 97 Squadron
Full Sutton	No 102 Squadron	Ludford Magna	No 104 Squadron
Carnaby	No 150 Squadron	Bardney	No 106 Squadron
Catfoss	No 226 Squadron	Coleby Grange	No 142 Squadron
Breighton	No 240 Squadron	Caistor	No 269 Squadron

North Luffenham Wing		Feltwell Wing	
Polebrook	No 130 Squadron	Feltwell	No 77 Squadron
North		Shepherds	
Luffenham	No 144 Squadron	Grove	No 82 Squadron
Harrington	No 218 Squadron	Tuddenham	No 107 Squadron
Folkingham	No 223 Squadron	Mepal	No 113 Squadron
Melton		North	
Mowbray	No 254 Squadron	Pickenham	No 220 Squadron

V-FORCE

Coningsby	No 9 Sqn Vulcan	Marham	No 207 Sqn Valiant
	No 12 Sqn Vulcan		No 214 Sqn Valiant
	No 35 Sqn Vulcan	Scampton	No 27 Sqn Vulcan
Cottesmore	No 10 Sqn Victor		No 83 Sqn Vulcan
	No 15 Sqn Victor		No 617 Sqn Vulcan
Finningley	No 18 Sqn Valiant	Waddington	No 44 Sqn Vulcan
	No 230 OCU Valiant		No 50 Sqn Vulcan
Gaydon	No 232 OCU		No 101 Sqn Vulcan
	Victor/Valiant		No 148 Sqn Valiant
Honington	No 55 Sqn Victor	Wittering	No 49 Sqn Valiant
	No 57 Sqn Victor		No 100 Sqn Victor
	No 90 Sqn Valiant		No 139 Sqn Victor
		Wyton	No 543 Sqn Victor

Serviceability and loading checks being completed on a Blue Steel Mk 1 stand-off weapon beneath a Vulcan B Mk 2, XL318, of No 617 Squadron; note that the undercarriage tyres are shrouded to avoid possible radiation contamination. The decision to discontinue development of the long-range Mark 2 version of this weapon set in train the events that ultimately ended any possibility of establishing a credible British nuclear deterrent employing manned aircraft. (Photo: Ministry of Defence)

Second World War ended, it was assumed that, with American assistance, Britain would have produced a nuclear weapon by the time a suitable turbojet-powered high-speed, bomber was ready for service. Two Operational Requirements, OR.229 and OR.230, were drafted, calling for medium- and long-range aircraft respectively; neither were to carry any defensive armament, but both were to be designed with the object of delivering a 10,000lb nuclear weapon.

Owing to the swingeing defence expenditure reductions, it soon became obvious that the long-range bomber was beyond the resources of both the Treasury and the aircraft industry for the foreseeable future, and OR.230 was held in abeyance. OR.229 was therefore quantified in Specification B.35/46 and issued to the Industry on 24 January 1947, attracting tenders from six manufacturers. Four of these were selected for prototype purchase.

Two of the designs were seen as relatively orthodox in concept and prototypes were ordered immediately, materialising as the Vickers Type 660 Valiant and the Short SA.4 Sperrin; the other two, the Avro Type 698 Vulcan and the Handley Page H.P.80 Victor, were of such advanced concept that much preliminary aerodynamic research was required, and were therefore not ordered until August 1952.

While the Sperrin fell by the wayside, on account of inadequate performance, the Valiant proved to be an attractive proposition, and was ordered into production as work continued to develop and test a British nuclear bomb, a task that was prolonged considerably following the passage of the American McMahon Act which forbade the release of any nuclear data by the USA to her allies — this despite the enormous contribution made by British scientists to the American wartime nuclear bombs. After a series of abrasive exchanges, the Ameri-

cans reluctantly agreed to provide engineering information, but left Britain to develop the physical operation of her own nuclear weapon.

The first British 25-kiloton nuclear device, mounted in the frigate HMS *Plym*, was successfully detonated off the Monte Bello Islands, Western Australia, on 3 October 1952. However, it was not until 1956 that British nuclear weapons were ready for testing. On 16 May that year a device, approximating to the 10,000lb Blue Danube 25-kiloton bomb, was mounted in a ground tower in the Monte Bello Islands and successfully detonated as RAF aircrews, flying in the vicinity, observed the test. (Five days later a Boeing B-52B, flying at about 50,000 feet, dropped the first American thermonuclear (hydrogen) bomb over Bikini Atoll in the Pacific.)

The Blue Danube was successfully detonated over the Maralinga Range, South Australia, on 11 October 1956, having been carried aloft by a Valiant bomber of No 49 (Bomber) Squadron. This was followed by the first British hydrogen weapon, a prototype Yellow Sun bomb, dropped by a No 49 Squadron Valiant south of Christmas Island in the Pacific on 15 May 1957.

The first Valiants had entered RAF service early in 1955 and, by the autumn of 1956, equipped five squadrons of Bomber Command. While No 49 Squadron was engaged in the nuclear weapon test programme, the other four Valiant squadrons were deployed to Malta to support the Suez campaign, mounted to safeguard international free passage through the Canal, but rendered abortive by badly-judged American opposition to the Anglo-French operations.

The Valiants flew raids over Egypt with loads of conventional iron bombs.

The Conservative Government's Defence White Paper, presented in the British Parliament by the Rt Hon Duncan Sandys, was one of those inept acts of government, referred to previously, ill-advised and inadequately prepared. Apart from prematurely seeking to end all production of manned fighters in favour of reliance upon surface-to-air missiles (in the development of which Britain was trailing badly), the Sandys' White Paper summarily cancelled the Avro Type 730, an eight-turbojet supersonic heavy bomber that had been designed ultimately to replace the Valiant/Vulcan/Victor trio — now universally referred to as the V-bombers.

With the early withdrawal of the American Washington bombers, Bomber Command came to rely heavily on the Canberra light bomber for a short period in the mid-1950s but, with the emergence of the Soviet Union as a major nuclear power and, as such, a very real threat to world stability, the policy of deterrence was accepted by the Western Alliance as apparently the only realistic safeguard of peace. The American Strategic Air Command represented the cornerstone of this deterrent force, possessing a truly awesome arsenal of huge Boeing B-52 'global' bombers as well as intermediate-range and intercontinental ballistic missiles with nuclear warheads, all targeted on cities, towns and military installations throughout the Soviet Union and the Communist bloc.

The British V-bombers were the only such aircraft available to NATO from a European nation, although with powerful American ground and air forces based in Europe, any aggression by the Soviet Union against NATO nations would have provoked an instant response by SAC's bombers and missiles.

This 'tripwire' response policy spurred the deployment of the V-force in Britain. This force amounted to 22 squadrons of bombers and was in place by 1963, based on ten major airfields as well as being capable of dispersal to 20 other airfields with operational readiness platforms in times of international tension. Also deployed in Britain between 1958 and 1963 were 60 American Thor intermediate-range ballistic missiles (IRBMs), manned by 20 RAF Squadrons. With a range of 1,500 miles, these missiles were, however, soon discarded as tactically unwieldy as, requiring authentication by an American officer at each weapon site, the firing reaction time was of the order of 15 minutes — time enough for every Thor to have been destroyed by incoming missiles.

In truth, the entire concept of the high-flying, manned bomber deterrent — both American and British — was invalidated when, on 1 May 1960, an American Lockheed U-2 reconnaissance aircraft, flying at 65,000 feet over Sverdlovsk in the Soviet Union, was shot down by Russian surface-to-air missiles, an altitude well above the maximum height at which American B-52s and RAF Vulcans and Victors would operate. It was immediately realised that high altitude penetration of Soviet airspace, whether for pre-emptive or retaliatory strikes, could be prevented by an efficient SAM defence, and that if manned bombers were to continue to be used, only an air-launched,

stand-off nuclear weapon had any chance of reaching its target.

At once the V-bombers were temporarily re-tasked with the low-level attack, to deliver free-fall, lay-down bombs, while alternative stand-off weapons were developed and introduced. The first of the British V-bombers to assume this rôle were the Valiants, as being the most vulnerable at high altitude. However, after only a short period, the Valiant was found to be suffering from potentially catastrophic fatigue weakness in its structure and had immediately to be withdrawn from bombing operations, although it continued to serve the V-force as a tanker aircraft in the in-flight refuelling rôle.

The first step taken to provide the two remaining V-bombers with suitable weapons was to modify the Yellow Sun thermonuclear bomb as a lay-down weapon, the Mark 2 version being released after a low-level approach and a steep climb to 12,000 feet. Another weapon introduced, the WE177, was an offset, toss-bomb, released at low level as the bomber executed a sharp turn to avoid overflying the target area. Both weapons were adopted while the Avro Blue Steel Mk 1, 100-mile-range stand-off weapon was developed; it was eventually introduced into service with Nos 27, 83 and 617 (Vulcan Mk 2) Squadrons at Scampton, and Nos 100 and 137 (Victor Mk 2) Squadrons at Wittering.

Blue Steel in its Mark 1 form was clearly of only limited value on account of its short range, and a much-improved Mark 2 was nearing introduction when it was cancelled by the British government in favour of the American Douglas

Skybolt, two of which were to have been carried under the wings of the Vulcan. When this weapons system was also cancelled (this time by the Americans themselves), the RAF's V-force was relieved of its strategic deterrent responsibility, this being henceforth assumed by the Royal Navy's submarine-launched Polaris missiles.

As the British Air Staff examined various options by which the RAF could continue to implement its responsibilities to NATO, following the cancellation by the Rt Hon Denis Healey of the BAC TSR-2 (see Chapter 8), the Vulcan and Victor continued to serve in the recently constituted Strike Command. In the meantime Handley Page Ltd had closed down, the penalty paid for Sir Frederick's refusal to join with one of the politically favoured aircraft manufacturing conglomerates, the British Aircraft Corporation or the Hawker Siddeley Group.

The Victor, after extensive modification, was redeployed in the tanker rôle, a task it continued to perform with great reliability until retired from the RAF in 1993. The Vulcan was eventually employed operationally during the short Falkland Islands campaign of 1982, 1,000lb iron bombs being dropped by a single aircraft on the airfield runway at Port Stanley, and Shrike anti-radiation missiles being discharged at enemy radar above the port. Both attacks represented a display of the Vulcan's remarkable capabilities, involving exceptionally long operational flights and frequent night air refuelling, the latter provided by relays of Victor tankers. Shortly after this operation the Vulcan was withdrawn from service.

Deployment of British Bomber Squadrons — 1 January 1950

Home Bases					
No 7 Sqn (H)	Avro Lincoln B.2	Upwood, Hunts	No 138 Sqn (H)	Avro Lincoln B.2	Scampton, Lincs
No 9 Sqn (H)	Avro Lincoln B.2	Binbrook, Lincs	No 139 Sqn (L)	D.H. Mosquito B.35	Coningsby, Lincs
No 12 Sqn (H)	Avro Lincoln B.2	Binbrook, Lincs	No 148 Sqn (H)	Avro Lancaster B.1	Upwood, Hunts
No 15 Sqn (H)	Avro Lincoln B.2	Wyton, Hunts	No 149 Sqn (H)	Avro Lincoln B.2	Mildenhall, Suffolk
No 35 Sqn (H)	Avro Lincoln B.2	Mildenhall, Suffolk	No 207 Sqn (H)	Avro Lincoln B.2	Mildenhall, Suffolk
No 44 Sqn (H)	Avro Lincoln B.2	Wyton, Hunts	No 214 Sqn (H)	Avro Lancaster B.1	Upwood, Hunts
No 49 Sqn (H)	Avro Lincoln B.2	Upwood, Hunts	No 617 Sqn (H)	Avro Lincoln B.2	Binbrook, Lincs
No 50 Sqn (H)	Avro Lincoln B.2	Waddington, Lincs			
No 57 Sqn (H)	Avro Lincoln B.2	Waddington, Lincs	*Germany*		
No 61 Sqn (H)	Avro Lincoln B.2	Waddington, Lincs	No 14 Sqn (L)	D.H. Mosquito B.35	Celle, Germany
No 83 Sqn (H)	Avro Lincoln B.2	Hemswell, Lincs			
No 90 Sqn (H)	Avro Lincoln B.2	Wyton, Hunts	*Middle East*		
No 97 Sqn (H)	Avro Lincoln B.2	Hemswell, Lincs	No 8 Sqn (L)	Bristol Brigand B.1	Khormaksar, Aden
No 100 Sqn (H)	Avro Lincoln B.2	Hemswell, Lincs	No 84 Sqn (L)	Bristol Brigand B.1	Habbaniya, Iraq
No 101 Sqn (H)	Avro Lincoln B.2	Binbrook, Lincs			
No 109 Sqn (L)	D.H. Mosquito B.35	Coningsby, Lincs	*Far East*		
No 115 Sqn (H)	Avro Lincoln B.2	Mildenhall, Suffolk	No 45 Sqn (L)	Bristol Brigand B.1	Tengah, Singapore

Fairey Spearfish

Intended as an ultimate replacement for the Barracuda, Herbert Eugene Chaplin's Spearfish was completed too late for service with the Fleet Air Arm during the War, and the planned production orders were cancelled after four of the seven prototypes had flown.

Specification O.5/43 was issued shortly after the first Fleet Air Arm squadrons began equipping with the American Grumman Avenger torpedo-bomber-reconnaissance aircraft in January 1943, an aircraft whose performance was superior to that of the Barracuda, largely on account of a more powerful engine, but also because the American aircraft carried its warload internally. Despite carrying a three-man crew, the Avenger was actually lighter than the Barracuda.

The approach of the powerful Centaurus engine to service status, however, opened up the possibility of producing a true multi-rôle naval strike aircraft, capable of dive and torpedo attack, mining, submarine search and strike and rocket-armed reconnaissance-strike. It was to be a large aircraft, and was ultimately intended to be embarked in the planned 45,000-ton *Gibraltar*-class fleet carriers (the so-called CVB, or battle carriers)[1]. Chaplin's design was about 10 per cent larger and 30 per cent heavier than the Barracuda, this being due to the internal stowage of all weapons (except the rocket projectiles which were to be mounted on zero-length, underwing launchers) and a much greater fuel load. Like the Barracuda, the Spearfish featured the successful Fairey-Youngman area-increasing aerofoil flaps, but these — as on the Firefly fighter — were now fully retractable into the wing when not required.

Other refinements included hydraulically-folding wings, an hydraulically-operated sliding canopy over the pilot's cockpit, the provision of Mark XV ASV radar in a retractable radome under the rear fuselage, and a massive, wide-track undercarriage which retracted outwards into the outer wing sections. The dorsal armament, comprising a pair of 0.50in Browning machine guns, was to be mounted in a remotely controlled Frazer Nash Type 95 barbette, although this was probably never fitted in the proto-

The first prototype Spearfish, RA356, was little more than an aerodynamic test aircraft, being unarmed and fitted with wing airbrakes. (Photo: The Fairey Aviation Co Ltd)

types. The pilot was provided with two forward-firing 0.50in Brownings.

The engine installation was exceptionally clean, with exhaust manifolds recessed into the sides of the front fuselage; a prominent oil cooler air

Type: Single-engine, two-seat, mid-wing monoplane carrier-borne multi-rôle torpedo strike aircraft.
Specifications: O.5/43 (and O.21/44).
Manufacturer: The Fairey Aviation Co Ltd, Hayes, Middlesex, and Heaton Chapel, Stockport, Lancashire.
Powerplant: One 2,585hp Bristol Centaurus 57 14-cylinder air-cooled sleeve-valve radial engine driving a 5-blade Rotol constant-speed propeller.
Dimensions: Span, 60ft 3in; length, 44ft 7in; height, 13ft 6in; wing area, 530 sq ft.
Weights: Tare, 15,200lb; all-up (maximum as bomber), 22,083lb.
Performance: Max speed, 292 mph at 14,000ft; climb to 10,000ft, 7 min 45 sec; range at 15,000ft, 1,040 miles; service ceiling, 25,000ft.
Armament: Two fixed forward-firing 0.50in Browning machine guns and intended to have two in remotely-controlled dorsal Frazer Nash Type 95 barbette. Bomb load of either four 500lb GP or AP bombs, one 1,800lb 18in torpedo, mines or depth charges carried internally, or up to sixteen 60lb rocket projectiles carried under the wings.
Prototypes: Eight (RA356, RA360 and RA363 built at Hayes; RN241, RN244, TJ175, TJ179, TJ184 scheduled to be built at Stockport). RA356 first flown by Flt Lt F H Dixon RAFO at Hayes on 5 July 1945; RN244, TJ175, TJ179 and TJ184 not flown. Planned production of 150 aircraft cancelled.

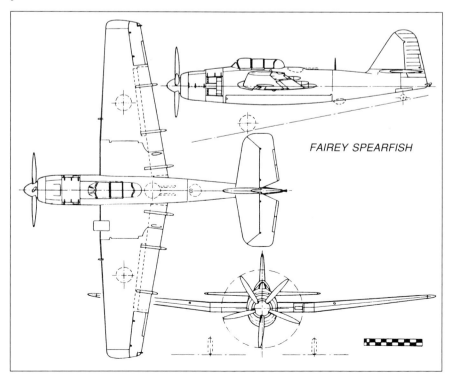

FAIREY SPEARFISH

---

[1] The three carriers of this class, *Gibraltar*, *Malta* and *New Zealand*, were all cancelled immediately after the end of the war with Japan in 1945.

Production of the Spearfish was to have been confined to the Fairey factory at Stockport, and the only Stockport-built prototype to have flown, RN241, was the closest to the production configuration. Both the underfuselage ASV Mk XV radome and the dorsal gun barbette, shown here apparently fitted, are thought to have been dummies. (Photo: The Fairey Aviation Co Ltd)

intake was located in the leading edge of the port inboard wing section.

Hydraulic servo-ailerons were planned for production aircraft, and although, as an interim expedient, pierced rectangular airbrakes were fitted in the upper and lower surfaces of the wings of the second and third prototypes, it was intended later to replace the Rotol five-blade constant-speed propeller with a reversing-pitch propeller as a form of airbrake to limit the diving speed to 260 knots.

Eight prototypes and 150 production aircraft were on order when the first Hayes-built prototype, RA356, made its maiden flight on 5 July 1945, flown by Flt Lt Foster Hickman Dixon RAFO,

Fairey's chief test pilot since 1942. This was followed by the first Stockport-built prototype, RN241, on 29 December 1945.

Cancellation of the *Gibraltar*-class carriers, and a reappraisal of the Fleet Air Arm's torpedo aircraft requirements, caused the Spearfish production orders to be cancelled before the end of 1945, but work on the two remaining Hayes-built aircraft went ahead at a slower rate, and these were flown in 1947 for purely research purposes; two further Stockport prototypes, RN244 and TJ179, were completed but not flown, and the two remaining Stockport prototypes were cancelled.

As early as 1944 it was seen that, with jet-powered naval fighters in the offing, the Centaurus-powered Spearfish was unlikely to enjoy a long service career, and Specification O.21/44 was issued, calling for much increased performance from an aircraft with the same load and rôle capabilities of the Spearfish. Fairey produced a considerably altered derivative of the earlier aircraft, power being provided by a tandem pair of Rolls-Royce Merlin engines driving co-axial three-blade propellers; the front engine was to be mounted under the pilot's cockpit, and the rear engine between the two cockpits. The engine radiators were to occupy the entire inboard wing section leading edges. Nothing came of this project as the Specification was withdrawn at the end of the War.

Short Sturgeon

Conceived at the same time as, and complementary to, the Fairey Spearfish as a high-performance, carrier-borne torpedo-bomber-reconnaissance aircraft, the Short Sturgeon was intended to operate from the new 45,000-ton *Gibraltar*-class aircraft carriers, planned to enter commission in the late 1940s.

Specification S.6/43 defined a requirement for a naval strike torpedo-bomber-reconnaissance aircraft, and to this Short tendered two designs, one with a single Centaurus engine, the other powered by a pair of Merlins. The latter was preferred, and a new Specification, S.11/43, was drawn up around a design produced under the direction of C T P Lipscombe, who had been appointed Short's chief designer after Arthur Gouge's departure to Saunders-Roe Ltd. In October 1943 a contract was raised with Short for three prototypes.

Almost immediately the torpedo-carrying requirement was deleted from the requirements (it being assumed that this

The second Sturgeon Mk 1 prototype RK791 landing at Sydenham, Belfast, after its maiden flight on 18 May 1948; the pilot was John Stanley Booth. (Photo: Short Bros & Harland Ltd)

would be more adequately satisfied by the Fairey Spearfish). The Short design went ahead (later to be named the Sturgeon) as an orthodox twin-engine, mid-wing aircraft with Alclad monocoque construction with fabric-covered control surfaces (the latter in spite of a maximum speed expected to be more than 350 mph), and an exceptionally strong but light airframe was achieved, bearing in mind the stressing demands of carrier landings.

The three-man crew was accommodated in two separate compartments, the pilot alone occupying a cockpit above the front wing spar, while the navigator and radio operator were situated in a cabin aft of the rear spar. Fuel was carried in the wing centresection, which was built integrally with the engine nacelles. These mounted a pair of 2,080hp Rolls-Royce Merlin 140s with two-speed superchargers and with radiators buried in the wing centresection leading edges; contraprops were considered necessary to minimise the aircraft's overall width with wings folded (this being limited to 20 feet).

To cope with the high vertical descent rate during carrier landings, a very sturdy undercarriage was designed and produced by Rubery Owen-Messier, and the highly-stressed wing spar joints were cast in nickel-chrome steel alloy to withstand an ultimate load of 75 tons/sq in. Sliding Zap flaps occupied the entire wing trailing edge between the ailerons, these being hydraulically actuated, as were the undercarriage retraction and wing folding. A deck arrester hook was fitted aft of the tailwheel.

By the time Geoffrey Tyson flew the first prototype Sturgeon, RK787, at Rochester on 7 June 1946, not only had the large carriers been abandoned, but all the aircraft intended to operate from them as well. The Sturgeon prototypes, however, on account of their ingenious approach to very demanding carrier operating requirements, were reprieved, and the second aircraft, RK791, was transferred to Belfast for completion according to plan. Carrier trials were conducted aboard HMS *Victorious* and the Sturgeons acquitted themselves extremely well.

This outstanding carrier-compatibility resulted in the aircraft being re-tasked for the target-towing rôle, the Sturgeon TT Mk 2 eventually entering production as the subject of the former bomber contract. The third bomber Mark 1 prototype, completed as VR363, served as the Mark 2 target tug prototype, and 24 production aircraft were built, eventually serving with Nos 703, 728 and 771 Squadrons of the Fleet Air Arm. Five of these were later stripped of their deck landing accoutrements and, as TT Mark 3s, served ashore at Hal Far, Malta, until October 1958.

Type: Twin-engine, three-crew, mid-wing monoplane carrier-borne bomber-reconnaissance aircraft (later target-tug).

Air Ministry Specifications: S.11/43.

Manufacturer: Short Bros Ltd, Rochester, Kent, and Belfast.

Powerplant: Two 2,080hp Rolls-Royce Merlin 140 12-cylinder liquid-cooled in-line engines driving 6-blade Rotol contraprops.

Dimensions: Span, 59 ft 11in (folded 19ft 10in); length, 44ft 0in; wing area, 518.4 sq ft.

Weights: Tare, 18,126lb; all-up (designed), 24,000lb.

Performance: Max speed, 352 mph at 16,800ft; service ceiling, 28,800ft.

Armament: Two or four fixed forward-firing 0.50in Browning machine guns. Bomb load of either one 1,000lb or two 500lb bombs, or four 250lb Torpex depth charges and up to sixteen 60lb rocket projectiles.

Prototypes: Two S Mark 1 prototypes, RK787 and RK791; RK787 first flown by Geoffrey Tyson at Rochester, Kent, on 7 June 1946. (A third Mk 1 prototype, RK794, was completed as the first TT Mk 2 prototype, VR363.) No production as a bomber.

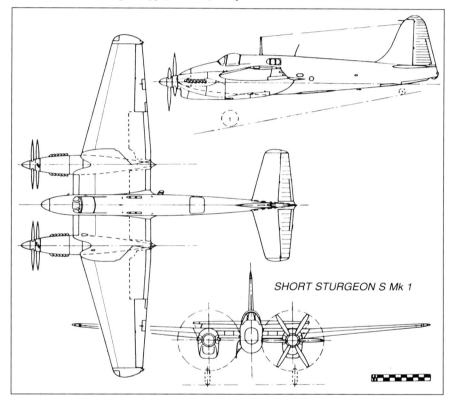

SHORT STURGEON S Mk 1

Avro Types 696/716 Shackleton

With front-line service spanning forty years, the Avro Shackleton was the outcome of a design originated by Roy Chadwick to Specification R.5/46 for a maritime reconnaissance aircraft suit-

A Shackleton MR Mk 2 of No 37 Squadron engaged in bombing operations on the borders of the Aden Protectorate in the 1960s. (Photo: R C B Ashworth)

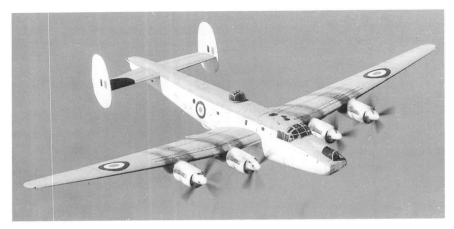

A standard Shackleton MR Mk 2, showing well the characteristic annular cowlings of the Rolls-Royce Griffon engines and the extremely spacious fuselage contours. (Photo: via R C B Ashworth)

able for service in the Pacific theatre. It employed wings similar to those of the Lincoln, as well as many components of the Tudor airliner, but featured an entirely new stressed skin fuselage, wider and deeper than those of the previous bombers.

Powered by four 2,450hp Rolls-Royce Griffon engines (Mk 57A inboard and Mk 57 outboard), driving six-blade contraprops, the prototype Shackleton GR 1, VW126, was flown by James Harold Orrell OBE, Avro's chief test pilot, at Woodford on 9 March 1949. 77 production MR Mk 1s followed and entered service with ten squadrons of Coastal Command in the maritime reconnaissance rôle, beginning with No 120 Squadron at Kinloss in April 1951.

The MR Mk 2 (of which 69 examples were produced) introduced improved gun armament and a semi-retractable ventral radome with improved sea search radar. In 1971 twelve of these aircraft were extensively modified to incorporate APS-20 search radar to enable the Shackleton to assume the airborne early warning rôle, joining No 8 Squadron at Kinloss in January 1972.

The Shackleton MR Mk 3 was introduced to provide greater all-round capabilitiy. The wing planform was improved, wingtip fuel tanks and nose-wheel undercarriage introduced, and a soundproofed wardroom provided for a relief crew on extended maritime patrols. The dorsal gun turret was deleted, and the range of weapons extended considerably (including provision to mount underwing rocket projectiles). Power was provided by four Griffon 57A piston engines, to which were added

a pair of small 2,500lb-thrust Rolls-Royce Viper 203 turbojets in the rear of the outboard piston engine nacelles to assist take-off and climb under overload conditions.

Although by far the greater part of the Shackleton's service was in the maritime reconnaissance and airborne early warning rôles, the aircraft came to be employed both for transport and bombing duties, as well as weather reconnaissance, and a number of T Mk 4 trainers was provided by modifying elderly MR 1s and MR 1As to carry the Mark 3's radio and navigation equipment, and

these served with the Maritime Operational Training Unit at Kinloss.

No 37 Squadron, began equipping with Shackleton MR 2s in 1953 at Luqa, Malta, in 1953 but moved to Aden in August 1957 where, in due course, it divided its activities between providing bombing support (usually armed with 500-pounders) for British ground forces defending the perimeter of the Aden Protectorate against hostile Yemeni forces, keeping watch on the increasing Soviet maritime presence in the Indian Ocean, and imposing a maritime blockade on ships attempting to supply Rhodesia, following that country's. unilateral declaration of independence. The Squadron was eventually disbanded in September 1967. AEW Shackletons continued in service for a further 24 years.

The accompanying data table refers to the Shackleton MR Mk 2, unless otherwise stated.

Type: Four-engine, ten-crew, mid-wing monoplane maritime bomber-reconnaissance aircraft.
Air Ministry Specification: R.5/46 (prototypes) and 42/46 (production).
Manufacturer: A V Roe & Co Ltd, Middleton, Manchester, and Woodford, Cheshire.
Powerplant: Four 2,450hp Rolls-Royce Griffon 57A 12-cylinder liquid-cooled supercharged in-line engines driving 6-blade DH Hydromatic contraprops.
Dimensions: Span, 120ft 0in; length, 87ft 3in; height, 16ft 9in; wing area, 1,421 sq ft.
Weights: Tare, 52,000lb; all-up, 86,000lb.
Performance: Max speed, 296 mph at 16,000ft; service ceiling, 21,400ft; maximum range, 4,300 miles.
Armament: Gun armament of two 20mm guns in nose and two in midships dorsal turret. Bomb load of up to 14,000 lb, comprising mines, depth charges and/or sonobuoys, or 1,000lb or 500lb GP bombs.
Prototypes: Three Mark 1 prototypes, VW126, VW131 and VW135 (VW126, which also served as the Mark 2 prototype, was first flown by J H Orrell at Woodford on 9 March 1949); first MR Mark 3, WR970, first flown on 2 September 1955.
Production: A total of 188 production Shackletons was built, comprising 77 Mark 1s, 69 Mark 2s and 42 Mark 3s (of which 8 were supplied to the South African Air Force).
Summary of RAF Service: Shackletons of the RAF served with Nos 8, 37, 38, 42, 120, 201, 203, 204, 205, 206, 210, 220, 224, 228, 240 and 269 Squadrons. As far as is known, only No 37 Squadron flew them in the bombing rôle operationally. They also flew with No 236 OCU (later the MOTU), and the Air Sea Warfare Development Unit.

A Shackleton AEW Mk 2 of No 8 Squadron, WR963. With the tailwheel undercarriage, the huge radome could only be located under the aircraft's nose, necessitating a shortened weapons bay. (Photo: Simon Barnes)

English Electric Canberra

When Specification B.3/45 was drafted, some weeks before the end of the War, the only jet bomber encountered by the Allies had been the German Arado Ar 234, a fast twin-engine aircraft without swept wings, examples of which would shortly be examined as enemy airfields were overrun. Britain was the only Allied nation to possess any operational experience with a turbojet-powered aircraft, the Gloster Meteor twin-engine fighter. And when the first B.3/45 Canberra prototype appeared in 1949 it seemed outdated already, when compared with the American Boeing XB-47 six-jet swept-wing bomber which had flown more than two years earlier. Yet America was to build over 400 Canberras for the USAF, some of which were still giving first-line service a quarter of a century later — long after the B-47 had disappeared from the USAF's inventory. This was the measure of the basic soundness of Britain's first jet-powered light bomber.

As eventually issued, Specification B.3/45 called for an aircraft with the same bomb load as the Mosquito B XVI (4,000lb) and with a Lancaster's normal radius of action (800 miles). Its operating height was to be in excess of 30,000 feet, and its structure was to be capable of withstanding a load factor of 5g. At English Electric (a company that had built hundreds of bombers during the War, but none of its own design) William Edward Willoughby Petter CBE — formerly technical director at Westland Aircraft Ltd — decided to base his design on an unswept wing of low aspect ratio and a thickness-chord ratio of 12 per cent, which could be constructed without recourse to heavy spars and still meet the stressing requirements. He originally intended to employ a single, fuselage-mounted turbojet of 13,000lb-thrust (then being proposed by Rolls-Royce) but, on account of complications anticipated with the air intakes of such an installation, decided instead to adopt

The first B.3/45 Canberra prototype, VN799, after the fin and rudder had been modified to the shape adopted in the subsequent B Mark 2 production version. (Photo: Simon Barnes)

the familiar Meteor configuration. Two of the new 6,500lb-thrust Rolls-Royce AJ.65 axial-flow turbojets (soon to be named the Avon) were therefore mounted in the wings, set in three ring-frames, two in the wing spars and one forward of the main spar.

The three-man crew was accommodated in a single pressurised cabin in the extreme nose, forward of the large bomb bay; the pilot occupied an ejector seat on the centreline of the aircraft, with the navigator and bomb aimer in similar seats, side-by-side, immediately behind him. The bomb aimer could move forward to a prone position in the front of the cabin to use his bombsight. All three seats were Martin-Baker Mark 1s.

Fuel was carried in large tanks in the upper half of the centre fuselage above the bomb bay which was designed to accommodate two 'triplet' bomb carriers, each with three 1,000lb bombs. Almost all systems employed were of wartime technology, with manual controls, gaseous oxygen for the crew, visual bombsight, VHF radio, IFF Mark III, Rebecca and G-H. Almost the only concession to advancing technology was the small tail warning radar, codenamed Orange Putter, in the extreme tail.

The first of four prototypes (referred to as A.1s), the two-seat VN799, was taken aloft by Wg Cdr Roland Prosper ('Bee') Beamont DSO* DFC*, English Electric's chief test pilot, on Friday 13 May 1949. Apart from being painted overall in 'PRU blue', this aircraft was distinguishable from subsequent examples in having a rounded top to its rudder and a small dorsal extension to the fin; it was also powered by 6,500lb-thrust RA.2 Avon engines. At the time of this first flight it had been intended that the Canberra would enter service as a two-seater equipped with a radar bombing system but, when this did not materialise, the design was changed to accommodate a bomb aimer with a visual bombsight located in a transparent nose, these changes being included in subsequent aircraft.

Probably produced as an insurance against delays in Avon engine production, the second prototype, VN813, was powered by 5,500lb-thrust Rolls-Royce Nene centrifugal-flow turbojets; however, as no such problems arose, all other Canberras were built with Avons.

VN799 was flown by Beamont at the 1949 SBAC Display at Farnborough, and his subsequent demonstrations were

The Canberra B 2 prototype VX165 shows off its exceptionally clean lines. The two 'skylights' in the top of the fuselage aft of the cockpit are set in a frangible panel through which the seats of the navigator and bomb aimer were ejected in an emergency. (Photo: The English Electric Co Ltd)

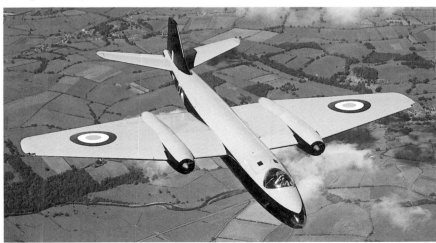

Left: *A Canberra B 6, WH968 of No 12 (Bomber) Squadron at Gibraltar. The provision of special sun canopies was essential for these aircraft in the tropics to prevent excessive cabin temperatures from rendering electronic equipment unserviceable and to enable servicing crews to work without too much discomfort.* (Photo: R C B Ashworth)

Below: *A Canberra B 16, WT369 (originally a B 6) of No 6 Squadron at Idris, Libya, in August 1964. This version was the only one to feature Blue Shadow radar and was unique to No 6 Squadron.* (Photo: R C B Ashworth)

probably instrumental in attracting the interest of the United States and Australia, both of which countries negotiated licences to build Canberras (the Glenn L Martin company eventually producing 403, designated B-57s, and the Commonwealth Aircraft company of Melbourne, 48). Four further prototypes had been ordered, and the first two of these, VX165 and VX169, served as precursors of the main production variant, the Canberra B Mk 2, prepared to Specification B.5/47, of which 412 were built (including batches contracted with A V Roe & Co Ltd, Handley Page Ltd, and Short Brothers & Harland, Ltd, see accompanying table).

The first production Canberra B Mk 2 was flown on 8 October 1950, and No 101 (Bomber) Squadron, formerly flying Lincolns at Binbrook, was warned to begin re-equipping early the following year, the first three aircraft being taken on charge in January 1951.[1]

The outbreak of war in Korea in 1950, and its major involvement of United Nations forces, had taken the

[1] Not May 1951, as fairly widely recorded elsewhere. The Squadron achieved its full complement of Canberras in May.

British government by surprise, and the annual defence appropriations provided no contingency for the acceleration of production of new aircraft. When, however, the Socialist government was defeated in the General Election the following year, the new Conservative administration sought to rectify matters by introducing a system of 'super priority' — the Canberra being one of the beneficiaries, even though the system exacerbated administrative chaos among the manufacturers of less favoured aircraft.

Fewer than 80 Canberra 2s were completed in 1951, and only one other Squadron, No 9, began taking deliveries in May, also at Binbrook. With pro-

duction getting underway at Shorts and Avro, the next year saw five more Canberra bomber squadrons equipped. The B Mark 2 was powered by the 7,500lb-thrust RA.3 Avon Mark 101 so that, with the 100-series engine also destined for the new Hawker Hunter transonic fighter, it was necessary to open new production lines for this engine with Bristol, Napier and Standard Motors.

In the main, Canberra 2s replaced Lincolns, Mosquitos and Washingtons in the early 1950s, thereby giving a much greater sense of purpose to the annual defence exercises over Britain. The days were over when Meteors and Vampires could simply intercept 'enemy' Lincolns with the greatest of ease and, before the arrival of the Hunter F Mk 4, the Canberra squadrons had matters much their own way. The first Canberra Squadron to join the 2nd Tactical Air Force in Germany was No 149, which flew out of Cottesmore to Ahlhorn on 24 August 1954, having

WH967 was one of a batch of former Canberra B 6s, converted to B 15s and provided with underwing Nord AS.30 ASMs and their associated avionics at the British Aircraft Corporation's Samlesbury factory. (Photo: Ministry of Aviation)

discarded its Washingtons; a month later it moved to Gutersloh. And the first to be based permanently in the Middle East was No 73 Squadron at Akrotiri, Cyprus, which gave up its Venom fighter-bombers to become a light bomber squadron — continuing to fly Canberras until 1969.

No 73 Squadron's aircraft were by no means the first Canberras to fly in the Middle East, however, as the Suez crisis of October 1956 had prompted the despatch of home-based bombers from the United Kingdom; No 10 Squadron had been the first to bomb targets in Egypt, flying from Malta, on 31 October, being followed by no fewer than ten other Canberra squadrons which operated temporarily from either Malta or Cyprus.

The next bomber version of the Canberra was the so-called target marker Mark 5 equipped with blind bombing radar, intended to carry a 5,000lb nuclear weapon (for which the cover name, target marker, was employed to disguise the operational rôle of this and other similarly-tasked aircraft; it was not a codename *per se*). The B Mk 5, designed to Specification B.22/48, introduced the Avro Mk 109 engine with triple-breech cartridge starters, and a new wing structure forward of the main spar to enable 450 gallons of additional fuel to be carried in each wing, thereby increasing the maximum range with bomb load to about 2,500 miles. To support the greater load and increase the runway footprint, larger mainwheels and more powerful brakes were introduced.

Little has been published authoritatively about the tactical nuclear weapon referred to above, and it may indeed have been an American weapon known to have been compatible with the 2nd TAF Canberras. Owing to the dual national authority demanded by the Americans to deliver these weapons, there was clearly little to be gained in proceeding with the Canberra as a nuclear weapon carrier in the tactical rôle until British weapons became available. The Canberra B 5 was therefore abandoned after a single prototype, VX185 (one of the PR Mk 3 prototypes), had been modified. It is said, without official confirmation or otherwise, that a British tactical nuclear weapon, Red Beard, may have been compatible with the Canberra.

The Canberra B 6, incorporating most of the B 5 modifications (including the Avon 109, but not the weapons

system), entered service with No 101 (Bomber) Squadron at Binbrook in June 1954, and went on to serve with a total of 14 squadrons. A variant of this version was the B (I) Mark 6 intruder which equipped No 213 Squadron from March 1956. This retained the normal Canberra nose and crew stations, but incorporated a pack of four 20mm Hispano or 30mm Aden cannon with 2,000 rounds under the rear bomb cell; the forward triplet of 1,000lb bombs could still be carried, as well as two 1,000lb bombs or rocket launchers under the wings.

Type: Twin-engine, three-crew, mid-wing light bomber.

Air Ministry Specifications: B.3/45, B.5/47 and B.22/48. (T.2/49 for Trainers)

Manufacturers: English Electric Co Ltd, Preston, Lancs; A V Roe & Co Ltd., Woodford, Cheshire; Handley Page Ltd, Radlett, Herts; Short Brothers & Harland Ltd, Belfast; Commonwealth Aircraft Factory, Fishermen's Bend, Melbourne, Australia; Glenn L Martin Co, Baltimore, Maryland, USA.

Powerplant: B Mk 2. Two 6,500lb-thrust Rolls-Royce Avon Mk 101 axial-flow turbojets. B Mks 6, 15 and 16. 7,500lb-thrust Avon Mk 109 turbojets.

Dimensions: Span (without tiptanks), 64ft 0in; length, 65ft 6in; height, 15ft 7in; wing area, 960 sq ft.

Weights: Tare, 22,265lb; normal all-up, 43,204lb (max overload, 53,000lb).

Performance: Max speed, 605 mph between sea level and 14,000ft (Mach 0.78), 541 mph at 40,000ft (Mach 0.82); service ceiling, 48,000ft; max combat radius with 6,000lb bomb load, 1,105 miles.

Armament: No gun armament. Normal bomb load, six 1,000lb bombs.

Prototypes: Four (to B.3/45), VN799, VN813, VN828 and VN850. VN799 first flown by Wg Cdr R P Beamont on 13 May 1949.

Production: A total of 1,352 Canberras was built (including 48 in Australia and 403 by Martin in the USA). The 901 Canberras built in the United Kingdom included 412 B Mk 2s (202 by English Electric, 75 by Avro, 75 by Handley Page and 60 by Short), 32 PR Mk 3s, 75 T Mk 4s, 106 B Mk 6, 79 PR Mk 7, 135 B(I) Mk 8s, 23 PR Mk 9s, 16 B (I) Mk 12s and one T Mk 13. Numerous aircraft were converted to other versions, and many aircraft were sold overseas to Argentina, Australia, Ecuador, Ethiopia, France, Germany, India, New Zealand, Peru, Rhodesia, South Africa, Sweden and Venezuela.

Summary of Canberra Bomber Service with RAF: Canberra B Mk 2s served with Nos 6, 9, 10, 12, 15, 18, 21, 27, 32, 35, 40, 44, 45, 50, 51, 57, 59, 61, 73, 76, 85, 90, 97, 98, 100, 101, 102, 103, 104, 109, 115, 139, 149, 151, 192, 199, 207, 245, 249, 360, 361, 527, 542 and 617 Squadrons; B Mk 6s with Nos 6, 9, 12, 21, 76, 100, 101, 109, 139, 213, 249, 360, 542 and 617 Squadrons; B and E Mk 15s with Nos 32, 45, 73, 100 and 249 Squadrons; and B Mk 16s with No 6 Squadron. The principal Canberra bomber training unit was No 231 OCU at Bassingbourn.

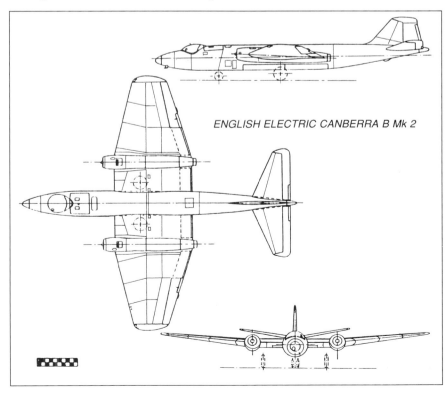

ENGLISH ELECTRIC CANBERRA B Mk 2

The former Canberra PR 3 and B 5 prototype, VX185, here modified as the prototype B(I)8 intruder prototype, showing the offset fighter-type pilot's cockpit canopy. This version was exported to India in large numbers as the Canberra Mk 58. (Photo: English Electric Co Ltd)

No further Canberra bombers were built from scratch. However, two other versions, the B 15 and B 16, were produced by modifying earlier aircraft. These introduced Fairey powered controls (first seen in the Canberra PR Mk 9 — which also introduced the 10,000lb-thrust Avon 200-series engines). The B 15 was built for the Akrotiri Strike Wing (comprising Nos 32, 73 and 249 Squadrons) and for No 45 Squadron, based at Tengah, Singapore. Equipment included Decca Doppler radar, three cameras and Nord AS.30 underwing missiles. A variant of the Mark 15 was the E 15, issued to No 100 Squadron in September 1972 for calibration of ground radio, radar and target facilities.

Finally the Canberra B 16, of which 19 examples were converted by Marshalls of Cambridge Ltd from Mark 6s, carried Blue Shadow radar, these aircraft being flown by No 6 Squadron from Akrotiri between January 1962 and January 1969.

Canberras were flown with a wide range of experimental engine installations, although in most instances the photo reconnaissance versions were employed. The Canberra also attracted large orders from overseas, apart from the licence contracts mentioned above. By far the largest number was supplied to India, and at one time that nation's main striking force comprised over 70 Mark 58 intruders, and these saw constant action during the various bitter conflicts with Pakistan and China. The Australian Canberra B 20s operated in Malaya, and flew in action during the Vietnam war, based at Phan Rang with the USAF 35th Tactical Fighter Wing. And a Canberra of the Argentine air force was shot down by British forces during the Falkland Islands campaign of 1982.

Just as the Lancaster and Halifax bombers created a powerful camaraderie among their wartime crews, so the truly classic Canberra became a symbol of *esprit de corps* among the many hundreds of postwar bomber crews.

The accompany data table refers to the Canberra B Mark 6 except where stated otherwise.

Representative of the many Canberra engine test beds was WF 909, a B Mark 2 flown with a de Havilland Gyron Junior DGJ.1 turbojet in the starboard engine nacelle. This 7,100lb-thrust turbojet was scheduled for the Blackburn Buccaneer S Mk 1 naval strike aircraft. (Photo: Author's Collection)

Fairey Gannet

Submarine activity during the Second World War, particularly by the German navy, involving operations at considerable distances from base ports and entirely new tactics and equipment, focused attention on the need to develop dedicated anti-submarine aircraft, particularly those capable of being embarked in fleet and small aircraft carriers. As already related, the venerable Swordfish, which had given such a remarkable account of itself as a torpedo bomber, found itself employed almost exclusively in the anti-submarine rôle in the last months of the War.

Specification GR.17/45 was therefore issued, calling for a two-seat carrier-borne aircraft equipped with specialised search radar capable of detecting and tracking very small objects, such as a submarine snorkel, or the conning tower of a submarine at long range, as well as the weapons to destroy submarines either surfaced or submerged; among the latter would be the small, airborne homing torpedo.

Three companies, Fairey, Blackburn and Short, submitted tenders, and two prototypes of each were ordered. The Fairey design, which went ahead under the leadership of H E Chaplin, was initially intended to be powered by the proposed Rolls-Royce Tweed double-propeller-turbine. This was abandoned in 1947, and in due course, at Fairey's suggestion, Armstrong Siddeley came up with coupled Mamba turbines. The 2,950ehp Double Mamba ASMD.1 drove a pair of co-axial, counter-rotating propellers through a common gearbox with clutch gear that enabled the pilot to shut

Still without the third crew member's cockpit, the second Gannet prototype, VR557, with its submarine search radome lowered, shows off the extent of its weapon bay. (Photo: The Fairey Aviation Co Ltd)

down one engine, thereby conserving fuel for extended range; in other words the aircraft would combine the security and load carrying ability of two engines with the compactness of a single-engine deck-operating aircraft. The aircraft featured a large weapons bay, later further enlarged to be able to accommodate two of the new homing torpedoes. Due, however, to uncertainty as to the need for a third crew member, the first Fairey prototype merely made space allowance for such.

The first prototype, VR546, was first flown at Aldermaston on 19 September 1949 by Gp Capt Richard Gordon Slade OBE. However, although the radical engine arrangement proved perfectly sound, a series of handling problems dogged the flight trials for many months, being associated with the difficulty in coping with the wide range of flight conditions that stemmed from the different power configurations available from the two engines, to which were added the different flight conditions bestowed by the Fairey-Youngman flaps. A third prototype, WE488, had been ordered and, by the time this was flown, most of the handling problems had been overcome, but it had also been decided to include the third crew member and to enlarge the weapons bay still further.

Such was the importance attached to introducing the Gannet into service that it was afforded the 'super-priority' status, and 100 production aircraft were ordered in 1951. However, Service and carrier trials (aboard HMS *Illustrious* and the light fleet carrier HMS *Albion*) brought to light further difficulties, which not even the addition of auxiliary finlets to the tailplane fully cured. It was also found that the Mamba engines suffered compressor stalling in certain conditions, and the early production Gannets were grounded for two months while modifications were introduced to the propeller controls.

The first four Gannet AS 1s were eventually handed over to the Fleet Air Arm on 5 April 1954 (100 American Grumman Avenger AS Mk 4s having been acquired as interim equipment). The first operational Gannet Squadron, No 826 (Lt-Cdr G F Birch RN) took on a complement of eight AS Mk 1s in

Type: Twin coupled-engine, three-seat, mid-wing anti-submarine/AEW carrier-borne turboprop aircraft.

Air Ministry Specification: GR.17/45

Manufacturer: The Fairey Aviation Co Ltd, Hayes, Middlesex, and Stockport, Lancs.

Powerplant: AS Mk 1. One 2,950ehp Armstrong Siddeley Double Mamba Mk 100 coupled-turboprop driving co-axial counter-rotating 4-blade propellers. AS Mk 4. 3,035ehp Double Mamba Mk 101.

Dimensions: Span, 54ft 4in (19ft 6in folded); length, 43ft 0in; height, 13ft 8½in; wing area, 482.8 sq ft.

Weights: Tare, 15,069lb; max all-up, 21,600lb.

Performance: Max speed, 310 mph; service ceiling, 25,000ft; range, 940 miles.

Armament: Two homing torpedoes and three depth charges; one 2,000lb, two 1,000lb or four 500lb bombs; provision for underwing rocket projectiles.

Prototypes: Three to GR.17/45, VR546, VR557 and WE488; VR546 first flown at Aldermaston on 19 September 1949 by Gp Capt R G Slade.

Production: Excluding the above three prototypes, a total of 349 Gannets was built, comprising 180 AS Mk 1s (116 at Hayes and 64 at Stockport), 35 T Mk 2s (all at Hayes), 44 AEW Mk 3s (all at Hayes), 82 AS Mk 4s (58 at Hayes and 24 at Stockport), and 8 T Mk 5s (all at Hayes). A small number of AS Mk 6s was converted from AS Mk 4s. Of the above, 18 Gannets were supplied to Indonesia, 36 to the Royal Australian Navy, and 16 to the German *Marineflieger*.

Summary of Fleet Air Arm Service. Gannet AS Mk 1s, 4s and 6s served with the following Fleet Air Arm Squadrons, Nos 700, 703, 703X, 719, 724, 725, 737, 744, 796, 810, 812, 814, 815, 816, 817, 820, 824, 825, 826, 831, 847, 849 and 1840.

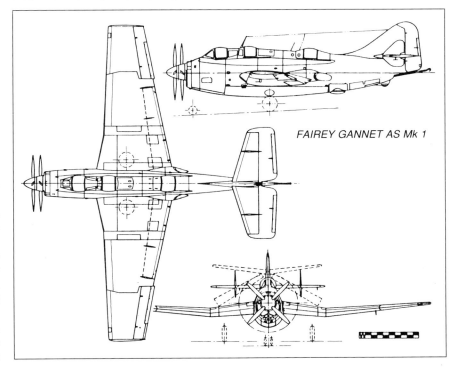

FAIREY GANNET AS Mk 1

A Gannet AEW Mk 3, XL427/044 of No 849B (Early Warning) Squadron, normally embarked in the light fleet carrier HMS Centaur *during the early 1960s.* (Photo: Simon Barnes)

January 1955 and embarked in the newly modernised carrier HMS *Eagle* in June that year for a short spell in the Mediterranean. Early Gannets were also delivered to the Royal Australian Navy, serving aboard the carriers HMAS *Melbourne* and *Sydney* with Nos 816 and 817 Squadrons.

In due course a total of nine operational squadrons of the Fleet Air Arm, and No 1840 Squadron of the RNVR, flew Gannet AS 1s, and a trainer version, the T 2, began delivery in 1955. In 1956 a new anti-submarine version, the AS Mk 4, was introduced to cater for increased equipment weight, the prototype being flown at Northolt on 12 March. Following tropical trials in Libya, the first Squadron, No 824 (Lt-Cdr L D Urry, RN) re-equipped later that year, embarking in HMS *Ark Royal* the following January.

Powered by the 3,035ehp Double Mamba 101, the AS Mk 4 was indistinguishable externally from the AS 1, but another version, the AEW Mk 3 (whose development had begun much earlier) was extensively redesigned. An enormous radome was mounted under the fuselage in place of the weapons bay, the 3,875ehp Double Mamba 112 engines were moved forward so as to exhaust beneath the wing root leading edge and the vertical tail surfaces were revised to be more angular. Two EW radar operators replaced the former crew members, being accommodated in a new cabin amidships without the transparent dorsal hatch. The first AEW 3 was flown on 20 August 1958, and this variant went on to serve with No 849 Squadron, replacing American Douglas Skyraider AEW Mk 1s and providing radar warning for HM carriers *Ark Royal, Centaur, Eagle, Hermes*

and *Victorious* between February 1960 and December 1978.

Returning to the anti-submarine Gannets, AS 4s eventually equipped nine operational squadrons of the Fleet Air Arm and, as the earlier AS 1s became redundant, 18 ex-FAA Gannets were supplied to Indonesia. These had been purchased by Fairey from the Ministry of Supply as AS 1s and T 2s and were then modified to AS 4 and T 5 standard for export. Fifteen newly-built AS 4s and a T 5 were diverted to the German *Kriegsmarine* in 1958 as the Federal Republic began rebuilding its armed forces in preparation for being admitted to NATO.

Anti-submarine Gannet 4s continued to serve with the Fleet Air Arm's operational squadrons until 1966 when, in May that year, No 849 Squadron gave up its AS 4s to concentrate on AEW duties. The same month, a lesser-known version, the Gannet ECM Mark 6, was also withdrawn from active service. A small number of these aircraft had been converted from Mark 4s, and served with No 831 (Electronic Warfare) Squadron at Watton, Norfolk, and, on being disbanded on 16 May, the personnel transferred to No 360 Squadron, RAF.

Blackburn Y.A.7, Y.A.8 and Y.B.9

The Blackburn tender to Specification GR.17/45 followed much the same design pattern as the Fairey Gannet; moreover, George Petty's original choice of engine, in this case the Napier Double Naiad, was also frustrated by cancellation. However, because it was likely that the Double Mamba would become available to Blackburn only after the Fairey prototypes had been completed (this engine having, after all, been produced at Fairey's suggestion),

Blackburn was permitted to complete its two prototypes (designated Y.A.7) with single Rolls-Royce Griffon 56 piston engines driving six-blade contraprops. A third prototype was to be built with the Double Mamba, this being referred to as the Y.B.1.

Like the Fairey aircraft, the Blackburn design featured an inverted gull

wing so as to limit the length of the undercarriage, but it seems likely that Petty anticipated directional control problems and incorporated a sharply dihedralled tailplane from the outset; this also kept the elevators clear of the disturbed airflow aft of the high-lift flaps during landing. The Y.A.7 also featured the large retractable search

The Blackburn Y.A.7, WB781, powered by a Griffon 56 piston engine; the 'jet pipe' aperture on the side of the fuselage was used as the radiator cooling air exit. (Photo: RAF Museum, Neg No P006411)

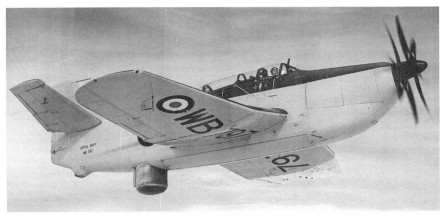

The Y.B.1, WB797, with the ventral radome lowered, being flown by P G Lawrence. As shown here, the aircraft was modified after the 1950 SBAC Display, being fitted with 8-blade co-axial propellers, and extended wingtips (the wings folded Z-fashion), but these changes were to no avail in the subsequent competitive trials with the Fairey Gannet and Short S.B.3. (Photo: Blackburn & General Aircraft Ltd, Neg No 1682, dated 12 September 1950)

radar's radome aft of a huge weapons bay, although it may be significant that at no time was any mention made in Blackburn's records of the Y.A.7's ability to carry the homing torpedoes specified.

The two-seat Y.A.7, WB781, made its maiden flight in the hands of P G Lawrence MBE at Brough on 20 September 1949, followed by preliminary carrier trials aboard HMS *Illustrious* on 8 February 1950. It is clear that, despite the tailplane's dihedral, WB781 encountered directional control problems, as the second aircraft, WB788 (which flew on 3 May 1950, also with Griffon piston engine), featured much enlarged vertical tail surfaces, although the base of the rudder was raised to enable the fuselage to be lengthened. The wing leading edge was given a small angle of sweepback, and (like the Gannet) the aircraft now included accommodation for a third crew member, all three being situated under a long transparent enclosure, the two radar operators in tandem, facing each other, aft of the pilot. With these extensive modifications, the second aircraft's designation was changed to Y.A.8.

In fact the Double Mamba-powered Y.B.1, WB797, was not far behind, and was first flown by Lawrence on 19 July 1950, making its first public appearance at the Naval Air Display at Lee-on-Solent on 26 August 1950, after which it was shown at the SBAC Display at Farnborough the following month.

When compared with the Fairey Gannet (and the Short S.B.3), the Blackburn Y.B.1 attracted general criticism of the crew disposition, and it was found to be impossible to load some of the naval weapons specified (again, no mention was made of torpedoes), owing to the low ground clearance of the weapons bay doors. There was little that could be done to improve the crew stations as a feature of the engine installation was the position of the tailpipes (higher and further forward than in the Gannet), which prevented inclusion of an enclosed cabin.

Failure to win a production contract under GR.17/45 was a bitter disappointment for Blackburn, and certainly aggravated the financial position of the company for several years owing to the general dearth of military contracts— partly as a result of the 'super-priority' status afforded elsewhere.

Type: Y.A.7. Single piston engine, two-seat, mid-wing monoplane experimental ship-borne anti-submarine aircraft. Y.B.1. Twin-engine, three-seat, mid-wing monoplane ship-borne anti-submarine turboprop aircraft.
Air Ministry Specification: GR.17/45.
Manufacturer: Blackburn Aircraft Ltd, Brough, Yorks.
Powerplant: Y.A.7 and Y.A.8. One 2,000hp Rolls-Royce Griffon 12-cylinder in-line piston engine driving 6-blade contraprops. Y.B.1. One 2,950ehp Armstrong Siddeley Double Mamba Mk 100 coupled-turboprop driving coaxial counter-rotating 8-blade propellers.
Dimensions: Y.B.1. Span, 44ft 2in (19ft 6in folded); length, 42ft 8in; height, 16ft 9in.
Weight: Y.B.1. All-up (no warload), 13,091lb
Performance: Y.B.1. Maximum speed, 320 mph at 10,000ft.
Prototypes: One Y.A.7, WB781, first flown 20 September 1949; one Y.A.8, WB788, first flown 3 May 1950; and one Y.B.1, WB797, first flown 19 July 1950. No production.

Short S.B.3

The proposal by Short Brothers and Harland Ltd under the terms of Specification GR.17/45 was not entered until 1948, at about the time that the Rolls-Royce Tweed and Napier Double Naiad coupled turbines were first reported to be on the point of being discontinued. There is little doubt but that it occurred to Lipscombe (while still in charge of design at Rochester) that with the ground apparently being cut from under the Fairey and Blackburn projects, a more orthodox adaptation of the Short Sturgeon torpedo bomber, powered by two single Mamba turboprops, stood a very good chance of succeeding if entered under GR.17/45. After all, the aircraft

The ill-fated Short S.B.3 WF632 at about the time of its first flight at Sydenham, Belfast, in August 1950. (Photo: Short Brothers & Harland Ltd, Neg No AC/2/545)

already possessed many of the features of the proposed anti-submarine requirement — three-man crew, deck landing strength factors and folded-wing dimensions within the stated limits. Above all, having already flown in prototype form, the Sturgeon had displayed excellent performance and handling qualities.

David Keith-Lucas had already taken over as chief designer at Shorts in Belfast (the design offices at Rochester having closed) when the new proposals were endorsed by the Air Ministry in 1949, and a new, supplementary Specification, M.6/49, covering the adapted Sturgeon, was issued, and two prototypes were ordered. Much of the Sturgeon's structure remained unchanged but, in order to accommodate the large search radar and its operators, the front fuselage was deepened considerably so that the two radar operators occupied a cabin forward of and below the pilot's cockpit, the scanner being enclosed in a large, fixed — that is, not retractable — chin radome.

The first S.B.3 (without weapons bay) was flown at Sydenham by Tom Brooke-Smith on 12 August 1950, and it was shown at the SBAC Farnborough Display the following month. However, from the outset it was obvious that the aircraft had lost almost every vestige of the Sturgeon's handling qualities, much of which had been attributed to the twin contraprops and their lack of torque, particularly with one engine stopped. The S.B.3's Mambas exhausted asymmetrically and obliquely, and their single-shaft turbines' speed and efflux varied widely with power demand, with the consequence that the pilot had constantly to be correcting for the slightest change in throttle setting — making landing a nightmare of coarse, destabilising trim changes.

So fundamental were these shortcomings that, although the second S.B.3 prototype almost reached the flight stage, it was never flown. The entire project was abandoned and the two aircraft were scrapped early in 1951.

Type: Twin-engine, three-crew, mid-wing monoplane ship-borne anti-submarine aircraft.
Specification: GR.17/45 and M.6/49.
Manufacturer: Short Brothers & Harland Ltd, Belfast, N Ireland.
Powerplant: Two 1,475ehp Armstrong-Siddeley Mamba ASMa3 axial-flow turboprops driving 4-blade propellers.
Dimensions: Span, 59ft 11in; length, 44ft 9in; wing area, 520.6 sq ft.
Weights: Tare, 15,252lb; all-up, 23,600lb.
Performance: Max speed, 320 mph at 10,800ft; max range, 715 miles.
Armament: 2,620lb max weapon load, comprising bombs, depth charges, mines and/or sonobuoys, and possibly two homing torpedoes.
Prototypes: Two, WF632 (first flown by Tom Brooke-Smith on 12 August 1950) and WF636 (not flown). No production.

Vickers Types 660/758 Valiant

The outstanding success of the de Havilland Mosquito as a fast, unarmed, long-range, high altitude bomber in the last eighteen months of the War, the demonstrated operational practicability of the turbojet engine, and the advent of the nuclear bomb all combined to encourage the British Air Staff to draft requirements for aircraft of advanced but similar concept with which to equip Bomber Command in the foreseeable future.

Before the end of 1945 two such operational requirements, OR.229 (Medium Range) and OR.230 (Long Range), were drafted, each calling for aircraft capable of penetrating enemy defences at high altitude, of evading interception by means of their high speed, and of delivering, if necessary, a nuclear weapon. It was assumed that the latter would be made available by America (in recognition of the significant rôles played by British scientists in developing the weapons dropped on Japan to end the Second World War); in the longer term Britain would de-

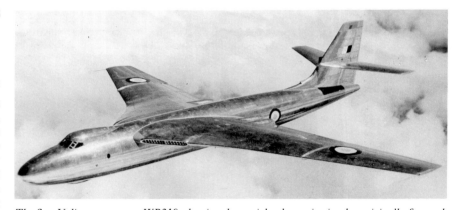

The first Valiant prototype, WB210, showing the straight-slot engine intakes originally featured. Unlike the Canberra, only the pilots in the V-bombers were provided with ejector seats. (Photo: Author's Collection)

velop her own nuclear arsenal.

Selected design leaders in the aircraft industry were invited to consider the broad design parameters of such aircraft (in particular that outlined in OR.229), and a draft Specification, B.35/46, was issued on 24 January 1947, calling for proposals to be tendered for a high-speed bomber capable of carrying a 10,000lb 'special weapon' and, alternatively, at least an equivalent weight of conventional bombs over a range of 3,600 miles. Of the six design tenders received, four were deemed to merit prototype purchase, those from Vickers and Short being less radical than those from Avro and Handley Page, and therefore prototypes were straightway ordered from the first two companies, while the others (being promised contracts in the future) embarked on aerodynamic research to explore the viability of their proposals.

Not that the Vickers design was in any respect pedestrian for, by the standards of its day, it was an impressive undertaking both aerodynamically and structurally — the more so when one recalls the pervading austerity of those postwar years and the painful cutbacks made in the aircraft industry. The airframe's primary structure was centred on a

One of the small number of Valiant B (PR) Mk 1s, XD823, which served with No 543 (Strategic Reconnaissance) Squadron at Wyton. Note the 'spectacle-type' engine air intakes and the refuelling probe in the nose; these features and the row of vortex generators on the outer wings were about the only external evidence of modifications applied after the prototypes first appeared. (Photo: A V Roe & Co Ltd)

massive backbone member extending along the top of the fuselage, to which light-alloy high-tensile formers, spaced by high-tensile stringers, were attached, the whole being covered by flush-riveted stressed skins. The bomb load was suspended from the sturdy backbone member, which branched at right angles to incorporate ring frames which encircled the turbojet engines in the wing roots. At the outer extremities of these branch spars were attached the outer wing main spars. A large pressure cabin (the largest single component of the airframe, and manufactured by Saunders-Roe), accommodating all crew members, occupied the entire nose.

The wing was designed with modest sweepback, possessing compound sweep on the leading edge, thereby providing large root chord and enabling the four Rolls-Royce Avon engines to be buried inside the inboard wing sections without exceeding a thickness-chord ratio of 12 per cent.

The tail surfaces were also swept, the tailplane being located high on the fin so as to be clear of the engine efflux. A nosewheel undercarriage was incorporated, the large main legs each carrying paired wheels in tandem and retracting outwards into the outer wing sections. Electrics were employed in all systems except the nosewheel steering

and the wheel brakes.

Manufacturing techniques, new to Vickers, were introduced, sculpture milling being employed to produce the wing centresection spar web plates, while powered stretching and forming tools were used to fashion large skin panels.

The Air Ministry prepared a separate Specification, B.9/48, to cover the Vickers prototypes, the first (Type 660), WB210, being first flown by 'Mutt' Summers, accompanied by Gabe Robb ('Jock') Bryce, from the grass airfield at Wisley, Surrey, on 18 May 1951. The following month the aircraft was officially named the Valiant — the first of the three great bombers that would equip the RAF for much of the ensuing Cold War.

All seemed to be going smoothly with the test programme when, on 12 January 1952, WB210 was lost during in-flight engine restart tests, when a fire in the port wing proved uncontrollable. The second prototype (Type 667), WB215,

was, however, flown on 11 April that year.

An initial production order for 25 (Type 706) Valiant B Mk 1s (WP199-WP223) had been placed in April 1951, the first five examples being earmarked for continuing development trials. These aircraft differed most noticeably in being provided with enlarged 'spectacle-type' engine intakes to allow for the greater mass flow of the more powerful RA.7 Avons now fitted.

Before the Valiant B 1 entered service, a new prototype version appeared, the Type 673 Mark 2 low-level night pathfinder, WJ954. First flown by Bryce, accompanied by Brian Trubshaw, on 4 September 1954, this aircraft was painted in high-gloss black overall, but it differed from the Mark 1 in that the main undercarriage components, each unit now carrying four wheels, retracted rearwards into large Küchemann bodies extending aft from the wings immediately outboard of the engines. The

The sole Valiant B Mk 2 low-level night pathfinder, WJ954, showing the large fairings aft of the wings into which the eight-wheel main undercarriage units retracted. (Photo: via R C B Ashworth)

A dummy Blue Danube plutonium bomb being dropped by Valiant B Mk 1 WP223 of No 90 (Bomber) Squadron, flown by Sqn Ldr C P Norfolk over Jurby range in about 1960. Approximate dimensions of the weapon were: length 24ft, diameter 5ft 8in. The photo was taken by the crew of a chase aircraft. Note the Orange Putter tail warning radome. (Photo: By courtesy of No 90 Squadron)

overriding reason for the change of undercarriage retraction was the need to strengthen considerably the wing structure (particularly in the region of the former wheel bays) so as to withstand the potentially destructive gust loads imposed during high-speed, low-level flying. The sinister-looking black bomber made a profound impression at the 1954 SBAC Display, but Air Staff interest in it was short-lived as the almost inevitable defence appropriation cuts forced the low-level pathfinder rôle to be abandoned, a decision which was, for the Valiant at least, unfortunate, as will be shown.[1]

---

[1] The decision was also taken just as the Royal Aircraft Establishment was about to commence a series of important trials to investigate the nature of low-level gusts and their effect on high-speed low-level flying aircraft. These were to have a considerable bearing on aircraft design and might have enabled relatively inexpensive modifications to be made in the Valiant's structure.

The remaining twenty of the first production Valiant B 1s were assigned to No 138 (Bomber) Squadron, which was re-formed on 1 January 1955 under Wg Cdr R G W Oakley at Gaydon, Warwickshire, as well as to a Valiant Operational Conversion Unit, formed simultaneously at the same airfield, and shortly afterwards designated No 232 OCU.

A second Valiant Squadron, No 543, was re-formed at Gaydon in July 1955. This Squadron had originally been a photographic reconnaissance squadron during the Second World War, flying Spitfires and Mosquitos, and when re-formed with Valiants it was tasked with strategic reconnaissance once more. It moved to its long-term base at Wyton in November that year, taking with it a new sub-variant of the Valiant, the B (PR) Mk 1 (Type 710), equipped with a wide range of reconnaissance cameras.

By the time of the Suez crisis of October 1956, Valiants had reached four

further Squadrons, and Nos 138, 148, 207 and 214 were deployed to Malta to carry out heavy bombing attacks with conventional bombs on Egyptian airfields during the Anglo-French operations.

Another Squadron, No 49 (which had received Valiants at Wittering in May 1956) had, at the time of Suez, become engaged in the long awaited trials of an air-dropped British nuclear weapon (Operation Buffalo), the 10,000lb Blue Danube free-fall plutonium bomb, when a prototype weapon was dropped from Valiant B 1 WZ366, captained by Sqn Ldr E J G Flavell, over the Maralinga range in South Australia on 11 October that year.

The same Squadron was involved in the first live drop of Britain's first thermonuclear (hydrogen) bomb, Operation Grapple, when, on 15 May 1957, Valiant B 1 XD818, captained by Wg Cdr K G Hubbard, released the weapon

A Valian B(K) Mk 1 tanker aircraft, WZ376, refuelling an Avro Vulcan of the V-force in the early 1960s. Note the large underwing fuel tanks on the Valiant, which also carries a nose probe, enabling it also to be refuelled in flight. This procedure later became commonplace during bombing operations, as was evident during the Falkland Islands campaign of 1982. (Photo: Flight Refuelling Ltd, Neg No M631)

in the vicinity of Christmas Island in the Pacific. This was a prototype of what, in a year's time, would carry the codename Yellow Sun, though it would only be destined for the Avro Vulcan and Handley Page Victor; the Valiant squadrons would be be assigned the Blue Danube.

Production of the Valiant was run down as the much superior Avro Vulcan entered service with Bomber Command in July 1957. Nevertheless the Vickers aircraft remained an active element of the fast-growing V-Force that now represented Britain's contribution to the Western Alliance's nuclear deterrent. In April 1962 two Valiant Squadrons, Nos 90 at Honington and No 214 at Marham, took on a number of Valiant in-flight refuelling tankers, designated, B (K) Mk 1s, their task being to enable other aircraft of the V-Force — Valiants as well as Vulcans and Victors — to extend their operational range, either on operational sorties or on long-distance flights, particularly to the Far East. The tanker aircraft were equipped with large underwing tanks as well as two extra fuel tanks in the bomb bays. To enable the Valiant bombers and strategic reconnaissance aircraft to take on fuel from the tankers, almost all the late production aircraft were equipped with refuelling probes extending from the nose.

However, events had already occurred that would enforce early retirement of the Valiant. The shooting down by a surface-to-air missile of an American U-2 high altitude intelligence-gathering aircraft, while flying above 60,000 feet over the Soviet Union during 1960, demonstrated emphatically the vulnerability of the RAF's V-Force, and particularly the Valiant, whose operational ceiling was well below the height at which the U-2 had been shot down.

As Valiants donned low altitude camouflage to assume the low-level nuclear strike rôle, and new radar and weapon delivery systems were quickly introduced to enable the other V-bombers to deliver their fusion weapons without over-flying their target, the Valiant squadrons (seven were still operational) embarked on a rigorous programme of low-flying training.

This intensive training continued until December 1964 when a routine examination of a squadron Valiant disclosed the onset of fatigue fissures in the wing mainspar; a hurried check with a dozen other aircraft disclosed the same symptoms, and within two months the entire Valiant force had been grounded;

the cost of dismantling every aircraft's primary wing structure and replacing the spars would have been prohibitive. Moreover, with plans already being laid for the Royal Navy's Polaris missile submarines to assume the rôle of Britain's nuclear deterrent in the foreseeable future, there could be no worthwhile operational task for the Valiant and all surviving aircraft

Type: Four-engine, five/seven-crew, swept shoulder-wing, strategic reconnaissance/bomber/tanker aircraft.

Air Ministry Specifications: OR.230, B.9/48 from B.35/46.

Manufacturer: Vickers-Armstrongs Ltd, Weybridge and Wisley, Surrey.

Powerplant: Prototypes (B.9/48). Four 6,500lb-thrust Rolls-Royce Avon RA.3 (100-series) axial-flow turbojets. B Mk 1. 7,500lb-thrust RA.7. B (PR) Mk 1 and B 2. 9,500lb-thrust Avon RA.14. B (K) Mk 1. 10,000lb-thrust Avon RA.28 (200-series).

Dimensions: Span, 114ft 4in; length, 108ft 3in; height, 32ft 2in; wing area, 2,362 sq ft.

Weights: Tare, 75,881lb; max all-up, 140,000lb.

Performance: Max speed, 567 mph at 30,000ft (Mach 0.85); service ceiling, 54,000ft; max range with underwing tanks, 4,500 miles.

Armament: No gun armament. Bomb load comprised either one 10,000lb nuclear weapon (Blue Danube) or twenty-one 1,000lb iron bombs. (For long range reconnaissance or ferry flights, two fuel tanks each of 1,615 Imp gal capacity could be carried in the bomb bay.)

Prototypes: One Type 660, WB210, first flown by Capt Joseph Summers accompanied by G R Bryce at Wisley on 18 May 1951. One Type 667, WB215, first flown at Wisley on 11 April 1952. One Type 673 Valiant B 2, WK954, first flown by G R Bryce and E B Trubshaw on 4 September 1953.

Production: A total of 104 Valiants was built, including the above prototypes: WP199-WP223, between WZ361 and WZ405, and between XD812 and XD875. (WP199-WP203 were pre-production aircraft.)

Summary of Service: Valiants served with No 7 Squadron between December 1956 and September 1962 at Honington and Wittering; No 18 Squadron between December 1958 and March 1963 at Finningley; No 49 Squadron between May 1956 and December 1964 at Wittering and Marham; No 90 Squadron between March 1957 and February 1965 at Honington (becoming a tanker squadron with B (K) Mk 1s from April 1962); No 138 Squadron between February 1955 and April 1962 at Gaydon and Wittering; No 148 Squadron between July 1956 and April 1965 at Marham; No 199 (Countermeasures) Squadron between June 1957 and December 1958 at Honington, then becoming No 18 Squadron; No 207 Squadron between 1956 and February 1965 at Marham; No 214 Squadron between January 1956 and February 1965 at Marham (becoming a tanker squadron with B (K) Mk 1s from April 1962); and No 543 (Strategic Reconnaissance) Squadron between July 1955 and February 1965 at Gaydon and Wyton (with B (PR) Mk 1s). Valiants also served with No 232 OCU at Gaydon.

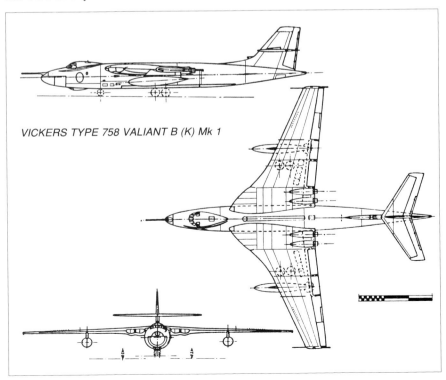

VICKERS TYPE 758 VALIANT B (K) Mk 1

were scrapped.

The Valiant was a contemporary of the de Havilland Comet 1 airliner, another fine aircraft that was also to suffer extinction owing to what was, at the time, unpredicted fatigue failure of metals under constant stress. What was ironic in the case of the Valiant was that a version had been produced, ten years before the discovery of the onset of fatigue, that had been designed with low-altitude fatigue resistance uppermost in the designer's mind. This appears to have been a classic example of a decision having been taken on financial grounds without a clear understanding of the operational ramifications involved, only to be burdened by an infinitely more costly *débâcle* resulting from that state of ignorance.

The first Short Sperrin, VX158, at the time of its first flight. (Photo: A J Jackson Collection)

Short S.A.4 Sperrin

Short's tender to Specification B.14/46, the outline design of which was undertaken in 1947 while Lipscombe's project staff was still at Rochester, was the least imaginative of the four tenders eventually submitted, yet it displayed some ingenuity. Lacking a modern, company-owned wind tunnel and not being privy to the records of German wartime swept-wing research, Lipscombe opted to retain an unswept wing, fully realising that performance would have to be traded for ease and speed of production. This policy was, alas, to be compromised by the decision to move the Company's aircraft design and production facilities from Rochester to Belfast in 1958.

The aircraft's massive slab-sided fuselage incorporated a very large bomb bay, 30 feet long, 10 feet deep and 10 feet wide; the five-man crew was accommodated together in a pressure cabin in the nose, only the pilot being provided with an ejector seat, the other crew members having to escape in an emergency down a chute which also served as the cabin's entry hatch.

The four Rolls-Royce Avon turbojets were mounted in pairs, each pair occupying a single nacelle, the engines being arranged one above the other. The wing possessed no dihedral, but the tailplane was angled sharply up to be clear of the engine efflux. The main undercarriage components, each carrying four wheels, retracted inwards, rotating about a trunnion immediately inboard of the engine nacelles, while the twin-wheel nose unit, mounted below the pressure cabin and aft of the 'improved-H_2S' nose radome, retracted rearwards. A 4,000lb/sq in British Messier hydraulic system serviced flap operation, air brakes, dive brakes, wheel brakes, undercarriage retraction and bomb doors. A total of 6,170 gallons of fuel was contained in fourteen wing tanks and eight located in the fuselage (fore and aft of the bomb bay), all being of the self-sealing type.

Three prototypes were built, including a structural test specimen.

The move to Belfast delayed the design work by about four months, and the first flight by VX158 did not take place at Aldergrove until 10 August 1951, with Tom Brooke-Smith at the controls. By then, of course, the first Valiant prototype had been flying for three months and was already the beneficiary of the 'super-priority' programme. The Sperrin, therefore, had become superfluous, even as an interim jet bomber, but went on to attend the 1951 SBAC Farnborough Display in September that year.

During flight trials with VX158 aileron flutter was experienced at 42,000 feet and the maximum speed was limited to Mach 0.78, although the Sperrin was probably capable of reaching about 0.82. The second aircraft, VX161, was flown

VX161 flying in October 1952, showing the engine configuration; also just discernible are the bomb doors, which give an idea of the size of the bomb bay. (Photo: Short Brothers & Harland Ltd, dated 13 October 1952)

on 12 August 1952, and was subsequently used for dropping trials with concrete dummies of new bombs, including the Blue Danube plutonium weapon.

In 1955 VX158 was experimentally fitted with a 15,000lb-thrust de Havilland Gyron DGy.1 turbojet in the lower half of the port engine nacelle. This powerful engine was being developed in parallel with the Bristol Olympus and the Rolls-Royce Conway to provide power for the inevitable generation of supersonic military and research aircraft then under consideration. The single Gyron installation was first flown on 7 July 1955, and was followed on 26 June 1956 by a second Gyron in the starboard nacelle; these two configurations were shown at the 1955 and 1956 SBAC Displays respectively .

The 1957 Defence White Paper caused the Gyron programme to be abandoned, however, and in 1958 both Sperrins were scrapped. They had, in truth, served little purpose, having been compromised from the outset as much by Short's own vicissitudes — the move to Belfast and the company's lack of tunnel facilities — as by the considerable efforts made by Vickers, Avro and Handley Page to meet similar requirements.

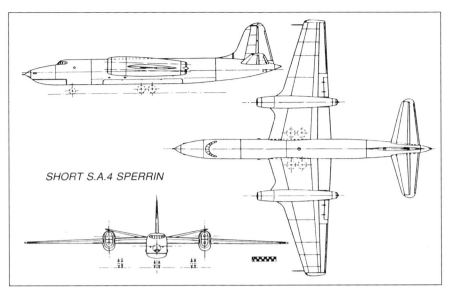

SHORT S.A.4 SPERRIN

Type: Four-engine, five-crew, shoulder-wing medium range strategic bomber.
Air Ministry Specification: B.14/46
Manufacturer: Short Brothers & Harland Ltd, Belfast, Northern Ireland.
Powerplant: Four 6,500lb-thrust Rolls-Royce Avon RA.3 axial-flow turbojets. Experimentally flown with two Avons and two 15,000lb-thrust de Havilland DGy.1 Gyron axial-flow turbojets.
Dimensions: Span, 109ft 0in; length, 102ft 4in; wing area, 1,663 sq ft.
Weights: Tare, 72,000lb; all-up, 115,000lb.
Performance: Max speed, 514 mph at 36,000ft (Mach 0.78); max range, 3,860 miles; max altitude reached, 42,000ft.
Armament: No gun armament. Either one 10,000lb bomb or sixteen 1,000lb iron bombs.
Prototypes: Two, VX158 and VX161; VX158 first flown at Aldergrove by Tom Brooke-Smith on 10 August 1951. VX161 first flown on 11 April 1953. No production.

Avro Type 698 Vulcan

Recognised from the outset as being considerably in advance of the designs tendered by Vickers and Short to Specification B.14/46, both aerodynamically and as a manufacturing undertaking, Roy Chadwick's very large delta-wing Type 698 design became the subject of a research programme that spanned four years. Much of it was undertaken as a private venture at the expense of the Hawker Siddeley Group between 1946 and 1949 (amounting to over £2 million), owing to the repeated reductions in Government research funding between 1946 and 1950.

Before he could learn that his tender had been accepted by the Air Ministry, Avro's great chief designer was to lose his life on 23 August 1947 when, following incorrect assembly of the aileron circuit on the Type 689 Tudor 2 proto-

The all-white prototype Avro 698, VX770, showing the almost perfect delta planform flown before encountering high altitude buffeting. (Photo: Bristol Aeroplane Co, Neg No MA161)

type, the aircraft crashed on take-off at Woodford; the pilot, S A Thorn, was also killed. Leadership of the design staff then passed to Stuart Duncan Davies, who survived the accident, an engineer of long experience who had been at Vickers under Rex Pierson during the 1920s and had worked under Sydney Camm at Hawker in the early 1930s before joining Avro in 1938. Chief project engineer was J G Willis (later G A Whitehead) and chief aerodynamicist, Eric Priestley (later J Roy Ewans).

The company was informed on 27

November 1947 that, subject to a revision of B.14/46 (re-issued the following year as B.35/46), two prototype Type 698 aircraft would be ordered, with a view to placing it in production approximately two years hence. During the year that followed this news, detail design of the Type 698 was completed, it being intended that power would be provided by four Bristol BE.10 two-spool turbojets (later named the Olympus), whose design was just beginning at Filton under Dr Stanley Hooker OBE, and which was expected to develop around 12,000lb-thrust.

The Type 698's plain delta wing was basically a two-spar structure with leading-edge sweepback of 52 degrees, the tail surfaces being confined to a single swept fin and rudder. With a wing root chord of no less than 46 feet, it proved possible to achieve a semi-span thickness/chord ratio of 10 per cent, this being sufficient to enclose the 40-inch diameter Olympus engines. Flying controls comprised two ailerons and two elevators on each wing, and two pairs of rotating-flap airbrakes were located above and below the wing inboard sections.

A Dowty nosewheel undercarriage was employed, its main units retracting forwards into the wings outboard of the engines, each massive magnesium-alloy cast leg carrying an eight-wheel bogie with Maxaret anti-skid units; the twin-wheel nose unit retracted rearwards aft of the crew cabin (being mechanically shortened during retraction so as to limit the size of the retraction bay).

The five-man crew comprised two pilots, a tactical navigator, a radar operator and an air electronics operator, the pilots being provided with Martin-Baker ejector seats and the other three being seated immediately behind, facing aft. In the extreme nose was located the advanced H2S radar with its 80-inch rotating scanner. A 24-foot diameter braking parachute was housed in the rear fuselage cone.

In order to investigate the control and stability characteristics of the delta aircraft, Avro built five one-third scale research delta replicas of the Type 698, designated Type 707s, of which two were covered by Ministry of Supply funds and defined in Air Ministry Specifications E.15/48 and E.10/49. All were powered by single Rolls-Royce Derwent turbojets and each was designed to explore specific flight regimes, two being low-speed aircraft, two high-speed, and one a two-seat familiarisation aircraft.

Two prototype Type 698s (VX770 and VX777) were duly ordered, together with 25 production aircraft (XA889-XA913), in 1950. Because the Olympus was not expected to be ready in time, the first aircraft, now named the Vulcan, was provisionally fitted with 6,500lb-thrust Avon RA.3 engines and made its maiden flight on 30 August 1952 with Roland John Falk OBE, AFC*, Avro's chief test pilot, at the controls. A week later, at the SBAC Farnborough Display, the same pilot astonished the crowds by rolling the big aeroplane — despite the relatively limited power then available.

VX770 was then fitted with four 8,000lb-thrust Armstrong Siddeley Sapphire engines as an insurance against further delays with the Olympus but, in the event, this engine was ready for the second Vulcan prototype, which was flown on 3 September 1953, powered by four 9,750lb-thrust Olympus Mk 101s.

The first production Vulcan B Mark 1 (XA889) was flown on 4 February 1955, also powered by Olympus Mk 101s. However, when this aircraft was flown by the A & AEE at Boscombe Down, it was shown that buffeting commenced if g was pulled at high altitude, a phenomenon thought likely to reduce the fatigue life of the aircraft's structure. To overcome this, Avro designed a new wing leading edge profile incorporating a 'kink' which, while maintaining the effective overall sweep angle, introduced reduced sweep from 52 to 42 degrees inboard, but increased the sweepback outboard. This proved to be a wholly effective remedy when flown on the second prototype, VX777, and those production Vulcans which had already been completed were accordingly modified.

On gaining CA Release, Vulcan B 1s were delivered to Finningley in May 1956, where they entered service with No 230 Operational Conversion Unit, tasked with preparing crews for operational squadrons, the first of which, No 83, took delivery of its Vulcans at Waddington in July 1957.

Production of the Vulcan B 1 eventually amounted to 45 aircraft, of which

Vulcan B Mk 2s, mostly of No 83 (Bomber) Squadron, on the runway at Scampton, probably early in 1961, before the full QRA procedure was adopted. Note the prominent wing leading edge kink and the enlarged tail fairing. No 83 Squadron was one of those later to equip with Blue Steel stand-off bombs.(Photo: A V Roe & Co Ltd, Neg No C/1/36)

A Vulcan 1 trials aircraft, XA903, flying at fairly high altitude with a Blue Steel stand-off bomb. In service the Vulcan B Mark 2 was equipped to carry these weapons, which were to be of only limited value on account of their short range. (Photo: A V Roe & Co Ltd, Neg No C798)

five were set aside for development work. The planned programme to equip four squadrons by the summer of 1960 was completed after Nos 83, 101, 617 and 44 Squadrons had each received their UE of eight aircraft. However, in December 1960 No 83 Squadron was re-equipped with the Vulcan B Mk 2 (see below) and, after limited re-engineering on their airframes, the discarded B 1s were delivered to No 50 Squadron, which re-equipped at Waddington in August 1961.

The entry of the Vulcan into squadron service in 1957 coincided with the successful dropping of the first Yellow Sun prototype megaton bomb by a Valiant, and within a year production examples were being delivered to the Waddington Vulcan Wing. It was a popular cliché of the period that the destructive power of just one Yellow Sun weapon (with Red Snow warhead) was greater than the total wrought by Bomber Command during the Second World War.

With Britain's nuclear deterrent being concentrated, for logistic reasons, on just ten major bases, it was clearly vital that in the event of a nuclear attack becoming imminent, the Vulcans —

Another Vulcan Mark 1, XA902, was relegated to engine test work, in this instance being flown with Rolls-Royce Spey turbofans, eventually destined to power the American McDonnell Douglas F-4K Phantom fighters, ordered for the RAF after successive British governments had terminated the development of indigenous aircraft. (Photo: Rolls-Royce Ltd, Neg No HP7322)

armed with the Yellow Sun weapons — should be able to disperse in the shortest possible time. To enable this to be achieved, the squadrons adopted a readiness state known as Quick Reaction Alert (QRA) at times of international tension; the aircraft were lined up on operational readiness platforms (ORPs) alongside the main base runways, their crews aboard, and capable of getting airborne in a matter five minutes or less — a capability that steadily improved as the power output of the Olympus engines increased as new versions were introduced.

Meanwhile, one of the early Vulcan B 1s, XA891, set aside for development work, had flown with the first of the 16,000lb-thrust Olympus 200-series engines. This considerable increase in power allowed significant improvements to be made in the aircraft to enhance its all-round operating performance. To begin with, it enabled the compound-swept wing leading edge to be extended to increase the aircraft's operating ceiling and expand the performance envelope and still avoid outer wing flutter;

also increased was the wing span. A Rover auxiliary power unit was added in order to render the new Vulcan B Mk 2 independent of outside services; provision for in-flight refuelling was made by the addition of a probe in the nose of the aircraft, enabling the bomber to reach potential targets anywhere in the world within range of a tanker base.

The rapid advance in electronic warfare technology made it imperative for the Vulcan to carry a wide range of ECM equipment, both of an active as well as a passive nature. The B Mk 2 therefore featured a much enlarged tail cone which accommodated an improved radar warning receiver, while chaff dispensers were added beneath the engines.

At the same time provision was made to carry the new British stand-off weapon, the Avro Blue Steel, in effect a small unmanned aircraft with a range of about 150 miles, carrying a megaton warhead. This enabled the aircraft to attack targets well inside enemy territory without overflying a heavily defended area and therefore proved vital owing to the extensive Russian surface-to-air missile

A Vulcan B Mk 2, XL426/ G-VJET, bearing the fin marking of the Waddington Wing. After the retirement of the Vulcan from service during the 1980s, several examples were offered for sale, but the cost of keeping such an aircraft in flying condition was considered to be prohibitive. (Photo: Simon Barnes)

(SAM) defences known to be deployed throughout the Soviet Union in the early 1960s.

Vulcan B Mk 2s, of which 89 examples were built, equipped nine squadrons during the 1960s, and included a sub-variant, the strategic reconnaissance SR Mk 2, which carried a wide range of photographic and electronic sensors, including RWR antennae located in a long rectangular fairing on top of the fin. SR Mark 2s equipped No 27 (Bomber) Squadron at Waddington from November 1973 onwards.

A plan to equip the Vulcan B Mk 2 with the American Douglas Skybolt air-launched ballistic missile came to nothing when the Americans cancelled the programme. Two aircraft, XH537 and XH538, had been modified to carry a pair of these large weapons under the wings, and successful dropping trials, using inert missiles, were carried out in Britain. Equally abortive was a proposal to introduce a much enlarged 'Phase 6' Vulcan with an all-up weight of 350,000lb and powered by four 23,500lb-thrust Olympus 23 turbojets, each aircraft loaded with no fewer than six Skybolts. While on the subject of very powerful Olympus engines, a Vulcan B Mk 1, XA894, was modified to mount a single 30,000lb-thrust Olympus 320 under the fuselage, this engine being intended for the BAC TSR-2 low-level bomber. (This aircraft blew up on the ground during engine running tests, and another engine failed while bench-running, blasting the roof off the test house.)

Just how effective the Russian air defences were became evident in 1960, when an American high altitude reconnaissance aircraft was shot down by a SAM deep inside the Soviet Union while flying at over 60,000 feet. This, as well as the growing realisation that air-launched nuclear weapons carried by high-flying manned aircraft were becoming outdated in the early 1960s, led to the decision to convert the RAF's entire V-Force to the very-low-level

penetration rôle, the Vulcans being re-equipped with new weapons, such as the Yellow Sun Mark 2 and the WE-177 lay-down, off-set and 'over-the-shoulder' weapons. Carried at low level during the approach to the target, these weapons were released as the aircraft executed accurately computed pull-ups or turns when still well short of the immediate target area.

Of all the V-bombers, the Vulcan proved the most robust, the Valiant being found to have suffered serious fatigue faults after only a short period serving in the low-level rôle; the Victor also suffered its share of misfortune.

These setbacks, however, proved to be superfluous when it was decided that, from 1968, Britain's nuclear deterrent responsibilities would be transferred to the Royal Navy, Polaris IRBMs being launched from a new class of super submarine.

By the beginning of the 1980s few of the Vulcans were still in service, and were due to be phased out completely as soon as the new Panavia Tornado multi-rôle aircraft could be introduced into service. Just how ill-advised this policy was, by reason of ignoring Britain's other overseas responsibilities, was to be demonstrated during the Falkland Islands campaign (Operation Corporate) of April-June 1982.

At the time of the Argentine occupation of the Falkland Islands the Vulcan

Type: Four-engine, five-crew, delta-wing monoplane medium-range strategic bomber.

Air Ministry Specification: B.14/46 (from OR.229), B.35/46 (Issue 2), E.15/48 and E.10/49 (Research).

Manufacturer: A V Roe & Co Ltd, Middleton, Manchester, and Woodford, Cheshire.

Powerplant: Prototypes. Four 6,500lb-thrust Rolls-Royce Avon RA.3 axial-flow turbojets; 7,500lb-thrust Armstrong Siddeley Sapphire ASSa.6 axial-flow turbojets; 9,750lb-thrust Bristol Olympus Mk 101; 15,000lb-thrust Rolls-Royce Conway RCo.7. B Mark 1. 9,750lb-thrust Olympus Mk 100; 11,000lb-thrust Olympus Mk 101; 12,000lb-thrust Olympus Mk 102; 13,400lb-thrust Olympus Mk 104. B Mark 2. 16,000lb-thrust Olympus Mk 200; 17,000lb-thrust Olympus Mk 210; 20,000lb-thrust Olympus Mk 301. Experimental. 30,000lb-thrust Olympus BOL.22R with reheat; Rolls-Royce Spey turbofan.

Dimensions: B Mark 1. Span, 99ft 0in; length, 97ft 1in; height, 26ft 6in; wing area, 3,554 sq ft. B Mark 2. Span, 111ft 0in; length, 100ft 1in; height, 27ft 2in; wing area, 3,964 sq ft.

Weight: B Mark 2. Max take-off, over 200,000lb.

Performance: B Mark 2A. Max speed, 645 mph (Mach 0.98) above 36,000ft; never-exceed speed at sea level, Mach 0.94; service ceiling, 55,000ft; cruise-climb absolute ceiling, 60,000ft; max range at low-level, unrefuelled, 3,450 miles.

Armament: Twenty-one 1,000lb iron bombs, one Avro Blue Steel Mk 1 stand-off bomb (150-mile stand-off range) or one free-fall Yellow Sun Mk 2 megaton-yield or WE-177 lay-down nuclear weapon.

Prototypes: Two Type 698 prototypes, VX770 and VX777; VX770 first flown by Wg Cdr R Falk on 30 August 1952; VX777 first flown on 3 September 1953. VX777 became prototype of B Mk 2 and as such was first flown on 31 August 1957.

Production: A total of 45 Vulcan B Mark 1s and 1As was built (commencing XA889), followed by 89 B Mark 2s (commencing XH533).

Summary of Service: Vulcan B Mark 1s served with the following Squadrons: No 44 at Waddington from August 1960 to November 1967; No 50 at Waddington from August 1961 to November 1966; No 83 at Waddington from July 1957 to August 1960; No 101 at Finningley and Waddington from January 1958 to January 1968; and No 617 at Scampton from May 1958 to July 1961. B Mark 2s served with the following Squadrons: No 9 at Coningsby, Cottesmore, Akrotiri and Waddington from April 1962; No 12 at Coningsby and Cottesmore from July 1962 to December 1967; No 27 at Scampton from April 1961 to March 1972 (followed by Vulcan SR Mk 2s at Waddington from November 1973); No 35 at Coningsby, Cottesmore, Akrotiri and Scampton from January 1963; No 44 at Waddington from November 1967; No 50 at Waddington from December 1965; No 83 at Scampton from December 1960 to August 1969; No 101 at Waddington from January 1968; and No 617 at Scampton from September 1961.

squadrons of the Waddington Wing were warned to prepare for possible long-distance bombing operations. Such operations would entail complete dependence upon the Victor tanker squadrons to provide in-flight refuelling, a procedure that had dropped out of use almost a decade earlier. Five Vulcans were made ready, and the Carousel inertial navigation equipment was installed to provide the accurate positioning required to refuel at night. Training flights were hurriedly arranged and flown over the United Kingdom.

In the event, three Vulcans were deployed to Wideawake airfield on Ascension Island, and two of them, XM597 and XM607, flew raids —

codenamed Black Buck — against the Falkland Islands on 30 April, 4 May, 31 May, 3 June and 12 June. Each attack, flown by a single Vulcan, involved a round-trip flight of 7,700 miles, the aircraft carrying a full load of twenty-one 1,000lb bombs for the attacks on Stanley airfield on 30 April and 4 May. Each Vulcan sortie required a back-up Vulcan in case of unserviceability in the attacking aircraft, and no fewer than eleven Victor tankers, including an airborne standby. The attacking Vulcan was refuelled five times on the outward flight and once on the return journey (the Victors themselves being refuelled ten times between them).

The third and fourth attacks were

made against the Argentine Skyguard radar using anti-radar Shrike missiles carried on hastily improvised underwing pylons, and the final sortie, on 12 June, was an attack on Argentine troop positions close to Port Stanley using radar air-burst bombs.

These operations, representing the longest point-to-point bombing raids in history by the air force of any nation, tested crews and aircraft to the limit and constituted extraordinary feats of organisation and airmanship, particularly for the three Vulcan captains directly involved in the raids, Sqn Ldr Neil McDougall[1], Sqn Ldr John Reeve and Flt Lt Martin Withers.

A colossal effort went into the operations, which represented only a relatively small part of Operation Corporate. Nevertheless, the Black Buck raids graphically demonstrated the ability of RAF Strike Command to attack the Argentine homeland had the need arisen. For this reason the Argentine Dassault Mirage III interceptor fighters were withdrawn from operations over the islands to stand defence of the mainland and, two days after the last Black Buck attack on 12 June, the Argentine forces on the Falkland Islands surrendered.

---

[1] During the attack of 3 June, Sqn Ldr McDougall had been obliged to loiter over the target area for half an hour while waiting for the Argentine radar to be switched on before he could attack. During the vital refuelling on the return flight the Vulcan's nose probe broke off preventing a full load of fuel being received. An extremely difficult emergency landing was successfully made at Rio de Janeiro, after which it was found that the Vulcan's tanks contained sufficient fuel for barely five minutes' flying.

AVRO TYPE 698 VULCAN B Mk 2

Handley Page H.P.80 Victor

Third of the V-bomber trio to enter service, the Handley Page H.P.80 Victor was to serve the longest, not being finally retired from RAF Strike Command until 1993, although by then its illustrious manufacturer had long since gone out of business, victim of its

own founding father's determination to remain independent of the dominant conglomerates.

Designed under the joint leadership

of Reginald Spencer Stafford and Godfrey Henry Lee, the H.P.80 was, with the Avro 698 Vulcan, considered to be too radical when first tendered to

The first Victor prototype, WB771, in its grey and black livery for the 1953 SBAC Display at Farnborough. (Photo: A J Jackson Collection)

Specification B.35/46 to justify an immediate order for prototypes, both Sir Frederick Handley Page and the Air Staff anticipating a fairly long period of research. Indeed, a tunnel model of 1947 shows the aircraft with a crescent-shaped wing, wingtip fins and rudders and a slab, all-moving tailplane on top of a very short tailfin, this tailplane being intended solely for trimming purposes. The fuselage was of circular section, and the four turbojet engines would be enclosed within a wing whose root thickness/chord ratio was expected to be about 14 per cent.

By the time work was underway to examine the benefit of wingtip control surfaces, and the likelihood of wing flutter, Gustav Lachmann (who was still working in an advisory capacity) appears to have favoured a much taller tailfin so as to retain longitudinal control at low speeds, with the tailplane raised accordingly. With a conventional rudder now logically admissible, the wingtip controls became superfluous.

At the same time, namely early 1948, it was decided to build a 40 per cent scale research aircraft, the H.P.88, reproducing the crescent wing and the tall T-tail configuration. This aircraft, to be built by Blackburn and General Ltd at Brough, featured a Supermarine Swift's fuselage with a 5,500lb-thrust Rolls-Royce Nene 3 turbojet, the whole aircraft being defined in a special research Specification, E.6/48. With a span of 40 feet, the wings combined three progressive angles of leading edge sweep, 48½ degrees on the inboard section, 37½ degrees at semi-span, and 26¾ degrees on the outboard section; a small, swept single-piece, all-moving tailplane was mounted high on the swept fin and rudder.

The H.P.88 was first flown by Flt Lt

Gatrell Richard Ian Parker DFC*, AFC, DSM, a Blackburn pilot, at Brough on 21 June 1951, about fourteen months later than scheduled. While this aircraft served to confirm much of what had been learned from tunnel work on the finite H.P.80, it broke up in the air low over Stansted airfield on 26 August killing the pilot, Douglas Broomfield, having flown no more than 14 hours, during which time it had been cleared for flight up to 550 mph.

By then construction of the first H.P.80 was underway, two prototypes, WB771 and WB775, having been ordered on 26 April 1948. The aircraft was planned from the start to be powered by what, in 1947, was referred to as the Metrovick F.9, a 6,800lb-thrust axial-flow turbojet. In 1948 development of this engine was taken over by Armstrong Siddeley Motors Ltd as the Sapphire which, when the time came for installation in WB771, was delivering 7,500lb-thrust. Like the Vulcan's Bristol Olympus engines, four of these Sapphires were

enclosed in the wing roots, closely paired on each side with root leading-edge air intakes. The wings of the H.P.80, now named the Victor, were to be fitted with Fowler trailing-edge flaps, Krüger nose flaps, elevons and speed brakes in order to retain good handling qualities at low speed in an aircraft that was to be the greatest load-carrier of the three V-bombers, and by a considerable margin (and marginally the fastest), such was the inherent efficiency of the new wing-form. (An early production Victor was inadvertently to exceed Mach 1 in a shallow dive at high altitude during 1957.)

Also central to the original design was the provision of an enormous bomb compartment which, as no definitive dimensions were yet available of the nuclear weapon to be carried, was intended to be able to accommodate either one 22,000lb Grand Slam-type or two 12,000lb Tallboy-type DP bombs; more prosaically thirty-five 1,000lb GP bombs could be carried in the fuselage bay with

Above: *Victor B Mk 1A, XH648, possibly of No 57 (Bomber) Squadron, releases its load of thirty-five 1,000lb iron bombs over a practice range in the United Kingdom. The bombs were stacked in groups of seven in the bomb bay, evidence of which can be seen in the salvo dropping pattern.* (Photo: Handley Page Ltd, Neg No A36-256)

Left: *The fourteenth production Victor B 1, XA930, in the overall white finish adopted to reflect the heat flash from a nuclear explosion. This aircraft is equipped with an in-flight refuelling probe over the cockpit, and underwing fuel tanks; the long fairings over the inboard wing trailing edge enclose the guide rails for the large Fowler flaps.* (Photo: A J Jackson Collection, dated October 1959)

The ill-fated Victor B Mk 2, XH668, distinguishable by its blunt tailcone and ECM cooling system heat interchanger intake at the base of the fin. The wing pitot-static heads, the loss of one of which proved catastrophic, can be clearly seen. (Photo: Handley Page Ltd, Neg No A36/198)

space to spare. Having been informed that the nuclear weapon was likely to weigh 'about 10,000lb' the Handley Page designers simply scaled down the 12,000-pounder and came up with a bay capable of mounting four such weapons; unfortunately the Blue Danube turned out to be a particularly bulky weapon, so that only one such bomb could be carried. To permit take-off in overload conditions, it was planned to make provision to mount a pair of 8,000lb-thrust de Havilland Spectre rockets under the wing roots, these being jettisoned after take-off.

The H₂S Mark 9 scanner, associated with a navigation and bombing computer, was located under the nose in a very large radome beneath the pressurised cabin. The customary five-man crew (comprising two pilots, a tactical navigator, a radar operator and an air electronics operator) was situated on one level, only the pilots being provided with ejection seats. In respect of the latter emergency equipment, the Air Minstry instructed Handley Page to investigate the provision of an escape capsule encompassing the entire nose and which should be explosively detached in a dire emergency, and descend by parachute; this system was ruled out on account of a prohibitive weight penalty.

The first production Victor B Mark

1, XA917, made its maiden flight at Radlett on 1 February 1956 and, like the Valiant and Vulcan, the first five such aircraft were set aside for development work and trials. XA920, for instance, underwent production assessment at Boscombe Down. Production of the Victor had gone ahead in spite of entrenched opposition by the Treasury, which advocated exclusive standardisation on the Vulcan.[1] This course was strongly and successfully opposed by the Air Ministry, constantly worried that a serious and fundamental deficiency might come to light after an aircraft had entered service — pointing to the recent experience with the ill-fated Supermarine Swift.

RAF Victors first equipped 'A' Squadron of No 232 Operational Con-

---

[1] An early production Victor B Mark 1 cost £820,000, including engines and embodiment loan items, of which some £450,000 covered airframe and flying systems. By comparison a fully-equipped Vulcan B Mk 1 costed out at £1,002,000. Mark 2 versions of each aircraft which survived in service until the 1980s had cost an average of slightly over £3.6m each in manufacture, systems and equipment updates, replacement engines and airframe fatigue inspection.

version Unit at Gaydon, five early production examples being delivered shortly before the end of 1957; early in the New Year four further aircraft, specially equipped with Yellow Aster reconnaissance radar, were also delivered on which to convert ex-No 543 (Strategic Reconnaissance) Squadron Valiant crews. Aircraft and crews then moved to Wyton to form the Radar Reconnaissance Flight. As far as is known, these early reconnaissance Victors, which carried an extensive range of electronic sensors, apart from Yellow Aster, were not accorded a separate designation, and never featured in any of the conversion programmes — suggesting that much of their work was of a clandestine nature.

The first Squadron to equip with Victor B Mark 1s was No 10 at Cottesmore in April 1958, followed in September that year by No 15 at the same station. Thus the Victor entered service just as the first Yellow Sun megaton nuclear weapons were reaching the Service, but it was perhaps natural that the two Vulcan squadrons, which had been awaiting the weapon for several months, should become operational

XL158 after being converted to a B Mark 2R, still wearing its white anti-flash finish and serving with No 139 Squadron. It carries the Blue Steel stand-off bomb and is fitted with Küchemann wing fairings. Note the greatly enlarged heat exchanger intake at the base of the fin. (Photo: C H Barnes Collection)

Another No 139 Squadron Victor B 2R, XL512 this time photographed in August 1973, painted in low-level camouflage scheme and carrying large underwing fuel tanks in addition to the Blue Steel weapon. Both this and the aircraft shown in the previous photograph were later converted to K Mark 2 refuelling tankers. (Photo: A J Jackson Collection)

with it first. Nos 10 and 15 Squadrons, therefore, worked up with conventional bombing training for much of 1958, with production Victor 1s of a second batch starting to arrive in service by the time a third Squadron, No 57, re-equipped, this time at Honington in Suffolk.

With the V-force now approaching its planned strength, and as 60 Douglas Thor IRBMs were deployed in four Wings in Yorkshire and East Anglia, attention turned to updating early production Victors, as well as introducing a Mark 2 version. As early as 1957 Handley Page learned that development of the Sapphire engine was about to be terminated with the result that, if the Victor was to keep pace with the Vulcan, whose Olympus was being progressively uprated, an alternative engine would have to be found for the Handley Page bomber. With virtually all Olympus production allocated to the Vulcan (not to mention the TSR-2 — should it ever materialise), and the de Havilland Gyron abandoned at the end of the 1950s, the only other available engine in the 15,000-20,000lb-thrust category was the Rolls-Royce Conway turbofan.

Thus, when the proposed 14,000lb-thrust Sapphire 9 was abandoned, and despite Sir Frederick's reluctance to adopt the Rolls-Royce by-pass engine, Stafford suggested embarking on an interim 'Phase 2A' Victor with Conways and the wing span increased to 120 feet. The wing centresection modifications would be confined to deeper air intakes to cater for the 17,250lb-thrust Conway R.Co.11s' increased mass flow.

At the same time 24 Victor B 1s were modified to become B 1As, the principal external difference being a shorter and blunter tail cone enclosing ECM equipment with a radar scanner; internally, however, the crew stations were revised,

and powerful transformers installed (requiring a glycol cooling system) for the new ECM equipment. Delivery of these Victor 1As, beginning with No 57 Squadron, was completed by February 1961.

The first Victor B 2, XH668, had been flown by John Allam on 20 February 1959, and in June that year was passed to Boscombe Down for a series of familiarity flights by A & AEE pilots. On 20 August, however, the aeroplane was lost in an accident off the Pembrokeshire coast during investigation of the buffet boundaries during turns at Mach 0.94 at 52,000 feet — manoeuvres at the extreme limits of the flight envelope. No radio message was received before the aircraft disappeared from ground radar, and the nature and cause of the accident remained a mystery for many weeks. Only after the most extensive salvage operation ever undertaken, during which almost 600,000 fragments of the aircraft were recovered from the sea bed and reassembled at the RAE, was it deduced that buffet vibration of the Victor's wing tips in a high speed turn had caused the starboard wingtip pitot static head to come adrift. The loss of this pressure head would have caused spurious data to be fed to the Mach trimmer and stall detector, which in turn would have depressed the pitching controls, causing an instantaneous nose down attitude; this catastrophic manoeuvre when flying at Mach 0.94 caused the Victor to disintegrate; all five crew members perished. The cost to remedy the fault was pennies rather than pounds.

By the time the Victor B 2 reached Nos 139 and 100 Squadrons in February and May 1962 respectively, the whole future of the V-force had been thrown into doubt when it became evident that neither the Vulcan nor Victor could

operate above the effective ceiling of Soviet surface-to-air missiles. The cancellation of the American Douglas Skybolt air-launched ballistic missile (which was being considered for the Victor as well as the Vulcan) and the purchase of Polaris submarine-launched missiles heralded the end of Britain's air-launched nuclear deterrent before the end of that decade.

Running some two years behind the Vulcan production schedule, the Victor B 2 accordingly suffered heavier cutbacks, despite being somewhat superior in performance and load-carrying to the Avro bomber, 28 aircraft being cancelled and only 34 delivered. Thus Nos 100 and 139 were the only bomber Squadrons to fly Blue Steel-equipped Victor B 2s, and these aircraft underwent progressive improvement. The B 2R (R=retrofit) were fitted with 20,600lb-thrust R.Co 17 Conway Mk 201 engines, which in turn resulted in the maximum take-off weight being raised to 223,000lb, for which it was normal to employ a pair of 8,000lb-thrust de Havilland Spectre assisted take-off rockets. Red Steer ECM equipment was fitted, as were very large underwing fuel tanks. Apart from these tanks, the most obvious external additions were Küchemann bodies above the wing trailing edges (these having been shown to delay the formation of shock waves at high subsonic speed); the fairings were also considered to be conveniently located to discharge ECM chaff.

Nine Victor B(SR) Mk 2s were produced for No 543 (Strategic Reconnaissance) Squadron at Wyton, beginning delivery in May 1965, these aircraft being equipped to carry F49 Mk 4, F89 Mk 3 and F96 Mk 2 cameras, sideways-looking radar, Red Neck reconnaissance radar and up to 72 8-inch photo-flashes. With a range of 3,300 miles at high altitude and a maximum ceiling of over 62,000 feet, it was said that a single Victor could photograph every ship in the Mediterranean in the course of a single sortie.

The discovery of serious fatigue cracks in the Vickers Valiant's wing spars, and the grounding of these aircraft early in 1965 — three years earlier than anticipated — led to every available Victor B 1 and B 1A undergoing immediate conversion to the air-refuelling tanker rôle. As a matter of urgency, the first six aircraft were fitted with two hose-drogue pods under the wings only (as the Victor B (K) Mk 1A), and delivered to No 55 Squadron in mid-1965. The next eleven conversions from former B 1s included a retractable hose-drogue in the Victor's bomb-bay to provide three-point refuelling as Victor K 1s, while fourteen B 1As, similarly converted, became K 1As. By the end of 1966 Nos 55, 57 and 214 Squadrons were all operational with Victor K 1s and 1As.

The Victor B 2Rs were all phased out of service in 1968, a move as much dictated by the imminent introduction of the Royal Navy's Polaris missiles as by the uncertainty of Handley Page's future. The company had run into financial difficulties during its development of the Jetstream light commercial turboprop transport and, despite the injection of capital from a number of sources, including an American company which acquired a controlling interest, Handley Page was compulsorily wound up on 27 February 1970 when the American backer withdrew its support.

Sir Frederick Handley Page had died on 21 April 1962, at a time when a suggested merger with the Hawker Siddeley Group might have avoided the Victor B 2 cancellations, and it was therefore all the more poignant that, when a contract was issued in October 1969 for the conversion of 24 Victor B 2Rs to K Mk 2 tankers, the aircraft were delivered to Hawker Siddeley Aviation Ltd at Woodford (formerly A V Roe & Co Ltd) in 1970 for the work to be carried out.

After No 214 Squadron was disbanded in January 1977, Nos 55 and 57 Squadrons continued to provide all in-flight refuelling services for Strike Command's Buccaneers, Harriers and Jaguars, being joined later by BAC VC-10s and Lockheed TriStars as Victor numbers gradually diminished. Indeed, as described on pages 384–385, almost the entire strength of the Victor tanker fleet was deployed to Ascension Island during Operation Corporate (the recovery of the Falkland Islands from Argentine forces) in 1982, in the first place to enable the Black Buck Vulcans to reach and bomb enemy forces in the islands,

Type: Four-engine, five-crew, mid-wing monoplane air-refuellable strategic bomber/reconnaissance/tanker aircraft.

Air Ministry Specifications: B.14/46 (from OR.229), B.35/46, E.6/48 (research), B.128 (production).

Manufacturer: Handley Page Ltd, Cricklewood, London, and Radlett, Herts.

Powerplant: Prototypes. Four 7,500lb-thrust Metrovick F.9/Armstrong Siddeley Sapphire axial-flow turbojets. B Mark 1. 11,050lb-thrust Armstrong Siddeley ASSa.7 Sapphire. B Mark 2. 17,250lb-thrust Rolls-Royce RCo.11 Conway Mk 200 turbofans. B Mark 2R. 20,600lb-thrust RCo.17 Conway Mk 201 turbofans. Overload optional assisted take-off with two 8,000lb-thrust de Havilland Spectre rocket motors.

Dimensions: B Mk 1. Span, 110ft 0in; length, 114ft 11in; height, 28ft 1½in; wing area, 2,406 sq ft. B Mk 2. Span, 120ft 0in; length, 114ft 11in; height, 30ft 1½in; wing area, 2,597 sq ft.

Weights: B Mk 1. Max all-up, 205,000lb. B Mk 2. Max all-up, 216,000lb. B Mk 2R. Tare, 114,240lb; max all-up, 223,000lb.

Performance: B Mk 1. Max speed, 627 mph above 36,000ft (Mach 0.95); max unrefuelled range, 6,000 miles; operational cruise-climb ceiling, 56,000ft. B Mk 2R. Max speed, 647 mph above 36,000ft (Mach 0.98).

Armament: B Mk 1. One '10,000lb' Yellow Sun Mk 1 megaton bomb, one 22,000lb Grand Slam-type bomb, two 12,000lb Tallboy-type bombs, three 10,000lb iron bombs, thirty-five 1,000lb iron bombs or seventeen 2,000lb Type S sea mines. Maximum load could be up to 48 'short' 1,000lb bombs, but RAF limit was 35. B Mk 2R. Normal weapon was Avro Blue Steel Mk 1 megaton stand-off bomb.

Prototypes: Two, WB771 and WB775. WB771 first flown at Boscombe Down by Sqn Ldr H G Hazelden DFC* on 24 December 1952; WH775 first flown on 11 September 1954.

Production: A total of 50 Victor B Mk 1s was built: XA917-XA941 (25) and between XH587 and XH667 (25); 34 B Mk 2s were built: XH668-XH675 (8) and between XL158 and XM718 (26). 24 B Mk 1As were produced as conversions from B Mk 1s in XH range; 11 K Mk 1s were converted from B Mk 1s in XH range. 6 B Mk 1A (K2P), previously B (K) Mk 1A conversions. 14 K Mk 1A were converted from B (K) Mk 1A in XH range. 21 B Mk 2R were converted from B Mk 2; 9 B (SR) Mk 2 were converted from B Mk 2; and 24 K Mk 2 were converted from B Mk 2 and B (SR) Mk 2.

Summary of Service: Victor B Mk 1s served with the following Squadrons: No 10 from April 1958 to March 1964 at Cottesmore; No 15 from September 1958 to October 1964 at Cottesmore; No 55 (also with B Mk 1As) from October 1960 to March 1967 at Honington and Marham; No 57 (also with B Mk 1As) from March 1959 to June 1966 at Honington and Marham; and No 543 from May 1965 to December 1966 at Wyton. Victor K Mk 1s, K Mk 1As and K Mk 2s served with No 55 Squadron from December 1966 to October 1993 at Marham, No 57 Squadron from June 1966 to 1992 at Marham, and No 214 Squadron from July 1966 to January 1977 at Marham. Victor B Mk 2s served with No 100 Squadron from May 1962 to September 1968 at Wittering, and No 139 Squadron from February 1962 to December 1968 at Wittering. Victor B (SR) Mk 2s served with No 543 Squadron from December 1965 to May 1974 at Wyton. Victors also flew with No 232 OCU.

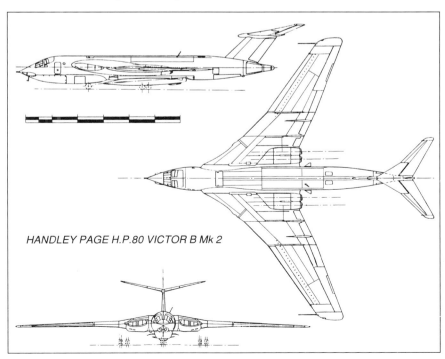

HANDLEY PAGE H.P.80 VICTOR B Mk 2

No 55 Squadron's Victor K 2, XH671, at Marham after Operation Desert Storm. Finished in desert camouflage, it carries a nose tally of 42 operational tanker sorties (the majority of them involving the replenishment of RAF Tornados and Jaguars). (Photo: Simon Barnes)

and later to refuel RAF Hercules transports *en route* to the Falklands.

The last Victor K 2s were honourably retired from service when No 55 Squadron was disbanded at Marham on 15 October 1993. The Squadron had established a record in the Royal Air Force, the Victor having served longer with one squadron than any other operational aircraft in the Service's history. Bearing in mind the numerous setbacks, repeated hostile political attempts to curtail its development and the final demise of its illustrious manufacturer, the Victor was aptly named. In the context of the subject of this work, as the longest-serving and heaviest load-carrying bomber the RAF ever flew, the Victor was indeed a classic aeroplane.

Short S.B.6 Seamew

David Keith-Lucas' quaint Short S.B.6 was the outcome of a Naval Staff requirement, set out in Specification M.123, for an uncomplicated but rugged carrier-borne anti-submarine aircraft, capable of operating from small fleet carriers in poor sea and weather conditions. This requirement came about at the dawn of the Cold War, as concern was being expressed at the Soviet Union's growing underwater fleet. To meet this threat, it had been thought likely that NATO member countries would avail themselves of war-surplus light carriers, such as the Royal Navy's 13,000-ton *Theseus*-class and the American CVL *Independence* class of 11,000 tons, and would wish to equip their naval forces with relatively inexpensive anti-submarine aircraft from Britain. In the event HM carriers *Venerable*, *Warrior*, *Magnificent* and *Powerful* were supplied to Holland and Canada, and USS *Belleau Wood* and *Langley* to France, over a period of ten years. However, by the time that most of the ships were re-commissioned, the Short S.B.6 had fallen by the wayside, a victim of its own shortcomings as well as the ravages of the British Treasury.

Ungainly in appearance, the S.B.6 Seamew was powered by a single Mamba turboprop, and featured a very deep fuselage with the two-man crew situated well forward in tandem cockpits. The midships section of the fuselage accommodated a large weapons bay, and the broad-chord, low-aspect-ratio wings were hydraulically folded outboard of a fixed,

The first Seamew prototype XA209, possibly before its first flight on 23 August 1953, when it was damaged, but later repaired. (Photo: Short Bros & Harland Ltd, Neg No AC/2/1469)

long-travel undercarriage. A large search radar scanner was mounted directly below the pilot, the tailpipe of the engine passing to starboard of the radome. A deck arrester hook, on a long arm, was located aft of the tailwheel, folding upwards beneath the rudder. A large rectangular tailplane and elevator were situated partway up the fin.

Three prototypes, XA209, XA213 and XA216 were ordered (the last-named being set aside as a structural test specimen), and XA209 was first flown by Sqn Ldr Walter Runciman at Sydenham on 23 August 1953, only to be badly damaged in an accident during landing. The aircraft was repaired, but subsequent flight trials showed that all the flying controls were overbalanced and poorly harmonised; there was inade-

Type: Single-engine, two-seat, mid-wing monoplane ship-borne anti-submarine aircraft.
Air Ministry Specification: M.123
Manufacturer: Short Brothers & Harland Ltd, Sydenham, Belfast.
Powerplant: One 1,590shp Armstrong Siddeley Mamba ASM.6 turboprop engine driving Rotol 4-blade propeller.
Dimensions: Span, 55ft (folded 26ft 1in); length, 41ft 0in; wing area, 550 sq ft.
Weights: Tare, 9,795lb; normal all-up, 14,400lb.
Performance: Max speed, 235 mph at 10,500ft; range, 750 miles.
Armament: Total weapon load, 1,844lb, comprising either four depth charges or 20 sonobuoys (internally) in addition to eight marine markers and six rocket projectiles carried under the wings.
Prototypes: Three, XA209, XA213 and XA216; XA209 first flown by Sqn Ldr Walter J Runciman at Sydenham on 23 August 1953; XA213 flew carrier trials aboard HMS *Bulwark* in 1955; XA216 was set aside as structural test specimen.
Production: Work started on 24 Seamews (XE169-XE192); 19 were completed, but only seven had been delivered to and accepted by the Royal Navy when further production was cancelled in May 1957.
Service: A total of six Seamew AS 1s served with No 700 Squadron (Trials and Requirements Unit) of the Fleet Air Arm at Lossiemouth between November 1957 and March 1958.

quate elevator control to correct the nose-down change of trim when the flaps were lowered, and airflow breakdown occurred at the junction of tailplane and fin. To alleviate the nose-down trim-change, large fixed semi-span slats were added to the wing leading edge outboard of the wing fold, while the airflow breakdown was cured by introducing tailplane root nose vents which exhausted into the elevator nose gap.

The Seamew was certainly a tricky aeroplane to fly, yet its general performance and agility, as demonstrated by Runciman, prompted the placing of an order for 41 production aircraft in February 1955, of which a number were a Mark 2 version, intended for service with RAF Coastal Command, with low-pressure tyres and without deck-landing equipment.

Carrier trials were flown by XA213 during 1955 aboard HMS *Bulwark* as the first six development aircraft were completed, these being delivered to No 700 Squadron, the Fleet Air Arm's Trials and Requirements Unit (commanded by Lt-Cdr D G Halliday RN, and later Lt-Cdr P M Lamb DSC, AFC, RN). Two other Seamews, flown by Short and A & AEE pilots, completed catapult trials and further deck landings aboard HMS *Warrior* in 1956.

The following year, however, the Sandys Defence White Paper — issued and employed by the British government to justify swingeing cuts in defence expenditure — caused further work on the Seamew to be suspended. Short Brothers & Harland had already been permitted to seek export orders among European nations, and an RAF Seamew Mark 2, WE175, had been prepared for demonstration work. Unfortunately, shortly after returning from a sales and demonstration tour of Italy, Yugoslavia and Germany, Runciman was killed while giving a demonstration at Sydenham when the aircraft g-stalled in a low-level roll and crashed inverted.

Deployment of British Bomber Squadrons — 1 January 1955

Home Bases

No 7 Sqn (H)	Avro Lincoln B.2	Upwood, Hunts
No 9 Sqn (M)	E.E. Canberra B.2	Binbrook, Lincs
No 10 Sqn (M)	E.E. Canberra B.2	Scampton, Lincs
No 12 Sqn (M)	E.E. Canberra B.2	Binbrook, Lincs
No 15 Sqn (M)	E.E. Canberra B.2	Cottesmore, Rutland
No 18 Sqn (M)	E.E. Canberra B.2	Scampton, Lincs
No 21 Sqn (M)	E.E. Canberra B.2	Scampton, Lincs
No 27 Sqn (M)	E.E. Canberra B.2	Scampton, Lincs
No 35 Sqn (M)	E.E. Canberra B.2	Marham, Norfolk
No 40 Sqn (M)	E.E. Canberra B.2	Wittering, Northants
No 44 Sqn (M)	E.E. Canberra B.2	Cottesmore, Rutland
No 49 Sqn (H)	Avro Lincoln B.2	Upwood, Hunts
No 50 Sqn (M)	E.E. Canberra B.2	Binbrook, Lincs
No 57 Sqn (M)	E.E. Canberra B.2	Cottesmore, Rutland
No 61 Sqn (M)	E.E. Canberra B.2	Wittering, Northants
No 76 Sqn (M)	E.E. Canberra B.2	Wittering, Northants
No 83 Sqn (H)	Avro Lincoln B.2	Hemswell, Lincs
No 90 Sqn (M)	E.E. Canberra B.2	Marham, Norfolk
No 97 Sqn (H)	Avro Lincoln B.2	Hemswell, Lincs
No 100 Sqn (M)	E.E. Canberra B.2/6	Wittering, Northants
No 101 Sqn (M)	E.E. Canberra B.6	Binbrook, Lincs
No 109 Sqn (M)	E.E. Canberra B.2	Hemswell, Lincs
No 115 Sqn (M)	E.E. Canberra B.2	Marham, Norfolk
No 139 Sqn (M)	E.E. Canberra B.2/6	Hemswell, Lincs
No 148 Sqn (H)	Avro Lincoln B.2	Upwood, Hunts
No 199 Sqn (M)	E.E. Canberra B.2	Hemswell, Lincs
No 207 Sqn (M)	E.E. Canberra B.2	Marham, Norfolk
No 617 Sqn (M)	E.E. Canberra B.2	Binbrook, Lincs

Germany

No 102 Sqn (M)	E.E. Canberra B.2	Gutersloh
No 103 Sqn (M)	E.E. Canberra B.2	Gutersloh
No 149 Sqn (M)	E.E. Canberra B.2	Gutersloh

Deployment of British Bomber Squadrons — 1 January 1960

Home Bases

No 7 Sqn (H)	Vickers Valiant B.1	Honington, Suffolk
No 9 Sqn (M)	E.E. Canberra B.6	Coningsby, Lincs
No 10 Sqn (H)	Handley Page Victor B.1	Cottesmore, Rutland
No 12 Sqn (M)	E.E. Canberra B.6	Coningsby, Lincs
No 15 Sqn (H)	Handley Page Victor B.1	Cottesmore, Rutland
No 18 Sqn (H)	Vickers Valiant B.1	Finningley, Yorks
No 35 Sqn (M)	E.E. Canberra B.2	Upwood, Hunts
No 49 Sqn (H)	Vickers Valiant B.1	Wittering, Northants
No 57 Sqn (H)	Handley Page Victor B.1	Honington, Suffolk
No 76 Sqn (M)	E.E. Canberra B.6	Upwood, Hunts
No 83 Sqn (H)	Avro Vulcan B.1	Waddington, Lincs
No 90 Sqn (H)	Vickers Valiant B.1	Honington, Suffolk
No 101 Sqn (H)	Avro Vulcan B.1	Finningley, Yorks
No 138 Sqn (H)	Vickers Valiant B.1	Wittering, Northants
No 148 Sqn (H)	Vickers Valiant B.1	Marham, Norfolk
No 207 Sqn (H)	Vickers Valiant B.1	Marham, Norfolk
No 214 Sqn (H)	Vickers Valiant B.1	Marham, Norfolk
No 245 Sqn (M)	E.E. Canberra B.2	Tangmere, Sussex
No 617 Sqn (H)	Avro Vulcan B.1	Scampton, Lincs

Germany

No 16 Sqn (BI)	E.E. Canberra B.(I) 8	Laarbruch
No 59 Sqn (BI)	E.E. Canberra B.(I) 8	Geilenkirchen
No 88 Sqn (BI)	E.E. Canberra B.(I) 8	Wildenrath
No 213 Sqn (BI)	E.E. Canberra B.(I) 6	Bruggen

Cyprus

No 6 Sqn (M)	E.E. Canberra B.6	Akrotiri
No 32 Sqn (M)	E.E. Canberra B.2	Akrotiri
No 73 Sqn (M)	E.E. Canberra B.2	Akrotiri
No 249 Sqn (M)	E.E. Canberra B.6	Akrotiri

Singapore

No 45 Sqn (M)	E.E. Canberra B.2	Tengah

H — Heavy bomber; M — Medium bomber; BI — Bomber-interdictor.

8. UNDER THE RADAR

The delivery of bombs by aeroplanes flying fast and very low in order to avoid detection entered the tactics manuals before the Second World War was a month old, and within a year special radar, capable of 'seeing' low-flying aircraft at ranges up to fifty miles away, was in service.

When the major powers acquired nuclear weapons, carried by manned aircraft (as distinct from ballistic missiles), the natural tactic was to deliver them from high altitude, not only to render interception more difficult, but to capitalise from the much lower fuel consumption of the turbojet at high altitude. With flight refuelling a commonplace practice in the United States Air Force, the American Strategic Air Command provided a truly global nuclear bombing deterrent. To this the RAF contributed a European element through NATO, its V-bombers being tied to bases in the United Kingdom, while France, which opted to leave the military arm of the Organisation in 1966, created her own independent nuclear strike force.

As has already been explained in the previous chapter, recording the relatively short-lived fortunes of the RAF's three strategic nuclear bombers, the Soviet Union, becoming increasingly aware that high-flying American reconnaissance aircraft were regularly violating Russian airspace, took effective steps to knock down these aircraft, thereby demonstrating that, if it could destroy the reconnaissance aircraft, it could also

counter any threat that might be posed by the bombers of Strategic Air Command and, by implication, those of the V-force.

For a further short period, therefore, the Valiant, Vulcan and Victor were switched to the low-level bombing rôle until, one by one, they succumbed to the potentially crippling effects of structural fatigue brought on by the punishing stresses of low flying. In order to deliver the Yellow Sun and other free-fall nuclear weapons, entirely new tactics, such as toss-bombing, over-the-shoulder and offset laydown were introduced in an effort to avoid the necessity to over-fly the extensive SAM defences that ringed potential strategic targets behind the Iron Curtain, should war with the Soviet Union occur.

This new phase of low-level strike tactics, with all their attendant countermeasures — both active and passive — began during the Vietnam war, the nature and disposition of the targets demanding that almost every bombing strike, whether carried out at high or low level, would involve in-flight refuelling, frequently more than once on each sortie.

For NATO nations, and for Britain in particular, this new style of bombing operations introduced a profound change in offensive strategy. The short-lived and costly deployment of American Douglas Thor IRBMs in East Anglia was quickly seen to be unmanageable (owing to the political niceties demanded by joint ownership of the missiles).

Moreover, there could be no question of Britain or, for that matter, European NATO nations collectively, being able to sustain a war, even on the scale of Vietnam, let alone a Third World War in the accepted sense, without continuing dependence on the United States. Most of the continental European nations preferred, despite the oft-repeated lessons of history, to resort to that politically convenient, but militarily impractical, panacea called collective security.

In the absence, therefore, of any suggestion that European nations might consider increasing individual defence funding, Britain opted to develop and produce an advance nuclear strike aircraft, precisely tailored to the 'tripwire' reaction to a Russian advance through central Europe. Thus was born the ill-fated TSR-2 project, with which the British Air Staff, apparently oblivious of the recent progressive decimation of the aircraft industry (as well as the intransigence of an unsympathetic Treasury), became utterly besotted.

At the outset TSR-2's requirement for a so-called Canberra replacement, set out in OR.339, defined the need for an aircraft that, being capable of short-field performance, could be deployed to relatively rudimentary, dispersed bases in western France from which to launch deep strikes at low level against key targets close behind the Iron Curtain, employing tactical nuclear weapons, and with a good chance of survival. (It is not known whether the French were enthusiastic about this plan or, indeed, whether they were privy to the TSR-2's original *raison d'être*; with the French withdrawal from NATO in 1966, this consideration became academic.)

TSR-2 failed on account of circumstances that were almost certainly predictable from the outset. Being the product of one half of the aircraft industry, and therefore the subject of acrimony in the other, the internecine quarrelling that rumbled for half a decade in the Service, in Parliament and in

Relatively little of reliable authority has been published about tactical nuclear weapons, and the '2,000lb special weapon' here shown recessed into the underfuselage of a Buccaneer of the Fleet Air Arm in 1966 has been variously described as a nuclear depth charge or Red Beard. (Photo: Fleet Air Arm Museum)

In the face of much early scepticism, the multi-national Panavia Tornado proved what could be achieved by several countries working in unison, simply by eliminating interference from politicians through the mutual agreement of threats to invoke huge financial penalties imposed on any party that reneged on carefully scheduled 'memoranda of understanding'. (Photo: British Aerospace, Warton, Neg No AW/FA752)

the aircraft and aero-engine industries generated all the conditions necessary for self-destruction. After all, the socialist party — traditionally opposed to military 'over-strength' — was waiting in the wings, so that when the Conservatives, themselves bankrupt of any realistic defence policy, pressed their own self-destruct button in parliamentary leadership squabbling and the Profumo scandal, the Wilson administration, when elected in 1964, lost no time in cancelling TSR-2 outright.

The aircraft itself was certainly very advanced in concept — more so than the American General Dynamics F-111 — but the resources it had demanded were, for Britain, prodigious. And neither the Ministry of Defence nor the industry itself possessed the administrative machinery to cope with the task of steering the project through to a successful conclusion (such American inventions as Critical Path Analysis were studiously ignored by the industry's sexagenarian boards of directors).

Cancellation of TSR-2 (together with that of every other advanced military project being pursued by the industry) not only left a mental vacuum in the Air Staff, but brought about the dismissal of almost a third of the industry's workforce through redundancy during the following two years, a situation that was exacerbated when the same socialist government opted first to purchase the American F-111 strike aircraft — and then had to pay huge cancellation costs when it changed its mind — and then decided to buy the McDonnell Douglas F-4 Phantom fighter-bomber, an aeroplane already technologically fifteen years old.

Cancellation of those cornerstone projects had its restorative side effects. It demonstrated that, in competition with the American manufacturing giants, no individual European nation's aircraft industry could 'go it alone' on a major project. Development of a supersonic airliner, to be undertaken as a joint Anglo-French project, had been spared from cancellation — probably more on

account of the political colour of the British manufacturer's parliamentary constituency than any faith in the aircraft's likely commercial viability. Following on this was the proposal to develop jointly an Anglo-French strike fighter, the SEPECAT Jaguar, an enterprise which was administered in a way that prevented, by legal methods and threats of massive penalties, the possibility of unilateral withdrawal by either Britain or France.

This was the background to the events that led to the concept of a Multi-Rôle Combat Aircraft (MRCA), a project whose origin was the product of discussions between Germany, Italy, Holland, Belgium and Canada, aimed at developing a Lockheed F-104G Starfighter replacement — discussions which, therefore, did not involve Britain in the early stages, as the RAF had not been equipped with Starfighters. Britain, on the other hand, had failed to reach agreement with France on the sharing of work on a tactical strike aircraft employing variable geometry, and entered the discussions on the MRCA late in the 1960s. These took an unexpected turn when the operational emphasis shifted towards the bombing and reconnaissance rôles, the air combat rôles being almost entirely excluded. This particularly appealed to Britain, whose remaining V-bombers were of declining operational value. Only the Victor appeared to possess a long-term future as a refuelling tanker. Moreover, as Britain, and in particular the British Aircraft Corporation, possessed greater design and research experience in variable geometry (the so-called swing-wing), it transpired that the major share of design authority for the new MRCA aircraft would be vested in BAC — which had also enjoyed the fruits of international collaboration on the SEPECAT Jaguar. As the likely cost of this project began to dawn

on the politicians from the smaller countries, Belgium and Holland withdrew, followed later by Canada, whose military responsibilities in Europe were, after all, additional to those on the other side of the Atlantic.

In due course the MRCA progressed towards flight stage, kept firmly on course by a statutory programme of Memoranda of Understanding, that is to say a succession of decision points in the programme beyond which the project would not proceed without unanimous agreement by all parties. If any nation opted to withdraw, a penalty would be required to be paid, and this penalty would progressively increase in order to reimburse the remaining nations for the money already invested. This system had the advantage of transcending national politics, and rewarded the nations who persevered to a successful outcome in the shared manufacture of the entire production run.

The MRCA, which became the Panavia Tornado, proved to be a masterpiece of industrial and technical collaboration which lasted for more than twenty years, and provided the likely pattern for future projects. It possessed the advantage over American aircraft of being optimised for operational circumstances in Europe. By reducing the possibility of interference by extraneous, self-opinionated but minor politicians who had proliferated in certain European capitals, the whole project was kept almost entirely within the forecast costs and timescale.

Britain, whose share in the Tornado project amounted to the manufacture of the front fuselage, engine installation and tail unit (as well as design leadership), began introducing the interdictor-strike version into service with the RAF in 1981, and it seems probable that both the bomber and fighter versions (the latter unique to the RAF among the

European partners) will remain in service beyond the turn of the century. It is an exceptionally expensive aeroplane, though in terms of its operational flexibility (the bottom line in the MRCA concept), it represents excellent cost-effectiveness, a fact already demonstrated during its participation in the Gulf War of 1992.

Deployment of British Bomber Squadrons — 1 January 1965

Home Bases			*Germany*		
No 9 Sqn (H)	Avro Vulcan B.2	Cottesmore, Rutland	No 3 Sqn (BI)	E.E. Canberra B.(I) 8	Geilenkirchen
No 12 Sqn (H)	Avro Vulcan B.2	Cottesmore, Rutland	No 14 Sqn (BI)	E.E. Canberra B.(I) 8	Wildenrath
No 27 Sqn (H)	Avro Vulcan B.2	Scampton, Lincs	No 16 Sqn (BI)	E.E. Canberra B.(I) 8	Laarbruch
No 35 Sqn (H)	Avro Vulcan B.2	Cottesmore, Rutland	No 213 Sqn (BI)	E.E. Canberra B.(I) 6	Bruggen
No 44 Sqn (H)	Avro Vulcan B.1/B.1A	Waddington, Lincs			
No 50 Sqn (H)	Avro Vulcan B.1/B.1A	Waddington, Lincs	*Cyprus*		
No 55 Sqn (H)	H.P. Victor B.1A	Honington, Suffolk	No 5 Sqn (M)	E.E. Canberra B.16	Akrotiri
No 57 Sqn (H)	H.P. Victor B.1A	Honington, Suffolk	No 32 Sqn (M)	E.E. Canberra B.15	Akrotiri
No 83 Sqn (H)	Avro Vulcan B.2	Scampton, Lincs	No 73 Sqn (M)	E.E. Canberra B.15	Akrotiri
No 90 Sqn (H/T)	Vickers Valiant B.(K)1	Honington, Suffolk	No 249 Sqn (M)	E.E. Canberra B.16	Akrotiri
No 100 Sqn (H)	H.P. Victor B.2	Wittering, Northants			
No 101 Sqn (H)	Avro Vulcan B.1/B.1A	Waddington, Lincs	*Singapore*		
No 139 Sqn (H)	H.P. Victor B.2	Wittering, Northants	No 45 Sqn (M)	E.E. Canberra B.15	Tengah
No 148 Sqn (H)	Vickers Valiant B.1	Marham, Norfolk			
No 207 Sqn (H)	Vickers Valiant B.1	Marham, Norfolk			
No 214 Sqn (H/T)	Vickers Valiant B.(K)1	Marham, Norfolk			
No 543 Sqn (SR)	H.P. Victor B.1	Wyton, Hunts	H — Heavy bomber; M — Medium bomber; H/T — Heavy bomber		
No 617 Sqn (H)	Avro Vulcan B.2	Scampton, Lincs	tanker; BI — Bomber-interdictor; SR — Strategic Reconnaissance.		

Blackburn B.103 Buccaneer

Barry Laight's Buccaneer was the outcome of Blackburn's tender to an Admiralty Requirement, NR/A.39, issued for an exceptionally advanced carrier-borne naval strike aircraft capable of operating close to the speed of sound at very low level. Implicit in this requirement was an extremely robust airframe, not only to withstand deck-landing on a pitching carrier, itself demanding a low approach speed, but also to withstand the punishing stresses imposed during low-level manœuvres, such as toss-bomb delivery.

From more than a dozen tenders, some of them as imaginative as Laight's design, the Blackburn B.103 — coming from a manufacturer with a long and distinguished tradition of naval aircraft — was selected. When detail design started, information was becoming available from America on what was to be known as 'area rule', whereby design of the aircraft fuselage avoids sharp variations in the total cross-sectional area, to delay the drag-rise as speed approaches Mach 1. Application of the area rule was

Buccaneers XK488 and XK489 of the unusually large development batch flying from Holme-on-Spalding Moor, Yorkshire, in 1959. (Photo: Hawker Aircraft Ltd, Neg No FAS.48/60)

manifest in the B.103 by the bulged shaping of its rear fuselage, resulting in a limitation of the crew stresses induced by low level turbulence. To withstand the stresses on the airframe, entirely new manufacturing techniques were adopted, including sculptural milling of the wing structure from solid billets and the machining of structural members from steel forgings.

In order to maintain control down to very low speeds — a demanding problem with a thin swept wing and tail — a system of 'super-circulation' was included by blowing hot air, bled for the engines, over the control surfaces to energise the boundary-layer, a system

that reduced the minimum flying speed by some 14 mph.

No fewer than twenty prototypes and development aircraft were ordered, the Sapphire engines originally planned being replaced by 7,100lb-thrust de Havilland Gyron Junior turbojets. Each of the early aircraft introduced new features, the eighth and subsequent machines being built in production jigs. The first B.103 (or NA.39 as it was more often called before the name Buccaneer was adopted) was flown at the RAE's airfield at Bedford by Derek Whitehead on 30 April 1958. The fourth aircraft introduced powered wing-folding, the fifth featured a rotating bomb door, the

An early Buccaneer S 1 in the Fleet Air Arm's white anti-flash finish. The bulky 'area-ruled' rear fuselage accommodated the nav/attack avionics while the long tail cone divided laterally to form petal-type airbrakes. The Buccaneer was unique in being the only advanced combat aircraft, conceived as a naval aircraft, to be introduced into front-line service with the RAF. (Photo: Blackburn Aircraft Ltd, Neg Ref No 18357)

sixth a flight refuelling probe. The ninth Buccaneer was the first to be fully equipped with the weapon and nav/attack system, housed in the rear fuselage bulge.

After carrier trials, which began aboard HMS *Victorious* on 19 January 1960, first deliveries were made to No 700Z Squadron at Lossiemouth (under Cdr A J Leahy RN), formed as the Buccaneer Intensive Trials Unit. Entering operational service as the Buccaneer S Mk 1, production aircraft first joined No 801 Squadron (Lt-Cdr E R Anson RN) at Lossiemouth in July 1962, being subsequently embarked in HMS *Victorious* for service in the Far East. No 809 Squadron (Lt-Cdr A J Leahy MBE, DSC, RN) received S Mk 1s in January 1963 and later flew from both HMS *Victorious* and *Eagle*. No 800 Squadron (Lt-Cdr R D

Lygo RN) equipped with Buccaneers in March 1964 and accompanied HMS *Victorious* to the Far East, while No 803 Squadron (Lt-Cdr M J A Hornblower RN) became the Buccaneer Headquarters Squadron in July 1967 at Lossiemouth, but also provided four aircraft which were sent out to join HMS *Hermes* in the Far East. The aircraft embarked in HMS *Eagle* were tasked in March 1966 with operating a blockade in the Mozambique Channel against oil tankers attempting to supply Rhodesia, after that country's declaration of independence.

Despite the Buccaneer 1's undoubted operational superiority, it possessed inadequate power to enable it to be catapulted from a carrier at maximum weight, and had to be launched with much reduced fuel load and subsequently refuelled by another Buccaneer.

To overcome this handicap a new version, the S Mk 2, powered by 11,100lb-thrust Rolls-Royce Spey turbofans, was developed, the first example being the tenth of the original development aircraft, XK526; it was first flown on 17 May 1963. This version subsequently served in the Fleet Air Arm with the former Buccaneer S Mk 1 squadrons during the late 1960s and the 1970s.

With the defence cut-backs of the 1960s, cancellation of the TSR-2 and of government plans to buy American General Dynamics F-111s, the Royal Air Force was without a tactical strike aircraft in the short term and, as the Royal Navy's fixed-wing air arm was progressively run down, so fairly large numbers of Buccaneer S Mk 2s became available. And it should be appreciated that, despite its age, this aircraft had hitherto represented one of the most advanced low-level strike aircraft in the world, and its ability to withstand air loads of 6g at very low level was probably unsurpassed for a decade.

Thus, in addition to 26 Spey-powered aircraft, newly ordered, 62 ex-Fleet Air Arm Buccaneer Mark 2s were transferred to RAF charge. The first RAF Squadron, No 12 at Honington, was equipped initially with ex-naval

Above: *During 1988-90 some of the oldest RAF (and naval) squadrons celebrated their 75th anniversaries; this Buccaneer of No 208 Squadron was painted in display colours which included a large sphinx on the tail, commemorating the Squadron's long association with the Middle East.* (Photo: via R C B Ashworth)

Right: *Buccaneer S 2B XX885 'Sky Pirates', complete with Pave Spike underwing pod, on its return from Operation Desert Storm. Most participating RAF aircraft acquired personalised nose art.* (Photo: Simon Barnes)

Mark 2s, armed with Martel ASMs and, in due course was tasked with the anti-shipping strike rôle. No 15 Squadron received S Mark 2Bs, also at Honington, in October 1970, this aircraft designation being applied to newly-built aircraft equipped with Martel. No 15 moved to Laarbruch in Germany, where it was joined by No 16 Squadron with Buccaneers in June 1972. Taking its place at Honington, No 208 Squadron was equipped with Buccaneer S 2As, armed for the overland strike rôle.

RAF Germany's Buccaneers were adaptable to carry tactical nuclear weapons or, alternatively, a wide range of conventional weapons from 1,000lb parachute-retarded bombs to laser-guided Paveway bombs with Pave-Spike designator pods. They were not, however, provided with in-flight refuelling equipment.

By the time of the Gulf War in 1991, the Buccaneer had almost disappeared from RAF service, a small number of S Mk 2Bs remaining at Lossiemouth. About ten of these aircraft were deployed to Saudi Arabia to perform the important laser designator rôle, their Westinghouse AV/AVQ-23E Pave Spike equipment being used to guide not only their own Paveway laser bombs, but also those of accompanying Tornados of the RAF. After arrival at Muharraq on 26 January, their first strike sortie was flown on 1 February against a bridge over the Euphrates, this being 'marked' by Buccaneers for Tornados, whose six Paveway bombs destroyed it. In a war that was characterised by the most advanced operational technology, the success of the Buccaneer — which had been conceived almost forty years earlier (albeit in a wholly different environment) — provides ample testimony to the soundness of the original design's concept and execution.

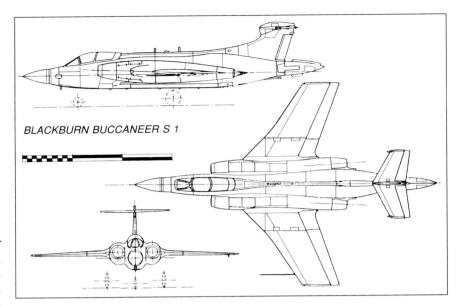

BLACKBURN BUCCANEER S 1

Type: Twin-engine, two-seat, mid-wing monoplane low-level strike bomber.
Air Ministry Specification: M.148 (from Admiralty Requirement NR/A.39)
Manufacturer: Blackburn & General Aircraft Ltd, Brough, East Yorkshire.
Powerplant: Prototypes and S Mk 1. Two 7,100lb-thrust de Havilland (later Bristol-Siddeley) Gyron Junior axial-flow turbojets. S Mk 2. Two 11,100lb-thrust Rolls-Royce RB.168-1A Spey Mk 101 turbofans.
Structure: Multi-spar folding wings with reinforced sculpturally-milled skins with spars and ribs manufactured from single-piece steel forgings. Three-section fuselage incorporating 'area rule'. Boundary-layer control by super-circulation. Rotary bomb bay.
Dimensions: Mk 2. Span, 44ft 0in; length, 63ft 5in; height, 16ft 3in; wing area, 515 sq ft.
Weight: S Mk 2. Max take-off, 62,000lb.
Performance: Max speed at sea level, 654 mph (Mach 0.85); normal range at 36,000ft without in-flight refuelling, 2,300 miles.
Armament: Up to 16,000lb of ordnance, typically comprising four 1,000lb iron bombs in bomb bay and four triple carriers under the wings, each with three 1,000lb bombs; alternatively four BL755 cluster bombs carried internally, plus one AIM-9B Sidewinder AAM for self-defence, AN/ALQ-101 jamming pod, a Pave Spike designator for, say, two 1,000lb Paveway laser-guided bombs.
Prototypes: 20 aircraft in prototype/development batch, XK486-XK491 and XK523-XK536; XK486 first flown on 30 April 1958 by Lt-Cdr D J Whitehead AFC and BJ Watson.
Production: A total of 189 production Buccaneers was built: S Mk 1, 40: between XN922 and XN973; S Mk 2, 84: XN974-XN983, XT269-XT288, between XV152 and XV361 and XV864-XV869; S Mk 2B, 49: XW525-XW550, XW986-XW988, XX885-XX901 and XZ430-XZ432. 16 Buccaneer S Mk 50s were built for the South African Air Force.
Summary of Service: Fleet Air Arm. Buccaneer S Mk 1s served with Nos 700, 736, 800, 801, 803 and 809 Squadrons between August 1961 and December 1970, and S Mk 2s served with the same Squadrons between April 1965 and December 1978. They served aboard the fleet carriers HMS *Ark Royal, Eagle, Hermes* and *Victorious*. Royal Air Force: Buccaneer S Mk 2s and 2Bs served with Nos 12, 15, 16, 208 and 216 Squadrons between October 1969 and 1992, Nos 12, 208 and 216 operating in the maritime strike rôle. Buccaneers also equipped No 237 OCU, this unit also providing an operational in-flight refuelling facility.

British Aircraft Corporation TSR-2

Conceived as a Canberra replacement in its long-range interdiction and reconnaissance rôles, the British Aircraft Corporation's TSR-2 was the winning tender to Operational Requirement 339, initially issued late in 1956. Implicit in this was Air Staff frustration that the Canberra was a first-generation aircraft with only modest subsonic performance and little foreseeable development potential. Just as disagreeably, it possessed poor airfield performance which demanded a programme of major airfield extension in the United Kingdom.

OR.339 envisaged an aircraft which embraced long-range, high supersonic performance at all, but particularly at very low altitudes, short-field operating capability, inertial navigation and precision nuclear weapon delivery. There was, moreover, more than a suggestion that the aircraft would be considered in the long term as a replacement for the V-force — itself still some way short of its planned strength.

Such an aircraft would obviously demand enormous research, design and

The TSR-2 XR219 during its tenth flight. The trails from the wings were said to have been caused by condensation of the flap-blowing air while flying at low airspeeds. (Photo: British Aerospace Neg No AW/FA508)

manufacturing resources, far beyond those of a single British company, and this factor did much to influence a re-structuring of the aircraft industry, as it was recognised that the manufacturer that possessed the most extensive resources and experience would immediately assume effective domination of the industry. The Hawker Siddeley Group was, in 1957, potentially such a conglomerate and, in order to provide effective competition within the industry, the British Aircraft Corporation Ltd was formed in February 1960, bringing together the aircraft, electronic and weapon interests of the Bristol Aeroplane Company, the English Electric Company and Vickers Ltd.

Because OR.339 was necessarily vague in its earliest form, the Requirement was re-issued several times with fundamental variations in its equipment and performance demands, with the result that a total of 21 design tenders was received from the industry over a two-year period. From proposals by Vickers, English Electric, Avro, Short, Handley Page, Gloster and Hawker, the final choice was made from the designs tendered by Vickers and Avro, the former ultimately being selected.

As it eventually emerged, the TSR-2 was a large, shoulder-wing, two-seat aircraft powered by a pair of Bristol Olympus two-spool turbojets whose early versions had entered production in 1953 for the Avro Vulcan. With reheat this engine was expected eventually to develop some 33,000lb thrust, and was also scheduled to power the Anglo-French Concorde supersonic airliner.

The TSR-2's wing was of delta planform with 60 degree leading-edge sweepback and exceptionally low thickness/chord ratio. It was manufactured throughout using integrally-machined skin-stringer panels; except for the tips, which were angled sharply downwards, the wing incorporated full-span blown flaps but possessed no dihedral. The engine intakes featured variable, half-conical centre shock-bodies, and the twin tandem-wheel main undercarriage units, with a Maxaret anti-skid system, retracted forwards into the engine intake fairings.

The vertical tail was a single-piece,

all-moving slab surface, as were the tailerons, which operated together for pitch control and differentially in roll by means of electronically-controlled Hobson hydraulic jacks.

The two crew members were situated in tandem in the very long nose, both being provided with rocket-powered

Martin-Baker 8VA low-level ejector seats. Operational systems were based on a central Elliott digital computer, functioning on data from a Ferranti inertial platform, forward-looking radar, EMI sideways-looking radar, Decca Doppler and Smith's air-data system. Computer output supplied information to the Elli-

Type: Twin-engine, two-seat, shoulder-wing monoplane tactical strike/reconnaissance aircraft.

Air Staff Requirement: (G) OR.339 and GOR.343

Manufacturer: British Aircraft Corporation Ltd, Weybridge, Surrey, and Warton, Lancashire.

Powerplant: Two 30,610lb-thrust Bristol Siddeley Olympus 320 turbojets with reheat and variable, half-cone, shock-body intakes.

Structure: Construction largely of aluminium-copper alloys with areas of aluminium-lithium and titanium alloys; integrally-stiffened machined skins widely employed.

Dimensions: Span, 37ft 0in; length, 89ft 0in; height, 24ft 0in; wing area, 700 sq ft.

Weights: Tare, 48,900lb; normal all-up, 80,000lb (96,000lb overload).

Performance: (Approx. figures). Max speed, 1,485 mph above 36,000ft (Mach 2.25), 850 mph at 100 ft (Mach 1.1); operating ceiling, 54,000ft; hi-hi combat radius, 1,150 miles with 2,000lb bomb load (800 miles, lo-lo radius).

Armament: Up to 6,000lb of nuclear or conventional weapons carried internally, and provision for up to 4,000lb of fuel or ordnance on four underwing pylons.

Prototypes: One prototype, XR219, first flown by Wg Cdr R P Beamont on 27 September 1964 at Boscombe Down; several other prototypes commenced and production of 30 aircraft negotiated, but all cancelled on 6 April 1965.

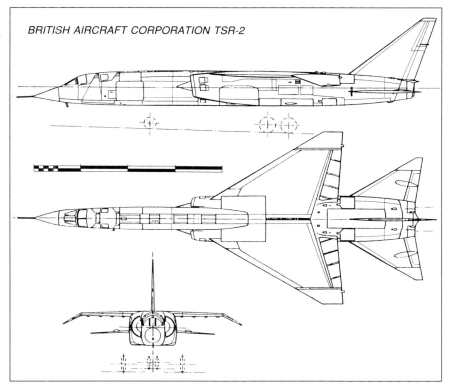

BRITISH AIRCRAFT CORPORATION TSR-2

With blown flaps extended, XR219 lands after its fourth flight. Just visible are the open suction-relief doors on the outer lips of the engine intakes, and the airbrakes (not fully closed) on the rear fuselage shoulders. (Photo: British Aerospace Neg No AW/FA298)

ott autopilot, the weapon-arming and release systems, the pilot's Rank-Cintel head-up display and Ferranti moving-map display, and to the navigator's instrument displays.

Despite re-issue of the Requirement (re-termed GOR.339 and later GOR.343) in 1959, the decision to accept the combined Vickers/English Electric TSR-2 tender had been made on 1 January that year, when long-lead instructions to proceed with 20 development aircraft was given. In 1953 this was followed by an order for 30 production aircraft, the total cost of these aircraft, their development, equipment, engines and their associated research, being quoted on a cost-plus basis of £690million — an unbelievably high figure and one that dwarfed any previous defence programme.

Engine development, in particular, was beset by problems, due largely to the wholly unsuspected phenomena engendered by the punishing demands on the military Olympus, not made on the Concorde airliner's engines. For instance, a low-pressure shaft failed, owing to the onset of fatigue, at near full-power during ground-running, causing the engine to disintegrate and blowing the Avro Vulcan test bed to smithereens.

Not all of the engine's shortcomings had been rectified when the TSR-2 XR219 made its first flight at Boscombe Down in the hands of Wg Cdr R P Beamont on 27 September 1964. The engines were therefore severely limited both in performance and flight time. Nor was the undercarriage cleared for retraction on the maiden flight. In truth, the writing was on the wall, and efforts had been made to fly XR219 as soon as safely possible, if only to persuade politicians of all shades that the aircraft represented a worthwhile answer to the Air Staff's demands.

There was no doubt but that the TSR-2 was an exceptionally advanced aeroplane which, unlike current and planned American aircraft, had been designed with European operations in mind.

Aerodynamically, it was a genuine Mach 3 aircraft. However, owing to consideration of kinetic heating limitations, its predominantly aluminium-alloy construction and the engine and intake design, it was necessarily limited to Mach 2.35 — a figure that XR219 never approached. Not that this limitation constituted an operational handicap, the decision on cancellation being made solely on political and economic grounds. Yet the question remains unanswerable: Would any British government have been able to justify the enormous costs — which would have had to be borne for many years to come — of a weapon whose ultimate value would have been strategically limited? For whatever reason, ideological or economic, the socialist Secretary of State for Defence, the Rt Hon Denis Healey PC MBE MP, announced the cancellation of the entire project early in 1965.

The folly (in the broadest sense of the word) of the TSR-2 lay firmly in the minds of the Air Staff, who ignored all the signs of potential disaster, both political and economic, in pursuing the project after the British (Conservative) government's future long-term attitude towards the Royal Air Force's strategic rôle had been made clear in the Defence White Paper of 1957, ill-conceived though that infamous document proved to be.

Deployment of British Bomber Squadrons — 1 January 1975

Royal Air Force
Home Bases

No 9 Sqn (H)	H.S. Vulcan B.2	Waddington, Lincs
No 12 Sqn (S)	H.S. Buccaneer S.2B	Honington, Suffolk
No 27 Sqn (SR)	H.S. Vulcan SR.2	Waddington, Lincs
No 35 Sqn (H)	H.S. Vulcan B.2	Scampton, Lincs
No 44 Sqn (H)	H.S. Vulcan B.2	Waddington, Lincs
No 50 Sqn (H)	H.S. Vulcan B.2	Waddington, Lincs
No 55 Sqn (H/T)	H.P. Victor K.2	Marham, Norfolk
No 57 Sqn (H/T)	H.P. Victor K.2	Marham, Norfolk
No 101 Sqn (H)	H.S. Vulcan B.2	Waddington, Lincs
No 208 Sqn (S)	H.S. Buccaneer S.2A	Honington, Suffolk
No 214 Sqn (H/T)	H.P. Victor K.1A	Marham, Norfolk
No 617 Sqn (H)	H.S. Vulcan B.2	Scampton, Lincs

Germany

No 15 Sqn (S)	H.S. Buccaneer S.2B	Laarbruch
No 16 Sqn (S)	H.S. Buccaneer S.2B	Laarbruch

Fleet Air Arm

No 809 Sqn (S)	H.S. Buccaneer S.2C and S.2D	Honington, Suffolk

H — Heavy Bomber; S — Strike Bomber; SR — Strategic Reconnaissance; H/T — Heavy Bomber Tanker; H.S. — Hawker Siddeley Aviation Ltd; H.P. — Handley Page Ltd.

Panavia Tornado

The second British Tornado prototype, 03/XX947, carrying a warload of six 1,000lb bombs, combat drop tanks and a countermeasures pod. (Photo: British Aerospace Neg No 42190)

Britain's participation in the original 'Multi-Rôle Combat Aircraft' programme came about quite fortuitously and contrary to logical reasoning — or so it might seem. The American/German Lockheed F-104G Starfighter had been in service for more than half a decade and used fundamentally ten-year-old technology; yet it was already within sight of the necessity for replacement with the eight NATO air forces with which it served (of which the Royal Air Force was not one). Whether that fighter had served the various purposes for which it had been adopted is open to doubt, but it has to be remembered that the F-104 had not been designed for the European operational environment, and the extensive adaptation which it underwent could never have been more than a relatively short-term compromise. Bearing in mind that much of Europe's aircraft industry was, in the 1960s, still only slowly recovering from the War's devastation, it seemed unlikely that a consortium of manufacturers would be able to develop and manufacture an advanced tactical aircraft capable of matching the swiftly advancing technology of the two super-powers.

Britain was, at that time, engaged in a collaborative venture with France to produce a tactical strike fighter which emerged as the SEPECAT Jaguar, in which the British Aircraft Corporation (BAC) occupied a subordinate rôle in the design and development, having had its TSR-2 cancelled, and therefore expressed its tactical needs rather late in the day. Yet the SEPECAT project was never intended to be more than a battlefield support aircraft (apart from an abortive French attempt to introduce it as a carrier-borne strike fighter).

BAC, having suffered what might be termed a post-TSR-2 recession, was examining means by which much the same rôle as that of the cancelled project might be undertaken by a smaller and much less costly aircraft, at the same time fully accepting that no modern military aircraft stood the slightest chance of commercial viability without considerable work-sharing among other European partners.

The early investigations, conducted under the leadership of I A M Hall, seemed to confirm that by adopting a variable-sweep wing and accepting the necessity to carry the ordnance externally, the natural process of electronic miniaturisation would enable the fuel, equipment and weapons to be accommodated in an aircraft about half the weight and size of the TSR-2. As a further consequence, engines of more modest power would suffice to provide Mach 2-plus performance at altitude.

Encouraged by the smooth progress of the SEPECAT collaboration, BAC entered preliminary discussions with France to extend the partnership to include the development of what came to be known as the AFVG (Anglo-French Variable-Geometry) aircraft. However, it soon became evident that France, having recently withdrawn from NATO, would only agree to a joint venture if her industry again took the dominant design and development share of a project based on the Dassault Mirage G8 — a circumstance that was not acceptable to Britain owing to BAC's accumulated extensive research into variable geometry.

Simultaneously, in January 1968, the Air Force Chiefs of Staff of Germany, Italy, Belgium, Holland and Canada decided to establish a permanent joint working group (JWG) to formulate the requirements for a long-term strike aircraft to replace the F-104G, known initially as the MRA (Multi-Rôle Aircraft), and later the MRCA (Multi-Rôle Combat Aircraft).

BAC, having failed to negotiate a joint venture with France, prepared a design project — the BVG (British Variable-Geometry) aircraft — and with this the RAF Chief of the Air Staff, Air Chief Marshal Sir John Grandy GCB, KBE, DSO, gained admission of British members to the JWG. On 17 July 1968 the First Memorandum of Understanding was signed by politicians of Germany, Italy and Britain, covering the Conceptional Phase of the MRCA. Between this date and 14 May 1969, when the Definition Phase commenced, Canada and Belgium withdrew from the project, opting to join with Denmark, Norway and Greece in the eventual purchase of suitable off-the-peg American aircraft.

During the Definition Phase, which established the basis of the share of manufacturing to be undertaken by the various nations, Holland expressed concern at the growing complexity and cost of the proposed aircraft and also withdrew from the enterprise, leaving just Britain, Germany and Italy. This was considered to be the minimum level of international participation that could possibly undertake what was to become the most costly European defence venture ever.

Meanwhile, design and manufacture of the first RB.199 turbofan engine was well underway at Rolls-Royce's Bristol factory, as the British, German and Italian prime contractors were announced as being BAC, Messerschmitt-Bölkow-Blohm (MBB) and Aeritalia, respectively, these three companies' responsibilities being co-ordinated by a tri-national parent, Panavia Aircraft GmbH, located at Munich. Broadly speaking,

The first production batch Tornado GR 1, ZA354, used for flight trials of the JP-233 runway denial weapon. These weapons were used very effectively, though not without loss among RAF crews, during the early stages of Desert Storm. (Photo: British Aerospace plc).

BAC would undertake manufacture of the front fuselage, tail unit and engine installation, MBB the centre fuselage and Aeritalia the wings. British sub-contractors would produce such items as the air data computer, head-up and head-down displays, wheels and wheelbrakes, autopilot, fuel cells, in-flight refuelling system and auxiliary power unit. The multi-mode nose radar was the only significant item not de-signed in Europe, being produced by the American company, Texas Instruments. The Rolls-Royce RB.199 engines would in due course be manufactured jointly by Rolls-Royce (Bristol), MTU (Mo-toren und Turbinen-Union) and Fiat.

Allocation and testing of the ten prototypes would be undertaken strictly on the basis of ultimate production-sharing between the three nations, Brit-ain producing five aircraft (one of which would be a dual-control trainer and one allocated as a static test airframe), Ger-many three and Italy two. Likewise the board of management, based in Munich,

was staffed (under a chairman in rota-tion) by British, German and Italian members, the British representatives in 1972 being Alan H C Greenwood, deputy chairman, Edward Loveless, deputy managing director and programme manager, B O Heath, systems engineer-ing, and R P Beamont, flight test pro-gramme manager.

The prototype 01, shortly to be offi-cially named the Panavia Tornado, was first flown at Manching, Germany, by Paul Millett (the project's senior test pilot) with Nils Meister in the rear cockpit, on 14 August 1974, and was allocated to general handling and per-formance assessment. It was followed by the first British aircraft, 02/XX946, flown by Paul Millett at Warton, Lancs, on 30 October 1974, this time with Pietro Trevisan in the rear cockpit. The next aircraft, 03/XX947, flown by David Eagles at Warton on 5 August 1975, was the first trainer and undertook the spin-ning trials (and, later, trials of the in-flight refuelling system). Prototype 06/

XX948, flown by Eagles on 20 Decem-ber 1975, was the first Tornado to be fitted with the 27mm Mauser cannon; the last British flying prototype, 08/XX950, was flown by Millett on 15 July 1976.

The nine flying prototypes were fol-lowed by six development aircraft — three German, two British and one Italian. The British Tornado P12/XZ630 was flown by Tim Ferguson and Roy Kenward on 14 March 1977 and under-took weapon release trials for the RAF at Boscombe Down, while P15/XZ631, flown on 24 November 1978, underwent supersonic flutter, gun-firing and other weapons clearance trials. The latter air-craft was also the first completed to full RAF production standard.

Meanwhile plans were underway to establish a Tornado flying training unit, the Tri-national Tornado Training Unit (TTTU) at Cottesmore under Gp Capt M G Simmonds, it being intended that Tornado pilots and navigators (as well as a high proportion of ground tradesmen and women) from all three nations would undergo training here. Accord-ingly, the first production batch of aircraft included twelve Tornado GR Mark 1s and eleven GR 1(T)s, all these aircraft being intended for delivery to Cottesmore. The first, ZA320, arrived there on 1 July 1980.

The first student training course opened at Cottesmore on 5 January 1981, being composed of RAF and *Luftwaffe* crews who had already com-pleted two or three tours of duty in fast jets (Phantoms, F-104Gs, Buccaneers or Harriers); their instructors had already completed a training-conversion course at Manching under the guidance of test pilots.

Above: *ZA592/G of No 9 Squadron at Honington landing from a practice bombing sortie, with thrust-reverser buckets, landing flaps, slats, spoilers and Krüger flaps all ex-tended; the aircraft has been updated by the addition of under-nose laser equipment. (Photo: MAP Neg No 121/383)*

Right: *A batch 4 Tornado GR 1, ZD848/BC of No 14 Squadron at Bruggen, Germany, in September 1985. (Photo: RAF Bruggen)*

While the TTTU undertook relatively little applied flying training, both the *Luftwaffe* and the RAF opened weapon conversion units, the *Waffenausbildungs Kommando* at Erding, and the Tornado Weapons Conversion Unit (TWCU, commanded by Wg Cdr Duncan Griffiths) at Honington (Gp Capt Mike Shaw). The first aircraft delivered to Honington were of the second production batch.

The first bomber squadron in the RAF to receive Tornados was No 9 (Bomber) Squadron (Wg Cdr Peter Gooding AFC) at Honington, whose 13 aircraft were delivered during the first five months of 1982, this station having been provided with Phase 3 hardened aircraft shelters. Typical of the sort of training flight undertaken by UK-based Tornado squadrons was a simulated attack on Akrotiri, Cyprus, involving a cruise-climb out to 24,000 feet (during which the aircraft was refuelled twice by Victor tankers), a visual low-level 'attack' on the RAF base, and a single in-flight refuelling on the high-level return flight. Carrying a pair of 330-gal underwing tanks, the Tornado, crewed by Flt Lt Ian Dugmore and Sqn Ldr Mike Holmes, navigator, flew 4,954 miles in 12 hours 10 minutes.

No 617 Squadron, based at Marham, was the next to equip with Tornados, under the command of Wg Cdr Tony Harrison early in 1983, having been reformed in January that year. In October 1984 aircraft of this famous Squadron flew to Ellsworth Air Force Base in South Dakota to participate in the USAF's Strategic Air Command Bombing Competition. In the course of this eight-week exercise (Operation Pairie Vortex), 617 Squadron Tornados, flown by Sqn Ldr Peter Dunlop and Flt Lt Steve Legg respectively, took the first two places in the Curtis E LeMay Trophy, while Sqn Ldr Dunlop won the John C Meyer Trophy — the long-awaited contest between the Tornado and the General Dynamics F-111.

The third British-based Tornado Squadron, No 27 (based at Marham under the command of Wg Cdr John Grogan), received second- and third-batch Tornados in May 1983, and it was this Squadron's turn in 1985 to attend the SAC Bombing Competition at Ellsworth. Even bettering No 617's triumph of the previous year, Flt Lt Dave Beveridge and Sqn Ldr Mal Prissick gained first and second places in the Curtis E LeMay, and Sqn Ldr Barry

Holding and Flt Lt John Plumb took the top two places in the Mayer.

By the end of 1983 trials of a new weapon had been completed and this, the Hunting JP-233 runway-denial weapon, entered the RAF's armoury in 1985. This store, of which the Tornado normally carried two under the fuselage, weighed 5,148lb and carried 215 HB876 area-denial mines in the forward section

and 30 SG367 parachute-retarded runway-cratering sub-munitions. These munitions would be discharged either as a salvo or in quick succession as the pilot flew low along a target runway, typically at 500 knots and 200 feet.

Other weapons compatible with the Tornado included the 1,000lb Paveway Mk 13/15 laser-guided bomb and 1,000lb Mk 83 retarded bomb, while other

---

Type: Twin-engine, two-seat, variable-geometry, shoulder-wing monoplane tactical strike/reconnaissance aircraft.

Manufacturers: International parent conglomerate. Panavia Aircraft GmbH, Munich, Germany. British Aerospace PLC, Warton, Lancashire; Messerschmitt-Bölkow-Blohm GmbH, Munich, Germany; Aeritalia p.a., Turin, Italy.

Powerplant: Two 16,800lb-thrust Turbo-Union RB199-34R Mk 103 turbofans with reheat and thrust-reversal systems.

Structure: Construction primarily of aluminium-alloys with integrally-stiffened machined skins; major-load components, such as wing carry-through box, of electron-beam welded titanium-alloy.

Dimensions: Span, (fully spread) 45ft 7½in, (fully swept) 28ft 2½in; length, 54ft 10¼in; height, 19ft 6¼in; wing area, 322.9 sq ft.

Weights: Tare, 31,065lb; max take-off, 60,000lb.

Performance: Max speed, 1,460 mph above 36,000ft (Mach 2.2); 710 mph at 200ft (Mach 0.92); climb to 30,000ft, 1 min 55 sec; radius of action (max ordnance, hi-lo-lo-hi sortie, unrefuelled), 810 miles.

Armament: Nominal max weapon load, 19,840lb. Two 27mm IWKA Mauser cannon with 360 rounds. Up to eight 1,000lb iron bombs carried under fuselage; two JP-233 runway-denial munition dispensers, Paveway laser-guided bombs, or any of a wide range of ASMs, retarded and fire bombs; four wing stations adaptable to carry two 330 Imp gal fuel tanks, chaff/flare dispensers, Pave Spike pods, data link pods, etc.

Prototypes: Four British prototypes, XX946, XX947, XX948 and XX950. XX946 first flown by Paul Millett and Pietro Trevisan at Warton on 30 October 1974.

Summary of Production (British): A total of 218 Tornado GR 1/1A/1Ts was built in the first five production batches (plus two prototypes updated to production standard): 23 (between ZA319 and ZA362), 55 (between ZA504 and ZA614), 68 (between ZA365 and ZA494), 54 (between ZD707 and ZD896) and 18 (from ZD996); subsequent production of at least 25 aircraft (between ZG705 and ZG794). Mid-life update conversions to GR Mk1B and GR Mk 4 in hand.

Summary of RAF Service: Tornado GR Mk 1s served with the following Squadrons: No 2 at Laarbruch and Marham, No 9 at Bruggen, No 12 at Lossiemouth, No 14 at Bruggen, No 15 (Reserve, tactical weapons conversion) at Laarbruch and Honington, No 16 (Reserve) at Lossiemouth, No 17 at Bruggen, No 27 at Marham, No 31 at Bruggen and No 617 at Marham; GR Mk 1As served with No 2 Squadron at Laarbruch and Marham. Tornados also served with the TTTE, Strike Attack Operational Evaluation Unit, TOEU, and DRA, Bedford.

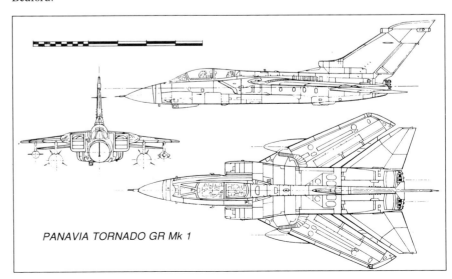

PANAVIA TORNADO GR Mk 1

Left: *Saudi Arabia placed substantial orders for Tornado interdictor strike and fighter aircraft in 1985, the first of 20 of the former, No 701, shown here, making its first flight in February 1986. By the time of Desert Storm these aircraft had acquired sand camouflage overall.* (Photo: Chris Riding, British Aerospace plc)

Below: *ZA354 during flight trials of ALARM anti-radiation missiles, seven of which are being carried in addition to BOZ 107, Sky Shadow and 220-gal combat tanks.* (Photo: British Aerospace Neg No AW/FH827)

stores could include the Philips BOZ-107 chaff/flare dispenser and Marconi ARI 23246/1 Skyshadow automatic, programmable active jamming pod.

RAF Squadrons based in Germany that were to receive the Tornado were Nos 15 (re-equipped on 5 July 1983 under Wg Cdr Barry Dove) at Laarbruch, No 16, also at Laarbruch, and the four Squadrons formerly flying Jaguars at Brüggen, Nos 14, 17, 20 and 31. The last, No 14, received its Batch 4 aircraft in 1985.

All these Squadrons were still serving in 1991 when, under the auspices of the United Nations, an international air force was assembled in Saudi Arabia for operations against Iraq in the event that diplomatic pressure failed to bring about the withdrawal of that state's armed forces from Kuwait. Apart from the deployment of RAF Tornado F Mk 3 fighters, which undertook high-altitude CAP sorties during the preliminary phase (Desert Shield), interdictor-strike Tornado GR 1s from several RAF Squadrons were despatched, and it was the latter force that was tasked in the early stages of the war itself (Desert Storm) to attack the Iraqi air bases (among them the old RAF station at Habbaniya) with the Hunting JP-233 weapons. Apart from a limited stock of laser-guided bombs, which were initially considered to be unsuitable for runway denial, the

JP-233s were deemed to be ideal for use by the Tornados. However, in the first two or three days' extremely hazardous operations at very low level (employing their terrain-following radar) over the

Iraqi airfields, five Tornados were lost to ground fire, a loss rate that was considered to be too high in relation to the number deployed. Towards the end of the brief war phase, however, the Tor-

Above: *An early Tornado GR 1 of No 27 Squadron at Marham before being updated with laser nose and the addition of an in-flight refuelling probe. The elephant motif on the RWR tail fairing recalls the Squadron's association with the Martinsyde Elephant aircraft during the First World War.* (Photo: British Aerospace Neg No AW/CN 34725)

Left: *A Tornado Squadron that celebrated its 75th anniversary in 1990 was No 17, whose gauntlet fin marking on ZD742/CZ recalls the Squadron's association with the Gloster Gauntlet fighter of the mid-1930s.* (Photo: Simon Barnes)

Shortly after its return from Saudi Arabia and participation in Desert Storm, ZA410 features a flight refuelling probe on the side of the nose, laser designator fairing, a self-defence Sidewinder missile on the inboard tank pylon, and three 220-gal combat tanks, not to mention the sharkmouth nose painting. (Photo: Simon Barnes)

nado strike aircraft, flying at a more circumspect height, achieved outstanding bombing accuracy using their laser-guided bombs against the important bridges over the Euphrates and pinpoint targets elsewhere.

In the absence of any announcement of an intended Tornado replacement, it seems likely that this superb and undeniably very costly aircraft will continue in RAF service until well into the 21st century. However, in the aftermath of the Soviet Union's fragmentation, poli-

tically-motivated steps have been taken to reduce the Tornado force, and all the German-based squadrons have been withdrawn to the United Kingdom, some of them being disbanded. Most of the surplus aircraft have been delivered

into long-term storage, and these aircraft will progressively undergo mid-life up-date programmes (involving power-plant, equipment and weapons) to re-enter service as the Tornado GR Mk 4 during the second half of the 1990s.

Deployment of British Bomber Squadrons — 1 April 1993

(75th Anniversary of the Formation of the Royal Air Force)

Home Bases

No 2 Sqn[1]	Panavia Tornado GR 1A	Marham, Norfolk
No 13 Sqn[2]	Panavia Tornado GR 1A	Honington, Suffolk
No 15 Sqn[3]	Panavia Tornado GR 1	Honington, Suffolk
No 27 Sqn[4]	Panavia Tornado GR 1	Marham, Norfolk
No 208 Sqn[5]	H.S. Buccaneer S 2B	Lossiemouth, Grampian
No 617 Sqn[6]	Panavia Tornado GR 1	Marham, Norfolk

Germany

No 9 Sqn	Panavia Tornado GR 1	Bruggen
No 14 Sqn	Panavia Tornado GR 1	Bruggen
No 17 Sqn	Panavia Tornado GR 1	Bruggen
No 31 Sqn	Panavia Tornado GR 1	Bruggen

[1]   Three aircraft detached to Dhahran, Saudi Arabia
[2]   Tactical reconnaissance; strike rôle secondary
[3]   Given Reserve status; was previously TWCU
[4]   Scheduled to move to Lossiemouth to become No 12 Sqn
[5]   Scheduled to re-equip with Tornado GR 1B with Reserve status
[6]   Scheduled to move to Lossiemouth

APPENDIX: THE CAPITAL SHIP BOMB

During the period 1936-39, when the British armed forces underwent rapid expansion, an impassioned debate continued between the Naval and Air Staffs on the nature of priority targets for British bombers in the event of war with Germany. The Admiralty maintained that, with the known German warship building programme underway, attention must be paid to the immediate destruction of the enemy's major warships (of over 10,000 tons), of which it seemed likely that about eight could well be in commission by 1940, with at least three others following soon after. Such a fleet, if deployed piecemeal against British mercantile shipping on the high seas, would constitute a major threat to the survival of Great Britain, particularly as it was suspected that Germany would also pursue the widespread use of submarines.

This cogent argument, expressed with growing vehemence by Admiral Sir Roger Backhouse, First Sea Lord before the War, and taken up with even greater vigour by Admiral Sir Dudley Pound on his appointment to this post on 12 June 1939, led to the accelerated development of the 2,000lb AP bomb, which had been the principal 'heavy weapon' for which the forthcoming RAF four-engine bombers had been designed. (It is also relevant to remark here that those heavy bombers were also originally required to carry torpedoes.) Moreover, a significant proportion of operational training, undertaken by Bomber Command during the last twelve months before the outbreak of war, was centred on attacks against shipping in port and against the ports and docking facilities. This was to

be reflected by the nature of early wartime RAF bombing attacks against the German Navy.

Early trials of and operations with the 2,000lb AP bomb appeared to be encouraging, the weapon possessing good ballistic qualities, and therefore capable of accurate aiming; it proved capable of penetrating most deck armour, but was found to possess an extremely unreliable fuse (it being estimated that only about 20 per cent of bombs detonated on impact during the first three months of operation).

One of the most ardent protagonists of a much improved and heavier anti-warship bomb was the Scientific Advisor to Winston Churchill, Professor Frederick Lindemann (created Lord Cherwell in 1941), who expressed the belief that conventional armour-piercing bombs expended too much energy piercing the ship's deck or superstructure without reaching or significantly damaging the sub-surface structure and bilges. It was suggested that if a bomb could penetrate the deck intact and then, on the Neumann principle, explosively discharge its own substantial projectile onwards and through the bilges, the heaviest naval vessels could be sunk by bombs.

The Capital Ship Bomb (CSB) was accordingly conceived and developed on this principle, two versions of the weapon — of 38in and 45in diameter respectively — being ordered. It consisted of an outer case in the nose of which was seated a hardened-steel disc; a thin, mild-steel nose cap was welded to the front, its blunt profile being intended to limit the bomb's terminal velocity. A

long striker tube, containing a Cordtex initiator, passed through the centre of the bomb and extended forward of the nose cap carrying a special fuse, and rearwards to two small exploder tubes each containing detonators and pistols.

After trials had been carried out to discover the nose fuse most likely to withstand the initial deck impact (it was originally intended that the bomb would descend by parachute but, after a serious accident, it was decided to dispense with this), a full-scale trial was held at Boscombe Down on 8 May 1942, witnessed by Lord Cherwell and senior officers from the Ordnance Board, Research & Development (Arm.4), HQ Bomber Command and No 5 Group, and the RAE. A Lancaster, L7529 (the third production Mark 1), had been selected as the prototype CSB carrier, its bomb bay being enlarged by bulging the doors, this modification being referred to as 'the provisioning mod' in order to disguise its true purpose, though it was not an official codename[1].

The bomb was dropped over a hardened target at Porton but, owing to its very poor aerodynamic shape, proved to be impossible to aim accurately and consequently missed the target and fell in open gorseland; its remains could not be recovered immediately as it had fallen in a chemically contaminated area. Examination of film taken of the trial, however, suggested that the bomb had functioned satisfactorily, and production examples were delivered before the end of July to No 106 (Bomber) Squadron, commanded by Wg Cdr Guy Penrose Gibson, for operational use. This Squadron, regarded as No 5 Group's 'operational laboratory' unit, was then currently

---

[1] This unofficial designation also came to refer to a number of other Lancasters to which modifications were made, including those to enable the aircraft to carry the 8,000lb HC bomb, some of which were further modified by removal of the bomb doors altogether in order to accommodate the Upkeep 'bouncing bomb', introduced a year later.

A 45in Capital Ship Bomb mounted on an adapted 4,000lb bomb trolley; the 45in version was designed in several variations, including a weapon weighing 6,959lb filled with Torpex intended for use against Japanese capital ships. (Photo: Air Ministry, A & AEE, Ref No 9974)

receiving special Lancasters, modified to carry the new 8,000lb HC bomb which it had been warned to introduce into service, and four of these aircraft were further slightly modified to accommodate the CSB.

The first of an intended series of attacks on German ports was ordered on the night of 27/28 August 1942 against the docks at Gdynia, where it was thought that the German battlecruiser *Gneisenau* was on the point of breaking out into the Atlantic. The German aircraft carrier *Graf Zeppelin* was also said to have been floated out of her dock in the port. Three aircraft took part in the raid, led by Wg Cdr Gibson, but this proved a total failure owing to unexpected cloud over the target; it did however appear to confirm, from the large flashes seen, that the detonating system functioned satisfactorily.

Nevertheless, the unpredictable behaviour of the bomb (and the difficulties of aiming) were not the only reasons for a feeling of unease that began to permeate the upper echelons of Bomber Command. Yet the CSB, and its operational drawbacks (for instance, it could not be dropped from above 10,000 feet as it was expected to 'topple' as a result of unstable ballistics, and this would have prevented the fuse from functioning on impact), unquestionably provoked fierce controversy surrounding all manner of fundamental facets of Bomber Command's operations. For one thing, it tended to strengthen Sir Arthur Harris' suspicion of purely academic scientists and their lack of understanding of operational requirements[2] — a suspicion that was only reconciled after the success of the Upkeep mines a year later. The CSB was the first 'special weapon, carried by a special squadron against a special type of target', circumstances which appeared to run counter to the RAF's disdain for any suggestion of operational élitism.

Yet, with Harris' approval, and ultimate acclaim, No 617 Squadron became just such an élite bombing unit, formed as it was, to all intents and purposes, out of No 106 Squadron (which had, for a year, been engaged in several operational tasks of much the same character and hazard as those later assumed by No

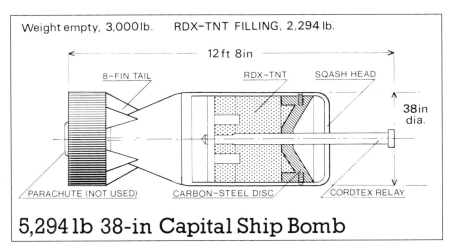

5,294 lb 38-in Capital Ship Bomb

617) with its illustrious commanding officer and many of its aircraft captains and crews.

The CSB did not die an immediate death, and production and development continued for a further six months, 35 examples of the 45in TNT/RDX version being delivered to No 115 Squadron, and production going ahead with a 38in version, apparently intended for Halifax units (however, it is now known that no Halifax was ever flown with a CSB, despite reports to the contrary). It is said that two examples of an improved version were dropped by No 115 Squadron in 1943, but no details of such use has been found. A total of six different CSB weapons was developed, their weights ranging from about 4,700lb to over 6,000lb, depending on their diameter (38in or 45in) and the constituents of their explosive filling.

Raid on Gdynia, 27/28 August 1942 by three Lancasters of No 106 (Bomber) Squadron.

Three aircraft carried out an attack on units of the German Navy at Gdynia, including the *Gneisenau* and *Graf Zeppelin*, reported to be anchored or in dock at the port. Special air bombers were carried, including Sqn Ldr Richardson and W/Off Naylor from the Armament School at Manby, who were conversant with the Stabilised Automatic Bombsight. The target was, however, badly obscured by cloud and, despite an intensive search, the ships were not seen, and the bombs were dropped on the dock area. Aircraft were modified with enlarged bomb bays, although Wg Cdr Gibson's aircraft carried only 1,000-pounders. Mid-upper gun turrets were removed, but the gunners were carried as extra observers. The aircraft were airborne from 19.55 until 05.50hr.

W4118. Loaded with six 1,000lb RDX bombs. Made 12 runs over target area and finally dropped bombs from 8,000ft. Bursts seen in the dock area.

Wg Cdr G P Gibson	Pilot
Sgt R F Crossley	Flight Engineer
Plt Off F Ruskell	Navigator
Sqn Ldr Richardson	Special Air Bomber
Plt Off R E G Hutchinson	Wireless Operator
Flt Lt W B Oliver	Mid-upper Gunner
Plt Off J F Wickens	Rear Gunner

R5574. Loaded with one 5,500lb CS bomb. Bombed docks from 8,500ft in 9/10ths cloud after searching for half an hour. No results seen except for huge flash.

Flt Lt W N Whamond	Pilot
Sgt J P Humphreys	Flight Engineer
F/Sgt R G McLelland	Navigator
Sgt B R McNair	Special Air Bomber
Sgt J R Hanson	Wireless Operator
Sgt B E Sutton	Mid-upper Gunner
Sgt E R Clarke	Rear Gunner

R5551. Loaded with one 5,500lb CS bomb. Docks located through 5/10ths cloud and bombed from 8,500ft on supposed position of *Graf Zeppelin*; very large explosion seen. Results not known.

Flt Lt J V Hopgood	Pilot
Sgt C Brennan	Flight Engineer
Sgt W P Bates	Navigator
W/Off A Naylor	Special Air Bomber
Sgt D B Gibson	Wireless Operator
Sgt J Hobson	Mid-upper Gunner
F/Sgt W Merrick	Rear Gunner

---

[2] The pith and content of correspondence which passed between Harris, the Under-Secretary of State for Air and the Directorate of Research make interesting reading. (Ref AVIA18/909 and AIR14/974 at PRO)

Glossary of Abbreviations and Acronyms

AAC — Army Air Corps
AACU — Anti-Aircraft Co-operation Unit
A & AEE — Aeroplane and Armament Experimental Establishment
AAF — Auxiliary Air Force
AAPC — Anti-Aircraft Practice Camp
AAS — Air Armament School
AASF — Advance Air Striking Force
ABC — Airborne Cigar
AC — Air Component
ACAS — Assistant Chief of the Air Staff
ACC — Army Co-operation Command
ACDU — Army Co-operation Development Unit
ACM — Air Chief Marshal
AD — Aircraft Depot
ADC — Air Data Computer
AEAF — Allied Expeditionary Air Force
AEE — Aeroplane Experimental Establishment
AES — Aeroplane Experimental Station
AEW — Airborne Early Warning
AFC — Air Force Cross
AFDU — Air Fighting Development Unit
AFEE — Airborne Forces Experimental Establishment
AFM — Air Force Medal
AFS — Advanced Flying School
A & GS — Armament & Gunnery School
AGLT — Automatic Gun-Laying Turret
AGS — Air Gunners' School
AHQ — Air Headquarters
AID — Aeronautical Inspection Department
AIEU — Armament and Instrument Experimental Unit
Air Cdre — Air Commodore
AM — Air Ministry, or Albert Medal (as post-nominal letters)
AMC — Armed Merchant Cruiser
AMX — Amatol Explosive
ANS — Air Navigation School
AOC — Air Officer Commander
AOC in C — Air Officer Commanding-in-Chief
AOS — Air Observers' School
AP — Armour Piercing
APC — Armament Practice Camp
APDU — Air Photographic Development Unit
APU — Auxiliary Power Unit
ARC — Aeronautical Research Council
ARD — Aircraft Repair Depot
AS — Anti-Submarine
ASM — Armstrong Siddeley Motors Ltd
ASR — Air-Sea Rescue
ASRTU — Air-Sea Rescue Training Unit
ASS — Air Signals School
AST — Air Service Training Ltd
ASU — Aircraft Storage Unit
ASV — Air-to-Surface Vessel (Search Radar)
ASWDU — Air-Sea Warfare Development Unit
ATA — Air Transport Auxiliary
ATC — Armament Training Camp
ATDU — Air Torpedo Development Unit
ATS — Armament Training Station
AVM — Air Vice-Marshal
AWA — Sir W G Armstrong Whitworth Aircraft Ltd
BABS — Beam Approach Beacon System
BAC — British Aircraft Corporation
BADU — Blind Approach Development Unit
BAe — British Aerospace plc
BAS — Beam Approach School
BATDU — Blind Approach Training and Development Unit
BATF — Beam Approach Training Flight

BATS — Beam Approach Training Schools
BBU — Bomb Ballistics Unit
BCBS — Bomber Command Bombing School
BCDU — Bomber Command Development Unit
BCIS — Bomber Command Instructors' School
BDU — Bomber Development Unit
BEF — British Expeditionary Force
BER — Beyond Economical Repair
BGS — Bombing and Gunnery School
BLC — Boundary-layer Control
BLEU — Blind Landing Experimental Unit
BP — Boulton and Paul (later Boulton Paul Ltd)
BSDU — Bomber Support Development Unit
BT — Bomber Transport
CA — Coastal Area (also Controller, Air)
Capt — Captain
CAS — Chief of the Air Staff
CAW — College of Air Warfare
CBE — Central Bomber Establishment
CBE — Commander of the Order of the British Empire
CBU — Cluster Bomb Unit
CC — Coastal Command
CCDU — Coastal Command Development Unit
CD Flt — Coastal Defence Flight
Cdr — Commander
Cdre — Commodore
CF — Communications Flight
CFS — Central Flying School
CGM — Conspicuous Gallantry Medal
CGS — Central Gunnery School
CLE — Central Landing Establishment
CLS — Central Landing School
CNS — Central Navigation School
CO — Commanding Officer
C of A — Certificate of Airworthiness
Col — Colonel
Comms. — Communications
COS — Chiefs of Staff
COW — Coventry Ordnance Works
CS — Communications Squadron
CSB — Capital Ship Bomb
CSE — Central Signals Establishment
CU — Conversion Unit
CUAS — Cambridge University Air Squadron
DArmD — Directorate of Armament Development
DBF — Destroyed by Fire
DBOps — Directorate of Bombing Operations
DBR — Damaged Beyond Repair
DC — Dual Control(s)
DCAS — Deputy Chief of the Air Staff
Deld — Delivered
DFC — Distinguished Flying Cross
DFM — Distinguished Flying Medal
DGRD — Director General, Research and Development
DH — de Havilland
DP — Deep Penetration
DSC — Distinguished Service Cross
DSM — Distinguished Service Medal
DSO — Distinguished Service Order
DTD — Directorate of Technical Development
DWI — Directional Wireless Installation
EAAS — Empire Air Armament School
EANS — Empire Air Navigation School
ECDU — Electronic Countermeasures Development Unit
ECFS — Empire Central Flying School
ECM — Electronic Countermeasures

E & RFTS — Elementary and Reserve Flying Training School
EEC — English Electric Co Ltd.
EFS — Empire Flying School
EFTS — Elementary Flying Training School
ERS — Empire Radio School
ETPS — Empire Test Pilots' School
EWS — Electrical and Wireless School
FAA — Fleet Air Arm
FEAF — Far East Air Force
FECS — Far East Communications Flight
FE Flt — Far East Flight
FF — First Flight
FFAF — Free French Air Force
Fg Off — Flying Officer
FIDO — Fog Investigation and Dispersal Operation
FIS — Flying Instructors' School
FL — Forced Landing
Flt Lt — Flight Lieutenant
Flt Sgt — Flight Sergeant
FP — Ferry Pool
FPP — Ferry Pilots' Pool
FRL — Flight Refuelling Ltd
FRU — Fleet Requirements Unit
FTC — Flying Training Command
FTS — Flying Training School
FTU — Ferry Training Unit
FU — Ferry Unit
GAC — Gloster Aircraft Company Ltd
Gardening — Minelaying by aircraft
GC — George Cross
GCB — Knight Grand Cross of the Order of the Bath
Gee — Airborne Navigation aid with ground transmitter
G-H — Blind bombing radar equipment
GIS — Glider Instructors' School
GM — George Medal
GOTU — Glider Operational Training Unit
GP — General Purpose
Gp Capt — Group Captain
GPEU — Glider Pilots' Exercise Unit
GR — General Reconnaissance
GRU — General Reconnaissance Unit
GTS — Glider Training School
H_2S — Airborne navigation and target identification radar aid.
HAD — Home Aircraft Depot
HAL — Hawker Aircraft Ltd
HC — High Capacity, Heavy Case (bombs)
HCF — Home Communications Flight
HE — High Explosive
HGCU — Heavy Glider Conversion Unit
HCU — Heavy Conversion Unit
HMS — His (or Her) Majesty's Ship
HP — Handley Page Ltd
HQ — Headquarters
HUD — Head-up Display
HxCF — Halifax Conversion Flight
IA — Inland Area
IAF — Indian Air Force
ICBM — Intercontinental Ballistic Missile
IDE — Instrument Design Establishment
IFF — Identification of Friend or Foe
ILS — Instrument Landing System
IN — Inertial Navigator
IRBM — Intermediate-range Ballistic Missile
JASS — Joint Anti-Submarine School
JWE — Joint Warfare Establishment
KBE — Knight Commander of the Order of the British Empire

KCB	Knight Commander of the Order of the Bath	
KCIE	Knight Commander of the Order of the Indian Empire	
LC	Light Case (bombs)	
LFS	Lancaster Finishing School	
LNSF	Light Night Striking Force	
LRDU	Long Range Development Unit	
Lt, Lieut	Lieutenant	
Lt Col	Lieutenant Colonel	
Lt Cdr	Lieutenant Commander	
MAEE	Marine Aircraft Experimental Establishment	
MAP	Ministry of Aircraft Production	
MC	Military Cross, also Medium Capacity (bomb), also Main Computer	
Met Flt	Meteorological Flight	
MEW	Ministry of Economic Warfare	
Mk	Mark	
MM	Military Medal	
MoD	Ministry of Defence	
Monica	Airborne warning radar equipment	
MoS	Ministry of Supply	
MR	Maritime Reconnaissance	
MRA	Multi-Rôle Aircraft	
MRCA	Multi-Rôle Combat Aircraft	
MU	Maintenance Unit	
NFF	Night Flying Flight	
NGTE	National Gas Turbine Establishment	
Nickelling	Leaflet-dropping by aircraft	
NPL	National Physical Laboratory	
NTP	New Types Park (Hendon)	
NTU	Navigation Training Unit	
OADF	Overseas Aircraft Delivery Flight	
OAFU	(Observers) Advanced Flying Unit	
OBE	Order of the British Empire	
Oboe	Blind bombing radar equipment	
OCU	Operational Conversion Unit	
OM	Order of Merit	
OR	Operational Requirement	
OTS	Officers' Training School	
OTU	Operational Training Unit	
OUAS	Oxford University Air Squadron	
PAFU	(Pilots) Advanced Flying Unit	
PD	Packing Depot	
PDU	Photographic Development Unit	
PFF	Pathfinder Force	
PFU	Parachute Flying Unit	

Pink Pansy	Target-marking bomb	
Plt Off	Pilot Officer	
PRO	Public Record Office	
PRU	Photographic Reconnaissance Unit	
PTS	Parachute Testing Section (also Parachute Training School)	
PV	Private Venture	
QRA	Quick Reaction Alert	
RAAF	Royal Australian Air Force	
R & D	Research and Development	
RAE	Royal Aircraft Establishment	
RAF	Royal Aircraft Factory (if prior to 1918), otherwise Royal Air Force	
RAFC	Royal Air Force College, Cranwell	
RAFFC	Royal Air Force Flying College	
RAFG	Royal Air Force, Germany	
RAFRO	Royal Air Force Reserve of Officers	
RAFVR	Royal Air Force Volunteer Reserve	
RCAF	Royal Canadian Air Force	
RDX	Research Department Explosive	
RFC	Royal Flying Corps	
RIAF	Royal Indian Air Force	
RL	Royal Laboratory	
RNAS	Royal Naval Air Service (or Station, after 1918)	
RNZAF	Royal New Zealand Air Force	
R-R	Rolls-Royce Ltd	
RRE	Royal Radar Establishment	
RSU	Repair and Salvage Unit	
RWE	Radar Warfare Establishment	
RWR	Radar Warning Receiver	
SAC	Strategic Air Command (American)	
SAM	Surface-to-Air Missile	
SBC	Small Bomb Carrier	
S of AC	School of Army Co-operation	
SAAF	South African Air Force	
SAN	School of Air Navigation	
SAP	Semi-Armour Piercing	
SASO	Senior Air Staff Officer	
SBAC	Society of British Aircraft Constructors (later Aerospace Companies)	
SD	Special Duties	
SDU	Signals Development Unit	
SF	Station Flight	
SFPP	Service Ferry Pilot Pool	
SFTS	Service Flying Training School	
SGR	School of General Reconnaissance	
SIU	Signals Intelligence Unit	

SMR	School of Maritime Reconnaissance	
SNC	School of Naval Co-operation	
SOC	Struck off Charge	
S of P	School of Photography	
S of TT	School of Technical Training	
Sqn Ldr	Squadron Leader	
SRAF	Southern Rhodesian Air Force	
STS	Seaplane Training School	
TACAN	Tactical Air Navigation	
TAF	Tactical Air Force	
TB	Torpedo Bomber	
TCU	Transport Conversion Unit	
TCDU	Transport Command Development Unit	
TDF	Torpedo Development Flight	
TDU	Torpedo Development Unit	
TFR	Terrain-Following Radar	
TFU	Telecommunications Flying Unit	
TI	Trial Installation, or Target Indicator	
TOC	Taken on Charge	
TOCU	Tornado Operational Conversion Unit	
TOEU	Tornado Operational Evaluation Unit	
Torpex	Underwater explosive	
TRE	Telecommunications Research Establishment	
TT	Target Towing	
TTTE	Tri-National Tornado Training Unit	
TTU	Torpedo Training Unit	
TTS	Technical Training School	
TURP	Training Unit and Reserve Pool (Middle East)	
TWCU	Tornado Weapons Conversion Unit	
UE	Unit Establishment	
UKVG	United Kingdom Variable Geometry (aircraft)	
ULAS	University of London Air Squadron	
USAS	United States Air Service	
USAAC	United States Army Air Corps	
USAAF	United States Army Air Force	
USAF	United States Air Force	
VC	Victoria Cross	
VCAS	Vice-Chief of the Air Staff	
VIP	Very Important Person	
WDCF	Western Desert Communications Unit	
Wg Cdr	Wing Commander	
WOC	Written off Charge	
W/Off	Warrant Officer	
W/T	Wireless Telegraphy	

Some Bomber-Related Operations and Codenames

Airborne Cigar	British 38-42 megacycle VHF jamming transmitter.
Arabian Nights	Codename of 1942 '1,000 bomber raids'.
Argument	Combined RAF/USAAF bombing campaign against German aircraft industry, 1944-45.
Bellicose	RAF Shuttle Bombing operations to North Africa, 20/24 June 1943.
Black Buck	Bombing strikes by Vulcans during Falkland Islands campaign, 1982.
Blue Boar	Reported to have been a British guided bomb.
Blue Danube	First operational British plutonium bomb.
Blue Steel	Stand-off weapon equipping V-Force bombers.
Buffalo	Dropping trials of first British atomic bomb (*Blue Danube*) over Maralinga Range, Australia, 11 October 1956.
Catechism	RAF bombing attacks on the *Tirpitz* at Tromso.
Chastise	Attacks on German dams by No 617 Squadron, 16/17 May 1943.
Crossbow	Bombing operations against German V-weapon sites, 1944.
Desert Storm	United Nations action against Iraq, 1992, involving low-level airfield strikes by RAF Tornado GR 1s.
Exodus	Repatriation of ex-POWs by air, 1945.
Firedog	RAF bombing on communist terrorists during Malayan emergency, 1949-52.

Gomorrah	RAF heavy bomber raids on Hamburg, July-August 1943.
Grapple	Dropping trials of first British hydrogen bomb 400 miles south of Christmas Island, Pacific.
Manna	Food drop by Bomber Command to Dutch civilians, 1945.
Margin	Lancaster attack on MAN Factory, Augsburg, 17 April 1942.
Millenium	1,000-bomber raid on Cologne, 30/31 May 1942.
Obviate	Lancaster attack on *Tirpitz*, October 1944.
Orange Putter	Postwar tail warning rader for bombers.
Pointblank	Bombing Directive by Allied Chiefs of Staff, 1943.
Prairie Vortex	1984 USAF Bombing Competition, Ellsworth Air Force Base, South Dakota
Red Beard	Reported to have been a tactical nuclear weapon.
Red Neck	Low-level reconnaissance radar for Victor.
Robinson	Lancaster attack on Le Creusot, 17 October 1942
Taxable	Air-mounted radar spoof by Lancasters on eve of D-Day, 6 June 1944.
Upkeep	Bouncing mine dropped by No 617 Squadron during dams raid, 17 May 1943.
Village Inn	British wartime tail warning and gun-laying radar.
Yellow Aster	Reconnaissance radar in Victor and Valiant B(PR) aircraft.
Yellow Sun	British hydrogen bomb equipping V-Force bombers.

INDEX